THIS

TIME

IS

DIFFERENT

THIS TIME IS DIFFERENT

*Eight Centuries
of Financial Folly*

CARMEN M. REINHART
KENNETH S. ROGOFF

Princeton University Press

Princeton and Oxford

Library of Congress Cataloging-in-Publication Data

Reinhart, Carmen M.
This time is different : eight centuries of financial folly /
Carmen M. Reinhart, Kenneth S. Rogoff.
p.   cm.
Includes bibliographical references and index.
ISBN 978-0-691-14216-6 (hardcover : alk. paper)
1. Financial crises—Case studies.   2. Fiscal policy—
Case studies.   3. Business cycles—Case studies.
I. Rogoff, Kenneth S.   II. Title.
HB3722.R45   2009
338.5'42—dc22
2009022616

British Library Cataloging-in-Publication Data is available

This book has been composed in Goudy text
with Trade Gothic and Century italic by
Princeton Editorial Associates, Inc., Scottsdale, Arizona

Printed on acid-free paper. ∞

press.princeton.edu

Printed in the United States of America

3   5   7   9   10   8   6   4

To William Reinhart,
Juliana Rogoff,
and Gabriel Rogoff

CONTENTS

CONTENTS

TABLES

FIGURES

BOXES

─────

PREFACE

This book provides a quantitative history of financial crises in their various guises. Our basic message is simple: We have been here before. No matter how different the latest financial frenzy or crisis always appears, there are usually remarkable similarities with past experience from other countries and from history. Recognizing these analogies and precedents is an essential step toward improving our global financial system, both to reduce the risk of future crisis and to better handle catastrophes when they happen.

If there is one common theme to the vast range of crises we consider in this book, it is that excessive debt accumulation, whether it be by the government, banks, corporations, or consumers, often poses greater systemic risks than it seems during a boom. Infusions of cash can make a government look like it is providing greater growth to its economy than it really is. Private sector borrowing binges can inflate housing and stock prices far beyond their long-run sustainable levels, and make banks seem more stable and profitable than they really are. Such large-scale debt buildups pose risks because they make an economy vulnerable to crises of confidence, particularly when debt is short term and needs to be constantly refinanced. Debt-fueled booms all too often provide false affirmation of a government's policies, a financial institution's ability to make outsized profits, or a country's standard of living. Most of these booms end badly. Of course, debt instruments are crucial to all economies, ancient and modern, but balancing the risk and opportunities of debt is always a challenge, a challenge policy makers, investors, and ordinary citizens must never forget.

In this book we study a number of different types of financial crises. They include sovereign defaults, which occur when a government fails to meet payments on its external or domestic debt obligations or both. Then there are banking crises such as those the world has experienced in spades in the late 2000s. In a typical major banking crisis, a nation finds that a significant part of its banking sector has become insolvent after heavy investment losses, banking panics, or both. Another important class of crises consists of exchange rate crises such as those that plagued Asia, Europe, and Latin America in the 1990s. In the quintessential exchange rate crisis, the value of a country's currency falls precipitously, often despite a government "guarantee" that it will not allow this to happen under any circumstances. We also consider crises marked by bouts of very high inflation. Needless to say, unexpected increases in inflation are the de facto equivalent of outright default, for inflation allows all debtors (including the government) to repay their debts in currency that has much less purchasing power than it did when the loans were made. In much of the book we will explore these crises separately. But crises often occur in clusters. In the penultimate text chapter of the book we will look at situations—such as the Great Depression of the 1930s and the latest worldwide financial crisis—in which crises occur in bunches and on a global scale.

Of course, financial crises are nothing new. They have been around since the development of money and financial markets. Many of the earliest crises were driven by currency debasements that occurred when the monarch of a country reduced the gold or silver content of the coin of the realm to finance budget shortfalls often prompted by wars. Technological advances have long since eliminated a government's need to clip coins to fill a budget deficit. But financial crises have continued to thrive through the ages, and they plague countries to this day.

Most of our focus in this book is on two particular forms of crises that are particularly relevant today: sovereign debt crises and banking crises. Both have histories that span centuries and cut across regions. Sovereign debt crises were once commonplace among the now advanced economies that appear to have "graduated" from periodic bouts of government insolvency. In emerging markets, however, recurring (or serial) default remains a chronic and serious disease. Banking crises, in contrast, remain a recurring problem everywhere. They are an equal-opportunity menace, affecting rich and poor countries alike. Our banking crisis investigation takes us on a tour from bank runs and bank failures in Europe during the Napoleonic Wars to the recent global financial crises that began with the U.S. subprime crisis of 2007.

Our aim here is to be expansive, systematic, and quantitative: our empirical analysis covers sixty-six countries over nearly eight centuries. Many important books have been written about the history of international financial crises,[1] perhaps the most famous of which is Kindleberger's 1989 book *Manias, Panics and Crashes*.[2] By and large, however, these earlier works take an essentially narrative approach, fortified by relatively sparse data.

Here, by contrast, we build our analysis around data culled from a massive database that encompasses the entire world and goes back as far as twelfth-century China and medieval Europe. The core "life" of this book is contained in the (largely) simple tables and figures in which these data are presented rather than in narratives of personalities, politics, and negotiations. We trust that our visual quantitative history of financial crises is no less compelling than the earlier narrative approach, and we hope that it may open new vistas for policy analysis and research.

Above all, our emphasis is on looking at long spans of history to catch sight of "rare" events that are all too often forgotten, although they turn out to be far more common and similar than people seem to think. Indeed, analysts, policy makers, and even academic economists have an unfortunate tendency to view recent experience through the narrow window opened by standard data sets, typically based on a narrow range of experience in terms of countries and time periods. A large fraction of the academic and policy literature on debt and default draws conclusions based on data collected since 1980, in no small part because such data are the most readily accessible. This approach would be fine except for the fact that financial crises have much longer cycles, and a data set that covers twenty-five years simply cannot give one an adequate perspective on the risks of alternative policies and investments. An event that was rare in that twenty-five-year span may not be all that rare when placed in a longer historical context. After all, a researcher stands only a one-in-four chance of observing a "hundred-year flood" in twenty-five years' worth of data. To even begin to think about such events, one needs to compile data for several centuries. Of course, that is precisely our aim here.

In addition, standard data sets are greatly limited in several other important respects, especially in regard to their coverage of the types of government debt. In fact, as we shall see, historical data on domestically issued government debt is remarkably difficult to obtain for most countries, which have often been little more transparent than modern-day banks with their off–balance sheet transactions and other accounting shenanigans.

The foundations of our analysis are built on a comprehensive new database for studying international debt and banking crises, inflation, and currency crashes and debasements. The data come from Africa, Asia, Europe, Latin America, North America, and Oceania (data from sixty-six countries in all, as previously noted, plus selected data for a number of other countries). The range of variables encompasses, among many other dimensions, external and domestic debt, trade, national income, inflation, exchange rates, interest rates, and commodity prices. The data coverage goes back more than eight hundred years, to the date of independence for most countries and well into the colonial period for several. Of course, we recognize that the exercises and illustrations that we provide here can only scratch the surface of what a data set of this scope and scale can potentially unveil.

Fortunately, conveying the details of the data is not essential to understanding the main message of this book: we have been here before. The instruments of financial gain and loss have varied over the ages, as have the types of institutions that have expanded mightily only to fail massively. But financial crises follow a rhythm of boom and bust through the ages. Countries, institutions, and financial instruments may change across time, but human nature does not. As we will discuss in the final chapters of this book, the financial crisis of the late 2000s that originated in the United States and spread across the globe—which we refer to as the Second Great Contraction—is only the latest manifestation of this pattern.

We take up the latest crisis in the final four chapters before the conclusion, in which we review what we have learned; the reader should find the material in chapters 13–16 relatively straightforward and self-contained. (Indeed, readers interested mainly in lessons of history for the latest crisis are encouraged to jump directly to this material in a first reading.) We show that in the run-up to the subprime crisis, standard indicators for the United States, such as asset price inflation, rising leverage, large sustained current account deficits, and a slowing trajectory of economic growth, exhibited virtually all the signs of a country on the verge of a financial crisis—indeed, a severe one. This view of the way into a crisis is sobering; we show that the way out can be quite perilous as well. The aftermath of systemic banking crises involves a protracted and pronounced contraction in economic activity and puts significant strains on government resources.

The first part of the book gives precise definitions of concepts describing crises and discusses the data underlying the book. In the construction of our data set we have built heavily on the work of earlier scholars. However, our data set also includes a considerable amount of new material from diverse primary and secondary sources. In addition to providing a systematic dating of external debt and exchange rate crises, the appendixes to this book catalog dates for domestic inflation and banking crises. The dating of sovereign defaults on domestic (mostly local-currency) debt is one of the more novel features that rounds out our study of financial crises.

The payoff to this scrutiny comes in the remaining parts of the book, which apply these concepts to our expanded global data set. Part II turns our attention to government debt, chronicling hundreds of episodes of default by sovereign nations on their debt to external creditors. These "debt crises" have ranged from those related to mid-fourteenth-century loans by Florentine financiers to England's Edward III to German merchant bankers' loans to Spain's Hapsburg Monarchy to massive loans made by (mostly) New York bankers to

Latin America during the 1970s. Although we find that during the modern era sovereign external default crises have been far more concentrated in emerging markets than banking crises have been, we nevertheless emphasize that even sovereign defaults on external debt have been an almost universal rite of passage for every country as it has matured from an emerging market economy to an advanced developed economy. This process of economic, financial, social, and political development can take centuries.

Indeed, in its early years as a nation-state, France defaulted on its external debt no fewer than eight times (as we show in chapter 6)! Spain defaulted a mere six times prior to 1800, but, with seven defaults in the nineteenth century, surpassed France for a total of thirteen episodes. Thus, when today's European powers were going through the emerging market phase of development, they experienced recurrent problems with external debt default, just as many emerging markets do today.

From 1800 until well after World War II, Greece found itself virtually in continual default, and Austria's record is in some ways even more stunning. Although the development of international capital markets was quite limited prior to 1800, we nevertheless catalog the numerous defaults of France, Portugal, Prussia, Spain, and the early Italian city-states. At the edge of Europe, Egypt, Russia, and Turkey have histories of chronic default as well.

One of the fascinating questions raised in our book is why a relatively small number of countries, such as Australia and New Zealand, Canada, Denmark, Thailand, and the United States, have managed to avoid defaults on central government debt to foreign creditors, whereas far more countries have been characterized by serial default on their external debts.

Asian and African financial crises are far less researched than those of Europe and Latin America. Indeed, the widespread belief that modern sovereign default is a phenomenon confined to Latin America and a few poorer European countries is heavily colored by the paucity of research on other regions. As we shall see, precommunist China repeatedly defaulted on international debts, and modern-day India and Indonesia both defaulted in the 1960s, long before the first postwar round of Latin defaults. Postcolonial Africa has a default record that looks as if it is set to outstrip that of any previously emerging market region. Overall, we find that a systematic quantitative examination of the postcolonial default records of Asia and Africa debunks the notion that most countries have avoided the perils of sovereign default.

The near universality of default becomes abundantly clear in part II, where we begin to use the data set to paint the history of default and financial crises in broad strokes using tables and figures. One point that certainly jumps out from the analysis is that the fairly recent (2003–2008) quiet spell in which governments have generally honored their debt obligations is far from the norm.

The history of domestic public debt (i.e., internally issued government debt) in emerging markets, in particular, has largely been ignored by contemporary scholars and policy makers (even by official data providers such as the International Monetary Fund), who seemed to view its emergence at the beginning of the twenty-first century as a stunning new phenomenon. Yet, as we will show in part III, domestic public debt in emerging markets has been extremely significant during many periods and in fact potentially helps resolve a host of puzzles pertaining to episodes of high inflation and default. We view the difficulties one experiences in finding data on government debt as just one facet of the general low level of transparency with which most governments maintain their books. Think of the implicit guarantees given to the massive mortgage lenders that ultimately added trillions to the effective size of the U.S. national debt in 2008, the trillions of dollars in off–balance sheet transactions engaged in by the Federal Reserve, and the implicit guarantees involved in taking bad assets off bank balance sheets, not to mention unfunded pension and medical liabilities. Lack of transparency is endemic in government debt, but the difficulty of finding basic historical data on central government debt is almost comical.

Part III also offers a first attempt to catalog episodes of overt default on and rescheduling of domestic public debt across more than a century. (Because so much of the history of domestic debt has largely been forgotten by scholars, not surprisingly, so too has its history of default.) This phenomenon appears to be somewhat rarer than external default but is far too common to justify the extreme assumption that governments always honor the nominal face value of domestic debt, an assumption that dominates the economics literature. When overt default on domestic debt does occur, it appears to occur in situations of greater duress than those that lead to pure external default—in terms of both an implosion of output and a marked escalation of inflation.

Part IV broadens our discussion to include crises related to banking, currency, and inflation. Until very recently, the study of banking crises has typically focused either on earlier historical experiences in advanced countries, mainly the banking panics before World War II, or on modern-day experiences in emerging markets. This dichotomy has perhaps been shaped by the belief that for advanced economies, destabilizing, systemic, multicountry financial crises are a relic of the past. Of course, the recent global financial crisis emanating out of the United States and Europe has dashed this misconception, albeit at great social cost.

The fact is that banking crises have long plagued rich and poor countries alike. We reach this conclusion after examining banking crises ranging from Denmark's financial panic during the Napoleonic Wars to the recent first global financial crisis of the twenty-first century. The incidence of banking crises proves to be remarkably similar in the high- and the middle- to low-income countries. Banking crises almost invariably lead to sharp declines in tax revenues as well as significant increases in government spending (a share of which is presumably dissipative). On average, government debt rises by 86 percent during the three years following a banking crisis. These indirect fiscal consequences are thus an order of magnitude larger than the usual costs of bank bailouts.

Episodes of treacherously high inflation are another recurrent theme. No emerging market country in history has managed to escape bouts of high inflation. Indeed, there is a very strong parallel between our proposition that few countries have avoided serial default on external debt and the proposition that few countries have avoided serial bouts of high inflation. Even the United States has had a checkered history, including in 1779, when the inflation rate approached 200 percent. Early on across the world, as already noted, the main device for defaulting on government obligations was that of debasing the content of the coinage. Modern currency presses are just a technologically advanced and more efficient approach to achieving the same end. As a consequence, a clear inflationary bias throughout history emerges. Starting in the twentieth century, inflation spiked radically higher. Since then, inflation crises have stepped up to a higher plateau. Unsurprisingly, then, the more modern period also has seen a higher incidence of exchange rate crashes and larger median changes in currency values. Perhaps more surprising, and made visible only by a broader historical context, are the early episodes of pronounced exchange rate instability, notably during the Napoleonic Wars.

Just as financial crises have common macroeconomic antecedents in asset prices, economic activity, external indicators, and so on, so do common patterns appear in the sequencing (temporal order) in which crises unfold, the final subject of part IV.

The concluding chapter offers some reflections on crises, policy, and pathways for academic study. What is certainly clear is that again and again, countries, banks, individuals, and firms take on excessive debt in good times without enough awareness of the risks that will follow when the inevitable recession hits. Many players in the global financial system often dig a debt hole far larger than they can reasonably expect to escape from, most famously the United States and its financial system in the late 2000s. Government and government-guaranteed debt (which, due to deposit insurance, often implicitly includes bank debt) is certainly the most problematic, for it can accumulate massively and for long periods without being put in check by markets, especially where regulation prevents them from effectively doing so. Although private debt certainly plays a key role in many crises, government debt is far more often the unifying problem across the wide range of financial crises we examine. As we stated earlier, the fact that basic data on domestic debt are so opaque and difficult to obtain is proof that governments will go to great lengths to hide their books when things are going wrong, just as financial insti-

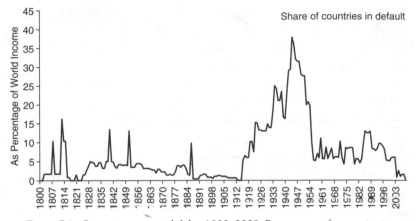

Figure P.1. Sovereign external debt, 1800–2008: Percentage of countries in external default or restructuring weighted by their share of world income.

tutions have done in the contemporary financial crisis. We see a major role for international policy-making organizations, such as the International Monetary Fund, in providing government debt accounts that are more transparent than those available today.

Our immersion in the details of crises that have arisen over the past eight centuries and in data on them has led us to conclude that the most commonly repeated and most expensive investment advice ever given in the boom just before a financial crisis stems from the perception that "this time is different." That advice, that the old rules of valuation no longer apply, is usually followed up with vigor. Financial professionals and, all too often, government leaders explain that we are doing things better than before, we are smarter, and we have learned from past mistakes. Each time, society convinces itself that the current boom, unlike the many booms that preceded catastrophic collapses in the past, is built on sound fundamentals, structural reforms, technological innovation, and good policy.

Given the sweeping data on which this book has been built, it is simply not possible to provide textural context to all the hundreds of episodes the data encompass. Nevertheless, the tables and figures speak very powerfully for themselves of the phenomenal recurrent nature of the problem. Take figure P.1, which shows the percentage of countries worldwide, weighted by GDP, that have been in a state of default on their external debt at any time.

The short period of the 2000s, represented by the right-hand tail of the chart, looks sufficiently benign. But was it right for so many policy makers to declare by 2005 that the problem of sovereign default on external debt had gone into deep remission? Unfortunately, even before the ink is dry on this book, the answer will be clear enough. We hope that the weight of evidence in this book will give future policy makers and investors a bit more pause before next they declare, "This time is different." It almost never is.

ACKNOWLEDGMENTS

A book so long in the making generates many debts of gratitude. Among those who helped is Vincent Reinhart, who consulted on the economic and statistical content and edited and re-edited all the chapters. He also provided the anecdote that led to the book's title. Vincent worked for the Federal Reserve for almost a quarter century. Back around the time of the collapse of the hedge fund Long-Term Capital Management in 1998, which seemed like a major crisis then but seems less so given recent events, he attended a meeting of the board of governors with market practitioners. A trader with an uncharacteristically long memory explained, "More money has been lost because of four words than at the point of a gun. Those words are 'This time is different.'"

A special debt of gratitude is owed to Jane Trahan for her extremely helpful and thorough editing of the manuscript, and to our editor at Princeton University Press, Seth Ditchik, for his suggestions and editorial guidance throughout this process. Ethan Ilzetzki, Fernando Im, Vania Stavrakeva, Katherine Waldock, Chenzi Xu, and Jan Zilinsky provided excellent research assistance. We are also grateful to Peter Strupp and his colleagues at Princeton Editorial Associates for skillfully negotiating all the technical details of producing this volume.

Preamble: Some Initial Intuitions on Financial Fragility and the Fickle Nature of Confidence

This book summarizes the long history of financial crises in their many guises across many countries. Before heading into the deep waters of experience, this chapter will attempt to sketch an economic framework to help the reader understand why financial crises tend to be both unpredictable and damaging. As the book unfolds, we will take other opportunities to guide interested readers through the related academic literature when it is absolutely critical to our story. Rest assured that these are only short detours, and those unconcerned with economic theory as an engine of discovery can bypass these byways.

As we shall argue, economic theory proposes plausible reasons that financial markets, particularly ones reliant on leverage (which means that they have thin capital compared to the amount of assets at stake), can be quite fragile and subject to crises of confidence.[1] Unfortunately, theory gives little guidance on the exact timing or duration of these crises, which is why we focus so on experience.

Perhaps more than anything else, failure to recognize the precariousness and fickleness of confidence—especially in cases in which large short-term debts need to be rolled over continuously—is the key factor that gives rise to the this-time-is-different syndrome. Highly indebted governments, banks, or corporations can seem to be merrily rolling along for an extended period, when *bang!*—confidence collapses, lenders disappear, and a crisis hits.

The simplest and most familiar example is bank runs (which we take up in more detail in the chapter on banking crises). We talk about banks for two reasons. First, that is the route along which the academic literature developed. Second, much of our historical data set applies to the borrowing of banks and of governments. (Other large and liquid participants in credit markets are relatively new entrants to the world of finance.) However, our examples are quite illustrative of a broader phenomenon of financial fragility. Many of the same general principles apply to these market actors, whether they be government-sponsored enterprises, investment banks, or money market mutual funds.

Banks traditionally borrow at short term. That is, they borrow in the form of deposits that can be redeemed on relatively short notice. But the loans they make mostly have a far longer maturity and can be difficult to convert into cash on short notice. For example, a bank financing the expansion of a local hardware store might be reasonably confident of repayment in the long run as the store expands its business and revenues. But early in the expansion, the bank may have no easy way to call in the loan. The store owner simply has insufficient revenues, particularly if forced to make payments on principal as well as interest.

A bank with a healthy deposit base and a large portfolio of illiquid loans may well have bright prospects over the long term. However, if for some reason, depositors all try to withdraw their funds at once—say, because of panic based on a false rumor that the bank has lost money gambling on exotic mortgages—trouble ensues. Absent a way to sell its illiquid loan portfolio, the bank might simply not be able to pay off its panicked depositors. Such was the fate of the banks in the classic movies *It's a Wonderful Life* and *Mary Poppins*. Those movies were rooted in reality: many banks have shared this fate, particularly when the government has not fully guaranteed bank deposits.

The most famous recent example of a bank run is the run on the United Kingdom's Northern Rock bank. Panicked depositors, not satisfied with the British government's partial insurance scheme, formed long queues in September 2007. The broadening panic eventually forced the British government to take over the bank and more fully back its liabilities.

Other borrowers, not just banks, can suffer from a crisis of confidence. During the financial crisis that started in the United States in 2007, huge financial giants in the "shadow banking" system outside regulated banks suffered similar problems. Although they borrowed mainly from banks and other financial institutions, their vulnerability was the same. As confidence in the investments they had made fell, lenders increasingly refused to roll over their short-term loans, and they were forced to throw assets on the market at fire-sale prices. Distressed sales drove prices down further, leading to further losses and downward-spiraling confidence. Eventually, the U.S. government had to step in to try to prop up the market; the drama is still unfolding, and the price tag for resolution continues to mount.

Governments can be subject to the same dynamics of fickle expectations that can destabilize banks. This is particularly so when a government borrows from external lenders over whom it has relatively little influence. Most government investments directly or indirectly involve the long-run growth potential of the country and its tax base, but these are highly illiquid assets. Suppose, for example, that a country has a public debt burden that seems manageable given its current tax revenues, growth projections, and market interest rates. If the market becomes concerned that a populist fringe candidate is going to win the next election and raise spending so much that the debt will become difficult to manage, investors may suddenly balk at rolling over short-term debt at rates the country can manage. A credit crisis unfolds.

Although these kinds of scenarios are not everyday events, over the long course of history and the broad range of countries we cover in this book, such financial crises occur all too frequently. Why cannot big countries, or even the world as a whole, find a way to put a stop to crises of confidence, at least premature ones? It is possible, but there is a rub. Suppose a world government agency provided expansive deposit insurance to protect every worthy borrower from panics. Say there was a super-sized version of the International Monetary Fund (IMF), today's main multilateral lender that aims to help emerging markets when they run into liquidity crises. The problem is that if one provides insurance to everyone everywhere, with no conditions, some players are going to misbehave. If the IMF lent too much with too few conditions, the IMF itself would be bankrupt in short order, and financial crises would be unchecked. Complete insurance against crises is neither feasible nor desirable. (Exactly this conundrum will face the global financial community in the wake of the latest financial crisis, with the IMF's lending resources having been increased fourfold in response to the crisis while, at the same time, lending conditionality has been considerably relaxed.)

What does economic theory have to say about countries' vulnerability to financial crises? For concreteness, let us focus for now on governments, the main source of the crises examined in this book. Economic theory tells us that if a government is sufficiently frugal, it is not terribly vulnerable to crises of confidence. A government does not have to worry too much about debt crises if it consistently runs fiscal surpluses (which happens when tax receipts exceed expenditures), maintains relatively low debt levels, mostly borrows at longer-term maturities (say ten years or more), and does not have too many hidden off–balance sheet guarantees.

If, in contrast, a government runs large deficits year after year, concentrating its borrowing at shorter-term maturities (of say one year or less), it becomes vulnerable, perhaps even at debt-burden levels that seemingly should be quite manageable. Of course, an ill-intentioned government could try to reduce its vulnerability by attempting to issue large amounts of long-term debt. But most likely, markets would quickly catch on and charge extremely high interest rates on any long-dated borrowing. Indeed, a principal reason that some governments choose to borrow at shorter maturities instead of longer maturities is precisely so that they can benefit from lower interest rates as long as confidence lasts.

Economic theory tells us that it is precisely the fickle nature of confidence, including its dependence on the public's expectation of future events, that makes it so difficult to predict the timing of debt crises. High debt levels lead, in many mathematical economics models, to "multiple equilibria" in which the debt level might be sustained

—or might not be.[2] Economists do not have a terribly good idea of what kinds of events shift confidence and of how to concretely assess confidence vulnerability. What one does see, again and again, in the history of financial crises is that when an accident is waiting to happen, it eventually does. When countries become too deeply indebted, they are headed for trouble. When debt-fueled asset price explosions seem too good to be true, they probably are. But the exact timing can be very difficult to guess, and a crisis that seems imminent can sometimes take years to ignite. Such was certainly the case of the United States in the late 2000s. As we show in chapter 13, all the red lights were blinking in the run-up to the crisis. But until the "accident," many financial leaders in the United States—and indeed many academics—were still arguing that "this time is different."

We would like to note that our caution about excessive debt burdens and leverage for governments is different from the admonitions of the traditional public choice literature of Buchanan and others.[3] The traditional public finance literature warns about the short-sightedness of governments in running fiscal deficits and their chronic failure to weigh the long-run burden that servicing debt will force on their citizens. In fact, excessive debt burdens often generate problems in the nearer term, precisely because investors may have doubts about the country's will to finance the debt over the longer term. The fragility of debt can be every bit as great a problem as its long-term tax burden, at times even greater.

Similar fragility problems arise in other crisis contexts that we will consider in this book. One of the lessons of the 1980s and 1990s is that countries maintaining fixed or "highly managed" exchange rate regimes are vulnerable to sudden crises of confidence. Speculative attacks on fixed exchange rates can blow up overnight seemingly stable long-lived regimes. During the period of the successful fix, there is always plenty of this-time-is-different commentary. But then, as in the case of Argentina in December 2001, all the confidence can collapse in a puff of smoke. There is a fundamental link to debt, however. As Krugman famously showed, exchange rate crises often have their roots in a government's unwillingness to adopt fiscal and monetary policies consistent with maintaining a fixed exchange rate.[4] If speculators realize the government is eventually going to run out of the resources needed to back the currency, they will all be looking to time their move out of the currency in anticipation of the eventual crash. Public debts do not always have to be explicit; contingent government guarantees have been at the crux of many a crisis.

Certainly countries have ways of making themselves less vulnerable to crises of confidence short of simply curtailing their borrowing and leverage. Economic theory suggests that greater transparency helps. As the reader shall see later on, governments tend to be anything but transparent when it comes to borrowing. And as the financial crisis of the late 2000s shows, private borrowers are often little better unless government regulation forces them to be more transparent. A country with stronger legal and regulatory institutions can certainly borrow more. Indeed, many scholars consider Britain's development of superior institutions for making debt repayment credible a key to its military and development successes in the eighteenth and nineteenth centuries.[5] But even good institutions and a sophisticated financial system can run into problems if faced with enough strains, as the United States has learned so painfully in the most recent crisis.

Finally, there is the question of why financial crises tend to be so painful, a topic we take up mainly in the introduction to chapter 10 on banking crises. In brief, most economies, even relatively poor ones, depend on the financial sector to channel money from savers (typically consumers) to investment projects around the economy. If a crisis paralyzes the banking system, it is very difficult for an economy to resume normal economic activity. Ben Bernanke famously advanced bank collapse as an important reason that the Great Depression of the 1930s lasted so long and hit so hard. So financial crises, particularly those that are large and difficult to resolve, can have profound effects. Again, as in the case of multiple equilibria and financial fragility, there is a large economic theory literature on the topic.[6] This strong connection between financial markets and real economic activity, particularly when financial markets cease to function, is what has made so many of the crises we consider in this book such spectacular historic events. Consider, in contrast, the collapse of the tech stock bubble in 2001. Although technology stocks soared and collapsed, the effect on the real economy was only the relatively mild recession of 2001. Bubbles are far more dangerous when they are fueled by debt, as in the case of the global housing price explosion of the early 2000s.

Surely, the Second Great Contraction—as we term the financial crisis of the late 2000s, which has spread to nearly every region—will have a profound effect on economics, particularly the study of linkages between financial markets and the real economy.[7] We hope some of the facts laid out in this book will be helpful in framing the problems that the new theories need to explain, not just for the recent crisis but for the multitude of crises that have occurred in the past, not to mention the many that have yet to unfold.

THIS

TIME

IS

DIFFERENT

- PART I -

FINANCIAL CRISES:
AN OPERATIONAL PRIMER

The essence of the this-time-is-different syndrome is simple. It is rooted in the firmly held belief that financial crises are things that happen to other people in other countries at other times; crises do not happen to us, here and now. We are doing things better, we are smarter, we have learned from past mistakes. The old rules of valuation no longer apply. Unfortunately, a highly leveraged economy can unwittingly be sitting with its back at the edge of a financial cliff for many years before chance and circumstance provoke a crisis of confidence that pushes it off.

- 1 -

VARIETIES OF CRISES
AND THEIR DATES

Because this book is grounded in a quantitative and historical analysis of crises, it is important to begin by defining exactly what constitutes a financial crisis, as well as the methods—quantitative where possible—by which we date its beginning and end. This chapter and the two that follow lay out the basic concepts, definitions, methodology, and approach toward data collection and analysis that underpin our study of the historical international experience with almost any kind of economic crisis, be it a sovereign debt default, banking, inflation, or exchange rate crisis.

Delving into precise definitions of a crisis in an initial chapter rather than simply including them in a glossary may seem somewhat tedious. But for the reader to properly interpret the sweeping historical figures and tables that follow later in this volume, it is essential to have a sense of how we delineate what constitutes a crisis and what does not. The boundaries we draw are generally consistent with the existing empirical economics literature, which by and large is segmented across the various types of crises we consider (e.g., sovereign debt, exchange rate). We try to highlight any cases in which results are conspicuously sensitive to small changes in our cutoff points or where we are particularly concerned about clear inadequacies in the data. This definition chapter also gives us a convenient opportunity to expand a bit more on the variety of crises we take up in this book.

The reader should note that the crisis markers discussed in this chapter refer to the measurement of crises within individual countries. Later on, we discuss a number of ways to think about the international dimensions of crises and their intensity and transmission, culminating in our definition of a global crisis in chapter 16. In addition to reporting on one country at a time, our root measures of crisis thresholds report on only one type of crisis at a time (e.g., exchange rate crashes, inflation, banking crises). As we emphasize, particularly in chapter 16, different varieties of crises tend to fall in clusters, suggesting that it may be possible, in principle, to have systemic definitions of crises. But for a number of reasons, we prefer to focus on the simplest and most transparent delineation of crisis episodes, especially because doing otherwise would make it very difficult to make broad comparisons across countries and time. These definitions of crises are rooted in the existing empirical literature and referenced accordingly.

We begin by discussing crises that can readily be given strict quantitative definitions, then turn to those for which we must rely on more qualitative and judgmental analysis. The concluding section defines *serial default* and the *this-time-is-different syndrome*, concepts that will recur throughout the remainder of the book.

Crises Defined by Quantitative Thresholds: Inflation, Currency Crashes, and Debasement

Inflation Crises

We begin by defining inflation crises, both because of their universality and long historical significance and because of the relative simplicity and clarity with which they can be identified. Because we are interested in cataloging the extent of default (through inflating debt away) and not only its frequency, we will attempt to mark not only the beginning of an inflation or currency crisis episode but its duration as well. Many high-inflation spells can best be described as chronic—lasting many years, sometimes dissipating and sometimes plateauing at an intermediate level before exploding. A number of studies, including our own earlier work on classifying post–World War II exchange rate arrangements, use a twelve-month inflation threshold of 40 percent or higher as the mark of a high-inflation episode. Of course, one can argue that the effects of inflation are pernicious at much lower levels of inflation, say 10 percent, but the costs of sustained moderate inflation are not well established either theoretically or empirically. In our earlier work on the post–World War II era, we chose a 40 percent cutoff

4

because there is a fairly broad consensus that such levels are pernicious; we discuss general inflation trends and lower peaks where significant. Hyperinflations—inflation rates of 40 percent *per month*—are of modern vintage. As we will see in chapter 12 on inflation crises (especially in table 12.3), Hungary in 1946 (Zimbabwe's recent experience notwithstanding) holds the record in our sample.

For the pre–World War I period, however, even 40 percent *per annum* is too high an inflation threshold, because inflation rates were much lower then, especially before the advent of modern paper currency (often referred to as "fiat" currency because it has no intrinsic value and is worth something only because the government declares by fiat that other currencies are not legal tender in domestic transactions). The median inflation rates before World War I were well below those of the more recent period: 0.5 percent per annum for 1500–1799 and 0.71 percent for 1800–1913, in contrast with 5.0 percent for 1914–2006. In periods with much lower average inflation rates and little expectation of high inflation, much lower inflation rates could be quite shocking and traumatic to an economy—and therefore considered crises.[1] Thus, in this book, in order to meaningfully incorporate earlier periods, we adopt an inflation crisis threshold of 20 percent per annum. At most of the main points at which we believe there were inflation crises, our main assertions appear to be reasonably robust relative to our choice of threshold; for example, our assertion that there was a crisis at any given point would stand up had we defined inflation crises using a lower threshold of, say, 15 percent, or a higher threshold of, say, 25 percent. Of course, given that we are making most of our data set available online, readers are free to set their own threshold for inflation or for other quantitative crisis benchmarks.

Currency Crashes

In order to date currency crashes, we follow a variant of an approach introduced by Jeffrey Frankel and Andrew Rose, who focus exclusively on large exchange rate depreciations and set their basic threshold (subject to some caveats) as 25 percent per annum.[2] This definition is the most parsimonious, for it does not rely on other variables such as reserve losses (data governments often guard jealously —sometimes long delaying their publication) and interest rate hikes (which are not terribly meaningful in financial systems under very heavy government control, which was in fact the case for most countries until relatively recently). As with inflation, the 25 percent threshold that one might apply to data from the period after World War II—at least to define a severe exchange rate crisis—would be too high for the earlier period, when much smaller movements constituted huge surprises and were therefore extremely disruptive. Therefore, we define as a currency crash an annual depreciation in excess of 15 percent. Mirroring our treatment of inflation episodes, we are concerned here not only with the dating of the initial crash (as in Frankel and Rose as well as Kaminsky and Reinhart) but with the full period in which annual depreciations exceeded the threshold.[3] It is hardly surprising that the largest crashes shown in table 1.1 are similar in timing and order of magnitude to the profile for inflation crises. The "honor" of the record currency crash, however, goes not to Hungary (as in the case of inflation) but to Greece in 1944.

Currency Debasement

The precursor of modern inflation and foreign exchange rate crises was currency debasement during the long era in which the principal means of exchange was metallic coins. Not surprisingly, debasements were particularly frequent and large during wars, when drastic reductions in the silver content of the currency sometimes provided sovereigns with their most important source of financing.

In this book we also date currency "reforms" or conversions and their magnitudes. Such conversions form a part of every hyperinflation episode in our sample; indeed it is not unusual to see that there were several conversions in quick succession. For example, in its struggle with hyperinflation, Brazil had no fewer than four currency conversions from 1986 to 1994. When we began to work on this book, in terms of the magnitude of a single conversion, the record holder was China, which in 1948 had a conversion rate of three million to one. Alas, by the time of its completion, that record was surpassed by

6

TABLE 1.1

Defining crises: A summary of quantitative thresholds

Crisis type	Threshold	Period	Maximum (percent)
Inflation	An annual inflation rate of 20 percent or higher. We examine separately the incidence of more extreme cases in which inflation exceeds 40 percent per annum.	1500–1790 1800–1913 1914–2008	173.1 159.6 9.63E+26[a]
Currency crash	An annual depreciation versus the U.S. dollar (or the relevant anchor currency— historically the U.K. pound, the French franc, or the German DM and presently the euro) of 15 percent or more.	1800–1913 1914–2008	275.7 3.37E+9
Currency debasement: Type I	A reduction in the metallic content of coins in circulation of 5 percent or more.	1258–1799 1800–1913	−56.8 −55.0
Currency debasement: Type II	A currency reform whereby a new currency replaces a much-depreciated earlier currency in circulation.	The most extreme episode is the recent Zimbabwean conversion at a rate of ten billion to one.	

[a]In some cases the inflation rates are so large (as in Hungary in 1946, for example) that we are forced to use scientific notation. Thus, E+26 means that we have to add zeroes and move the decimal point twenty-six places to the right in the 9.63 entry.

Zimbabwe with a ten-billion-to-one conversion! Conversions also follow spells of high (but not necessarily hyper) inflation, and these cases are also included in our list of modern debasements.

The Bursting of Asset Price Bubbles

The same quantitative methodology could be applied in dating the bursting of asset price bubbles (equity or real estate), which are commonplace in the run-up to banking crises. We discuss these crash episodes involving equity prices in chapter 16 and leave real estate crises for future research.[4] One reason we do not tackle the issue here is that price data for many key assets underlying financial crises, particularly housing prices, are extremely difficult to come by on a long-term cross-country basis. However, our data set does include housing prices for a number of both developed and emerging market countries over the past couple of decades, which we shall exploit later in our analysis of banking crises.

Crises Defined by Events: Banking Crises and External and Domestic Default

In this section we describe the criteria used in this study to date banking crises, external debt crises, and domestic debt crisis counterparts, the last of which are by far the least well documented and understood. Box 1.1 provides a brief glossary to the key concepts of debt used throughout our analysis.

Banking Crises

With regard to banking crises, our analysis stresses events. The main reason we use this approach has to do with the lack of long-range time series data that would allow us to date banking or financial crises quantitatively along the lines of inflation or currency crashes. For example, the relative price of bank stocks (or financial institutions relative to the market) would be a logical indicator to examine. However, doing this is problematic, particularly for the earlier part of our sample and for developing countries, where many domestic banks do not have publicly traded equity.

Another idea would be to use changes in bank deposits to date crises. In cases in which the beginning of a banking crisis has been marked by bank runs and withdrawals, this indicator would work well, for example in dating the numerous banking panics of the

---

BOX 1.1
Debt glossary

External debt   The total debt liabilities of a country with foreign creditors, both official (public) and private. Creditors often determine all the terms of the debt contracts, which are normally subject to the jurisdiction of the foreign creditors or to international law (for multilateral credits).

Total government debt (total public debt)   The total debt liabilities of a government with both domestic and foreign creditors. The "government" normally comprises the central administration, provincial governments, federal governments, and all other entities that borrow with an explicit government guarantee.

Government domestic debt   All debt liabilities of a government that are issued under and subject to national jurisdiction, regardless of the nationality of the creditor or the currency denomination of the debt; therefore, it includes government foreign-currency domestic debt, as defined below. The terms of the debt contracts can be determined by the market or set unilaterally by the government.

Government foreign-currency domestic debt   Debt liabilities of a government issued under national jurisdiction that are nonetheless expressed in (or linked to) a currency different from the national currency of the country.

Central bank debt   Not usually included under government debt, despite the fact that it usually carries an implicit government guarantee. Central banks usually issue such debt to facilitate open market operations (including sterilized intervention). Such debts may be denominated in either local or foreign currency.

1800s. Often, however, banking problems arise not from the liability side but from a protracted deterioration in asset quality, be it from a collapse in real estate prices (as in the United States at the outset of the 2007 subprime financial crisis) or from increased bankruptcies in the nonfinancial sector (as in later stages of the financial crisis of the late 2000s). In this case, a large increase in bankruptcies or nonperforming loans could be used to mark the onset of the crisis. Unfortunately, indicators of business failures and nonperforming loans are usually available sporadically, if at all, even for the modern period in many countries. In any event, reports of nonperforming loans are often wildly inaccurate, for banks try to hide their problems for as long as possible and supervisory agencies often look the other way.

Given these data limitations, we mark a banking crisis by two types of events: (1) bank runs that lead to the closure, merging, or takeover by the public sector of one or more financial institutions (as in Venezuela in 1993 or Argentina in 2001) and (2) if there are no runs, the closure, merging, takeover, or large-scale government assistance of an important financial institution (or group of institutions) that marks the start of a string of similar outcomes for other financial institutions (as in Thailand from 1996 to 1997). We rely on existing studies of banking crises and on the financial press. Financial stress is almost invariably extremely great during these periods.

There are several main sources for cross-country dating of crises. For the period after 1970, the comprehensive and well-known studies by Caprio and Klingebiel—the most updated version of which covers the period through 2003—are authoritative, especially in terms of classifying banking crises into systemic versus more benign categories. Kaminsky and Reinhart, and Jácome (the latter for Latin America), round out the sources.[5] In addition, we draw on many country-specific studies that pick up episodes of banking crisis not covered by the multicountry literature; these country-specific studies make an important contribution to this chronology.[6] A summary discussion of the limitations of this event-based dating approach is presented in table 1.2. The years in which the banking crises began are listed in appendixes A.3 and A.4 (for most early episodes it is difficult to ascertain exactly how long the crisis lasted).

External Debt Crises

External debt crises involve outright default on a government's external debt obligations—that is, a default on a payment to creditors of a loan issued under another country's jurisdiction, typically (but not always) denominated in a foreign currency, and typically held mostly by foreign creditors. Argentina holds the record for the largest default; in 2001 it defaulted on more than $95 billion in external

TABLE 1.2
Defining crises by events: A summary

Type of crisis	Definition and/or criteria	Comments
Banking crisis Type I: systemic (severe) Type II: financial distress (milder)	We mark a banking crisis by two types of events: (1) bank runs that lead to the closure, merging, or takeover by the public sector of one or more financial institutions and (2) if there are no runs, the closure, merging, takeover, or large-scale government assistance of an important financial institution (or group of institutions) that marks the start of a string of similar outcomes for other financial institutions.	This approach to dating the beginning of banking crises is not without drawbacks. It could date crises too late, because the financial problems usually begin well before a bank is finally closed or merged; it could also date crises too early, because the worst of a crisis may come later. Unlike in the case of external debt crises (see below), which have well-defined closure dates, it is often difficult or impossible to accurately pinpoint the year in which the crisis ended.
Debt crisis External	A sovereign default is defined as the failure of a government to meet a principal or interest payment on the due date (or within the specified grace period). These episodes include instances in which rescheduled debt is ultimately extinguished in terms less favorable than the original obligation.	Although the time of default is accurately classified as a crisis year, in a large number of cases the final resolution with the creditors (if it ever did take place) seems indeterminate. For this reason we also work with a crisis dummy that picks up only the first year.
Domestic	The definition given above for an external debt crisis applies. In addition, domestic debt crises have involved the freezing of bank deposits and/or forcible conversions of such deposits from dollars to local currency.	There is at best some partial documentation of recent defaults on domestic debt provided by Standard and Poor's. Historically, it is very difficult to date these episodes, and in many cases (such as those of banking crises) it is impossible to ascertain the date of the final resolution.

11

debt. In the case of Argentina, the default was managed by reducing and stretching out interest payments. Sometimes countries repudiate the debt outright, as in the case of Mexico in 1867, when more than $100 million worth of peso debt issued by Emperor Maximilian was repudiated by the Juarez government. More typically, though, the government restructures debt on terms less favorable to the lender than were those in the original contract (for instance, India's little-known external restructurings in 1958–1972).

External defaults have received considerable attention in the academic literature from leading modern-day economic historians, such as Michael Bordo, Barry Eichengreen, Marc Flandreau, Peter Lindert, John Morton, and Alan Taylor.[7] Relative to early banking crises (not to mention domestic debt crises, which have been all but ignored in the literature), much is known about the causes and consequences of these rather dramatic episodes. The dates of sovereign defaults and restructurings are those listed and discussed in chapter 6. For the period after 1824, the majority of dates come from several Standard and Poor's studies listed in the data appendixes. However, these are incomplete, missing numerous postwar restructurings and early defaults, so this source has been supplemented with additional information.[8]

Although external default dates are, by and large, clearly defined and far less contentious than, say, the dates of banking crises (for which the end is often unclear), some judgment calls are still required, as we discuss in chapter 8. For example, in cataloging the number of times a country has defaulted, we generally categorize any default that occurs two years or less after a previous default as part of the same episode. Finding the end date for sovereign external defaults, although easier than in the case of banking crises (because a formal agreement with creditors often marks the termination), still presents a number of issues.

Although the time of default is accurately classified as a crisis year, in a large number of cases the final resolution with the creditors (if it ever was achieved) seems interminable. Russia's 1918 default following the revolution holds the record, lasting sixty-nine years. Greece's default in 1826 shut it out of international capital markets for fifty-three consecutive years, and Honduras's 1873 default had a comparable duration.[9] Of course, looking at the full default episode is useful for characterizing borrowing or default cycles, calculating "hazard" rates, and so on. But it is hardly credible that a spell of fifty-three years could be considered a crisis—even if those years were not exactly prosperous. Thus, in addition to constructing the country-specific dummy variables to cover the entire episode, we have employed two other qualitative variables aimed at encompassing the core crisis period surrounding the default. The first of these records only the year of default as a crisis, while the second creates a seven-year window centered on the default date. The rationale is that neither the three years that precede a default nor the three years that follow it can be considered a "normal" or "tranquil" period. This technique allows analysis of the behavior of various economic and financial indicators around the crisis on a consistent basis over time and across countries.

Domestic Debt Crises

Domestic public debt is issued under a country's own legal jurisdiction. In most countries, over most of their history, domestic debt has been denominated in the local currency and held mainly by residents. By the same token, the overwhelming majority of external public debt—debt under the legal jurisdiction of foreign governments—has been denominated in foreign currency and held by foreign residents.

Information on domestic debt crises is scarce, but not because these crises do not take place. Indeed, as we illustrate in chapter 9, domestic debt crises typically occur against a backdrop of much worse economic conditions than the average external default. Usually, however, domestic debt crises do not involve powerful external creditors. Perhaps this may help explain why so many episodes go unnoticed in the mainstream business and financial press and why studies of such crises are underrepresented in the academic literature. Of course, this is not always the case. Mexico's much-publicized near-default in 1994–1995 certainly qualifies as a "famous" domestic default crisis, although not many observers may realize that the bulk of the problem debt was technically domestic and not external. In fact, the government debt (in the form of *tesobonos*, mostly short-term debt instruments repayable in pesos linked to the U.S. dollar), which was on the verge of default until the country was bailed out by the International Monetary Fund and the U.S. Treasury, was issued under domestic Mexican law and therefore was part of Mexico's domestic debt. One can only speculate that if the *tesobonos* had not been so widely held by nonresidents, perhaps this crisis would have received far less attention. Since 1980, Argentina has defaulted three times on its domestic debt. The two domestic debt defaults that coincided with defaults on external debt (1982 and 2001) attracted considerable international attention. However, the large-scale 1989 default that did not involve a new default on external debt—and therefore did not involve nonresidents—is scarcely known in the literature. The many defaults on domestic debt that occurred during the Great Depression of the 1930s in both advanced economies and developing ones are not terribly well documented. Even where domestic defaults are documented in official volumes on debt, it is often only footnotes that refer to arrears or suspensions of payments.

Finally, some of the domestic defaults that involved the forcible conversion of foreign currency deposits into local currency have occurred during banking crises, hyperinflations, or a combination of the two (defaults in Argentina, Bolivia, and Peru are in this list). Our approach to constructing categorical variables follows that previously described for external debt default. Like banking crises and unlike external debt defaults, for many episodes of domestic default the endpoint for the crisis is not easily established.

Other Key Concepts

Serial Default

Serial default refers to multiple sovereign defaults on external or domestic public (or publicly guaranteed) debt, or both. These defaults may occur five or fifty years apart, and they can range from wholesale default (or repudiation) to partial default through rescheduling (usually stretching interest payments out at more favorable terms for the debtor). As we discuss in chapter 4, wholesale default is actually quite rare, although it may be decades before creditors receive any type of partial repayment.

The This-Time-Is-Different Syndrome

The essence of the this-time-is-different syndrome is simple.[10] It is rooted in the firmly held belief that financial crises are things that happen to other people in other countries at other times; crises do not happen to us, here and now. We are doing things better, we are smarter, we have learned from past mistakes. The old rules of valuation no longer apply. The current boom, unlike the many booms that preceded catastrophic collapses in the past (even in our country), is built on sound fundamentals, structural reforms, technological innovation, and good policy. Or so the story goes.

In the preamble we have already provided a theoretical rationale for the this-time-is-different syndrome based on the fragility of highly leveraged economies, in particular their vulnerability to crises of confidence. Certainly historical examples of the this-time-is-different syndrome are plentiful. It is not our intention to provide a catalog of these, but examples are sprinkled throughout the book. For example, box 1.2 exhibits a 1929 advertisement that embodies the spirit of "this time is different" in the run-up to the Great Depression, and box 6.2 explores the Latin American lending boom of the 1820s, which marked the first debt crisis for that region.

A short list of the manifestations of the syndrome over the past century is as follows:

1. The buildup to the emerging market defaults of the 1930s

Why was this time different?   *The thinking at the time: There will never again be another world war; greater political stability and strong global growth will be sustained indefinitely; and debt burdens in developing countries are low.*

15

BOX 1.2
The this-time-is-different syndrome on the eve of the Crash of 1929

FAMOUS WRONG GUESSES
IN HISTORY
when all Europe guessed wrong

The date—October 3rd, 1719. The scene—*Hotel de Nevers*, Paris. A wild mob—fighting to be heard. "Fifty shares!" "I'll take two hundred!" "Five hundred!" "A thousand here!" "Ten thousand!" Shrill cries of women. Hoarse shouts of men. Speculators all—exchanging their gold and jewels or a lifetime's meager savings for magic shares in John Law's Mississippi Company. Shares that were to make them rich overnight.

Then the bubble burst. Down—down went the shares. Facing utter ruin, the frenzied populace tried to "sell". Panic-stricken mobs stormed the *Banque Royale*. No use! The bank's coffers were empty. John Law had fled. The great Mississippi Company and its promise of wealth had become but a wretched memory.

Today you need not guess.

HISTORY sometimes repeats itself—but not invariably. In 1719 there was practically no way of finding out the *facts* about the Mississippi venture. How different the position of the investor in 1929!

Today, it is inexcusable to buy a "bubble" —inexcusable because unnecessary. For now every investor—whether his capital consists of a few thousands or mounts into the millions —has at his disposal facilities for obtaining the *facts*. Facts which—as far as is humanly possible—eliminate the hazards of speculation and substitute in their place sound principles of investment.

STANDARD STATISTICS
200 VARICK ST.
New York, New York (now the home of Chipotle Mexican Grill)

Saturday Evening Post, September 14, 1929

Note: This advertisement was kindly sent to the authors by Professor Peter Lindert.

The major combatant countries in World War I had built up enormous debts. Regions such as Latin America and Asia, which had escaped the worst ravages of the war, appeared to have very modest and manageable public finances. The 1920s were a period of relentless global optimism, not dissimilar to the five-year boom that preceded the worldwide financial crisis that began in the United States in mid-2007. Just as global peace was an important component of the 2000s dynamic, so was the widely held view that the experience of World War I would not soon be repeated.

In 1929, a global stock market crash marked the onset of the Great Depression. Economic contraction slashed government resources as global deflation pushed up interest rates in real terms. What followed was the largest wave of defaults in history.

2. The debt crisis of the 1980s

Why was this time different?

The thinking at the time: Commodity prices are strong, interest rates are low, oil money is being "recycled," there are skilled technocrats in government, money is being used for high-return infrastructure investments, and bank loans are being made instead of bond loans, as in the interwar period of the 1920s and 1930s. With individual banks taking up large blocks of loans, there will be incentive for information gathering and monitoring to ensure the monies are well spent and the loans repaid.

After years of secular decline, the world experienced a boom in commodity prices in the 1970s; commodity-rich Latin America seemed destined to reap enormous profits as world growth powered higher and higher prices for scarce material resources. Global inflation in the developed world had led to a long period of anomalously low real interest rates in rich countries' bond markets. And last but not least, there had been essentially no new defaults in Latin America for almost a generation; the last surge had occurred during the Great Depression.

Many officials and policy economists spoke very approvingly of the loans from Western banks to developing countries. The banks were said to be performing an important intermediation service by taking oil surpluses from the Organization of Petroleum Exporting Countries and "recycling" them to developing countries. Western banks came into the loop because they supposedly had the lending and monitoring expertise necessary to lend en masse to Latin America and elsewhere, reaping handsome markups for their efforts.

17

The 1970s buildup, like so many before it, ended in tears. Steeply higher real interest rates combined with a collapse of global commodity prices catalyzed Mexico's default in August 1983, and shortly thereafter the defaults of well over a dozen other major emerging markets, including Argentina, Brazil, Nigeria, the Philippines, and Turkey. When the rich countries moved to tame inflation in the early 1980s, steep interest rate hikes by the central banks hugely raised the carrying costs of loans to developing countries, which were typically indexed to short-term rates (why that should be the case is an issue we address in the chapter on the theory of sovereign debt). With the collapse of global demand, commodity prices collapsed as well, falling by 70 percent or more from their peak in some cases.

3. The debt crisis of the 1990s in Asia

Why was this time different?   *The thinking at the time: The region has a conservative fiscal policy, stable exchange rates, high rates of growth and saving, and no remembered history of financial crises.*

Asia was the darling of foreign capital during the mid-1990s. Across the region, (1) households had exceptionally high savings rates that the governments could rely on in the event of financial stress, (2) governments had relatively strong fiscal positions so that most borrowing was private, (3) currencies were quasi-pegged to the dollar, making investments safe, and (4) it was thought that Asian countries never have financial crises.

In the end, even a fast-growing country with sound fiscal policy is not invulnerable to shocks. One huge weakness was Asia's exchange rate pegs against the dollar, which were often implicit rather than explicit.[11] These pegs left the region extremely vulnerable to a crisis of confidence. And, starting in the summer of 1997, that is precisely what happened. Governments such as Thailand's ultimately suffered huge losses on foreign exchange intervention when doomed efforts to prop up the currency failed.[12] Korea, Indonesia, and Thailand among others were forced to go to the International Monetary

Fund for gigantic bailout packages, but this was not enough to stave off deep recessions and huge currency depreciations.

4. The debt crisis of the 1990s and early 2000s in Latin America

Why was this time different?   *The thinking at the time: The debts are bond debts, not bank debts. (Note how the pendulum swings between the belief that bond debt is safer and the belief that bank debt is safer.) With orders of magnitude more debt holders in the case of bonds than in the case of international banks, countries will be much more hesitant to try to default because renegotiation would be so difficult (see instance 2 earlier).*

During the early 1990s, international creditors poured funds into a Latin American region that had only just emerged from a decade of default and stagnation. The credit had been channeled mainly through bonds rather than banks, leading some to conclude that the debts would be invulnerable to renegotiation. By spreading debt claims out across a wide sea of bond holders, it was claimed, there could be no repeat of the 1980s, in which debtor countries had successfully forced banks to reschedule (stretch out and effectively reduce) debt repayments. Absent the possibility of renegotiation, it would be much harder to default.

Other factors were also at work, lulling investors. Many Latin American countries had changed from dictatorships to democracies, "assuring greater stability." Mexico was not a risk because of the North American Free Trade Agreement, which came into force in January 1994. Argentina was not a risk, because it had "immutably" fixed its exchange rate to the dollar through a currency board arrangement.

Eventually, the lending boom of the 1990s ended in a series of financial crises, starting with Mexico's December 1994 collapse. What followed included Argentina's $95 billion default, the largest in history at that time; Brazil's financial crises in 1998 and 2002; and Uruguay's default in 2002.

5. The United States in the run-up to the financial crisis of the late 2000s (the Second Great Contraction)

Why was this time different?

The thinking at the time: Everything is fine because of globalization, the technology boom, our superior financial system, our better understanding of monetary policy, and the phenomenon of securitized debt.

Housing prices doubled and equity prices soared, all fueled by record borrowing from abroad. But most people thought the United States could never have a financial crisis resembling that of an emerging market.

The final chapters of this book chronicle the sorry tale of what unfolded next, the most severe financial crisis since the Great Depression and the only one since World War II that has been global in scope. In the intervening chapters we will show that the serial nature of financial crises is endemic across much of the spectrum of time and regions. Periods of prosperity (many of them long) often end in tears.

- 2 -

DEBT INTOLERANCE:
THE GENESIS OF SERIAL DEFAULT

Debt intolerance is a syndrome in which weak institutional structures and a problematic political system make external borrowing a tempting device for governments to employ to avoid hard decisions about spending and taxing.

This chapter lays out a statistical framework for thinking about serial default in terms of some countries' inability to resist recurrent exposure to debt default relapses. The reader wishing to avoid the modest amount of technical discussion in the next two chapters can readily skip ahead to the chapter on external default without any important loss of continuity.

Debt intolerance is defined as the extreme duress many emerging markets experience at external debt levels that would seem quite manageable by the standards of advanced countries. The duress typically involves a vicious cycle of loss in market confidence, spiraling interest rates on external government debt, and political resistance to repaying foreign creditors. Ultimately, default often occurs at levels of debt well below the 60 percent ratio of debt to GDP enshrined in Europe's Maastricht Treaty, a clause intended to protect the euro system from government defaults. Safe debt thresholds turn out to depend heavily on a country's record of default and inflation.[1]

Debt Thresholds

This chapter constitutes a first pass at understanding why a country might be vulnerable to recurrent default, then proceeds to form a quantitative measure of vulnerability to marginal rises in debt, or "debt intolerance."

Few macroeconomists would be surprised to learn that emerging market countries with overall ratios of public debt to GNP above, say, 100 percent run a significant risk of default. Even among advanced countries, Japan's debt of about 170 percent of its GNP (depending on the debt definition used) is considered problematic (Japan holds massive foreign exchange reserves, but even its net level of debt of about 94 percent of GNP is still very high).[2] Yet emerging market default can and does occur at ratios of external debt to GNP that are far lower than these, as some well-known cases of external debt default illustrate (e.g., Mexico in 1982, with a ratio of debt to GNP of 47 percent, and Argentina in 2001, with a ratio of debt to GNP slightly above 50 percent).

Our investigation of the debt thresholds of emerging market countries begins by chronicling all episodes of default or restructuring of external debt for middle-income countries for the years 1970–2008, where default is defined along the lines described in chapter 1 on definitions of default.[3] This is only our first pass at listing sovereign default dates. Later we will look at a far broader range of countries across a far more sweeping time span. Table 2.1 records the external debt default dates. For each middle-income country, the table lists the first year of the default or restructuring episode and the ratios of external debt to GNP and external debt to exports at the end of the year of the credit event, that is, when the technical default began.[4] Obviously the aforementioned defaults of Mexico in 1982 and Argentina in 2001 were not exceptions, nor was the most recent default, that of Ecuador in 2008. Table 2.2, which is derived from table 2.1, shows that external debt exceeded 100 percent of GNP in only 16 percent of the default or restructuring episodes, that more than half of all defaults occurred at levels below 60 percent, and that there were defaults against debt levels that were below 40 percent of GNP in nearly 20 percent of the cases.[5] (Arguably, the thresholds of external debt to GNP reported in table 2.1 are biased upward because the ratios of debt to GNP corresponding to the years of the credit events are driven up by the real depreciation in the ex-

TABLE 2.1

External debt at the time of default: Middle-income countries, 1970–2008

	Year of default or restructuring	Ratio of external debt to GNP at the end of the year of default or restructuring	Ratio of external debt to exports at the end of the year of default or restructuring
Albania	1990	16.6	98.6
Argentina	1982	55.1	447.3
	2001	50.8	368.1
Bolivia	1980	92.5	246.4
Brazil	1983	50.1	393.6
Bulgaria	1990	57.1	154.0
Chile	1972	31.1	n.a.
	1983	96.4	358.6
Costa Rica	1981	136.9	267.0
Dominican Republic	1982	31.8	183.4
Ecuador	1984	68.2	271.5
	2000	106.1	181.5
	2008	20.0	81.0
Egypt	1984	112.0	304.6
Guyana	1982	214.3	337.7
Honduras	1981	61.5	182.8
Iran	1992	41.8	77.7
Iraq	1990	n.a.	n.a.
Jamaica	1978	48.5	103.9
Jordan	1989	179.5	234.2
Mexico	1982	46.7	279.3
Morocco	1983	87.0	305.6
Panama	1983	88.1	162.0
Peru	1978	80.9	388.5
	1984	62.0	288.9
Philippines	1983	70.6	278.1
Poland	1981	n.a.	108.1
Romania	1982	n.a.	73.1
Russian Federation	1991	12.5	n.a.
	1998	58.5	109.8
South Africa	1985	n.a.	n.a.
Trinidad and Tobago	1989	49.4	103.6
Turkey	1978	21.0	374.2
Uruguay	1983	63.7	204.0
Venezuela	1982	41.4	159.8
Yugoslavia	1983	n.a.	n.a.
Average		69.3	229.9

Sources: Reinhart, Rogoff, and Savastano (2003a), updated based on World Bank (various years), *Global Development Finance*.

Notes: Income groups are defined according to World Bank (various years), *Global Development Finance*. n.a., not available. Debt stocks are reported at end of period. Hence, taking the ratio of debt to GNP at the end of the default year biases ratios *upward*, because in most cases defaults are accompanied by a sizable depreciation in the real exchange rate.

TABLE 2.2
External debt at the time of default: Frequency distribution, 1970–2008

Range of ratios of external debt to to GNP at the end of the first year of default or restructuring (percent)	Percentage of total defaults or restructurings in middle-income countries
< 40	19.4
41–60	32.3
61–80	16.1
81–100	16.1
>100	16.1

Sources: Table 2.1 and authors' calculations.

Notes: Income groups are defined according to World Bank (various years), *Global Development Finance*. These shares are based on the cases for which we have data on the ratios of debt to GNP. All cases marked "n.a." in Table 2.1 are excluded from the calculations.

change rate that typically accompanies such events as locals and foreign investors flee the currency.

We next compare profiles of the external indebtedness of emerging market countries with and without a history of defaults. Figure 2.1 shows the frequency distribution of external debt to GNP for the two groups of countries over 1970–2008. The two distributions are very distinct and show that defaulters borrow more than nondefaulters (even though their ratings tend to be worse at equal levels of debt). The gap between external debt ratios in emerging market countries with and without a history of default widens further when ratios of external debt to exports are considered. It appears that those that risk default the most when they borrow (i.e., those that have the highest debt intolerance levels) borrow the most, especially when measured in terms of exports, their largest source of foreign exchange. It should be no surprise, then, that so many capital flow cycles end in an ugly credit event. Of course, it takes two to tango, and creditors must be complicit in the this-time-is-different syndrome.

We can use these frequency distributions to ask whether there is a threshold of external debt to GNP for emerging economies beyond which the risk of experiencing extreme symptoms of debt intolerance rises sharply. (But this will be only a first step because, as we

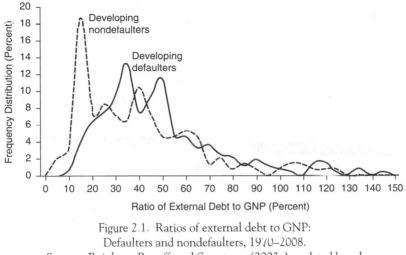

Figure 2.1. Ratios of external debt to GNP:
Defaulters and nondefaulters, 1970–2008.
Sources: Reinhart, Rogoff, and Savastano (2003a), updated based
on International Monetary Fund, *World Economic Outlook*, and
World Bank (various years), *Global Development Finance*.

shall see, differing levels of debt intolerance imply very different
thresholds for various individual countries.) In particular, we highlight that countries' repayment and inflation histories matter significantly; the worse the history, the less the capacity to tolerate debt.
Over half of the observations for countries with a sound credit history
are at levels of external debt to GNP below 35 percent (47 percent of
the observations are below 30 percent). By contrast, for those countries with a relatively tarnished credit history, levels of external debt
to GNP above 40 percent are required to capture the majority of observations. Already from tables 2.1 and 2.2, and without taking into
account country-specific debt intolerance factors, we can see that
when the external debt levels of emerging markets are above 30–35
percent of GNP, risks of a credit event start to increase significantly.[6]

Measuring Vulnerability

To operationalize the concept of debt intolerance—to find a way to
quantitatively measure a country's fragility as a foreign borrower—

we focus on two indicators: the sovereign ratings reported by *Institutional Investor* and the ratio of external debt to GNP (or of external debt to exports).

The *Institutional Investor* ratings (IIR), which are compiled twice a year, are based on survey information provided by economists and sovereign risk analysts at leading global banks and securities firms. The ratings grade each country on a scale from zero to 100, with a rating of 100 given to countries perceived as having the lowest likelihood of defaulting on their government debt obligations.[7] Hence, one may construct the variable 100 minus IIR as a proxy for default risk. Unfortunately, market-based measures of default risk (say, based on prices at which a country's debt trades on secondary markets) are available only for a much smaller range of countries and over a much shorter sample period.[8]

The second major component of our measure of a country's vulnerability to lapse or relapse into external debt default consists of total external debt, scaled alternatively by GNP and exports. Our emphasis on total external debt (public plus private) in this effort to identify a sustainable debt is due to the fact that historically much of the government debt in emerging markets was external, and the small part of external debt that was private before a crisis often became public after the fact.[9] (Later, in chapter 8, we will extend our analysis to incorporate domestic debt, which has become particularly important in the latest crisis given the large stock of domestic public debt issued by the governments of many emerging markets in the early 2000s prior to the crisis.) Data on domestic private debt remain elusive.

Table 2.3, which shows the panel pairwise correlations between the two debt ratios and the *Institutional Investor* measures of risk for a large sample of developing economies, also highlights the fact that the different measures of risk present a very similar picture of different countries' relative rankings and of the correlation between risk and debt. As expected, the correlations are uniformly positive in all regional groupings of countries, and in most instances they are statistically significant.

TABLE 2.3

Risk and debt: Panel pairwise correlations, 1979–2007

	100 − *Institutional Investor* ratings (IIR)
Correlations with ratio of external debt to GDP	
Full sample of developing countries	0.45*
Africa	0.33*
Emerging Asia	0.54*
Middle East	0.14
Western Hemisphere	0.45*
Correlations with ratio of external debt to exports	
Full sample of developing countries	0.63*
Africa	0.56*
Emerging Asia	0.70*
Middle East	0.48*
Western Hemisphere	0.47*

Sources: Reinhart, Rogoff, and Savastano (2003a), updated based on World Bank (various years), *Global Development Finance,* and *Institutional Investor.*

Note: An asterisk (*) denotes that the correlation is statistically significant at the 95 percent confidence level.

Clubs and Regions

We next use the components of debt intolerance (IIR and external debt ratios) in a two-step algorithm mapped in figure 2.2 to define creditors' "clubs" and regions of vulnerability. We begin by calculating the mean (47.6) and standard deviation (25.9) of the ratings for 90 countries for which *Institutional Investor* published data over 1979–2007, then use these metrics to loosely group countries into three clubs. Those countries that over the period 1979–2007 had an average IIR at or above 73.5 (the mean plus one standard deviation) form club A, a club that comprises countries that enjoy virtually continuous access to capital markets—that is, all advanced economies. As their repayment history shows (see chapter 8), these countries are the least debt intolerant. The club at the opposite extreme, club C, is comprised of those countries whose average IIR is below 21.7 (the mean minus one standard deviation).[10] This "cut-off" club includes countries whose primary sources of external financing are grants and official loans; countries in this club are so debt intolerant that markets only sporadically give them opportunities to borrow. The remaining countries are in club B, the main focus of our analysis, and exhibit varying degrees of vulnerability due to debt intolerance. These countries occupy the "indeterminate" region of theoretical debt models, the region in which default risk is nontrivial and where self-fulfilling runs are a possible trigger to a crisis. (We will return many times to the theme of how both countries and banks can be vulnerable to loss of creditor confidence, particularly when they depend on short-term finance through loans or deposits.) Club B is large and includes both countries that are on the cusp of "graduation" and those that may be on the brink of default. For this intermediate group of countries—whose debt intolerance is not so high that they are simply shut out of debt markets—the degree of leverage obviously affects their risk.

Hence, in our second step we use our algorithm to further subdivide the indeterminate club B into four groups ranging from the least to the most vulnerable to symptoms of debt intolerance. The least vulnerable group includes the (type I) countries with a 1979–2007 average IIR above the mean (47.6) but below 73.5 and a ratio of external debt to GNP below 35 percent (a threshold that, as we have discussed, accounts for more than half the observations of nondefaulters over 1970–2008). The next group includes (type II) countries with an IIR above the mean but a ratio of external debt to GNP that is above 35 percent. This is the second least vulnerable group, that is, the group second least likely to lapse into an external debt crisis. The group that follows encompasses (type III) countries with an IIR below the mean but above 21.7 and an external debt below 35 percent of GNP. Finally, the most debt-intolerant group—the group most vulnerable to an external debt crisis—is comprised of those (type IV) countries with an IIR below the mean and external debt levels above 35 percent of GNP. Countries in the type IV group can easily get bounced into the no-access club. For example, in early 2000 Argentina's IIR was about 44 and its ratio of external debt to

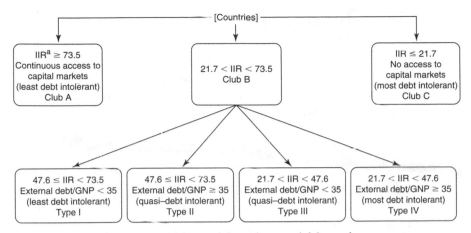

Figure 2.2. Definition of debtors' clubs and external debt intolerance regions.
[a]IIR, average long-term value for *Institutional Investor* ratings.

GNP was 51 percent, making it a type IV country. But by 2003 Argentina's rating had dropped to about 15, indicating that the country had "reverse-graduated" to club C. As we shall see (chapter 17), countries do not graduate to higher clubs easily; indeed, it can take many decades of impeccable repayment and sustained low debt levels to graduate from club B to club A. Falling from grace (moving to a more debt-intolerant range) is not a new phenomenon. It remains to be seen whether after the latest crisis club A loses some members.

The simple point underlying these definitions and groupings is that countries with a history of institutional weakness leading to recurrent default (as reflected in low IIR ratings) tend to be at high risk of experiencing "symptoms" of debt intolerance even at relatively low levels of debt. But both the "patient's" vulnerability to debt and the dose of debt are relevant to the risk of symptoms (default).

Reflections on Debt Intolerance

The sad fact related in our work is that once a country slips into being a serial defaulter, it retains a high and persistent level of debt intolerance. Countries can and do graduate, but the process is seldom fast or easy. Absent the pull of an outside political anchor (e.g., the European Union for countries like Greece and Portugal), recovery may take decades or even centuries. As of this writing, even the commitment device of an outside political anchor must be regarded as a promising experimental treatment in overcoming debt intolerance, not a definitive cure.

The implications of debt intolerance are certainly sobering for sustainability exercises that aim to see if, under reasonable assumptions about growth and world interest rates, a country can be expected to shoulder its external debt burdens. Such sustainability exercises are common, for example, in calculating how much debt reduction a problem debtor country needs to be able to meet its obligations on its remaining debt. Failure to take debt intolerance into account tends to lead to an underestimation of how easily unexpected shocks can lead to a loss of market confidence—or of the will to repay—and therefore to another debt collapse.

Is debt intolerance something a country can eventually surmount? Or is a country with weak internal structures that make it intolerant to debt doomed to follow a trajectory of lower growth and higher macroeconomic volatility? At some level, the answer to the second question has to be yes, but constrained access to international capital markets is best viewed as a symptom, not a cause, of the disease.

The institutional failings that make a country intolerant to debt pose the real impediment. The basic problem is threefold.

- First, the modern literature on empirical growth increasingly points to "soft" factors such as institutions, corruption, and governance as far more important than differences in ratios of capital to labor in explaining cross-country differences in per capita incomes.
- Second, quantitative methods suggest that the risk-sharing benefits to capital market integration may also be relatively modest. (By "capital market integration" we mean the de facto and de jure integration of a country's financial markets with the rest of the world. By "risk-sharing benefits" we mean benefits in terms of lower consumption volatility.) And these results pertain to an ide-

alized world in which one does not have to worry about gratuitous policy-induced macroeconomic instability, poor domestic bank regulation, corruption, or (not least) policies that distort capital inflows toward short-term debt.[11]

- Third, there is evidence to suggest that capital flows to emerging markets are markedly procyclical (that is, they are higher when the economy is booming and lower when the economy is in recession). Procyclical capital inflows may, in turn, reinforce the tendency in these countries for macroeconomic policies to be procyclical as well. The fact that capital inflows collapse in a recession is perhaps the principal reason that emerging markets, in contrast to rich countries, are often forced to tighten both fiscal policy and monetary policy in a recession, exacerbating the downturn.[12] Arguably, having limited but stable access to capital markets may be welfare improving relative to the boom-bust pattern we so often observe. So the deeply entrenched idea that the growth trajectory of an emerging market economy will be hampered by limited access to debt markets is no longer as compelling as was once thought.

The aforementioned academic literature does not actually paint sharp distinctions between different types of capital flows—for instance, debt, equity, and foreign direct investment (FDI)—or between long-term versus short-term debt. Practical policy makers, of course, are justifiably quite concerned with the exact form that cross-border flows take, with FDI generally thought to have properties preferable to those of debt (FDI tends to be less volatile and to spin off indirect benefits such as technology transfer).[13] We generally share the view that FDI and equity investment are somewhat less problematic than debt, but one wants to avoid overstating the case. In practice, the three types of capital inflows are often interlinked (e.g., foreign firms will often bring cash into a country in advance of actually making plant acquisitions). Moreover, derivative contracts can blur the three categories. Even the most diligent statistical authority may find it difficult to accurately separate different types of foreign capital inflows (not to mention the fact that, when in doubt, some countries prefer to label a particular investment FDI to make their vulnerabilities seem lower). Given these qualifications, however, we still believe that the governments of advanced countries can do more to discourage excessive dependence on risky nonindexed debt relative to other forms of capital flows.[14] Finally, it should be noted that short-term debt—typically identified as the most problematic in terms of precipitating debt crises—facilitates trade in goods and is necessary in some measure to allow private agents to execute hedging strategies. Of course, one can plausibly argue that most of the benefits of having access to capital markets could be enjoyed with relatively modest ratios of debt to GNP.

All in all, debt intolerance need not be fatal to growth and macroeconomic stability, but it is still a serious impediment. However, the evidence on serial default presented in this book suggests that to overcome debt intolerance, policy makers need to be prepared to keep debt levels low for extended periods of time while undertaking more basic structural reforms to ensure that countries can eventually digest higher debt burdens without experiencing intolerance. This applies not only to external debt but also to the reemerging problem of domestic government debt. Policy makers who face tremendous short-term pressures will still choose to engage in high-risk borrowing, and for the right price, markets will let them. But understanding the basic problem should at least guide a country's citizens, not to mention international lending institutions and the broader international community, in making their own decisions.

In our view, developing a better understanding of the problem of serial default on external debt obligations is essential to designing better domestic and international economic policies with regard to crisis prevention and resolution. Although further research is needed, we believe a good case can be made that debt intolerance can be captured systematically by a relatively small number of variables, principally a country's own history of default and high inflation. Debt-intolerant countries face surprisingly low thresholds for external borrowing, beyond which risks of default or restructuring become significant. With the explosion of domestic borrowing that occurred at the turn of the twenty-first century, on which we present new data in this book, the thresholds for external debt almost certainly fell even from the low levels of a decade earlier, as we shall discuss in chapter 11. Our initial results suggest that the same factors that determine external debt intolerance, not to mention other manifestations of debt intolerance such as domestic dollarization (de facto or de jure substitution of a foreign currency for transactions or indexation of financial instruments), are also likely to impinge heavily on domestic debt intolerance.

Finally, whereas debt-intolerant countries need badly to find ways to bring their ratios of debt to GNP to safer ground, doing so is not easy. Historically, the cases in which countries have escaped high ratios of external debt to GNP, via either rapid growth or sizable and prolonged repayments, have been very much the exception.[15] Most large reductions in external debt among emerging markets have been achieved via restructuring or default. Failure to recognize the difficulty in escaping a situation of high debt intolerance simply through growth and gently falling ratios of debt to GNP is one of the central errors underlying many standard calculations employed both by the private sector and by official analysts during debt crises.

At the time of this writing, many emerging markets are implementing fiscal stimulus packages that mirror efforts in the advanced economies in order to jump-start their economies. Our analysis suggests that in the "shadow of debt intolerance" such measures must be viewed with caution, for widening deficits leave countries uncomfortably close to debt thresholds that have been associated with severe debt-servicing difficulties. Going forward, after the global financial crisis of the late 2000s subsides, a challenge will be to find ways to channel capital to debt-intolerant countries in nondebt form to prevent the cycle from repeating itself for another century to come.

- 3 -

A GLOBAL DATABASE
ON FINANCIAL CRISES
WITH A LONG-TERM VIEW

One would think that with at least 250 sovereign external default episodes during 1800–2009 and at least 68 cases of default on domestic public debt, it would be relatively straightforward to find a comprehensive long-range time series on public sector debt. Yet this is not the case; far from it. Government debt is among the most elusive of economic time series.

Having defined crises and taken a first pass at analyzing vulnerability to serial default, we now turn to the core of the book, the data set. It is this lode of information that we mine in various ways to explain events. This chapter presents a broad-brush description of the comprehensive database used in this study and evaluates its main sources, strengths, and limitations. Further documentation on the coverage and numerous sources of individual time series by country and by period is provided in appendixes A.1 and A.2. Those are devoted, respectively, to the macroeconomic time series used and the public debt data (which together form the centerpiece of our analysis).

This chapter is organized as follows. The first section describes the compilation of the family of time series that are brought together from different major and usually well-known sources. These series include prices, modern exchange rates (and earlier metal-based ones), real GDP, and exports. For the recent period, the data are primarily found in standard large-scale databases. For earlier history we relied on individual scholars or groups of scholars.[1] Next we describe the data that are more heterogeneous in both their sources and their methodologies. These are series on government finances and individual efforts to construct national accounts—notably nominal and real GDP, particularly before 1900. The remaining two sections are devoted to describing the particulars of building a cross-country, multicentury database on public debt and its characteristics, as well as the various manifestations and measurements of economic crises. Those include domestic and external debt defaults, inflation and banking crises, and currency crashes and debasements. Constructing the database on public domestic and external debt can best be described as having been more akin to archaeology than to economics. The compilation of crisis episodes has encompassed the use of both mechanical rules of thumb to date a crisis as well as arbitrary judgment calls on the interpretation of historical events as described by the financial press and scholars in the references on which we have drawn, which span more than three centuries.

Prices, Exchange Rates, Currency Debasement, and Real GDP

Prices

Our overarching ambition in this analysis is to document the incidence and magnitude of various forms of expropriation or default through the ages. No such study would be complete without taking stock of expropriation through inflation. Following the rise of fiat (paper) currency, inflation became the modern-day version of currency "debasement," the systematic degradation of metallic coins that was a favored method of monarchs for seizing resources before the development of the printing press. To measure inflation, we generally rely on consumer price indexes or their close relative, cost-of-living indexes. For the modern period, our data sources are primarily the standard databases of the International Monetary Fund: *International Financial Statistics* (IFS) and *World Economic Outlook* (WEO). For pre–World War II coverage (usually from early 1900s or late 1800s), *Global Financial Data* (GFD), several studies by Williamson,[2] and the Oxford Latin American Economic History Database (OXLAD) are key sources.[3]

For earlier periods in the eight centuries spanned by our analysis, we rely on the meticulous work of a number of economic historians who have constructed such price indexes item by item, most often by city rather than by country, from primary sources. In this regard, the scholars participating in the Global Price and Income History Group project at the University of California–Davis and their counterparts at the Dutch International Institute of Social History have been an invaluable source of prices in Asia and Europe.[4] Again, the complete references by author to this body of scholarly work are given in the data appendixes and in the references. For colonial America, *Historical Statistics of the United States* (HSOUS, recently updated) provides the U.S. data, while Richard Garner's Economic History Data Desk: Economic History of Latin America, the United States and the New World, 1500–1900, covers key cities in Latin America.[5]

On the Methodology Used in Compiling Consumer Price Indexes

When more than one price index is available for a country, we work with the simple average. This approach is most useful when there are price series for more than one city for the same country, such as in the pre-1800s data. When no such consumer price indexes are available, we turn to wholesale or producer price indexes (as, for example, for China in the 1800s and the United States in the 1720s). Absent any composite index, we fill in the holes in coverage with individual commodity prices. These almost always take the form of wheat prices for Europe and rice prices for Asia. We realize that a single commodity (even if it is the most important one) is a relative price rather than the aggregate we seek, so if for any given year we have at least one consumer (or cost-of-living) price series and the price of wheat (or rice), we do not average the two but give full weight to the composite price index. Finally, from 1980 to the present, the International Monetary Fund's *World Economic Outlook* dominates all other sources, because it enforces uniformity.

Exchange Rates, Modern and Early, and Currency Debasement

The handmaiden to inflation is, of course, currency depreciation. For the period after World War II, our primary sources for exchange rates are IFS for official rates and *Pick's Currency Yearbooks* for market-based rates, as quantified and documented in detail by Reinhart and Rogoff.[6] For modern prewar rates GFD, OXLAD, HSOUS, and the League of Nations' *Annual Reports* are the primary sources. These are sometimes supplemented with scholarly sources for individual countries, as described in appendix A.1. Less modern are the exchange rates for the late 1600s through the early 1800s for a handful of European currencies, which are taken from John Castaing's *Course of Exchange*, which appeared twice a week (on Tuesdays and Fridays) from 1698 through the following century or so.[7]

We calculated the earlier "silver-based" exchange rates (trivially) from the time series provided primarily by Robert Allen and Richard Unger, who constructed continuous annual series on the silver content of currencies for several European currencies (for other sources see individual tables in the data appendixes, which list individual authors).[8] The earliest series, for Italy and England, begins in the mid-thirteenth century. As described in appendix A.1.4, these series are the foundation for dating and quantifying the "debasement crises"—the precursors of modern devaluations, as cataloged and discussed in chapter 11.

Real GDP

To maintain homogeneity inasmuch as it is possible for such a large sample of countries over the course of approximately two hundred years, we employ as a primary source Angus Maddison's data, spanning 1820–2003 (depending on the country), and the version updated through 2008 by the Groningen Growth and Development Centre's Total Economy Database (TED).[9] GDP is calculated on the basis of purchasing power parity (PPP) in 1990.[10] TED includes, among other things, series on levels of real GDP, population, and GDP per capita for up to 125 countries from 1950 to the present. These countries represent about 96 percent of the world's population. Because the smaller and poorer countries are not in the database, the sample represents an even larger share of world GDP (99 percent). We do not attempt to include in our study aggregate measures of real economic activity prior to 1800.[11]

To calculate a country's share of world GDP continuously over the years, we sometimes found it necessary to interpolate the Maddison data. (By and large, the interpolated GDP data are used only in forming weights and percentages of global GDP. We do not use them for dating or calibrating crises.) For most countries, GDP is reported only for selected benchmark years (e.g., 1820, 1850, 1870). Interpolation took three forms, ranging from the best or preferred practice to the most rudimentary. When we had actual data for real GDP (from either official sources or other scholars) for periods for which the Maddison data are missing and periods for which both series are available, we ran auxiliary regressions of the Maddison GDP series on the available GDP series for that particular country in order to interpolate the missing data. This allowed us to maintain cross-country comparability, enabling us to aggregate GDP by region or worldwide. When no other measures of GDP were available to fill in the gaps, we used the auxiliary regressions to link the Maddison measure of GDP to other indicators of economic activity, such as an output index or, most often, central government revenues—for which we have long-range continuous time series.[12] As a last resort, if no potential regressors were available, we used interpolation to connect the dots of the missing Maddison data, assuming a constant annual growth rate in between the reported benchmark years. Although this method of interpolation is, of course, useless from the vantage point of discerning any cyclical pattern, it still provides a reasonable measure of a particular country's share of world GDP, because this share usually does not change drastically from year to year.

Exports

As is well known, export data are subject to chronic misinvoicing problems because exporters aim to evade taxes, capital controls, and currency restrictions.[13] Nevertheless, external accounts are most often available for a far longer period and on a far more consistent basis than are GDP accounts. In spite of problems resulting from misinvoicing, external accounts are generally considered more reliable than most other series on macroeconomic activity. The postwar export series used in this study are taken from the International Monetary Fund (IMF), whereas the earlier data come primarily from GFD and OXLAD. Official historical statistics and assorted academic studies listed in appendix A.1 complement the main databases. Trade balances provide a rough measure of the country-specific capital flow cycle, particularly for the earlier periods, from which data on capital account balances are nonexistent. Exports are also used to scale debt, particularly external debt.

Government Finances and National Accounts

Public Finances

Data on government finances are primarily taken from Mitchell for the pre-1963 period and from Kaminsky, Reinhart, and Végh and sources they have cited for the more recent period.[14] The Web pages of the central banks and finance ministries of the many countries in our sample provide the most up-to-date data. For many of the countries in our sample, particularly in Africa and Asia, the time series on central government revenues and expenditures date back to the colonial period. Details on individual country coverage are presented in appendix table A.1.7. In nearly all cases, the Mitchell data go back to the 1800s, enabling us to calculate ratios of debt to revenue for many of the earlier crises.

The European State Finance Database, which brings together data provided by many authors, is an excellent source for the larger European countries for the pre-1800 era, because it offers considerable detail on government revenues and expenditures, not to mention extensive bibliographical references.

National Accounts

Besides the standard sources, such as the IMF, the United Nations, and the World Bank, which provide data on national accounts for the post–World War II period (with different starting points depending on the country), we consult other multicountry databases such as OXLAD for earlier periods. As with other time series used in this study, the national account series (usually for the period before World War I) build on the efforts of many scholars around the world, such as Brahmananda for India, Yousef for Egypt, and Baptista for Venezuela.[15]

Public Debt and Its Composition

As we have already emphasized, finding data on domestic public debt is remarkably difficult. Finding data on defaults on domestic debt is, not surprisingly, even more problematic. In this volume we catalog more than seventy instances of outright default on domestic debt dating back to the early 1800s. Yet even this tally is probably a considerable understatement.[16]

For the advanced economies, the most comprehensive data come from the Organisation for Economic Co-operation and Development (OECD), which provides time series on general government debt since 1980. However, these data have several important limitations. They include only a handful of emerging markets. For many advanced economies (Greece, Finland, France, and the United Kingdom, to name a few), the data actually begin much later, in the 1990s, so the OECD data on public debt provide only a relatively short time series. Moreover, only total debt is reported, with no particulars provided regarding the composition of debt (domestic versus foreign) or its maturity (long-term versus short-term). Similarly, to consider the IMF's well-known *World Economic Outlook* database as extending to public debt requires a stretch of the imagination.[17] Data are provided only for the G-7 and only from 1980 onward (out of 180 countries covered in the WEO).

The most comprehensive data on public debt come from the World Bank's *Global Development Finance* (GDF, known previously as the World Debt Tables). It is an improvement on the other databases in that it begins (for most countries) in 1970 and provides extensive detail on the particulars of external debt. Yet GDF also has serious limitations. No advanced economies are included in the database (nor are newly industrialized countries, such as Israel, Korea, or Singapore) to facilitate comparisons. Unlike data from the IMF and the World Bank for exchange rates, prices, government finances, and so on, the database includes no data prior to 1970. Last but certainly not least, these data cover only external debt. In a few countries, such as Côte d'Ivoire or Panama, external debt is a sufficient statistic on government liabilities because the levels of domestic public debt are relatively trivial. As we shall show in chapter 7, however, domestic debt accounts for an important share of total government debt for most countries. The all-country average share oscillated between 40 and 80 percent during 1900–2007.[18]

In search of the elusive data on total public debt, we examined the archives of the global institutions' predecessor, the League of Nations, and found that its *Statistical Yearbook: 1926–1944* collected information on, among other things, public domestic and external debt. Although neither the IMF nor the World Bank continued this practice after the war, the newly formed United Nations (UN) inherited the data collected by the League of Nations, and in 1948 its Department of Economic Affairs published a special volume on public debt spanning 1914–1946. From that time onward, the UN continued to collect and publish the domestic and external debt data on an annual basis in the same format used by its prewar predecessor in its *Statistical Yearbook*. As former colonies became independent nations, the database expanded accordingly. This practice continued until 1983, at which time the domestic and external public debt series were discontinued altogether. In total, these sources yield time series that span 1914–1983 for the most complete cases. They cover advanced and developing economies. For the most part, they also disaggregated domestic debt into long-term and short-term components. To the best of our knowledge, these data are not available electronically in any database; hence, obtaining it required going to the original publications. These data provide the starting point for our public debt series, which have been (where possible) extended to the period prior to 1914 and since 1983.

For data from the period prior to 1914 (including several countries that were then colonies), we consulted numerous sources, both country-specific statistical and government agencies and individual scholars.[19] Appendix A.2 provides details of the sources by country and time period. In cases for which no public debt data are available for the period prior to 1914, we approximated the foreign debt stock by reconstructing debt from individual international debt issues. These debenture (debt not secured by physical collateral or assets) data also provide a proximate measure of gross international capital inflows. Many of the data come from scholars including Miller, Wynne, Lindert and Morton, and Marichal, among others.[20] From these data we construct a foreign debt series (but it does not include total debt).[21] This exercise allows us to examine standard debt ratios for default episodes of several newly independent nations in Latin America as well as Greece and important defaults such as that of China in 1921 and those of Egypt and Turkey in the 1860s and 1870s. These data are most useful for filling holes in the early debt time series when countries first tap international capital markets. Their usefulness (as measures of debt) is acutely affected by repeated defaults, write-offs, and debt restructurings that introduce disconnects between the amounts of debt issued and the subsequent debt stock.[22]

For some countries (or colonies in the earlier period) for which we have only relatively recent data for total public debt but have reliable data going much further back on central government revenues and expenditures, we calculate and cumulate fiscal deficits to provide a rough approximation of the debt stock.[23]

To update the data for the time since 1983, we rely mostly on GDF for external debt, with a few valuable recent studies facilitating the update.[24] Last but certainly not least are the official government sources themselves, which are increasingly forthcoming in providing domestic debt data, often under the IMF's 1996 *Special Data Dissemination Standard*, prominently posted at the IMF's official Web site.[25]

Global Variables

We label two types of variables "global." The first are those that are genuinely global in scope, such as world commodity prices. The second type consists of key economic and financial indicators for the world's financial centers during 1800–2009 that have exerted a true global influence (in modern times, the U.S. Federal Reserve's target policy interest rate is such an example). For commodity prices, we have time series since the late 1700s from four different core sources (see appendix A.1). The key economic indicators include the current account deficit, real and nominal GDP, and short- and long-term interest rates for the relevant financial center of the time (the United Kingdom prior to World War I and the United States since then).

Country Coverage

Table 3.1 lists the sixty-six countries in our sample. We include a large number or African and Asian economies, whereas previous studies of the same era typically included at most a couple of each. Overall, our data set includes thirteen African countries, twelve Asian countries, nineteen European countries, and eighteen Latin American countries, plus North America and Oceania. (Our sample excludes many of the world's poorest countries, which by and large cannot borrow meaningful amounts from private sector lenders and virtually all of which have effectively defaulted even on heavily subsidized government-to-government loans. This is an interesting subject for another study, but here we are mainly interested in financial flows that, at least in the first instance, had a substantial market element.)[26]

As the final column of table 3.1 illustrates, our sample of sixty-six countries indeed accounts for about 90 percent of world GDP. Of course, many of these countries, particularly those in Africa and Asia, have become independent nations only relatively recently (see column 2). These recently independent countries have not been exposed to the risk of default for nearly as long as, say, the Latin American countries, and we have to calibrate our intercountry comparisons accordingly.

Table 3.1 flags which countries in our sample may be considered "default virgins," at least in the narrow sense that they have never outright failed to meet their external debt repayment obligations or rescheduled on even one occasion. One conspicuous grouping of countries includes the high-income Anglophone nations, Australia, Canada, New Zealand, and the United States. (The mother country, England, defaulted in earlier eras, as we have already noted.) In addition, none of the Scandinavian countries, Denmark, Finland, Norway, and Sweden, has defaulted, nor has Belgium or the Netherlands. And in Asia, Hong Kong, Korea, Malaysia, Singapore, Taiwan, and Thailand have all avoided external default. Admittedly, two of these countries, Korea and Thailand, managed to avoid default only through massive IMF loan packages during the last debt crisis of the 1990s and otherwise suffered much of the same trauma as a typical defaulting country. Of the default-free Asian countries, only Thailand existed as an independent state before the end of World War II; others have had the potential for default for only a relatively short time. Default or restructuring of domestic public debt would significantly reduce the "default virgin" list, among other things eliminating the United States from the roster of nondefaulters. For example, the abrogation of the gold clause in the United States in 1933, which meant that public debts would be repaid in fiat currency rather than gold, constitutes a restructuring of nearly all the government's domestic debt. Finally, one country from Africa, Mauritius, has never defaulted or restructured.

It is notable that the nondefaulters, by and large, are all hugely successful growth stories. This begs the question "Do high growth rates help avert default, or does averting default beget high growth rates?" Certainly we see many examples in world history in which very rapidly growing countries ran into trouble when their growth slowed.

Of course, governments can achieve de facto partial default on nominal bond debt simply through unanticipated bursts of inflation, as we discuss later, in chapters 11 and 12. Governments have

TABLE 3.1
Countries' share of world GDP, 1913 and 1990

| Region and country | Year of independence (if after 1800) | Share of world real GDP (1990 Geary-Khamis dollars) | |
		1913	1990
Africa			
Algeria	1962	0.23	0.27
Angola	1975	0.00	0.03
Central African Republic	1960	0.00	0.01
Côte d'Ivoire	1960	0.00	0.06
Egypt	1831	0.40	0.53
Kenya	1963	0.00	0.10
Mauritius*	1968	0.00	0.03
Morocco	1956	0.13	0.24
Nigeria	1960	0.00	0.40
South Africa	1910	0.36	0.54
Tunisia	1957	0.06	0.10
Zambia	1964	0.00	0.02
Zimbabwe	1965	0.00	0.05
Asia			
China		8.80	7.70
Hong Kong*		n.a.	n.a.
India	1947	7.47	4.05
Indonesia	1949	1.65	1.66
Japan		2.62	8.57
Korea*	1945	0.34	1.38
Malaysia*	1957	0.10	0.33
Myanmar	1948	0.31	0.11
Philippines	1947	0.34	0.53
Singapore*	1965	0.02	0.16
Taiwan*	1949	0.09	0.74
Thailand*		0.27	0.94
Europe			
Austria		0.86	0.48
Belgium*	1830	1.18	0.63
Denmark*		0.43	0.35
Finland*	1917	0.23	0.31
France		5.29	3.79
Germany		8.68	4.67
Greece	1829	0.32	0.37
Hungary	1918	0.60	0.25
Italy		3.49	3.42
Netherlands*		0.91	0.95

(continued)

TABLE 3.1 Continued

Region and country	Year of independence (if after 1800)	Share of world real GDP (1990 Geary-Khamis dollars)	
		1913	1990
Europe (continued)			
Norway*	1905	0.22	0.29
Poland	1918	1.70	0.72
Portugal		0.27	0.40
Romania	1878	0.80	0.30
Russia		8.50	4.25
Spain		1.52	1.75
Sweden*		0.64	0.56
Turkey		0.67	1.13
United Kingdom		8.22	3.49
Latin America			
Argentina	1816	1.06	0.78
Bolivia	1825	0.00	0.05
Brazil	1822	0.70	2.74
Chile	1818	0.38	0.31
Colombia	1819	0.23	0.59
Costa Rica	1821	0.00	0.05
Dominican Republic	1845	0.00	0.06
Ecuador	1830	0.00	0.15
El Salvador	1821	0.00	0.04
Guatemala	1821	0.00	0.11
Honduras	1821	0.00	0.03
Mexico	1821	0.95	1.91
Nicaragua	1821	0.00	0.02
Panama	1903	0.00	0.04
Paraguay	1811	0.00	0.05
Peru	1821	0.16	0.24
Uruguay	1811	0.14	0.07
Venezuela	1830	0.12	0.59
North America			
Canada*	1867	1.28	1.94
United States*		18.93	21.41
Oceania			
Australia*	1901	0.91	1.07
New Zealand*	1907	0.21	0.17
Total sample: 66 countries		93.04	89.24

Sources: Correlates of War (n.d.), Maddison (2004).

Note: An asterisk (*) denotes no sovereign external default or rescheduling history. n.a., not available. Several of these countries that have avoided external default (such as the United States) have not escaped from a default or rescheduling of their domestic debt. (See chapter 7.)

many ways to partially default on debts, and many types of financial crises over the years have taken their character from the government's choice of financing and default vehicle. The fact that government debt can be a common denominator across disparate types of crises will become even more clear when we take up the links between crises in chapter 16.

- PART II -

SOVEREIGN EXTERNAL DEBT CRISES

Most countries in all regions have gone through a prolonged phase
as serial defaulters on debt owed to foreigners.

- 4 -

A DIGRESSION ON THE THEORETICAL UNDERPINNINGS OF DEBT CRISES

In this book we chronicle hundreds of episodes in which sovereign nations have defaulted on their loans from external creditors. These "debt crises" range from defaults on mid-fourteenth-century loans made by Florentine financiers to England's Edward III to those on massive loans from (mostly) New York bankers to Latin America during the 1970s. Why do countries seem to run out of money so often? Or do they?

Former Citibank chairman (1967–1984) Walter Wriston famously said, "Countries don't go bust." In hindsight, Wriston's comment sounded foolish, coming just before the great wave of sovereign defaults in the 1980s. After all, he was the head of a large bank that had deeply invested across Latin America. Yet, in a sense, the Citibank chairman was right. Countries do not go broke in the same sense that a firm or company might. First, countries do not usually go out of business. Second, country default is often the result of a complex cost-benefit calculus involving political and social considerations, not just economic and financial ones. Most country defaults happen long before a nation literally runs out of resources.

In most instances, with enough pain and suffering, a determined debtor country can usually repay foreign creditors. The question most leaders face is where to draw the line. The decision is not always a completely rational one. Romanian dictator Nikolai Ceauşescu single-mindedly insisted on repaying, in the span of a few years, the debt of $9 billion owed by his poor nation to foreign banks during the 1980s debt crisis. Romanians were forced to live through cold winters with little or no heat, and factories were forced to cut back because of limited electricity.

Few other modern leaders would have agreed with Ceauşescu's priorities. The Romanian dictator's actions are especially puzzling given that the country could presumably have renegotiated its debt burden, as most other developing countries eventually succeeded in doing during the crisis of the 1980s. By the same token, modern convention holds that a debtor country should not have to part with rare national treasures to pay off debts. During Russia's financial crisis in 1998, no one contemplated for a moment the possibility that Moscow might part with art from the Hermitage museum simply to appease Western creditors.[1]

The fact that lenders depend on a sovereign nation's willingness to repay, not simply its ability to repay, implies that sovereign bankruptcy is a distinctly different animal than corporate bankruptcy. In corporate or individual bankruptcy, creditors have well-defined rights that typically allow them to take over many of the debtor's assets and put a lien on a share of its future income. In sovereign bankruptcy, creditors may be able to do the same on paper, but in practice their enforcement power is very limited.

This chapter provides an analytical framework that allows us to think more deeply about the underpinnings of international debt markets. Our goal here is to provide not a comprehesive survey of this extensive literature but a broad overview of issues.[2] Readers mainly interested in understanding the historical experience might choose to skip this chapter. In some respects, however, the analysis of this chapter lies at the heart of everything that follows. Why on earth do foreign creditors ever trust countries to repay their debt anyway, especially when they have been burned so regularly in the past? Why would domestic residents in emerging markets ever entrust their money to banks or local currency when they, too, have been burned so often? Why do explosions of global inflation occur sometimes, such as in the early 1990s, when forty-five countries had inflation rates over 20 percent, and not during other periods, such as the early 2000s, when only a couple had such high inflation rates?

These are not simple questions, and they are the subject of huge debate among economists. We do not come close to providing complete answers; the social, political, and economic problems underpinning default are simply too complex. If future generations of researchers do resolve these issues, perhaps the topic of this book will become moot and the world will finally reach an era in which we can say, "This time really *is* different." However, history is littered with instances in which people declared premature victory over such thorny issues.

We first concentrate on what is perhaps the most fundamental "imperfection" of international capital markets, the lack of a supernational legal framework for enforcing debt contracts across borders. This is an abstract way of saying that if the government of Argentina (a country sporting a famous history of serial default) borrows money from a U.S. bank and then defaults, the bank's options for direct enforcement of its claims are limited. To sharpen our discussion of the international aspects of the problem, we will temporarily ignore political and economic divisions within the borrowing country and simply treat it as a unified actor. Thus we will ignore domestic public debt (debt borrowed by the government from its own citizens or from local banks).

It may seem strange to those unfamiliar with economic modeling to group a government and its population together as a unified actor. In altogether too many countries, governments can be kleptocratic and corrupt, with national policies dictated by the political elite rather than by the average citizen. Indeed, political disunity is often a key driver of sovereign defaults and financial crises. The fact that the U.S. subprime crisis became much worse in the run-up to the country's 2008 election is quite typical. Preelection posturing and postelection uncertainty routinely exacerbate the challenge of developing a coherent and credible policy response. Brazil's massive 2002 financial crisis was sparked in no small part by investors' concerns regarding a shift from the centrist government of then-president Fernando Henrique Cardoso to the more populist policies of the opposition leader Luiz Inácio Lula da Silva. The irony, of course, is that the left-leaning winner ultimately proved more conservative in his macroeconomic governance than investors had feared or, perhaps, some of his supporters had hoped.

Sovereign Lending

If the reader has any doubt that willingness to pay rather than ability to pay is typically the main determinant of country default, he or she need only peruse our earlier table 2.2. The table shows that more than half of defaults by middle-income countries occur at levels of external debt relative to GDP below 60 percent, when, under normal circumstances, real interest payments of only a few percent of income would be required to maintain a constant level of debt relative to GDP, an ability that is usually viewed as an important indicator of sustainability. Expressed as a percentage of exports or government revenues, of course, payments would typically be several times higher, as we will illustrate later. But even so, a workout would be manageable over time in most cases except during wartime, especially if the country as a whole were clearly and credibly committed to gradually increasing exports over time to a level commensurate with eventual full repayment.

The centrality of willingness to pay rather than ability to pay is also clear when one looks back several hundred years to international lending during the sixteenth, seventeenth, and eighteen centuries (what we term the early period of default). Back then, the major borrowers were countries such as France and Spain, which commanded great armies of their own. Foreign investors could hardly have expected to collect through force. As Michael Tomz reminds us, during the colonial era of the nineteenth century, superpowers did periodically intervene to enforce debt contracts.[3] Britain routinely bullied and even occupied countries that failed to repay foreign debts (for example, it invaded Egypt in 1882 and Istanbul in the wake of Turkey's 1876 default). Similarly, the United States' "gunboat diplomacy" in Venezuela, which began in the mid-1890s, was motivated in part by debt repayment concerns. And the U.S. occupation of Haiti beginning in 1915 was rationalized as necessary to collect debt. (Box 5.2 explains how debt problems led the independent nation of Newfoundland to lose its sovereignty.)

In the modern era, however, the idea of using gunboat diplomacy to collect debts seems far-fetched (in most cases). The cost-benefit analysis simply does not warrant governments' undertaking such huge expenses and risks, especially when borrowing is typically diversified across Europe, Japan, and the United States, making the incentives for an individual country to use military force even weaker.

What carrots or sticks, then, can foreign creditors actually hold over sovereign borrowers? This question was first posed coherently in a classic paper by Jonathan Eaton and Mark Gersovitz, who argued that in a changing and uncertain world there is a huge benefit to countries in having access to international capital markets.[4] In early times, capital market access might have enabled countries to get food during times of an exceptionally bad harvest. In modern times, countries may need to borrow to fight recessions or to engage in highly productive infrastructure projects.

Eaton and Gersovitz argued that the benefits of continued capital market access could induce governments to maintain debt repayments absent any legal system whatsoever to force their cooperation. They based their analysis on the conjecture that governments need to worry about their "reputation" as international borrowers. If reneging on debt damages their reputation, governments will not do so lightly. The Eaton and Gersovitz approach is appealing to economic theorists, especially because it is relatively institution-free. (That is, the theory is "pure" in that it does not depend on the particulars of government, such as legal and political structures.) In principle, the theory can explain sovereign borrowing in the Middle Ages as well as today. Note that the reputation argument does not say simply that countries repay their debts now so they can borrow even more in the future. If that were the case, international borrowing would be a Ponzi scheme with exploding debt levels.[5]

This "reputation approach" has some subtle problems. If the whole edifice of international lending were built simply on reputation, lending markets might be even more fragile than they actually are. Surely fourteenth-century Italian financiers must have realized that England's Edward III might die from battle or disease. What would have become of their loans if Edward's successor had had very different goals and aspirations? If Edward had successfully conquered France, what need would he have had for the lenders in the future?[6]

If institutions really do not matter, why, over most of history, has the external debt of emerging markets been denominated largely in foreign currency and written so that it is adjudicated in foreign courts?

Bulow and Rogoff raised another important challenge to the notion that institutions and international legal mechanisms are unimportant in international lending.[7] Countries may, indeed, be willing to repay debts to maintain their right to borrow in the future. But at some point, England's debt burden would have had to reach a point at which the expected value of repayments on existing debt exceeded any future borrowing. At some point, a country must reach its debt limit. Why wouldn't Edward III (or his successor) have simply declared the Italian debts null and void? Then England could have used any payments it *might* have made to its financiers to build up gold reserves that could be used if it experienced a shortfall in the future.

The reputation approach therefore requires some discipline. Bulow and Rogoff argue that in modern times sophisticated investing strategies (e.g., those used in foreign stock markets) might offer as good, or almost as good, a hedge against default as any potential stream of foreign lending. In another work, Bulow and Rogoff contend that instead of relying simply on reputation, repayment of much foreign borrowing, especially by emerging markets, might be enforced by the legal rights of creditors in the lenders' own countries.[8] If a country tried to move to self-insurance, many of the investments it might need to make would involve overseas purchases. Creditors might not be able to seize assets directly in the borrowing country, but, armed with sufficient legal rights, they might well be able to seize the borrower's assets abroad, particularly in their own countries, but potentially also in other countries with highly developed legal systems. Of course, the right to seize assets abroad will also make it difficult for a defaulting country to borrow from other international lenders. If a country defaults on foreign bank A and then attempts to borrow from foreign bank B, bank B has to worry whether bank A will attempt to enforce its prior claim when it comes time for the country to repay. In this sense, the reputation and legal approaches are not so different, though the resemblance can become significant when it comes to policy questions about how to design and operate the international financial system. For example, establishing an international bankruptcy court to replace domestic courts may be virtually irrelevant if legal rights are of little consequence in any event.

Emphasizing legal rights also leads one to focus on other costs besides being cut off from future borrowing. A government contemplating default on international loans must also contemplate the potential disruption to its trade that will result from the need to reroute trade and financing to circumvent creditors. Fourteenth-century England depended on selling wool to Italian weavers, and Italy was the center of the trade in spices, which England desired to import. Default implied making future trade with and through Italy difficult, and surely this would have been costly. Nowadays, trade and finance are even more closely linked. For example, most trade, both within and across countries, is extremely dependent on very short-term bank credits to finance goods during shipment but prior to receipt. If a country defaults on large long-term loans, creditor banks can exert significant pressure against any entity that attempts to finance trade credits. Countries can deal with this problem to some extent by using government foreign exchange reserves to help finance their trade. But governments are typically ill equipped to monitor trade loans at the microeconomic level, and they cannot easily substitute their own abilities for bank expertise. Last but not least, creditors can enforce in creditor countries' courts claims that potentially allow them to seize any defaulter country's goods (or assets) that cross their borders. Bulow and Rogoff argue that, in practice, creditors and debtors typically negotiate a partial default so that one seldom actually observes such seizures.

At some level, neither the reputation-based model of Eaton and Gersovitz nor the institutional approach of Bulow and Rogoff seems quite adequate to explain the scale and size of international lending or the diversity of measures creditors bring to bear in real-life default situations. Trade depends not only on legal conventions but also on political resistance to tariff wars and on a broader exchange of people and information to sustain business growth and development.

Indeed, whereas a country's reputation for repayment may have only limited traction if construed in the narrow sense defined by Eaton and Gersovitz, its reputation interpreted more broadly—for instance, for being a reliable partner in international relations—may be more significant.[9] Default on debt can upset delicate balances in national security arrangements and alliances, and most countries typically have important needs and issues.

In addition to loans, foreign direct investment (FDI) (for example, when a foreign company builds a plant in an emerging market) can also be important to development. A foreign company that wants to engage in FDI with a defaulting country will worry about having its plant and equipment seized (a prominent phenomenon during the 1960s and 1970s; examples include Chile's seizure of its copper mines from American companies in 1977 and the nationalization of foreign oil companies' holdings in the early 1970s by the Organization of Petroleum-Exporting Countries). A debt default will surely cast a pall over FDI, costing the debtor country not only the capital flows but also the knowledge transfer that trade economists find typically accompanies FDI.[10]

In sum, economists can find arguments to explain why countries are able to borrow abroad despite the limited rights of creditors. But the arguments are surprisingly complex, suggesting that sustainable debt levels may be fragile as well. Concerns over future access to capital markets, maintaining trade, and possibly broader international relations all support debt flows, with the relative emphasis and weights depending on factors specific to each situation. That is, even if lenders cannot directly go in and seize assets as in a conventional domestic default, they still retain leverage sufficient to entice a country to repay loans of at least modest size. We can dismiss, however, the popular notion that countries pay back their debts so that they can borrow even more in the future. Ponzi schemes cannot be the foundation for international lending; they must eventually collapse.

How does the limited leverage of foreign creditors relate to the fragility of confidence we emphasized in the preamble? Without going into great detail, it is easy to imagine that many of the models and frameworks we have been alluding to produce highly fragile equilibria in the sense that there are often multiple outcomes that can be quite sensitive to small shifts in expectations. This fragility comes through in many frameworks but is most straightforwardly apparent in cases in which highly indebted governments need to continuously roll over short-term funding, to which we will turn next.

Illiquidity versus Insolvency

We have emphasized the important distinction between willingness to pay and ability to pay. Another important concept is the distinction between a country that faces a short-term funding problem and one that is not willing and/or able to service its debts indefinitely. In most of the literature, this distinction is typically described as the difference between "illiquidity and insolvency." Of course, the reader now understands that this literal analogy between country and corporate debt is highly misleading. A bankrupt corporation may simply not be able to service its debts in full as a going concern. A country defaulter, on the other hand, has typically made a strategic decision that (full) repayment is not worth the necessary sacrifice.

Often governments borrow internationally, either at relatively short horizons of one to three years or at longer horizons, at interest rates linked to short-term international debt. Why borrowing tends to be relatively short term is a topic of its own. For example, Diamond and Rajan contend that lenders want the option of being able to discipline borrowers that "misbehave," that is, fail to invest resources, so as to enhance the probability of future repayment.[11] Jeanne argues that because short-term borrowing enhances the risk of a financial crisis (when often debt cannot be rolled over), countries are forced to follow more disciplined policies, improving economic performance for debtor and creditor alike.[12] For these and other related reasons, short-term borrowing often carries a significantly lower interest rate than longer-term borrowing. Similar arguments have been made about borrowing in foreign currency units.

In either event, when a country borrows short term, not only is it faced with financing interest payments (either through its own resources or through new borrowing) but it must also periodically roll over the principal. A liquidity crisis occurs when a country that is

59

both willing and able to service its debts over the long run finds it-self temporarily unable to roll over its debts. This situation is in con-trast to what is sometimes casually labeled an "insolvency" problem, one in which the country is perceived to be unwilling or unable to repay over the long run. If a country is truly facing merely a liquidity crisis, a third party (for example, a multilateral lending organization such as the International Monetary Fund) can, in principle, make a short-term bridge loan, with no risk, that will keep the borrower on its feet and prevent it from defaulting. Indeed, if creditors were fully convinced that a country had every intention of repaying its debts over the longer term, the debtor would hardly be likely to run into a short-term liquidity problem ever again.

Sachs illustrates an important caveat.[13] Suppose that the money a country borrows is provided by a large group of lenders, each of which is small individually. It may be in the collective interest of the lenders to roll over short-term debt. Yet it can also produce equi-librium if all lenders refuse to roll over the debt, in which case the borrowing country will be forced into default. If no single lender can provide enough money for the country to meet its payments, there may be both a "default" and a "no-default" equilibrium. The exam-ple given by Sachs is, of course, a very good illustration of the theme of financial fragility and the vulnerability of debtors to the "this-time-is-different" syndrome. A borrower can merrily roll along as long as lenders have confidence, but if for some (possibly extraneous) reason confidence is lost, then lending collapses, and no individual lender has the power or inclination to stave it off.

The concept of illiquidity versus insolvency is one we already illustrated in the preamble with bank runs and one that we will see again in other guises. Technically speaking, countries can sometimes be exposed to "multiple equilibria," implying that the difference be-tween a case in which a country defaults and one in which it does not default can sometimes be very small. For a given structure of debt and assuming all actors are pursuing their self-interest, there can be very different outcomes depending on expectations and confidence.

Theorists have developed many concrete examples of situa-tions in which default can occur as a result of a "sunspot" that drives a country from a no-default to a default equilibrium.[14] The possible existence of multiple equilibria and the idea that investors may temporarily become skittish about a country can also play an important role in rationalizing intervention into sovereign lending crises by the governments of creditor countries and international institutions. The danger, of course, is that it is not always easy to distinguish between a default that was inevitable—in the sense that a country is so highly leveraged and so badly managed that it takes very little to force it into default—and one that was not—in the sense that a country is fundamentally sound but is having difficulties sustaining confidence because of a very temporary and easily solvable liquidity problem. In the heat of a crisis, it is all too tempting for would-be rescuers (today notably multilateral lenders such as the IMF) to persuade themselves that they are facing a confidence problem that can be solved with short-term bridge loans, when in fact they are confronting a much more deeply rooted crisis of solvency and willingness to pay.

Partial Default and Rescheduling

Until now, we have somewhat glossed over the point of exactly what constitutes default. In practice, most defaults end up being partial, not complete, albeit sometimes after long negotiations and much acrimony. Creditors may not have the leverage (from whatever source) to enforce full repayment, but they typically do have enough leverage to get at least something back, often a significant share of what they are owed. Even the most famous cases of total default have typically ended in partial repayment, albeit often quite small and many decades later. Russia's Bolshevik government refused to repay Tsarist debts in 1918, but when Russia finally re-entered the debt markets sixty-nine years later, it had to negotiate a token payment on its defaulted debt.

In most cases, though, partial repayment is significant and not a token, with the amount repaid presumably determined by the types of complex cost-benefit considerations we have already been discussing. Precisely because partial repayment is often the result of long and contentious negotiations, interested bystanders often get sucked in. For example, Bulow and Rogoff show how well-intentioned third parties such as international lending institutions (e.g., the IMF) or the governments of creditor countries may be gamed into making side payments to facilitate a deal, much as a realtor may cut her commission to sell a house.[15] Country borrowers and their creditors potentially have bargaining power vis-à-vis outside parties if failed negotiations interfere with trade and cause broader problems in the global financial system, such as contagion to other borrowers.[16] As we have noted, the creation of the IMF since World War II has coincided with shorter but more frequent episodes of sovereign default. This phenomenon is quite consistent with the view that default episodes occur even more frequently than they otherwise might, because both lenders and borrowers realize that in a pinch they can always count on subsidies from the IMF and the governments of creditor countries. (Later literature has come to term this gaming of third parties with deep pockets the "moral hazard" of international lending.)

A bargaining perspective on sovereign default also helps explain why, in addition to outright defaults (partial or complete), we include "reschedulings" in our definition of sovereign defaults. In a typical rescheduling, the debtor forces its creditors to accept longer repayment schedules and often interest rate concessions (relative to market interest rates). The ratings agencies (including Moody's and Standard and Poor's) rightly regard these episodes as negotiated partial defaults in which the agreed rescheduling minimizes the dead-weight costs of legal fees and other expenditures related to a more acrimonious default in which a country and its creditors simply walk away from the table, at least for a time. Our data set does make a distinction between reschedulings and outright defaults, although from a theoretical perspective the two are quite similar.

One final but critical point is this: the fact that countries sometimes default on their debt does not provide prima facie evidence that investors were irrational. For making loans to risky sovereigns, investors receive risk premiums sometimes exceeding 5 or 10 percent per annum. These risk premiums imply that creditors receive compensation for occasional defaults, most of which are only partial anyway. Indeed, compared to corporate debt, country defaults often lead to much larger recoveries, especially when official bailouts are included.

We do not want to overemphasize the rationality of lenders. In fact, there are many cases in which the very small risk premiums charged sovereign nations are hardly commensurate with the risks involved. High-risk borrowers, of course, not only have to face interest rate risk premiums on their borrowing but often bear significant deadweight costs if debt problems amplify recessions in the event of default. For borrowers the this-time-is-different mentality may be even more costly than for creditors, but again we will need to revisit this issue in a broader calculus of default.

Odious Debt

Another deep philosophical issue, in principle relevant to thinking about international lending, surrounds the notion of "odious debt." In the Middle Ages, a child could be sent to debtors' prison if his parents died in debt. In principle, this allowed the parent to borrow more (because the punishment for failure to repay was so great), but today the social norms in most countries would view this transfer of debt as thoroughly unacceptable. But of course nations do borrow intertemporally, and the children of one generation may well have to pay off the debts of their parents. At the end of World War II, the gross domestic debt of the United States reached more than 100 percent of GDP, and it took several decades to bring it down to a more normal 50 percent of GDP.

The doctrine of odious debt basically states that when lenders give money to a government that is conspicuously kleptomaniacal and corrupt, subsequent governments should not be forced to honor it. Jayachandran and Kremer argue that one can modify standard reputation models of debt to admit a convention of not honoring odious debt, and that this can be welfare improving.[17] However, there is quite a bit of controversy about whether odious debt can be clearly delineated in practice. Everyone might agree that if the leaders of a country engaged in genocide were to borrow to finance their military, the lenders should recognize the debt as odious and at risk of default in the event of a regime change. However, one can imagine global bureaucrats arguing over, say, whether debt issued by the United States is odious debt, in which case, of course, the concept would not provide sufficient discrimination to be useful in practice. The practical guidelines regarding odious debt must be sufficiently narrowly construed so as to be implementable. In practice, though, weaker versions of odious debt do, perhaps, have some relevance. The circumstances under which a debt burden is accumulated can affect a debtor's view of "fairness," and therefore its willingness to pay. On occasion, the international community may also be willing to treat debtors more gently in these circumstances (at the very least by giving them greater access to subsidized bridge loans).

Domestic Public Debt

If the theory of external sovereign debt is complex, the theory of domestic public debt is even more so. For the purposes of this discussion, we will assume that domestic public debt is denominated in domestic currency, adjudicated within the issuing country, and held by domestic residents. Of these three strictures, the only one that is really absolute in our definition in chapter 1 is the assumption that the debt is adjudicated by domestic authorities. Beginning, perhaps, with Argentina's U.K. pound–denominated "internal" bonds of the late nineteenth century, there have been a number of historical examples in which domestic debt has been indexed to foreign currency (mostly famously the *tesobono* debt issued by Mexico in the early 1990s and the precedents noted in box 7.1), and in recent years that phenomenon has become more prevalent. As more emerging markets have moved to liberalize their capital markets, it has become increasingly common for foreign residents to hold domestic public debt. The nuance that both foreign and domestic residents may hold a certain type of debt can be relevant, but we will set this nuance aside to simplify our discussion.[18]

Domestic debt is debt a country owes to itself. In Robert Barro's famous Ricardian model of debt, domestic public debt does not matter at all, for citizens simply increase their savings when debt goes up to offset future taxes.[19] Barro's analysis, however, presumes that debt will always be honored, even if savings patterns are not homogeneous and debt repayments (as opposed to repudiations) favor some groups at the expense of others. This presumption begs the question as to why political outcomes do not periodically lead countries to default on domestic debt, and assumes away the question as to why anyone lends to governments in the first place. If old people hold most of a country's debt, for example, why don't young voters periodically rise up and vote to renege on the debt, starting anew with a lower tax for the young at the cost of less wealth for the elderly?

One of the more startling findings in part III of this book, on domestic debt, is that such outright defaults occur far more often than one might imagine, albeit not quite as often as defaults on sovereign external debt. Governments can also default on domestic public debt through high and unanticipated inflation, as the United States and many European countries famously did in the 1970s.

What, then, anchors domestic public debt? Why are domestic bondholders paid anything at all? North and Weingast argue that a government's ability to establish political institutions that sustain large amounts of debt repayment constitutes an enormous strategic advantage by allowing a country to marshal vast resources, especially in wartime.[20] They argue that one of the most important outcomes of England's "glorious revolution" of the late 1600s was precisely a framework to promote the honoring of debt contracts, thereby conferring on England a distinct advantage over rival France. France, as we shall see, was at the height of its serial default era during this period. The Crown's ability to issue debt gave England the huge advantage of being able to marshal the resources needed to conduct warfare in an era in which combat was already becoming extremely capital intensive.

In democracies, Kotlikoff, Persson, and Svensson suggest that domestic debt markets might be a convention that can be sustained through reputation, much as in the Eaton and Gersovitz model of sovereign external debt.[21] Tabellini, in a related article, suggests that debt might be sustainable if young voters care sufficiently about older voters.[22] All of these theories, and others for the case in which the government is a monarchy rather than a democracy, are built around the assumption that debt markets are self-sustaining conventions in which the costs and benefits narrowly match up to ensure continuous functioning. Yet, as we have discussed, the incentives for repayment of any kind of government debt probably involve broader issues than just the necessity of smoothing out tax receipts and consumption. Just as failure to honor sovereign debt might conceivably trigger broader responses in international relations outside the debt arena, so might domestic default trigger a breakdown in the social compact that extends beyond being able to borrow in the future. For one thing, in many economies government debt is not simply a means for governments to smooth tax receipts but a store of value that helps maintain the liquidity of credit markets. Governments may periodically default on their debts, but in most countries the record of private firms is even worse.

Financial repression can also be used as a tool to expand domestic debt markets. In China and India today, most citizens are extremely limited as to the range of financial assets they are allowed to hold, with very low-interest bank accounts and cash essentially the only choices. With cash and jewelry at high risk of loss and theft and very few options for accumulating wealth to pay for retirement, healthcare, and children's education, citizens still put large sums in banks despite the artificially suppressed returns. In India, banks end up lending large amounts of their assets directly to the government, which thereby enjoys a far lower interest rate than it probably would in a liberalized capital market. In China, the money goes via directed lending to state-owned enterprises and infrastructure projects, again at far lower interest rates than would otherwise obtain. This kind of financial repression is far from new and was particularly prevalent in both advanced and emerging market economies during the height of international capital controls from World War II through the 1980s.

Under conditions of financial repression, governments can, of course, potentially obtain very large amounts of resources by exploiting to the fullest their monopoly over savings vehicles. However, as we will show later, domestically issued debt has flourished in many emerging markets even when financial repression has been quite limited, for example, during the decades before World War II.

We will defer further discussion of domestic debt until we look at the issue empirically in chapters 7–9. There we will also show that there is an important interaction between sovereign debt and domestic debt. Again, as in the case of sovereign external debt, the issue of multiple equilibria often arises in models of domestic debt.[23]

Conclusions

In this chapter we have given a brief overview of the key concepts governing sovereign debt and default, as well as other varieties of crises including currency and banking crises. This chapter, while admittedly abstract, has addressed fundamental questions about international financial crises. We will return to some of these themes later in the book as our expansive new data set helps to cast light on some of the more difficult questions.

In many regards, the theoretical work on the underpinnings of international lending and capital markets raises the question of why defaults are not more frequent. Even Venezuela, the modern-day sovereign default champion, with ten episodes since it achieved independence in 1830, still averages eighteen years between new defaults. If crises recurred almost continuously, the this-time-is-different mentality would seldom manifest itself: every time would be the same, borrowers and lenders would remain constantly on edge, and debt markets would never develop to any significant degree, certainly not to the extent that spectacular crashes are possible. But of course, economic theory tells us that even a relatively fragile economy can roll along for a very long time before its confidence bubble bursts, sometimes allowing it to dig a very deep hole of debt before that happens.

- 5 -

CYCLES OF SOVEREIGN DEFAULT ON EXTERNAL DEBT

*P*olicy makers should not have been overly cheered by the absence of major external sovereign defaults from 2003 to 2009 after the wave of defaults in the preceding two decades. Serial default remains the norm, with international waves of defaults typically separated by many years, if not decades.

Recurring Patterns

We open our tour of the panorama of financial crises by discussing sovereign default on external debt, which, as we have just been analyzing theoretically, occurs when a government defaults on debt owed to foreigners. (Some background on the historical emergence of sovereign debt markets is provided in box 5.1.)

Figure 5.1 plots the percentage of all independent countries in a state of default or restructuring during any given year between 1800 and 2008 (for which our data set is most complete). For the world as a whole (or at least those countries with more than 90 percent of global GDP, which are represented by our data set), the relatively short period of few defaults before the late 2000s can be seen as typical of the lull that follows large global financial crises. Aside from such lulls, there are long periods when a high percentage of all countries are in a state of default or restructuring. Indeed, figure 5.1 reveals five pronounced peaks or default cycles.

The first such peak was during the Napoleonic Wars. The second ran from the 1820s through the late 1840s, when at times nearly half the countries in the world were in default (including all

---

BOX 5.1
The development of international sovereign debt markets
in England and Spain

Modern debt institutions as we now understand them evolved gradually. This was particularly the case with domestic borrowing, in which the relationship between taxes, repayments, and power was historically often blurred. Loans were typically highly nontransparent, with ill-specified interest rates and repayment schedules and often no specific dates on which principal repayments would be made. A king's promise to "repay" could often be removed as easily as the lender's head. Borrowing was frequently strongly coercive in nature. Early history is replete with examples of whole families who were slaughtered simply to seize their lands and other wealth. In thirteenth-century France, the Templars (of Crusades fame) were systematically exiled by the French kings, who seized their wealth.

In medieval times, the church enforced usury laws that were intended to prevent Christians from lending to each other at interest. Of course, non-Christians, especially Jews, were allowed to lend, but this gave sovereigns access to only a very small pool of their nation's total funds. In order to gain access to larger wealth pools, borrowers (sometimes with the help of theologians) had to think of ways to try to circumvent church law. During this period, international lending markets were sometimes helped by the device of having a borrower repay in a stronger, more stable currency than was specified in the original loan, perhaps repaying in currency that was not being as aggressively debased. Of course, such devices are tantamount to paying interest, yet they were often viewed as acceptable.

By far the most sophisticated early financial markets appeared in the Italian city-states of Genoa, Florence, and Venice in the late thirteenth century. (See, for example, the excellent discussions of MacDonald or Ferguson.)[1] Early loans took the guise of "repayable taxes," but soon the system evolved to the point at which sovereign loans were sufficiently transparent that a secondary market developed.

As historian Carlo Cipolla has emphasized, the first true international debt crisis had its roots in loans made by Italian merchants to England starting in the late thirteenth century.[2] In that era, it was Italy that was the developed financial center and England the developing nation rich in natural resources, especially sheep's wool. As we have already discussed, a sequence of Italian loans helped finance various stages of a long series of wars between England and France. When Edward III of England defaulted in 1340 after a series of military failures, the news reached Florence quickly. Because the major banks had lent heavily to Edward, a bank run hit Florence's economy. The whole affair played out in slow motion by modern standards, but one major Italian lender, the Peruzzi Bank, went bankrupt in 1343, and another, the

Bardi Bank, did in 1346. Thus England, like so many emerging markets in later eras, went through the trauma of sovereign external default (and more than once) before it eventually "graduated" to the status of nondefaulter. Before its graduation, England was to experience several more episodes of government debt restructurings; however, these more recent credit events involved only domestic debt—as we will document.

Indeed, England did not truly cast off its status as a serial defaulter until the Glorious Revolution in 1688, which led to a substantial strengthening of Parliament's power. As North and Weingast argued in their seminal work, this provided, for the first time, a self-renewing institution that stood behind British debt. Weingast further argued that the Bank of England, by providing a bureaucratic "delegated monitor" to oversee the government's debt service, provided the key instrument through which Parliament expressed its power.[3] Certainly a number of other factors helped support Britain's success, including the government's practice of using short-term debt to finance wars, then converting the debt to longer-term debt after each war's conclusion. Short-term financing of wars makes sense, of course, because uncertainty over the war's conclusion forces the government to pay a premium, which it will not want to lock in. The issuance of long-term debt also facilitated an active secondary market that helped make English debt liquid, a point underscored by Carlos et al.[4] Finally, it cannot be overemphasized that one of the main factors underlying England's relatively pristine repayment record is the country's remarkable success in its many wars. As we have already seen with regard to the early British monarchs, nothing causes debt failure to the extent that war failure does. We will return to the issue of graduation toward the end of this book.

Prior to 1800, few nations other than England had achieved the capacity to build up significant international debts and then default on them. To achieve large-scale serial default requires a sufficient store of wealth to keep convincing each new generation of creditors that the earnings needed to repay the debt will eventually be available (that this time it will be different) and that the country is sufficiently stable to ensure that it will be around to make the payments. After 1800, thanks to rapid global income growth in the wake of the Industrial Revolution as well as to Britain's capacity for spinning off excess savings, many countries began to fulfill the wealth criteria. Prior to 1800, aside from the early Italian cities, plus Portugal and Prussia on one occasion each, only France and Spain commanded the resources and stability to engage in big-time international defaults. And default they did, Spain six times by our count and France eight, as we illustrate in this chapter.

Spain's first string of defaults, in 1557, 1560, 1575, and 1596 under Philip II (1556–1598), have been extensively studied and debated by economic historians, as have the later and far uglier episodes that occurred under Philip II's successors in 1607, 1627, and 1647. The Spanish experience illustrates a number of issues that have continually recurred in later cases of serial default. Spain is also extremely important historically as the last country to threaten the domination of Europe until Napoleon.

Prior to the sixteenth century, Spain was sufficiently diffuse and its regions' finances sufficiently tenuous that large-scale international borrowing was not feasible. The discovery of the New World changed all that. Spectacular lodes of silver were found in Mexico and Peru, with truly massive amounts beginning to arrive in Europe by the 1540s. The huge increase in revenues greatly enhanced the power of the king, who was no longer so reliant on domestic tax revenues, which required the cooperation of Parliament. At the same time, the influx of precious metals, especially silver, had a huge inflationary impact on prices in Europe.

Spain's newfound wealth made it relatively easy for its monarchs to raise money by borrowing, and borrow they did. Leveraging seemed to make sense given the possibility of dominating Europe. King Philip's various military adventures against the Turks and the Dutch, and then his truly disastrous decision to launch the "Invincible Armada" against England, all required huge sums of money. Financiers including wealthy Flemish, German, and Portuguese investors, Spanish merchants, and especially Italian bankers were willing to lend significant sums to Spain given a sufficient risk premium. At any one time, the Spanish Crown typically owed its creditors roughly half of a year's revenues, although on occasion the amount exceeded two years' income. Of course, as we summarize in table 6.1, Spain did indeed default on its debts, repeatedly.

of Latin America). The third began in the early 1870s and lasted for two decades. The fourth began in the Great Depression of the 1930s and extended through the early 1950s, when again nearly half of all countries stood in default.[5] The final default cycle in the figure encompasses the debt crises of the 1980s and 1990s in the emerging markets.

Indeed, when one weights countries by their share of global GDP, as in figure 5.2, the lull in defaults after 2002 stands out even more against the preceding century. Only the two decades before World War I—the halcyon days of the gold standard—exhibited tranquility anywhere close to that of 2003–2008.[6] Looking forward, one cannot fail to note that whereas one- and two-decade lulls in defaults are not at all uncommon, each lull has invariably been followed by a new wave of defaults.

71

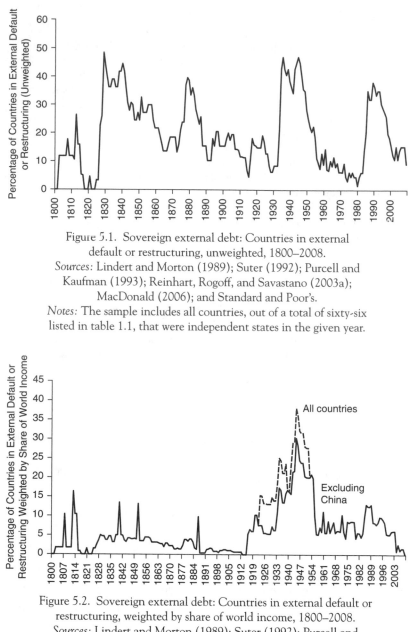

Figure 5.1. Sovereign external debt: Countries in external default or restructuring, unweighted, 1800–2008.
Sources: Lindert and Morton (1989); Suter (1992); Purcell and Kaufman (1993); Reinhart, Rogoff, and Savastano (2003a); MacDonald (2006); and Standard and Poor's.
Notes: The sample includes all countries, out of a total of sixty-six listed in table 1.1, that were independent states in the given year.

Figure 5.2. Sovereign external debt: Countries in external default or restructuring, weighted by share of world income, 1800–2008.
Sources: Lindert and Morton (1989); Suter (1992); Purcell and Kaufman (1993); Reinhart, Rogoff, and Savastano (2003a); Maddison (2004); MacDonald (2006); and Standard and Poor's.
Notes: The sample includes all countries, out of a total of sixty-six listed in table 1.1, that were independent states in the given year. Three sets of GDP weights are used, 1913 weights for the period 1800–1913, 1990 weights for the period 1914–1990, and 2003 weights for the period 1991–2008.

Figure 5.2 also shows that the years just after World War II were the peak, by far, of the largest default era in modern world history. By 1947, countries representing almost 40 percent of global GDP were in a state of default or rescheduling. This situation was partly a result of new defaults produced by the war but also partly due to the fact that many countries never emerged from the defaults surrounding the Great Depression of the 1930s.[7] By the same token, the defaults during the Napoleonic Wars are seen to have been as important as those in any other period. Outside of the crisis following World War II, only the peak of the 1980s debt crisis nears the levels of the early 1800s.

As we will see when we look at the experiences of individual countries in chapter 6, serial default on external debt—that is, repeated sovereign default—is the norm throughout every region in the world, including Asia and Europe.

Default and Banking Crises

A high incidence of global banking crises has historically been associated with a high incidence of sovereign defaults on external debt. Figure 5.3 plots the (GDP-weighted) share of countries experiencing a banking crisis against the comparably calculated share of countries experiencing a default or restructuring in their external debt (as in figure 5.2). Sovereign defaults began to climb with the onset of World War I (as did banking crises) and continued to escalate during the Great Depression and World War II (when several advanced economies joined the ranks of the defaulters). The decades that followed were relatively quiet until debt crises swept emerging markets beginning in the 1980s and 1990s.[8]

The channels through which global financial turbulence could prompt more sovereign debt crises in emerging markets are numerous and complex. Some of these channels are as follows:

- Banking crises in advanced economies significantly drag down world growth. The slowing, or outright contraction, of economic activity tends to hit exports especially hard, limiting the avail-

73

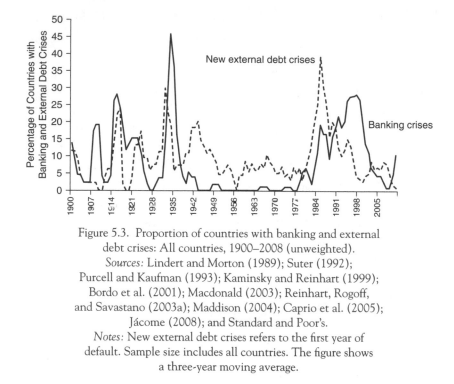

Figure 5.3. Proportion of countries with banking and external
debt crises: All countries, 1900–2008 (unweighted).
Sources: Lindert and Morton (1989); Suter (1992);
Purcell and Kaufman (1993); Kaminsky and Reinhart (1999);
Bordo et al. (2001); Macdonald (2003); Reinhart, Rogoff,
and Savastano (2003a); Maddison (2004); Caprio et al. (2005);
Jácome (2008); and Standard and Poor's.
Notes: New external debt crises refers to the first year of
default. Sample size includes all countries. The figure shows
a three-year moving average.

ability of hard currency to the governments of emerging markets
and making it more difficult to service their external debt.

• Weakening global growth has historically been associated with declining world commodity prices. These reduce the export earnings
of primary commodity producers and, accordingly, their ability to
service debt.

• Banking crises in global financial centers (and the credit crunches
that accompany them) produce a "sudden stop" of lending to
countries at the periphery (using the term popularized by Guillermo
Calvo).[9] Essentially, capital flows from the "north" dry up in a manner unrelated to the underlying economic fundamentals in emerging
markets. With credit hard to obtain, economic activity in emerging market economies contracts and debt burdens press harder
against declining governmental resources.

- Banking crises have historically been "contagious" in that investors withdraw from risk-taking, generalize the experience of one country to others, and reduce their overall exposure as their wealth declines. The consequences are clearly deleterious for emerging markets' ability both to roll over and to service external sovereign debt.
- Banking crisis in one country can cause a loss of confidence in neighboring or similar countries, as creditors look for common problems.

As of this writing, it remains to be seen whether the global surge in financial sector turbulence of the late 2000s will lead to a similar outcome in the sovereign default cycle. The precedent in figure 5.3, however, appears discouraging on that score. A sharp rise in sovereign defaults in the current global financial environment would hardly be surprising.

Default and Inflation

If a global surge in banking crises indicates a likely rise in sovereign defaults, it may also signal a potential rise in the share of countries experiencing high inflation. Figure 5.4, on inflation and default (1900–2007), illustrates the striking positive co-movement of the share of countries in default on debt and the share experiencing high inflation (defined here as an annual rate above 20 percent). Because inflation represents a form of partially defaulting on government liabilities that are not fully indexed to prices or the exchange rate, this observed co-movement is not entirely surprising.[10]

As chapter 12 illustrates, default through inflation became more commonplace over the years as fiat money displaced coinage as the principal means of exchange. In effect, even when we focus on the post-1900 era of fiat money (Figure 5.4), this pattern is evident. That is, a tight relationship between inflation and outright external default is of fairly modern vintage. For 1900–2007, the simple pair-

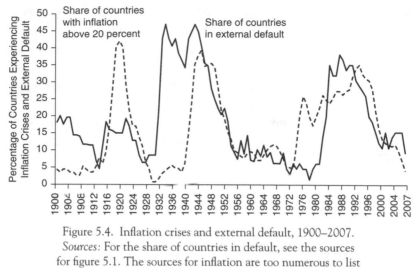

Figure 5.4. Inflation crises and external default, 1900–2007.
Sources: For the share of countries in default, see the sources
for figure 5.1. The sources for inflation are too numerous to list
here but are given in appendix A.1 by country and period.
Notes: Inflation crises are years in which the annual inflation rate
exceeds 20 percent per annum. The probabilities of both inflation
and default are simple unweighted averages. Correlations: 1900–2007,
0.39; excluding the Great Depression, 0.60; 1940–2007, 0.75.

wise correlation coefficient is 0.39; for the years after 1940, the correlation nearly doubles to 0.75.

This increased correlation can probably be explained by a change in the willingness of governments to expropriate through various channels and the abandonment of a gold (or other metallic) standard rather than by a change in macroeconomic influences. In Depression-era defaults, deflation was the norm. To the extent that such price-level declines were unexpected, debt burdens became even more onerous and detrimental to economic performance. This relationship is the essence of Irving Fisher's famous "debt-deflation" theory.[11] As a corollary to that theory, an adverse economy presumably makes sovereign default more likely. In contrast, a higher background rate of inflation makes it less likely that an economy will be pushed into a downward deflationary spiral. That defaults and inflation moved together positively in the later part of the post–World War II period probably indicates that governments are now more willing to resort to both to lighten their real interest burdens.

Inflation conditions often continue to worsen after an external default.[12] Shut out from international capital markets and facing collapsing revenues, governments that have not been able to restrain their spending commensurately have, on a recurring basis, resorted to the inflation tax, even in its most extreme hyperinflationary form.

Global Factors and Cycles
of Global External Default

We have already seen from figures 5.1 and 5.2 that global financial conflagration can be a huge factor in generating waves of defaults. Our extensive new data set also confirms the prevailing view among economists that global economic factors, including commodity prices and interest rates in the countries that are financial centers, play a major role in precipitating sovereign debt crises.[13]

We employed a range of real global commodity price indexes over the period 1800–2008 to assess the degree of co-movement of defaults and commodity prices. Peaks and troughs in commodity price cycles appear to be leading indicators of peaks and troughs in the capital flow cycle, with troughs typically resulting in multiple defaults.

As Kaminsky, Reinhart, and Végh have demonstrated for the postwar period and Aguiar and Gopinath have recently modeled, emerging market borrowing tends to be extremely procyclical.[14] Favorable trends in countries' terms of trade (meaning high prices for primary commodities) typically lead to a ramping up of borrowing. When commodity prices drop, borrowing collapses and defaults step up. Figure 5.5 is an illustration of the commodity price cycle, split into two periods at World War II. As the upper panel of the figure broadly suggests for the period from 1800 through 1940 (and as econometric testing corroborates), spikes in commodity prices are almost invariably followed by waves of new sovereign defaults. The

77

lower panel of figure 5.5 calibrates the same phenomenon for the 1940s through the 2000s. Although the association can be seen in the post–World War II period, it is less compelling.

As observed earlier, defaults are also quite sensitive to the global capital flow cycle. When flows drop precipitously, more coun-

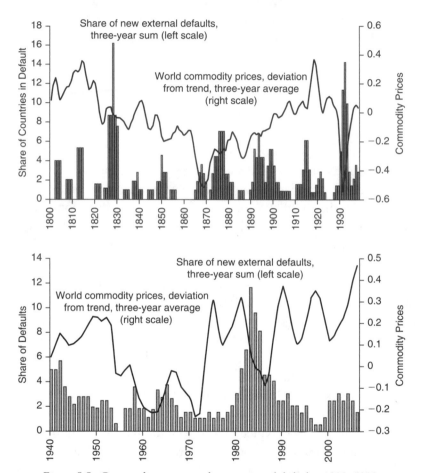

Figure 5.5. Commodity prices and new external defaults, 1800–2008.
Sources: Gayer et al. (1953); Boughton (1991); *The Economist* (2002); International Monetary Fund (various years), *World Economic Outlook;* and the authors' calculations based on the sources listed in appendixes A.1 and A.2. *Notes:* "New external defaults" refers to the first year of default. Because of the marked negative downward drift in commodity prices during the sample period, prices are regressed against a linear trend so as to isolate the cycle.

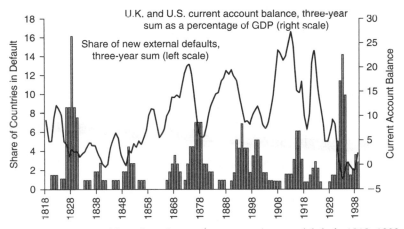

Figure 5.6. Net capital flows from financial centers and external default, 1818–1939.
Sources: Imlah (1958), Mitchell (2003a, 2003b), Carter et al. (2006),
and the Bank of England.
Notes: The current account balance for the United Kingdom and the United States
is defined according to the relative importance (albeit in a simplistic, arbitrary way)
of these countries as the financial centers and primary suppliers of capital to the
rest of the world: for 1818–1913, the United Kingdom receives a weight of 1
(United States, 0); for 1914–1939, both countries' current accounts are equally
weighted; for the period after 1940, the United States receives a weight equal to 1.

tries slip into default. Figure 5.6 documents this association by plotting the current account balance of the financial centers (the United Kingdom and the United States) against the number of new defaults prior to the breakdown of Bretton Woods. There is a marked visual correlation between peaks in the capital flow cycle and new defaults on sovereign debt. The financial centers' current accounts capture the pressures of the "global savings glut," for they give a net measure of excess center-country savings rather than the gross measure given by the capital flow series in our data set.

An even stronger regularity found in the literature on modern financial crises is that countries experiencing sudden large capital inflows are at high risk of experiencing a debt crisis.[15] The preliminary evidence here suggests that the same is true over a much broader sweep of history, with surges in capital inflows often preceding external debt crises at the country, regional, and global levels since 1800, if not before.

We recognize that the correlations captured by these figures are merely illustrative and that different default episodes involve many different factors. But aside from illustrating the kind of insights that can be achieved from such an extensive data set, the figures do bring into sharp relief the vulnerabilities of countries to global business cycles. The problem is that crisis-prone countries, particularly serial defaulters, tend to overborrow in good times, leaving them vulnerable during the inevitable downturns. The pervasive view that "this time is different" is precisely why this time usually is *not* different and why catastrophe eventually strikes again.

The capital flow cycle illustrated in figure 5.6 can be seen even more tellingly in case studies of individual countries, but we do not have the space here to include these.

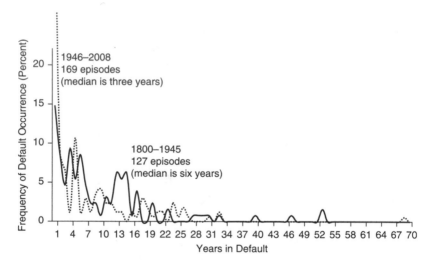

Figure 5.7. Duration of external default episodes, 1800–2008.
Sources: Lindert and Morton (1989); Suter (1992); Purcell and Kaufman (1993); Reinhart, Rogoff, and Savastano (2003a); MacDonald (2006); Standard and Poor's; and the authors' calculations.
Notes: The duration of a default episode is the number of years from the year of default to the year of resolution, be it through restructuring, repayment, or debt forgiveness. The Kolmogorov-Smirnov test for comparing the equality of two distributions rejects the null hypothesis of equal distributions at the 1 percent level of significance.

The Duration of Default Episodes

Another noteworthy insight from the "panoramic view" has to do with the observation that the median duration of default episodes in the post–World War II period has been half their length during 1800–1945 (three years versus six years, as shown in figure 5.7).

The charitable interpretation of this fact is that crisis resolution mechanisms have improved since the bygone days of gunboat diplomacy. After all, Newfoundland lost nothing less than its sovereignty when it defaulted on its external debts in 1936, ultimately becoming a Canadian province (see box 5.2); Egypt, among other countries, became a British "protectorate" following default.

A more cynical explanation points to the possibility that when bailouts are facilitated by multilateral lending institutions such as the International Monetary Fund, creditors are willing to cut more

---

BOX 5.2
External default penalized: The extraordinary case of
Newfoundland, 1928–1933

Just as governments sometimes broker a deal to have a healthy bank take over a bankrupt one, Britain pushed sovereign but bankrupt Newfoundland to be absorbed by Canada.

Newfoundland's fiscal march toward default between 1928 and 1933 can be summarized as follows:

Year	Total public debt (millions)	Ratio of debt to revenue	Interest payments as a share of revenues
1920	n.a.	n.a.	0.20
1928	79.9	8.4	0.40
1929	85.5	8.6	0.39
1930	87.6	7.6	0.36
1931	87.6	9.0	0.44

Year	Total public debt (millions)	Ratio of debt to revenue	Interest payments as a share of revenues
1932	90.1	11.4	0.59
1933	98.5	12.6	1.58

Sources: Baker (1994); League of Nations (various years), *Statistical Yearbook;* and the authors' calculations.

Note: The ratio of total debt to revenue at the time of external default, for an average of 89 episodes, is 4.2. n.a., not available.

Specific events hastened this march:

Time frame or date	Event
1928–1933	Fish prices collapsed by 48 percent, newsprint prices by 35 percent. The value of total exports fell by 27 percent over the same period, imports by 44 percent.[16]
Early 1931	Debt service difficulties began in earnest when the government had to borrow to service its debts.
February 17, 1933	The British government appointed a commission to examine the future of Newfoundland and in particular on the financial situation and the prospects therein.
October 4, 1933	The first recommendation of the commission was to suspend the existing form of government until such time as the island became self-supporting again.
December 21, 1933	The Loan Act was passed giving up sovereignty to avoid the certainty of default.

Between 1928 and 1933, government revenues, still largely derived from customs duties, declined and the ratio of debt to revenue climbed (see the above table). Also, demands for relief payments were increasing, occasioned by the failures of fisheries in 1930–1932. The cost of debt servicing was becoming unbearable.

Well before debt servicing difficulties became manifest in 1931, Newfoundland's fiscal finances were treading on precarious ground. Persistent fiscal deficits throughout the relatively prosperous 1920s had led to mounting (mostly external) debts. The ratio of public debt to revenues, around 8 at the outset of the Great Depression, was twice as high as the ratios of debt to revenue in about ninety default episodes! By 1932, interest payments alone absorbed the lion's share of revenues. A default seemed inevitable. Technically (and only technically), Newfoundland did not default.

As David Hale observes: "The Newfoundland political history of the 1930s is now considered to be a minor chapter in the history of Canada. There is practically no awareness of the extraordinary events which occurred there. The British parliament and the parliament of a self-governing dominion agreed that democracy should be subordinate to debt. The oldest parliament in the British Empire, after Westminster, was abolished and a dictatorship was imposed on 280,000 English-speaking people who had known seventy-eight years of direct democracy. The British government then used its constitutional powers to steer the country into a federation with Canada."[17]

Though not quite to the same extreme as Newfoundland, Egypt, Greece, and Turkey sacrificed partial sovereignty (as regards government finance, at least) to England following their nineteenth-century defaults. The United States established a fiscal protectorate in the Dominican Republic in 1907 in order to control the customs house, and then it occupied the country in 1916. The United States also intervened in Haiti and Nicaragua to control the customs houses and obtain revenue for debt servicing. Such were the days of gunboat diplomacy.

---

slack to their serially defaulting clients. The fact remains that, as Eichengreen observes in several contributions, the length of time separating default episodes in the more recent period (since World War II) has been much shorter. Once debt is restructured, countries are quick to releverage (see the discussion of the Brady plan countries in box 5.3).[18]

BOX 5.3
External default penalized! The case of the missing "Brady bunch"

Is it realistic to assume that a problem debtor country can achieve a "debt reversal" from a high ratio of debt to GDP to a low ratio simply through growth, without a substantial debt write-down? One attempt to do so was the issuance of Brady bonds, U.S. dollar–denominated bonds issued by an emerging market, collateralized by U.S. Treasury zero-coupon bonds. Brady bonds arose from an effort in the 1980s to reduce the debt of developing countries that were frequently defaulting on loans. The bonds were named for Treasury Secretary Nicholas Brady, who promoted the program of debt reduction. Participating countries were Argentina, Brazil, Bulgaria, Costa Rica, the Dominican Republic, Ecuador, Jordan, Mexico, Morocco, Nigeria, Peru, the Philippines, Poland, Uruguay, and Vietnam.

Identifying Debt Reversals

To identify episodes of large debt reversals for middle- and low-income countries over the period 1970–2000, Reinhart, Rogoff, and Savastano selected all episodes in which the ratio of external debt to GNP fell 25 percentage points or more within any three-year period, then ascertained whether the decline in the ratio was caused by a decrease in the numerator, an increase in the denominator, or some combination of the two.[19] The algorithm they used yielded a total of fifty-three debt reversal episodes for the period 1970–2000, twenty-six of them corresponding to middle-income countries and another twenty-seven to low-income countries.

The Debt Reversal Episodes

Of the twenty-two debt reversals detected in middle-income countries with emerging markets, fifteen coincided with some type of default or restructuring of external debt obligations. In six of the seven episodes that did not coincide with a credit event, the debt reversal was effected mainly through net debt repayments; in only one of these episodes (Swaziland, 1985) did the debt ratio decline primarily because the country "grew" out of its debts! Growth was also the principal factor explaining the decline in debt ratios in three of the fifteen default or restructuring cases: those of Morocco, Panama, and the Philippines. Overall, this exercise shows that countries typically do not grow out of their debt burden, providing yet another reason to be skeptical of overly sanguine standard sustainability calculations for debt-intolerant countries.

Of those cases involving credit events, Egypt and Russia obtained (by far) the largest reduction in their nominal debt burden in their restructuring deals. Two Asian countries that experienced crises (Korea and Thailand) engineered the largest debt repayments among the episodes in which a credit event was avoided.

Conspicuously absent from the large debt reversal episodes were the well-known Brady restructuring deals of the 1990s. Although the algorithm used by Reinhart, Rogoff, and Savastano picks up Bulgaria, Costa Rica, Jordan, Nigeria, and Vietnam, larger countries such as Brazil, Mexico, and Poland do not show up in the debt reversal category.

The Puzzle of the Missing "Brady Bunch": An Episode of Fast Releveraging

Reinhart, Rogoff, and Savastano traced the evolution of external debt in the seventeen countries whose external obligations were restructured under the umbrella of the Brady deals in the late 1980s. From this analysis of the profile of external debt, it became clear why the debt reversal algorithm used by

Reinhart, Rogoff, and Savastono did not pick up twelve of the seventeen Brady deals:

- In ten of those twelve cases, the decline in the ratio of external debt to GNP produced by the Brady restructurings was smaller than 25 percentage points. In fact, in Argentina and Peru, three years after the Brady deal the ratio of debt to GNP was higher than it had been in the year prior to the restructuring!
- By the year 2000, seven of the seventeen countries that had undertaken a Brady-type restructuring (Argentina, Brazil, Ecuador, Peru, the Philippines, Poland, and Uruguay) had ratios of external debt to GNP that were higher than those they had experienced three years after the restructuring, and by the end of 2000 four of those countries (Argentina, Brazil, Ecuador, and Peru) had debt ratios that were higher than those recorded prior to the Brady deal.
- By 2003, four members of the Brady bunch (Argentina, Côte D'Ivoire, Ecuador, and Uruguay) had once again defaulted on or restructured their external debt.
- By 2008, less than twenty years after the deal, Ecuador had defaulted twice. A few other members of the Brady group may follow suit.

In the chapter that follows, we document the extensive evidence of the repeated (or serial) nature of the default cycle by country, region, and era. In so doing we include some famous episodes as well as little-documented cases of default or restructuring in the now-advanced economies and in several Asian countries.

- 6 -

EXTERNAL DEFAULT
THROUGH HISTORY

Today's emerging market countries did not invent serial default—that is, repeated sovereign default. Rather, a number of today's now-wealthy countries had similar problems when they were emerging markets. Serial default on external debts is the norm throughout every region in the world, including Asia and Europe.

The perspective offered by the scale (across time) and scope (across countries) of our data set provides an important payoff in understanding defaults: it allows us to see that virtually all countries have defaulted on external debt at least once, and many have done so several times during their emerging market-economy phase, a period that typically lasts at least one or two centuries.

The Early History of Serial Default:
Emerging Europe, 1300–1799

Today's emerging markets can hardly claim credit for inventing serial default. Table 6.1 lists the number of defaults, including the default years, between 1300 and 1799 for a number of now-rich European countries (Austria, England, France, Germany, Portugal, and Spain).

Spain's defaults established a record that as yet remains unbroken. Indeed, Spain managed to default seven times in the nineteenth century alone after having defaulted six times in the preceding three centuries.

With its string of nineteenth-century defaults, Spain took the mantle for most defaults from France, which had abrogated its debt obligations on eight occasions between 1500 and 1800. Because

TABLE 6.1
The early external defaults: Europe, 1300–1799

Country	Years of default	Number of defaults
Austria	1796	1
England	1340, 1472, 1594*	2*
France	1558, 1624, 1648, 1661, 1701, 1715, 1770, 1788	8
Germany (Prussia)	1683	1
Portugal	1560	1
Spain	1557, 1575, 1596, 1607, 1627, 1647	6

Sources: Reinhart, Rogoff, and Savastano (2003a) and sources cited therein, MacDonald (2006).

Note: The asterisk (*) denotes our uncertainty at this time about whether England's default was on domestic or external debt.

during episodes of external debt default the French monarchs had a habit of executing major domestic creditors (an early and decisive form of "debt restructuring"), the population came to refer to these episodes as "bloodletting."[1] The French finance minister Abbe Terray, who served from 1768 to 1774, even opined that governments should default at least once every hundred years in order to restore equilibrium.[2]

Remarkably, however, despite the trauma the country experienced in the wake of the French Revolution and the Napoleonic Wars, France eventually managed to emerge from its status as a serial defaulter. France did not default in the nineteenth or twentieth century, nor has it (so far, anyway) in the twenty-first century. Therefore, France may be considered among the first countries to "graduate" from serial default, a subject considered in more detail in box 6.1. Austria and Portugal defaulted only once in the period up to 1800, but each then defaulted a handful of times during the nineteenth century, as we will see.

Two centuries after England defaulted under Edward III, King Henry VIII engaged in an epic debasement of the currency, effectively defaulting on all the Crown's domestic debts. Moreover, he seized all

---

BOX 6.1

France's graduation after eight external defaults, 1558–1788

French finances were thoroughly unstable prior to 1500, thanks in part to spectacular periodic debasements of the currency. In 1303 alone, France debased the silver content of its coins by more than 50 percent. At times, French revenues from currency manipulation exceeded that from all other sources.[3]

The French monarchy began to run up debts starting in 1522 with Francis I. Eventually, as a result of both extremely opaque financial accounting and continuing dependence on short-term finance, France found itself quite vulnerable when Philip II of Spain upset financial markets with his decision to default in 1557. Just as in modern financial markets, where one country's default can spread contagiously to other countries, the French king, Henry II, soon found himself unable to roll over short-term debt. Henry's efforts to reassure lenders that he had no intention to follow Philip's example by defaulting helped for a while, but by 1558 France had also been forced to default. The crash of 1557–1560 was an event of international scope, radiating throughout much of Europe.[4]

France's immediate problem in 1558 may have been the Spanish default, but its deeper problem was its failure to develop a less opaque system of finances. For example, Francis I systematically sold public offices, in effect giving away future tax revenues in exchange for upfront payments. Corruption was rampant. As a result of the center's loss of control over tax revenue, France found itself constantly rocked by defaults, including many smaller ones in addition to the eight defaults listed in table 6.1.

The War of the Spanish Succession (1701–1714) led to an explosion of debts that especially crippled France, given the difficulties the center faced in ramping up tax revenues. These massive war debts led to some of the most studied and celebrated financial experimentation in history, including the Mississippi and South Sea bubbles memorialized in Charles Kindleberger's classic book on bubbles, manias, and panics.[5]

The final French defaults of the eighteenth century occurred in 1770 and 1788.[6] The default in 1770 followed the Seven Years' War (1756–1763), in which financially better-developed England simply escalated (requiring ever-greater government resources) beyond the capacity of the financially underdeveloped French government to keep up.

Technically, 1788 was the year of France's last default, although, as we will see, postrevolutionary France experienced an epic hyperinflation that effectively led to the elimination of virtually all debts, public and private. Still, what is remarkable about the further course of French history is how the country managed to graduate and avoid further outright defaults.

the Catholic Church's vast lands. Such seizures, often accompanied by executions, although not strictly bond defaults, certainly qualify as reneging on sovereign obligations if not exactly international debt.

Capital Inflows and Default:
An "Old World" Story

The capital flow cycle emerges strikingly in figure 6.1, which is based on seventeenth-century Spain. The figure illustrates how defaults often follow in the wake of large spikes in capital inflows (which often roll in during the euphoria that accompanies the sense that "this time is different").

External Sovereign Default after 1800:
A Global Picture

Starting in the nineteenth century, the combination of the development of international capital markets and the emergence of a number of new nation-states led to an explosion in international defaults.

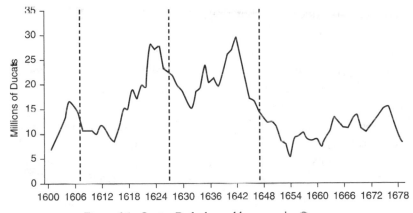

Figure 6.1. Spain: Defaults and loans to the Crown,
1601–1679 (three-year moving sum).
Sources: Gelabert (1999a, 1999b), European State Finance Database (Bonney n.d.).
Note: Defaults of 1607, 1627, and 1647 are represented by vertical lines.

Table 6.2 lists nineteenth-century episodes of default and reschedul-ing in Africa, Europe, and Latin America. We have already explained in chapter 4 why, from a theoretical perspective, debt reschedulings are effectively negotiated partial defaults. The issue is so fundamen-tal here that we feel obliged to expand further, particularly under-scoring why rescheduling is also akin to outright default from a practical perspective

Practitioners rightly view reschedulings as negotiated partial defaults for essentially two reasons. The first reason, of course, is that debt reschedulings often involve reducing interest rates, if not prin-cipal. Second, and perhaps more important, international debt re-schedulings typically saddle investors with illiquid assets that may not pay off for decades. This illiquidity is a huge cost to investors, forcing them to hold a risky asset, often with compensation far be-low the market price of risk. True, investors that have held on to de-faulted sovereign debt for a sufficient number of years—sometimes decades—have often eventually earned a return similar to what they would have earned by investing in relatively risk-free bonds issued by financial centers (the United Kingdom or, later, the United States) over the same period. Indeed, a number of papers have been written showing precisely such calculations.[7]

Although the similarity of these earnings is interesting, it is important to underscore that the right benchmark is the return on high-risk illiquid assets, not highly liquid low-risk assets. It is no coin-cidence that in the wake of the U.S. subprime mortgage debt crisis of 2007, subprime debt sold at a steep discount relative to the expected value of future repayments. Investors rightly believed that if they could pull their money out, they could earn a much higher return elsewhere in the economy provided they were willing to take illiquid positions with substantial risk. And of course they were right. Investing in risky illiquid assets is precisely how venture capital and private equity, not to mention university endowments, have succeeded (until the late 2000s) in earning enormous returns. By contrast, debt reschedulings at negotiated below-market interest rates impose risk on the creditor with none of the upside of, say, a venture capital investment. Thus, the dis-

TABLE 6.2

External default and rescheduling: Africa, Europe, and Latin America, nineteenth century

Country, date of independence[a]	Years of default and rescheduling			
	1800–1824	1825–1849	1850–1874	1875–1899
Africa				
Egypt, 1831				1876
Tunisia			1867	
Europe				
Austria-Hungary	1802, 1805, 1811, 1816		1868	
France	1812			
Germany				
Hesse	1814			
Prussia	1807, 1813			
Schleswig-Holstein			1850	
Westphalia	1812			
Greece, 1829		1826, 1843	1860	1893
The Netherlands	1814			
Portugal		1828, 1837, 1841, 1845	1852	1890
Russia		1839		1885
Spain	1809, 1820	1831, 1834	1851, 1867, 1872	1882
Sweden	1812			
Turkey				1876
Latin America				
Argentina, 1816		1827		1890
Bolivia, 1825				1875
Brazil, 1822				1898
Chile, 1818		1826		1880
Colombia, 1819		1826	1850, 1873	1880
Costa Rica, 1821		1828	1874	1895
Dominican Republic, 1845			1872	1892, 1897, 1899
Ecuador, 1830		1826	1868	1894
El Salvador, 1821		1828		1898
Guatemala, 1821		1828		1876, 1894, 1899
Honduras, 1821		1828	1873	
Mexico, 1821		1827, 1833, 1844	1866	1898
Nicaragua, 1821		1828		1894
Paraguay, 1811			1874	1892
Peru, 1821		1826		1876
Uruguay, 1811				1876, 1891
Venezuela, 1830		1826, 1848	1860, 1865	1892, 1898

Sources: Standard and Poor's, Purcell and Kaufman (1993), Reinhart, Rogoff, and Savastano (2003a) and sources cited therein.

[a]The years are shown for those countries that became independent during the nineteenth century.

tinction between debt reschedulings—negotiated partial defaults—and outright defaults (which typically end in partial repayment) is not a sharp one.

Table 6.2 also lists each country's year of independence. Most of Africa and Asia was colonized during this period, giving Europe and Latin America a substantial head start on the road to fiscal profligacy and default. The only African countries to default during this period were Tunisia (1867) and Egypt (1876). Austria, albeit not quite so prolific as Spain, defaulted a remarkable five times. Greece, which gained its independence only in 1829, made up for lost time by defaulting four times. Default was similarly rampant throughout the Latin American region, with Venezuela defaulting six times and Colombia, Costa Rica, the Dominican Republic, and Honduras defaulting four times.

Looking down the columns of table 6.2 also gives us a first glimpse of the clustering of defaults regionally and internationally. Note that a number of countries in Europe defaulted during or just after the Napoleonic Wars, whereas many countries in Latin America (plus their mother country, Spain) defaulted during the 1820s (see box 6.2 for a summary of Latin America's early days in international markets). Most of these defaults were associated with Latin America's wars of independence. Although none of the subsequent clusterings have been quite so pronounced in terms of the number of countries involved, notable episodes of global default occurred from the late 1860s to the mid-1870s and again from the mid-1880s through the early 1890s. We look at this clustering a bit more systematically later.

Next we turn to the twentieth century. Table 6.3 shows defaults in Africa and Asia, including the many newly colonized countries. Nigeria, despite its oil riches, has defaulted a stunning five times since achieving independence in 1960, more often than any other country over the same period. Indonesia has defaulted four times. Morocco, counting its first default in 1903 during an earlier era of independence, also defaulted three times in the twentieth century. India prides itself on having escaped the Asian crisis of the 1990s

---

BOX 6.2
Latin America's early days in international capital markets, 1822–1825

Borrowing by the newly independent (or newly invented) nations of Latin America between 1822 and 1825 is reflected in the following table:

State	Total value of bonds issued in London, 1822–1825 (£)
Argentina (Buenos Aires) ·	3,200,000
Brazil	1,000,000
Central America	163,300
Chile	1,000,000
Gran Colombia (Colombia, Ecuador, Venezuela)	6,750,000
Mexico	6,400,000
Peru	1,816,000
Poyais	200,000

Sources: Marichal (1989) and the authors.

The volatile and often chaotic European financial markets of the Napoleonic Wars had settled down by the early 1820s. Spain had, in quick succession, lost colony after colony in Central and South America, and the legendary silver and gold mines of the New World were up for grabs.

Forever engaged in an endless quest for higher yields, London bankers and investors were swept away by silver fever. The great demand in Europe for investment opportunities in Latin America, coupled with new leaders in Latin America desperate for funds to support the process of nation building (among other things), produced a surge in lending from (mostly) London to (mostly) Latin American sovereigns.[8]

According to Marichal, by mid-1825 twenty-six mining companies had been registered in the Royal Exchange. Any investment in Latin America became as coveted as South Sea shares (by 1825 already infamous) had been a century earlier. In this "irrationally exuberant" climate, Latin American states raised more than 20 million pounds during 1822–1825.

"General Sir" Gregor MacGregor, who had traveled to Latin America and fought as a mercenary in Simon Bolivar's army, seized the opportunity to convince fellow Scots to invest their savings in the fictitious country of Poyais. Its capital city, Saint Joseph (according to the investment prospectus circulated at the time), boasted "broad boulevards, colonnaded buildings, and a splendid domed cathedral." Those who were brave and savvy enough to cross the Atlantic and settle Poyais would be able to build sawmills to exploit the native forests and establish gold mines.[9] London bankers were also impressed with such prospects of riches, and in 1822 MacGregor (the Prince of

Poyais) issued a bond in London for £160,000 at a price of issue to the public of £80, well above the issue price for the first Chilean bond floated.[10] The interest rate of 6 percent was the same as that available to Buenos Aires, Central America, Chile, Greater Colombia, and Peru during that episode. Perhaps it is just as well that Poyais faced the same borrowing terms as the real sovereigns, for the latter would all default on their external debts during 1826–1828, marking the first Latin American debt crisis.

(thanks in part to massive capital controls and financial repression). In point of fact, it has been forced to reschedule its external debt three times since independence, albeit not since 1972. Although China did not default during its communist era, it did default on external debt in both 1921 and 1939.

Thus, as table 6.3 illustrates, the notion that countries in Latin America and low-income Europe were the only ones to default during the twentieth century is an exaggeration, to say the least.

Table 6.4 looks at Europe and Latin America, regions in which, with only a few exceptions, countries were independent throughout the twentieth century. Again, as in the earlier tables, we see that country defaults tend to come in clusters, including especially the period of the Great Depression, when much of the world went into default; the 1980s debt crisis; and the 1990s debt crisis. The last of these episodes saw somewhat fewer technical defaults thanks to massive intervention by the official community, particularly the International Monetary Fund and the World Bank. Whether these massive interventions were well advised is a different issue that we will set aside here. Notable in table 6.4 are Turkey's five defaults, Peru's six, and Brazil's and Ecuador's seven. Other countries, too, have had as many defaults.

So far we have focused on the number of defaults, but this measure is somewhat arbitrary. Default episodes can be connected, particularly if the terms of debt restructuring are harsh and make relapse into default almost inevitable. In these tables we have tried to exclude obviously connected episodes, so when a follow-on default occurs within two years of an earlier one, we count the two defaults

TABLE 6.3
Default and rescheduling: Africa and Asia, twentieth century to 2008

Country, date of independence[a]	Years of default and rescheduling			
	1900–1924	1925–1949	1950–1974	1975–2008
Africa				
Algeria, 1962				1991
Angola, 1975				1985
Central African Republic, 1960				1981, 1983
Côte d'Ivoire, 1960				1983, 2000
Egypt				1984
Kenya, 1963				1994, 2000
Morocco, 1956	1903			1983, 1986
Nigeria, 1960				1982, 1986, 1992, 2001, 2004
South Africa, 1910				1985, 1989, 1993
Zambia, 1964				1983
Zimbabwe, 1965			1965	2000
Asia				
China	1921	1939		
Japan		1942		
India, 1947			1958, 1969, 1972	
Indonesia, 1949			1966	1998, 2000, 2002
Myanmar, 1948				2002
The Philippines, 1947				1983
Sri Lanka, 1948				1980, 1982

Sources: Standard and Poor's, Purcell and Kaufman (1993), Reinhart, Rogoff, and Savastano (2003a) and sources cited therein.
[a]The years are shown for those countries that became independent during the twentieth century.

as one episode. However, to gain further perspective into countries' default histories, we next look at the number of years each country has spent in default since it achieved independence.

We begin by tabulating the results for Asia and Africa in table 6.5. For each country, the table gives the year of independence,

TABLE 6.4
Default and rescheduling: Europe and Latin America, twentieth century to 2008

Country, date of independence[a]	Years of default and rescheduling			
	1900–1924	1925–1949	1950–1974	1975–2008
Europe				
Austria		1938, 1940		
Germany		1932, 1939		
Greece		1932		
Hungary, 1918		1932, 1941		
Poland, 1918		1936, 1940		1981
Romania		1933		1981, 1986
Russia	1918			1991, 1998
Turkey	1915	1931, 1940		1978, 1982
Latin America				
Argentina			1951, 1956	1982, 1989, 2001
Bolivia		1931		1980, 1986, 1989
Brazil	1902, 1914	1931, 1937	1961, 1964	1983
Chile		1931	1961, 1963, 1966, 1972, 1974	1983
Colombia	1900	1932, 1935		
Costa Rica	1901	1932	1962	1981, 1983, 1984
Dominican Republic		1931		1982, 2005
Ecuador	1906, 1909, 1914	1929		1982, 1999, 2008
El Salvador	1921	1932, 1938		
Guatemala		1933		1986, 1989
Honduras				1981
Mexico	1914	1928		1982
Nicaragua	1911, 1915	1932		1979
Panama, 1903		1932		1983, 1987
Paraguay	1920	1932		1986, 2003
Peru		1931	1969	1976, 1978, 1980, 1984
Uruguay	1915	1933		1983, 1987, 1990, 2003
Venezuela				1983, 1990, 1995, 2004

Sources: Standard and Poor's, Purcell and Kaufman (1993), Reinhart, Rogoff, and Savastano (2003a) and sources cited therein.

Note: The World War II external debts of the Allied countries to the United States were repaid only by mutual agreement, notably that of the United Kingdom. Technically, this debt forgiveness constitutes a default.

[a]The years are shown for those countries that became independent during the twentieth century.

TABLE 6.5

The cumulative tally of default and rescheduling: Africa and Asia,
year of independence to 2008

Country	Share of years in default or rescheduling since independence or 1800[a]	Total number of defaults and/or reschedulings
Africa		
Algeria	13.3	1
Angola	59.4	1
Central African Republic	53.2	2
Côte d'Ivoire	48.9	2
Egypt	3.4	2
Kenya	13.6	2
Mauritius	0.0	0
Morocco	15.7	4
Nigeria	21.3	5
South Africa	5.2	3
Tunisia	5.3	1
Zambia	27.9	1
Zimbabwe	40.5	2
Asia		
China	13.0	2
Hong Kong	0.0	0
India	11.7	3
Indonesia	15.5	4
Japan	5.3	1
Korea	0.0	0
Malaysia	0.0	0
Myanmar	8.5	1
The Philippines	16.4	1
Singapore	0.0	0
Sri Lanka	6.8	2
Taiwan	0.0	0
Thailand	0.0	0

Sources: Authors' calculations, Standard and Poor's, Purcell and Kaufman (1993), Reinhart, Rogoff, and Savastano (2003a) and sources cited therein.

[a]For countries that became independent prior to 1800, the calculations are for 1800–2008.

the total number of defaults and reschedulings (using our measure), and the share (percentage) of years since 1800 (or since independence, if more recent) the country has spent in a state of default or rescheduling. It is notable that, although there have been many defaults in Asia, the typical default has been resolved relatively quickly. Only China, India, Indonesia, and the Philippines spent more than 10 percent of their independent lives in default (though of course on a population-weighted basis, those countries make up most of the region). Africa's record is far worse, with several countries having spent roughly half their time in default. Certainly one of the main reasons that African defaults are less celebrated than, say, Latin American defaults is that the debts of African countries have typically been relatively small and the systemic consequences less acute. These circumstances have not made the consequences any less painful for Africa's residents, of course, who must bear the same costs in terms of sudden fiscal consolidation and reduced access to credit, often accompanied by higher interest rates and exchange rate depreciation.

Table 6.6 gives the same set of statistics for Europe and Latin America. Greece, as noted, has spent more than half the years since 1800 in default. A number of Latin American countries spent roughly 40 percent of their years in default, including Costa Rica, the Dominican Republic, Mexico, Nicaragua, Peru, and Venezuela.

The same prevalence of default has been seen across most European countries, although there has been a great deal of variance, depending especially on how long countries have tended to remain in default (compare serial debtor Austria, which has tended to emerge from default relatively quickly, with Greece, which lived in a perpetual state of default for over a century). Overall, one can see that default episodes, while recurrent, are far from continuous. This wide spacing no doubt reflects adjustments that debtors and creditors make in the wake of each default cycle. For example, today many emerging markets are following quite conservative macroeconomic policies. Over time, though, this caution usually gives way to optimism and profligacy, but only after a long lull.

One way of summarizing the data in tables 6.5 and 6.6 is to look at a timeline giving the number of countries in default or re-

TABLE 6.6

The cumulative tally of default and rescheduling: Europe, Latin America,
North America, and Oceania, year of independence to 2008

Country	Share of years in default or rescheduling since independence or 1800[a]	Total number of defaults and/or reschedulings
Europe		
Austria	17.4	7
Belgium	0.0	0
Denmark	0.0	0
Finland	0.0	0
France	0.0	8
Germany	13.0	8
Greece	50.6	5
Hungary	37.1	7
Italy	3.4	1
The Netherlands	6.3	1
Norway	0.0	0
Poland	32.6	3
Portugal	10.6	6
Romania	23.3	3
Russia	39.1	5
Spain	23.7	13
Sweden	0.0	0
Turkey	15.5	6
United Kingdom	0.0	0
Latin America		
Argentina	32.5	7
Bolivia	22.0	5
Brazil	25.4	9
Chile	27.5	9
Colombia	36.2	7
Costa Rica	38.2	9
Dominican Republic	29.0	7
Ecuador	58.2	9
El Salvador	26.3	5
Guatemala	34.4	7
Honduras	64.0	3
Mexico	44.6	8
Nicaragua	45.2	6

(continued)

TABLE 6.6 Continued

Country	Share of years in default or rescheduling since independence or 1800[a]	Total number of defaults and/or reschedulings
Latin America (*continued*)		
Panama	27.9	3
Paraguay	23.0	6
Peru	40.3	8
Uruguay	12.8	8
Venezuela	38.4	10
North America		
Canada	0.0	0
United States	0.0	0
Oceania		
Australia	0.0	0
New Zealand	0.0	0

Sources: The authors' calculations, Standard and Poor's, Purcell and Kaufman (1993), Reinhart, Rogoff, and Savastano (2003a) and sources cited therein.

[a]For countries that became independent prior to 1800, the calculations are for 1800–2008.

structuring at any given time. We have already seen such a timeline in figure 5.1 in terms of the total number of countries and in figure 5.2 in terms of the share of world income. These figures illustrate the clustering of defaults in an even more pronounced fashion than do our debt tables that mark first defaults.

Later, in chapter 16, we will take a deeper and more systematic look at what truly constitutes a global financial crisis.

- PART III -

THE FORGOTTEN HISTORY OF
DOMESTIC DEBT AND DEFAULT

For most countries, finding data, even a couple of decades old, on domestic public debt is an exercise in archaeology.

- 7 -

THE STYLIZED FACTS OF
DOMESTIC DEBT AND DEFAULT

Domestic debt is a large portion of countries' total debt; for the sixty-four countries for which we have long-range time series, domestic debt averages almost two-thirds of total public debt. For most of the sample, these debts have typically carried a market interest rate except during the era of financial repression after World War II.

Domestic and External Debt

In part I we discussed the surprisingly exotic nature of our long-range sixty-four-country data set on domestic debt. Indeed, only recently have a few groups of scholars begun constructing data for the contemporary period.[1]

Figure 7.1 plots the share of domestic debt in total public debt for 1900–2007. It ranges between 40 and 80 percent of total debt. (See appendix A.2 for data availability by country.) Figures 7.2 and 7.3 break this information out by regions. The numbers in these figures are simple averages across countries, but the ratios are also fairly representative of many of the emerging markets in the sample (including now-rich countries such as Austria, Greece, and Spain when they were still emerging markets).[2] As the graphs underscore, our data set includes significant representation from every continent, not just a handful of Latin American and European countries, as is the case in most of the literature on external debt.

Of course, the experience has been diverse. For advanced economies, domestic debt accounts for the lion's share of public sector liabilities. At the other extreme, in some emerging markets, especially

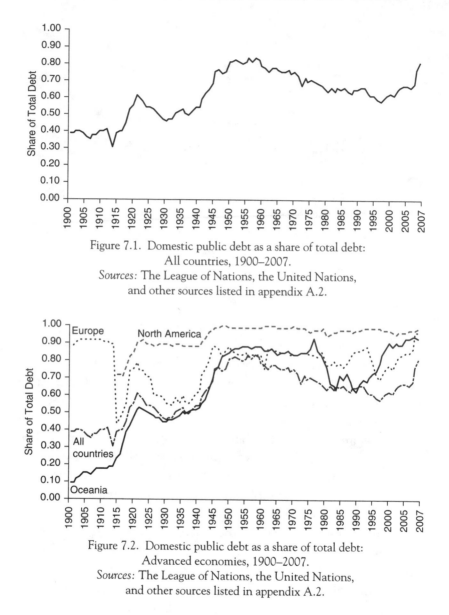

Figure 7.1. Domestic public debt as a share of total debt:
All countries, 1900–2007.
Sources: The League of Nations, the United Nations,
and other sources listed in appendix A.2.

Figure 7.2. Domestic public debt as a share of total debt:
Advanced economies, 1900–2007.
Sources: The League of Nations, the United Nations,
and other sources listed in appendix A.2.

in the 1980s and 1990s, domestic debt markets were dealt a brutal blow by many governments' propensity to inflate (sometimes leading to hyperinflation). For instance, in the years following the hyperinflation of 1989 to 1990, domestic debt accounted for 10 to 20 percent of Peru's

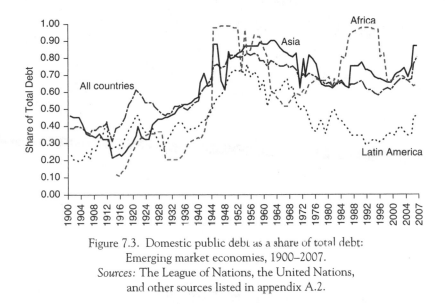

Figure 7.3. Domestic public debt as a share of total debt:
Emerging market economies, 1900–2007.
Sources: The League of Nations, the United Nations,
and other sources listed in appendix A.2.

public debt. Yet this was not always so. The early entries in the League of Nations data from the end of World War I show that Peru's domestic debt at the time accounted for about two-thirds of its public sector debt, as was then the case for many other countries in Latin America. Indeed, the share was even higher in the 1950s, when the world's financial centers were not engaged in much external lending.

Maturity, Rates of Return, and Currency Composition

In addition to showing that domestic public debt is a large portion of total debt, the data also dispel the belief that until recently emerging markets (and developing countries) had never been able to borrow long term. As figure 7.4 shows, long-term debt constitutes a large share of the total debt stock over a significant part of the sample, at least for the period 1914–1959. For this subperiod, the League of Nations/ United Nations database provides considerable detail on maturity structure. It may come as a surprise to many readers (as it did to us) that the modern bias toward short-term debt is a relatively recent phe-

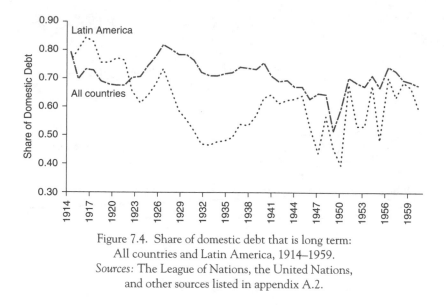

Figure 7.4. Share of domestic debt that is long term:
All countries and Latin America, 1914–1959.
Sources: The League of Nations, the United Nations,
and other sources listed in appendix A.2.

nomenon, evidently a product of the "inflation fatigue" of the 1970s
and 1980s.

Also not particularly novel was the fact that many emerging
markets began paying market-oriented interest rates on their domestic debt in the decade before the 2007 financial crisis. Of course, during the post–World War II era, many governments repressed their
domestic financial markets, with low ceilings on deposit rates and
high requirements for bank reserves, among other devices, such as directed credit and minimum requirements for holding government
debt in pension and commercial bank portfolios. But in fact, interest
rate data for the first half of the twentieth century shows that financial repression was neither so strong nor so universal. As table 7.1
shows for the years 1928–1946 (the period for which we have the best
documentation), interest rates on domestic and external debt issues
were relatively similar, supporting the notion that the interest rates
on domestic public debt were market determined, or at least reflected
market forces to a significant extent.

A final issue has to do with the extent of inflation or foreign
currency indexation. Many observers viewed Mexico's famous issuance of dollar-linked domestic debt in the early 1990s (the so-

106

TABLE 7.1

Interest rates on domestic and external debt, 1928–1946

Country	Range of interest rates (percent)	
	Domestic debt issues	External debt issues
Argentina	3–6	$3^1/_2$–$4^1/_2$
Australia	2–4	3.375–5
Austria	$4^1/_2$–6	5
Belgium	$3^1/_2$–5	3–7
Bolivia	$^1/_4$–8	6–8
Brazil	4–7	4–7
Bulgaria	4–$6^1/_2$	7–$7^1/_2$
Canada	1–$5^1/_2$	$1^1/_4$–$5^1/_2$
Chile	1–8	$4^1/_2$–7
Colombia	3–10	3–6
Costa Rica	6	5–$7^1/_2$
Denmark	$2^1/_2$–5	$4^1/_2$–6
Ecuador	3	4–8
Egypt	$2^1/_2$–$4^1/_2$	$3^1/_2$–4
Finland	4–$5^1/_2$	$2^1/_2$–7
Germany	$3^1/_2$–7	$5^1/_2$–6
Greece	3–9	3–10
Hungary	$3^1/_2$–5	3–$7^1/_2$
India	3–$5^1/_2$	3–$5^1/_2$
Italy	$3^1/_2$ 5	No external debt
Japan	$3^1/_2$–5	4–$6^1/_2$
The Netherlands	$2^1/_2$–6	No external debt
New Zealand	$2^1/_2$–4	$2^1/_2$–5
Nicaragua	5	4–5
Poland	3–7	3–7
Portugal	2.1–7	3–4
Romania	$3^1/_2$–5	4–7
South Africa	$3^1/_2$–6	$3^1/_2$–6
Spain	$3^1/_2$–6	3–4
Sweden	$2^1/_2$–$4^1/_2$	No external debt
Thailand	$2^1/_2$–$4^1/_2$	$4^1/_2$–7
Turkey	$2^1/_2$–$5^1/_2$	$6^1/_2$–$7^1/_2$
United Kingdom	$1^1/_2$–4	No marketable external debt
United States	$1^1/_2$–$2^1/_2$	No external debt
Uruguay	5–7	$3^1/_2$–6
Venezuela	3	3

Source: United Nations (1948).

Notes: Rates on domestic issues are for long-term debt, because this facilitates comparison to external debt, which has a similar maturity profile. The higher interest rates are the most representative.

called *tesobonos*) as a major innovation. As the thinking went, this time was truly different. We know by now that the situation was nothing new; Argentina had issued domestic government bonds in the late 1800s that were denominated in pounds sterling, and Thailand had issued dollar-linked domestic debt in the 1960s. (See box 7.1 for the case studies and the appendixes for sources.)[3]

We can summarize what we know about domestic debt by noting that over most of history, for most countries (especially emerg-

---

BOX 7.1
Foreign currency–linked domestic debt: Thai *tesobonos?*

Our time series on domestic debt covers sixty-four of the sixty-six countries in the sample and begins in 1914 (and in several cases much earlier). During this lengthy period, domestic debt has been almost exclusively (especially prior to the 1990s) denominated in the domestic currency and held predominantly by domestic residents (usually banks). However, there have been notable exceptions that have blurred the lines between domestic and foreign debt. Some examples follow.

Mexican Dollar-Linked Domestic Debt:
The "Infamous" Tesobonos

As part of an inflation stabilization plan, in the late 1980s the Mexican peso was tied to the U.S. dollar via an official preannounced exchange rate band; de facto, it was a peg to the U.S. dollar. In early 1994, the peso came under speculative pressure following the assassination of presidential candidate Luis Donaldo Colosio. To reassure (largely) U.S. investors heavily exposed to Mexican treasury bonds that the government was committed to maintaining the value of the peso, the Mexican authorities began to link to the U.S. dollar its considerable stock of short-term domestic debt by means of "tesobonos," short-term debt instruments repayable in pesos but linked to the U.S. dollar. By December 1994, when a new wave of speculation against the currency broke out, nearly all the domestic debt was dollar denominated. Before the end of the year, the peso was allowed to float; it immediately crashed, and a major episode of the twin currency and banking crises unfolded into early 1995. Had it not been for a then-record bailout package from the International Monetary Fund and the U.S. government, in all likelihood Mexico would have faced default on its sovereign debts. The central bank's dollar reserves had been nearly depleted and would not suffice to cover maturing bonds.

Because the *tesobonos* were dollar linked and held mostly by non-residents, most observers viewed the situation as a replay of August 1982, when Mexico had defaulted on is external debt to U.S. commercial banks. A nontrivial twist in the 1995 situation was that, if default proceedings had been necessary, they would have come under the jurisdiction of Mexican law. This episode increased international awareness of the vulnerabilities associated with heavily relying on foreign currency debt of any sort. The Mexican experience did not stop Brazil from issuing copious amounts of dollar-linked debt during the run-up to its turbulent exit from the *Real* Plan. Surprisingly, Mexico's earlier crisis had not raised concerns about the validity or usefulness of debt sustainability exercises that focused exclusively on external debt. Domestic government debt would continue to be ignored by the multilaterals and the financial industry for nearly another decade.

Argentine U.K. Pound–Denominated "Internal" Bonds of the Late Nineteenth and Early Twentieth Centuries

The earliest emerging market example of modern-day foreign currency–linked domestic debt widely targeted at nonresidents that we are aware of comes from Argentina in 1872.[4] After defaulting on its first loans in the 1820s, Argentina remained mostly out of international capital markets until the late 1860s. With some interruptions, most famously the Barings crisis of 1890, Argentina issued numerous external bonds in London and at least three more placements of domestic (or internal, as these were called) bonds in 1888, 1907, and 1909. Both the external and internal bonds were denominated in U.K. pounds. About a century later, after Argentina had fought (and lost) a long war with chronic high inflation, its domestic debts (as well as its banking sector) would become almost completely dollarized.[5]

Thailand's "Curious" Dollar-Linked Debt of the 1960s

Thailand is not a country troubled by a history of high inflation. Two large devaluations occurred in 1950 and 1954, and they had some moderate inflationary impact, but the situation during the late 1950s and early 1960s could hardly be described as one that would have fostered the need for an inflation hedge, such as indexing debts or issuing contracts to a foreign currency. Yet for reasons that remain a mystery to us, between 1961 and 1968 the Thai government issued dollar-linked domestic debt. During this period, domestic debt accounted for 80–90 percent of all government debt. Only about 10 percent of the domestic debt stock was linked to the U.S. dollar, so at no point in time was the Thai episode a case of significant "liability dollarization." We do not have information as to who were the primary holders of the domestic dollar-linked debt; perhaps such data might provide a clue as to why it came about in the first place.

ing markets), domestic debt has been a large and highly significant part of total debt. Nothing about the maturity structure of these debts or the interest rates paid on them lends justification to the common practice of ignoring them in calculations of the sustainability of external debt or the stability of inflation.

We acknowledge that our data set has important limitations. First, the data generally cover only central government debt. Of course, it would be desirable to have long-range time series on consolidated government debt, including state and local debt and guaranteed debt for quasi-public agencies. Furthermore, many central banks across the world issue debt on their own, often to sterilize foreign exchange intervention.[6] Adding such data, of course, would only expand the perception of how important domestic public debt has been.

We now take up some important potential applications of the data.

Episodes of Domestic Default

Theoretical models encompass a wide range of assumptions about domestic public debt. The overwhelming majority of models simply assume that debt is always honored. These include models in which deficit policy is irrelevant due to Ricardian equivalence.[7] (Ricardian equivalence is basically the proposition that when a government cuts taxes by issuing debt, the public does not spend any of its higher after-tax income because it realizes it will need to save to pay taxes later.) Models in which debt is always honored include those in which domestic public debt is a key input in price level determination through the government's budget constraint and models in which generations overlap.[8] There is a small amount of literature that aims to help us understand why governments honor domestic debt at all.[9] However, the general assumption throughout the literature is that although governments may inflate debt away, outright defaults on domestic public debt are extremely rare. This assumption is in stark contrast to the literature on external public debt, in which the government's incentive to default is one of the main focuses of inquiry.

110

In fact, our reading of the historical record is that overt de jure defaults on domestic public debt, though less common than external defaults, are hardly rare. Our data set includes more than 70 cases of overt default (compared to 250 defaults on external debt) since 1800.[10] These de jure defaults took place via a potpourri of mechanisms, ranging from forcible conversions to lower coupon rates to unilateral reduction of principal (sometimes in conjunction with a currency conversion) to suspensions of payments. Tables 7.2–7.4 list these episodes. Figure 7.5 aggregates the data, plotting the share of countries in default on domestic debt each year.

Our catalog of domestic defaults is almost certainly a lower bound, for domestic defaults are far more difficult to detect than defaults on international debt. Even the widespread defaults on domestic debt during the Great Depression of the 1930s in both advanced and developing economies are not well documented. As a more recent example, consider Argentina. Between 1980 and 2001, Argentina defaulted three times on its domestic debt. The two defaults that coincided with defaults on external debt (in 1982 and 2001) did attract considerable international attention. However, the large-scale 1989 default, which did not involve a new default on external debt, is scarcely known outside Argentina.

Some Caveats Regarding Domestic Debt

Why would a government refuse to pay its domestic public debt in full when it can simply inflate the problem away? One answer, of course, is that inflation causes distortions, especially to the banking system and the financial sector. There may be occasions on which, despite the inflation option, the government views repudiation as the lesser, or at least less costly, evil. The potential costs of inflation are especially problematic when the debt is relatively short term or indexed, because the government then has to inflate much more aggressively to achieve a significant real reduction in debt service payments. In other cases, such as in the United States during the Great Depression, default (by abrogation of the gold clause in 1933)

TABLE 7.2

Selected episodes of domestic debt default or restructuring, 1740–1921

Country	Dates	Commentary
Argentina	1890	This default also extended to several "internal" bonds. These bonds, although not issued in London, were denominated in a foreign currency (£s) and marketed abroad—the forerunners of the Mexican *tesobonos* of the 1990s.
China	March 1921	A consolidated internal debt plan was used to deal with arrears on most government bonds since 1919.
Denmark	January 1813	During the crisis, foreign debts were serviced but domestic debt was reduced by 39 percent.
Mexico	November 30, 1850	After the restructuring of foreign debt in October of that year, domestic debt, which accounted for 60 percent of total public debt, was cut roughly in half.
Peru	1850	Domestic colonial debts were not canceled; debt prices collapsed, and this debt was finally restructured.
Russia	December 1917–October 1918	Debts were repudiated and gold in all forms was confiscated, followed by confiscation of all foreign exchange.
United Kingdom	1749, 1822, 1834, 1888–1889	These were among several conversions of debt into lower coupon rates. The reductions in rates were mostly 0.5–1.0 percent in these episodes.
United States	January 1790	Nominally, interest was maintained at 6 percent, but a portion of the interest was deferred for ten years.
United States (nine states)	1841–1842	Three states repudiated their debts altogether.
United States (states and many local governments)	1873–1883 or 1884	By 1873, ten states were in default. In the case of West Virginia, settlement was as late as 1919.

Sources: Many sources were used in constructing this table. All are listed in the references.

TABLE 7.3
Selected episodes of domestic debt default or restructuring, late 1920s–1950s

Country	Dates	Commentary
Bolivia	1927	Arrears of interest lasted until at least 1940.
Canada (Alberta)	April 1935	This was the only province to default and the default lasted for about ten years.
China	1932	In this first of several "consolidations," the monthly cost of domestic service was cut in half. Interest rates were reduced to 6 percent (from more than 9 percent), and amortization periods were approximately doubled.
Greece	1932	Interest on domestic debt was reduced by 75 percent starting in 1932; domestic debt was about one-fourth of total public debt.
Mexico	1930s	Service on external debt was suspended in 1928. During the 1930s, interest payments included "arrears of expenditure and civil and military pensions."[a]
Peru	1931	After suspending service on external debt on May 29, Peru made "partial interest payments" on domestic debt.
Romania	February 1933	Redemption of domestic and foreign debt was suspended (except for three loans).
Spain	October 1936– April 1939	Interest payments on external debt were suspended; arrears on domestic debt service accumulated.
United States	1933	The gold clause was abrogated. In effect, the United States refused to pay Panama the annuity in gold that was due to Panama according to a 1903 treaty. The dispute was settled in 1936, when the United States paid the agreed amount in gold *balboas*.

(continued)

113

TABLE 7.3 Continued

Country	Dates	Commentary
United Kingdom[b]	1932	Most of the outstanding debt from World War I was consolidated into a 3.5 percent perpetual annuity.
Uruguay	November 1, 1932– February 1937	After suspending redemption of external debt on January 20, redemptions on domestic debt were likewise suspended.
Austria	December 1945	The schilling was restored, with a limit of 150 per person; the remainder were placed in blocked accounts. In December 1947, large amounts of previously blocked schillings were invalidated and rendered worthless. Fifty percent of deposits were temporarily blocked.
Germany	June 20, 1948	Monetary reform limited each person to 40 Deutschemark, along with partial cancellation and blocking of all accounts.
Japan	March 2, 1946–1952	After inflation, one-to-one exchange of bank notes for new issue was limited to 100 yen per person. Remaining balances were deposited in blocked accounts.
Russia	1947	The monetary reform subjected privately held currency to a 90 percent reduction.
	April 10, 1957	Domestic debt (about 253 billion rubles at the time) was repudiated.

Sources: Many sources were used in constructing this table. All are listed in the references.

[a]League of Nations (various years), *Statistical Abstract.*

[b]World War II debts to the United States were only partially repaid, by mutual agreement. Technically, this debt forgiveness constitutes a default.

TABLE 7.4

Selected episodes of domestic debt default or restructuring, 1970–2008

Country	Dates	Commentary
Africa		
Angola	1976, 1992–2002	
Cameroon	2004	
Congo (Kinshasa)	1979	
Gabon	1999–2005	
Ghana	1979, 1982	The country defaulted on central bank notes (in the context of conversion to a new currency).
Liberia	1989–2006	
Madagascar	2002	
Mozambique	1980	
Rwanda	1995	No external default.
Sierra Leone	1997–1998	
Sudan	1991	
Zimbabwe	2006	With maturities of less than a year for more than 98.5 percent of domestic debt, it was restructured.
Asia		
Mongolia	1997–2000	
Myanmar	1984, 1987	
Sri Lanka	1996	No external default.
Solomon Islands	1995–2004	
Vietnam	1975	
Europe and the Middle East		
Croatia	1993–1996	
Kuwait	1990–1991	
Russia	1998–1999	This was the largest local currency debt default (US$39 billion) since that in Brazil in 1990.
Ukraine	1998–2000	Bond maturities were unilaterally extended.
Western Hemisphere		
Antigua and Barbuda	1998–2005	

(continued)

115

TABLE 7.4 Continued

Country	Dates	Commentary
Western Hemisphere (*continued*)		
Argentina	1982, 1989–1990, 2002–2005	U.S. dollar–denominated debt was forcibly converted to peso debt.
Bolivia	1982	Deposits in U.S. dollars were forcibly converted into local currency. Foreign currency deposits were again allowed in 1985 as part of the stabilization plan when capital controls were lifted.
Brazil	1986–1987, 1990	Abrogation of inflation-linked indexes was embedded in the original contracts. The largest default (US$62 billion) occurred in 1990.
Dominica	2003–2005	
Dominican Republic	1975–2001	
Ecuador	1999	
El Salvador	1981–1996	This is the only case in Latin America in which a default on domestic debt was *not* accompanied by external default.
Grenada	2004–2005	
Mexico	1982	Dollar deposits were forcibly converted to pesos.
Panama	1988–1989	Domestic suppliers' credit, wages, and civil and military pensions were in arrears.
Peru	1985	Deposits in U.S. dollars were forcibly converted into local currency. Foreign currency deposits were allowed again in 1988.
Surinam	2001–2002	
Venezuela	1995–1997, 1998	

Sources: Many sources were used in constructing this table. All are listed in the references.

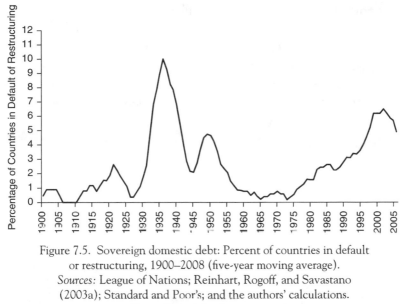

Figure 7.5. Sovereign domestic debt: Percent of countries in default
or restructuring, 1900–2008 (five-year moving average).
Sources: League of Nations; Reinhart, Rogoff, and Savastano
(2003a); Standard and Poor's; and the authors' calculations.
Notes: Unweighted aggregates.

was a precondition for reinflating the economy through expansion-
ary fiscal and monetary policy.

Of course, there are other forms of de facto default (besides
inflation). The combination of heightened financial repression with
rises in inflation was an especially popular form of default from the
1960s to the early 1980s. Brock makes the point that inflation and
reserve requirements are positively correlated, particularly in Africa
and Latin America.[11] Interest rate ceilings combined with inflation
spurts are also common. For example, during the 1972–1976 external debt rescheduling in India, (interbank) interest rates in India
were 6.6 and 13.5 percent in 1973 and 1974, while inflation spurted
to 21.2 and 26.6 percent. These episodes of de facto default through
financial repression are not listed among our de jure credit events.
They count at all only to the extent that inflation exceeds the 20 percent threshold we use to define an inflation crisis.[12]

Clearly, the assumption embedded in many theoretical models, that governments always honor the nominal face value of debt,

117

is a significant overstatement, particularly for emerging markets past and present. Nevertheless, we also caution against reaching the conclusion at the opposite extreme, that governments can ignore powerful domestic stakeholders and simply default at will (de jure or de facto) on domestic debt. We will now proceed to explore some implications of the overhang of large domestic debt for external default and inflation.

- 8 -

DOMESTIC DEBT: THE MISSING LINK
EXPLAINING EXTERNAL DEFAULT
AND HIGH INFLATION

Recognizing the significance of domestic debt can go a long way toward solving the puzzle of why many countries default on (or restructure) their external debts at seemingly low debt thresholds. In fact, when previously ignored domestic debt obligations are taken into account, fiscal duress at the time of default is often revealed to be quite severe.

In this chapter we also show that domestic debt may explain the paradox of why some governments seem to choose inflation rates far above any level that might be rationalized by seignorage revenues leveraged off the monetary base. (Loosely speaking, if a government abuses its currency monopoly by promiscuously printing currency, it will eventually drive the demand for its currency down so far that it actually takes in less real revenue from currency creation than it would at a lower level of inflation.) Although domestic debt is largely ignored in the vast empirical literature on high inflation and hyper-inflation, we find that in many cases the hidden domestic public debt was at least the same order of magnitude as base money (currency plus private bank deposits at a government's central bank) and sometimes a large multiple of that amount.

Understanding the Debt Intolerance Puzzle

We begin by revisiting the conventional wisdom on external debt default and its implications for debt sustainability exercises and debt default thresholds. Indeed, in the 250 episodes of default on external debt in our database, it is clear that domestic debt loomed large across the vast majority of them. Table 8.1 gives the ratio of both external debt and total debt (including domestic and external liabilities) relative to government revenues on the eve of many of the most notable defaults of the nineteenth and twentieth centuries. We normalize debt by means of government revenues because data on nominal GDP is sketchy or nonexistent for the nineteenth-century default episodes. (For many countries, standard sources do not provide anything close to a continuous time series for GDP for the nineteenth century.)[1] Exports, which make sense as the main basis for assessing a country's ability to service external debt owed to foreigners, are perhaps less important than government revenues once domestic public debt is added to the calculus of debt sustainability.

Looking more broadly at our sample, figure 8.1 is based on the eighty-nine episodes of external default from 1827 to 2003 for which we have full data on external debt, total debt, and revenues. We see that in all regions except Latin America, external debt has typically accounted for less than half of total debt during the year a country has defaulted on external debt; for Latin America, the average ratio has been higher but still only 60 percent.

TABLE 8.1
Debt ratios at the time of default: Selected episodes

Country	Year of default	Ratio of external public debt to revenue	Ratio of total public debt to revenue
Mexico	1827	1.55	4.20
Spain	1877	4.95	15.83
Argentina	1890	4.42	12.46
Germany	1932	0.64	2.43
China	1939	3.10	8.96
Turkey	1978	1.38	2.69
Mexico	1982	3.25	5.06
Brazil	1983	0.83	1.98
Philippines	1983	0.23	1.25
South Africa	1985	0.09	1.32
Russia	1998	3.90	4.95
Pakistan	1998	3.32	6.28
Argentina	2001	1.59	2.62

Sources: See appendixes A.1 and A.2.

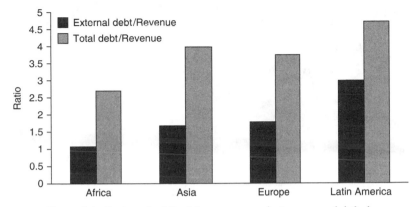

Figure 8.1. Ratios of public debt to revenue during external default:
Eighty-nine episodes, 1827–2003.
Sources: The League of Nations, Mitchell (2003a, 2003b), the
United Nations, and others sources listed in appendixes A.1 and A.2.

Thus, uncovering data on domestic debt suggests at least a partial answer to a basic question asked throughout the literature on international debt: Why do the governments of emerging markets tend to default at such stunningly low levels of debt repayment and ratios of debt to GDP?[2] In chapter 2, for example, we discussed evidence that serial defaulters tend to default at ratios of debt to GDP that are below the upper bound of 60 percent set by the euro area's Maastricht Treaty.[3] In fact, taking into account domestic public debt, the anomaly largely disappears.

Figures 8.2 and 8.3 give us a different perspective on the data by providing the frequency distribution (simple and cumulative) of external debt to GDP and of total debt to GDP across all the episodes of external debt in our sample for which we have full data. As the figures illustrate, the ratios of external debt to government revenue are massed at a much smaller average than are the ratios of total debt to government revenue during the year of an external default, with a mean of 2.4 versus 4.2. This order-of-magnitude difference is consistent across individual episodes (as table 8.1 highlights for some well-known cases). It is also consistent across regions and time.

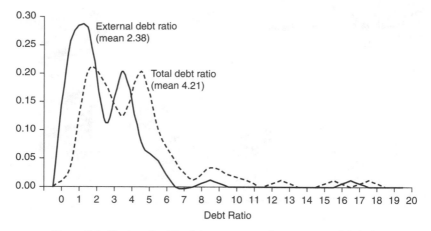

Figure 8.2. Ratios of public debt to revenue during external default:
Frequency of occurrence, 1827–2003.

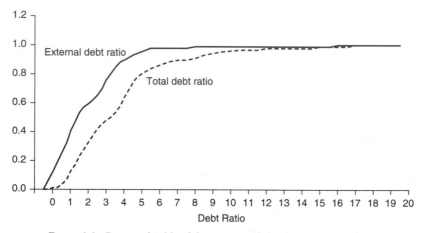

Figure 8.3. Ratios of public debt to revenue during external default:
Cumulative frequency of occurrence, 1827–2003.
Sources: The League of Nations, Mitchell (2003a, 2003b), the United Nations,
other sources listed in appendixes A.1 and A.2, and the authors' calculations.
Note: Kolmogorov-Smirnov, 31.46; significant at 1 percent.

Obviously, if domestic debt were trivial, the frequency distribution of the total debt ratio at the time of default should overlap
that of domestic debt. That is, we should find that domestic debt
is quite a small share of total debt on the eve of default. But this is

hardly the case, and a standard battery of tests rejects this hypothesis across the board.[4]

Domestic Debt on the Eve and in the
Aftermath of External Default

Domestic debt is not static around external default episodes. In fact, the precrisis buildup in domestic debt often shows the same frenzied increases in the run-up to external default as foreign borrowing does. The pattern is illustrated in figure 8.4, which depicts debt accumulation during the five years before and during external default across all the episodes in our sample.

Presumably, the co-movement of domestic and foreign debt is a product of the same procyclical behavior of fiscal policy documented by previous researchers.[5] As has been shown repeatedly over time, the governments of emerging markets are prone to treat favorable shocks as permanent, fueling a spree in government spending and borrowing that ends in tears.[6] Figure 8.4 does not continue past the default date. If it did, we would see that countries often continue

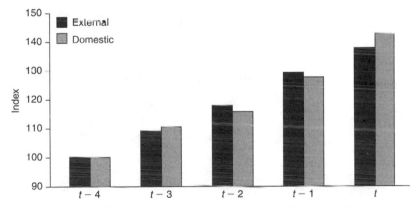

Figure 8.4. The run-up in government domestic and external debt on the eve of external default: Eighty-nine episodes, 1827–2003.
Sources: The League of Nations, the United Nations, and other sources listed in appendixes A.1 and A.2.
Note: The year of the default is indicated by *t*; *t* − 4 = 100.

123

to run up domestic public debt after they have been shut off from international capital markets.

Precommunist China (figure 8.5) provides an interesting and instructive example of why domestic debt often builds up in the aftermath of external defaults. Prior to its two major defaults in 1921 and 1939, China's government relied almost exclusively on external debt. But as access to foreign borrowing dried up, the government, still faced with the need to fund itself, was forced to rely on internal domestic borrowing, despite the underdeveloped state of China's financial markets. So it is hardly surprising that public domestic debt exploded in the aftermath of both incidents. By the mid-1940s, China's government relied almost exclusively on domestic debt.

The Literature on Inflation and the "Inflation Tax"

Another area of the literature that has, by and large, ignored domestic debt is the empirical work on high inflation and hyperinflation.

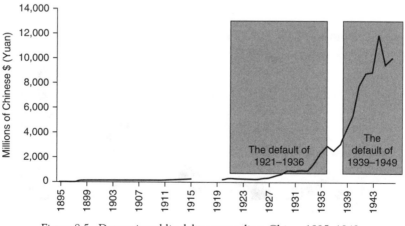

Figure 8.5. Domestic public debt outstanding: China, 1895–1949.
Sources: Huang (1919); Cheng (2003); the United Nations,
Department of Economic Affairs (various years),
Statistical Yearbook, 1948–1984; and the authors' calculations.
Note: Data for 1916–1919 are missing.

124

Ever since Cagan, researchers have concentrated on a government's incentives to gain seignorage revenues from the monetary base.[7] Indeed, a recurring paradox in this literature has to do with why governments sometimes seem to increase inflation above and beyond the seignorage-maximizing rate. Many clever and plausible answers to this question have been offered, with issues of time consistency and credibility featuring prominently. However, we submit that the presence of significant domestic public debt may be a major factor overlooked, especially considering—as we have already discussed—that a large share of debt was often long term and nonindexed. We do not refer simply to the study of rare hyperinflation episodes but equally to the much more common phenomenon of high and moderately high inflation as studied, for example, by Dornbusch and Fischer and by many others since.[8] Although there are literally hundreds of empirical papers on inflationary finance in developing countries and postconflict economies, domestic debt is rarely mentioned, much less employed in time series analysis.

Defining the Tax Base: Domestic Debt or the Monetary Base?

As in the literature on external debt, the implicit assumption is that domestic public debt is relatively unimportant. But is this a good approximation? Table 8.2 suggests that in many important episodes domestic debt has been a major factor in a government's incentive to allow inflation, if not indeed the dominant one.[9] Thus a comparison of actual inflation rates to any hypothetical "seignorage-maximizing rate," calculated only off the monetary base, may often be beside the point.

For example, we see from table 8.2 that when inflation first spiked to 66 percent in Germany in 1920 after World War I, domestic debt was almost triple the size of the monetary base. In the case of Brazil, domestic debt was almost 20 times the size of the money base.[10]

The importance of domestic debt is hardly confined to episodes of hyperinflation. Table 8.2 lists a number of high-inflation

125

TABLE 8.2
Inflation and domestic public debt: Selected episodes, 1917–1994

Country	Year	Rate of inflation	Ratio of domestic debt to GDP	Ratio of base money to GDP	Ratio of domestic debt to total domestic liabilities
		Some episodes of hyperinflation			
Argentina	1989	3,079.5	25.6	16.4	61.2
Brazil	1987	228.3	164.9	9.8	94.4
	1990	2,947.7	155.1	7.1	95.6
Germany	1920	66.5	52.6	19.4	73.0
	1923	22,220,194,522.37	0.0	0.0	1.0
		Episodes of high inflation			
Greece	1922	54.2	53.0	34.3	60.7
	1923	72.6	41.3	32.7	55.9
Italy	1917	43.8	79.1	24.1	76.6
	1920	56.2	78.6	23.5	77.1
Japan	1944	26.6	236.7	27.8	89.5
	1945	568.1[a]	266.5	74.4	78.2
Norway	1918	32.5	79.3	86.4	47.9
	1920	18.1	106.9	65.6	62.3
The Philippines	1981	13.1	10.4	6.6	61.1
	1984	46.2	11.0	13.9	44.2
Turkey	1990	60.3	14.7	7.4	66.6
	1994	106.3	20.2	7.1	73.9

Sources: See appendixes A.1 and A.2.

Notes: "Money" and "debt" refer to the levels at the beginning of each episode. The episodes of hyperinflation meet the classic Cagan definition.

[a]This episode does not meet the classic Cagan definition.

episodes as well. Domestic public debt was almost 80 percent of Japan's total domestic liabilities (including currency) in 1945, when inflation went over 500 percent. In all of the cases listed in table 8.2, domestic public debt has been at least the same order of magnitude as the monetary base (with the exception of the case of Norway, where it was slightly below that in 1918).

The "Temptation to Inflate" Revisited

Precise calculations of the gain to governments of inflating away the real value of their debt require considerably more information on the maturity structure of the debt and interest payments than is available in our cross-country data set. A critical piece of knowledge is the extent to which inflation is expected or not. In addition, one needs to understand bank reserve requirements, interest rate regulations, the degree of financial repression, and other constraints to make any kind of precise calculation. But the fact that domestic nominal debt has been so great compared to the base money across so many important episodes of high inflation suggests that debt needs to be given far more attention in future studies.[11]

We have now discussed some of the potential links among external default, inflation, and domestic debt, and emphasized that default through inflation is an important component of the domestic default calculus. In the next chapter we turn our attention to some features of the domestic versus external default cross-country experience that have hitherto remained unexplored.

- 9 -

DOMESTIC AND EXTERNAL DEFAULT: WHICH IS WORSE? WHO IS SENIOR?

We have shown that the amount of domestic debt is large in general, particularly in episodes of external default or high inflation. Clearly, in trying to understand how crises play out, it would be helpful to better understand the relative seniority of domestic and foreign debt. This section is an attempt to provide a first pass in looking at some key characteristics of the data. Clearly, the way crises play out is going to differ across countries and time. Many factors, such as the independence of the central bank and exchange rate regime, are likely to be relevant. Nevertheless, a few simple comparisons of the trajectory of output and inflation during the run-up to and the aftermath of domestic and external defaults are revealing.[1]

Our calculations can be taken as only suggestive for several reasons. One is simply that there is no comprehensive database on overt domestic debt defaults prior to our own, much less on de facto defaults. Although we are confident that we have a relatively complete picture of external defaults and episodes of high inflation in our sample, we simply do not know how many episodes of domestic default we may have missed, even restricting attention to de jure defaults. In this chapter we provide a broad indication of how clear episodes of domestic default or restructuring are hidden in the historical archives. Thus, our list of domestic defaults is surely a lower bound on the actual incidence.

Finally, but worthy of discussion, our approach is systematic in documenting the *incidence* of default but is silent about the *magnitude* of default. Even though our database on public debt can provide valuable insight on the magnitude of the original default or restructuring, it would be a stretch of the imagination to suggest that these data provide a snapshot of the subsequent restructuring nuances or the actual recovery rates. With these caveats in mind, a number of results stand out.

Real GDP in the Run-up to and the Aftermath of Debt Defaults

First, how bad are macroeconomic conditions on the eve of a default? Unambiguously, output declines in the run-up to a default on domestic debt are typically significantly worse than those seen prior to a default on external debt. As highlighted in figures 9.1 and 9.2, the average cumulative decline in output during the three-year run-up to a domestic default crisis is 8 percent. The output decline in the year of the domestic debt crisis alone is 4 percent; the comparable average decline for external debt events is 1.2 percent. To compare the antecedents of domestic and external defaults, we performed a variety of tests for individual years, as well as for the cumulative change in the window prior to default. The latter test comprised a total of 224 observations for domestic crises (that is, the number of annual observations in advance of domestic crises) and 813 for external crashes (again, years multiplied by number of crises).

As noted earlier, the results have to be interpreted with care, for many domestic episodes are twin default crises and, as a consequence, output is also suffering from limited access to external credit (if there is any at all).

Inflation in the Run-up to and the Aftermath of Debt Defaults

The comparable exercise for the inflation rate yields even starker differences (figures 9.3 and 9.4). Inflation during the year of an external default is on average high, at 33 percent.[2] However, inflation truly gallops during domestic debt crises, averaging 170 percent in the year of the default.[3] After the domestic default, inflation remains

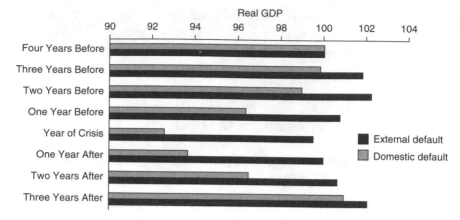

Figure 9.1. Real GDP before, during, and after domestic
and external debt crises, 1800–2008.
Sources: Maddison (2004), Total Economy Database (2008),
and the authors' calculations.
Note: Real GDP is indexed to equal 100 four years before the crisis.

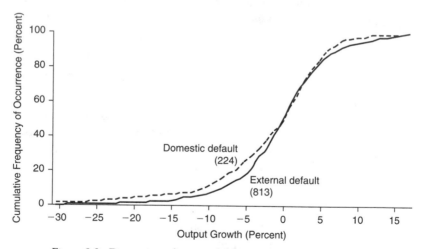

Figure 9.2. Domestic and external debt crises and real GDP, three
years before crisis and year of crisis, 1800–2008.
Sources: Maddison (2004), Total Economy Database (2008),
and the authors' calculations.
Notes: The Kolmogorov-Smirnov test (K-S test) is used to determine whether
two data sets differ significantly. The K-S test has the advantage of making no
assumption about the distribution of data. The test is nonparametric and
distribution free. Here Kolmogorov-Smirnov, 8.79; significant at 1 percent.

130

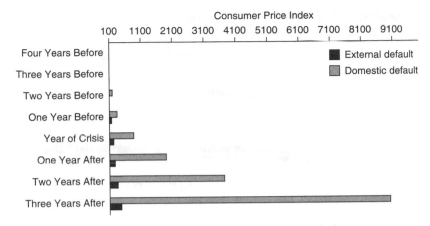

Figure 9.3. Consumer prices before, during, and after
domestic and external debt crises, 1800–2008.
Sources: International Monetary Fund (various years), *International
Financial Statistics* and *World Economic Outlook;* additional sources
listed in appendix A.1; and the authors' calculations.
Note: Consumer prices are indexed to equal 100 four years before the crisis.

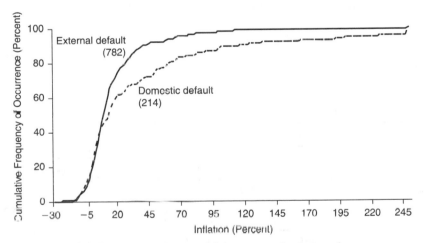

Figure 9.4. Domestic and external debt crises and inflation, three years
before crisis and year of crisis, 1800–2008.
Sources: International Monetary Fund (various years), *International
Financial Statistics* and *World Economic Outlook;* additional sources
listed in appendix A.1; and the authors' calculations.

131

at or above 100 percent in the following years. Not surprisingly, default through inflation goes hand in hand with domestic default— before, during, and after the more explicit domestic expropriations. The extensive scholarly literature on inflation has been silent on this point.[4] We conclude that overt domestic default tends to occur only in times of severe macroeconomic distress.

A more analytical approach in comparing real GDP growth and inflation across episodes of domestic and external debt defaults is shown in table 9.1. The columns of the table provide sample averages of economic growth and inflation in the run-up to and the after-

TABLE 9.1
Output and inflation around and during debt crises

	Means tests					
	Average real GDP growth			Average inflation		
	Domestic	External	Difference	Domestic	External	Difference
$t-3$	−0.2	1.8	−2.0*	35.9	15.6	20.3*
$t-2$	−0.9	0.4	−1.3	38.3	14.6	23.7*
$t-1$	−2.6	−1.4	−1.2	68.0	15.0	53.0*
t (crisis)	−4.0	−1.2	−2.8*	171.2	33.4	137.8*
$t+1$	1.2	0.4	0.8	119.8	38.2	81.6*
$t+2$	3.0	0.7	2.3*	99.2	28.9	70.2*
$t+3$	4.6	1.4	3.2*	140.3	29.1	111.2*
$t-3$ to t	−1.9	−0.1	−1.8*	79.4	19.7	59.7*
$t+1$ to $t+3$	2.9	0.8	2.1*	119.8	32.1	87.7*

	Kolmogorov-Smirnov tests for the equality of two distributions					
	Number of observations		K-S	Number of observations		K-S
	Domestic	External	statistic	Domestic	External	statistic
$t-3$ to t and $t+1$ to $t+3$	224	813	8.8*	214	782	20.0*

Sources: International Monetary Fund (various years), *International Financial Statistics* and *World Economic Outlook*; Maddison (2004); Total Economy Database (2008); additional sources listed in appendixes A.1 and A.2; and the authors' calculations.

Notes: Means *t*-tests assume unknown and unequal variances. The year of default is indicated by *t*. An asterisk (*) denotes that the difference is statistically significant at the 1 percent level. The critical value of the Kolmogorov-Smirnov test at the 1 percent significance level is 5.16.

math of defaults on the two types of debt. The bottom row reports the results of a Kolmogorov-Smirnov test, which is a statistical test of the equality of two frequency distributions. Both real growth and inflation behave distinctly differently around domestic defaults than around external ones.

The Incidence of Default on Debts Owed to External and Domestic Creditors

To shed some light on the incidence of expropriation of residents versus nonresidents, we constructed four time series for the period 1800–2006, showing the probability of external default (or the share of countries in our sample that are in external default in a given year); the comparable statistic for domestic default episodes; the probability of an inflation crisis (defined here as the share of countries in any given year during the more than two hundred years of our sample in which the annual rate of inflation exceeded 20 percent); and the sum of the incidence of high inflation and domestic default, which summarizes the expropriation of the holdings of domestic residents.[5]

Figure 9.5 shows the probability of external default versus the comparable statistic for domestic default through either inflation or explicit default. Table 9.2 presents some summary statistics on the underlying data. During the early period and up to World War II, the incidence of external default was higher than it was later.[6] Specifically, for 1800–1939, the probability of external default was about 20 percent versus 12 percent for domestic residents. For the entire sample, there was no statistically significant difference in the incidence of default on debts to domestic creditors versus foreigners. With the widespread adoption of fiat money, inflation apparently became the more expedient form of expropriation. As a result, the incidence of taxing domestic residents increased after World War II.[7]

Figure 9.6 plots the probability of domestic default as a share of the probability of default. A ratio above 0.5 implies that domestic creditors do worse, while a ratio below 0.5 implies that foreigners do worse.

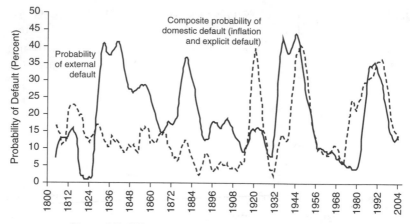

Figure 9.5. Who is expropriated, residents or foreigners?
The probability of domestic and external default, 1800–2006.
Sources: International Monetary Fund (various years), *International Financial Statistics* and *World Economic Outlook;* Maddison (2004); Total Economy Database (2008); additional sources listed in appendix A.1; and the authors' calculations.

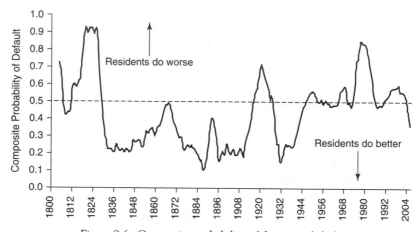

Figure 9.6. Composite probability of domestic default
as a share of the total default probability, 1800–2006.
Sources: International Monetary Fund (various years), *International Financial Statistics* and *World Economic Outlook;* Maddison (2004); Total Economy Database (2008); additional sources listed in appendix A.1; and the authors' calculations.

134

TABLE 9.2

Who gets expropriated, residents or foreigners? Preliminary tests for the
equality of two proportions (binomial distribution), 1800–2006

	The two samples	1800–2006	1800–1939	1940–2006
$n_1 = n_2$	Number of observations (years) over which the probability of external and domestic default was calculated	207	139	66
p_1	Probability of external default	0.1975	0.2048	0.1823
p_2	Composite probability of domestic default[a]	0.1505	0.1202	0.2138
$p_1 - p_2$	Difference	0.0470	0.0846	–0.0315
Z-test		1.2625	1.9122*	–0.4535
	Significance level	0.1034	0.0279	0.6749
Who was expropriated more, residents or foreigners?		Same	Foreigners	Same

Sources: International Monetary Fund (various years), *International Financial Statistics* and *World Economic Outlook*; Maddison (2004); Total Economy Database (2008); additional sources listed in appendixes A.1 and A.2; and the authors' calculations.

Notes: This table answers the question "Has the likelihood of expropriation of domestic residents increased in the recent period (i.e., from 1800–1939 to 1940–2006)?" The answer is "Yes!" Z-test, 1.4716; level of significance, 0.0706**; the year of default is indicated by t. The test statistic for the equality of two proportions is calculated as follows:

$$Z = \frac{(p_1 - p_2)}{\left\{ P(1-P)\left[\frac{1}{n_1} + \frac{1}{n_2} \right] \right\}^{1/2}}, \text{ where } P = \frac{p_1 n_1 + p_2 n_2}{n_1 + n_2}$$

[a]The composite probability of domestic default is defined as the probability of explicit default of domestic debt plus the probability of an inflation crisis (i.e. default through inflation).

* denotes significance at the 5 percent level.

** denotes significance at the 1 percent level.

Certainly, this admittedly very crude first pass at the evidence does nothing to dissuade us from our prior belief that domestic debt is often held by important political stakeholders in debtor countries and cannot always be lightly dismissed as strictly junior debt, a point highlighted by Allan Drazen.[8]

Table 9.2 allows us to look more systematically at the difference in the treatment of domestic residents and foreigners over time. It reports sample averages of the probability of domestic and external defaults for the entire period from 1800 to 2006 and two subperiods split at World War II. As is stated in the notes to the table, the probability that domestic residents would be expropriated was higher in the postwar period.

Summary and Discussion of Selected Issues

In the past few chapters we have provided an extensive new cross-country data set on a key macroeconomic variable that governments often manage to keep remarkably hidden from view: domestic public debt. We have also presented what we believe to be the first attempt at a cross-country international catalog of historical defaults on domestic public debt, spanning two centuries and sixty-six countries.

Our first look at the data suggests that researchers need to revisit the empirical literature on the sustainability of external government debt and on governments' incentives to engage in high inflation and hyperinflation, taking into account the newly uncovered data on domestic public debt and, where possible, broader definitions of government or government-guaranteed debt. Of course, how domestic debt impacts inflation and external default will vary across episodes and circumstances. In some cases, domestic debt is eliminated through high inflation; in other cases, governments default on external debt.

How did domestic public debt in emerging markets fall off many economists' radar screens? Many researchers, aware only of the difficulties of emerging markets in issuing debt in the ultra-high-inflation 1980s and 1990s, simply believed that no one would ever voluntarily lend in domestic currency to the kleptocratic government of an emerging market. Surely no one would trust such a government to resist inflating such debt down to nothing. The logical implication was that domestic currency public debt must not exist. True, a few researchers have contemplated the possibility. Alesina and Tabellini, for example, considered a theoretical case in which domestic debt was honored ahead of external debt.[9] But absent any data or even any awareness of the earlier existence of significant quantities of domestic public debt in virtually every country (even during its emerging market phase), these isolated examples have had no great impact on the mainstream academic or policy literature.

The lack of transparency exhibited by so many governments and multilateral institutions in failing to make time series on domestic debt easily available is puzzling. After all, these governments routinely tap domestic and foreign markets to sell debt. In general, uncertainty about a government's past repayment performance is more likely than not going to raise risk premiums on new issuances. Even more puzzling is why global investors do not insist on historical information relevant to the value of securities they may purchase. Any credit card company will want to know a consumer's purchase and repayment history, what kind of debt burdens the consumer has managed in the past, and under what circumstances. Surely historical information is equally relevant to governments.

One can only surmise that many governments do want capital markets to fully recognize the risks they are running by piling on debt and debt guarantees due to their fear of having to pay much higher financing costs. Publishing historical data will make investors ask why current data cannot be made equally available. Still, one would think a strong case could be made for less profligate governments to open up their books more readily and be rewarded for doing so by lower interest rates. This transparency, in turn, would put pressure on weaker borrowers. Yet today even the United States runs an extraordinarily opaque accounting system, replete with potentially costly off-budget guarantees. In its response to the most recent financial crisis, the U.S. government (including the Federal Reserve Board) took huge off-balance sheet guarantees onto its books, arguably taking on liabilities that, from an actuarial perspective—as evaluated at the time of the bailout—were of the same order of magnitude as, say, expenditures on defense, if not greater. Why so many governments do not make it easier for standard databases to incorporate their debt histories is an important question for future academic and policy research.

From a policy perspective, a plausible case can be made that an international agency would be providing a valuable public good if it could enforce (or at least promote) basic reporting requirements and transparency across countries. Indeed, it is curious that today's multilateral financial institutions have never fully taken up the task of systematically publishing public debt data, especially in light of these agencies' supposed role at the vanguard of warning policy makers and investors about crisis risks. Instead, the system seems to have forgotten about the history of domestic debt entirely, thinking that today's blossoming of internal public debt markets is something entirely new and different.[10] But as our historical data set on domestic central government debt underscores with surprising force, nothing could be further from the truth. Indeed, we have reason to believe that with our data we have only touched the tip of the iceberg in terms of fully understanding public sector explicit and contingent liabilities.

- PART IV -

BANKING CRISES, INFLATION, AND CURRENCY CRASHES

Countries can outgrow a history of repeated bouts with high inflation, but no country yet has graduated from banking crises.

- 10 -

BANKING CRISES

Although many now-advanced economies have graduated from a history of serial default on sovereign debt or very high inflation, so far graduation from banking crises has proven elusive. In effect, for the advanced economies during 1800–2008, the picture that emerges is one of serial banking crises.

Until very recently, studies of banking crises have focused either on episodes drawn from the history of advanced countries (mainly the banking panics before World War II) or on the experience of modern-day emerging markets.[1] This dichotomy has perhaps been shaped by the belief that for advanced economies, destabilizing, systemic, multicountry financial crises are a relic of the past.[2] Of course, the Second Great Contraction, the global financial crisis that recently engulfed the United States and Europe, has dashed this misconception, albeit at great social cost.

As we will demonstrate in this chapter, banking crises have long impacted rich and poor countries alike. We develop this finding using our core sample of sixty-six countries (plus a broader extended sample for some exercises). We examine banking crises ranging from Denmark's financial panic during the Napoleonic Wars to the recent "first global financial crisis of the twenty-first century." The incidence of banking crises proves to be remarkably similar in both high-income and middle- to low-income countries. Indeed, the tally of crises is particularly high for the world's financial centers: France, the United Kingdom, and the United States. Perhaps more surprising still are the qualitative and quantitative parallels across disparate income groups. These parallels arise despite the relatively pristine modern-day sovereign default records of the rich countries.

For the study of banking crisis, three features of the data set underlying this book are of particular note. First, to reiterate, our data on banking crises go back to 1800. Second, to our knowledge, we are the first to examine the patterns of housing prices around major banking crises in emerging markets, including Asia, Europe, and Latin America. Our emerging market data set facilitates comparisons across both duration and magnitude with the better-documented housing price cycles in the advanced economies, which have long been known to play a central role in financial crises. We find that real estate price cycles around banking crises are similar in duration and amplitude across the two groups of countries. This result is surprising given that almost all other macroeconomic and financial time series (on income, consumption, government spending, interest rates, etc.) exhibit higher volatility in emerging markets.[3] Third, our analysis employs the comprehensive historical data on central government tax revenues and central government debt compiled (as detailed in chapter 3). These data afford a new perspective on the fiscal consequences of banking crises—notably emphasizing the implications for tax revenue and public debt, which are far more substantive than the usual narrower focus in the literature, bailout costs.

We find that banking crises almost invariably lead to sharp declines in tax revenues, while other factors leading to higher deficits can include the operation of automatic fiscal stabilizers, countercyclical fiscal policy, and higher interest payments due to elevated risk premiums and rating downgrades (particularly, but not exclusively, for emerging markets). On average, during the modern era, real government debt rises by 86 percent during the three years following a banking crisis. (That is, if central government debt was $100 billion at the start of a crisis, it would rise to $186 billion after three years, adjusted for inflation.) These fiscal consequences, which include both direct and indirect costs, are an order of magnitude larger than the usual bank bailout costs. The fact that the magnitudes are comparable in advanced and emerging market economies is again quite remarkable. Obviously, both bailout costs and other fiscal costs depend on a host of political and economic factors, especially the policy response and the severity of the real shock that, typically, triggers the crisis.[4]

A Preamble on the Theory of Banking Crises

Banking Crises in Repressed Financial Systems

Our sample includes basically two kinds of banking crises. The first is common in poor developing countries in Africa and elsewhere, although it occasionally surfaces in richer emerging markets, such as Argentina. These crises are really a form of domestic default that governments employ in countries where financial repression is a major form of taxation. Under financial repression, banks are vehicles that allow governments to squeeze more indirect tax revenue from citizens by monopolizing the entire savings and payments system, not simply currency. Governments force local residents to save in banks by giving them few, if any, other options. They then stuff debt into the banks via reserve requirements and other devices. This allows the government to finance a part of its debt at a very low interest rate; financial repression thus constitutes a form of taxation. Citizens put money into banks because there are few other safe places for their savings. Governments, in turn, pass regulations and restrictions to force the banks to relend the money to fund public debt. Of course, in cases in which the banks are run by the government, the central government simply directs the banks to make loans to it.

Governments frequently can and do make the financial repression tax even larger by maintaining interest rate caps while creating inflation. For example, this is precisely what India did in the early 1970s when it capped bank interest at 5 percent and engineered an increase in inflation of more than 20 percent. Sometimes even that action is not enough to satisfy governments' voracious need for revenue savings, and they stop paying their debts entirely (a domestic default). The domestic default forces banks, in turn, to default on their own liabilities so that depositors lose some or all of their money. (In some cases, the government might actually have issued deposit insurance, but in the event of default it simply reneges on that promise, too.)

143

Banking Crises and Bank Runs

True banking crises, of the variety more typically experienced in emerging markets and advanced economies, are a different kind of creature. As we mentioned in the preamble, banks' role in effecting maturity transformation—transforming short-term deposit funding into long-term loans—makes them uniquely vulnerable to bank runs.[5] Banks typically borrow short in the form of savings and demand deposits (which can, in principle, be withdrawn at short notice). At the same time, they lend at longer maturities, in the form of direct loans to businesses, as well as other longer-dated and higher-risk securities. In normal times, banks hold liquid resources that are more than enough to handle any surges in deposit withdrawals. During a "run" on a bank, however, depositors lose confidence in the bank and withdraw en masse. As withdrawals mount, the bank is forced to liquidate assets under duress. Typically the prices received are "fire sale" prices, especially if the bank holds highly illiquid and idiosyncratic loans (such as those to local businesses about which it has far better information than other investors). The problem of having to liquidate at fire sale prices can extend to a far broader range of assets during a systemic banking crisis of the kind we focus on here. Different banks often hold broadly similar portfolios of assets, and if all banks try to sell at once, the market can dry up completely. Assets that are relatively liquid during normal times can suddenly become highly illiquid just when the bank most needs them.

Thus, even if the bank would be completely solvent absent a run, its balance sheet may be destroyed by having to liquidate assets at fire sale prices. In such a case, the bank run is self-fulfilling. That is, it is another example of multiple equilibria, similar in spirit to when a country's creditors collectively refuse to roll over short-term debt. In the case of a bank run, it is depositors who are effectively refusing to roll over debt.

In practice, banking systems have many ways of handling runs. If the run is on a single bank, that bank may be able to borrow from a pool of other private banks that effectively provide deposit insurance to one another. However, if the run affects a broad enough range of institutions, private insurance pooling will not work. An example of such a run is the U.S. subprime financial crisis of 2007, because problematic mortgage assets were held widely in the banking sector. Exchange rate crises, as experienced by so many developing economies in the 1990s, are another example of a systemic financial crisis affecting almost all banks in a country. In crises represented by both of these examples, it is a real loss to the banking system that eventually sets off the shock. The shock may be manageable if confidence in the banking sector is maintained. However, if a run occurs, it can bankrupt the entire system, turning a damaging problem into a devastating one. Diamond and Dybvig argue that deposit insurance can prevent bank runs, but their model does not incorporate the fact that absent effective regulation, deposit insurance can induce banks to take excessive risk.[6]

Bank runs, in general, are simply one important example of the fragility of highly leveraged borrowers, public and private, as discussed in the preamble to this book. The implosion of the U.S. financial system during 2007–2008 came about precisely because many financial firms outside the traditional and regulated banking sector financed their illiquid investments using short-term borrowing. In modern financial systems, it is not only banks that are subject to runs but also other types of financial institutions that have highly leveraged portfolios financed by short-term borrowing.

Why Recessions Associated with Banking Crises Are So Costly

Severe financial crises rarely occur in isolation. Rather than being the trigger of recession, they are more often an amplification mechanism: a reversal of fortunes in output growth leads to a string of defaults on bank loans, forcing a pullback in other bank lending, which leads to further output falls and repayment problems, and so on. Also, banking crises are often accompanied by other kinds of crises, including exchange rate crises, domestic and foreign debt crises, and inflation crises; we will explore the coincidence and timing of crises in more detail in chapter 16. Thus, one should be careful not to interpret this first pass at our long historical data set as definitive evidence of the causal effects of banking crises; there is a relatively new area in which much further work is yet to be done.

That said, the theoretical and empirical literature on how financial crises can impact real activity is extremely broad and well developed. One of the most influential studies was reported in 1983 by Bernanke, who argued that when nearly half of all U.S. banks failed in the early 1930s, it took the financial system a long time to rebuild its lending capacity. According to Bernanke, the collapse of the financial system is a major reason that the Great Depression persisted, on and off, for a decade rather than ending in a year or two as a normal recession does. (Bernanke, of course, became Federal Reserve chairman in 2006 and had a chance to put his academic insights into practice during the Second Great Contraction, which began in 2007.)

In later work with Mark Gertler, Bernanke presented a theoretical model detailing how the presence of imperfections in the financial market due to asymmetric information between lenders and borrowers can result in an amplification of monetary policy shocks.[7] In the Bernanke-Gertler model, a decrease in wealth (due, say, to an adverse productivity shock) has an outsized effect on production as firms are forced to scale back their investment plans. Firms are forced to scale back on investment because, as their retained earnings fall, they must finance a larger share of their investment projects via more expensive external financing rather than by means of relatively cheap internal financing. Recessions cause a loss in collateral that is then amplified through the financial system.

Kiyotaki and Moore trace out a similar dynamic in a richer intertemporal model.[8] They show how a collapse in land prices (such as occurred in Japan beginning in the early 1990s) can undermine a firm's collateral, leading to a pullback in investment that causes a further fall in land prices, and so on.

In his 1983 article, Bernanke emphasized that the collapse of the credit channel in recessions is particularly acute for small and medium-sized borrowers who do not have name recognition and therefore have far less access than larger borrowers to bond and equity markets as an alternative to more relationship-oriented bank finance. Many subsequent papers have confirmed that small and medium-sized borrowers do suffer disproportionately during a recession, with a fair amount of evidence pointing to the bank lending channel as a central element.[9] We will not dwell further on the vast theoretical literature on financial markets and real activity except to say that there is indeed significant theoretical and empirical support for the view that a collapse in a country's banking system can have huge implications for its growth trajectory.[10]

We now turn to the empirical evidence. Given the vulnerability of banking systems to runs, combined with the theoretical and empirical evidence that banking crises are major amplifiers of recessions, it is little wonder that countries experience greater difficulties in outgrowing financial crises than they do in escaping a long history of sovereign debt crises. In the latter it is possible to speak of "graduation," with countries going for centuries without slipping back into default. But thus far, no major country has been able to graduate from banking crises.

Banking Crises: An Equal-Opportunity Menace

As shown earlier, the frequency of default (or restructuring) on external debt is significantly lower in advanced economies than in emerging markets. For many high-income countries, that frequency has effectively been zero since 1800.[11] Even countries with a long history of multiple defaults prior to 1800, such as France and Spain, present evidence of having graduated from serial default on external debt.

The second column in tables 10.1 and 10.2 highlights the vast difference in the experience of sovereign default between emerging markets (notably in Africa and Latin America but even in several countries in Asia) and high-income Western Europe, North America, and Oceania. The third column of tables 10.1 and 10.2 presents the analogous calculation for each country for banking crises (i.e., the number of years in banking crises, according to the extended data set developed here, divided by the number of years since the

TABLE 10.1
Debt and banking crises: Africa and Asia, year of independence to 2008

Country	Share of years in default or rescheduling since independence or 1800	Share of years in a banking crisis since independence or 1800
Africa		
Algeria	13.3	6.4
Angola	59.4	17.6
Central African Republic	53.2	38.8
Côte d'Ivoire	48.9	8.2
Egypt	3.4	5.6
Kenya	13.6	19.6
Mauritius	0.0	2.4
Morocco	15.7	3.8
Nigeria	21.3	10.2
South Africa	5.2	6.3
Tunisia	9.6	9.6
Zambia	27.9	2.2
Zimbabwe	40.5	27.3
Asia		
China	13.0	9.1
India	11.7	8.6
Indonesia	15.5	13.3
Japan	5.3	8.1
Korea	0.0	17.2
Malaysia	0.0	17.3
Myanmar	8.5	13.1
The Philippines	16.4	19.0
Singapore	0.0	2.3
Sri Lanka	6.8	8.2
Taiwan	0.0	11.7
Thailand	0.0	6.7

Sources: Authors' calculations; Purcell and Kaufman (1993); Kaminsky and Reinhart (1999); Bordo et al. (2001); Reinhart, Rogoff, and Savastano (2003a) and sources cited therein; Caprio et al. (2005); Jácome (2008); and Standard and Poor's. See also appendix A.2.

Note: For countries that became independent prior to 1800, the calculations are for 1800–2008.

TABLE 10.2
Debt and banking crises: Europe, Latin America, North America,
and Oceania, year of independence to 2008

Country	Share of years in default or rescheduling since independence or 1800	Share of years in a banking crisis since independence or 1800
Europe		
Austria	17.4	1.9
Belgium	0.0	7.3
Denmark	0.0	7.2
Finland	0.0	8.7
France	0.0	11.5
Germany	13.0	6.2
Greece	50.6	4.4
Hungary	37.1	6.6
Italy	3.4	8.7
The Netherlands	6.3	1.9
Norway	0.0	15.7
Poland	32.6	5.6
Portugal	10.6	2.4
Romania	23.3	7.8
Russia	39.1	1.0
Spain	23.7	8.1
Sweden	0.0	4.8
Turkey	15.5	2.4
United Kingdom	0.0	9.2
Latin America		
Argentina	32.5	8.8
Bolivia	22.0	4.3
Brazil	25.4	9.1
Chile	27.5	5.3
Colombia	36.2	3.7
Costa Rica	38.2	2.7
Dominican Republic	29.0	1.2
Ecuador	58.2	5.6
El Salvador	26.3	1.1
Guatemala	34.4	1.6
Honduras	64.0	1.1
Mexico	44.6	9.7
Nicaragua	45.2	5.4
Panama	27.9	1.9
Paraguay	23.0	3.1

(continued)

149

TABLE 10.2 Continued

Country	Share of years in default or rescheduling since independence or 1800	Share of years in a banking crisis since independence or 1800
Latin America (*continued*)		
Peru	40.3	4.3
Uruguay	12.8	3.1
Venezuela	38.4	6.2
North America		
Canada	0.0	8.5
United States	0.0	13.0
Oceania		
Australia	0.0	5.7
New Zealand	0.0	4.0

Sources: Authors' calculations; Purcell and Kaufman (1993); Kaminsky and Reinhart (1999); Bordo et al. (2001); Reinhart, Rogoff, and Savastano (2003a) and sources cited therein; Caprio et al. (2005); Jácome (2008); and Standard and Poor's. See also appendix A.2.

country won independence, or since 1800 if it achieved independence earlier). One striking observation from the tables is that the average length of time a country spends in a state of sovereign default is far greater than the average amount of time spent in financial crisis. A country can circumvent its external creditors for an extended period. It is far more costly to leave a domestic banking crisis hanging, however, presumably due to the crippling effects on trade and investment.

Tables 10.3 and 10.4 present a different perspective on the prevalence of banking crises. The second column tallies the number of banking crises (rather than the number of years in crisis) since a country's independence or 1800; the third column narrows the window to the post–World War II period. Several features are worth noting. *For the advanced economies over the full span, the picture that emerges is one of serial banking crises.* The world's financial centers—the United Kingdom, the United States, and France—stand out in this regard, with 12, 13, and 15 episodes of banking crisis since 1800, respectively. The frequency of banking crises dropped off markedly for the advanced economies and the larger emerging markets alike after

World War II. However, all except Portugal experienced at least one postwar crisis prior to the recent episode. When the recent wave of crises is fully factored in, the apparent drop will likely be even less pronounced. Thus, *although many now-advanced economies have graduated from a history of serial default on sovereign debt or very high inflation*

TABLE 10.3
Frequency of banking crises: Africa and Asia, to 2008

Country	Number of banking crises since independence or 1800	Number of banking crises since independence or 1945
Africa		
Algeria	1	1
Angola	1	1
Central African Republic	2	2
Côte d'Ivoire	1	1
Egypt	3	2
Kenya	2	2
Mauritius	1	1
Morocco	1	1
Nigeria	1	1
South Africa[a]	6	2
Tunisia	1	1
Zambia	1	1
Zimbabwe	1	1
Asia		
China	10	1
India[a]	6	1
Indonesia	3	3
Japan	8	2
Korea	3	3
Malaysia	2	2
Myanmar	1	1
The Philippines	2	2
Singapore	1	1
Sri Lanka	1	1
Taiwan	5	3
Thailand	2	2

Sources: Authors' calculations, Kaminsky and Reinhart (1999), Bordo et al. (2001), Caprio et al (2005), and Jácome (2008). See also appendix A.2.

[a]For South Africa the calculations are for 1850–2008; for India they are for 1800–2008.

151

TABLE 10.4
Frequency of banking crises: Europe, Latin America,
North America, and Oceania, to 2008

Country	Number of banking crises since independence or 1800	Number of banking crises since independence or 1945
Europe		
Austria	3	1
Belgium	10	1
Denmark	10	1
Finland	5	1
France	15	1
Germany	8	2
Greece	2	1
Hungary	2	2
Italy	11	1
The Netherlands	4	1
Norway	6	1
Poland	1	1
Portugal	5	0
Romania	1	1
Russia	2	2
Spain	8	2
Sweden	5	1
Turkey	2	2
United Kingdom	12	4
Latin America		
Argentina	9	4
Bolivia	3	3
Brazil	11	3
Chile	7	2
Colombia	2	2
Costa Rica	2	2
Dominican Republic	2	2
Ecuador	2	2
El Salvador	2	2
Guatemala	3	2
Honduras	1	1
Mexico	7	2
Nicaragua	1	1
Panama	1	1
Paraguay	2	1
Peru	3	1

TABLE 10.4 Continued

Country	Number of banking crises since independence or 1800	Number of banking crises since independence or 1945
Latin America (*continued*)		
Uruguay	5	2
Venezuela	2	2
North America		
Canada	8	1
United States	13	2
Oceania		
Australia	3	2
New Zealand	1	1

Sources: Authors' calculations, Kaminsky and Reinhart (1999), Bordo et al. (2001), Caprio et al. (2005), and Jácome (2008).

Note: For countries that became independent prior to 1800, the calculations are for 1800–2008.

(*above 20 percent*), so far graduation from banking crises has proven elusive. As we will show later, the same applies to currency crashes. Indeed, tables 10.1–10.4 illustrate that despite dramatic differences in recent sovereign default performance, the incidence of banking crises is about the same for advanced economies as for emerging markets. It also should be noted that as financial markets have developed in the smaller, poorer economies, the frequency of banking crises has increased.[12]

Tables 10.5 and 10.6 summarize, by region, the evidence on the number of banking crises and the share of years each region has spent in a banking crisis. Table 10.5 starts in 1800. (The table includes postindependence crises only, which explains why emerging markets have lower cumulative totals.) Table 10.6 gives the evidence for the period since 1945.

Whether the calculations are done from 1800 (table 10.5) or from 1945 (table 10.6), on average there are no significant differences in either the incidence or the number of banking crises between advanced and emerging economies; indeed banking crises plague both sets of countries. In fact, prior to World War II, the ad-

TABLE 10.5
Summary of the incidence and frequency of banking crises,
1800 (or independence) to 2008

Region or group	Share of years in a banking crisis since independence or 1800	Number of banking crises
Africa	12.5	1.7
Asia	11.2	3.6
Europe	6.3	5.9
Latin America	4.4	3.6
Argentina, Brazil, and Mexico	9.2	9.0
North America	11.2	10.5
Oceania	4.8	2.0
Advanced economies	7.2	7.2
Emerging economies	8.3	2.8

Sources: Based on tables 10.1–10.4.

Notes: Advanced economies include Japan, North America, Oceania, and all European countries not listed below as part of emerging Europe. Emerging economies include Africa, all Asian countries except Japan, Latin America, and emerging Europe (Hungary, Poland, Romania, Russia, and Turkey).

TABLE 10.6
Summary of the incidence and frequency of banking crises,
1945 (or independence) to 2008

Region or group	Share of years in a banking crisis since independence or 1945	Number of banking crises
Africa	12.3	1.3
Asia	12.4	1.8
Europe	7.1	1.4
Latin America	9.7	2.0
Argentina, Brazil, and Mexico	13.5	3.0
North America	8.6	1.5
Oceania	7.0	1.5
Advanced economies	7.0	1.4
Emerging economies	10.8	1.7

Sources: Based on tables 10.1–10.4.

Notes: Advanced economies include Japan, North America, Oceania, and all European countries not listed below as part of emerging Europe. Emerging economies include Africa, all Asian countries except Japan, Latin America, and emerging Europe (Hungary, Poland, Romania, Russia, and Turkey).

vanced economies with their more developed financial systems were more prone to banking crises than were many of their smaller low-income counterparts.[13] Of course, it can be plausibly argued that smaller countries used foreign creditors as their bankers, and therefore the string of defaults on external debts might have been domestic banking crises had they more developed financial sectors.

Banking Crises, Capital Mobility, and Financial Liberalization

Also consonant with the modern theory of crises is the striking correlation between freer capital mobility and the incidence of banking crises, as shown in figure 10.1. The figure is highly aggregated, but a breakdown to regional or country-level data reinforces the message of the figure. *Periods of high international capital mobility have repeatedly produced international banking crises, not only famously, as they did in the 1990s, but historically.* The figure plots a three-year moving average of the share of all countries experiencing a banking crisis on the right-hand scale. On the left-hand scale we have graphed the index of international capital mobility, using the same design principle as Obstfeld and Taylor, both updated and cast back in time, to cover our full sample period.[14] Although the Obstfeld-Taylor index may have its limitations, we feel it nevertheless provides a concise summary of complicated forces by emphasizing de facto capital mobility based on actual flows.

For the period after 1970, Kaminsky and Reinhart have presented formal evidence of the link between crises and financial liberalization.[15] In eighteen of the twenty-six banking crises they studied, the financial sector had been liberalized within the preceding five years, usually less. In the 1980s and 1990s, most liberalization episodes were associated with financial crises of varying severity. In only a handful of countries (for instance, Canada) did liberalization of the financial sector proceed smoothly. Specifically, Kaminsky and Reinhart present evidence that the probability of a banking crisis conditional on financial liberalization having taken place is higher than the unconditional probability of a banking crisis. Using

155

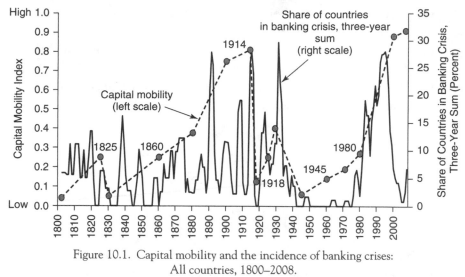

Figure 10.1. Capital mobility and the incidence of banking crises:
All countries, 1800–2008.
Sources: Kaminsky and Reinhart (1999), Bordo et al. (2001),
Obstfeld and Taylor (2004), Caprio et al. (2005), and the authors' calculations.
Notes: This sample includes all countries (even those not in our core sample
of sixty-six). The full listing of the dates of banking crises appears in appendixes
A.3 and A.4. This figure shows that the recovery in equities is far swifter than
that of the housing market. On the left-hand scale we updated our favorite
index of capital mobility, admittedly arbitrary but a concise summary of
complicated forces. The dashed line shows the index of capital mobility
given by Obstfeld and Taylor (2004), backcast from 1800 to
1859 using the same design principle they used.

a fifty-three-country sample for the period 1980–1995, Demirgüç-
Kunt and Detragiache also show, in the context of a multivariate
logit model, that financial liberalization has an independent negative effect on the stability of the banking sector and that this result
is robust across numerous specifications.[16]

The stylized evidence presented by Caprio and Klingebiel suggests that inadequate regulation and lack of supervision at the time of
liberalization may play a key role in explaining why deregulation and
banking crises are so closely entwined.[17] Again, this is a theme across developed countries and emerging markets alike. In the 2000s the United
States, for all its this-time-is-different hubris, proved no exception, for
financial innovation is a variant of the liberalization process.

Capital Flow Bonanzas, Credit Cycles, and Asset Prices

In this section we examine some of the common features of banking crises across countries, regions, and time. The focus is on the regularities among cycles in international capital flows, credit, and asset prices (specifically, housing and equity prices).

Capital Flow Bonanzas and Banking Crises

One common feature of the run-up to banking crises is a sustained surge in capital inflows, which Reinhart and Reinhart term a "capital flow bonanza." They delineate a criterion to define a capital flow bonanza (roughly involving several percent of GDP inflow on a multiyear basis), catalog (country-by-country) "bonanza" episodes for 1960–2006, and examine the links between bonanza spells and banking crises.[18] They employ the crises as defined and dated in appendix A.3.[19]

From the dates of banking crises and capital flow bonanzas, two country-specific probabilities can be calculated: the unconditional probability of a banking crisis and the probability of a banking crisis within a window of three years before and after a bonanza year or years—that is, the conditional probability of a crisis. If capital flow bonanzas make countries more crisis prone, the conditional probability of a crisis, P(Crisis Bonanza), should be greater than the unconditional probability, P(Crisis).

Table 10.7 reproduces a subset of the results given by Reinhart and Reinhart that are relevant to banking crises.[20] It presents aggregates of the country-specific conditional and unconditional probabilities for three groups (all countries, high-income countries, and middle- and low-income countries). *The probability of a banking crisis conditional on a capital flow bonanza is higher than the unconditional probability.* The bottom row of table 10.7 provides the share of countries for which P(Crisis Bonanza) = P(Crisis) as an additional indication of how commonplace it is across countries to see bonanzas associated with a more crisis-prone environment. The majority of countries (61 percent) register a higher propensity to experience a banking crisis around bonanza periods; this percentage would be

157

TABLE 10.7
The effect of a capital flow bonanza on the probability of a
banking crisis in a sixty-six country sample, 1960–2007

Indicator	Percentage of countries
Probability of a banking crisis	
Conditional on a capital flow bonanza (three-year window)	18.4
Unconditional	13.2
Difference	5.2*
Share of countries for which the conditional probability is greater than the unconditional probability	60.9

Source: Reinhart and Reinhart (2009, tables 2 and 4), and authors' calculations.
Notes: The window encompasses three years before the bonanza (see Reinhart and Reinhart 2009, table 2), the year (or years if these are consecutive) of the bonanza, and the three years following the episode. The asterisk (*) denotes significance at the 1 percent confidence level.

higher if one were to include post-2007 data in the table. (Many countries that have experienced the most severe banking crises during the late 2000s also ran large sustained current account deficits in the run-up to the crisis. These include many developed countries, such as Iceland, Ireland, Spain, the United Kingdom, and the United States.)

These findings on capital flow bonanzas are also consistent with other identified empirical regularities surrounding credit cycles. Mendoza and Terrones, who examine credit cycles in both advanced and emerging market economies using a very different approach from that just discussed, find that credit booms in emerging market economies are often preceded by surges in capital inflows. They also conclude that, although not all credit booms end in financial crisis, most emerging market crises were preceded by credit booms. They link credit booms to rising asset prices, an issue we turn to next.[21]

Equity and Housing Price Cycles and Banking Crises

In this section we summarize the literature on asset price bubbles and banking crises, extending it to incorporate new data on housing

158

prices in emerging markets, as well as data on the crises that are currently unfolding in advanced economies.

The now-infamous real estate bubble in the United States that began to deflate at the end of 2005 occupies center stage as a culprit in the recent global financial crisis. But the Second Great Contraction is far from unique in that regard. In an earlier work, we documented the trajectory in real housing prices around all the post–World War II banking crises in advanced economies, with particular emphasis on the "Big Five" crises (Spain, 1977; Norway, 1987; Finland and Sweden, 1991; and Japan, 1992).[22] The pattern that emerges is clear: a boom in real housing prices in the run-up to a crisis is followed by a marked decline in the year of the crisis and subsequent years. Bordo and Jeanne, also studying the advanced economies during 1970–2001, found that banking crises tend to occur either at the peak of a boom in real housing prices or right after the bust.[23] Gerdrup presented a compelling narrative of the links between Norway's three banking crises from the 1890s through 1993 and the booms and busts in housing prices.[24]

Table 10.8 illustrates the magnitudes and durations of the downturns in housing prices that have historically accompanied major banking crises in both advanced and emerging economies. Although the links between developed-country banking crises and the housing price cycle have been examined both in our earlier work and in numerous other papers (most frequently case studies), this is the first time systematic evidence has been provided on the behavior of housing prices in emerging market economies around some of their major banking crises. The crisis episodes include the "Big Six" Asian crises of 1997–1998 (Indonesia, Korea, Malaysia, the Philippines, Thailand, and the much-buffeted Hong Kong).

Other episodes in emerging markets have included Argentina's megacrisis in 2001–2002 and Colombia's 1998 crisis, which produced the worst recession since the national income accounts began to be tabulated in the early 1920s. In the conjuncture of recent crises we include Hungary in addition to the advanced economies that have recently had housing market bubbles (Iceland, Ireland, Spain, the United Kingdom, and the United States).[25]

TABLE 10.8

Cycles of real housing prices and banking crises

Country	Year of crisis	Peak	Trough	Duration of downturn	Magnitude of decline (percent)
Advanced economies: The Big Five					
Finland	1991	1989:Q2	1995:Q4	Six years	−50.4
Japan	1992	1991:Q1	Ongoing	Ongoing	−40.2
Norway	1987	1987:Q2	1993:Q1	Five years	−41.5
Spain	1977	1978	1982	Four years	−33.3
Sweden	1991	1990:Q2	1994:Q4	Four years	−31.7
Asian economies: The Big Six					
Hong Kong	1997	1997:Q2	2003:Q2	Six years	−58.9
Indonesia	1997	1994:Q1	1999:Q1	Five years	−49.9
Malaysia	1997	1996	1999	Three years	−19.0
Philippines	1997	1997:Q1	2004:Q3	Seven years	−53.0
South Korea[a]	1997		2001:Q2	Four years	−20.4
Thailand	1997	1995:Q3	1999:Q4	Four years	−19.9
Other emerging economies					
Argentina	2001	1999	2003	Four years	−25.5
Colombia	1998	1997:Q1	2003:Q2	Six years	−51.2
Historic episodes					
Norway	1898	1899	1905	Six years	−25.5
United States	1929	1925	1932	Seven years	−12.6
Current cases					
Hungary	2008	2006	Ongoing	Ongoing	−11.3
Iceland	2007	November 2007	Ongoing	Ongoing	−9.2
Ireland	2007	October 2006	Ongoing	Ongoing	−18.9
Spain	2007	2007:Q1	Ongoing	Ongoing	−3.1
United Kingdom	2007	October 2007	Ongoing	Ongoing	−12.1
United States	2007	December 2005	Ongoing	Ongoing	−16.6

Sources: Bank for International Settlements and the individual country sources described in appendixes A.1 and A.2.

[a]Data series too short to mark peak.

Two features stand out from the summary statistics presented in table 10.8. First is the persistence of the cycle in real housing prices in both advanced economies and emerging markets, typically for four to six years.[26] The second feature that stands out from table 10.8 is that *the magnitudes of the declines in real housing prices around banking crises from peak to trough are not appreciably different in emerging and advanced economies.* This comparability is quite surprising given that most macroeconomic time series exhibit drastically greater volatility in emerging markets; therefore, it merits further attention.[27] Certainly the first results presented here from comparisons of housing price booms and busts around the dates of banking crises appear to provide strong support for the contention that banking crises are an equal-opportunity menace.

The prolonged housing price downturns following financial crises are in stark contrast to the behavior of real equity prices, as illustrated in figure 10.2, in which the pattern of decline and recovery is more V-shaped. (The figure shows only emerging markets, but, as we shall detail later in part V, equity prices exhibit a similar V-shaped recovery in advanced countries.)

The figure shows the evolution of real equity prices from four years prior to a crisis to three years afterward. As the figure makes plain, equity prices typically peak before the year of a banking crisis and decline for two to three years as the crisis approaches and, in the case of emerging markets, in the year following the crisis. The recovery is complete in the sense that three years after the crisis, real equity

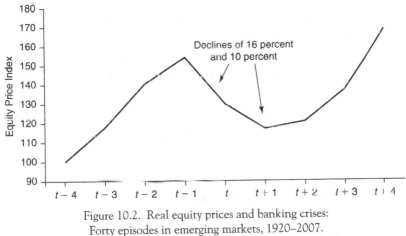

Figure 10.2. Real equity prices and banking crises:
Forty episodes in emerging markets, 1920–2007.
Sources: Global Financial Data (n.d.) and the authors' calculations.
Notes: Four of the forty episodes were from before World War II
(1921–1929). The year of the crisis is indicated by t; $t - 4 = 100$.

161

prices are on average higher than at the precrisis peak. However, post-crisis Japan offers a sobering counterexample to this pattern, because in that country equity prices only marginally recovered to a much lower peak than the precrisis level and have subsequently continued to drift lower.

One can conjecture that one reason major banking crises are such protracted affairs is that these episodes involve the real estate market's persistent cycle in a way that "pure stock market crashes"— for instance, Black Monday in October 1987 or the bursting of the information technology (IT) bubble in 2001—do not.[28]

Overcapacity Bubbles in the Financial Industry?

Philippon has analyzed the expansion of the financial services sector (including insurance) in the United States, which averaged 4.9 percent of GDP during 1976–1985 and rose to 7.5 percent during 1996–2005.[29] In his paper he argues that this gain was not sustainable and that a decline of at least 1 percent of GDP was probable. In the wake of the subprime crisis, the shrinkage of the financial sector during 2008 and 2009 is proving to be significantly larger. The precrisis explosion and postcollapse implosion of the financial sector surrounding a banking crisis are also not new or unique to the United States.

Figure 10.3 plots the number of banks in the United States in the run-up to and the aftermath of the Great Depression. Perhaps the bubble in equity and real estate prices also extended to the number of financial institutions. This expansion in the number of financial institutions in the run-up to a crisis and contraction in its aftermath have been evident during other banking crises—especially in those cases in which financial liberalization preceded the crisis.

The Fiscal Legacy of Financial Crises Revisited

Looking at the fiscal and growth consequences of banking crises, we again find some surprising parallels between developed countries and emerging markets. Our analysis of the fiscal consequences, in partic-

162

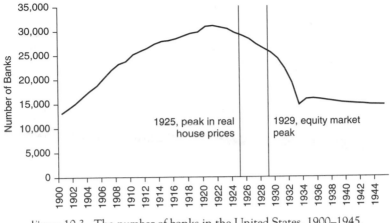

Figure 10.3. The number of banks in the United States, 1900–1945.
Source: Carter et al. (2006).

ular, is a sharp departure from the previous literature, which has focused almost entirely on imputed "bailout costs" to the government,
which, as we will argue, are extremely difficult to measure. Instead,
we focus on the fiscal costs to the central government, particularly
the huge buildup in debt that follows banking crises. We are able to
do so by tapping the extensive new cross-country data set on annual
domestic debt that underlies the research for this book, data we have
already exploited in earlier chapters. These data allow us to show the
remarkable surge in debt that occurs in the wake of a crisis.

The Elusive Concept of Bailout Costs

As we have noted, much of the literature on episodes of banking crisis focuses on estimating the ultimate fiscal costs of the bailouts (see,
for example, an excellent discussion by Frydl and various papers published by Norges Bank).[30] However, estimates of bailout costs vary
markedly across studies, depending on the methodology, and vary
even more across time, depending on the length of the horizon used
to calculate the fiscal impact of the crisis, a point stressed by Frydl.[31]

Table 10.9 presents the upper and lower bounds of estimates
of the bailout costs for some of the better-known banking crises in
both advanced and emerging economies in nearly all regions. The

163

TABLE 10.9
Creative accounting? Bailout costs of banking crises

Country, beginning year	Estimated bailout cost as a percentage of GDP		
	Upper bound	Lower bound	Difference
Argentina, 1981	55.3	4.0	51.3
Chile, 1981	41.2	29.0	12.2
Ghana, 1982	6.0	3.0	3.0
Japan, 1992	24.0	8.0	16.0
Norway, 1987	4.0	2.0	2.0[a]
The Philippines, 1984	13.2	3.0	10.2
Spain, 1977	16.8	5.6	11.2
Sweden, 1991	6.4	3.6	2.8
United States (savings and loan crisis), 1984	3.2	2.4	0.8

Sources: Frydl (1999) and sources cited therein.

[a]Norges Bank (2004) argues that the Norwegian government ultimately made a small profit from the banking resolution.

discrepancies across estimates are large and, in some cases, staggering. Among the "Big Five" crises in advanced economies since World War II, the differences in estimated bailout costs for Japan and Spain, for instance, are 16 and 11 percent of GDP, respectively. Furthermore, as noted by Vale, if the costs are calculated over a longer time horizon after the crisis, the picture that emerges is even more at odds with the higher-end estimates; it shows that the Norwegian government actually made a small profit on the banking resolution due to the later sale of shares in the nationalized banks.[32]

In what follows, we argue that this nearly universal focus on opaque calculations of bailout costs is both misguided and incomplete. It is misguided because there are no widely agreed-upon guidelines for calculating these estimates. It is incomplete because the fiscal consequences of banking crises reach far beyond the more immediate bailout costs. These consequences mainly result from the significant adverse impact that the crisis has on government revenues (in nearly all cases) and the fact that in some episodes the fiscal policy reaction to the crisis has also involved substantial fiscal stimulus packages.

Growth in the Aftermath of Crises

The fact that most banking crises, especially systemic ones, are associated with economic downturns is well established in the empirical literature, although the effects on some key variables, such as housing and government debt and fiscal finances, more broadly, are much less studied.[33] Figure 10.4 shows output for the advanced economies as a group, as well as those that have experienced the "Big Five" crises (Japan, the Nordic countries, and Spain), while figure 10.5 augments this analysis with a comparable summary of the postwar banking crises in emerging markets. As before, t denotes the year of the crisis. Interestingly, the figures show a steeper decline but a somewhat faster comeback in growth for emerging markets than for the advanced economies. It is beyond the scope of this book to ascertain the longer-run growth consequences of banking crises (it is too difficult to delineate the end of banking crises, and growth is simply too complex a subject to mix in here). Nevertheless, this postcrisis pattern is noteworthy because growth (important in its own right) has nontrivial implications for fiscal balances, government debt, and the broader cost and consequences of any financial crisis.

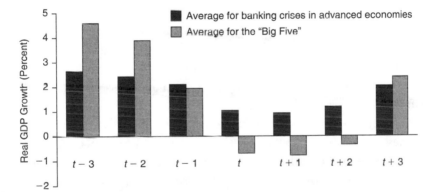

Figure 10.4. Real GDP growth per capita (PPP basis)
and banking crises: Advanced economies.
Sources: Maddison (2004); International Monetary Fund
(various years), *World Economic Outlook;* Total Economy
Database (2008), and the authors' calculations.
Notes: Episodes of banking crisis are listed in appendix A.3.
The year of the crisis is indicated by t.

165

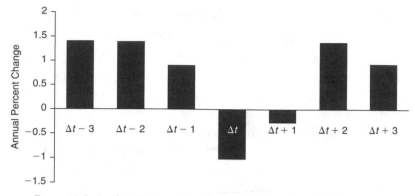

Figure 10.5. Real GDP growth per capita (PPP basis) and banking crises:
Emerging market economies (112 episodes).
Sources: Maddison (2004); International Monetary Fund (various years), *World Economic Outlook;* Total Economy Database; and the authors' calculations.
Notes: Episodes of banking crisis are listed in appendixes A.3 and A.4.
The year of the crisis is indicated by t.

*Beyond Bailout Costs: The Impact of a
Crisis on Revenues and Debt*

Since World War II the most common policy response to a systemic banking crisis (in both emerging and advanced economies) has been to engineer (with varying degrees of success) a bailout of the banking sector, whether through purchases of bad assets, directed mergers of bad banks with relatively sound institutions, direct government takeovers, or some combination of these. In many cases such actions have had major fiscal consequences, particularly in the early phases of the crisis. However, as we have emphasized repeatedly, banking crises are protracted affairs with lingering consequences in asset markets—notably real estate prices and the real economy. It is no surprise, then, that government revenues are adversely and significantly impacted by crises.

As noted, several studies have traced the adverse impacts of banking crises on economic activity; what these studies have left unexplored are the direct consequences of the recession on government finances—specifically, tax revenues. Figure 10.6 plots the average pattern in annual real revenue growth three years before, during, and

166

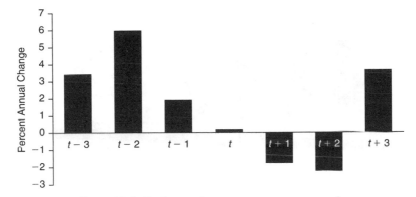

Figure 10.6. Real central government revenue growth
and banking crises: All countries, 1800–1944.
Sources: Revenues are from Mitchell (2003a, 2003b). For the numerous
country-specific sources of prices, see Reinhart and Rogoff (2008a)
Notes: The figure shows that the toll on revenue from crises is not
new. Central government revenues are deflated by consumer prices. There
were a total of eighty-six episodes of banking crisis during 1800–1940 for
which we have revenue data. The year of the crisis is indicated by *t*.

three years after a crisis for a total of eighty-six banking crises during
1800–1944 for which we have complete revenue data.[31]

A comparable exercise is shown in figure 10.7 for all 138
banking crises since World War II. The patterns of the pre- and postwar samples have not been identical but have been strikingly similar.
Annual revenue growth was robust in the years leading up to the banking crisis, weakened significantly in the year of the crisis, and subsequently posted declines in the years immediately following the onset
of the crisis. For the prewar episodes, revenues declined on average for
two years, while for the postwar crises the revenue slump has extended
to the third year.

*Parallels in Revenue Losses between
Emerging Markets and Developed Economies*

Again, the parallels in revenue losses between developed countries
and emerging markets have been striking. Figure 10.8 shows the revenue declines surrounding banking crises for the advanced countries
across the entire sample, with the "Big Five" postwar crises listed sep-

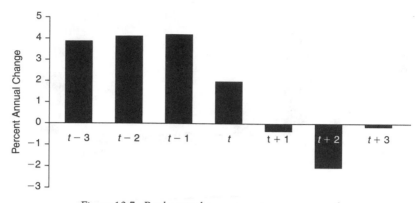

Figure 10.7. Real central government revenue growth
and banking crises: All countries, 1945–2007.
Sources: Revenue information is taken from Mitchell (2003a, 2003b). For the
numerous country-specific sources of prices, see Reinhart and Rogoff (2008a).
Notes: The figure shows that bailout costs are only part of the story of why public
debt surges after a crisis. Central government revenues are deflated by consumer
prices. There were a total of 138 banking crises during 1945–2008 for which we
have revenue data. The year of the crisis is indicated by t.

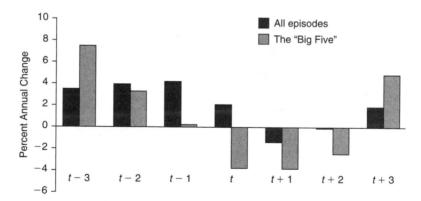

Figure 10.8. Real central government revenue growth
and banking crises: Advanced economies, 1815–2007.
Sources: Revenue information is taken from Mitchell (2003a, 2003b). For the
numerous country-specific sources of prices, see Reinhart and Rogoff (2008a).
Notes: Central government revenues are deflated by consumer prices.
The year of the crisis is indicated by t.

arately. Generally revenue growth resumes (from a lower base) starting in the third year after a crisis. Advanced economies exhibit a stronger inclination to resort to stimulus measures to cushion economic activity, as seen most spectacularly in the aggressive use of infrastructure spending in Japan during the 1990s. Emerging markets, more debt intolerant and more dependent on the vagaries of international capital markets for financing, are far less well poised to engage in countercyclical fiscal policy. Nevertheless, the effect of a crisis on the trajectory of taxes is broadly similar between the types of countries. Figure 10.9 shows revenue declines around banking crises for emerging markets for the entire sample. The average revenue drop is actually quite similar to that of the "Big Five" crises, although the recovery is faster—in line with a swifter recovery in growth, as discussed in the preceding section.

Government Debt Buildup in the Aftermath of Banking Crises

To obtain a rough approximation of the impact of a crisis on government finances, we use the historical data on central government debt compiled in appendix A.2, as discussed earlier. It is important

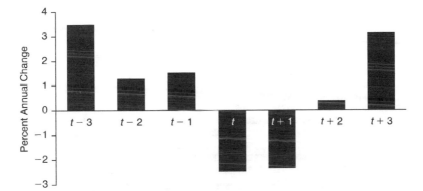

Figure 10.9. Real central government revenue growth
and banking crises: Emerging market economies, 1873–2007.
Sources: Revenue information is from Mitchell (2003a, 2003b). For the
numerous country-specific sources of prices, see appendix A.1.
Notes: The figure shows that the toll on revenue adds to the debt.
Central government revenues are deflated by consumer prices.
The year of the crisis is indicated by t.

169

to note that these data provide only a partial picture, because the entire country, including states and municipalities (not just the central government), is affected by the crisis. Also, typically during these episodes, government-guaranteed debt expands markedly, but this tendency does not show up in the figures for central governments.

With these caveats in mind, figure 10.10 presents a summary of the evolution of debt in the aftermath of some of the major postwar crises in both advanced and emerging markets.

Not surprisingly, taken together, the bailout of the banking sector, the shortfall in revenue, and the fiscal stimulus packages that have accompanied some of these crises imply that there are widening fiscal deficits that add to the existing stock of government debt. What is perhaps surprising is how dramatic the rise in debt is. *If the stock of debt is indexed to equal 100 at the time of the crisis* (t), *the average experience is one in which the real stock of debt rises to 186 three years after the crisis. That is to say, the real stock of debt nearly doubles.*[35] Such increases in government indebtedness are evident in emerging and advanced economies alike, and extremely high in both. Arguably, the true legacy of banking crises is greater public indebtedness—far

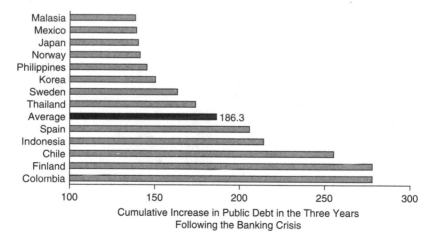

Figure 10.10. The evolution of real public debt following major postwar crises: Advanced and emerging markets.
Source: Reinhart and Rogoff (2008c). *Note:* The stock of debt is indexed to equal 100 in the year of the crisis (central government debt only).

170

over and beyond the direct headline costs of big bailout packages.[36] (Obviously, as we noted earlier, the rise in public debt depends on a whole range of political and economic factors, including the effectiveness of the policy response and the severity of the initial real economic shock that produced the crisis. Nevertheless, the universality of the large increase in debt is stunning.)

Living with the Wreckage: Some Observations

Countries may, perhaps, "graduate" from serial default on sovereign debt and recurrent episodes of very high inflation (or at least go into remission for extremely long periods), as the cases of Austria, France, Spain, and other countries appear to illustrate. History tells us, however, that graduation from recurrent banking and financial crises is much more elusive. And it should not have taken the 2007 financial crisis to remind us of that fact. Out of the sixty-six countries in our sample, only Austria, Belgium, Portugal, and the Netherlands managed to escape banking crises from 1945 to 2007. During 2008, however, even three of these four countries were among those to engage in massive bailouts.

Indeed, the wave of financial crises that began with the onset of the subprime crisis in the United States in 2007 has dispelled any prior notion among academics, market participants, or policy makers that acute financial crises are either a thing of the past or have been relegated to the "volatile" emerging markets. The this-time-is-different syndrome has been alive and well in the United States, where it first took the form of a widespread belief that sharp productivity gains stemming from the IT industry justified price-earnings ratios in the equity market that far exceeded any historical norm.[37] That delusion ended with the bursting of the IT bubble in 2001. But the excesses quickly reemerged, morphing into a different shape in a different market. The securitization of subprime mortgages combined with a heavy appetite for these instruments in countries such as Germany, Japan, and major emerging markets like China fueled the perception that housing prices would continue to climb forever. The new delusion was that "this time is different" because there were new markets, new instruments, and new lenders. In particular, financial engineering was thought to have tamed risk by better tailoring exposures to investors' appetites. Meanwhile, derivatives contracts offered all manner of hedging opportunities. We now know how the latest popular delusion unraveled. We will return to the more recent financial crisis, the Second Great Contraction, in chapters 13–16.

In sum, historical experience already shows that rich countries are not as "special" as some cheerleaders had been arguing, both when it comes to managing capital inflows and especially when it comes to banking crises. The extensive new data set on which this book is based includes data on housing prices in some key emerging markets as well as data on revenue and domestic debt that date back almost a century for most countries and more for many. Surprisingly, not only are the frequency and duration of banking crises similar across developed countries and middle-income countries; so too are quantitative measures of both the run-up to and the fallout from such crises. Notably, for both groups the duration of declines in real housing prices following financial crises is often four years or more, and the magnitudes of the crashes are comparable. One striking finding is the huge surge in debt that most countries experience in the wake of a financial crisis, with central government debt typically increasing by about 86 percent on average (in real terms) during the three years following the crisis.

This chapter has emphasized the huge costs of recessions associated with systemic banking crises. It is important to emphasize, however, that in the theory of banking crises (discussed briefly in the introduction to this chapter), they are seen as an amplification mechanism and not necessarily as an exogenous causal mechanism. When a country experiences an adverse shock—due, say, to a sudden drop in productivity, a war, or political or social upheaval—naturally banks suffer. The rate of loan default goes up dramatically. Banks become vulnerable to large losses of confidence and withdrawals, and the rates of bank failure rise. Bank failures, in turn, lead to a decrease in credit creation. Healthy banks cannot easily cover the loan portfolios of failed banks, because lending, especially to small and medium-sized businesses, often involves specialized knowledge and relationships.

Bank failures and loan pullbacks, in turn, deepen the recession, causing more loan defaults and bank failures, and so on.

Modern economies depend on sophisticated financial systems, and when banking systems freeze up, economic growth can quickly become impaired or even paralyzed. That is why mass bank failures can be so problematic for an economy and why countries in crisis that fail to fix their financial systems—such as Japan in the 1990s—can find themselves going in and out of recession and performing below potential capacity for years.

Although there is a well-developed theory of why banking failures are so problematic in amplifying recessions, the empirical evidence we have provided does not, in itself, decisively show that banks are the only problem. The kind of real estate and stock price collapses that surround banking crises, as documented here, would have very substantial adverse effects even in the absence of a banking collapse. As we will see in chapter 16 on the varieties of crisis, many other kinds of crises—including inflation, exchange rate, and domestic and sovereign default crises—often hit in coincidence with banking crises, especially the most severe ones. Thus what we have really shown here is that severe banking crises are associated with deep and prolonged recessions and that further work is needed to establish causality and, more important, to help prioritize policy responses. Nevertheless, the fact that recessions associated with severe banking crises are so consistently deep and share so many characteristics has to serve as a key starting point for future researchers as they attempt to untangle these difficult episodes.

- 11 -

DEFAULT THROUGH DEBASEMENT:
AN "OLD WORLD" FAVORITE

*A*lthough *inflation really became a commonplace and chronic problem only with the widespread use of paper currency in the early 1900s, students of the history of metal currency know that governments found ways to "extract seignorage" from the currency in circulation long before that. The main device was debasement of the content of the coinage, either by mixing in cheaper metals or by shaving down coins and reissuing smaller ones in the same denomination. Modern currency presses are just a more technologically advanced and more efficient approach to achieving the same end.*[1]

Kings, emperors, and other sovereigns have found inventive ways to avoid paying debts throughout recorded history. Winkler gives a particularly entertaining history of early default, beginning with Dionysius of Syracuse in Greece of the fourth century B.C.[2] Dionysius, who had borrowed from his subjects in the form of promissory notes, issued a decree that all money in circulation was to be turned over to the government, with those refusing subject to the pain of death. After he collected all the coins, he stamped each one-drachma coin with a two-drachma mark and used the proceeds to pay off his debts. Although we do not have any data from the period, standard price theory makes the strong presumption that general price levels must have soared in the aftermath of Dionysius's swindle. Indeed, classical monetary theory suggests that, all else equal (including a country's production), prices should double with a doubling of the money supply, meaning an inflation rate of 100 percent. In practice, the level of inflation might have been greater, assuming that the financial chaos and uncertainty that must have hit Syracuse led to a decrease in output at the same time the money supply was being doubled.

Whether or not this innovation had a precedent we do not know. But we do know that the example of Dionysius included several elements that have been seen with startling regularity throughout history. First, inflation has long been the weapon of choice in sovereign defaults on domestic debt and, where possible, on international debt. Second, governments can be extremely creative in engineering defaults. Third, sovereigns have coercive power over their subjects that helps them orchestrate defaults on domestic debt "smoothly" that are not generally possible with international debt. Even in modern times, many countries have enforced severe penalties on those violating restrictions on capital accounts and currency. Fourth, governments engage in massive money expansion, in part because they can thereby gain a seignorage tax on real money balances (by inflating down the value of citizens' currency and issuing more to meet demand). But they also want to reduce, or even wipe out, the real value of public debts outstanding. As noted in chapter 8, as obvious as the domestic debt channel is, it has been neglected in many episodes because the data have not been readily available.

For economists, Henry VIII of England should be almost as famous for clipping his kingdom's coins as he was for chopping off the heads of its queens. Despite inheriting a vast fortune from his father, Henry VII, and even after confiscating the church's assets, he found himself in such desperate need of funds that he resorted to an epic debasement of the currency. This debasement began in 1542 and continued through the end of Henry's reign in 1547 and on into that of his successor, Edward VI. Cumulatively, the pound lost 83 percent of its silver content during this period.[3] (The reader should note that by "debasement" we mean reduction in the silver or gold content of coins, as opposed to inflation, which measures their purchasing power. In a growing economy, a government might be able to slowly debase its coins without lowering their purchasing power because the public will demand more coins as the cost of transactions grows.)

Tables 11.1 and 11.2 provide details on the timing and magnitude of currency debasements across a broad range of European countries in 1258–1799 during the era before the development of paper currency and in the 1800s, the period of transition to paper money.

TABLE 11.1

Expropriation through currency debasement: Europe, 1258–1799

Country, currency	Period covered	Cumulative decline in silver content of currency (percent)	Largest debasement (percent) and year		Share (percentage) of years in which there was a debasement of the currency (a reduction in the silver content)	
					All	15 percent or greater
Austria, Vienna, kreuzer	1371–1499	–69.7	–11.1	1463	25.8	0.0
	1500–1799	–59.7	–12.5	1694	11.7	0.0
Belgium, hoet	1349–1499	–83.8	–34.7	1498	7.3	3.3
	1500–1799	–56.3	–15.0	1561	4.3	0.0
France, livre tournois	1258–1499	–74.1	–56.8	1303	6.2	0.4
	1500–1789	–78.4	–36.2	1718	14.8	1.4
Germany						
Bavaria-Augsburg,	1417–1499	–32.2	–21.5	1424	3.7	1.2
pfennig	1500–1799	–70.9	–26.0	1685	3.7	1.0
Frankfurt, pfennig	1350–1499	–14.4	–10.5	1404	2.0	0.0
	1500–1798	–12.8	–16.4	1500	2.0	0.3
Italy, lira fiorentina	1280–1499	–72.4	–21.0	1320	5.0	0.0
	1500–1799	–35.6	–10.0	1550	2.7	0.0
Netherlands						
Flemish grote	1366–1499	–44.4	–26.0	1488	13.4	5.2
	1500–1575	–12.3	–7.7	1526	5.3	0.0
Guilder	1450–1499	–42.0	–34.7	1496	14.3	6.1
	1500–1799	–48.9	15.0	1560	4.0	0.0
Portugal, reis	1750–1799	25.6	–3.7	1766	34.7	0.0
Russia, ruble	1761–1799	–42.3	–14.3	1798	44.7	0.0
Spain						
New Castile, maravedis	1501–1799	–62.5	–25.3	1642	19.8	1.3
Valencia, dinar	1351–1499	–7.7	–2.9	1408	2.0	0.0
	1500–1650	–20.4	–17.0	1501	13.2	0.7
Sweden, mark ortug	1523–1573	–91.0	–41.4	1572	20.0	12.0
Turkey, akche	1527–1799	–59.3	–43.9	1586	10.5	3.1
United Kingdom, pence	1260–1499	–46.8	–20.0	1464	0.8	0.8
	1500–1799	–35.5	–50.0	1551	2.3	1.3

Sources: Primarily Allen and Unger (2004) and other sources listed in appendix A.1.

TABLE 11.2
Expropriation through currency debasement: Europe, nineteenth century

Country	Period covered	Cumulative decline in silver content of currency (percent)	Largest debasement (percent) and year		Share (percentage) of years in which there was a debasement of the currency (a reduction in the silver content)	
					All	15 percent or greater
Austria	1800–1860	−58.3	−55.0	1812	37.7	11.5
Germany	1800–1830	−2.2	−2.2	1816	3.2	0.0
Portugal	1800 1855	−12.8	−18.4	1800	57.1	1.8
Russia	1800–1899	−56.6	−41.3	1810	50.0	7.0
Turkey	1800–1899	−83.1	−51.2	1829	7.0	7.0
United Kingdom	1800–1899	−6.1	−6.1	1816	1.0	0.0

Sources: Primarily Allen and Unger (2004) and other sources listed in appendix A.1.

The tables illustrate how strikingly successful monarchs were in implementing inflationary monetary policy via currency debasement. The United Kingdom achieved a 50 percent reduction in the silver content of its currency in 1551, Sweden achieved a debasement of 41 percent in 1572, and Turkey's amounted to 44 percent in 1586. The Russian ruble experienced a debasement of 14 percent in 1798 as part of the country's war-financing effort. The third column of each table looks at cumulative currency debasement over long periods, often adding up to 50 percent or more. Table 11.2 looks at the statistics for European countries during the nineteenth century; outliers include Russia's debasement of 57 percent in 1810 and Austria's of 55 percent in 1812, both related to the economic strains associated with the Napoleonic Wars. In 1829, Turkey managed to reduce the silver content of its coins by 51 percent.

The pattern of sustained debasement emerges strikingly in figure 11.1, which plots the silver content of an equally weighted average of the European currencies in our early sample (plus Russia and

Figure 11.1. Changes in the silver content of the currency, 1765–1815:
Austria and Russia during the Napoleonic Wars.
Sources: Primarily Allen and Unger (2004) and other
sources listed in appendix A.1.3.

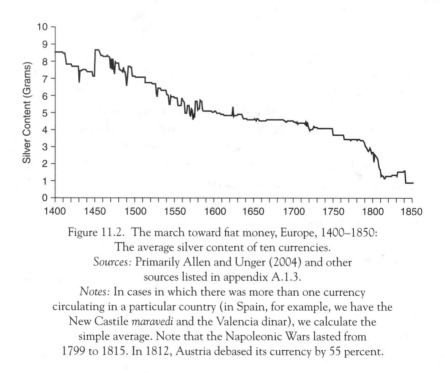

Figure 11.2. The march toward fiat money, Europe, 1400–1850:
The average silver content of ten currencies.
Sources: Primarily Allen and Unger (2004) and other
sources listed in appendix A.1.3.
Notes: In cases in which there was more than one currency
circulating in a particular country (in Spain, for example, we have the
New Castile *maravedi* and the Valencia dinar), we calculate the
simple average. Note that the Napoleonic Wars lasted from
1799 to 1815. In 1812, Austria debased its currency by 55 percent.

Turkey). Figure 11.2 shows what we refer to as "the march toward fiat money" and illustrates that modern inflation is not as different from debasement as some might believe. (The reader will recall that fiat money is currency that has no intrinsic value and is demanded by the public in large part because the government has decreed that no other currency may be used in transactions.)

Perhaps it may seem excessive to devote so much attention here to currency debasement when financial crises have long since moved on to grander and more extravagant schemes. Yet the experience of debasement illustrates many important points. Of course, it shows that inflation and default are nothing new; only the tools have changed. More important, the shift from metallic to paper currency provides an important example of the fact that technological innovation does not necessarily create entirely new kinds of financial crises but can exacerbate their effects, much as technology has constantly made warfare more deadly over the course of history. Finally, our study of debasement reinforces the point that today's advanced economies once experienced the same kind of default, inflation, and debasement traumas that plague many emerging markets today.

- 12 -

INFLATION AND MODERN
CURRENCY CRASHES

*If serial default is the norm for a country passing through the emerging
market state of development, the tendency to lapse into periods of high and
extremely high inflation is an even more striking common denominator.[1]
No emerging market country in history, including the United States (whose
inflation rate in 1779 approached 200 percent) has managed to escape
bouts of high inflation.*

Of course, the problems of external default, domestic default,
and inflation are all integrally related. A government that chooses to
default on its debts can hardly be relied on to preserve the value of
its country's currency. Money creation and interest costs on debt all
enter the government's budget constraint, and in a funding crisis, a
sovereign will typically grab from any and all sources.

In this chapter we begin with a helicopter tour (so to speak)
of our entire cross-country inflation data set, which, to our knowledge, spans considerably more episodes of high inflation and a
broader range of countries than any previously existing body of data.
We then go on to look at exchange rate collapses, which are very
strongly correlated with episodes of high inflation. In most cases, high
inflation and collapsing exchange rates result from a government's
abuse of its self-proclaimed monopoly on currency issuance. In the
final section of this chapter, we look at how, in the aftermath of
high inflation, this monopoly over currency (and sometimes over
the broader payments system) often becomes eroded through widespread acceptance and/or indexation of a hard currency alternative,
or "dollarization." Just as banking crises have persistent adverse consequences on the economy, so does high inflation.

A key finding that jumps out from our historical tour of inflation and exchange rates is how difficult it is for countries to escape a history of high and volatile inflation. Indeed, there is a strong parallel between escaping a history of high inflation and escaping a history of serial default, and of course the two are often interwined.

An Early History of Inflation Crises

However spectacular some of the coinage debasements reported in tables 11.1 and 11.2, without question the advent of the printing press elevated inflation to a whole new level. Figure 12.1 illustrates the median inflation rate for all the countries in our sample from 1500 to 2007 (we used a five-year moving average to smooth out cycle and measurement errors). The figure shows a clear inflationary bias throughout history (although of course there are always periods of deflation due to business cycles, poor crops, and so on). Starting in the twentieth century, however, inflation spiked radically. (We note that our inflation sample goes back to the 1300s for countries such as

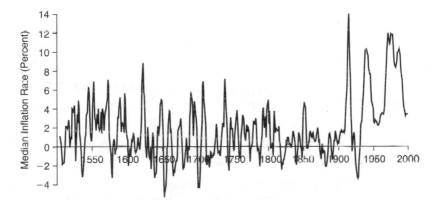

Figure 12.1. The median inflation rate: Five-year moving average
for all countries, 1500–2007.
Sources: Given the long period covered and the large number of countries included, consumer prices (or cost-of-living indexes) are culled from many different sources. They are listed in detail by country and period in appendix A.1.

181

France and England, but in order to achieve a broader and more uniform comparison, we begin here in 1500.)

In the three tables in this chapter we look at country inflation data across the centuries. Table 12.1 presents data for the sixteenth through eighteenth centuries over a broad range of currencies. What is stunning is that every country in both Asia and Europe experienced a significant number of years with inflation over 20 percent during this era, and most experienced a significant number of years with inflation over 40 percent. Take Korea, for example, for which our data set begins in 1743. Korea experienced inflation over 20 percent almost half the time until 1800 and inflation over 40 percent almost a third of the time. Poland, for which our data go back to 1704, experienced similar percentages. Even the United Kingdom had over 20 percent inflation 5 percent of the time, going back to 1500 (and this is probably an underestimate, because official figures of inflation during World War II and its immediate aftermath are widely thought to be well below the levels of inflation that actually prevailed). The New World colonies of Latin America experienced frequent bouts of high inflation long before their wars of independence from Spain.

Modern Inflation Crises: Regional Comparisons

Table 12.2 looks at the years 1800–2007 for thirteen African countries and twelve Asian countries. South Africa, Hong Kong, and Malaysia have notably the best track records in resisting high inflation, though South Africa's record extends back to 1896, whereas Hong Kong's and Malaysia's go back only to 1948 and 1949, respectively.[2]

Most of the countries in Africa and Asia, however, have experienced waves of high and very high inflation. The notion that Asian countries have been immune to Latin American–style high inflation is just as naïve as the notion that Asian countries were immune to default crises up until the Asian financial crisis of the late 1990s. China experienced inflation over 1,500 percent in 1947,[3] and Indonesia over 900 percent in 1966. Even the Asian "tigers,"

TABLE 12.1

"Default" through inflation: Asia, Europe, and the "New World," 1500–1799

Country	Period covered	Share of years in which inflation exceeded		Number of hyperinflations[a]	Maximum annual inflation	Year of peak inflation
		20 percent	40 percent			
Asia						
China	1639–1799	14.3	6.2	0	116.7	1651
Japan	1601–1650	34.0	14.0	0	98.9	1602
Korea	1743–1799	43.9	29.8	0	143.9	1787
Europe						
Austria	1501–1799	8.4	6.0	0	99.1	1623
Belgium	1501–1799	25.1	11.0	0	185.1	1708
Denmark	1749–1799	18.8	10.4	0	77.4	1772
France	1501–1799	12.4	2.0	0	121.3	1622
Germany	1501–1799	10.4	3.4	0	140.6	1622
Italy	1501–1799	19.1	7.0	0	173.1	1527
The Netherlands	1501–1799	4.0	0.3	0	40.0	1709
Norway	1666–1799	6.0	0.8	0	44.2	1709
Poland	1704–1799	43.8	31.9	0	92.1	1762
Portugal	1729–1799	19.7	2.8	0	83.1	1757
Spain	1501–1799	4.7	0.7	0	40.5	1521
Sweden	1540–1799	15.5	4.1	0	65.8	1572
Turkey	1586–1799	19.2	11.2	0	53.4	1621
United Kingdom	1501–1799	5.0	1.7	0	39.5	1587
The "New World"						
Argentina	1777–1799	4.2	0.0	0	30.8	1780
Brazil	1764–1799	25.0	4.0	0	33.0	1792
Chile	1751–1799	4.1	0.0	0	36.6	1763
Mexico	1742–1799	22.4	7.0	0	80.0	1770
Peru	1751–1799	10.2	0.0	0	31.6	1765
United States	1721–1799	7.6	4.0	0	192.5	1779

Sources: Given the long period covered and the large number of countries included, consumer prices (or cost-of-living indexes) are culled from many different sources. They are listed in detail by country and period in appendix A.1.

[a]Hyperinflation is defined here as an annual inflation rate of 500 percent or higher (this is not the traditional Cagan definition).

TABLE 12.2
"Default" through inflation: Africa and Asia, 1800–2008

Country	Beginning of period covered	Share of years in which inflation exceeded		Number of years of hyperinflation[a]	Maximum annual inflation	Year of peak inflation
		20 percent	40 percent			
Africa						
Algeria	1879	24.1	12.0	0	69.2	1947
Angola	1915	53.3	44.6	4	4,416.0	1996
Central African Republic	1957	4.0	0.0	0	27.7	1971
Côte d'Ivoire	1952	7.3	0.0	0	26.0	1994
Egypt	1860	7.5	0.7	0	40.8	1941
Kenya	1949	8.3	3.3	0	46.0	1993
Mauritius	1947	10.0	0.0	0	33.0	1980
Morocco	1940	14.9	4.5	0	57.5	1947
Nigeria	1940	22.6	9.4	0	72.9	1995
South Africa	1896	0.9	0.0	0	35.2	1919
Tunisia	1940	11.9	6.0	0	72.1	1943
Zambia	1943	29.7	15.6	0	183.3	1993
Zimbabwe	1920	23.3	14.0	Ongoing	66,000	
Asia						
China	1800	19.3	14.0	3	1,579.3	1947
Hong Kong	1948	1.7	0.0	0	21.7	1949
India	1801	7.3	1.5	0	53.8	1943
Indonesia	1819	18.6	9.6	1	939.8	1966
Japan	1819	12.2	4.8	1	568.0	1945
Korea	1800	35.3	24.6	0	210.4	1951
Malaysia	1949	1.7	0.0	0	22.0	1950
Myanmar	1872	22.2	6.7	0	58.1	2002
The Philippines	1938	11.6	7.2	0	141.7	1943
Singapore	1949	3.4	0.0	0	23.5	1973
Taiwan	1898	14.7	11.0	0	29.6	1973
Thailand	1821	14.0	7.5	0	78.5	1919

Sources: Given the long period covered and the large number of countries included, consumer prices (or cost-of-living indexes) are culled from many different sources. They are listed in detail by country and period in appendix A.1.

[a]Hyperinflation is defined here as an annual inflation rate of 500 percent or higher (this is not the traditional Cagan definition).

Singapore and Taiwan, experienced inflation well over 20 percent in the early 1970s.

Africa, perhaps not surprisingly, has a considerably worse record. Angola had inflation over 4,000 percent in 1996, Zimbabwe already over 66,000 percent by 2007, putting that country on track to surpass the Republic of the Congo (one of the poor developing countries divorced from global private capital markets that is not included in our sample), which has experienced three episodes of hyperinflation since 1970.[4] And for 2008 Zimbabwe's inflation rate would be seen to have been even worse.

Finally, table 12.3 lists the inflation rates for 1800 through 2008 for Europe, Latin America, North America, and Oceania. The European experiences include the great postwar hyperinflations studied by Cagan.[5] But even setting aside hyperinflations, countries such as Poland, Russia, and Turkey have experienced high inflation an extraordinarily large percentage of the time. In modern times, one does not think of Scandinavian countries as having outsize inflation problems, but they too experienced high inflation in earlier eras. Norway, for example, had an inflation rate of 152 percent in 1812, Denmark 48 percent in 1800, and Sweden 36 percent in 1918. Latin America's post–World War II inflation history is famously spectacular, as the table illustrates, with many episodes of peacetime hyperinflations in the 1980s and 1990s. Latin America's poor performance looks less unique, however, from a broader perspective in terms of countries and history.

Even Canada and United States have each experienced an episode of inflation over 20 percent. Although U.S. inflation never again reached triple digits after the eighteenth century, it did reach 24 percent in 1864, during the Civil War. (Of course, the Confederacy of the South did achieve triple-digit inflation with its currency during the Civil War, which the break-away states ultimately lost.) Canada's inflation rate reached 24 percent as well during 1917. In all of table 12.3, we can see that only New Zealand and Panama have experienced no periods of inflation over 20 percent, although New Zealand's inflation rate reached 17 percent as recently as 1980 and Panama had 16 percent inflation in 1974.

TABLE 12.3
"Default" through inflation: Europe, Latin America, North America, and Oceania, 1800–2008

Country	Beginning of period covered	Share of years in which inflation exceeded		Number of years of hyperinflation[a]	Maximum annual inflation	Year of peak inflation
		20 percent	40 percent			
Europe						
Austria	1800	20.8	12.1	2	1,733.0	1922
Belgium	1800	10.1	6.8	0	50.6	1812
Denmark	1800	2.1	0.5	0	48.3	1800
Finland	1861	5.5	2.7	0	242.0	1918
France	1800	5.8	1.9	0	74.0	1946
Germany	1800	9.7	4.3	2	2.22E + 10	1923
Greece	1834	13.3	5.2	4	3.02E + 10	1944
Hungary	1924	15.7	3.6	2	9.63E + 26	1946
Italy	1800	11.1	5.8	0	491.4	1944
The Netherlands	1800	1.0	0.0	0	21.0	1918
Norway	1800	5.3	1.9	0	152.0	1812
Poland	1800	28.0	17.4	2	51,699.4	1923
Portugal	1800	9.7	4.3	0	84.2	1808
Russia	1854	35.7	26.4	8	13,534.7	1923
Spain	1800	3.9	1.0	0	102.1	1808
Sweden	1800	1.9	0.0	0	35.8	1918
Turkey	1800	20.5	11.7	0	115.9	1942
United Kingdom	1800	2.4	0.0	0	34.4	1800
Latin America						
Argentina	1800	24.6	15.5	4	3,079.5	1989
Bolivia	1937	38.6	20.0	2	11,749.6	1985
Brazil	1800	28.0	17.9	6	2,947.7	1990
Chile	1800	19.8	5.8	0	469.9	1973
Colombia	1864	23.8	1.4	0	53.6	1882
Costa Rica	1937	12.9	1.4	0	90.1	1982
Dominican Republic	1943	17.2	9.4	0	51.5	2004
Ecuador	1939	36.8	14.7	0	96.1	2000
El Salvador	1938	8.7	0.0	0	31.9	1986
Guatemala	1938	8.7	1.4	0	41.0	1990
Honduras	1937	8.6	0.0	0	34.0	1991
Mexico	1800	42.5	35.7	0	131.8	1987
Nicaragua	1938	30.4	17.4	6	13,109.5	1987
Panama	1949	0.0	0.0	0	16.3	1974
Paraguay	1949	32.8	4.5	0	139.1	1952
Peru	1800	15.5	10.7	3	7,481.7	1990

TABLE 12.3 Continued

Country	Beginning of period covered	Share of years in which inflation exceeded		Number of years of hyperinflation[a]	Maximum annual inflation	Year of peak inflation
		20 percent	40 percent			
Latin America (*continued*)						
Uruguay	1871	26.5	19.1	0	112.5	1990
Venezuela	1832	10.3	3.4	0	99.9	1996
North America						
Canada	1868	0.7	0.0	0	23.8	1917
United States	1800	1.0	0.0	0	24.0	1864
Oceania						
Australia	1819	4.8	1.1	0	57.4	1854
New Zealand	1858	0.0	0.0	0	17.2	1980

Sources: Given the long period covered and the large number of countries included, consumer prices (or cost-of-living indexes) are culled from many different sources. They are listed in detail by country and period in appendix A.1.

[a]Hyperinflation is defined here as an annual inflation rate of 500 percent or higher (this is not the traditional Cagan definition).

As in the case of debt defaults, the early years following the 2001 global recession proved to be a relatively quiescent period in terms of very high inflation, although a number of countries (including Argentina, Venezuela, and of course Zimbabwe) did experience problems.[6] Many observers, following the same logic as with external default, have concluded that "this time is different" and that inflation will never return. We certainly agree that there have been important advances in our understanding of central bank design and monetary policy, particularly in the importance of having an independent central bank that places a heavy weight on inflation stabilization. But, as in the case of debt defaults, experience suggests that quiet periods do not extend indefinitely.

Figure 12.2 plots the share of countries that were having inflation crises (defined as an annual inflation rate of 20 percent or higher) in any given year (1800–2007) over four panels for Africa, Asia, Europe, and Latin America, respectively. None of the regions

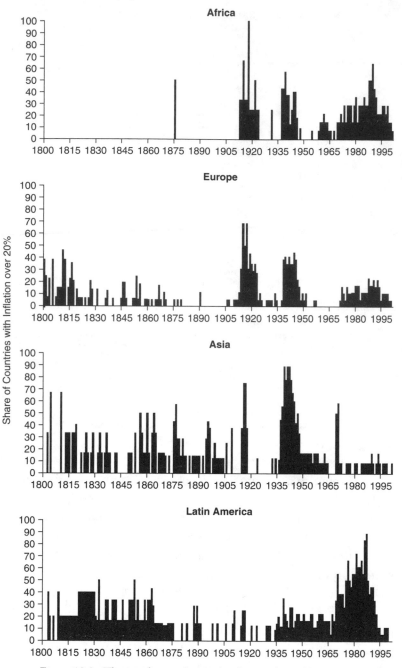

Figure 12.2. The incidence of annual inflation above 20 percent:
Africa, Asia, Europe, and Latin America, 1800–2007.

188

has had a particularly pristine inflation history. After World War II, the incidence of high inflation has been greater in Africa and Latin America than in other regions, with this trend intensifying during the 1980s and 1990s. The worldwide ebb in inflation is still of modern vintage; we will see if inflation resurfaces again in the years following the financial crisis of the late 2000s, particularly as government debt stocks mount, fiscal "space" (the capacity to engage in fiscal stimulus) erodes, and particularly if a rash of sovereign defaults in emerging markets eventually follows.

Currency Crashes

Having discussed currency debasement and inflation crises, including a long exposé on exchange rate crashes at this stage seems somewhat redundant. Our database on exchange rates is almost as rich as that on prices, especially if one takes into account silver-based exchange rates (see the appendixes for a detailed description). Although we will not go into detail here, a more systematic analysis of the data set will show that, by and large, *inflation crises and exchange rate crises have traveled hand in hand in the overwhelming majority of episodes across time and countries (with a markedly tighter link in countries subject to chronic inflation, where the pass-through from exchange rates to prices is greatest).*

When we look at exchange rate behavior, we can see that probably the most surprising evidence comes from the Napoleonic Wars, during which exchange rate instability escalated to a level that had not been seen before and was not to be seen again for nearly a hundred years. This is starkly illustrated in figures 12.3 and 12.4, with the former depicting the incidence of peak currency depreciation and the latter showing median inflation. The figures also show a significantly

---

Sources: Given the long period covered and the large number of countries included, consumer prices (or cost-of-living indexes) are culled from many different sources. They are listed in detail by country and period in appendix A.1.

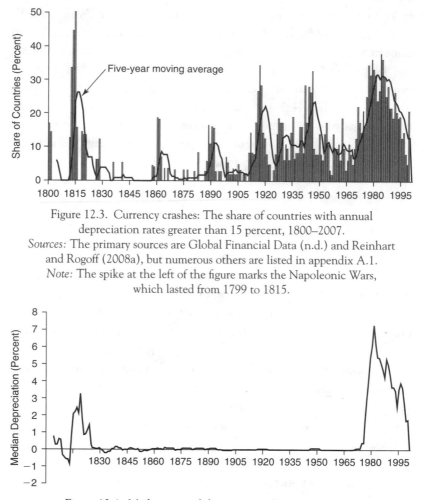

Figure 12.3. Currency crashes: The share of countries with annual
depreciation rates greater than 15 percent, 1800–2007.
Sources: The primary sources are Global Financial Data (n.d.) and Reinhart
and Rogoff (2008a), but numerous others are listed in appendix A.1.
Note: The spike at the left of the figure marks the Napoleonic Wars,
which lasted from 1799 to 1815.

Figure 12.4. Median annual depreciation: Five-year moving
average for all countries, 1800–2007.
Sources: The primary sources are Global Financial Data (n.d.) and Reinhart
and Rogoff (2008a), but numerous others are listed in appendix A.1.
Note: The spike at the left of the figure marks the Napoleonic Wars,
which lasted from 1799 to 1815.

higher incidence of crashes and larger median changes in the more
modern period. This should hardly come as a surprise, given the prominent exchange rate crises in Mexico (1994), Asia (1997), Russia
(1998), Brazil (1999), and Argentina (2001), among other countries.

The Aftermath of High Inflation and Currency Collapses

Countries with sustained high inflation often experience dollarization, a huge shift toward the use of foreign currency as a transaction medium, a unit of account, and a store of value. From a practical perspective, this can imply the use of foreign hard currency for trade or, even more prevalently, the indexation of bank accounts, bonds, and other financial assets to foreign currency (what we have termed elsewhere in joint work with Savastano as "liability dollarization").[7] In many cases, a sustained shift toward dollarization is one of the many long-term costs of episodes of high inflation, one that often persists even if the government strives to prevent it. A government that has grossly abused its monopoly over the currency and payments system will often find this monopoly more difficult to enforce in the aftermath. Reducing dollarization and regaining control of monetary policy is often one of the major aims of disinflation policy after a period of elevated inflation. Yet de-dollarization can be extremely difficult. In this short section we digress to look at this important monetary phenomenon.

Successful disinflations generally have not been accompanied by large declines in the degree of dollarization. In fact, the top panel of figure 12.5 shows that the degree of dollarization at the end of the period of disinflation was the same as or higher than at the time of the inflation peak in more than half of the episodes. Moreover, the decrease in the degree of dollarization in many of the other episodes was generally small. This persistence of dollarization is consistent with the evidence on "hysteresis" found by the studies based on a narrower measure of domestic dollarization. In this context, *hysteresis* simply refers to the tendency for a country that has become dollarized to remain so long after the original reasons for the shift (usually excessive inflation on domestic currency) have abated.

The persistence of dollarization is a regularity that tends to be associated with countries' inflation histories. In fact, countries that had repeated bouts of high inflation over the past few decades generally exhibited a higher degree of dollarization in the late 1990s than did countries with better inflationary histories (figure 12.5,

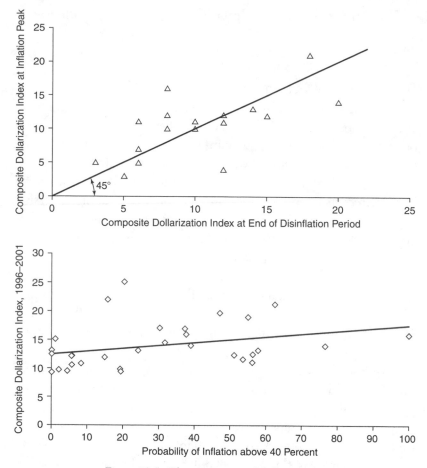

Figure 12.5. The persistence of dollarization.
Source: Reinhart, Rogoff, and Savastano (2003b).
Notes: The top panel shows that disinflation has had no clear effects on the degree of dollarization. "End of disinflation period" is defined as the year when the inflation rate fell below 10 percent. The bottom panel shows that current levels of dollarization are related to a country's history of high inflation. Unconditional probability computed with monthly data on inflation for the period 1958–2001.

lower panel). Interpreting the (unconditional) probability of high inflation used in figure 12.5 as a rough measure of the credibility of a monetary policy gives us some insights as to why achieving low inflation is generally not a sufficient condition for a rapid decrease in the degree of dollarization; namely, a country with a poor inflationary history will need to maintain inflation at low levels for a long period before it can significantly reduce the probability of another inflationary bout.[8] This is yet another parallel to the difficulties a country faces in graduating from debt intolerance.

One can also show a relationship between current levels of dollarization and countries' exchange rate histories. Parallel market exchange rates and pervasive exchange controls have been the norm rather than the exception in countries with histories of high inflation. Conversely, very few countries with hard pegs and unified exchange rates have experienced bouts of high inflation.[9] The evidence thus suggests a link between current levels of dollarization and countries' past reliance on exchange controls and multiple currency practices.

Undoing Domestic Dollarization

We have shown that reducing inflation is generally not sufficient to undo domestic dollarization, at least at horizons of more than five years. Nevertheless, some countries have managed to reduce their degree of domestic dollarization. To identify those countries, it is useful to treat separately cases in which the reduction in domestic dollarization originated in a decline in locally issued foreign currency public debt from those that originated in a decline in the share of foreign currency deposits in broad money.

The few governments in our sample that managed to dedollarize their locally issued foreign currency obligations followed one of two strategies: they either amortized the outstanding debt stock on the original terms and discontinued the issuance of those securities, or they changed the currency denomination of the debt—sometimes, but not always, using market-based approaches. One example of the former strategy is Mexico's decision to redeem in U.S. dollars all the dollar-linked *tesobonos* outstanding at the time of its December 1994 crisis (using the loans it received from the International Monetary Fund and the United States) and to cease issuing domestic foreign

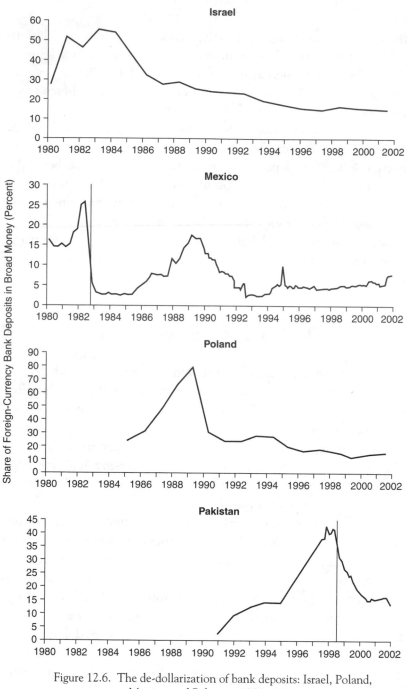

Figure 12.6. The de-dollarization of bank deposits: Israel, Poland, Mexico, and Pakistan, 1980–2002.

194

currency–denominated bonds thereafter. A recent example of the latter is Argentina's decision in late 2001 to convert to domestic currency the government bonds that it had originally issued in U.S. dollars (under Argentine law).

Decreases in domestic dollarization caused by declines in the share of foreign currency deposits to broad money are more common in our sample. To identify only those cases in which the reversal of deposit dollarization was large and lasting, we searched for all episodes in which the ratio of foreign currency deposits to broad money satisfied the following three conditions: (1) experienced a decline of at least 20 percent, (2) settled at a level below 20 percent immediately following the decline, and (3) remained below 20 percent until the end of the sample period.

Only four of the eighty-five countries for which we have data on foreign currency deposits met the three criteria during the period 1980–2001: Israel, Poland, Mexico, and Pakistan (figure 12.6). In sixteen other countries, the ratio of foreign currency deposits to broad money declined by more than 20 percent during some portion of 1980–2001. However, in some of these countries—for instance, in Bulgaria and Lebanon—the deposit dollarization ratio settled at a level considerably higher than 20 percent following the decline. And in the majority of the other cases (twelve out of the sixteen) the dollarization ratio initially fell below the 20 percent mark but later rebounded to levels in excess of 20 percent.[10] Some forms of dollarization are even more difficult to eradicate. At present between one-half and two-thirds of mortgage loans in Poland (one of the relatively more successful de-dollarizers) are denominated in a foreign currency, mostly Swiss francs.

In three of the four cases that met our three conditions for a large and lasting decline of the deposit dollarization ratio, the rever-

---

Source: See appendix A.1.
Notes: In the panel on Mexico, the vertical line marks the point, in 1982, at which there was a forcible conversion of foreign currency bank deposits. In the panel on Pakistan, the vertical line marks the point, in 1998, at which there was a forcible conversion of foreign currency bank deposits.

195

sal started the moment the authorities imposed restrictions on the convertibility of dollar deposits. In Israel, in late 1985 the authorities introduced a one-year mandatory holding period for all deposits in foreign currency, making those deposits substantially less attractive than other indexed financial instruments.[11] By contrast, in Mexico in 1982 and Pakistan in 1998, the authorities forcibly converted the dollar deposits into deposits in domestic currency, using for the conversion an exchange rate that was substantially below (i.e., more appreciated than) the prevailing market rate.

Interestingly, not all the countries that introduced severe restrictions on the availability of dollar deposits managed to lower the deposit dollarization ratio on a sustained basis. Bolivia and Peru adopted measures similar to those of Mexico and Pakistan in the early 1980s, but after some years of extreme macroeconomic instability that took them to the brink of hyperinflation, both countries eventually allowed foreign currency deposits once again, and they have since remained highly dollarized despite their remarkable success in reducing inflation.

Even in the countries where the restrictions on dollar deposits have thus far led to a lasting decline of deposit dollarization, the costs of de-dollarization were far from trivial. In Mexico, capital flight nearly doubled (to about US$6.5 billion per year), bank credit to the private sector fell by almost half in the two years that followed the forced conversion of dollar deposits, and the country's inflation and growth performance remained dismal for several years.[12] As for Pakistan, it is too soon to tell whether its compulsory de-dollarization of 1998 will prove permanent or whether it will eventually be reversed, as was the case in Bolivia and Peru—and in Argentina in its 2001–2002 forcible "pesoization."

This chapter has covered a great deal of ground, etching the highlights of the world's fascinating history of inflation and exchange rate crashes. Virtually every country in the world, particularly during its emerging market phase, has experienced bouts of inflation, often long-lasting and recurrent. Indeed, the history of inflation shows how profoundly difficult it is for countries to permanently graduate from a history of macroeconomic mismanagement without having occasional but very painful relapses. High inflation causes residents to minimize their exposure to further macroeconomic malfeasance for a very long time. Their lower demand for domestic paper currency reduces the base on which the government can secure inflation revenues, making it more painful (in fiscal terms) to restore low inflation. A destabilizing exchange rate dynamic is a natural corollary. In extreme cases, citizens may find ways to more aggressively circumvent the government's currency monopoly by using hard currency, or the government may find itself forced to guarantee the hard currency indexation of bank deposits and other liabilities in an effort to restore the payments system. This weakening of the government's currency monopoly can also take a long time to outgrow.

- PART V -

THE U.S. SUBPRIME MELTDOWN AND THE SECOND GREAT CONTRACTION

How relevant are historical benchmarks for assessing the trajectory of a modern global financial crisis? In this part of the book we draw on our historical data set to develop benchmarks for measuring the severity of the crisis in terms of both the run-up to it and the possible evolution of its aftermath. A few years back, many people would have said that improvements in financial engineering and the conduct of monetary policy had done much to tame the business cycle and limit the risk of financial contagion. But the recent global financial crisis has proven them wrong.

When the "subprime financial crisis" (as it was initially called) began to unfold in the summer of 2007, a cursory reading of the global financial press would have led one to conclude that the world economy was moving through dark and uncharted waters. Indeed, after events took a decided turn for the worse in the early fall of 2008, much of the commentary took on an apocalyptic tone usually reserved for a threat that could potentially end civilization (as we know it). Yet, had policy makers looked at the recent history of financial crises, they would have found that it provided an important qualitative and quantitative perspective on how to gauge the evolution of the crisis.

In the next four chapters we will attempt to do exactly that, drawing on past experiences for analogies and making use of our data set to establish quantitative benchmarks. Because many of our readers may want to begin with the most recent crisis, we have done our best to make this part of the book relatively self-contained, reviewing and repeating main themes from earlier chapters as necessary.

In the first of these chapters, chapter 13, we will begin with an overview of the history of banking crises that is tailored to give the reader a perspective of the current crisis. We will pay particular attention to the debate on the massive global current account imbalances that preceded the crisis and, some would say, helped trigger it. As we will show, the outsized U.S. borrowing from abroad that occurred prior to the crisis (manifested in a sequence of gaping current account and trade balance deficits) was hardly the only warning signal. In fact, the U.S. economy, at the epicenter of the crisis, showed many other signs of being on the brink of a deep financial crisis. Other measures such as asset price inflation, most notably in the real estate sector, rising household leverage, and the slowing output—standard leading indicators of financial crises—all revealed worrisome symptoms. Indeed, from a purely quantitative perspective, the run-up to the U.S. financial crisis showed all the signs of an accident waiting to happen. Of course, the United States was hardly alone in showing classic warning signs of a financial crisis, with Great Britain, Spain, and Ireland, among other countries, experiencing many of the same symptoms.

In the next chapter, chapter 14, we will extend the comparison between the past crises and the recent one by examining the aftermath of severe financial crises. To expand our data set, we will bring in a number of relatively well-known episodes in emerging markets. As we have seen in chapter 10, on banking crises, emerging markets and developed countries experience surprisingly similar outcomes in the wake of financial crises (at least in a number of core areas), so this would seem to be a reasonable exercise. For most of the chapter the crises we use as our comparison group will be postwar crises, but toward the end of the chapter we will make comparisons with the Great Depression. One can plausibly argue that macroeconomic policy was much too passive in the early stages of the Great Depression. Indeed, efforts to maintain balanced budgets in the wake of declining tax revenues were likely deeply counterproductive, while reluctance to abandon the gold standard contributed to deflation in many countries. Still, the comparisons are important because no other financial crisis since the Great Depression has been nearly as global in nature.

In the chapter that follows, chapter 15, we will explore the links that transmit crises across countries, ranging from financial links to trade to common factors such as technology and geopolitical shocks. We will also make a distinction between high-velocity or "fast-and-furious" factors that transmit crises across borders very quickly—for instance, via stock markets—and low-velocity or "slow-burn" factors whereby transmission takes somewhat longer.

In the last of these four chapters, chapter 16, we look at the recent crisis from a global perspective. This chapter will be a culmination of all that has gone before it. Our expansive data set spanning nearly all regions allows us to offer a working definition of a global financial crisis. In addition, our analysis of the different kinds of crises described in this book allows us to develop a new crisis index that essentially aggregates the number of different crises each country is experiencing across the globe. Thus chapter 16 is quite crucial in bringing together the entire spectrum of crises we consider in this book. Even though the most recent crisis does not appear likely to come close to the severity of the Great Depression of the 1930s, readers may nevertheless find the comparisons sobering.

- 13 -

THE U.S. SUBPRIME CRISIS:
AN INTERNATIONAL AND
HISTORICAL COMPARISON

This chapter begins with a broad-brush "pictorial" overview of the global incidence of banking crises through the past century, taking advantage of the expansive amount of data collected for this book. Our aim is to place the international situation of the late 2000s, the "Second Great Contraction," in a broader historical context.[1] We will then go on, in this chapter and the next, to look at how the late-vintage U.S. subprime financial crisis compares with past financial crises. Broadly speaking, we will show that both in the run-up to the recent crisis and in its aftermath (as of the writing of this book), the United States has driven straight down the quantitative tracks of a typical deep financial crisis.

In addition to making our quantitative comparisons in this chapter, we will also discuss the re-emergence of the this-time-is-different syndrome—the insistence that some combination of factors renders the previous laws of investing null and void—that appeared on the eve of the meltdown. This task is not particularly difficult, for the remarks and written works of academics, policy makers, and financial market participants in the run-up to the crisis provide ample evidence of the syndrome. We will place particular emphasis on the debate over whether massive borrowing by the United States from the rest of the world prior to the crisis should have been seen as a critical warning sign.

A Global Historical View of the
Subprime Crisis and Its Aftermath

Before focusing on the Second Great Contraction, which began in 2007, it will be helpful to review the incidence of banking crises over a broader span of history, which we first examined in chapter 10. A closer look at those data shows that the earliest banking crisis in an advanced economy in our sample is that of France in 1802; early crises in emerging markets befell India in 1863, China (in several episodes) during the 1860s–1870s, and Peru in 1873. Because in this chapter we are interested in making broad cross-country comparisons, we will focus mainly on data for the period since 1900, for they are sufficiently rich to allow a systematic empirical treatment.[2]

Figure 13.1 plots the incidence of banking crises among the countries in our sample (which the reader will recall accounts for about 90 percent of world income on the basis of purchasing power parity, or PPP). The graph is, in fact, based on the same data as figure 10.1 except that here we concentrate only on banking crises and not on capital mobility. As before, the figure shows the percentage of all independent countries that experienced a banking crisis in any given year from 1900 through 2008, taking a three-year moving average. As in figure 10.1 and a number of similar figures throughout the book, the tally in figure 13.1 weights countries by their share of global GDP so that crises in larger economies have a greater impact on the overall shape of the graph. This weighted aggregate is meant to provide a measure of the "global" impact of individual banking crises. Therefore, a crisis in the United States or Germany is accorded a much greater weight than a crisis in Angola or Honduras, all of which are part of our sixty-six-country sample. The reader should be aware that although we believe that figure 13.1 gives a fair picture of the proportion of the world in banking crisis at any one time, it is only a rough measure, because banking crises are of varying severity.

As we noted in chapter 10, the highest incidence of banking crises during this 109-year stretch can be found during the worldwide

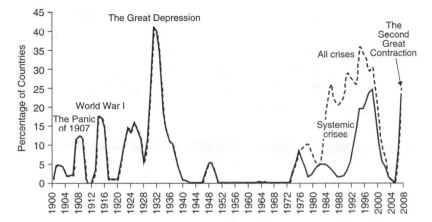

Figure 13.1. The proportion of countries with banking crises,
1900–2008, weighted by their share of world income.
Sources: Kaminsky and Reinhart (1999), Bordo et al. (2001),
Maddison (2004), Caprio et al. (2005), Jácome (2008), and the additional
sources listed in appendix A.3, which provides the dates of banking crises.
Notes: The sample size includes all sixty-six countries listed in table 1.1 that
were independent states in the given year. Three sets of GDP weights are used,
1913 weights for the period 1800–1913, 1990 weights for the period 1914–1990,
and finally 2003 weights for the period 1991–2008. The dotted line indicates
all crises, the solid line systemic crises (for instance, for the 1980s and 1990s,
the crises in the Nordic countries, then Japan, then the rest of Asia). The
entries for 2007–2008 indicate crises in Austria, Belgium, Germany,
Hungary, Japan, the Netherlands, Spain, the United Kingdom, and
the United States. The figure shows a three-year moving average.

Great Depression of the 1930s. Earlier, less widespread "waves" of
global financial stress were evident during and around the Panic of
1907, which originated in New York, as well as the crises accompanying the outbreak of the First World War. Figure 13.1 also reminds
us of the relative calm from the late 1940s to the early 1970s. This
calm may be partly explained by booming world growth but perhaps
more so by the repression of the domestic financial markets (in varying degrees) and the heavy-handed use of capital controls that followed for many years after World War II. (We are not necessarily
implying that such repression and controls are the right approach to
dealing with the risk of financial crises.)

205

As we also observed in chapter 10, since the early 1970s, financial and international capital account liberalization—reduction and removal of barriers to investment inside and outside a country—have taken root worldwide. So, too, have banking crises.[3] After a long hiatus, the share of countries with banking difficulties first began to expand in the 1970s. The break-up of the Bretton Woods system of fixed exchange rates, together with a sharp spike in oil prices, catalyzed a prolonged global recession, resulting in financial sector difficulties in a number of advanced economies. In the early 1980s, a collapse in global commodity prices, combined with high and volatile interest rates in the United States, contributed to a spate of banking and sovereign debt crises in emerging economies, most famously in Latin America and then Africa. High interest rates raised the cost of servicing large debts, which were often funded at variable interest rates linked to world markets. Falling prices for commodities, the main export for most emerging markets, also made it more difficult for them to service debts.

The United States experienced its own banking crisis, rooted in the savings and loan industry, beginning in 1984 (albeit this was a relatively mild crisis compared to those of the 1930s and the 2000s). During the late 1980s and early 1990s, the Nordic countries experienced some of the worst banking crises the wealthy economies had known since World War II following a surge in capital inflows (lending from abroad) and soaring real estate prices. In 1992, Japan's asset price bubble burst and ushered in a decade-long banking crisis. Around the same time, with the collapse of the Soviet bloc, several formerly communist countries in Eastern Europe joined the ranks of nations facing banking sector problems. As the second half of the 1990s approached, emerging markets faced a fresh round of banking crises. Problems in Mexico and Argentina (in 1994–1995) were followed by the famous Asian crisis of 1997–1998 and then the troubles of Russia and Colombia, among others.[4] That upswing in the banking crisis cycle was closed by Argentina in 2001 and Uruguay in 2002. A brief tranquil period came to an abrupt halt in the summer of 2007 when the subprime crisis in the United States began in earnest, soon transforming itself into a global financial crisis.[5]

As is well known, the U.S. financial crisis of the late 2000s was firmly rooted in the bubble in the real estate market fueled by sustained massive increases in housing prices, a massive influx of cheap foreign capital resulting from record trade balance and current account deficits, and an increasingly permissive regulatory policy that helped propel the dynamic between these factors (a pattern that we will quantify further). To place the housing bubble in historical perspective, figure 13.2 plots the now-famous Case-Shiller housing price index deflated by the GNP deflator (the picture is essentially unchanged if the consumer price index is used).[6] Since 1891, when the price series began, no housing price boom has been comparable in terms of sheer magnitude and duration to that recorded in the years culminating in the 2007 subprime mortgage fiasco. *Between 1996 and 2006 (the year when prices peaked), the cumulative real price increase was about 92 percent—more than three times the 27 percent cumulative increase from 1890 to 1996!* In 2005, at the height of the bubble, real housing prices soared by more than 12 percent (that was about six times the rate of increase in real per capita GDP for that year) Even the prosperous post–World War II decades, when demographic and income trends lent support to housing prices, pale in

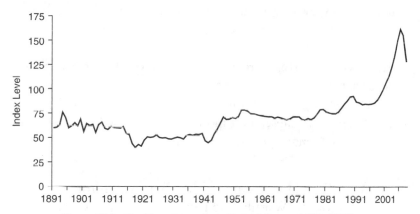

Figure 13.2. Real housing prices: United States, 1891–2008.
Sources: Shiller (2005), Standard and Poor's, and U.S. Commerce Department.
Notes: House prices are deflated by the GNP deflator. Real housing prices are indexed to equal 100 in 2000.

comparison to the pre-2007 surge in prices.[7] By mid-2007, a sharp rise in default rates on low-income housing mortgages in the United States eventually sparked a full-blown global financial panic.

The This-Time-Is-Different Syndrome and the Run-up to the Subprime Crisis

The global financial crisis of the late 2000s, whether measured by the depth, breadth, and (potential) duration of the accompanying recession or by its profound effect on asset markets, stands as the most serious global financial crisis since the Great Depression. The crisis has been a transformative moment in global economic history whose ultimate resolution will likely reshape politics and economics for at least a generation.

Should the crisis have come as a surprise, especially in its deep impact on the United States? Listening to a long list of leading academics, investors, and U.S. policy makers, one would have thought the financial meltdown of the late 2000s was a bolt from the blue, a "six-sigma" event. U.S. Federal Reserve Chairman Alan Greenspan frequently argued that financial innovations such as securitization and option pricing were producing new and better ways to spread risk, simultaneously making traditionally illiquid assets, such as houses, more liquid. Hence higher and higher prices for risky assets could be justified.

We could stop here and say that a lot of people were convinced that "this time is different" because the United States is "special." However, given the historic nature of the recent U.S. and global financial collapse, a bit more background will help us to understand why so many people were fooled.

Risks Posed by Sustained U.S. Borrowing from the Rest of the World: The Debate before the Crisis

Chairman Greenspan was among the legion that branded as alarmists those who worried excessively about the burgeoning U.S. current account deficit.[8] Greenspan argued that this gaping deficit, which reached more than 6.5 percent of GDP in 2006 (over $800 billion), was, to a significant extent, simply a reflection of a broader trend toward global financial deepening that was allowing countries to sustain much larger current account deficits and surpluses than in the past. Indeed, in his 2007 book, Greenspan characterizes the sustained U.S. current account deficit as a secondary issue, not a primary risk factor, one that (along with others such as soaring housing prices and the notable buildup in household debt) should not have caused excessive alarm among U.S. policy makers during the run-up to the crisis that began in 2007.[9]

The Federal Reserve chairman was hardly alone in his relatively sanguine view of American borrowing. U.S. Treasury Secretary Paul O'Neill famously argued that it was natural for other countries to lend to the United States given this country's high rate of productivity growth and that the current account was a "meaningless concept."[10]

Greenspan's successor, Ben Bernanke, in a speech he made in 2005, famously described the U.S. borrowing binge as the product of a "global savings glut" that had been caused by a convergence of factors, many of which were outside the control of U.S. policy makers.[11] These factors included the strong desire of many emerging markets to insure themselves against future economic crises after the slew of crises in Latin America and Asia during the 1990s and early 2000s. At the same time, Middle Eastern countries had sought ways to use their oil earnings, and countries with underdeveloped financial systems, such as China, had wanted to diversify into safer assets. Bernanke argued that it was also natural for some developed economies, such as Japan and Germany, to have high savings rates in the face of rapidly aging populations. All these factors together conspired to provide a huge pool of net savings in search of a safe and dynamic resting place, which meant the United States. Of course, this cheap source of funding was an opportunity for the United States. The question authorities might have wrestled with more was "Can there be too much of a good thing?" The same this-time-is-different argument appears all too often in the speeches of policy makers in emerging markets when their countries are experiencing massive capital inflows: "Low rates of return in the rest of the world are simply making investment in our country particularly attractive."

As money poured into the United States, U.S. financial firms, including mighty investment banks such as Goldman Sachs, Merrill Lynch (which was acquired by Bank of America in 2008 in a "shotgun marriage"), and the now defunct Lehman Brothers, as well as large universal banks (with retail bases) such as Citibank, all saw their profits soar. The size of the U.S. financial sector (which includes banking and insurance) more than doubled, from an average of roughly 4 percent of GDP in the mid-1970s to almost 8 percent of GDP by 2007.[12] The top employees of the five largest investment banks divided a bonus pool of over $36 billion in 2007. Leaders in the financial sector argued that in fact their high returns were the result of innovation and genuine value-added products, and they tended to grossly understate the latent risks their firms were taking. (Keep in mind that an integral part of our working definition of the this-time-is-different syndrome is that "the old rules of valuation no longer apply.") In their eyes, financial innovation was a key platform that allowed the United States to effectively borrow much larger quantities of money from abroad than might otherwise have been possible. For example, innovations such as securitization allowed U.S. consumers to turn their previously illiquid housing assets into ATM machines, which represented a reduction in precautionary saving.[13]

Where did academics and policy economists stand on the dangers posed by the U.S. current account deficit? Opinions varied across a wide spectrum. On the one hand, Obstfeld and Rogoff argued in several contributions that the outsized U.S. current account was likely unsustainable.[14] They observed that if one added up all the surpluses of the countries in the world that were net savers (countries in which national savings exceed national investment, including China, Japan, Germany, Saudi Arabia, and Russia), the United States was soaking up more than two out of every three of these saved dollars in 2004–2006. Thus, eventually the U.S. borrowing binge would have to unwind, perhaps quite precipitously, which would result in sharp asset price movements that could severely stress the complex global derivatives system.[15]

Many others took a similarly concerned viewpoint. For example, in 2004 Nouriel Roubini and Brad Setser projected that the U.S. borrowing problem would get much worse, reaching 10 percent of GDP before a dramatic collapse.[16] Paul Krugman (who received a Nobel Prize in 2008) argued that there would inevitably be a "Wile E. Coyote moment" when the unsustainability of the U.S. current account would be evident to all, and suddenly the dollar would collapse.[17] There are many other examples of academic papers that illustrated the risks.[18]

Yet many respected academic, policy, and financial market researchers took a much more sanguine view. In a series of influential papers, Michael Dooley, David Folkerts-Landau, and Peter Garber—"the Deutschebank trio"—argued that the gaping U.S. current account deficit was just a natural consequence of emerging markets' efforts to engage in export-led growth, as well as their need to diversify into safe assets.[19] They insightfully termed the system that propagated the U.S. deficits "Bretton Woods II" because the Asian countries were quasi-pegging their currencies to the U.S. dollar, just as the European countries had done forty years earlier.

Harvard economist Richard Cooper also argued eloquently that the U.S. current account deficit had logical foundations that did not necessarily imply clear and present dangers.[20] He pointed to the hegemonic position of the United States in the global financial and security system and the extraordinary liquidity of U.S. financial markets, as well as its housing markets, to support his argument. Indeed, Bernanke's speech on the global savings glut in many ways synthesized the interesting ideas already floating around in the academic and policy research literature.

It should be noted that others, such as Ricardo Hausmann and Federico Sturzenegger of Harvard University's Kennedy School of Government, made more exotic arguments, claiming that U.S. foreign assets were mismeasured, and actually far larger than official estimates.[21] The existence of this "dark matter" helped explain how the United States could finance a seemingly unending string of current account and trade deficits. Ellen McGrattan of Minnesota and Ed Prescott of Arizona (another Nobel Prize winner) developed a model to effectively calibrate dark matter and found that the explanation might plausibly account for as much as half of the United States' current account deficit.[22]

In addition to debating U.S. borrowing from abroad, economists also debated the related question of whether policy makers should have been concerned about the explosion of housing prices that was taking place nationally in the United States (as shown in the previous section). But again, top policy makers argued that high home prices could be justified by new financial markets that made houses easier to borrow off of and by reduced macroeconomic risk that increased the value of risky assets. Both Greenspan and Bernanke argued vigorously that the Federal Reserve should not pay excessive attention to housing prices, except to the extent that they might affect the central bank's primary goals of growth and price stability. Indeed, prior to joining the Fed, Bernanke had made this case more formally and forcefully in an article coauthored by New York University professor Mark Gertler in 2001.[23]

On the one hand, the Federal Reserve's logic for ignoring housing prices was grounded in the perfectly sensible proposition that the private sector can judge equilibrium housing prices (or equity prices) at least as well as any government bureaucrat. On the other hand, it might have paid more attention to the fact that the rise in asset prices was being fueled by a relentless increase in the ratio of household debt to GDP, against a backdrop of record lows in the personal saving rate. This ratio, which had been roughly stable at close to 80 percent of personal income until 1993, had risen to 120 percent in 2003 and to nearly 130 percent by mid-2006. Empirical work by Bordo and Jeanne and the Bank for International Settlements suggested that when housing booms are accompanied by sharp rises in debt, the risk of a crisis is significantly elevated.[24] Although this work was not necessarily definitive, it certainly raised questions about the Federal Reserve's policy of benign neglect. On the other hand, the fact that the housing boom was taking place in many countries around the world (albeit to a much lesser extent if at all in major surplus countries such as Germany and Japan) raised questions about the genesis of the problem and whether national monetary or regulatory policy alone would be an effective remedy.

Bernanke, while still a Federal Reserve governor in 2004, sensibly argued that it is the job of regulatory policy, not monetary policy, to deal with housing price bubbles fueled by inappropriately weak lending standards.[25] Of course, that argument begs the question of what should be done if, for political reasons or otherwise, regulatory policy does not adequately respond to an asset price bubble. Indeed, one can argue that it was precisely the huge capital inflow from abroad that fueled the asset price inflation and low interest rate spreads that ultimately masked risks from both regulators and rating agencies.

In any event, the most extreme and the most immediate problems were caused by the market for mortgage loans made to "subprime," or low-income, borrowers. "Advances" in securitization, as well as a seemingly endless run-up in housing prices, allowed people to buy houses who might not previously have thought they could do so. Unfortunately, many of these borrowers depended on loans with variable interest rates and low initial "teaser" rates. When it came time to reset the loans, rising interest rates and a deteriorating economy made it difficult for many to meet their mortgage obligations. And thus the subprime debacle began.

The U.S. conceit that its financial and regulatory system could withstand massive capital inflows on a sustained basis without any problems arguably laid the foundations for the global financial crisis of the late 2000s. The thinking that "this time is different"— because this time the U.S. had a superior system—once again proved false. Outsized financial market returns were in fact greatly exaggerated by capital inflows, just as would be the case in emerging markets. What could in retrospect be recognized as huge regulatory mistakes, including the deregulation of the subprime mortgage market and the

213

2004 decision of the Securities and Exchange Commission to allow investment banks to triple their leverage ratios (that is, the ratio measuring the amount of risk to capital), appeared benign at the time. Capital inflows pushed up borrowing and asset prices while reducing spreads on all sorts of risky assets, leading the International Monetary Fund to conclude in April 2007, in its twice-annual *World Economic Outlook,* that risks to the global economy had become extremely low and that, for the moment, there were no great worries. When the international agency charged with being the global watchdog declares that there are no risks, there is no surer sign that this time *is* different.

Again, the crisis that began in 2007 shares many parallels with the boom period before an emerging market crisis, when governments often fail to take precautionary steps to let steam out of the system; they expect the capital inflow bonanza to last indefinitely. Often, instead, they take steps that push their economies toward greater risk in an effort to keep the boom going a little longer.

Such is a brief characterization of the debate surrounding the this-time-is-different mentality leading up to the U.S. subprime financial crisis. To sum up, many were led to think that "this time is different" for the following reasons:

- The United States, with the world's most reliable system of financial regulation, the most innovative financial system, a strong political system, and the world's largest and most liquid capital markets, was special. It could withstand huge capital inflows without worry.
- Rapidly emerging developing economies needed a secure place to invest their funds for diversification purposes.
- Increased global financial integration was deepening global capital markets and allowing countries to go deeper into debt.
- In addition to its other strengths, the United States has superior monetary policy institutions and monetary policy makers.
- New financial instruments were allowing many new borrowers to enter mortgage markets.

- All that was happening was just a further deepening of financial globalization thanks to innovation and should not be a great source of worry.

The Episodes of Postwar Bank-Centered Financial Crisis

As the list of reasons that "this time is different" (provided by academics, business leaders, and policy makers) grew, so did the similarities of U.S. economic developments to those seen in other precrisis episodes.

To examine the antecedents of the 2007 U.S. subprime crisis (which later grew into the "Second Great Contraction"), we begin by looking at data from the eighteen bank-centered financial crises that occurred in the post–World War II period.[26] For the time being, we will limit our attention to crises in industrialized countries to avoid seeming to engage in hyperbole by comparing the United States to emerging markets. But of course, as we have already seen in chapter 10, financial crises in emerging markets and those in advanced economies are not so different. Later, in chapter 14, we will broaden the comparison set.

The crisis episodes employed in our comparison are listed in table 13.1.

Among the eighteen bank-centered financial crises following World War II, the "Big Five" crises have all involved major declines in output over a protracted period, often lasting two years or more. The worst postwar crisis prior to 2007, of course, was that of Japan in 1992, which set the country off on its "lost decade." The earlier Big Five crises, however, were also extremely traumatic events.

The remaining thirteen financial crises in rich countries represent more minor events that were associated with significantly worse economic performance than usual, but were not catastrophic. For example, the U.S. crisis that began in 1984 was the savings and loan crisis.[27] Some of the other thirteen crises had relatively little impact, but we retain them for now for comparison purposes. It will

TABLE 13.1
Post–World War II bank-centered financial crises
in advanced economies

Country	Beginning year of crisis
Severe (systemic) crises: The "Big Five"	
Spain	1977
Norway	1987
Finland	1991
Sweden	1991
Japan	1992
Milder crises	
United Kingdom	1974
Germany	1977
Canada	1983
United States (savings and loan)	1984
Iceland	1985
Denmark	1987
New Zealand	1987
Australia	1989
Italy	1990
Greece	1991
United Kingdom	1991
France	1994
United Kingdom	1995

Sources: Caprio and Klingebiel (1996, 2003), Kaminsky and Reinhart (1999), and Caprio et al. (2005).

soon be clear that the run-up to the U.S. financial crisis of the late 2000s really did not resemble these milder crises, though most policy makers and journalists did not seem to realize this at the time.

A Comparison of the Subprime Crisis with Past Crises in Advanced Economies

In choosing the variables we used to measure the U.S. risk of a financial crisis we were motivated by the literature on predicting financial crises in both developed countries and emerging markets.[28] This literature on financial crises suggests that markedly rising asset prices,

216

slowing real economic activity, large current account deficits, and sustained debt buildups (whether public, private, or both) are important precursors to a financial crisis. Recall also the evidence on capital flow "bonanzas" discussed in chapter 10, which showed that sustained capital inflows have been particularly strong markers for financial crises, at least in the post-1970 period of greater financial liberalization. Historically, financial liberalization or innovation has also been a recurrent precursor to financial crises, as shown in chapter 10.

We begin in figure 13.3 by comparing the run-up in housing prices. Period t represents the year of the onset of the financial crisis. By that convention, period $t - 4$ is four years prior to the crisis, and the graph in each case continues to $t + 3$, except of course in the case of the recent U.S. crisis, which, as of this writing and probably for some time beyond, will remain in the hands of the fates.[29] The figure confirms what case studies have shown, that a massive run-up in housing prices usually precedes a financial crisis. It is a bit disconcerting to note that, according to this figure, the run-up in housing prices in the United States exceeded the average of the "Big Five" financial crises, and the downturn appears to have been sharper (year $t + 1$ is 2008).

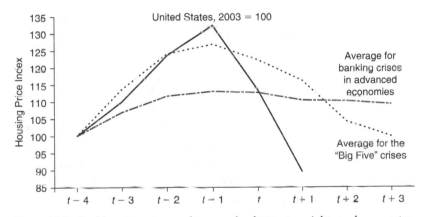

Figure 13.3. Real housing prices and postwar banking crises: Advanced economies.
Sources: Bank for International Settlements (2005); Shiller (2005); Standard and Poor's; International Monetary Fund (various years), *International Financial Statistics;* and the authors' calculations.
Notes: Consumer prices are used to deflate nominal housing price indices. The year of the crisis is indicated by t; $t - 4 = 100$.

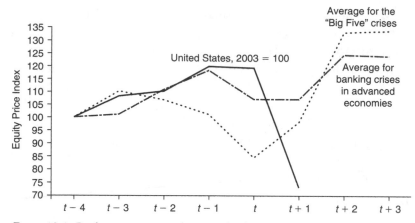

Figure 13.4. Real equity prices and postwar banking crises: Advanced economies.
Sources: Global Financial Data (n.d.); International Monetary Fund (various years), *International Financial Statistics*; and the authors' calculations.
Notes: Consumer prices are used to deflate nominal housing price indices. The year of the crisis is indicated by t; $t - 4 = 100$.

In figure 13.4 we look at real rates of growth in equity market price indexes.[30] We see that, going into the crisis, U.S. equity prices held up better than those in either comparison group, perhaps in part because of the Federal Reserve's aggressive countercyclical response to the 2001 recession and in part because of the substantial "surprise element" in the severity of the U.S. crisis. But a year after the onset of the crisis ($t + 1$), equity prices had plummeted, in line with what happened in the "Big Five" financial crises.

In figure 13.5 we look at the trajectory of the U.S. current account deficit, which was far larger and more persistent than was typical in other crises.[31] In the figure, the bars show the U.S. current account trajectory from 2003 to 2007 as a percentage of GDP, and the dashed line shows the average for the eighteen earlier crises. The fact that the U.S. dollar remained the world's reserve currency during a period in which many foreign central banks (particularly in Asia) were amassing record amounts of foreign exchange reserves certainly increased the foreign capital available to finance the record U.S. current account deficits.

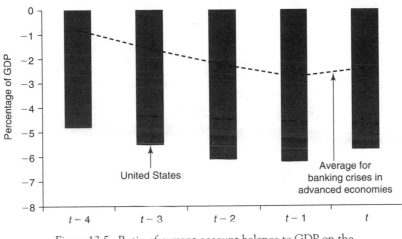

Figure 13.5. Ratio of current account balance to GDP on the
eve of postwar banking crises: Advanced economies.
Sources: International Monetary Fund (various years),
World Economic Outlook; and the authors' calculations.

Financial crises seldom occur in a vacuum. More often than
not, a financial crisis begins only after a real shock slows the pace of
the economy; thus it serves as an amplifying mechanism rather than
a trigger. Figure 13.6 plots real per capita GDP growth on the eve of
banking crises. The U.S. crisis that began in 2007 follows the same
inverted V shape that characterized the earlier crisis episodes. Like
equity prices, the response in GDP was somewhat delayed. Indeed,
in 2007, although U.S. growth had slowed, it was still more closely
aligned with the milder recession pattern of the average for all crises.

In 2008, developments took a turn for the worse, and the
growth slowdown became more acute. At the beginning of 2009, the
consensus—based on forecasts published in the *Wall Street Journal*—
was that this recession would be deeper than the average "Big Five"
experience. Note that in severe Big Five cases, the growth rate has
fallen by more than 5 percent from peak to trough and has remained
low for roughly three years.

Our final figure in this chapter, figure 13.7, illustrates the
path of real public debt (deflated by consumer prices).[32] Increasing

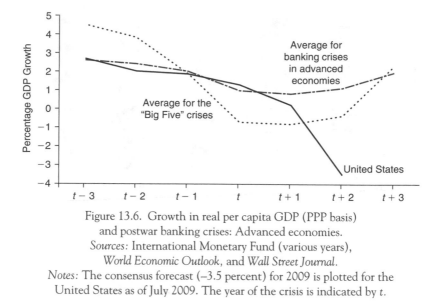

Figure 13.6. Growth in real per capita GDP (PPP basis)
and postwar banking crises: Advanced economies.
Sources: International Monetary Fund (various years),
World Economic Outlook, and *Wall Street Journal.*
Notes: The consensus forecast (−3.5 percent) for 2009 is plotted for the
United States as of July 2009. The year of the crisis is indicated by *t.*

public debt has been a nearly universal precursor of other postwar crises, although, as we will see in chapter 14, the buildup in debt prior to a crisis pales in comparison to its growth after the crisis has begun, for weak growth crushes tax revenues. The U.S. public debt buildup prior to the 2007 crisis was less than the Big Five average. Comparisons across private debt (which we have already alluded to for the United States) would be interesting as well, but unfortunately, comparable data for the range of countries considered here are not easy to obtain. In the case of the United States, the ratio of household debt to household income soared by 30 percent in less than a decade and could well collapse as consumers try to achieve a less risky position as the recession continues.

One caveat to our claim that the indicators showed the United States at high risk of a deep financial crisis in the run-up to 2007: compared to other countries that have experienced financial crises, the United States performed well with regard to inflation prior to 2007. Of course, the earlier crises in developed countries occurred during a period of declining inflation in the rich countries.

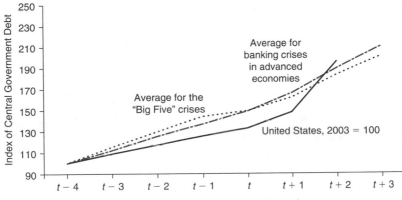

Figure 13.7. Real central government debt and postwar
banking crises: Advanced economies.
Sources: U.S. Treasury Department; International Monetary Fund
(various years), *International Financial Statistics;* appendixes A.1
and A.2 and sources cited therein; and the authors' calculations.
Note: Consumer prices are used to deflate nominal debt. The year
of the crisis is indicated by *t*; *t* − 4 = 100.

Summary

Why did so many people fail to see the financial crisis of 2007 coming? As to the standard indicators of financial crises, many red lights were blinking brightly well in advance. We do not pretend that it would have been easy to forestall the U.S. financial crisis had policy makers realized the risks earlier. We have focused on macroeconomic issues, but many problems were hidden in the "plumbing" of the financial markets, as has become painfully evident since the beginning of the crisis. Some of these problems might have taken years to address. Above all, the huge run-up in housing prices—over 100 percent nationally over five years—should have been an alarm, especially fueled as it was by rising leverage. At the beginning of 2008, the total value of mortgages in the United States was approximately 90 percent of GDP. Policy makers should have decided several years prior to the crisis to deliberately take some steam out of the system. Unfortunately, efforts to maintain growth and prevent significant sharp stock market declines had the effect of taking the safety valve off the pressure cooker. Of course, even with the epic proportions of this financial crisis, the United States had not defaulted as of the middle of 2009. Were the United States an emerging market, its exchange rate would have plummeted and its interest rates soared. Access to capital markets would be lost in a classic Dornbusch/Calvo–type sudden stop. During the first year following the crisis (2007), exactly the opposite happened: the dollar appreciated and interest rates fell as world investors viewed other countries as even riskier than the United States and bought Treasury securities copiously.[33] But buyer beware! Over the longer run, the U.S. exchange rate and interest rates could well revert to form, especially if policies are not made to re-establish a firm base for long-term fiscal sustainability.

- 14 -

THE AFTERMATH OF FINANCIAL CRISES

In the preceding chapter we presented a historical analysis comparing the run-up to the 2007 U.S. subprime financial crisis with the antecedents of other banking crises in advanced economies since World War II. We showed that standard indicators for the United States, such as asset price inflation, rising leverage, large sustained current account deficits, and a slowing trajectory of economic growth, exhibited virtually all the signs of a country on the verge of a financial crisis—indeed, a severe one. In this chapter we engage in a similar comparative historical analysis focused on the aftermath of systemic banking crises. Obviously, as events unfold, the aftermath of the U.S. financial crisis may prove better or worse than the benchmarks laid out here. Nevertheless, the approach is valuable in itself, because in analyzing extreme shocks such as those affecting the U.S. economy and the world economy at the time of this writing, standard macroeconomic models calibrated to statistically "normal" growth periods may be of little use.

In the previous chapter we deliberately excluded emerging market countries from the comparison set in order not to appear to engage in hyperbole. After all, the United States is a highly sophisticated global financial center. What can advanced economies possibly have in common with emerging markets when it comes to banking crises? In fact, as we showed in chapter 10, the antecedents and aftermath of banking crises in rich countries and in emerging markets have a surprising amount in common. They share broadly similar patterns in housing and equity prices, unemployment, government revenues, and debt. Furthermore, the frequency or incidence of crises does not differ much historically, even if comparisons are limited to the post–World War II period (provided that the ongoing global financial crisis of the late 2000s is taken into account). Thus, in this chapter, as we turn to characterizing the aftermath of severe financial crises, we include a number of recent emerging market cases so as to expand the relevant set of comparators.[1]

Broadly speaking, financial crises are protracted affairs. More often than not, the aftermath of severe financial crises share three characteristics:

- *First,* asset market collapses are deep and prolonged. Declines in real housing prices average 35 percent stretched out over six years, whereas equity price collapses average 56 percent over a downturn of about three and a half years.
- *Second,* the aftermath of banking crises is associated with profound declines in output and employment. The unemployment rate rises an average of 7 percentage points during the down phase of the cycle, which lasts on average more than four years. Output falls (from peak to trough) more than 9 percent on average, although the duration of the downturn, averaging roughly two years, is considerably shorter than that of unemployment.[2]
- *Third,* as noted earlier, the value of government debt tends to explode; it rose an average of 86 percent (in real terms, relative to precrisis debt) in the major post–World War II episodes. As discussed in chapter 10 (and as we reiterate here), the main cause of debt explosions is not the widely cited costs of bailing out and recapitalizing the banking system. Admittedly, bailout costs are difficult to measure, and the divergence among estimates from competing studies is considerable. But even upper-bound estimates pale next to actual measured increases in public debt. In fact, the biggest driver of debt increases is the inevitable collapse in tax revenues that governments suffer in the wake of deep and prolonged output contractions. Many countries also suffer from a spike in the interest burden on debt, for interest rates soar, and in a few cases (most notably that of Japan in the 1990s), countercyclical fiscal policy efforts contribute to the debt buildup. (We note that calibrating differences in countercyclical fiscal policy across countries can be difficult because some countries, such as the Nordic countries, have

powerful built-in fiscal stabilizers through high marginal tax rates and generous unemployment benefits, whereas other countries, such as the United States and Japan, have automatic stabilizers that are far weaker.)

In the last part of the chapter, we will look at quantitative benchmarks from the period of the Great Depression, the last deep global financial crisis prior to the recent one. The depth and duration of the decline in economic activity were breathtaking, even by comparison with severe postwar crises. Countries took an average of ten years to reach the same level of per capita output as they enjoyed in 1929. In the first three years of the Depression, unemployment rose an average of 16.9 percentage points across the fifteen major countries in our comparison set.

Historical Episodes Revisited

The preceding chapter included all the major postwar banking crises in the developed world (a total of eighteen) and put particular emphasis on the ones dubbed the "Big Five" (those in Spain, 1977; Norway, 1987; Finland, 1991; Sweden, 1991; and Japan, 1992). It is quite clear from that chapter, as well as from the subsequent evolution of the 2007 U.S. financial crisis, that the crisis of the late 2000s must be considered a severe Big Five–type crisis by any metric. As a result, in this chapter we will focus on severe systemic financial crises only, including the Big Five crises in developed economies plus a number of famous episodes in emerging markets: the 1997–1998 Asian crises (in Hong Kong, Indonesia, Korea, Malaysia, the Philippines, and Thailand); that in Colombia in 1998; and Argentina's 2001 collapse. These are cases for which we have all or most of the relevant data to allow for meaningful quantitative comparisons across key indicator variables, such as equity markets, housing markets, unemployment, growth, and so on. Central to the analysis are historical housing price data, which can be difficult to obtain and are critical for assessing the recent episode.[3] We also include two earlier historical cases for which we have housing prices: those of Norway in 1899 and the United States in 1929.

The Downturn after a Crisis:
Depth and Duration

In figure 14.1, based on the same data as table 10.8, we again look at the bust phase of housing price cycles surrounding banking crises in the expanded data set. We include a number of countries that experienced crises from 2007 on. The latest crises are represented by bars in dark shading, past crises by bars in light shading. The cumulative decline in real housing prices from peak to trough averages 35.5 percent.[4] The most severe real housing price declines were experienced by Finland, Colombia, the Philippines, and Hong Kong. Their crashes amounted to 50 to 60 percent, measured from peak to trough. The housing price decline experienced by the United States during the latest episode at the time of this writing (almost 28 percent in real terms through late 2008 according to the Case-Shiller index) is already more than twice that registered in the United States during the Great Depression.

Notably, the duration of housing price declines has been quite long lived, averaging roughly six years. Even excluding the extraordinary experience of Japan (with its seventeen consecutive years of real housing price declines), the average remains more than five years. As figure 14.2 illustrates, the equity price declines that accompany banking crises are far steeper than are housing price declines, albeit shorter lived. The shorter duration of a downturn compared with real estate prices is perhaps unsurprising given that equity prices are far less inertial. The average historical decline in equity prices has been 55.9 percent, with the downturn phase of the cycle lasting 3.4 years. As of the end of 2008, Iceland and Austria had already experienced peak-to-trough equity price declines far exceeding the average of the historical comparison group.

226

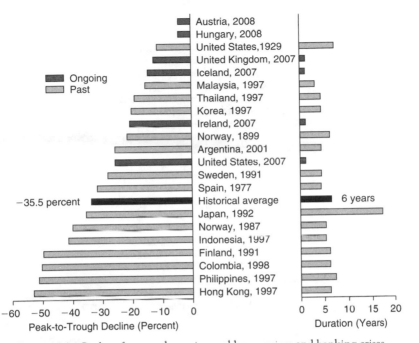

Figure 14.1. Cycles of past and ongoing real house prices and banking crises.
Sources: Appendixes A.1 and A.2 and sources cited therein.
Notes: Each banking crisis episode is identified by country and the beginning year of the crisis. Only major (systemic) banking crisis episodes are included, subject to data limitations. The historical average reported does not include ongoing crisis episodes. For the ongoing episodes, the calculations are based on data through the following periods: October 2008, monthly, for Iceland and Ireland; 2007, annual, for Hungary; and Q3, 2008, quarterly, for all others. Consumer price indexes are used to deflate nominal house prices.

In figure 14.3 we look at increases in unemployment rates across the historical comparison group. (Because the unemployment rate is classified as a lagging indicator, we do not include the most recent crisis, although we note that the U.S. unemployment rate has already risen by 5 percentage points from its bottom value of near 4 percent.) On average, unemployment rises for almost five years, with an increase in the unemployment rate of about 7 percentage points. Although none of the postwar episodes has rivaled the rise in un-

227

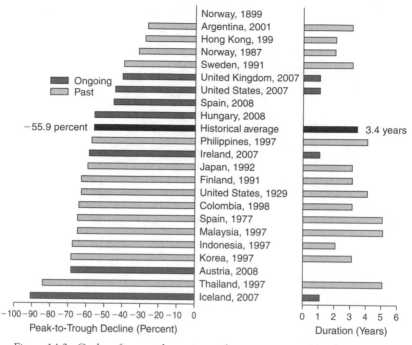

Figure 14.2. Cycles of past and ongoing real equity prices and banking crises.
Sources: Appendixes A.1 and A.2 and sources cited therein.
Notes: Each banking crisis episode is identified by country and the beginning year of the crisis. Only major (systemic) banking crisis episodes are included, subject to data limitations. The historical average reported does not include ongoing crisis episodes. For the ongoing episodes, the calculations are based on data through December 2, 2008. Consumer price indexes are used to deflate nominal equity prices.

employment of more than 20 percentage points experienced by the United States during the Great Depression, the employment consequences of financial crises are nevertheless strikingly large in many cases. For emerging markets the official statistics likely underestimate true unemployment.

Interestingly, figure 14.3 reveals that when it comes to banking crises, the emerging markets, particularly those in Asia, seem to do better in terms of unemployment than the advanced economies. (An exception was seen in the deep recession experienced by Colombia in 1998.) Although there are well-known data issues involved in

228

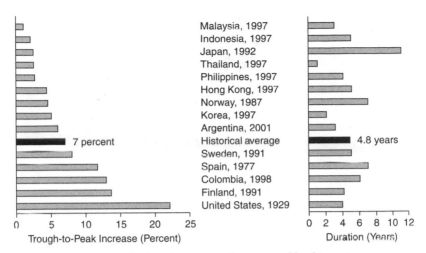

Figure 14.3. Cycles of past unemployment and banking crises.
Sources: Organisation for Economic Co-operation and Development;
International Monetary Fund (various years), *International Financial Statistics;*
Carter et al. (2006); various country sources; and the authors' calculations.
Notes: Each banking crisis episode is identified by country and the
beginning year of the crisis. Only major (systemic) banking crisis episodes
are included, subject to data limitations. The historical average reported
does not include ongoing crisis episodes.

comparing unemployment rates across countries,[5] the relatively poor
performance in advanced countries suggests the possibility that greater
(downward) wage flexibility in emerging markets may help cushion
employment during periods of severe economic distress. The gaps in
the social safety net in emerging market economies, compared to industrial ones, presumably also make workers more anxious to avoid
becoming unemployed.

In figure 14.4 we look at the cycles in real per capita GDP
around severe banking crises. The average magnitude of declines, at
9.3 percent, is stunning. Admittedly, as we noted earlier, for the post–
World War II period, the declines in real GDP have been smaller for
advanced economies than for emerging market economies. A probable explanation for the more severe contractions in emerging
market economies is that they are prone to abrupt reversals in
the availability of foreign credit. When foreign capital comes to a

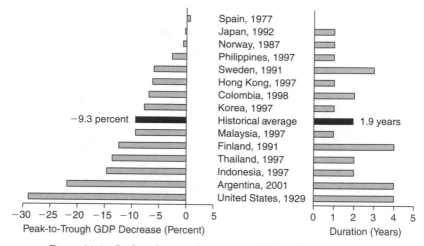

Figure 14.4. Cycles of past real per capita GDP and banking crises.
Sources: Total Economy Database (TED), Carter et al. (2006),
and the authors' calculations.
Notes: Each banking crisis episode is identified by country and the beginning
year of the crisis. Only major (systemic) banking crisis episodes are included,
subject to data limitations. The historical average reported does not include
ongoing crisis episodes. Total GDP in millions of 1990 U.S. dollars
(converted at Geary Khamis PPPs) divided by midyear population.

"sudden stop," to use the phrase popularized by Rudiger Dornbusch
and Guillermo Calvo, economic activity heads into a tailspin.[6]

Compared to unemployment, the cycle from peak to trough
in GDP is much shorter, only two years. Presumably this is partly because potential GDP growth is positive and we are measuring only absolute changes in income, not gaps relative to potential output. Even
so, the recessions surrounding financial crises are unusually long compared to normal recessions, which typically last less than a year.[7] Indeed, multiyear recessions usually occur only in economies that require
deep restructuring, such as that of Britain in the 1970s (prior to the advent of Prime Minister Margaret Thatcher), Switzerland in the 1990s,
and Japan after 1992 (the last due not only to its financial collapse but
also to the need to reorient its economy in light of China's rise). Banking crises, of course, usually require painful restructuring of the financial system and so are an important example of this general principle.

The Fiscal Legacy of Crises

Declining revenues and higher expenditures, owing to a combination of bailout costs and higher transfer payments and debt servicing costs, lead to a rapid and marked worsening in the fiscal balance. The episodes of Finland and Sweden stand out in this regard;
the latter went from a precrisis surplus of nearly 4 percent of GDP to
a whopping 15 percent deficit-to-GDP ratio. See table 14.1.

Figure 14.5 shows the increase in real government debt in
the three years following a banking crisis. The deterioration in government finances is striking, with an average debt increase of more
than 86 percent. The calculation here is based on relatively recent
data from the past few decades, but recall that in chapter 10 of this
book we take advantage of our newly unearthed historical data on
domestic debt to show that a buildup in government debt has been
a defining characteristic of the aftermath of banking crises for over a
century. We look at the percentage increase in debt rather than in

TABLE 14.1

Fiscal deficits (central government balance) as a percentage of GDP

Country, crisis year	Year before the crisis	Peak deficit (year)	Increase or decrease (–) in the fiscal deficit
Argentina, 2001	−2.4	−11.9 (2002)	9.5
Chile, 1980	4.8	−3.2 (1985)	8.0
Colombia, 1998	−3.6	−7.4 (1999)	3.8
Finland, 1991	1.0	−10.8 (1994)	11.8
Indonesia, 1997	2.1	−3.7 (2001)	5.8
Japan, 1992	−0.7	−8.7 (1999)	9.4
Korea, 1997	0.0	−4.8 (1998)	4.8
Malaysia, 1997	0.7	−5.8 (2000)	6.5
Mexico, 1994	0.3	−2.3 (1998)	2.6
Norway, 1987	5.7	−2.5 (1992)	7.9
Spain, 1977[a]	−3.9	−3.1 (1977)	−0.8
Sweden, 1991	3.8	−11.6 (1993)	15.4
Thailand, 1997	2.3	−3.5 (1999)	5.8

Sources: International Monetary Fund (various years), Government Financial Statistics and World Economic Outlook, and the authors' calculations.

[a]As shown in figure 14.4, Spain was the only country in our sample to show a (modest) increase in per
capita GDP growth during the postcrisis period.

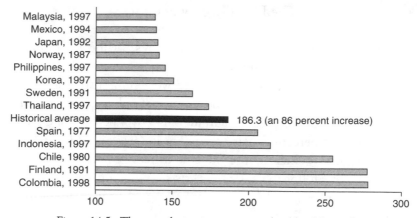

Figure 14.5. The cumulative increase in real public debt in the
three years following past banking crises.
Sources: Appendixes A.1 and A.2 and sources cited therein.
Notes: Each banking crisis episode is identified by country and the beginning year
of the crisis. Only major (systemic) banking crisis episodes are included, subject to
data limitations. The historical average reported does not include ongoing crisis
episodes, which are omitted altogether, because these crises began in 2007 or later,
and the debt stock comparison here is with three years after the beginning of the
banking crisis. Public debt is indexed to equal 100 in the year of the crisis.

debt relative to GDP because sometimes steep output drops compli-
cate the interpretation of debt-to-GDP ratios. We have already emphasized but it bears being stated again, the characteristically huge
buildup in government debt is driven mainly by a sharp falloff in tax
revenue due to the deep recessions that accompany most severe financial crises. The much-ballyhooed bank bailout costs have been,
in several cases, only a relatively minor contributor to the postcrisis
increase in debt burdens.

Sovereign Risk

As shown in figure 14.6, sovereign default, debt restructuring, and/or
near default (avoided by international bailout packages) have been
a part of the experience of financial crises in many emerging markets;
therefore, a decline in a country's credit rating during a crisis hardly

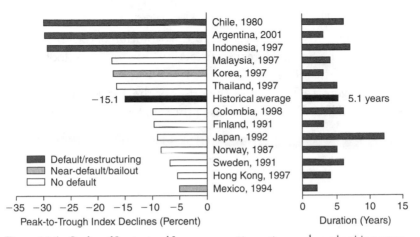

Figure 14.6. Cycles of *Institutional Investor* sovereign ratings and past banking crises.
Sources: Institutional Investor (various years) and the authors' calculations.
Notes: Institutional Investor's ratings range from 0 to 100,
rising with increasing creditworthiness.

comes as a surprise. Advanced economies, however, do not go unscathed. Finland's sovereign risk rating score went from 79 to 69 in the space of three years, leaving it with a score close to those of some emerging markets! Japan suffered several downgrades from the more famous rating agencies as well.

Comparisons with Experiences from the First Great Contraction in the 1930s

Until now, our comparison benchmark has consisted of postwar financial crises. The quantitative similarities of those crises with the recent crisis in the United States, at least for the run-up and early trajectory, have been striking. Yet, in many ways this "Second Great Contraction" is a far deeper crisis than others in the comparison set, because it is global in scope, whereas the other severe post–World War II crises were either country-specific or at worst regional. Of course, as we will discuss in more detail in chapter 17, policy authorities reacted somewhat hesitantly in the 1930s, which may also

233

explain the duration and severity of the crisis. Nevertheless, given the lingering uncertainty over the future evolution of the crisis of the late 2000s (the Second Great Contraction), it is useful to look at evidence from the 1930s, the First Great Contraction.

Figure 14.7 compares the crises of the 1930s with the deep post–World War II crises in terms of the number of years over which

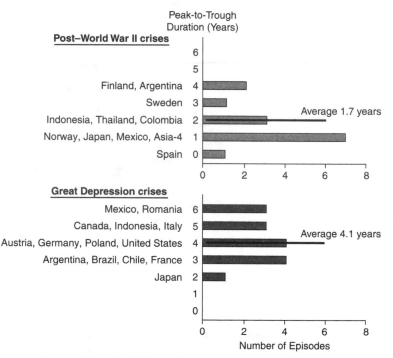

Figure 14.7. The duration of major financial crises: Fourteen
Great Depression episodes versus fourteen post–World War II
episodes (duration of the fall in output per capita).
Sources: Appendix A.3 and the authors' calculations.
Notes: The fourteen postwar episodes were those in Spain, 1977; Norway, 1987;
Finland, 1991; Sweden, 1991; Japan, 1992; Mexico, 1994; Indonesia, Thailand,
and (grouped as Asia-4 in the figure) Hong Kong, Korea, Malaysia, and
Philippines, all 1997; Colombia, 1998; and Argentina, 2001. The fourteen
Great Depression episodes were comprised of eleven banking crisis episodes
and three less systemic but equally devastating economic contractions in
Canada, Chile, and Indonesia during the 1930s. The banking crises were
those in Japan, 1927; Brazil, Mexico, and the United States, all 1929;
France and Italy, 1930; and Austria, Germany, Poland, and Romania, 1931.

234

output fell from peak to trough. The upper panel shows postwar crises including those in Colombia, Argentina, Thailand, Indonesia, Sweden, Norway, Mexico, the Philippines, Malaysia, Japan, Finland, Spain, Hong Kong, and Korea—fourteen in all. The lower panel shows fourteen Great Depression crises, including those in Argentina, Chile, Mexico, Canada, Austria, France, the United States, Indonesia, Poland, Brazil, Germany, Romania, Italy, and Japan.

Each half of the diagram forms a vertical histogram. The number of years each country or several countries were in crisis is measured on the vertical axis. The number of countries experiencing a crisis of any given length is measured on the horizontal axis. One sees clearly from the diagram that the recessions accompanying the Great Depression were of much longer duration than the postwar crises. After the war, output typically fell from peak to trough for an average of 1.7 years, with the longest downturn of four years experienced by Argentina and Finland. But in the Depression, many countries, including the United States and Canada, experienced a downturn of four years or longer, with Mexico and Romania experiencing a decrease in output for six years. Indeed, the average length of time over which output fell was 4.1 years in the Great Depression.[8]

It is important to recognize that standard measures of the depth and duration of recessions are not particularly suitable for capturing the epic decline in output that often accompanies deep financial crises. One factor is the depth of the decline, and another is that growth is sometimes quite modest in the aftermath as the financial system resets. An alternative perspective is provided in figure 14.8, which measures the number of years it took for a country's output to reach its precrisis level. Of course, after a steep fall in output, just getting back to the starting point can take a long period of growth. Both halves of the figure are stunning. For the postwar episodes, it took an average of 4.4 years for output to claw its way back to precrisis levels. Japan and Korea were able to do this relatively quickly, at only 2 years, whereas Colombia and Argentina took 8 years. But things were much worse in the Depression, and countries took an average of 10 years to increase their output back to precrisis levels, in part because no country was in a position to "export its way to re-

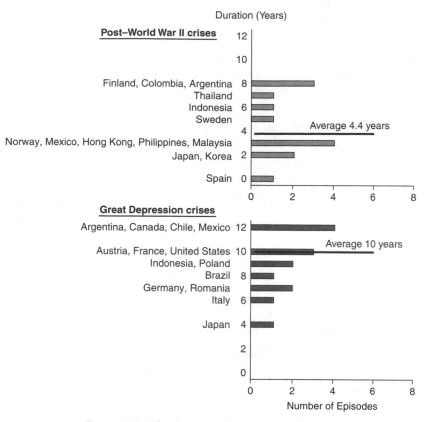

Figure 14.8. The duration of major financial crises:
Fourteen Great Depression episodes versus fourteen post–World War II
episodes (number of years for output per capita to return to its precrisis level).
Sources: Appendix A.3 and the authors' calculations.
Notes: The fourteen postwar episodes were those in Spain, 1977; Norway, 1987;
Finland, 1991; Sweden, 1991; Japan, 1992; Mexico, 1994; Hong Kong, Indonesia,
Korea, Malaysia, the Philippines, and Thailand, all 1997; Colombia, 1998; and
Argentina, 2001. The fourteen Great Depression episodes were comprised of
eleven banking crisis episodes and three less systemic but equally devastating
economic contractions in Canada, Chile, and Indonesia. The banking crises
were those in Japan, 1927; Brazil, Mexico, and the United States, all 1929;
France and Italy, 1930; and Austria, Germany, Poland, and Romania, 1931.
The precrisis level for the Great Depression was that of 1929.

236

covery" as world aggregate demand imploded. The figure shows, for example, that the United States, France, and Austria took 10 years to rebuild their output to its initial pre-Depression level, whereas Canada, Mexico, Chile, and Argentina took 12. Thus, the Great Depression era sets far more daunting benchmarks for the potential trajectory of the financial crisis of the late 2000s than do the main comparisons we have been making to severe postwar crises.

As we will show in chapter 16, the unemployment increases in the Great Depression were also far greater than those in the severe post–World War II financial crises. The average rate of unemployment increase was about 16.8 percent. In the United States, unemployment rose from 3.2 percent to 24.9 percent.

Finally, in figure 14.9 we look at the evolution of real public debt during the crises of the Great Depression era. Interestingly, public debt grew more slowly in the aftermath of these crises than it did

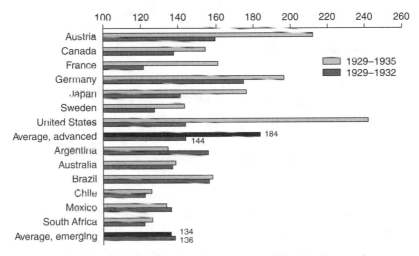

Figure 14.9. The cumulative increase in real public debt three and six years following the onset of the Great Depression in 1929: Selected countries.
Sources: Reinhart and Rogoff (2008b) and sources cited therein.
Notes: The beginning years of the banking crises range from 1929 to 1931. Australia and Canada did not have a systemic banking crisis but are included for comparison purposes, because both also suffered severe and protracted economic contractions. The year 1929 marks the peak in world output and hence is used as the marker for the beginning of the Depression episode.

237

in the severe postwar crises. In the Depression, it took six years for real public debt to grow by 84 percent (versus half that time in the postwar crises). Some of this difference reflects the very slow policy response that occurred in the Great Depression. It is also noteworthy that public debt in emerging markets did not increase in the later stages (three to six years) following the crises. Some of these emerging markets had already drifted into default (on both domestic and external debts); others may have faced the kind of external constraints that we discussed in connection with debt intolerance and, as such, had little capacity to finance budget deficits.

Concluding Remarks

An examination of the aftermath of severe postwar financial crises shows that these crises have had a deep and lasting effect on asset prices, output, and employment. Unemployment increases and housing price declines have extended for five and six years, respectively. Real government debt has increased by an average of 86 percent after three years.

How relevant are historical benchmarks in assessing the trajectory of a crisis such as the global financial crisis of the late 2000s, the Second Great Contraction? On the one hand, authorities now have arguably more flexible monetary policy frameworks, thanks particularly to a less rigid global exchange rate regime. And some central banks showed an aggressiveness early on by acting in a way that was notably absent in the 1930s or in the latter-day Japanese experience. On the other hand, we would be wise not to push too far the conceit that we are smarter than our predecessors. A few years back, many people would have said that improvements in financial engineering had done much to tame the business cycle and limit the risk of financial contagion. And as we saw in the final section of this chapter, the Great Depression crises were far more traumatic events than even the more severe of the post–World War II crises. In the Depression, it took countries in crisis an average of ten years for real per capita GDP to reach its precrisis level. Still, in the postwar crises it has taken almost four and a half years for output to reach its pre-crisis level (though growth has resumed much more quickly, it has still taken time for the economy to return to its starting point).

What we do know is that after the start of the recent crisis in 2007, asset prices and other standard crisis indicator variables tumbled in the United States and elsewhere along the tracks laid down by historical precedent. It is true that equity markets have since recovered some ground, but by and large this is not out of line with the historical experience (already emphasized in chapter 10) that V-shaped recoveries in equity prices are far more common than V-shaped recoveries in real housing prices or employment. Overall, this chapter's analysis of the postcrisis outcomes for unemployment, output, and government debt provides sobering benchmark numbers for how deep financial crises can unfold. Indeed, our post–World War II historical comparisons were largely based on episodes that were individual or regional in nature. The global nature of the recent crisis has made it far more difficult, and contentious, for individual countries to grow their way out through higher exports or to smooth the consumption effects through foreign borrowing. As noted in chapter 10, historical experience suggests that the brief post-2002 lull in sovereign defaults is at risk of coming to an abrupt end. True, the planned quadrupling of International Monetary Fund (IMF) resources, along with the apparent softening of IMF loan conditions, could have the effect of causing the next round of defaults to play out in slow motion, albeit with a bigger bang at the end if the IMF itself runs into broad repayment problems. Otherwise, as we have mentioned repeatedly, defaults in emerging market economies tend to rise sharply when many countries are simultaneously experiencing domestic banking crises.

- 15 -

THE INTERNATIONAL DIMENSIONS OF THE SUBPRIME CRISIS: THE RESULTS OF CONTAGION OR COMMON FUNDAMENTALS?

In the preceding two chapters we emphasized the similarities between the latest financial crisis (the Second Great Contraction) and previous crises, especially when viewed from the perspective of the United States at the epicenter. Of course, the crisis of the late 2000s is different in important ways from other post–World War II crises, particularly in the ferocity with which the recession spread globally, starting in the fourth quarter of 2008. The "sudden stop" in global financing rapidly extended to small- and medium-sized businesses around the world, with larger businesses able to obtain financing only at much dearer terms than before. The governments of emerging markets are similarly experiencing stress, although as of mid-2009 sovereign credit spreads had substantially narrowed in the wake of massive support by rich countries for the International Monetary Fund (IMF), which we alluded to in the previous chapter.[1]

How does a crisis morph from a local or regional crisis into a global one? In this chapter we emphasize the fundamental distinction between international transmission that occurs due to common shocks (e.g., the collapse of the tech boom in 2001 or the collapse of housing prices in the crisis of the late 2000s) and transmission that occurs due to mechanisms that are really the result of cross-border contagion emanating from the epicenter of the crisis.

In what follows we provide a sprinkling of historical examples of financial crises that swiftly spread across national borders, and we offer a rationale for understanding which factors make it more likely that a primarily domestic crisis fuels rapid cross-border contagion. We use these episodes as reference points to discuss the bunching of banking crises across countries that is so striking in the late-2000s crisis, where both common shocks and cross-country linkages are evident. Later, in chapter 16, we will develop a crisis severity index that allows one to define benchmarks for both regional and global financial crises.

Concepts of Contagion

In defining contagion, we distinguish between two types, the "slow-burn" spillover and the kind of fast burn marked by rapid cross-border transmission that Kaminsky, Reinhart, and Végh label "fast and furious." Specifically, they explain:

> We refer to contagion as an episode in which there are significant *immediate* effects in a number of countries following an event—that is, when the consequences are *fast and furious* and evolve over a matter of hours or days. This "fast and furious" reaction is a contrast to cases in which the initial international reaction to the news is muted. The latter cases do not preclude the emergence of gradual and protracted effects that may cumulatively have major economic consequences. We refer to these gradual cases as *spillovers*. *Common* external *shocks*, such as changes in international interest rates or oil prices, are also not *automatically* included in our working definition of contagion.[2]

We add to this classification that common shocks need not all be external. This caveat is particularly important with regard to the recent episode. Countries may share common "domestic" macroeconomic fundamentals, such as housing bubbles, capital inflow bonanzas, increasing private and (or) public leveraging, and so on.

Selected Earlier Episodes

Bordo and Murshid, and Neal and Weidenmier, have pointed out that cross-country correlations in banking crises were also common during 1880–1913, a period of relatively high international capital mobility under the gold standard.[3] In table 15.1 we look at a broader time span including the twentieth century; the table lists the years during which banking crises have been bunched; greater detail on the dates for individual countries is provided in appendix A.3.[4] The famous Barings crisis of 1890 (which involved Argentina and the United Kingdom before spreading elsewhere) appears to have been the first episode of international bunching of banking crises; this was followed by the panic of 1907, which began in the United States and quickly spread to other advanced economies (particularly Denmark, France, Italy, Japan, and Sweden). These episodes are reasonable benchmarks for modern-day financial contagion.[5]

Of course, other pre–World War II episodes of banking crisis contagion pale when compared with the Great Depression, which also saw a massive number of nearly simultaneous defaults of both external and domestic sovereign debts.

Common Fundamentals and the Second Great Contraction

The conjuncture of elements related to the recent crisis is illustrative of the two channels of contagion: cross-linkages and common shocks. Without doubt, the U.S. financial crisis of 2007 spilled over into other markets through direct linkages. For example, German and Japanese financial institutions (and others ranging as far as Kazakhstan) sought more attractive returns in the U.S. subprime market, perhaps owing to the fact that profit opportunities in domestic real estate were limited at best and dismal at worst. Indeed, after the fact, it became evident that many financial institutions outside the United States had nontrivial exposure to the U.S. subprime market.[6] This is a classic channel of transmission or contagion, through which a crisis in one country spreads across international borders. In the present context, however, contagion or spillovers are only part of the story.

That many other countries experienced economic difficulties at the same time as the United States also owed significantly to the

TABLE 15.1

Global banking crises, 1890–2008: Contagion or common fundamentals?

Years of bunching in banking crises	Affected countries	Comments
1890–1891	Argentina, Brazil, Chile, Portugal, the United Kingdom, and the United States	Argentina defaulted and there were runs on all Argentine banks (see della Paolera and Taylor 2001); Baring Brothers faced failure.
1907–1908	Chile, Denmark, France, Italy, Japan, Mexico, Sweden, and the United States	A drop in copper prices undermined the solvency of a trust company (quasi-bank) in New York.
1914	Argentina, Belgium, Brazil, France, India, Italy, Japan, Netherlands, Norway, the United Kingdom, and the United States	World War I broke out.
1929–1931	Advanced economies: Belgium, Finland, France, Germany, Greece, Italy, Portugal, Spain, Sweden, and the United States Emerging markets: Argentina, Brazil, China, India, and Mexico	Real commodity prices collapsed by about 51 percent during 1928–1931. Real interest rates reached almost 13 percent in the United States.
1981–1982	Emerging markets: Argentina, Chile, Colombia, Congo, Ecuador, Egypt, Ghana, Mexico, the Philippines, Turkey, and Uruguay	Between 1979 and 1982, real commodity prices fell about 40 percent. U.S. real interest rates hit about 6 percent— their highest readings since 1933. The decade-long debt crisis in emerging markets began.
1987–1988	Many small, mostly low-income countries; Sub-Saharan Africa was particularly hard hit	These years marked the tail-end of a nearly decade-long debt crisis.
1991–1992	Advanced economies: the Czech Republic, Finland, Greece, Japan, and Sweden	Real estate and equity price bubbles in the Nordic countries and Japan burst;

(continued)

TABLE 15.1 Continued

Years of bunching in banking crises	Affected countries	Comments
	Other countries: Algeria, Brazil, Egypt, Georgia, Hungary, Poland, Romania, and the Slovak Republic	many transition economies coped with liberalization and stabilization.
1994–1995	Argentina, Bolivia, Brazil, Ecuador, Mexico, and Paraguay Others countries: Azerbaijan, Cameroon, Croatia, Lithuania, and Swaziland	The Mexican "tequila crisis" dealt the first blow to the surge in capital inflows to emerging markets since the early 1990s.
1997–1999	Asia: Hong Kong, Indonesia, Malaysia, the Philippines, Taiwan, Thailand, and Vietnam Other countries: Brazil, Colombia, Ecuador, El Salvador, Mauritius, Russia, Turkey, and Ukraine	The second blow was dealt to capital flows to emerging markets.
2007–present	Germany, Hungary, Iceland, Ireland, Japan, Spain, the United Kingdom, the United States, and others	The U.S. subprime real estate bubble—and other real estate bubbles in advanced economies—burst.

Sources: Based on chapters 1–10 of this book.

fact that many of the features that characterized the run-up to the subprime crisis in the United States were present in other advanced economies as well. Two common elements stand out. First, many countries in Europe and elsewhere (Iceland and New Zealand, for example) had their own home-grown real estate bubbles (figure 15.1). Second, the United States was not alone in running large current account deficits and experiencing a sustained "capital flow bonanza," as shown in chapter 10. Bulgaria, Iceland, Ireland, Latvia, New Zealand, Spain, and the United Kingdom, among others, were importing capital from abroad, which helped fuel a credit and asset price boom.[7] These trends, in and of themselves, made these countries vulnerable to the usual nasty consequences of asset market crashes and capital flow reversals—or "sudden stops" a là Dornbusch/Calvo—irrespective of what may have been happening in the United States.

Direct spillovers via exposure to the U.S. subprime markets and common fundamentals of the kind discussed abroad have addi-

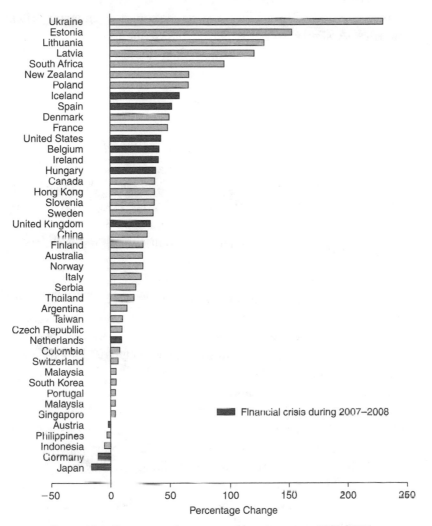

Figure 15.1. Percentage change in real housing prices, 2002–2006.
Sources: Bank for International Settlements and the sources listed in appendix A.1.
Notes: The China data cover 2003–2006.

tionally been complemented with other "standard" transmission channels common in such episodes, specifically the prevalence of common lenders. For example, an Austrian bank exposed to Hungary (as the latter encounters severe economic turbulence) will curtail lending not only to Hungary but to other countries (predominantly in Eastern Europe) to which it was already making loans. This will transmit the "shock" from Hungary (via the common lender) to other countries. A similar role was played by a common Japanese bank lender in the international transmission of the Asian crisis of 1997–1998 and by U.S. banks during the Latin American debt crisis of the early 1980s.

Are More Spillovers Under Way?

As noted earlier, spillovers do not typically occur at the same rapid pace associated with adverse surprises and sudden stops in the financial market. Therefore, they tend not to spark immediate adverse balance sheet effects. Their more gradual evolution does not make their cumulative effects less serious, however.

The comparatively open, historically fast-growing economies of Asia, after initially surviving relatively well, were eventually very hard hit by the recessions of the late 2000s in the advanced economies. Not only are Asian economies more export driven than those of other regions, but also their exports have a large manufactured goods component, which makes the world demand for their products highly income elastic relative to demand for primary commodities.

Although not quite as export oriented as Asia, the economies of Eastern Europe have been severely affected by recessions in their richer trading partners in the West. A similar observation can be made of Mexico and Central America, countries that are both highly integrated with and also significantly dependent on workers' remittances from the United States. The more commodity-based economies of Africa and Latin America (as well as the oil-producing nations) felt the effects of the global weakness in demand through its effect on the commodity markets, where prices fell sharply starting in the fall of 2008.

A critical element determining the extent of the damage to emerging markets through these spillover effects is the speed at which the countries of the "north" recover. As cushions in foreign exchange reserves (built in the bonanza years before 2007) erode and fiscal finances deteriorate, financial strains on debt servicing (public and private) will mount. As we have noted, severe financial crises are protracted affairs. Given the tendency for sovereign defaults to increase in the wake of both global financial crises and sharp declines in global commodity prices, the fallout from the Second Great Contraction may well be an elevated number of defaults, reschedulings, and/or massive IMF bailouts.

- 16 -

COMPOSITE MEASURES OF FINANCIAL TURMOIL

In this book we have emphasized the clustering of crises at several junctures both across countries and across different types of crises. A country experiencing an exchange rate crisis may soon find itself in banking and inflation crises, sometimes with domestic and external default to follow. Crises are also transmitted across countries through contagion or common factors, as we discussed in the previous chapter.

Until now, however, we have not attempted to construct any quantitative index that combines crises regionally or globally. Here, in keeping with the algorithmic approach we have applied to delineating individual financial crisis events, we will offer various types of indexes of financial turbulence that are helpful in assessing the global, regional, and national severity of a crisis.

Our financial turbulence index reveals some stunning information. The most recent global financial crisis—which we have termed the "Second Great Contraction"—is clearly the only global financial crisis that has occurred during the post–World War II period. Even if the Second Great Contraction does not evolve into the Second Great Depression, it still surpasses other turbulent episodes, including the breakdown of Bretton Woods, the first oil shock, the debt crisis of the 1980s in the developing world, and the now-famous Asian crisis of 1997–1998. The Second Great Contraction is already marked by an extraordinarily global banking crisis and by spectacular global exchange rate volatility. The synchronicity of the collapses in housing markets and employment also appears unprecedented since the Great Depression; late in this chapter we will show little-used data from the Great Depression to underscore this comparison.

The index of financial turbulence we develop in this chapter can also be used to characterize the severity of regional crisis, and here we compare the experiences of different continents. The index shows how misinformed is the popular view that Asia does not have financial crises.

This chapter not only links crises globally but also takes on the issue of how different varieties of crisis are linked within a country. Following Kaminsky and Reinhart, we discuss how (sometimes latent) banking crises often lead to currency crashes, outright sovereign default, and inflation.[1]

Finally, we conclude by noting that pulling out of a global crisis is, by nature, more difficult than pulling out of a multicountry regional crisis (such as the Asian financial crisis of 1997–1998). Slow growth in the rest of the world cuts off the possibility that foreign demand will compensate for collapsing domestic demand. Thus, measures such as our index of global financial turbulence can potentially be useful in designing the appropriate policy response.

Developing a Composite Index of Crises: The BCDI Index

We develop our index of crisis severity as follows. In chapter 1 we defined five "varieties" of crises: external and domestic sovereign default, banking crises, currency crashes, and inflation outbursts.[2] Our composite country financial turbulence index is formed by simply summing up the number of types of crises a country experiences in a given year. Thus, if a country did not experience any of our five crises in a given year, its turbulence index for that year would be zero, while in a worst-case scenario (as in Argentina in 2002, for instance) it would be five. We assign such a value for each country for each year. This is what we dub the BCDI index, which stands for banking (systemic episodes only), currency, debt (domestic and external), and inflation crisis index.

Although this exercise captures some of the compounding dimensions of the crisis experience, it admittedly remains an incomplete measure of its severity.[3] If inflation goes to 25 percent per annum (meeting the threshold for a crisis by our definition), it receives the same weight in the index as if it went to 250 percent, which is obviously far more serious.[4] This binary treatment of default is similar to that of the rating agency Standard and Poor's (S&P), which lists countries as either in default or not in default. The S&P index (and ours) take account of debt crisis variables. For example, Uruguay's relatively swift and "market-friendly" restructuring in 2003 is assigned the same value as the drawn-out outright default and major "haircut" successfully imposed on creditors by its larger neighbor, Argentina, during its 2001–2002 default. Nevertheless, indexes such as S&P's have proven enormously useful over time precisely because default tends to be such a discrete event. Similarly, a country that reaches our crisis markers across multiple varieties of crises is almost surely one undergoing severe economic and financial duress.

Where feasible, we also add to our five-crises composite a "Kindleberger-type" stock market crash, which we show separately.[5] In this case, the index runs from zero to six.[6] Although Kindleberger himself did not provide a quantitative definition of a crash, Barro and Ursúa have adopted a reasonable benchmark for defining asset price collapses, which we adopt here. They define a stock market crash as a cumulative decline of 25 percent or more in real equity prices.[7] We apply their methods to the sixty-six countries covered in our sample; the starting dates for equity prices are determined by data availability, as detailed on a country-by-country basis in the data appendixes. Needless to say, our sample of stock market crashes ends with a bang in the cross-country megacrashes of 2008. As in the case of growth collapses, many (if not most) of the stock market crashes have coincided with the crisis episodes described here (chapters 1 and 11). "Most" clearly does not mean all; the Black Monday crash of October 1987 (for example) is not associated with a crisis of any other stripe. False signal flares from the equity market are, of course, familiar. As Samuelson famously noted, "The stock market has predicted nine of the last five recessions."[8] Indeed, although global stock markets continued to plummet during the first part of 2009 (past the end date of our core data set), they then rose markedly in the second quarter of the year, though they hardly returned to their precrisis level.

Beyond sovereign events, there are two other important dimensions of defaults that our crisis index does not capture directly. First, there are defaults on household debt. These defaults, for instance, have been at center stage in the unfolding subprime saga in the United States in the form of the infamous toxic mortgages. Household defaults are not treated separately in our analysis owing to a lack of historical data, even for advanced economies. However, such episodes are most likely captured by our indicator of banking crises. Banks, after all, are the principal sources of credit to households, and large-scale household defaults (to the extent that these occur) impair bank balance sheets.

More problematic is the incidence of corporate defaults, which are in their own right another "variety of crisis." This omission is less of an issue in countries where corporations are bank-dependent. In such circumstances, the same comment made about household default applies to corporate debt. For countries with more developed capital markets, it may be worthwhile to consider widespread corporate default as yet another variety of crisis. As shown in figure 16.1, the United States began to experience a sharp run-up in the incidence of corporate default during the Great Depression well before the government defaulted (the abrogation of the gold clause in 1934). However, it is worth noting that corporate defaults and banking crises are indeed correlated, so our index may partially capture this phenomenon indirectly. In many episodes, corporate defaults have also been precursors to government defaults or reschedulings as governments have tended to shoulder private sector debts.

An Illustration of the Composite at a Country Level

The Argentine crisis of 2001–2002 illustrates how crises may potentially reinforce and overlap one another. The government defaulted on all its debts, domestic and foreign; the banks were paralyzed in a "banking holiday" when deposits were frozen indefinitely; the exchange rate for pesos to U.S. dollars went from one to more than three practically overnight; and prices went from declining (with deflation running at an annual rate of –1 percent or so) to inflating at

251

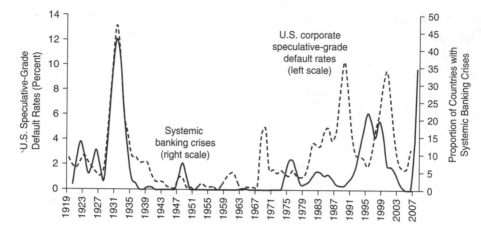

Figure 16.1. The proportion of countries with systemic banking
crises (weighted by their share of world income) and U.S.
corporate speculative-grade default rates, 1919–2008.
Sources: Kaminsky and Reinhart (1999), Bordo et al. (2001), Maddison (2004),
Caprio et al. (2005), Jácome (2008), *Moody's Magazine* (various issues), and
additional sources listed in appendix A.3, which provides banking crises dates.
Notes: The sample includes all sixty-six countries listed in table 1.1 that were
independent states in the given year. Three sets of GDP weights are used, 1913
weights for the period 1800–1913, 1990 weights for the period 1914–1990, and
finally 2003 weights for the period 1991–2008. The entries for 2007–2008 list crises
in Austria, Belgium, Germany, Hungary, Japan, the Netherlands, Spain, the United
Kingdom, and the United States. The figure shows two-year moving averages.

a rate of about 30 percent (by conservative official estimates). We
might add that this episode qualifies as a Barro-Ursúa growth collapse
(per capita GDP fell by about 20 to 25 percent), and real stock prices
crashed by more than 30 percent, along the lines of a Kindleberger-
type crash episode.

World Aggregates and Global Crises

To transition from the experience of individual countries to a world
or regional aggregate, we take weighted averages across all countries
or for a particular region. The weights, as discussed earlier, are given
by the country's share in world output. Alternatively, one can calculate an average tally of crises across a particular country group using
a simple unweighted average. We will illustrate both.

Historical Comparisons

Our aggregate crisis indexes are the time series shown for 1900–2008 in figures 16.2 and 16.3 for the world and for the advanced economies. The advanced economies aggregate comprises the eighteen high-income countries in our sample, while the emerging markets group

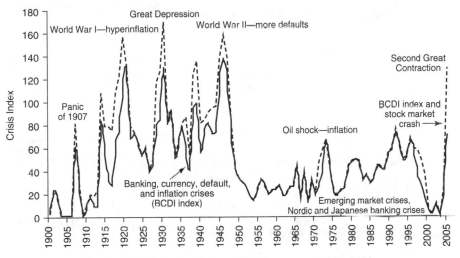

Figure 16.2. Varieties of crises: World aggregate, 1900–2008.
Source: The authors' calculations.

Notes: The figure presents a composite index of banking, currency, sovereign default, and inflation crises and stock market crashes (weighted by their share of world income). The banking, currency, default (domestic and external), and inflation composite (BCDI) index can take a value between zero and five (for any country in any given year) depending on the varieties of crises occurring in a particular year. For instance, in 1998 the index took on a value of 5 for Russia, which was experiencing a currency crash, a banking and inflation crisis, and a sovereign default on both domestic and foreign debt obligations. This index is then weighted by the country's share in world income. This index is calculated annually for the sixty-six countries in the sample for 1800–2008 (shown above for 1900 onward). In addition, we use the definition of a stock market crash given by Barro and Ursúa (2009) for the twenty-five countries in their sample (a subset of the sixty-six-country sample except for Switzerland) for the period 1864–2006; we update their definition of a crash through December 2008 to compile our banking, currency, default (domestic and external), and inflation composite (BCDI +) index. For the United States, for example, the index posts a reading of 2 (banking crisis and stock market crash) in 2008; for Australia and Mexico it also posts a reading of 2 (currency and stock market crash).

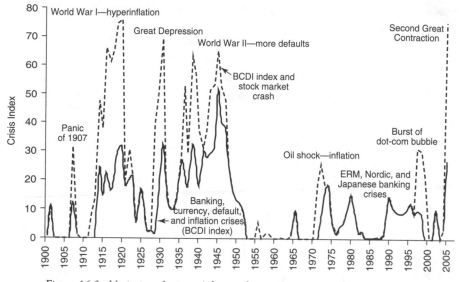

Figure 16.3. Varieties of crises: Advanced economies aggregate, 1900–2008.
Source: The authors' calculations.

Notes: This figure presents a composite index of banking, currency, sovereign default, and inflation crises and stock market crashes, weighted by their share of world income. The banking, currency, default (domestic and external), and inflation composite (BCDI) index can take a value between zero and 5 (for any country in any given year) depending on the varieties of crises taking place in a particular year. For instance, in 1947 the index took on a value of 4 for Japan, which was experiencing a currency crash, an inflation crisis, and a sovereign default on both domestic and foreign debt obligations. This index is then weighted by the country's share in world income. This index is calculated annually for the eighteen advanced economies (includes Austria but not Switzerland) in the Reinhart-Rogoff sample for 1800–2008 (shown above for 1900 onward). In addition, we use the definition of a stock market crash given by Barro and Ursúa (2009) for eighteen advanced economies (includes Switzerland but not Austria) for the period 1864–2006; we update their definition of a crash through December 2008 to compile our banking, currency, default (domestic and external), and inflation composite (BCDI +) index. For the United States and the United Kingdom, for example, the index posts a reading of 2 (banking crisis and stock market crash) in 2008; for Australia and Norway it also posts a reading of 2 (currency and stock market crash). ERM is exchange rate mechanism of the euro system.

254

aggregates forty-eight entries from Africa, Asia, Europe, and Latin America. The indexes shown are weighted by a country's share in world GDP, as we have done for debt and banking crises.[9] The country indexes (without stock market crashes) are compiled from the time of each country's independence (if after 1800) onward; the index that includes the equity market crashes is calculated based on data availability.

Although inflation and banking crises predated independence in many cases, a sovereign debt crisis (external or internal) is, by definition, not possible for a colony. In addition, numerous colonies did not always have their own currencies. When stock market crashes (shown separately) are added to the BCDI composite, we refer to it as the BCDI +.

Figures 16.2 and 16.3 chronicle the incidence, and to some degree the severity, of varied crisis experiences. A cursory inspection of these figures reveals the very different patterns of the pre–World War II and postwar experiences. This difference is most evident in figure 16.3, which plots the indexes for eighteen advanced economies. The prewar experience was characterized by frequent and severe crisis episodes ranging from the banking crisis–driven "global" panic of 1907 to the debt and inflation crises associated with World War II and its aftermath.[10]

The postwar periods offered some bouts of turbulence: the inflationary outbursts that accompanied the first oil shocks in the mid-1970s, the recessions associated with bringing down inflation in the early 1980s, the severe banking crises in the Nordic countries and Japan in the early 1990s, and the bursting of the dot-com bubble in the early 2000s. However, these episodes pale in comparison with their prewar counterparts and with the global contraction of 2008, which has been unparalleled (by a considerable margin) in the sixty-plus years since World War II (figure 16.3). Like its prewar predecessors, the 2008 episode has been both severe in magnitude and global in scope, as reflected by the large share of countries mired in crises. Stock market crashes have been nearly universal. Banking crises have emerged as asset price bubbles have burst and high degrees of leverage have become exposed. Currency crashes against the U.S. dollar in advanced economies took on the magnitudes and volatilities of crashes in emerging markets.

A growing body of academic literature, including contributions by McConnell and Perez-Quiros and Blanchard and Simon, had documented a post-mid-1980s decline in various aspects of macroeconomic volatility, presumably emanating from a global low-inflation environment. This had been termed "a Great Moderation" in the United States and elsewhere.[11] However, systemic crises and low levels of macroeconomic volatility do not travel hand in hand; the sharp increases in volatility that occurred during the Second Great Contraction, which began in 2007, are evident across asset markets, including real estate, stock prices, and exchange rates. They are also manifestly evident in the macroeconomic aggregates, such as those for output, trade, and employment. It remains to be seen how economists will assess the Great Moderation and its causes after the crisis recedes.

For many emerging markets, the Great Moderation was a fleeting event. After all, the debt crisis of the 1980s was as widespread and severe as the events of the 1930s (figure 16.3). These episodes, which affected Africa, Asia, and Latin America in varying degrees, often involved a combination of sovereign default, chronic inflation, and protracted banking crises. As the debt crisis of the 1980s settled, new eruptions emanated from the economies of Eastern Europe and the former Soviet Union in the early 1990s. The Mexican crisis of 1994–1995 and its repercussions in Latin America, the fierce Asian crisis that began in the summer of 1997, and the far-reaching Russian crisis of 1998 did not make for many quiet stretches in emerging markets. This string of crises culminated in Argentina's record default and implosion in 2001–2002.[12]

Until the crisis that began in the United States in the summer of 2007 and became global in scope a year later, emerging markets enjoyed a period of tranquility and even prosperity. During 2003–2007, world growth conditions were favorable, commodity prices were booming, and world interest rates were low, so credit was cheap. However, five years is too short a time span to contemplate extending the "Great Moderation" arguments to emerging markets; in effect, the events of the past two years have already rekindled volatility almost across the board.

Regional Observations

We next look at the regional profile of crises. In figures 16.2 and 16.3 we looked at averages weighted by country size. So that no single country will dominate the regional profiles, the remainder of this discussion focuses on unweighted simple averages for Africa, Asia, and Latin America. In figures 16.4–16.6 we show regional tallies for 1800–2008 for Asia and Latin America and for the post–World War II period for the more newly independent African states.

For Africa, the regional composite index of financial turbulence begins in earnest in the 1950s (figure 16.4), for only South Africa (1910) was a sovereign state prior to that period. However, we do have considerable coverage of prices and exchange rates for the years following World War I, so numerous preindependence crises (including some severe banking crises in South Africa) are dated and included for the colonial period. The index jumps from a low that is close to zero in the 1950s to a high in the 1980s. The thirteen African

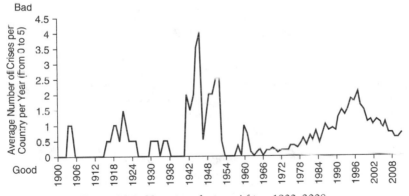

Figure 16.4. Varieties of crises: Africa, 1900–2008.
Source: The authors' calculations based on sources listed in appendixes A.1–A.3.

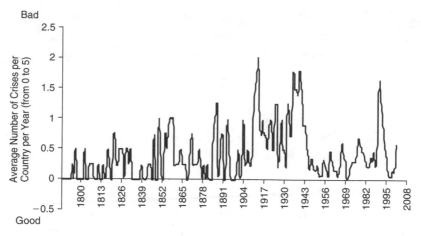

Figure 16.5. Varieties of crises: Asia, 1800–2008.
Source: The authors' calculations based on sources listed in appendixes A.1–A.3.

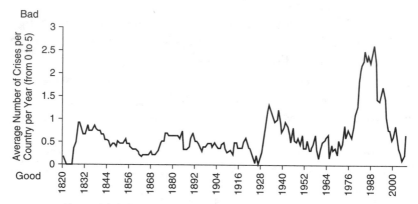

Figure 16.6. Varieties of crises: Latin America, 1800–2008.
Source: The authors' calculations based on sources listed in appendixes A.1–A.3.
Notes: The hyperinflations in Argentina, Bolivia, Brazil, Nicaragua, and Peru sharply increase in the index (reflected in the spike shown for the late 1980s and early 1990s) because all these episodes register a maximum reading of 5.

countries in our sample had, on average, two simultaneous crises during the worst years of the 1980s. In all cases, except that of Mauritius, which has neither defaulted on nor restructured its sovereign debts, the two crises could have been a pairing of any of our crisis varieties. The decline in the average number of crises in the 1990s reflected primarily a decline in the incidence of inflation crises and the eventual (if protracted) resolution of the decade-long debt crisis of the 1980s.

The regional composite index of financial turbulence for Asia (figure 16.5) spans 1800–2008, for China, Japan, and Thailand were independent nations throughout this period. Having gained independence almost immediately following World War II, the remaining Asian countries in the sample then join in the regional average. The profile for Asia highlights a point we have made on more than one occasion: the economic claim of the superiority of the "tigers" or "miracle economies" in the three decades before the 1997–1998 crisis was naïve in terms of the local history. The region had experienced several protracted bouts of economic instability by the international standards of the day. The most severe crisis readings occurred during the period bracketed by the two world wars. In that period, China saw hyperinflation, several defaults, more than one banking crisis, and countless currencies and currency conversions. Japan had numerous bouts of banking, inflation, and exchange rate crises, culminating in its default on its external debt during World War II, the freezing of bank deposits, and its near-hyperinflation (approaching 600 percent) at the end of the war in 1945.

Perhaps Latin America would have done better in terms of economic stability had the printing press never crossed the Atlantic (figure 16.6). Before Latin America's long struggle with high, hyper-, and chronic inflation took a dark turn in the 1970s, the region's average turbulence index reading was very much in line with the world average. Despite periodic defaults, currency crashes, and banking crises, the average never really surpassed one crisis per year, in effect comparing moderately favorably with those of other regions for long stretches of time. The rise of inflation (which began before the famous debt crisis of the 1980s, the "lost decade") would change the relative and absolute performance of the region until the second half of the 1990s. During Latin America's worst moments in the late 1980s —before the 1987 Brady plan (discussed earlier in box 5.3) restructured bad sovereign debts and while Argentina, Brazil, and Peru were mired in hyperinflation—as we can see from the index, the region experienced an average of almost three crises a year.[13]

Defining a Global Financial Crisis

Although the indexes of financial turbulence we have developed can be quite useful in assessing the severity of a global financial crisis, we need a broader-ranging algorithm to systematically delineate true crises so as to exclude, for example, a crisis that registers high on the global scale but affects only one large region. We propose the working definition of a global financial crisis found in box 16.1.

Global Financial Crises: Economic Effects

We next turn to two broad factors associated with global crises, both of which are present in the recent-vintage global contraction: first, the effects of the crisis on the level and the volatility of economic activity broadly defined and measured by world aggregates of equity prices, real GDP, and trade; and second, its relative synchronicity across countries, which is evident in asset markets as well as trends in trade, employment, and other economic sectoral statistics, such as

---

BOX 16.1

Global financial crises: A working definition

Broadly speaking, a global crisis has four main elements that distinguish it from a regional one or a less virulent multicountry crisis:

1. One or more global financial centers are mired in a systemic (or severe) crisis of one form or another. This "requirement" ensures that at least one affected country has a significant (although not necessarily dominant) share in world GDP. Crises in global financial centers also directly or indirectly affect financial flows to numerous other countries. An example of a financial center is a lender to other countries, as the United Kingdom was to "emerging markets" in the 1820s lending boom and the United States was to Latin America in the late 1920s.
2. The crisis involves two or more distinct regions.
3. The number of countries in crisis in each region is three or greater. Counting the number of affected countries (as opposed to the share of regional GDP affected by crisis) ensures that a crisis in a large country—such as Brazil in Latin America or China or Japan in Asia—is not sufficient to define the crisis episode.
4. Our composite GDP-weighted index average global financial turbulence is at least one standard deviation above normal.

Selected episodes of global, multicountry, and regional economic crisis

Episode	Type	Global financial center(s) most affected	At least two distinct regions	Number of countries in each region
The crisis of 1825–1826	Global	United Kingdom	Europe and Latin America	Greece and Portugal defaulted, as did practically all of newly independent Latin America.
The panic of 1907	Global	United States	Europe, Asia, and Latin America	Notably France, Italy, Japan, Mexico, and Chile suffered from banking panics.
The Great Depression, 1929–1938	Global	United States and France	All regions	With the exception of high inflation, no other crisis manifestation was present.
Debt crisis of the 1980s	Multicountry (developing countries and emerging markets)	United States (affected, but crisis was not systemic)	Developing countries in Africa, Latin America, and to a lesser extent Asia	Sovereign default, currency crashes, and high inflation were rampant.
The Asian crisis of 1997–1998	Multicountry, extending beyond Asia in 1998	Japan (affected, but by then it was five years into the resolution of its own systemic banking crisis)	Asia, Europe, and Latin America	Affected South-east Asia initially. By 1998, Russia, Ukraine, Colombia, and Brazil were affected.
The Global Contraction of 2008	Global	United States, United Kingdom	All regions	Banking crises proliferated in Europe, and stock market and currency crashes versus the dollar cut across regions.

Source: Earlier parts of this book.

housing. The emphasis of our discussion is on the last two global crises, the Great Depression of the 1930s and the Second Great Contraction, for which documentation is most complete. Obviously, looking at this broad range of macroeconomic data gives us a much more nuanced picture of a crisis.

Global Aggregates

The connection between stock prices and future economic activity is hardly new. The early literature on turning points in the business cycle, such as the classic by Burns and Mitchell, documented the leading-indicator properties of share prices.[14] Synchronous (across-the-board) and large declines in equity prices (crashes) characterized the onset of the episode that became the Great Depression and somewhat more belatedly the recent global crisis. Figure 16.7 plots an index of global stock prices for 1929–1939 and for 2008–2009 (to the present). For the more recent episode, the index accounts for about 70 percent of world equity market capitalization and covers seven distinct regions and twenty-nine countries. Stock prices are deflated by world consumer prices. The data for 1928–1939 are constructed using median inflation rates for the sixty-six-country sample; for 2007–2009 they are taken from the end-of-period prices published in the *World Economic Outlook*.[15] The years 1928 and 2007 marked the cycle peak in these indices.

The decline in equity markets during 2008 and beyond match the scale (and the cross-country reach) of the 1929 crashes. It is worth noting that during the crisis of the 1930s equity ownership worldwide was far more limited than it has become in the twenty-first century; the growth of pension funds and retirement plans and the ascent of an urban population have increased the links between household wealth and equity markets.

In much the same spirit as figure 16.7, figure 16.8 plots real per capita GDP (weighted by world population) for various country groupings for the two global crises.[16] The aggregate for Europe corresponds to Maddison's twelve-country population-weighted aggregate;[17] the index for Latin America is comprised of the region's eight

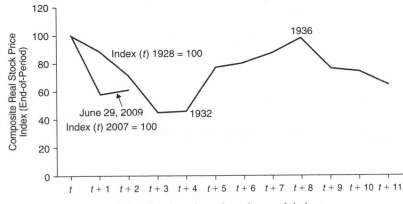

Figure 16.7. Global stock markets during global crises:
The composite real stock price index (end of period).
Sources: Global Financial Data (GFD) (n.d.); Standard and Poor's;
International Monetary Fund (various years), *World Economic Outlook;*
and the authors (details provided in appendix A.1).
Notes: The world composite stock price index was taken from GFD for 1928–1939
and from S&P for 2007–2009. The S&P Global 1200 index covers seven distinct
regions and twenty-nine countries and captures approximately 70 percent of the
world market capitalization. Stock prices are deflated by world consumer prices.
For 1928–1939 these have been constructed using median inflation rates for the
sixty-six-country sample; for 2007–2009 these have been taken from the *World
Economic Outlook* end-of-period prices. The years 1928 and 2007 marked the
cycle peak in these indexes. The year of the crisis is indicated by *t*.

largest countries. The year 1929 marked the peak in real per capita
GDP for all three country groupings. The current data come from the
World Economic Outlook. When all this information is taken together, it is difficult to reconcile the projected trajectory in real GDP,
particularly for emerging markets, and the developments of 2008
through early 2009 in equity markets.

As for trade, we offer two illustrations of its evolution during
the two global crises. The first of these (figure 16.9) is a reprint of an
old classic titled "The Contracting Spiral of World Trade: Month by
Month, January 1929–June 1933." This inward spiral appeared in the
World Economic Survey, 1932–1933, which in turn reprinted it from
another contemporary source.[18] The illustration documents the 67
percent decline in the value of trade as the Depression took hold. As

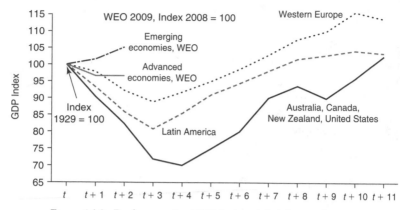

Figure 16.8. Real per capita GDP during global financial crises:
Multicountry aggregates (PPP weighted).
Sources: Maddison (2004); International Monetary Fund (various years),
World Economic Outlook; and the authors (details provided in appendix A.1).
Notes: The Europe aggregate corresponds to Maddison's twelve-country
population-weighted aggregate; the Latin America index is comprised
of the region's eight largest countries. The years 1929 and 2008 marked
the peak in real per capita GDP for all three country groupings.
The year of the crisis is indicated by *t*.

has been extensively documented, including by contemporaneous
sources, the collapse in international trade was only partially the
byproduct of sharp declines in economic activity, ranging from about
10 percent for Western Europe to about 30 percent for Australia,
Canada, New Zealand, and the United States.[19] The other destructive factor was the worldwide increase in protectionist policies in the
form of both trade barriers and competitive devaluations.

Figure 16.10 plots the value of world merchandise exports for
1928–2009. The estimate for 2009 uses the actual year-end level for
2008 as the average for 2009; this yields a 9 percent year-over-year
decline in 2009, the largest one-year drop since 1938.[20] Other large
post–World War II declines are in 1952, during the Korean War, and
in 1982–1983, when recession hit the United States and a 1930s-scale
debt crisis swept through the emerging world. Smaller declines occurred in 1958, the bottom of a recession in the United States; in 1998,
during the Asian financial crisis; and in 2001, after September 11.

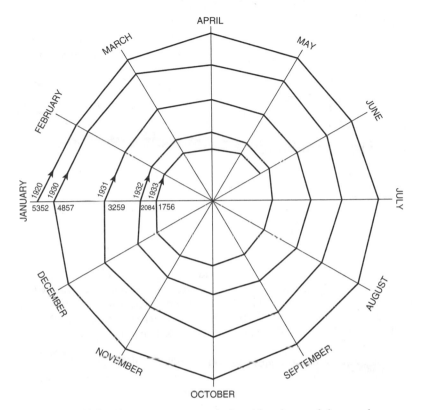

Figure 16.9. The contracting spiral of world trade month by month,
January 1929–June 1933.
Source: Monatsberichte des Österreichischen Institutes für
Konjunkturforschung 4 (1933): 63.

Cross-Country Synchronicity

The performance of the global aggregates provides evidence that a crisis has affected a sufficiently large share of the world's population and/or countries. However, because the information is condensed into a single world index, it does not fully convey the synchronous nature of global crises. To fill in this gap, we present evidence on the performance of various economic indicators during the most recent previous global crisis. Specifically, we present evidence on the changes in unemployment and indexes of housing activity, exports, and currency movements during 1929–1932.

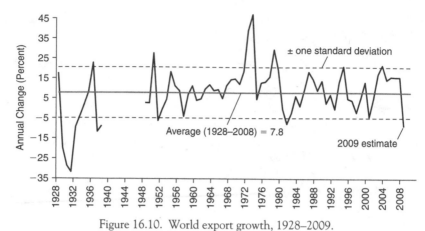

Figure 16.10. World export growth, 1928–2009.
Sources: Global Financial Data (GFD) (n.d.); League of Nations (various years),
World Economic Survey; International Monetary Fund (various years),
World Economic Outlook; and the authors (see notes).
Notes: No world aggregate is available during World War II. The estimate for
2009 uses the actual year-end level for 2008 as the average for 2009; this yields
a 9 percent year-over-year decline in 2009, the largest postwar drop. Other
large post–World War II declines were in 1952, during the Korean War, and
in 1982–1983, when recession hit the United States and a 1930s-scale debt
crisis swept through the emerging world. Smaller declines occurred in 1958,
the bottom of a recession in the United States; in 1998, during the Asian
financial crisis; and in 2001, after September 11.

The massive collapse in trade at the height of the Great Depression was already made plain by the two figures displaying world
aggregates. Figure 16.11 adds information on the widespread nature
of the collapse, which affected countries in all regions, low-, middle-,
and high-income alike. In other words, the world aggregates are truly
representative of the individual country experience and are not
driven by developments in a handful of large countries that are
heavily weighted in the world aggregates. Apart from wars that have
involved a significant share of the world either directly or indirectly
(including the Napoleonic Wars), such across-the-board synchronicity is not to be found in the data.

Cross-country synchronicity is not limited to variables for
which one would expect close cross-country co-movement, such as
international trade or exchange rates. The construction industry,

266

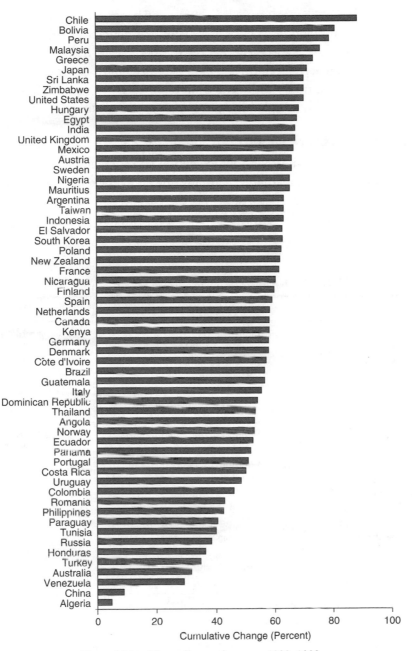

Figure 16.11. The collapse of exports, 1929–1932.
Sources: The individual country sources are provided in appendix A.1;
the authors' calculations were also used.

which lies at the epicenter of the recent boom-bust cycle in the United States and elsewhere, is usually best characterized as being part of the "nontraded sector." Yet the decline in housing-related construction activity during 1929–1932 was almost as synchronous as that seen in trade, as illustrated in table 16.1.

With both traded and nontraded sectors shrinking markedly and consistently across countries, the deterioration in unemployment reported in table 16.2 should come as no surprise. Unemployment increases almost without exception (no comparable 1929 data are available for Japan and Germany) by an average of 17 percentage points. As in the discussion of the aftermath of the postwar crises in the preceding chapter, the figures reflect differences in the defini-

TABLE 16.1
Indexes of total building activity in selected countries (1929 = 100)

Country	Indicator	1932
Argentina	Permits (area)	42
Australia	Permits (value)	23
Belgium	Permits (number)	93
Canada	Permits (value)	17
Chile	Permits (area)	56
Colombia	Buildings completed (area)	84
Czechoslovakia	Buildings completed (number)	88
Finland	Buildings completed (cubic space)	38
France	Permits (number)	81
Germany	Buildings completed (rooms)	36
Hungary	Buildings completed (number)	97
Netherlands	Buildings completed (dwellings)	87
New Zealand	Buildings completed (value)	22
South Africa	Buildings completed (value)	100
Sweden	Buildings completed (rooms)	119
United Kingdom	Permits (value)	91
United States	Permits (value)	18
Average		64

Memorandum item: September 2005 peak = 100:

United States	Permits (number)	25[a]

Sources: League of Nations, *World Economic Survey* (various issues), Carter et al. (2006).
Note: Note the differences in the definition of the indicator from country to country.
[a]Through February 2009.

TABLE 16.2
Unemployment rates for selected countries, 1929–1932

Country	1929	1932	Increase
Australia	11.1	29.0	17.9
Austria	12.3	26.1	13.8
Belgium	4.3	39.7	35.4
Canada	5.7	22.0	16.3
Czechoslovakia	2.2	13.5	11.3
Denmark	15.5	31.7	16.2
Germany	n.a.	31.7	n.a.
Japan	n.a.	6.8	n.a.
Netherlands	7.1	29.5	22.4
Norway	15.4	30.8	15.4
Poland	4.9	11.8	6.9
Sweden	10.7	22.8	12.1
Switzerland	3.5	21.3	17.8
United Kingdom	10.4	22.1	11.7
United States[a]	3.2	24.9	21.7
Average	8.2	25.0	16.8

Sources: League of Nations (various issues), *World Economic Survey;* Carter et al. (2006).
Note: The figures reflect differences in the definition of unemployment and in the methods of compiling the statistics, so cross-country comparisons, particularly of the levels, are tentative.
[a]Annual averages.

tion of unemployment and in the methods of compiling the statistics; hence cross-country comparisons, particularly of the levels, are tentative.

Some Reflections on Global Crises

Here we pause to underscore why global financial crises can be so much more dangerous than local or regional ones. Fundamentally, when a crisis is truly global, exports no longer form a cushion for growth. In a global financial crisis, one typically finds that output, trade, equity prices, and other indicators behave qualitatively (if not quantitatively) much the same way for the world aggregates as they do in individual countries. A sudden stop in financing typically not only hits one country or region but to some extent impacts a large part of the world's public and private sectors.

Conceptually, it is not difficult to see that for a country to be "pulled" out of a postcrisis slump is far more difficult when the rest of the world is similarly affected than when exports offer a stimulus. Empirically, this is not a proposition that can be readily tested. We have hundreds of crises in our sample, but very few global ones, and, as noted in box 16.1, some of the earlier global crises were associated with wars, which complicates comparisons even further.

More definitively, it can be inferred from the evidence of so many episodes that recessions associated with crises (of any variety) are more severe in terms of duration and amplitude than the usual business cycle benchmarks of the post–World War II period in both advanced economies and emerging markets. Crises that are part of a global phenomenon may be worse still in the amplitude and volatility (if not duration) of the downturn. Until the most recent crisis, there had been no postwar global financial crisis; thus, by necessity the comparison benchmarks are prewar episodes. As to severity, the Second Great Contraction has already established several postwar records. The business cycle has evidently not been tamed.

The Sequencing of Crises: A Prototype

Just as financial crises have common macroeconomic antecedents in terms of asset prices, economic activity, external indicators, and so on, common patterns also appear in the sequencing (temporal order) in which crises unfold. Obviously not all crises escalate to the extreme outcome of a sovereign default. Yet advanced economies have not been exempt from their share of currency crashes, bouts of inflation, severe banking crises, and, in an earlier era, even sovereign default.

Investigating what came first, banking or currency crises, was a central theme of Kaminsky and Reinhart's "twin crises" work; they also concluded that financial liberalization often preceded banking crises; indeed, it helped predict them.[21] Demirgüç-Kunt and Detragiache, who employed a different approach and a larger sample, arrived at the same conclusion.[22] Reinhart examined the link between currency crashes and external default.[23] Our work here has investigated the connections between domestic and external debt crises, inflation crises and default (domestic or external), and banking crises and external default.[24] Figure 16.12 maps out a "prototypical" sequence of events yielded by this literature.

As Diaz-Alejandro narrates in his classic paper about the Chilean experience of the late 1970s and early 1980s, "Goodbye Financial Repression, Hello Financial Crash," financial liberalization simultaneously facilitates banks' access to external credit and more risky lending practices at home.[25] After a while, following a boom in lending and asset prices, weaknesses in bank balance sheets become manifest and problems in the banking sector begin.[26] Often these problems are more advanced in the shakier institutions (such as finance companies) than in the major banks.

The next stage in the crisis unfolds when the central bank begins to provide support for these institutions by extending credit to them. If the exchange rate is heavily managed (it does not need to be explicitly pegged), a policy inconsistency arises between supporting the exchange rate and acting as lender of last resort to troubled institutions. The numerous experiences in these studies suggest that (more often than not) the exchange rate objective is subjugated

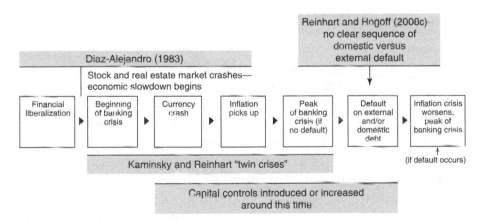

Figure 16.12. The sequencing of crises: A prototype.
Sources: Based on empirical evidence from Diaz-Alejandro (1985), Kindleberger (1989), Demirgüç-Kunt and Detragiache (1998), Kaminsky and Reinhart (1999), Reinhart (2002), and Reinhart and Rogoff (2004, 2008c), among others.

to the role of the central bank as lender of last resort. Even if central bank lending to the troubled financial industry is limited in scope, the central bank may be more reluctant to engage in an "interest rate defense" policy to defend the currency than would be the case if the financial sector were sound. This brings the sequence illustrated in figure 16.12 to the box labeled "Currency crash." The depreciation or devaluation of the currency, as the case may be, complicates the situation in (at least) three ways: (1) it exacerbates the problem of the banks that have borrowed in a foreign currency, worsening currency mismatches;[27] (2) it usually worsens inflation (the extent to which the currency crisis translates into higher inflation is highly uneven across countries, for countries with a history of very high and chronic inflation usually have a much higher and faster pass-through from exchange rates to prices);[28] and (3) it increases the odds of external and domestic default if the government has foreign currency–denominated debt.

At this stage, the banking crisis either peaks following the currency crash (if there is no sovereign credit crisis) or keeps getting worse as the crisis mounts and the economy marches toward a sovereign default (the next box in figure 16.12).[29] In our analysis of domestic and external credit events we have not detected a well-established sequence between these credit events. Domestic defaults have occurred before, during, and after external defaults, in no obvious pattern. As regards inflation, the evidence presented in chapter 9 all points in the direction of a marked deterioration in inflation performance after a default, especially a twin default (involving both domestic and foreign debt). The coverage of our analysis summarized here does not extend to the eventual crisis resolution stage.

We should note that currency crashes tend to be more serious affairs when governments have been explicitly or even implicitly fixing (or nearly fixing) the exchange rate. Even an implicit guarantee of exchange rate stability can lull banks, corporations, and citizens into taking on heavy foreign currency liabilities, thinking there is a low risk of a sudden currency devaluation that will sharply increase the burden of carrying such loans. In a sense, the collapse of a currency is a collapse of a government guarantee on which the private sector might have relied, and therefore it constitutes a default on an important promise. Of course, large swings in exchange rates can also be traumatic for a country with a clear and explicit regime of floating exchange rates, especially if there are substantial levels of foreign exchange debts and if imported intermediate goods play an important role in production. Still, the trauma is typically less, because it does not involve a loss of credibility for the government or the central bank. The persistent and recurring nature of financial crises in various guises through the centuries makes us skeptical about providing easy answers as to how to best avoid them. In our final chapter we sketch out some of the issues regarding the prospects for and measurement of graduation from these destabilizing boom-bust cycles.

Summary

This chapter has greatly extended our perspective of crises by illustrating quantitative measures of the global nature of a crisis, ranging from our composite index of global financial turbulence to comparisons of the aftermath of crises between the Great Depression of the past century and the recent Second Great Contraction. We have seen that by all measures, the trauma resulting from this contraction, the first global financial crisis of the twenty-first century, has been extraordinarily severe. That its macroeconomic outcome has been only the most severe global recession since World War II—and not even worse —must be regarded as fortunate.

- PART VI -

WHAT HAVE WE LEARNED?

There is nothing new except what is forgotten.
—Rose Bertin

- 17 -

REFLECTIONS ON EARLY WARNINGS, GRADUATION, POLICY RESPONSES, AND THE FOIBLES OF HUMAN NATURE

We have come to the end of a long journey that has taken us from the debt defaults and debasements of preindustrial Europe to the first global financial crisis of the twenty-first century the Second Great Contraction. What has our quantitative tour of this history revealed that might help us mitigate financial crises in the future? In chapter 13, on the run-up to the 2007 subprime financial crisis, we argued that it would be helpful to keep track of some basic macroeconomic series on housing prices and debt and calibrate them against historical benchmarks taken from past deep financial crises. But can one say more? In this chapter we begin by briefly reviewing the nascent "early crisis warning system" literature. We acknowledge that it can claim only modest success to date, but based on the first results here, we would argue that there is tremendous scope to strengthen macro prudential supervision by improving the reporting of current data and by investing in the development of long-dated time series (our basic approach here) so as to gain more perspective on patterns and statistical regularities in the data.

For starters, cross-country data on debt that covers long spans of time would be particularly useful. Ideally, one would have decades or even centuries of data in order to perform statistical analysis. We have taken a significant step here by exploiting previously little-known data on public debt for more than sixty countries for nearly one hundred years (and in some cases longer). But for most countries our long-dated time series includes only central government debt, not state and provincial debt. It would be helpful to have broader measures that take into account the debt of quasi-state companies and implicit debt guarantees. It would also be extremely help-ful to have long-dated time series on consumer, bank, and corporate debt. We recognize that gathering such information will be very dif-ficult for most countries, but it is our firm belief that much more can be done than has been accomplished to date. And whereas the hous-ing price series used here (in chapters 10, 13, 14, and 16) is a con-siderable improvement over earlier studies in making use of a broad range of countries, including emerging markets, it would be very use-ful to expand the data to include more countries and a longer time period.

The second section of this concluding chapter explores the potential role of multilateral financial institutions such as the Inter-national Monetary Fund in helping to gather and monitor data on domestic public debt, housing prices, and other matters. It is utterly remarkable that as of this writing no international agency with global reach is providing these data or pressuring member states to provide it. We argue that even with better data on risks, it would probably be extremely desirable to create a new independent international insti-tution to help develop and enforce international financial regula-tions. Our argument rests not only on the need to better coordinate rules across countries but also on the need for regulators to be more independent of national political pressures.

In the third section of the chapter we revisit the theme of "graduation" that comes up again and again throughout the book. How can emerging markets graduate from a history of serial default on sovereign debt and from recurrent bouts of high inflation? A cen-tral conclusion is that graduation is a very slow process, and con-gratulations are all too often premature.

We conclude the chapter with a range of broader lessons.

On Early Warnings of Crises

In earlier chapters we described some of the characteristic ante-cedents of banking crises and links between various types of crises (for instance, between banking and external debt crises or between inflation and debt crises). It is beyond the scope of this book to engage in a full-fledged analysis of early warning systems to anticipate the onset of banking, currency, or debt crises. Following the famous Mexican crisis of 1994–1995 and the even better-known Asian crisis of 1997–1998, a sizable body of empirical literature emerged representing an attempt to ascertain the relative merits of various macroeconomic and financial indicators in accurately "signaling" a crisis ahead of time.[1] These works reviewed a large body of indicators and adopted a broad array of econometric strategies and crisis episodes, with some modest success. Notably, as we have already discussed, the early literature had to be built on the very limited databases then available, which lacked key time series for many countries. In particular, data on real estate markets, a critical element of many bubble and overleverage episodes, are simply absent from most of the existing crisis warning literature because until now these data were not adequate.

Because the data set underlying the present book encompasses the prerequisite information on residential housing prices for a large number of advanced economies and emerging markets, spanning nearly all regions, we can now focus on filling in this important gap in the early warnings literature.[2] Our exercise, as regards housing prices, is not meant to be definitive. Specifically, we followed the approach proposed by Kaminsky and Reinhart in several of their contributions, the so-called signals approach, to examine where in the pecking order of indicators housing prices fit.[3] Table 17.1 presents some of the highlights of the signals approach exercise for banking and currency crises. We did not revisit, update, or enlarge the sample of crisis episodes with regard to the other indicators. Our contribution is to compare the performance of housing prices to that of the other indicators commonly found in this literature.

For banking crises, real housing prices are nearly at the top of the list of reliable indicators, surpassing the current account balance and real stock prices by producing fewer false alarms. Monitoring developments in the prices of this asset has clear value added for helping us to anticipate potential banking crisis scenarios. For predicting currency crashes, the link with the real estate price cycle is

TABLE 17.1

Early warning indicators of banking and currency crises: A summary

Indicator rank (best to worst)	Description	Frequency
Banking crises		
Best		
Real exchange rate	Deviations from trend	Monthly
Real housing prices[a]	Twelve-month (or annual) percentage change	Monthly, quarterly, annually (depending on country)
Short-term capital inflows/GDP	In percentage points	Annually
Current account balance/ investment	In percentage points	Annually
Real stock prices	Twelve-month percentage change	Monthly
Worst		
Institutional Investor (II) and Moody's sovereign ratings	Change in index	Biannually (II), monthly (Moody's)
Terms of trade	Twelve-month percentage change	Monthly
Currency crashes		
Best		
Real exchange rate	Deviations from trend	Monthly
Banking crisis	Dichotomous variable	Monthly or annually
Current account balance/GDP	In percentage points	Annually
Real stock prices	Twelve-month percentage change	Monthly
Exports	Twelve-month percentage change	Monthly
M2 (broad money)/ international reserves	Twelve-month percentage change	Monthly
Worst		
Institutional Investor (II) and Moody's sovereign ratings	Change in index	Biannually (II), monthly (Moody's)
Domestic-foreign interest differential (lending rate)[b]	In percentage points	Monthly

Sources: Kaminsky, Lizondo, and Reinhart (1998), Kaminsky and Reinhart (1999), Goldstein, Kaminsky, and Reinhart (2000), and the authors' calculations.

[a]This is the "novel" variable introduced here.

[b]This is not to be confused with a domestic-foreign interest rate differential such as that seen in the Emerging Market Bond Index spread.

not as sharp, and housing prices do not score as well as a proxy of overvaluation of the real exchange rate as does a banking crisis or the performance of the current account and exports.

The signals approach (or most alternative methods) will not pinpoint the exact date on which a bubble will burst or provide an obvious indication of the severity of the looming crisis. What this systematic exercise can deliver is valuable information as to whether an economy is showing one or more of the classic symptoms that emerge before a severe financial illness develops. The most significant hurdle in establishing an effective and credible early warning system, however, is not the design of a systematic framework that is capable of producing relatively reliable signals of distress from the various indicators in a timely manner. The greatest barrier to success is the well-entrenched tendency of policy makers and market participants to treat the signals as irrelevant archaic residuals of an outdated framework, assuming that old rules of valuation no longer apply. If the past we have studied in this book is any guide, these signals will be dismissed more often that not. That is why we also need to think about improving institutions.

The Role of International Institutions

International institutions can play an important role in reducing risk, first by promoting transparency in reporting data and second by enforcing regulations related to leverage.

It would also be extremely helpful to have better and clearer information on government debt and implicit government debt guarantees in addition to more transparent data on bank balance sheets. Greater transparency in accounting would not solve all problems, but it would certainly help In enforcing transparency, there is a huge role for international institutions—institutions that have otherwise foundered for the past two decades seeking their place in the international order. For governments, the International Monetary Fund (IMF) could provide a public good by having an extremely rigorous standard for government debt accounting that included implicit guarantees and off–balance sheet items.

The IMF's 1996 initiative, the *Special Data Dissemination Standard*, provides a major first step, but much more can be done in this regard. One has only to look at how opaque the United States government's books have become during the 2007 financial crisis to see how helpful an outside standard would be. (The Federal Reserve alone has taken trillions of dollars of difficult-to-price private assets onto its books, but during the depths of the crisis it refused to disclose the composition of some of these assets even to the U.S. Congress. This assumption of assets was admittedly an extraordinarily delicate and sensitive operation, yet over the long run systematic transparency has to be the right approach.) The task of enforcing transparency is far more easily said than done, for governments have many incentives to obfuscate their books. But if the rules are written from outside and in advance of the next crisis, failing to follow the rules might be seen as a signal that would enforce good behavior. In our view, the IMF can play a more useful role by prodding governments into being forthcoming about their borrowing positions than it can by serving as a firefighter once governments have already gotten into trouble. Of course, the lesson of history is that the IMF's influence before a crisis is small relative to its role during a crisis.

We also strongly believe that there is an important role for an international financial regulatory institution. First, cross-border flows of capital continue to proliferate, often seeking light regulation as much as high rates of return. In order to have meaningful regulatory control over modern international financial behemoths, it is important to have some measure of coordination in financial regulation. Equally important, an international financial regulator can potentially provide some degree of political insulation from legislators who relentlessly lobby domestic regulators to ease up on regulatory rule and enforcement. Given that the special qualifications needed to staff such an institution are extremely different from those prevalent in any of the current major multilateral lending institutions, we believe an entirely new institution is needed.[4]

Graduation

Our analysis of the history of various types of financial crises raises many important questions (and provides considerably fewer answers). Possibly the most direct set of questions has to do with the theme of "graduation," a concept that was first introduced in our joint work with Savastano and that we have repeatedly emphasized throughout this book.[5] Why is it that some countries, such as France and Spain, managed to emerge from centuries of serial default on sovereign debt and eventually stopped defaulting, at least in a narrow technical sense? There is the prerequisite issue of what exactly is meant by graduation. The transition from "emerging market" to "advanced economy" status does not come with a diploma or a well-defined set of criteria to mark the upgrade. As Qian and Reinhart highlight, graduation can be defined as the attainment and subsequent maintenance of international investment-grade status; the emphasis here is on the maintenance part.[6] Another way of describing this criterion for graduation would be to say that the country has significantly and credibly reduced its chances of defaulting on its sovereign debt obligations. If it ever was a serial defaulter, it no longer is, and investors recognize it as such. Gaining access to capital markets is no longer a stop-and-go process. Graduation may also be defined as the achievement of some minimum threshold in terms of income per capita, a significant reduction in macroeconomic volatility, and the capacity to conduct countercyclical fiscal and monetary policies or, at a minimum, move away from the destabilizing procyclical policies that plague most emerging markets.[7] Obviously, these milestones are not unrelated.

If graduation were taken to mean total avoidance of financial crises of any kind, we would be left with no graduating class. As we have noted earlier, countries may "graduate" from serial default on sovereign debt and recurrent episodes of very high inflation, as the cases of Austria, France, Spain, and others illustrate. History tells us, however, that graduation from recurrent banking and financial crises is much more elusive. And it should not have taken the 2007 financial crisis to remind us. As noted in chapter 10, out of the sixty-six countries in our core sample, only a few had escaped banking crises since 1945, and by 2008 only one remained. Graduation from currency crashes also seems elusive. Even in the context of floating exchange rates, in which concerted speculative attacks on a peg are no longer an issue, the currencies of advanced economies do crash (i.e., experience depreciations in excess of 15 percent). Admittedly, whereas countries do not outgrow exchange rate volatility, those with more developed capital markets and more explicitly flexible exchange rate systems may be better able to weather currency crashes.

Once we adopt a definition of graduation that focuses on the terms on which countries can access international capital markets, the question that follows is how to make this concept operational. In other words, how do we develop a "quantitative" working measure of graduation? A solid definition of graduation should not be unduly influenced by "market sentiment." In the run-up to major crises in Mexico (1994), Korea (1997), and Argentina (2001), these countries had all been widely portrayed by the multilateral organizations and the financial markets as poster children for—sterling examples of—graduation.

Tackling this complex issue is beyond the scope of our endeavors here. Our aim is to provide a brief snapshot of what "debtors' club" (as defined in chapter 2) countries belong to and a "big picture" of how perceptions of the chances of sovereign default have changed during the past thirty years. To this end, table 17.2 lists all the countries in our sample (and their respective dates of independence). The third column presents the *Institutional Investor* sovereign ratings for sixty-two of the sixty-six countries in our sample for which ratings are available. It is safe to assume that with the notable exceptions of Hong Kong and Taiwan, all the countries that are not rated fall into club C (countries permanently shut out of international private capital markets). The next column shows the changes in the ratings from 1979 (the first year during which *Institutional Investor* published the results of their biannual survey of market participants) to March 2008.

Candidates for graduation should not only meet the criteria for "club A," with an *Institutional Investor* rating of 68 or higher, but should also show the "right slope." Specifically, these countries should

TABLE 17.2

Institutional Investor ratings of sixty-six countries: Upgrade or demotion, 1979–2008

Country	Year of independence (if after 1800)	Institutional Investor rating, 2008 (March)	Change in rating from 1979 to 2008 (+ indicates improvement)
Africa			
Algeria	1962	54.7	–3.9
Angola	1975	n.a.	
Central African Republic	1960	n.a.	
Côte d'Ivoire	1960	19.5	–28.7
Egypt	1831	50.7	16.8
Kenya	1963	29.8	–15.8
Mauritius*	1968	56.3	38.3
Morocco	1956	55.1	9.6
Nigeria	1960	38.3	–15.8
South Africa	1910	65.8	3.8
Tunisia	1957	61.3	11.3
Zambia	1964	n.a.	.
Zimbabwe	1965	5.8	–18.0
Asia			
China		76.5	5.4
Hong Kong*		n.a.	
India	1947	62.7	8.5
Indonesia	1949	48.7	–5.0
Japan		91.4	–5.5
Korea*	1945	79.9	8.7
Malaysia*	1957	72.9	2.6
Myanmar	1948	n.a.	
The Philippines	1947	49.7	4.0
Singapore*	1965	93.1	14.2
Taiwan*	1949	n.a.	
Thailand*		63.1	8.4
Europe			
Austria		94.6	8.9
Belgium*	1830	91.5	5.7
Denmark*		94.7	19.4
Finland*	1917	94.9	20.0
France	943	94.1	3.0
Germany		94.8	–3.5
Greece	1829	81.3	18.7
Hungary	1918	66.8	4.2

(continued)

TABLE 17.2 Continued

Country	Year of independence (if after 1800)	*Institutional Investor* rating, 2008 (March)	Change in rating from 1979 to 2008 (+ indicates improvement)
Europe (*continued*)			
Italy		84.1	10.3
The Netherlands*		95.0	5.3
Norway*	1905	95.9	7.0
Poland	1918	73.0	23.5
Portugal		84.8	32.8
Romania	1878	58.4	3.6
Russia		69.4	−9.4
Spain		89.6	19.3
Sweden		94.8	10.6
Turkey		52.0	37.2
United Kingdom*		94.0	3.4
Latin America			
Argentina	1816	41.9	−20.5
Bolivia	1825	30.3	−1.3
Brazil	1822	60.6	4.3
Chile	1818	77.4	23.2
Colombia	1819	54.7	−6.0
Costa Rica	1821	52.3	7.6
Dominican Republic	1845	36.1	−0.3
Ecuador	1830	30.9	−22.3
El Salvador	1821	46.6	33.7
Guatemala	1821	41.3	19.7
Honduras	1821	31.5	12.4
Mexico	1821	69.3	−2.5
Nicaragua	1821	19.3	8.9
Panama	1903	57.1	11.6
Paraguay	1811	29.7	−13.7
Peru	1821	57.7	27.0
Uruguay	1811	48.8	7.8
Venezuela	1830	43.1	−29.3
North America			
Canada*	1867	94.6	1.1
United States*		93.8	−5.1
Oceania			
Australia*	1901	91.2	3.5
New Zealand*	1907	88.2	10.0

Sources: Institutional Investor (various years), the authors' calculations, and Qian and Reinhart (2009).
Notes: An asterisk (*) denotes no history of sovereign external default or rescheduling; n.a., not available.

show an overall improvement in their ratings from thirty years ago. Countries like Turkey have shown a substantial improvement in their ratings over time, but their current status still falls below the threshold of club A—advanced economy status. Others, such as Mexico on the basis of its 2008 score, meet club A criteria but have seen a deterioration in their rating from what it was in 1979. Figure 17.1 plots the change in the *Institutional Investor* ratings (the last column of table 17.2) and highlights the countries with the potential for graduation. These include Chile, China, Greece, Korea, and Portugal (Malaysia and Poland are more borderline cases whose most recent ratings are just below the threshold for club A). Absent from this list are African countries and practically all of Latin America. This exercise is meant to be illustrative rather than definitive, for the question of who graduates from "emerging market or developing" status and why should remain at the forefront of development economics.

Some Observations on Policy Responses

The persistent and recurrent nature of the this-time-is-different syndrome is itself suggestive that we are not dealing with a challenge that can be overcome in a straightforward way. In its different guises, this syndrome has surfaced at one time or another in every region. No country, irrespective of its global importance, appears immune to it. The fading memories of borrowers and lenders, policy makers and academics, and the public at large do not seem to improve over time, so the policy lessons on how to "avoid" the next blow-up are at best limited. Danger signals emanating from even a well-grounded early warning system may be dismissed on the grounds that the old rules of valuation no longer apply and that the "Lucas critique" is on our side. (The Lucas critique, named for Robert Lucas, known for his work on macroeconomic policy making, says that it is naïve to try to predict the effects of a change in economic policy entirely on the basis of relationships observed in historical data, especially highly aggregated historical data.)

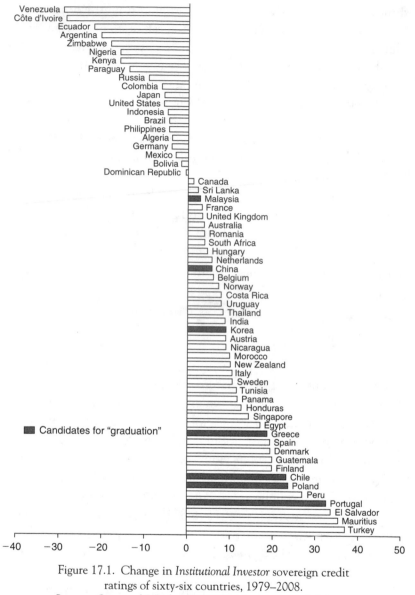

Figure 17.1. Change in *Institutional Investor* sovereign credit
ratings of sixty-six countries, 1979–2008.
Sources: Qian and Reinhart (2009) and sources cited therein.
Note: Malaysia and Poland are included as graduation candidates,
but these are "borderline" cases.

Even if crises are inevitable, there must at least be some basic insights that we can gather from such an extensive review of financial folly. We have already discussed the importance of developing better time series data for studying the history of financial crises, the central premise of this book. In what follows we highlight some further insights.

First, as regards mitigating and managing debt and inflation crises:

- Having a complete picture of government indebtedness is critical, for there is no meaningful *external* debt sustainability exercise that does not take into account the magnitude and features of outstanding *domestic* government debt, ideally including contingent liabilities.
- Debt sustainability exercises must be based on plausible scenarios for economic performance, because the evidence offers little support for the view that countries simply "grow out" of their debts. This observation may limit the options for governments that have inherited high levels of debt. Simply put, they must factor in the possibility of "sudden stops" in capital flows, for these are a recurrent phenomenon for all but the very largest economies in the world.
- The inflationary risks to monetary policy frameworks (whether the exchange rate is fixed or flexible) also seem to be linked in important ways to the levels of domestic debt. Many governments have succumbed to the temptation to inflate away domestic debt.

Second, policy makers must recognize that banking crises tend to be protracted affairs. Some crisis episodes (such as those of Japan in 1992 and Spain in 1977) were stretched out even longer by the authorities by a lengthy period of denial. Fiscal finances suffer mightily as government revenues shrink in the aftermath of crises and bailout costs mount. Our extensive coverage of banking crises, however, says little about the much-debated issue of the efficacy of stimulus packages as a way of shortening the duration of the crisis and cushioning the downside of the economy as a banking crisis unfolds. Pre–World War II banking crises were seldom met with counter-cyclical fiscal policies. The postwar period has witnessed only a hand-ful of severe banking crises in advanced economies. Before 2007, explicit stimulus measures were a part of the policy response only in the Japanese crisis. In the numerous severe banking crises in emerg-ing markets, fiscal stimulus packages were not an option, because governments were shut out of access to international capital markets. Increases in government spending in these episodes primarily re-flected bailout outlays and markedly rising debt servicing costs. It is dangerous to draw conclusions about the effectiveness of fiscal stim-ulus packages from a single episode. However, the surge in govern-ment debt following a crisis is an important factor to weigh when considering how far governments should be willing to go to offset the adverse consequences of the crisis on economic activity. This mes-sage is particularly critical to countries with a history of debt intol-erance, which may meet debt servicing difficulties even at relatively moderate levels of debt.

Third, on graduation, the greatest policy insight is that pre-mature self-congratulations may lead to complacency and demotion to a lower grade. Several debt crises involving default or near-default occurred on the heels of countries' ratings upgrades, joining the OECD (e.g., Mexico, Korea, Turkey), and being generally portrayed as the poster children of the international community (e.g., Ar-gentina in the late 1990s prior to its meltdown in late 2001).

The Latest Version of the This-Time-Is-Different Syndrome

Going into the recent financial crisis, there was a widespread view that debtors and creditors had learned from their mistakes and that financial crises were not going to return for a very long time, at least in emerging markets and developed economies. Thanks to better-informed macroeconomic policies and more discriminating lending practices, it was argued, the world was not likely to see a major wave of defaults again. Indeed, in the run-up to the recent financial crisis, an oft-cited reason as to why "this time is different" for the emerging markets was that their governments were relying more on domestic debt financing.

But celebrations may be premature. They are certainly uninformed by the history of the emerging markets. Capital flow and default cycles have been around since at least 1800, if not before in other parts of the globe. Why they would end anytime soon is not obvious.

In the run-up to the recent crisis, in the case of rich countries one of the main this-time-is-different syndromes had to do with a belief in the invincibility of modern monetary institutions. Central banks became enamored with their own versions of "inflation targeting," believing that they had found a way both to keep inflation low and to optimally stabilize output. Though their successes were founded on some solid institutional progress, especially the independence of the central banks, those successes seem to have been oversold. Policies that appeared to work perfectly well during an all-encompassing boom suddenly did not seem at all robust in the event of a huge recession. Market investors, in turn, relied on the central banks to bail them out in the event of any trouble. The famous "Greenspan put" (named after Federal Reserve Chairman Alan Greenspan) was based on the (empirically well-founded) belief that the U.S. central bank would resist raising interest rates in response to a sharp upward spike in asset prices (and therefore not undo them) but would react vigorously to any sharp fall in asset prices by cutting interest rates to prop them up. Thus, markets believed, the Federal Reserve provided investors with a one-way bet. That the Federal Reserve would resort to extraordinary measures once a collapse started has now been proven to be a fact. In hindsight, it is now clear that a single-minded focus on inflation can be justified only in an environment in which other regulators are able to ensure that leverage (borrowing) does not become excessive.

The lesson of history, then, is that even as institutions and policy makers improve, there will always be a temptation to stretch the limits. Just as an individual can go bankrupt no matter how rich she starts out, a financial system can collapse under the pressure of greed, politics, and profits no matter how well regulated it seems to be.

Technology has changed, the height of humans has changed, and fashions have changed. Yet the ability of governments and investors to delude themselves, giving rise to periodic bouts of euphoria that usually end in tears, seems to have remained a constant. No careful reader of Friedman and Schwartz will be surprised by this lesson about the ability of governments to mismanage financial markets, a key theme of their analysis.[8] As for financial markets, Kindleberger wisely titled the first chapter of his classic book "Financial Crisis: A Hardy Perennial."[9]

We have come full circle to the concept of financial fragility in economies with massive indebtedness. All too often, periods of heavy borrowing can take place in a bubble and last for a surprisingly long time. But highly leveraged economies, particularly those in which continual rollover of short-term debt is sustained only by confidence in relatively illiquid underlying assets, seldom survive forever, particularly if leverage continues to grow unchecked. This time may seem different, but all too often a deeper look shows it is not. Encouragingly, history does point to warning signs that policy makers can look at to assess risk—if only they do not become too drunk with their credit bubble–fueled success and say, as their predecessors have for centuries, "This time is different."

DATA APPENDIXES

APPENDIX A.1
MACROECONOMIC TIME SERIES

This appendix covers the macroeconomic time series used; a separate appendix (appendix A.2) is devoted to the database on government debt.

Abbreviations of Frequently Used Sources and Terms

Additional sources are listed in the tables that follow.

BNB	Banque Nationale de Belgique
DIA	Díaz et al. (2005)
ESFDB	European State Finance Database
GDF	World Bank, *Global Development Finance* (various issues)
GFD	Global Financial Data
GNI	Gross national income
GPIHG	Global Price and Income History Group
IFS	International Monetary Fund, *International Financial Statistics* (various issues)
II	*Institutional Investor*
IISH	International Institute of Social History
KRV	Kaminsky, Reinhart, and Végh (2003)
Lcu	local currency units
MAD	Maddison (2004)
MIT	Mitchell (2003a, 2003b)
NNP	Net national product

OXF	Oxford Latin American Economic History Database		
RR	Reinhart and Rogoff (years as noted)		
TED	Total Economy Database		
WEO	International Monetary Fund, *World Economic Outlook* (various issues)		

TABLE A.1.1
Prices: Consumer or cost-of-living indexes (unless otherwise noted)

Country	Period covered	Sources	Commentary
Algeria	1869–1884	Hoffman et al. (2002)	Wheat prices
	1938–2007	GFD, WEO	
Angola	1914–1962	MIT	
	1991–2007	WEO	
Argentina	1775–1812	Garner (2007)	Buenos Aires only
	1864–1940	Williamson (1999)	
	1884–1913	Flandreau and Zumer (2004)	
	1900–2000	OXF	
	1913–2000	DIA	
	1913–2007	GFD, WEO	
Australia	1818–1850	Butlin (1962), Vanplew (1987), GPIHG	New Wales, food prices
	1850–1983	Shergold (1987), GPIHG	Sydney, food
	1861–2007	GFD, WEO	
Austria	1440–1800	Allen (2001)	Vienna
	1800–1914	Hoffman et al. (2002)	Wheat prices
	1880–1913	Flandreau and Zumer (2004)	
	1919–2007	GFD, WEO	
Belgium	1462–1913	Allen (2001)	Antwerp
	1835–2007	GFD, WEO	
Bolivia	1936–2007	GFD, WEO	
Brazil	1763–1820	Garner (n.d.)	Rio de Janeiro only
	1830–1937	Williamson (1999)	Rio de Janeiro only
	1861–2000	DIA	
	1912–2007	GFD, WEO	

296

TABLE A.1.1 Continued

Country	Period covered	Sources	Commentary
Canada	1867–1975	Statistics Canada (StatCan)	
	1910–2007	GFD, WEO	
Central African Republic	1956–1993	MIT	
	1980–2007	WEO	
Chile	1754–1806	Garner (2007)	Santiago only
	1810–2000	DIA	
	1900–2000	OXF	
	1913–2007	GFD, WEO	
China	1644–2000	Lu and Peng (2006)	Rice prices
	1867–1935	Hsu	Wholesale prices
	1926–1948	GFD, WEO	
	1978–2007		
Colombia	1863–1940	Williamson (1999)	
	1900–2000	OXF	
	1923–2007	GFD, WEO	
Costa Rica	1937–2007	GFD, WEO	
Côte d'Ivoire	1951–2007	GFD, WEO	
Denmark	1748–1800	Hoffman et al. (2002)	Wheat prices
	1815–2007	GFD, WEO	
Dominican Republic	1942–2000	OXF	
	1980–2007	WEO	
Ecuador	1939–2007	GFD, WEO	
Egypt	1859–1941	Williamson (2000a)	
	1913–2007	GFD, WEO	
	1915–1999	GFD	
El Salvador	1937–2000	OXD	
	1980–2007	WEO	
Finland	1860–2001	Finnish Historical National Accounts	
	1980–2007	WEO	
France	1431–1786	Allen (2001)	
	1840–1913		
	1807–1935	Dick and Floyd (1997)	Retail prices
	1840–2007	GFD, WEO	

(continued)

TABLE A.1.1 Continued

Country	Period covered	Sources	Commentary
Germany	1427–1765	Allen (2001)	Munich
	1637–1855	Hoffman et al. (2002)	Wheat prices
	1820–2007	GFD, WEO	
Greece	1833–1938	Kostelenos et al. (2007)	GDP deflator
	1922–2007	GFD, WEO	
Ghana	1949–2007	GFD, WEO	
Guatemala	1938–2000	OXD	
	1980–2007	WEO	
Honduras	1938–2000	OXD	
	1980–2007	WEO	
Hungary	1923–2007	GFD, WEO	
India	1866–2000	DIA	
	1873–1939	Williamson (2000b)	
	1913–2007	GFD, WEO	
Indonesia	1820–1940	Williamson (2000b)	
	1948–2007	GFD, WEO	
Italy	1548–1645	Allen (2001)	Naples
	1734–1806		
	1701–1860	deMaddalena (1974)	Wheat prices, Milan
	1861–2007	GFD, WEO	
Korea	1690–1909	Jun and Lewis (2002)	Rice prices in the southern region of Korea
	1906–1939	Williamson (2000b)	
	1948–2007	GFD, WEO	
Japan	1600–1650	Kimura (1987)	Rice prices, Osaka
	1818–1871	Bassino and Ma (2005)	Rice prices, Osaka
	1860–1935	Williamson (2000b)	
	1900–2007	GFD, WEO	
Kenya	1947–2007	GFD, WEO	
Malaysia	1948–2007	GFD, WEO	
Mauritius	1946–2007	GFD, WEO	

TABLE A.1.1 Continued

Country	Period covered	Sources	Commentary
Mexico	1786–1821	Garner (2007)	Zacatecas
	1877–1940	Williamson (1999)	
	1918–2007	GFD, WEO	
Morocco	1939–2007	GFD, WEO	
Myanmar (Burma)	1870–1940	Williamson (2000b)	
	1939–2007	GFD, WEO	
The Netherlands	1500–1800	Van Zanden (2005)	
	1800–1913	Van Riel (2009)	
	1880–2007	GFD, WEO	
New Zealand	1857–2004	Statistics New Zealand	
	1980–2007	WEO	
Nicaragua	1937–2007	GFD, WEO	
Nigeria	1953–2007	GFD, WEO	
Norway	1516–2005	Grytten (2008)	
	1980–2007	WEO	
Panama	1939–2000	OXD	
	1980–2007	WEO	
Paraguay	1938–2007	GFD, WEO	
	1750–1816	Garner (2007)	Potosi
Peru	1790–1841	Garner (2007)	Lima
	1800–1873	DIA	
	1913–2000		
	1980–2007	WEO	
The Philippines	1899–1940	Williamson (2000b)	
	1937–2007	GFD, WEO	
Poland	1701–1815	Hoffman et al. (2002)	Oat prices, Warsaw
	1816–1914	Allen (2001)	Warsaw
	1921–1939	GFD, WEO	
	1983–2007		
Portugal	1728–1893	Hoffman et al. (2002)	Wheat prices
	1881–1997	Bordo et al. (2001)	
	1980–2007	WEO	

(*continued*)

TABLE A.1.1 Continued

Country	Period covered	Sources	Commentary
Romania	1779–1831	Hoffman et al. (2002)	Wheat prices, Wallachia
	1971–2007	WEO	
Russia	1853–1910	Borodkin (2001)	Wheat and rye flour prices, St. Petersburg
	1880–1913	Flandreau and Zumer (2004)	
	1917–1924	GFD, WEO	
	1927–1940		
	1944–1972		
	1991–2007		
Singapore	1948–2007	GFD, WEO	
South Africa	1895–2007	GFD, WEO	
Spain	1500–1650	Hamilton (1969)	Valencia
	1651–1800	Hoffman et al. (2002)	Prices of wheat, eggs, and linen
	1800–2000	DIA	
	1980–2000	WEO	
Sri Lanka	1939–2007	GFD, WEO	
Sweden	1732–1800	Hoffman et al. (2002)	Wheat prices
	1800–2000	Edvinsson (2002)	
	1980–2007	WEO	
Taiwan	1897–1939	Williamson (2000b)	
	1980–2007	WEO	
Thailand (Siam)	1820–1941	Williamson (2000b)	
	1948–2007	GFD, WEO	
Tunisia	1939–2007	GFD, WEO	
Turkey	1469–1914	Pamuk (2005)	Istanbul
	1854–1941	Williamson (2000a)	
	1922–2007	GFD, WEO	
United Kingdom	1450–1999	Van Zanden (2002)	Southern England
	1781–2007	GFD, WEO	
United States	1720–1789	Carter et al. (2006)	Wholesale prices

TABLE A.1.1 Continued

Country	Period covered	Sources	Commentary
	1774–2003	Carter et al. (2006)	
	1980–2007	WEO	
Uruguay	1870–1940	Williamson (1999)	
	1929–2000	OXF	
	1980–2007	WEO	
Venezuela	1830–2002	Baptista (2006)	
	1914–2007	GFD, WEO	
Zambia	1938–2007	GFD, WEO	
Zimbabwe	1920–1970	MIT	
	1930–2007	GFD, WEO	

TABLE A.1.2
Modern nominal exchange rates (domestic currency units per U.S. dollar and other currencies noted)

Country	Period covered	Source	Other relevant rates
Algeria	1831–2007	GFD, IFS	French franc, euro
Angola	1921–2007	GFD, IFS	
Argentina	1880–1913	Flandreau and Zumer (2004)	French franc
	1885–2007	GFD, IFS	
Australia	1835–2007	GFD, IFS	U.K. pound
Austria	1814–2007	GFD, IFS	U.K. pound, German mark
Belgium	1830–2007	GFD, IFS	French franc
Bolivia	1863–2007	GFD, IFS	
Brazil	1812–2007	GFD, IFS	U.K. pound
Canada	1858–2007	GFD, IFS	U.K. pound

(continued)

301

TABLE A.1.2 Continued

Country	Period covered	Source	Other relevant rates
Central African Republic	1900–2007	GFD, IFS	French franc
Chile	1830–1995	Braun et al. (2000)	U.K. pound
	1878–2007	GFD, IFS	
China	1848–2007	GFD, IFS	U.K. pound
Colombia	1900–2000	OXF	U.K. pound
	1919–2007	GDF, IFS	
Costa Rica	1921–2007	GDF, IFS	
Denmark	1864–2007	GDF, IFS	U.K. pound, German mark
Dominican Republic	1905–2007	GDF, IFS	
Ecuador	1898–2000	OXF, Pick (various years)	
	1980–2007	IFS	
Egypt	1869–2007	GFD, IFS	U.K. pound
El Salvador	1870–2007	GFD, IFS	
Finland	1900–2007	GFD, IFS	German mark
France	1619–1810	ESFDB, Course of the Exchange	U.K. pound
	1800–2007	GFD, IFS	U.K. pound, German mark
Germany	1698–1810	ESFDB, Course of the Exchange	U.K. pound
	1795–2007	GFD, IFS	
Greece	1872–1939	Lazaretou (2005)	U.K. pound, German mark
	1901–2007	GFD, IFS	
Guatemala	1900–2007	GFD, IFS	
Honduras	1870–2007	GFD, IFS	
Hungary	1900–2007	GFD, IFS	Austrian schilling
India	1823–2007	GFD, IFS	U.K. pound
Indonesia	1876–2007	GFD, IFS	Dutch guilder

302

TABLE A.1.2 Continued

Country	Period covered	Source	Other relevant rates
Italy	1816–2007	GFD, IFS	U.K. pound, German mark
Japan	1862–2007	GFD, IFS	U.K. pound
Kenya	1898–2007	GFD, IFS	U.K. pound
Korea	1905–2007	GFD, IFS	Japanese yen
Malaysia	1900–2007	GFD, IFS	U.K. pound
Mauritius	1900–2007	GFD, IFS	U.K. pound
Mexico	1814–2007	GFD, IFS	U.K. pound, French franc
	1823–1999	GFD	
Morocco	1897–2007	GFD, IFS	French franc, euro
Myanmar (Burma)	1900–2007	GFD, IFS	U.K. pound
The Netherlands	1698–1810	ESFDB, Course of the Exchange	U.K. pound
	1792–2007	GFD, IFS	German mark
New Zealand	1892–2007	GFD, IFS	U.K. pound
Nicaragua	1912–2007	GFD, IFS	
Nigeria	1900–2007	GFD, IFS	U.K. pound
Norway	1819–2007	GFD, IFS	Swedish krona, German mark
Panama	1900–2007	GFD, IFS	
Paraguay	1900–2000	OXD	Argentine peso
	1980–2007	IFS	
Peru	1883–2007	GFD, IFS	U.K. pound
The Philippines	1893–2007	GFD, IFS	Spanish peseta
Poland	1916–2007	GFD, IFS	
Portugal	1750–1865	Course of the Exchange	Dutch grooten
	1794–2007	GDF, IFS	U.K. pound, German mark

(continued)

TABLE A.1.2 Continued

Country	Period covered	Source	Other relevant rates
Romania	1814–2007	GFD	
	1900–2000	OXF, IFS	
	1921–2007	GDF, IFS	
Singapore	1834–2007	GFD, IFS	U.K. pound
South Africa	1900–2007	GFD, IFS	U.K. pound
Spain	1814–2007	GFD, IFS	German mark
Sri Lanka	1900–2007	GFD, IFS	U.K. pound
Sweden	1814–2007	GDF, IFS	U.K. pound, German mark
Taiwan	1895–2007	GDF, IFS	U.K. pound, Japanese yen
Thailand (Siam)	1859–2007	GFD, IFS	U.K. pound
Tunisia	1900–2007	GFD, IFS	French franc
Turkey	1859–2007	GFD, IFS	U.K. pound
United Kingdom	1619–1810	ESFDB, Course of the Exchange	French franc
	1660–2007	GFD, IFS	
United States	1660–2007	GFD, IFS	
Uruguay	1900–2007	GFD, IFS	
Venezuela	1900–2007	GFD, IFS	
Zambia	1900–2007	GFD, IFS	U.K. pound
Zimbabwe	1900–2007	GFD, IFS	U.K. pound

TABLE A.1.3
Early silver-based exchange rates (domestic currency units per U.K. penny)

Country	Period covered	Source	Currency, commentary
Austria	1371–1860	Allen and Unger (2004)	Kreuzer, Vienna
Belgium	1349–1801	Korthals Altes (1996)	Hoet
France	1258–1789	Allen and Unger (2004)	Livre tournois
Germany	1350–1830	Allen and Unger (2004)	Composite pfennig
Italy	1289–1858	Malanima (n.d.)	Lira fiorentina
Netherlands	1366–1800	Allen and Unger (2004), Van Zanden (2005)	Composite
Portugal	1750–1855	Godinho (1955)	Reis
Russia	1761–1840	Lindert and Mironov (n.d.)	Common ruble
Spain	1351–1809	Allen and Unger (2004)	Composite
Sweden	1523–1573	Söderberg (2004)	Mark ortug
Turkey	1555–1914	Ozmucur and Pamuk (2002)	Akche

TABLE A.1.4

The silver content of currencies

Country	Period covered	Sources	Currency, commentary
Austria	1371–1860	Allen and Unger (2004)	Kreuzer, Vienna
Belgium	1349–1801	Korthals Altes (1996)	Hoet
France	1258–1789	Allen (2001), Allen and Unger (2004)	Livre tournois
Germany	1350–1798	Allen (2001), Allen and Unger (2004)	Pfennig, Frankfurt
	1417–1830	Allen (2001), Allen and Unger (2004)	Pfennig, Augsburg
Italy	1289–1858	Malanima (n.d.)	Lira fiorentina
The Netherlands	1366–1575	Allen and Unger (2004)	Flemish grote
	1450–1800	Van Zanden (2005)	Guilder
Portugal	1750–1855	Godinho (1955)	Reis
Russia	1761–1840	Lindert and Mironov (n.d.)	Common ruble
	1761–1815		Assignatzia
Spain	1351–1650	Allen and Unger (2004)	Dinar, Valencia
	1501–1800		Vellon maravedis, New Castile
	1630–1809	Allen and Unger (2004)	Real
Sweden	1523–1573	Soderberg (2004)	Mark ortug
Turkey	1555–1914	Ozmucur and Pamuk (2002)	Akche
United Kingdom	1261–1918	Allen and Unger (2004)	Penny
United States	1800–1979	Allen and Unger (2004)	Dollar

TABLE A.1.5
Index of nominal and real gross national product and output (domestic currency units)

Country	Period covered	Source	Commentary
Algeria	1950–2007	GFD, WEO, IFS	
Angola	1962–2007	GFD, WEO, IFS	
Argentina	1884–1913	Flandreau and Zumer (2004)	Nominal
	1875–2000	DIA	Index of total production (1995 = 100)
	1900–2000	OXF	Real (base = 1970)
	1900–2007	GFD, WEO	
Australia	1798–2007	GFD, WEO	Nominal
	1820–2000	DIA	Index of total production (1995 = 100)
Belgium	1835–2007	BNB, Centre d'études économiques de la Katholieke Universiteit Leuven	Nominal
Bolivia			
Brazil	1861–2007	GFD, WEO	Nominal
	1850–2000	DIA	Index of total production (1995 = 100)
	1900–2000	OXF	(Base = 1970)
Canada			
Chile	1810–2000	DIA	Index of total production (1995 = 100)
China (NNP)	1962–1999	GFD	
Colombia	1900–2000	OXF	Real (base = 1970)
	1925–1999	GFD	
Costa Rica	1947–1999	GFD	
Côte d' Ivoire			

(*continued*)

TABLE A.1.5 Continued

Country	Period covered	Source	Commentary
Denmark	1818–1975	Nordic Historical National Accounts	
Egypt	1886–1945	Yousef (2002)	
	1952–2007	GFD, WEO	
	1821–1859	Landes (1958)	Cotton output
Finland	1860–2001	Nordic Historical National Accounts	
Greece	1833–1939	Kostelenos et al. (2007)	
	1880–1913	Flandreau and Zumer (2004)	
GNI	1927–1999	GFD	
	1948–1999	GFD	
India	1900–1921	GFD	
	1948–2007	GFD, WEO	
	1861–1899	Brahmananda (2001)	Real, per capita
	1820–2000	DIA	Index of total production
Indonesia	1815–1913	Van Zanden (2006)	Java
	1910–1970	Bassino and Van der Eng (2006)	
	1921–1939	GFD	
	1951–1999	GFD	
	1911–1938	GFD	
	1953–1999	GFD	
Korea	1911–1940	Cha and Kim (2006)	Thousand yen, GNI also calculated
GNI	1953–1999	GFD	
Malaysia	1910–1970	Bassino and Van der Eng (2006)	
	1949–1999	GFD	
Mexico	1820–2000	DIA	Index of total production (1995 = 100)

TABLE A.1.5 Continued

Country	Period covered	Source	Commentary
Mexico (*continued*)	1900–2000	OXF	
	1900–2000	OXF	Real (base = 1970)
	1925–1999	GFD	
Myanmar (Burma)	1913–1970	Bassino and Van der Eng (2006)	
	1950–1999	GFD	
The Netherlands	1800–1913	National Accounts of the Netherlands	
Norway	1830–2003	Grytten (2008)	
Peru	1900–2000	OXF	Real (base = 1970)
	1900–2000	OXF	Nominal
	1942–1999	GFD	
The Philippines	1910–1970	Bassino and Van der Eng (2006)	
	1946–1997	GFD, WEO	
Russia	1885–1913	Flandreau and Zumer (2004)	Nominal
GNI	1928–1940	GFD	
	1945–1995	GFD	
	1979–1997	GFD	
	1992–1999	GFD	Production
South Africa	1911–1999	GFD	
Sri Lanka	1900–1970	Bassino and Van der Eng (2006)	
Sweden	1720–2000	Edvinsson (2002)	Real, per capita
	1800–2000	Edvinsson (2002)	Nominal and real
Taiwan	1910–1970	Bassino and Van der Eng (2006)	
Thailand (Siam)	1946–2007	GFD, WEO	
	1910–1970	Bassino and Van der Eng (2006)	
Turkey	1923–2005	GFD	Nominal
	1950–1999	GFD	
United Kingdom	1830–1999	GFD	GNI
	1948–1999	GFD	

(*continued*)

TABLE A.1.5 Continued

Country	Period covered	Source	Commentary
United States	1790–2002	Carter et al. (2006)	Real, per capita
	1948–1999	GFD	
Uruguay	1935–1999	GFD	
	1955–2000	OXF	
	1900–2000	OXF	Real (base = 1970)
GNI	1955–1999	GFD	
Venezuela	1830–2002	Baptista (2006)	
	1900–2000	OXF	Real (base = 1970)
	1950–2007	GFD, WEO	

TABLE A.1.6
Gross national product (PPP in constant dollars)

Country	Period covered	Source	Commentary
Algeria	1950–2005	MAD, TED	
	1820–2005	RR (2008a)	Interpolation 1821–1949
Angola	1950–2005	MAD, TED	
Argentina	1875–2000	DIA	Base = 1996
	1900–2005	MAD, TED	
	1870–2005	RR (2008a)	Interpolation 1871–1899
Australia	1820–2006	MAD, TED	
Austria	1870–2006	MAD, TED	
	1820–2006	RR (2008a)	Interpolation 1821–1869
Belgium	1846–2006	MAD, TED	
	1820–2006	RR (2008a)	Interpolation 1821–1845
Bolivia	1945–2005	MAD, TED	
	1936–2005	RR (2008a)	Interpolation 1936–1944
Brazil	1820–2000	DIA	Base = 1996
	1870–2005	MAD, TED	
	1820–2005	RR (2008a)	Interpolation 1821–1869
Canada	1870–2006	MAD, TED	
	1820–2006	RR (2008a)	Interpolation 1821–1869
Central African Republic	1950–2003	MAD	
Chile	1810–2000	DIA	Base = 1996
	1820–2005	MAD, TED	
China	1929–1938	MAD, TED	
	1950–2006		
Colombia	1900–2005	MAD, TED	
Costa Rica	1920–2005	MAD, TED	
Denmark	1820–2006	MAD, TED	
Dominican Republic	1950–2005	MAD, TED	
	1942–2005	RR (2008a)	Interpolation 1942–1949

(*continued*)

311

TABLE A.1.6 Continued

Country	Period covered	Source	Commentary
Ecuador	1939–2005	MAD, TED	
	1900–2000	OXF	Base = 1970
	1900–2005	RR (2008a)	Interpolation 1900–1938
Egypt	1950–2005	MAD, TED	
	1820–2005	RR (2008a)	Interpolation 1821–1949
El Salvador	1900–2000	OXF	Base = 1970
Finland	1860–2006	MAD, TED	
	1820–2006	RR (2008a)	Interpolation 1821–1859
France	1820–2006	MAD, TED	
Germany	1850–2006	MAD, TED	
	1820–2006	RR (2008a)	Interpolation 1821–1849
Greece	1921–2006	MAD, TED	
	1820–2006	RR (2008a)	Interpolation 1821–1920
Guatemala	1920–2005	MAD, TED	
Honduras	1920–2005	MAD, TED	
Hungary	1824–2006	MAD, TED	
	1870–2006	RR (2008a)	Interpolation 1871–1923
India	1884–2006	MAD, TED	
	1820–2006	RR (2008a)	Interpolation 1821–1883
Indonesia	1870–2005	MAD, TED	
	1820–2005	RR (2008a)	Interpolation 1821–1869
Japan	1870–2006	MAD, TED	
	1820–2006	RR (2008a)	Interpolation 1821–1869
Kenya	1950–2005	MAD, TED	
Korea	1911–2006	MAD, TED	
	1820–2006	RR (2008a)	Interpolation 1821–1910
Malaysia	1911–2005	MAD, TED	
	1820–2006	RR (2008a)	Interpolation 1821–1910
Mauritius	1950–2005	MAD, TED	
Mexico	1900–2006	MAD, TED	
	1820–2006	RR (2008a)	Interpolation 1821–1899

TABLE A.1.6 Continued

Country	Period covered	Source	Commentary
Morocco	1950–2005	MAD, TED	
	1820–2005	RR (2008a)	Interpolation 1821–1949
Myanmar (Burma)	1950–2005	MAD, TED	
	1820–2005	RR (2008a)	Interpolation 1821–1949
Panama	1945–2005	MAD, TED	
	1939–2005	RR (2008a)	Interpolation 1939–1944
Paraguay	1939–2005	MAD, TED	
Peru	1895–2005	MAD, TED	
The Philippines	1902–2005	MAD, TED	
	1870–2005	RR (2008a)	Interpolation 1871–1901
Poland	1929–1938	MAD, TED	
	1950–2006		
	1870–2005	RR (2008a)	Interpolation 1871–1928
Portugal	1865–2006	MAD, TED	
	1820–2006	RR (2008a)	Interpolation 1821–1864
Romania	1926–1938	MAD, TED	
	1950–2006		
Russia	1928–2006	MAD, TED	
Singapore	1950–2005	MAD, TED	
	1820–2005	RR (2008a)	Interpolation 1821–1949
South Africa	1950–2005	MAD, TED	
	1905–2005	RR (2008a)	Interpolation 1905–1949
Spain	1850–2006	MAD, TED	
	1820–2005	RR (2008a)	Interpolation 1821–1849
Sweden	1820–2006	MAD, TED	
Thailand (Siam)	1950–2005	MAD, TED	
	1820–2005	RR (2008a)	Interpolation 1821–1949
Tunisia	1950–2005	MAD, TED	
	1820–2005	RR (2008a)	Interpolation 1821–1949
Turkey	1923–2005	MAD, TED	

(continued)

313

TABLE A.1.6 Continued

Country	Period covered	Source	Commentary
United Kingdom	1830–2006	MAD, TED	
	1820–2006	RR (2008a)	Interpolation 1821–1829
United States	1870–2006	MAD, TED	
	1820–2006	RR (2008a)	Interpolation 1821–1869
Uruguay	1870–2005	MAD, TED	
Venezuela	1900–2005	MAD, TED	
	1820–2005	RR (2008a)	Interpolation 1821–1899
Zambia	1950–2005	MAD, TED	
Zimbabwe	1950–2005	MAD, TED	
	1919–2005	MAD, TED	

Note: The information is also available on a per capita basis.

TABLE A.1.7
Central government expenditures and revenues
(domestic currency units unless otherwise noted)

Country	Period covered	Sources	Commentary
Algeria	1834–1960	MIT	Revenues begin in 1830
	1964–1975		
	1994–1996		
	1963–2003	KRV	
Angola	1915–1973	MIT	
	1980–2003	KRV	
Argentina	1864–1999	MIT	
	1880–1913	Flandreau and Zumer (2004)	
	1963–2003	KRV	
Australia	1839–1900	MIT	Revenues begin in 1824, for New South Wales and other provinces circa 1840
	1901–1997	MIT	Commonwealth
	1965–2003	KRV	

TABLE A.1.7 Continued

Country	Period covered	Sources	Commentary
Austria	1791–1993	MIT	Missing data for World Wars I and II
	1965–2003	KRV	
Belgium	1830–1993		Missing data for World War I
	1965–2003	KRV	
Bolivia	1888–1999	MIT	Revenues begin in 1885
	1963–2003	KRV	
Brazil	1823–1994	Instituto Brasileiro de de Geografia e Estatística, MIT	
	1980–2003	KRV	
Canada	1806–1840	MIT	Lower Canada
	1824–1840		Upper Canada
	1867–1995		Canada
	1963–2003	KRV	
Central African Republic	1906–1912	MIT	
	1925–1973		
	1963–2003	KRV	
Chile	1810–1995	Braun et al. (2000)	Base = 1995
	1857–1998	MIT	
	1963–2003	KRV	
China	1927–1936	Cheng (2003)	Nationalist government
	1963–2003	KRV	
Colombia	1905–1999	MIT	
	1963–2003	KRV	
Costa Rica	1884–1999	MIT	
	1963–2003	KRV	
Côte d'Ivoire	1895–1912	MIT	
	1926–1999		
	1963–2003	KRV	
Denmark	1853–1993	MIT	
	1965–2003	KRV	

(continued)

TABLE A.1.7 Continued

Country	Period covered	Sources	Commentary
Dominican Republic	1905–1999	MIT	
	1963–2003	KRV	
Ecuador	1884–1999	MIT	
	1979–2003	KRV	
Egypt	1821–1879	Landes (1958)	
	1852–1999	MIT	
	1963–2003	KRV	
El Salvador	1883–1999	MIT	
	1963–2003	KRV	
Finland	1882–1993	MIT	
	1965–2003	KRV	
France	1600–1785	ESFDB	
	1815–1993	MIT	
	1965–2003	KRV	
Germany (Prussia)	1688–1806	ESFDB	
Germany	1872–1934	MIT	Revenues end in 1942
	1946–1993		West Germany
	1979–2003	KRV	
Greece	1885–1940	MIT	Expenditure begins in 1833 and again in 1946
	1954–1993		
	1963–2003	KRV	
Guatemala	1882–1999	MIT	
	1963–2003	KRV	
Honduras	1879–1999	MIT	
	1963–2003	KRV	
Hungary	1868–1940	MIT	
India	1810–2000	MIT	
	1963–2003	KRV	
Indonesia	1821–1940	Mellegers (2006)	Netherlands East Indies, florins, high government

316

TABLE A.1.7 Continued

Country	Period covered	Sources	Commentary
	1816–1939	MIT	
	1959–1999		
	1963–2003	KRV	
Italy	1862–1993	MIT	
	1965–2003	KRV	
Japan	1868–1993	MIT	
	1963–2003	KRV	
Kenya	1895–2000	MIT	
	1970–2003	KRV	
Korea	1905–1939	MIT	Japanese yen
	1949–1997		South Korea
	1963–2003	KRV	
Malaysia	1883–1938	MIT	Malaya
	1946–1999		
	1963–2003	KRV	
Mauritius	1812–2000	MIT	
	1963–2003	KRV	
Mexico	1825–1998	MIT	
	1963–2003	KRV	
Morocco	1938–2000	MIT	Revenues also
			1920–1929
	1963–2003	KRV	
Myanmar (Burma)	1946–1999	MIT	
	1963–2003	KRV	
The Netherlands	1845–1993	MIT	
	1965–2003	KRV	
New Zealand	1841–2000	MIT	
	1965–2003	KRV	
Nicaragua	1900–1999	MIT	
	1963–2003	KRV	
Nigeria	1874–1998	MIT	
	1963–2003	KRV	

(continued)

TABLE A.1.7 Continued

Country	Period covered	Sources	Commentary
Norway	1850–1992	MIT	
	1965–2003	KRV	
Panama	1909–1996	MIT	
	1963–2003	KRV	
Paraguay	1881–1900	MIT	Revenues through 1902
	1913–1993		
	1963–2003	KRV	
Peru	1846–1998	MIT	
	1963–2003	KRV	
The Philippines	1901–2000	MIT	Missing data for World War II
	1963–2003	KRV	
Poland	1922–1937	MIT	
	1947–1993		Expenditure only
Portugal	1879–1902	MIT	
	1917–1992		
	1975–2003	KRV	
Romania	1883–1992	MIT	Expenditure begins in 1862
Russia	1769–1815	ESFDB	
	1804–1914	MIT	
	1924–1934		
	1950–1990		
	1931–1951	Condoide (1951)	National budget
Singapore	1963–2000	MIT	
South Africa	1826–1904	MIT	Natal began in 1850
	1905–2000		
	1963–2003	KRV	
Spain	1520–1553	ESFDB	Not continuous
	1753–1788		
	1850–1997	MIT	
	1965–2003	KRV	
Sri Lanka	1811–2000	MIT	
	1963–2003	KRV	

318

TABLE A.1.7 Continued

Country	Period covered	Sources	Commentary
Sweden	1881–1993	MIT	
	1980–2003	KRV	
Taiwan	1898–1938	MIT	
	1950–2000		
Thailand (Siam)	1891–2000	MIT	Revenue began in 1851
	1963–2003	KRV	
Tunisia	1909–1954	MIT	
	1965–1999		
	1963–2003	KRV	
Turkey	1923–2000	MIT	
	1963–2003	KRV	
United Kingdom	1486–1815	ESFDB	
	1791–1993	MIT	
	1963–2003	KRV	
United States	1789–1994	MIT	
	1960–2003	KRV	
Uruguay	1871–1999	MIT	
	1963–2003	KRV	
Venezuela	1830–1998	MIT	
	1963–2003	KRV	
Zambia	1963–2003	KRV	
Zimbabwe	1894–1997	MIT	
	1963–2003	KRV	

TABLE A.1.8
Total exports and imports (local currency units and U.S. dollar, as noted)

Country	Period covered	Sources	Currency, commentary
Algeria	1831–2007	GFD, WEO	
Angola	1891–2007	GFD, WEO	
Argentina	1864–2007	GFD, WEO	Lcu
	1885–2007	GFD, WEO	U.S. dollar
	1880–1913	Flandreau and Zumer (2004)	Exports
Australia	1826–2007	GFD, WEO	
Austria	1831–2007	GFD, WEO	
Belgium	1846–2007	GFD, WEO	
	1816–2007	GFD, WEO	U.S. dollar
Bolivia	1899–1935	GFD	Lcu
	1899–2007		U.S. dollar
Brazil	1821–2007	GFD, WEO	
	1880–1913	Flandreau and Zumer (2004)	Exports
Canada	1832–2007	GFD, WEO	Lcu
	1867–2007		U.S. dollar
Chile	1857–1967	GFD, WEO	Lcu
China	1865–1937	GFD, WEO	Lcu
	1950–2007		
Colombia	1835–1938		Lcu
	1919–2007	GFD, WEO	U.S. dollar
Costa Rica	1854–1938	GFD, WEO	Lcu
	1921–2007		U.S. dollar
Côte d'Ivoire	1892–2007	GFD, WEO	Lcu
	1900–2007		U.S. dollar
Denmark	1841–2007	GFD, WEO	Exports begin in 1818, lcu
	1865–2007		U.S. dollar
Ecuador	1889–1949	GFD, WEO	Lcu
	1924–2007		U.S. dollar
Egypt	1850–2007	GFD, WEO	Lcu
	1869–2007		U.S. dollar

TABLE A.1.8 Continued

Country	Period covered	Sources	Currency, commentary
El Salvador	1859–1988	GFD, WEO	Exports begin in 1854, lcu
	1870–2007		U.S. dollar
Finland	1818–2007	GFD, WEO	Lcu
	1900–2007		U.S. dollar
France	1800–2007	GFD, WEO	
Germany	1880–2007	GFD, WEO	
Ghana	1850–2007	GFD, WEO	Lcu
	1900–2007		U.S. dollar
Greece	1849–2007	GFD, WEO	Lcu
	1900–2007		U.S. dollar
Guatemala	1851–2007	GFD, WEO	
Honduras	1896–2007	GFD, WEO	
India	1832–2007	GFD, WEO	
Indonesia	1823–1974	GFD, WEO	Lcu
	1876–2007		U.S. dollar
Italy	1861–2007	GFD, WEO	
Japan	1862–2007	GFD, WEO	
Kenya	1900–2007	GFD, WEO	
Korea	1886–1936	GFD, WEO	Lcu
	1905–2007		U.S. dollar
Malaysia	1905–2007	GFD, WEO	Includes Singapore until 1955
Mauritius	1833–2007	GFD, WEO	Lcu
	1900–2007		U.S. dollar
Mexico	1797–1830	GFD, WEO	U.K. pound
	1872–2007		Lcu
	1797–1830		U.S. dollar
	1872–2007		
Morocco	1947–2007	GFD, WEO	
Myanmar (Burma)	1937–2007	GFD, WEO	
The Netherlands	1846–2007	GFD, WEO	

(continued)

TABLE A.1.8 Continued

Country	Period covered	Sources	Currency, commentary
Nicaragua	1895–2007	GFD, WEO	
Norway	1851–2007	GFD, WEO	
Panama	1905–2007	GFD, WEO	Lcu
Paraguay	1879–1949 1923–2007	GFD, WEO	U.S. dollar
Peru	1866–1952 1882–2007	GFD, WEO	Lcu U.S. dollar
The Philippines	1884–2007	GFD, WEO	
Poland	1924–2007	GFD, WEO	
Portugal	1861–2007	GFD, WEO	
Romania	1862–1993 1921–2007	GFD, WEO	Lcu U.S dollar
Russia	1802–1991 1815–2007	GFD, WEO	Lcu U.S. dollar
Singapore	1948–2007	GFD, WEO	
South Africa	1826–2007 1900–2007	GFD, WEO	Lcu U.S. dollar
Spain	1822–2007	GFD, WEO	
Sri Lanka	1825–2007 1900–2007	GFD, WEO	Lcu U.S. dollar
Sweden	1832–2007	GFD, WEO	
Taiwan	1891–2007	GFD, WEO	
Thailand (Siam)	1859–2007	GFD, WEO	
Turkey	1878–2007	GFD, WEO	
United Kingdom	1796–2007	GFD, WEO	
United States	1788–2007	GFD, WEO	
Uruguay	1862–1930 1899–2007	GFD, WEO	
Venezuela	1830–2007 1900–2007	GFD, WEO	
Zambia	1908–2007	GFD, WEO	
Zimbabwe	1900–2007	GFD, WEO	

TABLE A.1.9
Global indicators and financial centers

Country	Series	Period covered	Sources
United Kingdom	Current account balance/ GDP	1816–2006	Imlah (1958), MIT, United Kingdom National Statistics
	Consol rate	1790–2007	GFD, Bank of England
	Discount rate	1790–2007	GFD, Bank of England
United States	Current account balance/ GDP	1790–2006	Carter et al. (2006), WEO
	60- to 90-day commercial paper	1830–1900	Carter et al. (2006)
	Discount rate	1915–2007	GFD, Board of Governors of the Federal Reserve
	Federal funds rate	1950–2007	Board of Governors of the Federal Reserve
	Long-term bond	1798–2007	Carter et al. (2006), Board of Governors of the Federal Reserve
World	Commodity prices, nominal and real	1790–1850	Gayer, Rostow, and Schwartz (1953)
		1854–1990	Boughton (1991)
		1862–1999	*Economist*
		1980–2007	WEO
	Sovereign external default dates	1341–2007	Suter (1992), Purcell and Kaufman (1993), Reinhart, Rogoff, and Savastano (2003a), MacDonald (2006), Standard and Poor's (various issues)

TABLE A.1.10
Real house prices

Country	Period covered	Source	Commentary
Argentina	1981–2007	Reporte Immobiliario	Average value of old apartments, Buenos Aires
Colombia	1997:Q1–2007:Q4	Departamento Administrativo Nacional de Estadistica	New housing price index, total twenty-three municipalities
Finland	1983:Q1–2008:Q1	StatFin Online Service	Dwellings in old blocks of flats, Finland
	1970–2007	Bank for International Settlements	House price index, Finland
Hong Kong	1991:7–2008:2	Hong Kong University	Real estate index series, Hong Kong
Hungary	2000–2007	Otthon Centrum	Average price of old condominiums, Budapest
Iceland	2000:3–2008:4	Statistics Iceland	House price index, Iceland
Indonesia	1994:Q1–2008:Q1	Bank of Indonesia	Residential property price index, new houses, new developments, big cities
Ireland	1996:Q1–2008:Q1	ESRI, Permanent TSB	House prices, standardized, Ireland
Japan	1955:H1–2007:H2	Japan Real Estate Institute	Land prices, urban, residential index, Japan
Malaysia	2000:Q1–2007:Q4	Bank Negara	House price index, Malaysia
Norway	1970–2007	Bank for International Settlements	House price index, all dwellings, Norway
	1819–2007	Norges Bank	Housing prices, Norway
The Philippines	1994:Q4–2007:Q4	Colliers International: Philippines	Prime three-bedroom condominiums, Makati Central Business District

324

TABLE A.1.10 Continued

Country	Period covered	Source	Commentary
South Korea	1986:1–2006:12	Kookmin Bank	Housing price index
	2007:Q1–2008:Q1	Kookmin Bank	Housing price index
Spain	1990:Q1–2008:Q1	Banco de España	House price index, appraised housing, Spain
	1970–2007	Bank for International Settlements	House price index, appraised housing, Spain
Thailand	1991:Q1–2008:Q4	Bank of Thailand	House price index, single detached house
United Kingdom	1952:1–2008:4	Nationwide	Average house price, U.K.
	1970–2007	Bank for International Settlements	House price index, U.K.
United States	1890–2007	Standard and Poor's	Case-Shiller national price index, U.S.
	1987:Q1–2008:Q2	Standard and Poor's	Case-Shiller national price index, U.S.

TABLE A.1.11

Stock market indexes (equity prices) (local currency and U.S. dollars)

Country	Period covered	Country	Period covered
Argentina	1967–2008	Korea	1962–2008
Australia	1875–2008	Malaysia	1970–2008
Austria	1922–2008	Mexico	1930–2008
Belgium	1898–2008	The Netherlands	1919–2008
Brazil	1954–2008	New Zealand	1931–2008
Canada	1914–2008	Norway	1918–2008
Chile	1927–2008	Pakistan	1960–2008
Colombia	1929–2008	Peru	1932–2008
Denmark	1915–2008	The Philippines	1952–2008
Finland	1922–2008	Portugal	1931–2008
France	1856–2008	Singapore	1966–2008
Germany	1856–2008	South Africa, Union of	1910–2008
Greece	1952–2008	Spain	1915–2008
Hong Kong	1962–2008	Sweden	1913–2008
India	1921–2008	Switzerland	1910–2008
Ireland	1934–2008	Taiwan	1967–2008
Israel	1949–2008	United Kingdom	1800–2008
Italy	1906–2008	United States	1800–2008
Japan	1915–2008	Venezuela	1937–2008
Kenya	1964–2008	Zimbabwe	1968–2008

Source: Global Financial Data.

APPENDIX A.2
PUBLIC DEBT

This appendix covers the government debt series used, while appendix A.1 is devoted to the database on macroeconomic time series.

Abbreviations of Frequently Used Sources and Terms

Additional sources are listed in the tables that follow.

CLYPS   Cowan, Levy-Yeyati, Panizza, Sturzenegger (2006)
ESFDB   European State Finance Data Base
GDF   World Bank, *Global Development Finance*
GFD   Global Financial Data
IFS   International Monetary Fund, *International Financial Statistics* (various issues)
Lcu   local currency units
LM   Lindert and Morton (1989)
LofN   League of Nations, *Statistical Yearbook* (various years)
MAR   Marichal (1989)
MIT   Mitchell (2003a, 2003b)
RR   Reinhart and Rogoff (year as noted)
UN   United Nations, *Statistical Yearbook* (various years)
WEO   International Monetary Fund, *World Economic Outlook* (various issues)

TABLE A.2.1
Public debentures: External government bond issues

Country	Period covered	Sources	Commentary
Argentina	1824–1968	LM, MAR	Includes first loan
	1927–1946	UN	
Australia	1857–1978	LM, Page (1919)	
	1927–1946	UN	
Bolivia	1864–1930	MAR	
	1927–1946	UN	
Brazil	1843–1970	Bazant (1968), LM, MAR, Summerhill (2006)	Includes first loan
	1928–1946	UN	
Canada	1860–1919	LM	
	1928–1946	UN	
Chile	1822–1830	LM, MAR	Includes first loan
	1928–1946	UN	
China	1865–1938	Huang (1919), Winkler (1928)	
Colombia	1822–1929	MAR	
	1928–1946	UN	
Costa Rica	1871–1930	MAR	
Egypt	1862–1965	Landes (1958), LM	Includes first loan
	1928–1946	UN	
El Salvador	1922–1930	MAR	
	1928–1946	UN	
Greece	1824–1932	Levandis (1944)	Includes first loan (independence loan)
	1928–1939	UN	
Guatemala	1856–1930	MAR	
	1928–1939	UN	
Honduras	1867–1930	MAR	
India	1928–1945	UN	
Japan	1870–1965	LM	Includes first loan
	1928–1939	UN	

TABLE A.2.1 Continued

Country	Period covered	Sources	Commentary
Mexico	1824–1946	Bazant (1968), LM, MAR	Includes first loan
	1928–1944	UN	
Panama	1923–1930	UN	
	1928–1945	UN	
Peru	1822–1930	MAR	Includes first loan
	1928–1945	UN	
Russia	1815–1916	Miller (1926), Crisp (1976), LM	
South Africa	1928–1946	UN	
Thailand (Siam)	1928–1947	UN	
Turkey	1854–1965	Clay (2000), LM	Includes first loan
	1933–1939	UN	
Uruguay	1871–1939	MAR	
	1928–1947	UN	
Venezuela	1822–1930	MAR	Includes first loan
	1928–1947	UN	

TABLE A.2.2
Total (domestic plus external) public debt

Country	Period covered	Source	Commentary
Argentina	1863–1971	Garcia Vizcaino (1972)	Lcu
	1914–1981	LofN, UN	Lcu
	1980–2005	GFD, Jeanne and Guscina (2006)	
Australia	1852–1914	Page (1919)	
	1914–1981	LofN, UN	Lcu
	1980–2007	Australian Office of Financial Management	Lcu
Austria	1880–1913	Flandreau and Zumer (2004)	Lcu
	1945–1984	UN	Lcu
	1970–2006	Austrian Federal Financing Agency	Euro
Belgium	1830–2005	BNB, Centre d'études économiques de la KUL	Euro
Bolivia	1914–1953	LofN, UN	Lcu
	1968–1981		
	1991–2004	CLYPS	U.S. dollar
Brazil	1880–1913	Flandreau and Zumer (2004)	Lcu
	1923–1972	LofN, UN	Lcu
	1991–2005	GFD, Jeanne and Guscina (2006)	
Canada	1867–2007	Statistics Canada, Bank of Canada	Lcu
Chile	1827–2000	Diaz et al. (2005)	Lcu
	1914–1953	LofN, UN	Lcu
	1990–2007	Ministerio de Hacienda	U.S. dollar
China	1894–1950	Cheng (2003), Huang (1919), RR (2008c)	
	1981–2005	GFD, Jeanne and Guscina (2006) (2006)	
Colombia	1923–2006	Contraloria General de la Republica	Lcu
Costa Rica	1892–1914	Soley Güell (1926)	Lcu
	1914–1983	LofN, UN	Lcu
	1980–2007	CLYPS, Ministerio de Hacienda	U.S. dollar
Côte d'Ivoire	1970–1980	UN	Lcu

TABLE A.2.2 Continued

Country	Period covered	Source	Commentary
Denmark	1880–1913	Flandreau and Zumer (2004)	Lcu
	1914–1975	LofN, UN	Lcu
	1990–2007	Danmarks National Bank	Lcu
Dominican Republic	1914–1952	LofN, UN	Lcu
Ecuador	1914–1972	LofN, UN	Lcu
	1990–2006	Ministry of Finance	U.S. dollar
Egypt	1914–1959	LofN, UN	Lcu
	2001–2005	Ministry of Finance	Lcu
El Salvador	1914–1963, 1976–1983	LofN, UN	Lcu
	1990–2004	CLYPS	U.S. dollar
	2003–2007	Banco Central de Reserva	U.S. dollar
Finland	1914–1983	LofN, UN	Lcu
	1978–2007	State Treasury Finland	Lcu
France	1880–1913	Flandreau and Zumer (2004)	Lcu
	1913–1972	LofN, UN	Lcu
	1999–2007	Ministère du Budget, des comptes public	Lcu
Germany	1880–1913	Flandreau and Zumer (2004)	Lcu
	1914–1983	LofN, UN	Lcu
	1950–2007	Bundesbank	Lcu
Greece	1869–1893	Levandis (1944)	Not continuous, Lcu
	1880–1913	Flandreau and Zumer (2004)	Lcu
	1920–1983	LofN, UN	Lcu
	1993–2006	OECD	
Guatemala	1921–1982	LofN, UN	Lcu
	1980–2005	CLYPS	U.S. dollar
Honduras	1914–1971	LofN, UN	Lcu
	1980–2005	CLYPS	U.S. dollar
Hungary	1913–1942	LofN, UN	Lcu
	1992–2005	Jeanne and Guscina (2006)	

(continued)

TABLE A.2.2 Continued

Country	Period covered	Source	Commentary
India	1840–1920	Statistical Abstract Relating to British India	
	1913–1983	LofN, UN	Lcu
	1980–2005	Jeanne and Guscina (2006)	
Indonesia	1972–1983	UN	Lcu
	1998–2005	Bank Indonesia, GDF	
Italy	1880–1913	Flandreau and Zumer (2004)	Lcu
	1914–1894	LofN, UN	Lcu
	1982–2007	Dipartamento del Tesoro	Lcu
Japan	1872–2007	Historical Statistics of Japan, Bank of Japan	Lcu
Kenya	1911–1935	Frankel (1938)	U.K. pound
	1961–1980	LofN, UN	Lcu
	1997–2007	Central Bank of Kenya	Lcu
Korea	1910–1938	Mizoguchi and Umemura (1988)	Yen
	1970–1984	LofN, UN	
	1990–2004	Jeanne and Guscina (2006)	
Malaysia	1947–1957	UN	Lcu
	1976–1981		
	1980–2004	Jeanne and Guscina (2006)	
Mauritius	1970–1984	LofN, UN	Lcu
	1998–2007		Lcu
Mexico	1814–1946	Bazant (1968)	Not continuous
	1914–1979	LofN, UN	Lcu
	1980–2006	Direccion General de la Deuda Publica	
Morocco	1965–1980	UN	Lcu
The Netherlands	1880–1914	Flandreau and Zumer (2004)	Lcu
	1914–1977	LofN, UN	Lcu
	1914–2008	Dutch State Treasury Agency	Lcu
New Zealand	1858–2006	Statistics New Zealand, New Zealand Treasury	Lcu
Nicaragua	1914–1945	LofN, UN	Lcu
	1970–1983		
	1991–2005	CLYPS	U.S. dollar

TABLE A.2.2 Continued

Country	Period covered	Source	Commentary
Norway	1880–1914	Flandreau and Zumer (2004)	Lcu
	1913–1983	LofN, UN	Lcu
	1965–2007	Ministry of Finance	Lcu
Panama	1915–1983	LofN, UN	U.S. dollar
	1980–2005	CLYPS	U.S. dollar
Paraguay	1927–1947	LofN, UN	Lcu
	1976–1982		
	1990–2004	CLYPS	U.S. dollar
Peru	1918–1970	LofN, UN	Lcu
	1990–2005	CLYPS	U.S. dollar
The Philippines	1948–1982	LofN, UN	Lcu
	1980–2005	GFD, Jeanne and Guscina (2006)	
Poland	1920–1947	LofN, UN	
	1994–2004	GFD, Jeanne and Guscina (2006)	
Portugal	1851–1997	Instituto Nacional Estadisticas–Portuguese Statistical Agency	
	1914–1975	LofN, UN	Lcu
	1980–2007	Banco de Portugal	In euros from 1999
Russia	1880–1914	Crisp (1976), Flandreau and Zumer (2004)	French franc and lcu
	1922–1938	LofN, UN	Lcu
	1993–2005	Jeanne and Guscina (2006)	
Singapore	1969–1982	UN	Lcu
	1986–2006	Monetary Authority	Lcu
South Africa	1859–1914	Page (1919)	U.K. pound
	1910–1982	LofN, UN	Lcu
	1946–2006	South Africa Reserve Bank	Lcu
Spain	1504–1679	ESFDB	Not continuous
	1850–2001	Estadisticas Historicas de España: Siglos XIX–XX	Lcu
	1999–2006	Banco de España	Euro
Sri Lanka	1861–1914	Page (1919)	U.K. pound
	1950–1983	UN	Lcu
	1990–2006	Central Bank of Sri Lanka	Lcu

(continued)

TABLE A.2.2 Continued

Country	Period covered	Source	Commentary
Sweden	1880–1913	Flandreau and Zumer (2004)	
	1914–1984	LofN, UN	Lcu
	1950–2006	Riksgälden	Lcu
Thailand (Siam)	1913–1984	LofN, UN	Lcu
	1980–2006	Jeanne and Guscina (2006), Bank of Thailand	
Tunisia	1972–1982	LofN, UN	Lcu
	2004–2007	Central Bank of Tunisia	Lcu
Turkey	1933–1984	LofN, UN	Lcu
	1986–2007	Turkish Treasury	U.S. dollar
United Kingdom	1693–1786	Quinn (2004)	Total funded debt
	1781–1915	Page (1919), Bazant (1968)	1787–1815, not continuous
	1850–2007	U.K. Debt Management Office	
United States	1791–2007	Treasury Direct	
Uruguay	1914–1947	LofN, UN	Lcu
	1972–1984		
	1999–2007	Banco Central del Uruguay	U.S. dollar
Venezuela	1914–1982	LofN, UN	
	1983–2005	Jeanne and Guscina (2006)	
Zimbabwe	1924–1936	Frankel (1938)	U.K. pound
	1969–1982	UN	

TABLE A.2.3
External public debt

Country	Period covered	Source	Commentary
Algeria	1970–2005	GFD	U.S. dollar
Angola	1989–2005	GFD	U.S. dollar
Argentina	1863–1971	Garcia Vizcaino (1972)	Lcu
	1914–1981	LofN, UN	Lcu
	1970–2005	GFD	U.S. dollar
Australia	1852–1914	Page (1919)	
	1914–1981	LofN, UN	Lcu
	1980–2007	Australian Office of Financial Management	Lcu
Austria	1945–1984	UN	Lcu
	1970–2006	Austrian Federal Financing Agency	Euro
Belgium	1914–1981	LofN, UN	Lcu
	1992–2007		
Bolivia	1914–1953	LofN, UN	Lcu
	1968–1981		
	1970–2005	GFD	
	1991–2004	CLYPS	U.S. dollar
Brazil	1824–2000	Instituto Brasileiro de Geografia e Estatistica	U.K. pound and U.S. dollar
	1923–1972	LofN, UN	Lcu
	1970–2005	GFD	U.S. dollar
	1991–2005	Jeanne and Guscina (2006)	U.S. dollar
Canada	1867–2007	Statistics Canada, Bank of Canada	Lcu
Central African Republic	1970–2005	GFD	U.S. dollar
Chile	1822–2000	Díaz et al. (2005)	Lcu
	1970–2005	GFD	U.S. dollar
	1822–1930	RR (2008c)	Estimated from debentures
China	1865–1925	RR (2008c)	Estimated from debentures
	1981–2005	GFD	U.S. dollar

(continued)

TABLE A.2.3 Continued

Country	Period covered	Source	Commentary
Colombia	1923–2006	Contraloria General de la Republica	Lcu
Costa Rica	1892–1914	Soley Güell (1926)	Lcu
	1914–1983	LofN, UN	Lcu
	1980–2007	CLYPS, Ministerio de Hacienda	U.S. dollar
Côte d'Ivoire	1970–2005	GFD	U.S. dollar
Dominican Republic	1914–1952	LofN, UN	Lcu
	1961–2004	Banco de la Republica	U.S. dollar
Ecuador	1914–1972	LofN, UN	Lcu
	1970–2005	GFD	U.S. dollar
	1990–2007	Ministry of Finance	U.S. dollar
Egypt	1862–1930	RR	Estimated from debentures
	1914–1959	LofN, UN	Lcu
	1970–2005	GFD	U.S. dollar
France	1913–1972	LofN, UN	Lcu
	1999–2007	Ministère du Budget, des comptes public	Lcu
Germany	1914–1983	LofN, UN	Lcu
Greece	1920–1983	LofN, UN	Lcu
Guatemala	1921–1982	LofN, UN	Lcu
	1970–2005	GFD	U.S. dollar
	1980–2005	CLYPS	U.S. dollar
Honduras	1914–1971	LofN, UN	Lcu
	1970–2005	GDF	U.S. dollar
	1980–2005		U.S. dollar
Hungary	1913–1942	LofN, UN	Lcu
	1982–2005	GDF	U.S. dollar
	1992–2005	Jeanne and Guscina (2006)	
India	1840–1920	Statistical Abstract Relating to British India (various years)	
	1913–1983	LofN, UN	Lcu
	1980–2005	Jeanne and Guscina (2006)	

TABLE A.2.3 Continued

Country	Period covered	Source	Commentary
Indonesia	1972–1983	UN	Lcu
	1970–2005	GDF	U.S. dollar
Italy	1880–1913	Flandreau and Zumer (2004)	Lcu
	1914–1984	LofN, UN	Lcu
	1982–2007	Dipartamento del Tesoro	Lcu
Japan	1872–2007	Historical Statistics of Japan, Bank of Japan	Lcu
	1910–1938	Mizoguchi and Umemura (1988)	Yen
Kenya	1961–1980	LofN, UN	Lcu
	1970–2005	GDF	U.S. dollar
	1997–2007	Central Bank of Kenya	Lcu
Korea	1970–1984	LofN, UN	Lcu
	1970–2005	GDF	U.S. dollar
	1990–2004	Jeanne and Guscina (2006)	U.S. dollar
Malaysia	1947–1957	LofN, UN	Lcu
	1976–1981		
	1970–2005	GDF	U.S. dollar
	1980–2004	Jeanne and Guscina (2006)	
Mauritius	1970–1984	LofN, UN	Lcu
	1970–2005	GDF	U.S. dollar
	1998–2007	Bank of Mauritius	Lcu
Mexico	1814–1946	Bazant (1968)	Not continuous
	1820–1930	RR (2008c)	Estimated from debentures
	1914–1979	LofN, UN	Lcu
	1970–2005	GDF	U.S. dollar
	1980–2006	Direccion General de la Deuda Publica	
Morocco	1965–1980	UN	Lcu
	1970–2005	GDF	U.S. dollar
The Netherlands	1880–1914	Flandreau and Zumer (2004)	Lcu
	1914–1977	LofN, UN	Lcu
	1914–2008	Dutch State Treasury Agency	Lcu
New Zealand	1858–2006	Statistics New Zealand, New Zealand Treasury	Lcu

(*continued*)

TABLE A.2.3 Continued

Country	Period covered	Source	Commentary
Nicaragua	1914–1945	LofN, UN	Lcu
	1970–1983		
	1970–2005	GDF	U.S. dollar
	1991–2005	CLYPS	U.S. dollar
Norway	1880–1914	Flandreau and Zumer (2004)	Lcu
	1913–1983	LofN, UN	Lcu
	1965–2007	Ministry of Finance	Lcu
Panama	1915–1983	LofN, UN	U.S. dollar
	1980–2005	CLYPS	U.S. dollar
Paraguay	1927–1947	LofN, UN	Lcu
	1976–1982		
	1970–2005	GFD	U.S. dollar
	1990–2004	CLYPS	U.S. dollar
Peru	1822–1930	RR (2008c)	Estimated from debentures
	1918–1970	LofN, UN	Lcu
	1990–2005	CLYPS	U.S. dollar
	1970–2005	GFD	U.S. dollar
The Philippines	1948–1982	LofN, UN	Lcu
	1970–2005	GFD	U.S. dollar
Poland	1920–1947	LofN, UN	Lcu
	1986–2005	GFD	U.S. dollar
Portugal	1851–1997	Instituto Nacional Estadisticas– Portuguese Statistical Agency	
	1914–1975	LofN, UN	Lcu
	1980–2007	Banco de Portugal	In euros from 1999
Russia	1815–1917	RR (2008c)	
	1922–1938	LofN, UN	Lcu
	1993–2005	Jeanne and Guscina (2006)	
Singapore	1969–1982	UN	Lcu
South Africa	1859–1914	Page (1919)	U.K. pound
	1910–1983	LofN, UN	Lcu
	1946–2006	South Africa Reserve Bank	Lcu
Spain	1850–2001	Estadisticas Historicas de España: Siglos XIX–XX	Lcu
	1999–2006	Banco de España	Euro

TABLE A.2.3 Continued

Country	Period covered	Source	Commentary
Sri Lanka	1950–1983	UN	Lcu
	1970–2005	GFD	U.S. dollar
	1990–2006	Central Bank of Sri Lanka	Lcu
Sweden	1914–1984	LofN, UN	Lcu
	1950–2006	Riksgälden	Lcu
Thailand (Siam)	1913–1984	LofN, UN	Lcu
	1970–2005	GFD	U.S. dollar
	1980–2006	Jeanne and Guscina (2006), Bank of Thailand	Lcu
Tunisia	1970–2005	GFD	U.S. dollar
	2004–2007	Central Bank of Tunisia	Lcu
	1972–1982	LofN, UN	Lcu
Turkey	1854–1933	RR (2008c)	Estimated from debentures
	1933–1984	LofN, UN	Lcu
	1970–2005	GFD	U.S. dollar
	1986–2007	Turkish Treasury	U.S. dollar
United Kingdom	1914–2007	LofN, UN	Lcu
Uruguay	1871–1930	RR (2008c)	Estimated from debentures
	1914–1947, 1972–1984	LofN, UN	Lcu
	1970–2005	GFD	U.S. dollar
	1980–2004	CLYPS	U.S. dollar
Venezuela	1822–1842	RR (2008c)	Estimated from debentures, U.S. dollar
	1914–1982	LofN, UN	Lcu
Zambia	1970–2005	GFD	
Zimbabwe	1969–1982	UN	Lcu
	1970–2005	GFD	U.S. dollar

TABLE A.2.4
Domestic public debt

Country	Period covered	Source	Commentary
Argentina	1863–1971	Garcia Vizcaino (1972)	Lcu
	1914–1981	LofN, UN	Lcu
	1980–2005	GFD, Jeanne and Guscina (2006)	
Australia	1914–1981	LofN, UN	Lcu
	1980–2007	Australian Office of Financial Management	Lcu
Austria	1945–1984	UN	Lcu
	1970–2006	Austrian Federal Financing Agency	Euro
Belgium	1914–1983	LofN, UN	Lcu
	1992–2007	BNB, Centre d'études économiques de la KUL	
Bolivia	1914–1953	LofN, UN	Lcu
	1968–1981		
	1991–2004	CLYPS	U.S. dollar
Brazil	1923–1972	LofN, UN	Lcu
	1991–2005	GFD, Jeanne and Guscina (2006)	
Canada	1867–2007	Statistics Canada, Bank of Canada	Lcu
Chile	1827–2000	Díaz et al. (2005)	Lcu
	1914–1953	LofN, UN	Lcu
	1914–1946	UN	
	1990–2007	Ministerio de Hacienda	U.S. dollar
China	1894–1949	RR (2008c)	Lcu
Colombia	1923–2006	Contraloria General de la Republica	Lcu
Costa Rica	1892–1914	Soley Güell (1926)	Lcu
	1914–1983	LofN, UN	Lcu
	1980–2007	CLYPS, Ministerio de Hacienda	U.S. dollar
Côte d'Ivoire	1970–1980	UN	Lcu
Denmark	1914–1975	LofN, UN	Lcu
	1990–2007	Danmarks Nationalbank	Lcu

340

TABLE A.2.4 Continued

Country	Period covered	Source	Commentary
Dominican Republic	1914–1952	LofN, UN	Lcu
Ecuador	1914–1972	LofN, UN	Lcu
	1990–2006	Ministry of Finance	U.S. dollar
Egypt	1914–1959	LofN, UN	Lcu
	2001–2005	Ministry of Finance	Lcu
France	1913–1972	LofN, UN	Lcu
	1999–2007	Ministère du Budget, des comptes public	Lcu
Greece	1920–1983	LofN, UN	Lcu
	1912–1941	UN	
Guatemala	1921–1982	LofN, UN	Lcu
	1980–2005	CLYPS	U.S. dollar
Honduras	1914–1971	LofN, UN	Lcu
	1980–2005		U.S. dollar
Hungary	1913–1942	LofN, UN	Lcu
	1992–2005	Jeanne and Guscina (2006)	
India	1840–1920	Statistical Abstract Relating to British India (various years)	
	1913–1983	LofN, UN	Lcu
	1980–2005	Jeanne and Guscina (2006)	
Indonesia	1972–1983	UN	Lcu
	1998–2005	Bank Indonesia, GDF	
Italy	1880–1913	Flandreau and Zumer (2004)	Lcu
	1882–2007	Dipartamento del Tesoro	Lcu
	1894–1914	LofN, UN	Lcu
Japan	1872–2007	Historical Statistics of Japan, Bank of Japan	Lcu
	1914–1946	UN	
Kenya	1961–1980	LofN, UN	Lcu
	1997–2007	Central Bank of Kenya	Lcu
Korea	1970–1984	LofN, UN	Lcu
	1990–2004	Jeanne and Guscina (2006)	Lcu

(*continued*)

TABLE A.2.4 Continued

Country	Period covered	Source	Commentary
Malaysia	1947–1957	LofN, UN	Lcu
	1976–1981		
	1980–2004	Jeanne and Guscina (2006)	
Mauritius	1970–1984	LofN, UN	Lcu
	1998–2007	Bank of Mauritius	Lcu
Mexico	1814–1946	Bazant (1968)	Not continuous
	1914–1979	LofN, UN	Lcu
	1980–2006	Direccion General de la Deuda Publica	
Morocco	1965–1980	UN	Lcu
The Netherlands	1880–1914	Flandreau and Zumer (2004)	Lcu
	1914–1977	LofN, UN	Lcu
	1914–2008	Dutch State Treasury Agency	Lcu
New Zealand	1858–2006	Statistics New Zealand, New Zealand Treasury	Lcu
Nicaragua	1914–1945	LofN, UN	Lcu
	1970–1983		
	1991–2005	CLYPS	U.S. dollar
Norway	1880–1914	Flandreau and Zumer (2004)	Lcu
	1913–1983	LofN, UN	Lcu
	1965–2007	Ministry of Finance	Lcu
Panama	1915–1983	LofN, UN	U.S. dollar
	1980–2005	CLYPS	U.S. dollar
Paraguay	1927–1947	LofN, UN	Lcu
	1976–1982		
	1990–2004	CLYPS	U.S. dollars
Peru	1918–1970	LofN, UN	Lcu
	1990–2005	CLYPS	U.S. dollar
The Philippines	1948–1982	LofN, UN	Lcu
	1980–2005	GFD, Jeanne and Guscina (2006)	
Poland	1920–1947	LofN, UN	Lcu
	1994–2004	Jeanne and Guscina (2006)	Lcu

TABLE A.2.4 Continued

Country	Period covered	Source	Commentary
Portugal	1851–1997	Instituto Nacional Estadisticas–Portuguese Statistical Agency	Lcu
	1914–1975	LofN, UN	Lcu
	1980–2007	Banco de Portugal	In euros from 1999
Russia	1922–1938	LofN, UN	Lcu
	1993–2005	Jeanne and Guscina (2006)	
Singapore	1969–1982	UN	Lcu
	1986–2006	Monetary Authority	Lcu
South Africa	1859–1914	Page (1919)	U.K. pound
	1910–1983	LofN, UN	Lcu
	1946–2006	South Africa Reserve Bank	Lcu
Spain	1850–2001	Estadisticas Historicas de España: Siglos XIX–XX	Lcu
	1999–2006	Banco de España	Euro
Sri Lanka	1950–1983	UN	Lcu
	1990–2006	Central Bank of Sri Lanka	Lcu
Sweden	1914–1984	LofN, UN	Lcu
	1950–2006	Riksgälden	Lcu
Thailand (Siam)	1913–1984	LofN, UN	Lcu
	1980–2006	Jeanne and Guscina (2006), Bank of Thailand	Lcu
Tunisia	1972–1982	UN	Lcu
	2004–2007	Central Bank of Tunisia	Lcu
Turkey	1933–1984	LofN, UN	Lcu
	1986–2007	Turkish Treasury	U.S. dollar
United Kingdom	1914–2007	LofN, UN	Lcu
United States	1791–2007	Treasury Direct	Lcu
Uruguay	1914–1947	LofN, UN	Lcu
	1972–1984		
	1980–2004	CLYPS	U.S. dollar
Venezuela	1914–1982	LofN, UN	Lcu
	1983–2005	Jeanne and Guscina (2006)	Lcu
Zimbabwe	1969–1982	UN	Lcu

APPENDIX A.3
DATES OF BANKING CRISES

TABLE A.3.1
Banking crisis dates and capital mobility, 1800–2008

High-income countries		Middle-income countries		Low-income countries	
Country(ies)	Beginning year	Country(ies)	Beginning year	Country(ies)	Beginning year
Capital mobility: Low–moderate, 1800–1879					
France	1802				
France	1805				
United Kingdom	1810				
Sweden	1811				
Denmark	1813				
Spain, United States	1814				
United Kingdom	1815				
United States	1818				
United Kingdom, United States	1825				
United States	1836				
Canada, United Kingdom	1837				
United Kingdom	1847				
Belgium	1848				
United Kingdom, United States	1857			India	1863
Italy, United Kingdom	1866				
Austria, United States	1873	Peru	1873		
		South Africa	1877		
Capital mobility: High, 1880–1914					
Germany	1880				
France	1882	Mexico	1883		
United States	1884				
Denmark	1885				
Italy	1887				
France	1889				

TABLE A.3.1 Continued

High-income countries		Middle-income countries		Low-income countries	
Country(ies)	Beginning year	Country(ies)	Beginning year	Country(ies)	Beginning year
Portugal, United Kingdom, United States	1890	Argentina,* Brazil, Chile, Paraguay, South Africa	1890		
Germany, Italy, Portugal	1891				
Australia	1893	Uruguay	1893		
The Netherlands, Sweden	1897				
Norway	1898	Chile	1899		
Finland	1900	Brazil	1900		
Germany, Japan	1901				
Denmark, France, Italy, Japan, Sweden, United States	1907	Mexico	1907		
		Chile	1908		
		Mexico	1913	India	1913
Belgium, France,* Italy, Japan, the Netherlands, Norway,* United Kingdom, United States	1914	Argentina,* Brazil*	1914		

Capital mobility: Low, 1915–1919

		Chile*	1915		

Capital mobility: Moderate, 1920–1929

Portugal*	1920	Mexico	1920		
Finland, Italy, the Netherlands,* Norway*	1921			India	1921
Canada, Japan, Taiwan	1923	China	1923		
Austria	1924				
Belgium,* Germany*	1925	Brazil, Chile*	1926		
Japan, Taiwan	1927				
United States*	1929	Brazil, Mexico*	1929	India	1929

Capital Mobility: Low, 1930–1969

France, Italy	1930				
Austria, Belgium, Finland, Germany,* Greece, Norway, Portugal,* Spain,* Sweden,* Switzerland	1931	Argentina,* Brazil, China, Czechoslovakia, Estonia, Hungary, Latvia, Poland, Romania, and Turkey	1931		

(continued)

TABLE A.3.1 Continued

High-income countries		Middle-income countries		Low-income countries	
Country(ies)	Beginning year	Country(ies)	Beginning year	Country(ies)	Beginning year
Belgium*	1934	Argentina, China	1934		
Italy	1935	Brazil	1937		
Belgium,* Finland	1939				
				India*	1947
		Brazil	1963		
Capital mobility: Moderate, 1970–1979					
		Uruguay	1971		
United Kingdom	1974	Chile*	1976	Central African Republic	1976
Germany, Israel, Spain	1977	South Africa	1977		
		Venezuela	1978		
Capital mobility: High, 1980–2007					
		Argentina,* Chile,* Ecuador, Egypt	1980		
		Mexico, the Philippines Uruguay	1981		
Hong Kong, Singapore	1982	Colombia, Turkey	1982	Congo (Democratic Republic of), Ghana	1982
Canada, Korea, Kuwait Taiwan	1983	Morocco, Peru, Thailand	1983	Equatorial Guinea, Niger	1983
United Kingdom, United States	1984			Mauritania	1984
		Argentina,* Brazil,* Malaysia*	1985	Guinea, Kenya	1985
Denmark, New Zealand, Norway	1987	Bolivia, Cameroon, Costa Rica, Nicaragua	1987	Bangladesh, Mali, Mozambique, Tanzania	1987
		Lebanon, Panama	1988	Benin, Burkina Faso, Central African Republic, Côte d'Ivoire, Madagascar, Nepal, Senegal	1988
Australia	1989	Argentina,* El Salvador, South Africa, Sri Lanka	1989		
Italy	1990	Algeria, Brazil,* Egypt, Romania	1990	Sierra Leone	1990
Czech Republic, Finland, Greece, Sweden, United Kingdom	1991	Georgia, Hungary, Poland, Slovak Republic	1991	Djibouti, Liberia, Sao Tome	1991
Japan	1992	Albania, Bosnia-Herzegovina, Estonia, Indonesia	1992	Angola, Chad, China, Congo, Kenya, Nigeria	1992

346

TABLE A.3.1 Continued

High-income countries		Middle-income countries		Low-income countries	
Country(ies)	Beginning year	Country(ies)	Beginning year	Country(ies)	Beginning year
Macedonia, Slovenia	1993	Cape Verde, Venezuela	1993	Guinea, Eritrea, India, Kyrgyz Republic, Togo	1993
Capital mobility: High, 1980–2007					
France	1994	Armenia, Bolivia, Bulgaria, Costa Rica, Jamaica, Latvia, Mexico,* Turkey	1994	Burundi, Congo (Republic of), Uganda	1994
United Kingdom	1995	Argentina, Azerbaijan, Brazil, Cameroon, Lithuania, Paraguay, Russia, Swaziland,	1995	Guinea-Bissau, Zambia, Zimbabwe	1995
		Croatia, Ecuador, Thailand	1996	Myanmar, Yemen	1996
Taiwan	1997	Indonesia, Korea,* Malaysia, Mauritius, the Philippines, Ukraine	1997	Vietnam	1997
		Colombia,* Ecuador, El Salvador, Russia	1998		
		Bolivia, Honduras, Peru	1999		
		Nicaragua	2000		
		Argentina,* Guatemala	2001		
		Paraguay, Uruguay	2002		
		Dominican Republic	2003		
		Guatemala	2006		
Iceland, Ireland, United States, United Kingdom	2007				
Austria, Spain	2008				

Note: Appendix A.4 contains more information on episodes listed in this table and includes some selected milder episodes. An asterisk (*) denotes that the episode in question was associated with an output collapse as defined by Barro and Ursua (2008). However, many of the countries in our extended sample are not covered by Barro and Ursua.

APPENDIX A.4
HISTORICAL SUMMARIES
OF BANKING CRISES

TABLE A.4.1

Banking crises: Historical summaries, 1800–2008

Country	Brief summary	Year	Source
Albania	After the July 1992 cleanup, 31 percent of "new" banking system loans were nonperforming. Some banks faced liquidity problems due to a logjam of interbank liabilities.	1992	Caprio and Klingebiel (2003)
Algeria	Circulation limits led to suspended specie payments. Lack of mortgage banking institutes led banks to secure loans based on real estate; many were foreclosed to escape loss.	August 1870	Conant (1915), Reinhart and Rogoff (2008a)
	The share of banking system non-performing loans reached 50 percent.	1990–1992	Caprio and Klingebiel (2003)
Angola	Two state-owned commercial banks had insolvency problems.	1992–1996	Caprio and Klingebiel (2003)
Argentina	The operation of National Bank of the Argentine Republic was suspended; high levels of foreign debt, domestic credit, and imports led to reserve losses; the peso fell 27 percent, but the crisis was brief and had relatively little impact on industrial production.	January 1885	Conant (1915), Bordo and Eichengreen (1999)
	Banks made extensive loans, and real estate prices rose dramatically with the excess issue of bank notes. Land	July 1890–1891	Bordo and Eichengreen (1999), Conant (1915)

TABLE A.4.1 Continued

Country	Brief summary	Year	Source
	prices fell by 50 percent; and Bank of the Nation could not pay its dividend, leading to a run; and the peso fell 36 percent both years. In July 1890, every bank of issue was suspended, sending gold up 320 percent. In December 1890, the Bank of the Argentine Nation replaced the old Bank of the Nation.		
	Bad harvests and European demands for liquidity due to the war led to bank runs, with private banks losing 45 percent of deposits in two years	1914	Conant (1915), Bordo and Eichengreen (1999), Nakamura and Zarazaga (2001)
	The gold standard was ended, with insolvent loans building.	1931	della Paolera and Taylor (1999), Bordo et al. (2001)
	Huge loans to the government and nonperforming assets had been building for many years; finally all were taken over by the new Central Bank.	1934	della Paolera and Taylor (1999), Bordo et al. (2001)
	The failure of a large private bank (Banco de Intercambio Regional) led to runs on three other banks. Eventually more than seventy institutions—representing 16 percent of commercial bank assets and 35 percent of finance company assets—were liquidated or subjected to central bank intervention.	March 1980–1982	Kaminsky and Reinhart (1999), Bordo et al. (2001), Caprio and Klingebiel (2003)
	In early May, the government closed a large bank, leading to large runs, which led the government to freeze dollar deposits on May 19.	May 1985	Kaminsky and Reinhart (1999)
	Nonperforming assets accounted for 27 percent of aggregate portfolios and 37 percent of state banks' portfolios. Failed banks held 40 percent of financial system assets.	1989–1990	Bordo et al. (2001), Caprio and Klingebiel (2003)
	The Mexican devaluation led to a run on the banks, which resulted in an 18 percent decline in deposits between December and March. Eight	1995	Bordo et al. (2001), Reinhart (2002), Caprio and Klingebiel (2003)

(continued)

TABLE A.4.1 Continued

Country	Brief summary	Year	Source
	banks suspended operations, and three banks collapsed. Through the end of 1997, 63 of 205 banking institutions were closed or merged. In March 2001, a bank run started due to a lack of public confidence in government policy actions. In late November 2001, many banks were on the verge of collapsing, and partial withdrawal restrictions were imposed (*corralito*) and fixed-term deposits (CDs) were repro-grammed to stop outflows from banks (*corralon*). In December 2002, the *corralito* was lifted. In January 2003, one bank was closed, three banks were nationalized, and many others were reduced in size.	March 2001	Caprio and Klingebiel (2003), Jácome (2008)
Armenia	The Central Bank closed half the active banks; large banks continued to suffer from a high level of non-performing loans. The savings bank was financially weak.	August 1994–1996	Caprio and Klingebiel (2003)
Australia	A domestic lending boom showed the deteriorated quality of bank assets; a land boom and unregulated banking system led to speculation. Closure of Mercantile Bank in Australia and the Federal Bank of Australia meant that British deposits ran off. Bank share prices fell heavily, banks retrenched and stopped long-term loans, and many closed. The depression of the 1890s followed.	January 1893	Conant (1915), Bordo and Eichengreen (1999)
	Two large banks received capital from the government to cover losses.	1989–1992	Bordo et al. (2001), Caprio and Klingebiel (2003)
Austria	There was speculation in the economy; the crash of the Vienna Stock Exchange led firty-two banks and forty-four provincial banks to fail.	May 1873–1874	Conant (1915)

350

TABLE A.4.1 Continued

Country	Brief summary	Year	Source
	There were difficulties in the major bank; liquidation began in June.	1924	Bernanke and James (1990)
	The second-largest bank failed and merged with the major bank.	November 1929	Bernanke and James (1990)
	Creditanstalt failed, and there was a run of foreign depositors.	May 1931	Bernanke and James (1990)
Azerbaijan	Twelve private banks closed; three large state-owned banks were deemed insolvent, and one faced serious liquidity problems.	1995	Caprio and Klingebiel (2003)
Bangladesh	Four banks, accounting for 70 percent of credit, had 20 percent non-performing loans. From the late 1980s, the entire private and public banking system was technically insolvent.	1987–1996	Bordo et al. (2001), Caprio and Klingebiel (2003)
Belarus	Many banks were undercapitalized; forced mergers burdened some banks with poor loan portfolios.	1995	Caprio and Klingebiel (2003)
Belgium	There were two rival banks: the Bank of Belgium (created in 1835) and the Société Générale. Fear of war led to credit contraction. The Société tried to bankrupt the Bank of Belgium by redeeming large amounts of credit, weakening both. There were runs on Bank of Belgium; it did not suspend payment but appealed to the treasury for assistance.	December 1838–1839	Conant (1915)
	The Bank of Belgium resigned its function as state depository to the Société Générale; the Société felt the impact of the crisis and abandoned all branches except that at Antwerp.	1842	Conant (1915)
	The Société Générale suspended payments and lost the right of issue after the government demanded reform. The National Bank of Belgium was created.	February 1848	Conant (1915)

(continued)

351

TABLE A.4.1 Continued

Country	Brief summary	Year	Source
	There was public fear due to state decisions and burdens, but the Bank of Belgium reassured people by continuing payments (it raised the discount rate and placed restrictions on acceptance of commercial paper) —at great cost to commerce and the bank.	July 1870–1871	Conant (1915)
	Worldwide investors dumped assets and withdrew liquidity, pushing prices down and threatening financial institutions with failure. Stock exchanges around the world collapsed.	1914	Bordo et al. (2001)
	Systemic deflation led to a funding crisis.	1925–1926	Johnson (1998), Bordo et al. (2001)
	Rumors about the imminent failure of the Bank of Brussels, the largest bank, led to withdrawals from all banks. Later, expectations of devaluations led to withdrawals of foreign deposits.	May 1931	Bernanke and James (1990), Bordo et al. (2001)
	Failure of the Banque Belge de Travail developed into a general banking and exchange crisis.	1934	Bernanke and James (1990), Bordo et al. (2001)
	The economy was slowly recovering, although the prospect of war hampered investment decisions. Foreign exchange and gold reserves diminished dramatically.	1939	Bordo et al. (2001)
Benin	All three commercial banks collapsed, and 80 percent of banks' loan portfolios were nonperforming.	1988–1990	Caprio and Klingebiel (2003)
Bolivia	In October 1987, the central bank liquidated two of twelve state commercial banks; seven more reported large losses. In total, five banks were liquidated. Banking system nonperforming loans reached 30 percent in 1987 and 92 percent by mid-1988.	October 1987–1988	Kaminsky and Reinhart (1999), Caprio and Klingebiel (2003)
	Two banks, with 11 percent of banking system assets, closed in 1994. In 1995, four of fifteen domestic banks, with	1994	Caprio and Klingebiel (2003)

TABLE A.4.1 Continued

Country	Brief summary	Year	Source
	30 percent of banking system assets, experienced liquidity problems and suffered a high level of nonperforming loans. One small bank (with a market share of 4.5 percent of deposits) was intervened and resolved.	1999	Jácome (2008)
Bosnia and Herzegovina	The banking system suffered from a high level of nonperforming loans due to the breakup of the former Yugoslavia and the civil war.	1992–?	Caprio and Klingebiel (2003)
Botswana	Banks merged, liquidated, or recapitalized.	1994–1995	Caprio and Klingebiel (2003)
Brazil	There was a large amount of government borrowing and currency speculation; the government continually issued more notes. The National Bank of Brazil and Bank of the U.S. of Brazil merged into the Bank of the Republic of the U.S. of Brazil. The new bank retired the government's paper notes. Turmoil in the financial sector led to a decline in output.	December 1890–1892	Conant (1915), Bordo and Eichengreen (1999)
	There was a civil war and currency depreciation. A loan from Rothschild's in London helped, with an agreement made on settling the country's debt.	1897–1898	Conant (1915), Bordo and Eichengreen (1999)
	Inelastic coffee exports could not respond to currency depreciation; there was concentrated industry, limited competition, and slowed recovery from deflation. Liquidity injection did not help; deposits ran off, and loans were recalled.	1900–1901	Conant (1915), Bordo and Eichengreen (1999)
	Payments were suspended due to the difficulty of international remittance.	1914	Brown (1940), Bordo et al. (2001)
	The treasury supported large budget deficits by issuing notes for discount at the Banco de Brasil. High inflation and public dissatisfaction led to the	1923	Triner (2000), Bordo et al. (2001)

(continued)

TABLE A.4.1 Continued

Country	Brief summary	Year	Source
	reestablishment of the gold standard, and a new government reorganized the Banco de Brasil, making it the central bank. However, it failed to operate independent of political control. The banking sector contracted by 20 percent in the next three years due to diminished money supply.		
	Overaccumulation of capital came at the expense of urban workers, and the economic structures could not adjust to accommodate these pressures by changing wages. The economic crisis led to a political one, and a military coup resulted.	1963	Bordo et al. (2001)
	Three large banks (Comind, Maison Nave, and Auxiliar) were taken over by the government.	November 1985	Kaminsky and Reinhart (1999)
	Deposits were converted to bonds.	1990	Bordo et al. (2001), Caprio and Klingebiel (2003)
	In 1994, seventeen small banks were liquidated, three private banks were intervened, and eight state banks were placed under administration. The Central Bank intervened in or put under temporary administration forty-three financial institutions, and banking system nonperforming loans reached 15 percent by the end of 1997. Private banks returned to profitability in 1998, but public banks did not begin to recover until 1999.	July 1994–1996	Kaminsky and Reinhart (1999), Bordo et al. (2001), Caprio and Klingebiel (2003)
Brunei	Several financial firms and banks failed.	1986	Caprio and Klingebiel (2003)
Bulgaria	In 1995, about 75 percent of banking system loans were substandard. There was a banking system run in early 1996. The government stopped providing bailouts, prompting the closure of nineteen banks accounting for one-	1995–1997	Caprio and Klingebiel (2003)

TABLE A.4.1 Continued

Country	Brief summary	Year	Source
	third of sector assets. The surviving banks were recapitalized by 1997.		
Burkina Faso	Banking system nonperforming loans were estimated at 34 percent.	1988–1994	Caprio and Klingebiel (2003)
Burundi	Banking system nonperforming loans were estimated at 25 percent in 1995, and one bank was liquidated.	1994–1995	Caprio and Klingebiel (2003)
Cameroon	In 1989, banking system nonperforming loans reached 60–70 percent. Five commercial banks were closed and three restructured.	1987–1993	Caprio and Klingebiel (2003)
	At the end of 1996, nonperforming loans were 30 percent of total loans. Two banks were closed and three restructured.	1995–1998	Caprio and Klingebiel (2003)
Canada	The Bank of Upper Canada and Gore Bank suspended specie payments; a rebellion in Lower Canada led to suspension of payments.	1837	Conant (1915)
	A bank in Western Canada suspended payments, leading to financial panic. The Bank of Upper Canada failed; there was rapid growth in Ontario, and the bank lost capital in land speculation in 1857; it abandoned safe banking practices and made loans to lawyers, politicians, and the gentry.	September 1866	Conant (1915)
	There were several bank failures and a depression from 1874 to 1879.	September 1873	Conant (1915)
	Ontario Bank failed due to speculation in the N.Y. stock market; shareholders lost their entire investments.	October 1906	Conant (1915)
	A current account deficit and a crop failure meant that eastern banks were unwilling to ship funds west; banks raised their loan rates, cut lending, and limited credit to farmers. There was a short but sharp recession; Canadian banks borrowed dominion	January 1908	Conant (1915), Bordo and Eichengreen (1999)

(continued)

355

TABLE A.4.1 Continued

Country	Brief summary	Year	Source
	notes, and banks increased their note issue.		
	The Royal Bank acquired the Bank of British Honduras and Bank of British Guiana.	1912	Conant (1915)
	The Home Bank of Canada, with over seventy branches, failed due to bad loans.	1923	Kryzanowski and Roberts (1999), Bordo et al. (2001)
	Fifteen members of the Canadian Deposit Insurance Corporation, including two banks, failed.	1983–1985	Bordo et al. (2001), Caprio and Klingebiel (2003)
Cape Verde	At the end of 1995, commercial banks' nonperforming loans reached 30 percent.	1993	Caprio and Klingebiel (2003)
Central African Republic	Four banks were liquidated.	1976–1982	Caprio and Klingebiel (2003)
	The two largest banks, with 90 percent of assets, were restructured. Banking system nonperforming loans reached 40 percent.	1988–1999	Caprio and Klingebiel (2003)
Chad	The banking sector experienced solvency problems.	1980s	Caprio and Klingebiel (2003)
	Private sector nonperforming loans reached 35 percent.	1992	Caprio and Klingebiel (2003)
Chile	The bank currency system and gold standard were completely wrecked by the threat of war with the Argentine Republic. On July 5, growing exports of gold and the Bank of Chile's refusal to honor gold drafts led to a run on banks at Santiago and general suspicion of gold drafts. The government issued irredeemable paper money, constantly increasing the monetary supply for the next ten years, leading to a period of inflation and overspeculation.	July 1898	Conant (1915), Bordo and Eichengreen (1999)
	There were four years of inflationary measures following a stock market crash; the peso fell 30 percent during	1907	Conant (1915), Bordo and Eichengreen (1999)

TABLE A.4.1 Continued

Country	Brief summary	Year	Source
	the crisis, and the government loaned treasury notes to banks to prevent a financial sector crisis. Data concerning the ensuing recession are unavailable.		
	The entire mortgage system became insolvent.	1976	Bordo et al. (2001), Caprio and Klingebiel (2003)
	Three banks began to lose deposits; interventions began two months later. Interventions occurred in four banks and four nonbank financial institutions, accounting for 33 percent of outstanding loans. In 1983, there were seven more bank interventions and one *financiera*, accounting for 45 percent of financial system assets. By the end of 1983, 19 percent of loans were nonperforming.	1980	Kaminsky and Reinhart (1999), Bordo et al. (2001), Caprio and Klingebiel (2003)
China	Failure of a major silk-trading company in Shanghai led to the bankruptcies of many local banks.	1883	Cheng (2003)
	The postwar depression led many banks to fail.	1923–1925	Young (1971)
	Shanghai closed all Chinese banks for the duration of the war.	1931	Cheng (2003)
	The flight of silver led to a huge economic downturn and financial crisis; the two major banks came under government control and were reorganized.	1934–1937	Cheng (2003)
	China's four large state-owned commercial banks, with 68 percent of banking system assets, were deemed insolvent. Banking system nonperforming loans were estimated at 50 percent.	1997–1999	Caprio and Klingebiel (2003)
Colombia	Banco Nacional became the first of six major banks and eight financial companies to be intervened, accounting for 25 percent of banking system assets.	July 1982–1987	Kaminsky and Reinhart (1999), Bordo et al. (2001), Caprio and Klingebiel (2003)

(continued)

TABLE A.4.1 Continued

Country	Brief summary	Year	Source
	Many banks and financial institutions failed; capitalization ratios and liquidity decreased dramatically, and the total assets of the financial industry contracted by more than 20 percent.	April 1998	Reinhart (2002), Jácome (2008)
Congo, Democratic Republic of	The banking sector experienced solvency problems.	1982	Caprio and Klingebiel (2003)
	Four state-owned banks were insolvent; a fifth was recapitalized with private participation.	1991–1992	Caprio and Klingebiel (2003)
	Nonperforming loans reached 75 percent. Two state-owned banks liquidated, and two privatized. In 1997, twelve banks had serious financial difficulties.	1994–?	Caprio and Klingebiel (2003)
Congo, Republic of	A crisis began in 1992. In 2001–2002, two large banks were restructured and privatized. The remaining insolvent bank was being liquidated.	1992–?	Caprio and Klingebiel (2003)
Costa Rica	In 1987, public banks accounting for 90 percent of banking system loans were in financial distress, with 32 percent of loans considered uncollectable.	1987	Caprio and Klingebiel (2003), Bordo et al. (2001)
	The third largest bank, Banco Anglo Costarricense, a state-owned institution with 17 percent of deposits, was closed.	1994–1997	Bordo et al. (2001), Caprio and Klingebiel (2003), Jácome (2008)
Côte d'Ivoire	Four large banks (with 90 percent of banking system loans) were affected; three or four were insolvent, and six government banks closed.	1988–1991	Bordo et al. (2001), Caprio and Klingebiel (2003)
Croatia	Five banks, accounting for about half of banking system loans, were deemed insolvent and taken over by the Bank Rehabilitation Agency.	1996	Caprio and Klingebiel (2003)
Czechoslovakia	Withdrawal of foreign deposits sparked domestic withdrawals but no general banking panic.	July 1931	Bernanke and James (1990)

TABLE A.4.1 Continued

Country	Brief summary	Year	Source
Czech Republic	There have been several bank closings since 1993. In 1994–1995, 38 percent of banking system loans were non-performing.	1991–?	Caprio and Klingebiel (2003)
Denmark	The government declared that it could not redeem Deposit Bank's Courant notes at their original value; this was a form of bankruptcy that diminished its public debt because notes were held by the people. The new Royal Bank was established; Courantbank, Specie Bank, and Deposit Bank were abolished.	January 1813	Conant (1915)
	A financial crisis led the National bank to assume central bank responsibilities through the 1860s.	1857	Jonung and Hagberg (2002)
	Industrial Bank diverted half its capital stock to cover its losses; two provincial banks failed, leading to a lull in the banking business.	1877	Conant (1915), Jonung and Hagberg (2002)
	National Bank intervened to provide support for commercial and savings banks.	1885	Jonung and Hagberg (2002)
	An important bank failure led to suspension of Freeholders' Bank and bank runs on other institutions. The National Bank helped alleviate panic; it took on the five remaining banks and suspended the banks' liabilities.	February 1902	Conant (1915)
	Turbulence in the world markets and Germany and nonperforming assets led to decreased confidence. A consortium of five leading banks assisted and guaranteed the liabilities of weak banks, leading to a quick recovery.	1907	Conant (1915), Bordo and Eichengreen (1999), Jonung and Hagberg (2002)
	Banking crises lasted for many years due to reckless lending during the war and the international downswing in prices in the early 1920s.	1921	Bordo et al. (2001), Jonung and Hagberg (2002)
	The banks suffered liquidity problems that lasted until the gold standard was abandoned.	1931	Bordo et al. (2001)

(continued)

359

TABLE A.4.1 Continued

Country	Brief summary	Year	Source
	Two small banks collapsed, which shook the banking system, leading to moves to curb bank lending. The cumulative losses over 1990–1992 were 9 percent of loans; forty of sixty problem banks were merged.	March 1987–1992	Kaminsky and Reinhart (1999), Bordo et al. (2001), Caprio and Klingebiel (2003)
Djibouti	Two of six commercial banks ceased operations, and other banks experienced difficulties.	1991–1993	Caprio and Klingebiel (2003)
Dominican Republic	The third largest bank, with a market share of 7 percent of assets, was intervened.	1996	Jácome (2008)
	The 2003 banking crisis started with the intervention of the third largest bank, with a market share of 10 percent. Deposit withdrawals had already started by mid-2002 following allegations of fraud resulting from the discovery of hidden liabilities recorded in a parallel bank. Immediately afterward, the crisis extended to two other institutions (with an additional 10 percent of market share) featuring similar inappropriate accounting practices.	2003	Jácome (2008)
Ecuador	A program for exchanging domestic for foreign debt was implemented to bail out the banking system.	1981	Bordo et al. (2001), Caprio and Klingebiel (2003)
	A medium-sized bank, Banco de los Andes, with a market share of 6 percent of deposits, was intervened and then purchased by another private bank.	1994	Jácome (2008)
	Authorities intervened in several small financial institutions; by the end of 1995, thirty financial societies (*sociedades financieras*) and seven banks were receiving extensive liquidity support. In	1996	Bordo et al. (2001), Caprio and Klingebiel (2003)

360

TABLE A.4.1 Continued

Country	Brief summary	Year	Source
	early 1996, the fifth largest commercial bank was intervened.		
	Banks amounting to 60 percent of the banking system were intervened, taken over, or closed. Seven financial institutions, accounting for 25–30 percent of commercial banking assets, were closed in 1998–1999. In March 1999, bank deposits were frozen for six months. By January 2000, sixteen financial institutions, accounting for 65 percent of the assets, had either been closed (twelve) or taken over (four) by the governments. All deposits were unfrozen by March 2000.	April 1998–1999	Caprio and Klingebiel (2003), Jácome (2008)
Egypt	A crisis developed due to credit abuse and the issue of new securities.	March 1907	Conant (1915)
	There was a run on the Cairo and Alexandria branches of German banks.	July 1931	Bernanke and James (1990)
	The government closed several large investment companies.	January 1980–1981	Bordo et al. (2001), Reinhart (2002), Caprio and Klingebiel (2003)
	Four public banks were given capital assistance.	January 1990–1995	Bordo et al. (2001), Reinhart (2002), Caprio and Klingebiel (2003)
El Salvador	Nine state-owned commercial banks had nonperforming loans averaging 37 percent.	1989	Caprio and Klingebiel (2003)
	After a sharp stop in economic growth in 1996 associated with a terms-of-trade deterioration (a decline in coffee prices), the financial system was stressed from 1997 onward. A small- to medium-sized institution (Banco Credisa), with a 5 percent market share, was closed.	1998	Jácome (2008)

(continued)

361

TABLE A.4.1 Continued

Country	Brief summary	Year	Source
Equatorial Guinea	Two of the country's largest banks were liquidated.	1983–1985	Caprio and Klingebiel (2003)
Eritrea	Most of the banking system was insolvent.	1993	Caprio and Klingebiel (2003)
Estonia	Two medium-sized banks failed; the ensuing panic lasted until January 1931.	November 1930	Bernanke and James (1990)
	There were waves of general bank runs.	September 1931	Bernanke and James (1990)
	Insolvent banks accounted for 41 percent of financial system assets. Five banks' licenses were revoked, and two major banks were merged and nationalized while two more merged and were converted to a loan recovery agency.	1992–1995	Caprio and Klingebiel (2003)
	The Social Bank, with 10 percent of financial system assets, failed.	1994	Caprio and Klingebiel (2003)
	Three banks failed.	1998	Caprio and Klingebiel (2003)
Ethiopia	The government-owned bank was restructured, and nonperforming loans taken over.	1994–1995	Caprio and Klingebiel (2003)
Finland	A crisis in Russia and the Balkans and export prices put the finance sector at risk. The Bank of Finland extended loans and note issues, but the growth rate of real GDP still fell by 4 percent.	1900	Bordo and Eichengreen (1999)
	The country fared better than other Nordic countries because its currency was already severely devalued, which also eased economic recovery.	1921	Bordo et al. (2001), Jonung and Hagberg (2002)
	A recession began in 1929; many banks were stuck with large losses, which led to bankruptcies; the Bank of Finland facilitated loans and mergers.	1931	Bordo et al. (2001), Jonung and Hagberg (2002)

TABLE A.4.1 Continued

Country	Brief summary	Year	Source
	Financial stability was maintained, and GDP growth did not suffer much.	1939	Bordo et al. (2001), Jonung and Hagberg (2002)
	A large bank (Skopbank) collapsed on September 19 and was intervened. Savings banks were badly affected; the government took control of three banks that together accounted for 31 percent of system deposits.	September 1991–1994	Kaminsky and Reinhart (1999), Bordo et al. (2001), Jonung and Hagberg (2002), Caprio and Klingebiel (2003)
France	The Bank of France experienced a serious crisis.	1802	Conant (1915)
	The Bank of France had a debt of 68 million francs with only 0.782 million francs in specie; it used commercial paper, government bonds, and credit to buy specie (from the Spanish treasury). This occurred after the formation of a third coalition against France during preparations for Austerlitz; the victory at Austerlitz (December 2, 1805) restored much confidence.	September 1805–1806	Conant (1915)
	There were bankruptcies in Alsace.	December 1827–1828	Conant (1915)
	There were severe runs on banks in Paris after the Bank of Belgium failed.	December 1838–1839	Conant (1915)
	On March 24, 1848, notes from the Bank of France and departmental banks were declared legal tender; the need for a uniform paper currency led to the consolidation of local banks with the Bank of France (April 27 and May 2).	February 1848–1850	Conant (1915)
	There was a French panic after cotton speculation.	January 1864	Conant (1915)
	A French crisis developed after the failure of Credit Mobilier.	November 1867–1868	Conant (1915)

(*continued*)

TABLE A.4.1 Continued

Country	Brief summary	Year	Source
	Branches of the Bank of France suspended their operations. After surrender, Germany suspended the Bank of Strasburg, and the Bank of Prussia replaced the Bank of France in Alsace-Lorraine.	May 1871	Conant (1915)
	Speculation and financial innovation led to problems among banks; the Bank of France extended loans to smaller banks and borrowed from the Bank of England to replenish its reserves. Growth fell by 5 percent that year and failed to recover to the previous trend for a long time.	February 1882	Conant (1915), Bordo and Eichengreen (1999)
	A French financier attempted to corner the copper market, while the Comptoir d'Escompte discounted copper warrants; the product limits broke down and copper prices fell, so the Comptoir suffered heavy losses. The head committed suicide, leading to a run; sound assets could not satisfy liquidity demands. Comptoir appealed to the Bank of France for help; growth fell by 14 percent during the crisis.	March 1889	Conant (1915), Bordo and Eichengreen (1999)
	There was a French banking panic; there had been a depression in Bourse since the beginning of the Russo–Japanese War.	February 1904	Conant (1915)
	Trouble in the United States raised the global demand for gold and money; a majority of France's losses were in silver to its colonies. As a result, the visible impact on GDP growth was mild.	1907	Conant (1915), Bordo and Eichengreen (1999)
	Two major banks failed, and there were runs on provincial banks.	1930–1932	Bernanke and James (1990), Bordo et al. (2001)

TABLE A.4.1 Continued

Country	Brief summary	Year	Source
	Crédit Lyonnaise had serious solvency problems.	1994–1995	Bordo et al. (2001), Caprio and Klingebiel (2003)
Gabon	One bank temporarily closed in 1995.	1995	Caprio and Klingebiel (2003)
Gambia	In 1992, a government bank was restructured and privatized.	1985–1992	Caprio and Klingebiel (2003)
Georgia	Most large banks were virtually insolvent. About one-third of banking system loans were nonperforming.	1991	Caprio and Klingebiel (2003)
Germany	Hamburg Bank was rescued by the Austrian National Bank; this restored confidence and dispelled the crisis; Hamburg Bank repaid its loan in six months.	1857	Conant (1915)
	Triggered by Russia's crisis, stock prices in Berlin fell by 61 percent; the problem hit mortgage banks first, but discount banks provided liquidity. Dresdner Creditanstalt, the Bank of Leipzig, and Leipzig Bank failed. There was a modest slowdown in the rate of growth.	1901	Conant (1915), Bordo and Eichengreen (1999)
	There were twin crises in which banks were recapitalized or their deposits guaranteed by the government. Bank runs exacerbated troubles building since mid-1930; many banks were unable to make payments, and there was a bank holiday.	1931	Bernanke and James (1990), Bordo et al. (2001), Temin (2008)
	Giro institutions faced problems.	1977	Caprio and Klingebiel (2003)
Ghana	Seven out of eleven banks were insolvent; the rural banking sector was affected.	1982–1989	Bordo et al. (2001), Caprio and Klingebiel (2003)

(*continued*)

365

TABLE A.4.1 Continued

Country	Brief summary	Year	Source
	Nonperforming loans increased from 11 percent to 27 percent; two state-owned banks were in bad shape, and three others were insolvent.	1997	Bordo et al. (2001), Caprio and Klingebiel (2003)
Greece	The country defaulted on external debt and left the gold standard in place.	1931	Bordo et al. (2001)
	Localized problems required significant injections of public funds.	1991–1995	Bordo et al. (2001), Reinhart (2002), Caprio and Klingebiel (2003)
Guatemala	Two small state-owned banks had a high level of nonperforming operations and closed in the early 1990s.	1991	Caprio and Klingebiel (2003)
	Three small banks (Banco Empresarial, Promotor, and Metropolitano), with a market share of 7 percent of deposits, were intervened and later closed for not observing solvency requirements.	2001	Jácome (2008)
	The third largest bank, Bancafe (with 9 percent of deposits), was closed, followed by another small bank, Banco del Comercio (with 1 percent of deposits), a few months later.	2006	Jácome (2008)
Guinea	Six banks (with 99 percent of system deposits) were deemed insolvent.	1985	Caprio and Klingebiel (2003)
	Two banks were insolvent, and one other had serious financial difficulties, accounting for 45 percent of the market total.	1993–1994	Caprio and Klingebiel (2003)
Guinea-Bissau	At the end of 1995, 45 percent of commercial banks' loan portfolios were nonperforming.	1995	Caprio and Klingebiel (2003)
Honduras	A small bank, Bancorp, with 3 percent of deposits, was closed in September.	1999	Jácome (2008)

TABLE A.4.1 Continued

Country	Brief summary	Year	Source
	A small bank, Banhcreser, with 3 percent of market share, was closed.	2001	Jácome (2008)
	Two small banks, Banco Sogerin and Banco Capital, were intervened and taken over by the deposit insurance institution.	2002	Jácome (2008)
Hong Kong	Nine deposit-taking companies failed.	1982	Bordo et al. (2001), Caprio and Klingebiel (2003)
	Seven banks were liquidated or taken over.	1983–1986	Bordo et al. (2001), Caprio and Klingebiel (2003)
	One large investment bank failed.	1998	Caprio and Klingebiel (2003)
Hungary	There was a run on Budapest banks; there were foreign withdrawals and a bank holiday.	July 1931	Bernanke and James (1990)
	By the second half of 1993, eight banks (with 25 percent of financial system assets) were deemed insolvent.	1991–1995	Caprio and Klingebiel (2003)
Iceland	One of three state-owned banks became insolvent.	1985–1986	Bordo et al. (2001), Caprio and Klingebiel (2003)
	The government injected capital into the state-owned commercial bank.	1993	Bordo et al. (2001), Caprio and Klingebiel (2003)
India	The Bank of Bengal could not meet the demands for financing, which resulted in increased capitalization.	1863	Scutt (1904), Reinhart and Rogoff (2008a)
	There were crop failures and excessive obligations to European banks; silver replaced much of the gold.	April 1908	Conant (1915)
	The nonperforming assets of twenty-seven public banks were estimated at 20 percent in 1995.	1993–1996	Bordo et al. (2001), Caprio and Klingebiel (2003)

(continued)

367

TABLE A.4.1 Continued

Country	Brief summary	Year	Source
Indonesia	A large bank (Bank Summa) collapsed, triggering runs on three smaller banks.	November 1992	Kaminsky and Reinhart (1999)
	Nonperforming assets accounted for 14 percent of banking system assets, with more than 70 percent in state banks.	1994	Bordo et al. (2001), Caprio and Klingebiel (2003)
	Through May 2002, Bank Indonesia closed 70 banks and nationalized 13 out of 237. Nonperforming loans were 65–75 percent of total loans at the peak of the crisis and fell to about 12 percent in February 2002.	1997–2002	Caprio and Klingebiel (2003)
Ireland	There was a run on most Irish banks; Agricultural Bank failed in November.	November 1836–1837	Conant (1915)
	Tipperary Joint Stock Bank failed upon discovery that one director (John Sadlier) had systematically robbed the bank and falsified accounts.	February 1856	Conant (1915)
Israel	Almost the entire banking sector was affected, representing 60 percent of stock market recapitalization. The stock exchange closed for eighteen days, and bank share prices fell more than 40 percent.	1977–1983	Bordo et al. (2001), Caprio and Klingebiel (2003)
	Stocks of the four largest banks collapsed and were nationalized by the state.	October 1983	Reinhart (2002)
Italy	National Bank suspended specie due to the expectation of the Austro-Prussian War.	June 1866–1868	Conant (1915)
	Tiber Bank, the Italian Mortgage Bank Society, and the Naples Building Association were taken over by National Bank.	1887	Conant (1915)

TABLE A.4.1 Continued

Country	Brief summary	Year	Source
	There was a real estate boom and bust, bringing banks with it. A tariff war with France raised interest rates and helped to prick the land bubble. Growth slowed and did not pick up for five years.	1891	Bordo and Eichengreen (1999)
	The government overhauled the banking system by merging several banks and authorized expansions of credit, triggering a currency crisis. The lira depreciated, but the recessionary impact was mild.	January 1893	Conant (1915), Bordo and Eichengreen (1999)
	Financial speculation and mounting difficulties in New York, London, and Paris in 1906 put pressure on interest rates and pricked the financial bubble. A sharp drop in output followed.	1907	Bordo and Eichengreen (1999)
	Savings banks were on the verge of collapse; they were rescued by the three main issuing banks, which also supported industry during the war.	1914	Teichova et al. (1997), Bordo et al. (2001)
	The third and fourth largest banks became insolvent, partly due to overtrading during and after the war.	1921	Bordo et al. (2001)
	There were withdrawals from the largest banks; a panic ensued until April, when the government reorganized many institutions and took over bad industrial assets.	December 1930–1931	Bernanke and James (1990), Bordo et al. (2001)
	There were agricultural bank closures and savings and commercial bank mergers to such an extent that the Italian banking system appeared completely reorganized.	1935	Teichova et al. (1997), Bordo et al. (2001)
	Fifty-eight banks, with 11 percent of lending, merged with other institutions.	1990–1995	Bordo et al. (2001), Caprio and Klingebiel (2003)

(continued)

TABLE A.4.1 Continued

Country	Brief summary	Year	Source
Jamaica	A merchant banking group was closed.	1994–1997	Bordo et al. (2001), Caprio and Klingebiel (2003)
	FINSAC, a government resolution agency, assisted five banks, five life insurance companies, two building societies, and nine merchant banks.	1995–2000	Caprio and Klingebiel (2003)
Japan	The National Bank Act forced banks to accept the government's paper notes, causing nine or ten banks to fail.	1872–1876	Conant (1915)
	Deflationary measures depressed trade, and four national banks failed, five suspended operations, and ten were consolidated.	1882–1885	Conant (1915)
	There were trade deficits and reserve losses as well as significant output losses; growth fell by 6 percent in one year.	1901	Bordo and Eichengreen (1999)
	The Tokyo stock market crashed in early 1907, and there was global uncertainty; the Bank of Japan intervened for some banks and let other banks fail. The recession was severe.	1907	Bordo and Eichengreen (1999)
	Japan went off the gold standard.	1917	Bordo et al. (2001), Flath (2005)
	A Tokyo earthquake led to bad debts that shook the Bank of Tokyo and Chosen. They were restructured with government aid.	September 1923	Bernanke and James (1990)
	A banking panic led to tighter regulation. The failure of Tokyo Watanabe bank led to runs and a wave of failures; fifteen banks were unable to make their payments. The government's unwillingness to bail out the banks led to more uncertainty and other runs. The crisis resulted in bank consolidations.	April 1927	Bernanke and James (1990), Bordo et al. (2001)

370

TABLE A.4.1 Continued

Country	Brief summary	Year	Source
	Banks suffered from a sharp decline in stock market and real estate prices. In 1995, estimates of non-performing loans were $469–1,000 billion or 10–25 percent of GDP; at the end of 1998 they were estimated at $725 billion or 18 percent of GDP; and in 2002 they were 35 percent of total loans. Seven banks were nationalized, sixty-one financial institutions closed, and twenty-eight institutions merged.	1992–1997	Bordo et al. (2001), Caprio and Klingebiel (2003)
Jordan	The third largest bank failed.	August 1989–1990	Caprio and Klingebiel (2003)
Kenya	Fifteen percent of financial system liabilities faced liquidity and solvency problems.	1985–1989	Caprio and Klingebiel (2003)
	There were interventions in two local banks.	1992	Caprio and Klingebiel (2003)
	There were serious solvency problems with banks accounting for more than 30 percent of financial system assets.	1993–1995	Caprio and Klingebiel (2003)
	Nonperforming loans reached 19 percent.	1996	Caprio and Klingebiel (2003)
Korea	Financial deregulation led to an increase in the number of banks.	January 1986	Shin and Hahm (1998), Reinhart (2002)
	Through May 2002, five banks were forced to exit the market through a "purchase and assumption formula," 303 financial institutions (215 of them credit unions) shut down, and four banks were nationalized. Banking system nonperforming loans peaked between 30 and 40 percent and fell to about 3 percent by March 2002.	July 1997	Bordo et al. (2001), Reinhart (2002), Caprio and Klingebiel (2003)

(continued)

371

TABLE A.4.1 Continued

Country	Brief summary	Year	Source
Kuwait	About 40 percent of loans were nonperforming by 1986.	1983	Caprio and Klingebiel (2003)
Kyrgyz Republic	About 80–90 percent of banking system loans were doubtful. Four small banks closed in 1995.	1993	Caprio and Klingebiel (2003)
Lao People's Democratic Republic	Some banks experienced problems.	Early 1990s	Caprio and Klingebiel (2003)
Latvia	There was a run on banks with German connections; two large banks were hit especially hard.	July 1931	Bernanke and James (1990)
	Between 1995 and 1999, thirty-five banks saw their licenses revoked, were closed, or ceased operations.	1994–1999	Caprio and Klingebiel (2003)
Lebanon	Four banks became insolvent, and eleven resorted to Central Bank lending.	1988–1990	Caprio and Klingebiel (2003)
Lesotho	One of four commercial banks had nonperforming loans.	1988	Caprio and Klingebiel (2003)
Liberia	Seven out of eleven banks were not operational, accounting for 60 percent of bank assets.	1991–1995	Caprio and Klingebiel (2003)
Lithuania	In 1995, twelve small banks out of twenty-five banks were liquidated; three private banks (29 percent of banking system deposits) failed, and three state-owned banks were deemed insolvent.	1995–1996	Caprio and Klingebiel (2003)
Macedonia	About 70 percent of banking system loans were nonperforming. The government took over banks' foreign debt and closed the second largest bank.	1993–1994	Caprio and Klingebiel (2003)
Madagascar	Twenty-five percent of bank loans were deemed unrecoverable.	1988	Caprio and Klingebiel (2003)

TABLE A.4.1 Continued

Country	Brief summary	Year	Source
Malaysia	There were runs on some branches of a large domestic bank following the collapse of a related bank in Hong Kong. Insolvent institutions accounted for 3 percent of financial system deposits; marginally recapitalized and possibly insolvent institutions accounted for another 4 percent.	July 1985–1988	Kaminsky and Reinhart (1999), Bordo et al. (2001), Caprio and Klingebiel (2003)
	The finance company sector was restructured, and the number of finance institutions was reduced from thirty-nine to ten through mergers. Two finance companies were taken over by the Central Bank, including the largest independent finance company. Two banks—accounting for 14 percent of financial system assets—were deemed insolvent and were to be merged with other banks. Nonperforming loans peaked between 25 and 35 percent of banking system assets but fell to 10.8 percent by March 2002.	September 1997	Bordo et al. (2001), Reinhart (2002), Caprio and Klingebiel (2003)
Mali	The nonperforming loans of the largest bank reached 75 percent.	1987–1989	Caprio and Klingebiel (2003)
Mauritania	In 1984, five major banks had nonperforming assets in 45–70 percent of their portfolios.	1984–1993	Caprio and Klingebiel (2003)
Mauritius	The Central Bank closed two out of twelve commercial banks for fraud and irregularities.	1997	Caprio and Klingebiel (2003)
Mexico	The Mexican government borrowed widely and then suspended payments (June 1885); foreign investments fell, leading to a credit crisis and bank runs, and banks stopped	1883	Conant (1915)

(continued)

TABLE A.4.1 Continued

Country	Brief summary	Year	Source
	lending. National Bank and Mercantile Bank merged into National Bank of Mexico (Banamex) in 1884 to meet the government's demand for a loan.		
	National Bank absorbed Mexican Mercantile Bank, its main competitor.	1893	Conant (1915)
	There was a severe credit shortage due to the U.S. crash; banks could not collect debts; the Mexican Central Bank and many state banks failed. Other banks survived with federal assistance or by merging. The failures caused many bankruptcies and prevented economic activity. The government cautioned against overexpansion of credit; in February a circular warned against unsafe loans, and restrictions were imposed in June.	February 1908	Conant (1915)
	Payments were suspended after a run on the major banks.	1929	Bernanke and James (1990)
	There was capital flight; the government responded by nationalizing the private banking system.	1981–1982	Bordo et al. (2001)
	The government took over the banking system.	September 1982–1991	Kaminsky and Reinhart (1999), Caprio and Klingebiel (2003)
	Several financial institutions that held Ajustabonos were hurt by the rise in real interest rates in the second half of 1992.	October 1992	Kaminsky and Reinhart (1999)
	In 1994, nine banks were intervened and eleven participated in the loan/purchase recapitalization programs of thirty-four commercial banks. The nine banks accounted for 19 percent of financial system assets and were deemed insolvent. One percent of bank assets were owned by foreigners, and by 1998,	1994–1997	Bordo et al. (2001), Caprio and Klingebiel (2003), Jácome (2008)

TABLE A.4.1 Continued

Country	Brief summary	Year	Source
	18 percent of bank assets were held by foreign banks.		
Morocco	The banking sector experienced problems.	1983	Caprio and Klingebiel (2003)
Mozambique	The main commercial bank experienced solvency problems, which were apparent after 1992.	1987–1995	Caprio and Klingebiel (2003)
Myanmar	The largest state-owned commercial bank was reported to have large nonperforming loans.	1996–?	Caprio and Klingebiel (2003)
Nepal	In early 1988, the reported arrears of three banks, accounting for 95 percent of the financial system, averaged 29 percent of assets.	1988	Caprio and Klingebiel (2003)
The Netherlands	The Bank of Amsterdam closed by government decree; liquidation began in January and lasted many years.	December 1819–1829	Conant (1915)
	Discount rates were volatile and eventually reached a crisis high.	1897	Bordo et al. (2001), Homer and Sylla (1991)
	Temporary closure of the Amsterdam Exchange led to a sharp acceleration in the evolution of banking. Large commercial banks replaced older institutions, and many banks were taken over or replaced.	1914	't Hart et al. (1997), Bordo et al. (2001)
	Scores of banks failed, and many others experienced serious problems. The banking crisis resulted in banks' working more closely together and in more centralization. Banks financed industry more heavily after the war; after the crisis, industrial growth stalled.	1921	't Hart et al. (1997), Bordo et al. (2001)
	The major bank, Amsterdamsche Bank, took over another large bank, Noordhollandsch Land-bouwcrediet.	1939	Bordo et al. (2001)

(continued)

TABLE A.4.1 Continued

Country	Brief summary	Year	Source
New Zealand	One large state-owned bank, with 25 percent of banking assets, experienced solvency problems, with a high percentage of non-performing loans.	1987–1990	Bordo et al. (2001), Caprio and Klingebiel (2003)
Nicaragua	Banking system nonperforming loans reached 50 percent in 1996.	1987–1996	Caprio and Klingebiel (2003)
	Four out of eleven banks, representing about 40 percent of deposits, were intervened and sold to other financial institutions.	2000–2002	Jácome (2008)
Niger	In the mid-1980s, banking system nonperforming loans reached 50 percent. Four banks liquidated, three restructured in the late 1980s, and more restructured in 2002.	1983–?	Caprio and Klingebiel (2003)
Nigeria	In 1993, insolvent banks had 20 percent of banking system assets and 22 percent of deposits. In 1995, almost half the banks reported being in financial distress.	1992–1995	Bordo et al. (2001), Caprio and Klingebiel (2003)
	Distressed banks had 4 percent of banking system assets.	1997	Bordo et al. (2001), Caprio and Klingebiel (2003)
Norway	There was real estate speculation; the bubble burst when interest rates increased, and many banks failed. The Bank of Norway stepped in and prevented the crisis from spreading.	1898	Jonung and Hagberg (2002)
	Reckless lending during the war and the global downswing in the early 1920s causes bank instability.	1921–1923	Bordo et al. (2001), Jonung and Hagberg (2002)
	Norway abandoned the gold standard; the Norges Bank provided much support to smaller banks to prevent a systemic crisis. The situation was more successfully managed than the 1921 crisis.	1931	Bordo et al. (2001), Øksendal (2007)

TABLE A.4.1 Continued

Country	Brief summary	Year	Source
	Legislation introducing a tax on bank deposits led to many withdrawals.	1936	Bernanke and James (1990)
	Two regional savings banks failed. The banks were eventually merged and bailed out. The Central Bank provided special loans to six banks suffering from the recession of 1985–1986 and from problem real estate loans. The state took control of the three largest banks, with 85 percent of banking system assets.	1987–1993	Kaminsky and Reinhart (1999), Bordo et al. (2001), Jonung and Hagberg (2002), Caprio and Klingebiel (2003)
Panama	In 1988, the banking system had a nine-week banking holiday. The financial position of most state-owned and private commercial banks was weak, and fifteen banks ceased operations.	1988–1989	Caprio and Klingebiel (2003)
Papua New Guinea	Eighty-five percent of savings and loan associations ceased operations.	1989–?	Caprio and Klingebiel (2003)
Paraguay	The Bank of Paraguay and River Plate Bank suspended payments, and there was a severe run; gold prices increased 300 percent, and banks eventually liquidated.	1890	Conant (1915)
	The Government Superintendency intervened in most domestic private and public banks and in a number of finance companies by the end of 1998, including the largest bank and savings and loan institution. By the end of 1999, the banks were mostly foreign-owned, with over 80 percent of bank assets in foreign hands. All banks were deemed sound in 2000. Two banks, with about 10 percent of deposits, were intervened and closed in 1997. A medium-sized bank, with 6.5 percent of deposits, was closed in 1998.	1995–1999	Bordo et al. (2001), Caprio and Klingebiel (2003), Jácome (2008)

(continued)

377

TABLE A.4.1 Continued

Country	Brief summary	Year	Source
	The third largest bank, with nearly 10 percent of deposits, was intervened and closed.	2002	Caprio and Klingebiel (2003), Jácome (2008)
Peru	Gold coinage was suspended, and the country had a silver standard for twenty-five years.	1872–1873	Conant (1915), Reinhart and Rogoff (2008a)
	Two large banks failed. The rest of the system suffered from high levels of nonperforming loans and financial disintermediation following the nationalization of the banking system in 1987.	April 1983–1990	Kaminsky and Reinhart (1999), Bordo et al. (2001), Caprio and Klingebiel (2003)
	Capital outflows triggered a domestic credit crunch that unveiled solvency problems in a number of banks, including Banco Wiese, Banco Latino (16.7 percent and 3 percent of market share, respectively), and other smaller financial institutions. Bank resolution was applied to two banks (with nearly 21 percent of deposits). Instability also affected another six small banks (with 6.5 percent of deposits).	1999	Jácome (2008)
The Philippines	The commercial paper market collapsed, triggering bank runs and the failure of nonbank financial institutions and thrift banks. There were problems in two public banks accounting for 50 percent of banking system assets, 6 private banks accounting for 12 percent of banking system assets, 32 thrifts accounting for 53 percent of thrift banking assets, and 128 rural banks.	January 1981–1987	Kaminsky and Reinhart (1999), Bordo et al. (2001), Caprio and Klingebiel (2003)
	One commercial bank, 7 of 88 thrifts, and 40 of 750 rural banks were placed under receivership. Banking system nonperforming loans reached 12 percent by November 1998 and were expected to reach 20 percent in 1999.	July 1997–1998	Reinhart (2002), Caprio and Klingebiel (2003)

378

TABLE A.4.1 Continued

Country	Brief summary	Year	Source
Poland	Bank runs caused three large banks to stop payments; the bank shake-out lasted until 1927.	July 1926–1927	Bernanke and James (1990)
	There was a run on banks, especially those associated with Austrian Creditanstalt, representing spread of the Austrian crisis.	June 1931	Bernanke and James (1990)
	In 1991, seven of nine treasury-owned commercial banks (90 percent of credit), the Bank for Food Economy, and the cooperative banking system experienced solvency problems.	1991	Caprio and Klingebiel (2003)
Portugal	The Bank of Lisbon suspended payments; it had experienced a consistently troubled career because of its ties to the Portuguese government.	1828	Conant (1915)
	The Bank of Lisbon lost all credit, could not redeem its notes, and reorganized into the Bank of Portugal.	May 1846–1847	Conant (1915)
	Large budget deficits, the Barings crisis, and the Brazilian revolution led to currency depreciation. The government reneged on some domestic debt and renegotiated foreign debt to reduce interest payments. The crisis had a large impact on growth.	1890	Conant (1915), Bordo and Eichengreen (1999)
	Bank failures were common in the postwar economy.	1920	Bordo et al. (2001)
	Multiple bank failures occurred.	1923	Bordo et al. (2001)
	Portugal abandoned the gold standard.	1931–1932	Bordo et al. (2001)
Romania	German-controlled banks and other banks collapsed; there were heavy runs on banks.	July 1931	Bernanke and James (1990)

(continued)

TABLE A.4.1 Continued

Country	Brief summary	Year	Source
	In 1990, nonperforming loans reached 25–30 percent in the six main state-owned banks.	1990	Caprio and Klingebiel (2003)
Russia	The Bank of Russia closed in April; specie payments were suspended and never resumed. A permanent treasury deficit meant that several loans were necessary, and there was a hopeless credit situation.	April 1862–1863	Conant (1915)
	Skopine community bank garnered deposits from all over the empire but kept low reserves; the bubble burst in 1875 when it could not pay its deposits. There was limited communal banking after that.	1875	Conant (1915), Reinhart and Rogoff (2008a)
	Joint-stock commercial banks were loaded with nonperforming assets; many small banks failed, although large ones were protected by the state bank.	1896	Cameron (1967)
	The interbank loan market stopped working due to concerns about connected lending in many new banks.	August 1995	Caprio and Klingebiel (2003)
	Nearly 720 banks, representing half of those in operation, were deemed insolvent. The banks accounted for 4 percent of sector assets and 32 percent of retail deposits. Eighteen banks, holding 40 percent of sector assets and 41 percent of household deposits, were in serious difficulties and needed rescue.	1998–1999	Caprio and Klingebiel (2003)
Rwanda	One well-connected bank closed.	1991	Caprio and Klingebiel (2003)
Santo Domingo	The National Bank failed after unsuccessfully trying to adopt the gold standard; bank notes were not accepted anywhere.	1894	Conant (1915)

380

TABLE A.4.1 Continued

Country	Brief summary	Year	Source
Sao Tome and Principe	At the end of 1992, 90 percent of the monobank's loans were non-performing. In 1993, the mono-bank liquidated, and two new banks were licensed and took over most assets. In 1994, credit operations at one new bank were suspended.	1991	Caprio and Klingebiel (2003)
Scotland	Western Bank failed due to reckless banking practices. The bank made various bad loans to four firms; when discovered, the accounts were stopped and the firms closed. There was a panic on the stock exchange; depositors withdraw their accounts, and the bank failed.	October 1857–1858	Conant (1915)
	The City of Glasgow Bank failed due to the falsification of books for three years, with loans made to four firms; the failure ruined share-holders but not creditors.	September 1878–1880	Conant (1915)
	Bank of Scotland absorbed Caledo-nian Bank, and North of Scotland Bank absorbed Town and Country Bank.	March 1908	Conant (1915)
Senegal	In 1988, 50 percent of loans were nonperforming. Six commercial banks and one development bank (with 20–30 percent of financial system assets) closed.	1988–1991	Bordo et al. (2001), Caprio and Klingebiel (2003)
Sierra Leone	In 1995, 40–50 percent of banking system loans were nonperforming, undergoing bank recapitalization and restructuring.	1990	Caprio and Klingebiel (2003)
Singapore	Nonperforming loans rose to $200 million or 0.6 percent of GDP.	1982	Bordo et al. (2001), Caprio and Klingebiel (2003)

(continued)

TABLE A.4.1 Continued

Country	Brief summary	Year	Source
Slovakia	In 1997, unrecoverable loans were estimated at 101 billion crowns—about 31 percent of loans and 15 percent of GDP.	1991	Caprio and Klingebiel (2003)
Slovenia	Three banks (with two-thirds of banking system assets) were restructured.	1993–1994	Caprio and Klingebiel (2003)
South Africa	Trust Bank experienced problems.	December 1977–1978	Bordo et al. (2001), Reinhart (2002), Caprio and Klingebiel (2003)
	Some banks experienced problems.	1989	Caprio and Klingebiel (2003)
Spain	During the Peninsular War, Spain was occupied by France, and the Bank of St. Charles was essentially dead after 1814.	1814–1817	Conant (1915)
	The Bank of St. Charles reorganized into the Bank of Ferdinand.	July 1829	Conant (1915)
	The Bank of Isabella II (created by the government to punish the Bank of Ferdinand in 1844) and the Bank of Ferdinand consolidated into one, the Bank of Ferdinand. The Bank of Ferdinand bore the Bank of Isabella's debts and was completely at the mercy of the state. In 1848, with the cash reserve of the bank decreasing, circulation increasing, the government demanded more loans, the bank was a victim of theft and embezzlement. The government reorganized the bank into the Bank of Spain to resemble Bank of England.	February 1846–1847	Conant (1915)
	A number of Catalonian universal banks became insolvent, which eventually led to the failure of the most prominent and oldest credit	1920–1923	Bordo et al. (2001)

TABLE A.4.1 Continued

Country	Brief summary	Year	Source
	institutions, with the severest impact on Barcelona. Two major banks failed.	1924–1925	Bernanke and James (1990), Bordo et al. (2001)
	The country avoided the worst of the Great Depression by staying off the gold standard; it experienced runs, but the Bank of Spain could lend freely as a lender of last resort.	1931	Bordo et al. (2001), Temin (2008)
	The Bank of Spain began rescuing a number of smaller banks. In 1978–1983, 24 institutions were rescued, 4 were liquidated, 4 were merged, and 20 small and medium-sized banks were nationalized. These 52 banks out of 110, representing 20 percent of banking system deposits, were experiencing solvency problems.	1977–1985	Kaminsky and Reinhart (1999), Bordo et al. (2001), Caprio and Klingebiel (2003)
Sri Lanka	State-owned banks, comprising 70 percent of the banking system, were estimated to have nonperforming loans of 35 percent.	1989–1993	Caprio and Klingebiel (2003)
Swaziland	The Central Bank took over three other banks.	1995	Caprio and Klingebiel (2003)
Sweden	Depreciation of gold led to the Bullion Report (similar to the Report on Irish Currency of 1804).	January 1811	Conant (1915)
	There were severe banking crises.	1876–1879	Jonung and Hagberg (2002)
	The Riksbank Act made the Riksbank the central bank and gave it exclusive rights to issue bank notes.	1897	Bordo et al. (2001), Jonung and Hagberg (2002)
	There was a lending boom, and decreasing confidence in the stability of the banking system led to bank runs. Reserves depreciated,	1907	Bordo and Eichengreen (1999), Jonung and Hagberg (2002)

(continued)

383

TABLE A.4.1 Continued

Country	Brief summary	Year	Source
	but Riksbank extended loans to national banks. Output was negatively affected, but the economy recovered quickly.		
	One of severest banking crises in Swedish banking history occurred following a steep recession.	1922–1923	Jonung and Hagberg (2002)
	Banks tied to the financier Ivar Kreuger suffered after his death; the banks suffered large losses, but depositors were protected by the government and did not suffer from the failures.	1931–1932	Bordo et al. (2001), Jonung and Hagberg (2002)
	The Swedish government rescued Nordbanken, the second largest bank. Nordbanken and Gota Bank, with 22 percent of banking system assets, were insolvent. Sparbanken Foresta, accounting for 24 percent of banking system assets, intervened. Five of the six largest banks, accounting for over 70 percent of banking system assets, experienced difficulties.	November 1991–1994	Kaminsky and Reinhart (1999), Bordo et al. (2001), Jonung and Hagberg (2002), Caprio and Klingebiel (2003)
Switzerland	Switzerland could not obtain its supply of coin from France; bank clients rushed to redeem their notes for coin; the banks cut down discounts and loans, which led to an economic downturn.	July 1870–1871	Conant (1915)
	There was a wave of bank failures and consolidations.	1910–1913	Vogler (2001)
	Swiss banks were badly shaken by the German banking crisis; total assets shrank, and many banks restructured.	1931	Bordo et al. (2001), Vogler (2001)
	There was continued distress due to pressures from America and the Great Depression and due to the German banking crisis of 1931.	1933	Bordo et al. (2001), Vogler (2001)

TABLE A.4.1 Continued

Country	Brief summary	Year	Source
Taiwan	Four trust companies and eleven corporations failed.	1983–1984	Bordo et al. (2001), Caprio and Klingebiel (2003)
	The failure of Changua Fourth sparked runs on other credit unions.	July 1995	Bordo et al. (2001), Caprio and Klingebiel (2003)
	Banking system nonperforming loans were estimated at 15 percent at the end of 1998.	1997–1998	Bordo et al. (2001), Caprio and Klingebiel (2003)
Tajikistan	One of largest banks became insolvent, and one small bank closed.	1996–?	Caprio and Klingebiel (2003)
Tanzania	In 1987, the main financial institutions had arrears amounting to half their portfolios. The National Bank of Commerce, with 95 percent of banking system assets, became insolvent in 1990.	1987	Caprio and Klingebiel (2003)
Thailand	Following the stock market crash, one of the largest finance companies failed. The bailout of the financial sector began.	March 1979	Kaminsky and Reinhart (1999)
	Large losses in a finance company led to runs and government intervention. Authorities intervened in fifty finance and security firms and five commercial banks, with about 25 percent of financial system assets; three commercial banks (with 14 percent of commercial bank assets) were deemed insolvent.	October 1983–1987	Kaminsky and Reinhart (1999), Bordo et al. (2001), Caprio and Klingebiel (2003)
	As of May 2002, the Bank of Thailand shut down fifty-nine of ninety-one financial companies (13 percent of financial system assets and 72 percent of finance company assets) and one of fifteen domestic banks and nationalized four banks. A publicly owned assets manage-	May 1996	Bordo et al. (2001), Reinhart (2002), Caprio and Klingebiel (2003)

(continued)

TABLE A.4.1 Continued

Country	Brief summary	Year	Source
	ment company held 29.7 percent of financial system assets as of March 2002. Nonperforming loans peaked at 33 percent of total loans and were reduced to 10.3 percent of total loans in February 2002.		
Togo	The banking sector experienced solvency problems.	1993–1995	Caprio and Klingebiel (2003)
Trinidad and Tobago	Several financial institutions faced solvency problems, and three government-owned banks merged.	1982–1993	Caprio and Klingebiel (2003)
Tunisia	Most commercial banks were under-capitalized.	1991–1995	Caprio and Klingebiel (2003)
Turkey	There were runs on branches of German banks in the wake of the German crisis.	July 1931	Bernanke and James (1990)
	Three banks were merged with the state-owned Agriculture Bank and then liquidated; two large banks were restructured.	1982–1985	Bordo et al. (2001), Caprio and Klingebiel (2003)
	The start of the war led to massive withdrawals and a run on banks, prompting the government to guarantee all deposits.	January 1991	Kaminsky and Reinhart (1999)
	Three banks failed in April.	April 1994	Bordo et al. (2001), Caprio and Klingebiel (2003)
	Two banks closed, and nineteen banks have been taken over by the Savings Deposit Insurance Fund.	2000	Caprio and Klingebiel (2003)
Uganda	During 1994–1998, half the banking system faced solvency problems. During 1998–2002, various banks recapitalized and privatized or closed.	1994–2002	Caprio and Klingebiel (2003)
Ukraine	By 1997, 32 of 195 banks were being liquidated, while 25 others were undergoing financial rehabilitation. Bad loans amounted to 50–65 per-	1997–1998	Caprio and Klingebiel (2003)

386

TABLE A.4.1 Continued

Country	Brief summary	Year	Source
	cent of assets, even in some leading banks. In 1998, banks were further hit by the government's decision to restructure its debt.		
United Kingdom	There was mass speculation due to Napoleon's Berlin Decree. Many new country banks issued notes; excessive issue led to a severe fall on the London exchange; the treasury rescued the banks on April 11, 1811.	1810	Conant (1915)
	A good harvest and low prices led to speculation; a general depression of property prices affected production industries. Eighty-nine country banks went bankrupt; three hundred to five hundred ceased business, and there was an increased demand for Bank of England notes.	1815–1817	Conant (1915)
	Speculation in real and imaginary investments financed by unregulated country banking caused a bubble in stocks and Latin American foreign sovereign debt, followed by a stock market crash; six London banks closed (including Henry Thornton's Bank), and sixty country banks closed; there was a panic in London.	April 1825–1826	Conant (1915)
	Three banks failed in March 1837; the Bank of England gave generous advances to other banks to prevent a panic, but still they drifted toward bankruptcy. The country raised the discount rate and borrowed from France and Germany.	March 1837–1839	Conant (1915)
	The Irish Potato Famine and the railroad mania led to a steady drain on bullion; reduced resources led to a panic. Firms overextended	April 1847–1848	Conant (1915)

(continued)

TABLE A.4.1 Continued

Country	Brief summary	Year	Source
	into railroad endeavors and sugar plantations; they began failing, which led to bank failures.		
	The discovery of Australian and Californian gold fields led to massive speculation and then collapse, paralyzing finances throughout world (the crisis spread from the United States to Europe, South America, and the Far East). Most banks suspended operations; the Bank of England was the only source of a discount.	August 1857	Conant (1915)
	The Bank Act of 1844 was suspended to deal with the panic; demands were paid in gold. The Joint Stock Discount company failed, and various industries provided discounts.	May 1866	Conant (1915)
	There was a provincial bank crisis: the West of England and South Wales District Bank failed (December 9), and the City of Glasgow Bank failed (October 2) due to depressed confidence.	October 1878	Conant (1915)
	The House of Baring's portfolio was mostly in securities in Argentina and Uruguay. The Buenos Aires Water Supply and Drainage Company loan failed, but the Bank of England, assisted by the Bank of France and Russia, organized a rescue, which prevented Barings from failing. A short and mild recession followed.	November 1890	Conant (1915), Bordo and Eichengreen (1999)
	There was a "secondary" banking crisis.	1974–1976	Bordo et al. (2001), Caprio and Klingebiel (2003)
	Johnson Matthey Bankers failed.	1984	Caprio and Klingebiel (2003)
	The Bank of Credit and Commerce International failed.	1991	Caprio and Klingebiel (2003)
	Barings failed.	1995	Caprio and Klingebiel (2003)

388

TABLE A.4.1 Continued

Country	Brief summary	Year	Source
United States	State banks suspended specie payments due to the War of 1812, paralyzing the treasury's operations.	August 1814	Conant (1915)
	Forty-six banks were rendered insolvent due to demands for specie by Second Bank of the United States.	1818–1819	Conant (1915)
	Preceding England's crisis, the Bank of the United States and all other banks were brought to the verge of suspension.	January 1825	Conant (1915)
	Three banks failed; the Bank of England gave generous advances to other banks to prevent a panic. The failures began in New Orleans and New York and spread to other cities' banks.	1836–1838	Conant (1915)
	Second Bank of the United States liquidated; lenders were repaid, but shareholders lost all interest; twenty-six local banks failed.	March 1841	Conant (1915)
	The discovery of Australian and Californian gold fields led to massive speculation and then collapse, paralyzing finances throughout the world (the crisis spread from the United States to Europe, South America, and the Far East). Most banks suspended operations; the Bank of England was the only source of discount.	August 1857	Conant (1915)
	The government suspended specie payments until 1879, driving up the price of gold (which peaked in 1864) and all other retail items.	December 1861	Conant (1915)
	There was a U.S. panic due to the Civil War.	April 1864	Conant (1915)
	The Philadelphian banking firm Jay Cooke and Company failed, triggering a recession that lasted until 1877.	September 1873	Conant (1915)

(continued)

TABLE A.4.1 Continued

Country	Brief summary	Year	Source
	Weak commodity prices and a series of brokerage firm failures led to bank runs and suspended payments, mostly in the New York region. The output effects were mild.	May 1884	Conant (1915), Bordo and Eichengreen (1999)
	Monetary uncertainty and a stock market crash led to bank runs. Political action was taken to ameliorate the crisis; there was a severe decline in output, but the economy recovered quickly.	1890	Conant (1915), Bordo and Eichengreen (1999)
	There were global credit restrictions and domestic financial excesses, increasing the number of state banks, and a rising ratio of deposits to cash reserves set the stage for a crisis. Real estate and stock speculation bubbles burst; the crisis spread from New York nationwide. The growth rate fell by 9 percent per year. J. P. Morgan, the Bank of Montreal, and the treasury of New York replenished liquidity.	March 1907	Conant (1915), Bordo and Eichengreen (1999)
	The New York Stock Exchange closed until December in response to the war; however, a banking crisis was avoided by flooding the country with emergency currency to prevent hasty withdrawals.	July 1914	Bordo et al. (2001)
	During the Great Depression, thousands of banks closed; failures were correlated with particular Federal Reserve districts. The Bank of the USA failed in December 1930; between August 1931 and January 1932, 1,860 banks failed.	1929–1933	Bernanke and James (1990), Bordo et al. (2001)
	There were 1,400 savings and loan and 1,300 bank failures.	1984–1991	Bordo et al. (2001), Caprio and Klingebiel (2003)

TABLE A.4.1 Continued

Country	Brief summary	Year	Source
Uruguay	The National Bank failed.	1893	Conant (1915)
	There was a run on banks to redeem bank notes due to a government decree to reduce the circulation of notes.	September 1898	Conant (1915)
	Banco Mercantil failed. A wave of bank mergers and bankruptcies developed, driven by high real interest rates.	March 1971	Kaminsky and Reinhart (1999)
	A large-scale run on banks came in the wake of the Argentine devaluation, which marked the end of the Argentine *tablita*. The institutions affected accounted for 30 percent of financial system assets; insolvent banks accounted for 20 percent of financial system deposits.	March 1981–1984	Kaminsky and Reinhart (1999), Bordo et al. (2001), Caprio and Klingebiel (2003)
	The government-owned mortgage bank was recapitalized in December 2001. The banking system had 33 percent of its deposits withdrawn in the first seven months of 2002. In 2002, four banks (with 33 percent of total bank assets) were closed, and fixed-term deposits (CDs) were restructured and their maturity extended.	2002	Caprio and Klingebiel (2003), Jácome (2008)
Venezuela	There were notable bank failures in 1978, 1981, 1982, 1985, and 1986.	1978–1986	Bordo et al. (2001), Caprio and Klingebiel (2003)
	There were runs on Banco Latino, the country's second largest bank, which closed in January 1994. Insolvent banks accounted for 35 percent of financial system deposits. Authorities intervened in seventeen of forty-seven banks that held 50 percent of deposits, nationalized nine banks, and closed seven more in 1994. The government intervened in five more banks in 1995.	October 1993 1995	Kaminsky and Reinhart (1999), Bordo et al. (2001), Caprio and Klingebiel (2003), Jácome (2008)

(continued)

391

TABLE A.4.1 Continued

Country	Brief summary	Year	Source
Vietnam	Two of four large state-owned commercial banks (with 51 percent of banking system loans) were deemed insolvent; the remaining two experienced significant solvency problems. Several joint stock companies were in severe financial distress. Banking system nonperforming loans reached 18 percent in late 1998.	1997–?	Caprio and Klingebiel (2003)
Yemen	Banks suffered from extensive nonperforming loans and heavy foreign currency exposure.	1996–?	Caprio and Klingebiel (2003)
Zambia	Meridian Bank, with 13 percent of commercial bank assets, became insolvent.	1995	Caprio and Klingebiel (2003)
Zimbabwe	Two of five commercial banks had a high level of nonperforming loans.	1995	Bordo et al. (2001), Caprio and Klingebiel (2003)

NOTES

Preface

1. Notably those of Winkler (1928), Wynne (1951), and Marichal (1989).
2. More recently, there was Ferguson's (2008) excellent and equally engaging history of the foundations of currency and finance. See also MacDonald (2006).

Preamble: Some Initial Intuitions on Financial Fragility and the Fickle Nature of Confidence

1. See Shleifer and Vishny (1992) and Fostel and Geanakoplos (2008) for interesting technical analyses of how changing fortunes of optimists and pessimists can drive leverage cycles.
2. Classic articles on multiple equilibria and financial fragility include those of Diamond and Dybvig (1983) and Allen and Gale (2007) on bank runs, Calvo (1988) on public debt, and Obstfeld (1996) on exchange rates. See also Obstfeld and Rogoff (1996), chapters 6 and 9.
3. See Buchanan and Wagner (1977).
4. Krugman (1979).
5. See, for instance, North and Weingast (1988) and also Ferguson (2008).
6. See Bernanke (1983) and Bernanke and Gertler (1990), for example.
7. We term the recent global crisis the "Second Great Contraction" in analogy with Friedman and Schwartz's (1963) depiction of the 1930's Great Depression as "The Great Contraction." *Contraction* provides an apt description of the wholesale collapse of credit markets and asset prices that has marked the depth of these traumatic events, along with, of course, contracting employment and output.

Chapter 1   Varieties of Crises and Their Dates

1. See Reinhart and Rogoff (2004).
2. Frankel and Rose (1996).
3. Ibid.; Kaminsky and Reinhart (1999).
4. See Kaminsky and Reinhart (1999) for the construction of thresholds to date equity price crashes and Reinhart and Rogoff (2008b) for a depiction of the behavior of real estate prices on the eve of banking crises in industrialized economies.

5. See Kaminsky and Reinhart (1999), Caprio and Klingebiel (2003), Caprio et al. (2005), and Jácome (2008). For the period before World War II, Willis (1926), Kindleberger (1989), and Bordo et al. (2001) provide multicountry coverage on banking crises.

6. See Camprubri (1957) for Peru, Cheng (2003) and McElderry (1976) for China, and Noel (2002) for Mexico.

7. This is not meant to be an exhaustive list of the scholars who have worked on historical sovereign defaults.

8. Notably, that supplied by Lindert and Morton (1989), Suter (1992), Purcell and Kaufman (1993), and MacDonald (2006). Of course, required reading in this field includes Winkler (1933) and Wynne (1951). Important further readings include Eichengreen (1991a, 1991b, 1992), and Eichengreen and Lindert (1989).

9. At present, Honduras has remained in default since 1981.

10. Apparently an old saw in the marketplace is "More money has been lost because of four words than at the point of a gun. Those words are 'This time is different.'"

11. For example, during the mid-1990s Thailand claimed not to have a dollar peg but rather a peg to an (unspecified) basket of currencies. Investors could clearly see, however, that the basket did not contain much besides the dollar; the exchange rate of baht to dollars fluctuated only within narrow bands.

12. Central banks typically lose money in any unsuccessful intervention to prop up the currency because they are selling hard currency (e.g., dollars) in exchange for the local currency (e.g., baht). When the exchange rate for the local currency collapses, the intervening central bank suffers a capital loss.

Chapter 2   Debt Intolerance

1. Later, in chapter 8, we use new historical data on domestic public debt in emerging markets and find that it is a significant factor in some cases. However, introducing this consideration does not fundamentally change the remarkable phenomenon of serial default examined here.

2. The figures for Japan's level of debt relative to GDP are from International Monetary Fund, *World Economic Outlook*, October 2008.

3. Following the World Bank for some purposes, we divide developing countries according to their level of per capita income into two broad groups: middle-income countries (those with a GNP per capita in 2005 higher than US$755) and low-income countries. Most (but not all) emerging market economies with substantial access to private external financing are middle-income countries. Similarly, most (though not all) of the low-income countries do not have access to private capital markets and rely primarily on official sources of external funding.

4. Note that many of these default episodes lasted several years, as discussed in chapter 8.

5. Note that tables 2.1 and 2.2 measure *gross* total external debt because debtor governments have little capacity to tax or otherwise confiscate private citizens' assets held abroad. For example, when Argentina defaulted on US$95 billion of external debt in 2001, its citizens held foreign assets abroad estimated by some commentators at about US$120–150 billion. This phenomenon is not uncommon and was the norm in the debt crises of the 1980s.

6. Using an altogether different approach, an International Monetary Fund (2002) study on debt sustainability came up with external debt thresholds for developing countries (excluding the highly indebted poorest countries) that were in the neighborhood of 31 to 39 percent, depending on whether official financing was included or not. The results, which we will present later, suggest that country-specific thresholds for debt-intolerant countries should probably be even lower.

7. For particulars about the survey, see the September 2002 issue of *Institutional Investor* and their Web site. Though not critical to our following analysis, we interpret the ratings reported in each semiannual survey as capturing the risk of near-term default within one to two years.

8. One can use secondary market prices of external commercial bank debt, which are available for the time since the mid-1980s, to provide a measure of expected repayment for a number of emerging market countries. However, the Brady debt restructurings of the 1990s converted much of this bank debt to bond debt, so from 1992 onward the secondary market prices would have to be replaced by the Emerging Market Bond Index (EMBI) spread, which remains the most commonly used measure of risk at present. These market-based indicators introduce a serious sample selection bias: almost all the countries in the EMBI, and all the countries for which there is secondary debt price data for the 1980s, had a history of adverse credit events, leaving the control group of nondefaulters approximately the null set.

9. See the debt glossary (box 1.1) for a brief explanation of the various concepts of debt used in this study.

10. This exercise updates the work of Reinhart, Rogoff, and Savastano (2003a), who used thresholds based on a smaller sample of countries over 1979–2002.

11. Prasad, Rogoff, Wei, and Kose (2003) found that during the 1990s, economies that were de facto relatively financially open experienced, on average, a rise in consumption volatility relative to output volatility, contrary to the premise that the integration of capital markets spreads country-specific output risk. Prasad et al. also argue that the cross-country empirical evidence on the effects of capital market integration on growth shows only weak positive effects at best, and arguably none.

12. See Kaminsky, Reinhart, and Végh (2004) on this issue.

13. Of course, it was not always so. Prior to the 1980s, many governments viewed allowing foreign direct investment (FDI) as equivalent to mortgaging their futures, and hence preferred debt finance. And where FDI was more dominant (e.g., in oil and natural resources investment in the 1950s and 1960s), many countries eventually ended up seizing foreigners' operations later on, again leading to considerable trauma. Thus FDI should not be regarded as a panacea for poor growth performance.

14. Rogoff (1999) and Bulow and Rogoff (1990) argue that the legal systems of creditor countries should be amended so they no longer tilt capital flows toward debt.

15. The issues of debt reduction and debt reversal are taken up in box 5.3.

Chapter 3 A Global Database on Financial Crises with a Long-Term View

1. Detailed citations are in our references and data appendix.

2. See Williamson's "regional" papers (1999, 2000a, 2000b). These regional papers provided time series for numerous developing countries for the mid-1800s to before World War II.

3. For OXLAD, see http://oxlad.qeh.ox.ac.uk/. See also Williamson (1999, 2000a, 2000b).

4. See http://gpih.ucdavis.edu/ and http://www.iisg.nl/hpw/. Although our analysis of inflation crises begins in 1500, many of the price series begin much earlier.

5. HSOUS is cited in the references as Carter et al. (2006); Garner's Economic History Data Desk is available at http://home.comcast.net/~richardgarner04/.

6. Reinhart and Rogoff (2004).

7. See Richard Bonney's European State Finance Database (ESFDB), available at http://www.le.ac.uk/hi/bon/ESFDB/frameset.html.

8. Allen and Unger's time series, *European Commodity Prices 1260–1914*, is available at http://www2.history.ubc.ca/unger/htm_files/new_grain.htm. Sevket Pamuk has constructed comparable series for Turkey through World War I (see http://www.ata.boun.edu.tr/sevket%20pamuk.htm).

9. See Maddison (2004). The TED is available at http://www.ggdc.net/.

10. PPP is calculated using Geary-Khamis weights. The Geary-Khamis dollar, also known as the international dollar, is a hypothetical unit of currency that has the same purchasing power that the U.S. dollar had in the United States at a given point in time. The year 1990 is used as a benchmark year for comparisons that run through time. The Geary-Khamis dollar shows how much a local currency unit is worth within the country's borders. It is used to make comparisons both between countries and over time.

11. There are exceptions. For instance, Rodney Edvinsson's careful estimates for Sweden from 1720 to 2000 or HSOUS for the United States beginning in 1790 offers a basis from which to examine earlier economic cycles and their relation to crises.

12. It is well known that revenues are intimately linked to the economic cycle.

13. See, for example, calculations in the background material to Reinhart and Rogoff (2004), available on the authors' Web pages.

14. See Mitchell (2003a, 2003b) and Kaminsky, Reinhart, and Végh (2004).

15. See Brahmananda (2001), Yousef (2002), and Baptista (2006).

16. These numbers are a lower bound because they do not include the many sovereign defaults prior to 1800 and, as regards domestic defaults, we have only begun to skim the surface; see Reinhart and Rogoff (2008c).

17. This description comes from the IMF's Web site, http://www.imf.org/external/data.htm: "Download time series data for GDP growth, inflation, unemployment, payments balances, exports, imports, external debt, capital flows, commodity prices, more."

18. For some countries, such as the Netherlands, Singapore, and the United States, practically all public debt is domestic.

19. For Australia, Ghana, India, Korea, and South Africa, among others, we have put together debt data for much of the colonial period.

20. See Miller (1926), Wynne (1951), Lindert and Morton (1989), and Marichal (1989).

21. Flandreau and Zumer (2004) are an important data source for Europe, 1880–1913.

22. Even under these circumstances, they continue to be a useful measure of gross capital inflows; the earlier sample included relatively little private external borrowing or bank lending.

23. Indonesia prior to 1972 is a good example of a country where this exercise was particularly useful.

24. Jeanne and Guscina (2006) compiled detailed data on the composition of domestic and external debt for nineteen important emerging markets for 1980–2005; Cowan et al. (2006) performed a similar exercise for all the developing countries of the Western Hemisphere for 1980–2004. See Reinhart, Rogoff, and Savastano (2003a) for an early attempt to measure domestic public debt for emerging markets.

25. http://www.imf.org/.

26. The fact that some of the world's poorest countries often fail to fully repay their debts to official lenders cannot be construed as a financial crisis in the conventional sense, because the official lenders often continue to provide aid nevertheless. See Bulow and Rogoff (2005) for a discussion of the related issue of whether multilateral development banks would be better structured as outright aid agencies.

Chapter 4   A Digression on the Theoretical Underpinnings of Debt Crises

1. During the late 1920s, Stalin's collectivization of farms led to mass starvation, and Russia needed money to import grain. As a result, in 1930 and 1931 the country sold some of its art treasures to foreigners, including the British oil magnate Calouste Gulbenkian and the American banker Andrew Mellon. But Stalin surely did not contemplate using any of the proceeds to repay old Tsarist debts.

2. See Persson and Tabellini (1990) and Obstfeld and Rogoff (1996) for literature surveys.

3. Tomz (2007).

4. See Eaton and Gersovitz (1981).

5. If countries simply borrow ever greater amounts without ever repaying, levels of debt relative to income must eventually explode provided the world (risk-adjusted) real interest rate exceeds the country's long-term real growth rate, which generally appears to be the case both in practice and under reasonable theoretical restrictions.

6. More generally, the game theoretic approach to reputation detailed by Eaton and Gersovitz typically admits to a huge variety of equilibria (outcomes), all of which can be rationalized by the same reputation mechanism.

7. See Bulow and Rogoff (1989b).

8. See Bulow and Rogoff (1989a).

9. Bulow and Rogoff (1989b) present a simple example based on a tariff war; Cole and Kehoe (1996) place this argument in a more general setting.

10. Borensztein et al. (1998) examine the empirics of the relationship of FDI and economic growth.

11. See Diamond and Rajan (2001).

12. See Jeanne (2009)

13. See Sachs (1984).

14. See, for example, Obstfeld and Rogoff (1996, chapter 6).

15. See Bulow and Rogoff (1988a, 1989a).

16. The citizens of a creditor country (outside of banks) may realize gains from trade just as the citizens of the debtor country do. Or, in the case of an international lending agency such as the IMF, creditors and debtors may be able to induce payments based on the IMF's fear that a default will lead to contagion to other borrowers.

17. See Jayachandran and Kremer (2006).

18. See, for example, Broner and Ventura (2007).

19. See Barro (1974).

20. See North and Weingast (1988).

21. See Kotlikoff, Persson, and Svensson (1988)

22. See Tabellini (1991).

23. For example, see Barro and Gordon (1983).

Chapter 5   Cycles of Sovereign Default on External Debt

1. MacDonald (2006); Ferguson (2008).

2. Cipolla (1982).

3. North and Weingast (1988); Weingast (1997).

4. Carlos et al. (2005).

5. Kindleberger (1989) is among the few scholars who emphasize that the 1950s still has to be viewed as a financial crisis era.

6. This comparison weights defaulting countries by share of world income. On an un-weighted basis (so that, for example, the poorest countries in Africa and South Asia receive the same weight as Brazil or the United States), the period from the late 1960s until 1982 saw an even lower percentage of independent countries in default.

7. Kindleberger (1989) emphasizes the prevalence of default after World War II, though he does not provide quantification.

8. Note that in figure 5.2 the debt crises of the 1980s do not loom as large as the previous cycle of defaults, for only middle- and low-income countries faced default in the 1980s while, in addition to emerging market economies, several advanced economies defaulted during the Great Depression and several more defaulted during World War II.

9. Calvo (1998) credits the late Rudy Dornbusch, who quotes the old banking adage, "It is not the speed that kills you. It is the sudden stop" (Dornbusch et al. 1995).

10. Reinhart, Rogoff, and Savastano (2003b) illustrated that countries with a history of external defaults also had a poor inflation track record.

11. Fisher (1933).

12. Domestic defaults produce even worse inflation outcomes; see chapter 9.

13. See Calvo, Leiderman, and Reinhart (1993); Dooley et al. (1996); and Chuhan et al. (1998) for earlier papers quantifying the role of external factors influencing capital flows to emerging markets and their access to credit markets. On predicting defaults with domestic and some global factors, see Manasse and Roubini (2005).

14. See Kaminsky, Reinhart, and Végh (2004) and Aguiar and Gopinath (2007).

15. See the work of Reinhart and Reinhart (2009), who document the common occurrence of "capital inflow bonanzas" in the years preceding debt crises in emerging markets. It is of note that this analysis also shows that capital flow bonanzas precede banking crises in both advanced and emerging market economies.

16. For a fuller account of the episode, see Baker (1994).

17. Hale (2003).

18. Box 5.3 summarizes some of the results in Reinhart, Rogoff, and Savastano (2003a), which presents empirical evidence of this "quick-to-releverage" pattern.

19. Reinhart, Rogoff, and Savastano (2003a).

Chapter 6   External Default through History

1. See Reinhart, Rogoff, and Savastano (2003a); they thank Harold James for this observation.

2. Winkler (1933), p. 29. One wonders if Thomas Jefferson read those words, in that he subsequently held that "the tree of liberty must be refreshed from time to time with the blood of patriots and tyrants."

3. Macdonald (2006).

4. Ibid.

5. Kindleberger (1989).

6. Reinhart, Rogoff, and Savastano (2003a).

7. For example, see Mauro et al. (2006).

8. Latin American states were not the only ones borrowing at this time. Greece (still engaged in its struggle for independence), Portugal, and Russia were also issuing and placing pound-denominated bonds in London.

9. For a fascinating fact-based account of this enterprise that reads like fiction, see David Sinclair's 2004 book, *The Land That Never Was: Sir Gregor MacGregor and the Most Audacious*

Fraud in History. Of the 250 settlers who crossed the Atlantic en route to Poyais (which was supposedly on the Bay of Honduras, site of the present Belize), only 50 survived to tell the tale.

10. MacGregor was also able to raise an additional £40,000 through various channels for a total of £200,000, well above the £163,000 raised by the nonfictional Federation of Central American States during the 1822–1825 lending boom.

Chapter 7   The Stylized Facts of Domestic Debt and Default

1. Reinhart, Rogoff, and Savastano (2003a) drew on national sources to develop a data set for selected developing countries and emerging markets covering the years 1990–2002. More recently, Jeanne and Guscina (2006) provided detailed data on domestic debt for nineteen important emerging markets from 1980 to 2005. Cowan et al. (2006) provided data for all the countries in the Western Hemisphere from 1980 (or 1990) to 2004. Reinhart and Rogoff (2008a) described a companion database covering a broad range of related variables, including external debt, on which we also draw here.

2. Domestic public debt has never amounted to much in a few Latin American countries (Uruguay stands out in this regard), and public debt markets are virtually nonexistent in the CFA African countries (originally the *Colonies françaises d'Afrique*).

3. Of course, during the early years of the interwar period, many countries pegged their currencies to gold.

4. It should also be noted that until the past ten to fifteen years, most countries' external debt was largely public debt. Private external borrowing has become more significant only over the past couple of decades; see Prasad et al. (2003). Arellano and Kocherlakota (2008) developed a model of the relationship between private debt and external government default.

5. See chapter 12 for a discussion of the aftermath and consequences of high inflation.

6. See Calvo (1991) on these "perilous" practices.

7. See Barro (1974).

8. See Woodford (1995) on the former, Diamond (1965) on the latter.

9. For example, Tabellini (1991) or Kotlikoff et al. (1988).

10. Including a handful of very recent domestic defaults, the sample can in fact be extended to more than seventy domestic defaults.

11. Brock (1989). The average reserve requirements for developing countries in Brock's sample from 1960 to early 1980s ran at about 0.25, more than three times that for advanced economies.

12. Another subtle type of default is illustrated by the Argentine government's treatment of its inflation-indexed debt in 2007. Most impartial observers agree that during this period, Argentina's official inflation rate considerably understated its actual inflation because of government manipulation. This understatement represented a partial default on index-linked debt by any reasonable measure, and it affected a large number of bondholders. Yet Argentina's de facto domestic bond default did not register heavily in the external press or with rating agencies.

Chapter 8   Domestic Debt

1. One of the best standard sources is Maddison (2004).

2. For instance, Bulow and Rogoff (1988b); Reinhart, Rogoff, and Savastano (2003a).

3. See Reinhart, Rogoff, and Savastano (2003a).

4. For example, the Kolmogorov-Smirnov test rejects the hypothesis that the two frequency distributions are equal at the 1 percent level.

5. See Gavin and Perotti (1997) and Kaminsky, Reinhart, and Végh (2004) for evidence on procyclical macroeconomic policies. See also Aguiar and Gopinath (2007) for a model in which the procyclical behavior of the current account can be rationalized by the high ratio of permanent to transitory shocks in emerging markets.

6. Of course, today's rich countries experienced much the same problems in earlier eras—when they, too, were serial defaulters and they, too, exhibited highly procyclical fisal policy.

7. See Cagan (1956). Seignorage revenue is simply the real income a government can realize by exercising its monopoly on printing currency. The revenue can be broken down into the quantity of currency needed to meet the growing transactions demand at constant prices and the remaining growth, which causes inflation, thereby lowering the purchasing power of existing currency. The latter effect is generally referred to as the inflation tax. In a classic paper, Sargent (1982) includes data on central banks' holdings of treasury bills after World War I for five countries (Austria, Czechoslovakia, Germany, Hungary, and Poland). But of course, these debts are essentially a wash on the consolidated government balance sheet.

8. See Dornbusch and Fischer (1993).

9. Of course, the possibility of using unanticipated inflation to default on nominal debt is well understood in the theoretical literature, such as Barro (1983).

10. The case of Brazil is exceptional in that some of the debt was indexed to inflation, although lags in the indexation scheme still made it possible for the government to largely inflate away the debt with a high enough rate of inflation. Indeed, this appears to be exactly what happened, for the country lurched in and out of hyperinflation for many years.

11. Calvo and Guidotti (1992) developed a model of the optimal maturity structure of nominal debt whereby the government trades off flexibility (the option to inflate away long-term debt when under financial duress) versus its high credibility for maintaining a low inflation rate (achieved by having very short-term debt, which is more difficult to inflate away).

Chapter 9   Domestic and External Default

1. It should also be noted that other economic indicators (besides inflation and per capita GDP growth, which we examine in detail) would provide a richer answer to the broad question of how bad conditions have to be before a country should contemplate default. (Specifically, the impacts of domestic versus foreign default on social indicators relating to poverty, health, income distribution, and so on, are, in principle, bound to be quite different.)

2. It is hardly surprising that inflation rises in the aftermath of external default, especially given the typical massive exchange rate depreciation.

3. We have excluded Bolivia's 1982 domestic default from these averages, because inflation peaked at over 11,000 percent in the year before $(t-1)$ the domestic default.

4. Reinhart and Savastano (2003) discuss the forcible conversion of foreign currency bank deposits (as was also seen in Argentina in 2002) during the hyperinflations in Bolivia and Peru.

5. The United States, of course, is the modern exception. Virtually all U.S. debt is domestic (as the Carter bonds have matured). Yet about 40 percent is held by nonresidents (mostly central banks and other official institutions), and all is dollar denominated. Thus, inflation in the United States would also affect nonresidents.

6. The huge spike in external defaults in the 1820s was due to the much-studied first wave of sovereign defaults of the newly independent Latin American countries. But Greece and Portugal also defaulted at that time.

7. See figure 9.6.

8. Drazen (1998).

9. See Alesina and Tabellini (1990).

10. Beyond simply reporting debt data, international financial institutions such as the International Monetary Fund and the World Bank can also help with disseminating information on best practices (see, for example, the institutional evolution discussed in Wallis and Weingast 1988).

Chapter 10   Banking Crises

1. See Gorton (1988) and Calomiris and Gorton (1991) on banking panics before World War II; Sundararajan and Baliño (1991) for several case studies of emerging markets; and Jácome (2008) on banking crises in Latin America.

2. Studies that encompass episodes in both advanced and emerging economies include those of Demirgüç-Kunt and Detragiache (1998), Kaminsky and Reinhart (1999), and Bordo et al. (2001).

3. See, for instance, Agénor et al. (2000).

4. Reinhart and Rogoff (2008a, 2008c) show that output growth typically decelerates in advance of a crisis.

5. See Diamond and Dybvig (1983).

6. Ibid.

7. See Bernanke and Gertler (1990).

8. See Kiyotaki and Moore (1997).

9. See, for example, Bernanke and Gertler (1995).

10. See Bernanke et al. (1999).

11. This refers to default on external debt. The widespread abrogation of gold clauses and other forms of restructuring—on domestic debt—by the United States and other developed economies during the Great Depression of the 1930s are considered sovereign defaults on domestic debt (debt issued under domestic law).

12. As we have already acknowledged, our accounting of financial crises in poorer countries may be incomplete, especially for earlier periods, despite our best efforts.

13. To be precise, the advanced countries experienced 7.2 crises, on average, versus 2.8 for emerging market countries.

14. See Obstfeld and Taylor (2004).

15. See Kaminsky and Reinhart (1999).

16. See Demirgüç-Kunt and Detragiache (1998). See also Drees and Pazarbasioglu (1998) for an insightful discussion of the Nordic experience with financial liberalization.

17. See Caprio and Klingebiel (1996).

18. To define a capital flow bonanza, Reinhart and Reinhart (2009) settled on an algorithm that provided uniform treatment across countries but was flexible enough to allow for significant cross-country variation in the current account. Like Kaminsky and Reinhart (1999), they selected a threshold to define bonanzas that is common across countries (in this case, the 20th percentile of the sample). This threshold included most of the better known episodes in the literature but was not so inclusive as to label as a bonanza a more "routine" deterioration in the current account. Because the underlying frequency distributions vary widely across countries, the common threshold produces quite disperse country-specific cutoffs. For instance, in the case of relatively closed India, the cutoff to define a bonanza is a ratio of current account deficit

to GDP in excess of 1.8 percent, while for trade-oriented Malaysia the comparable cutoff is a ratio of deficit to GDP of 6.6 percent.

19. Reinhart and Reinhart performed comparable exercises for currency, debt, and inflation crises.

20. See Reinhart and Reinhart (2009).

21. See Mendoza and Terrones (2008). See also the work of Kaminsky and Reinhart (1999), who also examined the growth in real credit available to the private sector around both banking and currency crises.

22. See Reinhart and Rogoff (2008b). Each year refers to the beginning of the crisis.

23. See Bordo and Jeanne (2002).

24. See Gerdrup (2003).

25. Historical comparisons are hard to come by, because most real housing price series are of recent vintage, but we do include in this category two older episodes: that of the United States during the Great Depression and that of Norway at the turn of the century (1898).

26. See the work of Ceron and Suarez (2006), who estimate its average duration at six years.

27. For example, Agénor et al. (2000) provide evidence that output and real consumption are far more volatile in emerging markets; Kaminsky, Reinhart, and Végh (2003) present evidence that the amplitude of the cycle in real government spending is orders of magnitude greater in emerging markets.

28. This notion is consistent with the fact that house prices are far more inertial than equity prices.

29. See Philippon (2007).

30. See Frydl (1999) and Norges Bank (2004). See also Sanhueza (2001), Hoggarth et al. (2005), and Caprio et al. (2005).

31. A similar problem plagues work on determining the effectiveness of foreign exchange intervention by measuring the profitability of such market purchases or sales. The results depend significantly on the width of the time window and on implicit assumptions of the cost of financing. See Neely (1995).

32. See Vale (2004).

33. See, for instance, Frydl (1999), Kaminsky and Reinhart (1999), and especially Rajan et al. (2008), who examine the output consequences of the credit channel following banking crises using micro data. We note that, of the cases of output collapses studied by Barro and Ursúa (2008), virtually all are associated with banking crises.

34. Revenues (from Mitchell, 2003a, 2003b) are deflated by consumer price indexes; the numerous sources of these data are given on a country-by-country and period-by-period basis in appendix A.2.

35. Indeed, in some important cases, such as that of Japan, the accelerated debt buildup goes on for more than a decade, so the three-year cutoff grossly understates the longer-term consequences.

36. Note that figure 10.10 gives the percentage of change in debt rather than debt relative to GDP in order not to distort the numbers by the large falls in GDP that sometimes accompany crises. However, the same basic message comes across looking at debt relative to GDP instead. Note that the calculations are based on total central government debt.

37. An important question is how rare banking crises, through sudden changes in market liquidity, might amplify the effects on asset prices, as analyzed by Barro (2009).

Chapter 11   Default through Debasement

1. See, for example, Sargent and Velde (2003). Ferguson (2008) provides an insightful discussion of the early roots of money.
2. See Winkler (1928).
3. MacDonald (2006).

Chapter 12   Inflation and Modern Currency Crashes

1. Végh (1992) and Fischer et al. (2002) are essential readings for discussions of the literature on relatively modern inflation crises.
2. The dates in table 12.2 extend back prior to the time of independence for many countries, including, for example, Malaysia.
3. China, which invented the printing press well ahead of Europe, famously experienced episodes of high inflation created by paper currency in the twelfth and thirteen centuries. (For more on this subject, see, for example, Fischer et al. 2002.) These episodes are in our database as well.
4. Reinhart and Rogoff (2002).
5. Cagan (1956).
6. At the time of this writing, the "official" inflation rate in Argentina is 8 percent; informed estimates place it at 26 percent.
7. Reinhart, Rogoff, and Savastano (2003b).
8. The following section examines in detail the experience of countries that have recorded large declines in their degree of domestic dollarization, including in the context of disinflations.
9. Reinhart and Rogoff (2004) show that countries with dual exchange rate systems tend to have worse average growth performances and vastly worse inflation performances.
10. This pattern was particularly common in the second half of the 1990s among the transition economies (e.g., Azerbaijan, Belarus, Lithuania, and Russia) but was also present in other countries and periods—for instance, in Bolivia and Peru in the early 1980s and in Egypt in the mid-1990s.
11. See Bufman and Leiderman (1992).
12. See Dornbusch and Werner (1994).

Chapter 13   The U.S. Subprime Crisis

1. As indicated in note 7 to the preamble, we use the term "Second Great Contraction" after Friedman and Schwartz's (1963) depiction of the 1930s as "The Great Contraction." See also Felton and Reinhart (2008, 2009), who use the term "First Global Financial Crisis of the 21st Century."
2. See chapter 10 for further discussion.
3. We have explored this issue further in chapter 10.
4. Although China's heavy-handed capital controls shielded it from contagious currency crashes during Asia's turmoil, they did not protect it from a systemic and costly banking crisis emanating primarily from large-scale lending to inefficient and bankrupt state-owned enterprises.

5. Figure 13.1 does not fully capture the extent of the present upsurge in financial crises, for Ireland and Iceland (both of which are experiencing banking crises at the time of this writing) are not part of our core sixty-six-country sample.

6. The Case-Shiller index is described by Robert Shiller (2005) and in recent years has been published monthly in conjunction with Standard and Poor's (as described at their Web site, www.standardandpoors.com). The Case-Shiller index focuses on resales of the same houses and therefore is arguably a more accurate gauge of price movements than indexes that look at all sales. Of course, there are many biases even in the Case-Shiller index (e.g., it is restricted to major metropolitan areas). Nevertheless, it is widely regarded as the most accurate gauge of changes in housing prices in the United States.

7. The Case-Shiller index appears to paint a quite plausible history of housing prices, but as a caveat we note that construction of the series required a significant number of assumptions to interpolate data missing for some intervals, particularly prior to World War II.

8. The current account balance is basically a broader measure of the trade balance—imports minus exports—extended to include investment returns. Note that the current account represents the sum of both government and private borrowing flows from abroad; it is not the same thing as the government deficit. It is perfectly possible for the government to be running a fiscal deficit and yet for the current account to be in surplus, provided the private savings compensate.

9. Greenspan (2007).

10. *Economist Magazine*, "The O'Neill Doctrine," lead editorial, April 25, 2002.

11. Bernanke (2005).

12. See Philippon (2007).

13. Securitization of mortgages involves the bunching and repackaging of mortgage pools to transform highly idiosyncratic individual loans into more standardized products. Thus, to the extent that the U.S. current account was being driven by superior U.S. financial innovation, there was also nothing to worry about. Or so top U.S. financial regulators maintained.

14. See Obstfeld and Rogoff (2001, 2005, 2007).

15. Obstfeld and Rogoff (2001).

16. Roubini and Setser (2004).

17. Krugman (2007). Wile E. Coyote is the hapless character from Chuck Jones's *Road Runner* cartoons. His schemes invariably fail, and, as he runs off a cliff, there is a moment or two before the recognition sets in that nothing is below him.

18. See Obstfeld and Rogoff (2009) for a more detailed discussion of the literature; see also Wolf (2008).

19. Dooley et al. (2004a, 2004b).

20. Cooper (2005).

21. Hausmann and Sturzenegger (2007).

22. Curcuru et al. (2008) argue that the "dark matter" hypothesis is at odds with the data.

23. See Bernanke and Gertler (2001).

24. Bordo and Jeanne (2002), Bank for International Settlements (2005).

25. See Rolnick (2004).

26. We first noted the remarkable similarities between the 2007 U.S. subprime crisis and other deep financial crises in Reinhart and Rogoff (2008b), first circulated in December 2007. By the time of this writing, of course, the facts overwhelmingly support this reading of events.

Our sources have included Caprio and Klingebiel (1996 and 2003), Kaminsky and Reinhart (1999), and Caprio et al. (2005).

27. Later we look at some alternative metrics for measuring the depth of these financial crises, arguing that the traditional measure—fiscal costs of the bank cleanup—is far too narrow.

28. See, for example, Kaminsky, Lizondo, and Reinhart (1998) and Kaminsky and Reinhart (1999).

29. For the United States, as earlier in this chapter, house prices are measured by the Case-Shiller index. The remaining house price data were made available by the Bank for International Settlements and are described by Gregory D. Sutton (2002). Of course, there are many limitations to the international housing price data; they typically do not have the long history that allows for a richer comparison across business cycles. Nevertheless, they probably reasonably capture our main variable of interest, peak-to-trough falls in the price of housing, even if they perhaps exaggerate the duration of the fall, because they are relatively slow to reflect changes in underlying market prices.

30. For the United States, the index is the S&P 500.

31. According to Reinhart and Reinhart (2009), during 2005–2007 the U.S. episode qualified as a "capital flow bonanza" (i.e., a period of abnormally large capital inflows, which is a different way of saying above-average borrowing from abroad).

32. In principle, the rise in real public debt is determined by taking the rise in nominal public debt and adjusting for the rise that represents inflation in all prices.

33. See the conclusions of Reinhart and Reinhart (2008), who explain these changes in interest rates and exchange rates as anomalies for the United States—because the United States is too big to fail.

Chapter 14   The Aftermath of Financial Crises

1. Also included in the comparisons are two prewar episodes in developed countries for which we have housing price and other relevant data.

2. To be clear, peak-to-trough calculations are made on an individual series-by-series basis. The trough and peak dates are those nearest the crisis date and refer to the local (rather than global) maximum or minimum, following much the same approach pioneered by Burns and Mitchell (1946) in their classic study of U.S. business cycles. So for example, in the case of Japan's equity prices, the trough is the local bottom in 1995, even though the subsequent recovery in the equity market left prices well below their prior peak before the crisis (and that the subsequent troughs would see prices at lower levels still).

3. In chapter 10, we looked at financial crises in sixty-six countries over two hundred years, emphasizing the broad parallels between emerging markets and developing countries, including, for example, the nearly universal run-up in government debt.

4. The historical average, which is shaded in black in the diagram, does not include the ongoing crises.

5. Notably, widespread "underemployment" in many emerging markets and the vast informal sector are not fully captured in the official unemployment statistics.

6. Again, see Calvo (1998) and Dornbusch et al. (1995).

7. See International Monetary Fund (various years), World Economic Outlook, April 2002, chapter 3.

8. Other noteworthy comparisons and parallels to the Great Depression are presented in Eichengreen and O'Rourke (2009).

Chapter 15 The International Dimensions of the Subprime Crisis

1. The IMF, of course, is effectively the global lender of last resort for emerging markets, which typically face severe strains in floating new debt during a crisis. Given the quadrupling of IMF resources agreed to at the April 2, 2009, London meeting of the Group of 20 heads of state (including those of the largest rich countries and the major emerging markets), world market panic about the risks of sovereign default have notably abated. The IMF guarantees apply only to government debt, however, and risk spreads on the corporate debt of emerging markets remain elevated as of mid-2009, with rates of corporate default continuing to rise. It remains to be seen to what extent, if any, these debt problems will spill over to governments through bailouts, as they often have in the past.

2. Kaminsky, Reinhart, and Végh (2003); quote on p. 55, emphasis ours.

3. Bordo and Murshid (2001), Neal and Weidenmier (2003). Neal and Weidenmier emphasize that periods of apparent contagion can be more readily interpreted as responses to common shocks, an issue we return to in the context of the recent crisis. But perhaps the bottom line as regards a historical perspective on financial contagion is best summarized by Bordo and Murshid, who conclude that there is little evidence to suggest that cross-country linkages are tighter in the aftermath of a financial crisis for the recent period as opposed to 1880–1913, the earlier heyday of globalization in financial markets that they study.

4. Table 15.1 does not include the bunching of other "types" of crises, such as the wave of sovereign defaults during 1825 or the currency crashes or debasements of the Napoleonic Wars. Again, the indexes developed in chapter 16 will allow us to capture this kind of bundling of crises across both countries and types of crises.

5. See Neal and Weidenmier (2003) and Reinhart and Rogoff (2008a).

6. Owing to the opaqueness of balance sheets in many financial institutions in these countries, the full extent of exposure is, as yet, unknown.

7. See Reinhart and Reinhart (2009) for a full listing of episodes of capital inflow bonanzas.

Chapter 16 Composite Measures of Financial Turmoil

1. Kaminsky and Reinhart (1999).

2. The tally would come to six varieties of crises if we included currency debasement. We do not follow this route for two reasons: first, there are far fewer sources of data across countries (about a dozen or so) on the metallic content of their currencies; second, the printing press displaced debasement and decoupled currencies in circulation from a metallic base with the rise of fiat money. Because the period we analyzed for the turbulence composite was after 1800 (when our dating of banking crises begins in earnest), the exclusion of debasement crises is not as troublesome as for 1300–1799, when debasement was rampant.

3. This goes back to the dichotomous measures of crises that we (and most studies) employ. Of course, it is possible to consider additional gradations of crises to capture some measure of severity.

4. As noted, one could easily refine this measure to include three categories, say, high inflation (above 20 percent but less than 40), very high inflation (above 40 percent but less than 1,000), and hyperinflation (1,000 percent or higher).

5. Namely, crash episodes associated with international financial crises and turbulence (mostly in advanced economies).

6. Our list of economic crises does not include a growth collapse crisis as defined by Barro and Ursúa (2008, 2009), which is an episode in which per capita GDP falls cumulatively by 10 percent or more. An important share of the crisis episodes we identify are candidates for this definition as well. We examine this issue later. Nor does our composite index of financial turbulence necessarily include all "sudden stop" episodes as defined by Guillermo Calvo and co-authors in several contributions (see references). The reader will recall that a sudden stop is an episode in which there is an abrupt reversal in international capital flows, often associated with loss of capital market access. It is noteworthy that most systemic banking crises past and present (the 2007 U.S. subprime crisis is an exception) have been associated with sudden stops. The same could be said of sovereign external defaults.

7. Barro and Ursúa (2009). They identify 195 stock market crashes for twenty-five countries (eighteen advanced economies and seven emerging markets) over 1869–2006.

8. Samuelson (1966).

9. The reader will recall from earlier chapters that our sixty-six-country sample accounts for about 90 percent of world GDP.

10. It is important to note that Austria, Germany, Italy, and Japan remained in default for varying durations after the end of the war.

11. See McConnell and Perez-Quiros (2000) and Blanchard and Simon (2001).

12. As in nearly all previous historical crises in Argentina, the 2001–2002 episode was followed by a crisis in its small neighbor, Uruguay.

13. The hyperinflation episodes are the most notorious, obviously, but the share of countries in the region with an annual inflation rate above 20 percent, thereby meeting our threshold for a crisis, hit a peak of nearly 90 percent in 1990!

14. Burns and Mitchell (1946). For more recent treatments of the early warning properties of equity markets in the context of crises, see Kaminsky et al. (1998), Kaminsky and Reinhart (1999), and Barro and Ursúa (2009).

15. International Monetary Fund (various years), World Economic Outlook.

16. Eichengreen and O'Rourke (2009) add trade to highlight the similarities while noting the difference in monetary policy response (specifically, central bank discount rates).

17. Maddison (2004).

18. League of Nations (various years), World Economic Survey.

19. See, for example, League of Nations (1944).

20. Although we have reliable trade data for most countries during World War II, there are sufficient missing entries to make the calculation of the world aggregate not comparable to other years during 1940–1947.

21. Kaminsky and Reinhart (1999).

22. Demirgüç-Kunt and Detragiache (1998).

23. Reinhart (2002).

24. Reinhart and Rogoff (2004) also examined the relationship between currency crashes and inflation as well as the timing of currency crashes and capital control (specifically, dual or multiple exchange rates).

25. Diaz-Alejandro (1985).

26. In contrast to other studies of banking crises, Kaminsky and Reinhart (1999) provide two dates for each banking crisis episode—the beginning of a banking crisis and the later peak.

27. See Goldstein and Turner (2004).

28. See Reinhart, Rogoff, and Savastano (2003a).

29. The second and third effects of the depreciation or devaluation of the currency listed earlier are less of an issue for advanced economies.

Chapter 17 Reflections on Early
Warnings, Graduation, Policy Responses,
and the Foibles of Human Nature

1. On indicators for risk of currency crises, see Kaminsky, Lizondo, and Reinhart (1998); Berg and Pattillo (1999); Bussiere and Mulder (2000); Berg et al. (2004); Bussiere and Fratzscher (2006); and Bussiere (2007) and sources cited therein. For banking crises, see Demirgüç-Kunt and Detragiache (1998, 1999). For the twin crises (indicators of when a country is at risk of a joint banking and currency crisis), see Kaminsky and Reinhart (1999) and Goldstein, Kaminsky, and Reinhart (2000).

2. Ideally, one would also want comparable price data for commercial real estate, which played a particularly important role in the asset bubbles in Japan and other Asian economies in the run-up to their major banking crises.

3. Kaminsky, Lizondo, and Reinhart (1998) and Kaminsky and Reinhart (1999). The signals approach, described in detail by Kaminsky, Lizondo, and Reinhart (1998), ranks indicators according to their "noise-to-signal" ratios. When an indicator sends a signal (waves a red flag) and a crisis occurs within the following two-year window, it is an accurate signal; if no crisis follows the signal, it is a false alarm or noise. Hence the best indicators are those with the lowest noise-to-signal ratio.

4. We have argued the case for an international financial regulator in Reinhart and Rogoff (2008d).

5. See Reinhart, Rogoff, and Savastano (2003a).

6. Qian and Reinhart (2009).

7. See Kaminsky, Reinhart, and Végh (2004).

8. Friedman and Schwartz (1963).

9. See Kindleberger (1989).

REFERENCES

Agénor, Pierre-Richard, John McDermott, and Eswar Prasad. 2000. "Macroeconomic Fluctuations in Developing Countries: Some Stylized Facts." *World Bank Economic Review* 14: 251–285.

Aguiar, Mark, and Gita Gopinath. 2007. "Emerging Market Business Cycles: The Cycle Is the Trend." *Journal of Political Economy* 115 (1): 69–102.

Alesina, Alberto, and Guido Tabellini. 1990. "A Positive Theory of Fiscal Deficits and Government Debt." *Review of Economic Studies* 57: 403–414.

Allen, Franklin, and Douglas Gale. 2007. *Understanding Financial Crises*. Oxford: Oxford University Press.

Allen, Robert C. 2001. "The Great Divergence: Wages and Prices from the Middle Ages to the First World War." *Explorations in Economic History* 38 (4): 411–447.

———. n.d. *Consumer Price Indices, Nominal/Real Wages and Welfare Ratios of Building Craftsmen and Labourers, 1260–1913*. Oxford, England: Oxford University Press. Available at http://www.iisg.nl/hpw/data.php#europe.

Allen, Robert C., and Richard W. Unger. 2004. *European Commodity Prices, 1260–1914*. Oxford, England: Oxford University Press. Available at http://www2.history.ubc.ca/unger.

Arellano, Cristina, and Narayana Kocherlakota. 2008. "Internal Debt Crises and Sovereign Defaults." NBER Working Paper 13794. National Bureau of Economic Research, Cambridge, Mass. February.

Baker, Melvin. 1994. *The Second Squires Administration and the Loss of Responsible Government, 1928–1934*. Available at http://www.ucs.mun.ca/~melbaker/1920s.htm.

Bank for International Settlements. 2005. *Annual Report*. Basel: Bank for International Settlements.

Baptista, Asdrúbal. 2006. *Bases Cuantitativas de la Economía Venezolana, 1830–2005*. Caracas: Ediciones Fundación Polar.

Barro, Robert. 1974. "Are Government Bonds Net Wealth?" *Journal of Political Economy* 82 (6): 1095–1117.

———. 1983. "Inflationary Finance under Discretion and Rules." *Canadian Journal of Economics* 16 (1): 1–16.

———. 2009. "Rare Disasters, Asset Prices and Welfare Costs." *American Economic Review* 99 (1): 243–264.

Barro, Robert J., and David B. Gordon. 1983. "A Positive Theory of Monetary Policy in a Natural Rate Model." *Journal of Political Economy* 91 (August): 589–610.

Barro, Robert, and José F. Ursúa. 2008. "Macroeconomic Crises since 1870." NBER Working Paper 13940. National Bureau of Economic Research, Cambridge, Mass. April.

———. 2009. "Stock-Market Crashes and Depressions." NBER Working Paper 14760. National Bureau of Economic Research, Cambridge, Mass. February.

Bassino, Jean-Pascal, and Debin Ma. 2005. "Japanese Unskilled Wages in International Perspective, 1741–1913." *Research in Economic History* 23: 229–248.

Bassino, Jean-Pascal, and Pierre van der Eng. 2006. "New Benchmark of Wages and GDP, 1913–1970." Mimeo. Montpellier University, Montpellier, France.

Bazant, Jan. 1968. *Historia de la Deuda Exterior de Mexico: 1823–1946*. Mexico City: El Colegio de México.

Berg, Andrew, and Catherine Pattillo. 1999. "Predicting Currency Crises: The Indicators Approach and an Alternative." *Journal of International Money and Finance* 18: 561–586.

Berg, Andrew, Eduardo Borensztein, and Catherine Pattillo. 2004. "Assessing Early Warning Systems: How Have They Worked in Practice?" International Monetary Fund Working Paper 04/52. International Monetary Fund, Washington, D.C.

Bernanke, Ben S. 1983. "Nonmonetary Effects of the Financial Crisis in the Propagation of the Great Depression." *American Economic Review* 73 (June): 257–276.

———. 2005. "The Global Saving Glut and the U.S. Current Account Deficit." Speech given at the Homer Jones Lecture, St. Louis, Mo., April 14. Available at http://www.federalreserve.gov/boarddocs/speeches/2005/20050414/default.htm.

Bernanke, Ben S., and Mark Gertler. 1990. "Financial Fragility and Economic Performance." *Quarterly Journal of Economics* 105 (February): 87–114.

———. 1995. "Inside the Black Box: The Credit Channel of Monetary Policy Transmission." *Journal of Economic Perspectives* 9 (Fall): 27–48.

———. 2001. "Should Central Banks Respond to Movements in Asset Prices?" *American Economic Review* 91 (2): 253–257.

Bernanke, Ben S., and Harold James. 1990. "The Gold Standard, Deflation, and Financial Crisis in the Great Depression: An International Comparison." NBER Working Paper 3488. National Bureau of Economic Research, Cambridge, Mass. October.

Bernanke, Ben S., Mark Gertler, and Simon Gilchrist. 1999. "The Financial Accelerator in a Quantitative Business Cycle Framework." In *Handbook of Macroeconomics*, vol. 1A, ed. John Taylor and Michael Woodford. Amsterdam: North-Holland.

Blanchard, Olivier, and John Simon. 2001. "The Long and Large Decline in U.S. Output Volatility." *Brookings Papers on Economic Activity* 1: 135–164.

Bonney, Richard. n.d. European State Finance Database. Available at http://www.le.ac.uk/hi/bon/ESFDB/frameset.html.

Bordo, Michael D. 2006. "Sudden Stops, Financial Crises and Original Sin in Emerging Countries: Déjà vu?" NBER Working Paper 12393. National Bureau of Economic Research, Cambridge, Mass. July.

Bordo, Michael, and Barry Eichengreen. 1999. "Is Our Current International Economic Environment Unusually Crisis Prone?" In *Capital Flows and the International Financial System*. Sydney: Reserve Bank of Australia Annual Conference Volume.

Bordo, Michael, and Olivier Jeanne. 2002. "Boom-Busts in Asset Prices, Economic Instability, and Monetary Policy." NBER Working Paper 8966. National Bureau of Economic Research, Cambridge, Mass. June.

411

Bordo, Michael D., and Antu Panini Murshid. 2001. "Are Financial Crises Becoming Increasingly More Contagious? What Is the Historical Evidence?" In *International Financial Contagion: How It Spreads and How It Can Be Stopped*, ed. Kristin Forbes and Stijn Claessens. New York: Kluwer Academic. Pp. 367–406.

Bordo, Michael, Barry Eichengreen, Daniela Klingebiel, and Maria Soledad Martinez-Peria. 2001. "Is the Crisis Problem Growing More Severe?" *Economic Policy* 16 (April): 51–82.

Borensztein, Eduardo, José De Gregorio, and Jong-Wha Lee. 1998. "How Does Foreign Direct Investment Affect Economic Growth?" *Journal of International Economics* 45 (1): 115–135.

Borodkin, L. I. 2001. " Inequality of Incomes in the Period of Industrial Revolution: Is Universal Hypothesis about Kuznets's Curve?" *Russian Political cal Encyclopedia*. Moscow: Rosspen.

Bouchard, Léon. 1891. *Système financier de l'ancienne monarchie*. Paris: Guillaumin.

Boughton, James. 1991. "Commodity and Manufactures Prices in the Long Run." International Monetary Fund Working Paper 91/47. International Monetary Fund, Washington, D.C. May.

Brahmananda, P. R. 2001. *Money, Income and Prices in 19th Century India*. Dehli: Himalaya.

Braun, Juan, Matias Braun, Ignacio Briones, and José Díaz. 2000. "Economía Chilena 1810–1995, Estadisticas Historicas." Pontificia Universidad Católica de Chile Documento de Trabajo 187. Pontificia Universidad Católica de Chile, Santiago. January.

Brock, Philip. 1989. "Reserve Requirements and the Inflation Tax." *Journal of Money, Credit and Banking* 21 (1): 106–121.

Broner, Fernando, and Jaume Ventura. 2007. "Globalization and Risk Sharing." CREI Working Paper. Centre de Recerca en Economia Internacional, Barcelona. July.

Brown, William Adams. 1940. *The International Gold Standard Reinterpreted, 1914–1940*. New York: National Bureau of Economic Research

Buchanan, James, and Richard Wagner. 1977. *Democracy in Deficit: The Political Legacy of Lord Keynes*. Amsterdam: Elsevier.

Bufman, Gil, and Leonardo Leiderman. 1992. "Simulating an Optimizing

Model of Currency Substitution." *Revista de Análisis Económico* 7 (1): 109–124.

Bulow, Jeremy, and Kenneth Rogoff. 1988a. "Multilateral Negotiations for Rescheduling Developing Country Debt: A Bargaining-Theoretic Framework." *IMF Staff Papers* 35 (4): 644–657.

———. 1988b. "The Buyback Boondoggle." *Brookings Papers on Economic Activity* 2: 675–698.

———. 1989a. "A Constant Recontracting Model of Sovereign Debt." *Journal of Political Economy* 97: 155–178.

———. 1989b. "Sovereign Debt: Is to Forgive to Forget?" *American Economic Review* 79 (March): 43–50.

———. 1990. "Cleaning Up Third-World Debt without Getting Taken to the Cleaners." *Journal of Economic Perspectives* 4 (Winter): 31–42.

———. 2005. "Grants versus Loans for Development Banks." *American Economic Review* 95 (2): 393–397.

Burns, Arthur F., and Wesley C. Mitchell. 1946. *Measuring Business Cycles.* National Bureau of Economic Research Studies in Business Cycles 2. Cambridge, Mass.: National Bureau of Economic Research.

Bussiere, Matthieu. 2007. "Balance of Payments Crises in Emerging Markets: How 'Early' Were the Early Warning Signals?" European Central Bank Working Paper 713. European Central Bank, Frankfurt. January.

Bussiere, Matthieu, and Marcel Fratzscher. 2006. "Towards a New Early Warning System of Financial Crises." *Journal of International Money and Finance* 25 (6): 953–973.

Bussiere, Matthieu, and Christian Mulder. 2000. "Political Instability and Economic Vulnerability." *International Journal of Finance and Economics* 5 (4): 309–330.

Butlin, N. G. 1962. *Australian Domestic Product, Investment and Foreign Borrowing, 1861–1938/39.* Cambridge: Cambridge University Press.

Cagan, Philip. 1956. "The Monetary Dynamics of Hyperinflation in Milton Friedman." In *Studies in the Quantity Theory of Money,* ed. Milton Friedman. Chicago: University of Chicago Press. Pp. 25–117.

Calomiris, Charles, and Gary Gorton. 1991. "The Origins of Banking Panics: Models, Facts, and Bank Regulation." In *Financial Markets and Financial Crises,* ed. R. Glenn Hubbard. Chicago: University of Chicago Press for the National Bureau of Economic Research.

413

Calvo, Guillermo. 1988. "Servicing the Public Debt: The Role of Expectations." *American Economic Review* 78 (September): 647–661.

———. 1989. "Is Inflation Effective for Liquidating Short-Term Nominal Debt?" International Monetary Fund Working Paper 89/2. International Monetary Fund, Washington, D.C. January.

———. 1991. "The Perils of Sterilization." *IMF Staff Papers* 38 (4): 921–926.

———. 1998. "Capital Flows and Capital Market Crises: The Simple Economics of Sudden Stops." *Journal of Applied Economics* 1 (1): 35–54.

Calvo, Guillermo A., and Pablo Guidotti. 1992. "Optimal Maturity of Nominal Government Debt: An Infinite Horizon Model." *International Economic Review* 33 (November): 895–919.

Calvo, Guillermo A., Leonardo Leiderman, and Carmen M. Reinhart. 1993. "Capital Inflows and Real Exchange Rate Appreciation in Latin America: The Role of External Factors." *IMF Staff Papers* 40 (1): 108–151.

Calvo, Guillermo A., Alejandro Izquierdo, and Rudy Loo-Kung. 2006. "Relative Price Volatility under Sudden Stops: The Relevance of Balance Sheet Effects." *Journal of International Economics* 9 (1): 231–254.

Cameron, Rondo E. 1967. *Banking in the Early Stages of Industrialization: A Study in Comparative Economic History*. New York: Oxford University Press.

Camprubi Alcázar, Carlos. 1957. *Historia de los Bancos en el Perú, 1860–1879*. Lima: Editorial Lumen.

Caprio, Gerard Jr., and Daniela Klingebiel. 1996. "Bank Insolvency: Bad Luck, Bad Policy, or Bad Banking?" In *Annual World Bank Conference on Development Economics, 1996*, ed. Boris Pleskovic and Joseph Stiglitz. Washington, D.C.: World Bank. Pp. 79–104.

———. 2003. "Episodes of Systemic and Borderline Financial Crises." Mimeo. Washington, D.C.: World Bank. Available at http://go.world bank.org/5DYGICS7B0 (Dataset 1). January.

Caprio, Gerard, Daniela Klingebiel, Luc Laeven, and Guillermo Noguera. 2005. "Banking Crisis Database." In *Systemic Financial Crises*, ed. Patrick Honohan and Luc Laeven. Cambridge: Cambridge University Press.

Carlos, Ann, Larry Neal, and Kirsten Wandschneider. 2005. "The Origin of National Debt: The Financing and Re-Financing of the War of the Spanish Succession." University of Colorado Working Paper. University of Colorado, Boulder.

Carter, Susan B., Scott Gartner, Michael Haines, Alan Olmstead, Richard

414

Sutch, and Gavin Wright, eds. 2006. *Historical Statistics of the United States: Millennial Edition*. Cambridge: Cambridge University Press. Available at http://hsus.cambridge.org/HSUSWeb/HSUSEntryServlet.

Ceron, Jose, and Javier Suarez. 2006. "Hot and Cold Housing Markets: International Evidence." CEMFI Working Paper 0603. Center for Monetary and Financial Studies, Madrid. January.

Cha, Myung Soo, and Nak Nyeon Kim. 2006. "Korea's First Industrial Revolution, 1911–40." Naksungdae Institute of Economic Research Working Paper 2006–3. Naksungdae Institute of Economic Research, Seoul. June.

Cheng, Linsun. 2003. *Banking in Modern China: Entrepreneurs, Professional Managers, and the Development of Chinese Banks, 1897–1937*. Cambridge: Cambridge University Press.

Chuhan, Punam, Stijn Claessens, and Nlandu Mamingi. 1998. "Equity and Bond Flows to Asia and Latin America: The Role of Global and Country Factors." *Journal of Development Economics* (55): 123–150.

Cipolla, Carlo. 1982. *The Monetary Policy of Fourteenth Century Florence*. Berkeley: University of California Press.

Clay, C. G. A. 2000. *Gold for the Sultan: Western Bankers and Ottoman Finance 1856–1881: A Contribution to Ottoman and International Financial History*. London and New York: I. B. Tauris.

Cole, Harold L., and Patrick J. Kehoe. 1996. "Reputation Spillover across Relationships: Reviving Reputation Models of Debt." Staff Report 209. Federal Reserve Bank of Minneapolis.

Conant, Charles A. 1915. *A History of Modern Banks of Issue*. 5th ed. New York: G. P. Putnam's Sons.

Condoide, Mikhail V. 1951. *The Soviet Financial System: Its Development and Relations with the Western World*. Columbus: Ohio State University.

Cooper, Richard. 2005. "Living with Global Imbalances: A Contrarian View." Policy brief. Institute for International Economics, Washington, D.C.

Correlates of War. Militarized Interstate Disputes Database. http://correlates ofwar.org/.

Course of the exchange. Reported by John Castaing. Available at http://www .le.ac.uk/hi/bon/ESFDB/NEAL/neal.html.

Cowan, Kevin, Eduardo Levy-Yeyati, Ugo Panizza, and Federico Sturzenegger. 2006. "Sovereign Debt in the Americas: New Data and Stylized Facts." Working Paper 577. Research Department, Inter-American Development Bank, Washington, D.C. Available at http://www.iadb.org/res/pub_desc.cfm?pub_id=DBA-007.

Crisp, Olga. 1976. *Studies in the Russian Economy before 1914*. London: Macmillan.

Curcuru, Stephanie, Charles Thomas, and Frank Warnock. 2008. "Current Account Sustainability and Relative Reliability." *NBER International Seminar on Macroeconomics 2008*. Chicago: University of Chicago Press for the National Bureau of Economic Research.

Della Paolera, Gerardo, and Alan M. Taylor. 1999. "Internal versus External Convertibility and Developing-Country Financial Crises: Lessons from the Argentine Bank Bailout of the 1930s." NBER Working Paper 7386. National Bureau of Economic Research, Cambridge, Mass. October.

de Maddalena, Aldo. 1974. *Prezzi e Mercedi a Milano dal 1701 al 1860*. Milan: Banca Commerciale Italiana.

Demirgüç-Kunt, Asli, and Enrica Detragiache. 1998. "The Determinants of Banking Crises in Developing and Developed Countries." *IMF Staff Papers* 45: 81–109.

———. 1999. "Financial Liberalization and Financial Fragility." In *Annual World Bank Conference on Development Economics, 1998*, ed. Boris Pleskovic and Joseph Stiglitz. Washington, D.C.: World Bank.

Diamond, Douglas, and Philip H. Dybvig. 1983. "Bank Runs, Deposit Insurance, and Liquidity." *Journal of Political Economy* 91 (3): 401–419.

Diamond, Douglas, and Raghuram Rajan. 2001. "Liquidity Risk, Liquidity Creation and Financial Fragility: A Theory of Banking." *Journal of Political Economy* 109 (April): 287–327.

Diamond, Peter A. 1965. "National Debt in a Neoclassical Growth Model." *American Economic Review* 55 (5): 1126–1150.

Díaz, José B., Rolf Lüders, and Gert Wagner. 2005. "Chile, 1810–2000, La República en Cifras." Mimeo. Instituto de Economía, Pontificia Universidad Católica de Chile, Santiago. May.

Diaz-Alejandro, Carlos. 1983. "Stories of the 1930s for the 1980s." In *Financial Policies and the World Capital Market: The Problem of Latin American Countries*, ed. Pedro Aspe Armella, Rudiger Dornbusch, and Maurice Obstfeld. Chicago: University of Chicago Press for the National Bureau of Economic Research. Pp. 5–40.

———. 1984. "Latin American Debt: I Don't Think We Are in Kansas Anymore." *Brookings Papers in Economic Activity* 2: 355–389.

———. 1985. "Goodbye Financial Repression, Hello Financial Crash." *Journal of Development Economics* 19 (1–2): 1–24.

Dick, Trevor, and John E. Floyd. 1997. "Capital Imports and the Jacksonian Economy: A New View of the Balance of Payments." Paper presented at the Third World Congress of Cliometrics, Munich, Germany, July.

Dooley, Michael, Eduardo Fernandez-Arias, and Kenneth Kletzer. 1996. "Recent Private Capital Inflows to Developing Countries: Is the Debt Crisis History?" *World Bank Economic Review* 10 (1): 27–49.

Dooley, Michael, David Folkerts-Landau, and Peter Garber. 2004a. "An Essay on the Revived Bretton Woods System." *International Journal of Finance & Economics* 9 (4): 307–313.

———. 2004b. "The Revived Bretton Woods System: The Effects of Periphery Intervention and Reserve Management on Interest Rates and Exchange Rates in Center Countries." NBER Working Paper 10332. National Bureau of Economic Research, Cambridge, Mass. March.

Dornbusch, Rudiger, and Stanley Fischer. 1993. "Moderate Inflation." *World Bank Economic Review* 7 (1): 1–44.

Dornbusch, Rudiger, Ilan Goldfajn, and Rodrigo O. Valdés. 1995. "Currency Crises and Collapses." *Brookings Papers on Economic Activity* 26 (2): 219–293.

Dornbusch, Rudiger, and Alejandro Werner. 1994. "Mexico: Stabilization, Reform, and No Growth." *Brookings Papers on Economic Activity* 1: 253–315.

Drazen, Allan. 1998. "Towards a Political Economy Theory of Domestic Debt." In *The Debt Burden and Its Consequences for Monetary Policy*, ed. G. Calvo and M. King. London: Macmillan.

Drees, Burkhard, and Ceyla Pazarbasioglu. 1998. "The Nordic Banking Crisis: Pitfalls in Financial Liberalization." IMF Occasional Paper 161. International Monetary Fund, Washington, D.C.

Eaton, Jonathan, and Mark Gersovitz. 1981. "Debt with Potential Repudiation: Theory and Estimation." *Review of Economic Studies* 48 (2): 289–309.

Economist Magazine. 2002. "The O'Neill Doctrine." Lead editorial, April 25.

Edvinsson, Rodney. 2002. "Growth, Accumulation, Crisis: With New Macroeconomic Data for Sweden 1800–2000." Ph.D. dissertation, University of Stockholm, Sweden.

417

Eichengreen, Barry. 1991a. "Historical Research on International Lending and Debt." *Journal of Economic Perspectives* 5 (Spring): 149–169.

———. 1991b. "Trends and Cycles in Foreign Lending." In *Capital Flows in the World Economy*, ed. H. Siebert. Tübingen: Mohr. Pp. 3–28.

———. 1992. *Golden Fetters: The Gold Standard and the Great Depression 1919–1939*. New York: Oxford University Press.

Eichengreen, Barry, and Peter H. Lindert, eds. 1989. *The International Debt Crisis in Historical Perspective*. Cambridge, Mass.: MIT Press.

Eichengreen, Barry, and Kevin O'Rourke. 2009. "A Tale of Two Depressions." June 4. Available at http://www. voxeu.org.

European State Finance Database. Available at http://www.le.ac.uk/hi/bon/ESFDB/.

Felton, Andrew, and Carmen M. Reinhart. 2008. *The First Global Financial Crisis of the 21st Century*. London: VoxEU and Centre for Economic Policy Research. July. Available at http://www.voxeu.org/index.php?q=node/1352.

———. 2009. *The First Global Financial Crisis of the 21st Century, Part 2: June–December, 2008*. London: VoxEU and Centre for Economic Policy Research. Available at http://www.voxeu.org/index.php?q=node/3079.

Ferguson, Niall. 2008. *The Ascent of Money: A Financial History of the World*. New York: Penguin Press.

Fischer, Stanley, Ratna Sahay, and Carlos A. Végh. 2002. "Modern Hyper- and High Inflations." *Journal of Economic Literature* 40 (3): 837–880.

Fisher, Irving. 1933. "Debt-Deflation Theory of Great Depressions." *Econometrica* 1 (4): 337–357.

Flandreau, Marc, and Frederic Zumer. 2004. *The Making of Global Finance, 1880–1913*. Paris: Organisation of Economic Co-operation and Development.

Flath, David. 2005. *The Japanese Economy*. 2nd ed. Oxford: Oxford University Press.

Fostel, Ana, and John Geanakoplos. 2008. "Leverage Cycles and the Anxious Economy." *American Economic Review* 98 (4): 1211–1244.

Frankel, Jeffrey A., and Andrew K. Rose. 1996. "Currency Crashes in Emerging Markets: An Empirical Treatment." *Journal of International Economics* 41 (November): 351–368.

Frankel, S. Herbert. 1938. *Capital Investment in Africa: Its Course and Effects*. London: Oxford University Press.

Friedman, Milton, and Anna J. Schwartz. 1963. *A Monetary History of the United States, 1867–1960*. Princeton, N.J.: Princeton University Press.

Frydl, Edward J. 1999. "The Length and Cost of Banking Crises." International Monetary Fund Working Paper 99/30. International Monetary Fund, Washington, D.C. March.

Garcia Vizcaino, José. 1972. *La Deuda Pública Nacional*. Buenos Aires: EU-DEBA Editorial Universitaria de Buenos Aires.

Garner, Richard. 2007. "Late Colonial Prices in Selected Latin American Cities." Working Memorandum. Available at http://home.comcast.net/~richardgarner04/.

————. n.d. "Economic History Data Desk: Economic History of Latin America, United States and New World, 1500–1900." Available at http://home.comcast.net/~richardgarner04/.

Gavin, Michael, and Roberto Perotti. 1997. "Fiscal Policy in Latin America." *NBER Macroeconomics Annual* 12: 11–61.

Gayer, Arthur D., W. W. Rostow, and Anna J. Schwartz. 1953. *The Growth and Fluctuation of the British Economy, 1790–1850*. Oxford: Clarendon.

Gelabert, Juan. 1999a. "Castile, 1504–1808." In *The Rise of the Fiscal State in Europe, c. 1200–1815*, ed. R. J. Bonney. Oxford: Oxford University Press.

————. 1999b. "The King's Expenses: The Asientos of Philip III and Philip IV of Spain. In *Crises, Revolutions and Self-Sustained Growth: Essays in European Fiscal History, 1130–1830*, ed. W. M. Ormrod, M. M. Bonney, and R. J. Bonney. Stamford, England: Shaun Tyas.

Gerdrup, Karsten R. 2003. "Three Episodes of Financial Fragility in Norway since the 1890s." Bank for International Settlements Working Paper 142. Bank for International Settlements, Basel, Switzerland. October.

Godinho, V. Magalhaes. 1955. *Prix et Monnaies au Portugal, 1750–1850*. Paris: Librairie Armand Colin.

Global Financial Data. n.d. *Global Financial Data*. Available at https://www.globalfinancialdata.com/.

Global Price and Income History Group. Available at http://gpih.ucdavis.edu.

Goldstein, Morris. 2003. "Debt Sustainability, Brazil, and the IMF." Working Paper WP03-1. Institute for International Economics, Washington, D.C.

Goldstein, Morris, and Philip Turner. 2004. *Controlling Currency Mismatches in Emerging Markets*. Washington, D.C.: Institute for International Economics.

Goldstein, Morris, Graciela L. Kaminsky, and Carmen M. Reinhart. 2000. *Assessing Financial Vulnerability*. Washington, D.C.: Institute for International Economics.

Gorton, Gary. 1988. "Banking Panics and Business Cycles." *Oxford Economic Papers* 40: 751–781.

Greenspan, Alan. 2007. *The Age of Turbulence*. London and New York: Penguin.

Groningen Growth and Development Centre and the Commerce Department. 2008. Total Economy Database. Available at http://www.ggdc.net.

Grytten, Ola. 2008. "The Economic History of Norway." In *EH.Net Encyclopedia*, ed. Robert Whaples. Available at http://eh.net/encyclopedia/article/grytten.norway.

Hale, David. 2003. "The Newfoundland Lesson: During the 1930s, Long before the IMF, the British Empire Coped with a Debt Crisis in a Small Country. This Is a Tale of the Choice between Debt and Democracy. It Shouldn't Be Forgotten." *International Economy* (Summer). Available at http://www.entrepreneur.com/tradejournals/article/106423908.html.

Hamilton, Earl. 1969. *War and Prices in Spain, 1651–1800*. New York: Russell and Russell.

Hausmann, Ricardo, and Federico Sturzenegger. 2007. "The Missing Dark Matter in the Wealth of Nations and Its Implications for Global Imbalances." *Economic Policy* 51: 469–518.

Hoffman, P. T., D. S. Jacks, P. Levin, and P. H. Lindert. 2002. "Real Inequality in Europe since 1500." *Journal of Economic History* 62 (2): 381–413.

Hoggarth, Glenn, Patricia Jackson, and Erlend Nier. 2005. "Banking Crises and the Design of Safety Nets." *Journal of Banking & Finance* 29 (1): 143–159.

Homer, Sidney, and Richard Sylla. 1991. *A History of Interest Rates*. New Brunswick, N.J., and London: Rutgers University Press.

Hsu, Leonard Shih-Lien. 1935. *Silver and Prices in China: Report of the Committee for the Study of Silver Values and Commodity Prices*. Shanghai: Commercial Press.

Huang, Feng-Hua. 1919. *Public Debts in China*. New York: MAS.

Imlah, A. H. 1958. *Economic Elements in the Pax Britannica*. Cambridge. Mass.: MIT Press.

Institutional Investor. Various years. *Institutional Investor*.

Instituto Brasileiro de Geografia e Estadistica. 2007. *Estadisticas Historicas de Brazil*. Rio de Janeiro: Instituto Brasileiro de Geografia e Estadistica.

Instituto Nacional de Estatistica (Portuguese Statistical Agency). 1998. *Estadisticas Historicas Portuguesas*. Lisbon: INE.

International Institute of Social History. n.d. Available at http://www.iisg.nl/.

International Monetary Fund. 2002. "Assessing Sustainability." Available at http://www.imf.org/external/np/pdr/sus/2002/eng/052802.htm.

———. Various years. *International Financial Statistics*. Washington, D.C.: International Monetary Fund.

———. Various years. *World Economic Outlook*. Washington, D.C.: International Monetary Fund.

Jácome, Luis. 2008. "Central Bank Involvement in Banking Crises in Latin America." International Monetary Fund Working Paper 08/135. International Monetary Fund, Washington, D.C. May.

Jayachandran, Seema, and Michael Kremer. 2006. "Odious Debt." *American Economic Review* 96 (March): 82–92.

Jeanne, Olivier. 2009. "Debt Maturity and the International Financial Architecture." *American Economic Review*, forthcoming.

Jeanne, Olivier, and Guscina, Anastasia. 2006. "Government Debt in Emerging Market Countries: A New Dataset." International Monetary Fund Working Paper 6/98. International Monetary Fund, Washington, D.C. April.

Johnson, H. Clark. 1998. *Gold, France, and the Great Depression: 1919–1935*. New Haven, Conn.: Yale University Press.

Jonung, L., and T. Hagberg. 2002. "How Costly Was the Crisis?" Työväen Akatemia, Kauniainen. September.

Jun, S. H., and J. B. Lewis. 2002. "Labour Cost, Land Prices, Land Rent, and Interest Rates in the Southern Region of Korea, 1690–1909." Working Memorandum. Academy of Korean Studies, Seoul. Available at http://www.iisg.nl/hpw/korea.php.

Kaminsky, Graciela L., and Carmen M. Reinhart. 1999. "The Twin Crises: The Causes of Banking and Balance-of-Payments Problems." *American Economic Review* 89 (3): 473–500.

Kaminsky, Graciela L., J. Saul Lizondo, and Carmen M. Reinhart. 1998. "Leading Indicators of Currency Crises." *IMF Staff Papers* 45 (1): 1–48.

Kaminsky, Graciela L., Carmen M. Reinhart, and Carlos A. Végh. 2003. "The Unholy Trinity of Financial Contagion." *Journal of Economic Perspectives* 17 (4): 51–74.

———. 2004. "When It Rains, It Pours: Procyclical Capital Flows and Policies." In *NBER Macroeconomics Annual 2004*, ed. Mark Gertler and Kenneth S. Rogoff. Cambridge, Mass: MIT Press. Pp. 11–53.

Kimura, M. 1987. "La Revolucion de los Precios en la Cuenca del Pacifico, 1600–1650." Mimeo. Universidad Nacional Autonoma de México, Mexico City.

Kindleberger, Charles P. 1989. *Manias, Panics and Crashes: A History of Financial Crises*. New York: Basic Books.

Kiyotaki, Nobuhiro, and John Moore. 1997. "Credit Cycles." *Journal of Political Economy* 105: 211–248.

Kohlscheen, Emanuel. 2007. "Why Are There Serial Defaulters? Evidence from Constitutions." *Journal of Law and Economics* 50 (November): 713–729.

Korthals Altes, W. L. 1996. *Van L Hollands tot Nederlandse f*. Amsterdam: Neha.

Kostelenos, George, S. Petmezas, D. Vasileiou, E. Kounaris, and M. Sfakianakis. 2007. "Gross Domestic Product, 1830–1939." In *Sources of Economic History of Modern Greece*. Athens: Central Bank of Greece.

Kotlikoff, Lawrence J., Torsten Persson, and Lars E. O. Svensson. 1988. "Social Contracts as Assets: A Possible Solution to the Time-Consistency Problem." *American Economic Review* 7: 662–677.

Krugman, Paul. 2007. "Will There Be a Dollar Crisis?" *Economic Policy* 51 (July): 437–467.

Kryzanowski, Lawrence, and Gordon S. Roberts. 1999. "Perspectives on Canadian Bank Insolvency during the 1930s." *Journal of Money, Credit & Banking* 31 (1): 130–136.

Landes, David S. 1958. *Bankers and Pashas: International Finance and Economic Imperialism in Egypt*. Cambridge, Mass.: Harvard University Press.

Lazaretou, Sophia. 2005. "The Drachma, Foreign Creditors, and the International Monetary System: Tales of a Currency during the 19th and the Early 20th Centuries." *Explorations in Economic History* 42 (2): 202–236.

League of Nations. 1944. *International Currency Experience: Lessons of the Interwar Period.* Geneva: League of Nations.

———. Various years. *Statistical Abstract.* Geneva: League of Nations.

———. Various years. *Statistical Yearbook, 1926–1944.* Geneva: League of Nations.

———. Various years. *World Economic Survey, 1926–1944.* Geneva: League of Nations.

Levandis, John Alexander. 1944. *The Greek Foreign Debt and the Great Powers, 1821–1898.* New York: Columbia University Press.

Lindert, Peter H., and Boris Mironov. n.d. Ag-Content of the Ruble. Available at http://gpih.ucdavis.edu/.

Lindert, Peter H., and Peter J. Morton. 1989. "How Sovereign Debt Has Worked." In *Developing Country Debt and Economic Performance,* vol. 1, ed. Jeffrey Sachs. Chicago: University of Chicago Press. Pp. 39–106.

Lu, Feng, and Kaixiang Peng. 2006. "A Research on China's Long Term Rice Prices: 1644–2000." *Frontiers of Economics in China* 1 (4): 465–520.

MacDonald, James. 2006. *A Free Nation Deep in Debt: The Financial Roots of Democracy.* New York: Farrar, Straus, and Giroux.

Maddison, Angus. 2004. *Historical Statistics for the World Economy: 1–2003 AD.* Paris: Organisation for Economic Co-operation and Development. Available at http://www.ggdc.net/maddison/.

Malanima, Paolo. n.d. *Wheat Prices in Tuscany, 1260–1860.* Available at http://www.iisg.nl/.

Mamalakis, Markos. 1983. *Historical Statistics of Chile.* Westport, Conn.: Greenwood.

Manasse, Paolo, and Nouriel Roubini. 2005. "'Rules of Thumb' for Sovereign Debt Crises." IMF Working Paper 05/42. International Monetary Fund, Washington, D.C.

Marichal, Carlos. 1989. *A Century of Debt Crises in Latin America: From Independence to the Great Depression, 1820–1930.* Princeton, N.J.: Princeton University Press.

Mauro, Paolo, Nathan Sussman, and Yishay Yafeh. 2006. *Emerging Markets and Financial Globalization: Sovereign Bond Spreads in 1870–1913 and Today.* London: Oxford University Press.

McConnell, Margaret, and Gabriel Perez-Quiros. 2000. "Output Fluctuations in the United States: What Has Changed since the Early 1980's?" *American Economic Review* 90 (5): 1464–1476.

McElderry, Andrea Lee. 1976. *Shanghai Old-Style Banks, 1800–1935: A Traditional Institution in a Changing Society*. Ann Arbor: Center for Chinese Studies, University of Michigan.

McGrattan, Ellen, and Edward Prescott. 2007. "Technology Capital and the U.S. Current Accounts." Working Paper 646. Federal Reserve Bank of Minneapolis. June.

Mellegers, Joost. 2006. "Public Finance of Indonesia, 1817–1940." Working Memorandum. Indonesian Economic Development, International Institute of Social History, Amsterdam.

Mendoza, Enrique G., and Marco Terrones. 2008. "An Anatomy of Credit Booms: Evidence from the Macro Aggregates and Micro Data." NBER Working Paper 14049. National Bureau of Economic Research, Cambridge, Mass. May.

Miller, Margaret S. 1926. *The Economic Development of Russia, 1905–1914*. London: P. S. King and Son.

Mitchell, Brian R. 2003a. *International Historical Statistics: Africa, Asia, and Oceania, 1750–2000*. London: Palgrave Macmillan.

———. 2003b. *International Historical Statistics: The Americas, 1750–2000*. London: Palgrave Macmillan.

Mizoguchi, Toshiyuki, and Mataji Umemura. 1988. *Basic Economic Statistics of Former Japanese Colonies, 1895–1938: Estimates and Findings*. Tokyo: Toyo Keizai Shinposha.

Moody's Investor Service. 2000. "Historical Default Rates of Corporate Bond Issuers, 1920–1999." *Moody's Investor Service Global Credit Research*, special comment, January.

Morris, Stephen, and Hyun Song Shin. 1998. "Unique Equilibrium in a Model of Self-Fulfilling Currency Attacks." *American Economic Review* 88 (June): 587–597.

Nakamura, Leonard I, and Carlos E. J. M. Zarazaga. 2001. Banking and Finance in Argentina in the Period 1900–35. Federal Reserve Bank of Philadelphia Working Paper 01-7. Federal Reserve Bank of Philadelphia, Pa. June.

Neal, Larry, and Marc Weidenmier. 2003. "Crises in the Global Economy from Tulips to Today: Contagion and Consequences." In *Globalization in Historical Perspective*, ed. Michael Bordo, Alan M. Taylor, and Jeffrey Williamson. Chicago: University of Chicago Press. Pp. 473–514.

Neely, Christopher. 1995. "The Profitability of U.S. Intervention in the Foreign Exchange Markets." *Journal of International Money and Finance* 14: 823–844.

Noel, Maurer. 2002. *The Power and the Money—The Mexican Financial System, 1876–1932*. Stanford, Calif.: Stanford University Press.

Norges Bank. 2004. "The Norwegian Banking Crisis." Ed. Thorvald G. Moe, Jon A. Solheim, and Bent Vale. Occasional Paper 33. Norges Bank, Oslo.

North, Douglass, and Barry Weingast. 1988. "Constitutions and Commitment: The Evolution of Institutions Governing Public Choice in Seventeenth Century England." In *Empirical Studies in Institutional Change*, ed. L. Alston, P. Eggertsson, and D. North. Cambridge: Cambridge University Press.

Nurkse, Ragnar. 1946. *The Course and Control of Inflation: A Revue of Monetary Experience in Europe after World War I*. Geneva: League of Nations.

Obstfeld, Maurice. 1994. "The Logic of Currency Crises." *Cahiers Economiques et Monetaires* 43: 189–213.

———. 1996. "Models of Currency Crises with Self-Sustaining Features." *European Economic Review* 40 (April): 1037–1048.

Obstfeld, Maurice, and Kenneth S. Rogoff. 1996. *Foundations of International Macroeconomics*. Cambridge, Mass.: MIT Press.

———. 2001. "Perspectives on OECD Capital Market Integration: Implications for U.S. Current Account Adjustment." In *Global Economic Integration: Opportunities and Challenges*. Federal Reserve Bank of Kansas City, Mo. March. Pp. 169–208.

———. 2005. "Global Current Account Imbalances and Exchange Rate Adjustments." *Brookings Papers on Economic Activity* 1: 67–146.

———. 2007. "The Unsustainable U.S. Current Account Position Revisited." In *G7 Current Account Imbalances: Sustainability and Adjustment*, ed. Richard Clarida. Chicago: University of Chicago Press.

————. 2009. "The US Current Account and the Global Financial Crisis." Draft of a paper prepared for the Ohlin Lectures in International Economics, Harvard University.

Obstfeld, Maurice, and Alan Taylor. 2004. *Global Capital Markets: Integration, Crisis, and Growth*. Japan–U.S. Center Sanwa Monographs on International Financial Markets. Cambridge: Cambridge University Press.

Øksendal, Lars. 2007. "Re-Examining Norwegian Monetary Policy in the 1930s." Manuscript. Department of Economics, Norwegian School of Economics and Business Administration, Bergen.

Oxford Latin American Economic History Database. Available at http:// oxlad.qeh.ox.ac.uk/references.php.

Ozmucur, Suleyman, and Sevket Pamuk. 2002. "Real Wages and Standards of Living in the Ottoman Empire, 1489–1914." *Journal of Economic History* 62 (June): 292–321.

Page, William. 1919. *Commerce and Industry: Tables of Statistics for the British Empire from 1815*. London: Constable.

Pamuk, Sevket. 2005. "Prices and Wages in Istanbul, 1469–1914." Working Memorandum. International Institute of Social History, Amsterdam.

Persson, Torsten, and Guido Tabellini. 1990. *Macroeconomic Policy, Credibility and Politics*. London: Routledge.

Philippon, Thomas. 2007. "Why Has the U.S. Financial Sector Grown So Much? The Role of Corporate Finance." NBER Working Paper 13405. National Bureau of Economic Research, Cambridge, Mass. September.

Pick, Franz. Various years, 1955–1982. *Pick's Currency Yearbook*. New York: Pick.

Prasad, Eswar, Kenneth S. Rogoff, Shang-Jin Wei, and M. Ayhan Kose. 2003. "Effects of Financial Globalization on Developing Countries: Some Empirical Evidence." IMF Occasional Paper 220. International Monetary Fund, Washington, D.C.

Purcell, John F. H., and Jeffrey A. Kaufman. 1993. *The Risks of Sovereign Lending: Lessons from History*. New York: Salomon Brothers.

Qian, Rong, and Carmen M. Reinhart. 2009. "Graduation from Crises and Volatility: Elusive Goals." Working mimeograph. University of Maryland, College Park.

Quinn, Stephen. 2004. "Accounting for the Early British Funded Debt, 1693–1786." Working paper. Mimeograph. Texas Christian University.

426

Rajan, Raghuram, Enrica Detragiache, and Giovanni Dell'Ariccia. 2008. "The Real Effect of Banking Crises." *Journal of Financial Intermediation* 17: 89–112.

Reinhart, Carmen M. 2002. "Default, Currency Crises, and Sovereign Credit Ratings." *World Bank Economic Review* 16 (2): 151–170.

Reinhart, Carmen M., and Vincent R. Reinhart. 2008. "Is the U.S. Too Big to Fail?" VoxEU, November 17. Available at http://www.voxeu.com/index.php?q=node/2568.

———. 2009. "Capital Flow Bonanzas: An Encompassing View of the Past and Present." In *NBER International Seminar in Macroeconomics 2008*, ed. Jeffrey Frankel and Francesco Giavazzi. Chicago: Chicago University Press for the National Bureau of Economic Research. Pp. 1–54.

Reinhart, Carmen M., and Kenneth S. Rogoff. 2002a. "FDI to Africa: The Role of Price Stability and Currency Instability." In *Annual World Bank Conference on Development Economics 2002: The New Reform Agenda*, ed. Boris Pleskovic and Nicholas Stern. Washington, D.C.: World Bank/Oxford University Press. Pp. 247–282.

———. 2002b. "The Modern History of Exchange Rate Arrangements: A Reinterpretation." NBER Working Paper 8963. National Bureau of Economic Research, Cambridge, Mass. May.

———. 2004. "The Modern History of Exchange Rate Arrangements: A Reinterpretation." *Quarterly Journal of Economics* 119 (1): 1–48.

———. 2008a. "This Time Is Different: A Panoramic View of Eight Centuries of Financial Crises." NBER Working Paper 13882. National Bureau of Economic Research, Cambridge, Mass. March.

———. 2008b. "Is the 2007 U.S. Subprime Crisis So Different? An International Historical Comparison." *American Economic Review* 98 (2): 339–344.

———. 2008c. "The Forgotten History of Domestic Debt." NBER Working Paper 13946. National Bureau of Economic Research, Cambridge, Mass. April.

———. 2008d. "Regulation Should Be International." *Financial Times*, November 18.

———. 2009. "The Aftermath of Financial Crisis." *American Economic Review* 99 (2): 1–10.

427

Reinhart, Carmen M., and Miguel A. Savastano. 2003. "The Realities of Modern Hyperinflation." *Finance and Development*, June, 20–23.

Reinhart, Carmen M., Kenneth S. Rogoff, and Miguel A. Savastano. 2003a. "Debt Intolerance." *Brookings Papers on Economic Activity* 1 (Spring): 1–74.

———. 2003b. "Addicted to Dollars." NBER Working Paper 10015. National Bureau of Economic Research, Cambridge, Mass. October.

Rogoff, Kenneth. 1999. "Institutions for Reducing Global Financial Instability." *Journal of Economic Perspectives* 13 (Fall): 21–42.

Rolnick, Arthur J. 2004. "Interview with Ben S. Bernanke." *Region Magazine* (Minneapolis Federal Reserve), June. Available at http://www.minneapolisfed.org/publications_papers/pub_display.cfm?id=3326.

Roubini, Nouriel, and Brad Setser. 2004. "The United States as a Debtor Nation: The Sustainability of the US External Imbalances." Draft. New York University, New York. November.

Sachs, Jeffrey. 1984. *Theoretical Issues in International Borrowing*. Princeton Studies in International Finance 54. Princeton University, Princeton, N.J.

Samuelson, Paul. 1966. "Science and Stocks." *Newsweek*, September 19.

Sanhueza, Gonzalo. 2001. "Chilean Banking Crisis of the 1980s: Solutions and Estimation of the Costs." Central Bank of Chile Working Paper 104. Central Bank of Chile, Santiago.

Sargent, Thomas J. 1982. "The Ends of Four Big Hyperinflations." In *Inflation: Causes and Effects*, ed. Robert J. Hall. Chicago: University of Chicago Press.

Sargent, Thomas, and Francois Velde. 2003. *The Big Problem with Small Change*. Princeton, N.J.: Princeton University Press.

Scutt, G. P Symes. 1904. *The History of the Bank of Bengal*. Bengal: Bank of Bengal Press.

Shergold, Peter. 1987. "Prices and Consumption." In *Australian Historical Statistics*. Sydney: Fairfax, Syme and Weldon.

Shiller, Robert. 2005. *Irrational Exuberance*. 2nd ed. Princeton, N.J.: Princeton University Press.

Shin, Inseok, and Joon-Ho Hahm. 1998. "The Korean Crisis: Causes and Resolution." Korea Development Institute Working Paper. Prepared for the Korea Development Institute–East-West Center Conference on the Korean Crisis: Causes and Resolution, Hawaii. August.

428

Shleifer, Andrei, and Robert W. Vishny. 1991. "Liquidation Values and Debt Capacity: A Market Equilibrium Approach." *Journal of Finance* 47 (4): 1343–1366.

Sinclair, David. 2004. *The Land That Never Was: Sir Gregor MacGregor and the Most Audacious Fraud in History.* London: Headline.

Söderberg, Johan. 2004. "Prices in Stockholm: 1539–1620." Working Memorandum. International Institute of Social History, Amsterdam.

Soley Güell, Tomas. 1926. *Historia Monetaria de Costa Rica.* San Jose, Costa Rica: Imprenta Nacional.

Standard and Poor's Commentary. Various issues.

Summerhill, William. 2006. "Political Economics of the Domestic Debt in Nineteenth-Century Brazil." Working Memorandum. University of California, Los Angeles.

Sundararajan, Vasudevan, and Tomás Baliño. 1991. *Banking Crises: Cases and Issues.* Washington D.C.: International Monetary Fund.

Suter, Christian. 1992. *Debt Cycles in the World-Economy: Foreign Loans, Financial Crises, and Debt Settlements, 1820–1990.* Boulder, Colo.: Westview.

Sutton, Gregory D. 2002. "Explaining Changes in House Prices." *BIS Quarterly Review* (September): 46–55.

Tabellini, Guido. 1991. "The Politics of Intergenerational Redistribution." *Journal of Political Economy* 99 (April): 335–357.

Teichova, Alice, Ginette Kurgan–van Hentenryk, and Dieter Ziegler, eds. 1997. *Banking, Trade and Industry: Europe, America and Asia from the Thirteenth to the Twentieth Century.* Cambridge: Cambridge University Press.

Temin, Peter. 2008. "The German Crisis of 1931: Evidence and Tradition." *Cliometrica: Journal of Historical Economics and Econometric History* 2 (1): 5–17.

't Hart, Marjolein, Joost Jonker, and Jan Luiten van Zanden. 1997. *A Financial History of the Netherlands.* Cambridge: Cambridge University Press.

Tomz, Michael. 2007. *Reputation and International Cooperation: Sovereign Debt across Three Centuries.* Princeton, N.J.: Princeton University Press.

Total Economy Database. Available at http://www.conference-board.org/economics/database.cfm.

Triner, Gail D. 2000. *Banking and Economic Development: Brazil, 1889–1930.* New York: Palgrave Macmillan.

United Nations, Department of Economic Affairs. 1948. *Public Debt, 1914–1946*. New York: United Nations.

———. 1949. *International Capital Movements during the Inter-War Period*. New York: United Nations.

———. 1954. *The International Flow of Private Capital, 1946–1952*. New York: United Nations.

———. Various years. *Statistical Yearbook, 1948–1984*. New York: United Nations.

Vale, Bent. 2004. Chapter 1. In "The Norwegian Banking Crisis." Ed. Thorvald G. Moe, Jon A. Solheim, and Bent Vale. Occasional Paper 33. Norges Bank, Oslo.

Vanplew, W. 1987. *Australia: Historical Statistics*. Sydney: Fairfax, Syme and Weldon.

Van Riel, Arthur. 2009. "Constructing the Nineteeth-Century Cost of Living Deflator (1800–1913)." Working Memorandum. International Institute of Social History, Amsterdam.

Van Zanden, Jan Luiten. 2002. "Wages and the Cost of Living in Southern England (London), 1450–1700." Working Memorandum. International Institute of Social History, Amsterdam.

———. 2005. "What Happened to the Standard of Living before the Industrial Revolution? New Evidence from the Western Part of the Netherlands." In *Living Standards in the Past: New Perspectives on Well-Being in Asia and Europe*, ed. Robert Allen, Tommy Bengtsson, and Martin Dribe. New York: Oxford University Press.

———. 2006. "Economic Growth in Java, 1815–1930: The Reconstruction of the Historical National Accounts of a Colonial Economy." Working Memorandum. International Institute of Social History, Amsterdam.

Végh, Carlos A. 1992. "Stopping High Inflation: An Analytical Overview." *IMF Staff Papers* 91 (107): 626–695.

Velasco, Andres. 1996. "Fixed Exchange Rates: Credibility, Flexibility and Multiplicity." *European Economic Review* 40 (April): 1023–1036.

Vogler R. 2001. "The Genesis of Swiss Banking Secrecy: Political and Economic Environment." *Financial History Review* 8 (1): 73–84.

Wallis, John, and Barry R. Weingast. 1988. "Dysfunctional or Optimal Institutions: State Debt Limitations, the Structure of State and Local Governments, and the Finance of American Infrastructure." In *Fiscal Challenges: An Interdisciplinary Approach to Budget Policy*, ed. Elizabeth Garrett, Elizabeth Graddy, and Howell Jackson. Cambridge: Cambridge University Press. Pp. 331–363.

Wall Street Journal. Various issues.

Wang, Yeh-chien. 1992. "Secular Trends of Rice Prices in the Yangze Delta, 1638–1935." In *Chinese History in Economic Perspective*, ed. Thomas G. Rawski and Lillian M. Li. Berkeley: University of California Press.

Weingast, Barry, 1997. "The Political Foundations of Democracy and the Rule of Law." *American Political Science Review* 91 (2): 245–263.

Williamson, Jeffrey G. 1999. "Real Wages, Inequality, and Globalization in Latin America before 1940." *Revista de Historia Economica* 17: 101–142.

———. 2000a. "Factor Prices around the Mediterranean, 1500–1940." In *The Mediterranean Response to Globalization before 1950*, ed. S. Pamuk and J. G. Williamson. London: Routledge. Pp. 45–75.

———. 2000b. "Globalization, Factor Prices and Living Standards in Asia before 1940." In *Asia Pacific Dynamism, 1500–2000*, ed. A. J. H. Latham and H. Kawakatsu. London: Routledge. Pp. 13–45.

Williamson, John. 2002. "Is Brazil Next?" International Economics Policy Briefs PB 02-7. Institute for International Economics, Washington, D.C.

Willis, Parker H., and B. H. Beckhart, eds. 1929. *Foreign Banking Systems*. New York: Henry Holt.

Winkler, Max. 1928. *Investments of United States Capital in Latin America*. Cambridge, Mass.: World Peace Foundation.

———. 1933. *Foreign Bonds: An Autopsy*. Philadelphia: Roland Sway.

Wolf, Martin. 2008. *Fixing Global Finance*. Baltimore, Md.: Johns Hopkins University Press.

Woodford, Michael. 1995. "Price-Level Determinacy without Control of a Monetary Aggregate." *Carnegie-Rochester Conference Series on Public Policy* 43: 1–46.

World Bank. Various years. *Global Development Finance*. Washington D.C.: World Bank.

Wynne, William H. 1951. *State Insolvency and Foreign Bondholders: Selected Case Histories of Governmental Foreign Bond Defaults and Debt Readjustments*, vol. II. London: Oxford University Press.

431

Young, Arthur Nichols. 1971. *China's Nation-Building Effort, 1927–1937: The Financial and Economic Record.* Stanford, Calif.: Stanford University Press.

Yousef, Tarik M. 2002. "Egypt's Growth Performance under Economic Liberalism: A Reassessment with New GDP Estimates, 1886–1945." *Review of Income and Wealth* 48: 561–579.

References: National Sources

Australian Office of Financial Management
Austrian Federal Financing Agency
BNB (Banque Nationale de Belgique)
Banco Central del Uruguay
Banco Central de Reserva (El Salvador)
Banco de España
Banco de la Republica (Dominican Republic)
Banco de Portugal
Bank of Canada
Bank of Indonesia
Bank of Japan
Bank of Mauritius
Bank of Thailand
Bundesbank (Germany)
Central Bank of Kenya
Central Bank of Sri Lanka
Central Bank of Tunisia
Contraloria General de la Republica (Colombia)
Danmarks Nationalbank
Dipartamento del Tesoro (Italy)
Direccion General de la Deuda Publica (Mexico)
Dutch State Treasury Agency
Estadisticas Historicas de Espana: Siglos XIX–XX (Spain)
Finnish Historical National Accounts
Historical Statistics of Japan
Historical Statistics of the United States
Instituto Brasileiro de Geografia e Estatística

Ministère du Budget, des comptes public (France)
Ministerio de Hacienda (Chile)
Ministerio de Hacienda (Costa Rica)
Ministry of Finance (Ecuador)
Ministry of Finance (Egypt)
Ministry of Finance (Norway)
Monetary Authority (Singapore)
National Accounts of the Netherlands
New Zealand Treasury
Nordic Historical National Accounts
Organisation for Economic Co-operation and Development (for Greece)
Riksgalden (National Debt Office, Sweden)
South Africa Reserve Bank
State Treasury (Finland)
Statistical Abstracts Relating to British India
Statistics Canada
Statistics New Zealand
Treasury Direct (United States)
Turkish Treasury
U.K. Debt Management Office

NAME INDEX

Page numbers for entries occurring in boxes are suffixed by a b; those for entries in figures, by an f; those for entries in notes, by an n, with the number of the note following; and those for entries in tables, by a t.

SUBJECT INDEX

Page numbers for entries occurring in boxes are suffixed by a b; those for entries in figures, by an f; those for entries in notes, by an n, with the number of the note following; and those for entries in tables, by a t.

academic literature: on banking crises, focus of, xxxii, 141; data used in, xxvii–xxviii, 279; domestic public debt ignored in, xxxi, 109b, 110, 119, 124–25, 136–37; on indicators of crises, 216–17, 279; on types of capital flows, 30; on U.S. current account balance, 210–12

advanced economies: banking crises in, xxvi–xxvii, xxxii, 141–42, 147–55, 167–69, 223–24; data on public debt in, 40–41; debt intolerance in, 27; financial turbulence index for, 253, 254f, 255; transition from emerging market to, 283. *See also specific countries*

Africa: banking crises in, 143, 147, 148t, 151t, 154t; contagion of crises in, 246–47; data coverage of, 43, 45t; domestic public debt in, 105f, 399n2; external default in (*See* African external default); financial turbulence index for, 257–59, 257f; graduation in, 287; inflation crises after 1800 in, 182, 184t, 185, 187, 188f, 189. *See also specific countries*

African external default, xxxi; in 1800s, 91t, 92; in 1900s and 2000s, 92, 95t; countries with no history of, 44; time spent in, since independence, 95–98, 97t

aftermath, 223–39; of banking crises, xxxii, 162–71, 223–39; comparison of episodes of, 225–38; depth of downturn in, 226–30, 235; domestic public debt in, 123–24, 123f; duration of downturn in, 224, 226–30; of exchange rate crises, 191–93; external default in, 232–33, 233f; fiscal legacy in, 231–32, 231t, 232f; GDP in, 129, 130f; of Great Depression, 225, 233–38; of inflation crises, 180, 191–93; inflation rates in, 129–33, 131f, 132t; public debt in, 224–25, 231–32, 231t, 232f, 237–38; shared characteristics of, 224–30; of U.S. subprime crisis, 222, 405n33

Albania, banking crises in, 348t

Algeria: banking crises in, 348t

Angola: banking crises in, 348t; inflation crises in, 185

Annual Reports, League of Nations, 37

Argentina: banking crises in, 143, 159, 206, 225, 251, 348–50t; Barings crisis of 1890 in, 242; Brady bonds in, 83b, 85b; debt crisis of 1990s and early 2000s in, 19; debt intolerance of, 28–29; de-dollarization in, 195–96; domestic debt in, foreign currency–linked, 64, 108, 109b; domestic default by, 14, 111, 251,

ARCTIC

FOREST

AMERICAN

PRAIRIE

GREAT LAKES

NORTHEAST WOODLANDS

NORTH ATLANTIC COAST

APPALACHIAN HIGHLANDS

SOUTH ATLANTIC COAST AND PIEDMONT

SOUTHERN HILL COUNTRY

GULF COAST

The *Stories from Where We Live* Series

Each volume in the *Stories from Where We Live* series celebrates a North American ecoregion through its own distinctive literature. For thousands of years, people have told stories to convey their community's cultural and natural history. *Stories from Where We Live* reinvigorates that tradition in hopes of helping young people better understand the place where they live. The anthologies feature poems, stories, and essays from historical and contemporary authors as well as from the oral traditions of each region's indigenous peoples. Together they document the geographic richness of the continent and reflect the myriad ways that people interact with and respond to the natural world. We hope that these stories kindle readers' imaginations and inspire them to explore, observe, ponder, and protect the place they call home.

Please visit www.worldashome.org for a teaching guide to this book and more information on the *Stories from Where We Live* series.

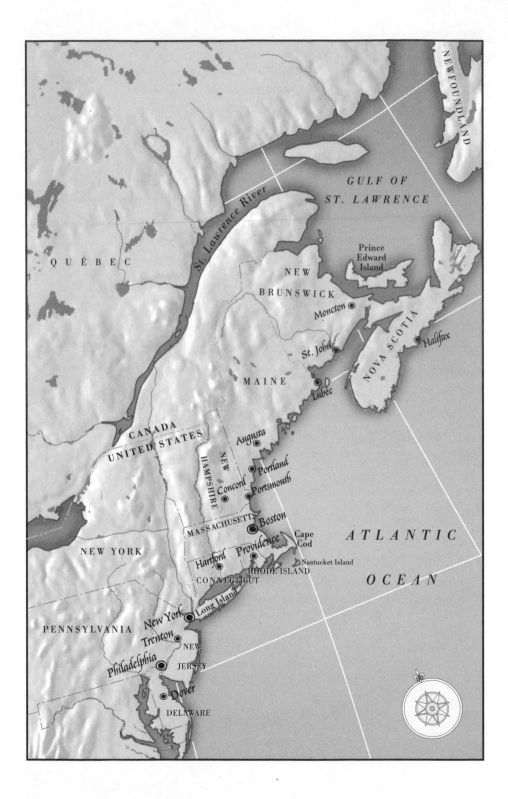

Stories from Where We Live

The North Atlantic Coast

EDITED BY SARA ST. ANTOINE

Maps by Paul Mirocha
Illustrations by Trudy Nicholson

MILKWEED EDITIONS

Published 2000 by Milkweed Editions
Printed in Canada
Jacket design by Paul Mirocha
Jacket and interior illustrations by Trudy Nicholson
Jacket and interior maps by Paul Mirocha
Interior design by Wendy Holdman
The text of this book is set in Legacy.
00   01   02   03   04   5   4   3   2   1
First Edition

Milkweed Editions, a nonprofit publisher, gratefully acknowledges support from our World As Home funders, Lila Wallace-Reader's Digest Fund; Reader's Legacy underwriter Elly Sturgis; and children's fiction funder, the James R. Thorpe Foundation. Other support has been provided by the Elmer L. and Eleanor J. Andersen Foundation; James Ford Bell Foundation; Bush Foundation; General Mills Foundation; Honeywell Foundation; Jerome Foundation; McKnight Foundation; Minnesota State Arts Board through an appropriation by the Minnesota State Legislature; Norwest Foundation on behalf of Norwest Bank Minnesota; Lawrence and Elizabeth Ann O'Shaughnessy Charitable Income Trust in honor of Lawrence M. O'Shaughnessy; Oswald Family Foundation; Ritz Foundation on behalf of Mr. and Mrs. E. J. Phelps Jr.; John and Beverly Rollwagen Fund of the Minneapolis Foundation; St. Paul Companies, Inc.; Star Tribune Foundation; Target Foundation on behalf of Dayton's, Mervyn's California and Target Stores; U.S. Bancorp Piper Jaffray Foundation on behalf of U.S. Bancorp Piper Jaffray; and generous individuals.

Library of Congress Cataloging-in-Publication Data

The North Atlantic coast / edited by Sara St. Antoine.—1st ed.
    p.   cm. — (Stories from where we live)
    ISBN 1-57131-627-2 (alk. paper)
        1. Atlantic Coast (New England)—Miscellanea—Juvenile literature. 2. Atlantic Coast (Middle Atlantic States)—Miscellanea—Juvenile literature. 3. Atlantic Coast (Canada)—Miscellanea—Juvenile literature. 4. Natural history—Atlantic Coast (New England)—Miscellanea—Juvenile literature. 5. Natural history—Atlantic Coast (Middle Atlantic States)—Miscellanea—Juvenile literature. 6. Natural history—Atlantic Coast (Canada)—Miscellanea—Juvenile literature.   I. St. Antoine, Sara, 1966-   II. Series.

F12.A74 N67 2000
974—dc21   00-036062

Stories from Where We Live
The North Atlantic Coast

Reapers and Sowers

Wild Lives

Appendixes: Ecology of the North Atlantic Coast

An Invitation

Have you ever held a shell to your ear and listened to its roar? No matter where you are, that sound can be enough to transport you to the edge of the sea—where the wind whistles and the waves crash.

We hope that this book will be a bit like that seashell. Pick it up and listen to what each of these authors has to say about life along the North Atlantic Coast. Maybe you'll start to feel like you're standing on the seashore. Or bobbing along on a lobster boat. Or watching snails shimmy up a stalk of marsh grass.

As the stories, essays, poems, and journals in this anthology make clear, the communities that line the coast from Newfoundland to Delaware are varied, life-filled places. They include tiny fishing villages, farming communities, college towns, and some of North America's biggest cities—including Boston and New York City. They comprise inlets, estuaries, city parks, mud flats, salt marshes, backyards, and barrier beaches. At the same time, these communities have a common bond in their proximity to the great Atlantic Ocean.

Stories from Where We Live—The North Atlantic Coast portrays this ecological region through the literature that is its alone. You probably know that people have been sharing stories about the place where they live for thousands of years. Maybe you've heard a local legend from long ago, or listened to your grandparents tell stories about your town from the days when they were young. We believe these stories are the key to helping us better understand—and appreciate—the world around us.

Stories help us recall the history of our communities and see the ways they have changed over time. They teach us about other people who live there. They remind us of the creatures that dive, fly, creep, and scuttle around us. They entice us to become explorers! And, in many cases, they inspire us to become caretakers of all that is wild and wonderful in our home community.

With that in mind, we've collected some of the stories of people who have inhabited the North Atlantic Coast over the centuries, from early Wampanoag Indians to eighteenth-century seafarers to contemporary teens. As you'll see, we've divided the anthology into four parts: "Adventures" recounts both lighthearted and thrilling moments of action and exploration along the Atlantic; "Great Places" brings to life some favorite wild sites; "Reapers and Sowers" shows ways that local people have drawn sustenance from—and nurtured—the natural world around them; and "Wild Lives" portrays the creatures making a home on land or at sea.

We hope you enjoy this homegrown literary collection. And whether you live along the Atlantic coast or are merely stopping in for an armchair visit, we hope you'll discover some of the reasons it's a fascinating and beloved place.

—Sara St. Antoine

Stories from Where We Live
The North Atlantic Coast

Adventures

Sail by the Moon

GRETCHEN WOELFLE

Iceboats have long been used for recreation on lakes and rivers where the ice freezes thick. This story takes place in the late 1800s. Today you can find enthusiastic iceboaters from Maine to Washington State—and in Canada and Europe, too.

On Chester Erskine's eleventh birthday, his father said, "It's time to build you an iceboat. I did it and so did your grandfather, and his father too."

"Will I have to sail her alone?" Chester asked.

"A-yuh," Father answered. "Maine boys do that."

Chester frowned. "Why wasn't I born in Boston?"

"You've got nothing to worry about, son," Father chuckled.

Every winter the two of them sailed from their farm at the head of Damariscotta Lake down toward the Narrows, where the lake fell into a river that ran to the sea. The iceboat whizzed faster than the wind that stung Chester's eyes and froze his cheeks. The blades scratched the ice and hissed past beaver lodges covered in snow. The beavers stayed warm inside. Chester kept warm sitting close to Father.

Over the years Father had guided Chester's hand in steering clear of jagged ice that could flip a boat. He showed Chester how to let out the sail and lean to the side when the wind tipped the boat on two runners. Father's gentle hand corrected all his mistakes.

Chester loved to sail in light breezes, but when a strong northwest wind blew, he gave Father the tiller. What if a big wind came up when he was sailing alone?

I'll be a year a-building, Chester thought. I won't think about it now.

Chester and Father cut pine trees in February. All spring they sawed and planed the planks. They made a frame for the boat in the shape of a cross, and strengthened it with two braces.

"Back in 1871 when I was a boy," declared Father, "an iceboat won a race against the New York-Chicago express train."

"Will mine go that fast?" asked Chester.

"Not quite," Father said. "Maybe as fast as the local train to Portland."

That's still too fast, Chester thought.

During the summer Chester nailed slats across the boat to make a platform. Then he sanded the wood as smooth as the lake in early morning. The summer sun raised a sweet smell from the sawdust. Winter seemed far away.

When maple leaves turned red and yellow, Chester filed three steel runners until they gleamed. Father helped him bolt one runner on each side, and one on a swivel in the back.

"She'll turn on a dime," Father said.

Chester wasn't sure he wanted to turn that fast. He knew what it took to turn a boat—minding the sail, steering just right, and keeping all three runners on the ice.

By the first snow, he had attached a tiller and sanded the mast.

"Are you ready to take her out?" Mother asked as they sewed the canvas sail.

"I suppose so," Chester mumbled.

"I remember when your father was tending a sickly calf and you drove the hay wagon to the barn, just in time to beat a thunderstorm. You didn't think you could handle the horses, but you did."

"Those horses just plodded through the field," protested Chester. "They didn't run as fast as a railroad train!"

"You've got a steady hand," replied Mother. "You'll do just fine."

One bright day in January their neighbor, Mr. Bond, came to visit. "They say the lake is frozen all the way across," he reported.

"Tomorrow you can launch your boat, son," Father said.

"Maybe I should walk across the lake to check the ice," Chester offered.

"Linwood Brewer's done it," said Mr. Bond. "He's the one that told me."

I would have found some thin ice, Chester thought.

Father and Mr. Bond helped Chester carry the iceboat from the barn to the lake. "She's ready to go," said Father.

"Don't you want to come along?" Chester asked him.

"No, she's all yours." Father clapped him on the shoulder.

Father and Mr. Bond played checkers while Chester set the table for midday dinner.

Mr. Bond ate two helpings of everything, including Mother's apple pie, still warm from the oven.

"Chester," said Father, "if you take Mr. Bond home in your iceboat, we can play checkers all afternoon."

Chester's apple pie sank in his stomach. How could he refuse? Mr. Bond lived directly across the lake, a three-mile walk on an icy road.

"I'll go if you're willing, Mr. Bond," Chester said.

"I grew up by the ocean and never sailed an iceboat," he replied.

"You'll make good ballast after this meal," Father said.

Everyone laughed but Chester. After dinner he walked down to the boat. He ran his hand over the smooth planks. The wind was light, and Mr. Bond was heavy. Things might go all right.

When Mr. Bond finally jumped Father's last king, he exclaimed, "This is my lucky day. I'll celebrate on Chester's iceboat!"

Chester wrapped a scarf around his neck and tucked the ends under his collar. He strapped spikes to his boots. Mr. Bond pulled a woolen cap over his bald head. Mother and Father came to see them off. The long afternoon shadows reached across the snow and down to the lake.

Chester walked out on the ice. It was so smooth and clear he could see his shadow in the mud below. Black ice, he thought, the fastest ice of the winter.

"You're sure Chester can sail alone?" asked Mr. Bond, getting on the boat.

Mother laughed. "Of course he can!"

"He's been practicing since he was six," Father added. "But mind the ice slabs, son. They can be dangerous."

Chester wanted to run away—to the house, to the barn, to the woods. Instead he shouted, "Here we go!" and pushed the boat onto the frozen lake, his spikes crunching as he ran. He leaped aboard and pulled in the sail.

Mr. Bond clutched the side as the boat shot forward. "Waaait . . ." His voice faded in the wind.

Chester strained to see ahead. He saw jagged ice and clutched the tiller, pushing it just an inch. The boat lurched to the right, skittish as a high-strung horse. As they bumped over the jagged ice, Chester realized he'd pushed the tiller the wrong way.

"Stupid mistake!" hissed Chester.

"Slooow dooown!" moaned Mr. Bond.

Chester pulled in the sail and the boat went faster. "Wrong again," he muttered. He let out the sail and the boat slowed.

He had to change course to get to Mr. Bond's house. "Coming about! Duck, Mr. Bond!"

This time he turned the tiller and worked the sail just right. He smiled at Mr. Bond, but his neighbor stared hard at the ice, his lips pressed tightly together.

He's more nervous than I am! Chester thought. He tried to chuckle but coughed instead. Cold wind stung his throat.

Ahead the ice had buckled and thrown big slabs up three, four, five feet high. His heart pounded. What would Father do? Chester sailed along the ice wall until he spied an opening.

"Coming about! Hold on!" he shouted. A side runner rose off the ice as the boat sailed through. Chips of ice stung their cheeks.

"Stop!" gasped Mr. Bond.

"Lean!" shouted Chester. Mr. Bond sat frozen. "Lean!" Chester shouted again. He pushed against Mr. Bond and the runner returned to the ice. The land rushed toward them.

"My house!" Mr. Bond pointed.

Chester let out the sail and dragged his spikes on the ice till the boat stopped. Mr. Bond stood up, his knees shaking.

"Thank you, Chester," he said. "It was a once in a lifetime experience . . . for me anyway."

Chester waved and pushed off again. The boat was lighter now, and faster. Daylight was nearly gone. He hunched his shoulders and peered around the sail.

He glided through the opening in the slabs of ice. Suddenly a gust of wind caught the back runner and lifted it off the ice. The boat began to spin. Chester's scarf flew across his eyes and disappeared. He grabbed the sides as the boat whirled round and round, the sail flapping angrily. Chester waited for the crash against the slabs and the jolt that would fling him out onto the ice.

What if the boat smashed to pieces? What if he broke his leg? Would he freeze to death on the lake?

Without thinking, Chester leaned back. He felt the back runner touch the ice. The boat kept spinning. He stretched his legs until his spikes gripped the ice and the boat slowed. Finally it stopped. He lay on his back and looked at the deep blue sky. He and Father had never had a boat flicker like this. But he'd done the right thing and saved the boat and himself from harm.

Chester walked back to find his scarf. As he wound it round his neck, he gazed at his boat. She was a beauty and he could sail her alone.

The wind filled the sails and he took off down the lake. For the first time, he saw the full moon shining bright. Ice mounds sparkled like heaps of diamonds.

Why go home yet? He could sail by the moon. The wind lifted a side runner. The boat leaped ahead. Chester clutched the tiller, then relaxed. He balanced the boat so the runner stayed a foot off the ice. He was floating, he was flying.

I could beat an express train! he thought.

Snow-clad pine trees glowed along the shore. The wind whistled in his ears. The runners scraped white across the black ice as Chester circled a small island. He passed a snowy mound and called, "Hello, beavers!"

He raced up the lake. "Faster," he called to the wind and laughed out loud in the frosty air. The moon lit up a path to lead him home.

Gretchen Woelfle *writes children's stories and environmental nonfiction in Venice, California. Her grandfather-in-law, Chester Erskine, was born in 1881 on a farm in Jefferson, Maine, on the shores of Damariscotta Lake. He grew up to be the fastest iceboater on the lake. He married Iva McArdle in 1907, and they moved to Connecticut. In 1939 they bought a small cottage on the lake, not far from the old Erskine farm. They spent every summer there till they died in 1967. Chester and Iva's sons, grandchildren, and great-grandchildren continue to visit the cottage each year. Chester's iceboat is long gone, but the Erskines still swim and sail on Damariscotta Lake during the summer.*

The Rescuer from Lime Rock

STEPHEN CURRIE

Lime Rock is a tiny island off the Newport coast that is now called Ida Lewis Rock in honor of its famous lighthouse keeper. Although the original tower light was officially discontinued in 1927, the light attached to the keeper's house is kept lit as an ongoing tribute to Ida Lewis.

Huge waves crashed against the shore. A cold wind raced across the ocean, sending spray everywhere. Rain mixed with snow and ice pelted down. If you had been in Newport, Rhode Island, on that March day back in 1869, you might have enjoyed the violent storm—from indoors!

On Lime Rock, a small island near Newport, Ida Lewis had been sneezing and coughing all afternoon. Ida was a lighthouse keeper. Each night she lit the huge lamp that guided ships safely into Newport Harbor. She had just propped her chilly bare feet next to the kitchen oven when she heard a cry. Ida knew what it meant: out on the ocean, a boat had tipped over.

Ida didn't hesitate. "I started right out, just as I was," she recalled years later: no shoes, no jacket, no hat. Ignoring her mother, who begged her to stay inside, Ida ran to the rowboat she kept on the beach. Far from shore, two men were struggling in the icy water. Could she reach them in time?

Quickly Ida slid her boat into the waves and began to row. It was hard work. The wind made steering almost impossible, and waves splashed over her every few seconds. Luckily Ida was strong and determined, and she never lost sight of her target. Little by little she worked her way through the storm toward the drowning men.

But getting there was only part of the problem. Bringing the men into the boat would be just as hard. Ida knew they would not be able to help themselves. First she stroked hard on one oar, turning the boat so its broad stern faced the struggling men. Then she braced her legs against the side of the boat and reached into the black, frigid water.

She had steered well. One of the men, nearly unconscious, was within reach. Seizing his hand, she turned him onto his back and pulled him toward her. Then she reached under his shoulders and locked her arms securely around his chest.

Ida balanced as steadily as she could in the rocking surf. With all her might, she heaved the man up and back. She pulled again, drawing more of his body over the side, but it took several lifts before his knees cleared the stern. Ida made sure he was still breathing. Then, leaving him at the bottom of the boat, she fished the other man out of the water, too.

Even now, the rescue was not over. Between the boat and safety lay a hundred yards of wind and waves. Shivering with cold, her strength almost gone, Ida rowed through the blinding spray. Again, her aim was perfect. One last pull on the oars, and she was safely on the beach. Ida had saved the men from certain drowning. Now she *really* had a reason to warm her feet.

Lime Rock saw plenty of boating accidents. Some people forgot to watch for rocks, and others went out when the wind and waves were too strong. Still others couldn't handle a boat properly. But few of the accident victims drowned. During fifty years of keeping the Lime Rock lighthouse, Ida single-handedly rescued seventeen people—and most of the other rescues were just as dangerous as this one.

In 1866, for instance, a soldier overturned his boat on a windy February night. Luckily Ida knew the harbor well. Using the lighthouse beam to guide her, Ida steered around jagged rocks and up to the struggling solider, then rowed him to safety.

Another winter, three farmers set off across the harbor in a leaky boat, trying to catch an escaped sheep that was swimming toward the ocean. When they capsized, Ida rowed out, pulled all three farmers into her own boat, and brought them to shore. Then she went back to save the sheep!

But Ida's bravest rescue of all didn't involve her boat. In 1881 two men who were walking across the frozen harbor fell through a patch of thin ice. Fortunately, Ida saw them from Lime Rock. She had to run a half mile across the treacherous ice and pull both of them out of the chilly water. She said many years later, "I never thought of danger when people needed help."

Living on a tiny island had taught Ida to be resourceful and independent. She had many jobs, from polishing the beacon lights to doing the laundry. She rowed her sister and brothers to school in Newport each morning and rowed back to pick them up every afternoon. And Ida had learned early on to do whatever had to be done. Her father had been Lime Rock's lighthouse keeper before her, but when he had a stroke and could no longer work, she took over. Not everyone approved. A few people felt that being a lighthouse keeper was unladylike, and some said that women were too weak to do the job properly—even while Ida was busy rescuing one person after another!

But Ida never cared what other people thought, nor did she believe that she was unusually brave. Although her rescues made her famous, she disliked the attention. "If there were some people out there who needed help," she told a writer, "I would get into my boat and go to them even if I knew I couldn't get back. Wouldn't you?" Like taking over for her father or rowing to Newport every school day, rescuing people was something that simply had to be done. "I just went," she said, "and that was all there was to it."

Stephen Currie *is the author of about forty books and many magazine articles. He lives with his family in upstate New York.*

The Ocean Is a Heartbeat

Mary Quigley

The ocean is a heartbeat.
Within circulates me,
a dolphin.
Seeing sound,
I split the waves in two,
quietly,
like
a lullaby.

A lullaby
is a heartbeat
for me,
a child.
Ocean music playing
from a shell
pressed upon my ear
as

I drift
on waves.

I drift,

to sleep.

Waves change,
a crashing pulse upon the shore.
The air feels different,

storm is coming.

Storm is coming.
Wake up!
Oatmeal and juice.
We need more food.
To the market for
bottled water,
peanut butter,
canned soup.
Don't forget
crackers and

Eat more
tuna fish.

tuna fish.

Catch twice as many tuna fish.
Must be ready to swim far,
dive deep,
do without,
and make it through the storm.
Mother nudges at my side,
helps me catch fish.
Water churns.

Wind churns.
Land,

water

merge,

foam.

Better go farther,

Better go farther,

deeper,

into

the ocean.

Below the churning waves
and flying debris
I hold my breath longer.
Lunging through the mix of
air and water,
I blast with
my blowhole,
clearing away the spray
to make way for a quick,
deep
breath.
Hold my breath.

away from
the ocean.

Hold my breath.
I hope the lights
don't go out as they
flicker.
Radio crackles and
fails.
Light candles.
Study map.
Mama and Papa pack and
we drive west,
beyond the waves
and flying debris.

Only to return again.

Only to return again.

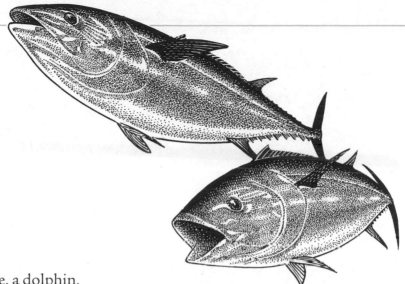

Me, a dolphin,
in the ocean,

Me, a child, on the
shore.

when the ocean is a heartbeat,
steady, pulsing.
And
Mama helps me catch
a fish.

Mama helps me catch
a fish.

Mary Quigley *is a wife, mother, and author with experience in teaching and nature study. She has supervised a program for academically at-risk youth and taught history to college students. She is frequently found enjoying a garden, museum, pond, or bookstore.*

Dorchester Days

ALICE STONE BLACKWELL

As a child, Alice Stone Blackwell lived with her parents on a high hill in Dorchester, Massachusetts, overlooking Boston to the north and the Atlantic Ocean to the east. Her parents were both suffragists, and her mother ran a newspaper devoted to women's issues. Alice's days were enlivened by her parents' activities and by the opportunities for adventure and play in the gardens, woods, and water near her home. She began the journal excerpted below in 1872 when she was fourteen years old.

March 20th

Wednesday. A strange and wonderful day; a mixture of clouds, sunshine, cold, and a wind that made the elms bend and crack, roared around the schoolhouse, made us all wild at recess, and blew me home after school in a wild whirl of skirts, coat, cloud, hair, hat and dust. Made tart crusts. Emma arrived under convoy of Mama, and was fed and seen to. She immediately set to work clipping slips for the *Journal* like a born editor.

April 26th

Friday. Awfully and outrageously hot. I could have Oh'ed for a lodge in a garden of cucumbers, for the first time this year. I went up with Miss Tucker to the house, did a wee bit of gardening and dug up part of the patch for my beans. There was a big wind toward evening, whirling weird white clouds of dust along the road, and Annie and I went out and got blown.

July 6th

Saturday. Had a beautiful sail with Mr. and Mrs. Campbell. They were to hoist a black flag, and I was put upon the watch for it, and wished it had been my pirate lover. When it appeared Papa, Mama, Mrs. Dennet and I drove down to the shore in the carriage, and found Mrs. C. sitting in the boat, her husband having gone up to the house to call us. When he came back we had a beautiful sail, lunching on cake and crackers, and landed on Moon island,* where we stayed just long enough for me to take a delightful bath. Moon Isl. reminds me of M[artha's] V[ineyard] only the cliffs are not high enough, and are grass grown. We landed at Squantum, where the carriage awaited us, and drove home with Mrs. Campbell.
Moon Island is now a peninsular extension of Squantum.

Sept. 20th

Friday. Clouds wind and sunshine. After school walked over to some beautiful woods in the direction of Milton, and got a lot of moss, partridge vines and sweet acorns.

Oct. 4th

Friday. Had the fullest intention of going Miltonward, but Emma Adams asked me to go out rowing, and I accepted with pleasure of course. Hattie went with us, and we all three raced to Commercial point. The boat was launched with some trouble, and we started out. It was delightful to be on blue water once more, and be able to dip my hand in the blessed brine. We had to come back at last, and I had leave to row one oar, which I liked. Hattie and Emma gave me contradictory orders, but I obeyed the Skipper of course. As we made for the pier, we ran aground in the mud. I pushed the boat off once, but it stuck again—fast. And the tide was still falling. And rowing, and pushing, and laughter and vexation, were of no use; we couldn't stir her a hair's breadth. A little crowd of men and boys collected on the wharf and watched us with great amusement. A man hailed us from one of the little vessels at anchor, and bawled to us to push off and row so and so. He might as well have told us to go to the moon; we *couldn't* push off; that was just it. Finally he came to our assistance in a wherry, took Hattie and me into his boat, and towing and pushing and tugging and grunting hauled our boat into the channel; paddled after an oar we had left stuck in the mud, received our thanks and paddled away. We only ran aground once more, and were triumphantly hauled up to the pier by a rope we flung to the men and boys thereon collected. We then retreated to a boat-house and exploded.

April 12th

Saturday. Went in to the dentist, and came out with Mamma through a heavy snowstorm. Mr. & Mrs. Horne and baby were on the platform, & Mamma offered to drive the two last up when our carriage came. Mr. H. said he would go on home and light the fire, and overtook me, I having started to walk up. We went on together, and the snowflakes were huge, as big as birds.

April 20th

Sunday. Went over to Chapel, walking with Fanny, whom I overtook. It was not as nice as in the afternoon, and there were few there. Rode over to Quincy Great Hill or Head with the folks. It is a glorious place—a great round hill with water all around it, and great cliffs that seemed almost like Martha's Vineyard. I watched my face in the blessed salt water, and heard the sound of it; but it was nearly spoiled by Edith's incessant noise and chatter, which gave me a headache.

May 14th

Wednesday. Went to music lesson. Cut dandelion greens in the evening with Miss Jones and Edie. Got letters from Kitty and Aunt Marian. Went out walking after supper with Edie, and walked a mile and a half in 30^m.

June 4th

Wednesday. Sent in a huge bunch of lilies of the valley to be divided among the girls in the printing office. I think it is such a pity the flowers should all be in one place and the people in another! We have more flowers than we know what to do with. Edie's last day here. She sent her goodbye to Miss Morse by me. Played croquet with her, and let her beat the last game, it being the last.

June 8th

Sunday. Rode over to the Quincy granite quarries with Papa and Mamma, and he & I climbed up to the top, saw the view and got 5 leaved ivy & ferns, also Solomon's seal & I an armfull of ~~colubines~~ wake robin—one huge specimen nearly half as long again as my arm, measuring from root to leaf tip. It is a lovely romantic place & I mean to go again.

July 28th

Monday. Flo arrived. I saw the queerest fog bank coming in from sea when I was on the house top watching. Went shopping in Boston with Mamma. We mutually begged each other to put on our tombstones

"Died of shopping with an unreasonable mother"

"Died of shopping with an impracticable daughter."

Alice Stone Blackwell *was the daughter of suffragists Lucy Stone and Henry Blackwell. She grew up to be a social reformer, writer, and editor.*

The Legend of Big Claw

JEFF W. BENS

for my father, David L. Bens, a great teller of stories

Block Island, where this story takes place, is known as "the island of hope" because so many of its remarkable natural areas—high cliffs, dunes, moorlands, salt ponds, marshes, beaches, and more—have been protected through the actions of its loyal residents.

Luther stood by the lobster traps at the Old Harbor docks, watching a ferry boat crossing from the mainland. His father had been captain of that boat, ferrying passengers from Point Judith, Rhode Island, out to Block Island and back again, every hour on the hour during the summer. A crowd of people lined the dock waiting for the ferry to land. Block Island was a funny place: for three seasons Luther could bike all over the island and hardly see anyone he didn't know, or hardly anyone period, but in the summer the island was packed with people from the mainland.

"Swarmed," with people, his Uncle Bill would say.

Jenny Swanson was from the mainland. Luther didn't think a lot about Jenny Swanson, but when he did his head went hot and his stomach felt like it would if he were falling off a cliff. He'd seen her only once. She had blonde hair and brown eyes and she wore a t-shirt for a rock band that neither Luther, nor the guy who ran the Block Island Music Shoppe, had ever heard of.

Jenny Swanson's family was renting Uncle Bill's house for the summer, and that's how Luther had met her. He and his little sister, Kate, had been biking along the road that went past the Mohegan Bluffs when Luther felt the air go out of his tire. Luther had a patch kit and a pump at home, but home was on the other side of the island, overlooking Great Salt Pond. So he and Kate went by his uncle's house to see if there was a pump in the garage. Jenny Swanson answered the door. She was pulling a green elastic from the ponytail in her hair. Her hair fell across her shoulders.

"My tire broke," Luther said. He felt his face go red.

Jenny Swanson laughed. Luther couldn't look at her. Kate got the pump and caught up with him. He was practically running his bicycle down the road.

"Hey, Captain!"

It was Uncle Bill, with a bait bucket in each hand.

"You look like you've seen a ghost," Uncle Bill said. Bill was wearing denim cutoff shorts and a hat that said "What's Cookin'?"

"I was just thinking," Luther said.

Uncle Bill's boat, named *Cathy's Cloud*, was a small one compared to the big boats that fished traps farther out to sea. Those boats were sometimes forty feet long and had diesel engines and depth sounders and radar and fished hundreds of traps. Bill's boat had a gasoline engine and a leaky place in the deck, and Luther could walk from bow to stern in ten paces.

His uncle didn't work a lot of lobster traps, but in August and early September he brought in enough lobster to pay Luther five dollars for a morning's help. His uncle let Luther tend a couple of traps. Luther had marked them with a green shamrock, because his family was Irish-American and because he loved the Boston Celtics.

They loaded up the boat and pushed back from the slip. Luther took a big breath and exhaled up toward the sun. He liked the way the ocean smelled, especially when he was out in the middle of it, not just lying on some beach. When they'd cleared the harbor, Uncle Bill let Luther take the wheel. Luther kept the course set from the compass. He knew how to read navigational maps if he ever needed to. His father had shown him.

They passed the Point Judith ferry as it neared the harbor, and Luther could see the passengers out on the deck—whole families in sunglasses throwing bread crumbs to hovering gulls. He'd ridden sometimes in the bridge of that ferry with his father. His father had died of cancer when Luther was seven, four years ago. In the end his father couldn't leave his own bed, though this is not the way Luther wanted to remember him.

Uncle Bill put a hand on Luther's shoulder. Luther relaxed his grip on the wheel.

"Maybe my new hauler will finally haul in old Big Claw." Uncle Bill raised his eyebrows a couple of times and pulled on his gloves. The hauler was a hydraulic pulley that lifted the traps from the ocean floor. Uncle Bill used to haul the traps up with his hands.

"Big Claw's got to be ten feet long by now," Luther said. He smiled a little. "You'd need bigger traps."

Uncle Bill laughed. Big Claw was famous among the lobstermen on the island. He was sort of like Block Island's own Loch Ness monster.

Luther's father had told Big Claw stories when Luther was little. They'd sit with his mother and Kate on the screen porch, looking out across Great Salt Pond. As the sun sank into the Atlantic, his father would light his pipe, and Luther would have a lemonade, and Kate would be hanging onto her stuffed horse, and his father would tell them about the time when Big Claw was small.

"When I was just a boy," his father would begin, "the Delancey boys pulled him up in their father's trap. He wasn't much of a lobster then, sort of a runt."

The blue heron, the one that was there every summer, would glide low along Great Salt Pond's shore. Later, when his father was unable to go for walks along the pond, Luther would give him reports on the herons, and the osprey with their gray wings, and the sniggling plovers.

"The Delancey boys were mean kids," his father would continue. "They sometimes liked to set two lobsters on the bait table and have them fight."

Luther's mother would shake her head at this point and smile. She'd heard the stories even more times than Luther.

"Big Claw didn't want to fight, but the Delancey boys made him, pushing him toward a big, mean-looking lobster, who snapped at him with its claws. 'Fight, fight!' the Delancey boys shouted. They poked at Big Claw and snapped him with elastic bands." Here his father would straighten up excitedly beside Luther on the couch, the way he always did when he came to the good part of a story. "The Delancey boys snapped Big Claw one too many times. Suddenly, Big Claw spun around

and chomped onto the big brother's thumb, then he swept the other lobster, mean as it was, right back into the water."

"And Big Claw?" Katie would ask, because she hadn't heard the story as often as Luther.

"The Delancey kid leapt to his feet, shook his hand, flung his arm out, 'Yowch!' But Big Claw hung on, until . . ."

Here his father would go quiet, slowly nodding his head, packing his pipe with his thumb.

"Until . . . ," Luther might say, because this part of the story always got to him.

"Until Big Claw made it back to the ocean. But his claw stayed clamped to the Delancey boy's thumb."

There were lots of Big Claw stories, near misses over the years. A few boats even claimed to have had him on board, but somehow Big Claw always managed to get away. Like Big Claw, the stories grew larger over the years. Whenever a trap was snapped from its buoy so the lobstermen couldn't haul it from the bottom of the ocean, it was Big Claw at work. He became the great lobster liberator! And his size! And that big crusher claw! In one story, Big Claw stood ready to signal the U.S. Navy should Axis warships sail into Narragansett Bay. This would have made Big Claw over fifty years old.

You could use just about anything for lobster bait. Uncle Bill used the cheapest fish he could find. Lobsters ate anything: fish, crabs, mussels, starfish, sea urchins, even each other. Luther sometimes felt bad about hauling up lobsters to cook them in a pot. But a person had to eat, and the fact that they sometimes ate each other made him feel like maybe they weren't the nicest creatures. Big Claw was different, though.

Uncle Bill leaned over the side of the boat and hooked the gaff around the first green, white, and orange buoy.

"Would you eat him?" Luther asked.

"Who?"

"Big Claw."

The cork line attached to the buoy was draped with sea kelp. "I'd sure as heck sell him. Fifty pounds at three dollars a pound." Bill hooked the line around his bright hydraulic hauler. "I don't know if I could eat him, though."

The hauler began to spin, slowly pulling the trap up from the bottom of the cove. Uncle Bill stood back and grinned.

"My bad back is smiling." He waved his arms at the water. "Rise, rise!"

There were two lobsters in the kitchen of his trap. They lifted the lobsters out, banded their claws, and measured them. Luther had his own gauge. A lobster couldn't be too small or too big. If it was you had to throw it back. Luther's lobster was a good one, shiny brown and about four pounds. He placed it in the cooler. Uncle Bill's lobster had eggs along the underside of the carapace. Uncle Bill took out his knife, cut a V-shaped notch in the lobster's tail flipper, and dropped her back into the water. The V-notch would let other lobstermen know that the lobster was a female. If you ate all the females, soon there'd be no lobsters left.

"That hauler is going to save my back twenty years of abuse." He looked at Luther. "And you can thank the summer rent from your girlfriend's family for that." Uncle Bill winked at him.

Luther thought, Katie and her big mouth.

Luther sat with his mother and Uncle Bill on the porch overlooking Great Salt Pond. Katie was standing at the water's edge. Luther's dog, Jump Shot, was turning circles and sniffing after fiddler crabs that popped in and out of their muddy holes. The sun sank into the waves.

Luther watched his sister, squawking now like a gull. There weren't a lot of kids on the island, but he had a couple of good friends, and Jump Shot. And when she wasn't acting like a jerk, Katie was OK, too. He'd even given her one of the fishing rods that his father had given him.

Luther and his father had fished the channel for flounder and mackerel. His father had shown him how to cast and troll, how to clean a fish, how to cook it in a frying pan outside over an open flame. Luther missed his father a lot, especially at night on the porch, when the sun was setting behind the cat-tails and the reeds.

His mother looked up from her book. "Uncle Bill and I are going to do a Labor Day clambake," she announced. "We'll need both of your help."

Uncle Bill always did a clambake for someone over Labor Day. There were a lot of ways to make money in the summer on Block Island.

"It's for the Swansons," his mother said. "You know, the doctor's family that rented Bill's house."

Jump Shot yelped. Luther watched a loon dive into the pond.

Luther didn't want to sit on the porch and talk about serving Jenny Swanson quahogs and corn. So he rode the loop, past the Mohegan bluffs where merlins rode warm air currents, effortlessly gliding high above the waves. If you got too close to the edge of the bluffs you were a goner; it was at least a hundred feet to the rocky beach below. Luther wheeled his bike near the edge of the bluff. Wind blew around his already curly hair. He threw a stone as far out as he could. He took a deep breath of ocean air.

In the harbor, a huge crowd gathered outside the Double Dip ice cream shop. Luther rode up to investigate. There must have been fifty people, mostly tourists on mopeds and families he did not recognize. But there were people he did recognize, too, and they seemed very excited. Maybe the Double Dip was giving away free samples. Little kids were up on their fathers' shoulders, laughing and pointing.

Luther saw Captain Murphy. Captain Murphy had one of

the big boats that took the mainlanders out for sea bass and bluefish.

"What's going on in there?" Luther asked.

"Luther! You won't believe it!" It was as if Captain Murphy had just seen Santa Claus come down the Harborview Fish House chimney. "The Johnson boat. In a fish net. They captured Big Claw!"

Luther didn't believe it. But seeing the excited crowd and the grin of disbelief on Captain Murphy's face, he decided to squeeze his way up the three short steps and onto the Harborview porch. It was true. There, in a tank in the window of the Harborview Fish House, was Big Claw himself, staring out at the crowd.

Mr. Languis, the owner of the fish house, was proudly tapping on the glass with his gold ring. "He's thirty-eight point seven pounds, and my guess is he's over forty years old."

Big Claw barely fit inside the tank. The hairy cilia on his legs looked like seaweed, and his shell was encrusted with barnacles. His crusher claw was forced up over his head. The claw itself must have weighed five pounds, its edges jagged like a knife. Inside the restaurant, little kids and even some adults were tapping at the tank, trying to get Big Claw's attention. A kid his age reached up and squeezed the tip of the crusher claw. Big Claw tried to pull away but couldn't. The kid laughed. His little sister laughed.

Maybe Big Claw remembered how he'd lost his other claw.

Maybe Big Claw thought he was going to be eaten.

Luther went inside.

"You're not going to eat him, are you, Mr. Languis?"

"That big lobster? Of course not. He draws the people in. I hope he'll last another forty years!" Mr. Languis carried an order to a table of diners, all of whom had lobster bibs tied underneath their chins. Luther leaned down to look at Big Claw. Big Claw just stared out the window toward the bay.

They held the clambake on the strip of beach in front of Uncle Bill's house. Being right on the beach was what made Uncle Bill's house so valuable. The house was always sort of a mess inside, but, as Uncle Bill put it, "I could raise pigs in there from October to May and still rent it out to the mainlanders." From the number of people that Luther saw packing the beaches on his bike ride over, he figured this was true. He'd nearly been hit by a moped and by a BMW with a Massachusetts license plate.

His mother had the jeep backed up to the flat rocks that lined the sandy part of the shore. In the back of the jeep were coolers full of quahogs, Uncle Bill's lobsters, fresh corn from the mainland, cherrystone clams, potatoes, lemons, big blocks of butter, and a brown bag full of parsley, onions, bay leaf, and sage. Luther looked out at the beach. Uncle Bill had dug the hole already. Beside it were two piles, one of driftwood and one of stone. They'd layer the pit with wood and stone, light it, then cook the food slowly in the fire.

Luther didn't see Jenny Swanson anywhere. He glanced quickly up at the house as he leaned his bike against his father's jeep. The sun and the ocean reflected in the windows. The bay was filled with sails. Luther's father had asked his mother to marry him during a sail, jumping into the water when she said yes. Luther liked to think of him this way, before he'd even known him, jumping into the water with his mother laughing and clapping her hands the way she did when she was happy.

"Luther!" Uncle Bill and his mother were hauling a big cooler down to the fire pit.

Luther hustled down to the beach.

The air had cooled. Some of the Swanson party was dancing now. The rest were roasting marshmallows in the embers of the fire pit. Luther was washing his hands in the ocean. He'd hauled a dozen trash bags full of shells and carcasses and gnawed corncobs up to the jeep, not to mention the recycling bags full of bottles and cans.

He'd watched Jenny Swanson for a lot of the clambake. Mostly she'd lain on a towel away from the rest of the party. Once he watched her swim. She'd come up from under a small wave coughing, like she'd swallowed water. She looked as if she didn't know where she was for a moment, and then she was looking straight at him. He wanted to talk with her, but he didn't have anything to say.

The water was warm around his hands, feet, and arms. He wanted to swim, but his mother had said he was to wait until he got home. He was an employee, not a guest, even if it was Uncle Bill's house. Near his toes, a bunch of hermit crabs were rolling around with the waves. One of them was too big for its shell. It would be looking for a new one soon. He picked it up. He felt the crab tickling his hand. He thought about Big Claw, all cooped up in his glass cage.

"You're the boy with the broken bicycle."

Luther turned. Jenny Swanson stood on the shore, not letting her feet get wet. She was holding a whole lobster tail that was split in two and dripping with butter.

The hermit crab dropped from Luther's hand. Luther

watched it float down through the water to the sand. "I had a flat." Luther didn't look up.

"My brother's got a BMX 9000. Maybe he'll let you ride it sometime."

Luther glanced at Jenny Swanson. She peeled some of the meat from the cracked lobster tail and put it in her mouth.

"I hate this island, don't you?" she said. "It's so boring." Butter dripped down her chin.

"I don't know," Luther said. And then he was walking quickly past her to his bike, resisting the urge to run. He knew what he had to do. His mother was sweeping the porch above the driveway. She called out Luther's name, but he did not answer. He got on his bike and sped away. He could phone Uncle Bill when he got home.

"He's a big lobster, isn't he?"

An elderly woman sat with her husband at the table in the Harborview Fish House nearest the tank. Luther tried to pretend he didn't hear her. Big Claw hadn't moved. Mr. Languis had put a filter and some sea plants in the tank, and a sign that read: "Big Claw—Monster from the Deep." Big Claw had positioned his head so that it was partially hidden by the plants.

Luther picked up the chair nearest him and set it next to the tank.

"Are you going to eat him up?" The woman was looking at Luther now. Luther was still in his shorts, and his t-shirt was stained with clam juice and wet with saltwater from the beach.

"No, ma'am," Luther said quickly. He had Kate's wagon just outside the door.

Luther wondered how much Jump Shot weighed; he'd picked her up before. He took a deep breath, sprang onto the chair, and plunged both arms down into the water. He tried not to think of what would happen if the plug slipped out of the crusher claw.

"Young man!" the old woman said, her eyes wide.

With one huge effort, Luther hoisted Big Claw from the tank, Big Claw's eight legs snapping, water splashing everywhere.

"Just a minute!" said her husband.

But Luther didn't stop. He charged out the restaurant door. He dropped Big Claw into the wagon. "Hold on, Big Claw," Luther said, and then he raced Kate's wagon across Ocean Avenue, rushing the lobster toward *Cathy's Cloud*.

Luther looked back once. Mr. Languis stood in the Fish House doorway, his arms folded across his chest.

Uncle Bill had the engine running. "Your mother's going to kill me," he hollered as he and Luther hurried the wagon onto the deck. Luther's heart was racing.

Cathy's Cloud sped away from the slip.

Luther watched Old Harbor get smaller, the people on the ferry dock and the crowded beaches shrinking, until he couldn't tell one person from another. Uncle Bill got on the CB radio and was laughing with someone as Luther wheeled the wagon toward the starboard edge. He carefully removed the wagon peg from the hinge of the crusher claw. And then he set Big Claw free.

❧

Jeff W. Bens *was raised in Massachusetts and currently teaches in the film department at the University of North Carolina School of the Arts.*

Cape Cod Girls

This chantey was probably written sometime in the nineteenth century. It was designed to lift the spirits and boost the energies of men hauling up their ship's anchor as they prepared to take to the sea.

Cape Cod girls don't use no combs,
Haul away, haul away;
They comb their hair with a codfish bone,
And we're bound away for Australia.

REFRAIN:
So heave her up my bully, bully boys,
Haul away, haul away;
Heave her up and don't ya' make a noise,
And we're bound away for Australia.

Cape Cod kids don't have no sleds,
Haul away, haul away;
They slide down the hill on a codfish head,
And we're bound away for Australia.

[Refrain]

Cape Cod cats don't have no tails,
Haul away, haul away;
They lost 'em all in a Northeast gale,
And we're bound away for Australia.

[Refrain]

Cape Cod ladies don't have no frills,
Haul away, haul away;
They're plain and skinny as a codfish gill,
And we're bound away for Australia.

So heave her up my bully, bully boys,
Haul away, haul away;
Heave her up and don't ya' make a noise,
And we're bound away for Australia.

Of Beaches, Bays, and My Boyhood with the Colonel

WILLIAM W. WARNER

Although most visitors to the New Jersey shore favor its sandy beaches,
budding adventurers can explore a wonderful variety of coastal habitats,
including salt marshes, dunes, bays, tidal flats, and barrier beaches—
thin strips of land that lie just off the coast.

Very little in my upbringing seems to have pointed toward a
love for our great Atlantic beaches, much less writing about
them. I was born and grew up in New York City in a house that
was without great books, without a father, and for some periods of the year, without a mother. In *loco patris,* I had only a
highly irascible step-grandfather. Colonel George Washington
Kavanaugh was his name, and he wanted to be known by all of
it. His most frequent utterance to me, apart from constant reminders that I was no blood kin, went something like this:
"Your father is a bum, your mother is running around with
every gigolo in Europe, so I suppose the spring can rise no
higher than its source."

So much for the Colonel, as my brother and I always called
him, and the genetic malediction he constantly laid on us. But
there was one thing the Colonel did for us for which we are
both eternally grateful. Come June every year he took our
family, such as it was, to a place called Spring Lake, a summer

resort on the New Jersey coast. Not that we especially liked the place. Our school mates all went "to the country" on vacations, and Spring Lake with its kiosked boardwalks, well-ordered streets, and great hotels with long porches and double rows of rocking chairs didn't seem very country to us. Reinforcing this impression was an institution known as the Bath and Tennis Club, where our contemporaries spent much of the day playing blackjack and sneaking cigarettes.

But at one end of the well-ordered streets, beyond the boardwalk and the great hotels, was an immense space. How immense I learned from my older brother, who at age nine or ten gave me my first taste for geography. "Look here," he said, showing me a world map and running his finger along the fortieth parallel, "there is nothing but the Atlantic Ocean between our beach and the coast of Portugal, four thousand miles away."

Suffice it to say that this bit of information, which was quite accurate, overwhelmed me. I soon began taking long walks along the beach, staring out at the ocean and dreaming of the day I might have a boat of my own to venture beyond the breakers and explore it. My brother shared this vision, although more in terms of a quest for better fishing. In due course we therefore built a crude box-shaped scow of heavy pine planking, painted it red, white, and green, and proudly named it the *Rex* after the great Italian ocean liner that was at the time one of the largest and most luxurious ships in the transatlantic passenger service. With the help of some of our huskier friends we grunted the *Rex* down the beach. The chosen day was fine, with a sprightly land breeze that did much to calm the breakers. Our plan was alternately to fish and paddle down to an inlet at the south end of Spring Lake that led into a small bay known as Wreck Pond. But after we were successfully launched, our friends all laughing and cheering us on, we found the *Rex* to be something less than seaworthy and quite difficult to paddle. In fact, the sprightly western breeze that had made our passage through the surf so easy was now rapidly carrying us out to sea—straight for Portugal, I could not help thinking—with a strength against which our best efforts were no match. The reader can guess what followed. Alarms were sounded, authorities were summoned, and we were rescued. "One more trick like this and I'm cutting you out of my will," the Colonel said to us when we were brought home, humiliated, by the Coast Guard.

Nevertheless, before the summer was over, my brother and I found we could explore the incongruously named Wreck Pond well enough by foot and bicycle. It was, in fact, what biologists call a complete estuarine system, in miniature. At its mouth was the tide-scoured inlet, constantly shifting its sandy course. Behind the inlet was a shallow bay, a labyrinth of marsh islands, and ultimately, well inland, a freshwater stream fed by a millpond bordered by pin oak and magnolia. Thanks to this complex we could do everything from netting crabs and small fish to stalking the marsh flats looking for shorebirds, muskrat, or an occasional raccoon. We could even catch small trout up by the millpond dam, graciously provided by the New Jersey state fish hatcheries. What a relief these occasions offered from the Bath and Tennis Club, what an escape from the Colonel! Wreck Pond, in short, became our private world.

But there were other worlds to conquer, as the saying goes, in particular a large blank space on maps of the coast that my brother and I had both noticed and wondered about. It appeared as a long finger of land pointing southward, a mere ribbon of land between the Atlantic Ocean and Barnegat Bay. Most remarkably, the southern part of the finger, below a cluster of closely spaced beach resorts, showed no signs of human settlement nor even a road, as far as we could tell. (The reader will understand how rare this was when I say that even in the 1930s, which is the time I speak of, much of the New Jersey coast was already a solid corridor of resort townships.) The blank space was called Island Beach. It had to be investigated, we agreed.

For this greater enterprise we borrowed a canoe, provisioned it with three days' worth of canned pork and beans, and left an ambiguous note concerning our intentions on the Colonel's pillow. But once again the Aeolian gods did not favor us. This time a wet east wind slammed us against the marshes of Barnegat Bay's western shore, so strongly, in fact, that we found we could only gain ground by wading in the shallows and pushing and pulling the canoe. There was one bright moment in this otherwise dismal effort, however. After rounding a sharp bend in one of the marsh islands we came upon a sheltered and relatively quiet cove. There to our amazement were four or five mink cavorting down a mud slide they had excavated in the marsh bank. Over and over they shot down the slide—head first, tail first, on their stomachs, on their backs—to splash into the water with splendid abandon. Well hidden by the tall cordgrass, we watched transfixed as the mink evidently scrambled up an underwater burrow, reappeared above on the marsh bank, shook their silvery wet coats, and repeated the process. Forever, it seemed, or what must have been at least ten minutes. I have never forgotten the sight, nor seen another mink slide since.

We passed what seemed like a sleepless night huddled under a tump of bushes in the cordgrass that offered little cover from intermittent rains. The next morning we set out again, very tired, under a hazy sun and on glassy calm waters. Island Beach seemed almost in sight on the far horizon to the east, although it was hard to be sure in the haze. Just as we began to ponder the wisdom of continuing our journey, a large and official-looking motorboat with a slanted red stripe on its bow came alongside, bearing instructions to take us in tow. "That does it!" the Colonel said to us two hours later when we were brought home again, humiliated but grateful, by the Coast Guard. "I'm cutting you both out of my will."

A few years later, when I was sixteen and my brother and I had gone our separate ways, I got to Island Beach. I got there in what today is known as an ORV, or off-road vehicle. But mine was quite different from current models. Mine was a splendid little ORV, in fact, for which I make no apologies. Unknown to the Colonel I had acquired a lightweight Ford Model-T beach-buggy prototype with a chopped down body, painted in salt-resistant aluminum and equipped with four enlarged wheel rims and tires, all for the sum of fifty dollars. My buggy was totally incapable of sustained driving in soft sand, having only the standard two-wheel drive and a weak one at that. It therefore could never charge up dunes or otherwise alter the beach topography. To operate it successfully on Island Beach it was necessary to travel at low tide only, along the wet and more compact swash sand of the forebeach. This meant driving along close to the surf, constantly dodging the biggest waves, in what proved to be a thoroughly exhilarating experience. One could do this, moreover, for ten glorious miles, ten miles of wind-plumed breakers rolling in from the Atlantic, ten miles with seldom another human being in sight. Sometimes there would be schools of marauding bluefish just beyond the surf, marked by sprays of small fish breaking the surface and the screams of wheeling gulls and terns. In such event I would jam on the brakes (stepping on the reverse gear pedal worked even better), grab my cane surf rod, and heave out a heavy lead-squid lure as far as possible. If your cast went far enough, you got your blue. By the time you brought him in and unhooked him, you had to jump back into the buggy and race on to catch up with the fast-moving school. For a boy of sixteen these were moments of pure bliss, of feeling at one with the sea and the sand.

There were other attractions. Often I would leave my fishing companions to their patient pursuits and explore the back beach. The dunes of Island Beach were low, but with steep rampartlike faces on their seaward side. Behind the ramparts were small hollows of smooth sand marked only with the delicate circular tracings made by the tips of swaying dune grass. Then came beach heather and thickets of sea myrtle, stunted cedar, holly, and scrub oak. Gain the highest point of land, perhaps no more than twenty feet above sea level, and the small world of Island Beach lay revealed before you. On the one side were the choppy waves of Barnegat Bay at its broadest, bordered by salt marsh and tidal flats that attracted great numbers of both migrant and resident shorebirds. On the other were the dunes, the white sand, and the Atlantic breakers stretching away to a seeming infinity. It was a small world, easy to comprehend, and I loved it from the beginning.

William W. Warner *is the author of* Beautiful Swimmers: Watermen, Crabs, and the Chesapeake Bay, *which won a 1977 Pulitzer Prize,* Distant Water: The Fate of the North Atlantic Fisherman, *and* Into the Porcupine Cave and Other Odysseys: Adventures of an Occasional Naturalist. *He lives in Washington, D.C.*

Log of the *Downit*

ADRIAN KINGSBURY LANE

Adrian Kingsbury Lane grew up exploring the waters off Noank, Connecticut, in a small boat. His hobby was the start of something big: he grew up to become a ship captain and sail the major oceans of the world. The following are excerpts from the journal he kept between the ages of eleven and thirteen. We've kept his original spellings.

April 30, 1932

Went with father to Ram Island. The wind was southerly and blew hard. It was quite ruff. We sailed over in about 5 tacks and back in one. We brought back a cargo of muscles and we explored the island and went wading. We landed on the north end of the island and came home from there in eight mi[nutes].

May 14

Went to Mouse Island with Jack & Donn [the dog]. Used double power. Buried treasure and got a cargo of crockery. Then we visited West Ledge but found no gulls' eggs. We explored both places.

June 16, 1932

Cruised around in the river with the mate who went ashore and I went [on] to North Cove and picked up W.H.W. who went with me to Sixpenny Island which we explored. Then we explored a little on Goat Point and went under sail to the opposite shore. Then we went home, having a bad time putting through the bridge where the tide was against us. Wind was E.

June 18, 1932

The *Swan* towed us up the river to N Cove where we went for crabs but got none. Then we went further up the river and got a cargo of lumber at Sixpenny & Mason Islands where we explored.

P.M. The *Swan* towed us to Ram Island where we got a cargo of muscles.

June 21, 1932

I rowed alone to Ram Island to find my hunting knife which I lost on the voyage before. I went over in 20 minutes and found it. On the way back, spotted Fred Galley bound for the island for strawberries. I also got a cargo of fish from the *Alicia Estes*.

August 10, 1932

(Not sure of the date.) Went handlining with the mate for crabs by Bakers [Enders Is.] Cove Bridge near red buoy. We caught eight which we had cooked and ate for supper. We used four lines and caught lots of eggers. We rowed.

Sat. Aug. 5 P.M. [1933]

Louis, Father, Mother, Elizabeth D. [and I] went on a picnic up to Ram Pt. [Mason Is.] in the *Swan* and took my boat as a tender with the engine. When we were eating our dinner we heard the fire whistle and then saw some smoke at Rat Wilbur's dock. It was Loren Ellis's dragger *Idelie* which burned, injuring H. H. Park and others. The boat was not damaged very bad. Louis and I took my boat down to see the fire (after it was over). When we got down there the engine stopped and we had to row back. I couldn't start it because the gas wasn't on. There was no wind and we had to tow the *Swan* home with the engine on my boat. When Louis and I were going down to Noank [with the tow], we saw a sort of fin in the water which soon disappeared. We thought it might be a sand shark or something.

[No date.]

Norton Jamieson, Louis Bradford and I rowed up the river to see if we could see any sharks. We found a draw bucket adrift.

Aug. 30, 1933

Walter & I rowed to Mystic Island for the day. We took our dinner. We went swimming and sailed my schooner [working model] and explored the Is. There were quite a few people there. We were the second to arrive & the last to leave (except some campers who had borrowed our tent). Walter tried to catch fish on a safety pin. We didn't succeed, but we got some muscles. We got some golden rod.

Sat. Sept. 30, 1933

The *Swan* and my boat went to F.I. [Fishers Island] where my boat was used to go ashore. We had the engine and towed the *Swan* part way over and most of the way back. The rest of the time the *Swan* towed my boat. We went down the Is. and up on top of Chocomont from where with my spyglass we could see the houses on Block Island and the lighthouse on Montauk Pt. We saw a two-masted lumber schooner going down the Sound when we were coming over. It was moon light when we got home. We saw some porpoise coming over.

Saturday. July 14 [1934]

Norton and I rowed over to Mason Is. We went up the creek and into the woods but found only green huckleberries. Then we went as much farther as we could and went up on the hill where we picked a quart of high bush blueberries and did some exploring. We had never been there before.

Adrian Kingsbury Lane *was a lieutenant in the U.S. Coast Guard during World War II, then spent sixteen more years skippering sailing vessels, including the world's largest sailing ketch, the* R/V Atlantis, *which he sailed for the Woods Hole Oceanographic Institute.*

A Summer in Brewster

HELEN KELLER

Helen Keller was born in Alabama in 1880. When she was seventeen months old, she fell ill with a fever that left her blind and deaf. She was later taught to communicate through sign language and to read braille. The following excerpt, taken from an autobiography written when Helen Keller was a sophomore in college, recounts an episode that occurred when she was eight years old.

Just before the Perkins Institution closed for the summer, it was arranged that my teacher and I should spend our vacation at Brewster, on Cape Cod, with our dear friend, Mrs. Hopkins. I was delighted, for my mind was full of the prospective joys and of the wonderful stories I had heard about the sea.

My most vivid recollection of that summer is the ocean. I had always lived far inland and had never had so much as a whiff of salt air; but I had read in a big book called "Our World" a description of the ocean which filled me with wonder and an intense longing to touch the mighty sea and feel it roar. So my little heart leaped high with eager excitement when I knew that my wish was at last to be realized.

No sooner had I been helped into my bathing-suit than I sprang out upon the warm sand and without thought of fear plunged into the cool water. I felt the great billows rock and sink. The buoyant motion of the water filled me with an exquisite, quivering joy. Suddenly my ecstasy gave place to terror; for my foot struck against a rock and the next instant there was a rush of water over my head. I thrust out my hands to grasp some support, I clutched at the water and at the seaweed which the waves tossed in my face. But all my frantic efforts were in vain. The waves seemed to be playing a game with me, and tossed me from one to another in their wild frolic. It was fearful! The good, firm earth had slipped from my feet, and everything seemed shut out from this strange, all-enveloping element—life, air, warmth and love. At last, however, the sea, as if weary of its new toy, threw me back on the shore, and in another instant I was clasped in my teacher's arms. Oh, the comfort of the long, tender embrace! As soon as I had recovered from my panic sufficiently to say anything, I demanded: "Who put salt in the water?"

After I had recovered from my first experience in the water, I thought it great fun to sit on a big rock in my bathing-suit and feel wave after wave dash against the rock, sending up a shower of spray which quite covered me. I felt the pebbles rattling as the waves threw their ponderous weight against the shore; the whole beach seemed racked by their terrific onset, and the air throbbed with their pulsations. The breakers would swoop back to gather themselves for a mightier leap, and I clung to the rock, tense, fascinated, as I felt the dash and roar of the rushing sea!

Helen Keller *devoted her life to social reform for people with disabilities, writing twelve books and winning numerous national and international honors.*

Great Places

Where the River Meets the Sea

JOHN FRANK

The winding current reaches wide
where the river meets the sea.
The air draws scent from the salted tide
where the river meets the sea.
The marsh grass sways from side to side,
the mud flats foam where the mollusks hide,
the herons fly in a long low glide
where the river meets the sea.

John Frank *resides in Kirkland, Washington, and is the author of three books for children.*

The Magic of the Flats

CLARE LEIGHTON

Mud flats are the vast plains you see along certain shorelines at low tide. Flat and a bit drab, they're not the sort of places most people find imme-diately attractive. But in this essay, Clare Leighton describes the wonders of the mud flats in such a way as to make just about anyone want to stop and take a closer look.

The best time to learn the world of the flats comes at the full of the moon. Then, for a few days in the Bay of Cape Cod, the big tides run high—nearly twelve feet at their peak—and, with the correspondingly extreme low, the water retreats far into the bay, exposing land that is never seen over the rest of the month.

This dramatically low tide occurs early in the day, when the morning light is clean and clear, giving a pearly beauty to the world.

The mud flats are forsaken and desolate, frequented only by a scattering of quahog rakers. During the summer, when the Cape is filled with vacationists, you seldom find any of the visitors out there. To them the sea is something in which to swim. When it withdraws from them at low tide, they wait until the water returns. And this is fortunate, for some of the special quality of the flats lies in the eerie solitude.

The flats hold a subtle, rather than an obvious, beauty. It is the beauty of uncountable gradations of tone and hue, of the sheen and polish of exposed wet sand at low water. It is a world of reflections upon the wet sand from the slanted light of the morning sky.

There is a sense of vastness on such a morning. This stretch of mud and sand, merging imperceptibly in the far distance into remote water, seems to extend into eternity. In such a light, time and space become intermingled; we can no longer distinguish one from the other.

But it is not only the muted, opalescent coloring of the wet sand, shimmering and glinting upon the bed of the withdrawn ocean, that holds such magic. There are uncountable variations of form here, too. For this is the whole earth in microcosm, with Lilliputian valleys and hills, gorges and plateaux. . . .

And then we walk out on these flats, so muddy that the feet sink deep beneath the surface, into soft black ooze. Seen from a distance they appear devoid of all life, and all interest. But what do we discover? This is no dead world of mud. It is a living, agitated world, filled with pulsating rhythm and movement. Scarcely anything here lies motionless, except the long-vacated, sharp-edged shells of oysters and clams, clumped upright in the wet sand and looking as prehistoric as Stonehenge.

Stand still in your path across this mud. The flats appear to move. They heave. They vibrate. And then you hear a strange sound against the silence around. . . .

Puzzled, I raise my eyes to the flats. Thin jets of water spout before me, like tiny fountains. The air sparkles as the sun catches them, tossing into them the colors of the rainbow. Sometimes they are flung far, and this spectrum-tinted water, bewitched by the early morning sun, describes great arcs across the mud.

What is it that causes this crazy happening?

It is the scallops. They lie here, countless in their numbers.

At this moment, when I am confused, still, by sight and sound and strange recollections from the past, the shellfish warden approaches me across the flats.

"A good scallop year," he informs me blandly, not knowing how he has smashed my fantasies. "Never seen so many scallops—not for years I haven't. Looks to me as if we'll have a real bumper season, come October and they've grown."

And then I see what is happening. It is a world of *Alice in Wonderland,* with the Walrus and the Carpenter and the Oysters. The uncountable scallops assume a fairy-tale quality, till you would feel little surprise were they suddenly to develop legs and feet and should walk and talk. They open and shut their shells, like a multitude of castanets, like a gigantic audience applauding the beauty of this earth on such a morning in late June.

But, too, they have a rude aspect to their behavior; they spit, as they open, in the manner of vulgar old men. They yawn, exposing that mighty muscle which is the part that we eat. Along the rim of each beautiful fluted shell they boast a row of brilliant turquoise-blue, green-edged, jewel-like eyes. Give them the slightest kick as they lie here in the mud at low tide, and they will retaliate by spitting you in the face. They imagine they are beneath the water, still, opening and shutting to breathe and propel themselves along the bay.

The scallop is never static. It is far more active and flexible than the heavy, uncouth quahog that noses its way downward into the mud and sand of the water bed. It has an adventurous spirit. The entire bay is its universe. And it is as beautiful of shape as it is mobile of movement, a delicate, graceful creature, the fluted shells subtly varied in color. And with this beauty it carries, too, the sense of history in its background; for did not the pilgrims of the Middle Ages adopt it as their symbol of pilgrimage?

Sometimes this sucking sound changes to a wheezing, squeezing noise, as the scallops force out the water before them, the better to propel themselves along. They do not even await disturbance, as does the razor fish, but act independently of all outside happenings.

Nothing is still here upon the flats, except the discarded clam and oyster shells; and even these ancient creatures are peopled with tiny sea snails perching on top of them, like Kings of the Castle in the game of a child. Over the floor of the sea swarm the hermit crabs, so minute and so active, trotting around on nervous little feet, or retiring into their shells to get sucked down deep into the bed of the wet sand. They creep among the colorless slabs of jellyfish, and the stranded shells, dull of hue against the rich scarlet of the frilly edged sponge that encrusts the oysters and clams.

. . . I walk further out into the bay, to join a friend who is raking for quahogs.

We scratch the surface of the mud

at the water's edge, or even down into the water-covered channels, for the hard-shelled clam, the quahog, as it is called on the Cape from the days when the Indians lived here and prized it as their food. It is an exciting harvest, like all harvests of the unseen. It is charged with speculation, like the digging of potatoes. Something hard resists the rake and you haul it up, secure between the prongs: there is your quahog. Or you dip your hand down into the muddied water—this water that blackens as you disturb it with the rake or with your feet—and bring it up. The wire basket, sitting there on the bed of the channel, three quarters submerged below the water, grows heavy with the quahogs. We lift it and place it near to our center of operation, as we move across the flats.

When the basket is full to the brim, we carry it to our staked bed. Scratching a shallow hole in the mud, we stick the quahogs vertically down, scarcely below the surface. The bed has the appearance of a vegetable garden, out here at sea, with its orderly rows. They might almost be onions that we plant, or daffodil bulbs. And now, as we place the clams into their new home, we watch them. After the first moment of stunned resistance they start to react according to their nature. With a gentle rocking movement they get themselves sucked down below the surface of the mud, drawing in their siphons and shutting their shells as they force out the water inside them in tiny jets. Come back here in a few more minutes and you will see nothing. They will have vanished below, settling themselves flat within their muddy beds. And all that can be seen will be the oyster shells, planted in this bed, shabby-colored and ancient-looking, so hoary of texture that they seem to antedate time.

The world of the flats has a seasonal element, every bit as

much as though it were the vegetable world of dry land, with the blooming and ripening of fruit or grain. The "set" of the oyster takes place in the spring or the early summer, and the little scallops in the bay reach maturity only in October. June and July pass, and I wander over the flats at the end of August. The morning is foggy. I seem to move in space, like a figure in an early Chinese landscape. I have lost all sense of dimension or element. It is already daylight, but the fog makes me recollect a walk I took many years before, at dusk, when the fog rolled in with the suddenness of the dropping of the curtain at the end of a play. That evening, as I stood there upon the flats, well out into the bay, I felt myself to be living upon an uninhabited planet. It was as I would imagine it to be, were I to wander upon the surface of the moon. My feet sank deep into mud, plunging to the calves of my legs. My mind knew that this was black mud, though my eyes could see little of the color. I waded into channels of water, to the knees, water filled with unperceived crabs. And suddenly, as I stood there, knee-deep in water and mud, I felt panic. It was an unashamed, animal panic, the terror of complete loss of direction, an aloneness in space, with the tide turning and the sea advancing, and my not knowing exactly where to walk. In this eerie, scarifying world, formless and lightless, extending into fog, blurred by fog and darkening dusk, I stood still. I searched the sky, but above me was nothing but fog.

"Stupid," I found myself saying. "Nobody in their senses would have done such an idiotic thing. Why, perhaps I'll have to stay here till the incoming tide, with the water lapping higher and higher up my legs and thighs. That will show me where I am. Then I can walk away from it. . . . But suppose I go in circles, as people are supposed to do when they are lost?"

In a queer way I found something exciting in the sense of utter loneliness. I knew that if I were to manage to reach land, I would have experienced something that was worth this panic and fear.

But things always seem to turn out right in the end. At the moment when panic was beginning to envelop me, I stood completely still and very slowly turned myself around. There must have been a sudden break in the thickening fog, for I saw a light in the distance before me. I walked towards it, my eyes fixed upon it, regardless of whether I trod upon crab or sharp-edged oyster shell, or sank deep to my knees in mud. I shall never know how long it took me to reach shore, for I had forsaken the habitual world of dry land, with its sense of time. But I fastened my eyes to that solitary light, till finally I found my feet were treading safely on sand.

All this has come back to me, as I wander across the flats on a foggy morning in late August. But it is a thin fog today, simplifying the curves of Egg Island, dark gray against the silver water. At any moment it will lift, disclosing the form of the flats and the patterning of the cool, swift-running channels. I cross Egg Island, to the far edge, past the green-tinged part that is covered with tattered sea lettuce, and the desolate, lifeless mud gives way to the strangest accumulation of razor fish shells. My feet crunch upon them, in their thousands, mud-obscured, lying there at all angles. And I wonder why it should be that they are here at this particular spot, and nowhere else. . . .

It is rich, varied, and beautiful, this world of the flats, this low-tide country of sand and mud. It may lack the dramatic violence of the Atlantic, but if you look closely at it, and stand still and listen, it will disclose immeasurable magic.

Clare Leighton *was born in London in 1898 and moved to the United States when she was forty. She spent many summers in Wellfleet, Massachusetts. A talented woodcut engraver, she illustrated her own books and many classics, and designed the stained-glass windows for the Wellfleet Methodist Church.*

Cranberry Cove

MÉLINA BROWN

Although wild cranberries were probably served at the first Thanksgiving, the cranberry we now eat—the American, or large, cranberry—is culti-vated. Cranberry cultivation began in Massachusetts in the early nine-teenth century and later spread to New Jersey, where this story takes place. When the cranberries are ready for harvesting, the fields are flooded, and brilliant red berries rise to the surface.

"Hop in the car," Dad said with a huge smile. He extended his arm in front of the door of a new, royal blue BMW, like those glittery women do on game shows.

"Where did you get the car, Dad?" I asked, noticing the shine of the body as well as the hubcaps. We usually rode the bus.

"Never mind. . . . It's ours for the weekend. Put your bag in-side and let's go for a ride!"

We cruised out of Atlantic City, leaving the high-rise ho-tels, casino billboards, neon lights, and car exhaust fumes be-hind. Living so close to the ocean would be great, if I could actually be next to it more. But Mama is always working at the restaurant and worries about me going places without her.

Sometimes I meet Dad near the casino where he works, and we walk along Atlantic City's famous boardwalk. It's not a bad place in the fall and winter. Even though seagulls are always screaming for food, you can smell a salty freshness in the air and feel a misty wind on your face. Frothy waves crash against the sand. But in the summer, zillions of tourists polka dot the beach and the air smells like popcorn, tanning oil, old cologne, dead fish, fried fish, french fries, and damp sand.

I was excited now about going out of town with Dad, but awfully curious. Even though it was my weekend to spend with him, we usually didn't go away. I wondered if Mama would be happy to have a long weekend to herself or if she'd be nervous about me going out of town without her.

"Where are we going?" I asked as we crossed another bridge.

"You'll see soon enough," was all Dad said before his curly black mustache stretched into another wide smile.

We watched the scene change from tall, shiny hotels to cottagelike motels to farmhouses and fields. But neither of us said a word. We just listened to the hip-hop beat blasting through custom speakers. This was some ride!

Trees appeared alongside the road, taller than the ones in town. We were on Route 563, headed toward the Pinelands. At least that's what the sign said. The sky opened up a bit and I noticed wavy hills, like sand dunes, only with less sand. A couple of hours later, Dad pulled onto a small, sandy road and we headed farther north. Then he stopped the car and said, "Let's stretch a bit."

I grabbed my jacket, even though it was pretty warm for October. I followed Dad's every move, not sure where we were going or why.

We walked through a mushy field of tall grass, almost up to my waist. I'm tall for a sixth grader, but nowhere near as tall as

Dad. This grass was high! Dad clamped my shoulder lightly, like he does when he's got something serious to tell me—like when he and Mama got divorced. "Troy," he had said then, "your mama and me are breaking up." As though they were only going together or something.

I wondered if he'd say something that serious this time too. But he didn't say anything. We walked on. I saw him looking at some tall trees with peeling strips of white and gray bark, like wisps of hair.

"That's paper birch," he said without looking at me.

His hand left my shoulder and he turned to watch a tall, skinny bird take off from its hiding place in a tuft of grass. When the bird fluttered and flapped its steel gray wings, it looked gawky. Its spindly legs stuck out behind it. But seconds later it was in the air, its long needlelike beak guiding it in a graceful glide. Dad noticed me noticing the bird.

"That's a blue heron," he explained.

I wondered how he knew the names of these things. He'd worked in the casino as long as I could remember.

The ground grew squishier and small pools of tea-colored water appeared. It was swampy, but not full of crocodiles or creepy creatures like swamps in the movies. It was open and wide here, not spooky at all.

"We're close now," Dad said.

"Close to what?" My heart was beating fast. I couldn't figure out where we were going.

"You'll see," was all Dad offered.

He's still smiling, I thought. So it can't be all that bad, whatever it is.

The air smelled fresh and piney, and just a little salty— different from the fishy food and exhaust smell of Atlantic

City. We climbed a small, sandy dune. Once at the top, I stopped and caught my breath. Dad turned to see my reaction as I looked down below.

A small sea of red stretched before me. Tiny, bright, red beads bobbed on top of the water. Sun sparkled through open patches, and it was so pretty it made me smile. I'd never seen such a spread of red.

"What is that, Dad?"

He laughed at me as though I'd made a joke. "Cranberries, Troy, my boy!" He laughed again. "That's where your cranberry jelly comes from."

I thought back to Thanksgiving, the last time I'd had cranberries. I'd been with Mama and her folks, Aunt Treecie and Uncle Clarence, and Serina. We'd had only the canned cranberry jelly, not the fresh cranberries Dad had always insisted on when he had lived with us. I never knew where they'd come from though.

We walked down closer to the water and I could see the details I'd missed. Small clusters of candy red berries floated and waved as the wind rippled through the water. They reminded me of tiny Christmas tree ornaments and lights decorating the swamp. I wondered if I'd become cranberry colored if I jumped in.

"Bet you never knew your dad used to come here all the time," Dad said, smiling again and turning to me for my reaction.

I didn't know what to say. So I waited for his explanation.

"You know I was born in Newark. But I grew up over here, in Burlington County."

I was surprised that he'd grown up here and I'd never known it. But was that why he brought me here?

"I used to love coming here when I was a boy," he went on. "Spring would come, and I'd pick me some blossoms from the bog when no one was looking. They looked like pink ribbons all curled up. We weren't supposed to mess with them, because that's what brings the money in— these cranberries. But, you gotta have a little fun. Know what I'm saying?"

He waited for me to answer, and I nodded my head. I wondered if he'd just brought me here to see where he used to live, or if there was more he had to tell me.

"Your grandfather, my father—it's too bad you didn't get to meet him before he died—he used to be a picker. Hard work, standing in the cold water all day. They use these big, blue roller-beater-like machines now, to get the berries off the stems and floating onto the water. They look kind of like over-sized lawn mowers."

Dad crouched down near the water and picked up a berry. He shook it in his fist and turned toward me again.

"Troy," he started, and I knew it was coming—the news he'd brought me here for. "I've decided to leave the city. Get away from that gambling life. Find me another job."

He eyed me with concern as my eyes widened with surprise. "I met someone, Troy. She's from here, too, and wants me to move back."

I let out a breath, relieved that he didn't have an incurable illness, or another son, or anything else. But this also meant he'd never get back together with Mama.

"Hey, little man. Don't look so shocked. It's not that far! You saw how long it took us to get here—barely a couple of hours." He tapped me under my chin. Usually, he does that to make me look down, and when I do, he laughs, "Gotcha! Made you look!" This time he didn't.

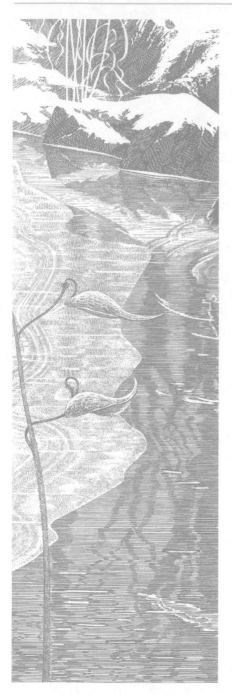

"Will I still get to see you?" I asked him.

"Course you will, Troy. That's not going to change. We'll still see each other just as much as we do now, and maybe even more, depending on what kind of job I find. And," he added with a smile, "you'll get to come here." He spread his arms wide, as if he were the King of Cranberries, and this was his kingdom.

He looked happier than I remembered seeing him in a long time, and I felt a little better, knowing I wouldn't lose him. I picked up a couple of berries and shook them in my fist as he'd done. Then I smiled.

"Soooo, what's her name?"

"*Now* you're interested in my life, hmmm? Well, I'm glad. She's a very nice woman." Dad smiled again.

"Aren't you going to tell me her name?" I asked, shaking the fist full of cranberries faster.

"She works at the state park, and—hey, don't cream me with cranberries!" Dad laughed and ran as I showered him with the remaining cranberries in my hand. He chased me as I scrambled up the hill, then lightly tackled me from behind. But instead of throwing me to the ground, he turned me around in a hug.

"Everything will work out, Troy. You'll see. Cranberries aren't that bad, are they?"

I nodded and smiled back, wondering what else I might discover about Dad, or about this land outside the city I never knew existed.

Mélina Brown was born in France, raised in Minnesota, and reincarnated in North Carolina. She attended the College of St. Thomas, the Sorbonne, and the University of North Carolina at Chapel Hill. Ms. Brown works as a school librarian much of the year and has written pieces that have appeared in Library Talk, Life Notes: Personal Writings by Contemporary Black Women, *and* Women's Words: A Journal of Carolina Writing.

Seascape

APRIL LINDNER

At low tide you can wade the cove
from Revere to Nahant, the warmed Atlantic
licking your knees, clouds of red algae
clinging to your calves. Along the damp
and wrinkled sand, sea worms curl
into pale rosettes, so many
they're difficult to miss. Keep leaning
against the current, trying to forget
the boulders worried down to rocks,
to pebbles, to the silt that wants
to suck you under. Let your feet
brush bottle tops and gutted clams
diminishing in the alchemy
of salt. A few miles out
a garbage scow shuttles its load,
dusky and slow as a seafaring mountain
against the bright sky. Keep north,
pocking the mud with temporary footprints
past gray-capped birds, half-breeds
of pigeon and gull, each one
declaring a small kingdom
with a stretch of its pterodactyl wings.

April Lindner, *who once lived on the north shore of Massachusetts, now teaches English at Wittenberg University in Ohio.*

Three Trees in the City

CECILE MAZZUCCO-THAN

Many of us visit beaches or protected areas to experience the natural wonders of the North Atlantic Coast. But what kinds of life can we find right outside our doors? In this essay, Cecile Mazzucco-Than shares her memories of city trees and a backyard wilderness.

I grew up in Bridgeport, Connecticut, a city of 130,000 people and three sixty-foot oak trees whose trunks were each about four feet in diameter. Actually, my neighborhood was lucky enough to have lots of trees, many of them oaks, but none were as big and beautiful as the three that stood in front of my parents' house.

The canopies of our three trees combined to form a dense shade that kept our house and front yard cool all summer. At twilight, my aunt would walk over from her own house two doors away, to sit on the shaded stoop with my parents and talk. My cousins and I hid behind the trees and ran around them. Although the front lawn was mostly mushrooms and moss, it was our stage and the trees were our biggest props. They were also our biggest fans. On summer evenings while our parents chatted quietly, we presented our three-person interpretation of *The Wizard of Oz*, and the trees applauded with a cool breeze.

In the autumn we'd rake up a haystack-high pile of leaves to jump in. Then we'd gather acorns and my dad would help us hollow them out—big ones for Popeye pipes and little ones that could fit in the caps of larger acorns for sets of Barbie dishes. If I was playing on the corner with my cousins when the sun went down and the streetlights flickered on, I ran toward the silhouette of a small house nestled under three giant trees.

When I was in fourth grade, my cousins and I used to sit on webbed lawn chairs in the garage during the summer thunderstorms and watch through the open door as the trees groaned and swayed in the wind. My cousins recounted certain scientific studies they had read proving oak trees attracted lightning. I always shivered appreciatively, but I knew these "scientific studies" were no more believable than a good ghost story.

When I began to read poetry, the trees became the village blacksmith's spreading chestnut or Evangeline's murmuring pines and hemlocks. Seeing the trees in the summer sunshine I could imagine the majesty of Ashley Wilkes's Twelve Oaks, and on a foggy Halloween night I could feel the terror of Ichabod Crane's lonely ride through Sleepy Hollow.

My dad had seen those same three oak trees when he was growing up in Bridgeport during the mid-1920s, long before our home was built, when the trees were part of a forest surrounding a small lake that my dad and his friends used to swim in. A stream and a waterfall connected it to a much larger lake only a few miles away. In those days, the larger lake served as a reservoir supplying drinking water to a large part of the city, and the small lake helped maintain the water level in the reservoir and prevent flooding in times of heavy rain.

The area around both lakes was protected, and my dad and his friends always ran the risk of being chased away. My dad had seen a different city, one where forests, lakes, and farmlands began at the end of the bus line. Where I saw rows of post-war Cape Cod homes, my dad had seen forests of American chestnut, walnut, and hazelnut.

I guess we were lucky the developer who built our house resolved to work around the three oaks. I don't know if developers were more conscientious in 1942, but they decided to preserve the small lake also. Despite the nearness of Main Street and the houses that crowded around the lake and side streets, I knew the joy of jumping into the clear water on a hot summer's day. The three trees and the lake brought *Wild Kingdom* out of my television set and into my backyard. Little fishes nipped my legs as I floated in the water. I watched painted turtles sun themselves on the concrete steps of the neighbor's landing, and I listened to bull frogs and crickets sing in the evening. Mallard ducks ate the bread I tossed to them and built their nests in the brambles around the roots of the huge, twisted old willow trees at the water's edge. I watched as the ducks defended their eggs from the muskrats, who were invisible except for the v-shaped ripples that they made as they swam through the water. Squirrels built nests in the oak trees, crows cackled from their topmost branches, and a red winged blackbird swooped down on anyone that dared walk under the high branch in one of the gnarled willows that cradled his nest.

When I was about eight or nine years old, my dad and I salvaged a half-submerged, ten-foot aluminum rowboat that had been floating in the lake for several weeks. We pulled it out of the water, across our landing, and into the backyard. We patched the hole in its bottom with metal plates, rubber gaskets, and short, sturdy carriage bolts. My father found oarlocks and a pair of oars and taught me to row. Soon my cousins and I could follow the turtles and the muskrats along the rocky banks of the lake.

We loved to glide across the lake to the opposite bank where three huge weeping willows grew so close to the water's edge that tough, red, stringy webs of their roots pushed through the stones lining the lake's banks and floated in thick, wide clumps on top of the water. We called it the Sargasso Sea. The roots made it almost impossible to dip the oars into the water, and the boat nearly beached itself on them as if they were sandbars. The willows' heavy branches sent hundreds of very thin, bright yellow, flexible branches cascading towards the water's surface. Each of these ribbonlike branches sported thousands of pairs of long, thin, lozenge-shaped leaves, pale green on one side and silver on the other, attached so tenuously to each branch that they danced in the wind. We loved to row under these branches and let them trail across the boat as we slowly moved through them. We pretended we were deep in the bayou with its trees dripping with Spanish moss.

I never realized how unique my experience of growing up in the city had been until many years later when I brought a friend from college home with me for a short visit. She grew up in Barcelona, one of the largest and most beautiful cities in all of Spain. When I told her I lived in the largest city in Connecticut, she thought she would feel at home. Barcelona, she said, is a city of cars and scooters, apartment buildings, shops, and churches. So is Bridgeport, I replied. As we rode the Main Street bus from the railroad station in the center of the downtown business district up to the North End where I lived, she could see from the shops, tall buildings, and apartment complexes that the cities were similar. However, once we got off the bus and walked up and down the side streets to the street where I lived, she thought my home was in the middle of a city park.

I introduced her to all my childhood joys. We sat on the front porch in the shade of the three oak trees; we rowed the boat into the Sargasso Sea and shivered as the curtains of Spanish moss trailed over us. I showed her how to hold a piece of bread in her hands and let the mallard ducks snatch it from her fingertips. Each time, she pulled her fingers back and squealed. Although Barcelona has many parks, she'd never done anything like this in the city.

She'd never seen trees as tall and strong as the three oaks that stood in front of our house, either. I told her how a fourth-grade Sunday school class inspired me to name them Shadrach, Mesach, and Abednego. The three trees refused to yield to the yards and asphalt streets and concrete sidewalks that surrounded them, threatened to knock them down and cover them over in the name of clean and progressive city life. Their tenacity reminded me of the Old Testament story of Daniel's three friends who stood firm in their faith and survived being thrown into an inferno. For the next twenty years as I grew up and went to high school, then college, and finally graduate school, I remained their Daniel fighting to save them from neighbors who would rather cut them down and burn their limbs than rake the leaves that fell from their branches in autumn.

While I lived with my parents and afterward when I returned home from college and grad school for summer vacations and holidays, I was forest ranger, conservationist, and arborist—the only obstacle between them and the fiery furnace—tirelessly raking their fallen leaves in October and urging our neighbors to enjoy the cool breeze and dense shade under their canopy in July. And then, when I was twenty-nine years old, I married a man with a job in another state. I knew I'd have to move away from my parents' home forever. Since my dad had passed away some years before and my mom couldn't live alone, I knew she'd have to move with us. That meant we'd have to sell my parents' home and with it, the three trees. And I wasn't sure the new owners would understand the importance of preserving them.

If Nationwide moved trees, I would have taken them with me. Before we packed up my mother's furniture and sold my parents' home, I even tried to think of a way to get the trees on a historical preservation list. I hoped the U.S. Department of the Interior would take over where I left off and the National Park Service would send over a forest ranger from time to time to check on them. Even at nearly thirty years old, I guess I was a bit naive about how unimportant very small and privately owned green space must seem to a federal government already overburdened by more pressing issues such as crime, poverty, and unemployment, and perhaps spoiled by the vast public riches of national parks such as Yosemite or the Grand Canyon.

However, my idea of getting the trees on a historical preservation list wasn't without precedent. I remembered a long-ago third grade field trip when the class piled into a sawed-off school bus and rode to the naked side of the city to look at a one hundred-year-old tree. It didn't have any notable history—not like the Charter Oak in Hartford. This tree was just a tree that had managed to survive despite the factories and six-family houses, the concrete and asphalt, and the dented Chevys double-parked between sidewalk and curb. It was big and gnarled, and its roots had twisted up beneath the pavement, lifting the concrete in places. We looked at it in wonder, and I remember being sure that my three oaks, though taller and straighter, were at least as old. But this tree was somehow put on a historical preservation list, and mine were not.

Although I have never returned to my former home, I heard from some well-meaning relatives that the people who bought our house cut down the three oak trees. The reason the new owners gave was that they owned several vehicles, but only one could fit in our garage. I'm sure at first they tried to wedge their pickup between one tree and the stockade fence the neighbor put up twenty years ago to keep our leaves from blowing onto her lawn. Then, after a backbreaking autumn of raking leaves, they might have rationalized that the trees took up space that could be used to park their truck, extra passenger car, and oversized camper. Without the trees, they could drive their vehicles right up to the side door and park them in a neat row.

I cannot imagine my parents' home without

the three oak trees or how anyone could look at their stumps and feel anything but pain. When I remember the trees now, seven years after I moved away from them, I remember my wedding day, the day the trees greeted me for the last time. I wore my mother's wedding gown of post-war satin the color of candlelight. As I stepped out the front door and onto the porch where my parents and my aunt had sat and watched us play so many years ago, the trees applauded once again, rustling in the cool breeze. Our neighbor across the street dropped his rake and ran inside his house to get his camera. I waited on the porch. On what truly was the happiest day of my life, in my mind I had to say good-bye to my three old friends.

When my husband brought his relatives back to my parents' house after the wedding, they couldn't stop looking at the three oak trees. One uncle walked halfway down the street to take a picture of one tree from root to crown. Some of these relatives came from Europe, long ago deforested. Others came from Malaysia, where a supercity squeezes the jungle, and others from Aruba, where no tree is taller than the squat divi-divi permanently bowed to the island breeze. None of them would have sacrificed one of our oaks for an additional parking spot.

While the wonders of the natural world from Malaysia to Aruba are showcased on *National Geographic,* the trees cut down in the city go unnoticed. In the shade of the oak trees and the cool of the pond, I learned to breathe deeply and tread softly and look at the natural world with awe and reverence while living in the largest city in Connecticut. This was my Amazon and my Sahara, a place as fragile and ecologically important as the rain forest or the desert. Perhaps, if Shadrach, Mesach, and Abednego had appeared on television, if the Discovery channel had told their story, they might have lived on to provide the new owner's children with Popeye pipes and Barbie dishes, piles of autumn leaves to jump into, and applause for the dreams playacted in their shade.

◞◞

Cecile Mazzucco-Than, *her husband, and her mom now live in Massachusetts in a home surrounded by a dozen sixty-foot pine trees. She has been writing since she was ten years old, and her essays have been published in popular magazines as well as scholarly journals.*

In New Jersey Once

Maria Mazziotti Gillan

In New Jersey once, marigolds grew wild.
Fields swayed with daisies.
Oaks stood tall on mountains.
Powdered butterflies graced the velvet air.

Listen. It was like that.
Before the bulldozers.
Before the cranes.
Before the cement sealed the earth.

Even the stars, which used to hang
in thick clusters in the black sky,
even the stars are dim.

Burrow under the blacktop,
under the cement; the old dark earth
is still there. Dig your hands into it,
feel it, deep, alive on your fingers.

Know that the earth breathes and pulses still.
Listen. It mourns. In New Jersey once, flowers grew.

Maria Mazziotti Gillan *is the founder and director of the Poetry Center at Passaic County Community College in Paterson, New Jersey, editor of the* Paterson Literary Review, *and coeditor with her daughter Jennifer Gillan of* Unsettling America: An Anthology of Contemporary Multicultural Poetry *(Viking/Penguin),* Identity Lessons: Contemporary Writing about Learning to be American *(Penguin/Putnam), and* Growing Up Ethnic in America *(Penguin/Putnam). This poem describes her memories of the neighborhood in Paterson where she lived as a child.*

New Hampshire Shore: Haiku

DIANE MAYR

low tide line—
footprints fill with water
washing me away

on the rocks
humming tunes for
periwinkles

roots grasp cliff
as if to balance leaves
pointing seaward

sandcastles
and mayflies gone
in a day

sea glass—
human debris returns
as treasure

found:
mermaid's purse empty
of its riches

Diane Mayr *has spent the past twenty-five years in New Hampshire and loves its eighteen miles of Atlantic coast. She's been a children's librarian for more than a dozen years and a writer for nearly as long. The mother of two children, Ms. Mayr also shares the house with two cats.*

The Fog Maiden's Necklace

GERALDINE MARSHALL GUTFREUND

Geologists say the islands of Maine are the tops of mountains and hills that have been submerged by the rising sea. But we like this explanation just as much.

Around the land of Maine are islands large and small, scattered in the sea as though they had been strewn haphazardly from the sky. Some days there is a misty gray fog that enfolds the land like a veil, and it is on these days that you can learn the secret of the Maine islands. For if you are lucky enough to be on such an island in such a fog, and if you sit quietly beneath a tall, blue-green spruce, the wind will whisper through the boughs and tell you the story of the fog maiden's necklace.

In the early time, when the spirits of land, sea, and sky had human forms, there was a beautiful maiden of fog. Often, the fog maiden would put on her dress and veil of gray mist, brush her long hair until it gleamed like softly burnished silver, and visit her brother, the sea, and her mother, the land.

Wherever she went, the fog maiden always wore her most precious possession, an intricate seashell necklace. In all the world there was no necklace like the fog maiden's; it was made of all the shells the sea could create. There were pearly white barnacles and violet blue mussels; even the small, speckled limpets had a place. But what the fog maiden loved most about the necklace was that all the colors of the rainbow sparkled in its shells.

One day, when the fog maiden was visiting her brother the sea, she saw a young fisherman pulling in his nets. He had black hair and sparkling green eyes the color of pine trees, and the fog maiden loved him with her whole heart.

But knowing that a spirit could never marry a mortal, she visited her sister the birch, who was very wise.

"How can I become a mortal maiden, so that I might marry the young fisherman?" asked the fog maiden.

"There is only one way," answered the birch in her wisest voice. "You must give your necklace back to the sea."

The fog maiden looked sadly down at her necklace. Its rainbow hues of pink and lavender shone as the sun peeked through the arms of the birch. "Surely," she pleaded, "there is another way."

"No, little sister," said the birch. "You carry all the magic of the sea, for good or for harm, in your necklace, and to become mortal, you must forsake that power."

"I will keep my necklace one more day," said the fog maiden finally. "Tomorrow, I will surely give it up gladly."

And as she went on her way, the birch whispered, "Tomorrow . . ."

But when tomorrow came, the necklace seemed even more beautiful than before, and although the fog maiden watched the young fisherman day after day and thought that her heart would break without him, she could not give her necklace back to the sea.

Then one day, the north wind and the sea began to argue about who was the stronger. They were soon tossing wildly in a fight. The fog maiden watched, terrified, as the young fisherman's boat was buffeted between the wind and the sea. The north wind swiped angrily at the sea, the sea lunged at the wind. Then the small boat overturned, and the fisherman was swept far out to sea.

He will perish, thought the fog maiden in despair. Then she held her necklace to her ear and listened carefully. A gentle voice was calling to her through the roar of wind and sea.

". . . all the magic of the sea, for good or for harm . . ."

The fog maiden knew what she must do. She took one last look at her beautiful seashell necklace, swiftly broke the strand that held it together, and watched the rainbow-colored shells dance to the sea.

As each shell touched the water, it became a bit of land until the sea was a patchwork of islands large and small.

The young fisherman had just enough strength to swim to the nearest of these islands. He lay there, exhausted, for a long while. Then, looking up, he saw a maiden with soft, gray eyes and mist in her hair. The fisherman loved the maiden at once. They were married that very day and made their home on that very island.

There they lived many long and happy years. Being a simple

man, the fisherman never did ask his wife where she had come from. But on days when the north wind blew a veil of fog across their island, he always brought a bunch of many-colored wildflowers home for his wife.

Taking the flowers, she would laugh happily, and her gray eyes would brighten. "Here they are," she would say, "all the colors of the rainbow!"

Geraldine Marshall Gutfreund *has published five books for children and more than fifty stories, articles, and poems for children and adults. She and her husband have two daughters, a dachshund dog, and a cat.*

Aye! no monuments

Rita Joe

Ai! Mu knu´kaqann,
Mu nuji-wi´kikaqann,
Mu weskitaqawikasinukl kisna
    mikekni-napuikasinukl
Kekinua´tuenukl wlakue´l
    pa´qalaiwaqann.

Ta´n teluji-mtua´lukwi´tij nuji-
kina´mua´tijik a.

Ke´kwilmi´tij,
Maqamikewe´l wisunn,
Apaqte´l wisunn,
Sipu´l;
Mukk kasa´tu mikuite´tmaqanmk
Wula knu´kaqann.

Ki´kelu´lk nemitmikl
Kmtne´l samqwann nisitk,
Kesikawitkl sipu´l.
Wula na kis-napui´kmu´kl
Mikuite´tmaqanminaq.

Nuji-kina´masultioq.
  we´jitutoqsip ta´n kisite´mekl

Wisunn aqq ta´n pa´qi-klu´lk,
Tepqatmi´tij Lnu weja´tekemk
  weji-nsituita´timk.

Aye! no monuments,
No literature,
No scrolls or canvas-drawn pictures
Relate the wonders of our yesterday.
How frustrated the searchings
    of the educators.

Let them find
Land names,
Titles of seas,
Rivers;
Wipe them not from memory.
These are our monuments.

Breathtaking views—
Waterfalls on a mountain,
Fast flowing rivers.
These are our sketches
Committed to our memory.
Scholars, you will find our art
In names and scenery,
Betrothed to the Indian
    since time began.

Rita Joe *lives in Eskasoni, Nova Scotia. She has published many of her poems and records of Micmac legends in the* Micmac News *and in* Bluenose Magazine. We Are the Dreamers *is her latest book.*

A Wild, Rank Place

HENRY DAVID THOREAU

Between 1849 and 1855, Henry David Thoreau took several trips to Cape Cod and wrote a book by that name that described what he found there. Today most people associate Cape Cod's beaches with scenic beauty and recreation. But the following excerpt reveals the raw and sometimes grisly side of the seashore in the nineteenth century.

It was even more cold and windy to-day than before, and we were frequently glad to take shelter behind a sand-hill. None of the elements were resting. On the beach there is a ceaseless activity, always something going on, in storm and in calm, winter and summer, night and day. Even the sedentary man here enjoys a breadth of view which is almost equivalent to motion. In clear weather the laziest may look across the Bay as far as Plymouth at a glance, or over the Atlantic as far as human vision reaches, merely raising his eyelids; or if he is too lazy to look after all, he can hardly help *hearing* the ceaseless dash and roar of the breakers. The restless ocean may at any moment cast up a whale or a wrecked vessel at your feet. All the reporters in the world, the most rapid stenographers, could not report the news it brings. No creature could move slowly where there was so much life around. The few wreckers were either going or coming, and the ships and the sand-pipers, and the screaming gulls overhead; nothing stood still but the shore. The little beach-birds trotted past close to the water's edge, or paused but an instant to swallow their food, keeping time with the elements. I wondered how they ever got used to the sea, that they ventured so near the waves. Such tiny inhabitants the land brought forth! except one fox. And what could a fox do, looking on the Atlantic from that high bank? What is the sea to a fox? Sometimes we met a wrecker with his cart and dog,—and his dog's faint bark at us wayfarers, heard through the roaring surf, sounded ridiculously faint. To see a little trembling dainty-footed cur stand on the margin of the ocean, and ineffectually bark at a beach-bird, amid the roar of the Atlantic! Come with design to bark at a whale, perchance! That sound will do for farmyards. All the dogs looked out of place there, naked and as if shuddering at the vastness; and I thought that they would not have been there had it not been for the countenance of their masters. Still less could you think of a cat bending her steps that way, and shaking her wet foot over the Atlantic; yet even this happens sometimes, they tell me. In summer I saw the tender young of the Piping Plover, like chickens just hatched, mere pinches of down on two legs, running in troops, with a faint peep, along the edge of the waves I used to see packs of half-wild dogs haunting the lonely beach on the south shore of Staten Island, in New York Bay, for the sake of the carrion there cast up; and I remember that once, when for a long time I had heard a furious barking in the tall grass of the marsh, a pack of half a dozen large dogs burst forth on to the beach, pursuing a little one which ran straight to me for protection, and I afforded it with some stones, though at some risk to myself; but the next day the little one was the first to bark at me. . . .

Sometimes, when I was approaching the carcass of a horse or ox which lay on the beach there, where there was no living creature in sight, a dog would unexpectedly emerge from it and slink away with a mouthful of offal.

The sea-shore is a sort of a neutral ground, a most advantageous point from which to contemplate this world. It is even a trivial place. The waves forever rolling to the land are too far-travelled and untamable to be familiar. Creeping along the endless beach amid the sun-squall and the foam, it occurs to us that we, too, are the product of sea-slime.

It is a wild, rank place, and there is no flattery in it. Strewn with crabs, horse-shoes, and razor-clams, and whatever the sea casts up,—a vast *morgue*, where famished dogs may range in packs, and crows come daily to glean the pittance which the tide leaves them. The carcasses of men and beasts together lie stately up upon its shelf, rotting and bleaching in the sun and waves, and each tide turns them in their beds, and tucks fresh sand under them. There is naked Nature, inhumanly sincere, wasting no thought on man, nibbling at the cliffy shore where gulls wheel amid the spray.

Henry David Thoreau *was born in Massachusetts in 1817 and devoted much of his life to the observation and celebration of the natural world. He is best known as the author of* Walden: or, Life in the Woods, *and "Civil Disobedience."*

Haiku, Spring Lake, New Jersey

PENNY HARTER

twilight fading
into dark, the sea foam
brightens

full moon—
from wave to wave
the same

moon wet beach—
where the wave recedes,
sandpipers

in back of
the fish market, buckets
of the summer moon

meteor shower—
the glimmer
of the surf

in her dream
grandmother arranges
seashells

Penny Harter *taught for many years in the New Jersey Poets-in-the-Schools program. She now teaches seventh and ninth grades at Santa Fe Preparatory School.*

The Great Marsh

JENNIFER ACKERMAN

According to the author, the marsh described here was created seven thousand years ago when rising ocean waters turned a valley of the Broadkill River into a small lagoon. Over time, the lagoon grew clogged with silt, which provided a foothold for grasses, which trapped soil in their roots to make the marsh.

Just before sunrise, low tide. I walk out into the marsh in the dark, stepping around chocolate brown pools agitated with the scratching and scuttling of fiddler crabs, past delicate marsh pinks, absent their color in the white-wash light. Waves of warm air waft up from the mudbanks bared by the outcreeping tide, a strong sulphur smell, not unpleasant. The beam of my flashlight catches the giant ghostly pale blossoms of the seashore mallow, *Kosteletzkya virginica*. I linger here for a moment, hoping to "shine" the eyes of a wolf spider, a species with mirrorlike membranes that reflect light.

The darkness of the marsh is not the close darkness of woods, where blackness pours up from between the trees, but a thin, liquid, open, far-reaching darkness that descends onto the grass. Silence stretches from horizon to horizon, broken only by the occasional call of a whippoorwill, a sound that carries easily over the flat topography, somehow amplified by the open acres of air and the drum-flat surface of the nearby bay. . . .

Pull up the blanket of marsh, give it a shake, and out would tumble coffee-bean snails, *Melampus bidentatus,* little half-inch creatures tinted with brown and green, as well as grasshoppers, beetles, ants, flies, and cinch bugs, which feed on *Spartina's* tender leaves, and plant hoppers, which suck its juices. Also fiddler crabs and mud crabs, oysters and dense clumps of ribbed mussels, which pave the mud along the creeks where the tide floods regularly. According to one study, this marsh supports more than three and a half million mussels per acre. Out, too, would tumble diamondback terrapins, turtles the size of a small skull, their segmented pentagons fused to form a leathery dome, their reptilian heads spotted like a leopard. The diamondback was once here in great numbers, but its sweet flesh made it a gastronomic delicacy and the target of tireless collectors.

The shake wouldn't loose such tenacious insiders as the larva of the common marsh fly, family Chloropidae, which lives in the stems of *Spartina* and eats the plant's tissue. (The adults are so small, only two or three millimeters long, that they are nearly invisible except when swarming.) Nor would it dislodge the larvae of the fierce-biting greenhead fly, whose singular appetites are described by John and Mildred Teal in *Life and Death of the Salt Marsh.* "The larvae are maggots, soft, elongate, leathery-skinned, lumpy individuals with a pair of organs for breathing air at one end and a pair of sharp jaws at the other. They wriggle through the mud eating anything they come across, including others of their kind. If a number of *Tabanus* maggots are put together in a dish, the end result is one fat, temporarily contented individual."

Here are some of the thirty or so species of fish that swim the waters of the Great Marsh: the small, glistening fish known as silversides, the four-spined stickleback, anchovy, northern pipefish, two kinds of herring, young striped bass, sea robins, summer flounder, naked gobies, striped mullet and white perch, eel, croaker, menhaden, northern kingfish, and three species of killifish, including the mummichog, a name that comes from a Narraganset word meaning "they go in great numbers."

The sun has reappeared above the cloud reef, a second bloom. In this low morning light the marsh looks different than it does under cloud cover or high sun, not a hazy watercolor wash, but a dazzling mosaic of distinctly different greens. The tide is sliding up the marsh slope, slithering into the creeks and spilling over between the blades of grass. The up, down, in, out of the tides makes this place dangerous—sometimes in-undating animals with lethal doses of saltwater, sometimes exposing them to a devastating high-and-dry death—but also inconceivably rich. The tides distribute food and flush out waste, encouraging rapid growth and quick decay. Adaptation to this pulse is the contract that all successful marsh creatures have signed with a country half land, half sea. When the ebbing tide bares the flats, hundreds of scraping chitinous legs and claws scribe the mud as fiddler crabs emerge from their burrows to search for bacteria, fungi, minute algae, and fer-menting marsh plants. Tiny star-shaped pigment cells dotting the crab's body obey the compounded rhythms of sun and tide. The cells contain granules of dark pigment, which dis-perse at daytime low tide, giving the crabs the color of the mudbank and thus protecting them from predators. At night the pigment granules shrink from the cell's reaches and cluster together, the color fades, and the crabs turn the pale ivory-white of moonlight. These changes occur every day at a different hour, synchronized with the tides.

Now, as the salt tide seeps up the mudbank, the fiddlers are waiting until the water reaches their knees before they disappear into their deep mud tunnels to wait out the deluge. Though they breathe air with a primitive lung beneath the edge of their shell, they can hole up in their burrows with no oxygen for long periods—for months in cold water—a feat that makes the limit of our own tolerance for organic variation seem narrow indeed. A few moments' loss of oxygen and we rapidly descend into unconsciousness.

Coffee-bean snails, too, are air-breathers, but they go up rather than down when the tide rises. Like ghost crabs and beach fleas, they are members of a race that is learning to live outside the sea. Somehow they anticipate rising tides, creeping up the stalks of grass well before the water arrives. They take a breath of air that will hold them for an hour or so if the drowning sea submerges them.

Spiders and insects such as grasshoppers keep company with the snail, scaling stems to escape the high tide. This habit exposes the climbers to the keen eyes and hungry beaks of birds. The Teals once described the scene of an especially high tide, insects hopping, jumping, and flying onto taller plants until "only the tallest grasses along the creeks mark the meandering channels and these grasses are weighted and bending at the tips, alive with insects. Sparrows and wrens from the marsh, buntings and warblers from the land, gulls and terns from the beach, and swallows, dip, fly, settle, and swim along the twisting lanes of helpless insects and gorge themselves." I've seen swallows swooping over the marsh, snatching insects from mid-air, then suddenly dodging a marsh hawk's hook and talon in a startling turnabout of predator and prey.

Sunlight to marsh grass to grasshopper to swallow to hawk: these are some of the links that compose the marsh web. Learning a place is like this, glimpsing the individuals, the pinpoint touches of color on the broad canvas, randomly splattered. You pick them out, sort them out, name them, then tumble them back into the landscape, and by reading and more observation, figure out how they fit together. As more spaces are filled in, the image or weave is revealed, the continuous meshing intimacy. It helps to have a native tutor, and a sense of the storyline, the narrative over time. In the marsh, the little rhythms of the day have a way of focusing attention on particular species, the way the slow, small meter of an Emily Dickinson poem brings each syllable into close-up.

Jennifer Ackerman *is a writer who specializes in natural history and the biological sciences.*

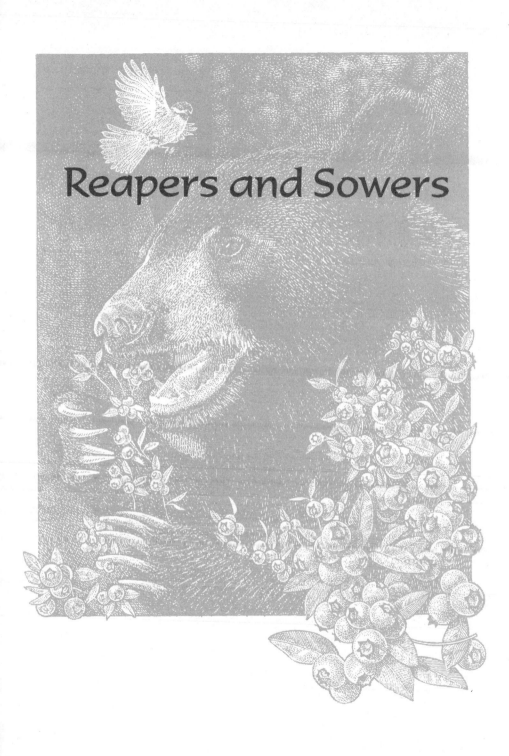

Reapers and Sowers

Blueberries

JIM GORMAN

Blueberries are a favorite food of bears, birds, and humans alike. They grow on heathlands and meadows along the North Atlantic Coast, and on blueberry farms, such as the one in this story.

It is August, and we know like birds where to find the ripe berries. We have come down Route 1 in Uncle Larry's old school bus, across the border into America, into the great state of Maine, where we used to live, Grammaw says, ninety years ago.

We are from the Micmac tribe, living in Nova Scotia now, twenty-eight of us on the bus, eleven adults not counting Grammaw, and the rest of us kids, mostly boys, but also Sister and me, two girls who have proven ourselves before, pickers with fast hands. "Twenty-eight sore backs tonight," says Uncle Larry. "Twenty-eight sore backs and fifty-six blue hands."

We arrive long before noon and are greeted by Mrs. Gable. Now it is her land, two hundred acres that slope toward the ocean. We have picked for her family for many years. She knows us, knows some of us by name.

I help Grammaw from the bus, and Mrs. Gable says, "All the rain has made them bigger this year, Grammaw. Bigger and juicier. It is a good year."

Grammaw puts out her hand and says, "It is a good year to be alive." Though she is losing her sight, she knows how to find the sun, the east, also the direction of the warm wind. She bows and says, "I can smell the ripeness. This year even the bears will not be hungry."

We join the other rakers on the barrens, a rocky plain with poor soil, limestone worn away to fine gravel. The blueberry thrives in it. The low bushes hug the ground, twisted in with weeds and prickers. You can kneel, you can crouch, or you can bend from the waist. Whatever way, a pain comes and lives in your back for all the days you are here.

Uncle Larry passes out the rakes. They look like dustpans or flour scoops, tin boxes with long tines. You face uphill and jab at the bushes with short strokes. You gather both berry and chaff as fast as you can, filling the buckets.

"Eight cents," Uncle Larry calls out. "Eight cents a pound this season. That's a good wage. I want to see some ten-dollar-a-day rakers."

Grammaw sits on a rock as we rake. The wind from the ocean lifts her thin hair. She should not have come this year. Both her body and her mind lean toward death. She counts with doubt and sometimes with bitterness each day she has outlived her daughter, our mother, who died in the winter last year. Some days Grammaw is not in this world of automobiles and electricity anymore, but drifts, sometimes here, sometimes in the world of long ago. She sits on the rock and talks again and again of Glooskap, the magic spirit, who has made all the animals and plants, made them useful to people.

The magic spirit, she says, gave us the blueberry rake, gave it first to the bear as a paw. Our people watched the bear, his powerful arm and long claws, then made their first rakes out of wood and bone, then gave both berry and rake to the white man.

But the white man has forgotten Glooskap, Grammaw says. The white man kills the bear. The white man passes his hands across the barrens and says, I own.

Grammaw says, "Only the white man needs to rake so many pounds, needs to feed so many mouths in his vast nation."

Uncle Larry speaks against her. They are like two ravens, and the rest of us smile at their squawking. Sister especially, who goes further than smiles, moving her lips with their speeches, mocking them both with her  eyes. She gets the boys to watch her. She is fourteen and easy to watch if you are a boy. I give her that look that Mother used to give her—Mother's pained face, Sister calls it—and she sticks out her tongue at me, her little sister, Mama's good girl.

The voices go on above us. "The white man pays well for the food that goes into his belly," Uncle Larry says.

"But the berries will run out, nephew, some day, both the berries and our people to pick them," Grammaw says.

"But they've made new bushes now that stand up high as your chest, Grammaw. They grow in any soil with berries big as grapes," he says.

"And as sour," she says. "Sour and without the healing magic."

The hours pass. I rake my bucket full several times. Filled, it weighs about twenty pounds: $1.60, three times, four times. Uncle Larry keeps a tally, and I am high on his list.

At sundown, he and the other men set up the tents. They are not teepees, but made of nylon, bright yellow and green. The Gable family has built new showers near the fields. They are proud, showing us, and we will use them someday, Uncle Larry says politely, but tonight we ride in the bus the seven miles to the ocean. I leap into the icy waves with a shriek, and the pain goes out of my back.

Almost. I lie in the tent while the others eat. At long last Sister returns, tossing the package from the store on the blanket next to me. "Uncle Larry drove me over," she says, "just the two of us in that stupid, rattling bus. I told him we needed magazines, and he bought my little story." She snaps her chewing gum as she talks and then blows a pink bubble, a broad-faced girl who seems to have no feelings, no low spots, no holes. "He bought the magazines too, and lucky he did. You could spend a day's picking on two magazines."

Sister gives me the pills and a drink, then breaks the cellophane and hands me a scented packet. "Cheer up, girly," she says. "Every girl gets surprised her first time. I did. But Uncle Larry doesn't know, and none of the boys do either—unless I tell them." Then she lies on the other blanket, a magazine open, flipping through pages of glossy models, touching their cheeks, their lips, with her blue fingers.

Grammaw does know. But when she comes to the tent, Sister is not there but gone, out with the boys. Grammaw crouches by me and says, "Your pain is not from the picking, is it, girl?" She has a cup of steaming water, and into it she drops what look like bits of dried blood. "Blueberry tea," she says. "Not this year's berries, but ones you save. This is better than mint for your pains." Her hands are warm and moist from the hot cup. She touches my forehead and then rubs my temples. Pulse to pulse I feel the blood in her fingers. I lean my head into her and say, "Rock me," and she does, whispering, "Your mammaw is still here, isn't she, in this wide brow of yours, and in how you work without resting. This day you raked with the fast hands of a child. This night you have the pains of a woman."

Jim Gorman *has published two chapbooks of stories and won an Ohio Arts Council Individual Artist Fellowship in fiction writing in 1996. He teaches at Otterbein College in Ohio and coordinates the Otterbein Community Poetry Workshop, which brings college students together with at-risk youth.*

Pauline Sings across the Rooftops

Julie Parson-Nesbitt

Summer bees, their soft voices
the sweet packages their legs carry
Pauline sings.

Falling leaf, wind in branches
nest apple the wind buries
Pauline sings:

Brother, brother, bumblebee
pirate sailor come to me
sail across our mother water
with gifts of gold and sandbox treasure.

Crocus bulb, cradle ember
firethorn and baby's thimble
quiet steps the street remembers
bagpipes calling dreams to waking
fly like flags across the rooftops
Pauline sings.

From your dream of windy bridges
tell us, tell us
in your subway lullaby

how you found us. We think you followed
snow falling through plane trees. We heard
you hopscotched here on sidewalk slate
to sky blue, turn around, turn around child
pebbles in your fingers,
turn around, turn around child.
Tell us the secret to pick up sticks so carefully
so the walls won't come tumbling down
tumbling tumbling down.

Sparrow-elf, cricket sister
we will bring you every pleasure:
blue balloons and yellow feathers
October moons and lady slippers.
Cry Pauline, we'll feed your hungers
we'll hang your crib with rainy roses
cry, cricket, cry.

Crocus bulb, cradle ember
you will bring us every pleasure
firethorn and wind in branches
quiet steps the street remembers
with your heart a fingered steeple
playground filled with children swinging
bagpipes calling dreams to waking
fly like flags across the rooftops

Pauline sings.

Julie Parson-Nesbitt *has received the Gwendolyn Brooks Poetry Award and two Academy of American Poets awards. Her poetry collection is* Finders *(West End Press). A Chicago writer, she has worked as a poet-in-the-schools and is executive director of the Guild Complex, a literary organization.*

Of the Sea

ANNE SPOLLEN

This story is based on a real person Anne Spollen knew as a child while living along Raritan Bay in Staten Island, New York.

The house on the Atlantic harbor beach was tiny—a shack, really—slanting to one side with shining bald patches on its exterior where decades of wind had detached shingles. Beneath the shingles lay speckled tar paper that glistened when sun touched the house. On a sunny day, motes of light combined with the surrounding seascape to give the shack an enchanted air, as if deep within its dank swell of wood there existed a kind of magic.

I had always wondered about the shack's owner. My parents told me he was a fisherman named Duke. That explained why I rarely saw him: fishermen rose before dawn to gather their day's catch. By the time he returned home, I had already left for school. I had seen him a few times during the summer, but we had never spoken. I longed to meet him and see the interior of his cottage.

One week in late summer, two unusual events occurred: we had six straight days of rain; and Monsey Rose, a cousin I had never met from upstate New York, came to stay with us. Monsey and I were almost the same age, and we liked each other right away. The day after she arrived, the weather cleared and we were able to venture outside.

We lived about a quarter mile up from the beach. Between our house and the sand lay a patch of marsh. Normally, the marshland consisted only of damp soil visited by a variety of birds. But now the constant rain had swollen its arteries to the point that Monsey Rose and I could paddle a rowboat through the cattails, down to the hem of the bay.

"Where I live, all we have is a reservoir," Monsey Rose said. "And no one is allowed to swim there."

"Then have you ever seen anything like this?" I asked, pointing over the side of the boat.

Monsey Rose turned to see the water at low tide, exposing a rich garden of mollusk, kelp, and sea grass. A squadron of gulls squalled, diving into the seabed in search of food. We stopped to watch the gulls for a moment.

"How can gulls stay in the air without flapping their wings?" Monsey asked.

"They're gliding on the wind," I told her. "I think they're graceful, don't you?"

Monsey nodded. We got out of the rowboat and lashed its bow to a log. Then we waded the last few feet to the sandy beach.

"What on earth is that?" Monsey asked, pointing to a horseshoe crab scuttling back from shore toward the water.

"It's one of these," I said. I picked up a dead horseshoe crab and turned it onto its back. With its undersides exposed, double rows of short, meaty claws hooked the air. "My dad says they haven't changed since prehistoric times."

"You mean they looked just like this to the dinosaurs?"

I nodded.

"We have nothing like this up where I live in Taconic Park," Monsey said. "Thank goodness."

We walked into the warm, fishy wind. At last we stood by Duke's cottage.

"Who lives here?" Monsey asked. "It's such a tiny house."

"A fisherman," I answered. "I only know his name is Duke."

"So you've never met him?"

"Never."

"Or seen the inside of his house?" Monsey asked.

"No, never."

"Do you suppose he's home now?" Monsey smiled slyly as she asked this.

I looked over to the side of his house where he usually tied his boat to a piling. It was gone.

"He must be out in the bay." I quickly scanned the water for any sight of his skiff, but he was evidently still far from shore.

"Do you think he'd mind if we just peeked around his yard a bit?" Monsey asked.

"Well . . . ," I stammered. I had always wanted to get a closer look at the cottage, but I feared that Duke would get back in time to catch us.

"Oh, c'mon, just for a minute," Monsey urged. She rounded the corner into Duke's yard.

I followed Monsey, still glancing over my shoulder for any sign of Duke. But once I saw his yard, I forgot to look back. "A garden!" I exclaimed. "Look at this, Monsey!"

Before us spread neat rows, alive with bursts of flowers, tomatoes, peppers, beans, and ruffles of edible greens as borders. "My mother has been trying to grow flowers in this sandy soil for years and she's never had any kind of luck. I wonder how he grew this garden on the beach."

"I don't know," Monsey said. "But look at this!" She held a large, dried crab shell filled with powder that looked like salt. "There are tiny pieces of bone in here!"

"Bones?" I peered inside the shell. "Are you sure?"

Monsey shrugged and put the shell down. "That's what it looks like to me. And look—here's a knife!"

She picked up the strangest looking knife I had ever seen. Several clamshells had been whittled down, then glued to a stick. The knife was large and looked dangerously sharp.

"This place is beginning to give me the creeps," I said.

"I just want to take one quick peek inside," Monsey said. "Are you sure he's not coming?"

I took another look at the bay. I saw a boat coming toward shore, but it was smaller than Duke's.

Monsey tiptoed over to Duke's window and cupped her hands around her eyes. "Is he married?" she called out.

"Not that I know of," I answered. "Why?"

"Come look," she said.

I walked over to the window and peered in next to Monsey. A painted and framed portrait of a young woman hung on the wall over the kitchen table. Beneath her Duke had placed a table setting, as if the young woman were about to step down from the painting and dine with him.

"What do you think is going on there?" I asked.

"Something really weird," Monsey said. "I'm ready to go back to the house. Are you?"

"Yes," I answered. I stepped away from the window and something pierced my toe. "Ouch!" I yelled, pulling my foot out of my sandal. A small puncture mark was clearly visible on my big toe.

"Are you okay?" Monsey asked.

"Yes, I'm fine." Carefully, I brushed sand from the area beneath me. I pulled at a smooth piece of bone, and up from the sand came a hinged jaw with two triangular teeth still embedded in the lower half. "This is what got me."

"That looks like a shark's jaw," Monsey said in disbelief.

I nodded. "Just think—I was bitten by a shark, and all I said was 'ouch!'"

"Let's go," Monsey said. "I've seen enough for one day."

"Me, too."

We were just about to turn the corner when we saw the shadow of a figure coming toward us. I wheeled around quickly. There, lashed to the piling, was Duke's boat. That must have been his boat on the bay after all. In the distance, the craft had looked smaller.

"Hurry, this way!" I whispered.

Monsey and I scampered down a sandy knoll to our boat and paddled back to the house as quickly as we could.

"I hope you girls didn't disturb any of that man's hard work," my mother said when we told her about the things we had found in Duke's garden. "And I'm sure there's a perfectly good explanation for everything else. In fact, I'd like to see this garden." She sighed, and I knew she was thinking about her most recently failed flower bed.

The following afternoon, when we were sure Duke would be home, my mother packed a batch of brownies. We walked the length of the cove to Duke's cottage.

"You girls are unusually quiet today," my mother remarked.

Monsey and I exchanged quick glances. Before we could answer, Duke waved from his garden. "Hello there!" he called.

"Hello," my mother said. "I'm Adele Ross."

"Yes," Duke said, "I know you. And I know this one," he said, looking directly at me. "You two live just up the street from the cove. In the gray house. But this young lady . . ."

"My cousin, Monsey Rose," I said.

I did not mean to stare, but the man standing before us appeared ancient, as if his skin were made of papyrus. His hooded eyelids were wrinkled and puckered as walnut shells.

"You were the girls I saw going down into the marsh yesterday. I meant to thank you for finding my chum grinder." In his hand was the jawbone. "This was a gift from a friend who does deep sea fishing."

"Are there sharks around here?" Monsey asked.

"Oh, not here. Way out in the sea."

Monsey looked relieved.

"What's a chum grinder?" I asked.

"Here, I'll show you." Duke placed a fish carcass over the lower jaw, then dragged the fish across the teeth. The fish shredded almost instantly. "See, now I have chum—ground-up fish that attracts fluke for my catch."

"Well, we brought something more appetizing than chum," my mother said as she offered the brownies to Duke. He smiled as he accepted the plate. "I hope you don't mind, but the girls described your garden. I was wondering how anything grows in this sandy soil."

"I enrich it with treasures from the sea," Duke replied. "I've spent years mixing seaweed, fish remains, soil, and even my kitchen scraps to make gold for this garden. The mixture changes the soil so I can grow almost anything in this little patch. And here," Duke picked up the shell containing the salty powder, "I grind the fluke bones and spread the powder on the soil."

We walked around the garden. He was right about using everything from the sea. He had lashed together horseshoe crab tails as stakes for his tomato and bean vines. Herbs grew between propeller blades. A thick crust of dried seaweed lay beneath his plants to fertilize his vegetables and keep weeds from taking root.

"I can show you how to layer the compost," Duke said to my mother. "If you girls could go inside for some plates and forks, I'd be willing to share these brownies. You can bring them right out here." He gestured to a picnic table he had crafted out of driftwood.

The first thing that struck me as I entered Duke's house

was the smell: fresh and salty at the same time, like the waters of the Atlantic. "You know, Monsey, it's almost like being in the ocean when you're inside here."

"That's because he's practically brought the ocean in here," she said. I walked over to where Monsey stood in the kitchen. Duke had separated his fishing lures and weights into different-sized clamshells. All of them were shelved on planks he had made out of driftwood. Knives, forks, and spoons were neatly housed in cleaned-out hulls of horseshoe crabs. "I hope he really cleaned those things," Monsey said.

He had. In fact, he had put a clear glaze of shellac over them. I looked around at the tiny house—just a main room, a kitchen, and a small bathroom—and almost wished we had a cottage like this on the ocean. Then I looked above the small table at the haunting portrait of the young woman.

We did not see Duke and my mother standing in the doorway. Duke held a watermelon he had just picked from his garden.

"That's my wife, girls. When I eat, I get lonesome for somebody. I talk to her picture like she's still here. She died not long after we got married. She was only twenty-three." Duke looked sad for a moment. Then he added, "Clara's body may not be here, but her spirit is with me always. Right here," he said, patting his chest over his heart.

"That's a lovely thought," my mother said.

Duke sighed. Then he leaned down and opened a kitchen drawer. He took out a knife just like the one Monsey had found in the yard. We watched as he deftly sliced through the watermelon.

We ate on Duke's picnic table, looking at the ocean. "You know, I don't own a television," Duke said as he gazed into the

bay. "I watch changes in the face of the sea for entertainment."
As orange fingers of sun rippled the surface of the water, we
could see what he meant. When we finished our watermelon,
Duke politely collected all our seeds and rinds for his compost
pile.

"Well, thank you for showing me how to build a compost
pile," my mother said.

"And thank you for the delicious watermelon," Monsey
and I added.

"Thank you for the brownies," Duke said. "Come back
anytime."

And we did go back, many times.

My mother began her compost pile the day of our first visit,
assigning Monsey and me the task of gathering seaweed and a
variety of shells and rocks that she used for decoration, borders, and soil enrichment. By the following summer, for the
first time, Mother had beds of vibrant flowers.

Anne Spollen *holds an M.A. in English literature and has taught
middle school for the past decade.*

Shells

WALLY SWIST

As she taught the alphabet,
my mother collected shells,
mounting polished conchs,
augers, sundials, and whelk
in a glass case on velvet.

As a child, I recited the alphabet
as waves rolled from the sea to land.
I have never lost the words
found in a harbor, the shells
brought home from the beach.

I still pocket them
as I walk the shore
and press some to my ear
so that I can listen again
to the beginning.

Wally Swist's *books of poetry include* The New Life *(Plinth Books, 1998) and* Veils of the Divine *(Hanover Press, 2001). His poems appear in such magazines as* Appalachia, Puckerbush Review, *and* Yankee. *He is a recipient of a fellowship from the Connecticut Commission on the Arts.*

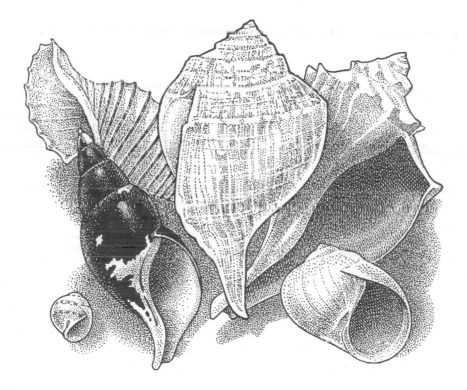

The Maize Doll

BETSY McCULLY COOPER

The place we call New York City has undergone many changes over the last four hundred years. This story takes us back to a time when New York was the home of the Lenape Indians, and gives us a glimpse of its transition to a burgeoning Dutch colony.

Lenapehoking: 1609, European time

It was the time of the Hunger, when the maize withered on the stalks and the earth became parched. One day a little girl found a stick that looked like a person, but when she brought it home, her parents shook their heads and told her to throw it away because it might be a bad spirit. The girl did as she was told and soon after fell into a fever. One night while she was ill, she dreamed that a shriveled old woman spoke to her to tell her that she must dress the stick and hold a dance and feast to honor Maize Maiden. Only in this way would Maize Maiden return and bless their crops. The next morning the girl got up and retrieved the stick, dressing it in maize husks to make a doll. Then the women and girls performed a dance. Sure enough, Maize Maiden returned, bringing with her the rains that watered the earth. The maize sprang up, and the people's health returned. In thanks, the people perform the Doll Dance every spring.

Having finished her tale, Old Story Woman sat silent, the

firelight flickering on her creased brown face and dancing in the dark pupils of her eyes. Her story sticks were arranged on the ground in the shapes of a doll and a maize stalk. The children seated around her in the Story Circle were caught in the spell of her story, Listening Girl most of all because she loved listening to stories. When a low rustling sound seemed to arise out of the shadows, the children shivered—until they saw Old Story Woman's hand emerge from under the folds of her skirt, holding a doll dressed in a cornhusk skirt: it was Ohtas, the Doll Being. Smiling, Old Story Woman spoke the words she always spoke at the end. "Never forget that you are of the Turtle Clan, people of water and land, the First People of this place, Lenapehoking." She rose, breaking the Story Circle.

Listening Girl got up slowly, reluctant to leave the warmth of the fire. Grandfather North was already blowing an icy breath, painting the leaves flaming colors. Soon, at the time of Leaf-Fall, her people would pack up and move away from their summer home on the Far Point by the Great Salt Water, upland to the Place of Tall Trees.

Listening Girl looked forward to the Snow Months. All the people of her clan came together then, living in the longhouses the men had built from hickory saplings and chestnut tree bark and greeting the Time of Snows with dancing and feasting. She couldn't wait to hear the stories the elders told when they gathered around the fire during the long winter nights. She always listened closely so that she could memorize the stories and pass them on to her children. Perhaps she would even become a Storyteller like Old Story Woman. But now, she thought as she walked toward her wigwam, there was much work to do to get ready for the move. She looked up into the night sky that glittered with stars like so many campfires.

Turning her gaze to Grandfather East, she looked for the Seven Sisters that her father said were the sign of the coming frost—and sure enough, there they were, dancing.

Listening Girl lifted the flap to her wigwam and crept to her sleeping mat. That night she dreamed that a green maize stalk grew way up to the sky, so close to the sun that her tassels caught fire. Then Grandfather North blew his icy breath, turning the tassel-flames to cinders that fell to the earth like snow, and wherever they fell, cornstalks and bean vines and pumpkins sprang up. Then she saw herself dancing in the Planting Field with Old Story Woman, both raising their hands to the sky to give thanks to Uncle Sun and to Thunderbird, who brought rain.

The next morning, as soon as the sunlight stole through the smoke hole, Listening Girl's eyes flew open. She could see her breath. She held the bearskin around her as she got up and slipped into her moccasins. Already her mother was up with the baby, tending the fire. When she saw that Listening Girl was up, she ladled thick hot maize porridge from the clay pot into a wood bowl and handed it to her. Listening Girl ate in silence, watching her mother comb out her long shiny black hair and braid it, weaving a white feather into one of the braids. They called her mother White Feather because she once had a dream of a white bird who gave her a feather and told her to heal her people. This was seen as a sign of a special gift, allowing her mother to become a medicine woman. She knew the powers of all the plants, and her people came to her for herbs and roots to cure their sickness. She always carried dried roots and herbs in a medicine pouch that she hung from her beaded sash. She motioned to her daughter to come over so she could comb and braid her hair. It was then that

Listening Girl told her mother of her dream. White Feather listened intently, worried by the burning cornstalk, then reassured at the last part. "That is a good dream, daughter; it means that you will be the Maize Maiden in the Doll Dance. You must tell Old Story Woman." Then she instructed her daughter to go wash up in the stream and meet her in the Planting Field.

As soon as Listening Girl stepped outside into the crisp air, she faced the Four Directions. To the East, Uncle Sun glowed like an ember through the mist that was rising from the ground. Listening Girl greeted Uncle Sun and thanked him for his light and warmth. To the South was the shimmering blue of the Great Salt Water, whose waves crashed on the shores of Rockaway and Canarsie. A wedge of geese flew low over the water, led by their *Sakima* or Chief Goose to the land of Grandmother South. She could clearly hear their honks. To the West, just across the Narrow Water, rose the green back of the island *Aquehonga*, place of high sandy banks, where her mother's kin lived. Beyond *Aquehonga* were the lands of the Raritan and Hackensack. To the North was *Mahicannituk*, the River That Flowed Both Ways.

She rejoiced in the beauty of her home—place of water and sky and many islands. Her village was set on a bluff overlooking the bay. Below was *Mocuny*, the low muddy place, where grasses taller than she rippled in the sea breezes. The reeds were no longer green, but now tan as deer hide. Atop a cattail, Wren sang his gurgly song. Bittern boomed loudly from her hiding place, "Gloong-KA-glunk! Gloong-KA-glunk!" The sea of grass was broken by several clearings Muskrat had made when he cut cattails and reeds to build his underwater wigwam. She could see the domed tops of the muskrat wigwams sticking up here and there in the water. At the water's edge, White Heron stood on one leg, her head cocked as she watched intently for killifish swimming in the shallows; in a blink of an eye, she extended her long neck and snapped up a fish for breakfast. Casting a shadow over the reeds, Hawk circled in the sky, hunting for his breakfast—perhaps a vole or white-footed mouse who scurried in the grasses. Listening Girl's attention was drawn by what appeared to be a whirling black cloud: it was a horde of blackbirds, ready to descend on their fields and steal their maize. Old Story Woman had taught that the Maize-Thief had brought the first grain of corn and first bean from the Creator to them, so they must respect Blackbird and not harm him.

Remembering that she must be in the Planting Field soon, she hurried to the stream, carefully picking her way along the path through the meadow so as not to step on any plants. Her mother had taught her that all plants are sacred and must be treated with respect. Soon, her mother would teach her the healing ways of plants and how to collect them. Many flowers and grasses had sprung up in the clearing her people had made here so they could build their houses and plant their fields. Goldenrods, asters, and gayfeathers brightened the meadow with their yellows and purples. She could hardly see the yellow wands of the goldenrod because they were covered with the orange-and-black wings of the Flowers-That-Fly. Other Winged Creatures browsed in the meadow flowers, buzzing and droning. The grasses and herbs were bursting with seeds, food for the little brown sparrows who flew up at her approach. She loved the songs of these birds in the spring, especially the sweet, clearly whistled notes of the one with the dark spot on its breast, singing joyfully from a tree branch.

Now the birds were silent, busily fattening up for the Snow Months.

In the soft mud of the stream bank, Listening Girl noted the tracks left by Red Fox, out hunting last night. Kneeling on the bank of the stream, she saw in its clear water schools of little silvery fish heading into the current; these were babies of the big fish who swam upstream from the Great Salt Water every spring, during the time of the Great Fish-Run. Her father and other men would cast their nets of woven reeds weighted with stones, and the fish would swim right into them. So many fish crowded the streams, her father told her, that a man could walk across the water on their backs! The shad were the first to arrive, followed by the great striped bass. The men would easily spear these fish, then split and clean and dry them over smoky fires on wooden racks they had set up on the beach. Of course, they would also bring some fresh fish home to their women to prepare, seasoning them with berries and herbs and baking them on hickory-wood planks set close to the fire.

A sudden sound of shouting broke her reverie. It was the voices of the old men and young boys who were on the beach below the bluff, where they were gathering and drying shellfish for winter use. Listening Girl jumped up and ran back through the meadow to the edge of the bluff. She was astonished to see what appeared to be a tall straight tree trunk tipped in clouds floating on the water. Then a second and a third tall cloud-tipped tree appeared, and then a floating island like an upside-down turtle shell, growing larger and closer. "Manitou! Manitou!" she murmured. "There is a powerful spirit at work here!" Before she could run to the Planting Field to alert the women and girls, they had dropped their tools and run out to the bluff. Old Story Woman emerged from her wigwam, looking out toward the water. She gasped. Listening Girl ran up to her. "What can it mean, Old Story Woman?" she asked.

"It is the Floating-Island-of-Winds my grandmother told me about, which one morning during the Moon-of-Seed-Sowing brought strange Men-with-Hair-on-Their-Faces. When they started to come ashore in a large canoe, Thunderbird blew a great wind over the Salt Water, forcing them to turn around and return to their Floating Island." Old Story Woman scanned the sky. "Today there will be no great wind, and they will come ashore. We must greet them with plenty of food and make them feel welcome. We will see what they want, but surely they will not want to harm the First People of Lenapehoking."

New Amsterdam, fifty solar years later (650 moons) . . .

When Anna woke up that morning, she wasn't sure where she was at first, but then she remembered: she and her mother, Sara, were visiting Grandma to help her prepare for market day, when the farm women gathered to sell their produce. Although a market was held every Saturday, the harvest market was special, for then the women traveled from all parts of New Netherland, bringing their handmade linens, laces, and woolens along with their farm produce. The Indian women also came to sell their wares, and the commerce between Dutch and Wilden was always lively. Her own mother had persuaded the governor to start the weekly market on the Strand, near the dock, and had even built a shed in her backyard to house the Indian women who came for the event. Because she spoke fluent Algonkian, she often served as translator between tribal representatives and government officials or traders. Relations between Indian and Dutch could get tense, and Sara was often able to smooth things over. Her diplomatic skills and warm hospitality made her esteemed by the local Indians—even the Hackensack chief, Oratani, called her a friend.

Anna peered at her mother through the linen curtains of her wall bed. Dressed in a blue linen gown, her hair braided and coiled beneath a white linen headdress, her mother was a handsome woman. She was busily loading a basket with earthenware crocks of preserves and pickles. Another basket was piled high with the fresh apples and pears that Anna had helped pick from Grandma's orchard.

Anna loved visiting Grandma's farm. Many a happy summer day she had spent taking walks with Grandma, going berry picking or mushroom hunting or collecting wild plants. Grandma seemed to know everything about plants. "That low plant growing on the ground is plantain," she would say, "what the Wilden call White Man's Foot because it seems to spring up wherever we walk! The leaves make a poultice for burns. That tall plant there with broad leaves and a fat seed pod is called the milkweed because of its bitter milky sap; its fluffy seed tassels stuff your pillow. The sweet leaves of purple bee balm make a soothing tea, and the roots of the aster, with its starlike purple flowers, make a good tea to cool a fever. Those sunflowers you see have a thick tuber that can be boiled and eaten—an Indian food. If you know where to look in the thickets by the stream—and if you let the sweet smell of its pealike flowers guide you—you can find the groundnut vine, whose meaty root is delicious." Once Anna asked her how she knew so much about plants. Annekje told her that every good Dutch housewife must know the uses of plants, if she is to tend to her family's ailments. "I learned from my mother, but when I came to this country, I could not find the plants I knew. Of course, I brought seeds from the old country to plant in my herb garden, but it was the Wilden who taught me about the wild plants, for they know the earth like their mother." Now, Annekje—whom the townspeople called Widow Bogart—was known to Dutch and Indian alike for her skills in healing.

"Where's Grandma?" Anna asked as she swung her legs out from under her feather quilt and over the sides of the bed.

Her mother answered, "Out to gather eggs from her chickens, with no help from you! So up with you, lazy bones, and help us get to market!"

Used to her mother's good-natured scolding, she happily complied. She needed no encouragement to get up on market day! Her grandmother's maid, Trina, dished out *suppone*—corn mush mixed with buttermilk and molasses—from the iron pot that hung over the hearth and set it on the wooden table. Anna ate quickly, then stepped outside to the well, where she could wash herself with the cool water she drew up in the wooden bucket. The sun was just rising over the fields like a piece of molten iron on the blacksmith's anvil, lighting up the bay. She could see Staten Island in the distance, and beyond that the highlands of Sandy Hook. A salty breeze rippled the marsh grasses below, where cows were grazing. In the mudflats, hogs rooted for shellfish.

The clomping of horse's hoofs and clatter of wheels startled Anna out of her reverie. It was time to go to market! Once everything was loaded, they were on their way, the two women and the girl sitting atop the cart seat facing backward so they could steady the baskets, while Grandma's bond servant Peter guided the horse along the road to the ferry.

The farms receded before Anna's eyes, field after field of stubble where wheat and tobacco had been harvested. Now men were cutting hay and stacking them into bales for winter feed, or repairing fences, or ploughing where they planned to put in winter wheat. Black men and white men worked these fields; the white men were bond servants who had to serve their time as field hands and servants in exchange for ship passage to the new country, and the black men were slaves brought from Africa and the West Indies to work company plantations. A few of the slaves, Anna knew, had been granted their freedom and a plot of land where they could raise their children.

At the ferry landing, Peter unloaded the cart and placed their baskets in ferryman Dircksen's boat. There was a good breeze, so the ferryman could put up his sail instead of having to row them across to New Amsterdam. Anna could see the town easily, with its fort and windmill overlooking the North and East Rivers, the Dutch flag flapping its orange and blue colors over the fort. Among the rows of shops and houses clustered near the dock, she could pick out her own house, one of the new two-story brick houses with a red tile roof and step gable. Her father, Hans, the town doctor, needed to live in the town center so that he could serve the soldiers, sailors, and white and Indian traders who frequented the dock. They were a rough lot, given to drinking and fighting, so Anna was not allowed to go alone among them. Still, she could watch from her window the ships coming in, bearing exotic cargo: spices and silk from the East Indies, tea from China, wine from Portugal, rum and sugar and molasses from the West Indies. This cargo would be unloaded, then the ships would take on new cargo—the furs, lumber, sacks of grain, and cured tobacco that were the products of the colony.

The dock was bustling with activity as men and women milled about, speaking all kinds of languages: Dutch, English, French, Italian, Portuguese, Algonkian dialects, and the languages of Africa. Indian agents were earnestly negotiating with Dutch traders over the price of the furs the Indians had brought from upriver to exchange for cloth and blankets, metal tools, and wampum, which was Indian money made from shell beads. Anna knew from her father—who often treated the Indians and saw the bad effects of liquor—that rum was often passed around to sweeten the deal, even though this was illegal.

Anna looked forward to seeing the Indian women at their booths because they always had a kind word for Sara's daughter and the most interesting things to sell besides. So after helping Sara and Annekje set out their wares, she scampered off, making her way through the crowds of excited children, barking dogs, squawking chickens, bleating lambs, and squealing pigs; past tables piled high with colorful vegetables and fruits, stacks of preserves and pickles, and neatly folded linen and lace. She found the women seated cross-legged on reed mats, dressed in dyed cloth skirts and blouses. They were older women—those who could be spared from the tasks of the harvest—who brought many wonderful things: fine-woven hemp baskets and bags, bayberry soaps and candles, maplewood spoons, calabash bowls, hickory-wood fish planks, neatly tied straw brooms, and beaded deerskin moccasins and sashes. There were foods, too: smoked oysters and clams, dried berries, maple sugar and syrup.

Anna's attention was drawn to an old woman who sat somewhat apart from the others and was dressed in traditional deerskin garb. She had bowls of dried herbs and maize dolls. She noticed that one of the dolls was larger than the others. It was made of a long piece of polished wood, with a knob that was carved into a woman's head, long silky black hair held by a headband, a deerskin blouse, cornhusk skirt, beaded sash, and moccasins.

"Is this for sale?" asked Anna.

"No, child, I bring doll for good fortune."

"My grandma told me that the maize doll brings good crops and health, and that the Indians have a Doll Dance to honor her."

"That is so," agreed the woman, who now eyed Anna with interest. "And how did your grandma learn this?"

"She says she learned much from the Indians in the old days—about wild plants that feed and heal us."

"Is she here, child?" Anna nodded. "Bring her to me, and tell her that I am old woman with herbs to sell."

Anna hurried back to her grandmother's booth and beckoned her to come. "There is a strange old woman who wants to see you; she makes maize dolls and has herbs to sell." Annekje's face lit up with the prospect of meeting a new Indian woman who knew herbs. Together, Anna and her grandmother walked back to see the maize-doll woman. When the two old women saw each other, a shock of recognition passed between them. Both brought their hands to their hearts in show of friendship, then exchanged greetings in Algonkian. Grandma turned to Anna. "Go, child, and help your mother. I'll be here awhile. Tonight I will have a long story to tell."

True to her word, Grandma told her story after supper at Sara's house, when the family gathered before the great hearth.

When I first came to New Netherland, your mother was just a tiny child. This place would be the only home she would know, but for me, newly married to a young farmer, I would find the new land strange and hard. Here the woods grew thickly, much of the ground was hilly and stony, and the marshes extended as far as the eye could see! I missed the flat lush meadows and fields of home, our neat houses and flower gardens all fenced round. Here we had to start from scratch: to cut the trees to make our houses; to drain the marsh to make pasture for our cattle; to clear the land for our crops. At first we lived like animals in the ground, in dugouts lined with bark and sod or reeds for roofs.

We could not have survived without our Wilden friends. We learned from them how to make wigwams of saplings and bark, where we could live until our houses were finished. They gave us maize and beans, which we planted in hills without need of ploughing. They taught us how to dry wild fruits and smoke meat and fish to preserve them. And they showed us the wild plants that would nourish us and heal us in times of sickness.

It was not long after we arrived here that your mother became ill. I did not know what to do, because it was a strange illness that my herbs could not help. One day, an Indian woman about my age came to my door. She had heard about my child's trouble and had come to offer help. Her mother had taught her the healing ways, she said, and she brought her medicine pouch. I decided to trust her.

She spent many days by Sara's side, feeding her teas and broth, rubbing her skin with salves made from plants, singing and chanting. Each day, Sara got better and was soon well. I was amazed and grateful. During that time, we spoke in broken Dutch and Algonkian. I learned that her home was at Nayack, not far from where I now live. When she was a girl about your age, she saw Hudson's boat come into the bay. She told me that after the white man came, her people became very sick, as if an ill wind had followed the sails of the white man's boats. She lost her mother, father, sister, and brother, and many of her kin to the terrible sickness. The medicine men and women were unable to cure their people. Some thought that the Great Spirit was angry with them because they had become greedy for the white man's goods, so they burned everything they had—and the sickness went away. She herself left the land that had been the home of her mothers as far back as memory could go. She went to live with kin on Staten Island, and married a young trader, and bore him three children. Her husband was often away upriver hunting for furs to supply the Dutch traders. He would go away for longer and longer times because the beaver and other fur animals moved farther and farther away. Sometimes her husband came home empty-handed. Then came the time of the Indian wars.

Our people were greedy for the land and wanted to see the Indians off the land, so our governor set tribe against tribe, arming some and not others. Warriors from different tribes would fight with each other over who had the right to the fur animals. But when they realized that we wanted them off their lands forever—that they weren't just signing a deed to share land rights—enemies formed alliances and struck back. They burned our farms and villages—this happened in my time, and I well remember the fires that raged through the land and the smoke that could be seen for miles. And I will never forget how Governor Kieft— evil man that he was—ordered a surprise attack on a group of Indians who had sought refuge in New Amsterdam from their enemies—how his soldiers set upon them like wolves in the dead of night, slaughtering men, women, and children in the innocence of their sleep! When the Indian wars were over, thousands of Dutch and Indian people had died. Her husband was among the dead.

She came to me with her children and asked to stay for awhile. Of course I welcomed her—as did my husband—for we owed her our daughter's life. She made a wigwam and camped on our farm. She and her children all helped with the farm chores—because the Wilden never take something for nothing. Sara became friends with her children and began to learn Algonkian, which is why she is so fluent now. My friend taught me many of the Indian medicine plants, and I shared my knowledge in return—but I could never learn in a summer as much as she had learned in her lifetime. At the end of summer, after the harvest, she and her children left to join her kin in the Far Country. And that is the last I saw of her until today.

Anna stared wide-eyed at the fire, whose reflection danced in her eyes. The gleaming tiles arrayed around the fireplace with their Biblical scenes could not hold her attention the way her grandmother's story had. "Why has she come back?" asked Anna.

"She wishes to pay her final respects to the dead who are buried in her homeland, before she joins her daughters on their journey westward, across the mountains."

"Why won't she stay here? Some Wilden still live at Nayack."

"She cannot remain in the land of the dead. She says that the land is no longer what she knew: the great trees are cut down, the white man's animals trample woods and marsh, and the wild animals are gone. Her people can no longer walk freely across their land because the fences block their way." Now her grandmother asked Anna to get her a bundle that lay on the table. Anna rose and fetched it, curious to know what was in it. It rustled when she carried it, as if it had dried herbs in it. Her grandmother unrolled the linen and took out a maize doll. "My friend wished for you to have this. She hopes that you will remember her story, and the story of the maize doll—and that you will tell it to your children." Anna gently took the doll into her hands.

"What is she called, Grandma, so I can remember her?"

"She says they called her Listening Girl when she was your age because she loved to listen to the stories of the elders; now they call her Storytelling Woman, because she tells the story of her people wherever they go, so their children do not forget."

That night, Anna lay with her doll beside her. She thought of the old woman and imagined how the land must have looked to her as a girl. She thought of what it must feel like to lose so much that you love. Then she fell into a dream. In the dream, she was holding the hands of an old woman who sometimes looked like Grandma, and sometimes like Grandma's friend. They were walking in a field, and the woman was telling her to walk gently so as not to harm Our Mother. There were tall cornstalks in the field, green with ripening ears of corn. The old woman and the girl danced around the corn, raising their hands to the sky. Then the girl found herself flying like a bird, with all the fields and woods and marshes and waters stretched out below her—and she was filled with the green, gold, and blue beauty of this place of many islands—beauty that was not hers to keep, but to guard, the way a bird keeps its nest against harm.

Note: Although this story is fictional, it is based on many true things. The Lenape, or Delaware, people once lived along the Middle Atlantic Coast between the Delaware and Hudson Rivers, which they called Lenapehoking. Listening Girl's village was Nayack, or "Far Point," on a bluff overlooking New York Bay in what is now Fort Hamilton, Brooklyn. Annekje and Sara were real Dutch women who were known for their extensive knowledge of medicinal herbs. Annekje's farm was located in Brooklyn, and the "road to the ferry" was later to be called Fulton Street. New Amsterdam is the Dutch name for Manhattan.

Betsy McCully Cooper *is a writer and teacher who calls New York City her home. For the past decade she has researched and written about the region's natural history.*

A Song for New-Ark

Nikki Giovanni

When I write I like to write . . . in total silence . . . Maybe total . . . silence . . . is not quite accurate . . . I like to listen to the notes breezing by my head . . . the grunting of the rainbow . . . as she bends . . . on her journey from Saturn . . . to harvest the melody . . .

There is no laughter . . . in the city . . . no joy . . . in the sheer delight . . . of living . . . City sounds . . . are the cracking of ice in glasses . . . or hearts in despair . . . The burglar alarms . . . or boredom . . . warning of illicit entry . . . The fire bells proclaiming . . . yet another home . . . or job . . . or dream . . . has deserted the will . . . to continue . . . The cries . . . of all the lonely people . . . for a drum . . . a tom-tom . . . some cymbal . . . some/body . . . to sing for . . .

I never saw old/jersey . . . or old/ark . . . Old/ark was a forest . . . felled for concrete . . . and asphalt . . . and bridges to Manhattan . . . Earth acres that once held families . . . of deer . . . fox . . . chipmunks . . . hawks . . . forest creatures . . . and their predators . . . now corral business . . . men and women . . . artists . . . and intellectuals . . . People . . . and their predators . . . under a banner of neon . . . graying the honest Black . . . cradling the stars above . . . and the earth below . . . turning to dust . . . white shirts . . . lace curtains at the front window ... automobiles lovingly polished ... Dreams ... encountering racist resistance ... New-Ark knows too much pain ... sees too many people who aren't special ... watches the buses daily ... the churches on Sunday ... the bars after midnight ... disgorge the unyoung ... unable ... unqualified ... unto the unaccepting ... streets ... I lived ... one summer ... in New-Ark ... New-Jersey ... on Belleville Avenue ... Every evening ... when the rats left the river ... to visit the central ward ... Anthony Imperiali ... and his boys ... would chunk bullets ... at the fleeing mammals ... refusing to recognize ... the obvious ... family ... ties ... I napped ... to the rat-tat-tat ... rat-tat-tat ... wondering why ... we have yet to learn ... rat-tat-tats ... don't even impress ... rats ...

When I write I want to write ... in rhythm ... regularizing the moontides ... to the heart/beats ... of the twinkling stars ... sending an S.O.S. ... to day trippers ... urging them to turn back ... toward the Darkness ... to ride the night winds ... to tomorrow ... I wish I understood ... bird ... Birds in the city talk ... a city language ... They always seem ... unlike humans ... to have something ... useful ... to say ... Other birds ... like Black americans ... a century or so ago ... answer back ... with song ... I wish I could be a melody ... like a damp ... gray ... feline fog ... staccatoing ... stealthily ... over the city ...

Nikki Giovanni *is the author of more than a dozen books of poetry and a professor at Virginia Polytechnic Institute and State University. Among many honors, she has been named woman of the year by* Mademoiselle, Ladies Home Journal, *and* Ebony *magazines.*

Fledgling Summer

Jennifer Stansbury

with special thanks to Monica Hansen

◆

People aren't the only ones who flock to Long Island's beaches in the summer. Many kinds of shorebirds gather on the beaches to lay their eggs and raise their young. In this essay, Jennifer Stansbury describes what it was like to spend a summer as a field biologist on Long Island studying roseate terns and other nesting birds.

◆

Even as a young girl, watching nature shows and playing in the woods around my house, I knew I wanted to be a biologist. In 1987 I had just finished college, and I was to spend one summer on Long Island, in a beach community not far from New York City. But it wasn't for a family vacation or a typical summer job. I had been hired by Joanna Burger, a research scientist and professor at Rutgers University in New Jersey, to collect data on terns. I saw this job as my introduction to a career as a scientist. I was excited, especially to work with an endangered species, but I was also scared. I wasn't sure of myself or whether I could do a good job.

Terns are shorebirds in the same family as gulls, but they are smaller, with black caps on their heads and forked tails.

Known for their long seasonal migrations, these long-lived birds have straight sharp bills and pointed wings ideal for diving for fish in the ocean. They live in crowded colonies on the beaches and marshes of the barrier islands. The main focus of the study was to compare the endangered roseate terns to the common terns that dominated the colony.

Joanna was coordinating her studies with those of her former graduate student Carl Safina, who had hired half a dozen interns for the summer. The interns had their own jobs to do, but they also had to take turns helping me with my daily task of weighing and measuring chicks. We traveled each work day from the main island to work on land owned and protected by the Nature Conservancy.

We were housed in an old castlelike mansion. I was the only one with a room on the third floor, which I accessed by a dark, narrow, turning stairway. It was spooky at night to climb those stairs alone to an isolated room. Once there, I could look out one narrow window squeezed between the thick stone walls of the "castle."

The place was dank, very much like an actual castle. But with its large rooms, turrets, and French doors, it hinted of splendor. And though I longed to take strolls in the evening to explore the grounds, I could not. The wooded property, now a wildlife sanctuary, consisted of swampy wetlands that produced swarms of large mosquitoes.

Every evening the large kitchen was a lively, bustling place as each of us prepared our separate meals. We took turns at the stove and the shower, and at telling of our adventures in the field.

The Birds

I remember the first time I saw the colony on Cedar Beach. Carl and Joanna drove me up from New Jersey, past the huge garbage dumps on Staten Island and over the long bridges that led to Long Island and the barrier island. The colony included hundreds of nesting pairs of common terns along with roseate terns, black skimmers, and other birds. Their nesting areas were surrounded by a fence that separated them from the adjacent public beach. It was spring, before the hordes of summer visitors came to escape their unair-conditioned houses. And it was before the flocks of birds, migrating north from the tropics, reached their most numerous. It seemed very peaceful and beautiful. Peaceful, that is, until we squeezed through a break in the fence into the birds' nesting area. The birds took to the air and mobbed us with screeching voices.

Once our summer field season began, we quickly became accustomed to the endless bombardment of hard pecks on our helmets and the constant high-pitched rasping of the birds defending their nests and young. Agile flyers, the terns would sometimes pull at the hair poking out from under my helmet at the nape of my neck. They even used their fecal matter as a weapon. We would go home covered with bird poop—a variety of colors and consistencies, depending on the types of fish the terns were eating. We'd get tan lines on our arms and legs in the shape of splatters. Even our data sheets were not spared. The birds had very good aim. Once I got hit with poop on the inside of my sunglasses but got nothing in my eye. It was especially tough when I was assigned to count the number of individuals mobbing at a particular time and location. Normally when we were weighing and measuring chicks in the nest, we would keep our heads down, tolerate the assault, and shout to the person right by us to be heard over the roar. But when I had to count the birds in the air, I had to expose my face to the onslaught. I could see them jockey for position, screaming when they'd get too close to each other or touch wings. Then they would take turns swooping down with a screech at me and a hit. The birds' impeccable aim would remind me to count with my mouth closed.

The birds were not trying to protect the entire colony, only their own young. So once we left the vicinity of their own nests, they would settle down. As we moved to the next section of the colony, we would rouse another group, inviting them to return the harassment we inflicted on them. I had thought birds were not intelligent creatures. Then Carl told us that the terns learned to recognize his vehicle and would begin mobbing him in the parking lot, before he even reached the colony. Interestingly, though, they would leave Joanna alone; she didn't even bother to wear a helmet. They must not have felt as threatened by her because she often came to sit and watch rather than disturb their nests as we were instructed to do daily.

I'd often wish I had time to sit and watch. I would have watched the terns' behavior—how they interacted with their neighbors, how they treated their young. I would have watched their sleek, streamlined bodies navigate the wind, the way they walked awkwardly on short legs with flat feet, and many other things. But there was no time for me to sit and watch. I had to check about a hundred roseate tern nests and fifty common tern nests each day I was in the field. And in my spare time, I had to estimate the percentage cover of plants near each nest on my list (and at random points too), estimate the number of mobbing adults, search for undiscovered roseate tern nests, and record the weather conditions. All this was important in order to learn as much as possible. Without information, there is no way to help an endangered species. But whenever I could, I'd search out a roseate adult circling around the perimeter of the mob of common terns. Less aggressive and more beautiful, with longer tails and blacker beaks, the roseates were stunning against the blue sky. When I'd spot one, the noise of the mob would go quiet in my head. This was why *I* was here.

Nesting

The terns' nests were scattered all over the beach—a varied habitat of flat, open ground between mounds and small dunes covered with beach grasses, broadleaf plants, and small shrubs. The nests consisted merely of shallow scrapes in the sand with the eggs sitting there in the open. Some of the depressions contained a few twigs, grass, or shells—almost as a token effort toward a true nest. Early in the season, a few nests got stepped on, crushing the eggs. It happened as easily as someone stepping backward to shift his weight. We quickly learned to watch our *every* step. I felt so awful, like we were huge clumsy intruders—and we were. I questioned our presence in the colony.

As part of our work, we had to learn to distinguish between the nests of the two species. Roseate terns usually sited their nests close to plants. These locations may have provided more protection from the heat or from aerial predators. Although the eggs of both roseates and common terns were speckled and blotchy, they differed slightly in color and shape. Also, the roseates usually laid one or two eggs per clutch, while many of the common terns laid three. Once the chicks hatched, it was much easier to tell them apart. Roseate chicks were gray, and their feathers were not as fluffy as those of the tawny yellow common tern chicks.

Monitoring the nests daily, I got to know each one, and I waited eagerly for the milestone of hatching as one waits for the first word or first step of a child. The same kind of excitement and happiness filled me when I witnessed a crack in a shell or a newly hatched chick, panting as it dried into a little fuzz ball. Likewise, I was saddened when some of the eggs never hatched. Also, I became fond of certain nests—the unusual three-egg clutch of a roseate, or a nest I myself had discovered. Every day I checked my nests for their progress and condition. The eggs were laid one or two days apart, so the chicks hatched one or two days apart. Thus the oldest chick of a clutch was always larger than its siblings.

As soon as a chick was born, we would band it. To do this well, without squeezing the leg or crimping the metal band, took practice. We had to make sure the band was smooth and could move up and down on the leg without injury. After the chicks were hatched, we would measure their weight and the lengths of their beaks, wing tips, and tarsus (the part where the band is placed, which is actually part of the foot), and record the time of day. We had to complete our task at each nest as quickly as possible so the attending adult could return to the young. The eggs and chicks needed shelter from the hot sun or the rain. Of course the adults, with their noise and dive-bombing, made sure we didn't forget to make haste, their confidence increasing as the summer wore on.

We banded some of the adults, too, but unlike the chicks, they had to be trapped first. With Carl's supervision, we placed traps that were like metal wire cages over three or four nests at a time, careful not to crush the eggs. Most of the adults would walk right into the trap as though it weren't there. We watched, and as soon as all the traps were sprung, we hurried to collect them. One at a time, we took the birds out, performed the usual measurements, banded, and released them. It was extra special for me to handle the adults, to see them up close and feel their soft feathers. But again, skill and care were in order. The birds were held gently but firmly by their legs and waist, with their wings tucked in. Carl told us to be careful not to squeeze their chests because their air passages, so crucial to flight, could easily be damaged.

We would always break for lunch by the ocean waves. I had a peanut butter and jelly sandwich every day because I liked nothing else, a juice box, and chips. It was such a relief after working all morning in the heavy heat and bright sand to actually see the ocean, cool off in the waves, and just sit for a spell. We enjoyed talking and watching the piping plover chicks follow their mother and forage for food along the water's edge. The tiny, very endangered birds had legs that moved in a blur beneath them, and they made the sweetest monotone sound, like a flute. It was always hard to pick up and head back to work.

Threats

The privilege of handling wild birds endeared them to me, but that only made things harder once nature showed me her cruelty. Sometimes a chick would begin its tiring task of cracking its eggshell, pecking to break free, then resting, and pecking again. Only it would never get out. Ants would discover the egg, its shell no longer intact. They would crawl through the hole in the shell and kill the chick—before it could see the sunlight or taste a fish, and long before it could meet the promise of flight. Sometimes a chick would suffer an ant attack after hatching, being painfully bitten all over by an unknown force, aware of nothing but its suffering.

The terns themselves were no more sympathetic. Nesting together in a colony afforded them some safety from predators, but their close proximity did not make them friendly neighbors. Things weren't too bad until the chicks were old enough to wander from their own scrapes in the sand. Parents chased away any chicks that were not their own. This behavior is expected in a colonial situation, but I was not prepared for the brutality of it. One day I noticed a chick, strangely alone. As I approached, I could see a bright red bead of blood on its head. It took me a moment to comprehend that the injury was caused by a neighboring adult. At that moment, my romantic notions of nature were gone.

On that day I became very grateful I didn't have to struggle and fight for my very life. Grateful I didn't have to worry about predators like the terns did—mammals by night, gulls by day. I remember being by the water at the end of the day, walking toward the beach house, and seeing a gull flying with a tern chick in its beak. It dropped it on the hard sand. Right then I hated the gulls. But I could not blame the scavengers for utilizing a helpless and plentiful food resource.

The terns also battled the weather. During a big storm midseason we humans retreated to the safety and comfort of the mansion, but the birds had to stick it out on the beach. Some didn't make it. Upon our return to the field, the beach was changed. Debris and sand had been shifted around. Some nests had been completely washed away.

Then, late in the season, when the chicks were nearing fledgling age, sickness swept across the colony. Victims were seen walking in circles, unable to control their movements, before they died. It became more clear why adults would be so determined to protect their own chicks from possibly infected neighbors.

Humans, too, posed a threat to the birds. Although the colony was fenced off, we occasionally had to chase people out of the nesting area anyway. They crossed it as a shortcut to the beach, unaware that they could easily tread on the eggs of endangered species. I'll admit that at times I was a bit envious of the beachgoers. They were there to play and relax. They could get in the water to cool off when I had to march the shadeless sand with poop all over me. But their bliss was in ignorance, and it was ignorance that was endangering these birds. The trash they carelessly left behind was hazardous to the birds and the other creatures that inhabit the ocean and shoreline.

The worst of it by far was the fishing line. I was exposed to the evils of the endless, unbreakable, invisible, indigestible stuff when a fishing line was found one day on the beach. It was stretched across the colony for about one third, or perhaps even half, of the nesting area's length. We gathered it up, untangling birds as we went. Only some were still alive. I remember one victim vividly: fishing line wrapped many times around its tarsus, cutting through bloody skin. We freed it, but we couldn't know if it would survive.

Summer's End

At the end of the season, the colony looked very different. Early on, there were eggs or chicks in the nests and adults flying above, but now there were birds running all over the ground, exercising and stretching their wings, trying to fly. The chicks were getting ready to join their parents on the migration. The interns and I were sent out with strings of bands. We were systematically to band as many birds as we could of the hundreds not included in the nest monitoring. No longer concerned with stepping on eggs, we ran, chasing juveniles who would often out maneuver us. Sometimes they would surprise us, and themselves, when, after trying to outrun us, they would take off into the air, and out of our reach. We'd have to give up that chase for another. Once we caught a runner, we would band it and gently toss it into the air. If it couldn't fly it would flap down to the ground, but once in a while, it would fly. It would fledge, right out of our hands. Imagine the feeling and the surprise of the first flight!

And then the field season was finished. I was glad to be done with the heat, the biting flies, and the stench of my clothes and data papers. Taking a final visit to the beach, I looked at the transformed colony, which I now saw as both nursery and battleground. I would miss the ocean, watching the terns in flight, and seeing the eggs nestled together in the sand. I would miss the killdeer calling me away from her nest, pretending she had a broken wing, only to fly and try again in a different spot. I would miss the tiny piping plovers, funny little puffballs on stilts, and the black skimmers standing together, still as statues.

It was also time to leave my summer sanctuary, the "castle" in the woods. I took my final drive out the winding gravel road. It was lined with towering rhododendrons, which when I had arrived were in full bloom. Now they were plain green. Science, I had learned, was not glamorous, or even glorious. It was tedious, disruptive, and unsure. But understanding nature was empowering. I had been privileged to walk the colony, and had proudly worn those splattered clothes.

❧

Jennifer Stansbury *is a biologist who now enjoys watching the behavior and development of her two young children at her home in Laramie, Wyoming.*

Golden-Crowned Kinglet

Tyler Cadman

This afternoon
as I sat in the woods,
the sun piercing the canopy,

I saw in the corner
of my eye a small bird
fluttering from branch to branch.

Chirping in its high voice
it drifted toward me,
vibrating the branches

as it landed,
touching down on the
branch next to me.

It cocked its head.
Its golden crest flashed in
the bright light.

For a magical moment it
looked me in the eye.
When it flew away

I wondered why
I do not make the time
for more moments

like
this
one.

Tyler Cadman *lives in Westport Island, Maine, and is a student at the Center for Teaching and Learning. He wrote "Golden-Crowned Kinglet" when he was twelve years old.*

Never Go Home without a Fish

GRETCHEN WOELFLE

This tale is based on an event that took place on Damariscotta Lake around 1850, but we suspect that even today one can find fishermen on the lakes of Maine exhibiting the same kind of stubborn persistence.

"Let's go fishing tomorrow," Christopher said to Uncle Johnathan.

"We'll pack our food tonight and leave before dawn," his uncle replied.

Uncle Johnathan never went home without a fish, so he carried enough food to last the whole day: bread, butter, and salt pork for breakfast; more of the same with cheese and apple pie for lunch; and doughnuts for snacks in between. "I don't weigh 260 pounds by eating light," Uncle Johnathan allowed.

At the shore Christopher cut saplings for fishing poles. "Thick as my index finger on one end, thin as a pencil on the tip," said Uncle Johnathan. They tied on twenty feet of linen line, then tied hooks on the end of the line.

Christopher rowed to their favorite cove. He filled a bucket with water and lowered a sieve into the lake. He threw bread crumbs on the surface, and soon a school of minnows swarmed to eat the crumbs. Christopher raised the sieve and dropped the minnows into the bucket.

"Good start," said Uncle Johnathan.

The sun rose as they baited their hooks, cast their lines, and watched a kingfisher dive for its breakfast.

Morning came and went.

No fish.

"Nothing's happening," complained Christopher.

"Fishing is mostly waiting," said his uncle as they rowed ashore for lunch.

Uncle Johnathan poked through the lunch bucket. "I'm tired of salt pork," he said. "Fried fish will taste mighty good for supper."

Uncle Johnathan got ready for a nap. He stuck his pole in the sand with a mess of sticks and string and a spare fish hook that would lift his hat if he got a bite.

"Never let the fish know you're sleeping," he said.

Christopher stuck his pole in the sand too, but he needed his hat for picking blueberries. He filled it nearly full, but the tiny berries tasted so good he ate half a hatful before Uncle Johnathan woke up.

"Save some for later," his uncle said. "We won't go home without a fish."

During the afternoon they anchored near a rock ledge and floated in the weeds. They rowed toward the narrows and fished with worms as well as minnows.

"I hate all this waiting," Christopher said. "I'm going for a swim." He swam round the boat. He dove underneath and thumped the bottom to give Uncle Johnathan a start. Finally he climbed back in.

"Good night for fishing," said his uncle looking to the sky.

"We can wait all night for a fish, right, Uncle Johnathan?" He tried to keep the excitement out of his voice.

They ate leftover lunch for supper and watched the sun set behind the hills. A breeze made orange and pink ripples on the water, and a great blue heron glided by.

"Hoo ooo ooo ooo," called a loon. "Hoo ooo ooo ooo," came an answer across the lake. Stars came out. Christopher picked out constellations—the Big Bear, the Little Bear, Leo the Lion.

"Tell me about the ice-skating contest," Christopher said. It was his favorite story, and it happened right here on the lake.

"All the other skaters were young and lean. I was middle-aged and fat." His uncle chuckled. "They dragged logs out onto the ice and took turns jumping. One log, then two, four, eight, twelve logs. They laughed every time I took my turn, but I laughed back."

Christopher could picture Uncle Johnathan heaving his big body from side to side, swinging his arms back and forth.

"At sixteen logs, only three skaters were left, and one was me. At nineteen logs, another man fell. Then there was just young Bill Bixby and me. We both jumped twenty logs. Then at twenty-one, Billy nicked his skate on the last log and skidded for fifty feet. You should have heard him howl. I cleared it. Then for good measure, I jumped over another one. Twenty-two logs. No one has ever beaten my record." He chuckled again.

"Life gives you things you never expect," Uncle Johnathan mused, "and sometimes it doesn't give you what you have every right to expect—like a fish for dinner!" He paused, then continued, "Hornpouts come out at night. They'll taste good for breakfast."

Uncle Johnathan kept fishing. Christopher lay down with his jacket under his head. The rocking boat lulled him to sleep. He awoke to hear Uncle Johnathan singing.

I'm lonesome since I crossed the hill,
And o'er the moor and valley;
Such heavy thoughts my heart do fill,
Since parting with my Sally.

I seek no more the fine and gay,
For each does but remind me
How swift the hours did pass away
With the girl I left behind me.

That was something Christopher didn't expect. He'd never heard his uncle sing before. The boy felt he was floating . . . above the boat . . . above the earth. . . . When he woke again, Uncle Johnathan was asleep, his fishing pole in his hand.

The moonlight wiggled on the lake like a giant silver snake. He swished his hand through the water. It felt warm. A bat whooshed past, and a solitary fish splashed across the lake. He remembered his uncle's lonesome song. Had Uncle Johnathan ever had a sweetheart?

Christopher lay down again. Mist swirled around the boat when he woke, but he saw a rosy glow in the east. Uncle Johnathan was still sleeping, his head on his chest.

The moon grew dim as the sky brightened. Finally the sun burst over the pine trees and blazed on the water, scattering the mist. Christopher jumped into the lake and came up hollering. The cold water chased the sleepiness from his body.

Uncle Johnathan woke with a start and dropped his fishing pole overboard. Christopher laughed so hard he swallowed water and started sputtering.

"When you're done laughing, would you mind fetching my pole?" his uncle asked. "It's floating away."

With a few strong strokes, Christopher caught the pole, then lay on his back and kicked back to the boat. "Never let a fish catch you sleeping, Uncle Johnathan."

"Humph," grunted his uncle, but the corners of his mouth turned up.

Christopher saw two soggy doughnuts and some blueberries in the bucket. "Blueberries or doughnuts?" Christopher asked.

"Save the best for last. We won't go home without a fish," his uncle said as he reached for a doughnut.

When would that be? thought Christopher. Would they stay out for days and nights until they caught a fish? At noon they ate the blueberries. Christopher's feet fell asleep. He rubbed them against the boat.

"Have you ever fished this long before?" asked Christopher.

"Nope." Uncle Johnathan pressed his lips together.

"Well," said the boy, "life gives us things we never expect."

Christopher was daydreaming about creamy fish chowder when he felt a tug on his line. A yellow perch thrashed about underwater, its golden flanks glittering in the sunlight.

"Easy there," his uncle said. Christopher pulled the line out, then brought it closer. The perch swam to the rocks. If the line snagged, the fish might get away.

Uncle Johnathan rowed so Christopher could pull the fish straight out of the water. His uncle caught the perch in the net, and Christopher dropped it in the pail.

"Well done," said Uncle Johnathan.

An arrow of orange afternoon light shot across the lake.

"Can we go home," Christopher asked, "if I give you my fish?"

Uncle Johnathan stared at his nephew. Christopher knew the answer: Uncle Johnathan had to catch his own fish.

A few minutes later Christopher cried, "I've got it! Uncle Johnathan, is there any salt pork left?"

"I'm not hungry."

"Is there?"

"Just a hunk of rind."

"Well then, we'll give the fish something *they* don't expect." Christopher took out his pocket knife. "I'll carve a frog with the pork rind!"

"By golly, why didn't I think of that?" exclaimed Uncle Johnathan.

"Because we've been saving the best till last," said the boy.

When Christopher had carved his frog, he scraped away the fat from under the legs. Then he shook it. The frog body was firm, but the legs wiggled. It might fool a fish.

Christopher attached the frog to the hook, and Uncle Johnathan pulled it to and fro on the water. It skittered among the lily pads.

Suddenly a fish grabbed for it. Uncle Johnathan pulled his line, but the fish got away.

"I'll row in a circle," Christopher said. "We know he's in there."

Back and forth Uncle Johnathan guided his frog. The lily pads trembled.

Splash! The fish bit the frog's leg, then vanished.

"Third time lucky," muttered Uncle Johnathan, pulling the frog a little quicker.

Snap! The fish grabbed the whole frog in its mouth. Uncle Johnathan eased him closer, then out of the water. It was a smallmouth bass, his favorite.

"Hooray for Uncle Johnathan!" shouted Christopher, stamping his feet.

His uncle looked at the two fish in the bucket. "Well, we've got our fish . . ."

Christopher chimed in, ". . . so we can go home!"

~⌣~

Gretchen Woelfle *writes children's stories and environmental nonfiction in Venice, California. Johnathan Ames, a distant relative of hers, really did weigh 260 pounds, did jump over twenty-two logs on ice skates, and did stay out for thirty-six hours until he caught a fish on Damariscotta Lake in Maine.*

The Beech Tree

W. D. Ehrhart

My neighbor leans across the fence
and gestures upward grandly, making
with his two arms a tiny human
imitation of a beech tree lifting
two hundred years of sprawling growth.
"Quite a tree you've got!" he says.
"By God, I wish I owned it."

But though it lives in my backyard,
this tree belongs to the squirrels
leaping branches just beyond my window.
"You'd like to catch us, but you can't,"
they seem to scold the tabby cat
that crouches daily with a patience
too dim to comprehend the squirrels
own this tree and will not fall.

It belongs to the robins that nested
last year in a high sheltered fork.

It belongs to the insects burrowing
beneath its aging bark like miners.

I'm just the janitor: raking leaves,
pruning limbs to keep them from collapsing
the garage roof next door or climbing
into bed beside my wife and me.

Possession is a curious thing:
some things are not for owning,
and I don't mind caring for a tree
that isn't mine. I take my pay
in April reawakening and summer shade.
Just now, I'm watching snow
collecting in the upper branches,
waiting for the robins to come home.

W. D. Ehrhart *is the author or editor of seventeen books of prose and poetry, most recently* Beautiful Wreckage: New and Selected Poems *from Adastra Press. He wrote "The Beech Tree" while waiting not only for the robins to come home but also for the arrival of his daughter Leela, who was born just days after the poem was written.*

Wild Lives

Glooskap and the Whale

Joseph Bruchac

This story comes from the Micmac, native peoples of Newfoundland and the Canadian Maritimes. According to Micmac legend, Glooskap was a giant, a trickster, and a creator. He was said to have slept across Nova Scotia, using Prince Edward Island for his pillow.

Long ago, Glooskap lived on an island. He came down to the shore, wanting to cross over to the mainland. He had no boat and the water was deep. So he began to sing a song:

> Podawawogan,
> Whale come and help me,
> Podawawogan,
> Help me to cross

His song had great power and soon a whale rose to the surface of the water and swam close in the deep water to the place where Glooskap stood. This whale, though, was not a big whale and Glooskap was a giant. Glooskap put one foot on the whale's back. As soon as he began to put his weight onto the whale it sank. Glooskap pulled his foot back.

"Thank you, brother," he said, "but you are not strong enough to carry me."

Then Glooskap sang his song again:

> Podawawogan,
> Whale come and help me,
> Podawawogan,
> Help me to cross

This time, the largest of all the whales came. It was a huge female, her blue back so wide that Glooskap could easily climb on board. Soon she was swimming through the waves, heading for the mainland.

This great whale, though, was worried about going aground. She knew that the water grew shallow close to the mainland. Glooskap, however, did not want to get his feet wet. Before long, they started to get close to shore.

"Can you see the land from my back?" the great whale said.

The land was now in sight, but Glooskap was afraid she would dive and leave him in the water if he told the truth.

"No," he said, "land is still out of sight. Swim faster, Grandmother, swim faster."

Then the whale began to swim faster. But as she swam, she looked down and she could see the shells of the clams below her. This frightened her, for she knew that meant the water was no longer so deep.

"Can you see the land from my back," she said, "doesn't it show itself like the string of a bow?"

"No," Glooskap said, "we're still far from land. Swim faster, Grandmother, swim faster."

Now the clams did not like Glooskap. He had gathered many of them and eaten them, making great mounds of empty shells on the shore. The clams began to sing:

You are close to land,
throw him off, thrown him off,
You are close to land,
throw him off, let him drown

"What are the clams singing?" the great whale said. She could not understand their language.

"Ah," Glooskap said, "I can understand them. They are saying to hurry, to hurry along. To hurry along for we're still far from shore."

"Then I must hurry," the whale said. She dove with her mighty tail—and found herself grounded up on the beach! She was stuck and could not get free.

Glooskap climbed from her back.

"Grandchild," the great whale said, "you have been my death. I will never swim in the sea again."

Glooskap shook his head. "No, Grandmother," he said. "I will not let you suffer. You will swim in the sea again." He pulled his great bow from his back and pushed with it against the great whale's head. He pushed her from the beach and back into the deep water again.

The whale was very happy. She leaped and danced in the waves, throwing great mountains of spray up as she breached. To this day the great whales dance that way, remembering how Glooskap pushed their grandmother back into the water. Then the whale turned back towards Glooskap.

"Grandchild," she said, "can you give me something?"

Glooskap took his pipe from his pouch. "I will give you this, Grandmother," he said.

The great whale took the pipe. To this day you may see the big whales blowing the smoke up into the air from that pipe which Glooskap gave their grandmother when she helped him come to the mainland.

◡

Joseph Bruchac *has authored more than fifty books for adults and children. Of part Abenaki descent, he is a scholar of Native American culture and was honored in 1999 with the Lifetime Achievement Award of the Native Writers' Circle.*

Starfish

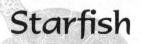

MARY OLIVER

In the sea rocks,
    in the stone pockets
        under the tide's lip,
            in water dense as blindness

they slid
    like sponges,
        like too many thumbs.
            I knew this, and what I wanted

was to draw my hands back
    from the water—what I wanted
        was to be willing
            to be afraid.

But I stayed there,
    I crouched on the stone wall
        while the sea poured its harsh song
            through the sluices,

while I waited for the gritty lightning
    of their touch, while I stared

down through the tide's leaving
where sometimes I could see them—

their stubborn flesh
lounging on my knuckles.
What good does it do
to lie all day in the sun

loving what is easy?
It never grew easy,
but at last I grew peaceful:
all summer

my fear diminished
as they bloomed through the water
like flowers, like flecks
of an uncertain dream,

while I lay on the rocks, reaching
into the darkness, learning
little by little to love
our only world.

⌣

Mary Oliver *is a Pulitzer Prize-winning poet and the author of more than seven poetry collections. She was born in Cleveland, Ohio, and has lived in Provincetown, Massachusetts, since 1964. She currently teaches at Bennington College.*

Otter Delight

DAVID SOBEL

River otters are energetic and playful, known for cavorting in the water and sliding headlong down stream banks. What would it be like to spend a day following in an otter's tracks? David Sobel tells us in this essay.

The tracks left the stream below the beaver pond and just above the waterfall. Perhaps the otter was avoiding my house, located near the base of the falls. More likely, she was taking a timeworn shortcut. Quick bounds up the bank were recorded in her tracks. Then, on level ground, her stride became syncopated: run, run, slide . . . run, run, slide. Her slides formed a carved trough of pliant snow; even going slightly uphill, she continued this rhythm. Across the lichened stone wall and then downhill, she executed a single glissade, sinuously slithering around trees, like water flowing along the path of least resistance. At the beaver pond below my house she rejoined the stream, moving onward.

Like brooks, otters move with effortless strength. They are always traveling, often covering ten miles in a day. Yet they take time to dawdle in eddies, careen down banks, and do corkscrew turns and double one-and-a-half gainers in pursuit of fish. I envy both their energy and their diversity of movement. While skiing, I try to imitate the thrust of otters in snow, streamlining forward, their legs clamped to their sides. If I could achieve the same purposeful thrust and remain spontaneously sensitive to the topography underfoot, my skiing would be perfect.

The otter that had jaunted past my house was probably traveling part of a winter circuit. In southern New Hampshire, where most bodies of water freeze hard from December to March, otters often need to range far afield to visit a variety of feeding spots. They search out warm springs, fast-water rapids, or active beaver ponds that allow them access to the under-ice world. This otter probably came across the divide from the Great White Swamp into Bailey Brook, past my house to Robb Marsh, then along the swampy reaches of the North Branch, into the Contoocook drainage, and up the Nubanusit to Spoonwood and the swamp. Or she might be traveling the North Branch and its numerous swampy setbacks. Her circuit might be up to forty miles around, taking up to two weeks to complete. And since otter populations average only one per six to ten square miles, this is probably the same individual that passed my house a month ago.

I set off a few days later to track the otter. The mid-February rains followed by a freeze had produced a hard and glassy ice. I skated the meandering marshy streams, through the muskrat and beaver swamps, following the frozen slush trail of the otter. The post-rain soggy snow had not slowed her progress. I could see sprays of slush from her sliding, frozen near her tracks. Underneath the sultry black ice, air bubbles were trapped eight inches beneath my feet. Using these bubbles, otters can stretch their under-ice time from the regular two-to-four minutes to an hour.

Approaching the rapids below Robb Marsh, I slowed down.

Piles of scaly and chitinous scat were evident near the ice's edge, but no otter. Evidently, she was eating perch, pickerel, and crayfish. Contrary to prevalent myths, otters do not solely eat game fish. In fact, an all-fish diet can kill an otter (piscivores, take note). Otters eat crayfish when it is available and a wide variety of forage fish as well as game fish. Being unselective, they also regularly dine on frogs, salamanders, and aquatic insects; they certainly are undeserving of their reputation as trout murderers. But because of the lack of variety in wintry food, this otter was taking primarily fish.

I skated with long, cutting strokes to the rapids two miles

distant and in time heard the noise of quick water ahead. I approached and peered around a willow thicket: there she was. She tossed her head back and chewed, fish bones grinding. Another bite and her head arched again, sniffing the air. She slipped into the icy water, and I could imagine her quick undulations propelling her forward toward a pickerel, the fish dashing for cover amid the bank sedges, red-maple roots, and mazes of beaver-felled poplars, the otter catching the faint glint of the pickerel's scales, hovering, darting, twisting, and grabbing it behind the head. She came back up on the ice in a liquid swoop, her whiskers twitching as she chomped down the Y-bones. I thought her food would preoccupy her enough to make her unaware of my presence, and I inched forward. She glanced in my direction and was underwater in an instant. She thrust her head through the surface as if standing on a rock and examined me for a moment, then dove and was gone.

I waited, but she had retired to a hideout beneath the ice, either to the abandoned beaver lodge nearby or the hollow created by a felled tree beneath the snow and ice. Otters thrive in these vegetative labyrinths. I remember creeping through such tunnels when I was young, and I tried to imagine swimming through them now in the gray-green gloom. She was down there, cleaning her fur, snuggling into the warm grass and mud.

I skated on to Ball Basin, an assemblage of swamps, marshes, and wide expanses of ice. Numerous stream basins opened like rooms onto the central sweep of ice. No otter was to be found, but at the upper reach of each marshy expanse there was an unusual playground. Each stream had frozen into a gentle-tiered ice floe, the rain and cold synthesized into a melted wedding cake. I herringboned my way to the top, lay down on my stomach, and streamlined my hands to my sides. Slithering down the ice floe, I pushed off from a frozen rock with my hip, following the icy contours of the stream and sharing the otter's sinuous grace for a moment.

David Sobel *directs the elementary teacher certification program at Antioch New England Graduate School. He is the author of several nonfiction books about children and the natural world, including* Children's Special Places, Beyond Ecophobia: Reclaiming the Heart in Nature Education, *and* Mapmaking with Children: Sense of Place Education for the Elementary Years.

Long Island Crow

Norbert Krapf

He soars darkly above cars
crawling bumper to bumper

toward Manhattan, glides in a circle
above treetops in the village park,

climbs above apartment complexes
toward a grove of oaks

on the highest ridge in the county.
He perches, gazes back down

at the valley, and caws forth
from the shadows of his brain

a thick forest in which morning
campfire smoke rises like mist.

Norbert Krapf *grew up in southern Indiana but has lived on Long Island since 1970. The director of the C. W. Post Poetry Center of Long Island University, he is the author of several books, including* Somewhere in Southern Indiana, Blue-Eyed Grass: Poems of Germany, *and the forthcoming* Bittersweet Along the Expressway. *He has a special interest in the relationship between literature and place.*

The Great Whale

Farley Mowat

In the winter of 1967, a seventy-foot whale became trapped in a pond in Burgeo, Newfoundland. The pond was connected to the Atlantic by a narrow channel that became deep enough for the whale to swim through during an unusually high tide. In the following excerpt, author and naturalist Farley Mowat responds to news of the whale's existence and to the rumor that local islanders have been taking shots at her for sport.

Early next morning I telephoned Danny Green, a lean, sardonic and highly intelligent man in his middle thirties who had been the high-lining skipper of a dragger but had given that up to become skipper, mate and crew of the little Royal Canadian Mounted Police motor launch. Danny not only knew—and was happy to comment on—everything of importance that happened on the Sou'west Coast, he was also familiar with and interested in whales. What he had to tell me brought my excitement to fever pitch.

"I'm pretty sure 'tis one of the big ones, Farley. Can't say what kind. Haven't seen it meself but it might be a Humpback, a Finner or even a Sulphur." He paused a moment. "What's left of it. The sports have been blasting hell out of it this past week."

As Danny gave me further details of what had been happening, I was at first appalled, then furious.

"Are they bloody well crazy? This is a chance in a million. If that whale lives, Burgeo'll be famous all over the world. *Shooting* at it! What the hell's the matter with the constable?"

Danny explained that our one policeman was a temporary replacement for the regular constable, who was away on leave. The new man, Constable Murdoch, was from New Brunswick. He knew nothing about Burgeo and not much about Newfoundland. He was hesitant to interfere in local matters unless he received an official complaint.

At my request, Danny put him on the phone.

"Whoever's doing that shooting is breaking the game laws, you know," I told him. "It's forbidden to take rifles into the country. Can't you put a stop to it?"

Murdoch was apologetic and cooperative. Not only did he undertake to investigate the shooting, he offered to make a patrol to Aldridges Pond and take me with him. However, Claire and I had already made other arrangements with two Messers fishermen, Curt Bungay and Wash Pink, who fished together in Curt's new boat. They were an oddly assorted pair. Young, and newly married, Curt was one of those people about whom the single adjective, "round," says it all. His crimson-hued face was a perfect circle, with round blue eyes, a round little nose, and a circular mouth. Although he was not fat, his body was a cylinder supported on legs as round and heavy as mill logs. Wash Pink was almost the complete opposite. A much older man, who had known hard times in a distant outport, he was lean, desiccated, and angular. And whereas Curt was a born talker and storyteller, Wash seldom opened his mouth except in moments of singular stress.

A few minutes after talking to Murdoch, Claire and I were under way in Curt's longliner. I was dithering between hope that we would find a great whale in the Pond, alive and well, and the possibility that it might have escaped or, even worse, have succumbed to the shooting. Claire kept her usual cool head, as her notes testify:

"It was blowing about 40 miles an hour from the northwest," she wrote, "and I hesitated to go along. But Farley said I would regret it all my life if I didn't. Burgeo being Burgeo, it wouldn't have surprised me if the 'giant whale' had turned out to be a porpoise. It was rough and icy cold crossing Short Reach but we got to Aldridges all right and sidled cautiously through the narrow channel. It was several hours from high tide and there was only five feet of water, which made Curt very nervous for the safety of his brand-new boat.

"We slid into the pretty little Pond under a dash of watery sunlight. It was a beautifully protected natural harbour ringed with rocky cliffs that ran up to the 300-foot crest of Richards Head. Little clumps of dwarfed black spruce clung in the hollows here and there along the shore.

"There was nobody and nothing to be seen except a few gulls soaring high overhead. We looked eagerly for signs of the whale, half expect-ing it to come charging out of nowhere and send us scurrying for the exit. There was no sign of it and I personally concluded it had left— if it had ever been in the Pond at all.

"I was ready to go below and try to get warm when somebody cried out that they saw something. We all looked and saw a long, black shape that looked like a giant sea-serpent, curving quietly out of the water, and slipping along from head to fin, and then down again and out of sight.

"We just stared, speechless and unbelieving, at this vast monster. Then there was a frenzy of talk.

"'It's a *whale* of a whale! . . . Must be fifty, sixty feet long! . . . That's no Pothead, not that one . . .'

"Indeed, it was no Pothead but an utterly immense, solitary and lonely monster, trapped, Heaven knew how, in this rocky prison.

"We chugged to the middle of the Pond just as the R.C.M.P launch entered and headed for us. Farley called to Danny Green and they agreed to anchor the two boats in deep water near the south end of the Pond and stop the engines.

"Then began a long, long watch during which the hours went by like minutes. It was endlessly fascinating to watch the almost serpentine coming and going of this huge beast. It would surface about every four or five minutes as it followed a circular path around and around the Pond. At first the circles took it well away from us but as time passed, and everyone kept perfectly still, the circles narrowed, coming closer and closer to the boats.

"Twice the immense head came lunging out of the water high into the air. It was as big as a small house, glistening black on top and fish-white underneath. Then down would go the nose, and the blowhole would break surface, and then the long, broad back, looking like the bottom of an overturned ship, would slip into our sight. Finally the fin would appear, at least four feet tall, and then a boiling up of water from the flukes and the whale was gone again.

"Farley identified it as a Fin Whale, the second largest

animal ever to live on earth. We could see the marks of bullets—holes and slashes—across the back from the blowhole to
the fin. It was just beyond me to even begin to understand the
mentality of men who would amuse themselves filling such a
majestic creature full of bullets. Why *try* to kill it? There is no
mink or fox farm here to use the meat. None of the people
would eat it. No, there is no motive of food or profit; only a
lust to kill. But then I wonder, is it any different than the
killer's lust that makes the mainland sportsmen go out in
their big cars to slaughter rabbits or ground-hogs? It just
seems so much more terrible to kill a whale!

"We could trace its progress even under water by the
smooth, swirling tide its flukes left behind. It appeared to be
swimming only about six feet deep and it kept getting closer to
us so we began to catch glimpses of it under the surface, its
white underparts appearing pale aqua-green against the
darker background of deep water.

"The undulations on the surface came closer and closer
until the whale was surfacing within twenty feet of the boats.
It seemed to deliberately look at us from time to time as if trying to decide whether we were dangerous. Oddly, the thought
never crossed my mind that *it* might be dangerous to us. Later
on I asked some of the others if they had been afraid of this,
the mightiest animal any of us was ever likely to meet in all our
lives, and nobody had felt any fear at all. We were too en-
thralled to be afraid.

"Apparently the whale decided we were not dangerous. It
made another sweep and this time that mighty head passed
right under the Mountie's boat. They pointed and waved and
we stared down too. Along came the head, like a submarine,
but much more beautiful, slipping along under us no more

than six feet away. Just then Danny shouted: 'Here's his tail! Here's his tail!'

"The tail was just passing under the police launch while the head was under *our* boat, and the two boats were a good seventy feet apart! The flippers, each as long as a dory, showed green beneath us, then the whole unbelievable length of the body flowed under the boat, silently, with just a faint slick swirl of water on the surface from the flukes. It was almost impossible to believe what we were seeing! This incredibly vast being, perhaps eighty tons in weight, so Farley guessed, swimming below us with the ease and smoothness of a salmon.

"Danny told me later the whale could have smashed up both our boats as easily as we would smash a couple of eggs. Considering what people had done to it, why didn't it take revenge? Or is it only mankind that takes revenge?"

Once she accepted the fact that our presence boded her no harm, the whale showed a strange interest in us, almost as if she took pleasure in being close to our two 40-foot boats, whose undersides may have looked faintly whale-like in shape. Not only did she pass directly under us several times but she also passed between the two boats, carefully threading her way between our anchor cables. We had the distinct impression she was lonely—an impression shared by the Hann brothers when she hung close to their small boat. Claire went so far as to suggest the whale was seeking help, but how could we know about that?

I was greatly concerned about the effects of the gunning but, apart from a multitude of bullet holes, none of which showed signs of bleeding, she appeared to be in good health. Her movements were sure and powerful and there was no bloody discoloration in her blow. Because I so much wished to believe it, I concluded that the bullets had done no more harm than superficial damage and that, with luck, the great animal would be none the worse for her ordeal by fire.

At dusk we reluctantly left the Pond. Our communion with the whale had left all of us half hypnotized. We had almost nothing to say to each other until the R.C.M.P launch pulled alongside and Constable Murdoch shouted:

"There'll be no more shooting. I guarantee you that. Danny and me'll patrol every day from now on, and twice a day if we have to."

Murdoch's words brought me my first definite awareness of a decision which I must already have arrived at below—or perhaps above—the limited levels of conscious thought. As we headed back to Messers, I knew I was committed to the saving of that whale, as passionately as I had ever been committed to anything in my life. I still do not know why I felt such an instantaneous compulsion. Later it was possible to think of a dozen reasons, but these were afterthoughts—not reasons at the time. If I were a mystic, I might explain it by saying I had heard a call, and that may not be such a mad explanation after all. In the light of what ensued, it is not easy to dismiss the possibility that, in some incomprehensible way, alien flesh had reached out to alien flesh . . . cried out for help in a wordless and primordial appeal which could not be refused.

Farley Mowat's *love of nature awoke at the age of fourteen when he took a trip to the Arctic with his uncle, an ornithologist. Since then he has written more than two dozen books about people and nature, including* An Owl in the Family *and* Never Cry Wolf. *The tragic fate of the trapped fin whale is described in his book,* A Whale for the Killing, *from which this excerpt is drawn.*

Persistent Haiku

ELISAVIETTA RITCHIE

The hurricane past,
the spider returns
to lace up the shattered wharf.

Elisavietta Ritchie *has published eleven books of poetry and two of short fiction and also works as a poet-in-the-schools. She lives in Broome's Island, Maryland.*

The Legend of the Mashpee Maiden

Elizabeth Reynard

Chief Red Shell, Historian of the Nauset Wampanoag Tribe, and Chief Wild Horse, Wampanoag Champion of Mashpee, told the author this story and "generously contributed" it to her book The Narrow Land.

In the long ago, there lived among the Wampanoag of the Mashpee Village, a maiden called Ahsoo. Her legs were like pipe-stems; her chin was pointed and sharp as the beak of a loon; her nose was humped and crooked; and her eyes were as big as a frightened deer's. Day after day she sat on a log and watched those around her. No one cared for her; none of the men desired her friendship. She was an idle, lazy maiden who would not work in a wigwam nor carry wood for a fire.

Although Ahsoo was ugly, no woman could equal her in singing. Birds paused on the bough to listen to her, and the river, running over rapids, almost ceased its flowing to hear the Mashpee Maiden. On a low hill near the river Ahsoo would sit and sing. Beasts of the forest, birds of the air, fish of the lakes came to hear. Maugua the Bear came, and even the great War Eagle; but Ahsoo was not afraid for she knew that they had only come to listen to her songs. The river at the foot of the hill became alive with fishes, journeying up from the South Sea to hear the voice of Ahsoo. Every animal, bird, and fish applauded in its own manner, since they all greatly desired that Ahsoo should continue.

There was a big trout, chief of all trout, almost as big as a man. Because of his size he could not swim up the river to hear Ahsoo sing. Every night he burrowed his nose further and further into the bank. At length he planed a long path inland and the seawater, following him closely, made Cotuit Brook. This chief of the trout loved Ahsoo and he could not see how ugly she was, for she always sang in the summer evenings after the sun went down. So he told her that she was pretty; and of course the Mashpee Maiden fell deeply in love with that trout. She told him how she loved him and invited him to visit her wigwam.

At this time, the Pukwudgee chief lived with his followers in the marshes near Poponesset Bay. He observed the Great Trout who was making a new brook for the use of the pygmy people, and one day the little chief overheard the trout lamenting because he could not have Ahsoo for a wife.

"The charming Mashpee Maiden and I love each other dearly," sighed the Monster Fish, "but, alas! neither of us can live without the other, and neither of us can live where the other lives."

The chief of the Pukwudgees was sorry for these lovers, so he changed the Maiden into a trout, and placed her in Santuit Pond. Then he told the Monster Fish to dig his way to the Pond, and have the Maiden for his wife. The Trout digged so hard and so fast that, when he reached Santuit Pond, he died of too much exertion; and the Maiden who had become a trout died of a broken heart. Indians found the defeated lovers, and buried them side by side in a large mound, called *Trout Grave*, near the brook dug by the Chief of Trout.

Elizabeth Reynard *was born in Boston in 1896 and was an associate professor of literature at Barnard College for many years. When she had a home in Chatham, Massachusetts, she gathered material for her book* The Narrow Land, *in which this story appears.*

Fire Island Walking Song

EUGENE F. KINKEAD

I know a large dune rat whose first name is Joe
And he skips beneath the boardwalk medium slow
Out to the edge where the daylight glisters
And he hasn't any brothers and he hasn't any sisters
And he hasn't any uncles and he hasn't any aunts
And he hasn't any Sunday-go-to-meeting pants.

Oh, he lives all alone in the big tall grassages
And through the brush piles he has secret passages.
He dines on moonbeams and washed-up scobbles
And he never has the toothache or the collywobbles.
He comes out at night and he dances by the sea
And he's a pretty nice dune rat, if you're asking me.

Eugene F. Kinkead, *a longtime staff writer for the* New Yorker, *also wrote books on urban wildlife and Central Park.*

Waxwings

HENRY BEETLE HOUGH

Although winter months on Martha's Vineyard are wet and cold, cedar waxwings, chickadees, and many other plucky birds are willing to ruffle up their feathers and wait out the wintry weather.

It's quite a thing to have a flock of cedar waxwings paying you a visit in the calm of January, and not a few Vineyarders have had that experience.

Cedar waxwings are larger than chickadees and more svelte—an exotic word being best for exotic-looking birds like these—and they are not individualists in the same sense. Your chickadee is quite a citizen and maintains his own goings and comings, although he doesn't at all object to company. But the waxwings come in numbers, work in numbers, and go away in numbers.

They have unbelievable smoothness and neatness. They are lissome (that's what svelte means) and they wear black on their faces as if provided with dominoes for a winter masquerade. Their heads are crested, and their wings splashed with a bit of red like sealing wax, as the books say, and occasionally you see this red on their tails too. But the tips of their tails look as if they had been dipped in yellow paint. Waxwings manage to be spectacular without appearing garish, indeed without even being noticeable, if you can figure that out. Of course, if you've seen a winter flock of these birds and just barely missed not seeing them while glancing right at them, you can understand perfectly.

Waxwings feed on berries at this time of year—cedar berries, bittersweet berries, bayberries, and so on. They will whip in and out of a vine in no time, or they will drift about in twos and threes, grazing the garden, checking up on old seed pods and so on.

A winter in New England, and thus a winter on the Vineyard, should be an empty season (so Californians think) but there is so much to fill it and give it distinction. There's always the likelihood of snow, that bulky commodity, and meantime the cedar waxwings supply their precise and spirited accent to our by no means scanty scene.

Henry Beetle Hough *lived on Martha's Vineyard for almost all his life. The editor of the* Vineyard Gazette *for nearly sixty years, he also wrote more than twenty books and worked for environmental causes. In 1979 he received the Environmental Award from the Massachusetts Conservation Council.*

Germantown Friends Cemetery

YVONNE

Among the meek

stone teeth

grey squirrel twirls

a seed

Yvonne *is the author of a three-volume epic:* Iwilla Soil *(1985),* Iwilla Scourge *(1986), and* Iwilla Rise *(1999). She was poetry editor at* Ms. *magazine from 1973–1986.*

A Moth Flies in Brooklyn

Thomas J. Campanella

*Cities can be surprisingly good places for tracking and observing wildlife.
As Thomas Campanella discovered as a boy, the trick is patience and a
curiosity about even small wild lives.*

Were an official tree chosen for Brooklyn, the honor would no
doubt go to *Ailanthus altissima*—stinking ash, tree-of-heaven,
ghetto palm, the tenacious weed of Betty Smith's 1943 novel,
A Tree Grows in Brooklyn. As a child raised in the Flatlands section of the borough, I never had to wander far to come upon a
clump or specimen of ailanthus. Down by the Belt Parkway
was my favorite stand, a venerable grove that filled an entire
embankment near Exit Eleven, beside the Flatbush Avenue
overpass. The ailanthus there reached bravely and greenly sky-
ward, in spite of the carbon monoxide and road salt and the
indelicacies of highway maintenance crews. And these hardy
trees were, unbelievably, home to a vigorous population of
Samia cynthia—silk worms descended from creatures brought
to America in the late nineteenth century, in the hope of creating a native silk industry. The venture failed, but the worms
survived and their hosts gained a secure foothold in the new
land.

As an avid chaser of butterflies and moths, I was fascinated by *cynthia*. It was not just a lost rustic, but truly a child of the city. My beloved *Golden Nature Guide, Butterflies and Moths,* was quite clear on this: the *cynthia* moth, it said, is "found mostly near cities from Boston to Washington, D.C." (Its range has since spread, presumably along with that of the ailanthus; the latest edition of *Butterflies and Moths* describes the moth's territory as stretching "south to Savannah, and west to Indiana.") The *Audubon Society Guide to North American Insects and Spiders* delineated *cynthia's* domain as "Major metropolitan areas . . . where ailanthus is found." I had found a bit of urban nature that seemed in a different league than the starlings and pigeons and other common urban creatures. The *cynthia* moth was enigmatic, rarely seen, and remarkably beautiful.

One afternoon, I took several of the plump, horn-studded caterpillars home and placed them in an old dry fish tank. Every few days I would replenish their supply of ailanthus leaves, until one day I found that the caterpillars had tucked themselves into husklike brown cocoons. Several weeks passed, and then one morning my breath was taken away: the cocoons had opened. Dewy-winged *cynthia* moths were resting on the twigs, their discarded hatcheries nearby. The insects waited for the fluids in their plump bodies to pump wingward, to unfurl the powdery sheets like petals in the morning sun. Hours passed, and the big moths slowly took form. Their regal wings spread nearly five inches now, painted in pastel pinks and browns, marked with the beautiful, haunting "eyes" characteristic of the family Saturniidae. Fine antennae, like newly unfurled fern fronds, hung at their heads. It seemed decidedly uncouth to name these magnificent insects "moths"—a term that brought to mind holey winter woolens and the grandmotherly aroma of moth balls.

I kept them only long enough to show my parents and friends what had become of the "worms," and then I released them into the Brooklyn sky. There were six or seven moths I let fly that day, all females. But one I kept behind.

I had always been thrilled to find traces of nature in my city. A cardinal on a neighbor's fence, a wild pheasant in the

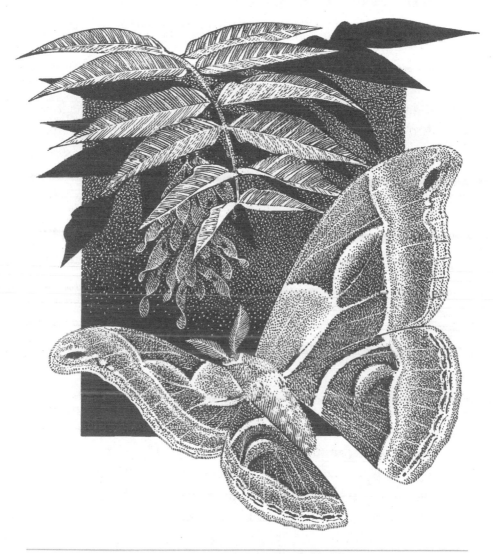

Gerritsen salt marshes, a flock of Canada geese hunkered down on the tawny March ballfields of Marine Park—these things I never expected to encounter as a Brooklyn child. When I did, nature, even in these wonderful forms, seemed reticent, on the defensive; it had to be searched out and flushed. And then, one night during the summer of the moths, nature in all its wild mystery came to me.

I had built a small cage for my last moth, from a section of coarse wire screen tacked to two wooden disks. That evening I took the cylindrical pen and placed it on a table in the garden. The moon silvered the staked tomatoes and pressed bold shadows of them into the russet brown garage wall. I sat and waited and watched, hoping that the newly emerged insect would attract a mate from the moonlit city sky. My *Golden Guide,* or some other trusty text, had hinted that such a thing would happen, that from as far as five miles away a mate would be called to join the female and together stoke the engines of life. As optimistic as I was, I suspected that the writers of my well-worn *Guides* had not Brooklyn (nor any city, for that matter) in mind when they wrote their evocative little essays.

I had fallen asleep on the chaise lounge in the backyard. My mother had placed a blanket on me and let me be with my moth. It was deeply quiet and still when I awoke; the moon was low and dim, but I could see in the pale of light that my companion was no longer alone. Through the wide gaps in the wire screen, the caged moth was locked in procreative embrace with a male she had lured out of the night sky. Her pheromones had conquered Brooklyn; a tiny bit of wildness had slipped into my presence, into this one small garden in the city. Led by its frondlike antennae, the visitor had glided over the tarred flat roofs of Flatlands, over the idling buses and parked cars, to be with my moth. It may have come from as far away as the Rockaways or Prospect Park, though I suspected it was just another lost child from Exit Eleven.

In the morning I set the last moth free. She would wander toward the ailanthus, I imagined, searching from a prospect high above the streets after the sun had gone down behind the row houses of south Brooklyn. Or maybe it was that the moth was simply heading home, guided by some unseen force to bed down her offspring in the rough grove by the acrid rush of the Belt Parkway.

Thomas J. Campanella *is an urbanist and cultural critic who has written about landscapes, cities, and the built environment around the world. He is currently completing a history of the American elm in New England, entitled* Republic of Shade.

Lunch with a Gull

VIRGINIA KROLL

I had lunch with a gull today.
It waddled up as if to say,
"Can you spare a bit of bread?"
It blinked its eyes and cocked its head.

We shared my sandwich and my pie.
We gladly gulped, the gull and I.
And afterward, we both took flight
With tummies heavy and hearts light.

Virginia Kroll *is the author of more than thirty books and sixteen hundred magazine articles for children. She lives in New York.*

Stranded

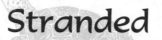

HENRY BESTON

In 1926, Henry Beston spent a year living in a small house he designed and built (and dubbed "the Fo'castle") on Coast Guard Beach in Eastham, Massachusetts. With only the crew of the nearby Nauset light-house for human company, Beston devoted most of his attention to the sea, the shore, and its many wild inhabitants. The following excerpt is taken from his account of that year, called The Outermost House.

On the next morning—it was sunny then, but still freezing cold—I chanced to go out for a moment to look at the marsh. About a mile and a half away, in one of the open channels, was a dark something which looked like a large, unfamiliar bird. A stray goose, perhaps? Taking my glass, I found the dark object to be the head of a deer swimming down the channel, and, even as I looked, there came to my ears the distant barking of dogs. A pair of marauding curs, out hunting on their own, had found a deer somewhere and driven the creature down the dunes and into the icy creeks. Down the channel it swam, and presently turned aside and climbed out on the marsh island just behind the Fo'castle. The animal was a young doe. I thought then, and I still believe, that this doe and the unseen creature whose delicate hoofprints I often found near the Fo'castle were one and the same. It lived, I believe, in the pines on the northern shore of the marsh and came down to the dunes at earliest dawn. But to return to its adventures: All afternoon I watched it standing on the island far out in the marsh, the tall, dead sea grass rising about its russet body; when night came, it was still there, a tiny spot of forlorn mammalian life in that frozen scene. Was it too terrified to return? That night a tide of unusual height was due which would submerge the islands under at least two feet of water and floating ice. Would the doe swim ashore under cover of darkness? I went out at midnight into my solitary world and saw the ice-covered marsh gleaming palely under a sky of brilliant stars, but could see nothing of the island of the doe save a ghostliness of salt ice along the nearer rim.

The first thing I did, on waking the next morning, was to search the island with my glass. The doe was still there.

I have often paused to wonder how that delicate and lovely creature endured so cruel a night, how she survived the slow rise of the icy tide about her poor legs, and the northwest gale that blustered about her all night long in that starlit loneliness of crunchy marsh mud and the murmur of the tides. The morning lengthened, the sun rose higher on the marsh, and presently the tide began to rise again. I watched it rising toward the refugee, and wondered if she could survive a second immersion. Just a little before noon, perhaps as the water was flooding round her feet, she came down to the edge of her island, and plunged into the channel. The creek was full of ice mush and of ice floes moving at a good speed; the doe was weak, the ice cakes bore down upon her, striking her heavily; she seemed confused, hesitated, swam here, swam there, stood still, and was struck cruelly by a floe which seemed to pass over her, yet on she swam, bewildered, but resolute for life. I had almost given up hope for her, when rescue came unexpectedly. My friend Bill Eldredge, it appeared, while on watch in the station tower the day before had chanced to see the beginning of the story, and on the second morning had noticed the doe still standing in the marshes. All the Nauset crew had taken an interest. Catching sight of the poor creature fighting for life in the drift, three of the men put off in a skiff, poled the ice away with their oars, and shepherded the doe ashore. "When she reached dry land, she couldn't rise, she was so weak, and fell down again and again. But finally she stood up and stayed up, and walked off into the pines."

⌒⌒

Henry Beston *was born in Quincy, Massachusetts, in 1888. He attended Harvard College, served as a French volunteer in World War I, and lived on a farm in Maine for the last forty years of his life.*

Pickering Beach

Marybeth Rua-Larsen

Every spring, migrating shorebirds land on beaches along the Delaware
Bay just as thousands of horseshoe crabs are coming ashore to lay their
eggs. The birds feast on the eggs to fuel their long flights to the Arctic.
Sometimes the birds will feed on an overturned adult horseshoe crab,
too, but most of the horseshoes successfully lay their eggs and return to
the water unharmed.

When May invades Delaware's shore, hundreds
of horseshoe crabs litter this battlefield,
some empty helmets cradled by salty sand,
others with exposed belly wounds, too weary
to roll themselves over and crawl

to the sea. Thousands of red knots, rusty
breasts at attention, slop the crab's
jellied eggs while ruddy turnstones, allies
who scour nest sites, dig for rations.
Belligerent laughing gulls join the next wave

of attacks, and though a few crabs arm wrestle air
for leverage, they are unequipped for combat.
We turn over one crab, watch it circle

sand, tug itself toward the sea.
There are too many to rescue.

Knots and turnstones, bellies
bursting, mobilize long camouflaged wings
toward the Arctic. Horseshoe crabs
crackle in the sun.

Marybeth Rua-Larsen *teaches English at the Lancaster Campus of Harrisburg Area Community College in Pennsylvania. She credits her growth as a poet to her participation in the Feminist Women's Writing Workshop in Geneva, New York.*

Roostwatch

Marie Winn

One day, Marie Winn discovered the Central Park "Bird Register"—a notebook filled with handwritten comments about wildlife sightings throughout New York City's biggest park. Curious about these creatures and their human admirers, she introduced herself to Central Park's bird-watching community. Soon she was one of the "Regulars" who visited the park nearly every day. The following excerpt describes one of the group's many close-up encounters with their wild neighbors.

The stars were bright in the city sky as I left my house for Central Park. Yet none of the winter constellations were out, though it was February, not the brilliant-eyed Charioteer nor Orion the Hunter with his three-studded belt. And where was Sirius the Dog Star, brightest of all heavenly objects in the winter sky? The earth had spent the long night rotating on its axis and now, as I set off for Central Park at the unearthly hour of 5:00 a.m., the stars of a different season had risen in the winter sky: the giant star Arcturus as bright as a little moon overhead, and Altair, Vega, and Deneb, the great triangle of the summer sky, shining almost as radiantly as on an evening in July.

Not only the stars seem out of season when one is out in the city before dawn. There is a languid, almost tropical feel to the place at that hour, like Bogart's Key Largo before the hurricane strikes. You know that the storm is coming, that in an hour or two those hushed empty streets will be full of cars and trucks and taxis and buses with maddened drivers blasting their horns, trading insults about each other's mothers and fathers; you know that those empty sidewalks will be full of people bumping into each other while failing to apologize. All hell is about to break loose, but at five in the morning the storm seems far away.

The streets were almost deserted as I walked toward my destination that morning: only a newspaper delivery man removing bundles from a car trunk, a doorman smoking outside an apartment house, and an old man sweeping in front of an all-night grocery to give a hint of the workaday world. Here and there another passerby, someone coming home from somewhere—a night of illicit love, an all-night vigil at a deathbed; someone on the way to somewhere—a train to catch, an early shift as short-order cook at a Greek coffee shop. I caught myself staring at one of those dawn walkers, wondering why he was out at such an hour, what his story was. I laughed to think what he'd say if he knew mine.

It began a few weeks earlier, on a freezing Sunday afternoon in January as Norma Collin was making her daily rounds of the Ramble. That's when she heard a loud tattoo coming from a nearby tree.

"I know that sound," she thought cheerfully, and within minutes she had found her bird: a downy woodpecker, the smaller and more common of Central Park's two resident woodpeckers (the red-bellied is the other, though a few hairy woodpeckers and flickers sometimes overwinter). The little bird was in a half-dead black cherry tree, drilling away at a short, stubby snag about ten feet from the ground.

The woodpecker was familiar, but its action was puzzling. It was not just drumming as woodpeckers often do, sending a message of love or war to another of its kind, nor was it extracting larvae or grubs from crevices in the bark. It was clearly making a hole.

Clinging to the reddish-brown, scaly bark with feet especially adapted for feeding on vertical surfaces—two toes pointing forward and two back—zygodactyl is the scientific term—while bracing itself with its stiffened, spinelike tail feathers, the woodpecker attacked the branch with a steady, rapid back-and-forth motion. It looked for all the world like a living black-and-white jackhammer. The cavity was already quite deep, and every so often the bird would briefly disappear within for a second or two, and then reappear to toss out billful after billful of sawdust, with a jaunty flick of its head at each toss.

What in the world is this bird up to? Norma wondered. It wasn't odd to see a woodpecker making a hole exactly the way this one was doing. But that was to be expected at the start of the breeding season, in April or May. Why was this bird excavating a hole in January? As she watched, she noted that the woodpecker was definitely a *he:* on the back of his head was a bright red patch, the only feature that distinguishes male downies from females. Well, maybe he's practicing for spring, she finally decided, and left it at that.

Norma had been observing the woodpecker for a good fifteen minutes and her fingers and toes were numb. She was looking forward to getting home and settling down with a nice cup of linden tea—she had picked the blossoms herself from a tree on Pilgrim Hill the previous spring. First, however, a quick stop at the Boathouse to write down her day's sightings in the Bird Register. During the excitement of the migration seasons a bird like a downy woodpecker is hardly even mentioned in the long lists of visitors that fill the Register's pages. But January is a month when the park's residents—woodpeckers, sparrows, blue jays, crows, titmice, and cardinals—take center stage. The downy woodpecker drilling a hole near lamppost 7631 was by far the most important sighting Norma had to report that day.

The next day Charles Kennedy, voracious reader of bird books and accumulator of arcane information about almost any natural history subject, came up with a possible explanation. He happened to have, among his huge number of bird books, one called *Woodpeckers of Eastern North America* written by an engaging amateur naturalist named Lawrence Kilham. That's where Charles got the idea that Norma's woodpecker must have been making a winter roost hole.

Roost holes, according to Kilham, offer a woodpecker insulation against cold and shelter from the wind. When the outside temperature is 17 degrees Fahrenheit it can be 11 degrees higher inside a roost hole, even higher if the woodpecker's body fits the cavity exactly. "The amount of energy . . . conserved may make the difference between survival and death during periods of extreme weather during winter," Kilham wrote.

A woodpecker's winter roost hole has advantages for birdwatchers as well: it offers anyone wishing to study the Picidae family an opportunity to locate its members dependably. "Just wait until an hour after sunrise, and the chances of locating a Downy or a Hairy in a reasonable time can be slim. . . . But in taking the trouble to be by a roost hole at dawn, I have had some of the best of birdwatching," wrote Kilham.

Yes! thought Charles, lover of eccentric projects. If Norma's discovery turns out to be a roost hole, we've got some serious woodpecker-studying to do.

It was almost 5:30 a.m. on that February morning by the time I arrived at Naturalists Gate, the park entrance at West 77th Street. The other five birdwatchers were already waiting and we entered the park at once. Though it was almost an hour before sunrise, day was beginning to break, and we didn't want to be late. Crossing the Upper Lobe at Bank Rock Bridge, we took a short path going south, and then east, taking us under the Rustic Arch with its buttresses of natural stone. Then we were in the woods, in the wilds of the Ramble.

A few moments later we arrived at the scraggly cherry tree. There we put down our knapsacks, took out our thermoses of coffee, and settled in for a wait. Roostwatch had officially begun.

The woods were silent and the roost hole was barely visible in the semi-darkness. Good. We'd arrived in time—every bird in the park was still asleep. Now we would keep a watch to see if a downy woodpecker was roosting within.

We waited and watched the day grow brighter. Around 6:00 a.m. we heard the first bird sounds—blue jays screaming in the distance. The roost hole was silent. Sunrise arrived at 6:24 a.m.—no sign of life at the cherry tree snag.

In truth, few of us had faith that there was a bird inside that neat hole, not even Charles, who is a dyed-in-the-wool optimist. I wasn't convinced that there even *was* such a thing as a roost hole, in spite of Kilham. After all, there had been downy woodpeckers in Central Park for as long as anyone could remember. Wouldn't someone have seen a roost hole by this time—Tom Fiore, for instance? And yet we must have had more than a little room for hope. Why else would we have been willing to spend all that time standing and waiting, our toes and fingertips freezing and puffs of smoke coming out of our mouths with every breath as the temperature hovered around 20 degrees?

Our little band waited on. If you get up at 4:15 in the morning you don't give up just like that. At 6:40 a.m. Charles said rather quietly: "Well, look who's there." The rest of us were deep in conversation. We looked up and saw a soft, fuzzy head filling up the roost hole entrance. The bird was decidedly morning-sleepy.

First the woodpecker stared straight ahead without moving, as if in a trance. After a minute or two he began to look up and down and up and down, more alert. Finally he seemed to fix his gaze directly at us. "What? You guys?" I imagined him thinking. "I have to put up with the sight of you and your binoculars all day long in the park. Now you're here when I get up in the morning too!"

He flew out—whoosh! It happened so fast we couldn't entirely believe what we'd seen. Was it a group delusion? No, everyone finally agreed, we had really seen a bird zip out of the hole. Charles looked at his watch. It was exactly 6:42 a.m.

The woodpecker alighted on a nearby dead branch and commenced a loud tattoo, a long unbroken drumroll. There were ten bursts of drumming, which Charles diligently timed. Each lasted about six seconds. Experts can identify a woodpecker by its drum pattern. The hairy woodpecker's roll is shorter and louder than a downy's, with a greater interval between each stroke. The yellow-bellied sapsucker starts with a short roll and ends with five or six distinct taps. Sapsuckers, by the way, appear in Central Park only during migration. Their grid-like rows of neat holes (for collecting sap) may be seen on the trunks of many park trees.

An active roost hole! Usually the excitement of birdwatching is based on unpredictability, for unpredictability breeds hope. As you stroll around with binoculars at the ready, you never know when something new and exciting, perhaps something rare or beautiful might show up. That's hope.

Now the pleasure was in the very predictability of the bird. Predictability breeds hope too, we discovered, the same sort of hope that each year's cycle of seasons inspires. It is somehow deeply fulfilling and hopeful to know that the phoebe will arrive in Central Park on March 13th every year, give or take a few days. Or that if you stand at a certain place at a certain time a particular bird will show up and perform a predictable action—like zipping in or out of a hole in a tree.

A small group of Regulars began to monitor the roost hole with regularity, both at dawn and at sunset when the bird flew in for the night. The essence of Roostwatch was timekeeping, making note of the bird's precise moment of entry and exit. This produced a fact, a concrete piece of data. Charles Kennedy, the major instigator of the project, loved facts. Above all he loved to time. He timed how long cardinals bathed in his brook under Balcony Bridge. He timed owl fly-outs, and mockingbird songs. He also loved to measure—the sticks in the ill-fated hawk nest, for example.

On March 16th, with an orange-red full moon setting in the west just before sunrise, woodpecker wake-up was at 6:01 a.m. On the evening of March 27th and the following morning, March 28th, the roostwatchers managed to document a woodpecker's full night of sleep. They watched the bird scoot in at 5:55 p.m. They returned the next morning—it hardly seemed worth going home, somebody quipped—and observed downy reveille: it was 5:46 a.m., one minute before sunrise. The bird had been in the roost hole for eleven hours and fifty-one minutes, Charles Kennedy announced.

On April 9th, a cold spring day, a new development at the early morning Roostwatch warmed the watchers' hearts if not their toes. A moment or two after the woodpecker emerged from his roost hole at 6:38 a.m. (the bird was not sleeping in that morning—Daylight Savings Time had commenced), another downy woodpecker materialized as if out of nowhere. Double vision. Only one bird had flown out of the hole, and now there were two woodpeckers climbing on a nearby branch. They looked identical but for one detail: no red patch on the newcomer's head. It was a female. "Yahoo!" exclaimed Charles, the eternal romantic.

After that, the female showed up regularly at Roostwatch, morning and evening. Before bedtime the two birds were often seen feeding in the vicinity, busily working the bark of nearby trunks and branches for whatever it is that woodpeckers extract from crevices—seeds, bugs, larvae. Then, as night began to fall the female would fly off somewhere—to her own roost hole, no doubt—and he would zip into his. In the morning the female was often on a nearby tree, waiting for her sweetheart to rise and shine.

April 28th was a warm, balmy spring day. Six roostwatchers had assembled for the evening roostwatch by 6:30 p.m. This time they did not reminisce about past vigils at the roost hole, those cold February and March waits. Tonight the talk was about the present, about the day's birds.

Spring migration was in full swing and the day had been a

glorious one: scarlet tanagers, rose-breasted grosbeaks, an orchard oriole, and a yellow-billed cuckoo had been sighted in the Ramble. Tom Fiore had heard a singing indigo bunting at 6:20 a.m. that very morning. The electric blue bird had been near the Belvedere Castle at the same place indigo buntings show up every year—near a patch of Kentucky bluegrass favored by that species. Tom had also sighted a least flycatcher making his "che-bek che-bek" call, the only way you can distinguish this bird from four other small, virtually identical flycatchers. Nineteen species of warblers had been seen so far that spring, and Tom had seen sixteen that very day.

Little leaves were already out on the scraggly cherry; soon they would obscure the roost hole. Somebody picked one and crushed it to demonstrate its bitter smell—cyanide! That evening the woodpecker took the longest time arriving.

He didn't show up until 7:30 p.m., later than ever before. The female arrived almost immediately after. The pair first flew from branch to branch of a nearby tree, making little chip sounds and feeding desultorily. At about 7:35 the female suddenly disappeared, and at 7:43—whoop!—into the hole whizzed the male. This time there was a round of applause from the assembled gang.

Night had fallen and the Regulars walked out of the park together. No matter how many times it had happened before, it still seemed incredible, incredible to have penetrated the secret life of a creature so *other*.

On the morning of May 3rd four watchers waited from 5:30 a.m. to 7:00 a.m. We waited and waited until the day was bright and clear, as clear as our knowledge that no bird was going to come out of the hole. Quite a few other birds showed up in the vicinity that morning—a great crested flycatcher and a wood thrush singing its enchanting song. Also seven species of warblers. Everything was lush and green. The knotweed was high as an elephant's eye. But the roost hole was empty.

The downy woodpecker and his mate failed to show up at the roost hole that evening, and the next. Gone. Obviously they had other business to take care of. This had been a winter roost hole, after all, and the winter was over.

Marie Winn *has published thirteen books and writes a column on nature and bird-watching for the* Wall Street Journal. *She spends part of every day in Central Park.*

Today

NADYA AISENBERG

Sailing home from the Barred Islands today
we saw two dolphins in tandem flash
That was enough for today
And tomorrow

Nadya Aisenberg *was an adjunct associate professor of women's studies at Brandeis University in Boston, Massachusetts, and the author of four nonfiction books.*

A White Heron

SARAH ORNE JEWETT

Written in the late 1800s, this story describes the widespread practice of collecting animal specimens for study or museum display. While such collecting has helped advance our understanding of biology and taxonomy, the practice is now highly regulated to protect wild species, especially rare ones. The white heron described in this story is probably a snowy egret, a bird that was nearly hunted to extinction by the end of the nineteenth century but that is now quite common throughout its range.

One

The woods were already filled with shadows one June evening, just before eight o'clock, though a bright sunset still glimmered faintly among the trunks of the trees. A little girl was driving home her cow, a plodding, dilatory, provoking creature in her behavior, but a valued companion for all that. They were going away from the western light, and striking deep into the dark woods, but their feet were familiar with the path, and it was no matter whether their eyes could see it or not.

There was hardly a night the summer through when the old cow could be found waiting at the pasture bars; on the contrary, it was her greatest pleasure to hide herself away among the high huckleberry bushes, and though she wore a loud bell she had made the discovery that if one stood perfectly still it would not ring. So Sylvia had to hunt for her until she found her, and call Co'! Co'! with never an answering Moo, until her childish patience was quite spent. If the creature had not given good milk and plenty of it, the case would have seemed very different to her owners. Besides, Sylvia had all the time there was, and very little use to make of it. Sometimes in pleasant weather it was a consolation to look upon the cow's pranks as an intelligent attempt to play hide and seek, and as the child had no playmates she lent herself to this amusement with a good deal of zest. Though this chase had been so long that the wary animal herself had given an unusual signal of her whereabouts, Sylvia had only laughed when she came upon Mistress Moolly at the swamp-side, and urged her affectionately homeward with a twig of birch leaves. The old cow was not inclined to wander farther, she even turned in the right direction for once as they left the pasture, and stepped along the road at a good pace. She was quite ready to be milked now, and seldom stopped to browse. Sylvia wondered what her grandmother would say because they were so late. It was a great while since she had left home at half past five o'clock, but everybody knew the difficulty of making this errand a short one. Mrs. Tilley had chased the hornéd torment too many summer evenings herself to blame any one else for lingering, and was only thankful as she waited that she had Sylvia, nowadays, to give such valuable assistance. The good woman suspected that Sylvia loitered occasionally on her own account; there never was such a child for straying about out-of-doors since the world was made! Everybody said that it was a good change for a little maid who had tried to grow for eight years in a crowded manufacturing town, but, as for Sylvia her-self, it seemed as if she never had been alive at all before she came to live at the farm. She thought often with wistful com-passion of a wretched dry geranium that belonged to a town neighbor.

"'Afraid of folks,'" old Mrs. Tilley said to herself, with a smile, after she had made the unlikely choice of Sylvia from her daughter's houseful of children, and was returning to the farm. "'Afraid of folks,' they said! I guess she won't be troubled no great with 'em up to the old place!" When they reached the door of the lonely house and stopped to unlock it, and the cat came to purr loudly, and rub against them, a deserted pussy, indeed, but fat with young robins, Sylvia whispered that this was a beautiful place to live in, and she never should wish to go home.

The companions followed the shady woodroad, the cow tak-ing slow steps, and the child very fast ones. The cow stopped long at the brook to drink, as if the pasture were not half a swamp, and Sylvia stood still and waited, letting her bare feet cool themselves in the shoal water, while the great twilight moths struck softly against her. She waded on through the brook as the cow moved away, and listened to the thrushes with a heart that beat fast with pleasure. There was a stirring in the great boughs overhead. They were full of little birds and beasts that seemed to be wide-awake, and going about their world, or else saying goodnight to each other in sleep twitters. Sylvia herself felt sleepy as she walked along. However, it was not much farther to the house, and the air was soft and sweet. She was not often in the woods so late as this, and it made her feel as if she were a part of the gray shadows and the moving leaves. She was just thinking how long it seemed since she first came to the farm a year ago, and wondering if everything went on in the noisy town just the same as when she was there; the thought of the great red-faced boy who used to chase and frighten her made her hurry along the path to escape from the shadow of the trees.

Suddenly this little woods-girl is horror-stricken to hear a clear whistle not very far away. Not a bird's whistle, which would have a sort of friendliness, but a boy's whistle, determined, and somewhat aggressive. Sylvia left the cow to whatever sad fate might await her, and stepped discreetly aside into the bushes, but she was just too late. The enemy had discovered her, and called out in a very cheerful and persuasive tone, "Halloa, little girl, how far is it to the road?" and trembling Sylvia answered almost inaudibly, "A good ways."

She did not dare to look boldly at the tall young man, who carried a gun over his shoulder, but she came out of her bush and again followed the cow, while he walked alongside.

"I have been hunting for some birds," the stranger said kindly, "and I have lost my way, and need a friend very much. Don't be afraid," he added gallantly. "Speak up and tell me what your name is, and whether you think I can spend the night at your house, and go out gunning early in the morning."

Sylvia was more alarmed than before. Would not her grandmother consider her much to blame? But who could have foreseen such an accident as this? It did not appear to be her fault, and she hung her head as if the stem of it were broken, but managed to answer "Sylvy," with much effort when her companion again asked her name.

Mrs. Tilley was standing in the doorway when the trio came into view. The cow gave a loud moo by way of explanation.

"Yes, you'd better speak up for yourself, you old trial! Where'd she tuck herself away this time, Sylvy?" Sylvia kept an awed silence; she knew by instinct that her grandmother did not comprehend the gravity of the situation. She must be mistaking the stranger for one of the farmer-lads of the region.

The young man stood his gun beside the door, and dropped a heavy game-bag beside it; then he bade Mrs. Tilley good-evening, and repeated his wayfarer's story, and asked if he could have a night's lodging.

"Put me anywhere you like," he said. "I must be off early in the morning, before day; but I am very hungry, indeed. You can give me some milk at any rate, that's plain."

"Dear sakes, yes," responded the hostess, whose long slumbering hospitality seemed to be easily awakened. "You might fare better if you went out on the main road a mile or so, but you're welcome to what we've got. I'll milk right off, and you make yourself at home. You can sleep on husks or feathers," she proffered graciously. "I raised them all myself. There's good pasturing for geese just below here towards the ma'sh. Now step round and set a plate for the gentleman, Sylvy!" And Sylvia promptly stepped. She was glad to have something to do, and she was hungry herself.

It was a surprise to find so clean and comfortable a little dwelling in this New England wilderness. The young man had known the horrors of its most primitive housekeeping, and the dreary squalor of that level of society which does not rebel at the companionship of hens. This was the best thrift of an old-fashioned farmstead, though on such a small scale that it seemed like a hermitage. He listened eagerly to the old woman's quaint talk, he watched Sylvia's pale face and shining gray eyes with ever growing enthusiasm, and insisted that this was the best supper he had eaten for a month; then, afterward, the new-made friends sat down in the doorway together while the moon came up.

Soon it would be berry-time, and Sylvia was a great help at picking. The cow was a good milker, though a plaguy thing to keep track of, the hostess gossiped frankly, adding presently that she had buried four children, so that Sylvia's mother, and a son (who might be dead) in California were all the children she had left. "Dan, my boy, was a great hand to go gunning," she explained sadly. "I never wanted for pa'tridges or gray squer'ls while he was to home. He's been a great wand'rer, I expect, and he's no hand to write letters. There, I don't blame him, I'd ha' seen the world myself if it had been so I could.

"Sylvia takes after him," the grandmother continued affectionately, after a minute's pause. "There ain't a foot o' ground she don't know her way ov⌣, and the wild creatur's counts her one o' themselves. Squer'ls she'll tame to come an' feed right out o' her hands, and all sorts o' birds. Last winter she got the jay-birds to bangeing here, and I believe she'd 'a' scanted herself of her own meals to have plenty to throw out amongst 'em, if I hadn't kep' watch. Anything but crows, I tell her, I'm willin' to help support,—though Dan he went an' tamed one o' them that did seem to have reason same as folks. It was round here a good spell after he went away. Dan an' his father they didn't hitch,—but he never held up his head ag'in after Dan had dared him an' gone off."

The guest did not notice this hint of family sorrows in his eager interest in something else.

"So Sylvy knows all about birds, does she?" he exclaimed, as he looked round at the little girl who sat, very demure but increasingly sleepy, in the moonlight. "I am making a collection of birds myself. I have been at it ever since I was a boy." (Mrs. Tilley smiled.) "There are two or three very rare ones I have been hunting for these five years. I mean to get them on my own ground if they can be found."

"Do you cage 'em up?" asked Mrs. Tilley doubtfully, in response to this enthusiastic announcement.

"Oh, no, they're stuffed and preserved, dozens and dozens of them," said the ornithologist, "and I have shot or snared every one myself. I caught a glimpse of a white heron three miles from here on Saturday, and I have followed it in this direction. They have never been found in this district at all. The little white heron, it is," and he turned again to look at Sylvia with hope of discovering that the rare bird was one of her acquaintances.

But Sylvia was watching a hop-toad in the narrow footpath.

"You would know the heron if you saw it," the stranger continued eagerly. "A queer tall white bird with soft feathers and long thin legs. And it would have a nest perhaps in the top of a high tree, made of sticks, something like a hawk's nest."

Sylvia's heart gave a wild beat; she knew that strange white bird, and had once stolen softly near where it stood in some bright green swamp grass, away over at the other side of the woods. There was an open place where the sunshine always seemed strangely yellow and hot, where tall, nodding rushes grew, and her grandmother had warned her that she might sink in the soft black mud underneath and never be heard of more. Not far beyond were the salt marshes and beyond those was the sea, the sea which Sylvia wondered and dreamed about, but never had looked upon, though its great voice could often be heard above the noise of the woods on stormy nights.

"I can't think of anything I should like so much as to find that heron's nest," the handsome stranger was saying. "I would give ten dollars to anybody who could show it to me," he added desperately, "and I mean to spend my whole vacation hunting for it if need be. Perhaps it was only migrating, or had been chased out of its own region by some bird of prey."

Mrs. Tilley gave amazed attention to all this, but Sylvia still watched the toad, not divining, as she might have done at some calmer time, that the creature wished to get to its hole under the doorstep, and was much hindered by the unusual spectators at that hour of the evening. No amount of thought, that night, could decide how many wished-for treasures the ten dollars, so lightly spoken of, would buy.

The next day the young sportsman hovered about the woods, and Sylvia kept him company, having lost her first fear of the friendly lad, who proved to be most kind and sympathetic. He told her many things about the birds and what they knew and where they lived and what they did with themselves. And he gave her a jack-knife, which she thought as great a treasure as if she were a desert-islander. All day long he did not once make her troubled or afraid except when he brought down some unsuspecting singing creature from its bough. Sylvia would have liked him vastly better without his gun; she could not understand why he killed the very birds he seemed to like so much. But as the day waned, Sylvia still watched the young man with loving admiration. She had never seen anybody so charming and delightful; the woman's heart, asleep in the child, was vaguely thrilled by a dream of love. Some premonition of that great power stirred and swayed these young foresters who traversed the solemn woodlands with soft-footed silent care. They stopped to listen to a bird's song; they pressed forward again eagerly, parting the branches,—speaking to each other rarely and in whispers; the young man going first and Sylvia following, fascinated, a few steps behind, with her gray eyes dark with excitement.

She grieved because the longed-for white heron was elusive, but she did not lead the guest, she only followed, and there was no such thing as speaking first. The sound of her own unquestioned voice would have terrified her,—it was hard enough to answer yes or no when there was need of that. At last evening began to fall, and they drove the cow home together, and Sylvia smiled with pleasure when they came to the place where she heard the whistle and was afraid only the night before.

Two

Half a mile from home, at the farther edge of the woods, where the land was highest, a great pine-tree stood, the last of its generation. Whether it was left for a boundary mark, or for what reason, no one could say; the woodchoppers who had felled its mates were dead and gone long ago, and a whole forest of sturdy trees, pines and oaks and maples, had grown again. But the stately head of this old pine towered above them all and made a landmark for sea and shore miles and miles away. Sylvia knew it well. She had always believed that whoever climbed to the top of it could see the ocean; and the little girl had often laid her hand on the great rough trunk and looked up wistfully at those dark boughs that the wind always stirred, no matter how hot and still the air might be below. Now she thought of the tree with a new excitement, for why, if one climbed it at break of day, could not one see all the world, and easily discover whence the white heron flew, and mark the place, and find the hidden nest?

What a spirit of adventure, what wild ambition! What fancied triumph and delight and glory for the later morning when she could make known the secret! It was almost too real and too great for the childish heart to bear.

All night the door of the little house stood open, and the whippoorwills came and sang upon the very step. The young sportsman and his old hostess were sound asleep, but Sylvia's great design kept her broad awake and watching. She forgot to think of sleep. The short summer night seemed as long as the winter darkness, and at last when the whippoorwills ceased, and she was afraid the morning would after all come too soon, she stole out of the house and followed the pasture path through the woods, hastening toward the open ground beyond, listening with a sense of comfort and companionship to the drowsy twitter of a half-awakened bird, whose perch she had jarred in passing. Alas, if the great wave of human interest which flooded for the first time this dull little life should sweep away the satisfactions of an existence heart to heart with nature and the dumb life of the forest!

There was the huge tree asleep yet in the paling moonlight, and small and hopeful Sylvia began with utmost bravery to mount to the top of it, with tingling, eager blood coursing the channels of her whole frame, with her bare feet and fingers, that pinched and held like bird's claws to the monstrous ladder reaching up, up, almost to the sky itself. First she must mount the white oak tree that grew alongside, where she was almost lost among the dark branches and the green leaves heavy and wet with dew; a bird fluttered off its nest, and a red squirrel ran to and fro and scolded pettishly at the harmless housebreaker. Sylvia felt her way easily. She had often climbed there, and knew that higher still one of the oak's upper branches chafed against the pine trunk, just where its lower boughs were set close together. There, when she made the dangerous pass from one tree to the other, the great enterprise would really begin.

She crept out along the swaying oak limb at last, and took the daring step across into the old pine-tree. The way was harder than she thought; she must reach far and hold fast, the sharp dry twigs caught and held her and scratched her like angry talons, the pitch made her thin little fingers clumsy and stiff as she went round and round the tree's great stem, higher and higher upward. The sparrows and robins in the woods below were beginning to wake and twitter to the dawn, yet it seemed much lighter there aloft in the pine-tree, and the child knew that she must hurry if her project were to be of any use.

The tree seemed to lengthen itself out as she went up, and to reach farther and farther upward. It was like a great mainmast to the voyaging earth; it must truly have been amazed that morning through all its ponderous frame as it felt this determined spark of human spirit creeping and climbing from higher branch to branch. Who knows how steadily the least twigs held themselves to advantage this light, weak creature on her way! The old pine must have loved his new dependent. More than all the hawks, and bats, and moths, and even the sweet-voiced thrushes, was the brave, beating heart of the solitary gray-eyed child. And the tree stood still and held away the winds that June morning while the dawn grew bright in the east.

Sylvia's face was like a pale star, if one had seen it from the ground, when the last thorny bough was past, and she stood trembling and tired but wholly triumphant, high in the tree-top. Yes, there was the sea with the dawning sun making a golden dazzle over it, and toward that glorious east flew two hawks with slow-moving pinions. How low they looked in the air from that height when before one had only seen them far up, and dark against the blue sky. Their gray feathers were as soft as moths; they seemed only a little way from the tree, and Sylvia felt as if she too could go flying away among the clouds. Westward, the woodlands and farms reached miles and miles into the distance; here and there were church steeples, and white villages; truly it was a vast and awesome world.

The birds sang louder and louder. At last the sun came up bewilderingly bright. Sylvia could see the white sails of ships out at sea, and the clouds that were purple and rose-colored and yellow at first began to fade away. Where was the white heron's nest in the sea of green branches, and was this wonderful sight and pageant of the world the only reward for having climbed to such a giddy height? Now look down again, Sylvia, where the green marsh is set among the shining birches and dark hemlocks; there where you saw the white heron once you will see him again; look, look! a white spot of him like a single floating feather comes up from the dead hemlock and grows larger, and rises, and comes close at last, and goes by the land-mark pine with steady sweep of wing and outstretched slender neck and crested head. And wait! wait! do not move a foot or a finger, little girl, do not send an arrow of light and conscious-ness from your two eager eyes, for the heron has perched on a pine bough not far beyond yours, and cries back to his mate on the nest, and plumes his feathers for the new day!

The child gives a long sigh and a minute later when a com-pany of shouting cat-birds comes also to the tree, and vexed by their fluttering and lawlessness the solemn heron goes away. She knows his secret now, the wild, light, slender bird that floats and wavers, and goes back like an arrow presently to his home in the green world beneath. Then Sylvia, well satisfied, makes her perilous way down again, not daring to look far below the branch she stands on, ready to cry sometimes because her fingers ache and her lamed feet slip. Wondering over and over again what the stranger would say to her, and what he would think when she told him how to find his way straight to the heron's nest.

"Sylvy, Sylvy!" called the busy old grandmother again and again, but nobody answered, and the small husk bed was empty, and Sylvia had disappeared.

The guest waked from a dream, and remembering his day's pleasure hurried to dress himself that it might sooner begin. He was sure from the way the shy little girl looked once or twice yesterday that she had at least seen the white heron, and now she must really be persuaded to tell. Here she comes now, paler than ever, and her worn old frock is torn and tattered, and smeared with pine pitch. The grandmother and the sportsman stand in the door together and question her, and the splendid moment has come to speak of the dead hemlock-tree by the green marsh.

But Sylvia does not speak after all, though the old grandmother fretfully rebukes her, and the young man's kind appealing eyes are looking straight in her own. He can make them rich with money; he has promised it, and they are poor now. He is so well worth making happy, and he waits to hear the story she can tell.

No, she must keep silence! What is it that suddenly forbids

her and makes her dumb? Has she been nine years growing, and now, when the great world for the first time puts out a hand to her, must she thrust it aside for a bird's sake? The murmur of the pine's green branches is in her ears, she remembers how the white heron came flying through the golden air and how they watched the sea and the morning together, and Sylvia cannot speak; she cannot tell the heron's secret and give its life away.

Dear loyalty, that suffered a sharp pang as the guest went away disappointed later in the day, that could have served and followed him and loved him as a dog loves! Many a night Sylvia heard the echo of his whistle haunting the pasture path as she came home with the loitering cow. She forgot even her sorrow at the sharp report of his gun and the piteous sight of thrushes and sparrows dropping silent to the ground, their songs hushed and their pretty feathers stained and wet with blood. Were the birds better friends than their hunter might have been,—who can tell? Whatever treasures were lost to her, woodlands and summer-time, remember! Bring your gifts and graces and tell your secrets to this lonely country child!

Sarah Orne Jewett *was born in 1840 in South Berwick, Maine, where she lived for most of her life. She published fourteen collections of stories, several volumes of verse, and a number of children's books before her death in 1909.*

Appendixes

~⌣~

Ecology of the
North Atlantic Coast

What Is an Ecoregion?

The *Stories from Where We Live* series celebrates the literature of North America's diverse *ecoregions*. Ecoregions are large geographic areas that share similar climate, soils, and plant and animal communities. Thinking ecoregionally helps us understand how neighboring cities and states are connected and makes it easier for people to coordinate the use and protection of shared rivers, forests, watersheds, mountain ranges, and other natural areas. For our part, we believe that ecoregions provide an illuminating way to organize and compare place-based literature.

While many institutions have mapped the world's ecoregions, no existing delineation of ecoregions (or similar unit, such as *provinces* or *bioregions*) proved perfectly suited to a literary series. We created our own set of ecoregions based largely on existing scientific designations, with an added consideration for regional differences in human culture.

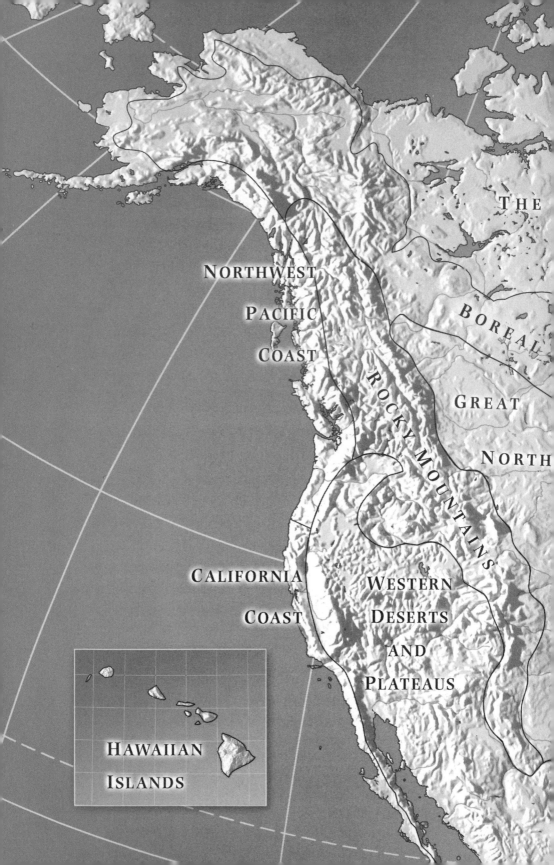

NORTHWEST

PACIFIC

COAST

THE

BOREAL

GREAT

NORTH

ROCKY MOUNTAINS

CALIFORNIA

COAST

WESTERN

DESERTS

AND

PLATEAUS

HAWAIIAN

ISLANDS

ARCTIC

FOREST

GREAT LAKES

NORTHEAST WOODLANDS

NORTH ATLANTIC COAST

AMERICAN

PRAIRIE

APPALACHIAN HIGHLANDS

SOUTH ATLANTIC COAST AND PIEDMONT

SOUTHERN HILL COUNTRY

GULF COAST

Defining the
North Atlantic Coast

Scientists have lots of ways of parceling out the North Atlantic Coast into manageable pieces. If you're a toe-dipping sort, you might appreciate knowing that water temperatures are noticeably colder north of Cape Cod, Massachusetts, than south of it. And water temperatures north of Cape Hatteras, North Carolina, are much colder than those to the south. The result is three distinct zones of water temperature. Some species of plants and animals are uniquely suited to just one or two of these zones; others can tolerate a range of water temperatures.

If you're a beachgoer, you may have observed another natural boundary along the North Atlantic Coast: the beaches from New York northward (not including Cape Cod and the islands) are generally rockier than the beaches to the south. That's because glaciers that advanced from the north more than twelve thousand years ago got no farther than New York City. Even though the glaciers are long gone, rocky shores are part of the enduring rubble they left behind.

Based solely on these two pieces of information, one might expect the southern boundary of our ecoregion to end with Cape Cod, New York, or Cape Hatteras. But that's where culture comes in. Delaware is generally more closely aligned with the culture of the northern states; after all, the Mason-Dixon line divides it from Maryland to the south and west. So, for that reason, our ecoregion extends south to the Delaware Bay.

Where that takes us is from the cold waters of Newfoundland, past the green hills of Prince Edward Island and the spruce-lined shores of New Brunswick and Nova Scotia, bumping along Maine's rocky coast, past New Hampshire's brief stretch of shoreline, around the arm of Cape Cod where oaks and pitch pine become more common, in and out of the inlets of Rhode Island, then winding west past the salt marshes and salt ponds of Connecticut, south to Manhattan and the barrier beaches of Long Island, along New Jersey's sandy shores, and slipping around the Delaware Bay to the eastern edge of the Delmarva Peninsula.

As large and diverse as this area is, its history, economy, and life-forms have all been shaped by the Atlantic Ocean is some way. Think fish, for example. Early Beothuk, Micmac, Wampanoag, and other native groups relied on the seas as a regular source of food. Sometime around 1000 A.D., Atlantic fisheries lured the first Viking ships from Iceland and Greenland over to the Newfoundland coast. Later, new methods of drying fish over fires prompted fishermen from Portugal, England, and other countries to set up seasonal camps on shore, leading the way for European exploration and settlement. Fish even played a key role in the life of the Pilgrims, who probably would not have survived their first winter if Chief Squanto hadn't taught them to catch shellfish, eels, and shad. Fish have given us place names –Alewife Brook, Cape Cod, and Halibut Beach, to name a few. And despite some serious declines in Atlantic fisheries, fish and shellfish continue to boost the economy of all the states and provinces that border the Atlantic, especially the Canadian Maritimes, Maine, Massachusetts, and Delaware.

In a similar way, proximity to the Atlantic has influenced everything from the region's architecture (weathered shingles and captain's walks) to its settlement patterns (note the bustling port towns) to its folklore (such as shipwreck stories and sea chanteys). For coastal dwellers, the ocean is not just part of the scenery: it's an active player in community life. It delivers welcome breezes and destructive storms. It creates sweet sandy beaches and then sweeps them back to sea. Most significant, it sets a tidal tempo by which many human communities –and all nearby ecological communities—organize their lives.

Habitats

Every wild creature that lives along the North Atlantic Coast is adapted in some way to conditions created by the sea. But not all species can tolerate the same conditions. The particular type of place where a creature finds the food, shelter, and space it needs to thrive is called its *habitat*. Not surprisingly, there are many different habitats along this northern coast—from small suburban backyards to the vast expanse of the open ocean. The following sections highlight some of the dominant wildlife habitats of this region and describe some of the plants and animals that live there.

Rocky Shores: Rocky shores dominate the North Atlantic Coast, especially from Canada to Maine. Over very long periods of time, the action of waves will weather these rocks into sandy beaches. For now, they offer dramatic views and a chance to witness the stratified strategy of rock-dwelling sea life.

If you visit the rocky shore during low tide, you may be able to pick out some of the different zones of life stretching from land to sea. High on the rocks is the *periwinkle zone,* an area submerged only during the very highest tides. Periwinkles are small sea snails. They may appear to be rooted in place, but in fact, they inch up and down the rock in response to the monthly high and low tides. Between the high-tide and low-tide mark lies the *barnacle zone,* where rock or acorn barnacles become most abundant. These are tough creatures who put up with pounding surf, predators, and winter ice. When you see them exposed to the air, their shells will usually be tightly closed. But when submerged, they open up like great hungry mouths and sweep in tiny plants and animals from the water. Below these barnacles and the low-tide line lies the *kelp zone*. Here long, strong kelp plants hold fast to the rocks against the constant push and pull of the waves. Around their base live a pack of other creatures, including mussels, spiny sea urchins, and oysters.

One other great place for viewing coastal creatures along rocky shores is in *tide pools*—shallow ponds left between the rocks at low tide. Size and location tend to determine who resides within a particular tide pool. You might see colorful starfish or sea anemones clinging to the rocks or catch a glimpse of rockpool shrimps darting through the water. (Examples: "New Hampshire Shore: Haiku"; "The Fog Maiden's Necklace.")

Sandy Beaches and Dunes: Visit a beach, and your first impression may be of a broad blank canvas: blue sky, blue waters, and tawny sand. Gulls and sunbathers may seem to be the only visible forms of life. But look again. Stand ankle deep, and you may be able to spot sand dollars, sea cucumbers, or other sun-sensitive organisms nestled in the sand beneath your feet. Then look at the surface of the water and you should be able to see bits of debris being tossed to the shore. That's the ocean's smorgasbord—bits of kelp and fish particles and tiny plants and animals—delivered wave after wave to the wet sand. Burrowed beneath your toes are worms that eat the sand and shellfish that suck in water to get to these nutritious morsels. If you can't find any of these burrowers, try looking for their holes. Or, look for shorebirds along the water's edge. Some skitter to and fro with the waves, dipping in the water for their meal. Others patrol the high-tide mark for the tasty jetsam left there.

Now head up the beach. Soon you'll reach the foredune—a hump of sand anchored by hardy beach grass. There's not much life here—the conditions are too windy and too dry. But just over the dune lie sheltered hollows where beach plum, beach heather, and bayberry take hold. Some of these hollows are even moist enough to harbor wild cranberries and other bog plants. Continue on and you may find miniature forests of cedar and pitch pine. Salty winds kill most of these trees' new growth, so they stay stunted. But they offer enough protection for rabbits, mice, songbirds, and more.

Come back at night to see more beach wildlife: ghost crabs creeping along the water's edge and shrimplike sandhoppers popping up from the sand. (Examples: "Of Beaches, Bays, and My Boyhood with the Colonel"; "Fledgling Summer"; "Fire Island Walking Song.")

Tidal Flats: Twice a day, the receding tide reveals sandy or muddy flats along many parts of the North Atlantic Coast. During the lowest tides of the month, the flats are at their most exposed. That's your best chance for seeing clams and other tidal inhabitants. But it won't be easy. All residents of the flats must endure the alternating extremes of flooding and complete exposure. Burrowing underground is usually their best way of avoiding sun and predators, such as black-bellied plovers, green crabs, and gulls. Some, like the razor clam, are such speedy diggers that you probably wouldn't even be able to catch one if you dug after it! (Examples: "The Magic of the Flats"; "Where the River Meets the Sea.")

Rivers and Lakes: Freshwater rivers and lakes along the North Atlantic are home to many creatures you won't find right at the seashore. Willows may grow along the shore, and trout and pickerel may meander

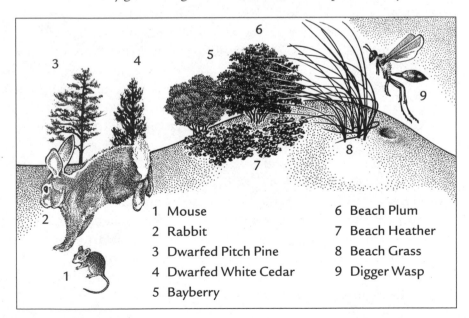

1 Mouse
2 Rabbit
3 Dwarfed Pitch Pine
4 Dwarfed White Cedar
5 Bayberry

6 Beach Plum
7 Beach Heather
8 Beach Grass
9 Digger Wasp

through the water. But you can still spot some ocean influences on many freshwater rivers in this region. For example, some coastal rivers rise and fall dramatically with the tides. And some boast saltwater fish—such as alewives and shad—that migrate between the ocean and inland water bodies at different points in their lives. Many fish also begin their lives in *estuaries,* which form the transition zone between these freshwater and saltwater environments. (Examples: "Never Go Home without a Fish"; "The Legend of the Mashpee Maiden.")

Salt Marshes: Just as people are attracted to a well-stocked kitchen, so are coastal organisms drawn to the nutrient-rich waters of the salt marsh. Here the tides deliver a regular supply of nutrients, which get trapped by salt-marsh grasses. As salt-marsh plants and animals grow, die, and decay, they add even more nutrients to the mud or sand below. If you visit a salt marsh, you're likely to spot some of the beneficiaries of this ample food supply. Snails cling to the cordgrass. Muskrats crawl along the ground, building domed lodges to protect themselves and their young. Herons and bitterns stand still among the reeds, while redwinged blackbirds, sparrows, and marsh wrens swoop overhead.

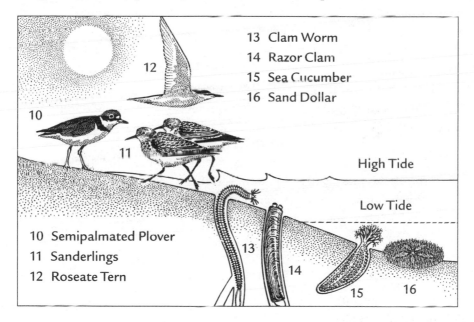

13 Clam Worm
14 Razor Clam
15 Sea Cucumber
16 Sand Dollar

12

10

11

High Tide

Low Tide

10 Semipalmated Plover
11 Sanderlings
12 Roseate Tern

13

14

15   16

You'll find salt marshes all along the North Atlantic Coast, where their presence is a blessing in all sorts of ways. Salt marshes provide a buffer against storm waves. They help purify coastal waters. They are twice as productive as most of our farms, producing food for hundreds of thousands of migrating waterfowl and countless other critters. And they're nursery grounds, where young ducklings, fiddler crabs, mussels, and many other creatures begin their lives. (Example: "The Great Marsh.")

Heathlands and Grasslands: Climb up the shore in certain parts of the North Atlantic Coast, and you may come across a heathland—an open meadow filled with low shrubs and wildflowers. The plants that live here are hardy: they can grow where the soil is poor and the air is laced with salt from the sea. If you visit the heathlands of Maine during the summer months, you may be in for a treat: wild blueberries! Heathlands are also the favored habitat of some rare bird species, including the short-eared owl.

Similar, but more rare, are the North Atlantic Coast's grasslands. Found in such places as Long Island, Nantucket, and Martha's Vineyard, these areas are like a pocket of prairie right next to the sea! In fact, some of these grasslands were once home to the heath hen, the East Coast's version of the prairie chicken. Today, ecologists are working to restore grasslands along the North Atlantic Coast. They won't be able to bring back the heath hen, but they can help other species that thrive in these grasslands, including the rare grasshopper sparrow. (Example: "Blueberries.")

Forests: While dwarfed forests of cedar, pitch pine, holly, and sassafras may be the norm near the dunes, tall trees are not absent from the North Atlantic Coast. In fact, impressive forests of spruce and fir still grow near the shore in parts of Canada and Maine. Farther south, oaks and hickories have sprouted on many of the lands that used to be farms. And pine-oak woodlands dominate the sandy, less fertile soils of this region. (Examples: "Otter Delight"; "A White Heron.")

Urban Parks: Even if you live in the city, you can see some of the North Atlantic's wildlife in nearby parks or even in a backyard tree! Many birds stop in city parks during fall and spring migrations. For example, New York City's Central Park is a haven for migrating warblers. Other creatures have been able to adapt to the urban environment. Raccoons and opossums feed on our scraps and trash. Peregrine falcons dive-bomb pigeons in the valleys between skyscrapers, much as they once caught prey between vertical cliffs. Gray squirrels, robins, and even red-tailed hawks have proven resilient to much of the hustle and bustle of urban life. But of course, the more we keep our urban lands and waterways safe, clean, and undisturbed, the better chance we'll have of keeping these and other creatures as our neighbors. (Examples: "Roostwatch"; "A Moth Flies in Brooklyn.")

Animals and Plants

It would take a whole book to describe the animals and plants of the North Atlantic Coast. So, we've simply listed below the organisms mentioned in this anthology and given a brief explanation, where necessary, of what they are.

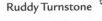

Birds: Birds fall into several big categories, which may help to keep them straight. The *swimmers,* such as mallards, loons, and Canada geese, stick close to the water. The *aerialists,* or flyers, are seabirds such as laughing gulls, herring gulls (which are sometimes called seagulls), black skimmers, and terns (including roseate terns and common terns). *Long-legged wading birds,* frequently found in marshes, include bitterns, great blue herons, green herons, and snowy egrets. Many *smaller wading birds* feed close to the ocean's edge. These include piping plovers, red knots, ruddy turnstones, sandpipers, and killdeer. Pheasants are an example of *fowl-like birds.* Hawks, ospreys, eagles, owls, and merlins (which are small falcons) are all *birds of prey,* or raptors. They have talons, sharp beaks, and terrific eyesight, helping them catch small rodents and other prey. *Perching birds* make up a large category that includes red-winged blackbirds, ravens, sparrows, crows, wrens, indigo buntings, warblers, golden-crowned kinglets, cedar waxwings, chickadees, starlings, pigeons, cardinals, scarlet tanagers, rose-breasted

Ruddy Turnstone

Golden-Crowned Kinglet

Merlin

grosbeaks, orchard orioles, yellow-billed cuckoos, least flycatchers, great crested flycatchers, wood thrushes, blue jays, titmice, robins, and mockingbirds. And finally, the *non-perching land birds* are kingfishers; downy, red-bellied, and hairy woodpeckers; flickers and yellow-bellied sapsuckers (which are woodpeckers, too); phoebes; and whippoorwills.

Fin Whale

Mammals:

Many people don't realize it, but dolphins, porpoises, and whales—including humpbacks, fins, sulphurs, potheads, and, biggest of all, the blue whale—are marine mammals. Some of the mammals living near the sea shore include beavers, mink, muskrats, otters, and raccoons. And the mammals of nearby parks and woodlands include squirrels, foxes, bears, white-footed mice, voles (another kind of rodent), chipmunks, rats, bats, and deer.

Marine Invertebrates: Marine invertebrates are sea creatures that don't have a backbone. You can group them in the following way. *Jellylike animals* include jellyfish and sea anemones. *Mollusks* include coffee-bean snails, whelks, conchs, augers, sundials, limpets, and periwinkles, as well as all the bivalves, or two-shelled organisms: clams, oysters, scallops, mussels, soft-shelled clams, razor clams, and quahogs.

Lobster

Knobbed Whelk

(Quahogs are called cherrystone clams when they're at their smallest, littlenecks when they're a bit bigger, and quahogs when they're full grown.) Lobsters, barnacles, fiddler crabs, hermit crabs, ghost crabs, mud crabs, sandhoppers (or beach fleas), and shrimp are all crustaceans, and they're in the same broader group as horseshoe crabs: the *arthropods.* The spiny skinned *echinoderms* include sea stars (or starfish), sea urchins, sea cucumbers, and sand dollars.

Freshwater and Terrestrial Invertebrates: Crayfish are freshwater invertebrates. Terrestrial invertebrates (those that live on land) include wolf spiders and other spiders, and *insects,* such as crickets, powdered butterflies, *cynthia* moths, mayflies, grasshoppers, bees, beetles, ants, chinch (or cinch) bugs, plant hoppers, and, of course, mosquitoes.

Reptiles and Amphibians: Painted turtles and diamondback terrapins are *reptiles.* That means they have claws on their feet and their skin is dry and scaly, and they lay their eggs on land. Salamanders, frogs, and toads are all *amphibians.* Clawless with moist skin, they lay their eggs in the water, and their young go through a change called metamorphosis as they develop into adulthood.

Diamondback Terrapin

Fish: Saltwater bony fish include tuna, cod (also called codfish or bacalao), shad, striped bass, sea bass, killifish (including mummichogs), bluefish, mackerel, silversides, sticklebacks, northern pipefish, eels, white perch, herrings, anchovies, menhadens, searobins, naked gobies, striped mullets, croackers, northern kingfish, flounders, and flukes. A "mermaid's purse" is the egg sac of a saltwater fish called a skate. *Freshwater bony fish*

Four-Spined Stickleback

Mermaid's Purse

include minnows, hornpouts, yellow perch, smallmouth bass, pickerel, salmon, and trout. (Some of the fish listed above spend portions of their lives in both fresh and saltwater environments.) Finally, sharks are in a category all their own: they're *cartilaginous fish*.

Plants: These are the *tall, broadleaf trees* mentioned in the readings: maple, oak, hickory, elm, magnolia, American chestnut, willow, poplar, black cherry, beech, linden, paper birch, walnut, holly, London planetree (a relative of the sycamore), and ailanthus (also known as tree-of-heaven). The *coniferous trees* include cedar, spruce, hemlock, and pine trees. *Smaller broadleaf shrubs* include rhododendron, low and high bush blueberry, cranberry, and bayberry. The following are, broadly speaking, *wildflowers:* dandelion, lady slipper, rose, cattail, aster, gayfeather, lily of the valley, plantain, milkweed, sunflower, purple bee balm, groundnut, wake-robin, marigold, daisy, Solomon's seal, partridgeberry, strawberry, huckleberry, goldenrod, rushes, cordgrass, beach grass, beach heather, sea myrtle, and knotweed.

Blueberries

Not all the plants mentioned in the readings are native to the North Atlantic Coast. For example, ailanthus, dandelions, sunflowers, marigolds, and daisies come from other regions (or continents) but have become common in this region over time.

Other: Mushrooms are a kind of *fungus*. Neither fungi, nor the group of organisms called *algae* are now considered part of the plant family. Algae range from tiny, single-celled organisms to large seaweeds, such as kelp. Sea lettuce is also a kind of algae. *Lichens* are made up of fungi living symbiotically with colonies of microscopic algae.

Stories by State
or Province

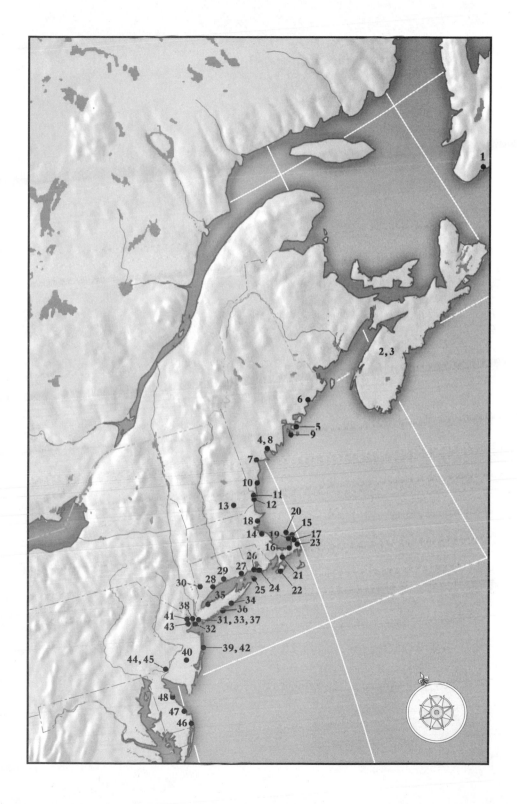

Parks and Preserves

Listed below are just a few of the many places where you can go to experience the wilder side of the North Atlantic Coast region. Please note: the phone numbers provided are sometimes for the park's headquarters, but often for a managing agency or organization. In any case, the people at these numbers can provide you with details about the area and directions for how to get there!

Connecticut

Audubon Center in Greenwich (Greenwich) 203-869-5272
Bluff Point State Park (Groton) 860-424-3200
Connecticut Audubon Center at Fairfield (Fairfield) 203-259-6305
Hammonasset Beach State Park (Madison) 203-245-2785
Lighthouse Point Park (New Haven) 203-946-8005
Stuart B. McKinney National Wildlife Refuge (Westbrook) 860-399-2513
Milford Point Bird Sanctuary (Milford) 203-878-7440

Delaware

Brandywine Creek State Park (Wilmington) 302-577-3534
Bombay Hook National Wildlife Refuge (Smyrna) 302-653-9345
Cape Henlopen State Parks (Lewes) 302-645-8983
Delaware Seashore State Park (Rehoboth Beach) 302-227-2800
Robert L. Graham/Nanticoke Wildlife Area (Laurel) 302-739-5297
Great Cypress Swamp (Selbyville) 302-653-2880
Killens Pond State Park (Felton) 302-284-4526
Little Creek Wildlife Area (Little Creek) 302-739-5297
Lums Pond State Park (Bear) 302-368-6989

Pea Patch Island (Delaware City) 302-834-7941
Prime Hook National Wildlife Refuge (Milton) 302-684-8419
Trap Pond State Park (Laurel) 302-875-5153
Norman G. Wilder Wildlife Area (Viola) 302-739-5297

Maine

Acadia National Park (Bar Harbor) 207-288-3338
Back Cove (Portland) 207-772-4994
Biddeford Pool/East Point Sanctuary (Biddeford) 207-781-2330
Cobscook Bay State Park (Dennysville) 207-726-4412
Gilsland Farm (Falmouth) 207-781-2330
Great Wass Island Preserve (Beals) 207-729-5181
Indian Point-Blagden Preserve (Bar Harbor) 207-729-5181
Machias Seal Island (contact boat companies in Jonesport:
    207-497-5933; Lubec: 207-733-5584; or Cutler: 207-259-4484)
Matinicus Island and Matinicus Rock (Matinicus) 207-366-3868
Monhegan Island (contact boat companies in Port Clyde:
    207-372-8848; Boothbay Harbor: 800-298-2284; or New Harbor:
    207-677-2026)
Petit Manan National Wildlife Refuge (Milbridge) 207-546-2124
Quoddy Head State Park (Lubec) 207-733-0911
Rachel Carson National Wildlife Refuge (Wells) 207-646-9226
Rachel Carson Salt Pond Preserve (New Harbor) 207-729-5181
Roque Bluffs State Park (Roque Bluffs) 207-255-3475
Scarborough Marsh (Scarborough) 207-781-2330
Wells National Estuarine Research Reserve (Wells) 207-646-1555
Wolfe's Neck Woods State Park (Freeport) 207-624-6080 (Nov.–Mar.)
    and 207-865-4465 (Apr.–Oct.)

Massachusetts

Blue Hills Reservation (Milton) 617-698-1802
Cape Cod National Seashore (extensive region on Cape Cod)
    508-255-3421
Daniel Webster Wildlife Sanctuary (Marshfield) 781-837-9400
Demarest Lloyd State Park (Dartmouth) 508-636-3298

Eastern Point Wildlife Sanctuary (Gloucester) 781-259-9500
Great Meadows National Wildlife Refuge (Sudbury and Concord)
     978-443-4661
Halibut Point State Park (Rockport) 978-546-2997
Marblehead Neck Wildlife Sanctuary (Marblehead) 978-887-9264
Martha's Vineyard (contact Chamber of Commerce: 508-693-0085 or
     Mass. Audubon Society: 508-627-4850)
Middlesex Fells Reservation (Stoneham) 617-727-5215
Monomoy National Wildlife Refuge (Chatham) 508-945-0594
Mount Auburn Cemetery (Cambridge) 617-547-7105
Nantucket Island (contact Chamber of Commerce: 508-228-1700 or
     Maria Mitchell Assoc.: 508-228-9198)
Parker River National Wildlife Refuge/Plum Island (Newburyport)
     978-465-5753
Plymouth Beach (Plymouth) 800-872-1620
Wellfleet Bay Wildlife Sanctuary (South Wellfleet) 508-349-2615

New Hampshire

Beaver Brook Association (Milford, Brookline, Hollis) 603-465-7787
Isle of Shoals (contact boat company: 603-431-5500 or 800-441-4620;
     or Audubon Society of N.H.: 603-224-9909)
Odiorne Point State Park (Rye) 603-436-8043

New Jersey

Bennett Bogs Preserve (Lower Township, Cape May County)
     908-879-7262
Cape May Point State Park (Cape May Point) 609-884-2159
Edwin B. Forsythe National Wildlife Refuge, Brigantine Division
     (Oceanville) 609-652-1665
Gateway National Recreation Area, Sandy Hook Unit (Highlands)
     732-872-5970
Great Bay Wildlife Management Area (Tuckertown) 609-259-2132
Great Swamp National Wildlife Refuge (Basking Ridge) 973-425-1222
Kearny Marsh (Kearny) 201-460-1700
McNamara Wildlife Management Area (Marmora) 609-292-2965

Parvin State Park (Vineland) 609-358-8616
Reed's Beach (Dennisville) 609-628-2103
Webb's Mill Bog (Whiting) 609-292-2965
Wharton State Forest (Batsto) 609-561-0024

New York

Central Park (New York City) 212-360-3444
Fire Island National Seashore (Patchogue) 516-289-4810
Gateway National Recreation Area, Jamaica Bay Unit (New York City-
    Queens) 718-318-4340
Long Pond Greenbelt (Sag Harbor) 516-367-3225
Montauk Point State Park (Montauk) 516-668-3781

Rhode Island

Beavertail State Park (Jamestown) 401-884-2010
Block Island (contact Chamber of Commerce: 401-466-2982)
Brenton Point State Park (Newport) 401-847-2400
Burlingame State Park (Charlestown) 401-322-7337
Great Swamp Wildlife Management Area (West Kingston)
    401-789-0281
Ninigret National Wildlife Refuge (Charlestown) 401-364-9124
Norman Bird Sanctuary (Middletown) 401-846-2577
George B. Parker Woodland (Coventry and Foster) 401-949-5454
Sachuest Point National Wildlife Refuge (Middletown) 401-847-5511
Sakonnet Point (Little Compton) 401-789-0281
Swan Point Cemetery (Providence) 401-272-1314
Trustom Pond National Wildlife Refuge (South Kingston)
    401-364-9124

Recommended Reading

Alden, Peter and Brian Cassie, et al. *The National Audubon Society Field Guide to the Mid-Atlantic States.* New York: Alfred A. Knopf, 1999.

Alden, Peter and Brian Cassie, et al. *The National Audubon Society Field Guide to New England.* New York: Alfred A. Knopf, 1998.

Amos, William H. *The Life of the Seashore.* New York: McGraw-Hill Book Company, 1966.

Bredeson, Carmen. *Tide Pools.* Danbury, Conn.: Franklin Watts, 1999.

Finch, Robert. *Smithsonian Guide to Natural America: Southern New England.* Washington D.C.: Smithsonian Books and New York: Random House, Inc., 1996.

Gosner, Kenneth L. and Roger Tory Peterson. *A Field Guide to the Atlantic Seashore.* Boston: Houghton Mifflin, 1999.

Hay, John and Peter Farb. *The Atlantic Shore: Human and Natural History from Long Island to Labrador.* New York: Harper and Row, 1966.

Kochanoff, Peggy. *Beachcombing the Atlantic Coast.* Missoula, Mont.: Mountain Press, 1997.

Martinez, Andrew J. *Marine Life of the North Atlantic: Canada to New England.* Camden, Maine: Down East Books, 1999.

Teal, John and Mildred. *Life and Death of the Salt Marsh.* New York: Ballatine Books, 1971.

Special Thanks

Seven years ago, in the inspiring company of Mount Abraham and a gaggle of nature writers, I happened upon the first ideas for this book. Since then, more people than I can name have helped me turn these ideas into the reality of a children's literary series. I hope the following list, however incomplete, helps to express my gratitude for this assistance.

First, a thanks to John Elder, Gary Paul Nabhan, Richard Nelson, Terry Tempest Williams, Chris Merrill, Laurie Lane-Zucker, and Jennifer Sahn for the thoughtful and ebullient company that so inspired me on that bright autumn weekend. Soon after, Olivia Gilliam listened and shared her gentle insights, and she left us too soon.

With heartfelt gratitude I thank the echoing green foundation for supporting my early work on this project, and for believing in young people's big, tenacious dreams. The echoing green community gave me practical guidance, and, most important, some lifelong friends.

Three cheers go to some of the teachers who are working to bring kids back in touch with the natural world, and who helped me test early curriculum ideas: Juanita Lavadie and Randy Thorne of Taos Pueblo School; Lynn Grimes of Turquoise Trail School in Santa Fe; Jen Fong, formerly of Bronx Green-Up; Karen Rogers Childress of Rural Resources in Greenville, Tennessee; and Alex Glass and Wyatt Weber of Watkins Elementary School in Washington, D.C.

When it came time to create this first anthology, several colleagues and friends offered expertise and assistance. Great thanks to Miriam Stewart and Robin Kelsey, perceptive readers; to E. Barrie Kavasch for reviewing our Lenape story; to Bruce Hammond of The Nature Conservancy for helping me get my ecological facts straight; to Jen Kretser and Priscilla Howell for inspired and enthusiastic feedback on the book's content and format; and to the many friends who shared with me their favorite North Atlantic literature.

Finally, deepest thanks go to the staff of Milkweed Editions, for undertaking and guiding this project; to Gary Paul Nabhan, for wise counsel and enduring faith; and to my best friend and best husband, Robin, for all things great and small.

Contributor Acknowledgments

Jennifer Ackerman, "The Great Marsh," excerpted from *Notes from the Shore* (New York: Viking Penguin, 1995), 114–15, 118–21. Copyright © 1995 by Jennifer Ackerman. Reprinted with permission from Viking Penguin, a division of Penguin Putnam Inc.

Nadya Aisenberg, "Today." Copyright © 2000 by Nadya Aisenberg. Printed with permission from the author.

Jeff W. Bens, "The Legend of Big Claw." Copyright © 2000 by Jeff W. Bens. Printed with permission from the author.

Henry Beston, "Stranded," excerpted from *The Outermost House* (New York: Rinehart & Company, 1928), 78–80. Copyright © 1928, 1949, 1956 by Henry Beston, © 1977 by Elizabeth C. Beston. Reprinted with permission from Henry Holt and Company, LLC.

Alice Stone Blackwell, "Dorchester Days," excerpted from *Growing Up in Boston's Gilded Age: The Journal of Alice Stone Blackwell, 1872–1874,* ed. Marlene Deahl Merrill (New Haven, Conn.: Yale University Press, 1990), 49, 66, 91, 109, 112–113, 162, 163, 169, 176, 177, 188. Copyright © 1990 by Yale University. Reprinted with permission from Yale University Press.

Mélina Brown, "Cranberry Cove." Copyright © 2000 by Mélina Brown. Printed with permission from the author.

Joseph Bruchac, "Glooskap and the Whale," in *Return of the Sun* (Freedom, Calif.: Crossing Press, 1990), 73–76. Copyright © 1990 by Joseph Bruchac. Reprinted with permission from The Crossing Press, P.O. Box 1048, Freedom, CA 95019.

Tyler Cadman, "Golden-Crowned Kinglet," in *River of Words: The Natural World as Viewed by Young People,* ed. Robert Hass (Berkeley, Calif.: River of Words, 1999), 11. Copyright © 1999 from River of Words. Reprinted with permission from River of Words Poetry and Art Contest.

Thomas J. Campanella, "A Moth Flies in Brooklyn," in *Orion Nature Quarterly* 13, no. 4 (Autumn 1994): 18–19. Copyright © 1994 by Thomas J. Campanella. Reprinted with permission from the author.

"Cape Cod Girls," on *Blow, Ye Winds in the Morning: A Celebration of the Sea,* recorded by The Revels, 1 Kendall Square #600, Cambridge, MA 02139.

Betsy McCully Cooper, "The Maize Doll." Copyright © 2000 by Betsy McCully Cooper. Printed with permission from the author.

Stephen Currie, "The Rescuer from Lime Rock," in *Cricket* 25, no. 5 (January 1998): 28–29. Copyright © 1998 by Stephen Currie. Reprinted with permission from the author.

W. D. Ehrhart, "The Beech Tree," in *Beautiful Wreckage: New and Selected Poems* (Easthampton, Mass.: Adastra Press, 1999), 141–42. Copyright © 1999 by W. D. Ehrhart. Reprinted with permission from the author.

John Frank, "Where the River Meets the Sea." Copyright © 2000 by John Frank. Printed with permission from the author.

Maria Mazziotti Gillan, "In New Jersey Once," in *Where I Come From: New and Selected Poems* (Toronto, Ontario: Guernica Editions, 1995, 1997), 27. Copyright © 1995, 1997 by Maria Mazziotti Gillan. Reprinted with permission from the author.

Nikki Giovanni, "A Song for New-Ark," in *Those Who Ride the Night Winds* (New York: William Morrow, 1983), 61–62. Copyright © 1983 by Nikki Giovanni. Reprinted with permission from Harper Collins Publishers, Inc.

Jim Gorman, "Blueberries," in *Will Work for Food* (Normal: Illinois Writers, Inc., 1993), 19–22. Copyright © 1993 by Jim Gorman. Reprinted with permission from the author.

Geraldine Marshall Gutfreund, "The Fog Maiden's Necklace," in *Cricket* 10, no. 6 (February 1983): 43–46. Copyright © 1983 by Geraldine Marshall Gutfreund. Reprinted with permission from the author.

Penny Harter, "Haiku, Spring Lake, New Jersey." Copyright © 2000 by Penny Harter. Printed with permission from the author. Fourth stanza of sequence previously published in *Haiku Southwest* 1, nos. 3–4 (July/October 1993): 1. Copyright © 1993 by Haiku Society of America. Reprinted with permission from the author.

Henry Beetle Hough, "Waxwings," in *Singing in the Morning and Other Essays about Martha's Vineyard* (New York: Simon and Schuster, 1951), 220–22. Copyright © 1951, renewed 1979 by Henry Beetle Hough. Reprinted with permission from Simon and Schuster, Inc.

Sarah Orne Jewett, "A White Heron," in *The Country of the Pointed Firs and Other Stories* (Garden City, N.Y.: Doubleday, 1956), 161–71.

Rita Joe, "Aye! no monuments," in *Poems of Rita Joe* (Sydney, Nova Scotia: Abanaki Press, 1979), 10. Copyright © 1979 by Rita Joe. Reprinted with permission from the author.

Helen Keller, "A Summer in Brewster," excerpted from *The Story of My Life* (Garden City, N.Y.: Doubleday, 1954), 51–52.

Eugene F. Kinkead, "Fire Island Walking Song," in the *New Yorker* 33, no. 28 (August 31, 1957): 51. Copyright © 1957 by Eugene F. Kinkead. Reprinted with permission from the *New Yorker*. All rights reserved.

Norbert Krapf, "Long Island Crow," in *Arriving on Paumanok* (Port Jefferson, N.Y.: Street Press, 1979), 8. Copyright © 1979 by Norbert Krapf. Reprinted with permission from the author.

Virginia Kroll, "Lunch with a Gull," in *Story Friends* 94, no. 7 (July 1999): 16. Copyright © 1999 by Virginia Kroll. Reprinted with permission from the author.

Adrian Kingsbury Lane, "Log of the *Downit*," excerpted from *Log of the Downit*, ed. Richard Knowles Morris (Noank, Conn.: Noank Historical Society, 1993), 4, 5, 8, 15, 16, 17, 22. Copyright © 1995 by Highlights for Children, Inc. Reprinted with permission from Highlights for Children, Inc., Columbus, Ohio.

Clare Leighton, "The Magic of the Flats," excerpted from *Where Land Meets Sea* (New York: Rinehart and Company, 1954), 41–42, 43–47, 50–53, 55. Copyright © 1954 by Clare Leighton. Reprinted with permission from Devin-Adair, Publishers, Inc., Old Greenwich, CT 06870. All rights reserved.

April Lindner, "Seascape." Copyright © 2000 by April Lindner. Printed with permission from the author.

Diane Mayr, "New Hampshire Shore: Haiku." Copyright © 2000 by Diane Mayr. Printed with permission from the author.

Cecile Mazzucco-Than, "Three Trees in the City." Copyright © 2000 by Cecile Mazzucco-Than. Printed with permission from the author.

Farley Mowat, "The Great Whale," excerpted from *A Whale for the Killing* (Boston: Little, Brown and Company, 1972), 124–29. Copyright © 1972 by Farley Mowat Limited. Reprinted with permission from Little, Brown and Company, Inc. and McClelland & Stewart, Inc., *The Canadian Publishers*.

Mary Oliver, "Starfish," in *Dream Work* (New York: Atlantic Monthly Press, 1986), 36–37. Copyright © 1986 by Mary Oliver. Reprinted with permission from the author.

Julie Parson-Nesbitt, "Pauline Sings across the Rooftops." Copyright © 2000 by Julie Parson-Nesbitt. Printed with permission from the author.

Mary Quigley, "The Ocean Is a Heartbeat." Copyright © 2000 by Mary Quigley. Printed with permission from the author.

Elizabeth Reynard, "The Legend of the Mashpee Maiden," in *The Narrow Land* (Cambridge, Mass.: Riverside Press, 1934), 31–33. Copyright © 1934 by Elizabeth Reynard. Reprinted with permission from the Chatham Historical Society, Chatham, Massachusetts.

Elisavietta Ritchie, "Persistent Haiku." Copyright © 2000 by Elisavietta Ritchie. Reprinted with permission from the author. Originally published in *Christian Science Monitor.*

Marybeth Rua-Larsen, "Pickering Beach." Copyright © 2000 by Marybeth Rua-Larsen. Printed with permission from the author.

David Sobel, "Otter Delight," in *Sanctuary: The Journal of the Massachusetts Audubon Society* 21, no. 5 (January 1982): 7–8. Copyright © 1982 by David Sobel. Reprinted with permission from the author.

Anne Spollen, "Of the Sea." Copyright © 2000 by Anne Spollen. Printed with permission from the author.

Jennifer Stansbury, "Fledgling Summer." Copyright © 2000 by Jennifer Stansbury. Printed with permission from the author.

Wally Swist, "Shells," in *The New Life* (West Hartford, Conn.: Plinth Books, 1998), 65. Copyright © 1998 by Wally Swist. Reprinted with permission from the author.

Henry David Thoreau, "A Wild, Rank Place," excerpted from *Cape Cod* (New York: Thomas Y. Crowell Company, 1961), 214–16.

William W. Warner, "Of Beaches, Bays, and My Boyhood with the Colonel," in *Heart of the Land: Essays on Last Great Places*, ed. Joseph Barbato and Lisa Weinerman (New York: Pantheon Books, 1994), 60–64. Copyright © 1994 by William W. Warner. Reprinted with permission from the author. Republished as "A Prologue, by the Sea," in *Into the Porcupine Cave and Other Odysseys: Adventures of an Occasional Naturalist* (Washington, D.C.: National Geographic Society, 1999).

Marie Winn, "Roostwatch," in *Red-Tails in Love* (New York: Pantheon Books, 1998), 153–61. Copyright © 1998 by Marie Winn. Reprinted with permission from Pantheon Books, a division of Random House, Inc.

About the Editor

Sara St. Antoine grew up in Ann Arbor, Michigan. She holds a bachelor's degree in English from Williams College and a master's degree in Environmental Studies from the Yale School of Forestry and Environmental Studies. Currently living in Cambridge, Massachusetts, she enjoys walking along the Charles River and seeing black-crowned night herons hunkered in the trees.

About the Illustrators

Paul Mirocha is a designer and illustrator of books about nature for children and adults. His first book, *Gathering the Desert*, by Gary Paul Nabhan, won the 1985 John Burroughs Medal for natural history. He lives in Tucson, Arizona, with his daughters, Anna and Claire.

Trudy Nicholson is an illustrator of nature with a background in medical and scientific illustration. She received her B.S. in Fine Arts at Columbia University and has worked as a natural-science illustrator in a variety of scientific fields for many years. She lives in Maryland.

The World As Home, the nonfiction publishing program of Milkweed Editions, is dedicated to exploring our relationship to the natural world. Not espousing any particular environmentalist or political agenda, these books are a forum for distinctive literary writing that not only alerts the reader to vital issues but offers personal testimonies to living harmoniously with other species in urban, rural, and wilderness communities.

Milkweed Editions publishes with the intention of making a humane impact on society, in the belief that literature is a transformative art uniquely able to convey the essential experiences of the human heart and spirit. To that end, Milkweed publishes distinctive voices of literary merit in handsomely designed, visually dynamic books, exploring the ethical, cultural, and esthetic issues that free societies need continually to address. Milkweed Editions is a not-for-profit press.

For more information on other books published by Milkweed Editions for intermediate readers, contact Milkweed at (800) 520-6455 or visit our website (www.milkweed.org).

Interior design by Wendy Holdman
The text is typeset in 12/16 point Legacy Book
by Stanton Publication Services, Inc.
Printed on acid-free, recycled 55# Frasier Miami Book paper
by Friesen Corporation

Follies *of* God

Follies *of* God

Tennessee Williams
and the Women of the Fog

JAMES GRISSOM

ALFRED A. KNOPF   New York
2015

THIS IS A BORZOI BOOK
PUBLISHED BY ALFRED A. KNOPF

Copyright © 2015 by James Grissom

All rights reserved. Published in the United States by Alfred A. Knopf,
a division of Random House LLC, New York, and in Canada
by Random House of Canada Limited, Toronto,
Penguin Random House companies.

www.aaknopf.com

Knopf, Borzoi Books, and the colophon are registered trademarks
of Random House LLC.

Grateful acknowledgment is made to HarperCollins Publishers for
permission to reprint "Youth" from *New and Collected Poems: 1931–2001*
by Czesław Miłosz, copyright © 1988, 1995, 2001 by Czesław Miłosz
Royalties, Inc. Reprinted by permission of HarperCollins Publishers.

Library of Congress Cataloging-in-Publication Data
Grissom, James.
Follies of God : Tennessee Williams and the Women of the Fog /
James Grissom. — First edition.
pages   cm
ISBN 978-0-307-26569-2 (hardcover) — ISBN 978-1-101-87465-3 (eBook)
1. Williams, Tennessee, 1911–1983—Criticism and interpretation.
2. Characters and characteristics in literature.   3. Women in literature.
I. Title.
PS3545.I5365Z666   2015   812'.54—dc23   2014021046

Jacket photograph courtesy of the
Cecil Beaton Studio Archive at Sotheby's
Jacket design by Carol Devine Carson
Book design by Cassandra J. Pappas

Manufactured in the United States of America
First Edition

Four women made the writing of this book possible:

Winnie Hubbard Grissom

Marian Seldes

Dr. Dale V. Atkins

Rose Byrnes

And one made it publishable:

Victoria Wilson

I have been very lucky. I am a multi-souled man, because I have offered my soul to so many women, and they have filled it, repaired it, sent it back to me for use.

—TENNESSEE WILLIAMS

Illustrations

Follies *of* God

One

P ERHAPS YOU can be of some help to me."
These were the first words Tennessee Williams spoke to me
in that initial phone call to my parents' home in Baton Rouge,
Louisiana. It was September of 1982, a fact I noted in a small blue book.
The book was new and had been purchased for an upcoming test in
World History that I would not be taking because Tennessee invited me
to lunch in New Orleans, and I accepted.

I know that pleasantries were exchanged, and he laughed a lot—a
deep, guttural, silly theatrical laugh—but the first quotation attributable to Tennessee Williams to me was the one I wrote in my small blue
book.

Perhaps you can be of some help to me.

How could I be of help to Tennessee Williams? How, when in fact
I had written to him, several months before, seeking *his* help? From
a battered paperback copy of *Who's Who in the American Theatre*, I
had found the address of his agent (Audrey Wood, c/o International
Famous Agency, 1301 Avenue of the Americas), and had written a
letter—lengthy and containing a photograph, and, I'm thankful, lost
to us forever—asking for his advice on a writing career. I wrote that his

work had meant the most to me; that I was considering a career in the theater. I also enclosed two short stories, both written for a class taken at Louisiana State University. It was a time I recall as happy: I was writing, and exploiting the reserves of the school's library and its liberal sharing policy with other schools. I was poring over books and papers that related to Tennessee and other writers I admired.

Tennessee (he told me, by the end of that first phone call, to call him Tenn) was in a horrible "knot of time." He asked me to imagine a knot of time, but time for me at that point was something from which I was seeking favors, something I was approaching. I did not feel a part of time yet, which can be somewhat attributable to growing up and living in Baton Rouge, a city detached from time, thought, or curiosity. Tenn acknowledged with a laugh that Baton Rouge was a city encased in gelatin.

Tenn, however, could see and feel a literal knot of time and people and places encircling him, choking him, pursuing him. While he told me that he could no longer dream, due to age, a lack of flexibility both glandular and creative, and the "monumental accretion of toxins self-administered," he was, comically, fully equipped to endure nightmares. His most frequent nightmare, one he had endured the night before he chose to call me, consisted of his slow, painful death by means of a massive knot, bearing the image of an enormous boa constrictor as well as an "artistic representation of a penis," encircling him and squeezing him into darkness and death. The scales of this boa were faces of people and covers of books and posters of plays (both his and others'), travel brochures of trips planned, taken, aborted. The faces of the people and the blurbs on the books and the posters all posed the same question: Where have you been?

This time knot was for Tenn a threat, an indictment, and a motivator, and he took it as a primarily positive occurrence. "This thing, this horror," he told me, "may very well allow me to write at my previous level of power, and it appears to be telling me to plunge into my memories, to plunder them. And those that are most vivid to me are in Louisiana."

Tenn believed that writers, all artists, had several homes. There was the biological place of birth; the home in which one grew up, bore witness, fell apart. There was also the place where the "epiphanies" began—a school, a church, perhaps a bed. Rockets were launched and an identity began to be set. There was the physical location where a writer sat each day and scribbled and hunted and pecked and dreamed and drank and cursed his way into a story or a play or a novel. Most importantly, however, there was the emotional, invisible, self-invented place where work began—what Tenn called his "mental theater," a cerebral proscenium stage upon which his characters walked and stumbled and remained locked forever in his memory, ready, he felt, to be called into action and help him again.

"I've got to get home."

When Tennessee Williams was young, when he could dream and felt that time was a destination awaiting his arrival, he would repair to this mental theater, a safe place that operated under his management, where he could close his eyes and open the stage curtains and be not only home, but working.

If you're a writer, you write. If you don't, you're dead. You have no home, no reason to be offered a seat at any table, and no reason to live.

No play written by Tennessee Williams, however, got its bearings until a fog rolled across the boards, from which a female form emerged.

"I do not know why this is," Tenn confessed to me, "but there is a premonitory moment before a woman, an important, powerful woman, enters my subconscious, and this moment is announced by the arrival of fog. Perhaps it is some detritus of my brain belching forth both waste and a woman. I do not know, but it comes with a smell, and it is the crisp, pungent smell of radiators hissing and clanking and rattling in rooms in New Orleans and St. Louis and New York. Rooms in which I wrote and dreamed and starved and fucked and cried and read and prayed, and perhaps all that action and all that steam creates both this fog and this woman.

"I have not seen the fog in years."

Tenn's primary activity, he told me, was "faking the fog." When he closed his eyes and summoned his mental theater, he could see the scuffed boards of the stage, the frayed, slow-moving curtains, smell the dust, and feel the excitement of drama forthcoming.

"When I was young," Tenn told me, "I never sought out a woman, a character. She came to *me*. She had a story to tell, urgently, violently, fervently. I listened and I identified, and I became her most ardent supporter and witness. I cannot get a witness for me and I cannot be a witness for anyone! I cannot find a woman who will speak to me on my stage."

So Tenn sought the women elsewhere, searched for fog in movie theaters, on television screens, and in the pages of magazines, in stacks of photographs. He failed to find fog in literature, because, he explained, "I am a very visual person. I need to have the shape and movement and *intent* of a woman before me."

In his homes, in hotel rooms, in lodges and athletic clubs and as a guest of others, Tenn would pull out his typewriter or his pad of paper (which he called the "pale judgment" awaiting his ministrations), move close to a television set, and wait for a woman to speak to him. With friends like Maria St. Just and Jane Smith, whose love for and patience with him were boundless, he would sit in movie theaters for up to three consecutive showings, because a "wisp" of fog was emanating from the screen.

"I have not seen the fog in years," Tenn repeated. "But your letter made me believe it still existed."

Writing early in the morning or deep into the night, Tenn kept his television set on, the volume set to low, a radio or a phonograph playing the music of people who had led him to fog-enshrouded stages in the past. An image would come across the screen and catch his eye, the volume would be raised, and a voice would speak to him. Tenn had notes and diagrams and plot outlines scrawled on envelopes, napkins, hotel stationery, menus from restaurants and diners and airport lounges. Once, he delicately constructed a plot outline on a paper tablecloth, which the waiter neatly folded and presented to him along with the check.

He consulted psychics, tarot-card readers, tea-leaf diviners. He placed himself in tubs of warm water and tried to experience rebirth, so that he could emerge from his liquid prison young and alert and full of creative and glandular flexibility, free forever of the impending time knot.

Time and the ever-present pale judgment haunted him, jeered at him, reproached him. In the home of a friend, a fellow writer, he once walked over to a desk holding a ream of white paper and violently pushed it to the floor, then shoved it from view behind a desk. "I will have none of that from you!" he admonished the pile of paper, and went on with his visit.

Where have you been? the scales of the time knot asked him.

"Well, where the hell have *you* been?" Tenn once yelled out. "I was very loyal to my women, to my plays, to the construct of words. Where are they? Oh, they're all on tour, baby, and I'm here with silence and clean air and a condemned theater. My heart and eyes are failing, but those gals are doing fine." In Tennessee's mind, Amanda and Blanche and Alma and Serafina and the Princess were errant daughters, each of whom who had been carefully listened to and coddled and husbanded by him, their "queer Lear," and were now on stages telling their stories—the stories that had come to him in the fog—and he was off on his heath, yelling and whining and drinking and fighting off the time knot.

"Sometimes," he told me during that first phone call, "I think the fog has been replaced by something else. I feel that there is a wind tunnel inside of my head, and inside my head, within my very brain, there are leaves flying about, and each leaf is an idea."

When I finally met Tenn, he placed two fingers on his forehead, as if pushing against the pressure within, and he told me that the nights were spent scurrying after these leaves, trying to catch and collect them and find some meaning and comfort in them. He had also come to believe that the specks in his eyes, darting and floating, were reflections of these leaves moving across his brain, and if he could only marshal them, calm them down, and make the many dots one whole entity, he would have a character, a play, a woman, an idea.

"I am incapable of containing it," he told me, "this mulch, this confetti, until I can find some form in which to place it. A shadow box of the cerebellum; a case of curiosities plucked from my subconscious; a brilliantly white page framed in gold that I can approach and admire for its order and cleanness and say to it, in front of it, 'Yes, I have something to add.'"

Because he believed that the spots in his eyes, the floaters in his vitreous humor, were actually reflections of his cerebral leaf storm, Tenn took to staring into white tablecloths, looking upon blank white walls, and facing the sky, blinking and rolling his eyes, hoping to focus and find a connection.

"I've heard of connecting the dots," he laughed, "but this is ridiculous.

"I try to approach the whiteness of the page, the pale judgment, as if I were a neophyte priest, and the paper is the host," Tenn confessed to me. "I approach it gingerly and ask it to be patient. I see upon it the darting leaves in my brain, and I pray they will alight on the page and have some meaning. Or I touch it gently, a frightened queer faced with his first female breast, a nipple that seeks attention and ministration. 'Forgive me,' I say to it, 'I don't know my way around these parts.'

"I start with anything—one lone sentence—and I ask the leaves, I ask the page, for the next line, the next phrase."

Sentence after sentence would follow, and Tenn would write them down, fervently, eagerly. Later, once we had met, once he had decided to trust me, I would write them down for him, and the bits of papers, the pages yanked from journals, and the old bills and envelopes—all littered with words—would pile up.

"I think we can help each other," Tenn told me in that first phone call.

Tenn admitted that he was repairing to bars, where jukeboxes sat in dusty corners ("I judge a place by the particular pattern of its dust," he told me: "dust often tells me I can be comfortable . . . or not"), and play, incessantly, songs that gave him something, that took him somewhere, that might ignite the clanking and rattling of radiators and produce a fog. Fumbling for coins in the sparse afternoons of dark, dusty bars, he listened to "If I Didn't Care," "Wichita Lineman," "Bridge over Troubled Water," "Haunted Heart," "Our Finest Hour," "The Long and Winding Road."

"One should discard immediately from one's life anyone who does not cry at the sound of these songs," Tenn told me. "These songs hurt the heart."

Once, he told me, he was driven to write on a series of napkins a letter to his mother, after hearing the Andrews Sisters sing "I'll Be with You in Apple Blossom Time."

I think of organza and linen. My nose pressed into her bosom, the slightly singed smell of where the iron pressed into the fabric. My face rubbed raw by the fabric.

Comfort/discomfort.

I am not moving.

Tell me something. Tell me anything.

When did you realize that to survive, you would need to stumble in the dark rooms of reality until you found a door, to a closet perhaps, that, once opened, held a dream, or a memory, and suddenly, Mama, you could face grocery lists and altar-society meetings, and congregation with my father and . . . me?

Tell me, Mama. What did you give to me, and where is it now?

Tenn believed that if he could get back to the intersection of Royal and Conti streets, or Dumaine and Bourbon, he could connect all those floaters in his brain, all those leaves, which he came to believe were memories unacknowledged, unrecognized.

Another night, sleepless, anxious, afraid of a visitation of the time knot, Tenn saw an actress on television and had an idea. He would later relay it to me, and I would write it on the menu of a praline shop.

A young man circles a small Southern town. Everyone has seen him. The older woman, living alone, nurses her memories of the young man she once loved, who died, taking with him her unrequited love, her desire for the surcease provided by the flesh, and a dark secret. Is this man walking about a ghost? He appears to the young man who sits in the public park at night, because he has heard there are assignations among the magnolias, buttocks pressed against the cool bases of the Confederate statues. This young man speaks to the phantom, who never responds, and who never submits to his longing. Is he real? Is he the desire most wanted and never found? The town becomes afraid of the young man. Is he responsible for the vandalisms, the small robberies, the sound of shattering glass in the still night?

Tenn would stare into tablecloths, bare walls, the noonday sky, and remember: "This is the white of the pale judgment which faces me every day. I think of piles of cocaine, beautifully white and pure, like sand on the beaches where I was beautiful and the days were long and fat with purpose. I can look into the cocaine, as I look into a white tablecloth, and I can see the spots that dance in my eyes, and they are like the leaves that whirl in my brain. If I can only connect them. If I can only find a means to use them.

"I pray to the emptiness that is the page," Tenn said, "and I pray to the emptiness that is my mind, and I ask that I be filled."

Tenn paused, then continued.

"Now, I can recall a summer in Italy, in a small *pensione*, simple and rustic, with the most luxurious towels. No grand hotel of Europe ever had such plush towels, as white as this tablecloth, fresh-smelling, nubby.

I remember that the shower had a loud, slow drain, and as you began to rub your body down with the towel, you would stand ankle-deep in warm, soapy water. The air was full of the smell of castile soap—those bars that are as large and as heavy as Baptist hymnals—and the sweet smell of onions and peppers slowly cooking in olive oil. When I would begin to dry my face, I would press the towel against my eyes and I would feel—and be—totally blind. There was blackness as stark as this cloth is white, and I was ankle-deep in the water, and I was casting off the poisons of the previous night, so I was not strong or sure on my feet, and the smells were there, and I would suddenly hear a woman's voice, hear her words, and she was reciting her Rosary, in Italian, a language that was still new to me, so I could only decipher a few words of her prayers, but I could hear, I could feel, her intent, her desire, and I could begin to write. That voice ultimately became the voice of Serafina [the primary character in *The Rose Tattoo*], and I just followed that voice from prayer to prayer, from room to room, and that woman and I completed that play, on a different evening, in a different setting, on a night that was balmy and smelled of lemons."

The memory of balmy evenings forced Tenn to reopen, then reclose his eyes, and remember a New Orleans summer, in a room where the shuttered windows were open to the humidity and the noise of the city, burning peanuts, hot chicory, and a blank page in front of him, but fog incoming. "I was poor and I was parched," Tenn laughed, "and there's a prayer everyone has memorized, and I took my last coin and I went to a Rexall's and I bought a lemonade, extra ice, and I drank it fast and hard, and it hurt and it healed, and I could only think *Rapture!* And Blanche DuBois had entered the picture, danced her way into the blank whiteness, and begun to live.

"Tell me," Tenn had wondered, "is it that I can't find the words? Is it that I have nothing more to share or to care deeply about? Or am I husbanding my niggardly treasures because I would rather have them surprise and comfort me in the deep of the night, scribbled on some scrap of paper, rather than fill the vast whiteness?

"I need you to understand three things," he told me. "Find the memories. Build words from those memories. Trust me, they will come. Finally, recognizing the worth of the words, separate the wheat from the chaff. That is all."

"That is all?" I asked.

"That is more than enough, baby! That is enough for a lifetime of fog and time knots."

Plans were made. I was to meet Tenn in Jackson Square, in front of St. Louis Cathedral ("Louie's Place," he called it), and we would have lunch, we would talk about writing, I would help him connect the dots that were flying about.

"I need to know that I mattered," Tenn told me, "and your letter led me to feel that I did. Surely, there must be others who can tell me that I mattered, that I was of some value." Tenn paused to cite, apparently from memory, two vituperative quotes from theater critics who had come to their separate conclusions that Tennessee Williams had never mattered; his work had been overrated; it was time to reevaluate him or discard him forever.

"One man felt it charitable," he continued, "to assume that the real Tennessee Williams had died, and all of my later plays, my work of two decades, had been perpetuated by a clever epigone, a paid hack carrying on the industrial entity known as Tennessee Williams!" He laughed and hacked a bit, recovered, and muttered, using a term I hadn't heard since childhood Sundays in revivals, "Good Lord, can I get a witness?"

"Do you need a witness?" I asked.

"Yes," Tenn quickly responded, "and I'll be yours. I've read your work and I'll champion it, and I'll be your witness."

He was full of energy now.

"Here is the importance of bearing witness. We do not grow alone, talents do not prosper in a hothouse of ambition and neglect and hungry anger; love does not arrive by horseback or prayer or good intentions. We need the eyes, the arms, and the witness of others to grow, to know that we have existed, that we have mattered, that we have made our mark. And each of us has a distinct mark that colors our surroundings, that flavors the recipe of 'experience' in which we find ourselves; but we remain blind, without identity, until someone witnesses us.

"How does the pretty girl know she is pretty? Her witnesses testify to the fact that she is unique, that her peers lack something in pigment or stature. How can we know that we have talent until our words or the manner in which we speak them moves someone? Makes them think outside the puny lines into which they've colored themselves? We can't know that we have the power to break these lines apart with thought until we have our first witness, that person who tells us what we have done.

"So we grow from being watched and felt and we grow from watching others, and we have to fight our way out of the blind alleys that we create by believing that a witness can be snorted from a mirror or can reside on the tip of a syringe or come tumbling from the mouth of a paid witness.

"No," he uttered, seemingly defeated, "I'm afraid that we can't continue to run from each other; I'm afraid that only in the company of these people, all of our witnesses, many of whom frighten us, can we learn who we are and what we've done.

"Jim, be my witness."

The following morning I got into a 1977 Chevy Malibu and drove the eighty miles to New Orleans from Baton Rouge with the memory of something Tennessee Williams had said to me.

"Perhaps you can be of some help to me."

HERE IS what I took with me on that trip from Baton Rouge to New Orleans: three small blue exam booklets. Soft-blue covers and lined pages. I took Berol pens. I did not take a tape recorder, because I was not a journalist and this was not a "story" or an "interview."

I wrote everything down. I am a dutiful student and there have been complaints that I rarely look up and into the face of my subject. I wrote when I was with Tennessee, and I wrote when I was away from him. I researched everything he mentioned or told me to study.

The blue books multiplied, and ultimately more than twenty were filled with notes. The books have long since deteriorated, their staples fallen away, their pages thinned and yellowed. The words from those books were transferred to pages typed on an IBM Selectric, then to pages created through an IBM word processor and on to Compaq and Dell computers. Some of the pages were given to those about whom Tenn spoke.

That day in September was slightly muggy, so I used the air conditioner in my car, and people throughout the Quarter were in shorts and light cotton shirts. There was a lingering feel of summer in the air. Nonetheless, Tenn was wearing an enormous coat of indeterminate fur, a large straw hat, and sunglasses: he seemed ready at any moment to

Tennessee Williams in Jackson Square, in the late 1970s, reciting poetry to the pigeons

endure a winter storm, imitate Rudy Vallee, or face the firing squad of a Latin American judicial system.

Before I could approach him, he turned, saw me, and smiled. "You must be Jim," he crooned. "You look utterly confused."

Tenn had been engaged in conversation with several people huddled in the Square, only a few feet from the bird-infested statue of Andrew Jackson, but he pulled from them quickly, put his arm around my shoulders and began walking toward the Quarter.

"I am most at home in the Quarter," he spoke to my right ear, but the conversation seemed decidedly one-sided, a monologue for his own edification. "Wonderful things have happened for me on Royal, of course. Nothing of any positive significance ever happens on Rampart. Have you felt that way?"

I explained that I was actually from Baton Rouge, the club-footed cousin to New Orleans, and my time in the Quarter had been solely as a tourist. I could not speak to any deep experience on Rampart Street, or any other street in the city.

"Let's try to change that while we're here!" he exulted. "But let's now eat something. Do you like the Court of Two Sisters?"

I admitted that I had never eaten there before.

"You'll love it. Wonderful food, courtly service, lovely people, food served in bowls the size of a dog's head, all the time in the world."

I was not able to get a look at Tenn's face until we stood in the dark, brick-lined passageway to the restaurant; a tiny shaft of sunlight streamed from the courtyard, and it fell across his face as if directed by an aging film star. Shadow obscured his prominent chin and neck, and his face held a high pinkness that made me think of Easter hams fresh from the oven. His mustache and beard were both trimmed short but looked askew, as if he had recently been resting flat on his face; there were hairs posing in quizzical fashion, curious as to their whereabouts. His lips were dry and flecked with white, and his tongue darted quickly and constantly across them, but never long enough to provide any moisture or comfort. Tenn's eyeglasses rested unevenly across the bridge of his nose, which was red, weltlike, as if the glasses had rested too heavily and abraded him. The lenses were coated with fingerprints. His eyes were bright and were confusing in that they could appear blue or green or a combination of the two; the lids were heavy, and he blinked at an alarming slowness. Nonetheless, they were not the eyes of an old or tired man—they appeared to be fighting against the flesh that held them.

The host and several waiters flocked around Tenn like bridesmaids cooing over a giddy bride; they were flush with compliments, praise, greetings. They all knew and loved Tenn, so they all loved me. I was embraced and led, a few steps behind Tenn, to a table in a dark corner, away from the bulk of the diners but still within view, our gustatory real estate of value to us and to the restaurant.

Tenn snapped his fingers, then pointed to a pitcher of water. A tall, elegant waiter brought to our table the pitcher and two large goblets and filled them. Tenn quickly and voraciously drank them. "Good God," he stated, spraying the table with fluid, "I was dying and didn't even know it." There was then a long, dramatic pause. "As is my wont."

I know that the waiter read us the specials and left us with menus. I don't remember any of what he said, and I know that we failed to order for some time. It was more important for Tenn to drink, and he signaled that he wanted a bottle of liquor left at the table, along with a bucket of ice. I chose iced tea, the house wine of the South.

Every eye and ear in the restaurant was trained on us.

"I would like to talk about prayer," Tenn said.

Prayer was introduced to me—and to Tenn—as a device to achieve what earthly vendors could not provide. Prayer opened up supernal supermarkets, opportunities; energies were shifted, and people we needed or wanted appeared.

I prayed to be accepted into the kingdom of heaven and I prayed whenever I plugged an appliance into an electrical socket, because I had been shocked at a young age doing so. I prayed to be left alone by school bullies, and I prayed to die young, because I believed that one remained forever at the age at which one died, and I didn't want to get to heaven and be too old to enjoy myself or to be able to move around with ease. More than anything else, I prayed to get out of Baton Rouge.

Tenn prayed for this same liberation, but his prayers came with a particular consecration: Tenn was raised in the cradle of the Episcopalian Church, his family serving the institution (on retainer to Christ, as he saw it), and his mother finding great strength in having and maintaining a high standing within its social confines. Deluded into thinking that his prayers would hold a higher power because of his connections, Tenn was bitter that they failed to remove him from his unfortunate place of residence.

"I awoke every morning," he told me, "enraged that I was not in Maine (I fancied Damariscotta, because I thought it might be like the Taj Mahal on the water, with silver maples in the background) or Paris or Los Angeles. I expressed grave disappointment as my mother's face hovered over me in the bed each morning. It should have been Gloria Swanson or Judith of Bethulia or any number of imaginary women I had conjured in the night. I came to see that my reality was St. Louis and oilcloth on the table and watery eggs and perpetual abuse by my father and other boys, so I found a new means of prayer and a new means of liberation."

Tenn explained to me that he had and loved a large radio throughout his childhood. The radio reminded him of a photograph he had once seen of a cathedral, and it became for him a holy relic, an object of great adoration, as esteemed as the church that gave him nothing on barren Sunday mornings. Tenn could not recall if the radio was made of cherry, walnut, or oak, but it was the first fine gift he had ever been given, and his first memories of reverence were of polishing this radio with lemon or verbena oil.

Deep in the night of his sleep, Tenn would hold the radio as he might have held a puppy or a stuffed animal, and he would listen to radio dramas, or parties over which band music wafted, and he could imagine other lives, other snatches of dialogue that could remove him from the reality of the life he endured.

"When I was young," Tenn told me, "and if I was particularly inappropriate, my father would punish me by sending me to bed early, demanding that I sit in my room with no illumination and reflect upon my maledictions. Having no access to my books or drawings, I would turn on the radio that sat by my bed and listen to the dramas that played there. I would hug the radio close to my body, the better to hide what I was doing from ears of enmity that lived around me, and also to better feel the vibrations of the action that was emanating from the radio—to feel the action of the airwaves enter my body. I became engaged to my imagination, and I loved the organ stings, the glissandos, the tiny dramas that used so much, so quickly.

"As I listened to these programs, I also husbanded a deep hatred for my father and for the God who had decided, in an attack of cruel capriciousness, to cast him as my father in our own tiny drama, which deprived me of so much, so quickly.

"I prayed a new prayer as I listened to these dramatic programs. I asked to be released from the prison that was my home, from the meanness that surrounded me. I utter this prayer every day, to this day. You'll learn," he explained to me, "that prayers are directed at us, at our souls, our gifts; and I was being released, I was being directed to a new reality.

"When my father was especially angry and fulsome in his rage, when I was especially effeminate or dreamy for his tastes, he would remove my radio from my room, and I was left with nothing but my imagination, my rage, and my pitiful prayer, thrown up to a God who directed, mercifully, my attention to the sounds outside my window—the scattered conversations of my neighbors, the sound of music and dramatic programs emanating from dozens of radios around the neighborhood, cast on spring or summer breezes, or encased in closed-for-winter homes. Faint or forceful, I would listen, and I would imagine the circumstances surrounding the shards of dialogue or music I could hear.

"I believe this was when I came to believe I could write. I believe this was the time when I could imagine that there might be a God.

"As the years have progressed, and as my maledictions have become pronounced and occasionally profitable, I still find myself in the dark, in the silence, listening and waiting, hoping and praying, beseeching that ever-capricious God to show me something, share something with me, cast upon the movie screen that hangs over my bed, or within the radio tubes that reside in my head, a narrative, a woman that I can follow and believe in and dream for and write about to pull me from that St. Louis bed of anger and fear and sadness. God, give me something, anything!"

A pause, a lick of the lips.

"Oil, as you may know, is most often found in our own backyards; euphoria deep within. Aren't we told that the kingdom of heaven is within us? I'm still looking, and my guides, my fearless and supernal Sherpas, are attempting to keep me on the right paths.

"As I stare into the darkness of my many nights and bad intentions, waiting for my mental proscenium to be lit, or for my above-bed screen to flicker with images, I think instead on those women—and a few men—who have been a constant source of inspiration and illumination; examples and extremes. I can't always recall the circumstances through which they came to dominate my thoughts and my earliest attempts to communicate, but I can remember their names, and I have created acts of idolatry for them all, an amended Stations of the Cross in which I recall their acts of alchemy, of kindness, of spiritual and imaginative valor. I hold the memory of these people as close to me as I held that radio, lost to me forever."

Tenn paused and looked into the courtyard, not for human contact, but for a distant spot into which he could stare and think. His eyes were lightly misted, but he brushed away any emotion, and returned his attentions to me.

"A few years ago," he continued, "a friend in publishing told me of a typeface bearing a most marvelous name: Friz Quadrata. Very bold, very stylish. I was given some samples of this typeface, and they were on a sheet of paper upon which you could press and they would stick to whatever you had devised for a communicative purpose. Pressure letters, they're called. What a lovely title that is: 'Pressure Letters.'

"I can waste a good day applying these pressure letters to surfaces of pale judgment that cry out for a story or a woman speaking to us, and I can fool myself that I am writing, that I am praying to that same fucking God again to allow me to hear the distant voices, the distant music, to bring forth words.

"I now imagine the names of my great influences, and I see them in this great and bold typeface, and I focus and I pray and I am not bitter. I am grateful that they have been in my life and continue to be in my life, and I hope to be of use to them again. To matter.

"If there is a God, I think that he realized upon creating the world, upon making the mud and man—the rudiments, the utilities of the world—he needed color and beauty and analysis of what he had made, and he made woman, not from dust of the earth or spit or rain or sweat, but from the bone of a man. Now there's a title, too: 'The Bone of a Man.'"

Another pause, a slight laugh.

"So God presented us with the follies of God, the great and immortal truth of his humor and comfort and care and taste. And at night, in the dark, without my radio, without my rosary, without a word to place on the pale judgment, I see, without effort, and with great peace, the names of these women in Friz Quadrata type on the screen above my bed or on the lids of my tired eyes. And I can dream, and I can sometimes write, but I can always, always believe again.

"And so, baby, that is proof enough for me that there are higher powers and better stations awaiting us—awaiting you—and a woman will lead us to them."

Tenn then picked up his menu and handed it to me. He pointed to it and said only one word: "Write."

Over the next twenty minutes or so, Tenn dictated to me the names of the people he wanted both of us to pray to, dream of, write for.

He called them the follies of God, and I wrote down the names.

The menu was soon covered with names, primarily women, and then Tenn offered me an assignment.

"I would like for you to ask these people if I ever mattered," he confessed. "I ask you to go to them because these people have mattered to me, and they keep me going—to the pale judgment, to face another day, to care again."

The tone of the lunch changed abruptly. I was no longer the rube from Baton Rouge seeking advice and counsel; I was his partner in a venture that would bolster us both. I would go to New York and I would go to these people with a message from Tenn, after which the topic of

Tenn mattering would be broached. I would then call or write Tenn and let him know what had been said.

"I am keeping the disease of bitterness firmly at bay," he said. "I've been to the bottom of that barrel, and I'm not going there again. I am no longer angry, baby. A little aggrieved, perhaps, but anger is a voracious cancer on the soul and the talent: it cripples the instincts, leaves you open to all manner of bad things."

Bitterness was kept at bay by a pronounced concentration on those people who had mattered to him, would matter again, and who might be of some value in pouring some fog on his mental proscenium and allowing some women to come forth and begin talking. He had taken an old rosary—given to him more than a decade earlier, when he had converted to Roman Catholicism—and he had renamed the mysteries and each bead along its length. There were no longer mysteries reserved for the crucifixion or the giving of water as the burdensome cross was carried. Instead there were beads bearing the memory and imagined visages of Jessica Tandy, Kim Stanley, Maureen Stapleton, Maria Tucci, Irene Worth, Marian Seldes, William Inge, Elia Kazan, John Guare—far too many names, so the beads had to be rotated, understudies taking over for leads, Beatrice Straight sometimes being called forward to take over the bead reserved for Geraldine Page, her memory caressed, recalled, blessed.

My assignment would be to knock on the doors of these people and relate to them what Tenn felt about them, then tarry and see if the thought was reciprocated, if they believed that Tenn mattered.

"There is very little that I can do well," he confessed. "I cannot have or care for a child. I cannot prepare a meal satisfactorily—the dishes never emerge at the appropriate times. I cannot even eat a meal when I would like to. Things are falling apart; I lack mental and glandular flexibility. My brain doesn't produce the creative fog, or words or sentences that share anything but the dusty refuse that resides in my skull. I cannot even be a friend for any sustained period of time, because my boundaries, always gently traced in sand—sands of madness—have been blown away and I can't retrace them. I cannot, you see, really do anything, can't relate to anything, but goddammit, I thought once, and I think still, that I can write. Can't I get a single witness to whom I once delivered pages and deliverance to say that I once mattered?"

I accepted the assignment. I took out my first blue book and began to take the notes, to receive the directions to find my way to the people who had mattered to Tenn.

"One more thing," Tenn interjected, as I began to write. "I would like to call you Dixie. It seems appropriate."

I nodded and returned to my blue book and the description of the first folly of God. I wrote her name: Maureen Stapleton.

Two

HER THEATRICAL LIFE began in circumstances similar to Tenn's: in the darkness, with a radio attached to her body and a deep desire to be transported.

"I'm a dumb broad," she would admit to me, "and I don't always know what I mean, and I don't always say what I should say, but I so understood what it meant to be transported. I wanted *out*! The radio was my first taste of an 'out there' that I had to get to, that I believed was a salvation of sorts; and later, I lived in the movies, looking for the same thing—that crazy belief that I could get *there* and away from . . . *this*."

Early on she was allowed access to the radio that resided in the living room, and she would continue to listen deep into the night. Later she was given her own radio, and while Maureen did not recall her model being as grand as Tenn's—there was no resemblance to cathedrals that she could recall—she did keep it near her, on the bedside table, and when she tried to imagine that a male actor in a radio serial was speaking directly to her, she would place it in the bed, right next to her face. "I believed," she told me, "I *had* to believe, that dreaming and praying and hoping would change things."

Maureen and Tenn would remain bonded—through many years and many circumstances—by their insistent belief that to dream was to change things; that to cast an ideal image into the mental theater (Maureen's was a huge Art Deco movie palace; Tenn's a stately theater meant for great plays) was to begin to change lives and paths. These were two friends who could meet at any time, under any circumstances, and begin to talk out their methods of escape.

Maureen and Tenn also shared what they laughingly called joint custody of a dreaming spine that would neither bend nor break. "It wasn't so much that Tennessee and I were committed to what we dreamed—we were—but we were also incapable, unable, unwilling to do anything else. I mean, what could we do? Attached to radios and mothers and dreams—what else was there for us to be? Had we failed . . . Well, we dreamers don't think about that. We push that away with another dream, another drink. I never gave up, because there was nothing else I could do or wanted to do, not because I have some incredible will of steel. I just didn't know what else I could possibly do. And maybe the misfits like me do better because we can't marry for money and be a sweet wife at the door at the end of the day; we can't become a terrific secretary; we can't sell anything but our dream of being an actress—we can't write or edit or search the world for those who can. We can't do a damn thing but wait for someone to write a part that speaks to us. And Tennessee could only write. It was all he really did well; it was all he could do where he felt comfort and power. It's not so much refusing to give up as just sidling along and repeatedly trying, repeatedly failing, until you get a break. And maybe I kept at it because I really wanted to piss off all those people who told me I wouldn't make it. And maybe I kept at it because I wanted to honor the kid who dreamed all this up. I don't know, but I kept at it. However you can manage it, keep at it. And Tennessee and I both kept at it, through a lot of thin, wet times, but we stuck it out. Tennessee and I had our movies and our mothers."

Maureen felt comfortable sharing her dreams with her mother and her aunts, single women who raised her in Troy, New York, when her father abandoned them. These women were angry, funny, fueled with an almost diabolical melancholy, and movies and weekly Mass were their methods of emotional release and comfort.

"I wanted my movies big and dumb and shiny," Maureen admitted. "Serious stuff was too much like life, too much like the drama that was my daily bread. I wanted shiny floors and dancing; singing; silly people who had lots of beautiful clothes and food and people who left to do wonderful things and came back and told stories. People only walked out to get better things to bring into your life; they didn't abandon the life—the cards—they'd been dealt. They coped and looked good. They didn't work at notions counters and drink too much beer and bitch into the night about injustice and Irish men. They had good lighting and futures, and that's what I wanted."

Maureen and Tenn never abandoned their nightly reveries: they both thrived in the darkness—it erased the unsatisfactory surroundings into which they had born, and in which they repeatedly found themselves. "We always got to the bad points," Maureen said, "so that we could get to the dreaming part, the getting-in-the-bed-and-sorting-things-out part, the understanding that we could do nothing else. And we always found each other, no matter how bad the times or how far apart we had become. And I still do this, and I still look for points of escape and entry."

Maureen paused and thought for a minute.

"I don't know how I thought I would do it," she confessed, "but I really thought that this fat little girl from Troy was going to be able to enter ballrooms or dining rooms or whatever setting I liked that night and introduce myself. I didn't grow up thinking I was especially adorable or likable, but I somehow thought that I would be understood by anybody on the 'other side,' the folks who had gotten *there*. I imagined that they had grown up hearing their mother cry herself to sleep; that they had been abandoned and rendered worthless by their fathers; that they didn't understand the rhythms and regulations of daily life, as I didn't. I thought they would embrace me and tell me I was home. And I *still* think this way, and so did Tenn—until the very end."

While Tenn loved his mother, he was frequently frustrated by her, irritated by her intrusions on his life and what he called his ambulatory dreaming, but what he most resented was that she never offered help. "My mother wanted very badly to help," Tenn told me. "Her desire was to help. She frequently told me and my sister that if she could only help, she would. She craved the ability to help and to love, but she didn't know how to do it. My mother gave me the dreams, and she infused me with so much passion and drama, not to mention an eye for a story, an eye for characters and details, but she couldn't hold me or love me in a way that made me feel safe for very long. This Maureen could do for me. Maureen always helped. Always. Not merely in the way that she could—that horrible, niggardly offer so many people make: 'I am doing what I can; I am doing what I think I should.' Maureen gave fully and immediately and consistently. Maureen broke her own bank to see to it that I was safe."

Maureen loved her mother, even if she failed to understand her, even if she resented her stubborn sadness. "Of course, I have *become* my mother," Maureen confessed. "We all do, I suppose, but I'm the same way. I can harbor a grudge or cry over an injustice my whole life, just sit and piss away my life on utter bullshit, and that's what she did, and I thought I knew better and would never do anything but head out for the shiny life. And whatever shiny life Tennessee and I dreamed for ourselves, we set a place, put aside a chair, for our mothers."

"The care and feeding and placement of mothers," Tenn told me, "has been one of my life's greatest obsessions."

Maureen fantasized that she would take her mother with her to the better places. They made a great pair, laughing at the same things, loving the same things, creating a commotion. "Until I had my kids," Maureen told me, "nothing gave me greater pleasure than sharing with my mother. My heart would swell until it hurt, and I would be dizzy with gratitude. I wanted her out of the same place I'd come from, but she didn't have the same drive to get out that I did. I think she found a level of comfort in her sad little corner."

And Tenn?

"Tenn kept writing plays," Maureen said, "and throwing pretty things at his mother, all in the hope that she would tell him he was a man, a grown-up, that he had done well. And on those soggy nights in the dark, I never heard from him that this had happened. I think that Edwina withheld praise until her last breath."

"Perhaps I stopped trying so hard to reach my mother, to have my mother love me," Tenn told me, "because Maureen came into my life. There were other women as well, but Maureen was the greatest, safest place to fall. By finding these women in my life, I no longer felt the great need to connect with and know my mother. I began to look outside of my mother's heart and my own biography for answers to things."

Maureen Stapleton was born on a cruelly hot day in June of 1925, a day so hot that her mother was momentarily comforted by the water that broke and cascaded down her legs, announcing the arrival of her daughter. Maureen loved to tell and retell the story of her mother, in her simple cotton shift, now spattered with water, and her legs shiny with expectant motherhood, rushing to give birth to her "perfect, pudgy" baby.

"I have always been known for my entrances," Maureen remarked drily.

She was equally known for her departures, for her long, frequently miserable absences from friends and family and work, but the primary damage seems always to have been self-inflicted. "No one creates more pernicious scenarios for herself than Mo," Tenn told me, using the favored nickname for the actress. "She is forever on the precipice of some horrendous disaster, and inevitably, she is the only person aware of it. And then," he remarked with wonder, "it just blows over, and becomes another of her rich anecdotes."

"Do not," Maureen told me once, after another so-called disaster in her life, "ever worry about me insofar as drama and food are concerned. I always get my share."

This ravenous need for drama, for attention, and—she was ashamed to admit—her desire to be rescued, and loved anew after her salvation, began at an early age.

"Tennessee and I truly loved each other," she said, "and we were bound by our love of the theater and movies and movie stars and comedy. And we were bound to each other particularly by our mothers: the way they raised us; the things they said, the things they never could say; the things they gave us. The dreaming nature, most of all."

"I have been very fortunate," Tenn told me. "I have been recognized and I have made a considerable amount of money being so recognized. But I cannot escape the persistent curiosity to know about what else exists in the world, and what things might have been like if the wheels of fate had shifted just a little bit on a given day. Whatever happens to me, I need to know that I can commiserate with a friend—particularly Maureen—and lie in the dark and wonder and marvel and cackle at how it happened and how it might have been better or worse or something entirely different. I know that this act of getting into a dark place with Maureen makes her my great friend, but I also think that the act of doing this, of being with her in these dreams, keeps me an artist. Maureen keeps me dreaming."

"Tennessee keeps me moving," Maureen told me. "He likes to dream, and so do I, but my dream is always to keep things moving. I can't bear stillness." Maureen could remember with clarity the fear she felt at the repetitiveness of her life, of the routines in her household, at her school, among her schoolmates; often feeling the need to scream, if only to break the monotony. "I sometimes felt," she said, "that if I didn't break up the routine of things, I would literally freeze, just turn into a pillar of salt or shit and be stuck in that same position for the rest of my life in a schoolroom or on a front porch in Troy, New York, and I would just create a racket to break things up, move me an inch or so farther from paralysis."

The fuel for her "rackets" was provided by the scenarios in films and on the radio, and Maureen began to spend more time alone in her room. "I needed to be alone with the stories," she told me, "so I could dream and find the little sliver of time and opportunity I could slip into." Maureen shared with Tenn a childhood and adolescence peppered with family concern for their solitude, their moodiness, their long stretches of silence and dreaming. "Why," Tenn asked me once, "is it so bad to dream? Why is the honor solely in submitting to reality? To what is present and ready? I never understood why I was odd for wanting to be detached." "I've got to tell you," Maureen marveled, "I would be hard-pressed to think of a happier time. The dreaming, I'm telling you, is the best. Screaming against paralysis is the greatest—it's all downhill from there."

Years later, as Tenn and Maureen, whom he came to call "the old shoe"—because he could always fit right into her rhythms, her schedule, her neuroses, and find understanding and comfort—began to realize that they had achieved, by happy accident, one of their goals: They had found an order to things, a means by which they could place what Tenn called a "black border of clarity" around events and emotions. They would find each other and submit to the ritual of holding each other in the dark, and analyze who they were and how they had gotten there. "I have never felt terribly comfortable with people," Tenn told me, "but I feel comfortable with Mo."

In our conversations Tenn would speak of words by great writers collecting like bricks or gems or stones, rising ultimately in a play or a novel or a story that could make him believe in writing and living. Tenn spoke of prayers that relied on beads or a specific number of steps or rituals, and he came to believe that they could lead him to peace or industry. However, the steps leading to Maureen's West Seventieth Street bedroom were also a ritual, a rite of "clearance and comfort," and Tenn felt better with each step toward that unmade but welcoming bed. "Let me tell you," Tenn told me, "Maureen did not keep an especially fit home, and the bed had seen its share of adventures, but in I went."

"We got into the bed," Maureen remembered, "and we got a radio, a transistor radio that I cadged from one of my kids, and we looked and looked for a drama, for music that might remind us of our childhood, and there was nothing! Just rock and roll and weather and religious nuts. I said, 'Honey, this ain't happening.'"

But Tenn had an idea: It was irrelevant what was *on* the radio. What mattered was what they *did* with what came on the radio. "After all," he reasoned, "we never knew what would pop up on the radios of our youth. Why know now?"

Tenn and Maureen lay in the bed for hours, speaking aloud when they saw or imagined another setting, another room, another reality. They would re-create this scenario, in various locales, with various radios, over the years.

"We didn't drink an ounce on those nights," she would say, "not an ounce. We might have gone to the bed drunk, but we had nothing once we got there and started dreaming. Jesus Christ, were those the only times we were comfortable or felt safe?"

"I tell you now," Tenn told me, "that at an advanced age, knowing many things, I can live and go on and try and fall and try again because there is a woman named Maureen Stapleton in this world."

Tennessee had an idea for a play, created expressly for Maureen.

He came to believe that he could complete a play—a play that *mattered*—if he could dictate it to me.

"The ideas are *here*," he would announce, pointing to his leaf-strewn cranium, ideas swirling out of control. "You and your young eyes, your eagerness, can help me get them *there*." He would point to the blue books or a menu or a tablecloth, and I would take dictation.

She lies in bed, fully dressed. Resplendently dressed, ready to receive. The room is plush, everything in its place, but the bed is a rumpled paradise of linens, undergarments, paperback novels, candy wrappers, handkerchiefs, pads of paper and pens, a multitude of pillows that will be used to prop her up when she is excited or to place over her head when she can't bear another moment of stimulation or boredom or what we call life.

She could be in Mississippi or Morocco; Nebraska or Nepal; Baltimore or Bangladesh.

It does not matter. She has the capacity to be wherever she needs to be.

Or did.

Her powers are beginning to fail her.

By her bedside are a phone and a large radio, very modern, with an enormous dial. If she turns it—and she does, with great skill and swiftness—she can tune into programs across the globe and across time. All of experience and extremity are within this radio.

The radio sometimes fails her.

She reaches for the phone on those occasions and calls several men from a list she has compiled over the years of the great fabulists, writers, and performers around the world.

"Talk to me," she'll say into the phone, and their voices will fill the room, the lights will dim, and through the scrim of the wall behind her bed we will see whatever scene they create together.

She lives in fear of satellite failures, program interruptions, inclement weather.

Radios fail, phone lines are inoperable.

She cannot bring herself to recall the hurricanes of the past, when all communication was lost and she was forced to dive deeply into her own reservoir of memory and painfully dredge up her entertainment, her arousal.

One evening, after an unsatisfactory encounter with a young novelist, whose stories have grown increasingly pale, she takes a break for dinner and to make notes for future phone mates.

There is a rumble of thunder.

She looks out the window and sees ominous clouds.

She quickly places calls to three of her best phone mates and asks them to be ready soon. A storm is approaching, and she has not gained surcease for the night.

She begins writing notes and becomes increasingly giddy at the prospect of the upcoming call. Which of the three should she call? Which one of the men would best handle the scenarios she was considering?

The room is plunged into darkness. The lights are out. The phones are dead.

She rushes to the window and we see her silhouette, outlined with lightning.

She rushes back to the phone, angrily jiggling the receiver.

"Hello? Hello?"

End of act 1.

"I think we can do something with this," Tenn told me. I kept the outline in my blue book, and we continued to talk.

I did not make contact with Maureen until the fall of 1991. I sent several letters to the West Seventieth Street address: one was returned and others were never answered. Ultimately, an editor told me that Maureen no longer lived at that address—she had moved to Lenox, Massachusetts—and he recommended I write to her through the auspices of Chen Sam, the press agent she shared with Elizabeth Taylor. I took the name and address and sent the letter.

However, my editor friend had butchered the name of the press agent, so that it read like the name of a Szechuan restaurant: the letter was sent in the care of Hang Cham, and this created such hysteria on the part of the press agent, and for Maureen, that my letter got a brisk reply.

"I laughed until I peed," Maureen told me, "so you can see that I'm easily amused. But you got my attention."

She was deeply disappointed to learn that mine was an honest gaffe, and not some bold and iconoclastic statement. Maureen had hoped to meet a twisted customer; instead she met a writer who wanted to talk about Tennessee.

"Oh well," she sighed, "you're in the door; do your stuff."

In that fall of 1991, the country—and, more explicitly, Maureen—was totally enmeshed in the Clarence Thomas hearings, and any phone conversations I wished to have with her had to be carefully arranged around this television coverage, her allotted drinks for the day, and the ministrations of a friend who had been drafted to care for her after a serious back injury.

"Hey," she blurted on the phone one day, "this guy wants *out*. I've had him here too long. You wanna come up and see after me?"

I had not yet met Maureen and did not feel sufficiently trained to care for her, with or without a back injury. I somehow knew that caring for Maureen required a very specific set of skills and strengths unknown to me. I could not imagine traveling to Lenox and serving as her masseur and provider of Blue Nun.

Maureen grumbled into the phone and told me that she was growing increasingly disappointed in me. I did not seem the bold person Tenn had loved and spent time with, much less had sent into the world to meet the people who had mattered to him. And yet she stuck with me, because, as she always said, "any friend of Tenn's is a friend of mine."

Maureen was tough and occasionally brutal in her assessments of herself and her peers. Like so many artists—and many considered her one, even if she did not—she had come to feel that she had wasted her life and her talents, and if she could look back on her career and find some good work, she immediately attributed it to Tennessee's writing or Harold Clurman's direction or a fluke or a newspaper strike or a diet she had been on or the fact that all of the other "cunts" (the term she insisted on using for her fellow actresses) had temporarily lost their senses and ceded the center of the stage to her.

Maureen might have been a dreamer, and she might have admitted that her addiction to fantasy was greater than her addiction to alcohol, but she demanded the truth from her friends and those with whom she worked. "I hate a soft sell," she told me. "Do not protect my feelings if I ask your opinion: I'm asking because I'm unsure; I'm asking because I know something's wrong. Tell me the truth. Be brutal. Help me."

Tenn had sent a copy of his play—dictated to me in a mad rush— and she had chastised him for it, calling it furtive and sentimental, a childish plea for affirmation. I learned on that day in 1991, when I traveled to Lenox, that Maureen had been called late at night after I had met Tenn in New Orleans, and in the confusing, raucous conversation, she had assumed that my arrival at her doorstop was imminent. "I thought you were coming to see me—and soon," she told me. "It wasn't unlike Tenn to tell me someone was coming, and it wasn't unlike me to agree to whatever he suggested. So I put away the Blue Nun and took a bath. What took you so long? I'd like to know. I took a fucking bath for you in 1982!"

Maureen had read the play and hadn't liked it, so Tenn read it to her, interrupting himself to explain the casting, the effect, the intention. Maureen hated the play—the "treatment," she called it, "jagged ideas"—and told him he was gasping for air, reaching, hoping, failing.

"You have a great desire to write," she told him, "and nothing to write about yet. Strip it down."

"The play?" Tenn asked.

"The desire," she replied. "The play you can burn."

"I hated to hurt him," Maureen said, "but I knew that as a friend, as someone he trusted and needed, as someone who dreamed and hoped with him, I needed to tell the truth. I also knew that I was dumping on a man who was already in deep trouble, scared, desperate. I tried to give him some positive criticism, some examples."

Maureen reminded Tenn of a conversation with Harold Clurman during rehearsals, in 1957, for *Orpheus Descending*. The play, Clurman had told Tenn, should be like your own hand. Clurman had held up his own firm, elegant, expansive hand, fingers flexed, the palm pink and healthy. Each finger, he recounted, was a memory, a snatch of time so real to you and utterly dear, whether sweet or evil, accidental or committed with intensive purpose. The fingers—the events—lead to the palm, which is the play, and those fingers have to—must—close over the palm. Clurman then curled his fingers over his palm into a tight fist. The events are tightly contained in the play; the play should be as tight as this fist, as powerful, as capable of restriction or damage. And at its conclusion, Clurman continued, the fingers unfurl, the angry redness recedes, the hand is open, a symbol of supplication. The effect has been achieved, and now there is release.

"And your play—this play," Clurman continued, "is like this." At which point he stood and danced a manic jig, both hands spastically splayed, fingers wiggling, frequently clapping together.

"Let me tell you," Maureen told me, "the point was made, and we sat there fucking slack-jawed. I told Tenn that story; he remembered it. He laughed and said he was going to work on his fists and his fogs. I hoped that I helped."

In our time together, Tenn would often raise his fist—clenched, as if extolling Black Power—and announce loudly, *"En avant!"*

It was impossible to engage Maureen on the topic of acting: it bored her senseless. While she had attended sessions at the Actors Studio for many years, she had, like so many others, turned mutinous toward its artistic director, Lee Strasberg, and had largely abandoned much of what she had once held true about its controversial Method.

"I don't think we need to know why we do things onstage," she said, "I really don't. I think we need to be trained to be ready for whatever comes up, and I fault the Studio for failing to adequately train us for a career of any variety or depth. We never worked on our voices or our bodies at the Studio, so when you get to be of a certain age, as certain assholes put it, you no longer have the muscles or the memory in your throat to get a sound for a period piece. I was never trained to move properly, to use my body as that 'vessel' so many speak of. So I think we spent too much time at the Studio delving into our brains and serving ourselves and not plays or audiences. And now," she announced, "I don't want to talk about the fucking Studio anymore. I spent way too much time there. We all did. We learned a lot and we grew, but it's also true that we wasted our time, but we felt glorious, positively glorious, about ourselves."

Maureen was quick to admit that she had little patience with what she called "ordinary, run-of-the-mill" analysis, of either one's art or one's psyche. "Granted, I'm a mess," she said, "and the messes are probably less likely to want to go into the crevices of the brain and see what's wiggling around in there, but I just think it's bullshit. I think I drink because I'm scared and bored most of the time, and booze livens things up for me. I don't think I have the courage to do the things I should do—like face responsibility, or become a full-fledged, grown-up woman—so I delay the taking of that responsibility with a drink or with a pill or with an act of amazingly stupid carnal courage. Is it important why I do it?"

Admitting that it was perhaps a form of folly, Maureen believed that her times alone, dreaming, or with Tennessee, dreaming in "tipsy tandem," were her only consistent and effective forms of self-improvement. "I may be a mess," she said, "and I may be crazy, but I had a great friend—Tennessee—and he had a great friend in me. For a long, long time. And that means something. Or it should."

In the summer of 1990, I had a series of telephone conversations with Marlon Brando. In those days before caller ID, when I simply picked up a ringing phone and took my chances, I heard the voice of Marlon Brando on the other end of the receiver.

"I want to talk about Tennessee," he told me.

I had several calls from Marlon over a period of several weeks. Brando was in what he called a catastrophic state at that time: his son was facing trial for the murder of his sister's boyfriend, and he was also

Maureen Stapleton and Marlon Brando, on the set of Sidney Lumet's *The Fugitive Kind* (1959), based on Tennessee's *Orpheus Descending.* "I think we were trying to stay sane during the shoot," Maureen said upon seeing this image.

taking on the process of writing his autobiography, and he wanted to talk about people and events that had been important to him. "Or should have been," he stressed repeatedly. *"Or should have been."* Brando called to talk about Tennessee Williams—and he did—but he also could not stop talking about Maureen Stapleton.

Marlon adored Maureen and compared her to a large box of Cracker Jacks: sweet, sticky, messy, simple, and, in its way, perfect. Both Tenn and Maureen remembered happy times with the mercurial and beautiful Brando, cluttered and loud and joyous, at the apartment he and Wally Cox shared on West Fifty-second Street. If Tenn and Maureen needed to regularly repair to a bed with a radio and some imaginative memory work, they could also find what Maureen called "a kind of joy and understanding" in Brando's apartment.

"We were young and alive and stupid and generous," Brando told me, "and we believed that anything could happen: Opportunities and new friends were all around us. There was no fear—for our talents or for our persons—and we were, all of us, committed to something big." Brando's apartment was always open, there was food, some wine, perpetual music (both from a phonograph and from the many clubs along the street, from which jazz wafted up to the skies), and everyone spoke of their music or their art or the scene on which they were working—or the passionate life they were seeking. The apartment had a unique open-admissions policy: all were allowed entrance a first time, but a return visit depended on your commitment to life in general and the life of the party within the apartment. "It was rampant," Tenn remembered. "And wonderful." "It was insane," Maureen remembered. "And glorious."

Tenn had known success by the time the parties were attended in the Brando apartment, but he wanted to be with the people he called "the strivers," and he marveled at their energy, their sense of community, their sense of freedom. "I wanted to remain a striver," Tenn told me. "I wanted to be creatively young, even if my flesh would not accommodate me. That apartment and those people helped me to keep dreaming the 'what if' and 'what else' scenarios I needed. I was so afraid and so timid for so long, and these people seemed to have no fears: they were loose and comfortable with their ideas and their minds and their food and their affection." Brando and his friends fascinated Tenn, but they also intimidated him. "They were all beautiful and young and unafraid to touch, to go for what they wanted," Tenn told me, "and I've never been able to accept that, to flow with that. I felt safe with Maureen—safe enough to look at the young strivers and follow their dreams, which were as fervent as mine, but which were not so much in the darkness; not so much the fragile dreams of a queer kid locked in his room, safe from enemies. These were active dreamers, fervent, angry—but joyously angry. They believed that they would make good work, make a difference, matter. Watching these people, I realized that God makes an artist. Face this now and hold the fact dear. There is nothing else to do about the equipment you had installed celestially, and there is absolutely not one single thing you can do about the equipment that your family, your place of birth and culturation, your surroundings, your history implant in you. You can tweak and lie and warp and weave, but you've got what you've got. But the art can come from the tweaking and the weaving. You can't change yourself, but you can change what you produce. He [Brando] was the most exquisite man I think I've ever seen. He smelled of activity and musk and wheat fields. His body was perfectly and powerfully developed, a specimen not often seen in those postwar years. He was built like a stevedore, but he had the most beautiful and fragile of faces—smooth, flawless skin; a full and sensuous mouth; luxuriant eyelashes; a sweet smile. I thought of murky fairy tales my mother had read to me as a child, in which unwary people wandered into forests and discovered magical creatures who combined human traits with animal, with flora, with elements."

"Tenn and I both needed those people, that education," Maureen said. "And I needed him by my side. Tenn made me feel safe. We needed each other."

"Maureen talks of being this shy, fat girl from Troy," Tenn remembered, "but I remember her as joyous, open, brave. She could talk to or seduce anyone; she tackled any role that was given to her—onstage or in a class—and soon she would be my Serafina, a part that was inspired to a great extent by my time in Italy and from my exposure to the fears of Maureen, as well as the warmth with which she covered and healed them."

"I think it was Tenn speaking to me, explaining Serafina to me, that made me feel so safe," Maureen said. "Safer than I ever felt—onstage or in life. It was like being on that bed. What the hell is going on? I always ask. And Tenn calmed me. Tenn had that ability. He could just look at you and say 'There is this woman, she lives in the Keys, and she takes in sewing on occasion. She doesn't always get her work done on time, but she is exquisite in her detail. Any Parisian house would be honored to have her on its staff. She is a mess, however. Her hair, her posture, her diction—all loose and out of control. She only has control with pins and scissors and material. She only has a sense of control when she surrenders hers to the Madonna, who resides on a shelf in her little house full of mannequins and material and melancholy and the scent and memory of a man almost always gone.' I was a mess," she admitted. "I wasn't doing very well. I didn't understand the play or the woman or why a mick from Troy, New York, was playing this virago."

What is a virago? Clurman asked her. Before she could answer, he

Stapleton and Tennessee (1975), happy and tipsy, and looking for an escape, where they could talk. "Even then," Maureen said, "we felt we were just getting things right, learning how to cope."

told her to forget what she thought it was and just play the woman. Maureen did not respond well to such direction, so she sought out Tenn and asked for his help.

"Tenn was a seducer," Maureen remembered. "He seduced with words, and he seduced by loving you so goddamned much. He just looked right through me and told me I could do it, but then he told me who and what I was playing and what I should be doing. He told me to stop thinking and to look into being. I was outside of myself, looking at Maureen playing this woman, rather than being this woman, and in that play—probably only in that play—I was fully alive and real and myself."

It wasn't only on the stage that Maureen gave of herself fully, however. She was a very present friend, and confessed that that period of time that became known as "the *Tattoo* years" were her happiest and fullest—as an actress, a friend, a woman. "Maureen always appears at the ideal time, so she is the angel we dream of, pray for, pine for, wait to see," Brando said. "People laugh at her and her ability—extraordinary ability—to find and secrete food on her person and that of her friends.

Everyone knows that food is not safe around Maureen—it finds its way to her home. What no one seems to add to the stories, to the jokes, is that she shares her bounty, and the food often found its way to my home, to the homes of my friends. On the street once—we were walking and talking and arguing and laughing—a child was crying, and Maureen pulled a piece of cake, wrapped in foil, from her purse. 'Where did you get that?' I asked. 'Jed Harris had an opening last night.' And that was that. Jed Harris opened a play, had an abundance of cake, and a crying child was calmed on the street by Maureen's gift. On that day, in that time, she was his angel." In the *Tattoo* years, there were many examples of this kindness, and Tenn admitted to me that Maureen often fed him or found him food, even though he was what he called "a so-called successful adult." "It wasn't the food," he told me. "It was Maureen. I wanted to see her and spend time with her. My hunger could get her to respond."

Brando was aware of the closeness that existed between Tenn and Maureen, and he was both perplexed by it and envious of it. "You tell me that Tennessee used to lie on a bed with her and talk things out. I can see that. It might be one of the wisest things Tennessee ever did—to have and to keep a friendship with Maureen. I never got on a bed with her to talk things out, but I have watched the sun rise many a morning as we were still trying to figure out life and work and our own battered hearts. Tennessee says he can believe in the world because there is a woman named Maureen Stapleton, and I can't be completely defeated in a world in which she lives."

Both Brando and Tenn asked Maureen—repeatedly, she claims—why she was so sweet, so giving.

Maureen waved away the question.

Tenn believed that it was her attempt to create for herself the narrative that biology and geography had denied her. "We are all fantasists creating the journal of the life we want to live, to read about, to leave behind. Life is a long revision, and Maureen and I share a similar—and odd—version of revision."

Brando saw it differently, however, and believed that things appear most vividly and consistently to those who most want them, and Maureen, more than anything else, wanted everyone to be happy. "She grew up with abandoned women and sad hopes, but her job was to cheer everyone up, goad them into going to the movies, urge them to bake a cake and have a party. Atlas with an apron, you could call her: holding up the world with some confiscated food, a huge heart, and a shoulder on which so many people have leaned and wept."

When I told Maureen what Marlon Brando had said of her, she was silent and still for a time. "Well," she quipped, "we must believe what Marlon tells us."

We sat in her kitchen for several more hours, talking and drinking Blue Nun. Every half hour or so she would ask me to reread what Marlon had told me on the telephone on a summer night in 1990. And I did. Over and over.

I was determined to talk to Maureen about acting, if only because Tenn had told me she was one of our greatest talents—big in gifts and in their sharing. This enraged Maureen, and it was the only occasion on which I saw her angry. "I know that you—and probably Tenn— want me to talk about Strasberg," Maureen said, "and I was betrayed by Strasberg; hurt by him. I don't want to live it, pick it apart, dissect it again. I did all that. I've been through all that. I'd like to forget it. All that you need to know about that time and that place has been given to you—by Tenn."

I had given her several books of notes I had made in my time with Tenn, and she had been up several nights reading them. She found the proper notes and shoved them across a table toward me. "That's why I don't want to talk about it."

"It" was the Actors Studio, which Maureen had needed and trusted, to which she had opened her heart and what she called her "wobbly talent," and she had believed in Lee Strasberg. "I not only bought and read the Bible that was Lee Strasberg, but I copied and bound the damned thing," she said. "And then everything collapsed. Or my eyes were opened. I don't know which."

The notes she pinpointed dealt with Marilyn Monroe.

Maureen looked me in the face and very flatly said: "I did not like what I saw there."

Here is what Tenn said about Marilyn Monroe at the Actors Studio:

"Marilyn was an example of the weak children who seek a guru. Having no balance in her life, having no family, having no understanding of the give-and-take that is daily life, she was drawn toward Mary Baker Eddy, Buddha, Jung, Freud, and finally, the gnomish Lee Strasberg, who specialized in adopting sexually confused, physically abused women and becoming the seemingly gentle father figure they desired. Strasberg lied to her and told her she was the new Duse; he told her she should play Nina; he told her to investigate O'Neill and Shakespeare. This was all folly, because Marilyn had no talent and no understanding, and it was folly because Strasberg only wanted access to and withdrawal privileges from fame.

"Only Strasberg got what he wanted.

"In that awful church in the West Forties, Marilyn sat, face upturned, checkbook open, heart confused, and believed that she might become the great actress Strasberg told her she could and should be. It was an evil, extended con game, and there were many witnesses. You will, no doubt, speak to some of them. It was during Marilyn's tenure at the Studio, and particularly after her death, that the exodus of the talented began from the Studio. The emperor had always been naked, but some of his adherents had finally invested in some spectacles and could see his puny endowments and the intentions he had for them.

"I wanted to love Marilyn: I fall for myths, too. She was fragile and she was beautiful and she was silly. She was the lost kitten in the rain, or the kittens who were born on Carson McCullers's bed in Nantucket— you wonder who will take care of them, because you know that she cannot, and you cry like the child you were who saw the dog run over and the town move on, uncaring and serious about getting their needs attended.

"Marilyn was also annoying and cloying and demanding. She knew her power and she abused it, but in the demonstration of it she degraded herself and she knew this, so the spiral of destruction deepened and intensified. Do not think for a moment that I do not see this in my own behavior and that of others: I am only offering a sobering lesson.

"When we can't imagine understanding or loving a God or some other myth of support, we attach ourselves to artistic symbols: the lost soul; the waif; the abused artist. This is all utter nonsense. Get to work. Work hard and well. Your troubles are no one's business but your own. Don't be a Pharisee extolling yourself on the street—take it inside; use it; share it; overcome it.

"I spoke to Arthur [Miller] only once about Marilyn, and it was during his exhumation of her [*After the Fall*, 1964]. I wondered if he was satisfied; I wondered if he had exorcised himself of her spirit and her toxins, and I wondered if he had expiated his own sins. He told me he thought he could help her, yes, but he wanted to buck the odds and be the homely, skinny, cerebral Jew who got the beauty queen; he wanted to be the bookish, pedantic, shy boy who introduced the beautiful and simple girl to books and plays and ideas and the act of thinking things out beyond the crotch and the nipples and the people with the cameras. Arthur wanted to be her savior, but he also wanted to be envied; he wanted attention; he wanted to be noticed; he wanted to expand his audience.

"I think Arthur Miller got what he wanted.

"It's fine to cry for Marilyn Monroe. I did, and I still do. She was tragic, but she was also lucky. There are beautiful, sad, dumb girls all over the world who endure worse than she did, but they never get to live on the screen or bathe in perfume or populate the dreams of people who love beauty or who love pain or who wonder what it must be like to possess such sexual power.

"Let her go. Look at the beauty, but move on. There is nothing else there. A pretty visage with a sad story."

Maureen was deeply affected by these words from Tenn, and she wanted to comment on them. "I love acting, and I needed it; but acting . . . no art on earth is a cure or a replacement. You have to have a life. You have to love and be betrayed and heal and move on and start all over again, and there is no church or book or slogan or some single person who can give you something that will make it all work for you. No one. But we all stupidly believed that we had found a secret, a way, a shortcut, to life or happiness or understanding.

"Marilyn Monroe," Maureen continued, "was a sweet girl. I know she was a woman, but I think of her as a girl. She had talent, but she was not the second coming. Lee and others at the Studio made her the second coming because they needed her to be this; they needed her to stay there and bring in the money and the attention. It was easy to be intimidated by Marilyn, and I was. She was so goddamned beautiful. Luscious. Sweet. But the intimidation disappeared fast, because she was so committed and so ready to get better. She listened like no one else, and she worked to the point of a migraine, and I would tell her to lighten up, go easy on yourself, but she couldn't: she wanted to be taken seriously; she wanted to get it right. I bitch about my upbringing, and my sad mother and sad aunts and no men around and nothing but dead ends all around, but I had love and food and the space and the silence to dream. Marilyn didn't have that. She told me once that she just wanted her own bedroom, her own bed, and a door she could close. And grass. Grass to run in. Trees to hug and flowers to pick. This was a girl who had nothing but the great gem that she was, and everyone got to hold and fondle that gem, and then put it back when they were done with it. She was happiest—for a time—when she married Arthur, and there was a country house and trees and fruit and flowers—and silence and doors." Maureen paused, her voice thick and low. "I just wish," she told me, "that we had spent more time helping her find the grass to run and the room with the door she could close. I wish more time had been spent helping her instead of pushing her. It can't always be about the art or the play or the dream in the dark: sometimes it's about the person who needs to be cared for. I felt that way about Marilyn, and I felt that way about Tennessee.

"That's how I feel about it all now," Maureen told me. "The emperor has no clothes. Let it go. There is nothing else there. Maybe we all dreamed too much for too long."

By the time I met Tenn in 1982, he felt that the roles had been reversed for him and for Maureen: he now felt lost and confused and bereft while she was soaring—or so he thought. Maureen had won an Oscar in the spring for her performance in the Warren Beatty film *Reds*. One year earlier she had been much ogled during the theatrical and show-business extravaganza that was the revival of Lillian Hellman's *The Little Foxes*, starring Elizabeth Taylor. Maureen was being offered many film and television roles. Tenn felt that she was now in a position to offer him aid and advice.

"I could never explain to him that I was still the same mess I'd always been," Maureen said, somewhat exasperated. "I was just getting paid a bit more; that's it. The work wasn't really any better. I certainly wasn't functioning any better. But Tenn believed that I was now connected, and he wanted me to make calls for him, to help him get his plays produced. He even wanted me to call Warren and get him some film work."

Maureen made none of the calls, but she did stay on the phone with her friend and tried to calm him, reassure him, and get him back to the pale judgment.

"His writing had become an ordeal," Maureen remembered. "Writing for him was like walking into gunfire—he knew he was going to be injured or killed, and he couldn't face it. He wanted someone to walk him through it. That's why he liked you."

Maureen was the first person to explain to me why Tenn had found my presence reassuring or necessary.

"I mean, you're great," she confessed, "and I like you, but you were gonna help him get the words on the page. Or so he thought." Maureen was exasperated by her friend, by his creation of so many steps and rituals and activities he needed to try to write, to believe he could write, to get in the mood. Journals were bought, begun, discarded. Prayers were written or learned, then forgotten. Everything was done but the writing. "He drove me crazy," Maureen told me. "What do you say to a friend who's afraid? I couldn't tell him he was driving me insane. I couldn't hurt him. I wanted him to know he was a great writer; that he could do it. But he . . . *had to do it*! He kept aiming for the writing, but he wasn't writing. He wasn't—God forgive me—writing well." Maureen would talk to Tenn deep into the night, in the measured and soothing tones he had reserved for her when he told her who Serafina was, where she lived, how she lived. Maureen offered to Tenn the hand she had offered that led him to Marlon Brando's apartment, full of young artists, fervent and fearless.

"I would say to him: 'Tenn, you are a playwright, an American playwright, born to us on March 26, 1911. Your words are magical, because they came to you as an escape from a world you couldn't handle, and while they are poetic and shot through with fantasy gold, they came to you through windows and across the fences of neighbors and overheard in offices of priests and around the kitchen tables of frustrated wives and mothers. The words in your plays are promises, and your plays are promises. We need you and we love you. Your writing is glorious and—fuck you—it mattered.'"

TENN AND I GOT UP from our table at the Court of Two Sisters. Lunch was over, and Tenn wanted me to join him at the Cathedral of St. Louis, which faces Jackson Square, the church in which Tennessee "received Christ."

The moment Tenn entered St. Louis Cathedral, he took a sharp left and slipped into its tiny, cluttered gift shop. "We are in the market for rosaries," Tenn announced, and the wan acolyte in charge pointed us toward a shelf on which rested a series of bags and boxes, as well as stainless-steel implements upon which were draped a variety of rosaries, cast of wood, ivory, onyx, and plastic, all in various sizes, from a laughably tiny version meant, perhaps, for a very young child, to one so large it could have been a wall hanging. Tenn was drawn to a moderate-sized black model that hung on a Styrofoam bust. "I like this one," he told the clerk, who then directed him to a lower shelf stacked with plastic bags. Tenn chose the first one that read "Holy Rosary/Black/Large," and pulled it open. The rosary fell into his welcoming palm, and we realized that its cross bore no Christ.

"This is a good sign," Tenn whispered. "A rosary with no Christ indicates that He is already on the job. This is very portentous." Tenn purchased the rosary—against the shocked, strong objections of the clerk, who called it damaged and ineffective—gave it to me, and we walked into the cathedral proper. When Tenn entered, he dramatically genuflected and made the Sign of the Cross. He remained in the position for some time, and I began to wonder if he was able to lift himself. I was not a Catholic, and I did not know the time allowed or required for such a gesture, but I also did not want to interrupt what might have been a sacred or obligatory rite. As I was considering which action to take, he lifted himself and grabbed my arm. He walked with purpose toward an array of red votive candles and looked for one that "reminded" him of Maureen. He chose one high and in the center, was unable to reach it, and asked me to light it.

Tenn surveyed the pews, looking for the perfect one, the absolute right one, for our purposes. "We must move quickly," he told me in a whisper. "We must do this before the candle has been extinguished."

We finally found a pew, fifth from the main altar, in the center of the cathedral, and we sat, or rather I sat and Tenn fell to his knees. He lowered his head to begin his prayer, but paused, turned to me, and said, "Write this down. I want you to take this to Maureen."

I pulled out my blue book and pen and waited.

In a few seconds, Tenn began to pray aloud.

"I found my voice, which is to say my salvation, in the dark, with a radio, or the voices of neighbors, and a pure hatred in my heart, and a prayer that I would be transported. I pray that you and others who dream, in a literal and a spiritual darkness, are transported, and I pray, and I know, that they will, on the other side of a stage or a backyard

The garden behind St. Louis Cathedral in New Orleans, with its statue of Christ throwing a shadow upon the building where Tennessee claimed he found Christ, sobriety, and the courage to continue

fence or on the farthest reaches of understanding, find a listener, some recognition, some feeling of usefulness.

"We wait here, Jesus, in a confluence of crises for voices to rise up. I pray that the fears that cripple the young eventually force them to walk when they can find no other progress; when their only movement is purely emotional, I pray that their artistic limbs will take them to people hungry for what they've observed, on the sidelines, silent and seeing.

"I pray that the world will always want a story to be told, and I pray that they will always be able to trust themselves and others strongly enough to hear and accept what others have experienced, lived through, and strained to turn into art that can be subsumed by the willing.

"I pray that we will care to be big—of heart, of soul, of pocket, of industry, of daring—to magnify who and what we are through whatever means we have—in art, in living, in being. This is a great undertaking; it has value; it has saved so many; it is dying, but it is always in the process of dying, and is always rescued by those who recognize its frailty, its grandeur, and its necessity. Our greatness often lies in saving something that will be of use to souls unknown to us.

"I pray that this boy finds these women, these struggling, wonderful agents of change and creation, and learns not only to dream but to love and to apply and to give and to matter.

"I pray that I have mattered to some, and that I will matter again. I offer this candle to Maureen in the belief that its light will serve primarily to remind her that she, more than so many, has loved, applied, given, and mattered.

"I am, God help us all, a writer, and I have nothing else but my voice, for which I offer up, to my enduringly patient God, my heartfelt thanks.

"Amen."

Tenn sat upright, leaned into me, and sighed. We looked at the altar, bathed in lovely amber light, and focused on the inscription ECCE PANIS ANGELORUM: Behold the bread of angels.

No more words were spoken. People came and prayed and left.

Tenn patted my hand, we got up, and I delivered him to his hotel. I drove back to Baton Rouge, with one blue book full, a menu covered with scribbles, and an assignment.

Three

ALONG ENTRY.

"A writer must admit to everyone—but primarily to himself—when he is unable to write, when he is unable to communicate, which is to say when he is unable to care. I have suffered no known incidents or accidents of the brain. I am unaware of any neurological maladies that might have pressed negatively upon my nerves or arteries, creating any blockage of feeling or movement. And yet I face the task of writing—not to mention the task of living—with a profound sense of apathy and anger, and they often alternate their entrances. A day may begin with my rage at the fog not coming over my mental boards, or it may begin lethargically, with my feeling that it might be best if the fogs remain offshore. But I write. I face the task every day. Pen to paper or keys to paper. Word upon word.

"I told you that I do not consider myself a religious man. I do not understand or try to understand the mysteries of Scripture or dogma or superstition or holy tradition. I use them. I try to understand them. I believe that if I count, as so many Catholics do, the injuries seared into the flesh of Jesus, count them, see them, feel them, adding them up, imagining their depth, they might be transformed into words.

"I imagine that words can become like the beads on the rosary, and I can count them, hold them in my hand and hold them in my mind, and hold them in my heart, and they can become images too. Images can become words, and words can become stones or steps that can lead me to a play.

"A woman appears only when images she deserves appear. My goal is to get to the images, to make my mind and my heart care enough to imagine a woman in a situation from which she must escape, and I can then hold out a means to do so for her.

"Which I can't do, because the essential act of caring has left me.

"This gives me no comfort.

"When I think of words as stones or steps, I'm reminded of another woman. Not a woman who ever inspired the fog, not a woman who ever altered the idea of theater for me, but a woman who altered my sense of what a writer could be.

"She was a stone against which I could rub my talent and feel that it became sharper, and I can now imagine, from a distance, armed only with memory and imagination, that she can do this for me again.

"Tough and sad and funny and angry and lonely. Lovely and ugly and elegant and rustic. A born pilgrim who built—stone by stone, word by word, step by step—an artist."

This was Tenn's description to me of Eva Le Gallienne.

I NEVER MET Eva Le Gallienne in person, and only spoke to her on the telephone twice, calls that were arranged by Kim Hunter during my first year in New York.

Le G, as she asked me to call her, had no interest in seeing anything Tenn had said about her, and she let out a derisive snort when I offered to show her notes on other actresses Tenn had mentioned to me.

"No time for all that," was what she told me. Le Gallienne could not be bothered to consider or "imagine" anything; she was, however, ready to be of assistance. "If I can help you," she told me, "I'll do it. I'll do what I can, but I don't want to talk about things that I can't understand or that I have no interest in trying to understand. I can talk about Tennessee, and I can talk about me. *So.*"

Le Gallienne had a habit—at least with me—of ending sentences with that one word, and it sounded as if it were both a firm conclusion—closing a subject—and also, with its slight lilt, a cue to move on to the next question or comment. While Tenn had warned me that she was

Eva Le Gallienne, circa 1920, perpetually working—
on herself, on designs—for her Civic Repertory
Theatre, which the young Tennessee followed with
great interest

formidable and often curt, my impression was of a curious, alert woman
eager to analyze and argue.

"If I may," she said to me early in our first phone call, "might I
suggest that you never easily accept the conclusions of others when it
comes to your work. I'm sure that Tennessee meant very well by telling
you about his experiences and his impressions, but those should not be
impressed upon you to such a degree that you begin to feel that his was
the only way, or that his are the only opinions that are truthful.

"He was a great writer," she continued, "but he was a flawed man.
Emulate the writer, not the man."

This laconic introduction was one that I had been prepared to expect
from Le Gallienne, because it mirrored the odd but important relationship Tenn shared with her. "She never bored me," Tenn had said to me,
"even when I expected her to do so. Even when I expected the worst

from her—judgments and self-aggrandizing attitudes and bitterness over spent gifts. But it never happened that way. She had a mind that was like a tough, tall broom that swept everything before it away, and what was left was a clean, bare floor, a screen, and you could then project onto it whatever you needed to rethink something, to begin again."

The first meeting between Tenn and Le Gallienne—or at least the one that Tenn could recall—had not gone well. Tennessee Williams was already a successful playwright—both *The Glass Menagerie* and *A Streetcar Named Desire* had been produced and published—and Le Gallienne admired his work, had studied it, and had, she admitted, taken notes.

"I felt that his talent was great enough to bear repetition of experience," Le Gallienne told me. "I cannot think of a greater thing that could be said to a writer, but I don't think he understood my statement. He looked bemused, even a little bored, but I wanted to tell him that those plays had altered me, had—now how can I say this?—uncomfortably forced me to accept some things about myself and about others that I might not have. This was great praise as I saw it, but I got the impression that it angered him, that he believed me to be a critic who wanted to show him where he needed improvement."

Tenn admitted that the meeting was tense and "decidedly odd." Tenn looked upon Le Gallienne, who was perhaps fifty years old when the meeting took place, as "ancient, of a different time," although he had great admiration for her work with the Civic Repertory Theatre, her championing of writers, and her own writing skill, which he knew from her autobiography, *At 33*. Tenn also held in great esteem what he called her "blunt-force sleekness" in handling her lesbianism, which she carried not as a burden or a dysfunction, but as another attribute she chose not to deny and which contributed to her work, just as much as her talent, her beauty, and her intelligence.

"I was not terribly educated about lesbians," Tenn admitted to me. "I had only a tertiary understanding of their trials through Radclyffe Hall and Mrs. Danvers [Judith Anderson's Sapphic servant in the Hitchcock film of *Rebecca*], and I had a not much better understanding of what we called the male homosexual. I was still in a bit of a maze in that regard, and Miss Le Gallienne appeared neither deranged nor incomplete."

Le Gallienne was, however, intimidating to Tenn: She was intelligent, a fact she chose not to hide, and she was opinionated, unafraid, in Tenn's eyes, to speak her mind to anyone. After she had made her remarks about studying Tenn's plays and making notes in their margins, Le Gallienne asked the young writer what he thought of Ibsen. This was of no small concern to Le Gallienne: she adored Ibsen, translated his works, studied him intently.

Recalling the encounter years later, Tenn could not help laughing. "I am a terrible reprobate, I'm afraid," he said. "I could not help myself, for I felt that a stern, spinsterish Shaker woman had taken it upon herself to emend my plays. I told her I had, indeed, read the plays of Mr. Ibsen, had seen them in numerous productions, and found them to be quite like the act of eating a box of soap flakes, when they were not like two months of Sundays in church."

Tenn cackled at the memory of his comment, but he also recalled that Le Gallienne did not dismiss or scorn him. Instead, they continued their discussion, and when they met again, years later, they picked up their friendship, such as it was, and kept talking.

"He was a child," Le Gallienne remembered, "and a nervous one. I knew he was performing for me, trying to be smart. I also felt he wanted an argument, a defense, from me. I refused to offer one. I wanted to talk about his work, about work in general.

"If you want to know about me," she told me, "you'll need to know that I want to work, and work is what motivates everything I do.

"*So.*"

Tenn believed that Eva Le Gallienne's autobiography, *At 33,* began with the following paragraph:

"At seven in the morning of January eleventh, 1899, a lusty and hideous baby was brought into the world to artistic parents. Bow bells sounded for the cockney baby, because, as is well-known, no baby born to bow bells can be anything but cockney. Thus began my first year."

That is not the first paragraph of *At 33,* but Le Gallienne liked it. "In some ways," she laughed, "it's better, it's tighter."

Tenn and Le Gallienne shared a love of dramatic entrances—and alliteration.

"My God," she once said, after I had recounted something he had said, "he really gets caught in the circle, doesn't he? I do it, too, searching for a rhythm."

Le Gallienne sympathized with Tenn's desperation for order, for a plan, a metaphor—anything onto which he could depend to get to the act of writing. However, she had never been able to display any patience—or to hold her barbed opinions—when Tenn began talking about rivers and streams and steps and stones.

"He had the talent," she all but shouted. "He had the gift. This was demonstrable; that could not be disproved. What he lacked, and what I believe he always lacked, was the foundation of discipline and respect that everyone needs to remain balanced and to function. When he was young and strong, he could fly on lots of dreams and little maintenance, but when I last saw him [a meeting Le Gallienne believed occurred in 1980], he was adrift, sad, diminished." Tenn had told her during that last meeting that he felt distracted. "*He* was the distraction," Le Gallienne quipped. "Tennessee Williams was the only thing that could destroy Tennessee Williams. And he did."

Could anything destroy Eva Le Gallienne? I was prompted to ask this question because Tenn had told me that she and her Civic Repertory Theatre had been launched with great fanfare and hope, only to fail. Le Gallienne's face and hands had been severely damaged in a fire at her home in Connecticut, and she had constructed ways to conceal both the scars and the nerve damage that had resulted. A film career that she had pursued, primarily for funds to continue working in the theater, had not prospered. After each of these setbacks—heavily chronicled and intently watched by Tenn—Le Gallienne had returned to her home in the country, regrouped, pondered, thought about things. "I am amazed at her resilience," Tenn told me. "I wish I had it."

"To live is to be destroyed," Le G told me. "There is no other way to get through life. We have to have hopes and we have to witness them being shattered; we have to love and we have to lose; we have to fail; we have to find ourselves depleted of faith. I have been destroyed repeatedly, but I have been able to recuperate; I have been able to mend myself; to love and to be loved; to find some other way of working.

"And this was absent in Tennessee Williams," she continued, "who believed in writing, and who once could write, but when that gift had been altered by his self-destruction, he could not recuperate, because he had never learned how to survive on his own. He used sex and liquor and drugs and amusements where he ought to have applied love and faith and work.

"I haven't worked—fully—as an actress in years, but this has not prevented me from finding other ways of being of some use and of some purpose." When she offered this summation of her life as an actress, Le Gallienne was ninety years old, and she felt that her ability to act "fully and freely" had disappeared some thirty years before our call took place, at some point in the early 1960s, when she launched another version of her repertory theater and tried yet again to take challenging works to people all across the country.

I was amazed that Le Gallienne had used that phrase "being of some use and of some purpose," and I told her that Tennessee had used it frequently, to the point where other actresses in whom he confided used it as well.

"It was first uttered by my father," Le Gallienne told me, referring to Richard Le Gallienne, a poet who worried that the bounties of nature and affection would pull him from his writing table. "He instilled in me the love of languages, the love of work, the love of nature," Le Gallienne said, "and he taught me that we needed to know our histories, to know everyone's histories. We are all perpetual students, and we are all perpetually ignorant—of something."

When we ended our first phone call, Le Gallienne told me that our conversation, as well as Tennessee's words I'd read to her from my notes, had reminded her of a little poem her father had written, and which was among the first she had memorized.

> At last I got a letter from the dead,
> And out of it there fell a little flower,—
> The violet of an unforgotten hour.

"This is what you've given me," Le Gallienne told me, "a violet from a fabled time; a gift from a great writer."

It was Eva Le Gallienne who instilled in Tenn a love for the words of Ralph Waldo Emerson, and in their earliest visits, Tenn could talk about Emerson and draw a line toward his interest—capricious at best—in Christian Science, Religious Science, and "a damnable tendency toward Christian positivism," as Le Gallienne remembered.

"His mother had given him a book once," Le Gallienne recalled, "and it was called *It Shall Be Done Unto You,* and with all that he should have been remembering and doing, snatches of that book stayed within his mind."

It took me many years and many searches of used bookstores to find a copy of *It Shall Be Done Unto You*, which, as Le Gallienne's memory has it, was given to Tenn not long after the success of *The Glass Menagerie*. "To keep him centered," Le Gallienne remembered. "On the straight and narrow."

The book is subtitled "A Technique of Thinking" and was written by Lucius Humphrey and published in 1936 by Duell, Sloan and Pearce. (It has since been reprinted as a paperback and "gift idea.") Tenn never mentioned the book to me by name, but Le Gallienne's vivid recollection of what it entailed—not to mention her scorn—led me to believe that much of what he remembered as his mother's "survival tips" derived from this book, and what he took from multiple readings he shared with many of the actresses I would ultimately meet.

For all of his dependence on psychoanalysis and its attendant prescriptions, all of the illegal substances ingested, the liquor, and the "happy subsuming" into the Roman Catholic Church in the late 1960s, many of Tenn's core beliefs concerning his mental rejuvenation stemmed from this book's teachings on creativity.

Tenn's obsession with work, and his fear that he might never again work well, was calmed by remembering what he called "the Creative Principle." In chapter 4, entitled "Be Ye Doers," there is a description of the division of the mind of man into three component parts, or phases. Each of these phases has distinct qualities peculiar to itself; each complements the activities of the others; and each is an extension of, and one with, the Creative Principle.

> The first and foremost phase is Creative Principle—God. It is the embodiment of all the known laws of creation, and not only expresses itself in the other two phases but also constitutes the highest phase of intelligence, our Super Mind, symbolized as the *Father*.
>
> The second phase, the "Christ Mind," manifests its distinct and peculiar quality in that it is at once conscious both of our God phase and also of the human phase. It is the conscious link between the two, and is symbolized as the *Son*.
>
> The third phase, our human mind, or the Habitual Mind, is distinct and peculiar in that it can, with understanding, use all three phases for the purpose of fulfilling its desires, or it can, by its ignorance, deprive itself of the privileges of the higher phases. Nearly all of us are motivated exclusively by the restricted ideas which arise from

the limited understanding of Habitual Mind. This Habitual Mind is the individual's accumulated consciousness—the aggregate of experiences arising from the reactions of inherited tendencies to environment and education. By relying solely upon habitual thinking we deprive ourselves of experiences we might otherwise have. In fact, most of us are running our lives today on one cylinder. I can of mine own self do nothing.

Tenn spoke often of the Habitual Mind, whose description he found in Humphrey's book, and of the Mortal Mind, which is a term attributed both to Mary Baker Eddy, the founder of Christian Science, and Phineas Quimby, the healer from whom, it is suggested, Eddy found her inspiration. Several times Tenn told me that the human race is governed by its imagination, a quote of Napoleon's that appears in the Humphrey book, preceding the following paragraph, one frequently quoted by Tenn to me and others: "By means of our thoughts and feelings we can unite ourselves with, and direct, Creative Energy. Therefore we should understand the vital necessity of forming the habit of thinking upon our thoughts and controlling them. Nothing in the world is more important than considered thinking. It is the practical means of consciously producing whatsoever we desire."

Eva Le Gallienne epitomized for Tenn the art of considered thinking. So too did Stella Adler, Edith Evans, Ruth Gordon, and a series of other actresses who served as a unique section of his redesigned Rosary, because the memory of them, the "habit of thinking upon their thoughts and actions," kept Tenn sane and balanced deep in the real and imagined night of his confusion: Julie Harris, Kim Hunter, Elizabeth Wilson, Frances Sternhagen, and Marian Seldes.

Le Gallienne held a high place among those actresses because she was tough and outspoken, and because she shared with Tenn the additional bonus of creating, of tapping into Creative Energy, while also carrying the secret and, as he imagined it, the shame of being "inverted." (I had never heard that term applied to a homosexual, and Tenn explained to me that it was the term his mother preferred. "She felt it was more sympathetic to their plight," Tenn said, "and it stated their sexual preference as if it were brown eyes or a cleft chin—or a cleft palate. An accident, a trick, of nature.")

Le Gallienne and I did not discuss her sexuality at great length, but she did not feel that it was a burden to be carried, nor did she feel that she had brought it forth often as a matter of pride or embarrassment. But Irene Worth told me that during their work together, Le Gallienne had told her, in confidence and with great tenderness, that she was a lesbian. "She thought I should know about it," Irene remembered, "as if it were narcolepsy or memory lapses—something that would impact our working relationship, our time together on the stage. It didn't matter to me at all," she continued, "but I did feel that she needed to tell people, some people."

Tenn believed that Le Gallienne escaped the many problems he had experienced with his homosexuality—or rather his homosexual relationships—because of her strict ordering of her life and her emotions. He spoke of her many journals filled with her tiny, elegant, spidery script, noting her thoughts, her readings, her activities, her plans. Le Gallienne did not let the "accumulated consciousness," the "garbage that clutters our minds and drags us down," as he saw it, to alter the Creative Principle. Their shared homosexuality could be categorized, via Humphrey, as "the reactions of inherited tendencies," and Tenn believed that Le Gallienne had trumped them, or had at least compartmentalized them, by virtue of her dogged discipline, her noting of every thought or action.

"What is religion?" Le Gallienne asked me. "A series of acts and intentions meant to honor, most of the time, one man: Jesus Christ. He is to be our example. What should Tennessee's religion have been? *Writing*. And what is writing comprised of? *Words*. He should have been in the habit of worshipping, collecting, studying words all the time."

When Tenn would meet with Le Gallienne, and in their phone calls in the last few years of his life, they would discuss writers and their works. The subject of Ibsen would be brought up. "I would quote Ibsen in his native tongue," Le Gallienne recalled, "and I would then translate it, noting the intention of the words, their placement, their meaning. There are no accidents in Ibsen, and if you divine his intentions, you can begin to see how a great writer thinks."

Tenn would follow this line of thinking for a time, and would even entertain Le Gallienne's request that he take apart his own works in this way. "He could then explain, with great clarity," Le Gallienne remembered, "what Blanche was doing and thinking, what her intentions were, and how the brutal swirl of circumstances delivered her to her safest, desired place."

But Tenn's mind would wander; he would grow tired of searching for the foundations and scaffolding of great works. His Habitual Mind would take over, and he would be hungry for gossip, for ideas, for affirmation.

"I would be fascinated in the beginning," Tenn told me, "of Le Gallienne telling me to begin each play with the title page, the name of the author, the date of publication." Stella Adler discussed plays in this manner as well, but she was far more passionate, far more sympathetic to the artistic temperament than Le Gallienne, who had about her, Tenn said, "the pure rigidity of a devoted teacher." Tenn liked, however, what the deconstruction of plays revealed. "Line upon line, word upon word, you see the bones," he marveled. "You see the intention, and it must be what musicians feel when they take notations—chords and notes on a page—and transform it into a piece of music, and it's a piece that makes you think of your mother, or a lover, or the sun on your young arms."

Recalling a conversation with Le Gallienne, and how she implored him to think of the words he wrote—that anyone wrote—as strings that were literally attached to people or ideas, Tenn became animated and emotional.

"I am seduced by the strings—in songs as well as in plays. The strings we attach to the people we love, the people who are in our works. The strings are feelings and memories—our memories. But they must be heard musically; they have to sound like orchestral strings to have their effect. The sound is what I imagine in moments of extreme intensity and vulnerability. I pray to have the ability to evoke through words what wonderful orchestral music can accomplish—or even tawdry jukebox ditties that pull out a string to move a person. I can recall times in my life when I would be walking down a street—a street in El Paso or Provincetown, Hollywood or New Orleans, Dallas or New York—and from a bar or an open window I might hear the sound of strings and with it a voice that competed with its cry, its teasing wail. It's a sound that stops me cold, literally. I stand there and I'm transported to another time in my life when I had a similar feeling, when my heart hurt so much, from longing or hunger or rage. I can remember being in that bed, in the dark, in St. Louis, sent to bed hungry by my father, my radio removed from my night table and hidden, and through the open windows all around our house, I could hear Jack Benny and *The Shadow* and *Lux Presents Hollywood* and strings! And those strings were saying to me that life was rotten, small, and worthless, but life, *this* life, could be escaped. Follow the strings.

"A friend lost his mother a few years ago," Tenn remembered. "She died in a nursing home that reeked of death and disinfectant, and my friend felt haunting in the halls, spirits discarded. When my friend's mother had been young, she had worn Mitsouko and Bellodgia, and her clothes, her handkerchiefs, the air that swirled around her, always carried these scents. My friend hated to see his mother in this condition, smelling of shit and unguents and pine oil. When my friend's mother died, he went to the nursing home to spend a few moments with her body, to bury her and any ill will he had harbored, to spend himself of some tears and some resentments. She was tiny and withered and fully dead, but the air hummed with energy and Mitsouko, and I wondered, my friend wondered, if the smell returned as she returned to her desired self, or if he felt compelled to remember her, even in an olfactory manner, as he knew her in happier times, and as he knew she would prefer to be. *That* is writing; those are strings. The strings tug at our hearts musically, and they also pull us, tightly and closely, to those things we've loved, those things we've lost, those things we pray will return— those things that are, God help us, who we are. That is what I hope the Creative Principle can be."

When I read those words to Le Gallienne, she cried, and she announced that I had been in the presence of a writer. "He still could do it," she said, "if he had wanted to. Tell me, where did those gorgeous images go?"

I had no idea if he eventually wrote them down, or if he ever took them to a pad of paper or a typewriter. He never mentioned those images to me again in our short time together—but they effortlessly came forth when he took thoughts he had, analyzed the feelings they generated, and expressed them in words that meant something to him.

"You see," Le Gallienne said, "if he had just gotten himself to a piece of paper, if he had just begun the act of capturing his feelings, he would have been able to write a play we would now be producing and loving and discussing. But what did he do instead?"

There was drinking and praying and talking and circular walks in the Quarter, and on every corner a search for the writer he had once been.

"He didn't believe in the pragmatic habit," Le Gallienne continued. "He was like that other Tom—the Tom in *The Glass Menagerie,* who wanted magic, who got lost in dreams. We all know what happens to people who descend into magic, don't we?"

No, I said.

"They disappear," she said.

Four

"**M**EMORY, OF COURSE, is unreliable, often evil, but it is the source of our identity."

That is the note I was given as Tenn and I began to walk around New Orleans one morning.

Tenn and I spent part of our second day together on foot and in my car, and because of the amount of time I spent behind the wheel, my notes were sporadic, composed at rest stops and when I returned home that evening. Tenn wanted to talk, exhume memories, and he needed someone to tell them to. He asked me to be that person.

I drove Tenn to the corner of Coliseum and Constantinople streets and parked in front of an ornate house, a whirl of pastel meringue. In this house he had been young and handsome and much appreciated. Promise was, he recalled, "written" all over him, and he was loved by the married man who lived here with his wife. Tenn was also liked by proper people who did not mind that this young and awkward writer often needed money and encouragement to keep heading to his writing table, which held a typewriter that was often pawned, and so intermittent handwritten pages would accumulate, and the secretary to this man—he was a professional man, very successful—would type up these notes and they were pristine, crisp.

Tenn learned to write during this fall he was remembering, during the war, but before he left for Hollywood, at the urging of his agent, Audrey Wood, to make enough money so that he would not need the love, prodding, and secrets of this married man.

"It wasn't a long-lived memory," Tenn recalled. "We met at an art gallery in the French Quarter, long gone, on Royal Street. It was an odd assemblage of people—the people who wanted the arts, enjoyed the arts, wanted to be artists, visual and verbal. He was handsome, softly handsome, which means that his looks weren't immediately present—they became evident through his kindness, his ability to be gentle. That's rare in a man—married or not—the ability to be gentle, the courage to move slowly and softly across the contours of a young queer."

Tenn's memories of this man included gifts of a Royal typewriter on which he had written portions of *Battle of Angels*, *The Glass Menagerie*, and *Streetcar*. Tenn tapped his wrist and recalled another gift: his first good watch, shiny and large and not his style, and pawned in Los Angeles, when he needed extra money to woo and impress a young Italian he met on the set of a Lana Turner film he remembered with laughter.

"Shiny toys for shiny boys." Tenn laughed. "I am at my most extravagant in pursuit of love and affection, and at my most niggardly in accepting either. And that," he said, pointing to my blue book, "is a point worth noting: a memory of value, if not comfort."

Los Angeles in 1943 was Tenn's next mental destination. On the corner of Coliseum and Constantinople, Tenn found himself instead mentally on Fountain Avenue, in front of the El Palacio Apartments, an explosion of broad strokes and architectural overstatements, enormous trees and hedges, overgrown and overheated. He was drawn there by its gaudy glamour and was dismayed that its cost was beyond his reach, even as it was close to so many men he had met and for whom he had fallen. ("Everybody," he told me, "has had a lover on Fountain Avenue.") Tenn would close his eyes and remember being driven around Hollywood or driving in a borrowed car up Fairfax until it passed Hollywood Boulevard and then crept up the hills, blooming into a series of zigzagging streets, and it was there that he knew a wealthy young man, an inheritor of money, who had come to what he always called "the Dream Factory" and whose house bulged with beautiful men, premium alcohol, and drugs. There did not seem to be a war raging anywhere, no shortages of any kind. The fabrics of the house were rich and clean, the food was abundant, and it was there that Tenn first tasted cocaine, which the host bought from a dealer out on Crenshaw, when he didn't buy it out of a slab of limestone on Argyle, or had to make a call—a long-distance call, the ultimate extravagance—to someone in the art department at Columbia who had connections, and who also, deep in the night, utilized the sets of the Three Stooges' soundstage to make high-end pornographic films with hopeful starlets and beautiful men, mostly black and Latin, "supremely sculpted" and frequently available to those, like the generous host, who wanted his guests happy in every way. High in those hills ("in every sense, I assure you!") you could stand in a curve, on the soft shoulder of that street, with its fragrant, rich name, and look out over all of downtown Los Angeles, and you could see it twinkle, and the lights were bright but they carried no sound, and everything seemed bathed in a lovely blue shade of night.

"No sound from the city," he remembered, "but so much from behind me, where the house hummed and trilled." Records were turned and dropped, and each cut would propel an emotion, a memory from one of the guests. "Little Brown Jug" was played over and over, and the guests danced.

Each time a record fell, Tenn could feel that a word dropped into his mind, then fell upon his mental stage, waiting to be accepted or rejected by whatever woman waited in the wings. Each time an ice cube dropped into his glass, an idea was stored away for future use, a sound or a smell catalogued for future reference. In his pants pocket were coins, and he rubbed them like worry stones, the ridges of quarters and dimes calming him, helping him in conversations with men, all so burnished and poised, all of them unaware of time and resources slipping, fading.

"You drop the word," Tenn said, "and it happens. You follow, word by word, brick by brick, bead by bead."

Tenn was happier at the parties of other struggling writers, hopeful actors. They had "pads" on Olive and Cherokee and Ivar, and the booze wasn't premium, but the talk was pitched at a higher level, and Tenn might wake up the next morning with someone who had a mind and an opinion of Clifford Odets or Ferenc Molnár or what might be coming up in a production that did not feature Lana Turner.

Tenn's favorite apartments were on Havenhurst, right off Sunset, which he urged me not to confuse with the Havenhurst Apartments, which were grand in the 1930s, but which by 1944 were already beginning to fade and to draw into their environs a number of retired, unwanted, or cash-strapped contract players, and a couple of sad bachelors who had also come to play in the Dream Factory, but had stayed too long for too little and now invited the young Tennessee Williams to their rooms to talk about past glories and to gently kiss him and hold him in their beds until he could sneak out and walk along Hollywood Boulevard, wondering when things would happen for him.

"The search for the 'click' might have begun then," Tenn said. "I spent my time in that city searching."

One of his worst experiences in the Havenhurst was the night he went to be with an older gentleman who had worked with Alla Nazimova and who agreed to introduce Tenn to Ruth Chatterton, who was then living in New York. He did not want to go, but ambition superseded desire that evening, a clear, pink night, as he recalled. His shoes clicked on the terrazzo floors; a fan hummed in the corner of the lobby; the garden was full of chattering ladies. Tenn had a sandwich in a brown paper bag, and he carried it with him into the man's apartment.

At work, at MGM, Tenn had found himself seated next to director Clarence Brown, who had eschewed the menu of the commissary and instead drew out from a leather satchel a sandwich wrapped in wax paper. Tenn watched the director—who had been Garbo's favorite—and was amazed to find that his lunch was that supreme Southern offering, pimiento cheese. Tenn struck up a conversation with Brown. Tenn's mother prided herself on her pimiento-cheese "spread," and the two men, one from Kentucky, the other deeply marinated in the ways of Mississippi and Louisiana, laughed over shared tastes. Ultimately, the director offered Tenn one half of his sandwich. Brown's wife or maid or cook spiked his spread with a dash of vinegar, giving it a kick that Tenn's remembered recipe lacked. Tenn praised the sandwich, and the men discussed films, actresses, and the theater.

The following day, Brown found Tenn again in the commissary and pulled from the satchel a sandwich wrapped in waxed paper. "For later," he said, "when you're writing."

This was the sandwich Tenn took to the Havenhurst.

After a grim session of wrestling and groping, ending in apologies and regrets, Tenn sat across from the man and, surrounded by an airless room full of musty books, a candelabra from a touring production, and a kitchenette that smelled of a moldy sponge and tuna fish, the man spied the bag and asked about it.

Trapped, Tenn offered the man half of the sandwich, and they sat together, each eating, drinking lukewarm ginger ale, and discussing Chekhov.

"It was one of the worst nights of my life," Tenn remembered. "The glorious gesture of Clarence Brown coming into contact with my resentful gesture toward that man, whose use to me was Ruth Chatterton's address."

Tenn remembered something of that night that had remained with him. "When I am most uncomfortable," he remembered, "when I find myself caught in a situation entirely absent of desire or interest, when I feel deprived of air, and the room grows small and silent and the walls seem to move toward me, the person who is threatening or boring to me appears closer than they should, and I resort to rubbing coins, or the legs of my pants, or, in that particular case, the waxed paper of Clarence Brown, which I turned into a warm, worn prayer cloth, patting, turning, until it was creased and worthless, but I saved it, and I took it with me—a reminder of what not to do, of what not to remember."

The memory of that night sent Ruth Chatterton into retirement, at least from Tenn's mental repertory. Tenn began to search for another actress to crowd his mind, inhabit his dreams, drop words.

A happier memory for Tenn was his time with the young Italian he met at MGM, a carpenter or electrician ("in some technical capacity"), early twenties, handsome, terribly sweet. "I am never so weak," he recalled, "than when I am in the presence of kind eyes. He had kind eyes." They talked of movies, of literature, and Tenn learned that the young man dreamed of directing. Tenn shared memories of conversations with Clarence Brown, which included directorial advice that had been shared with him by William Wyler and George Stevens. Tenn explained to him that Wyler had consulted with his cinematographer, Gregg Toland, over maneuvers that would draw the viewers'—the camera's—attention from the teeth and eyes of Patricia Collinge and the thespian limitations of Bette Davis in *The Little Foxes*. Collinge seemed to animate her teeth and eyes more fervently each day, and the oracular and dental exertions were driving Wyler to distraction. The solution was to consider Collinge primarily in two positions: when pathetic, she was to be shot from above, allowing her to look small and humble, defeated; when in reflection, thinking of past beauty and worth, she was to be shot in profile, as if dreaming, half a person, diminished.

Clarence Brown, one of the most acclaimed and stylish directors at MGM, who encouraged Tennessee—with words and sandwiches—during his brief tenure at the studio

George Stevens told Brown that the surest, simplest way to indicate that a character, especially a woman, was in doubt, in trouble, in need of an audience's sympathy, was to take the camera as high as it could go, and to slowly bring the lens to her level. The world was against her, but the audience had sought her out, found her, felt protective of her. Tenn remembered the visual of a woman as seen from above, and the young man also wrote it down, as he wrote down everything Tenn told him about his time on the set, his reading, his life. "Every woman I have ever met or known or loved," Tenn told me, "and every woman I have ever created, I have seen from above, sought out, found, coddled, loved, protected."

The young man, whose name Tenn could not recall, although he could recall the contours of his physique and the décor of his apartment, lived off Hollywood Boulevard, in a multi-dwelling house on Vista. Tenn decided, in the retelling, to call the man Mangia, because he was a wonderful and generous cook, and because his memories of their times together revolved around discussion of movies, sex, and food. "A trinity I would willfully worship today," Tenn quipped.

The apartment on Vista was one of four, and the home in which they sat had a wholesome, Andy Hardy look about it. The directions were simple—Vista, between Hollywood and Hawthorn—and Mangia had friends on surrounding streets with names like Sierra Bonita and Poinsettia Place. Another friend, who had access to marijuana, lived on Yucca. Luckier friends had advanced to dwellings on De Longpre and Harper; another was having an affair with a famous cinematographer who lived in a glorious wedding cake of a building on Fountain and Sweetzer.

The memory of these places became a Rosary for Tenn. Sierra Bonita. Poinsettia. Yucca. De Longpre. Harper. Sweetzer.

There was a Rosary of names for the streets, and the prayer Tenn had in his mind was to find and locate and coddle Miriam Hopkins, who had moved into the prominent position once held by Ruth Chatterton. "I was loved and I was loving in that time," Tenn said, "but my primary passion was to find Miriam Hopkins, an actress my mother and I loved, and for whom I felt I had dreamed a character."

I asked which character, but Tenn held up a hand and silenced me.

Tenn did not feel comfortable staying in Mangia's apartment when he left for work in the morning, making a call that was earlier than Tenn's. Tenn would stay in bed while Mangia prepared breakfast, only arising when it was completed. With morning slipping away, there was kissing and laughter and no time for a leisurely breakfast. Mangia had prepared sweet rolls, and they were still warm. The aroma of coffee filled the apartment. Two sweet rolls were placed in a brown paper bag and coffee was poured into a mug. "I'll bring it back after work," Tenn promised. Mangia left, and Tenn, without a car, and a couple of hours early for work, walked along Hollywood Boulevard, stopping at St. Thomas the Apostle Episcopal Church, where he ate the sweet rolls and sipped the coffee while looking at the altar and sharing the space with a handful of other early risers. Tenn said a prayer: bring me, please, to Miriam Hopkins.

Days later, on another walk, he discovered Camino Real, and the thought of walking that particular camino, in that particular time, gave him ideas. Walking that camino, he created a lady, a great lady, and her contours were growing more and more into those of Miriam Hopkins.

"Did Miriam Hopkins always exist?" Tenn asked. "Or did I dream her into being? Certainly no one needed her more."

Tenn had an epiphany: he had found Amanda Wingfield on the soft shoulder of that high street overlooking downtown Hollywood, blue lights and music and beautiful men and relaxed nerves and dreams of succeeding all around him, threatening and arousing him. "The album and the ice dropped," he said, "and the words and the idea dropped. Amanda stands in her environment, and in the distance she sees expansion and hope and light, and behind her she hears youth and merriment and the hope of flesh and folly. And she's right in the center, unable to move, unable to know where she's headed. She lives in both of the worlds, both of the visions: her glorious past, which was what that house high in the Hollywood hills must have seemed to me, shiny and clean and full of things I wanted but was afraid to seek, and ahead was the glory that was unattainable. For me, it would have required understanding how the movies worked, knowing how to move in those circles. For Amanda it required moving Tom and Laura toward jobs or mates who could provide for her a safe, clean room, full of air, with walls that didn't crowd, and space for her to remember."

Tenn fingered coins in his pocket, rubbed the waxed paper of Clarence Brown's sandwich, and held the warm mug in that church on Hollywood Boulevard.

Drop a memory. Drop a word. Words collect.

You go to Hollywood for some distinct reason. Even those born there are descendants of desire—the desire to be rich in money or movies or experience. Proximity to success is as powerful an incentive to be there as success itself, and the ambition and the craving give the city a buzz, the intensity of a hive, swirling with passion and avarice and occasional artistry. It was, Tenn remembered, a city glazed like a beautiful and perfectly unnecessary dessert.

Amanda Wingfield was Tenn's mother, and also the young Tennessee, standing on that high hill, dreaming. The love and comfort Tenn felt in Mangia's house, so different from the confusion he felt on the soundstages, where his work felt flat and forced, brought forth another version of himself, his mother, and an actress who had become an obsession. "Lady Torrance [in *Battle of Angels* and its later reworking as *Orpheus Descending*] was born in the intersections of my confusion," Tenn told me. "She had had desire, and she remembered it. She wanted desire again, but didn't know where to find it. She walked and she wandered and she prayed. She was in strange lands. There was silk but there was also the sun that could damage it, shrink it, destroy it. I had these thoughts and these desires, but I was searching for the female form onto which I could impress them all. And I found them. On a hill. On the Camino. In a prayer."

Tenn paused. "I could write then," he said. "I could connect things."

He paused again.

"I believe I can write again," he told me. "Thank you for indulging me."

I then drove to the Marigny, where one of the city's loveliest balconies beckoned to Tenn. "I believe that I can connect my memories, and reconstruct my life, my writing life," he confessed, "through the balconies of New Orleans. Much as [John] Cheever reconstructed a man's life through the connected swimming pools that held memories, that had access to the people and events that shaped his life."

Tenn turned to me as we continued to wait. "I'm thinking like a writer. Drop a memory, drop a word. Drop a memory, drop a word." He repeated the words like a mantra all through our drive to the Marigny.

Five

———————

A T THE CORNER of Elysian Fields and Royal, Tenn asked me to slow down as we looked up at a forbidding grey building festooned with yards of wrought iron—a wraparound balcony that seemed, to Tenn, to call out for an embrace, and on which he had been many times, many years ago.

There had been parties, celebrations, parades, kisses, followed with walks back home made slow and fuzzy by liquor, to apartments on Royal and Dumaine, squatter pads on Governor Nicholls and Touro.

"To be drunk and young," Tenn told me, "your lips slightly chafed from the attentions of someone you like or love, and to walk home, where, waiting like a loved and lonely pet, is a piece of paper in the typewriter, slightly curled, half-completed, waiting for your next move. And"—he flexed his fingers and made a fist—"the move comes. You complete the sentence, drop a memory, spread the remembrance across time and words, and make a gift of it to someone else.

"Take me down Royal," he said.

We moved well below ten miles per hour, but the day was lazy, there was no one on the sidewalks, only a few people on porches or crossing the streets that we navigated as if lost and confused; and while Tenn's eyes were frequently closed, his mind was alive as he ticked off names and dates and times and places.

Royal Street is populated by a series of houses amber or peach, cinnamon brown, slate grey, cerulean and turquoise, squat and stately—Necco wafers often shaded by trees that had burst through the mottled and cracked concrete of the sloped sidewalks. During several months in the forties, Tenn had walked this street, lived on this street, and his mind had been full of images of Miriam Hopkins.

"Whatever I have learned of any value," Tenn said, "has come to me from women and from photographs, and I consider films to be a form of photography. I need images of women to understand things." Tenn shared movies and their actresses with his mother and sister: it was a form of communication that always worked in his childhood—no

Miriam Hopkins was an idol to both Tennessee and his mother: a refined, intelligent, and talented Southern woman who was honest and comfortable with what Tennesse called "the finer things: she was surrounded by all the things I wanted."

codes or hidden messages were needed. "I was freest," Tenn said, "when I could live my life, understand my life, reorder my life, through the movies, and then through drama. And my mother was the same; my sister served us both." It was not an exaggeration, he told me, to think of those three—in their various locations—as a repertory company, working themes out, seeking clarity. "Life only made sense to my mother through dreaming," Tenn told me, "and I was the same, but I wanted to move on and out; I needed to see if the dreams had any value or traction: I needed to find some realization of a few dreams, and my motivation for some time was Miss Hopkins."

Tenn found a play—and a woman—in his mind. It would become *Battle of Angels,* and later it would turn into *Orpheus Descending,* but it began as a series of mental introductions he imagined between his mother and Hopkins. "I not only admired Hopkins for her work in films," Tenn said, "and for what I had heard of her stage work: I admired and sought her because she represented so many things that my mother admired." Hopkins had been born into comfortable circumstances in Georgia; her pedigree, Edwina often asserted, as she looked up from movie magazines she had cadged from the beauty parlor, was one of pristine Southern heritage. Hopkins was beautiful and funny and smart, and she filled her days with painting and cooking and golf and flying lessons and sewing and maintaining famous husbands and lovely homes. "This was the catechism I heard on Miss Hopkins," Tenn told me, "and I bought it, and I loved her, and I wanted to stay close to my mother and to my sister, even as my dreams pulled me farther and farther away."

Near the houses on Royal that meant so much to Tenn there had been coffee shops and restaurants and candy counters—confectionaries, they were called, social centers for those with short attentions and sweet teeth. Tenn imagined Miriam Hopkins bumped from her pedestal of privilege and waiting on the motley band of hungry and lonely people who sat on pink stools and sipped pastel drinks. A character was born.

"I adored Miriam Hopkins," Tenn told me, "for no other reason than that she answered my letters: she *responded.* She met with me and she talked to me and she encouraged me." Once at a Hollywood party, during Tenn's Mangia days and walks on the Los Angeles Camino Real and morning prayers in Episcopal churches, he had seen Hopkins—in the flesh, not through letters or phone calls—and he recalled that she had "that rapid and gooey Southern charm—which meant that she kissed me and welcomed me as a relative or automatic friend. We had things in common, she said. She simply could tell. I promised her my friendship and I promised her my play; she returned the offer of friendship. I cannot stress enough how important her vow would be."

Tenn held the image of Miriam Hopkins in his mind both during his writing hours and his "living, walking, surviving" hours. "She was an instrument of usefulness," Tenn told me. "There were no wasted hours, no unused gifts. I wanted to be that sort of person. And I learned then, during that process, that I am incapable of writing without the supervision—real or supernatural; intended or accidental—of a woman. Women give me the characters and the ideas and the language, and it is women who have brought me the food and the drink and the bits of cash to keep me going. I am entirely possible—by physical and artistic birth—because of women." Like so many of the women who influenced Tenn, Hopkins knew that it was her responsibility to expand her life and her options within it. Hopkins used her own talent and her own will—as well as her beauty and her charm—to reshape and conquer reality. Hopkins did not have Christian Science or an adherence to scholarship and tough professionalism to keep her moving and mattering, but she had all those hours in all those days, and she frequently told Tenn that life was his to shape.

Not long after their meeting at that Hollywood party, Tenn was back in New York, poor and desperate to complete his work, a task made difficult by the fact that he had, once again, pawned his typewriter. "The Royal typewriter had fallen on hard times," Tenn said. He had read in the newspapers that Miss Hopkins was in town, and he requested that they meet. Miss Hopkins cheerfully agreed, suggesting a chic restaurant. "There is no greater fear," Tenn said, "than accepting an invitation that is beyond your means—financially, emotionally, socially. But I was desperate, and I went. There was a hole in one of my shoes and another in my heart. If I possessed two dollars at that time, I was flush. I saw Miss Hopkins on the sidewalk—lovely, smooth, perfectly attired. Miss Edwina's eyes had trained me to look at a woman and to judge her character by her accessories, her deportment, her *equipage,* so to speak. I will never know if this was accidental or providential or what, but as I approached Miss Hopkins, as she turned and gave me her dazzling smile, I tripped and felt myself aiming for her feet. She caught me; there was a flurry of activity, patted shoulders, mother-hen cooings, and as I was being lifted up, I came face-to-face with Miss Hopkins and blurted out, 'Could I possibly borrow five hundred dollars?' I was shocked at my outburst, but she merely smiled, took my arm, and treated me to a feast of a lunch. Later in the day, she delivered to my sad apartment an envelope containing five hundred dollars, an amount that bought me several months of freedom, and released the Royal. Miriam Hopkins refused to call it a loan: it was, she said, a gift—for my gifts." Tenn's eyes misted at the memory, of seeking a woman who pleased his mother and who believed in him and who brought to life one of his women. "Is it a gift that I was lucky enough to bring into my life such women? If so, I accept it, and place it high in my estimation. Let no bad things be said about Miriam Hopkins."

AT ROYAL AND FRENCHMEN, Tenn asked that I stop and park, so that we could walk through Washington Square, a lush block that was blissfully empty, and there were faint wafts of music from the Quarter, snatches of radio and television transmission from the houses surrounding it. Frenchmen and Touro Streets held memories for Tenn of rent parties during the war years and beyond, happy neighbors eating and dancing and gratefully accepting crisp bills in return for a plate of food or a po' boy. The revelers were straight and gay, young and old, and Tenn could not remember being afraid; he felt open to express happiness and desire on a sunny street that smelled of crab boil and patchouli.

At Royal and Kerlerec, one can see the city downtown, one is closer to the Quarter and can hear it. At Royal and Esplanade stands a house much loved by Tenn, pristine and, as he put it, "glistening like a just-licked glans."

We walked Royal for a bit, looking at balconies beautiful and blighted, but we ultimately came to Royal and Marigny and its simple but elegant balcony, swirling around a faded, pea-green house that had once been home to people who had invited Tenn up to that elevated porch, where he sat and caught what breeze there might be, and talked, and dreamed.

In the time when he was on that balcony at Royal and Marigny, Tenn was happy. He had, as he put it, "ideas and a record player and a little money." Over and over, in the cooler months, he threw open the windows, and the air caught the linen curtains and they danced about—the animated arms, as he imagined, of the woman who was dominating his thoughts and his work. Tenn could smell coffee and night-blooming jasmine, and his record player repeatedly played "You Won't Be Satisfied (Until You Break My Heart)" by Doris Day and "Do I Worry?" by Tommy Dorsey, which asked in its lyrics

> *When evening shadows creep,*
> *Do I lose any sleep?*

To the record, crackling and popping from overuse, Tenn would yell, "Hell, no!" and continue typing, on the Royal typewriter on Royal Street. All seemed well. The work was good. Miriam Hopkins was still much loved, and she had served Tenn well in the creation of one role, Lady Torrance, with whom he was already growing impatient. "My mental repertory rotates swiftly," Tenn said, "and when I could dream and write, things moved quickly." Tenn now had another actress—and another character in his sights, and he had written to her, telling her he was interested in luring her talents into his world. "I had a world," he told me, "that I had dreamed, and then I had made it happen, in the mental theater, on the pale judgment, and it was now alive and real and felt right. Ready for the unveiling."

The actress was Lillian Gish, and from several calls to his agent, Tenn ascertained that she could be found on Cielo Drive in Los Angeles, high above Benedict Canyon, in a French country house with a wishing well. To that address—10050 Cielo Drive—Tenn sent a play called, at that time, as he remembered, *The Moon and the Royal Balconies.*

My introduction to Lillian Gish was made in 1989, by a portrait painter, then nearing eighty, named Dorothy Hart Drew. Drew lived in a penthouse triplex within the Beaux-Arts Building at West Fortieth Street and Sixth Avenue, directly across from the worst perimeter of Bryant Park, where assault and crack cocaine were both on ample display.

Dorothy Hart Drew was the woman with whom I first lived when I moved to New York City to finally meet the people Tenn had told me I should. The arrangement had been made by a friend, a Baton Rouge native who had once lived in New York, made a name and a small fortune as a model and TV personality (she was the Pirate Girl opposite

Lillian Gish at her home on Cielo Drive, above Benedict
Canyon, in the 1940s, at the time Tennessee imagined her
as Blanche DuBois, and mailed her a copy of the young,
unformed play that would be *A Streetcar Named Desire*

Jan Murray on the game show *Treasure Hunt*), then, after divorcing her
husband, had returned to her hometown and settled into comfort and
the persistent study of Christian Science. Her practitioner was also the
practitioner for Drew (mental mind and its maladies knowing nothing
of distance or time, one can be healed by a healer anytime, anywhere),
and she told my friend's practitioner that an aged friend needed a companion who would live with her—rent-free—and help with shopping
and cooking.

I wanted to get to New York, had a small amount of money to do so,
and felt I could not turn down the opportunity.

For two months I stayed in the apartment, a wonder of Louis Comfort Tiffany stained glass and bathrooms rimmed with gold-plated abalone shells, during which time I learned that my host had been a well-regarded sculptor and painter, had been close friends with the sculptors Anna Hyatt Huntington and Paul Manship, the latter having family in my hometown. Drew took news of this relationship, such as it was, as a good sign, and invited me to move in. All of this was done by phone—me in Baton Rouge; Drew in New York.

Once in this apartment, I learned a few other things: Drew and her sister, Lorna, had been great friends with Lillian and Dorothy Gish; Drew possessed only seven teeth in her head, necessitating a number of changes in the recipes I had brought along in my capacity as house chef; and she was a rabid anticommunist and virulent conservative, whose life, once her artwork had subsided, was consumed by ferreting out those people she was convinced were red or subversive, or who had grown successful through nefarious political means.

In my first few days in the apartment in the Beaux-Arts, I cleaned and began reworking recipes to make them softer, and in the evenings I read to Drew from *Science and Health* or from books like T. H. Robsjohn-Gibbings's *Mona Lisa's Mustache,* which eviscerated the modern-art movement, along with all of the attendant mystical and political insanity he believed was threatening the world's health and the survival of "good" art. I frequently had to stop what I was reading because his observations were so loony, and the book's margins were littered with notes from Drew.

I had the master bedroom in the apartment, a large suite that included a dressing room and the gold-plated bathroom. The second floor of the apartment was the split-level studio in which Drew now slept on a small bed wedged behind a grand piano, and which featured an enormous skylight through which one could look up Sixth Avenue all the way to Central Park; the first level consisted of three small rooms: an anteroom holding a small bed covered with a purple velvet coverlet and several large cardboard boxes, a tiny kitchen and bathroom with a slop sink in which Drew took her daily cleaning, and a large dining room with an enormous and burnished table on which were stacked hundreds of books, magazines, and boxes. It was at this table that Drew sat for up to twelve hours a day, listening to talk radio, smoking (an activity that prevented her from seeking membership in the mother church), and talking to her sister, Lorna, who had died at least a decade before. Drew occasionally interrupted her schedule to call radio programs and yell at the liberals.

On the wall by the bed in which she slept, Drew had written, boldly and neatly, the names and numbers of those she might need to reach quickly: her practitioner, her relatives, her Christian Science nurse, and the AM radio stations that carried her favorite programs. Above all of this information was written—also boldly and neatly—the following:

Cubism aims to destroy by designed disorder.
Futurism aims to destroy by the machine myth.
Dadaism aims to destroy by ridicule.
Expressionism aims to destroy by aping the primitive and insane.
Abstractionism aims to destroy by the creation of brainstorms.
Surrealism aims to destroy by denial of reason.

When I asked Drew about the lines written above her bed (they formed a sort of halo above her head when she slept), she told me that they were taken from a statement made in 1949 by her good friend Congressman George Dondero, before the House of Representatives. Drew had helped him write it. "We both knew that art was a weapon, the strongest weapon, used by Communists to undermine America. He, along with Joseph McCarthy, was my greatest friend and hero."

That night in my journal, I wrote "May you live in interesting times and interesting apartments."

Drew led me to the many dusty boxes in the anteroom and invited me to look through them. Inside I found many copies of *Red Channels*, the booklet that informed advertisers and network officials of those suspected of being under Communist influence or enjoying its support. There were many other magazines and books, but there were also hundreds of letters, all of them pertaining to the diligent removal from the "shores of this great country" of reds and pinks in the artistic community. Drew's letters were primarily a dance, a suggestive tango, between her and Dondero, a Republican from Michigan, who had first been elected to the House in 1932, and who admitted in one letter that the advent of Roosevelt and his New Deal had plunged him deeply into his "patriotic mission."

One of the letters, marked COPY, was dated 1956, and had been sent to Drew to illustrate Dondero's consistent commitment to stamping out modern art. The letter deals with the Republican's distaste for Eisenhower's weakness toward this menace, epitomized by his visit to the Museum of Modern Art on its twenty-fifth anniversary, at which he had "given them a slap on the back" and told them they should paint anything they felt like. Dondero wrote: "Frankly, I do not understand some of the statements made by the President regarding the Museum of Modern Art. Modern art is a term that is nauseating to me. We are in complete accord in our thinking regarding this subject and its connection with communism. No one is attempting to stifle self-expression, but we are attempting to protect and preserve legitimate art as we have always known it in the United States."

Dondero's statement before Congress, parts of which Drew had memorized, read in part:

> Mr. Speaker, quite a few individuals in art, who are sincere in purpose, honest in intent, but with only a superficial knowledge of the complicated influences that surge in the art world of today, have written me—or otherwise expressed their opinions—that so-called modern or contemporary art cannot be Communist because art in Russia today is realistic and objective.

Drew stopped me as I read this aloud to her to tell me that she was one of the "friends" referenced by Dondero, and she would later share with me the piles of correspondence in which she revealed suspicious and unacceptable artistic Americans.

"This glib disavowal," Dondero's address continued,

> of any relationship between Communism and so-called modern art is so pat and so spontaneous a reply by advocates of the "isms" in art, from deep, Red Stalinist to pale-pink publicist, as to identify it readily to the observant as the same old party-line practice. It is the party line of the left-wingers, who are now in the big money, and who want above all to remain in the big money, voiced to confuse the legitimate artist, to disarm the arousing academician, and to fool the public.

As I have previously stated, art is considered a weapon of Communism, and the Communist doctrinaire names the artist as a soldier of the revolution. It is a weapon in the hands of a soldier in the revolution against our form of government, and against any government or system other than Communism.

Drew interrupted to tell me that she had worked—and hoped to continue to work—to enlist soldiers of her own revolution, right-leaning "true" Americans who could cleanse and enhance "authentic" art in all media.

One of the most ardent soldiers of this revolution was Lillian Gish.

"Lillian," Drew told me, "is one of the greatest soldiers in the good revolution."

I asked Drew if Lillian Gish believed as she did about the influence of communism in the arts. "Well," she demurred, "I'm often disappointed in Lillian. She's very naïve, as you are. She can't believe that anyone who can produce art she likes could be someone she ought to hate, could be someone she ought to destroy." Nonetheless, Gish donated money and verbal support to both Dondero and Drew in their pursuits.

Drew was upset, however, that Gish respected Pablo Picasso, "a demented and diseased Communist and murderer and thief." Drew quoted again from Dondero:

> The artists of the "isms" change their designations as often and as read-ily as the Communist front organizations. Picasso, who is also a dada-ist, an abstractionist, or a surrealist, as unstable fancy dictates, is the hero of all the crackpots in so-called modern art.
>
> Léger and Duchamp are now in the United States to aid in the destruction of our standards and traditions. The former has been a con-tributor to the Communist cause in America; the latter is now fancied by the neurotics as a surrealist.

The gist of Dondero's and Drew's mission, the "pearl of great price," as Drew described it, was in the following paragraph:

> It makes little difference where one studies the record, whether of sur-realism, dadaism, abstractionism, cubism, expressionism, or futurism. The evidence of evil design is everywhere, only the roll call of the art contortionists is different. The question is, what have we, the plain American people, done to deserve this sore affliction that has been vis-

ited upon us so direly; who has brought down this curse upon us; who has let into our homeland this horde of germ-carrying art vermin?

Drew was moist-eyed as she claimed that she was one of the purest of the plain American people, as was Gish, as had been Dondero, and the mission continued. "I want you to talk to Lillian," she told me, "but not about the degenerate writer you knew, and who probably spoiled your brain about art and the world. I want you to talk to her about purity and the truth, about the way America was meant to be."

And that is how it was arranged that I should meet Lillian Gish.

DREW'S APARTMENT in the Beaux-Arts Building was grand but filthy, and at night, when the commercial tenants had left for the day, mice rushed up to the penthouse and executed a St. Vitus's dance across the wood floors, their claws clattering. In the morning there would be hundreds of droppings, and the pantry shelves would be askew.

Drew did not want Lillian Gish to see what had become of the apartment on West Fortieth Street—or its primary tenant, whose refusal to frequent the offices of doctors had led to the loss of her teeth and most of her hair. Drew would tie old blouses over her head, creating striking turbans, but she could not fashion new teeth, and she could not stop smoking, so she refused Lillian's suggestion of a visit to Fortieth Street, and sent me, alone, to East Fifty-seventh Street to meet the actress.

The apartment of Lillian Gish was as orderly as Drew's was chaotic—beautiful and quiet and controlled. Nothing was out of place in any of the rooms, on any of the shelves, on any of the tables, or, for that matter, in the mind of Miss Gish. She had planned for our visit by rereading my letters to her and the comments Tenn had made about her, about our trips up and down Royal Street, and about the original version of *A Streetcar Named Desire*, called *The Moon and the Royal Balconies*, in which she was to have played the lead character, a woman who eventually became Blanche DuBois.

"Oh, listen," Gish told me, "I don't believe in guilt or regret. I believe that they exist, that people are almost always struggling through one or the other, or both, but I don't see any value in honoring those emotions. However," she laughed, "I think Tennessee felt guilty that I didn't play that part, and I would be lying if I didn't tell you that I often wonder about my life—my professional life—if I had had the opportunity to be Blanche. Could I have done it? Could I have done it well? What or who would I be today if I had taken on that challenge?"

Gish was frail and tiny, and she showed difficulty in using her hands. She did not move from the chair in which she sat except to let me into the apartment and to see me off. Our first visit lasted about an hour, and my understanding is that it had been scheduled by Drew with James Frasher, Gish's manager, who was normally present for all of Gish's interviews, but who on this day had been called away. I sensed that Gish missed his presence, and that she might have been stronger had he been there. When Gish and I later had several phone conversations, she seemed more secure and comfortable—and opinionated—and I wonder if it might have been because Frasher was nearby, or because she didn't have to present herself in the composed and attractive manner she did when she met people face-to-face, with full makeup, Fortuny gown, and rigid focus.

"I hope," Gish told me, "that you don't think I am entirely in league with Dorothy on her views on art and politics. I am conservative by nature, but I think Dorothy became a bit unsettled early in her life. There was promise, but there was not the attention she felt she deserved. It was easier to imagine a conspiracy, a plan for which she was not suited or invited, than to face the fact that the work and the acclaim she felt she deserved had passed her by. This is very common in the arts; I've seen it often. Bitterness is horrible, and we can never know why things happen as they do. Faith is an enormous challenge, but it's all we have to keep going, and my faith is in God and the art I know and believe He has sanctioned for us, and in the role that art has in our life. I think art improves us, I think that it . . . Oh, what am I trying to say? It enlarges us and can act as a mirror, and that is valuable, and no one is a better example than Tennessee."

Gish admitted that she found Tenn odd when she first met him: he giggled to himself nervously and his clothes were worn and ill-fitting. She considered him handsome, but he had a nervous and persistent habit of placing his hands over his mouth or his forehead when he spoke; he frequently ran his fingers through his hair. Gish felt an immediate desire to comfort him, but she was shocked, then amused, by Tenn's defensive need to push away such affection with odd statements, declarations made only to disarm.

"He liked freaks," Gish told me, "and odd situations. Tragic situations. He was obsessed with homes in which murders had occurred. He never forgot that I had lived in the house where Charles Manson had those poor people killed." (This was the house at 10050 Cielo Drive in Los Angeles, where Tenn had mailed his play to Gish.) "He asked me if anything odd or scary had happened when I lived there; if the house was haunted. I told him I was perfectly happy there. The air was clear and sweet. The view was gorgeous. I rested and read and took care of myself. 'Yeah,' Tenn would say, 'but were there ever any apparitions or portents?'"

Tenn asked Gish once if she would like to accompany him to the freak shows on West Forty-second Street. On another occasion he invited her down to West Fourth Street, to rustle through a succession of what she called "junk shops" that the artist Joseph Cornell had told him about. Gish declined the first invitation but accepted the second.

"He was such a sweet boy, really," she remembered. "He loved pulling things out of boxes and bins, finding lost items, beautiful and sweet things that had once meant so much to someone. 'Look,' he said once, 'look at these pieces of jewelry.' They were nice pieces of costume jewelry, nothing extravagant, but one brooch was inscribed 'To my mother, who made me and loves me.' He cried when he found that, and he bought it. We had lunch later and he would take his purchases—jewelry, beads, a bag of marbles, old magazines, frayed playbills, books with sweet inscriptions—and spread them across the restaurant table. 'Who are these people? Where are they now?' He wanted to re-create their lives, to imagine what had happened on the day before and the day after these gifts had been given. He showed me a brooch with a lovely woman's face on it, and he said that was how he saw me, and it was how he saw me in his play: golden, creamy, wearing a tiara. We couldn't tell if it was meant to be a religious token or not, because it did vaguely resemble the Blessed Mother."

(On one of our days together, Tenn and I visited several antique shops on Magazine Street, and he bought some old rosary beads that had been made in Jerusalem, some votives, many old magazines—some of which featured the women I was being sent to meet—and tiny pieces of jewelry and religious items, which he gave me, along with instructions as to who should receive what and what I should say when I presented them. For Mildred Natwick he bought a poem of Mary Baker

Eddy's that had been decoupaged on a block of wood; and for Gish, he purchased a hand fan, from a New Orleans funeral home, on which was an image of the Blessed Mother, her arms outstretched, surrounded by gentle animals, all of them at rapt attention. Her face, creamy and beautiful, featured a mouth that strongly resembled Gish's. When I presented it to her, not long after she described the brooch he had found on their jaunt, she wept and asked that our meeting end. She apologized later, but admitted that seeing it had "made my heart hurt. I was pierced. I couldn't handle it. I felt loss I had forgotten I had known.")

Tenn had pored over the items he found, amazed at the worn report cards he found, with their comments and the signatures of parents, some of them grateful. "We so appreciate all that you've done with Billy," one might read. The teachers' rejoinder might have read, "Billy is coming along nicely. I would like him to try harder and calm down." "Where is Billy now?" Tenn wanted to know. Was he a simple boy who fidgeted and couldn't quite understand the letters that swam before his eyes or the numbers that never added up correctly? Another student, on another discarded item from some abandoned box of memories, had given his teacher a cheap, trick-shop tiara, and on a piece of cardboard paper he had written, "You Are My Queen." The cardboard paper also held the teacher's neat, adult handwriting. "I loved your tiara. It was so sweet of you." Why had the teacher given the carefully inscribed piece of paper back to the boy who had created it? Had the boy been hurt? What had happened to the tiara? Might it have been saved by the teacher, who was, perhaps, lonely, and now old, and who could take it out and remember that she had been loved and that someone had gone out and with his tiny allowance purchased this gift?

"He was obsessed with all of these dusty things," Gish told me. "I didn't understand it, but now I do. He was always searching for evidence of people who felt as he did. I guess we all do eventually, but I didn't feel safe doing it until I was older. You risk so much. You find things—not always in boxes of old things, but in memories or questions answered—that make you realize things about yourself. I think—no, I *know*—that I hid things from myself for a long time. I thought reflection was a waste of time. It required too much; it took you backward. Progress was something I was told to pursue and revere, and all I was supposed to reflect were qualities: love and mercy and forgiveness and charity. What I felt or what I wanted weren't worthy of my thoughts.

But being with Tennessee and seeing what he did with every day I spent with him—with everyone, I suppose—opened my eyes. You subsume all that you see and all that you've experienced. That is what he told me. I didn't know what 'subsume' meant, but he told me to look at everything, to think about everything. Everything we needed was all around us. All the stories we'd ever need. More than we could ever handle in terms of time and space and in emotional terms.

"Every day," she continued, "life has so much to show us: death and injury; birth and happiness; joy and the depths of grief; color and music and food and sensation. If we're open to it, if we let ourselves see and feel as much of it as we can, we have a fullness that is extraordinary. Tennessee Williams gave me that. Tennessee changed my life."

Tenn described to Gish a nightly event that took place in the apartment on Royal Street he had while writing the play he hoped she would inhabit. Wild cats roamed the Quarter at night, toppling garbage cans and fighting as they sought food. Some of the neighbors shot at them with guns or threw things or set traps, but most only wanted to stop the nightly disruptions. Tenn, working late into the night, with his records dropping and turned to a low volume, smoking and drinking Coca-Cola with ice he bought by the block and shattered with a knife or dropped to the floor, would hear the cats approaching and would go to his window and throw down pieces of chicken or fish to them, waiting below with upturned faces and rigid tails, eyes wide and glowing. Often Tenn would have a visitor, and the two of them would giggle at the cats, their ferocious hunger, the after-meal cleaning, their calmness, the way some of them, bellies full, plopped in the center of the street and stretched. Tenn and his friend would drop another record—usually Bach at this late hour—and slip into bed. If the night was cool, the windows would be open and the curtains, light and airy and now emblems of the arms of Lillian Gish, would billow and set, expand and retreat, the scent of jasmine and orange rinds and burnt-sugar residue from the street vendors and the water sloshed over the streets would rise up to the room and mingle with the scent of the friend who rested against Tenn, his neck against his lips and their legs rubbing both the cool sheets and each other, the hairs moving back and forth, a comfort and an arousal. Trains and boats could be heard in the air, and lights would play across the ceiling, and Tenn would think, This is a glorious time and these are glorious feelings and images and sensations. I want to take them deep within me, drop them as far into myself as I can, so that they can never be taken from me, never leave me, be a part of my identity forever. The records would drop and play, and Tenn would think: Remember the cats and the laughter. Drop it down low. Tenn would kiss and caress his friend and think, at every comfortable rub, Drop this memory of the comfort and the pleasure. From all the pleasure came a responsibility, and another happy event: to drop the memory on the page—the pale judgment—and not only share it, but further make it permanent.

"Tennessee taught me to commemorate not only every day," Gish told me, "but every emotion. We worked together and walked around together a lot, and whatever happened—a conversation about films; an argument about religion; a beautiful sunset; seeing paintings or hearing music that moved us—he would find a way to make it last, to make it a permanent part of us. A subsuming."

Gish was a student of Emanuel Swedenborg, and she and Tenn often discussed his writings, comparing them to the teachings passed to Tenn by his mother's book and constant urgings. Gish thought of one of his statements when she and Tenn were discussing memories and the act of subsuming them and sharing them and keeping them. In *Divine Providence,* Swedenborg writes: "It is also known that everything a person meditates in his reason arises from the love of bringing it into effect by means of his thought. . . . It is the very delight of reason to see from love the effect in thought, not the effect in its attainment."

"Tennessee had a theater in his head," Gish told me, "and he could have populated it with anyone or anything he wished. He was monumental, but he seemed never to believe that, or he forgot it, or he just stopped looking for people and their feelings and their lives and just subsumed himself, instead of all that was going on around him. I think he got lost, but not in the flurry of events that he loved when I knew him, but in desperate attempts to merely stay alive, to get up and try again."

Gish sent Tenn another statement from Swedenborg, this one from *Secrets of Heaven:* "Unless a person is prepared, that is, furnished with truths and goods, he can by no means be regenerated, still less undergo temptations. For the evil spirits who are with him at such a time excite his falsities and evils; and if truths and goods are not present, to which they may be bent by the Lord, and by which they may be dispersed, he succumbs."

Tenn claimed that the letter from Gish bearing this statement arrived when he was in Italy, visiting the film director Luchino Visconti. Tenn was despondent, utterly in agreement that he lacked the necessary truths and goods. Visconti, knowing of Tenn's descriptions from the past of good times and happy memories, both subsumed and set aside, commanded him to speak of some sensations and take them within. "Begin," he said, "with a description of the ceiling above the bed where you felt safe and happy, and circle the room. Drop every detail before you drop the memory."

Our discussions included more than the balconies of Royal Street and Lillian Gish, but when the early afternoon arrived, after a lunch that had included a large amount of wine, it was this actress, this "titanic sprite," as he called her, who was most on his mind. Tenn asked for the rosary he had given me, and I handed it over to him. He held it in his fist and closed his eyes, saying a silent prayer. When he opened his eyes, he began fingering the beads, editing the owners of each one. "This one," he told me, pointing to the fourth bead of the first decade, "belongs to Lillian Gish." Tenn began moving his fingers across the beads, but it was no known prayer he was speaking: he was naming names and attributes, truths and goods.

Six

TENN BEGAN the following morning with a confession.

"I want to explain something to you about Lillian Gish," he told me. "About all the women you are going to meet and, God willing, learn from. There are lessons in them all. They are golden apples, all of them. Some with poisonous seeds, but none of them are wholly poisonous, or they would not have been influential to you or inspiring to me. I promise not to send you to any entirely awful people. Well—" He stopped himself. "None of these people were entirely awful when I knew them and worked with them. But times—and people—change."

What I needed to understand was that everyone operates on many levels. It is entirely impossible to face the world "bare of face or bare of soul," as Tenn explained. All of us are coated in a series of myths and nostrums and superstitions, all of which create a particular person. "It won't be easy to understand people, ever," Tenn told me, "but our lives require us to keep trying."

What Tenn wanted me to know about Lillian Gish, whom he had presented to me as virginal and vital and supportive, was that she was "packed with a multitude of sins and superstitions" that might make me think he had misled me into seeking her.

"Lillian Gish frightened and annoyed me as often as she inspired

Bursting with health and gently beautiful, the biggest star in the life of Tennessee's mother, Lillian Gish (here in the mid-1930s) walked through the city with the writer, shopping and talking, and becoming the inspiration for *Portrait of a Madonna*.

me," Tenn confessed that morning, "but I remain grateful to her for what she taught me. What she taught me was the importance of fear—or, to be more precise, the importance of not allowing fear to rule your decisions."

Gish feared many things in her time with Tenn.

"She was terrified of being ignored," Tenn told me. "There is an extraordinary photograph Andy Warhol showed me. Lillian Gish is sitting with some of the glamorous, well-oiled people—Liza or Bianca or Jackie O. Or it could be Grace Jones or Monique Van Vooren or Lee Radziwill. It doesn't matter. These types of people are supremely interchangeable on the social circuit and represent a particular mood or circle or ambience. In the context of a club or a party, they are not real people. They are far more artificial than characters in a play, costumed and smeared with makeup and awaiting a cue and a follow light. But one goes. One must be seen. One must announce to the world that they are still dancing or writing or acting or staying sober or walking without assistance. A part is being played. A result is being sought. In this particular picture, Lillian sits, folding in upon herself, like a disused ventriloquist's dummy, eyes vacant. She is being ignored. She, in her sensible shoes and dowager's clothes, looks like the ladies' room attendant, and everyone else—Martha and Rudi and Paloma—are waiting for a warm towel or supplication, and there sits this small, frightened Episcopalian lady. Ignored.

"One ignores Lillian Gish at great risk," Tenn told me.

"You see," he explained, "her life—her role in life—has been ordained—demanded!—by God."

Lillian Gish had been born into a family of refinement and respectability, but her father was a wanderer, and he left his wife and two daughters, each of whom then descended upon a life on the stage. The Gish sisters often performed together, but they were also often separated, and Gish, "a frightened victim of abandonment," as she told me, was grief stricken whenever she was apart from Dorothy. Their reunions were lachrymose and operatic, and Lillian recalled being slapped once by her mother for carrying on so fulsomely.

During her early years, Gish was surrounded by actors, vaudevillians, jugglers, and gypsies. Her performing life began before she could read, and she loved to describe the ceremony, as she called it, of her mother reciting the required lines of dialogue to Lillian and her sister as they were bathed, as they ate dinner, as they prepared for sleep. The routine was repeated the following morning, through the making of beds, breakfast, and later, that night, the performance.

Gish cleaned up the chronology and the order of her life considerably for her autobiography and for later interviews, but in the time she spent with Tenn, she made the recitation of her life scabrous and scintillating, justifying the rogue nature of her mother (who was not above skimming tips off of restaurant tables or leaving hotel rooms deep in the night due to a lack of funds) by the understanding that she—and,

Lillian and Dorothy Gish. They were partners—
professionally and personally—from childhood; they spent
virtually every day together.

to a lesser extent, Dorothy—was being prepared for delivery to D. W.
Griffith and the greatest art form ever invented.

Gish had implanted in her mind the belief that the cinema was a
creation that had been prophesied in the Bible, the means by which the
multitude of tongues—that horrible Tower of Babel that was nothing
to Gish but the collective human inventory—could come to understand
each other, to live in harmony, to learn from and love each other.

Tenn loved Gish and he did not regret a moment of the time they
spent together; but, as he told me, he found her to be utterly divorced

from time or space or reality. "The Earth as we know it," Tenn explained, "bears no relation to Miss Gish. Or I should say: she respects it only as a prop, something Mr. Griffith commissioned for her to act upon. It is not a spinning planet in the cosmos; it does not provide a home to other people making their way or finding a purpose. The Earth and all of its inhabitants and all of its resources are placed in a particular order so that the destiny of Lillian Gish can be realized."

Order was her primary obsession, as Tenn saw it. Things had to be done in a particular way and at a particular time; but more importantly, *her* order, *her* placement, *her* billing needed always to be seen to, secured, given special treatment.

While Tenn conceded that her narcissism was colossal, he was quick to point out that her kindness and her concern—at least for him— always appeared to be genuine. Gish worried that he did not eat properly; she abhorred his clothes. She fussed over him, and the care she displayed pleased Tenn, and pleased his mother even more. "That I had a 'great lady,' which my mother believed Lillian Gish to be, taking care of me, gave her years of bragging rights."

However, even Gish's acts of kindness had their place. If she gave a donation to a charity, or provided tickets to the theater to a friend unable to afford them, or helped her "poor, addled, soggy sister" yet again, it was because of a plan crafted by God to put Lillian Gish in a position to be of use, to fulfill some destiny.

Dorothy Gish was not simply a depressive alcoholic who might require treatment or patience or love: she was a reminder, from God, that Lillian should refrain from drink, should eat the proper foods, should carve out time each day for slant boards and Delsarte exercises and blackstrap molasses and wheat germ. A sign had been sent and must be acknowledged and obeyed.

"Violently uneducated," as Tenn put it, Gish learned everything from the people with whom she worked, from sawdust carny workers to Griffith to David O. Selznick. Gish attempted to learn from John Gielgud, who took an interest in her as a stage actress. "She was very sweet," Gielgud told me, "but extraordinarily naïve. Quite spongelike, which is good, but she absorbed all the bad along with all the good, and her mind, which was sharp and retentive, remembered clichés, wives' tales, and myths equally as sharply as poetry, history, or sound advice. She was hungry to learn, but she was also hungry to be the center of attention, and I could never tell if her desire to learn was motivated by her need for knowledge or her need to be noticed."

Gielgud recalls working on *Hamlet* as a happy time, because Gish was, even in her mid-forties, ideal as Ophelia. "She was tiny and alabaster white, with those enormous, lovely, empty eyes," he remembered, "and it was easy to direct her, because one only had to push an emotion, as if it were a slide into a projector, across her mind. 'Be manic, darling.' And there she was twirling about the stage, limbs flying. 'Be contrite, darling,' and she would have made the devil himself weep. 'Be sweet and flirtatious, angel,' and you could hear the cooing from the gallery. She was an actress trained in adverbs and adjectives. She could not—did not—understand emotional motivation, subtext, layers. But if you threw her something—sad, horny, angry, confused—her entire body was transformed and every inch of her, every pore of her body, exuded the adjective you had provided."

A later stage experience with Gielgud, an adaptation of Dostoyevsky's *Crime and Punishment*, directed by the formidable Russian director Theodore Komisarjevsky, was not one he remembered as sweetly. "Komisarjevsky was a brilliant man," Gielgud recalled, "and very precise with some of the details of the play, which was good but misshapen. I think he respected the person who was Lillian Gish, but had very little use for the actress who was Lillian Gish. He clearly knew who she was and what she had done and what she meant, but he could not ascertain what she could do or what she could become for this production."

Understanding that Gish was an actress who needed to be fed words or direct actions she could emulate, Gielgud would meet with her and describe the scene with which she might be struggling. "Lillian was the sort of actress," Gielgud continued, "who wanted to be told something like 'We are in the wintry home of the old teacher. He is tired and near death and feels unloved. Sitting with him is his beloved and devoted daughter. She would do anything for him. She dotes and she worries and she prays. She knows he will die soon, but she does everything to hide this fact from him, and from herself.' That is not a scene from *Crime and Punishment*, I must add, but it illustrates how I spoke to her."

In her mid-fifties during the run of *Crime and Punishment*, Gish amazed her fellow players with her energy and her enthusiasm. She also wanted to be beautiful, and Komisarjevsky's directions for severity were meant to move her from the coquettish performance she was giving. He

John Gielgud, one of Tennessee's favorite people in theater, and a man patient and intelligent enough to help explain plays and actresses to him

wanted her hair covered; he wanted her less flirtatious. "What is with the cute?" he would ask Gielgud, who laughed at the fact that the Russian despised the concept of cute, which he labeled as solely American. "The cute I do not want."

Almost every day during the sharing of notes with the cast, Gish would raise her hand like a penitent student and ask if there were any for her: Komisarjevsky always left her out of the discussion periods. One day, spent and impatient, Komisarjevsky looked at her for a long time. "How can I improve my performance?" she asked, in the long silence.

"More rouge," he told her, and the discussion was over.

Lillian learned many things from D. W. Griffith that she rarely discussed in her writings or interviews, including virtually all of her political and cultural beliefs, primarily a Republicanism that embraced "the purity of the Nation," as Tenn recalled, and he was never sure if she was referring to the United States of America or Griffith's 1915 film *Birth of a Nation.*

Tenn was surprised to learn that Gish had been devastated when Gielgud was arrested, in 1953, on a morals charge. "Accosted in a men's room!" Gish had said. "I wasn't sure I could ever face him again." They remained friends, but she prayed for his "sickness" to be healed. Tenn had asked her if she hadn't known that her friend was homosexual. "Of course not!" she replied. "Such a good actor, and so successful. It never entered my mind."

Gish's surprise was not that Gielgud had been discovered in his perfidy in a public toilet (that was, after all, where those types did what they did), but that a man who had succeeded, who had earned her trust, could be *that way*. Tenn was amused and amazed to learn what Gish believed about homosexuals. "Mr. Griffith told me about the homosexuals we worked with," she explained. "I knew they existed. I knew they were there. We weren't to expose them or abuse them, but we were to avoid them. You see, Mr. Griffith told me that homosexuals—and drug addicts and alcoholics—had drifted away from the light, from the light of God, and they walked in pools of darkness, clouded from goodness, and they could hold you in the dark if you let them. I don't fear them or dislike them, but I pity them, and I pray for them."

Gish also believed that because of the darkness in which they lived and moved, they could never be seen—or photographed or understood—properly, so success and happiness could not come to them. Any male artist who floundered in his career or who drank or who had difficulties with his monthly expenses was probably *that way,* and the sins accruing to his condition were simply calling on him. When Tenn confessed to Gish that he, too, was homosexual, she hugged him and told him that it was fine to have the condition of homosexuality, but one could not indulge in the commission of homosexuality. "That is when the darkness begins," she told Tenn. "God gives us our weaknesses, but he also gives us the freedom of our choices. I can tell you haven't succumbed to the temptations because there is light around you."

"As long as I was a success," Tenn told me, "as long as John Gielgud or Alec Guinness or Cecil Beaton or Cole Porter or Noel Coward were doing well and earning knighthoods and large royalties and full houses, it was assumed by Miss Gish that we were chaste; we were good boys. When I succumbed to failure, when my plays were demoted to church basements and off-Broadway hallways, when my mind and my narratives were no longer clear, when phone calls were not returned, it was clear that I had fallen into the darkness and was fully *that way*."

And yet every time Tenn saw Gish at a party, at the theater, on the street, she embraced him and told him she was praying for him. "I want the light back on you," she would say. When I spoke to Gish about those hugs and those prayers, she remembered them sadly. "Oh," she exclaimed, "it's terrible to live so long and to see so many people lost to the darkness! We have our hungers and we succumb to them and we only incur greater hungers, stronger appetites. Once we feel we're owed the flesh, then we may feel we're owed the wine, then we may feel we're owed the protection and the aid of the government. 'Protect and husband me, for I'm special,' they seem to say, and soon you can't see them at all. They're just utterly lost. My sister was lost. Mr. Griffith was lost. They couldn't believe in their destinies any longer, and they sought comfort elsewhere. They sought it in alcohol, and it only served to douse the fire of their talent.

"Listen," she said to me, "the trees are loaded with fruit. Don't be tempted by it. Look above the trees, look heavenward. All hungers are filled from above."

Miss Gish, Tenn explained, walked the earth as if it were an enormous back lot, and high above the trees of which she spoke was cinematographer Billy Bitzer, shooting it beautifully, capturing every move she made, and next to him was Mr. Griffith, dry and full of light, making sure her every step was safe and sure.

"Do you know where the theater was born?" Lillian Gish asked me on the phone one day. "Do you know where the art of storytelling came from? Do you know where art came from?"

I admitted that I didn't know the answers to these questions.

In honoring God, she told me, in the preparation of the Eucharist, all art forms were born. "There, in the earliest days of worship," Gish continued, "the worshippers prepared the table, brought the water, brought the wine, carefully put down the finest cloth, made their prayers. Something more needed to be done, a sound made, a commemoration was required, and so people made a noise. They invented singing; they invented prayer. If someone was especially ecstatic, he might paint an image, draw an emblem. Man needed some way to express his love and gratitude and fear of God, and so he found a multitude of ways to do so.

"Each time you sit in a church and you watch the priests come forth and set the table and ring the bells and pray and consecrate, you're witnessing not only the Eucharist, but the commemoration of the invention of art, and every time we commit to our work in the arts, we have to honor Him, or it will fail to serve any of us."

Tenn knew of Gish's beliefs on the origins of art, and he indulged her, which is not to say that he believed similarly. "You know," he told me, "I'm afraid of many things, but my fear of God has never factored into my writing. My fear of the things that make us believe we *need* a God drive me to the pale judgment daily."

Tenn found a need for—and an inspiration in—Lillian Gish. He came to understand her, and came to see how she could be of use to him as a writer. "I did believe," he said, "that she could, in her way, drive me to be a better writer. Even if by forcing me to not live as she lived."

On their earlier trips to the stalls and the junk shops downtown, Tenn had purchased the items, then shared them with Gish; as he regaled her with the discarded finery and sentimental objects, she smiled and endured his questions as to their provenance. But Tenn decided to invite her to choose the items on their next foray.

The change was extraordinary.

"When Miss Gish found an object," Tenn told me, "no matter how tiny or dirty or damaged, it held the importance of one of Mr. Howard Carter's excavations." (Carter was the archaeologist who unearthed the tomb of King Tut, a discovery that fascinated Tenn.) "She would cry over the torn fan that some woman had once used to remain cool, perhaps while waiting for a lover to return. She would exclaim over the poem that had been inscribed in a tattered copy of Miss Browning's poems, imagining the couple that this book had belonged to, and all that had passed between them. The difference between my discoveries and Miss Gish's, you see, is that God had ordained her acquisitions, God had led her to the very items she would need for whatever purpose He would later proclaim."

Watching her with her wares, her face suffused with the happiness she knew from divine providence, ageless, capable of lightning-quick biographies of the previous owners of the items she now held, Tenn began to think of a way he could understand this woman before him. Girlish, lovely, pregnant with fantasy, visited perpetually by the beliefs instilled in her by Griffith, Delsarte, Swedenborg, and God Himself, Tenn saw a lovely woman untouched by time.

"To be happy is to be forever out of time's grasp."

Tenn was certain that Thornton Wilder had said that, was sure that it was a quote given to him once by Lillian Gish. When? In 1982 he could not remember exactly; but he did remember that on that day, on the Lower East Side, some time in the 1940s—was it 1944, the year they had seen *Since You Went Away?*—he had looked at Lillian Gish, free from the constant rush of time and worry, and thought of a woman, felt some fog rising, and a play came to him.

He would call it *Portrait of a Madonna*.

The one-act *Portrait* was a rewritten version of a play Tenn had completed in 1941. "The war year," he would recall, "and the play was not sufficient to its purposes." Constantly revised and discarded, carrying various titles, he picked it up again after making the acquaintance of Lillian Gish.

"The primary character grew softer due to Lillian's influence," Tenn recalled. "I originally envisioned a rather desiccated spinster playing with her gewgaws of the past, recalling past lovers, a drugstore Miss Havisham, but Lillian presented another visage: a woman preserved in fantasy, pickled by delusion, ageless, untouched by time or care or reality. Glowing a bit, suffused with an inner itinerary that bore no relation to her surroundings. This is a woman I know well. It is my mother, of course, and . . ."

Tenn paused and collected himself. His mother, Edwina, had died only two years before our meeting, and the event had still not become one he could manage or direct or label in a way that made handling it comfortable for him.

"My mother could not fill out the lineaments of this woman on her own," Tenn continued. "Lillian came along and at a café table, not far from the Brevoort, one of my favorite destinations in New York City, Lillian sat surrounded by her day's findings in the stores and the stalls, and a woman came to me."

Lucretia Collins, the title character of *Portrait of a Madonna*, is, as Tenn admitted, a recurring, obsessive archetype from which he was unable to escape. As he put it, this woman, a dramatic template, is a "neurotic fabulist with delusions of grandeur; a woman divorced from reality, and in perpetual pursuit of a dreamed-for, hoped-for world of her own creation; a lost soul, floundering on the shores of the real world, an honest-to-God fish out of water; a tough performer who decides, while floundering, while awaiting her own destruction, to, at the very least, put on a good show, scales shining, tail flapping, gasping forcefully until the end."

In the brisk one act that is *Portrait,* Lucretia Collins calls down to the manager of her shabby-genteel "moderately priced city apartment" to complain that "Richard," her persistent, imaginary tormentor, is back and taking advantage of her, "indulging his senses." Two men, a porter and an elevator operator, come to the room and look over her belongings, consigning some to a future Dumpster, but finding others potentially valuable or useful. As one oils Lucretia's aged turntable ("Freud incoming!" Tenn cracked to me about this device), the younger man thinks of taking the records for his own uses, since his girl has let him know that "it's better with music." Most of the items in the apartment are old magazines and newspapers, all covered with dust as thick as verdigris. From the magazines Lucretia clips pictures of elegance or innocence, emblems of a lost or dreamed time. At one point she clipped hundreds of images of the Campbell's Soup twins, their oversized, cherubic, and glistening faces totems of purity and gravity at its strongest, and placed them in a scrapbook, which she delivered to the Children's Hospital on Christmas Eve and Easter Sunday. ("I felt," Tenn explained, "that on these Christian holidays, we are trying to remember or become our ideal selves—at least in Christian theology, which is to say myth. We take this belief system—typically our first one—and we paste it upon all our intercourses with others and with life. Naturally, the sick and dying children would like to be as pneumatic and bright as the Campbell's Soup twins, and Lucretia gives them their symbol, their cartoonish icons, as an inspiration. We do what we can.") For her own needs and her own indulgences, Lucretia probably clips out images of elegant movie stars, princesses, models bathing in milk or mink—images she had hoped to fulfill, but which were denied her because she had pushed away the man with whom she would have liked to have around for the indulgence of her senses.

Tenn had explained to Gish that this was one of his greatest fears, and one of his most often repeated offenses. "I fear," he told me, "never experiencing love or appreciation or affection. On one level—on one day—I will believe myself unworthy of them, so my fears appear justified. On another day, I will very grandly believe I have been unjustifiably denied these things, deserve them in spades, and aggressively pursue them. The aggression I display at these times initially excites me, but afterwards—after the manic, muscular display—I am horrified. Like the regret and rubbish that surround a binge of drinking or drugs or repetitive rutting, I awake to guilt and apologies and a deeper retreat from everyone."

Tenn tried to explain to Gish that Lucretia had lived in a time when women were expected to wait passively—and often fruitlessly—for their desired men to express themselves, show up, and to care for them. Surely, he asked, she could understand this lost, lonely woman in this regard.

"I have never known this of a man," was Gish's reply. But, Tenn countered, you must have known frustration, even desperation, when your needs were not met. "At some point," Tenn told me he asked her, "you must have felt the need to be daring, even foolish, in reaching out to see that a need of yours, a desire of yours, was met?"

Gish replied that she didn't have needs, and desires were "guilt markers," a sign that you had neglected something or someone, and your conscience—"God's nudge to your ribs"—was exercising this emotion, unpleasant and aching like a hunger, until you attended to your duties. "Whenever you want something," she told me, "you really are wanting in some specific way. You're short in some department, and the lack is painful. You fill the lack with work, with service. You don't fill it with dreams or food or love or *things*."

Gish then described for me the reactions or emotions she had felt when, on the set of a film, a light, high above the soundstage, had flickered out, and a cool, small spot appeared on her face, unnoticed by the director, the other actors, the visitors to the set. Only Gish knew what had happened; she could *feel* it. She waited, however, to alert anyone to the failure until an ideal time appeared. "You don't disturb anything or anyone to get what you need," she told me. "There's no excuse for that." At other times, on stage or screen, a scene may have been altered so that lines or business were denied Gish, leaving her an observer to others. "My ego may have arisen," she said, "but what I needed to rise toward, what I needed to know as my message, was to give everything to the other actors, to fulfill what was needed *of* me, not *for* me. Happiness comes from such things, never from looking around for what will fulfill you or make you happy or make you noticed.

"I have," she insisted, "no needs, and I never feel the discomfort of desire, because I always do what I should and I always have what I need."

Tenn asked Gish how she felt at the conclusion of *Portrait,* when, after being calmed or "looked after" by the two black men, underlings sent to deal with the crazy woman repeatedly raped by her phantom lover, she is led away, by a distracted doctor and a curt nurse, to the state hospital. Delivered, Tenn stressed, to a horrible end.

Gish disagreed strongly. Lucretia Collins is not being delivered to anything, she insisted. Lucretia Collins *gave herself over* to this punishment.

Tenn was frustrated by what he saw as Gish's selective sympathies. Lucretia Collins, the seedling from which burst forth Blanche DuBois, was a victim only of her own sins and improper actions and desires. Both women, Tenn would later realize, had ample opportunities, in Gish's view, to right their ways and find happiness, to be comfortable, free of desire, respectable.

"She could not, or would not, conceive of people destroyed by circumstances beyond their control," Tenn told me, in amazement. "It reminded me of the perpetual argument—the rampant animosity—that existed between Carson McCullers and Flannery O'Connor, two demonically talented and aberrantly distorted women who shared a region but violently different views of what transpired there." McCullers saw the world as one of chance and circumstances beyond our control, wandering evil looking for characters to take to a stage it had designed and controlled. One's goal, one's hope, was to not be cast in one of the roles needed for this pitiless passion play, always packed with an audience, and performing every hour of every day. In O'Connor's view, evil only visited the deserving: some flaw, some significant neglect, had opened the door, perhaps several doors, to whatever horror now prevailed. Almost always it was a lack of God, an improper or puny penance that had led to the calamity, from which the "deserving, the observant" could learn their lesson.

Tenn saw a similar mind-set in Gish, particularly when charity was requested of her. The theater community was a close one—they looked out for their own. When actors and actresses, directors or designers, fell on hard times and weren't eating properly or being cared for or falling behind on their rent, the community would rally and ask for donations. Tenn, then in his thirties, had known poverty, but the poverty of youth, when resilience was a fairly strong defense against want, when there was hope, when windfalls were always forthcoming. In his time with Gish, Tenn first became aware of the sadness and want that had come to visit so many of the talents he had once admired so much. In their own "moderately priced city apartments" or hotels where plaster rained down like dandruff—an "architectural psoriasis"—he saw men and women who had worked for Belasco and McClintic and Ziegfeld cramped into tiny rooms with hot plates and molding playbills. Gish was always prompt and generous with checks and cash (as well as invitations to dinners and events) for those she felt deserved her help, but she could not help anyone whose desperate times they had brought on themselves. Alcoholics, drug addicts, "people of any intemperance" should not be helped, outside of prayer and distant concern. As she explained to Tenn: "You do not feed the shrew who will later devour the garden."

Gish would share, however, her wealth—of money, of time, of good cheer—with anyone who had been decreased by age or infirmity or changing times and values. The latter affected her most dramatically, given that so many of the people to whom she gave so much had worked with her in the silent-film industry, and their acting styles, their salability, and their beliefs, according to Gish, had been cast aside, disrespected.

As she told me, "Those were the people who built the temple in which we now work, and they were just rotting away, molding. Theaters and streets should have been named for them, but they were unable even to afford a closet with a hot plate."

One surprising person in whom Lillian Gish rarely—if ever—invested time or money was D. W. Griffith, living in tatty seclusion in the Knickerbocker Hotel in Hollywood, cast aside, Tenn said, like some botched model of taxidermy, drunk and bitter and raging at past associates by phone, when the service had not been disrupted for nonpayment.

Griffith, the man who had given both Lillian and Dorothy Gish their lives in film, who had, in the opinion of many, transformed cinema, who was, in Tenn's opinion, a "demented, savage, but brilliant master of narrative," and who had been, for a time, Lillian's lover, educator, and, as she told me, her "lodestar," was not deserving of her time, but quite deserving of his misery, because he had succumbed to liquor, to envy, to rage, and to desires and wants.

"He sat there," Gish told me, "in that awful room and took no pride in what he had done. He waited for a reward for his work, when the work *was* the reward. He asked of the world and himself 'What now?' after he had invented and shared the modern cinema with the world. He was one of the world's greatest storytellers, but he kept insisting on a bad ending—an unconvincing, undeserving end—for his own story. I owed him everything, but I couldn't give him my time, and I couldn't give him hope. But life, Hollywood, fate didn't destroy him. He destroyed himself. Openly, willfully."

As Tenn told me, "He transformed the world, and what he really wanted was a gold watch." His gold watch came in the form of an honorary Oscar, guilt money to a vanquished artist, but it did nothing to assuage Griffith. He wanted work, and on his terms. "Terms!" Gish snorted to me on the phone. "Terms and desires and needs. These are the bricks in the road to hell."

Tenn and Gish went one weekend to a festival of silent films, and the experience was annotated with comments from Gish on the ultimate fate of so many of the beautiful images that flickered on the huge screen. Bankruptcy, broken heart, drug addiction, homosexuality, botched abortion, car accident, pornography, suicide. At one point, Gish gasped and grabbed her chest. Tenn, expecting the worst—even after the long list of horrors—asked what had happened to the young and beautiful man on the screen.

"He," Gish sputtered, "he . . . went into real estate!"

Portrait of a Madonna is "respectfully dedicated to the talent and charm of Miss Lillian Gish," and Tenn fully felt she earned it.

When Tenn first presented *Portrait of a Madonna* to Gish, he hoped that one of the adjectives she might use to describe Lucretia Collins would be "heroic."

It was not.

As she told me in 1989, "Oh, she was so tragic! So lost. So utterly in the darkness, and what she wanted was to be loved and respected, but she had made mistakes that cast her deeply into darkness. She couldn't even stand the light of the sun, unable to see it as beautiful or nourishing or illuminating. To her it was a judgment, a revelation of who and what she really was: the spotlight of God shining down on her, exposing her, and offering a way out. But she ran from the truth, and she ran from the salvation. And then, with that elevator door crashing with the sound of a cage being snapped shut, she is placed into deep, perhaps eternal, darkness. It was a lovely and terrifying play."

"Lillian's influence upon the play," Tenn told me, "was to soften it. Lucretia, as filtered through Lillian, was more frantic, more flirtatious, frail, a moth not only flittering about the flame, but frequently flying right into it, emerging singed and tattered but determined to keep flying."

Tenn could see, however, that Lillian could never fully understand Lucretia, and she didn't play the role until 1957, more than a decade after Tenn presented it to her.

How was she in the role?

"She was brilliant as Lillian Gish passing judgment on this poor, unfortunate soul who gave herself over to the wrong people and the wrong desires," Tenn said.

Immediately upon completing and dedicating *Portrait,* Tenn began thinking of another play—and another role—that could be filled by Lillian Gish.

"Why, I'm sure you want to ask, did I want to continue to write for Lillian?" Tenn asked me. "Well, she fascinated me, and I wanted her approval. My own needs and desires got the better of me. I was determined to have her approve of me."

Tenn was also enamored of her beauty, that translucent skin, that long golden hair. "She was like something I had either dreamed or had remembered from some large, ornate book my mother had read to me as a child—a book of fairy tales or a biblical primer for children. In either she was virtuous and beautiful and perpetually in danger, too good for this earth, alien to ordinary people." Gish walked about the city with Tenn in ornate hats or with an umbrella, protecting her skin and her large, light eyes. "Talent, time, and skin," Tenn mused. "She protected them all fiercely, and they have all lasted well."

Tenn recalled that Gish had a "nice" but not terribly abundant sense of humor. Her propriety, and her determination to be sunny and productive, often placed her in situations that were funny. To sit with her in a theater near someone with an especially unpleasant body odor was something Tenn felt should have been captured on film. She *denied* the offense, because it could not interfere with the play or the film she *needed* to see. Around her, however, people laughed and writhed or moved. Lillian was oblivious. Gish was also often challenged by regal and ornate dining arrangements, foreign foods, but she plunged ahead, utterly serious even if utterly wrong. She adored stories of dining mishaps, and loved the story of Marion Davies's facial strap—a device placed beneath a wig to pull up sagging skin—coming undone and landing in her soup. The bowl was Lalique or Villeroy & Boch or bought from the estate of a

Hapsburg, but it now served a soiled facial strap. Davies soldiered on. At another party, during the making of *The Night of the Hunter,* the pendulous and free bosom of Shelley Winters kept grazing the top of her soup, her main course, her frothy dessert: her blouse, at least beneath the breasts, was a testament to both her eating habits and her posture.

Tenn imagined a funny, scattered woman of a certain age, once refined and destined for a good and respected and examined life, pretty and smart, capable of humor and sexuality, living in a lovely apartment on Royal Street, with one of its best balconies, and every inch covered with dust and trinkets she had collected through her living and through her pursuit of her fantasy life. Bibelots, trinkets, poems. Her desire for the respectable was as strong as her desire for the "indulgence of the senses," and she could admit that the reading of Elizabeth Barrett Browning was well and good, but sometimes a woman needed to be loved, appreciated, ogled.

Gish was not comfortable discussing sex or even things that could be labeled sensual. The fact that people loved and sought and were addicted to sex was a fact she skipped past mentally with the same quickness she displayed when she walked past the strip clubs and porno theaters in New York City. She would look, giggle, and shake her head, and move on. What fools these mortals be! What strange things ordinary people give themselves over to so often and to no good end!

Lillian Gish helped to get the new play, then called *The Moon and the Royal Balconies,* started, but Edwina Williams began to work her way in.

"My mother," Tenn told me, "was very much of her time, and she was very much aware of the role the 'fine' and 'refined' Southern woman must play in the strata. Nonetheless, my mother would often tell me, in bald terms, what women really wanted; and what women really wanted, above a secure station in life or church or the neighborhood, above a line of credit in the best stores and a lovely home, was the admiration, seemly or not, of men. You were loyal to one, but you could entice and entrance multitudes, and a lack of physical attractiveness and charm were deformities toward which she displayed no charity or patience. Many times I saw her speak to photographs in newspapers and magazines, or to images on the television, that displayed a less-than-comely woman, and she was outraged. 'An ugly woman,' she always maintained, 'has no reason whatsoever to be out and about. She should be ashamed of herself.'

Ugly women were created by God—or had managed to escape the grace of God—to become religious women; librarians; restorers of works of art, hidden behind the scenes with toxic chemicals, bleaching and refining paintings and sculpture. Some of them might write books or poems in the attic, but would manage, with great tact, to die before their faces could be exposed to a public that might not be able to reconcile their work with their lineaments. These women might also become cooks and maids, who would be grateful for the respite from judgmental eyes, and would pour all of the love they could not force or slaver over a man into pies and soups and casseroles and perfectly tended flower beds and shining bathrooms. 'I always prefer an ugly maid,' Edwina would say, 'because all of her pregnant and fulsome attention will be transferred to me.'"

Beauty was a gift from God. Charm was a gift that arose from a woman, like a scent, from the beauty of her character and the refinement of her mind. You were given the beauty, but you earned the charm. Charmless people baffled and enraged Edwina, and Tenn admitted that he found them curious as well, freaks of nature who, rather than possessing a third arm or a pinhead or hundreds of extra pounds of fat, simply shot through the world selfish and blunt and humorless, sating every immediate hunger. Every villain written by him, Tenn told me, could be said to possess as a primary sin the absence of charm. They were not gifted.

Edwina was also unafraid to share with her son the glories of sexual and sensual pleasure, although they were always given in the mode of a confession—secretive and giggly and flushed with delight.

"My mother told me that there were three occasions upon which a man should and could consign his women to their beds," Tenn said. "One occasion was upon the tragedies of war or illness or some other calumny visited upon his person. Another was his self-inflicted destruction—his unfaithfulness with his appendage or his finances or his time, a sort of spiritual and sensual suicide. The third was when a man took his woman to bed and, as Mother put it, 'stretched her out from here to Tupelo.' Then you stayed in bed, tired but happy, with a hot-water bottle, a movie magazine, and the ministrations of your devoted and ugly maid, who seethed with jealousy because she wasn't going to be stretched from here to anywhere, but she had to hand-wash the dainties and restock the basins where proof of her mistress's pleasure could be discerned."

As Edwina aged, she displaced her uses for sexual pleasure with the sensual ones—menial sins replacing the venial. Sensual pleasures were walks and visits with men, refined conversations, a helpful arm, a peck on the cheek, dinners and nice gifts. Perhaps some kissing, but nothing that would require the exertions of removing the Harry Houdini/ Rube Goldberg appliances that transformed her body into that of the younger, more nubile Edwina.

Nothing ruled out, however, mental sins, and they were always of the venial variety, and Edwina would sometimes remove her constrictive public armor, slather on some Bellodgia, put a record on the turntable, and take a "nap," during which she returned to a more robust form of male company. Tenn admitted that he enjoyed this activity too. Slumber in the afternoon, "a drink and a self-massage," he called it. Both he and his mother laughingly used the same term to describe their sensual times alone.

They both called them "reveries."

Seven

TENN ENCOURAGED ME to develop and maintain the ability to see things as a young and curious person. When he was walking city streets, dreaming of an actress, of a foggy stage, and a story waiting to be told, he felt young, his eyes were sharp. A note I scribbled read, "Jessica Tandy preserves young eyes," to which Tenn added that it was imperative that an artist remember the frightened and scabrous rube who first came to the big city and tried to achieve his dream. "I was happiest when I was dreaming of the achievement," Tenn confessed, "far happier than I was when I actually succeeded, and I miss those hungry and hopeful eyes of mine: eyes that were very similar to Jessie's. What we shared was our inbred lack of sophistication, and our mortal fear that we would be found out. Her salvation was in her eyes."

I found another entry, this one a quote from Proust: "The real voyage of discovery consists not in seeing new landscapes but in having new eyes." Tenn provided his own annotation: "You find yourself not by purchasing maps and setting across new lands, but by purchasing some quiet and restoring yourself to your young self, eyes open, ready to receive."

Jessica Tandy had a face that was delicate and beautiful and expressive: her skin, as thin and pale as onionskin, would literally sag when she was moved or shocked; conversely, her delight was often accompa-

Jessica Tandy, in the mid-1940s, as she
prepared to appear in Tennessee's *Portrait of a
Madonna,* her calculated audition for Blanche
DuBois

nied by a rosy glow that transformed her face into that of a young girl,
and her laugh was as delightful as that of a child. As she thought of the
similarities she shared with Tenn, she looked utterly devastated.

"I always knew that Tennessee Williams was my salvation," she whispered, "but I never dreamed that I was of any help to him. I wish I had
been more to him; I wish I could be more to *anyone.* That is something
else we had in common: our utter failure to believe ourselves worthy of
another's interest or affection."

The subject was changed, but several days later, as we walked on
the outskirts of Central Park, a few blocks from her home in the Hotel
Wyndham, Jessica returned to the subject of young eyes. "My mother
wanted me to succeed," she told me, "but she wanted me to succeed in

a distinguished manner. *Her* definition of 'distinguished,' mind you, what was distinguished in her eyes, but it was the manner in which I was trained. I was to be silent and kind and I should never forget the circumstances into which I was born, which were horrid. I should never forget that I was a nobody who succeeded because I used my brains and I taught myself breeding, but my ambitions should be kept to myself and carried out by others. This is something else Tennessee and I shared: we uncovered our secrets and our desires with those who were strong enough to see to it that we would have the opportunity to show up and shine, without ever being dirtied by the unseemly residue of ambition or negotiation or compromise. Our compromises were made within and for the work, but the doors that needed to be opened so that we could do our work were opened for us by others, and the reason we allowed others to be so in control of so much of our lives had to do with the fact that we always felt that the moment we entered into a situation with anyone of a better station—which in my case was virtually everyone—we would be discovered and asked to leave the room. I only felt comfortable in a situation where I was an actress working on a role, and Tennessee always told me that he only wanted to show up as the writer, to offer assistance with words. We were only gifted in our single area of expression, and otherwise we were totally lost and useless."

I asked Tandy once if she could describe herself, and I did so in the presence of her husband and frequent acting partner, Hume Cronyn. She laughed the beautiful, silvery laugh and responded that she was still, at heart, the young, frightened, rustic girl from "poverty and pretension," but also an alternate person, "who was patched together by desire and design." Cronyn interrupted and said to me, "You—or any outside observer—are in a better position to decide who Jessie really is. I don't think she can see herself clearly anymore." Jessica grew silent, and the delicate skin sagged. Under her breath she muttered, "As always, Hume has the last, correct word."

Tenn saw Jessica Tandy clearly. She was, to him, "Big Lady," the epitome of manners and refinement and kindness, always perfect in deportment and always available with the right word, the right sentiment, at the right time. "She was marvelous," Tenn admitted, "and to my mind, the ideal lady by Southern standards. Women in organza, with corsages, just the right dab of scent, behaving impeccably no matter the circumstances. Given the mess that I was when *Streetcar* began,

I latched onto Jessie with a most indecorous ferocity, and she kept me on balance. Initially, I loved her for the lady she was, and I didn't feel she was the actress that Blanche needed and deserved. I clung to her for her kindness, and she clung to me to be seen as deserving of my lovely Blanche."

I kept trying to imagine Jessica and Tenn in 1947, clinging to each other, working toward their goals, frightened of many of the same things, seeing this extraordinary play through young eyes; but I never could see them coming together, I never could imagine them having their corrosive self-images.

It was Elia Kazan, with his brutal and brusque vision, who told me why I was failing.

"You're seeing them with *your* young eyes," he said, "and you think they're great and wonderful. Don't be blinded by the gilding. Go back to the beginnings, and find the rubes they're speaking of. The greatness of these two people lies in how they got from their squalor—real or perceived—and became artists. Always go to the beginnings. The real person will always be found there."

On a walk through the French Quarter, Tenn pointed out to me the bars and restaurants that had once offered him hospitality. He pointed out the places in which he had lived and written, and he finally walked me to the actual streetcar named Desire, which stood outside of the old Federal Mint. He grew silent, and in the silence I asked him how the play had come to him. The question seemed to revive him. "Let's go to the water to talk," he suggested, and we went to the promenade across from Jackson Square that looks out over the Mississippi, and sat on a bench. The day was humid and the air was still, but there was a slight breeze coming off the brownish water, and Tenn felt calm looking out across it.

"*Streetcar*," he continued, "was my literary manifestation of my very present fear that I would not be able to support myself as a writer," he began, "and that I would be forced to fall upon the mercies and the coffers of people unsympathetic to my plight and to my needs. Which is to say, everyone—for no one really understands or sympathizes with artists until a profitable emission is seen and utilized. My family looked upon *me* for support, which only added to my neurotic obsessions with money, and who else could I search for sympathy, for food, for a roof over my head? As time went on, and I saw no ease of my debts or my fears, I became paralyzed with the fear that I would be sent to live with some relatives in Mississippi or the outermost regions of Louisiana: religious, rustic people who not only had no understanding of the artistic temperament or needs, but who probably felt that an artist was an aberration. How would I survive in their world? How would I earn my keep and my peace while leaning upon them to keep me alive and able to write? Would I have to give up completely my ambitions and become one of them, a toiler of the earth, or a volunteer in the rectory, or a day laborer, hiding my own reality behind a veneer of normality just to have a home? That is where *Streetcar* began. Within my very real, very possible fear that I would become a ward of venomous people who would rather see me destroyed than to survive."

As Tenn thought more about the play, his "fear-based fantasia," the main character became a woman who was an "amalgamation of me, my mother, my sister, and an actress [Lillian Gish] with whom I had become incongruously obsessed," and it was, as Tenn always insisted, the play "that grew the fastest, gave me the most satisfaction, and ultimately speaks more about me than any other. It is my clarion cry for survival, and I believe that it is heard by most everyone who sees or reads the play—if they have a heart and a shred of truth within them."

However, the version of *Streetcar* that reached Elia Kazan was not the theatrical landmark that, in Kazan's words, "propelled the American theater forward to an almost unimaginable degree." The play was, instead, "a diamond in the rough, a jewel thrown atop a dung heap. Everything that ultimately made it so brilliant was in there, I assure you," Kazan told me, "but the script was not focused. Anyone reading that script immediately knew that something remarkable, perhaps revolutionary, was going to occur when this play reached a stage. We just couldn't always believe that it *would* reach a stage, and the primary cause of our fear that it would not was Tennessee. And the primary cause of Tennessee's insanity and inability to focus in those early days of work on *Streetcar* had to do with the actress he had decided would be his Blanche."

That actress was not, of course, Jessica Tandy.

"When I first imagined a woman at the center of my fantasia," Tenn revealed to me, "I immediately saw the pure and buoyant face of Lillian Gish, and *Portrait of a Madonna,* which is *Streetcar* in postulant mode, was written for her and dedicated to her. It is, in every sense of the word, *her* play. My perceived knowledge of her, which is always very intimate with me, imbued that piece, and she was very taken with it. Her enthusiasm and her graciousness toward me led me to develop the play, and hers was the figure that walked out of the fog toward me.

"When I write," Tenn explained to me, "I am not myself, really. I cannot sit down at my typewriter or my pad of paper as Thomas Lanier Williams or Tennessee Williams or anybody at all, really. I need to completely erase all that I was thinking of and allow myself to be made captive to the creatures who actually lead me through my plays.

"My writing is very much of the automatic variety, almost incantatory," he continued. "Almost anyone observing me in this state would assume that I was dreaming or was the victim, perhaps, of some cerebral incident, but it is actually when I am most focused, and I do not understand it at all."

Tenn paused, looked at the water, and closed his eyes.

"As I close my eyes and think upon some recent series of events or a dream or a nightmare," Tenn told me, his hands pantomiming the act of typing, "a woman will appear to me. She will walk toward me and begin speaking and will, literally, lead me through what ultimately becomes a play. I do not need this process so much with stories, as I now feel my stories are the residue of plays best left abandoned. However, everything that is in one of my stories has been through the mental theater, has had a figure from the fog as its escort. And Lillian Gish was the escort who brought me to Blanche. I love her for this gift, and I love her for the journey she provided, but there was a point at which she abandoned me, or I abandoned her."

Tenn offered the analogy of a wedding he had once attended, in which the bride, a young girl, the product of a particularly acrimonious divorce, had been walked only halfway down the aisle by her errant father, then met by the dutiful mother, who had always been there for the daughter, and who now delivered her to the pastor, the groom, and the hoped-for, prayed-for good graces of a happy marriage. Lillian Gish had taken Tenn halfway down the aisle of his mental theater, and as he stood there "among the red chairs and the worn carpeting, somewhere around row L," he laughed, "I looked up at the stage, well lit but free of fog, and realized I had come to the theater on the wrong evening. The stage was empty. The woman had abandoned me. I looked to my left and Lillian was gone. I needed a new woman, a new escort. I could not be delivered to my stage, my altar, my hoped-for, prayed-for marriage of playwright and play.

"When I wrote *Menagerie*," Tenn continued, "I knew that Amanda was, at her core, my mother, but given that I could not countenance my mother's presence in the real and present world, I was certainly not going to allow her admission into my mental theater, so Amanda soon became part Miriam Hopkins and, later, very much Laurette Taylor, and those women are deeply invested in that character. With *Streetcar*, which was *Portrait of a Madonna*, and *The Poker Night*, and *Miss Blanche Thinks About Things*, and *The Moon and the Royal Balconies* before it finally found its moorings as *A Streetcar Named Desire*, I always imagined Lillian Gish in the leading role. I did not know her at all when she first entranced me, but I had become quite enchanted with her through her film appearances, and very early in my years in New York, young and impoverished both of pantry and of soul, I had seen her walking along Broadway, very happy and gay and smartly dressed, and I wanted so much to be in her mind-set, to have the comfort of accessories that were perfect, to have that sheen of happiness and wellness that she emanated. I recall that she caught my eye and smiled at me, a warm and open smile.

"I lived at the movie palaces in those days," Tenn said, "at a time when they *were* palaces: huge, gaudy buildings with secret alcoves for assignations or naps, and the utter neglect of the staff, who would allow you to sit for multiple viewings, and who would allow me cups of ice for my own liquids. There were always revivals of old films, and those films are really what inspired my own dreams and my own productions in my mental theater, for my women look like those cinematic women: pale and perfect and terribly demonstrative. Demonstrative they would have to be, as I am a most lazy person, and it is a strong woman who must pull me toward my conclusions."

Lillian Gish held Blanche DuBois—and its creator—firmly in her hands until Tenn began to rewrite and refashion the play under the forceful direction of Elia Kazan.

Forty-five years after this period, Kazan was candid in his assessment that Tennessee was, for a frighteningly long period of time, incapable of taking his diamond in the rough and transforming it into the play we now know. "He was, in an annoyingly honorable way, devoted to Lillian

Gish playing the part," Kazan explained. "He truly believed that since hers was the vision that was his first of Blanche, he would lose the character completely without her performance of it. I had great respect for Miss Gish, and her film legacy is not to be slighted, but she quite simply failed to understand any aspect of Blanche or any of the other characters in the play. Her intelligence was very simple, very openhearted, and Blanche was as alien to her as if she were playing a Martian, and in order to make her real, she applied an odd salad of philosophy and religion atop her head, and I simply couldn't stomach it. I was very harsh with Tennessee, and I told him that his play was being diluted daily by the presence of Miss Gish."

"I was digging far into the earth to find these characters," Tenn told me, "finding oil and bones and buried treasure, and far away, safe and pristine on the lip of this enormous hole I had dug into the human soul, stood Lillian Gish—remote and not at all a participant in what I was happily excavating."

It would be the job of both Tenn and his producer, Irene Mayer Selznick, to let Lillian Gish know that she would not be Blanche DuBois. Kazan confirmed this story, and recalls his own happiness when Tenn revealed that the play could go forward without his spiritual muse. "I'm only slightly ashamed to say that I was jubilant," Kazan confessed, "because, in the end, *A Streetcar Named Desire* is, and ever shall be, far more important than Miss Gish's feelings."

Tenn had no way of knowing that his play, which he revised extensively, was garnering attention in other quarters. "I thought I was typing in the dark," Tenn told me, "with occasional flashes of light from Kazan, who hovered and hummed and scratched through scenes with a Blackwing pencil." But there were others who were aware of this new play: Hume Cronyn and Jessica Tandy had heard of it—as bright and as destructive as fire, messy but potentially brilliant—and they were friends with its director. Jessica hungered for the part, and Cronyn shared her desire, which he expressed in various long-distance telephone conversations with Kazan. "I'll admit now," Kazan boasted, "that I was obnoxiously excited. I knew what this play could be, but my gloatings to Hume and Jessie were not because I ever saw Jessie in the role: I simply trusted Hume's wily intelligence and taste. However, if I should be recognized for nothing else in my life, I brought Blanche to Tennessee."

In one of the telephone conversations, Hume Cronyn asked for a copy of the play. "There isn't a play . . . yet," was Kazan's reply. However, Kazan did mail them a copy of *Portrait of a Madonna*.

"And the moment I read it," Jessica Tandy told me, "my life began. I was, for the first time in my life, unafraid to be ruthless in order to get something I wanted."

Jessica Tandy was thirty-seven years old when she first felt unafraid to be ruthless. "I'm the first to admit how idiotic it appears," she confessed, "that a morbidly shy and ashamed person should choose to go on the stage, but my fear of recognition was as the person Jessica Tandy, not as a character. Characters were what I was hiding behind, transforming myself into something or someone interesting, perhaps, or useful, but I wasn't even able to pursue roles for myself. I was—and to a degree still am—passive. I endure far more nonsense than anyone my age should, but I am emotionally paralyzed in so many ways, and whenever I feel myself getting a little confident, or feeling that I may be doing things fairly well and should be proud, I am immediately drawn back to poor little Jessie Alice Tandy, forever without."

Jessie Alice Tandy was born on June 7, 1909, in London. She recalls one of her earliest days in school, when her vital statistics were entered into her teacher's ledger, and she heard the words "Tandy 6-7-9" read aloud. "I thought those numbers, which were simply my birth date, were somehow a judgment, a rating of sorts," she remembered. "At even that young age—and I guess I was six or seven—I knew that we were poor, we didn't come from 'fine' people, and that I would be called upon to do more to simply acquire the most basic education or courtesies. I held that 'Tandy 6-7-9' in my head for years. It still makes me ashamed, and I can still hear it being called, and still remember my shame at what I thought was a public accounting."

Tandy's family was poor, and there was always a struggle for everything, but things seemed always to appear. "I now know," she told me, "that there was family and a few friends and neighbors who helped us; we all helped each other." However, when Tandy's father died of cancer when she was twelve, the family's finances, and their sense of identity, became even more precarious. "I don't even know how my mother kept us alive, my two brothers and me," she told me, and was clearly touched by the memories she held. "I have been fortunate for so long in having things, in not having to worry about so many things that were once entirely out of my reach, but even from my healthier perspective it becomes more amazing to me that my mother maintained a home and managed to instill in me a dream or a motive, however distorted it might have been."

Tandy's mother took on as many jobs as she could manage, and she was perpetually saving money to attend classes. "My mother," Tandy said one day, beaming, "was very American in her belief in self-improvement, so she constantly enrolled in classes: sewing, public speaking, cooking, whatever she could manage. And since she worked at a school for retarded and handicapped children, she was often offered free tuition. When she knew the tuition was free, she would ask if her daughter could join. And in one of those classes, I discovered Shakespeare."

Tandy recalled that the first class in which she became enamored by the sonnets of William Shakespeare was a public-speaking course, but after she displayed an affinity for reciting, she was referred to a course better suited for aspiring performers. "Mind you," she told me, "these 'aspiring' thespians were my mother's age, but they coddled me and treated me kindly as I worked on those sonnets, and I was truly transported."

Tandy was encouraged in her dramatic studies and eventually earned acceptance at the wonderfully Dickensian-sounding Ben Greet Academy, which, as she told me, "was no RADA or Central School, I assure you"; but the young, shy actress earned parts and respect. "I was, if nothing else, the most polite young girl in any acting school of that time," Tandy joked, and she was also, as was her tendency, "maddeningly passive. My reports from my teachers were always the same: 'Do more,' 'Define yourself,' 'Let us know how you see yourself,'" she remembered. "How could I come out and tell them that I had no idea of the answers to any of those questions? How can I tell you that today, when I am more than eighty years old, I *still* cannot answer those questions?"

Tandy found work, most of it execrable, as she recalls; but John Gielgud insisted that Tandy was far harder on herself than she deserved. "She was developing into a very ordinary repertory actress," Gielgud told me, "and she was very conscious of her diction, which was very much the style in the theater in the late twenties and early thirties. There was a great deal of artificiality abounding on the stages at that time, and what made Jessica fetching to me was her reticence, what I gather was her fear, in the performance of these minor plays. She had a realism that caught my eye: that it was fear was not known to me at the time, and it was irrelevant as well, for all I knew was that something interesting was going on with her."

Tandy also earned an admirer—the handsome actor Jack Hawkins, a burly and virile man who would succeed in the films *The Cruel Sea*, *The Bridge on the River Kwai*, *Lawrence of Arabia*, and *Zulu*. "He was a wonderful actor," said Tandy, "and he tried to be a sympathetic mate to me, but I was woefully unprepared for men." Tandy had spent her entire childhood helping her mother care for her two brothers, attending night classes with her mother, and dreaming of an escape. "I could literally see the cycles of each day," she remembered, "and as much as I admired my mother for attempting to see us become better, I also resented the metronome-like banality of each day and its tasks. I never dated or spent time with any men other than my brothers and those gentlemen who were with me in classes or who had been my cast members in plays, and none of them had ever shown the slightest interest in me. I also had no girlfriends to speak of, so I didn't even know that I was lacking anything by having no social life with boys. I was socially inept."

What drew her to Hawkins was a combination of his striking looks and his overwhelming confidence. "He seemed," she told me, "to be afraid of nothing, and entered every room unafraid, and was soon its most popular guest. He was the first person to whom I would share my fears of inadequacy, my shame at my upbringing. I told him that most London cabbies didn't even know where my house was—that was how distant and déclassé my home was. I could tell him that I came to the theater through an adult-education class, and suddenly he was telling me how poor he was and that his theater life had begun in children's pantomimes and playing Santa Claus for dying children in hospitals. I looked at him and felt I had found someone who could accept me and understand me."

Tandy and Hawkins were married in 1932 and would have a daughter two years later. "What I remember about that marriage were the constant pep talks that Jack gave me," Tandy said, "and the constant arguments about money." Tandy knew the cost of every item and kept an amazingly detailed itinerary in her head. "I tell myself that I'm not good at numbers or with finances," she confessed, "but I could stretch a little bit of money with great skill, although it wasn't a skill that gave one a great sense of pride." Hawkins, while not wealthy, felt that money was to be spent; he was bored with accounting and budgets, and he attempted to tell his wife that her inability to rise to being a great actress had its basis in her crippling sense of limitation. "He may well have been right," Tandy said, "but I couldn't change my ways. When I first got some decent, regular income to my name, do you know what I bought? Soap. When I told this story to John Gielgud, he assumed that I had bought some marvelous soap by Poiret or some French *parfumier*, but it was a simple box of glycerin soap from my local chemist. When Jack got a bit of money, he bought a car. I was horrified."

Tandy had also never learned the art of flirtation, of keeping a man interested, or of keeping a home intact. "My upbringing was about getting brothers out of bed, out of the house, and off to school or work," she admitted. "I didn't know about cooking or decorating or having unexpected friends drop in. I didn't like it when Jack brought people over; he didn't like it that there wasn't a stocked bar and food on the table. He wanted to go out every night, and I was this spinster sitting at home reading." In time Hawkins found social graces and affection elsewhere, and Tandy accepted it with little surprise. "I just assumed that I wasn't gifted in that way, so I would stay home with my daughter, and I would work on my acting."

Tandy's career remained stagnant, primarily, Gielgud recalls, because "Jessica didn't know how to make calls or ask for favors. She had had wonderful successes, but she had failed to realize that the blustery confidence that Jack had blown beneath her feet was what had gotten her through so many things, so she was adrift. Jessica as an actress and as a person is very incremental; she moves in small, delicate steps. It is fascinating to witness both as her acting partner and as her director, and I've been both. It is as if she is doling out her talents as stingily as she doled out her coins when she was growing up poor and terribly conscious of lack. Jessica feels that her talents are as limited now as her finances were then, so there is this dribble of talent that comes at you as she investigates a role, surveys her players, analyzes the text. She was this way when she was my Ophelia [in 1934], and she was this way when I directed her in *All Over* [in 1971]. As if working on a collage that will soon be immense, she starts in one tiny corner and adds snippet after snippet. This is fascinating when she has a role to which she can apply this technique, but it is utterly futile when one is sitting at home with a child and needs work."

A quartet of mutual admiration: Hume Cronyn, Jessica Tandy, Lillian
Gish, and John Gielgud, backstage at the Martin Beck Theater, after
a performance of Edward Albee's *A Delicate Balance* in which the
Cronyns starred, 1966

Jessica Tandy found her impetus to feel confident again in Hume
Cronyn, whom she met backstage in New York, in 1940, after a performance in a play called *Jupiter Laughs*. "It was not a good play," Tandy
remembered, "and I don't recall that I felt very good in my part, but he
was very effusive."

In fact, Cronyn recalled that he was *too* effusive. "I saw her and I
wanted her," Cronyn barked out one day in the living room of their
hotel suite. "I was stunned by her. I thought she was exquisite." Tandy
blushed as Cronyn said these things, but it was clear that, fifty years
later, she could recall the impact of his words. "I told her I would divorce
my wife, and she should divorce her husband," Cronyn told me, "and I
saw no reason why she couldn't." Cronyn was, according to Elia Kazan,
"the little Bantam of Broadway [who] had money, which meant he had
clothes and money for dining, which meant he had women, and he
was wonderfully cocky and smart and funny. I liked him immediately.

I would have liked to have been there when he began courting Jessica because they are so different."

"Hume terrified and appalled me in the beginning," Tandy told me. "He thought British actors were pretentious and British theater obsolete. He made fun of my having so many fears about money, and when I lost my last one hundred dollars"—which she had tucked into her girdle—"he made fun of my horror and peeled off two hundred-dollar bills and told me to shut up."

Eventually, Tandy had a moment with Cronyn when she told him that she was growing very fond of him, but that he was going to have to learn who and what she truly was, why she was fearful of certain things, and what he was destined to live with if he pursued her. "And I listened, and I agreed that it was all good," Cronyn said, and within weeks both Tandy and Cronyn filed for divorce so that they could begin their life together.

Whenever I spoke to Jessica, she would send Cronyn out of the room after a polite spell of a few minutes, because she felt he would take over the conversation, and because his opinions of people, including Tenn and others for whom Jessica held great affection, were harsh and unforgiving and offered without solicitation. However, one day when I called on them at the Wyndham, Cronyn met me in the lobby and took me up himself. In the elevator he told me what he felt I needed to know about Jessica Tandy.

"When I met her," he told me, "I not only had dreams of acting opposite her, but I wanted to scour the world for plays she could star in, and I wanted to produce and direct them. I believed then and I believe now that she is an extraordinary actress, and I feel that every movement she makes is beautiful and worth repeated viewings. I think she imbues every performance with her very ardent life story, and that is rare, and I wanted to be a part of it. And Jessica didn't know how to make it happen. I made it happen."

When the elevator doors opened onto their floor, Jessica was at the door to their suite, and she looked surprised to see the two of us together. "I can just imagine that Hume filled your ear in that ride," she teased. "You know I did," he told her, kissing her on the cheek. "But when has anything I've told anyone not been to their benefit?"

In New York Tenn was furiously revising *Streetcar*. "I knew what the play was *supposed* to be," Tenn told me, "but I couldn't bring all the disparate parts together. I relied heavily on Gadg [Kazan], and he made the play happen."

"What I did," Kazan told me, "was to remind Tennessee of where he was in his life when the inspiration for the play had come to him. I told him to remember the days when he didn't even have a nickel for the subway; the days without food; the sense of utter misery you could feel having nothing, and feeling that you couldn't get a break anywhere, from anybody."

Recalling these sensations was complicated. Tenn had enjoyed some financial ease from the production of *The Glass Menagerie,* and while not rich, he had a place to live and food and books. "Kazan told me to remove myself, as much as possible, from my comfort," Tenn told me, "and return to the young Tom who had first encountered Blanche in that fog." In his early days in New York, Tenn had been so broke that he had survived by cadging meals at the Automat, and his agent, Audrey Wood, would send him books, because "without books, I absolutely would die. I could forget about food if I had something marvelous to massage my mind." Once, in a volume of poetry, Wood had placed a twenty-dollar bill. "My God," Tenn enthused, "can you imagine the paroxysms I endured to be reading a poem *and* to have money flutter toward me? Oh Lord, that was heaven!"

Tenn began walking everywhere in the city, refusing subways, buses, and cabs. He walked the streets, cold and alone, and looked into warmly lit windows and felt he would never know the simplest comfort. He ate in the small, simple installments he had known in his poorest days, stretching bread and milk and cheese to their farthest limits, setting goals for himself as to how far three or five dollars could take him. He did not realize, at that time, that he was living his life in a similar fashion to that of Jessica Tandy.

"I was very happy then," Tenn told me, "so don't be afraid of lack. Obviously, I had control over my lack, and I had people who would have stepped in, but the creative energy that swept over me was remarkable."

As Kazan recalls, "*Streetcar* was very much a patchwork quilt at that time. We had the entrance of Blanche, which was very effective and poignant, and we had the sister, Stella, who, unlike Blanche, had not been calcified by her alleged Southern aristocracy. We did not yet have the powerful contrast of Stanley, and so I began to talk to Tenn about the

Producer Irene Mayer Selznick, Tennessee, Elia Kazan, and an unidentified man during a rehearsal for *A Streetcar Named Desire,* 1947

types of men he feared. As it happens, they were the type I envied and recoiled from as well: virile, earthy, pagans to Blanche's wobbly spiritual sense. Once Stanley was introduced, we could see that Stella willfully chose all of this carnality because she saw the deadness of Blanche's narcotized existence. When those ideas fell into Tennessee's head, *then* the play took off."

"And so I walked and I wrote," Tenn remembered, "and the play was like a wild dog on a leash, leading me headlong into places I not only didn't know existed, but which frightened the hell out of me, but Kazan approved, and I knew he was right. I must tell you," he said, "that without Elia Kazan, there would not have been a Tennessee Williams. Certainly not the Tennessee Williams who inspired you to write such a lovely letter seeking advice on becoming a writer. He *made* me a better writer, and not by rewriting my work, or forcing me to change a word, but rather by making me fully understand the responsibilities I owed to my talent and helping me to better understand the delicate and decidedly odd equipment that is within actors. I don't think that anyone ever had or ever will walk among us who had so broad an understanding of the human condition; the needs and abilities of actors; the possibilities and confines of theater; and the remarkable magic, true magic, that happens when you fully engage an audience in your act of discovery.

"Every writer should have so brilliant and honest a critic to champion their work," Tenn continued, "and Kazan's passion amazed me. He was ferociously hungry for stimulation, information, entertainment, joy, amazement. He was also fearless, which I am definitely not. There was nothing that terrified him, and he faced his fears, his enemies, his weaknesses with great boldness and strength, and was never happy with himself or his discoveries once he had obtained them.

"He loved fully," Tenn marveled, "but he also hated fully. There was nothing he hated more than dishonesty, and he always reminded me that one person's honesty was another's mendacity, and that there was brute courage and strength in the greatest effort made by even the weakest person, and the step was a monumental occasion that should not be lightly dismissed.

"He always worked on my plays by first letting me know that he believed in me, *he* knew what I was trying to do, but that we must now bring 'this lovely, this important play' to every mind receptive to it. I tend always to write too much—and to talk too much, can't you see?—and Kazan always admitted that he was the same, he understood this trait, but that we must remove the extraneous, the fatty, and reveal the lovely structure that lay beneath whatever we were working on. He loved to talk about the scaffolding that could come only after we had the strongest foundation, and he taught me how to give a play the strength onto which others could grow and contribute.

"He hated talk of themes, and insisted that from truth every condition known to man could derive," Tenn said, standing up, excited and imitating the director. " 'Let the future talk about your themes,' he might say, 'just write what is true, and everyone will find themselves.' To truly enrage him, you might suggest a *coup de théâtre*. 'The *audi-*

ence provides those,' he told me, 'not the director or the designer.' He nakedly thrust the characters, with all their flaws and their gifts, into the very faces and hearts of his audiences, and knew that they would provide the revolutionary moments, the fireworks.

" 'Show me a truly honest actor realizing the words of a truly honest writer,' he would say, 'and you have a revolution in the theater.'

"He hated stars who *performed* rather than *became,* and he couldn't understand why anyone wouldn't want endless aid and criticism, and no one sought it more than he did.

"I love him, but I had times when I hated him, because it is never easy or comfortable to be so revealed. We shared a fear of time wasted, love misunderstood, and he was unashamed of tears if he was moved or challenged. Both of us thought ourselves ugly, odd, out of place, and we both worked doggedly to not be thought of as lesser than those we admired.

"He helped me," Tenn continued, "to realize that everyone in *Streetcar* was right to fight for what they needed. The human need to survive is honorable; others may be destroyed, but everyone would understand that survival, its beauty and its fragility, received top priority. He saw the most touching moment in that play to be when Stella lies to Blanche as she is about to be led away to the hat factory. 'I'll go with you,' Stella says, but of course both realize the lie. She will *not* be there, and how many walks have we taken alone, when we begged for company and support? The need is to get Blanche out of the house and their lives so that their own lives can begin their own descent into fantasy: fantasy that will help them live with themselves—just as Blanche, just as I, have our fabulist devices to cope. That scene *was* the play, in Kazan's eyes. And he was right. And he cried like a baby every time he saw it.

"I never had the power of my earlier work once Kazan stopped being my director," Tenn said, then nodded as if to reinforce his statement, which he regretted but could not deny. "And I never had the joy of working in the theater once he moved on to other projects. I thought of him often, and I tried to be true to the standards he imparted to me, but no one can emulate something so original, so rare, and so brilliant.

"He is now as much a part of me, my work, as my own tired, grateful heart."

Twelve years later, when I was working in the Ecce Panis bakery on Madison Avenue, which was frequented by Kazan and his wife, I called him on the phone and read him the words that Tenn had shared with me. Kazan, seemingly so tough, dissolved into tears and, gasping, asked if he could hang up. Later, he would call me and say, "I am always amazed at what I was fortunate enough to be surrounded by, and the loss of these people is too much to bear. You will feel this one day yourself. Prepare yourself."

Jessica Tandy could remember clearly the day she read *Portrait of a Madonna*. "It pierced my heart," she told me. "Here was a character who had the same frightened sense of self as I did, who stumbled through life constantly afraid of discovery, clinging to her own methods of survival. It was me. With my obsessive counting of money, time, opportunities, experiences, I could understand wanting to impose a fantasy world where I actually was in control."

Cronyn called Kazan after hearing Tandy's estimation of the play, and even before he had read it himself, he wanted to produce it. "I didn't fully understand that *Portrait* was growing into *Streetcar*," Cronyn told me, "but Kazan informed me that Tennessee was working like a demon, and the play was growing greater by the day. I immediately realized that Jessie would be in *Streetcar*, but she would only have the opportunity if she was seen acting a part that was similar, so I mounted a production in Los Angeles of *Portrait*."

The production, financed and directed by Cronyn, played in a tiny theater to small but appreciative audiences. "The only audience member that mattered," Tandy confessed, "was Elia Kazan. Hume told me that once he saw me in *Portrait*, he would *see* me in *Streetcar*. Now I still had not read *Streetcar*; it was, as I recall it, an unfinished play. But my faith in Tennessee's talent and my faith in Hume, coupled with my incredible need for a part, led me strongly."

Kazan recalled the performance as "striking, and Jessica was clearly more of an actress than I had imagined. She was still far too reliant on effects—her voice was doing far too much to convey emotion or a change of moods, and her gestures were not entirely believable. But her ability to dissolve emotionally on the stage was phenomenal, and I knew that she could be our Blanche. I knew that she understood the lies we tell in order to survive, and that was an admission I was not getting from any other actress."

Kazan brought the news of Tandy's performance to Tenn, and he did not find a receptive author. "Tenn thought she was a phony British actress," Kazan recalled, "and he couldn't imagine her as Blanche. Ironically, he thought of Jessica as 'brittle,' and she is the last person to whom I would attribute that description."

But Tenn agreed to the casting of Jessica Tandy as Blanche, relying entirely on the judgment of Kazan. Once she had the part, she realized that she had another role that she craved: "I wanted—and needed—desperately to become Tennessee's friend," Tandy told me. "I realized that I would have to have him with me and for me if I was going to succeed."

Tandy suggested that she and Tenn have dinner together, and Tenn accepted.

"Big Lady and I formed an immediate mutual-admiration society," Tenn told me, and he recalled the meeting with great affection. Tandy recalled that, in her life, she had had three meetings with men where she freely revealed her secrets, what she saw as her shameful self, and those men were Jack Hawkins, Hume Cronyn, and Tenn. "We were comfortable and intimate from the beginning," Tandy told me, "although I was afraid of him, in the sense that his talent was, to me, so incredible, and yet I saw before me a boy, an overgrown child."

Tenn was in his self-imposed poverty, walking the streets of New York, and seeing life through the eyes of a person who would never survive without aid, who was perpetually changing masks to appear acceptable and to make life tenable, and it had given him a happiness he had not expected. While Tenn had Frank Merlo in his life, during this exercise in which he was delving into his own derelict past, he had made himself believe that he was completely alone.

Then Jessica Tandy entered his life.

"I was feeling even more confessional than I normally do," Tenn said, "and so our first meeting was full of disclosures. She revealed herself to me as utterly afraid and utterly unrefined, and we laughed at our mutual charade. Suddenly, I had a sister, a soul mate, along for the adventure of *Streetcar*." They each had the ability to make the other comfortable, to provide calmness. "Jessica could not imagine that she could ever pull off this role," Tenn admitted, "and what hung her up was the sexuality of Blanche. Jessica was not comfortable at all with flirtation, and she ran strenuously from seduction. She found Kazan a very strong, sexual force, and she feared his direction of those scenes where Blanche needed to be seductive and, later, conquered. So I worked with her on those instead."

"I was torn, also, between two Stellas," Jessica revealed. "Marlon was very much devoted to the teachings of Stella Adler, which were unknown to me, yet fascinating, and Kazan had begun an affair with Kim [Hunter, the play's Stella], so I felt adrift as an actress and as a woman. Marlon was an extraordinary actor and a beautiful man. No acting was required to tremble before him, but I could not easily face the Blanche who could effortlessly flirt with him, and I could not convince anyone that I was the Blanche who indiscriminately entertained men."

"What Jessica could believe," Tenn told me, "was that a woman—or anyone—can and will do anything to find surcease. 'Surcease' became our word. If Jessica could not play Blanche as a whore, she could play her as a woman who craved affirmation as a lovely, refined lady, and Jessica completely identified with that. When Jessica was nervous, she became terribly, terribly polite, she shook a bit, and she sought the nearest exit, and that is how I told her she should flirt with Stanley. Her Blanche might not have *wanted* Stanley in her bed—or any man—but she *needed* it. I told her to think 'castor oil,' not 'cock,' and as distasteful as both were, they ultimately did her a world of good."

When I repeated this to Tandy, she burst into her wonderful laugh and couldn't believe that Tenn had told me that. "I had forgotten that wonderful mental trick I played on myself," she giggled, "and only Tennessee could have given it to me in such a fashion and so freely."

Tenn invited Jessica to join him on his forays about the city, his "promenades of the poor," and she found it wonderful. "Even though we were both going home to comfortable places," she remembered, "and we had food and money, we fully fell into our fantasy of being unknown, unloved, unaware people, hopelessly wandering. We ate in greasy diners, allowing ourselves each sixty cents, and it brought back my entire life prior to Hume, who simply swept finances out of my head and my life. As we walked, Tenn would recite poems or talk about situations that might work in the play, and I could snatch, from the deepest parts of my mind, the sonnets I had loved so much, as well as long portions of *Hamlet* and *Henry V.* Tennessee reintroduced me to a vital part of my past, and a vital part of my person, and although we were both in our late thirties, on the cusp of an amazing experience, we were terribly, happily young. One of my fondest memories of that time with Tenn was going to his apartment and finding him flipping furiously through books. 'What are you doing?' I asked, and he admitted he was looking for money. He had found money once in a book—a gift—and I often stashed money in books, one of my eccentric habits. We laughed ourselves silly over that, and I remember Tenn telling me, 'Stay young, honey. It's all that will save us.' "

When *A Streetcar Named Desire* was published in hardcover, Tenn sent an inscribed copy to Jessica. Inside, he had slipped a crisp twenty-dollar bill onto which he had taped a small note. It read: "Don't spend it all in one place."

"Jessica took baby steps toward Blanche," Kazan recalled, "but goddammit, she got there. She was luminous, not only due to the fairness of her complexion, but from this fervent belief she manifested in the fantasies of Blanche DuBois. She was otherworldly, she was wonderfully correct and precise, and so when she sank to the level of Stanley Kowalski, you truly felt a woman you cared for had been degraded. When she arched her back and walked off at the end of the play, your heart broke, because someone very similar to your mother or your aunts or a beloved teacher was lost to us forever, and who could fathom what we might have gained had she stayed, if we had only been a bit more eager to be kind?"

Helping Jessica along in her baby steps were Tenn, Kazan—and Hume Cronyn. "I believe that Hume wanted a stronger role in the production," Tenn revealed, "and his presence was not pleasant. He was very protective of Jessica, but he was also quite dismissive of everyone else in the company, and he had to be told several times by Kazan that his presence was not appreciated. I never felt that Hume thought much of me: I think he was grateful that I had written a play that would help his wife, but I always felt like the most flagrant queer around him, as if he were trying to conduct a conversation with an armadillo, so strange was the concept."

Cronyn began making staging suggestions, and ultimately Tenn left rehearsals. If Tenn was in the theater, Kazan, sitting behind him, would report "Good news" on the entrance of Tandy, then "Bad news" on the entrance of Cronyn. "Believe me, we were a happy company when nothing but good news came in that door," Tenn said.

Jessica knew that maneuvers and machinations by Cronyn had led her to this moment, to this opportunity, but she deeply resented the belief, now a part of theater myth, that Cronyn had served as a merciless puppet master to this pliant actress. "Listen," she admonished me, in the presence of Cronyn, "you sit here talking to me because of Hume Cronyn and Tennessee Williams, but I was ready for anything—not only ready, but *hungry*. I can say now—after some success and a lifetime in the theater—that I cannot think of anything or anyone who could have *stopped* me from making a better life for myself in the theater. I was not going to be counting coins and opportunities in some council flat in my old age. Hume was simply the one who saw in me the potential to take on roles that no one else felt I deserved. I was not passive, however. I was an active participant in those things I pursued."

The most valuable lesson Jessica learned from *Streetcar* was to inhabit the mind of the playwright. "Because I became so close to Tennessee," she admitted, "each and every night that I said those words, I imagined myself with him, saying and defending his words, and it made all the difference in the world. I wanted Tennessee Williams to believe in me again, even if I was in a play not written by him. I would imagine us walking the streets of New York, so young, our eyes so full of possibility and wonder and that longing we were so soon forgetting, and I could make any playwright's work real to me.

"And when he died," Tandy said, her face crumbling, "and I had to say those words of Blanche's at his memorial service, it finally hit me that he was gone, that there was no smiling face, no set of young eyes, receiving my words, judging my input, and so I was devastated. I have loved my life in the theater, but now, after all these years, I can think of perhaps three experiences in the theater that fulfilled me or drew upon *half* of what I had as an actress. Tennessee said that *Streetcar* utilized all of his skills as a writer, and its production filled him with great satisfaction. It was also my greatest experience, but it only drew upon *some* of my reserves."

Jessica and I shared a love of poetry, and when I told her that I was emulating the walks that she and Tenn had made across the city, and that I was keeping my eyes young and trying to forget my bare pantry, she wanted to know which poems I was using. (She also, against my wishes, and with incredible stealth, managed to have food sent to me.)

One day, as I was reading a book of poems, I found something that appeared to have been written for and about the young Tennessee Williams. I was in Central Park, and I found a pay phone, called the Wyndham, and got Jessica on the phone, who promptly invited me up to her suite. The poem, by Czesław Miłosz, is called "Youth."

Your unhappy and silly youth.
Your arrival from the provinces in the city.
Misted-over windowpanes of streetcars,
Restless misery of the crowd.
Your dread when you entered a place too expensive.
But everything was too expensive. Too high.
Those people must have noticed your crude manners,
Your outmoded clothes, and your awkwardness.

There were none who would stand by you and say,

You are a handsome boy,
You are strong and healthy,
Your misfortunes are imaginary.

You would not have envied a tenor in an overcoat of camel hair
Had you guessed his fear and known how he would die.

She, the red-haired, because of whom you suffer tortures,
So beautiful she seems to you, is a doll in fire.
You don't understand what she screams with her lips of a clown.

The shapes of hats, the cut of robes, faces in the mirrors,
You will remember all that unclearly, as something from long ago,
Or as what remains from a dream.

The house you approach trembling,
The apartment that dazzles you—
Look, on this spot the cranes clear the rubble.

In your turn you will have, possess, secure,
Able to be proud at last, when there is no reason.

Your wishes will be fulfilled, you will gape then
At the essence of time, woven of smoke and mist,

An iridescent fabric of lives that last one day,
Which rises and falls like an unchanging sea.

Books you have read will be of use no more.
You searched for an answer but lived without answer.

You will walk in the streets of southern cities,
Restored to your beginnings, seeing again in rapture
The whiteness of a garden after the first night of snow.

I read the poem aloud to Jessica, and she was devastated. She cried as one might upon hearing of a great tragedy or the death of a loved one. We sat in her living room, crying and thinking of Tennessee Williams, and, I think, the youth of Jessie Alice Tandy. "That poem *is* Tennessee Williams," she whispered, and then she began to cry again. "Oh, Jim, was anyone ever there to help our friend? Did anyone ever reach out to hold him?"

Kim Hunter left me with the most potent image of the relationship between Jessica Tandy and Tennessee Williams. After the opening night of *Streetcar*, with its rapturous curtain calls and ovations, with the cast amazed at its own skill and good fortune, Tenn stood in the alleyway of the Ethel Barrymore Theatre smoking a cigarette. Close to the street were Hunter, several other members of the company, members of the press—a small mob. Tandy exited the theater from the stage door, which was several feet ahead of where Tenn was smoking, and when she arrived at the mob, she was unable to move forward, and stood there, a smile frozen on her face. Suddenly, from behind her, Tenn's voice boomed. "Step aside," he bellowed, "there's a great lady coming through." Without looking behind her, Tandy's face beamed, and as if choreographed, her hand slipped behind her back and fell into his, which he had stretched toward her at just the right moment. "In that moment," Hunter recalled, "was consummation. They had done it, and they were acknowledging it." All night long, through all the drinks and all the photos, Hunter kept looking over and seeing, too many times to recount, Jessica's hand in Tenn's.

Eight

I WAS UNFAMILIAR with the method of praying the Rosary, so Tenn purchased for me a small, blue booklet entitled "Pray the Rosary" and tried to explain, in his own way, the proper way to use this holy tool.

"Ignore these pages," he would say, dog-earing particular pages, and writing on others.

The act of the Rosary, as Tenn put it, had become a meditation on qualities, a pursuit of desires. The history, semantics, and directions offered by the book were unnecessary, beyond the colorful, rich illustrations, along with the remedial instruction it offered to the uninitiated. "I need words," Tenn said, "and I need visuals, and I need women. The beads are steps to walk; stones to build; women to inspire." The essentials: There are fifty-nine beads that comprise the rosary, or garland of roses, or "flowers at the feet of the Lady," as Tenn named it. *Flores para los muertos.* There is also a crucifix, on which is recited the Apostles' Creed, and above that a large bead, on which is recited the Our Father.

"You do what you want," Tenn told me. "Nothing of much good came from the Our Father. Use a quote that means something to you. Find a woman who moves you. We do what we can. We make our walks alone, scared but stoic, but we have our support systems, and prayer;

God, all myths, all ladders of hope. Fashion them to your fears. Fan your fog. Do what you can."

The mind of Tennessee Williams, as he put it, had always been full of female inspiration, feminine means of escape, salvation. "Women know where to look for the escapes we need," he said. "I suggest you follow a woman." Some of the women Tenn held in his thoughts as he tried to write were not close friends, but what he called teachers and examples. "They are of use to me in reminding me how I should act; how I should behave; how I should proceed."

When Tenn mentioned Lois Smith, he seemed to say, as if in prayer, "Ah, Lois Smith: lyric and rustic and pure; a grandmother's feather bed, comfortable and easy to sink into, but also barbed, full of opinions. At first sight, a haven, soft and pliant, but really an old Recamier piece covered with a more comfortable material. Oh, Lois, where have you been?"

Tennessee claimed that a still of Lois Smith from Elia Kazan's *East of Eden* (1955) hung above his typewriter for a number of years. "She is an inspiration to me," Tenn said.

Lois Smith possessed a soul that Tenn had earmarked for subsuming. She would be, he insisted, the gentlest spirit in the cabal of women to whom he was sending me, a virginal handmaiden to all that is "fair and clean and morally uplifting."

Tenn first saw her when she was twenty-four years old; he was forty-four. It was 1955, a good year, a "sitting-on-the-fence" year, with good things behind him, and the hope of greater things ahead. Despite the difference in their ages and experiences, Tenn felt that he was her inferior in judgment and he envied her equanimity, the glow that surrounded her and kept her employed in roles that called for vulnerability and gossamer charms.

"I liked her," Tenn said, "because I like ethereal women, but I can't really be friends with them because they really are not of the earth: they are Puck women, and their feet are nowhere where you need them— on the ground or on your back. What I truly admire are those women who are both ethereal and perfectly simple. I think Lois is this way. She's worldly, but she is also a Shaker woman stranded on the isle of Manhattan."

On a morning that had turned hot, Tenn and I were setting out for Decatur Street. We began our jaunt from the Café du Monde, and

Tennessee claimed that a still of Lois Smith from Elia Kazan's *East of Eden* hung above his typewriter for years. "She is an inspiration to me," Tenn said.

along the way stopped for pounds of coffee, items of negrobilia, chunks of pralines, a glance at a drugstore window that featured both vintage advertising and bold examples of soft-core pornography ("Medicine for some, I suppose," Tenn quipped), and, desiring a brief respite, a stop in the Central Grocery, where Tenn had a beer and one of the city's cherished muffuletta sandwiches, which he cut into four wedges and ate as carefully as he chose his words, which came forth at a slow, painful pace.

"I have begun a portion of our story that has me concerned," he said. "I don't know where to take it."

Tenn showed me the passage of a story inspired by Lois Smith. He allowed me to copy his attempt in my notebook. It read: "She had known from the time her childhood priest had told her so, that she carried within her a private altar, completely arrayed with all that was sacrosanct to her. Her daily duty, as well as her decision, was to polish the implements that lay on this altar, or to allow them to sit in dust and neglect, lonely, disabused, unserving in her quest for perfection."

"What I feel I am trying to say," Tenn admitted, "is that our redemption begins within, which is certainly not a new idea, but it's one that I, on a personal level, have faced myself. So I'm feeling a little punk tackling it on paper." He dismissed the problem of the story—not to say of redemption—and we continued our walk toward Decatur, which eventually led us to a fenced-in market that trafficked in terra-cotta ducks, fountains, Blessed Mothers, and a myriad of angels in earth tones, which hung on chain-link fences, their faces a bewildered judgment of their resting place. "This would be a great backdrop for Sebastian Venable," Tenn cracked, imagining his character from *Suddenly, Last Summer,* clad in tight-fitting white silk, his sinewy arms crossed, waiting, beneath the angels, for his prey. Tenn joked with the proprietor for a moment about the angels, then about the man's not having the remotest idea who he was. Tenn grew silent and picked up a cherub as white as a piece of divinity fudge and held it away from him, observing it as if it were some noble ruin recently uncovered, or as if he were the father of a particularly odd newborn.

"The rustic cherub," he mused. "A personality I've often searched for in my women, real and imagined. Anna Magnani was one. Maureen Stapleton is another. The most complex one—in my opinion—is Lois Smith. Let me tell you about her."

Before he began his description, Tenn purchased the rustic cherub, which the proprietor wrapped in cerulean paper. Tenn gave it to me, and I kept it above my desk for nearly ten years, until I gave it to Lois Smith, who had inspired its purchase.

Like so many of the women who inspired Tenn, Lois Smith's first exposure to theater was through a church, a fact that was vital to Tenn's understanding of her. "As I understand it," Tenn told me, "she is a Nazarene! Isn't that wonderful? Lois Smith, Nazarene." In notes Tenn made for what he called the Lois Smith story that he wanted us to write together, he made the following notes about Lois to help in the creation of a character.

She felt that she was always in that church in which she first felt happiness, and through the years, she has built within and around herself sanctuaries that promote peace and harmony, and [she] has made the theater something of a professed house of worship. It was not in her nature to find the ugly in life or situations, but she was not weak or restrained by ancient mores: she would, if she must, say what she felt.

She resides in a brilliantly white cocoon in which she placed herself gently, surrounded only by what was deemed absolutely necessary, which more often than not was merely her person.

There is within a lavish, hidden altar that everyone would be surprised she owned and loved and kept private to all but one other. With others she is apt to erect those pillars that announce her dismissal of a thought or a person who harbors thoughts that might disturb what she has fought to attain.

She wondered about people who lied. While she wouldn't let them into her life, she often thought about them, their motivations, their final, secret thoughts as they lay in bed in the dark, plotting their next move. What propelled them? Why did they choose to immerse themselves in the dank waters of deception when she herself longed for the clear creek of purity?

One day she hoped to find within herself that special something that would allow all other events to click, to move into some meaning that might explain her desires, her perpetual moving toward what she couldn't know, but was obsessed with.

In the margin of the last passage, Tenn had written some lines from a poem by the French poet Valery Larbaud, whose death had occurred during preparations for the premiere of *Orpheus Descending*, in which Lois played Carol Cutrere. Larbaud was an elegant man, fastidious, sickly, addicted to spas and arcane treatments. Tenn could imagine becoming this type of person, gulping supplements, surrendering to mud baths and enemas and the ministrations of muscular therapists. From this frail man came images that haunted Tenn, but all he could remember of his work was "My reader, my brother, place a heavy kiss on my forehead and my cheek and press upon my face, hollow and perfumed." These are the actual lines:

> *Oh, that some reader, my brother, to whom I speak*
> *Through this pale and shining mask,*
> *Might come and place a slow and heavy kiss*

On this low forehead and cheek so pale,
All the more to press upon my face
That other face, hollow and perfumed.

"All of our faces," Tenn said, "need the attention and the affection of some observer, some lover. We—as men, as people, as writers—do not exist or matter until someone believes enough to come closer, to examine, to praise, to hate, to let us know we have been observed. We can then fill the mask with our reactions."

I possessed all of these words, all of this information, for eight years, until I finally met Lois Smith myself, and sought to find out about her hidden altars and her masks. When I told her of my intention, she laughed heartily and said, "Oh, you brave and foolish young man! Well, come on!"

Tenn believed that Lois possessed a deep commitment to spiritual and physical well-being, and this became her shell, her armor. When I shared this observation with Lois, she quickly agreed. Yes, she admitted, the theater is a cruel place, occasionally populated by good people and great teachers, but for the most part unforgiving and harsh and "precipitate and foolish." What she has chosen to do is to remove herself from the utilitarian aspects of the theater—fund-raising, backstage gossip, tales of its imminent disintegration—and focus on the work, devote herself to the pursuit and the praise of what she finds worthy. Her opinions are true and often harsh, but they are brief. She moves on.

"I like to think of myself always as a rube, or a neophyte," she told me. "It keeps the experience as special and as wonderful as it was when I started, before I had my eyes opened—or my skin thickened."

Tenn had watched her during the production of *Orpheus Descending*, adored by its director, Harold Clurman, respected by the company, and absent from the turmoil surrounding the quality of the production. "I was so touched," Tenn told me, "by the manner in which she held the script: like a newly ordained priest holding his first host, or a young lover caressing the breast of a lover."

The production of that play was not a happy time, and the year in which it took place—1957—was one that Tenn relegated to a pile of memories he referred to as "bad times."

"It was not a good time," he remembered. "I was not well, and I did not feel that I contributed very much to Harold's direction, which is

something he wanted very much. He was a collaborator, a loud, screaming inspirer of people, from the stagehands to the set designer to the
playwright, and I was utterly mute in the face of his exhortations. I
failed the play and I failed Harold. I failed everybody."

When Tenn recounted the times of *Orpheus,* he remembered manic
discussions over coffee with the "wild-eyed, warmhearted Clurman"
and an increasingly bemused Maureen Stapleton, who, as Lady Torrance, felt adrift in what Tenn called his "murky sea of words." In the
midst of this confusion was the implacable Lois Smith.

"It takes years to gain that resolve, if one ever does," Tenn marveled,
"and here she had it while in her twenties. I was not a little impressed.
Such iron beneath so flawless an exterior; her silk had steel underpinnings."

Tenn claimed that he had brought about Lois's hiring in *Orpheus* by
virtue of his constant ravings about her talent in two previous productions: *The Young and Beautiful,* an adaptation of the stories of Sally
Benson, in which she played what Tenn called a "Middle American,
middle-class Gigi coming of age," and a revival of *The Glass Menagerie,*
in which she played Laura opposite the redoubtable but miscast Helen
Hayes. In that production, mounted at New York's City Center, which
Tenn likened to a cross between the New York Port Authority bus terminal and an offshoot of the Federal Theatre Project, Lois dispelled the
myth that Laura was an unplayable part, a symbol with no substance,
a device.

"She understood the part perfectly," Tenn said. "She revealed the
anger that rests beneath so fragile an exterior: the rage at one's imprisonment; the rage at the dissonance between what we see of a person and
what a person actually is, actually feels, actually wants. She proved that
Laura's fragility is as much a ruse as a defense. 'Take care of me; rescue
me. Pity me; dominate me. Remove me from my current station. Take
me—along with my crystal counterparts—off this shelf. Break me if
you must, but set me free.'

"Lois works in tiny movements," Tenn remembered. "Hers are not
the bold strides of a dancer, but the mincing, delicate steps of the geisha, and with each rehearsal she brought a new strength, a new dimension." If Lois Smith works in small spaces with tiny gestures, it is only
appropriate that another artist who worked in a similar fashion should
have offered an *homage* to her abilities. Joseph Cornell, whose intricate

shadow boxes held tiny objects that captured the essence of its subject, saw Lois in *The Young and Beautiful,* then went home to create a tribute. Lois at the time was pale, luminous, "supremely supple," as Tenn recalled. She seemed to be the epitome of burgeoning womanhood, and the Cornell piece, deep blue, painfully fragile, and bringing to mind a delicately mended Christmas ornament, captures the performance Lois gave in the play.

The box was given to Donald Windham and Sandy Campbell, friends of Cornell's and Lois's—and of Tenn's—with the stipulation that it be left in an open place. If Lois saw it and liked it, it was to be hers. It now resides in Lois's apartment.

"I used to wonder how Lois survived the theater and life," Tenn told me. "Then I remembered a lovely piece by Kierkegaard called 'Love Abides,' and it reminds me of Lois. She doesn't rely on anything but her own reserves for well-being. She doesn't need—like mother's milk or unguent—the affirmation of others. What keeps her going, as if it were blood, is love."

I found the Kierkegaard piece. It reads in part.

"Love never faileth"—it abides.

When a child has been away all day among strangers and now considers that it ought to go home, but is afraid to go alone, and yet really wants to stay as long as possible, it says to the older children, who perhaps wished to leave earlier, "Wait for me"; and so the older ones do as the child asks. When of two equals one is more advanced than the other, the latter says to the first, "Wait for me"; and so the second does what the first asks.

I had not read the above passage when Tenn recommended it, and I was unable to locate it during our brief time together. I asked him why this piece made him think of Lois. "It makes me think of her," Tenn said, "because Lois, every time I see her, and every time I think of her, brings to mind the face I saw and the feeling when I was forgiven, when I was given help, when I was safe. When there was love in the room.

"Kazan told me about her," Tenn told me. "He loved her work at the Studio, and he cast her in *East of Eden,* and I sought her out, and I got her, in every sense of the word." Kazan warned me to not stress her sweetness so much. "I think of her as fair," he said, "as opposed to sweet. There is no willfulness within her that makes her see the sweet. That's what I think sweet people are—willful, in denial, lacquering their true feelings with some notion of kindness or fairness. Lois is fair. Lois seeks all information, and she has a gift that I particularly envy: she is patient."

A case in point: the set of *East of Eden,* dominated by the talented but mercurial James Dean; the diabolically unbalanced Jo Van Fleet; the histrionic and challenging Barbara Baxley; the grand and indifferent Raymond Massey. Serving as the peacemakers on the film were Julie Harris and Lois Smith. "Think of the lions outside the [New York] Public Library," Kazan told me. "What are their names?" "Patience and Fortitude," I answered. "That's who they were. Lionesses determined to keep the peace, see the good, do the great. She [Lois] believes, she projects, and she receives." When Kazan learned that *The Glass Menagerie* was being revived for Helen Hayes, "I cringed," he told me. "As I might cringe if I heard that Danny Kaye was cast in a production of *Death of a Salesman.* There are people who have gifts insufficient to great works, and I place Hayes in that category. I hated to think of her as Amanda Wingfield. Yes, she was of value—her name on marquees drew in hordes, but the *wrong* hordes. I knew that she would distort that play. She distorted all plays, and subverted all of them to the contours of her own personality and intelligence. She *shrank* plays and opportunities and fellow players, and some saw this as intimacy or an ability to 'connect,' whatever that means. I thought if Helen Hayes was going to be Amanda, a role at which she had already failed [in London], it was imperative that Tennessee have a real actress, an actress capable of portraying a real person, in the play. I suggested Lois."

During that production of *The Glass Menagerie,* Tenn began to study Lois Smith, to imagine future possibilities.

Tenn wrote in the notes to the short story he was considering: "She was never burdened by the reserves she held within her, because they carried no weight. They rested right beneath her skin, alerted by her senses, her nerves, into action. Her reserves were instantly active when aroused, but they were never a burden because they were never lightly used, never abused, never ignored. They were husbanded and shared perfectly, and they were offered selflessly. There was never a possibility of burden."

In the margin, Tenn had written: "Light heart, light feet."

The Glass Menagerie is the play of Tenn's that was most often abused, badly directed, misunderstood. This baffled him, because his stage directions are lengthy and precise—and frequently ignored.

As Tenn explained to me, paragraph 3 of scene 1 reads: "The scene is memory and is therefore nonrealistic. Memory takes a lot of poetic license. It omits some details; others are exaggerated, according to the emotional value of the articles it touches, for memory is seated predominantly in the heart. The interior is therefore rather dim and poetic."

Offered this description of the scene—what Tenn called the "emotional lighting and design" of the piece—most directors ignore it; most actors in the piece fail to adapt their acting to fit the space in which they are working.

Kazan offered an explanation. "I think most directors resent a playwright directing from the page," he told me. "I might have reacted strongly, if I had been given the play when it was new. I might have pressured Tennessee to explain to me his descriptions, to make them clearer. I think that he would have done so, but [being] handed a script that is as precise as his is, down to the timing of ascending scenery, might have unleashed in me a resistance that would have harmed the play."

Tenn took the brunt of the blame for the original production of *Menagerie,* a bastard child of a production that had, in fact, four directors, none of them, in Tenn's estimation, up to the task. They were Eddie Dowling, who also produced and appeared as Tom; Margo Jones, the peripatetic director who founded a theater in Dallas, Texas, and became a strong supporter of Tenn's work; Tenn himself, who, when frustrated, would alter or remove the "fillips of failure" that Dowling and Jones had inserted into his play; and Laurette Taylor, the actress who was cast as Amanda Wingfield.

"Everyone remembers and reveres Taylor," Kazan told me, "but what no one talks about is what a mess the production was. If you focused on Laurette Taylor, you were transported. If you listened to the words of the play, if you allowed yourself to be moved by the extraordinary power and beauty of the play, you were altered forever. But if you went back time after time, as I did, and looked at the overall production, it was amateurish and forced and set, I think, a standard, a low standard, for that play for all time."

"Could I have been any clearer?" Tenn asked me, in reference to the opening lines of the play, in which Tom states, "Yes, I have tricks in my pocket, I have things up my sleeve. But I am the opposite of a stage magician. He gives you illusion that has the appearance of truth. I give you truth in the pleasant disguise of illusion. To begin with, I turn back time."

"I reverse time," Tenn continued, "and that is what all dreamers do. It is our earliest drug, don't you think? Clutching that radio in the dark, in the night. Praying your Rosary. A reverie in the night in your bed, held by someone who understands you. Light and time and space are altered. You are in control, if only for a fleeting speck of time. That is a mood to be sought, to be admired, and no one—I mean no one—gets it.

"Do not be fooled," he warned me. "The theater is not populated by dreamers."

Tom speaks again, a few moments later. "The play is memory. Being a memory play, it is dimly lighted, it is sentimental, it is not realistic. In memory everything seems to happen to music. That explains the fiddle in the wings."

"A dream with humor and music," Tenn told me, "and I usually get a set out of Odets and an acting style from the Philco Playhouse. I wrote a personal play in which I first gained a voice, and it has been tossed about like a whore at a frat party."

Lois Smith served as the soul and the vital center of the 1955 revival of *Menagerie*, making it a satisfactory experience for Tenn, as well as, he believed, an opportunity for people to reevaluate his play, whose reputation had suffered from the 1950 film version, which had featured a cast he called woefully inadequate. Gertrude Lawrence, Jane Wyman, Arthur Kennedy, Kirk Douglas. "All of them suitable for some purposes," Tenn admitted, "but not one of them appropriate for my play."

A play, Tenn told me, is extraordinarily delicate, a psychic heirloom delivered by its writer to audiences and actors with blind trust. "'How beautiful it is and how easily it can be broken,'" Tenn said, utilizing a quote from *Menagerie*, a play that is an attempt, through words cast upon the pale judgment, to enjoy some sense of atonement with his mother, his sister, and that "wayward, silly queer" known as Thomas Lanier Williams. "What you love you become," Tenn told me. "Of course we are also identified by those things and those people we hate.

Laurette Taylor, a mother on the stage in *The Glass Menagerie* and in life for Tennessee. "She understood me," Tenn said, "and was not repulsed."

Our identities are as fragile as the things we write, spoors of our psyche, if you will. We can't batter ourselves any longer with hatreds and wayward thoughts and wasted energies."

Tenn was aware again of the time knot, that ruthless and enormous serpent that had him firmly in its grip, crushing out time and energy and will. "I always believed I had lots of time," he told me, "and I also believed I had lots of patience. I believed myself grateful when anyone read or produced one of my plays, but I'm now unable to see productions that fail to understand what I sought to do. What I *needed* to do. I came to love—was required to come to love—my mother through the writing of *Menagerie*. You'll hear of prayers and vigils and excursions that allegedly open the mind and cleanse the soul, and that is what that play was for me. The walk along the Camino; the dip into holy waters at Lourdes; the agony in my own mental garden, and the weeds and the brambles were hatreds and anxieties and grudges collected. To make oneself capable of forgiveness and acceptance, one must be made terribly vulnerable, and I came to think of myself as crafted of glass: fragile, yes, but transparent. Here I am, flaws and all, but utterly clear and open. I have sinned. I have made mistakes. I have tricks in my pocket. I am human."

Lois Smith can make a person think of himself in this way, Tenn told me. So, too, could Laurette Taylor. The two actresses of two entirely different generations merged in Tenn's mind, and Smith became a "talisman" for him at a time when he felt he needed to defend his theatrical confession to his mother. "There is gentleness and there is greatness in Lois," Tenn told me. "I was fascinated by her, watching her. I began to train myself to write in the same manner as she moved through the world: gently, calmly, fully aware, unafraid to be bewildered, detailed to the point of obsession."

In the upper-right-hand corner of one page during our talks on Lois Smith and *The Glass Menagerie,* I wrote, "Napoleon House. First Sazerac cocktail," and I had placed a large star next to this quote from Tenn: "We lie in order to live, and in time our lives become the lie. The writer can see and understand the lies. He does so without judgment. Everything else emanates from this." I remember that Tenn watched me write his words in the book, then looked at me for a long time. "I'm going to make it as clear for you as I can," he promised, "but nothing will prove these points in the way experience will."

The primary point Tenn wished to make on that day, at that time, was that Lois Smith was his link—his only living link—to Laurette Taylor and to his mother. To focus on Lois, an actress and a woman he loved and admired, was to trick himself into believing that his mother was still with him, still loving him, protecting him, appreciating what he had been able to give her. "Lois is the lie, I suppose, that allows me and my mother to live together," Tenn said.

WHEN TENN BEGAN making notes for *The Glass Menagerie* in 1943, when he was thirty-two, he was utterly undistinguished, as he saw himself, spending most of his days in the movie theaters of whatever city in which he found himself, waking up in beds "of compromise and inces-

Two films seen repeatedly
by Tennessee in 1943 altered the
shape of *The Glass Menagerie:*
Ida Lupino (seen here with
Joan Leslie), in *The Hard Way,*
influenced his portrait of Amanda
Wingfield, and Jennifer Jones,
in *The Song of Bernadette,*
"threw a shade" on Laura.

sant farting, a constant morning-after of regret and failed promises."
Within him was something—a poem, a story, a play—but he could not
bring it toward him, and in all of our discussions about this play, he
always spoke of it as bobbing toward him as if on water, floating toward
him like a mist, coming at him like a dream, or fading in and out like a
scene from one of his beloved black-and-white films. "I could lose myself
in the cinema," he confessed, as we walked through New Orleans and
witnessed cineplexes and ugly, boxlike theaters that couldn't "possibly

hold a dream or one's attention for an afternoon or day." No matter his age or the number of spirits imbibed or pills swallowed, Tenn had an extraordinary memory for the films he watched in those years, and a remarkable facility for imitation of the stars, both male and female. "You have to realize that the cinema was my entire life for so long," he confessed, "so you mustn't feel ashamed at your young age to be lost and to wonder where or when inspiration will strike. It will strike if you let it. It will strike if you understand and accept that it may come from the most unexpected of places. There I was, more than a decade older than you are now, utterly lost, angry, frightened, and sitting in theaters, growing progressively drunker and happier, at whatever was playing at the time."

Those movie outings were not simply inspiration or entertainment: the theaters were very often meeting places. "My social life was also rooted in those theaters," he admitted, "for I wasn't likely to meet similarly afflicted persons in ordinary circumstances. I could not find people who shared my fascinations in the usual social snares, but there was a very heady underworld that lived its life in the dark, smoky, salty smelling environment of the cinema, all of us as pale as the images on the screen, and the artists among us suddenly seeing in the most remarkable of circumstances the inspiration for that one great poem or the solution to that maddening second act. I am fully convinced that the image—the special, hobbling image—of Laura Wingfield came to me from numerous viewings of Jennifer Jones in *The Song of Bernadette*. I seriously doubt that I could watch that film today without a boisterous round of hootings," he laughed, "but in that year, in that time, in my mind, it served to present me with the shadings of a character." Tenn also found some important elements of Amanda Wingfield in the performance of Ida Lupino in *The Hard Way,* in which the actress "brilliantly played a woman hell-bent on finding stardom through the more easily accepted trappings of another, all the while knowing that her own cunning had made it happen. While she had none of the canny and utterly artificial charm that Amanda—that my mother—used to such heady affect, that woman completely entranced me."

Even more potent than the characters were the images themselves, those many slow fades and wipes and calendar pages flipping by; split screens that compressed decades and multiple emotions into seconds. "Getting the damn thing on the page is what always kills me," Tenn admitted. "I may live with the characters, the plot, the entire play in my head and heart, but until I can find a way to make it live on paper, I'm lost, and filmic images, which I applied to the page, helped me to get *Menagerie* from the psyche to the page." Tenn's intense relationship with cinema coincided with his employment at Metro-Goldwyn-Mayer, which provided him with needed funds, but which depressed him, because "I never saw the magic, only the industry, and I needed the magic."

Tenn also wanted to please his mother; to impress her. "I began to think of gifts I could give to my mother," he told me. "I knew that my mother saved things—odd things—that helped her to remember what she was and what she could have been." The home of Edwina Williams had held paper and linen napkins on which had been written sentiments and phone numbers and poems; rose petals had been pressed into books; bottles of perfume—often never used—lined tables and shelves, and they were perpetually dusted and touched and fussed over. Each had a story and each had a place in her home until she died.

"Totems," Tenn told me. "I wanted to give to my mother something she could place on a shelf and love, something as fragile and as transparent as those perfume bottles. Something as beloved and fraught with meaning as those rose petals and those napkins."

Tenn's memory of the initial script of *The Glass Menagerie* is one of "heated but half-hearted intentions, overdirection by the playwright through pages of hoped-for effects, but through it all, a great deal of emotion, which I feel led to its being produced." While Audrey Wood found much to admire in *The Glass Menagerie,* and while Tenn felt it could finally allow him to be recognized as a writer, the play was "wobbly, unfelt," a vital and hungry animal looking for "a friendly lap and an unpunishing hand."

"Let me tell you my memory of St. Louis," Tenn said to me after many cocktails. "I think of a jar of snakes wrapped in lace and scented with vanilla. I *despised* my father, and every cruel act imagined in my plays emanates from his necrotic soul. I hated my mother for blandly accepting the mediocrity that was our life, and until I jumped on her train of outward-bound dreams, I hated her for moving out of the real world, where I felt she might have offered me some aid. I came to realize that my mother could only function in this world of illusions, could only survive if she could believe that one, that *any,* of these illusions might one day manifest itself. The writing of *Menagerie* taught me something very important about myself and about others. I believe, as I told you, that we lie in order to live, and in time, our lives become the lie. Our destiny depends on our lie: Is it benign and beneficial, or is it corrosive, bearing a cost none can bear?"

My blue book bore examples Tenn gave me of the lies we need to live, and he summed them up in his belief that "God will not come and save us. Life will not treat us fairly if we dutifully follow the rules. Our friends, the true ones who can be counted on one hand, might come to our aid, unless they are dressed and perfumed and waiting for their own gentleman caller to arrive. We are utterly, completely alone, and when I have been my most fragile, my most shattered, that has been when I have fully realized how vulnerable I am. Far more frightening is the realization that those on whom I often need to lean are equally fragile, and can be—and have been—plucked from my life with sickening swiftness. To face this, brutally and openly, would be for me to die, so I found my solace, my lie, in the illusion of writing, in which I could create alternate worlds with alternate people, and rule them beneficently. I was saved by writing, and later, when I was no longer able to love fully and clearly, and therefore could no longer write, I found solace, and still find it, in alcohol, drugs, in a multifaceted God who does as I choose. We are not created by God; our God is created by *us*. You cannot find salvation or solace anywhere until you find it in yourself, and it is there," he said, pointing to his heart, "that you then create your God.

"My mother found her happiness in her past," Tenn continued, "and it was one we all might covet—a past in which she was pretty and cosseted and appeared to hold promise. Perhaps that was her gift, her one niggardly ornament in life: a beginning in life that held promise. And suddenly the promise is gone, and reality has taken residence in her heart and head, and it is too much." So Tenn's mother retreated to sticky summer dances at Moon Lake, furtive kisses from men overwhelmed by her face in the moonlight, gardenia corsages rotting in the icebox, their lives as brief and fragile as the infatuations that warranted them. "And she drug us all with her to those places"—Tenn laughed—"and I knew her conquests as other boys might know baseball scores or the itinerary of Lindbergh. I could not know then, because I hated her, that my mother was allowing me into her heart, was giving me all she felt worthwhile about herself, wanted both to elevate herself in my eyes, in everyone's eyes, but also because she needed me to see her as she saw herself. She wanted to be loved."

When Tenn spoke of his mother, he would often stop, literally shake himself, laugh, and either change the subject or resume it with greater animation. "There's an old Southern saying, common among Negroes, in which they talk of their mothers after they've passed away. If you hear a song you associate with your mother; if you smell a scent that was distinctly hers; if you overhear a voice that reminds you of hers—you experience a pain deep within you, at your very core. They call it Mama Bones, and I felt it for the first time sitting in those theaters, watching those movies, and thinking 'I must tell Mama how outrageous Miriam Hopkins is,' or 'Bette Davis has totally incorporated the druggist's wife's mannerisms,' and I would feel this pain, and suddenly realize that the person with whom I wished to share these reactions, these observations, was someone I believed I hated. The person I thought I hated, and felt I didn't understand, had made me someone who could appreciate these images, these illusions, and who had probably made me a writer."

Tenn stood on a soft shoulder on a street high above Hollywood, heard the laughter of pretty boys and the repeated playing of "Little Brown Jug," and juggled coins in his pocket and thought of his mother. Tenn thought of her in the house on Vista with his lover, who cooked and cared for him and sent him off to work with hot coffee; he thought of her and the affection she had either misplaced or he no longer trusted.

Tenn walked the streets of Hollywood and wished he could have his mother with him. Tenn wished he could discuss Greta Garbo and Clarence Brown and Ruth Chatterton with her. "Thank God for the ability to think of characters, real or imagined," Tenn said, "when we are utterly trapped and are praying for a better scene."

Tenn began to cry as he related these memories of his mother. "I will tell you how I was able to begin to realize my love for my mother," he confessed, "how I came to understand her illusions. I could remember her falling asleep on the sofa, waiting for me to return home. Her exhaustion, or her submission to her dreams, was so severe that she would not hear me approach her, and I could look at her without the animating force of her stories, her performance, her illusions. I would then see the face of a child, the face of the girl dancing away her youth with her beaux. Pushing, pushing. Pushing away the reality she felt had cheated her of her due, and pushing me toward a better illusion for myself. I saw, most clearly, however, myself. And then she would wake up and begin talking, and she was in control, and she was masterly. But I recall the sweet, still face of a girl, and I came to love her with that image in my mind, and that image carried me to Amanda Wingfield."

I asked Tenn if he still thought of his mother, if he still experienced the sensation of Mama Bones. Tenn laughed and admitted that "everything has diminished with age, my darling, but my feelings for my mother and my sister pierce me daily, and it is no illusion that they center me and let me know who I am, and let me know that I have loved and have been loved, no matter how badly or clumsily."

In 1943 Tenn applied this love, clumsily, he admitted, to paper. Two years later, in the company of Laurette Taylor, the actress who would assume the role of his mother in *The Glass Menagerie*, he would experience the most profound and immediate and intimate love he had yet encountered.

He was not ready for it.

According to Tenn, *The Glass Menagerie* came to be, and still exists, is read, performed, and loved, because of Laurette Taylor, whose candor and "unfinished, uncensored" honesty elicited from those around her remarkable achievements, and because a writer named Tennessee Williams "wrote something quite remarkable and personal and sweet, if I may say so."

When Tenn talked about Laurette Taylor and the initial production of *The Glass Menagerie*, he frequently flipped the surnames, referring to "Taylor" in one anecdote and "Smith" in another. When I pointed this out, Tenn realized that he now conflated the two actresses because they had "inhabited and owned" this play, and had become imprinted, infinitely, upon his memories of his mother.

"Taylor immediately wanted to know who these people were," Tenn recalled, "and her demands were kind and intelligent, so that I trusted her and could share with her, but they were also supported by an uncanny and unyielding sense of her own talent and technique and place in the theater. Absolutely nothing escaped her attention or her merciless sense of detail, and she never hesitated to point out a discrepancy or an untruth in my work or in the work of the others.

"After all the talk and all the analysis, what ultimately matters is whether or not you reach the hearts of the audience," Tenn said, "and this Laurette taught me. That love that I spoke of—that is so important to the crafting of a play—extends in its production and must be carried through every performance. With Amanda I was purging myself of the hatred I had felt toward my mother and was left only with the very strong love I knew was there. So I loved her through the play. The strong, strange love—that for my sister, Rose—I poured into Laura, whose love for her brother is what truly hobbled her. I even found I could love Tom—myself—by showing him in constant turmoil in that lacy imprisonment. A prison is a prison. And the Gentleman Caller is every promise held out to those who seek one, who believe that there is one around the corner. The Gentleman Caller is religion and its God; the newspaper page that holds the horoscope and the society page. The Gentleman Caller tells us that we can be *here* right now, but the *there,* the glistening *over there* is possible and imminent and near. It's one novena, one afternoon reverie, one cocktail, one rubbing of the Clarence Brown waxed paper away."

When Lois Smith took on the role of Laura, she understood that her character was a performer as well. Amanda essays roles on the telephone, for the grocer, for the neighbors. Laura tackles the role of the victim, and searches for the love that we can often easily bestow on the sad and the abandoned. "Laura is the freak occurrence against which we pray," Tenn told me. "When you do your Rosary and pray for humility or a happy death, or zeal, you'll also pray to be delivered from flood, fire, or famine. You will also love, in a very peculiar and hateful way, all of those who have been visited by these things. Guilt, along with a sense that money invested toward the sad prevents tragedy from visiting our doorstep, also creates a fulsome affection toward the gimpy and the fat and the unprepossessing. Laura knows this—Lois Smith as Laura knew this—and so she perfects her daily performance of limitation and struggle, dusts her little symbols of beauty and imprisonment, and begs to be given a shelf on which she and her mother can live out their days, Amanda free of reality; Laura free of social intercourse with others. Surcease and silence.

"And so," Tenn continued, "what I learned from Laurette Taylor, from my mother, from *Menagerie* is that we—writers, people—only conquer when we love, because when we love, we see clearly what is in front of us, and what was our past, and what we own. So love your characters, and by doing so you may ultimately come to love yourself. Laurette told me she loved my mother *for* me while playing Amanda, and also expressed her love for her own mother through the performance. There was a lot of love in that play, and if an audience can't identify with these sad outcasts of Dixie, they can identify with those loves that destroyed them and those loves that liberated them.

"And as you can probably imagine, my love for my mother and sister defined and destroyed me, and my love for Laurette, and for my play, liberated me, and . . ."

And? I asked.

"I never realized that—truly realized that—until this moment, when I said it."

Tenn excused himself from the table at which we sat and was absent for more than half an hour.

On another page of the notes about *Menagerie*, I wrote, "What is at stake?" and I remember that Tenn had told me that the characters are racing against time, against which illusions are useless. Each character pursues a singular desire—security, acceptance, sexual pleasure, social standing—and each, as Tenn stated "with a clock ticking in their ears." Taylor explained her motivation in portraying Amanda as similar to a time when her daughter, Marguerite, was crying, and in her attempts to calm her child, Taylor made faces, bobbed balloons, found candy, and finally held the baby tightly and begged her to please stop crying. "She never forgot this manic desire," Tenn told me, "this spinning of many plates to calm and control someone she loved, and any mother or child could recognize her actions."

One afternoon, when Tenn was especially worried about his play, about many things, Taylor called out, "Light be the earth upon you, lightly rest," and Tenn recognized it as a line from Euripides. He also remembered his image of his mother, asleep and vulnerable and sweet, waiting for her errant son to return home. He shared this image with Taylor, who promptly decided that Amanda never falters in her impeccable performance, her affront to reality, when anyone can see her, but when reality makes its presence and its power known to her, when Tom goes to his assignations, when the Gentleman Caller falls from reach, when the attempt to sell subscriptions seem to be failing, her performance, her posture, and her face all momentarily—and frighteningly— would sag. "Every actress who ever saw Laurette in *Menagerie* wants to talk about that performance," Tenn boasted, "and every one of them remembered the shock of seeing her seem to come undone at the seams in those moments in the play. It was as if they were seeing a horrible mistake, the onset of illness or pain, perhaps, in the middle of an otherwise flawless performance."

The last notes about *The Glass Menagerie* are an exotic list, but I remember that it was a list of things that reminded Tenn of his mother and of Laurette Taylor, and included Judy Holliday, Giulietta Masina, and Maureen Stapleton, but also Bellodgia perfume, the scent of starched linen, a particular brand of scented face powder, and movies, late at night, when Tenn realized he wanted to discuss what he was watching, but his favorite partner in such things was gone, silent.

"Memory is what cures us of a loss," Tenn told me. "I was stupidly afraid of my memories for so long, because I was afraid to feel, but memories are the ultimate illusion—perhaps the final one—in that they allow us to believe that those we love are forever with us, within us, and now I no longer grasp for greatness, merely for feeling."

Tenn gave me Lois Smith—in the form of a rosary bead—because he believed in her purity and in her young eyes, both of which he felt I possessed but might lose. Tenn also adored her for her working habits on the two plays they worked on together, and whenever he saw her in films, on television, or onstage, he had the sense that a beloved relative had been spotted in a large crowd of strangers. He felt safe. "She has the effect on me similar to those coins in my pocket," Tenn told me, "or that damned piece of waxed paper I rubbed into oblivion in that musty apartment. She centers me."

Nine

A FTER TENN GAVE ME the name of Marian Seldes, he paused and tried to remember a poem, "a very old and haunting French poem." He could not recall much of it, but he described it in great detail, as well as the feeling it brought over him. It was a poem, he said, that reminded him of the dream state he required to write and to generate the fog. I found the poem years later.

> You are distant, alien—you are
> The night of fog,
> Foul drizzle over the faubourgs
> Where life is the earth's cold color,
> Where men have died untouched by passion.
> We have met already, you will recall,
> Yes, long since and unfortunately
> In some region of vellum and toccatas
> In the blue twilight of a quiet house,
> Windows of lassitude.
> —O. V. DE L. MILOSZ, "L'ETRANGÈRE"

"That poem," Tenn told me, "helps me to write and helps me to think of Marian Seldes."

The career of Marian Seldes began when she was a child, in her bedroom, late at night. It is appropriate that an actress of whom Tenn once said, "She came to me from a fog, as so many did, seemed unreal, unmoored, floating free from reality, the Duse of Fogs," should have come to the realization of her destiny within nocturnal reveries that involved delusion and a mirror.

During these night visits to another reality, Marian glimpsed herself—clad in a long, white nightgown—in a full-length mirror that threw back a reflection of someone far more glamorous and interesting. As she grew older, and began taking dance instruction, she would go to the roof of her parents' apartment building and reconstruct the day's steps, throwing her long arms heavenward, drawing down the moon, begging Providence for aid in the pursuit of purpose and beauty, lost in the ecstasy of being someone else, of being free from time.

All that Marian Seldes was during these activities—during the 1930s and 1940s—she still is today. She is someone free of time's grasp and calamity. She is still the obedient, whispering, hesitant daughter who grew up in comfort (physically, intellectually, spiritually) and was impatient for the night vapors to begin. She is, Tenn noted, lost to us forever. She is enslaved by fantasy.

Marian Seldes was born on August 23, 1928, in Manhattan. She once wrote that "a longing to move from my own time to my father's, to share in lives before my life . . . pulled me toward the theater." Her father's life was marked by glamour, erudition, and controversy. Gilbert Seldes was a writer of plays, novels, and irate letters to editors, corporations, and boards; an educator; a *provocateur;* a man who goaded F. Scott Fitzgerald to write, who evoked rapture in Marianne Moore, and with whom Tenn was frankly obsessed.

"I don't blame Marian for being besotted with her father," Tenn told me. "I am, too. Hers was the fantasy upbringing on the isle of Manhattan that all Dixiecrats dream of." Gilbert Seldes lent his keen eyes and generous wit to such publications as *The Dial, Esquire, The Saturday Evening Post,* and *The New Yorker.* The work for which he will most likely be remembered is *The Seven Lively Arts,* a book whose theme, according to Seldes, is that "entertainment of a high order existed in places not usually associated with Art, that the place where an object was to be seen or heard had no bearing on its merits, that some of Jerome Kern's songs in the *Princess* shows were lovelier than any number of operatic airs and that a comic strip printed on news pulp which would tatter and rumple in a day might be as worthy of a second look as a considerable number of canvasses at most of our museums."

Gilbert Seldes was married to a woman whose name—Alice—he despised, so he renamed her Amanda, and she is, by photographic account, the parent who bequeathed to Marian her height, her dark, thick hair, her alabaster coloring, and her expressive brows, which usually tell the whole story of her inner being. One friend advised, "Just look at her brows: *they* don't lie." Her mother, who was, in Marian's words, "lethargic and listless," also passed on to her daughter an almost neurotic obsession with time, which has exhibited itself most alarmingly in a tendency to scrutinize dictionaries to find especially comforting and useful definitions for the very word. Time is ruthless, and to be within a hairbreadth from opportunity is to spend one's entire life as a supernumerary when stardom may have been offered. There is about Marian's life a certain quality that reminds one of a distaff version of *Appointment in Samarra,* with her persistent fears of appointments missed, time not adequately used, changes not fully recognized and utilized. She walks about town with typed itineraries in her purse, each minute of every day accounted for, every thought recorded. She recoils at the thought that her absences from grade school and performances of Peter Shaffer's *Equus* are recorded, and she dreams of finding the books in which the damaging evidence is located, and blotting it out. She fears that incipient sloth will result in lost time or, worse, in its turning against her, having its way with her, leaving her without energy and plopped against pillows (like her mother), watching the rest of the world create and prosper. She says, "Life goes by. There does not seem to be enough time to accomplish in daily living, much less in a career, all that you want to. Your use of time defines the kind of person you are off the stage—and on. When you are in charge of that time—the time of your life—you are happy."

Tenn shared this obsession with Marian, even if he failed to possess or harness her discipline in reshaping it. "Time has—is having—its way with me," he said, "and I want to alter this trajectory. I don't know how, so I reflect on Marian; I think of her moving about the city—a vision in purple or blue—checking clocks, her watch, the location of the sun, and getting things done, sharing herself. I think I can do this."

Marian's prestidigitation with time has not only served her in terms of productivity and efficiency; it has also kept her firmly where both she and Tenn would like to be: in her father's time. When she walks about Manhattan, she is surrounded by wafts of a time gone by. She is apt to inspire one to think of elegant, elliptical short stories, Aubusson rugs, lunch in the ladies' section of Schrafft's, and an afternoon assignation beneath the Biltmore clock. This is no accident, no trick of the mind: it is an affect deliberately chosen by Marian, and held to with affection. Her demeanor will bring to mind (if you are lucky and have a long memory) Katharine Cornell, the actress who became so vast an influence on Marian—as did her husband and director, Guthrie McClintic—that Marian consumed portions of the actress's character as her own and bestowed her name on her only daughter.

Control of time can also keep you busy—hence there is no time for

Tall, dark, moody, "almost inordinately polite," Marian
Seldes fascinated Tennessee, and he thought of her often
when he sought a "lost but resolute" female character. Seldes,
seen here in *Ring Around Rosy,* a 1960 television drama.

idle thoughts or reflection to intrude. By preventing such an invasion on her happiness, which is stringently created each day, Marian can use ruses and defenses to distract her from the fact that the dream she began in that mirror so long ago was a lie: the theater she dreamed of does not exist.

And never did.

Every actress, Tenn repeatedly told me, has within her a mental theater, similar to the one he managed in his own mind. This theater is complete with a repertory company and a costume shop, as well as a dreamed audience: the perfect recipients of what one dreams to create and share. The interesting assignment for me, as Tenn saw it, was to discover how many of these actresses have come face-to-face with a theater life that in any way resembles the existence concocted by their inner fabulist, an entity Tenn claimed required perpetual stoking.

Of all the other actresses to whom Tenn sent me, none has had a longing to match that of Marian Seldes, and none has displayed so servile an attendance to and affection for the workings and workers of the theater arts. No description of Marian can be accused of smacking of hyperbole. She is truly a handmaiden in the temple of Art; she is the slave to her craft; she has made the theater her church and its peripheral activities her religion, the primary tenet being extracted from the writings of Robert Edmond Jones, who wrote:

> An artist must bring into the immediate life of the theater . . . images of a larger life. . . . Here is the secret of the flame that burns in the work of the great artists of the theater. They seem so much more aware than we are, and so much more awake, and so much more alive that they make us feel that what we call living is not living at all, but a kind of sleep. Their knowledge, their wealth of emotion, their wonder, their elation, their swift clear seeing surrounds every occasion with a crowd of values that enriches it beyond anything which we, in our happy satisfaction, had ever imagined. In their hands it becomes not only a thing of beauty, but a thing of power. And we see it all—beauty and power alike—as a part of the life of the theater.

It was Tenn's belief that an actress was forever frozen in that time when she had the epiphany, when she found a safe harbor in the theater.

For Marian there was the Christmas pageant at the Dalton School, in which she was employed as one of the three angels whose task it was to remain immobile in an alcove, their faces and bodies testaments of supplication and bliss. Swathed in royal blue and swatches of gold oilcloth, Marian felt upon her a light that was "brighter than the sun," as well as hundreds of eyes. She kept her own eyes steadfastly forward, her hands pressed together in adoration for a Christ in which she did not believe—except as a fellow player in this pageant. She says of that time, "I knew there was no heaven and thought there was no God, but there was loveliness and safety and a secret excitement in that time and place."

In keeping with her religious fervor, Marian discovered upon changing her costume that she had even been visited by stigmata, red marks searing her flesh as proof of her theatrical bondage, making her, as such, the Padre Pio of grade-school pageants. She says, "My religious training took place in a theater. It became the church of my life; existence there was as magical as what I dreamed of in the room with the mirror. It was the dream made real."

Life for Marian from that time on was a relentless pursuit of the theater, and it was through theatrical experience that she chose to view things, using drama as a sieve through which she ran each and every event of her life. As she became a young woman, grew attractive, and received attention from young men, she wondered if she, like women in plays and films, would ever be happy. She was perpetually making lists, charts, heartfelt pleas to become important in the theater. She feared that she would become stagestruck, and she did, looking upon the participants of the theater with a soft focus, imagining them superior, horrified that they might fail or have faults. Her comments about guests met at Katharine Cornell's home on Martha's Vineyard swoon with delirium (and with reason, since the guest lists included everyone from Billie Burke to the Lunts to Margot Fonteyn to Mainbocher to Marlene Dietrich), and she took each of the people she met as assignments, as challenges to amplify her character and her life, to take from them what would make her better and more valuable—to the world, to the theater, to herself.

"I want to love as fully as she does," Tenn told me, "and I want to have her young and loving eyes."

Marian's abilities to tell time—and therefore to control and manipulate it—to make love, and learn a part are the three things that alert her to the fact that she is no longer the awkward, shy child keeping scrap-books full of glowing items about her idols. As the years passed and opportunities for stardom and full creative expression did not come to her, she did not become bitter; instead, she substituted earnest—some would say dogged—work for the parts that would tap into the vast, dark recesses of her talent. The positive addiction she has adopted to assuage disappointment is to become the ideal worker, so she will make the record books by appearing in a play for over four years, never missing a performance (in Ira Levin's *Deathtrap,* from 1978 to 1982), when she would have preferred that the same books note her talent. Her utilitar-ian spirit has taken dominance over the intelligent actress who sees the lack of challenge in the theater she has pursued.

Robert Edmond Jones (who agreed to see the young Marian in his large, dark, imposing apartment, where he served her wisdom along with brandy cake and a glass of B&B) wrote, at precisely the time Mar-ian was graduating from her theater studies at the Neighborhood Play-house, that

> we all have our hopes and our dreams of a theater which is to be. But when we attempt to discuss the theater of the present day with any seriousness we discover at once that we have very little to discuss. What we are practicing today in the name of theater has almost nothing to do with the theater. It is so unrelated to real theater that sometimes it actually seems as if you would have to grow a new set of faculties to create theater with. This thing that I am saying is not a whim, nor a beef, nor a gripe. It is a fact. What we are taught to call theater today isn't theater at all. True theater isn't, with the rarest exceptions, to be found in our playhouses. It has gone out of the window. It has hidden itself bitterly away.

Tenn had said to me, "Here is your life lesson. You should know that there are people in the theater for whom the stage is all. They have not allowed the real, functioning part of their souls and hearts to develop, so all they can be is a thespian. Away from greasepaint and an excuse to emote, they are masks waiting for a human touch to allow them move-ment, a reason for being.

"This is what happened to Marian," he continued. "She got lost in a childhood mirror in which she could be someone else, in whose reflection she was an actress, something grand. And what we are left with is the prepubescent girl who only wants to extinguish the very real, very wonderful person she is, for she feels that, *au naturel,* she can never please anyone. Believing that she is ugly and knowing that she will never be the star of the theater she hoped to be, she allows herself to be abused by the theater, by its practitioners, by men, by friends.

"But," Tenn offered, smiling, "there is a fantasy Marian, who is erudite, glamorous, beautiful, and I have seen her become consumed by this fantasy at rehearsals and parties, but it truly thrives on the stage. The stage is her narcotic, which she needs to keep herself alive. The stage no longer functions as a means of communication, but a means of fulfilling some craven desire, gorging some inner lacuna that can never be filled. I think I have this in common with Marian. I'm dreaming as I live."

Because I had already met Marian (in the fall of 1978, on a theater trip to New York with my high-school drama club, during which I went backstage at the Music Box Theatre, where Marian was appearing in *Deathtrap,* and we became friends), Tenn armed me with special items for my visit with her. The first was a prayer to St. Joseph, which we had found stuck in a discarded and well-worn missal in St. Louis Cathedral. It was typed on a piece of onionskin paper, and read:

O glorious St. Joseph, model of those who are devoted to labor, obtain for me the grace to work in a spirit of penance for the expiation of my many sins; to work conscientiously, putting the call of duty above my inclinations; to work with thankfulness and joy, considering it an honor to employ and develop by means of labor the gifts received from God; to work with order, peace, moderation, and patience, never shrinking from weariness and trials; to work, above all, with purity of intention and with detachment from self, keeping unceasingly before my eyes death and the account I must give of time lost, talents unused, good omitted, and vain complacency in success, so fatal to the work of God. All for Jesus, all through Mary, all after your example, O patriarch Joseph; such shall be my watchword in life in death. Amen.

"I think this is perfect for Marian," Tenn had said.

Tenn purchased for Marian, in a gift shop on Magazine Street, an old rosary of wooden beads that had been made in Jerusalem, and when he gave it to me, he wrapped around it a piece of paper he had found in the cathedral: a tiny calling card that had been wedged against one of the statues and which was worn from penitential homage, a sign of wear that impressed Tenn. The card read: "Devote yourself to Marian Worship." On the opposite side, Tenn wrote: "I am no longer surprised by what karma does to me."

Marian Seldes was cast in the 1964 revival of *The Milk Train Doesn't Stop Here Anymore*, as Blackie, the secretary to Flora Goforth, the flamboyant center of the play, who is transcribing the memoirs of her rich and shattered life, when she is not being seduced and recruited by the Angel of Death, who arrives in the form of a man—"lovely and fertile and fleshly accessible"—named Christopher Flanders. A friend of opulent and devious qualities, called the Witch of Capri, visits and shares the psychic components of Flora. Blackie is the character who maintains, and can still recognize, what Tenn called "intercourse with the real world, with real people, seeking real results." Blackie is not a fabulist or a fraud: She needs a job and Flora needs a screen onto which she can project her image, the events of her life that, once collected, may tell her who and what she is before she is consigned to the "bone gallery." Blackie is that screen. Blackie is also Tenn. So is Flora. "I am almost everyone in that play," Tenn said. "Lost, confused, hungry, messy, mean."

Marian also became the screen for the production of *Milk Train*, which was being revived only a year after its original production, which had featured Hermione Baddeley, an actress of "enormous talent and ingenuity" lost in a cloud of "farts and Fracas," and Mildred Dunnock, one of Tenn's greatest friends, who had said, throughout rehearsals and the brief run, that "we were drowning, and instead of life preservers, we kept being thrown words that held nothing: no truth, no beauty, no meaning." A faint whiff of creativity arose from the script of *Milk Train*, like the fog of dry ice, but the production was a mess. Tenn, convinced that his play—and the story it told—had merit, began to revise it even as it was being performed. The British director Tony Richardson, fresh from directing the film *Tom Jones,* and much lauded for his stage work with John Osborne, decided, for reasons never made clear to anyone, to revive and to salvage this play, which, he told Tenn, held more meaning than any he had read in some time.

"He wanted to be my savior," Tenn told me, "or rather, the savior of

Hermione Baddeley and Mildred Dunnock in the first Broadway
production of *The Milk Train Doesn't Stop Here Anymore,* in 1963,
a nightmare that the revival—and Marian Seldes—helped to exorcise
for Tennessee in 1964. "The play never worked," Tennessee said,
"but at least Marian threw some good dirt on it."

Milk Train, and I cannot tell you why. He spoke eloquently and at great
length about what he hoped to do with the play, about what the play
meant to him, but I could never discern any of his intentions or desires
in the completed production. As a director, he was like the flirt who
talks sweet and rubs fast on the dance floor, but who takes you home
and consummates nothing. In fact, pants never hit the floor."

A great impetus for reviving *Milk Train* was the opportunity to
cast Tallulah Bankhead in the role of Flora Goforth. "Tony loved the
idea—the very camp idea—of directing Tallulah in this part, which
he believed to have been based on her. It is true that there are elements
of Tallulah in Flora, but there are elements of people like Tallulah in
many of my plays, because people like Tallulah—hothouse flowers bred
in the garden of Narcissus—grow all across the world. I have known
many. There is a great deal of my mother in Flora, but also Ruth Ford

[who played the Witch of Capri in the revival] and Miriam Hopkins and Ina Claire and Ruth Chatterton. Uta Hagen and Elaine Stritch and Judith Anderson and Elizabeth Ashley. And Tallulah. And any number of aunts and grand ladies I listened to and learned from in St. Louis and Louisiana."

People like Flora Goforth do not fear death by organ failure; they do not fear the actual act of death and whatever judgment awaits: they fear that failure will visit the production of life that they have written, produced, directed, and star in, frequently above the title, the fray, and the law. These women tend to be very "rich-blooded," as Tenn put it, aware of the station they have designed and to which they have assigned themselves. There is a great deal of effort in maintaining the "ruse of living" when you are one of these grand creatures, people who cannot actually create or understand art—literature, music, painting, sculpture—but who can sculpt and enhance their persons to become ambulatory, dilatory works of art. "They have a richness of voice," Tenn said, "cultivated by repetition. They have a way of moving their heads and bodies, cultivated by time spent in front of a mirror. They are hesitant in their beliefs, because they have no real soul or sense of self. Well, they have no self to speak of! They have to wait to see what others think of something, then they weigh in. They must be outré in their desires and allegiances, but they also must align themselves with bourgeois loves, because that is where the traffic is, and the traffic holds people—an audience.

"These are very tiring women," Tenn continued, "but fascinating. The role they have created for themselves has been cast and is played continuously. Christopher Flanders and Blackie are paid audience members to Flora. We all need an audience, even as we approach our final curtain. And every fabulist like Flora needs to be surrounded by people who are not yet bold enough to create an identity, a life, a self through the machinations of imagination. Blackie admires Flora, even as she grows impatient with her and doesn't understand her at all times. Blackie, you see, is very much like Marian Seldes. This is no facile statement. Marian Seldes makes herself a better person so that everyone can benefit. Marian needs a Flora Goforth—and, I might add, a Tallulah Bankhead—to learn what one should and should not do. She needs a Tallulah to serve and to honor, and she did." Marian loved Tallulah for what she had been and for her stardom and her glamour and her daring. Marian also feared Tallulah as if she were an infectious agent: the drinking, the drugs, the nakedness, the lost memory, the lack of discipline were dangerous elements that Marian came to believe might be catching. Marian also had her young daughter around during out-of-town tryouts, and she must have wondered what the girl thought of the marcescent diva.

Tenn believed that Marian gave the only legitimate performance in the revival of *Milk Train,* seeking to play a real person rather than a construct or a symbol or a camp icon. The original production had been designed as a Kabuki nightmare by Jo Mielziner, but everyone, especially Richardson, wanted a simpler, starker production, so Rouben Ter-Arutunian, a handsome, manic designer, kept some elements of Kabuki but stuck them within a set that Tenn believed bore elements of German expressionist, Art Deco, and WPA "mentalities."

"The original production had possessed an ornate and absurd set," Tenn related, "and the revival possessed an ornate and absurd cast. Whatever had been extreme and silly about the original had been contained, for the most part, within inanimate objects—sets, costumes, lighting effects. Now the extreme and silly had been thrust front and center with the cast."

In addition to Bankhead, Seldes, and Ford, Richardson completed the primary cast with Tab Hunter, the handsome blond star of such films as *Battle Cry* (1955), *Lafayette Escadrille* (1957), and the Hollywood version of the Broadway musical *Damn Yankees* (1958). "He was mobile cotton candy," Tenn remembered, "pretty and weightless and dumb. Beware the pretty idol in career rehabilitation." Richardson was mad for Hunter, flirted with him outrageously, marveled at his beauty. Tenn was distressed by the relationships that developed through that brief production. Richardson and Bankhead never understood each other and gave each other no more than perfunctory notice. The relationship that fascinated Tenn was that between Marian Seldes and his play. "She taught me how to love what was flawed and frightening," Tenn said, "and she taught me how to remain calm and caring in a time of confusion. I did not write *Milk Train* as an avant-garde exercise. That play, like all of my plays, was a very real manifestation of my present thoughts, and they took a turn toward the grotesque, toward the Grand Guignol, because that is where my mind was, my thoughts, my feelings. I think I speak for a great many people when I say that we were in confusing times then. Kennedy was murdered during our rehearsal period [of the revival]. I would run out for a sandwich and coffee and blacks had commandeered the luncheon counters and the cash registers. I was over fifty and afraid that my powers, always capricious, were waning. All around me my compatriots were floundering, wondering if we had a theater to which we could report for work. Bill Inge was falling apart in some house above the Hollywood Hills. Arthur Miller was drinking some bitter cup of forgiveness with Kazan at Lincoln Center and producing tracts [*After the Fall, Incident at Vichy*] disguised as plays, given a sense of importance, attention paid, because he came from a gilded age and had a dead movie star on his résumé and within his inventory."

Tenn was also addicted to a series of pills and was "taking them in, my murderous Eucharist," with a variety of alcoholic concoctions. "I needed to feel something to write," Tenn said, "but I had reached a point where I could no longer feel anything too strongly with any comfort. It was a numb age, but I wrote truthfully from within and about that numb age, and while Herbert Machiz [the director of the 1963 *Milk Train*] sought to emulate my garish and frightening turn of mind with costumes and sets that he thought complemented it, Richardson subverted the entire play into a big, camp joke. He thought we should laugh at Flora, I suppose, because he laughed at Tallulah, who he thought was outrageous and idiotic and some relic from another time. Well, Flora— and Tallulah—are you and me. Tony Richardson, I would imagine, is having his Flora Goforth times right about now and is probably feeling some sense of identification with her. But at that time, bright with his own brilliance, he simply saw an excuse to throw some glitter in the air and entertain the boys."

Richardson was not alone in his sabotage, however. Tallulah Bankhead was soiling the stage as ferociously—and far more openly—than its director.

Born in Alabama finery in 1902, Tallulah Bankhead had been one of the voices he had heard on radios cradled in the dark—in bedrooms, cubbyholes at the YMCA, in hotel suites. Bankhead epitomized for Tenn the stylish New York, and he imagined that she would be as crisp and scintillating as the person he had assembled from memories and sounds over the years. Tenn adored Bankhead, saw her talent, wanted it—like his—to be revived, to be noticed.

Bankhead's theatrical successes were firmly behind her when she

Tennessee's mother kept photographs of Tallulah
Bankhead in scrapbooks and folded into books—
including the Bible—because the Alabama-born
actress epitomized Southern finery and Broadway
glamour. Tennessee was elated to meet her and
work with her—initially.

tackled the role of Blanche, in 1956. Her Regina in *The Little Foxes* and
her Sabina in *The Skin of Our Teeth* were performances Tenn recalled as
incandescent. "Even her voice on the radio, as she repeated the role of
Regina," he remembered, "was the work of a real actress." But as Tenn
would later learn, Herman Shumlin, the director of *Foxes,* and Kazan,
her director for *Skin of Our Teeth,* were perpetually atop the actress, giving her line readings, herding her into rehearsals and into constricted
places on the stage.

"If you told her what to do and where to do it," Kazan remembered,
"she was effective, but it was persistent, backbreaking work."

As Tenn would sadly learn, however, Bankhead could no longer
sustain a performance throughout an evening, and she was incapable

of investing any veracity into a character. "I think an important point is often forgotten," Tenn told me, "and that is that Tallulah was a great actress—was capable of being a great actress. She certainly was a great theatrical personality, and the cult—the frenzy—that surrounded her cannot truly be understood by those who didn't know of, hear of, or attend to that phenomenon."

All Bankhead had, and trusted, by the time of *Milk Train* was faith in her public, who dutifully attended her performances and enjoyed a relationship, "a persistent conversation," with her as she struggled. "Toward the end," Tenn remembered, "no intelligent playwright ever trusted her, because her pact was with the public—that slavering, fanatical public. It is inconceivable to us now to realize that there was an actress, a theater actress, who had throngs of fans lined up to watch her eat, shop, and walk down a street. And the theaters! They throbbed and pounded like sports arenas, and there was always that glorious moment—and I use the term facetiously—in Coward, Barry, and, God help us, Williams—when she broke character and beamed out at the audience. 'It's all for you, darlings,' she transmitted. Maddening but fascinating, and so exciting for the boys. No one cut a figure across a stage like she did. She could upstage a crucifixion with the right dress, and she would gladly do so, if the pay was sufficient."

Milk Train was a mess. Actors did not bother to bring too many personal effects into their dressing rooms; one brought a sample-size box of soap flakes and a travel-size tube of toothpaste. Everyone knew they would not be employed—in what Mildred Dunnock called "the sad salvation of Tennessee Williams"—for very long.

"Tennessee wanted his play produced," Seldes told me, "and he wanted us to do our best, and so I did, and so, I think, did everyone else in the play, to the best of their ability. I loved Tennessee; I loved Tallulah; I loved everyone in that play, and I'm happy if I gave Tennessee some happiness or balance during that time."

"My mistake with so many of the plays of that time," Tenn told me, "and it really began with *Milk Train,* was in presenting my new plays along the same lines, with some of the same people, as the earlier ones. So everyone came and expected *Menagerie* or *Streetcar* or *Cat,* and when these gilded gorgons came on, spouting dark humor and beating back time with all the tools in their arsenals, audiences were perplexed.

"I disliked Alan Schneider," he continued, "when he directed *Slap-*

stick Tragedy [in 1966]. He claimed he understood most of my humor, but he cast the play with brilliant actresses"—Margaret Leighton, Kate Reid, Zoe Caldwell—"and then proceeded to direct them in a play of an entirely different tone. *Slapstick* is an absurd play; so is *Milk Train*. You may openly and perhaps correctly identify them as products of a diseased mind, but I wrote truthfully about what I saw and felt. The plays, however, were directed as if they were naturalistic, kitchen-sink dramas, and this baffled me in the matter of Schneider, who had so shrewdly cast Buster Keaton in the work of Beckett. *That* was terribly subversive and effective, but in our work together, he cast actresses from whom audiences were expecting something altogether different, and they sat there dumbstruck and angry. If I agreed to a production today, I would insist on a cast of true clowns," he told me, and rattled off the names of a number of actresses who would amuse and discomfit an audience: Carol Burnett, Jo Anne Worley, Ruth Buzzi, Joan Rivers. "Let them think they're in for a few laughs," he told me, "then show them what is really beneath the clown-white makeup. That is what life is. That is what life was for me at that time, and that is what I wrote."

Milk Train might have worked with a comedienne in the lead role, Tenn believed, and it might have worked if there had not been so much effort placed on forcing a camp sensibility into it. "It's a morbid play," Tenn told me, "and its humor arises from the attempts we all understand to keep death at bay. We are all spinning around, trying to stay alive, and that is as funny as it is sad as it is futile. That's the play. He [Richardson] didn't get it."

"Oh, my!" Seldes said. "I don't think anyone *got* it. I tried to get it, but it was like holding mercury in your hand or making a suit out of meringue. There were so many problems: a lack of trust between Tallulah and Tony, and Tennessee's inability to be there all the time, ready to work, ready to trust. He gave away so much of his work to everyone, and never fought to make his work the best it could be. He gave up, so why shouldn't Tony? What could he do?"

Prepare to be misunderstood, Tenn told me repeatedly. The production of *Milk Train* set off two decades of his not being understood or properly respected, of his placing his hopes in the wrong people at the wrong times. Upon the closing of *Milk Train* (after four days), Tenn immediately began to revise it again. He tinkered with it for years, and kept recasting it in his mind. He joked that our relationship, such as it was, resembled that between Flora Goforth and Blackie.

"Blanche told us she depended upon the kindness of strangers," Tenn said, "but in fact she had never in her life ever met a kind stranger. She dreamed she might, and she hoped that such flattery might convince her captor to be the kind stranger of her dreams. I came to depend, in that time, upon the kindness and the example of sane women, balancing women: Marian, of course; Lois Smith, of course; and three others."

I pressed Tenn for more information on Marian Seldes and Lois Smith. With both actresses there was much admiration and affection, but no stories of lunches or talks or evenings discussing the future of the world; dreams; means of escape.

Tenn paused, then asked what I was looking for.

"What, ultimately, was the lesson taught to you by these two women?" I asked.

Tenn paused; his face grew red. He calmed down and leaned closer to my face, ready to tell me not so much what these two women had taught him, but of what they had reminded him.

"Let me explain something to you: no one owes any of us anything other than respect, some courtesy, and the amount of time they deem necessary to hear our story, see our dance, judge our gifts. That is all. I operated for many years under the common delusion that artists are sensitive creatures who require husbanding, cosseting, extreme care to function in the brutal world. This is utter bullshit: all human beings thrust into the act of living require the same amounts of love and kindness and patience, and I came to see that when I adopted the pose of the walking wounded, when I referred to myself as an open scab walking the mean streets, I was asking for forgiveness for the multitude of sins for which I was guilty: ugliness, laziness, a lack of discipline, the inability to make the words and the women that came to me work fully.

"I was asking for a break I did not deserve at all. You either are a good person or a good writer or a good actor or you are not. You cannot then apply a collage of sickness and neuroses to your person and ask for exemptions. It is unfair; it is dishonest. Make this decision today: Will you be a good and honest writer, or would you rather be famous, loved, noticed? Tell me, because there are different paths for these two divergent goals. The decision to be a true artist is lonelier and slower, but it will lead to better work and, I think, a better life. Very rarely you will be a good and honest writer and also know a little comfort and some attention and the well wishes of a crowd. This is very rare."

That lesson, Tenn told me, came from Smith and Seldes.

Ten

"THE ONLY JOY in the world is to begin," wrote Cesare Pavese, one of Tenn's favorite writers, an Italian poet and a suicide, whose poems and diary entries Tenn recalled from a forced but fervent memory. Long before Tenn had read this Pavese sentiment, he had overheard his grandfather and other church elders and members offer the same advice, in different forms, to a variety of grieving, curious, or confused parishioners. "I like balance and order," Tenn told me, "and my first memory of seeking it was in the act of beginning again, after an event had made solid footing and thinking an impossibility."

Unimportant and virtually invisible (or so he believed), Tenn moved about the rectory and the church property with freedom and easy access. The church always smelled of polishing oil—touches of lemon and verbena—and the flowers that were tended daily by the women of a flower guild. The church—as well as refined St. Louis life—operated through a series of guilds, clubs, organizations, and societies, and each had its leaders, its rules, and its methods of "mattering and ordering." Tenn eavesdropped on the women of the flower guild, each flower thrust into Styrofoam or water accompanied by a judgment, an aphorism, or a sentiment served with a sign. "They had the world in the crosshairs and by the short hairs," Tenn remembered. "They had the answer to everything." The women came to their functions dressed formally and with frills, their faces caked with powder, which flaked and smeared in the summer months, and the reapplication of powder and rouge and lipstick rendered them cartoonish by the time afternoon refreshments were served. Tenn could remember that the air smelled of their perfumes—flowery, musky, heavy—their starched apparel, their lavender-scented underthings. Their cups and napkins were smeared with stains of crimson, amber, blood orange, Chinese red, brick red: they had left their mark by dint of opinion, perfume, cosmetics, and influence. The flower arrangements grew higher and bigger the more fervent their demeanor or their resolve. Their primary complaint? Things were moving too fast. The world was simply too confusing. "These were my first female characters," Tenn said. "They had invented their own stages—church, society, the home, my imagination—and they fascinated me."

When death visited a parishioner, calls were made and these women appeared. Some were sent to comfort the widowed spouse; others were dispatched to divert the attentions of children, the weak, the simple, or older survivors who might not be able to handle the news, and so were given information in tiny installments, like drops of sugar water to hummingbirds. Tenn could remember cries and screams beginning in the parlor of a home, followed by howls from the backyard swing, and then sniffles in driveways and along sidewalks circling the home that death had now visited.

"Death has come to our community," Tenn's grandfather would always state, in sermons and bulletins and conversations meant to comfort. The term always horrified Tenn, and he passed on this fear to many of his characters, most of whom recognized that death, like a wayward misfit with a gun and a grudge, was prowling the neighborhoods—of real estate and psyche—and waited for the open door, the unlatched window, the friendly gesture to gain entrance and make his visit permanent.

Death propelled the community into action. Those who had been sent to inform and to console were now joined by those who sought to explain, to bring order and balance to the unsettled. Another group brought food, trying in vain to get the grieving to eat, to store up their strength "for what lay ahead." Tenn remembered their sunken chests and vacant eyes at the mention of this event or the destination known as "what lies ahead." There was never any answer provided to their questions as to what this would be, but it was a requirement that they have faith, and that they bring to the tasks strength that would serve them and their family well.

"We wait and we have faith that whatever He may bring to us, He will also bring us the aid we need": so said Tenn's grandfather. The vagueness infuriated Tenn. "I began to see the cruelty in the casseroles and the confessions; the refreshments and the sweet hugs and aphorisms," he told me. "There was no clarity, no concrete answers, just a vague cloud of words and phrases and prayers that we were to cling to and hope would serve as armor when 'the time' came, when 'what lies ahead' knocked at the door still resounding from the knock that had brought death or disease or doubt."

There had been a woman, normally composed and in control of her senses and her wardrobe and her mind, who had been brought into the office of his grandfather to be told her husband had been killed in an automobile accident. Tenn could remember her screams, the smeared lipstick, the hat that fell to the floor, its veil pointing upward, as if in confusion at the disorder and discord that had erupted. Her screams demanded answers, cried out for revenge or clarification, damned the automobile (progress, the world changing), repeatedly asked if her informants were sure of what they spoke.

All that was given to her were muttered Scriptures, affirmations that His way is greater than ours, that there is an answer and a blessing in all things. An obscenity flew from the fine woman's mouth—one of the first Tenn could remember hearing, although he knew immediately that its utterance was verboten—and the group moved in closer, a constricting circle of censorship and comfort.

"They pressed that lady down," Tenn remembered, "and I realized right then, as a child, that no amount of service to a flower guild, no award for hymns sung or cookies baked or casseroles scooped or sick parishioners visited, was enough to prepare you for what life has waiting for you. We seek order and answers in the rituals, in the order, in belonging—strength in numbers. We behave well and we take care of things. We seek and then we follow the natural and proper order of things in our homes, our communities, and our churches, and when 'what lies ahead' now lies before you, walls and floors melt into nothingness, people become obstructions that prevent you from running toward—what?"

Tenn turned to me and asked me to write down, once, "We are in this alone," and then, three times:

How to begin
How to begin
How to begin

The woman who had lost her husband in that accident, who had demanded answers and had shouted an obscenity in the offices of an Episcopalian rectory (a mighty and pregnant sin), never recuperated, and Tenn could never look at her in the same way. "She's gone from us," Tenn's mother said. "She just broke apart, and lost her faith." Tenn's grandfather would ascribe this loss of faith to the fact that the woman had loved her husband—and all that he represented—more than she had loved the Lord. "Her relationship with her husband was too strong and too dependent," he explained at dinner one evening. "Perhaps God took him away because he was lonely for her. Now she'll develop the relationship with God that had suffered in the past. We ignore God at our own peril."

Tenn remembered the woman as formidable, a "Big Lady," proper and well-dressed and assured of her place in all communities, societies, guilds. She was the type of woman he would describe to Jessica Tandy and Geraldine Page, to help them become this woman, to be assured, to know who she was. This woman had dressed impeccably. "Shiny buttons," Tenn remembered, "and silky skin and every hair in place. A large, proud bosom. A flash of gold." The woman had lovely handwriting, and Tenn had loved to read her letters to his mother, and had once asked her to write something, anything, so he could admire the swoops and the flows of her penmanship. She made mints in her kitchen, pouring the fondant onto a large, oval piece of marble, forming perfect rounds onto which she placed a flower of pink icing, a bit of green for a stem. She had told Tenn that each flower, each bit of icing that dripped from the bag, was a prayer, perhaps a kiss, to the person who would enjoy the candy.

Order and control: "Whatever I have learned of life and order and the method of coping," Tenn told me, "has come from women, and from the earliest days of my life." In order for him to understand things,

Tenn felt he had to "walk into a woman's mind, and see what could be done, what could be fashioned."

Tenn watched the woman shrink from lack of interest in food, her body lost in the fabrics that had once proudly enclosed her body. It was never believed that she was lost in grief, shattered at losing a husband of nearly four decades. She had merely lost her faith, and she drifted away. Her eyes never met another's. Her appearances at the flower guild ended.

"This is why you need faith," Tenn's mother told him, and that is when Tenn remembered that he began to pray, to beg for order, to be buffeted for "what lay ahead."

On some occasions of death, the body of the deceased would be brought to the church and prepared for presentation at the funeral service. Tenn's grandfather would, of course, officiate, but he was attended by yet another guild of ladies, who sought to bring order and comfort to this awful occurrence. There were candles to be lit and particular linens, starched and perfect and blindingly white, to be placed in a certain way at a certain time. Each act, timed and holy, announced to the bewildered that there was control and understanding in this house, in this act, in this world.

Tenn remembered all of the prayers, and his childhood was full of times when he was led to pray for the Increase of the Military, for Fruit ful Seasons, for Congress and Courts of Justice, for Fair Weather, and always *In Time of Calamity,* a prayer he remembered as a title, emblazoned as if in neon, calamity a particular time set aside like the flower guild meetings or a bridge lesson or a beauty-parlor appointment.

O God, merciful and compassionate, who are ever ready to hear the prayers of those who put their trust in Thee; Graciously hearken to us who call upon Thee, and grant us Thy help in this our need; through Jesus Christ our Lord. Amen.

So much grievous suffering, so much fear and doubt, all of it remembered by Tenn as being surrounded by the smell of perfumes and flowers and candle wax and lemon and verbena and starched linen, and all of it failing to answer even the simple questions of this wandering child, listening to adults in moments of emotional extremity and "horrible human strain," as he stole cookies from the church kitchen and looked at the stained-glass windows for some sign that there really was a God to whom everyone was reaching.

"This is what I came to realize," Tenn told me. "We spend too much time throwing our prayers up in the air and hoping that an answer, a miracle, will fall from above and explain everything. The lessons, the prayers answered, are right here. They are in front of us and we can learn from them." They rest, Tenn told me, within women. All of life's lessons hold a feminine form. Men may carry out what has been learned from the lessons, but the instructions—"like life itself"—came from a woman.

Tenn wanted me to go to these life lessons, these "ambulatory answered prayers," and learn from them not only for my own sake, but for him as well. Tenn wanted me to ask them if he had mattered to them; he wanted their advice, their strength, their order and balance. "They say God is in the details," Tenn said, "and these particular women are those details. Use the beads if you wish, but by all means use the examples I'm about to give you. Women who help me to reach balance and order, and who allow me to believe I can begin again."

Frances Sternhagen first came to Tenn's attention in the 1950s, when she began to be praised for a series of sharp, intelligent, and stylish performances that were offered primarily in off-Broadway theaters that Tenn compared to "well-meaning closets." Sternhagen, who typically asks everyone to immediately call her Frannie, was a blonde of average height who, onstage and in character, gave Tenn the appearance of height, of great bones holding up skin that knew care and breeding, and she cut through characters and their lines, as well as the stages on which she acted, like a piercing and jeweled scimitar. "I loved her immediately," Tenn told me. "She was like some heavily buffed apple, shiny and good for you, that had been placed on the stage as if it were the teacher's desk, and everything around her became immediately superfluous."

As Tenn explained it to me, "I believe she came to particular fruition as an actress when she began to get better parts and greater challenges. She was remarkable in a double bill of Harold Pinter plays that were gorgeously produced, delicately and frighteningly performed, and which made absolutely no sense whatsoever: in other words, quintessential Pinter. If you should ever meet Ms. Sternhagen, long before you ask her any questions about life, love, and the literature that is the-

The radiant, positive face of Frances Sternhagen
was one that Tennessee sought on the stage and
at most theatrical events and openings. Tennessee
and Sternhagen were both avid swimmers and
converts to Catholicism. "I think we are on to
some good things," Tennessee said.

ater, ask her for me what the hell *The Room* was supposed to be about. I
would like to know. She played it like she did, but she is quite nefarious."

When I met and came to know Frances Sternhagen, she did not
claim to know what Pinter's *Room* was about, even though the playwright was present for rehearsals. "He just told us to play it as we felt it,"
she told me. "Your truth is the play's truth. So . . . I don't know what
it is about, I really don't, but I played the woman as if she were present
in a very real situation and something was terribly urgent for her. I suppose it worked, but I don't feel that I am necessarily nefarious. I'm just
an actress working. We look for the truth as the character sees it. I don't
find this extraordinary."

The evening's second play was *A Slight Ache,* in which Frannie played
Flora, who, along with her husband, observes a stranger in their garden.

They bring him into their perfectly lit and appointed home, and he sits, silent and passive, as they share their stories with him. There is discussion of lawns and the ideal marmalade and lives of order and balance; but Flora is decidedly off-balance, and she comes to love, to the best understanding she possesses, this stranger, and her devotion to and need for him unnerved Tenn. At one point, Flora throws her arms around this man and exclaims, "I'm going to keep you!"

"I was changed by that performance," Tenn remembered, "because here was a woman of a certain standing, who played by the rules, belonged to the guilds and the societies, but who had always wanted, and had never received, answers to some big questions, such as: What is love? Will I find it? She clearly had not had sufficient outlets for her passions; so when this man arrived, and for reasons known only to her unique heart and her unique eyes and her unique glands, she felt what she took to be love for him. And she leapt for it. She sought to possess it. She needed someone to tell her story to."

There was another prayer—or rather a portion of one—from the Book of Common Prayer that came to Tenn's mind when he thought of Frannie in the Pinter play, and when he remembered maiden aunts and young, frightened women praying that they may find a companion, love, acceptance, desire. The line Tenn remembered was: "We commend to Thy fatherly goodness all those who are any ways afflicted, or distressed, in mind, body, or estate; that it may please Thee to comfort and relieve them, according to their several necessities. . . ."

Those "several necessities" haunted Tenn from childhood until the day I met him, fresh into his eighth decade. What were the several necessities, and were they all worthy of comfort and relief and "prompt succor"? "I will never know," Tenn admitted. "None of us will ever know, but in that performance, I thought, and I cried, and I spent some time in touch with my own necessities, and I prayed and hoped for comfort. I found some small measure of it in her performance, and I would have to say that is the highest praise I can offer. She put me in touch with my needs and partially filled them."

Tenn continued to follow Frannie's career, asking questions of women who worked with her and whom he admired, like Colleen Dewhurst and Maureen Stapleton and Madeleine Sherwood. Who was this Frances Sternhagen? Tenn was delighted to discover that one of Frannie's first professional assignments was playing Laura in *The Glass*

Menagerie, in summer stock, when she was only eighteen. "So she truly is mine," he said.

"Bigger and better roles came to her in the 1970s, and that is when she came to me in corporeal form," Tenn recounted. "I was being honored by the Drama Desk, a group of people who always seemed to know who I was, but I always found myself feigning recognition, even as they fed and feted me. I always felt like a man arriving in a foreign train station and being fulsomely greeted by strangers, and thinking that I must go ahead and go home with them and nod in agreement at their statements.

"I am very bad about being disingenuous when I am praised," Tenn confessed.

It was at this Drama Desk "scene," as Tenn characterized it, that he ultimately made fleshly contact with Frannie. By all accounts Tenn was miserable at the event, at which he was being rewarded for "surviving, apparently," and Frannie was being honored for her featured performance in Peter Shaffer's *Equus*. Tenn admitted that he was both mildly drunk and solidly stoned that evening, and he remembered "gaudy colors and loud patterns and perfumes and Sterno," and he was not happy. "I had not had a good time of it," he recalled. His most recent plays had not succeeded, either by his own standards or by those of the critics or actors he admired. *The Red Devil Battery Sign* was having a difficult and painful birth, and the revivals of *A Streetcar Named Desire* produced in 1973 for a twenty-fifth-anniversary celebration he didn't fully welcome or understand had been, in his estimation, abortive or unpleasant or amateurish. "I felt like an old failure," he told me, "and the idea of being given a plaque or a medal for hanging on, muddling through, was not something I desired or wanted."

But?

"Well," he laughed, "I am very bad about being disingenuous when I am praised, and the praise was running erratically and in small spurts."

Tenn recalled that he was placed, for the duration of the event, on a large and uncomfortable wicker chair of vast proportions. "It proceeded to make a waffle out of my buttocks," he remembered, "and each time I moved in it to achieve some sense of balance and comfort, it creaked and shifted, and as I was on a raised platform of sorts, displayed like a war criminal or an especially succulent duck in Chinatown, my shiftings drew attention."

Drunk, stoned, uncomfortable, his tongue darting about his parched lips like a startled chameleon, Tenn endured, watching people "largely unknown to me" receive their awards. "I creaked and shifted and swayed," he recounted, "which is when I saw Frannie's face, which exhibited so much sympathy toward my plight and my discomfort. She would smile at me as if to imply that my ordeal would soon be over, and I found myself pulling her toward me, literally and figuratively, and she got me through that night—with her kindness, yes; with her support, yes—as we stood with our awards, which we held as if they were dead babies, and my grace and gratitude were directed toward her. Not merely for that evening—awful and draining as it was—but for the memory of so many evenings I'd spent with her genius."

Tenn would continue to seek Frannie's company within the confines of a theater, but he never attempted a personal relationship. "I thought of it," he confessed, "but I wanted to enter a relationship that was based on work, and I could never find a woman—faked from the fog or of natural derivation—that could serve her."

Tenn claimed that he kept mental and actual notes on actresses he loved and admired, and he wondered how it might appear if these notes should ever be discovered. Tenn noted their physical characteristics, their age, his impressions. "In Frannie's case," Tenn told me, "I was making a case—to myself, to the universe, and on her behalf—that she should come to inhabit a play of mine, and to enter my life."

When Tenn had his encounter with Frannie at the Drama Desk Awards in the spring of 1975, Frannie was forty-five, but she appeared "buoyant, ageless," and she was at an awkward age for the visions he was having of women on his mental proscenium. "She was too young for the victims I was imagining," he said, "and she was much too vital to be a mother or an aggressor. I couldn't place her."

Tenn imagined that Frannie was a rich and "polished" woman. He knew that she had been born in Washington, D.C., the daughter of a judge, "well-placed from all I can ascertain," and she had attended the Madeira School and Vassar College, where she soon came to dominate the drama department. During the run of *Equus*, Frannie's mother had died, necessitating a leave of absence during which she managed the estate. Anthony Perkins, who was playing the lead role in the play at the time (having succeeded Anthony Hopkins), marveled at this fact with Tenn. "Tony was quite obsessed with money and muscles and meat,"

Tenn told me. "Any one of those three subjects was likely to set him off for some time, and he spoke at some length about Frannie's alleged wealth, which might have embarrassed him, given that he was among the least generous of people."

Frannie then entered a special niche of actresses Tenn reserved in his notes—the rich and removed. Tenn placed Frannie next to Beatrice Straight, born to the fortunes of the Whitneys, and "so far removed from the cares and frictions of the world" that he adored and envied her greatly. Frannie, however, laughed when told of this perception Tenn had held of her. Her life was comfortable, but her education was provided by wealthy relatives who wanted her to do well. The settling of the estate was, like the acts of the women in all those guilds of Tenn's childhood, a series of actions and rites that might help Frannie come to grips with the loss of her mother, and with the new direction her life was now likely to take.

"What tends to make people think of Frannie as rich," Marian Seldes told me, "is her generosity. She gives freely and fully, as if there was no want in her life. She gives richly." Frannie also operates from what Tenn called a "rich heart," which he imagined was routinely stocked by her devotion to the Catholic faith, to which she converted when she married her husband, the actor Thomas Carlin. "Frannie radiates goodness," Tenn told me, and the knowledge that she was a member of the Roman Catholic Church played some part in Tenn's own conversion. "I imagined if it passed the exacting eyes and senses of Frannie Sternhagen," he explained, "I could do something with it."

Frannie's religious beliefs were not the only thing that helped her rise from the bonds of a cruel world, with its exacting God of no answers, its endless rites and passages and disorder: like Tenn, she was an ardent swimmer. "I wonder if her special sense of balance derives from her habit of swimming," Tenn asked. "No one seems to know that I am never far from a body of water. I always urge my theatrical compatriots to swim—many in the hopes that they will drown, of course—but primarily to know the bliss that comes when you are freed from the heavy bonds of the earth, of being rooted in a particular time and place. It is often cruel that we find ourselves where we are, and with whom, but you can feel utterly insignificant and free, floating there in the water, gazing at the sky, thinking. You can feel wonderfully superior once you hit dry land, knowing, as others cannot, that you've been free for a minute and came back of your own volition. I think that Frannie knows the value of pulling away from this scene we work in. It isn't always healthy."

In the memory book Tenn kept on Frances Sternhagen, there was no darkness or doubt: Frannie was perpetually sunny and balanced and ready to work. Frannie was representative of all that Tenn hoped he could become, and the pages of the memory book were all happy and full of rites free of superstition. It surprised Frannie that Tenn never mentioned the fact that she had six children with Thomas Carlin, that the family was raised in New Rochelle, and that Frannie's life, both in and out of the theater, revolved around these seven people and the house they shared. "I always felt," Frannie told me, "that everything I did, or wanted to do, was filtered first through what was needed at home, by the needs of the children and my husband. Maybe my superstition was that if I always thought fully and lovingly about my family, everything else would take care of itself. All would be well."

Frannie's church attendance, her walk to a nearby body of water for a swim, her reading, her particular rites of life, were all to make herself a stronger and better mother, person, and, finally, actress. "Whatever I do in the day," she told me, "goes into the mix and winds up on the stage, so I knew I had to watch what entered my head and my heart. I didn't want to spoil. I only wanted to bring good into a situation."

Perpetually curious, Frannie continues to study other religions and philosophies, and while she treasures her daily Mass and the prayers that came to her as a new Catholic, she picks up bits and pieces that help her "get it going and get it together." She is all about action, direct but polite, no flab, no fuss. One friend noted that when Frannie developed celiac disease, and could no longer consume gluten, it was probably only another attempt on her part to streamline and condense her life; there was now more time to focus on the things that mattered; fewer foods to worry about, more time at hand. Frannie is very much about getting on with things.

The only thing about her life shared with me that caused her pain was the alcoholism of her husband, particularly when she realized that a letter he wrote to alcohol, on the advice of a counselor, was a passionate, unbridled love letter. "I don't know if he ever felt as ardently for me as he did alcohol," Frannie confessed, "and it hurt me; it embarrassed me. It was full and free and unashamed, and Tom was often shy and reserved, so this was a very concerted effort, a break from his normal means. I still wonder if there is a human being on earth who could inspire so much devotion and dependency. I guess I always will."

Thomas Carlin died, of a heart attack, at 11:11 a.m., a time and a numerical construction that continue to haunt and follow Frannie. Once when we were together, racing toward Grand Central Station, where she hoped to catch a train home to New Rochelle, she glanced at her watch. She stopped, stunned and shocked. Her watch read 11:11, and it gave her pause. November 11th is also a reminder, and, perhaps, a prayer, a rite of passage, something to help her begin to keep living, to keep going.

"I think lies of a certain nature are better than truth," Frannie said one day. She was thinking of a time when her presence in the hospital with her young son was forcing him to stay awake so he could be with her. Frannie didn't want to leave him, but she recognized that he needed sleep, so she lied and told him it was better that she leave. He slept, but Frannie wept once she was away from the side of her child. This was, to her, the good lie. "There has never been a trying time that didn't push me toward the good things that would help me and others get through them. Maybe it's my German background, but when a challenge arises, I think to myself that it should be investigated, studied, pondered, conquered. I never come out the other end of it anything but better."

To watch Frannie was a distinct and intelligent pleasure for Tenn. He felt he could see her brain at work, that her intelligence—one he described as "astringent"—fueled her every action. "Her control of her self and her material," Tenn told me, "is so firm—so rooted in theatrical correctness and her own sanity—that I immediately relax when she commands a stage, because I know that energy will be directed in the right places. No actress can elevate meretricious theater, but a good actress can elevate *me*, momentarily, from a meretricious theatrical experience. And Frannie has done this for me many times. What I always feel is that she focuses well and intelligently; she shares fully and freely; she laughs at the right things and the right people; she knows when to leave when a scene isn't good."

Tenn paused for a moment and then laughed, solidly and loudly. "She also has," he continued, "and this took me by surprise, a great ass. Watch her in *Outland,* a perfectly outré sci-fi thing with Sean Connery.

She runs with great grace and alacrity through a labyrinth of hallways and hairy men, and in these white pants one glimpses a perfectly wonderful ass. I was looking at hers; not at Sean Connery's.

"So," Tenn surmised, "Frannie is also an agent of change."

Tenn smiled at the thought, then remembered another prayer of his childhood, one he never heard from his grandfather, in the city of St. Louis. It was a prayer for those persons going to sea. Tenn thought of it for Frannie Sternhagen the swimmer. Tenn could only recall snatches of it, because he never heard it offered in a church, but only in explanation by his grandfather and from reading the Book of Common Prayer:

We commend to Thy almighty protection, Thy servant, for whose preservation on the great deep our prayers are desired. Guard him, we beseech Thee, from the dangers of the sea, from sickness, from the violence of enemies, and from every evil to which he may be exposed. Conduct him in safety to the haven where he would be, with a grateful sense of Thy mercies.

"I offered that prayer to the memory of Hart Crane," Tenn told me, "wishing I had thought to utter it before he felt he needed to lose himself deep in the sea, to drown away whatever was pressing upon him. I offer it to Frances Sternhagen, who helps me to stay above the water, to place words, like stones, one on top of the other, to move forward, to begin again."

Tenn told me he would offer the prayer to no others.

"That prayer is taken," he told me. "My heart and its plea have done all they can."

Julie Harris was an actress who never worked with Tennessee Williams, save for a recording of *The Glass Menagerie* for which she took on the role of Laura. Tenn had few memories of it, as he exerted all of his energies and concerns toward Montgomery Clift, who, as Tom, sputtered and frayed and held everyone in the shaky palm of his hand. "I would look at him," Tenn remembered, "and think to myself, 'Not only can he not play this part, or any part, but he is worthless at living.' And near him, almost always, would be Julie, a hand at his back, on his arm, smiling at him. She was serving a purpose for him similar to what Jessica had done for me: holding him up, helping him to see what he had been, nursing him through."

Harris had created pages in Tenn's theatrical memory book almost from the onset of his own New York debut. A costume designer of "a malignant camp sensibility" told him of a marvelous and unformed young actress who was a member of the company of Eva Le Gallienne's *Alice in Wonderland.* That production appeared in 1947, and it was approximately one year later that Tenn had an audience with Le Gallienne. The two of them discussed Julie Harris.

"What I told him then," Le Gallienne remembered, "was that the intention was there, but the equipment was lacking. The voice was inadequate." Tenn recalled that another "power" in the theater referred to Harris as "an unshelled peanut," dry and perhaps void of a center or substance.

Harris continued to work.

One of the happiest times in Tenn's life was his 1949 revision of *Summer and Smoke,* composed by typewriter and occasionally by longhand at one end of a dining table. At the other end sat Carson McCullers, who was laboriously adapting her novel *The Member of the Wedding* to the stage. Both plays were suffused with longing—of their playwrights as well as their protagonists—and both were, like the prayers and rites of Tenn's childhood, progressive and fearful and full of stones laid, metaphorical linens folded and applied, flowers plunged through psychic Styrofoam.

"If I reread *Summer and Smoke,*" Tenn remembered, "I can feel, and almost see, the writer that I was in that time and at that place. Alma moves fearfully and slowly but purposefully toward her desire. Alma comes to respect her need for love, for physical pleasure, for an acceptance of her gifts, no matter how niggardly or unnecessary they may appear. Alma is a woman who would have no problem finding a place on altar guilds or prayer councils, and her baked goods would always find a place at the tables of the best clubs, but her amatory gifts go begging, and her carnal desires, which she examines and recognizes in solitude, in darkness, grow stronger and hungrier as they find themselves attended to by only her own hands and ministrations. Alma moves slowly, each step a brick, perfectly shaped and sanded and placed in a wall that blocks what she finds unpleasant, and then, later in the play, each step a small scalpel that scoops away the plaster and the bricks of this wall, through which she hopes she can walk and find what she needs."

Alma Winemiller has at her core a young woman named Julie Harris.

The prologue to *Summer and Smoke* begins in the park near the angel of the fountain, at dusk. It is May, in the

> first few years of this century. . . . Alma, as a child of ten, comes into the scene. She wears a middy blouse and has ribboned braids. She already has the dignity of an adult; there is a quality of extraordinary delicacy and tenderness or spirituality in her, which must set her distinctly apart from other children. She has a habit of holding her hands, one cupped under the other in a way similar to that of receiving the wafer at Holy Communion. This is a habit that will remain with her as an adult. She stands like that in front of the stone angel for a few moments; then bends to drink at the fountain.

I brought a copy of *Summer and Smoke* to my meetings with Tenn, and he took the book and pulled the pages back, cracking the spine, and reading it as if it were something he had forgotten, or a work he had only heard of and had finally obtained. He read and reread passages, and pointed to the prologue. "If I spaced this differently," he said, "and added a few things, it could be a poem. Was I imagining Julie Harris when I wrote this? When I showed my pages to Carson—and she showed hers to me—did my Alma mingle and mate with her Frankie Addams?"

Tenn could not answer that question, but he recalled that when he was introduced to Harris prior to the premiere of *The Member of the Wedding,* he felt he was seeing a version—short-haired, blunt-fingered, and freckled—of his Alma. "There is a radiation of goodness and urgency that surrounds Julie Harris," Tenn told me. "She is fervent and fulsome, and there is an element of hysteria that never fully develops into anything dangerous or destructive, because, I believe, once she steps toward the lip of oblivion or unwise action, her love of life and people, her basic decency, pulls her back, and she again walks among us."

This element of hysteria gave to Harris a sheen of sadness that Tenn could always sense and identify. When he later learned that Harris had lost a brother to suicide—as Tenn had lost his sister to medical tampering and madness—he felt a stronger bond with her, and whenever he witnessed Harris in a scene that called for a sense of attraction to or

Julie Harris was clear of prejudice and pretension, wise, and unafraid to tell Tennessee how to improve his work and his life. Watching her rehearse as Frankie Addams in Carson McCullers's *Member of the Wedding* was, for Tenn, a master class in acting, writing, living.

dependency on another person, he was moved to write "strongly and well." Harris transmitted to Tenn both a sense of attachment and the "shattering sense of disorientation we all know and feel when we are snatched from home, or our concept of home. She has the most incredible ability to make me feel the utter barrenness of life that has lost its bearings, and then she can smile or begin again, and I want to live another thirty years and see what might happen."

Tenn joked that I was "the King of Prefaces," but he labeled himself, among other things, "the Regent of Revisions": he loved nothing more than the act of deconstructing an earlier play, short story, or essay. Maria

St. Just recounted how she had once found him, in his studio in Key West, revising an essay he had written for the *New York Times* to commemorate the opening of *Orpheus Descending*. When St. Just pointed out what she saw as the absurdity of revising, "tampering with," a piece that had been published months before and was now lining cages or had itself been revised into pulp or mulch, Tenn's response was quick and blunt: "It is never absurd to try to get it right."

Words on a page and thoughts in one's mind, Tenn believed, should always be revised, improved, analyzed, explained. A writer's work could always be improved, a thought clarified. Revisions were "metaphysical and spiritual" as well as literary, and he was heavily influenced by the working habits and writing style of McCullers, a woman Tenn admitted could be difficult, but who worked "with the ferocity of a demon and the delicacy of an angel," and under whose spell Tenn had finalized the script of the play.

At lunch one day in the French Quarter, Tenn thought it best to invoke his friend and "geographical collaborator" Carson McCullers by quoting from memory (so "ruined but still holding the greatest of the gems") the lines of her prose that had meant the most to him. With the exception of the opening line from her *Ballad of the Sad Café* ("The town itself is dreary"), it is impossible to find any of Tenn's quotes in the collected works of Carson McCullers. It is also possible that McCullers would resent the synopses Tenn offered of her novels and short stories; but in the months and years following my time with Tenn, as I read and reread works he had told me to study and emulate, as I looked through stacks in libraries and private collections, it became clear that Tenn had deeply personal relationships and reactions to works that moved him, and he reshaped and rewrote their words to suit his own needs.

The Member of the Wedding began, for Tenn, with this paragraph:

I wonder if you can remember that green and crazy summer when Frankie turned twelve years old and realized that she was a person who was joined to nothing at all. It was a terribly long summer, as all seasons are unbearably long to the young, when time is abundant and choices are few, and she could see that during the weeks of that summer she had belonged to no club, was a member of nothing, and was not even comfortable with her position in her odd and small family. Frankie's mother was dead and her father was absent, forgetful, busy, and like most adults around children, uncomfortable, impatient, unfeeling unless there was some extremity of emotion. The trees that summer were dizzying in their color and their size—Frankie wanted to feel, and to be, as rich and as ripe as those trees. The sun would hit those trees and you could be blinded. The same sun would bear down on the grey sidewalks of the town and they would glitter like glass or the baubles Frankie had won one earlier, better summer at the State Fair. Dizzying, dazzling. Lovely words. Lovely ideas. Would they ever apply to Frankie?

It was McCullers, Tenn claimed, who wrote the following:

Do not search for the human soul. It moves with alacrity and capriciousness, and it does not wish to be located, looked over. It operates best when its owner is in doubt, plagued with questions, stranded. Some believe that it hovers above a person, visible to mystics and saints and people trained in the dark arts, but more believe that it is deep within, and you can feel it react and constrict when tragedy approaches or when great happiness is felt. Part of the soul atrophies in moments of great extremity, and if it is subject to too much, it dies. The soul cannot endure too much sadness or happiness. Its ideal home is one of equilibrium. No one has yet determined what the soul actually does for a person, but like an appendix or tonsils, it lies there, thought of, written about, pondered over, waiting to explode or disappear.

These words, these thoughts, which Tenn believed derived from his friend, often kept him focused and hoping to write. McCullers's influence on Tenn was, in his own words, formidable—she was a writer of extremity, as he was, and her ability to "observe, fully and painfully, a person in isolation" was her greatest gift as a writer. Her greatest gift as a housemate—and as a person who shared his writing space—was her painstaking approach to each and every word, every single sentence and paragraph, even though she was adapting a work that had already worked well as a novel, and whose contours and shadows she knew well.

"She approached the work as one totally new to her," Tenn remembered, "and she agonized over the placement of words, emphasis, the ideal place for a blackout or a dash of humor or a sparkle of violence or melodrama." McCullers loved melodrama, but only if it was earned. "She used to say to me," Tenn continued, "that if you show a reader

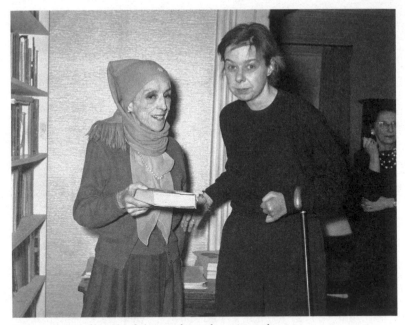

Carson McCullers (right) was the only writer whose company
Tennessee could tolerate when he was working, and his visit with her,
in Nantucket, remained one of the handful of happy times he could
recall. McCullers hosted a party in her Nyack home in 1959 for Isak
Dinesen (seen here, left), an occasion that was a bit grander than the
"fun squalor" of her times with Tennessee—but, she told him, his name
came up often during the festivities.

or an audience a baby-sized casket, and ten minutes later the group
begins to tell jokes or sing a hymn, that's melodrama, but it's earned.
People need to live again, to begin again, and they reach for whatever
represents for them life or color or the dazzle. 'Dazzle' to my mother
meant nice soap or perfume, gorgeous flowers in a bed outside or in her
best vase or on her bosom. Carefully applied powder and dinner with
a nice man. Life continues. The dazzle returns." For Carson it was the
company of a sympathetic listener, or a reader who had been moved
or altered by her work. She was devastated by failure, even if it was
imaginary, anticipated. She was convinced that the critics would savage her for being lazy by adapting her novel to the stage, so she typed
and she smoked and she sighed. Her most comfortable position was a
crouch in which she was warding off blows, and the blows were always
forthcoming, and they were always earned. She would reread her work

and wonder why she'd written a scene or a character as she had. While she could exhibit pride in certain sections of her work, more often than not she wished she could rewrite each book line by line. This obsession was one she shared with the man who sat opposite her at that table, keys clacking and pages coming at a fast pace.

"We could never have been so close for so long," Tenn said, "if we had been working on original pieces, but adaptation could survive the presence of another. Carson was moving her novel to the stage, and I was finalizing a play that had been in at least three different earlier versions. Carson would stop me every hour or so and ask me to read what she had done, and I would show her my pages. I knew that I was doing right by Miss Alma if Carson sniffled or if she told me that I was 'killing' her. And Frankie was the tomboy Alma might have been if she had not been raised in that oppressive, doily-infested house."

Tenn had made the acquaintance of Carson McCullers by writing her a fan letter, one as fulsome and sweet as the one I had written to him. "And mine was successful," he remembered, "as yours was. She could feel in me, as I did in you, a sympathetic reader, a seeker, someone lost and worth finding, someone with a soul contracting." Their earlier meeting, perhaps in 1946, was in Nantucket, and Tenn remembered those times as deliriously happy, full of "the dazzle": gorgeous weather, abundant food, the pages of pale judgment filling up daily, the company of people who fulfilled all mental and physical needs. Tenn was in love with "buoyant, brown" Pancho Rodriguez at that time, and the house at 31 Pine Street was full of laughter and argument and the scent of crab boil and patchouli, on which Carson was overly dependent. "The house was always full of patchouli clouds," Tenn recalled, "and the pocked wooden floors held a thin layer of patchouli dust. Our footprints were visible on the floor at all times, and every breeze, every move, sent it up in a sweet-smelling cyclone." In the kitchen on Pine Street, Carson experimented with odd dishes, like a soupy version of mashed potatoes into which were blended olives and onions, and Tenn, Carson, and Pancho would eat the concoction while reading aloud the works of Hart Crane, D. H. Lawrence, and Chekhov. "We would eat and drink and smoke and read," Tenn told me, "until Pancho would tug at the cuff of my pants, and then it was time to fuck." The curtains were light and made of linen and they floated on a breeze. "It was like the time on Royal Street," Tenn reminded me, "with the right breezes and good music—we had a record player on Pine Street, too—and soft, warm skin in the night. And cats." While the cats of Royal Street had mewled from below waiting for food, on Pine Street a rainstorm and a broken window convinced a pregnant cat to take up residence on Carson's bed, where she delivered her brood. "We cared for the kittens," Tenn said, "and to everything else, we could add tenderness to the season."

Tenn had been deeply affected by Carson's second novel, *Reflections in a Golden Eye,* for which he would later write an introduction. He made no attempt to quote from it, but he spoke at great length about the descriptions of Private Ellgee Williams, the soldier who stoked the desires of the sleepy Southern town.

"I felt she had found out about me," Tenn told me, "and was writing about someone I recognized. It felt as though portions of my journal had been purloined by this young girl, and I was amazed and embarrassed." While Tenn could criticize the fact that *Reflections,* like *Ballad of the Sad Café,* opened with a statement of the locale's dullness, he exulted over the descriptions of the town's foliage and the eyes and thoughts of its characters:

The soldier in this affair was Private Ellgee Williams. Often in the late afternoon he could be seen sitting alone on one of the benches that lined the sidewalk before the barracks. This was a pleasant place, as here there was a long double row of young maple trees that patterned the lawn and the walk with cool, delicate, windblown shadows. In the spring the leaves of the trees were a lucent green that as the hot months came took on a darker, restful hue. In late autumn they were flaming gold. Here Private Williams would sit and wait for the call to evening mess. He was a silent young soldier and in the barracks he had neither an enemy nor a friend. His round sunburned face was marked by a certain watchful innocence. His full lips were red and the bangs of his hair lay brown and matted on his forehead. In his eyes, which were of a curious blend of amber and brown, there was a mute expression that is found usually in the eyes of animals. At first glance Private Williams seemed a bit heavy and awkward in his bearing. But this was a deceptive impression; he moved with the silence and agility of a wild creature or a thief. Often soldiers who had thought themselves alone were startled to see him appear as from nowhere by their sides. His hands were small, delicately boned, and very strong. . . . Private Williams did not smoke, drink, fornicate, or gamble.

Although Tenn did not attempt to quote this passage from *Reflections in a Golden Eye,* he laughingly recalled that at the time the novel was written, he was certainly engaged in the four qualities that held no interest for his literary doppelgänger. "Oh, we smoked, and we drank, and we fornicated, and we gambled. Oh, how we gambled!"

In what way? I asked.

"In the only way that matters," Tenn replied. "With our hearts planted on the pale judgment, risking exposure and ridicule. Gambling it all, line by line, in a cloud of patchouli dust."

Tenn applied tiny but decisive cuts and the occasional "bloodletting" to the 1949 revision of *Summer and Smoke.* He gave to Alma a more delicate entrance, allowing her to build slowly toward her neurasthenia, which he felt had been too obvious in the premiere production, something that might have been attributable to the actress, Margaret Phillips, who created the role. "She was a lovely but certifiably insane woman," Tenn told me. "She accepted direction as if it were a dagger to the heart. She took everything personally, instantly. Her Alma was ready for the hat factory in scene 1; there was no layer of Southern proprietary holding in this cascade of illness and regret and passion that was building and boiling. She was oozing—no, she was drenched— once the lights were up."

When I met with José Quintero, the director who staged the revival at Circle in the Square four years after the failed Broadway production, he remembered the alterations to the play as thematic rather than as literary, and his recollection was that Tenn wrote the original version of *Summer and Smoke* in the presence of McCullers, not the revision, which was actually brought forth in the rehearsals for the revival, which now featured a young and brilliant actress named Geraldine Page.

"I think you need to realize something," Quintero told me. "Tenn's chronology is very romantic, and he revises it as often as he does his work. I understand that he needs to think of that time with Carson as the time during which he improved or 'saved' *Summer and Smoke,* but the play was pretty much set by the time I was called in to direct it. We altered a lot, and the name Julie Harris was bandied about a lot by Ten-

José Quintero, the passionate and incisive director of the off-Broadway revival of *Summer and Smoke*. Tennessee felt comfortable with Quintero, and allowed him to make suggestions and revisions to his play. "I think it can be said that José improves people," Tennessee said.

nessee, much to the annoyance of Gerry, who was convinced that we wanted her to emulate Julie. Tenn needed to destroy the memory of the original production, which I had seen, and which was not good, so he began to speak of the 'restoration,' as he called it, in much larger terms, with entire acts and whole pages ripped out and apart. But the script did not change much. The emphasis changed entirely, but I don't recall great changes in the text."

Tenn's notes for *Summer and Smoke* are exacting, and Quintero did his best, in the cramped playing space of the original, downtown Circle in the Square, to accommodate them. Tenn wrote:

As the concept of a design grows out of reading a play I will not do more than indicate what I think are the most essential points.

First of all—*The Sky*. There must be a great expanse of sky so that the entire action of the play takes place against it. This is true of interior as well as exterior scenes. But in fact there are no really interior scenes, for the walls are omitted or just barely suggested by certain necessary fragments such as might be needed to hang a picture or to contain a doorframe.

During the day scenes the sky should be a pure and intense blue (like the sky of Italy as it is so faithfully represented in the religious paintings of the Renaissance) and costumes should be selected to form dramatic color contrasts to this intense blue which the figures stand against. (Color harmonies and other visual effects are tremendously important.)

In the night scenes, the more familiar constellations, such as Orion and the Great Bear and the Pleiades, are clearly projected on the night sky, and above them, splashed across the top of the cyclorama, is the nebulous radiance of the Milky Way. Fleecy cloud forms may also be projected on this cyclorama and made to drift across it.

So much for *The Sky*.

Now we descend to the so-called interior sets of the play. There are two of these "interior" sets, one being the parlor of an Episcopal Rectory and the other the home of a doctor next door to the Rectory. The architecture of these houses is barely suggested but is of an American Gothic design of the Victorian era. There are no actual doors or windows or walls. Doors and windows are represented by delicate frameworks of Gothic design. These frames have strings of ivy clinging to them, the leaves of emerald and amber. . . . There should be a fragment of wall in back of the Rectory sofa, supporting a romantic landscape in a gilt frame. In the doctor's house there should be a section of wall to support the chart of anatomy. Chirico has used fragmentary walls and interiors in a very evocative way in his painting called *Conversation Among the Ruins*.

Now we come to the main exterior set which is a promontory in a park or public square in the town of Glorious Hill. Situated on this promontory is a fountain in the form of a stone angel, in a gracefully crouching position with wings lifted and her hands held together to form a cup from which water flows, a public drinking fountain. The stone angel of the fountain should probably be elevated so that it appears in the background of the interior scenes as a symbolic figure (Eternity) brooding over the course of the play. *This entire exterior set may be on an upper level, above that of the two fragmentary interiors.* I would like all three units to form an harmonious whole like one complete picture rather than three separate ones. . . .

Everything possible should be done to give an unbroken fluid quality to the sequence of scenes.

Finally, the matter of music. One basic theme should recur and the points of recurrence have been indicated here and there in the stage directions.

The notes are marked "Rome, 1948," but Quintero recalls those directions being expanded for the revival in 1952. In New Orleans, in 1982, Tenn recalled those stage notes, and told me it was one of his most autobiographical pieces of writing.

The rectory described in the stage notes is the one in which he spent those formative years of his childhood, haunting the dark, oiled hallways, hiding beneath Gothic eaves, eavesdropping on adults and watching the actions of the ladies of the church.

The sky, that oppressive sky "as large and as unyielding and unfeeling as the back of an absentminded God," was an image he claimed he cadged from McCullers. "All those green, dizzying summers that Carson wrote of," he recounted, "all those slanting rays of the sun, were held against and fueled from an expansive sky, and the sky is a judgment, an eternal witness to all of our struggles. I came to feel that Frankie Addams looked at the sky and saw it as proof that the world was large—it stretched for millions of miles, perhaps even back in time. There had to be places and people to which she could escape and find friendship and acceptance and membership in a club or a society, and the friends you did have didn't die suddenly, and people weren't betrayed and people didn't lie. I always felt that Carson's people were always in the longest line of all time—like something from a George Tooker painting—and the window would slam shut when they finally had their number called. Horribly hopeful and naïve, you just held your breath for the disappointment that was to come.

"My Alma, on the other hand," he continued, "sees the sky above Glorious Hill as a rebuke. Look at this tiny toy town of perfect lawns and manicured women and order and balance applied to all of those things for which there can never be order and balance. The body is dead and now lies in a room attended to by people who cover it in linen and bathe its limbs and mutter prayers for its proper deliverance. The body is still dead, and its survivors still devastated, but the prayers continue. Food is delivered, comfort murmured, backs and hands patted. Casseroles and cards and comforting words. A beautifully handwritten note at the top of which a hole has been punched, a piece of pink ribbon pulled through it: a prayer for healing you can hang from a wall. All of this comfort, all of this attention comes down upon you and smothers you and ties you closer to the town; your roots sink ever deeper into its soil, even though you never felt loved or welcomed here. And there is the huge sky, laughingly reminding you that there is so much out there in the world beyond Glorious Hill, places to go, people to meet, passions to be plumbed, and here you are, a ribboned prayer on the wall, a corset to be tied, a church social to be attended, at which you will serve sandwiches without crust or complaint, and you die some more, your soul constricted beneath that girdle and beneath that sky.

"And that is Alma," Tenn told me, "and that is me."

Carson McCullers gave him that image, and Tenn claimed that Julie Harris magnified it, first with her performance in *The Member of the Wedding,* and then through other transformational appearances that made him think of her as an emotional pilgrim, completely lost until she is able to inhabit a character, a person utterly real to her, and to whom she is in complete service.

Tenn imagined that Julie Harris, like Frances Sternhagen, came from wealth and the protections it offered. He envied her Grosse Pointe, Michigan, upbringing, her attendance at Yale, her ability to appear unaffected by the mundane practicalities of daily life—bills, meetings, meals, frayed furniture, appliances. "I think that she rises above it all," Tenn believed, "and casts aside what she can't—or shouldn't—use in her work."

It is true that Harris was born in Grosse Pointe and attended the Yale School of Drama, but she laughed when I told her that Tenn imagined her untouched by life. "I happily live," she told me, in a suite at the Hotel Wyndham, where she resided during the short run, in 1991, of *Lucifer's Child,* a one-woman show about Isak Dinesen, "and I also happily bear the scars for having done so."

Tenn had purchased a gift for Julie in the French Quarter. In a voodoo shop, he passed up a number of amulets, skulls, animal skins, beads, and candles to find a tiny and lovely photograph of a dark-skinned girl encased in bright material. It was clearly handmade, and Tenn asked the proprietor about its provenance. "It's from Milagro," he was told. "What does that mean?" Tenn asked. "It means it's powerful," was the response, so Tenn bought it for Julie, and I held it for almost nine years before giving it to her.

She wept and told me that she had recently attended church services for the Easter season. "In one church," she remembered, "the cross had been made bare, the Christ figure removed. This was not a time for sadness, for he had arisen and was in his place. He will be back on that cross in time, of course, for us to look upon and grimace and love and try to understand, but for now he's away and all is well. I look at this," she said, looking down at the icon, "and I know that Tennessee Williams is dead, and I know that this is devastating to me, but he's on no cross at all—he is arisen, and he arises every time a play of his is read in a bedroom or a classroom or a library; every time it is produced in a basement or a high school or a theater. They can't hurt my friend anymore. He's gone from all of this."

TO FULLY APPRECIATE a Julie Harris or a Frances Sternhagen, Tenn explained to me, one must have in one's company a Kim Hunter. "I adore Kim," Tenn told me, "and there is about her a rudimentary quality that is very appealing—and very necessary at times. But there has never been a sense of liftoff with Kim. She is very dutiful and very intelligent, but there is nothing within her that wants to push at the confines of a character or the wall of the theater. She is very pliant, and I learned a lot about life and women and the theater working with her, but it has never occurred to me to seek to inhabit her skin or mind to find a woman to speak to me."

It requires a certain bravery—or recklessness—to read the above directly to the woman about whom it was said, but I did so, in the summer of 1989, in Hunter's apartment at 42 Commerce Street, at the top of an incredibly steep staircase, where she stood, smiling, radiant, asking, "Is this intimidating or what? I think it would be rude to not wait for you here, but it is very off-putting." Hunter and her husband, Robert Emmett, welcomed me and talked about Tennessee Williams and everything else that came up in a seven-hour conversation. Hunter, who was an avid cook, had prepared a lovely meal, which she claims was inspired entirely by Paul Bocuse. (Hunter had also written an autobiographical cookbook called *Loose in the Kitchen,* a copy of which she gave me before I left.) I liked her instantly, as Tenn told me I would. Theirs had been a short but intense time spent together—the production of *A Streetcar Named Desire,* in which she created the part of Stella—but they were always able to pick up quickly and intimately, usually through a late-night phone call, when Tenn would call and confess that he felt lost. (Tenn may have never inhabited Hunter's skin or mind, but he frequently inhabited her ear and her apartment, where he was cared for, listened to, loved.) Tenn had explained to me that he found her "loving and rational and calm," but Hunter scoffed at that and said that she thought that Tenn called her because she represented a happy and productive time.

"The time of *Streetcar,*" she remembered, "was blazing with life and work, good work, and success and fulfillment, and he could call me and we could remember that time. If it got him back to a place where he could work or think or feel good about himself, I'm happy about that, but I'm not a pillar of sanity or balance. I was a memory of a happy time, and I don't think he felt comfortable picking up a phone and calling Jessie or Karl [Malden] or Marlon—and even before Vivien Leigh died, Tenn didn't have a rapport with her. He thought she was a bit of a machine, an acting machine, and she didn't have time for his doubts or concerns. She had her own problems; she didn't have time for Tennessee Williams's problems. I didn't, either, but I loved him."

When Kim Hunter came into the life of Tennessee Williams, she was known as a film actress who had been signed to a contract with David O. Selznick, and who had appeared in *The Seventh Victim,* which Tenn loved as a camp horror film, and the Michael Powell–Emeric Pressburger film *Stairway to Heaven,* with its Art Deco ethereality of the afterlife. Both films amused Tenn, but he couldn't quite see how the comely, slightly round young actress featured in them could be his Stella Kowalski.

"Kazan was mad for her," Tenn told me. "I don't know how they met or when, but she was presented to me as a virtual *fait accompli.*" Irene Mayer Selznick, who produced *Streetcar,* claims that Hunter was a "property" much bragged about by her ex-husband, David O. Selznick, and that is how she came to meet her and have her read for the role. "Elia Kazan," Irene Selznick told me forcibly, "took what was presented to him, and I was the very active producer of that play."

Hunter herself couldn't recall how she came to be cast in the play, but she was very open about the fact that she and Kazan conducted an affair—not terribly discreetly—during the time of *Streetcar,* and the fact embarrassed her. "It was foolish and very dramatic," she remembered. "I was a very young twenty-five, with one marriage collapsing,

Kim Hunter was a young mother overseeing a hectic household, but she always made time and space for Tennessee, inviting him for meals and holding him up when he doubted his talent. "She was, I guess, a sort of sister," Tennessee said.

and my career seemed to be without focus. Kazan was all about focus, and he passed it on to me. He *pasted* it on me, and he got me into the Actors Studio, where he and Robert Lewis really taught me what acting was about. They opened my mind; they told me what I should read and see and hear. All of that was good. I should have left it at that, but I also fell madly for Kazan, which was easy to do. He shaped me on the stage, and he shaped me in the bedroom. That experience—that experience of *A Streetcar Named Desire*—completely changed me in every way, artistically, sexually, intellectually."

Both Tenn and Hunter conceded that her performance grew incredibly under Kazan's tutelage. "There was an unabashed amateurishness to Kim's performance in the early days," Tenn remembered. "She had it in her head that Stella was nervous, jumpy, and so she remained—one note and one dimension—for the length of the play. I admired her tenacity and her ability to concentrate on that one aspect, but the performance was abrasive and thin. Whatever Kazan did, it worked."

"He spoke to me as an adult," Hunter revealed. "He sat me down and explained the full text of the play, and he compared the four [major] characters in the play to people we knew in common. Kazan believed that there were a limited number of people, or archetypes, in the world, and our individual personalities determined how we lived and how our personalities were revealed. He allowed me to see that I shared a great deal in common with Stella. I also came to see some similarities I shared with Blanche. He led me to realize that no one, and no action, could or should be alien to me."

The conversations I had with Hunter were very much like the phone calls Tenn shared with her when he called "deep in the blues" and needed some balance. "He wanted to hear that he was a good writer," Hunter said, "and he wanted me to know that I had meant something to him, that he meant something to me. He wanted to talk about our human bond, the world being connected by our similarities, our shared fears and dreams. I think he called me when he had gotten a bad review or he had been rejected by a lover. He needed to hear from someone who looked up to him, who wouldn't judge him. He needed to hear from someone who had grown up—grown in every way—right in front of him, and because of one of his plays."

Kim Hunter openly addressed the issue of her not having a sense of liftoff, in Tenn's eyes. "I would have to agree with him," she confessed, "but let's look at the facts." After the Broadway production of *Streetcar*, Hunter gave a praised performance in *Darkness at Noon*, Sidney Kingsley's adaptation of Arthur Koestler's novel, and another in the film version of *Streetcar*, for which she won the Oscar as Best Supporting Actress. "There was a good and clear line going," Hunter recalled. "And then the bottom fell out of everything."

The event to which she referred was the blacklist: Hunter's name appeared in *Red Channels,* and film producers were urged to reconsider casting her. In 1953 alone, she knew of seven film roles for which she was wanted (including the one ultimately played by Donna Reed in *From Here to Eternity*) and about which she received polite but evasive calls changing the dates and times. Soon the calls ended altogether. Hunter found work in the theater, but films and television were almost completely blocked to her. Her role in the 1956 film *Storm Center* was given to her solely because Bette Davis (an actress who admired Hunter and who had accepted her Oscar) demanded her inclusion. "Bette Davis told the producers and the studio that I was in or she was out," Hunter told me. "She thought that the blacklist would only be broken if the stars, the people with power, stood up and refused to be bullied any longer. That is what ultimately happened, and Bette was among the first, at least in my experience, to go to bat for actors." Davis also wrote letters—and checks—on Hunter's behalf in the hopes of getting her back on track. When I spoke to Bette Davis by phone—about Hunter and about other things—she agreed with Tenn's assessment of her friend's career, but she was quick to point out the circumstances. "You have to think of Kim's career as having suffered a sort of amputation," Davis told me. "We will never know what she might have done if that ludicrous blacklist hadn't happened. Those were years where she would have grown in film roles, elevated to starring roles on the stage, but she was pushed to the side, was a bit scared. Stunted! That's what I mean to say. She was an injured actress."

One other person sent checks and notes of encouragement to Hunter during the time of the blacklist: Tennessee Williams. Hunter recalled that a recurring line from all of the notes was "I need you; hold on."

Hunter did not wish to reveal too much about herself to me, or to anyone else. When she looked at notes I had made of my time with other actresses, she admitted that she would never be as forthcoming. "If I wanted to tell as much as those women," she told me, "I would write my own book. I'll tell you some things, and that's it."

Those areas she was willing to discuss—her affair with Kazan, her phone calls with Tenn, and the spotty but loving relationship they had—led to free and full conversations, but she was far more comfortable talking about books and plays and food, and I was invited back many times to the apartment. And on one occasion, when a play she especially liked, called *The Sum of Us,* was playing at the Cherry Lane Theatre—which was housed in the building next to Hunter's—she invited me into her bedroom. "Come and lie down," she said. "Don't be nervous."

There was nothing romantic about the request: she wanted me to listen to the play, which reverberated through the wall above her bed. On several occasions, we would lie there and listen to the muffled second act, and occasionally Robert Emmett would join us; but before the conclusion and the curtain calls, he would repair to the kitchen. When the play was over, and Hunter and I would leave the bedroom, we would find dessert and a *New York Times* at our places on the table, waiting for us. I loved being in their company, and I trusted everything she told me about the theater, even as I regretted that she didn't want to say anything more about her life.

We were talking one evening over dinner when I mentioned my bizarre living arrangements. I was still in my early months of living in

New York, and was staying with Dorothy Hart Drew. When I mentioned the artist's name, Hunter literally gasped, then looked in disbelief at her husband. It had been Dorothy Hart Drew, under the direction of Congressman George Dondero, who had written a letter to Hunter in 1952, urging her to name names to the House Un-American Activities Committee, as well as to "repent" her ways. In time a call came to Hunter's apartment: it was Drew, castigating her for taking her "God-given talent" and allowing it to be misused by Communists. Hunter told the woman on the phone, "a certifiable loon," to go immediately to hell.

Remembering the conversation—and the woman—Hunter began to laugh, a lovely, girlish laugh, then a boisterous, full-throated one. "What are the odds?" she asked me and her husband. "What are the fucking odds? He's living with Dorothy Hart Drew. Sometimes I don't think life is a mystery at all. It's a slapstick comedy constantly replayed, over and over! And here we are again!"

Tenn and I discussed all of these things—and all of these people—on one afternoon in New Orleans. Clearly inspired, he returned to his hotel room and composed a poem about our conversation, and he showed it to me, some parts typed, some handwritten, lines crossed out, written over, inserted, transposed. I could not read it, so Tenn read it aloud to me, and I wrote it down.

When I was very young, I would sit, alone and in the darkness,
Facing a first day of school, or a funeral, or a baptism,
And I would not know what to expect or how to behave.
And I would think of you.
You were the memory I called on.
I don't know why I had this ritual, alone and in the darkness,
But I was afraid, and I believed that some ritual, like all the rituals,
Would help me to make some sense of what was to come.
And I would think of you.
You were the memory I called on.
Nothing beneath this cruel and blind sky can ever hurt a person,
Who has seen the light and the color and the heat that comes from this
*   sky.*
And you saw the gifts and the blessings in the funeral, the baptism,
*   the beating.*

Anything can be altered with kindness, a scent, a reading from Crane
    or a Sousa waltz.
If I can't imagine any of these things,
If I can't recall the horns of that Gershwin record,
Or the poem about creative manifestation,
Or the scent of my baby's back, scrubbed, smooth, touched by breeze
    and affection.
I'm going to think of you.
You're going to be the memory I call on.
When I was very young and sat alone and in the darkness,
I could not have known that you would be a part of my life, invested
    in my heart.
I imagined you on those dark nights, and that was my ritual.
Creating friends, partners, who would know what to say and how to
    feel.
Who would dance in a cloud of perfumed powder,
Who would write a sentence about love that could help me accept that
    I had seen it,
Who would display it toward another person so that I could accept that
    it was real.
Who would give to me, just hand it to me, and say "I love you."
I'm thinking of you.
You are my memory.
There seemed so much time then, when I dreamed you, in the
    darkness.
I was frightened of time, then, not knowing what it would introduce
    or take away.
But I'm afraid now as I watch it recede, slink away, droop like a
    drunken come-on or an old man's neck.
I want to bring it back and tell it what I've seen, through your eyes.
I want to bring it back and sing it the songs I've heard from your lips.
I want to bring it back and take care of it, as you took care of me.
When the curtains lifted and brought us the scent of sand and salt.
When the words came easy and often so that we could tell each other
    how lucky we were.
When we could talk and no one was alone and in the darkness.
I will always think of you.
You are always a part of my memory.

Because of you there will be hope for the frightened child in the dark.
They haven't met you yet, but they will.
They may have to dream you into existence, but they'll find you.
Traces of you will be in their happy memories.
The days may dawn as a judgment—of our souls, our work, our right
*   to live,*
And the nights may press down on us like a bad debt,
But I go back to the young person I think I once was,
The young person who dreamed you up and then found you.
I will always think of you.
You are my memory.

Tenn told me that he wrote the poem as if imagining a sturdy, bare piece of tapestry. Julie Harris was a large and strong needle, made of gold, and Frances Sternhagen was a strong string of brilliant thread, multicolored, that he used as he plunged the needle through the tapestry and created the poem. Kim Hunter was a bright and luminous white thread, needed to set off the colors around it.

I closed my book, hugged Tenn in Jackson Square, found my car, and drove home.

Eleven

I HAD NOT BEEN home for more than thirty minutes when the telephone rang. It was Tenn, and he was apologetic: he felt he had terminated our conversation far too abruptly. Might he explain why?

I propped the receiver against the left side of my head and wrote what
he said, but he was speaking to me from a location full of voices and
music and clattering plates and cutlery, and his thoughts raced about
madly. My notes are full of dashes and dots, an improvised shorthand
that make it impossible for me to quote him directly. Here is the essence
of what he told me that night in that phone call.

The discussion of Carson McCullers and the pairing of his mind
with that of another writer had led his thoughts to William Inge. The
life and death of William Inge weighed upon Tenn tremendously, and
the prayers and rituals he had cobbled together to help him write and
learn to live by the lies that fuel our days, the "manic and masturba-
tory steps and apologies for surviving," were always accompanied by an
image of Inge's haunted and beautiful eyes, clear and long-lashed; his
arms, which Tenn remembered as lightly furred and warm and strong;
and that high forehead, like something out of a Tenniel drawing by way
of an Arrow shirt advertisement.

"Bill and I were rubes," Tenn told me. "Rustic and golden by way
of the fire of ambition and sexual fear, and both somewhat retarded,

in a tertiary manner, by means of our time spent in the Midwest, a dry and flat terrain in which secretive souls such as ours could never hide and touch and dream and compose the life we hoped to live." Tenn had benefited from his time in the South, "full of shadow and moist heat and the forced intimacies born out of a need to remain cool, to get through the night." The South had been the "great rock" for Tenn, the rock upon which he felt he could build his new identity, and he liked to think that he was able, fitfully, to provide Bill Inge some shadow time beneath his rock, a "splotch of darkness in which he could relax and reveal himself to me, to himself. Call me St. Peter," Tenn quipped, "and from beneath my rock, Bill Inge began to be built."

Tenn and Bill Inge met in St. Louis in 1944, when he considered himself a "raw and angry" person, bruised by the reaction of Boston critics and audiences to *Battle of Angels,* and conflicted about his brief time in Hollywood, where he had loved the weather, the money, the easy physicality and humor of his Italian lover, and access to MGM and routes and locales that held so many memories for him of films he had loved. Foremost on his mind, however, was that he was a failure as a writer. "I felt terribly old," he told me, remembering himself at thirty-three, "the words and the characters so close to the surface, so ready to be exposed and shared, and yet I knew I hadn't been fully free with whatever talent I might have had."

Inge, himself a frustrated writer, was working as a reporter and critic for the *St. Louis Star-Times* and requested an interview with Williams, "a young and promising playwright sprung from our own environs," as Tenn remembered it laughingly. "As you know," Tenn told me, "and as I keep saying, I am very disingenuous when I am being feted." Tenn agreed to the interview and remembered the electric current that coursed between and around the two men, who began their time together in great propriety, sitting in separate spaces in the famed S curve taught to aspiring models and proper young ladies at the John Robert Powers school, smoking, smiling—emblems of professionalism. This pose broke down in what Tenn recalled as less than an hour, and they became "fast and rampant," exchanging "sensations and fluids, and vowing to each other a devotion to a prepared and examined death." Tenn paused for a moment and told me to be sure and write the words as a title: *A Prepared and Examined Death.*

William Inge, a natural playwright, but a man, according to Tennessee, utterly alien in the world, afraid of virtually everything. They were only comfortable in Inge's apartment, discussing art, theater, and music.

"I won't hide anything from you," Tenn said. "I'll tell you everything. Perhaps it will be of some help to you."

When Tenn first walked into the small apartment kept by William Inge in St. Louis, he noticed a piece of onionskin paper, folded in half and taped to the wall above his typewriter. On the page was written *"Le monde est fait pour aboutir à un beau livre."* The translation: *"The world was made in order to result in a beautiful book."* The quote came from Mallarmé, a poet unknown to Tenn.

"I was taken by this man instantly," Tenn remembered, "but I began to feel far more passionate as I looked about his monkish little apartment, the important books, the stark devotion to work, and this quote, in French. Here was a man like me: a frightened rube, tiptoeing toward his work, his passions, himself. Straining so hard in every direction, tight and tense and ready to fire if only a target existed."

Tenn and Inge also shared a belief—morbid but embraced with a brio that made it appear joyous—that they were each on a short-term lease on Earth, and everything needed to be consumed and burnt off in pursuit of the few works they could manage before they fulfilled the destiny of a prepared and examined death.

In the midst of a pusillanimous America in the midst of a World War, Tenn and Inge had cast their minds back to the avant-garde 1920s, a "great flowering of aberrant minds," the "diseased diaspora" of restless Americans who settled in Paris and threw off the trappings of the puritanical states that had shaped and rejected them. "We were much taken by Harry Crosby," Tenn told me, "and we wanted to latch on to some of the fire he had harnessed. We knew the great burning would come for us eventually, but we wanted the white heat of the fire, the illumination of the flames, before we were engulfed."

Crosby, the son of great Bostonian wealth, had witnessed carnage and death as an ambulance driver in the First World War, and as Tenn would later learn in conversations with Malcolm Cowley and others who had known the young man, he had created, in the grey and wet hills of France and the blood-slicked halls of army hospitals and tents, his own religion, one that would best fill the emptiness he now felt, with so many young men like himself maimed so quickly, so senselessly. "He wanted grandeur," Tenn recounted, "and he found it, initially, in the religion he fashioned in which he worshipped the sun, which might ignite some life inside the deadly shell he now inhabited. Looking upon the blanched corpses of young soldiers, he imagined the sun, angry at times, but also pulsing with life, beaming over their bodies, and he wrote, 'Lost things were warm with beauty,' and 'The sun is our God and . . . death is our marriage.'" Marriage for Crosby, as Tenn intuited him, existed between men and women, men and men, men and literature, men and art, men and the locales they lived in, and the people fate and their own will had determined would be their neighbors or friends. Everything moved according to the cycles of the sun: the farmer knew to turn his soil according to solar charts; the sea responded to its mighty determination; and death, prepared and examined, should be timed to guarantee one's deliverance, one's ascendancy to the sun. "Fly into the sun," Tenn remembered Crosby urging all artists. "Sun/Speed/ Darkness/Death—these are the cycles of life as we know it. Inhabit the sun, be a person of light, burn out fast." Crosby founded the Black Sun Press, which published Hart Crane, the poet who most influenced Tenn's own thoughts and approaches to writing. "In those early years," Tenn remembered, "I never began notes on a play, a poem, a short story, without rereading all of Hart Crane, thinking of him, trying to be with him on the deck of that ship from which he slipped from us forever. He fell to the bottom of the sea, but I think he was actually flying into the sun, seeking to find his ultimate membership among those who might understand him, those who, like him, could only be destroyed on this planet." In life the mind of Hart Crane raced and scattered, but Tenn imagined that there was calm and quiet "and no jarring distractions or rejections" on the cool floor of the Gulf of Mexico, whose waters had always been a part of Tenn's life, the source of frolics on vacations or fear when storms arose, and which was now the final resting place for his favored poet. Tenn had kept a jar of water from the Gulf on his writing desk for years, and even as he hocked typewriters and changed addresses, the cloudy water traveled with him. Tenn's lover Pancho Rodriguez, when told of the provenance of the water, replied that he had always thought it was holy water, blessed in some way. "It is," Tenn replied, "and it was."

TENN FELT for a brief time that he and Bill Inge might be able to bond and become a working and loving unit—bold writers drawing words from the sun and throwing them back up and toward their fiery source. "We wanted so much to love and be loved, to meld with someone who loved as we did. We could transgress in spirit. We wanted to change things; we wanted to blow away the plays that we found boring, that didn't speak to us; we were queer and finding ways to be so openly and freely and with some sense of enjoyment. In those ways we were pushing against things as they were, but our work was very simple and orderly in comparison with the men who were fueling our dreams."

Both Tenn and Inge felt old and failed when they met, but Inge was on the cusp of thirty-one, and Tenn was thirty-three. "We were much older than our years," Tenn admitted. "We had ambition, but we were mentally and physically slack."

Tenn was not typically attracted to a man with Inge's attributes, but he assured me that the sexual response he felt for the writer was instant and genuine. This response grew as he observed Inge at work and realized that he possessed a sense of discipline that was as strong as his confidence was weak. "He wrote and wrote," Tenn remembered, "and then he shredded and burned. I have no idea how many reams of paper he filled with plays and stories and then destroyed. He could walk proudly and erect toward an idea, but then he flinched and fell away when he began to read it over and consider it."

Tenn thought of the characters in his plays as being observed from a great height, and he confessed to Lillian Gish that what helped him the most in moving toward his strongest female characters was watching, over and over, those D. W. Griffith films in which his brilliant cinematographer, Billy Bitzer, risking life and limb, rose high above the sets and the actors and most of the lot, to reveal the characters, all of humanity, scrambling like ants across "this sticky plate we call Earth, soiled with our plans and our beliefs." Tenn could close in on his female protagonist and race toward a conclusion once he could imagine the situation in which she was placed and see it, God-like, from a great height, the "seat of Fate, which carries in its cushion foresight and perspective," and then, once we know that she seeks a rescue from the reality that keeps battering her (Blanche), love and relocation that are both forever out of her grasp (Alma), and identity that will give her a secure perch in her environment (Serafina), he could zoom in tight on the woman, allowing us to better see her place and her predicament.

William Inge, on the other hand, had no sense of distance or great height: he saw the situation in which his female characters were set in small, mincing steps "from the toaster to the sink," as Tenn put it, from the utterly sexless twin bed to the lavatory, from the phone to the back porch where a dog was pitifully called, pudgy thighs patted in the hopes that the dog (youth, love, promise) would come bounding out of the hedge and life could return to a schedule easily managed and freckled with affection.

There were no sweeping panoramas from which we could see where Lola and Doc Delaney of *Come Back, Little Sheba* lived or had been or where they were headed. We discovered their biographies and their grievances and regrets at the pace one would find while reading faded, frequently folded letters, the kind that the mothers of both playwrights saved, tied with ribbon, collected, pulled from beneath beds as vindication or damning evidence. "Bill Inge's mother referred to letters from her husband, her beaux, her children, bill collectors, as if they were Scripture," Tenn told me. "Her placement in the world could be proven or solidified by a letter from a handsome man from 1935. She was very much like my mother, encased in a past that was both real and fantasy, a terrible mixture of what might have been, what was imagined, and what should have been given to them. Their sense of entitlement—or rather their outrage at entitlements snatched away from them—was epic, horrible, and Bill and I both grew up suffocating on this scent of rot and retribution."

Inge was literally frozen in his actions, having been so coddled and watched over by his mother, Maude, that he had a habit of looking around for permission or physical clearance if he simply needed to rise from a chair, even if he was alone. Tenn could remember pretending to be asleep and watching Inge, in his own apartment, move with the careful steps and exaggerated quietude of a burglar or a "man made of glass, awaiting the next loud noise or powerful movement that might shatter him." Tenn assumed he moved with such quiet agility as a courtesy to his presumed sleep, but even when preparing a meal or showing him pages of a play, he moved with an irritating slowness that tried Tenn's patience.

Inge found drama and death in household appliances and daily toiletries. His older brother, Luther, recalled by the playwright as young and handsome and recently married, had nicked himself while shaving, introducing into his body a rare blood poisoning that took his life. Inge had desired Luther, a fact that filled him with considerable dread, even as he admitted spying on his brother as he showered and shaved. The act of watching Luther shave was Inge's first memory of erotic pleasure, as he sat on the closed toilet seat and watched his older, naked brother at the bathroom mirror. Inge had resented Luther's leaving the family to marry, and now he had left the earth altogether, his body a waxy off-white in the coffin, "the color of maggots," as Inge described it to Tenn. "Bill Inge wondered his entire life if his eroticization of his brother's shaving had infused it with some horrible and evil power," Tenn told me, and in Inge's novel *My Son Is a Splendid Driver,* he wrote what Tenn considered to be one of his most honest sentences: "Sex was as fearful as black magic to all of us." Sex—both the act of intercourse and the pursuit and deification of various acts—had destroyed Harry Crosby, and perhaps Hart Crane. These were erotic, inverted men—amatory mentors to Inge and Tenn. Sex, therefore, had to be denied, repressed, rerouted. Little Billy Inge, as he was known, took to imitation, dressing up as a refined dowager or one of the female film stars he loved, doted on by his mother, detested by his father, held like a treasured doll by his older sister, Helene. "Performance trumped consummation," Tenn surmised.

Tenn discovered his love of imitation, shared with his mother, Edwina, in the sickbed, as they pored over comic books, movie magazines, and gossip columns in various newspapers. "My mother would become the columnist, the film star," Tenn remembered, "and this was extraordinary, because the films were silent. We did not know the caliber or timbre of Constance Talmadge's voice; we could only assume that Garbo was deep-voiced. So we improvised, often attributing to a film star—say, Pola Negri or Lillian Gish—the voice of the church pianist or the girl at the grocery store with a harelip. I must say we got the voices right more often than not."

Tenn's fantasies were fostered in the darkness of the illnesses that visited him as a child, which he told me included scarlet fever, "virulent rashes," and "breakdowns of nervous and digestive systems." Tenn admitted that he welcomed, even feigned, outbreaks of illness when he dreaded school or encounters with his father, and off he would be whisked to his sickbed. "There was no threat of the radio being taken by my father in the darkness of sickness," Tenn told me, "and my mother liked to take care of me, to get away from her own barren life by laughing and performing with me."

Both mothers hated their husbands and resented the skimpy, hateful lives they had provided. Inge grew up in a Kansas that was becoming an oil metropolis, and Harry Ford Sinclair had become a millionaire from his investments in oil exploration, creating the famed Sinclair Oil, whose logo haunted Billy Inge: it was the wealth and the freedom he hoped for, for himself and his mother. Rumor had it that Sinclair had shot himself in the foot in order to gain an insurance settlement, which he then invested in oil. Inge and his mother fantasized about a perfectly placed bullet—in a foot or a thigh or an elbow—that might produce for them a chunk of money that would make their lives better. Or, maybe, a deadly bullet sunk into the body of the hated father, Luther Sr. The thought of this, as well as of the plans that would be necessary, would send Billy and his mother into gales of laughter, which were often silenced by the barbed statements of the intended victim.

Finances were tight in both the Inge and the Williams household. Tenn's father never shared the bulk of his paychecks with his family, so Edwina took on a variety of "suitable and respectable" means of bringing extra funds into the house. She was also not above writing to well-off relatives for financial aid, citing illnesses that did not exist or departures from her husband, which were hoped for but had not yet been scheduled. Inge's mother took in boarders for extra income, and she and her son obtained extra entertainment, laughing at the predilections of certain men and women who took up residence with them. Some tenants drank, others had odd eating habits and squirreled away chocolates or maple candy, which Billy and his mother would find and consume when they snooped in the rooms. Inge first encountered pornography in the bureau drawers of a male tenant. His mother snatched the pictures away from him and replaced them beneath the socks and shirts, but Inge returned and looked at the blurred black-and-white images and saw for the first time the male form in its fullness and its beauty. He would later see it in its all-too-real state of decline when he watched the man whose magazines and photographs he had purloined: he had an enormous inguinal hernia, which he would forcefully push from his groin up into its proper placement, then attach a truss, a contraption with wires and heavy laces, which he would ask Billy to help him pull tightly and into place. Inge was always aware that there was incipient "decay, decline, and disappointment" waiting to visit the body. Inge could never imagine that his own body could give another pleasure, and Tenn recalled that their times together were awkward and would never have advanced except for the fact that he became aggressive and all but demanded sex. "The exception," Tenn recalled, "was when liquor was introduced," at which time Bill was amorous and skillful and bold. But with the morning, and sobriety, guilt would set in, the furtive movements would return, the cat burglar would tiptoe into the bathroom, where tiles and sinks and strops and razors presaged death, where the kitchen held the prospect of odd boarders or angry encounters with his father. "His life," Tenn told me, "his very apartment, his every step, was haunted by phantoms, bogeymen who might beat him or ask him to help him into a truss or show him pictures of naked men, or his mother, ready to dress him in her Sunday finery and put on a show. It amazes me now that he could even get up in the morning and get things done."

Tenn and Bill liked to lie in bed naked, smoking and reading and talking. They both knew large swatches of Hart Crane by memory, and because each was influenced by films and drew inspiration from repeated viewings of those they liked, they loved this section from *The Bridge:*

I think of cinemas, panoramic sleights
With multitudes bent toward some flashing scene
Never disclosed, but hastened to again,
Foretold to other eyes on the same screen . . .

"I think," Tenn told me, "that we took this as a sign from our poet that we were not misguided in seeking comfort and impulse from the cinema." Both of them would re-create scenes from films they had seen over and over, and they thought of films as ephemeral, burned away in an instant. In the days before television, and in cities that did not harbor a revival house or a curious university, films came and disappeared. You could often find an abbreviated and recast version of a film you'd liked on *Lux Radio Theatre* or *Academy Award Theater*, then recline in the dark, breathing in the nicotine and the musk on a lover's neck and reveling in having Bette Davis or Jean Arthur or Claudette Colbert emanating from the radio by your bed. These were among the happiest times with Bill Inge, laughing and remembering films or deconstructing plays.

"We knew that the hymen had not yet been broken on the twentieth century," Tenn said. "Eugene O'Neill had his greatness, but he was very much of the previous century, and so many of the other plays being done were British and pale and careful, or American and written in the British style. Aborted babies encased in amber or framed in gilt. Lifeless. Here we were, a nation at war, and here we were, two queers under the influence of rebels who worshipped the sun and appetites and new ways of speaking and writing, and we were also too careful. We weren't smart enough to blow the conventions of the theater, but I think we were creeping toward something."

Tenn believed that the revolutions lurking within him and Bill Inge were not so much structural as emotional. You could keep your characters in the kitchen or the living room, talking things out, arguing about grocery bills and prom dresses and typing classes, but the subtext, the ground on which they all stood and argued and dreamed, was loaded with land mines and shards of glass, and every corner hid shadows and secrets. Watching Bill Inge creep around the city of St. Louis, his own apartment, his own bed, navigating his own body with apology and fear, Tenn came to see that Tom in *The Glass Menagerie* was a perfect blending of the two men who had found each other—frightened, hesitant queers who lost themselves in movies and booze, and could only enjoy the flesh of another man while tipsy and in the shadows of an ornate alcove of a movie theater, accompanied by the sounds of Barbara Stanwyck or Gary Cooper or the music of Miklós Rózsa. Sexual acts in balconies or alleyways managed to blur in the account ledger Tenn kept of conquests and adventures; they allowed him the pleasure of men and movies, but they failed to be real, so they failed to disappoint. He expected only a quick blast of warmth and pleasure, and then came the parting. In Hollywood, he had enjoyed the openness of his time with his Italian on Vista, but he had also known that the time was limited—he would be called away from his odd temporary assignment at MGM and have to face the work that still felt thin to him. With Bill Inge, he knew he needed to get back to work on *Menagerie* and make it work and salvage the reputation he felt had been soiled by the failure of *Battle of Angels*, but he allowed himself time to observe both Inge and his own reactions when he was with him.

"I allowed myself to be slow with him," Tenn remembered. "I wanted to see all that there was of Bill Inge, and primarily there was fear."

When they discussed Hart Crane, Inge obsessed over the fact that Crane was coddled and fawned over and pressed upon by his mother. Born to wealth ("They were rich in chocolate," Tenn told me), he had no material worries, other than those his sexual desires presented. "He seemed to know at an early age that he wanted to be with men," Tenn said, "and he knew at an early age of the risks this presented. He was ridiculed and beaten frequently." Crane's mother was an adherent of Christian Science, a religion that was first presented to Tenn through his study of the poet. Inge was horrified at the thought that Crane's mother, seeking to heal her son of his desires for men and liquor, had poisoned him against his own passions by continually telling him that God had not created him in this aberrant image. There was no man but perfect man, and perfect man does not lie down with another. In notes that Tenn made for a play he was considering about Crane, he wrote of a mother physically holding her son down and asking him to deny all that he was and all that he felt. "Both of our mothers did this to us, in their way," Tenn said, "but neither of them secured the services of God or Divine Mind to set us straight, so to speak. We were simply told to be good and respectable gentlemen, to present good and noble faces to the public. We could dress up and camp up in privacy with our mothers, but the world needed to see two men who may have been writers, but who could have passed for members of the Rotary Club."

Tenn spent only a short time with Bill Inge in St. Louis, in that apartment of good books and posters and a Scottie dog named Lula Belle, who may have been the only creature around whom Inge felt any sense of comfort. Inge would later have to give up the dog when he moved to another locale (one not predisposed to animals), and Tenn would recall that he received calls of despair from Inge about this. "Thus was born Sheba," Tenn said, referring to the lost dog for whom Lola Delaney pines and calls on that forlorn back porch. "Bill believed that all of his life he had been abandoned and betrayed by everyone," Tenn continued, "but with the relinquishment of his beloved dog, he was finally a member of the betraying class." Within all of those rooms of the houses he built for his plays, with their memories and soiled furniture and seemingly mundane daily activities that could kill, Inge now added the ghosts of pets abandoned or dead, and his characters were haunted by pillows where they once sat or felt phantom sensations on legs they had once rubbed against. "I am an obsessive person myself," Tenn concluded, "but Bill worked the dog angle longer than was necessary, in my opinion."

Bill Inge visited Tenn both in Chicago and in New York, to see the new shape of *The Glass Menagerie* and to spend more time together—in and out of bed. "He had been teaching a lot of dumb coeds," Tenn remembered, "and writing reviews of touring productions and local dramatic societies, and his mind was becoming sclerotic."

Openly enthusiastic about Tenn's writing, he no longer considered him a promising playwright, but a genius, and he began to talk to Tenn about his literary future. "I was in my own particular hell with *Menagerie*, so I was probably dismissive. I know that I pushed Bill away, as well as his script. I just couldn't be bothered, and I was not in a mind in which I wanted to read someone's work and figure out how to improve it: I was trying to improve my own." Tenn preferred that they spend lazy mornings in bed, reciting poetry. "It was an aimless, wasted time," he recalled, "but I was happy while I was in it. It was only when he was gone that I saw that there was nothing gained from the time. It was selfish snuggling, really. I drained the little affection from Bill that he could share, and then I wanted to get back to the play. I was looking for a lover, and I got an apprentice."

Time passes and a play, *Farther Off from Heaven,* is sent to Tenn. It is from Bill Inge, and it is a "sepia-toned Valentine," a sweet and slight little play that will later become *The Dark at the Top of the Stairs,* a family drama about overdue bills and an absent and unfaithful husband, confused adolescents, sudden death—all played out within and about a seemingly perfect midwestern home in a postcard-ready town. "But poison pulses in the blood of all the characters," Tenn told me. "No one is to be trusted; appearances are both deceiving and wicked and carefully constructed, like the piecrusts of the worn and defeated mother. I did not care for it, but I passed it along to Audrey Wood, who passed on it."

Wood's rejection of the play sent Inge into a torrent of anger and depression—and voluminous drinking. "I was already myself something of a drinker," Tenn told me, "and I was amazed with the amount of drinking he was doing." Inge visited Tenn in New York around this time—right as Tenn was completing *A Streetcar Named Desire*—and "Bill was a mess." Not only was Inge drinking heavily, but he was engaging in that "laughable series of tricks" long employed by alcoholics—frequent showers, copious quantities of the powder used in barbershops, chewing gum, and Sen-Sen—all in a vain attempt to diminish the odor of alcohol and sweat that was oozing from his pores. "He had grown flabby," Tenn remembered, "and lined. His eyes were ancient, witness to God knows how many trials and horrors." Tenn was now involved with Frank Merlo, but he still arranged for trysts with Inge. "I wanted the comfort I had once known with him," Tenn said, not happy with his admission. "I wanted the warmth and the sweetness, but he was now weak and girlish and passive. He slept and he smelled and he whined." Tenn pulled away from Inge and wondered if he would have to "suffer the sad declivity he had become" any longer.

Farther Off from Heaven found a home with Margo Jones and her theater in Dallas, creating a rift between Tenn and Jones. "Now our conversations included Bill," Tenn said, "and I didn't like that. I'm dying with *Summer and Smoke,* for instance, and Margo keeps telling me about the new play Bill is writing. I seemed incapable of transmitting to Margo how little I cared about any of this."

The play Inge was working on was *Come Back, Little Sheba,* and after a production at the Westport Country Playhouse that Tenn heard about from a number of people, including Eva Le Gallienne, it came to Broadway, where it was a success. Inge had built a home of rooms full of phantoms and dangerous memories, and a couple, Lola and Doc, defeated and desiccated because they had succumbed, as we often do, to the transitory glories of youth—muscles and taut flesh and dewy faces. Romance renders us blind to all that we can lose when we fall into a bed under which rests a ticking clock and a few explosives. Babies are lost and replaced by a dog, Sheba, upon whom Lola can bestow the love that Doc now finds repellent. An impotent alcoholic, he had been forced to abandon his plans for medical school and has become a chiropractor, a trade that Tenn remembered was a notch or two above witch doctor or back-alley abortionist at the time Inge wrote his play. Doc serves the lower middle class, who often cannot pay, so he barters, coming home with poultry and vegetables and crocheted afghans. To boost their finances, Doc and Lola rent out a room to a young college student, who is pretty and bright and ambitious—a young Lola, brought right into that house to haunt and humiliate them. A boyfriend visits, and he is handsome and muscular and he can throw the javelin—long and hard and thick and strong—farther than anyone else, causing it to land in the ground with a groan and quiver. "I introduced the ambulatory penis in the form of Stanley Kowalski," Tenn told me, "and Bill brought it onstage in the form of a piece of athletic equipment. The good-looking guy was an aside, but the talk of his arms and his javelin . . . well, the point was made."

So much youth, so much sex, and the Delaney household is again full of the resentments that had been hidden beneath heavy meals, mindless chatter, alcohol, and that damned dog, which—Inge told the actress who created the part, Shirley Booth—was frequently dressed in clothes and held as if it were a baby. All masks are ripped away, and Doc drinks the sherry that Lola, in an act of simpleton cruelty, has kept in the kitchen cupboard. He lunges at her with a knife, hoping, as Inge told Tenn, "to cauterize, at long last, this cancer, this Lola, from his life, from the horrible, sagging body that once housed a brain and a soul."

"The play worked," Tenn admitted, sounding surprised as he said so, "and I must admit I was surprised, and not a little envious. It had never occurred to me that Bill could write, or that he would find success. I was not entirely sure how I should react, and I doubt that I did anything honorable or direct. I'm sure I felt threatened. I know that I was told I should feel threatened. So many people told me I had someone gaining on me. But I must admit that I had one primary thought as I watched that play, and as I read it several times: I had lost a sweet lover and gained a dangerous rival."

For nearly a decade, from 1950, when *Come Back, Little Sheba* opened on Broadway, until 1957, when *The Dark at the Top of the Stairs* premiered, becoming the fourth play to be included in a volume of his collected plays, William Inge enjoyed a series of what Tenn called "seamless successes." Tenn resented the failure of so many critics to ask tough questions of Inge, while he felt he was routinely held to a higher standard.

The film version of *Sheba* earned Shirley Booth both an Oscar and the Best Actress prize at the Cannes Film Festival. As Tenn was suffering both the failure of *Camino Real* and what he felt was the dismissive attitude of its director, Elia Kazan, Inge's *Picnic*, which Tenn claimed to have read more than five times, offering revisions and advice—most of it unheeded—earned Inge the Pulitzer Prize and was sold to Columbia's Harry Cohn for more than a quarter of a million dollars. The film version of the play, released in 1955, and starring William Holden and Kim Novak, was a box-office success and earned two Oscars. *Bus Stop*, which opened on Broadway as *Picnic* was still in movie theaters, was pitted against Tenn's *Cat on a Hot Tin Roof* for most of the season's prizes; and in 1957 Elia Kazan ("My director!" Tenn exclaimed to me) agreed to direct *The Dark at the Top of the Stairs,* a play that Tenn, in a meeting in 1956, had told Inge to discard. (Tenn recounted all of this information as seriously as he did the mysteries of the Rosary: they were ingrained in his memory.) "That play never worked for me," Tenn told me, "in any form at all, and I told him so. His response was to find and use Kazan, to plaster over the holes and pockmarks in the foundation and walls of that particular house he had constructed, and make it work one way or the other. I was not amused."

When I broached this subject with Kazan, he remembered how amazed he had been at Tenn's pettiness. "Tennessee never should have possessed for a moment any fear that any other playwright, any other writer, might have presented to him," Kazan told me. "He felt very threatened by Inge, and I could never understand it. Bill Inge literally trembled at the thought and the presence of Tennessee. 'Idolatry' is the word I am most apt to use as a description, and Tennessee was very dismissive of him. He went through the script of *Dark,* ridiculing virtually every line and scene and pressuring me to remove myself from the

Elia Kazan and William Inge on the set of *Splendor in the Grass* (1961). Tennessee introduced the playwright to Kazan, and later envied the success the two of them shared. "I was not yet comfortable in the role of mentor," Tennessee confessed.

production, allegedly for the sake of my reputation, but really, I think, because he saw Bill as intruding, once again, as always, on his turf."

An article written by Robert Brustein for *Harper's* magazine served as a cruel and oddly fortuitous wish fulfillment for Tenn. "It was a barbaric piece," Tenn remembered, "and I was soon enough to suffer my own injuries by virtue of Mr. Brustein's malicious pen, but it was the first, the only, piece that asked the questions of Bill that I had raised in our conversations. Brustein's was the only critical piece that pointed out precisely what Bill was up to play after play, scene after scene."

Titled "The Men-Taming Women of William Inge," the piece opened with this salvo: "Considering the modesty—one is tempted to say the mediocrity—of his work, it is clear that the excitement over Inge has been inspired by something other than the intrinsic value of his plays." After disemboweling *Come Back, Little Sheba; Picnic; Bus Stop;* and *The Dark at the Top of the Stairs,* Brustein presents his thesis: "Specifically, Inge's basic plot line revolves around a heroine threatened either with violence or sexual aggression by a rambunctious male. Both terrified and attracted by him, she tries to escape his influence until she learns that, despite his apparent confidence, he is riddled with doubts, loneliness, and need. Once he has confessed this, he loses his ogre quality and the woman is able to domesticate him without difficulty."

"Exactly!" Tenn said he exclaimed upon reading the piece. "Bill Inge neuters his men through the offices and the orifices of his wan women, and peace reigns in the house. The oilcloth-covered table groans with pies and roasts and the husband squeezes the waist of his good wife, soaking dishes and his truss in the kitchen slop." Tenn boasted that his men were emasculated in a more "realistic" way, as Val Xavier in *Orpheus Descending* and Chance Wayne in *Sweet Bird of Youth* can attest, and that, as in life, the "strong and the sure, the brutal and the willful" prevail. Inge's view, Tenn believed, was dishonest, an attempt on the part of Inge to bear witness to what had escaped him all his life: domestic harmony, a home in which he was loved, a planet, like the sun of Harry Crosby, to which he could ascend and rule, while Tenn was blunt enough to know and to reveal that what we often must face instead is the cold ocean floor of Hart Crane to find any level of release. "At all other times," Tenn insisted, "we submit, we forbear. We do not walk lovingly into arms that fail to excite, that pin us down, that serve as fleshly straitjackets."

As Brustein wrote of Inge, "Marriage demands, in return for its spiritual consolations, a sacrifice of the hero's image (which is the American folk image) of maleness. He must give up his aggressiveness, his promiscuity, his bravado, his contempt for soft virtues, and his narcissistic pride in his body and attainments, and admit that he is lost in the world and needs help."

This portion of the article was particularly apt, a deeply personal and sharp observation of how Maude Inge had raised her son to adapt and behave, "holding down her son and asking him to relinquish all of the things about a man that he either desires or is proud to possess or has earned," Tenn explained. "His goal should be to submit to the particular insane and feminine notion of the 'good man,' absent any sexual pleasure or curiosity, any desire to question his place in the world or his rights among his family or his peers. I found—and I find—this repellent in his work."

Tenn admitted that he found guilty satisfaction in the Brustein article, and in reports that Inge broke down on the phone with the critic and with friends, for whom he asked advice. "I have never sought advice when I failed," Tenn boasted. "I have asked, as I have asked you, to find out if my work ever mattered, if what I have written ever possessed any level of importance among the people I'm sending you to look over and learn from. Never, however, has it occurred to me—nor would it—to call someone, dry-eyed or not, and ask them how I should write, ask them if I could write."

All of the pain that William Inge experienced in the last fifteen years of his life, from the publication of the Brustein article in 1958 until his suicide in 1973, could have been avoided, Tenn believed, if only he had listened to his inner voice—and to Tenn—and written the play that *Picnic* was supposed to be, and deserved to be.

Originally called *Front Porch,* the play that came to be known as *Picnic* began as what Tenn described as "postcards of despair, sepia-toned, seemingly gentle, but depicting harsh realities in the so-called gentle heartland." The women of the play, even Madge, the town's beauty, find disappointment in their pursuits of companionship, with both men and women. "As I remember it," Tenn told me, "you could not trust anyone, whether you were looking for a dance, a necking session, a look at last week's homework or a cobbler recipe." Lives of desperation were being lived in this town, and activity—butter-churning, church socials, PTA meetings, picnics, dress fittings—all served, vainly, to fill the horrible void that resided in the center of each character. The women had their pies and their gossip, their days ending in exhaustion when the radio transmission concluded and only a pop and a hiss emanated, and sleep, another diversion, came to end their day. The men boasted of financial or sexual conquests, fish caught, marriages avoided, touchdowns remembered. Bragging or charming their way through a day, the town's frayed schedules are shattered when Hal, a "priapic construction," enters the town. Hal's rampant sexuality, "hovering like heat rising from asphalt," unmoors the women, who had long forgotten the joys of a "good rutting," and the men are threatened, their bodies turned to fat, their jowls expanded, and their hairlines in swift retreat. Madge, who shares her home with her mother—"another of Bill's dry, tired domestic slaves"—her tomboyish sister, Millie, and a series of plump, mother-hen women who amble in and out discussing sewing patterns and the weather and the upcoming picnic and the crowning of the "Neewollah Queen" (the Halloween Queen), the pivotal social event of the town, and the event that will serve to bring the play's characters toward their emotional conclusions. The play that Tenn read, at some point in 1952 as he remembered it, had all of the characters "missing the romantic and sexual trains they had hoped to board." Madge and Hal do not run off together, as the town's women help the young girl realize that he is a loser and a drifter, and nothing good would come from congress with him; Rosemary, the town's spinster schoolteacher, fails to convince Howard, the unprepossessing salesman, to settle down with her and give her an identity different from that of old maid. The original play ended with the women scattered across the stage, one at a clothesline, another tending a garden, and Madge and her mother, deep in despair, simply looking ahead—at nothing—as the lights dimmed.

"It was brutal," Tenn said, "but it was true, and Bill vowed that it would be the conclusion that would appear on a New York stage." Almost immediately Inge was encouraged to give the play a happier conclusion. He had hoped to retain Harold Clurman as the play's director, but he proved to be unavailable or uninterested. Elia Kazan was involved in a film and had already committed to Tenn's *Camino Real.* Joshua Logan was then suggested, and Tenn was immediately against it. "I was never impressed with Josh Logan the man or Josh Logan the director," Tenn told me. "He operated under the delusional notion that we were similar in nature, being Southern and queer and all, but I found his taste deplorable, and I urged Bill to find another director, even if it meant postponing the play."

But Bill Inge did not believe in or understand postponement, and he imagined, not without some veracity, that Tenn might not have his interests at heart. Inge was not excited about Logan, whose reputation rested on musicals like *Annie Get Your Gun* and *South Pacific* (which he also co-wrote and for which he won a Pulitzer Prize) and light entertainments like *Mister Roberts,* but he was available and was quick to move ahead with the play, even as he told Inge that it had to be rewritten. "Logan told him," Tenn told me, "that the original ending would have the audience in an uproar. They would storm the stage! The audience must have romance, they must believe the myth that hopes are rewarded and every season brings, along with death and the rotation of crops, a new batch of love and sex to brighten the soul and the complexion." Logan fought for the revision, and Tenn visited rehearsals at one point to see how things were faring.

And he saw Elizabeth Wilson. Cast as the town's newest schoolteacher, Christine Schoenwalder, Wilson had a small part, but she was a "tall, shiny woman, with coal-black hair, perfect posture, and a look on her face that conveyed that she was patient with the shenanigans, but she recognized their foolishness." As arguments raged all around her, Wilson would repair to the sidelines, taking no part in the discussions, refusing to engage with the other actors in conversations about the direction of the play.

"Bill," Tenn said to Inge one day, "take as your role model that young actress over there," pointing to Wilson. "Imagine yourself committed but distant; passionate but professional. Do what is right."

Tenn offered the greatest gift he could imagine: a woman to shape and inspire Bill Inge. "I pushed a woman, a teacher, toward him, as I would have wished someone would do for me. A gift, a rope to pull me from the waters."

Exhausted by phone calls and visits from Logan, Audrey Wood, and various producers and friends, Inge ultimately relented and had Madge follow Hal out of town, but he managed to make it a Pyrrhic victory: what would Madge gain in the company of this man? And look at the women on the porches, alone and back to canning peaches, headed for another night of restless sleep. There was the whistle of dry air across the stage as the curtain descended, but most audiences cheered that Madge "found love and release."

"I thought the play was now silly," Tenn said, "which of course meant it had to succeed mightily, which it did." Tenn suffered the power of his own honesty about love and myth when his *Camino Real* was met with puzzlement and empty seats, while *Picnic* satisfied audiences for nearly five hundred performances.

Elia Kazan disagrees, however. "I think the girl has to leave town," he said, "even if she dries up and dies in some other awful town: she has at least taken ownership of her life, has driven a stake in the ground and told the world, 'Here I am. Let's see what I can do.' And in her own way, she has shaken up the town, reminding them of what love and lust can look like and accomplish. She has devastated her mother, who now has the younger daughter, who is probably destined to join the other gentle midwestern lesbians, teaching civics and gym, and whose hands and knees will ultimately give out, so that sewing is no longer possible. Hell, Madge and Hal may have to come back to the town, full of strip malls, and care for the old lady. The play is a tragedy no matter how you revise it, but I don't know that it worked any better with the bleaker ending. But it worked. I saw it. I don't respect it, but it worked. It was a Valentine that had fallen from a girl's purse and been stepped on, and you could see the dusty, insensitive footprint across its lacy contours."

Tenn's jealousy and vehement judgments against *Picnic* perplexed Kazan, given that two years later, with *Cat on a Hot Tin Roof,* Tenn would make changes to his own play that made those Inge made to his pale in comparison. "Tenn speaks of honest emasculation," Kazan laughed, "but Jesus, what he did to *Cat*! It's what I wanted, and I think I was right, but he acquiesced far more than Inge did. Far more."

Bill Inge's emasculation, both personal and professional, was a play, Tenn said, "of multiple acts and multiple attempts at mutilation," and it required a number of instruments: alcohol, a lack of faith in himself and his talents, and a woman who would make Hart Crane's Christian Science mother look like the girl on the Art Nouveau candy box Madge Owens was meant to be.

"Oh, Lord," Tenn said, "I kept telling Bill to look at Elizabeth Wilson and learn from her balance and her calm, and instead he flew right into a toxic cyclone, sat himself right down on a fence of barbed wire, and waited for . . . I don't know what he was waiting for, but what came couldn't have been what anybody wanted."

Twelve

H ER NAME WAS Barbara Baxley.

It is impossible to write of her without spraying an inordinate number of literary bullets, because in the telling and the living of her life she was wild and disparate and spread about in many places. Her mind was like those cluttered desks owned by people who can nonetheless find any item you might request. Barbara's mind was populated by years of memories, regrets, ambitions, and encounters, and they were related without regard to chronology or relevance. In the telling of her stories, Barbara would glow with happiness or rage or enlightenment. It was this quality that led Tenn to liken Barbara to the "firefly, because it flits about so mercilessly, and you're amazed by its phosphorescence, and you wonder if the flight can be sustained." When I asked Tenn if this reference was to Barbara's stage work, he said that it wasn't, for while he had the highest regard for the work she had done for him and for William Inge, he felt that her greatest performance was the one she pulled off in life.

"Barbara doesn't want to be here, you know," Tenn told me. "I think she turned off to life in 1973, when Bill killed himself. I think Bill took a huge piece of her with him, and I'll never be able to let him get away with that; I'll have a hatred for him forever because of the destruction he caused her. I know that she never loved a man as she loved Bill, and she gave herself to him indiscriminately, and he abused that. He had an intelligent, captive acolyte in Barbara, and he threw her to the ground with great force, first with his actions against her—like refusing to cast her in his plays, then refusing to marry her—and then by killing himself, which was his way of saying, 'All your efforts were in vain. You weren't enough to make my life worth living.' He sought affection, not arousal, so he could 'function' with Barbara. He wanted to be wanted, and if he found that acceptance, he felt he was done. There was very little revision applied toward Bill's sexual activities; he offered no rewrites or improvements or deletions. Once he felt you wanted him, he was no longer present. I think that with me he found comfort, acceptance, but it was two writers holding each other—holding each other up and holding each other in bed, music on the radio and plots coursing through our heads. Bill used to say that he hoped he'd get his resistances weakened when he was older or richer or better-known, and I finally told him that if he was really smart, he'd learn that you either have a healthy approach to sex or you don't. I do not believe in analysis and I do not believe in miracles of the libido. Bill was career-driven, and he should have learned to love and depend on his friends more. And besides, few marriages are based on sex, anyway. The strongest ones are usually between two people who act as if they were good friends away at summer camp, sharing pocket change and suntan lotion. Barbara offered him that, as well as freedom to write and read and spend time alone, which is vital for a writer, and was mandatory for Bill. The biggest mistake of his life was in abandoning her."

When I broached the subject of Inge with Barbara, she was surprisingly unemotional and uninvolved. She spoke candidly and unhesitatingly. When I remarked on this, she said, "Well, all the deeper feelings were buried with Bill. Now the retelling is just trivia; it's not information about anyone I know."

BARBARA MET INGE accidentally, and in fact she couldn't remember exactly where the first encounter took place, but she thought that it had been at a party thrown by Lee Strasberg during the run of *Come Back, Little Sheba*. Barbara admired Inge and wanted to meet him, because she had liked his play, and wanted to be "in his world, his theatrical world, which I understood. I came from country people, prairie people,

Barbara Baxley, seen here in the 1960 film *The Savage Eye,* entered into a strange triangle with Tennessee and William Inge. She was a true friend, a brilliant actress, and a woman almost diabolically driven to destroy her career and herself.

who used few words, worked hard, and hid a lot of secrets. Those secrets would often explode, but more often than not, they were swept under rugs of denial or alcohol or sexual outbursts. Life always returned to the pillars of the community: family, work, church. All was forgotten, or all was attempted to be forgotten."

Barbara also found Inge attractive, as Tenn had, and she was surprised to learn that he was a homosexual. "He looked at a woman," Barbara remembered, "or rather, he looked at *me,* with so much affection and understanding. I felt a sexual attraction for him—and from him—that very first time." Baxley and Inge began seeing each other socially and sporadically, and in 1953, after Baxley had had success replacing Jean Arthur in *Peter Pan* and Julie Harris in *I Am a Camera,* she was deemed "appropriate escort material" for Inge to openings of plays, museum outings, and, finally, his bed. "I was not frightened," Barbara told me. "I am not someone who is shy or afraid of a challenge, and I believed that the affection I felt for Bill, which soon developed into love, would transform both of us, and everything we did together." Baxley also imagined a fruitful partnership between playwright and actress. "I wanted us to be together for everything," she told me. "All the way down the line. Heart. Home. Bed. Theater. Film. Death."

Tenn noticed the pairing and gave his blessing. The awkward man and lover Tenn had known in Bill Inge would profit from finding creative and spiritual solace from a woman (as Tenn always did) along with sexual and domestic comforts (which Tenn understood were lost to him).

Inge approved Barbara as Kim Stanley's understudy as Cherie in *Bus Stop,* a role she would assume many times, as Stanley had alerted both Inge and the play's director, Harold Clurman, that she had no intention of playing the part for very long. As Barbara put it, "She would start to feel all stretched out from a part, and she was afraid of becoming 'Little Miss Xerox,' so she never stayed very long. Thank God for me." Inge came to feel that Barbara brought things to the role that had been unexamined by the brilliant but mercurial Stanley. "I thought I'd died and gone to heaven," Barbara would later say of her time in that production, "but I'd really walked into an alley that was completely blind, littered with all sorts of shit. I thought I was taking on a role that would change my career, and it did: I was immediately seen as a leading actress, not just a gifted supporting character actress or a replacement. But it came with a price, and the price was Bill."

BARBARA BAXLEY'S FINGERPRINTS are all over *The Dark at the Top of the Stairs.* I was told this by Elia Kazan, who directed the play, and who saw Baxley at many of the readings and the rehearsals, and it was confirmed by Barbara, who told me that the play was "jointly autobiographical," blending elements of both her life and those of Inge and some of his childhood neighbors. Barbara was turned down for the leading role of Cora, a hybrid of herself and her mother, because her name was not considered sufficient to sell the play: the part went to Teresa Wright. Barbara would play the role in the national tour, however, and the revisions to the play continued on the road.

"Truth is very powerful," Barbara told me, "but it is also very elusive: It slips away, changes form. Bill and I kept feeling the truth move around and alter, and we kept getting ahead of it and improving the play. That may have been the most creative and intense time I'd ever known in the theater."

Barbara's immersion into the world of Bill Inge created a rift between her and Tenn, one that would continue until their collaboration on *Period of Adjustment.* "Tenn never liked for me to be with Bill," Barbara said. "Tenn was very possessive with almost anyone, but he always felt that Bill had sidled into the theater not only on his coattails, but by way of his bed, his immediate sexual needs." Inge served for Tenn several clearly delineated purposes—sexual comfort, conversation with a passionate reader and writer, the devotion of an acolyte. Tenn never imagined that Inge would become a successful playwright, and he never fully accepted it when it became a reality. "Tenn thought Bill was a dreamer," Barbara said. "Although he was only a couple of years younger than Tenn, he was always seen as a kid, a yahoo, someone definitely beneath Tenn's station in life and the theater."

While Tenn had encouraged the relationship between Baxley and Inge, he was not happy when he saw that it was "taking hold." When Tenn was told of the solidity of the affair—during the many meetings he had with Inge over the proper final act of *Picnic*—he was livid, then quickly became dismissive. "He thought it was a Method-actor sort of thing," according to Barbara. "I was trying something out, and Bill was ready for someone else to lie in bed with him and listen to music and smoke and talk about literature. But I see now that Tenn felt that Bill was taking one more thing from him. I had, after all, been in Tenn's life first." Tenn came to resent the gift he felt he made to Inge of Barbara Baxley.

There would soon be—briefly—a Williams-Inge-Baxley triangle, as Tenn, during a brutal rehearsal period of *Camino Real,* again sought the comfort of his "carnal collaborator." Tenn would visit Inge at his apartment, and Baxley on several occasions had the "horrible, bizarre" experience of leaving Tenn at the National Theatre, where she was tackling the role of Esmeralda in *Camino,* only to arrive at Inge's apartment to see Tenn, in a bathrobe, sitting in the kitchen, smoking and laughing with Inge. "I was trying to be good and true in my performance as Esmeralda," Barbara told me, "and then I was trying to be good in my performance as Bill's lover. Both parts were impossible, unplayable, but I kept showing up, kept trying, kept getting caught up in it all."

The meetings between Tenn and Inge came to an end, but not because of any ultimatum issued by Baxley. A pivotal and poisonous moment occurred not long after the opening night of *Camino Real,* a night that included not only poor reviews, but vitriolic arguments that flared between Tenn and Kazan, Tenn and Cheryl Crawford, the play's producer, and Tenn and Baxley, who had the temerity to remind him— the playwright of a failed play—that he had sought the advice of Bill Inge for help in making his play more accessible to audiences. "Tenn *had* asked Bill for help," Barbara told me. "*Camino* is wonderful, and I loved it. I love it still. But it was not always clear in its intentions, and it was not like anything Broadway had seen before. It was very dense, very rich. It required some knowledge of its characters. It isn't a play you can walk into, plop down, and start watching. You have to think. Bill kept telling Tenn to put a spine in the play, some bones on which to hang the lovely pictures he had made, and Tenn took his advice and tried to make his play stronger, to give it a stronger foundation."

Tenn took as much of Inge's advice as he could, applied it where he thought it worked, but the play failed nonetheless. Kazan remembers a trying time with the play, but he assigned himself a great deal of its failure. "I wasn't as present as I should have been," he confessed. "I had a lot on my mind, and my life was as shattered and fragmented and full of hallucinatory images as *Camino.* I did what I could, but it was halfhearted at best. I sat in the theater on opening night, and my mind suddenly expanded with ideas on how to improve the production and the play. Too late."

The "poisonous" moment that ended the interactions among Tenn, Inge, and Baxley was when Inge attempted to comfort Tenn. "Bill only wanted to console Tenn," Baxley told me. "He put his arm around Tenn, and that was very bold for Bill, very unlike him, as he was not easily demonstrative. He told Tenn that things would be okay, that he was sorry it hadn't gone well, and Tenn responded as if Bill had wrapped a serpent around his neck." Tenn pushed Inge away

"They didn't speak, except in brief, social occasions, for years," Barbara told me. "And I did not try to patch things up, because, without Tenn around, Bill was a bit stronger, a bit sweeter: he was all mine. And without Bill around, Tenn could spend all of his time with Frank, as he should, because Frank loved him, wanted nothing, took nothing."

Speaking of that time, Tenn told me that the experience of *Camino*

Real was a "slap in the face, a comeuppance, evidence of an angry and stingy God," who was alerting the writer to the fact that resources were limited, talent waned, and time was running out. "That was one of the first times," Tenn confessed, "that I began to think that a trip to visit Hart Crane, deep in the Gulf, might be a pleasant vacation to book. As a writer I was perfectly dry, and I wanted to take to the waters, the permanent waters."

"I needed William Inge very strongly after so much time with Tennessee Williams," Barbara told me. *Camino Real* had made her not only hungry for, but appreciative of, "straight, clean, propulsive narrative. It is true that Bill's work had fewer layers than Tenn's, but it's also true that there is immediate engagement with Bill's work: you get it. You may hate it; you may look down on it, but you get it. You understand it. *Camino* was lovely and haunting, but it was like a literary vortex: you got lost; you got confused. People would tell me they were moved at scenes, and then they were abandoned and had to fight to return to the feeling they had had."

Alone with Bill Inge, Baxley sought to give him the greatest gifts she felt she could bestow: she would give her lover herself—her entire biography and history and heart—and she would urge Bill Inge to place in it the heart, the domestic heart, of Tennessee Williams, a former lover whose affection and attention he had lost. This is how *The Dark at the Top of the Stairs* came to be written.

The Dark at the Top of the Stairs is the story of the Flood family, who are, according to Baxley, a "nice, middle-class midwestern family who are figurines, not of glass, as Tenn created, but sturdier bisque, frozen in one appropriate expression, resting on little doilies in what would seem a perfect environment, but the tables on which they rest are scarred, eaten by termites, ready to fall. Bill was really channeling Tenn, or trying to channel him. He used a spare and strong line of narrative—the one he had tried to throw out to Tenn during *Camino*—and he inserted it into a tender portrait of his family and mine."

The father of the family, Rubin, loses his job as a salesman, one that provided the family with security, and which kept him on the road, jovial and grandiose and unfaithful. Rubin Flood was the absent and feared father that had dominated the lives of both Tenn and Inge, and his returns, with hugs and occasional gifts, are dreaded by the sensitive, sissy son, who is bullied by his classmates and neighbors, and welcomed by the daughter, who is coming into her own sexually and socially and loves her father, whom she sees as strong and attractive, "a force of nature," as Barbara put it, "a literal flood, of words and emotions and feelings." The mother of the family, Cora, is thin of emotion, voice, patience. She runs a house with efficiency but no warmth. Affection has perpetually disappointed her, either because it was never reciprocated or because it led to the children, who need her fulsomely and give her no sense of satisfaction. Cora has wealthy family members who remind her of what she could have had and could have been. Although Rubin has provided a home for his family, and always addresses their needs, if not their desires, Cora views his inability to give them "things that shine and change a person, pretty things and happy times," as especially niggardly, a withholding of affections. Cora and Rubin no longer attempt anything but rudimentary physical contact, and their discussions are all about busted appliances, frayed rugs, and the dress their daughter will need for her first school dance. They worry about their sissy son: "Billy Inge, in every way," Barbara pointed out, "who runs to his mother and asks for help, who would love to have the town visited by a tornado, if only to prevent the torture of Monday mornings at school, when the bullying began again."

The Flood house, loveless, joyless, and airless, pushes the father and daughter outside of its walls for some comfort and diversion. Rubin reacquaints himself with Mavis, the town's beautician and an alleged women of promiscuous gifts, with whom he can be "gentle and open and served"; and the daughter finds a new friend, a young Jewish boy whose mother, a famous actress, has plunked him, alone and wild with imagination, in this dry little town for his education.

Barbara Baxley was Cora Flood in that she retreated when most hurt and withdrew sex when she couldn't face a man, but she was more fully Mavis, an open, nonjudgmental, sexually free woman who felt most comfortable affirming the prowess and the promise of her man. "You were my Mavis," Bill Inge told Barbara, and he went to her for approval of every line the character uttered, and he tried in vain to earn the role for her in the 1960 film version. (It went, instead, to Angela Lansbury.)

The Flood home is a mortuary of memories and resentment, and it was modeled on the St. Louis apartment of Tenn's *Glass Menagerie.* "It wasn't supposed to look like the Wingfield home," Barbara said, "but it was the same in nature, in its feel. People twirled fruitlessly in the home, dreaming, plotting to leave or to grow or to feel. The flood of emotions that are headed toward that house, to drown everyone in it, led to the family surname, and Bill wondered if 'Wingfield' was an ironic statement on Tom's ability to fly away from the home, while the wingless birds—those without a dream—remain on the ground, flapping and flailing and dying."

The writing of *The Dark at the Top of the Stairs* was a contest for William Inge. As a boy his head had become lodged in the banister of the family staircase, and the boy and his mother and sister became panicked; the young Billy Inge screamed in terror. Rubbing his back and neck, Inge's mother gently talked him out of his trap, all along praising him for being a "big and good boy, a little man." "Bill always remembered that," Barbara told me, "the day his mother told him to grow up, and let him know he could rescue himself—but only, it seems, if a woman was there to rub and console and praise him."

Once freed, the embarrassed Inge ran up the stairs to his room. He was left undisturbed, but he remained embarrassed by the event. The play was his announcement to the world that he was no longer afraid, he no longer needed his mother to rub his head and neck and tell him he was a big boy. Like Tom Wingfield, who had to flee his mother to grow and to be himself, Bill Inge, through the writing of *Dark*, let his mother, Maude, go, let her return to her own dreams and plots, and he got himself out of his troubles. "He had me," Barbara said, "so he could let go of his mother."

As was often the case, Inge soared while Tenn fumbled. As *Dark* was succeeding on Broadway, Tenn had a small success off-Broadway with *Garden District,* an evening of two one-act plays—a smaller score. "Bill Inge was perpetually plundering my toy box," Tenn told me, "and I was against a wall on which I could not imagine a mural and against which I could not imagine an escape."

When the script of *The Dark at the Top of the Stairs* was published, William Inge dedicated it to Tennessee Williams.

Tenn was not amused.

The Dark at the Top of the Stairs would be William Inge's last successful play, as well as the last one his mother would ever see or read: Maude Inge died in 1958. "The attack by Brustein, and then the death of his mother, unhinged him," Barbara told me, "but then he grew very calm and began thinking of ways to remember her, to love her again." Inge had lost his mother, and eternally. Tenn, however, was still alive, still in the corners of Inge's mind. The "final act of love" Inge constructed for both Maude Inge and Tennessee Williams was *A Loss of Roses*.

The story of the play: It is Depression-era Kansas, where Helen and Kenny, a widowed mother and her twenty-one-year-old son, cobble together a modest living with minor jobs and major sacrifices. Kenny is attractive and hungry for sexual and intellectual adventure, seeking the former with the town's randiest girls. Into this home arrives Lila, a former neighbor who had once done household work for Helen and Kenny, babysitting the boy, and who now visits the town with the touring company of actors she has joined. Brassy and free and funny, Lila deeply arouses Kenny, who wants to hear of her travels and who would like to sample the experience she has gained with a variety of men across the country. "This was Bill's fantasy," Barbara told me. "When he knew that I had slept with Marlon Brando, or any other men he found attractive, he had a greater interest in sleeping with me. He wanted to gain access to men he found attractive in whatever way he could, and that was often through me." Kenny presented himself to the world as heterosexual, but Inge wrote him with the knowledge that he was most aroused at getting from Lila not what she offered physically but what she had experienced physically with others. "That was Bill's religion, if you will," Barbara told me. "He didn't want to get God through Jesus Christ, or to be entered by Jesus, or to give his soul to something above: he wanted to be consumed by a furtively sought, fantasized sex, one that had been prayed for, hoped for, imagined."

Kenny aggressively moves on Lila, his former babysitter, and she resists him, to a point. "Like Bill, Kenny arouses the women around him," Barbara told me. "It's the classic pity fuck: 'I can help this confused man, and I do find my saving him sexually to be attractive, even if I know that it will bring me nothing but grief.'" As Kenny moves toward the desired Lila, he fashions a means of leaving his mother, who wants him to be independent, stand on his own, move along, but who is horrified that he has made inappropriate advances toward Lila, even as she is relieved to discover that her son has "normal" male urges.

"It is far beyond time for the son to leave that house," Kazan told me. "It was so clearly the experience of Bill Inge and his mother: the clinging affection, the staying too long, the incongruity of a young man stuck at home with his mother, acting as a surrogate husband." Kazan had been offered *A Loss of Roses,* but he rejected it, not merely because he was consumed with Tenn's *Sweet Bird of Youth* and the film *Wild River,* but because he couldn't imagine a coherent theatrical shape for the play, and he couldn't conceive of coaxing Inge to tell the play's whole truth. "He gave us this dinky, dime-store Oedipal story," Kazan continued, "and it comes at you with the delicacy of a train. The real story—of the play Bill wanted to write, and of the life Bill had led—is that the boy is queer. This terrifies the mother and it intrigues Lila, the tent-show actress who has not only had her honor and her body sullied, but who is drawn to the only people in her circus world who have ever shown her any sensitivity—the queers, the freaks. I would have been interested in a play that had this boy—in the middle of a truly unique and intense circle—pulled and coddled from these two very different women, both of whom had raised him and were now trying to raise him up toward manhood. Instead, we get a horny little stud who, for reasons that no one can accept, is at home with Mommy, henpecked, docile, horny after dinner."

Inge set the play in the Depression, in Kansas, because that was the time he recalled with his mother, dreaming of finding riches, of escaping the dry, flat land and the corrosive attentions of "the father-husband monster," the name Inge had applied to Luther Inge. Kenny tries to be both son and provider to his mother, and when he is feeling strongest, when he has begun to make sexual advances toward Lila, he presents his mother with an expensive watch, for which he has laboriously saved: it is a replacement for a watch given to her by her late husband, and the mother refuses it. "Bill never loved or understood his father," according to Barbara, "and all he could ultimately give him was money, which he did. There was some rapprochement between the idea of his father and himself when he stepped in and began to care for Maude, when he metaphorically turned to his father and announced, 'I'll take it from here.'" Bill always loved *The Glass Menagerie,* but he hated that only Tom gets away, only Tom leaves the suffocating apartment and the mother's past. Bill decided that in *Roses,* everyone finds their freedom. This does not mean they find happiness: Bill always maintained—as did Tenn—that it is a myth that freedom means happiness. It doesn't. It usually means that you're now free to make colossal mistakes, ruin your own life in your own style and on your own time—but you're free. Bill was not going to leave Helen and Lila—as Tom had left Amanda and Laura—in the dark, literally and metaphorically."

At the conclusion of *A Loss of Roses,* Kenny realizes it is folly to pursue a life with Lila, but it is equally impossible to live in the house with his mother. He leaves to begin his own life, with whatever sexual roles he is most comfortable playing. Helen, free for the first time in her life of domestic obligations, may become a new person, or she may drift away entirely. Lila, offered employment that may include blue movies and stag shows, leaves the town and the sweet boy who made her feel like both a lady and an instrument of sexual pleasure. On her way out of the neighborhood where she once lived, she sees a young girl heading for the local school, with a bunch of roses in her hand, a gift for the teacher. Lila recalls that she had once taken roses to her grade-school teacher, and later in the day, sharing this experience with classmates, she had been punished and humiliated by the teacher. Hurt by this action, Lila had wanted her roses back: she felt the gift had been voided. "That was crafty," Kazan said. "Roses are symbols of purity and innocence and romantic intention. If they are red, they can be symbols of womanhood, menstruation, fecundity. Rose also happens to be the name of Tennessee's poor sister, who, when she expressed herself—wildly, crazily—was lobotomized. Lila gives of herself, gives the roses, and that is her purity and her innocence and her sweetness, but when she speaks out, when she is most herself, she is slapped down, silenced. Not lobotomized, but traumatized."

Barbara urged Bill to include some sort of homage, in any way he could manage, to Luther Inge, and so Kenny learns, as he is trying to replace and remove from memory the dead and distant father, that his father had died saving his life. "There was too much compressed in too little a space of time," Kazan told me. "The boy learns he cannot have Lila or his mother; he decides he should get out on his own; his mother rejects and resents the boy's attempts to push the father out of memory, and is told that he was actually something of a saint, saving the kid and losing his own life; and then they all bravely face their bleak futures. Great issues and great themes, but presented in an inferior way."

The inclusion of a subplot concerning the father—seen initially as unlovable, but actually the victim of a loving and risky act—was another effort on the part of William Inge to tackle something of which Tenn felt incapable: love for his father. "That was the hardest part of the play," Barbara told me. "Bill always knew that Tenn had forced himself to love or to understand his mother in *The Glass Menagerie,* and Bill hoped to achieve the same dramatic and personal release with this tribute. It wasn't fully realized in the play because Bill couldn't fully deal with it."

Herbert Machiz, who had directed some of Tenn's off-Broadway works, was approached and did not respond. Even Joshua Logan, with whom Inge had tense relations and for whom he had little respect, was approached. He, too, turned it down. Ultimately, Barbara suggested Daniel Mann, who had done well by Inge with both stage and screen versions of *Come Back, Little Sheba,* and by Tenn with *The Rose Tattoo.* There was no question of casting: Inge had written Lila for Barbara Baxley, and he had written Helen for Shirley Booth, with whom he had forged a tender, if not close, relationship during *Sheba.* For the role of Kenny, it was Kazan, through the urging of Stella Adler, who recommended a young actor named Warren Beatty. "I remember Stella's words to this day," Barbara told me. " 'He's smart and he's stunning and you'll believe that these two women—along with all the women in the town—are fighting for some time with him.' "

Mann, however, was a poor choice to direct, because, according to Kazan, "he wasn't a terribly good director, which is a detriment to begin with, but he also could only build on something good. He had no ability at all to reshape a play, to shift focus, to talk to a playwright and coerce him to alter something that wasn't working. He was a passive director: he showed up and followed the lead, generally a female star. You can't go too terribly wrong when Shirley Booth or Anna Magnani [whom he directed in the film version of *The Rose Tattoo*] or Maureen Stapleton is the focus. Those women directed whatever had Danny Mann's name plastered on it. He was a gofer with a DGA membership."

Daniel Mann also did not care for Barbara Baxley, and flatly refused to cast her as Lila, a part that had been written for her. "He had heard I was difficult," Barbara said, "and I thought, 'Well, okay, so much for my suggesting him for the job. We'll just get another director.' " That did not happen. To everyone's amazement, Bill Inge agreed with Mann and told Baxley that he "was going another way."

"I was devastated," said Barbara, "and that ended my relationship with Bill for a number of years. I had been aware of his many weaknesses over the years, but I always believed—stupidly—that he would stand up for me, defend me."

Carol Haney, a singer and dancer who had won a Tony Award for her role in *The Pajama Game,* and who had begun a career as a director and choreographer, was chosen to play the role. "That was ludicrous," Tenn told me, "because she became a cartoon. It was like when Imogene Coca on *Your Show of Shows* would play a *femme fatale.* You would fall out of your seat laughing, and that's what happened with Haney. She was a sexless beanpole of a girl, and every line became a laugh line. There was no sexual tension, and I would have thought Warren Beatty could look at a credenza and force it to lubricate. There was nothing with Haney."

Shirley Booth came to hate her part, which she realized, correctly, was a supporting role, and she quit when the play was rehearsing out of town. She was replaced with Betty Field, touted as a "William Inge actress" because of her roles in the film versions of *Picnic* and *Bus Stop;* but whatever allure or appeal Field had possessed in the days when her husband Elmer Rice had written *Dream Girl* for her were gone. Suitably fat and tired for the role of Helen, she was unfocused, inaudible, and unable to understand her character.

A Loss of Roses closed in less than a month, but turned a profit nonetheless, thanks to a film sale. (The film, renamed *The Stripper,* would star Joanne Woodward and be released in 1963.) Warren Beatty earned a Tony nomination for his performance as Kenny—a triumph of "priapic appeal," according to Tenn.

Alone on opening night, Inge wrote a letter to Tenn, begging forgiveness ("For *what* I could never surmise," said Tenn) and alluding to the prepared and examined death they had discussed so many years ago. Tenn offered no reply, in any form, to the letter.

"Life is so odd," Tenn told me. "I only came to be reconciled with Bill Inge through failure and tragedy. Failure and tragedy and friendship—our odd Holy Trinity."

Inge now lived in California, having renounced New York, where, he claimed, there was the scent of failure on every corner, and deception in the eyes of everyone he saw. California had brought him the success he thought he wanted: he earned an Oscar for his screenplay for *Splendor in the Grass,* directed by Kazan, and he bragged to friends that young actors circled around him for advice, stories, affirmation. Inge lived at 1440 Oriole Drive, in the Hollywood Hills, what he called "the bird street," a residential homage to Tenn, who was forever known as "Bird" or, to Inge, "the Glorious Bird." The address might bring him luck, he thought, an amulet via address to tap into the greater talents of his friend; but his writing was torturous, and his drinking became, as Tenn put it, "Olympian, outrageous." "He tried to dry out," Baxley told me. "He went to fat farms and health clinics and took vitamins and tried to walk around California. He could always give a regimen about two weeks, and then he would go on a bender that was stronger than the last."

"There was a period of time," Tenn explained to me, "when Bill and I compared battle scars, which is to say, we talked about our failures, and we came to a level of understanding and comfort that was close to what we had when we first met."

Inge would rethink and reshape *A Loss of Roses, Natural Affection,* and *Where's Daddy?,* while Tenn would mount defenses for the quality inherent in *The Milk Train Doesn't Stop Here Anymore, Slapstick Tragedy, The Seven Descents of Myrtle, In the Bar of a Tokyo Hotel.* "What we had, I now see," Tenn said, "was a Rosary of failures, and if we had had some beads to work, we certainly would have, expanding characters, hiring new directors, altering dialogue. In our phone calls and in meetings we had, we imagined our lives as successful writers and fully integrated people."

When Tenn and Inge got together, they would repair to the bedroom, lying "on bed" talking, holding each other. There was no longer even a pretense of romance, only of comfort, and there was a feeling, this time, that a final watch was in effect: they were no longer the young, dreaming writers with Mallarmé quotes on the wall or Harry Crosby's fiery sun to look to for inspiration. "This was a sweet form of Extreme Unction," Tenn said, "final rites for our talents and for our friendship, but we were back to the old days, and I told Barbara to do the same when she went to visit him. 'Just hold him. Talk to him. Treat him like a writer. Tell him the failures were some sort of mistake, not his fault.' This was, of course, what I was also telling people to say to me as well."

William Inge began to write novels: They were met with mixed reviews, and he attempted suicide. "If I can't write any longer," he told Tenn, "why do anything any longer, like live?" Inge's sister, Helene, was sent for and moved into his house. Inge had turned to mysticism, religion, the occult. One spirit diviner contacted his long-dead and much-loved brother; another his mother, who told him she was appalled at the condition in which he was keeping his home. "Was that all she said?" Tenn asked. "Yes," Inge replied. "Mother always told me I never took care of my things."

Inge threw some runes for Tenn to divine his own future. It was not good. "Somehow my future included an alphabet that was missing several vital letters," Tenn said. "I never could figure out how Bill got this from a velvet bag of little blocks, but it felt as genuine as anything else I was consulting at the time."

Both writers investigated Catholicism at the same time, with Tenn ultimately converting to his own design of the Roman faith, while Bill found comfort in the prayers and the ritual. Ultimately, Inge would claim comfort from a faith that was described to him by Tenn after an encounter with Anne Sexton.

Sexton, a poet of "sensitive and suicidal intent," as Tenn put it, had come to his attention through Robert Lowell, who told Tenn that she was a strong but dangerous talent. "He added that I was such a thing myself," Tenn told me, "so I felt compelled to read her work, which I found fascinating. She had managed to tap into the same fears and self-hatreds I understood so well. We both loved music, and we both hated to be too close to anyone. She loved me, or said she did, so something of a relationship was established."

In 1969 Sexton was working on her first—and only—play, *Mercy Street*. She sent Tenn the script, asking for his advice on any revisions he thought necessary. Tenn read the play and admired it, envied what he called its "epic scope and chilling fatality." Tenn made no notes, even though Sexton had requested them: all she got was his praise, both for the text and for the decision to cast Marian Seldes ("my wise and tender servant") in the role based on Sexton. Told by Tenn to adhere to Seldes, Sexton did so, wearing a pair of shoes given to her by the actress, which cushioned her feet against the Manhattan sidewalks, watching her every move, even imitating her speech patterns. Tenn even told her they looked like sisters: tall, raven-haired, pale, like "a duo of seers from medieval vaudeville."

Tenn became obsessed with Sexton's poetry, and he called the poet at her home in Massachusetts several times, telling her he was looking for peace or God or some comfort. Sexton told him he would be better off taking the advice of her therapist, who said that God, whatever that was, was deep in her typewriter. "And so," Tenn told me, "I went to my machine, my *deus ex machina* every day, looking for God. I was typing toward God." Tenn urged Bill Inge to search for the same God in the same way.

Tenn took copies of Sexton's books to Inge and read them to him on his cluttered bed, the drapes drawn, traffic on Sunset Boulevard sounding as if it were hundreds of miles away. The central air-conditioning hummed. Bill Inge survived on soft food and televised sermons. "I wanted to tell him stories when there had been a future for us," Tenn said, "because we both wanted to know if we still had a future, if we still could dream and write and matter." The stories were told in the language of Anne Sexton, "severe and strained and seared into the mind and on the page." Although the room was dark and no reflections were available, Tenn asked his friend to imagine bouncing lights on the ceiling, and to each one he should attach a thought, drop a memory. 'Look upward and latch on to whatever happy memory or need arises.' This activity lulled Bill Inge into sleep. The next day, according to Tenn, Inge had scribbled some notes on a pad for a play that was based on their conversations of the previous evening. Tenn was enraged by the notes, and he destroyed them not long after he discovered them. He left abruptly and would never see William Inge again.

Back in New York, Tenn began writing a play about his "shattered" friends Bill Inge and Anne Sexton. "For so many years, I had resented the competition that had been brought to me by Bill. I loved and wanted and needed the comfort he brought instead, and I failed to understand that the competition from his plays grew stronger and asked the same questions I had. I see now a large and golden bed—golden by the memories that are happy and remind me that we were once young and time was an ally, and by the ministrations of a Jo Mielziner who is not dead but ready to cast one of his lemony sunsets on a bad memory— and Bill and I are there and songs of our time are playing on a radio that can't be taken from us by our bad actions or our misguided erotic affections. We speak of plays and novels and paintings and stories told. We both understand that stories are what get us up in the morning and to sleep at night. Myth and fable and the simple story of a woman who has a breakdown making a grocery list; myth and legend and the image of a young man attempting to outrun an imagined team of athletes, hoping for a victory on the field. He's trying to outrun the truth and the power of his feelings, and the only victory, he realizes, late in the game, is death or a life suspended in lies of action or of liquid. Alcohol builds for us an amber gel into which we can submerge our minds, but our minds fight the action, like the kittens the lady down the street used to place in burlap sacks, stuffing them into garbage pails of warm water, drowning them, keeping the yards and the streets clean, and the children screaming. The truth wants to win.

"And a woman—Anne Sexton, tall and dark and serious—walks through that window with the billowing curtains, and on the street below, happier cats roam and mewl. She is fine with the image of two male lovers relaxing, and asks for a cigarette. She sits and smokes deeply. 'Time is wasting,' she reminds the men. 'There won't be much more time for nights like this.'

"Anne Sexton walks into my dreams now, as she walked into my life in the late sixties, a dead decade, when my brain had been submerged in amber, my limbs on a course of action separate from that for which my brain had arranged an itinerary. Sexton never doubted my talent, never doubted the worth of what I might be trying to do. She only doubted the ability we had to stay on the job, to endure the rigors of our employment, to keep marshaling our puny endowments to keep providing the poems and the plays.

" 'We have our limits,' she always told me. 'We run against and away from the limits.' But the limbs don't always work, and to get the mind working, I need liquor and pills and powders and help from the saints and the legends who lived before us. What should I do?

"As she did in Manhattan in 1969, Anne Sexton tells me—and a slumbering Bill Inge—the same things in that timeless dream: 'I don't believe in looking so high. There's nothing up or out there that can help us. We're earthbound now, and there is help right here, right now. Not for me, but for you.' "

"I LOOK BACK NOW," Tenn said, "and I remember that on that bed, in that cold, dark room, Bill and I were both men—queer men—who spent our lives creating the perfect woman—or perfect women— who would make us whole and happy and operational. This is true in both our work as writers and as men." What the two men kept seeing in imagined reflections on the ceiling, what the dropped memories revealed, were women—those kind women who had supported and inspired them all their lives. There was no hope in money or awards or production of a play, but a female friend, a soft shoulder, a kind voice, embraces Tenn called "the rescue in the dark night with a mother's cool palm," was what they most wanted. Tenn recalled nights in that room when he and Inge exchanged recipes for the ideal woman: If Edwina Williams could not give Tenn warmth and unconditional love, he would find it with Maureen Stapleton or Marian Seldes or Elizabeth Ashley; if he needed someone to champion his work without "daggers of doubt," he would call on Stella Adler, Eva Le Gallienne. Inge replaced Maude Inge with Eileen Heckart and Barbara Baxley and Elizabeth Wilson—strong women who would fight off his bullies and keep him safe, get him back to work, tell him he was loved, a "good boy." All through the night they added quarters and halves of certain women, until they might get the formula right.

"The construction of the ideal woman, either from flesh or the fog, is what I do," Tenn said, "and I came to see that it was also what Bill did." Tenn realized, he confessed, that Inge had been—could have been—his soul mate, the male friend he felt he was never able to cultivate or endure.

"Wisdom arriving late is particularly brutal," Tenn told me.

IN THE SUMMER of 1973, Tenn discovered again the joys and the benefits of cocaine, and he consumed a great deal of it as he tried to write and as he watched the televised hearings concerning the Watergate scandal and the presidency of Richard M. Nixon. "I was unable," he told me, "to know what was real that summer of 1973. I kept confusing my play with the Watergate hearings, and conversations with friends with the testimonies of various pudgy men at that green, felt-covered table, with cocklike microphones sticking up in their faces. I came to believe that Mo Dean was the manifestation of Wallace Stevens's emperor of ice cream, although she had whipped-cream hair, a sort of clitoral baked Alaska. I had dinner with Harold Clurman one night and could not tell if he was the man who had once directed my plays or Senator Sam Ervin. I kept asking Clurman questions about Watergate, about Haldeman and Ehrlichman, and he ultimately left, something for which I do not blame him at all."

It was during this time that both Barbara Baxley and Maureen Stapleton called Tenn to tell him that Bill Inge had entered a "terminal" phase. Inge was constantly drunk, seriously abusing pills. His sister, Helene, informed Tenn that there were hundreds of pills underneath her brother's mattress. Tenn agreed to call his friend, in the hope of steering him off an obvious suicide course.

"We talked for a long time," Tenn told me. "I wasn't as high as I usually was. I talked to him about writers who might help him, who might inspire him to find the God in his own typewriter. I quoted to him from Joan Didion, who had the lapidary toughness we both loved and could never accomplish. I would read sentences from *Play It as It Lays* and show him how marvelous they were. I would describe how the paragraphs were broken up, how the words looked against the page. I read to him—from books and from memory—Bill Goyen's *The House of Breath*. I reminded him of the majesty and the mystery of Goyen's people, of how surprised we could still be by ourselves and others." Tenn attempted several other calls to Bill Inge, but he wouldn't come to the phone. Tenn would speak to Helene, and he would hear Bill's labored breathing in the background, listening on an extension, the inevitable click when he hung up, and he would wonder what Bill was up to. Regretting that he had destroyed Bill's notes for a play, Tenn tried to re-create them. He imagined making them a gift to his friend, so he wrote, under the manic snowiness of cocaine, a fast version of what he had remembered.

Tenn was unable to type fast enough: William Inge committed suicide on June 10, 1973, stumbling out to his garage, climbing into his immaculate and rarely used car, and turning on the engine. Inge had always been a nervous driver—his passengers never felt comfortable being in a car with him. His novel *My Son Is a Splendid Driver* held a title that was ironic to his friends.

Tenn wondered if his friend found, in that car, at long last, the comfort and peace that he always believed a prepared and examined death would bring. "I wondered," Tenn said, "if he thought of all the teasing he had endured, all the misunderstandings, all the gifts he had offered and that had gone begging for a loving recipient, and I hoped that he could let it all go, perfumed by carbon monoxide, falling into a deep and final sleep." One of the notes Inge had made for his play had read: "My final comfortable place will be one in which my mind will contain no memories except of being held and hugged and pulled up and away from harm. Everything else will fall away."

Tenn returned to New York and to a writing table that contained two piles of pale judgment: typing paper and cocaine. He would write and snort in marathon sessions. On or near July 4th, friends became worried about him and called to see how he was doing. Maureen Stapleton tells me that his words flew from his mouth so quickly that she had no idea what he was saying. She urged him to lay off the drugs, drink some coffee, and watch some TV. "And I got my ass over there from wherever I was supposed to be," she told me. "I did what we always did for each other: dropped everything and went to see about my crazy friend." Stapleton fed him coffee and Chinese food "to soak up the poisons," and they turned on the television. "It was a fucking double feature," Stapleton told me. "*Picnic*, of course, which, because of the timing, made us cry like babies. I saw so much in that film that I had never seen and will never see again, and Tenn and I were basket cases." The second film was *The Music Man*, and "it saved us. We could laugh and live again. That musical was a world that Bill Inge wanted to join, but didn't really understand. Bill Inge's Harold Hill would have been fucking his mother and wearing ladies' panties, and the women of the town, led by Hermione Gingold, would have been eating school-children. Tenn and I watched the movie knowing the underside of it, and it saved us."

Stapleton stayed the night, boiling coffee and throwing out cocaine. "The plumbing was paranoid and jumpy," she quipped, "but Tenn began to calm down." Stapleton got into bed with Tenn and they began, once again, to talk things out. At one point Tenn began to cry and Stapleton cradled him. Tenn was asking, over and over, "Who will take care of Tennessee now?" Tenn asked it repeatedly, and just as often Stapleton would reply, "Baby, I have no fucking idea, but I'm here now."

Tenn returned to his typewriter "occasionally visited by God," and took breaks to watch the never-ending saga of Watergate. He was joined in the watching, via phone, by Carrie Nye and Kate Reid, who were filming Maxim Gorky's *Enemies* in upstate New York, where they often refused to report to the set during good moments of testimony. At one point, while working on a poem that had come to him in a dream, he phoned Anne Sexton to read it to her.

"She was polite but without praise," Tenn told me. "She told me what was good about it, but that was only about a quarter of it. I told her I would throw it out and start over, even as it killed me to do so. 'Yeah,' she said, 'but that's being a poet. Gutting and sewing up and smiling through the shit.'"

The Watergate hearings came to an end. Richard M. Nixon resigned the presidency in August of 1974. Gerald Ford assumed the presidency, assuring the citizenry that "our long national nightmare is over." Tenn liked the quote and wrote it down, for the title of either a play or a poem or a short story. He thought he should call Sexton and ask her what she thought.

On October 4, 1974, Anne Sexton put on her mother's fur coat and walked out to her garage and got into her not-so-immaculate car and turned on the engine. Tenn liked to think that the mother's coat smelled of Arpège or Norman Norell or Bellodgia, to soften the thick but welcoming smell of carbon monoxide. "I hope she felt that the coat was her mother's arms," Tenn told me. "I hope that, like Bill, she went with ease and a sense of peace."

Thinking of William Inge and Anne Sexton in New Orleans with me, Tenn came up with an idea for a poem. He dictated the following, in fits and starts, over several hours, to me:

So tell me, if you can, if you will, is there peace?
In the deep or the dark, wherever you ran,
Is what we wanted and needed there? To own, sense, or lease?
I would follow you—think of it—will if I can.

Somewhere—in my memory, of course—is a noisy café, full of smoke
*   and laughter*
And questions that find a reply—gifts that find a happy recipient.
All of us sought answers in machines and medicines,
Not trusting people or the God who had hastily created them,
Who made them empty, if occasionally pretty and useful.
We found comfort in beds that held no sex, in which nothing would be
*   born*

But resentment. If we couldn't be held in bed by a lover, we could be
* held by a story.*
I have a new story now, one I wish I could share with you, but you ran
* ahead of me*
As you often did. In my story there are tomorrows with no fear and
* typewriters that*
Are full of Gods and extra letters, to help us tell our side of things, to
* reach out and*
Fill up all these people we keep meeting and losing.
I hope you're full now, your stories complete and neatly typed and
* indexed with the*
endings you craved, wrapped in your mother's arms or sitting by the
* sink,*
Heart and life expanding, the blood on the tiles innocent and pure,
* so unlike your thoughts.*
This café will have music soon, I think, and the instruments will
* always sound out the clearest*
notes, the purest tones. There is celebration in the air, for all that
* you did and all that you left behind. The sound is faint now,*
* considerate for your slumber, your need for quiet, but the sound*
* will grow, a party will begin, and you'll join us, and you'll be*
* welcomed, and you will join the sound of the music with your*
* voices.*
This is whatever it is. Notes. Thoughts. A poem.
It is not, and never will be, a farewell.

When Tenn had finished the poem, I asked him what I should do
with it. He asked that I give it to Barbara Baxley, if and when I ever
met her.

Thirteen

TENN WAS a different person after discussing Bill Inge: organized, focused, hurried. I would not know until many years later that he had returned to his hotel room and made a phone call, deep in the night, to Elia Kazan, to share some ideas about *Camino Real,* to score some points. Tenn was scratching at scabs, digging in what Kazan called "the dirt of that garden we had neglected so long ago." Kazan had been critical of Tenn in that call, lamenting his wasting of time, the blurred thinking, the failure of faith, and he told his friend to leave him alone, to get back to work.

Tenn handed me a small piece of paper on which was written: "Intention is the hard, straight line on which you should be walking. Let it lead you where it wants to."

I read the note, twice, and then looked to Tenn for an explanation. He then handed me several sheets of paper on which he had crafted a family tree of characters.

The tree of characters was populated with the names of actresses we had already discussed, and whose names I had scribbled on the menu from our lunch that first day. In the middle of the tree, straddling it somewhat, I saw my name and Tenn's. Mine was followed by a question mark.

"I no longer know where this is going," Tenn told me, and since the statement was made as he gestured toward the cluttered shopping bag, I wasn't sure if he was referring to a particular project, our course of action, or his life as a writer.

"I'm alone now," he explained, and he soon made it clear that he meant in his current hotel room, which no longer housed the person, never named, with whom he had traveled to New Orleans. It was the first time I learned that during our discussions across the city, someone had sat, somewhere, waiting for his return; and since Tenn had arrived each morning with examples of writing or descriptions of calls made to various people at all hours, there could not have been much interaction or discussion between them. Nonetheless, Tenn described this person, a young man, a writer, as a distraction and a nuisance, who needed to "sort out his own things, in his own way—something I could say for both of us as well."

Our time together was now limited, Tenn explained. He had been writing all night, and he learned that his work could not continue with his given inventory. His mind seemed to him now to have grown smaller, poorly maintained. As people age and are moved to smaller, tighter, ignored spaces, one can find an armoire, a night table, a chair—emblems of the house they had once lived in fully, happily. These pieces of furniture, still beautiful, vintage and proud, stood next to the bedpan and the hospital bed and the plastic flowers from the inattentive front desk of the hospice in which they now sat. "This is my theater," Tenn told me, savagely slapping his forehead. "It is dark and dusty and it is no longer in the beautiful building, but housed in some small, dark artery, dusty and ignored. But good pieces are still scattered about." The good pieces were not chairs or desks but characters, women looking for a writer to help them out of their predicament, to give them voice, to get the fog rolling.

One of the first pages to come out of Tenn's shopping bag was an outline of sorts, jagged and fast, of a memoir he now hoped to write. Tenn had published his memoirs only a few years prior to our meeting. I had read them and we had hurriedly discussed them. It was not a book of which he was proud; it was an effort he had avoided, rushed through, skimmed over, and forgotten about. He had not been honest in the book, not fully, and he had not marshaled his talents and his thoughts toward its completion. "It was a project created to give me momentum," he admitted, "to allow me to continue as a writer, to inject myself into the flow of things, to be noticed." The book was full of anecdotes of what he had done and what he had thought, but he now wanted to write a book that would be, as his notes attested, "a document of the elements that made me write and made me want to share my thoughts and my fears with others. A testament to the people who led me to the act of writing and allowed me to complete it."

In the margins were references to the house at Coliseum and Constantinople, the balconies of Royal Street, the stage directions of *Summer and Smoke,* the days and nights spent with Lillian Gish and on the soft shoulders of streets high above Los Angeles. Tenn was, in his thoughts, in his words, and in his notes, continually circling the same locations, the same people, the same themes.

"I'm drowning," he confessed, "and I know that. I know there's a reason that I keep returning to those memories, those points of departure, but I don't know what it is. I can't progress from the memories and the notes and the dreams, all of which give me hope and that intense warmth and brackish recognition that I know precede the truth of things."

Tenn paused for a moment, fingering the pages in the bag.

"I've approached this terribly," he told me. "Entirely inappropriate. I've wandered. I have not been truthful. I want to try another method, another project."

I did not understand what the new project would be, or the method needed to complete it. I did not ask for clarification.

The name that took the top position on the tree of characters, Tenn's family of function, was that of Geraldine Page, an actress to whom Tenn had made numerous references, but who had always been pushed aside, saved for later, when time and energy might be more abundant. Page, like Tenn, had a history in Missouri, a state and a mind-set that both had escaped and that both reflected upon with the same mixture of humor and embarrassment.

Born in a city called Kirksville in 1924, Page always quipped to Tenn that it was full of churches and crayons—that was her primary memory. Like another rustic yet supernal actress—Lois Smith—Page found her first outlet as an actress in a church, finding her greed for the attention and for more and more lines to learn in direct opposition to the humility and grace she was supposed to search and yearn for within the walls of what she called a "square and stark and solid" building. Thirteen years younger than Tenn, Page was the "little sister of the dramatic arts" to the older playwright, and if he didn't always trust her opinions and her intentions off the stage (she could be niggardly with her affections and her opinions, and she burned off boring situations and people like an athlete burns off fat), Tenn never failed to ask her how things were operating on the stage, both with plays in which she starred and with those he would beg her to read. Page, in a fashion similar to that employed by Laurette Taylor in *The Glass Menagerie,* had an ability to shift the focus of a play toward its leading female character, and as with Taylor, this was not done in an attempt to garnish all of the attention or the acclaim. "She recognized that the women I had written into my plays, and which I had asked her to play, were the center of the play, the scaffolding of the building I had constructed," Tenn told me. "So she always made sure that the intentions grew from her, radiated from her position."

Tenn crafted a statement (as he titled it) for me to present to Page, in the hopes that she would read or hear it and then call on Tenn to write for her, or she might call to recommend some means of improving himself. This is what Tenn wrote:

She has the mind of a writer, which is, I assure you, the highest compliment I could pay her. She was also unafraid of honesty or silence, two things I always think of when I think of her. She didn't need approval or find comfort in silly talk or empty conversations that bond people together: She came to work and to work well. She wore herself out. Shaw writes something in his preface to *The Doctor's Dilemma,* I think, that always makes me think of Gerry: "Use your health, even to the point of wearing it out. That is what it is for. Spend all you have before you die; and do not outlive yourself." Gerry used everything, and she was not afraid to ask everyone around her to use everything as well. She had an understanding of why we were all gathered together to create theater that I have only found in perhaps two or three other people. She did not take a lot of things seriously, but she certainly took her work seriously, and she took herself seriously in the ruthless pursuit of getting her work to the highest level of accomplishment.

Geraldine Page is a great actress. That is not a statement one makes freely. It wasn't that she simply had talent—everyone has some bit of talent, a speck of something sparkly—she had a genius, a maddening intellect that came with a supernatural vision—of people and things. She pushed me. We argued. We worked it out. She made me a better writer and she made my plays better plays. Friendship? I wouldn't say so: I don't think of leaning on Gerry's shoulder or calling her up in the middle of the night for comfort and a few laughs. But I would call her—and I have called her—to remind me of why we do this, why we matter, why we have to get it right.

Geraldine Page is all about getting it right, and just above that goal is getting it brilliant, which she does. A solitary genius.

When Page read the notes, she snorted, look stunned, smiled softly at me. "I tried to be a friend to Tennessee," she told me. "I really did, but there was always a thick wall around him, defenses and artifice and deflections. Maybe that's what I also have; maybe that's what he's talking about. I will say that I thought I was being a friend when he called me, when he sought me out, but I was never enough: I could never give him what he needed, and what he needed was ludicrous, because he wanted a simple answer or a simple method to get himself together and to work and to mean something to people. And there is no simple way. There is no *one* way!"

Page noticed a quote from Oscar Wilde in the upper-right-hand corner of his notes: "She lives the poetry she cannot write." "Why is that here?" she asked.

I told her that Tennessee had struggled to recall this quote as he spoke of her, an actress he certainly adored, but a woman he never came to understand. "I'm a dreamer," he told me. "I anticipate events, emotions, outcomes, and I am always disappointed. Gerry does not dream until a task is at hand, and she dreams with the assistance of a writer and a director and a design crew, so her dreams find manifestation, even if she is never satisfied with the final presentation. I could learn so much from her. I haven't learned yet to not dream of or for anything unless it is directly related to work, to survival, to getting by. The people in our daily midst are not deserving of our dreams. We must be like Gerry and walk and move and take care of daily events, but we must not commit to these activities our priceless ability to transform through a dream."

"I have no idea what he means," Page confessed. "I think that we dream precisely to work and to survive, but I also think we dream too much. Tennessee dreamed too much. The dreams took over. It is, I

Geraldine Page in the 1961 film version of *Summer and Smoke*, much as she first appeared to Tennessee a decade earlier in the off-Broadway production of the play. Page was intense, driven, and, in Tennessee's words, "obsessive about working and observing."

suppose, what we must do initially: dream. We dream our way into a fantasy and we dream our way out of whatever town or situation or identity we found at birth, and we craft a new one. When we craft a way out and a way forward, the dreamer is replaced, I guess, by the worker, the craftsman.

"When I get a script, the dreams of the writer are a gift to me, to open and unravel and play with. I don't dream when I act—I guess I expect a lot, I work toward a lot, but I do not imagine or dream an outcome or a reaction. What I try to do instead is take the writer's dream—like with Tennessee's work—and meld it with images and feelings I've noticed throughout my life. Maybe I'm melding the dreams of the writer with the waking, walking dream of life to create a part. Who knows what people are thinking about when they walk around or do their daily chores? Is that dreaming? Hoping? Expecting?

"But you see, dreaming is a negative thing, in a way, and I think Tennessee's dreaming—that lifelong plunge into darkness—was a negative thing. Dreams come when we're asleep or unconscious or drugged or near death. We see white light and dead friends and relatives in a sort of dream when the brain recedes. It's very poetic, but it's not a state in which I care to work. I need all of my senses when I'm working. I need to remember and to be alive and afraid and able to edit and censor and evaluate. There's an age to dream, and I'm past that. So was Tennessee. So are you. The dreams are the first act, I guess. The overture. And the work begins. One should always be beginning to work. And then you allow others to dream."

Page came to Tenn through the ministrations of José Quintero, who had been assigned to direct the revival of *Summer and Smoke,* a reclamation of Tenn's play, a rebuke to the failure that had been presented on Broadway by Margo Jones, whose affections Tenn now rejected, and who had been pushed to the mental sidelines. "Tennessee had a particularly sharp ability to remove from his line of vision, and from his thoughts, anyone who had, in his opinion, failed to serve his theatrical aspirations," Quintero told me. "The revival of *Summer and Smoke* had a cloud over it, of revenge and of settling scores. Tennessee was determined to show audiences and critics that it was a play that worked, that it was a fine piece of literature, that it could move people. These were points he reiterated over and over, after which he would tell me—in clear terms—that these wonderful attributes had been degraded by the limitations and prejudices of the director. I had very little trust handed to me by Tennessee during our time on *Summer and Smoke.* I don't think that he appreciated—and certainly never acknowledged—my contributions to the play until the reviews were in and the play was well-received, and this is, of course, ludicrous. Tennessee could trust an actress, a designer, a composer simply on the basis of how their contributions made him feel. He would point to his heart and tell me that the primary critic—that bruised and knowing heart—had passed the crucial judgment. He did not extend the same courtesy, by way of his heart, to his directors—certainly not to me, not at that time."

Given that he did not trust Quintero, whose work was largely unknown to him, Tenn did not approve initially of his casting choice for the role of Alma, a woman who, more than Blanche DuBois, was a reflection of the playwright's "errant and hungry heart."

"It has become a sort of concrete truth that I am Blanche," Tenn said, "but I am much more like Alma, peeking through actual and metaphysical curtains, spying on the things I want to love and to feel and to have, but afraid to get much farther than the porch. My porch is the stage, I suppose, or the pale judgment, where I can place stage directions and characters and move them about in a fashion that is more to my liking than those presented by my limitations and my fears. Blanche, I suppose, is Alma after years of denial and needs unfurnished. Blanche is Alma beyond that porch, the lacy curtains through which she has peered now tied about her head, a mantilla she will tell people came from some nobleman from Barcelona who had hoped to marry her. We lie when we cannot love, when we are not loved. Alma has learned only to lie to herself, to keep believing that she is worthy of love, that she may one day possess it. Her delusions have not taken root in the land beneath her feet."

Tenn wanted an actress of great strength who could also convey the ethereal and "spiritual nobility" of Alma Winemiller, and Geraldine Page, an actress who had spent most of her professional time on stages outside of New York, did not seem ideal for this purpose. "Geraldine burned with intelligence, with concentration," Quintero remembered. "This is a quality that she had even at that age, at that stage of her development, and it was very disconcerting when it was not in the service of a character. It could create the appearance of arrogance or coldness. I came to know and to love her very much, so I could see what she was actually thinking or doing, but I think that when I presented her to Tennessee, he looked at her as a temporary diversion before we got back to seriously casting the part."

Tenn recalled the first meeting with Page as one in which she interviewed *him;* she dominated the conversation. Quintero confirmed this, but added that Tenn's passivity may have been born out of his conviction that she would never play the part, and that he was simply briefly entertaining the curiosity of a rube. "She was very sharp, of mind and of feature," Tenn told me. "She was almost violently scrubbed, very pale, almost bleached looking." Page arrived wearing no makeup, not because she had begun to imagine the physical characteristics of Alma Wine-miller, but because it was simply not her style to dress up and powder down. As she told me, "I wanted to come to Tennessee as a blank slate. I wanted him to look at me and ask me to become whatever he wanted, and I would have, and I could have. I can glow or show any particular emotion you might need, but I had no interest, and still have no interest, in smearing on makeup and scent and certain clothes to show you a character. That's not character; that's costuming. I walked in there as an actress, ready to work."

Geraldine Page had only recently celebrated her twenty-seventh birthday when she met with Tennessee Williams, but he recalled that she could have been fifteen or she could have been forty. She arrived with her hair pulled back from her face and fastened into a bun, which was appropriate for Tenn's concept of Alma, but as the conversation progressed, Page's hair, shiny and brown and abundant, fell to her shoulders and she ran her fingers through it, both nervously and flirta-tiously; she lashed it about like a whip; put strands of it in her mouth and chewed; she draped a shank of it over her eyes as if in embarrass-ment. "She seemed to orchestrate her oddness," Tenn told me. "She did not present herself to me as an attractive woman, but as she spoke and as she explained herself and her understanding of the play, her features changed, the color rose in her cheeks, her mouth might shift from a sneer to a ravishing smile."

Page possessed hands that never sat in her lap or stood still. They flew like speed-injected doves across her face, up in the air, over her mouth, which seemed to be the orifice from which some truth was always likely to emerge. "I focused on her mouth and her chin," Tenn told me. "She seemed to be terribly self-conscious of her mouth, but her teeth were fine—she was not hiding some dental catastrophe. Her smile could be lovely or it could be too strong, almost demented in its demonstration. Her hands were lovely. They reminded me of a porcelain box that had once rested on my mother's dressing table: a jewelry box on top of which rested these lovely porcelain hands, clasped together in resignation or prayer or death—I never knew. Geraldine Page had those hands, and she kept them in flight, all about her, energy and diversion."

Quintero laughed at the description of Page's hands. "Someone somewhere is writing a dissertation at some wonderful drama school on Geraldine Page's hands," he quipped. "I know from directing her and from being her friend that her hands were the instruments that she felt kept her from pursuing things both good and bad. If she was harboring some negative thought about something, you would find her pressing her fingers into her forehead or her temples, to suppress or push away the thoughts. If she sat on the edge of an opinion she might regret expressing, she would place her hand over her mouth, to keep it housed where it couldn't hurt anyone."

Page also became embarrassed when praised or aroused or exhilarated, and she grew flushed and would bring her hands over her face, to hide her delight and to defuse any criticism or examination that her joy might invite. "I never felt comfortable showing my pleasure," Page told me. "I thought it unseemly, and I thought I would be criticized."

Both José Quintero and Lee Strasberg, with whom Page studied at the Actors Studio, would instruct her to control her hands, with Strasberg going so far as to tie them, with rope, to either her sides or a chair. (The story varies, and when I met Page she refused to discuss Lee Strasberg at all.) "I wanted her face and her intentions to show," Quintero told me. "The story was always in Geraldine's face. It was also in her hands, but I wanted her to combine all of her methods of storytelling, all of her limbs, to become the great actress I knew, even then, that she was."

But on that day when Geraldine Page first met Tennessee Williams, she had no control over her body or her hair or her hands, and as the meeting progressed, and Page's hair and blouse and demeanor altered and loosened and moved about, Tenn came to see that she could be Alma. "She asked the right questions," Tenn remembered. "There was no waste of time, or energy, or intelligence. She cut right to the point. She begged for nothing."

When I read those words to Page, more than three years after Tenn had given them to me, she cut me off and said, forcefully, "I never begged for anything, except piano lessons, which my parents couldn't afford. I got the lessons and I loved them, but I did not become a pianist; I never conquered that instrument or the world of music. I learned not to beg. Never beg for anything. Earn it. Demand it. Seek it. Never beg for it. You see, I knew I was meant to be Alma. I knew I was meant to play those parts. I knew that it was my time. I had to trust that people would see that. But I didn't beg. I never, ever begged. What I'm trying to say is that nothing was ever *given* to me, and nothing that really matters in the world ever is. You earn it in that special time of your life when everything combines to make you prove yourself."

That day in 1952, when Geraldine Page met Tennessee Williams, was that special time of her life, and she admitted that she was not terribly shy or polite about making it work out to her satisfaction.

From the notes in Tenn's shopping bag:

There is a place to which I once had swift and easy access. This is not a geographical location, but a psychic one, I suppose. It swirls with memory and a generous if not always healthy need to share these memories. I do not understand how I came to possess so much extraneous thought and fear, but it drags me away from this place to which I would like to return.

Several lines were crossed out, to the point that I couldn't read them, and then the thread continued.

Just jump, my brain tells me. Take the thought, take the intention, and place it on the page, share it, see what happens. But my heart is full of fear, and I hold back. What if? What if? Years ago this was the question in classes, and actors asked "What if?" and imagined things "as if" and found new dimensions to their work and to themselves. Here I am, old and stiff and afraid, and I need that flexibility and forcefulness that I envy in so many others. I need to develop an intolerance for fear. I need to stop wasting my time on the edge of writing and caring and simply do both of those things. I had no fear once about testing the tolerance of others with what I had witnessed, and now I'm afraid to even discuss my hopes with an aspirant with whom I walk and talk and write in circles. We dream and we hope and we bring nothing to the page or to the point.

This was the first time I had seen myself mentioned in the notes Tenn made during our time together. Later in the notes, after stating his desire to return to discipline and intention, Tenn writes of his phone call with Elia Kazan:

He was right, of course. It is time to get back to work and back to the point. I was brought back to the memories and the examples of the people who had made me want to write, and I held them as beads in prayer, but Gadg was right to note that I had earned the beads, and I had them and I could use them, but I had also acquired a barnacle on my boat, and travel was now impossible. I'm weighed down by many things, and some of them may be permanent impositions, but some I can cast off quickly and painlessly and get back to the pale judgment.

It is in my best interests now to leave New Orleans.

I never said anything to Tenn about these particular notes, and I chose to believe that there was no malice or regret in what he wrote. I returned the notes to him and we resumed our conversations. Our talks now were focused and frenzied. Tenn was very clearly on a deadline.

"Do you remember when we discussed the stage directions to *Summer and Smoke*?" Tenn asked me. We were in a room at the Royal Orleans, one that had clearly not been housing him for very long: there were no clothes in the closet; the soaps in the bathroom were still wrapped; other than a pile of folders on the television set, every surface was pristine. A portable typewriter, installed by a bellman, sat on a folding table, which Tenn immediately moved within inches of the television set. The day was hot and the room was air-conditioned to an Arctic degree and the room service was swift and obsequious. I found the notes and read them back to Tenn.

"I was really trying to bring Geraldine back into my consciousness," he explained. "The stage directions were important, and they clarified my intention, but I really wanted Gerry in the room, in my mind, moving me toward the work."

Tenn thought of Geraldine Page as the finest, sharpest needle, capable of piercing any fabric and creating any number of patterns. I thought I had heard him say this of another actress in another context, but I took the notes and I listened.

"The play is a pattern," he continued, "a pattern by Simplicity or McCall's, and the actress cuts and shapes the crisp paper of the pattern and attaches it to the fabrics, and the fabric is all that she brings to the part. It is her life and her experience and her unique take on all that passes before her. Read that back to me."

I read it back to him.

Tenn handed me several folded pieces of paper. "Type those notes when you get a chance," he told me. "It's television work." The work was not toward some play for television, but observations he had made of things recently seen on TV—"sparks," he called them, material for the fog.

> I found last night, in an episode of *Hazel,* in the gait of Shirley Booth, the intention of Amanda Wingfield. [Booth had assumed the role of Amanda on CBS *Playhouse* some fifteen years prior to this note, but Tenn claimed no memory of that production.]
>
> The voice of Polly Holliday is the voice of so many aunts and fine ladies of my childhood, joined in guilds and societies and secrets and resentments, and I could follow her to a resolution.
>
> I can endow, if I wish, the theater and the work I create for the theater, with the power and the love I once held for it.

I put the notes aside and turned to Tenn, who was snapping his fingers at me.

"Do you have the notes on the Mexican artists?" Tenn asked me. "The ones I studied for *Camino Real*?" I reached into my backpack and found the notes and I read them to Tenn. When I was finished, he paused, thought, then looked at me.

"I think there might be a way," he said, slowly and seriously, "that we can apply all of that to a play for Geraldine. Or a memoir."

Geraldine Page had read *Summer and Smoke* several times before she met with Tenn to discuss the possibility of playing Alma. Page admitted to José Quintero that she had seen the Broadway production twice, cringing each time at what she called its "lost possibilities." My time with Page was severely limited, lasting less than half an hour, and it took place backstage at the Promenade Theater on the Upper West Side, where she was appearing in Sam Shepard's *A Lie of the Mind.* I was in New York for only a few days, catching some plays and seeing some friends and beginning to craft plans to move to the city. I saw the play and, when it was over, asked a theater staff member where I might wait to see Miss Page. The young man nonchalantly waved me toward a door in the lobby, and once I opened the door I was face-to-face with Geraldine Page, still in costume, preparing to head to her dressing room, and a bit startled at my sudden arrival. I told her that I had met Tennessee Williams three years earlier and that I had something from him that I wanted to read to her. Page's eyebrows shot up to her hairline and she let out a gruff laugh, but she looked around for some chairs for us and she sat and looked at me, her demeanor sending forth the message "Proceed." She put one of her expressive hands under her chin and she stared at me. I got about two sentences into the notes Tenn had dictated to me about her when she suddenly and viciously grabbed the page from my hand. "I'll read it myself!" she said, but I saw that she was crying, was terribly moved, and as she read, her hand found mine and she caressed it. Over and over as she read, she said, "Why? Why?" She finished reading and looked at me and began talking, telling me her reactions to what Tenn had said and what she thought I needed to know.

I could not write anything down as she spoke, because she never let go of my hand.

Geraldine Page was an accumulator of ideas and images and memories, and she often joked that her mind was as cluttered as her home, and both were stuffed with interesting and loved and rare things. Page hated inactivity, idle minds or chatter, conversations for which there was no point or theme or purpose. Tenn thought that she possessed, along with Marian Seldes, one of the strongest obsessions with time he had ever encountered, but Quintero disagreed with that assessment. "She wasn't obsessed with time running out, or time having its way with her," he told me, "but she did believe that every single thing, every moment, should serve toward some bigger purpose, so she was prone to asking a room of people what they were up to, and really mean it, and really want an answer. You could have drinks and talk about things, but the conversation needed to be, had to be, intelligent and open and *about* something."

She had no patience or sympathy for unintelligent, unexamined people or situations, and in that first encounter, Page let Tenn know that *Summer and Smoke*, on Broadway, had been two of her least favorite things: thoughtless and unclear. "And I agreed with her," Tenn told me. Page admired Tenn's extensive stage directions in the play's script, and she marveled at his use of language. "Trust me," she told me, "I knew all about Alma—as much as I could at that age. But I felt that Tennessee was acting as both the writer and the director of his play. I came to feel this way even more as I read more of his plays, but I tried to let him know that what made Alma was entirely here"—she pointed to her heart —"and here," as she pointed to her head. "It's not in her hands or her hair or the color of her dress or the way she holds her prayer book. There was so much projection and labeling in both the script and the direction of that play. It couldn't breathe. It didn't move. It was so cloudy and heavy and thick with symbolism and 'meaning' that you lost the whole thing."

Quintero and Page formed a partnership of sorts, because both believed in the play and lamented the abuse it had endured in its initial production, and both saw in it the potential to showcase their talents. "That play allowed us both to grow as artists," Quintero told me, "and we both knew that would happen when we pursued it. We had both looked at the Margo Jones production slack-jawed with shock. It was a very bad stock production, and I began to think of casting it properly and directing it almost immediately. When I found Geraldine, I knew precisely how the production would look and sound and be received."

From Tenn's notes on Page:

She suffered nothing except the insult and negligence that is attached to all matters of love and attraction. She had no fear of beginning, of jumping off where she should, over and over, to get to where she needed to be. I would like to emulate her in her impatience with delusion. I delude myself all the time, still, and it offers me no reward. I do not believe that she ever saw the benefit of delusion, and so never suffered its various harms.

Nearly every actress I came to meet in the course of finding the people who had mattered to Tennessee Williams would ask who else was on the list, who else was on that menu from the Court of Two Sisters. They wanted to know what Tennessee had said about them, about the other talent in the arena, and they did not wait to share their own opinions of those named. The exception was Geraldine Page. She did not ask for names or the comments of others, and she did not care to hear how I had come to the Promenade Theater to find her. She responded immediately to what I had brought her and sought to help me find out something about the writer with whom I had spent time; and yet she, more than any other actress in Tenn's index of follies, was the one others wished to discuss, jumped to praise, tried to understand.

Page's talent has been described in a variety of ingenious ways. Her work on a part has been compared to photography, in which the tray of chemicals is the play or the various intentions of the playwright, the

After studying numerous film stars, including
Bette Davis and one of Tennessee's favorites, Ruth
Chatterton, Geraldine Page felt comfortable in
applying the armor she needed to become Alexandra
Del Lago of *Sweet Bird of Youth*, in both the 1959
play and the 1962 film, for which she sat for this
photograph.

director, and the designers, and the photographic paper is the actress, who surrenders to the liquid and a sharp image magically and suddenly appears. Her emotional intensity has been compared to a singer capable of holding a particular note for an astonishingly long time, leaving an audience on edge, wondering if the artist can survive such a commitment, then marveling when the note ends and a new note is pursued, held, conquered. Her impossibly high standards of conduct and creativity have led her to be compared to any number of wild and ferocious animals, the female of said species all too eager to maim or kill those who would trespass on her grounds or usurp her authority.

"Her ego was wrapped securely in getting the part right and serving the playwright," Elia Kazan told me. "I respected that about her and I thought very highly of her gifts, but I did not find her easy or terribly inspiring when we worked together on *Sweet Bird of Youth*." He found her courteous and professional, but also set in her ways. "She knew the character of the Princess before we ever had a rehearsal. She understood her emotionally; she knew where the scars were and how the heart operated and what the eyes saw and did not see. All of that was set, and all of that was, for the most part, true and correct to the play. She only lacked confidence in her appearance, in her movement. She did not believe herself to be beautiful or to have the composure—or should I say 'comportment'?—of a movie star, of a grand lady who got what she wanted."

Tenn was helpful in that regard, describing the physical movements of the actresses "born to drama and convinced that the world had been brought into existence to ease their passage toward perfumed comfort," and showed her how they moved. Tenn's time with Tallulah Bankhead and Miriam Hopkins showed him how nearsighted actresses, too vain to be seen wearing eyeglasses, sidled against men or railings or walls to wend their way about town or a party or a premiere. "Their confidence was such that they did not hesitate one bit," Tenn remembered. Their creamy beauty and smooth transitions would lead them wherever they must go, and it was irrelevant that they had no idea whom they were passing. Their importance was so great that they would be sought out, as they always were. Tenn stood with Page and showed her the walk, slightly somnambulistic, slow, sure. "I always thought of what Geraldine did with her walk to be Lillian Gish by way of Rossetti's *Blessed Damozel* right through to John Everett Millais's great painting *Ophelia*," he laughed, remembering that Page listened to his references, then waved him away. "Tennessee always gave too much too quickly and too indiscriminately," she remembered. "His ideas were fulsome and rich and perfect, but he had no concept of how I might be working or thinking or feeling, and he would just pile on all of this stuff. He couldn't understand that I—or any other actress—might want to discover some things on our own. We weren't there solely to emulate images or visions he had entertained."

Kazan took Page's natural impatience and told her to use it to convey the imperious rush that surrounded all of Alexandra Del Lago's activities. "She literally jumped, as if with joy, when I gave her that direction," Kazan remembered. "It was so perfect and immediate and it altered her performance. Blind and beautiful and willful and in a hurry. Seeking to be sated at all times. I think that may have been all that I said to her in that production. The rest was hair, lips, dresses, sounds. I had to show her how to yelp in a way that was sexy rather than shrill. Everything else was some sort of covenant between her and Tennessee."

"One doesn't teach Geraldine Page anything," Tenn told me. "You do your work and you are aware that she is observing you. She picks and studies and ponders what you do and what you didn't do and comes away with an idea or a philosophy or the knowledge of something, but she doesn't share it with you, unless it can be transmitted through a part, unless she can show you through a gesture or an act she has imagined for a character."

"I do not like to talk," Page told me, as if to explain her reticence at my questions, even though she gave me her address and her phone number and asked me to call her as I progressed with whatever it was this project might turn into. "You have to hold on to what you have and what you've picked up," she explained. "I was never one to talk about what I'd done or seen. I guess I never thought anyone cared what I thought about things, and I came to believe, as I think most shy and solitary people do, that things increased in value if they were hidden and kept in a special place and brought out at special times. I mean, you don't put up a wreath or a tree until it's Christmas, and you're presumably celebrating something big and important. It means something when the tree goes up and the candles are lit and people are in the house. You do something like that every Tuesday and it soon comes to mean nothing. It's a joke or some desperate act of a sick mind to hold on to all the Christmases of the world and time. I feel that way about memories or images or experiences: they have their place and their time, and our responsibility toward them is to keep them special and to use them well. All I have, really, to bring to a role is that history of experience, those stories."

Tenn wrote in his notes:

In a box I have all of these snapshots of my life, old, sepia-toned photographs and newer, stiffer instant photographs of parties with friends I've often forgotten. In another box I have old toys and ornaments that can transport me to Missouri or Mississippi or Louisiana, to 1923 or 1937 or 1943. There is an album on which one can find "Little Brown Jug" and I play this song on this album and I can smell citrus and remember a cool breeze rising up a hill full of lupine. There is a crocheted doily made by my mother and I can look at the thread and remember her hands moving as she made it, and I hold it in my hand and here is my mother and what year is it? Here is a spool of thread, almost used up, old, worthless, but I took this spool of thread with me thinking that it could be unraveled and hold me to a place where I did not always find love, but where I always felt somewhat wise in searching for it.

Geraldine Page made Tenn aware of thread, an artistic thread that connected all artists. "I suppose it runs through all of us," he told me, "and from this psychic fabric we create what we create when we create it. It is husbanded by us, shared by us. We often abuse it; we far more frequently craft it into and onto items that hold no shape or offer any comfort, so we pull it apart again and wait for a receptive fabric or canvas into which we can press it. Again and again. Over and over."

Tenn had me read these notes, both scribbled and typed, several times, asking me to edit and revise sentences as I went along. "What I want to impress on you," he told me, "is the need to husband your talent, which is housed in such a fragile and fickle vessel. We destroy ourselves every day, and then we rebuild. Some of us can survive this damage and use it to some good effect—through work or sympathy or charity or awareness. I do not have this ability, and my failure to be a good steward of my talent led to many clashes with Geraldine, who is a fearsome guardian of her work, of her mental theater, from which emerge her characters, which are crafted from something I can only call majestic. Hers is a titanic talent; her vision is frightening—I don't think that I could withstand being in its line for very long. She has an intellect that I would match against that of anyone else in the world, and it is attached to a talent that is something like a ton of dynamite bearing a one-inch wick. It explodes frequently and beautifully, and it is lethal to be stupid in its path."

Writers, Tenn explained, "create scratches on pieces of paper. We hope and we dream. We try to locate those moments in our life when things happened and we were left stranded and stunned and wonder-

ing and asking 'Why?' To these scratches some people bring blood and
flesh and perfume picked up from having stood in places long enough
to catch an essence, a memory, of life. Geraldine Page poured blood and
flesh into my pages—and the pages of others—and left me wondering
'Why?'"

Tenn asked me to type up his notes, and I began working on the
typewriter he had borrowed. The ribbon was new and it blurred and
several keys stuck, so typing was slow and tortured, and the table on
which the machine sat wobbled as I continued. Tenn remarked that it
was growing late; it was time for dinner. Perhaps room service should
be called. I did not know if he intended to include me in his plans,
but he had me look at the menu for what I might want. He was aware
of my surprise, because he told me that although it was late, he had
other things to say about Geraldine Page, and he wanted me to stay and
handle those notes.

Tenn spoke into the night about Page's performances. "If I knew
how," he told me, "if I had the gifts of the greatest magicians or sages or
warlocks, I would wish that I could transport you to the theaters all over
the world in which I've seen the great performances."

On an index card stuck into the corner of Tenn's bureau mirror
was typed the following: "The most exquisite prayer in the world is the
memory of beauty, of art created and shared in space and air and time
in which we lived, for a moment, within its reach." It was attributed
to Luchino Visconti, with whom Tenn had worked on the film *Senso,*
whom Tenn had loved, and to whom he had made one of his desperate
phone calls, in the supernal hours, alone and mad, looking for a release,
a reason to continue.

"Visconti gave me back my life more times than I can recall," Tenn
told me. "He was the first artist I ever encountered who was also regal,
both of carriage and of ancestry. Visconti had a nobility in his pursuit of art that I've never encountered in anyone else. An emulation of
him would serve as a great line of intention to place at your feet. His
passions—for life, for work, for people, for spirits—were large and grand
and generous, but they never got him away from his purposes. When I
was at my most desperate—in person, by phone, by wire, by letter—he
always calmly put me back into the position of postulant, talking about
experiences we've shared, the prayer of art: The nights with Pasolini.

Luchino Visconti, stage and film director with
whom Tennessee had what he called a "close and
sweet relationship." Visconti taught Tennessee how
to analyze his characters—from their place of birth
to their dialect to the style of shoes they might wear.
"No one was safe around him," Tennessee said. "He
saw through every layer a person might have."

Callas onstage. Laurette Taylor. Jean Cocteau. Jean Renoir. E. M. For-
ster. I told him of the actresses I'd shared air with—women with whom
he'd never shared proximity."

Tenn described for Visconti (and for me) the sight of Geraldine
Page, in a play called *Mid-Summer,* arriving home late in the evening,
exhausted, her face and ankles bulging from weight and fatigue and
despair, her eyes blurry, the lid of one eye twitching, an alabaster hand
rising to hold it down, keep it still. The woman is met by her children,
who are happy to see her home from work and bearing food. The children tear into the food, ripping apart bread and meat and fruit, and the
mother laughs and sighs, her hand over her heart, her lips clamped tight
to ward off tears. She needs and wants the food, but her maternal

instinct, her large and savage heart, recognize the need to share, so she gives it to her children, who then clamber off to bed, sated, calmed for one more day, assured of survival; and Page, as this mother, looks into the empty bag, sniffs it, imagines what might have been eaten, looks off into the distance, and the scene ends.

"I cannot tell you the name of that play's writer," Tenn told me. (Her name was Vina Delmar, and the director was Paul Crabtree; both are as lost to the rubble of time as the theater, the Vanderbilt, in which the play ran.) "I cannot even tell much about the rest of the play, these poor people in a hotel room at the turn of the century. But I can tell you about Geraldine Page's posture and her voice and the strangled cry she stifled when she was sad when she couldn't be, and which she let out when she needed to get something that might mean another hour of life, such as it was."

Tenn had believed that actors were incapable of thought in their acting, that perhaps they were discouraged from displaying this action in their work. American actors, he felt, demonstrated, indicated, spoke, moved, and all intentions, all motivations, all desires had been worked out prior to performance—in study with an acting coach, perhaps, or in discussions with a therapist. Nothing, however, appeared to Tenn to happen in real time in that shared space. This began to change for him with Taylor in *The Glass Menagerie*, where one saw a woman range from deliquescence to giddiness to machination to panicked improvisation in a matter of minutes. It happened again with Brando in *Streetcar*—a human being caught in all the gaudy abundance of his being. "Marlon never did anything physical twice," Tenn told me. "He let his body sweat and move as nature chose on that stage, and he hitched or removed his shirt accordingly. He scratched where it itched, in that time, in that moment. He wiped real sweat off of his brow in real time, regardless of where he was in the script. He dragged life and thought onto that stage."

No one, however, in Tenn's estimation, brought the process of thought and intention to the stage as Geraldine Page did.

"I wrote a play called *Summer and Smoke*," Tenn told me. "I endured a production of that play in 1948, knew every word, comma, semicolon, exclamation point. And yet what I saw on the stage was alien to me, strange, unfelt. I did not recognize that play in the flat badness with which it was presented. When it was done again, almost four years later, I still knew every word, comma, semicolon, exclamation point, and I fought to have each and every one of them properly emphasized and retained. I fought to have some semblance of my vision retained in that tiny space downtown. I fought with José to assure the truth of the play. I was there, is what I'm trying to say, and yet all the times I watched that play, from a seat, from the back of the theater, from behind a pillar, in the company of an usher, it came to me new over and over. What I think Geraldine did was to subsume my own fears and fantasies of life and sex and self-destruction and shove them into her own skin and mannerisms, and then she played with them—which is to say, she responded in ways that were appropriate for the reactions or incentives she was given onstage each night. There was nothing frozen or rigid about her work: she understood that Alma, that all people, may operate from the same fears and patterns each day, but each day calls for a new means of pursuit, of preying, of getting what you need."

There was the memory of Page endowing the actor playing John with so astounding an ability of arousal that the audience became uncomfortably complicit in her unsound pursuit of him. "Tenn wanted to know how she did that," Quintero told me. "He wanted to know if she looked at the actor and imagined cocks sticking out of every pore on his body, and Geraldine was horrified at that thought: She understood that there was power in sex, that we needed sex, but she also knew that it's not enough to just want a man; it's not enough to want some physical action. The need extends beyond the act of sex. It's the fulfillment of a great and longstanding lack, so Geraldine looked at John and imagined that he had the heart or the kidney or the lung she would need to live throughout the week. The words and the actions of the play indicated that the need was sexual and emotional, but there was not, to Geraldine's thinking, any great way of portraying that, so she took it higher. Alma's full, total survival depended on John and what he could give her. Alma's pact at the conclusion of the play—and, later, in the film—was a sad and puny one: she would submit to the mere physicality of a union with a man, and maybe he was simply cock and form and function, and it was chilling to see Alma on that level. You recognized her demotion from crazed romantic to avaricious victim."

Tenn had once described to Visconti, late into a Roman night, the effect of watching a young and pliant and joyously sexual James Dean dancing and swaying, clad in a robe and bearing scissors, taunting an unyielding yet clearly amused and intrigued Geraldine Page, her back hard but her eyes eagerly taking in the boy's body. The play was *The Immoralist*, based on the novel by André Gide; and to the play's director, Daniel Mann, Page described, from her reading of Gide's work, a religion of male beauty to which she nightly converted and submitted. When she looked at James Dean on that stage, he was her God, his body her Eucharist, and her soul empty and ready to be filled with his gifts. Offstage she found Dean to be gifted but silly, undisciplined, and spoiled.

Visconti asked Tenn to demonstrate the dance performed by Dean, as well as the reactions of Page, and he later incorporated elements of this re-creation into his film *The Damned,* in which Helmut Berger bandies his male beauty about like a new toy, which some find captivating and playful and others as dangerous as the impending Nazism that presses down on the film's characters.

Tenn had me write on three index cards the names Luchino Visconti and Lee Strasberg and Kim Stanley. I wedged them into the mirror of his bureau, and was told that they would crop up later, "if needed."

"Geraldine Page suffered no one outside the confines of her own home," Tenn believed. "Her nature was soft and passive in social and professional situations. She was not one to make scenes; she tended to drift away, to move onto other subjects and other people. She shifted focus, and anyone who bored or angered or threatened her was suddenly relegated to an area where no harm could come to her." Maureen Stapleton referred to Page as the "gauzy ghost," a woman whose soul seemingly left her body when she no longer felt the need to be present. When I mentioned this to Page in our meeting, she laughed, and that hand went over her mouth, her characteristic gesture when she felt she had been found out. "I wish I could be bolder with people," she confessed, "but I'm not the type of person who can announce that I'm unhappy or furious or tapped out. I always think it's better to get away. I never felt I had to announce my absence. I think my absences spoke for themselves."

Fourteen

T HIS NARRATIVE," Tenn wrote in those pages he left behind in the hotel room, "what I call my fog, which I need to see rolling across my boards again, comes only to those who dream it into existence, who need it, who honor it. Any narrative that has found a home in my mental theater has been a literary orphan, and I gave it a home. One needs to be a suitable recipient of the narrative, the fog. I am no longer suitable to receive. Am I, to quote Paul Tillich, too proud to receive? Or have I debased the dreaming part of myself? Find the places where I once dreamed. Take young eyes and fear nothing."

Tenn had written next to this passage the name Joan Didion, and farther down he wrote that

> streets and counties and trees and winding roads deep in the pines of Mississippi belong forever to Faulkner; any map of Hawaii has among its arteries the memories and the experiences of James Jones; the street on which I stood high in the Hollywood Hills holds my memory of standing there and feeling young and on the verge of not only a city of dreams and possibilities and beauty, but a play about loving home and leaving home, and that city belongs to Joan Didion now. They have dreamed the strongest about those places, and those places belong to them, respond to them, produce for them.

My places were emotional, primarily. I wrote of locales in which I had lived, or in which I imagined I could live, but the topography was primal and sexual and terminal. It bore no distinct architecture or design or dialect. It was merely human and in peril, which is to say universal. But on Royal and Coliseum and Vista—streets I cannot relinquish—I found my places and I dreamed a narrative. Can I go there and find it again?

Below this Tenn had written: "Pare down. Make it matter. Widen the margins. Increase the stakes."

I do not know if his note concerned what he had written or what he felt he needed to do personally, because throughout are notes about the reordering of his mind, his body, his living quarters. Particular notebooks were required. Pens with the finest points would allow him the maximum speed to get onto paper what he felt was imminent. "Pray for fog!" he wrote over and over, in excitement, next to paragraphs that pleased him. Alcohol consumption should be limited to the "white waters," since they caused him less upset and lost time. Heavy meals no longer interested him; they "bogged him down" and kept him up late, gassy and anxious. "I adore the Mexican spirit," he wrote, "and I am most comforted by soft Mexican skin, but the cuisine of that country leads me to the most ignominious conclusions." It was vital that the odor of pine not be present in the apartment in New York or hotel rooms or any place he hung his "hungry hat": it unnerved him, reminded him of hospitals and the house on Oriole where William Inge grew cold and sad and kept loitering in the garage, until he "finally maneuvered his smoothest drive, straight down a road that held his firmest intention."

There was a man, a drug dealer, who might be able to provide Tenn with various grades of cocaine, which to his mind should be, like tea or coffee, labeled as "Morning Blend," "Evening Blend," and "Blend Blend."

"I need a significant bump in the morning," he wrote. "Nothing works or moves, and the first few lines force the blood into operation, the mind becomes nimble." Later in the day, energy was called for, "nothing too manic or forced, and when sleep beckons I would like to be in a position to accept," and when parties or dinners or social occasions were necessary, panes of time through which he passed fearing peril at every step, he wanted a "bold, white friend" to come along for the ride, "helping me laugh and move and hold in my pockets a few laughs, a crumb of inspiration."

I did not spend time with Tenn as a reporter: my eyes and ears were trained for the inspiration I hoped he would provide. I was not out for a story. I was not equipped emotionally or professionally for the gathering of facts outside my direct line of vision, what Tenn called my "charming purview." And yet I knew that the frequent visits to bathrooms (he especially loved the ones in the Cabildo and in Tujague's restaurant) involved pills and powders. The tabletops of the hotel room and the porcelain countertop in the bathroom appeared to have been utilized by a manic baker, and while I knew that Tenn was becoming impatient with our time together, and that he needed to get back to some serious work and be surrounded by people he had known for years, both Elia Kazan and Maria St. Just would tell me that his trip to New Orleans, like so many before it, to so many other cities, had been precipitated or terminated because of the balance of his chemical inventory. An actress with whom Tenn occasionally enjoyed the use of cocaine, and the waves of fervent nostalgia and brainstorming it engendered, told me that once he got back to New York from our time together, he placed an order, through her, for an ounce of cocaine. "The good stuff," he told her. "I have a lot of work to do, and it feels good, and I don't." Tenn had told her that during the days he spent with me in New Orleans, he had been using less cocaine than usual. "This sweet boy," he told her, was so ignorant and open and fervent that his visits were as invigorating as two or three or four fat tracks of cocaine.

On another page, in a recounting of a conversation he and I had had about writers we both admired, Tenn had written: "Had I ever been this naïve? Had I ever loved words and the patterns they made on a page or on a heart or on the mind as this boy does? Ignorance is often sexual and deadly and poisonously addictive. It is often treacherous and mean, and you share space with it at great risk. I have never known it to be so exhilarating, so capable of allowing me to see things as I did when young and open and utterly unaware of so many things."

I had wanted to be of some help to Tenn, but I hadn't known how. I learned in those notes that it was by knowing nothing and asking, as he wrote, "always, over and over, 'What do you mean?' I don't know what I mean! But I keep trying to tell him." And in the margin, next to this entry, one word: "Lunacy!"

Tenn had asked me, early in our encounters, if I had paid any particular attention to the physical characteristics of the women I hoped might inspire characters in my work. I hadn't thought much about it, but Tenn clearly had, for all of his writing life, and in our time together. There were six pages bulging with descriptions of every part, angle, and style of actress, along with analyses of what certain eyes, lips, and teeth implied or portended.

Of an actress who hailed from St. Louis and who had appeared in one of his plays in an off-Broadway production, Tenn wrote that she had

an alarming, starkly unappealing lack of proportion of face and head, like something Goya might have imagined or Picasso in making a political or social point. One eye is overwhelmingly larger than the other and it was even glazed and a bit askew: the eye of a specimen in an autopsy report. Her teeth appear to be rotting and her gums are an unhealthy shade of red, far too large, and serving as host to a set of teeth that are little more than squatters in a head that covers a mind that alternates between rich-girl sweetness and avaricious ambition. I want to trust her, and I want to like her. She is fulsome in her praise of me and my work. She claims to have known both my mother and my sister, and I try to imagine a link between us that extends beyond the confines of the theater, but I cannot trust her. There remains the old myth, rooted in my childhood, that one should not trust those with one small, mean, dead eye, or the teeth of a mummy rooted, perilously, in the dark gums of some voodoo priestess.

In the margins Tenn imagined a short story he might call "Mummy Teeth and a Tiny Eye," and on the opposite side of the page, he wrote a few sentences, which began

The boy smelled perfume, a heavy floral scent, before he smelled the woman who sat in a chair before him. She was young and softly pretty, tired but polite, and she nodded her head toward him, and extended a hand: she hoped he would sit in the chair opposite him, beside which was a table that held a Bible and a small, burning candle. It was a bug candle, citron and chemicals to keep the mosquitoes, big and black and mean, away from their pale skins. Her clothes were colorful and neatly pressed and clean, but a smell, musky and oppressive and unpleasant, arose from her, pushing against him as persistently as the heat and the desire he had to know what lay ahead for him.

The sentences were scratched through and Tenn had added an editorial comment: "Too much like Truman," a reference, I later learned, to Capote's short piece "Dazzle," which had been given prominent placement in *Esquire*. There were dozens of pages upon which Tenn began profile pieces that he believed might make for a similar collection. One was headed "The Heat of the Cinema," and had some of the details Tenn had told me about the time he had spent in the balconies of opulent movie theaters, sleeping and drinking and watching movies over and over, meeting men with similar interests, and heading home

with a sandwich and a bottle of milk, the genesis of a hangover, and an urge to type something, anything, that might have the manic energy and the clean narrative line of what I had just seen. Silver and black and flashing images and ideas coming so fast and sharp. Take the vocal thread provided by Gladys George and have her hover over an errant and queer son; admonish him; fog rolls in.

Four lines down he appeared to start the piece anew and wrote:

Film is, in and of itself, an explosive object. Film is a medium that is dangerous in so many ways—injected with silver, poisons, odd recipes to capture, enhance, and transmit illusion. So I am very much alive and present and pregnant—with fear and joy and anticipation when I watch a film. It is for me an act of not only capturing a past event—the event of performance and collaboration—but a living, very kinetic act: the film spools and crackles and shines.

Every film is exciting to me, for the best and worst reasons. Films I've loved in the past are new to me because I keep discovering details that fascinate me. I am a writer who was very much shaped by movies, far more than literature and theater. Film came into my life and my consciousness long before I had ever heard of Chekhov or Ibsen or Shakespeare or Strindberg. Flaubert and Turgenev were brought to me at a time when I had seen certain films more than fifty times. I am a student, a lover, a product of films.

On another page, Tenn wrote, "Jim should know more about this," then continued:

The one requisite attribute that I always notice among film stars is hunger. There is a ravenous quality to film stars that is deeply sexual, deeply disturbing. I don't think that a person acquires this quality through training: I think it lodges within the system of a person through experience and expression, and I think it begins in childhood, with the development of multiple lacunas that must be filled. Hungers that must be sated. Every film star I ever met, particularly those of the female persuasion (this would include several film actors, obviously), has a core of obsessive connection, by which I mean a craving to connect with each and every person upon contact. This is not always done in an obvious manner, as a Joan Crawford or Bette Davis might be—and have been—with me: a cloying and yet abrasive manner that shifts them to the center of attention. Rita Hayworth was overtly sexual, playful, as was Doris Day, in an entirely different style.

Rapid style is what William Wyler told me all actresses had. They adapt with awesome rapidity and rapacity. Shall I be a slut? Shall my lips be moist? What is my motivation, indeed! An actress becomes whatever she must to be needed, and a film actress, in order to survive, must become whatever she must to be needed and salable and desired. This is some heavy shit. What is especially admirable is the manner in which they take their hungers, their needs, their collective angers and styles, and compress them all into an entity that can then be sold, like soda or lipstick or turtle wax, and give it to a roomful of strangers and . connect.

Barbara Stanwyck has volumes of rage and regret within her tiny frame, and the years of repression bubble and spew up through her body and rest tightly and elegantly right behind her two front teeth. Her words barely fit through this slit that her mouth becomes—I mean a slit created by tension and emotion, not by actually compressing her lips, which are always available and approachable. She is coiled, right down to her vowels, by both rage and resignation. Within my memory of every Stanwyck performance is her slow cocking of the head, the raising of an eyebrow, the languid droop of her lids—resignation, acceptance, revenge. Big emotions, small gestures, an ultimate victory.

A lifetime of grievances and lusts and allegiances contained in a flick of the head or hand, a sassy walk, a cinched waist. But always winning, striding forcefully toward victory. She doesn't always get (or want) the guy or the company or the love of a child. She might even lose her mind or her life. Her victory is won from the audience—who admire, crave, and fear her. She has never not had us where she wanted us, and she has never been far from where she always wanted to be—at the hot, dead center of our attention. I only met her once. I saw her several times, at dismal affairs: premieres, parties, burnished hallways of film supplication. (Which is to say, an appointment with a producer.) She was introduced to me by, of all people, Gertrude Lawrence, who had just endured, shall we say, an embarrassment of poor intentions and rich irony at a screening of *The Glass Menagerie*. Stanwyck was gracious and laconic; very tiny, very chic, very controlled. But I met her! I doubt I made much of an impression, for I was not only speechless, but I was the author of a play that had just served as a suppository. But I saw the eyes, the lips. Contact was made.

Another page held writing that was markedly neater than the others: it was a report, a presentation of sorts, for me. In the upper-right-hand corner was an address in the East Forties of New York, and in underlined capital letters Tenn had written: TURTLE BAY, HEPBURN, KATHARINE.

This, you see, is true rapid style, willful and consistent and permanent. The life is the performance, the gestures strokes of color on canvas, every word an aria reaching the upper reserves, every opinion a new school of philosophy seeking adherents. Ego and energy and effort. All the time. A wily but limited intelligence. Facts for her are things to be bent and molded toward her needs and ignored if they fail to satisfy or flatter. Her mind, clear and primed at all times for conquest, has been compressed and cajoled, like the foot of a geisha, into a particular size and shape that will get her to the sound stage, the theater, the center of attention.

Another page: "The Center of Attention: The Only Known Address for an Actress."

A list of hands, with Kim Hunter, Betsy Palmer, and Nan Martin earning honors for having the longest, boniest hands, rendering them unsuitable as sympathetic heroines. "Poor Betsy Palmer," Tenn wrote. "I liked her and I felt she might have had some talent, which she squandered. She took on Alma, but her hands were too broad and long and hard. They were not the hands of a supplicant."

He harbored a fascination with the complexion of Glenda Jackson, an actress he found to be diabolically gifted and intelligent, and with whom he hoped to work, on a new piece, as he couldn't fathom her placement in an existing play. But he was amazed to discover that she was "blotchy and shiny, her face liberally littered with the pimples of a teenager and pores as large and open as the eyes of startled kittens." With her face clean of makeup, Tenn found Jackson to be shy, soft-spoken, reticent, but once she had assembled her "formidable *maquillage* and a shiny, defensive wig," she became a lovely and confident and dismissive "grand lady, as confident behind her mask of liquids and powders and paints as we had been as children behind our masks of goblins and criminals and cretins, haunting the streets on Halloween night. New identities, new personalities."

Age was a judgment as well as a biological and inevitable fact. Skin sagged and faded in accordance with spiritual valor or its absence; eyes betrayed nothing, or would reveal one's interests and intention. A down-turned mouth might connote cruelty and disappointment, or it might be a calling card left after the visitation of tragedy, physical or psychic; therefore, Beatrice Straight's "hard, thin, southward-bound" mouth was due to her realization that her vast family fortune guaranteed her nothing but curiosity and lengthy visitations from the needy, while Catherine Deneuve's "frosty, firm bite" was due to her having witnessed the violent death of her sister, actress Françoise Dorléac. (That this did not, in fact, actually happen did not deter Tenn. "The event has been developed on her face as if it were a photograph," he insisted.)

I needed to look closely at eyes and lips, both on a personal basis and before I began to write a character possessing the same features. "Keep a journal of those elements that please, annoy, or alarm you," he told me. "As a writer, whatever you believe about a person is true." In real life, however, where interaction with skin and sinew is necessary, what is true is highly subjective, and it needs to be sought out. The reality of all people, Tenn believed, could be discerned through eyes, hands, and voice. "I find that the soul of a person, their honest and expressed beliefs and desires, are shown through these attributes," he wrote, and he gave me examples of the types of voices that not only pleased him aesthetically but also helped him to create characters, to write, to live. Tenn was partial to voices that from experience and "sensual awareness" sounded as if some form of mastication were taking place with the words spoken. Edith Evans sounded to him always as if she were gargling a jar of sour balls; and Helen Mirren, an actress known at that time primarily for her blond good looks, was someone he trusted to do well, if only because when she spoke, her words flowed like the ejaculate that would appear if she had managed to fellate a vat of marmalade. "I see that this is both a physical and a sexual impossibility," Tenn told me, "but I believe that my auditory point is made."

Tenn bemoaned the fact that voices of stage actors and actresses were no longer given the place of importance that once existed: a lovely voice was at one time an inducement to seek employment as an actress, and Guthrie McClintic had once told Tenn that the voice of an actress was an indicator of talent to come, talent perhaps hidden, talent waiting to be coaxed from within. McClintic's wife, Katharine Cornell, had one of the voices that pleased Tenn greatly—deep and rich and slightly mournful. Cornell seduced vowels, and her sentences, especially in her performance in *Antony and Cleopatra,* tended to end with a nearly imperceptible gasp, as if the completion of that particular act of spoken art had been slightly beyond her abilities. "It was riveting," Tenn remembered, "and although I know it was the trick of a skilled actress, it was done well, and I bought it. I learned to hear and to understand that play—that type of play—by virtue of how she parsed and shared her sentences."

Jessica Tandy and Julie Harris, two actresses Tenn admired, had, in fact, poor voices: thin and high-pitched, prone to scratching the ear if intense emotions were called for. Both learned to compensate through the use of facial expressions and the manipulation of their bodies to convey feelings and effects their voices could not evoke. In a long section Tenn wrote about the Actors Studio, he revealed that his chief criticism was the school's disdain and disregard for the development of its students' voices and bodies. "Their ids and their egos and their maladjustments were heavily scrutinized and valued," he wrote, "but their voices were no better, no stronger, no more capable of expressing the multitude of themes contained in the great works than when they first harbored a dream of acting. They sound, always and forever, like the eager and intense students of an urban high school."

Talent and beauty both bore expiration dates and short shelf lives unless a concerted series of efforts were maintained to keep the heart and the mind growing and learning and loving, unless a "heartfelt intention" was supported. Tenn was amazed by those women who seemed to have landed upon a fast track to "early deaths of potential and possibilities," but he told me to be wary of them, for they had earned their rapid decomposition.

I found an assignment within the pages: Tenn wanted me to write a short story in which a person begins as attractive or ugly and steadily reverses course, without any descriptions of physical change. "Do it all through characterization," he wrote. "Do it all with words." All of us change, he kept reminding me, even if only through our own perceptions. Remain alert: "Wariness," he told me, "is a gift."

I discovered that Tenn had come to these pages after our days together and had continued his study of the subjects we'd covered, so I could read that Geraldine Page and Estelle Parsons were "long-term" artists, solid in ways that so many others were not, even as they had "clear indications of neuroses and those concomitant illnesses of the theater." Page and Parsons were good women to study in contrast to Kim Stanley, whose talents were short term, aging from birth, and wasting more rapidly than fish in the glare of a summer sun. Katharine Hepburn was a "willful and resourceful star," striving always to become an actress, with limited results, but her stamina was such that Tenn sent me to see her. "A gilded and willful retardation is a valuable asset," he assured me. "It is never easy to believe in oneself. Bend the facts; change the narrative. You must always remind yourself that you must win. Katharine Hepburn, while living and moving, appears always to have won. Find out how she has done this."

"Investigate any and all myths," Tenn wrote, circling the admonition. All of those people in pursuit of the arts or show business or attention (or all three) will have had their time in the duck press of egos, which is to say they have seen reality and it holds no place for them. This is a truth almost impossible to bear for most people, but a particularly difficult one for actresses, who, unlike writers, have no pale judgment to sit before and scribble upon: their scratches are made on their own psyches and the doors of agents and producers. The isolation of the actress leads her to investigate other realms from which she might find comfort or counsel to help her weather the realm into which she has been born and in which she seeks employment. Any number of gods, goddesses, gurus, shamans, therapists, nutritionists, card readers, and trainers will be called on to give her faith and courage. The metaphysical as well as the theatrical résumés of these women would most likely be padded, Tenn warned, and I should look into their systems of support. "You might learn something you can use," he assured me, "and you will definitely understand them better, and you will learn if any of it has helped them to matter."

Places are made, created, protected. No one writes a play or has it produced without struggles that deserve a story, and no actress builds a body of work without some sacrifice and subterfuge that reveal as much about her, if not more, than any performance given. There were no accidents that Tenn could conceive. People moved to the locations that would best serve their desired narrative. They altered their appearances, their résumés, their diets, their peccadilloes. They married well or they did not marry at all. They said what needed to be said when it served a purpose, unless they were Geraldine Page, Estelle Parsons, or Zoe Caldwell, three women who brandished brutal gifts of honesty like "ploughshares or the cocks of captors." On three separate occasions in these pages, Tenn urged me to be like Page and Parsons and eliminate and ignore the people and the works that were not serious, worthy, deserving of one's time. As I studied these women, on whom he desired reports, delivered by phone or by mail, I should believe nothing, stay longer than I might want to, look for the facts that had been altered, the man behind the curtain who was pulling the strings. "The man behind the curtain is the id," Tenn wrote, "and he only appears when someone is tired. Wear them out."

Above all else, be tough. Actresses, Tenn assured me, were both deserving of and inured to abuse, in the form of broken promises, phone calls unreturned, representation precipitately canceled when returns dwindled or personalities chafed, when the soul pulled the face and body into the forms they now deserved. "If they give you trouble," he told me, "call me and I'll see what I can do. Otherwise, be dismissive and abrupt, and they'll do whatever you want them to. They will notice the shift of focus, and they will assume they deserve it, and they will endow you with some sort of power forever denied them, and you will get what you need."

The bottom line: find a voice and use it to give to others. On a neatly folded piece of onionskin paper, Tenn wrote directly to me:

What I want you to know is that I needed to be heard through my art; later to avenge through it. And then I was dependent upon it, because it was all that kept me alive. Now I see that the anger I felt for so long about the gawky queer that I was seems entirely misguided. I was indeed a gawky queer, but I was a cosseted, husbanded, much-loved gawky queer, and my anger soon dissipated, and I was ready to fill my work with the gratitude and the love that has been shown to me by these remarkable women—those who inspired my plays and those who inhabited them. And now, ironically, I have no voice. I have a voice to share with you the names of these women and the generosity I hold for them, but I lack the voice to praise them or to write for them or to say what frightens me the most. I am desperate to give, to share, to love. But *I* destroyed my voice. I wasted energies on emotions unfounded and unfocused. I want my *voice*, Jim. I *need* my voice. Don't lose yours. Speak truthfully and fearlessly, and for God's sake, give. Give everything you have. I miss nothing more than giving. All other diminishments and declivities I can suffer. But I remain a gift unwanted in every quarter, and I most want to give.

The final entry within was titled "Strangers on a Train," but it had nothing to do with the Alfred Hitchcock film. Instead, Tenn wrote:

I have always felt as if I traveled through life on one train, while, on an alternate track an alternate train, of my own creation, moved along with me. This alternate train followed me through my life and still does—but it is populated with those people I might wish to know or to be, and it stops at those destinations I might have preferred over the itinerary fate and folly have dealt me. So many of the women I have known and admired—and feared and ridiculed—have had similar travel arrangements. I used to think, as I held on to my strap, on the train I did not choose, that if I hoped enough, dreamed enough, I might make the move to that other train. In living my life in this foolish way, I came to realize that every encounter in my life, and therefore in my plays, had at its core a feverish desire, a longing, perhaps a futile one, almost always a futile one, as I think on it. But I came to see that this desire is nothing more than prayer. True prayer. When I fell to the depths and sought help from the religious, they sought to teach me the art of prayer, and I dutifully followed along, eager to learn and to be saved. Then I saw that what they most envied, most desired, was that energetic and stupidly hopeful desire I had manifested, eyes closed, on that damn train of mine.

In the margin: "You are on this train with me now. I know that I contradict myself and may appear angry, but I do my work with love, and I ask that you do the same. God help you."

Fifteen

IN THE TIME that I knew her, Jo Van Fleet arose every morning and had a cup of coffee and a glass of wine, the latter consumed before a large, framed poem written in her honor by Ben Belitt. As she told me often, she could read this poem and feel better about herself because she had "once been noticed and appreciated." The wine might have made her feel a little lighter about the loads she insisted others had given her to carry, but the poem helped her in her daily insistence that she had been great, had possessed a talent that startled actors, audiences, playwrights, and at least one poet, who had come to be friends with her when he was a faculty member at Bennington along with William Bales, Jo's husband. "People used to notice me," Jo would say, and she would set her mouth in a sneer that is visible in all of her screen performances, most noticeably as James Dean's mother in *East of Eden,* for which she received an Oscar in 1956. "Poor Jo," Tenn had said. "She makes that sneer and it's as if she's smelling the rotting of her soul."

The Belitt poem made her feel appreciated, but so did the words Tenn had said about her, and when I typed them up and gave them to her, she began to carry them with her in a canvas tote bag that she took with her on her walks about the city. On occasion, she would also place her Oscar, now tarnished and a bit mottled, in this bag, and off she would go, to regale shopkeepers, her dining companions in local cafeterias, and the booksellers outside Zabar's with this treasure, and everyone would marvel at the opportunity to hold this recognized prize. (Once, when a man who sat near us in a diner was holding the Oscar and improvising an acceptance speech, Jo muttered, almost inaudibly, "I wish it gave me as much pleasure as it does him.") Then she would hurriedly stuff it back in her tote bag and be on her way.

Her daily trip was almost always the same. She would leave her apartment, at Riverside Drive and Seventy-eighth Street and slowly—oh, God, how slowly!—walk down to Ninth Avenue and Fifty-first Street, to St. Clare's Hospital. Her husband, once a dancer and a longtime instructor at many colleges, was now confined to a hospital bed, a victim of Alzheimer's, and on several occasions Jo asked me to accompany her. Jo would say the same things to the same people every time ("Hi, I'm Jo Van Fleet, and I'm here to see my husband," "I used to be a great actress, you know") and she would introduce me, telling them I was very important and I was going to reintroduce her to a theatrical world that had forgotten what real acting was like.

We would then go up to William Bales's room, where he lay, stunned and silent, although he would often clearly recognize Jo and would try to speak. Most times, however, Jo simply kissed him on the forehead, put her tote bag on the floor, and sat in a chair by his bedside. She would begin by telling him all that she had done, but mostly she would complain that no one was helping her. ("I called Colleen again. She's head of Actors Equity, but she won't help me. She's such a liar. Anne and Eli brought me some food, but I didn't like it. They don't care about my needs.") Eventually, she would tire of this litany, and she would stand and pace the room for a minute or two, then turn toward the bed and transform herself. Although she was then in her mid-seventies, was in poor health, and drank heavily throughout the day, Jo would proceed to recite Shakespeare sonnets, a monologue from *Camino Real* (a role she created on Broadway, and which she delivered perfectly), lines from her films *East of Eden* and *Wild River,* as well as nursery rhymes and songs that Jo and Bill had sung to their son, Michael.

In these performances, of which I witnessed only three, Jo became an actress again, and she clearly relished the opportunity to perform. "You see," Tenn had told me, "an actress will create an opportunity to act at every occasion. The ordering of a meal in a restaurant will have all the texture or range or drama of an O'Neill play or a Wagnerian opera.

They give it their all, because they live in a business—a culture—that rarely requires even a minimum of what they believe they can give."

So in that little hospital room, Jo acted again, and if her husband attempted to speak, or if he appeared to cry, she felt that she had done well, had provided a service to an appreciative audience. When I would compliment her on her recitation of a particular sonnet, she would stand tall, thank me, but add in her astringent voice ("all bile and citrus and pride," Tenn had called it), "That's sweet, but you're young and stupid and have no idea of what I can do."

Jo would pick up her tote bag and begin the long walk home. Sometimes we exchanged words; more often than not we walked in silence. On one of our walks home after a hospital visit, we were standing at an intersection when Jo looked over at a newsstand and read that Tony Perkins had AIDS. Jo had loved Tony, had worked with him onstage in *Look Homeward, Angel* and on film in *This Angry Age,* and I heard her yelp with pain before I saw the headline. Jo dropped her bag and began crying, walking in circles, confused. Passersby looked on at this tiny woman and laughed, thinking they were merely witnessing a crazy New Yorker having a spell. When Jo noticed their laughter, she turned on them and yelled, "I'm crying for you, don't you see? Because you don't get that it's all shit! Life is nothing but shit!"

AMID THEIR LAUGHTER, Jo picked up her bag and we began walking again. Mildred Natwick lived in a sunny penthouse apartment on Park Avenue, lemony and spotless and elegant. Tenn had never worked with Miss Natwick, but he adored her, sought her out at openings and auditions, visited her backstage, and claimed that Guthrie McClintic had told him that a season with Millie was worth more than a decade with doctors. "Guthrie was convinced that Millie had healing powers," Tenn told me, "but when I questioned her about them, she assured me that the powers belonged to Mary Baker Eddy, and she was merely a conduit. I went home and looked up 'conduit,' but it didn't seem to apply to the actress I knew."

Each morning Millie read her Bible Lesson from the *Christian Science Quarterly,* which comprised selections from the King James Bible and others from Eddy's *Science and Health with Key to the Scriptures.* Millie did not like to discuss her religion, and indeed I knew her for many months before she would talk openly about it with me. "I mean," she would say, in that sweet, quizzical voice of hers, "they don't ask Helen Hayes about the Roman Catholic faith, and they shouldn't, but when anyone learns of my beliefs, they think I'm an expert. I'm merely a student. Edith Evans"—also a Christian Scientist—"used to say, 'Millie, just go on being perfect and they won't ask any more questions. They'll just follow you around and get the point.' But I hardly think myself perfect."

After her lesson, which she surmised took her anywhere from forty-five minutes to an hour, Millie would ready herself for her day. As she did so, she would recite the Scientific Statement of Being: "There is no life, truth, intelligence, or substance in matter . . ." But her favorite passage, and the one to which she would cling whenever she was faced with pain or illness or doubt or depression, was: "All is infinite Mind, and its infinite manifestation, Man."

Once, when I was having a difficult time, Millie was instantly helpful, in ways both practical and supernal. Millie had an easy and cheerful generosity, which blended effortlessly with her dignified reserve, and the recipient never felt discomfort or judgment. Because she always noted her gratitude for anything you had done for her, her aid to you was simply, in her words, "fair and deserved," and she would always add, "Let's make nothing of this as quickly as possible." Her devotion to Christian Science had freed her from the tyranny of illness and pain, she admitted, but it continued to help her address the question of who she was and what she was intended to become. Although Millie was in her late seventies when I began to spend time with her, she was actively involved in "the act of becoming," and she was endlessly interested in reaching her goal of being "utterly in the Mind and out of the body."

When Tenn and I were walking in the French Quarter, we stopped in a small antiques shop that had once been, he swore, a gay bar for young men who appreciated older men. "So it is in the lease that it must remain in the trade of antiquities," he quipped, then walked to the rear of the store to use the bathroom. The proprietor said nothing, only warmly shaking Tenn's hand as he began to leave the store. As we were walking out, Tenn noticed a small, decoupaged square on which was a prayer written by Mary Baker Eddy. Tenn purchased it, which surprised both me and the proprietor, but he gave it to me to give to Millie when

I met her. "I think," Tenn said, "that the words of this woman have helped Millie to realize herself."

When I gave the gift to Millie, eight years after Tenn had purchased it, Millie was moved and embarrassed, and only said, "I would like to think that I became something, but I'm not yet all that I could have been or should have been." She looked at me and smiled, clearly closing the subject, but I knew somehow that she would return to it.

"Millie is loved and wonderful," Tenn told me, "but she has within her, I think, a rage as to what might have been. I believe that she, like all of us, has a deep hurt, a gash, a wound, that she chooses to cure or remove with a positive agenda, where others exploit this wound, or reveal this wound, to achieve uniqueness or attention or surcease. I would like to know how she takes care of herself, and what she feels led her to this obsessive need to purify and reshape herself. How muddy can her waters be?"

Millie was always active. She saw plays and operas and exhibitions. She visited friends with cheer and aid. She attended and hosted parties. She took a huge interest in whatever presented itself to her, but I could see that as she did these things, she was fully engaged in her inner reconstruction. When I told her about Tenn's analogy about our lives being two trains running simultaneously, she laughed like a delighted little girl, and agreed immediately. "That is so true," she said, "and I'm the dotty old woman who always misses her stop. But I'm okay, because I would rather keep traveling."

Mildred Natwick was born in Baltimore, early in the twentieth century (she was cagey with the date) into what she called relative comfort; and while attending college, she finally admitted to her parents that she wanted to be an actress. "I was beautifully raised by my parents," Millie told me, "and I never felt a lack of anything, but it was not until the day they gave me their blessing to be an actress that I felt accepted, loved, assured." Early in her career, Millie became a favorite of Joshua Logan, who cast her in several plays in repertory, which led her to her Broadway debut in 1932. While that was a propitious date in her life, far more important was her meeting Guthrie McClintic and Katharine Cornell. "If Christian Science gave me the foundation for life and living," Millie told me late in our relationship, "then I can tell you that Guthrie and Katharine gave me the foundation for a life in the theater." While Millie

Mildred Natwick was almost Quaker-like in
appearance and demeanor—calm, kind, virtually
invisible—but her acting reminded Tennessee of
finely spun crystal, and he frequently sought out
her clear mind and persistent cheer.

would never have said disparaging things about herself and others, she
alluded to the fact that she had lacked confidence in her appearance, but
that these doubts had been cleared away by Cornell. "Katharine Cornell
was a great beauty," Millie told me, "and her beauty came not from jars
or camouflage, but from within. Mary Baker Eddy tells us that to have
more beauty we must have less illusion and more soul, and this was
manifested in her. She looked at me one day and she said . . ." Millie
paused, laughed, blushed, and then continued. "She said, 'Millie, your
face is a comfort to me and to others. Its beauty is the beauty you find
in things that loved ones have given you. And I like to see you coming.'
So I knew—how could I not?—that I would never be as appealing as
Katharine Cornell, but I trusted her so much as a friend and an actress
that I felt if she didn't mind seeing me coming, I wasn't insane to think
I could walk on a stage."

Millie appeared in several productions with Cornell, but her great-est triumphs were in plays not affiliated with her mentor. "And I rather liked that," Millie admitted, "because it meant that I could be sur-prised by a visit from Katharine when I least expected it, offering the perfect words, as only she could supply them." Millie created the role of Madame Arcati in Noel Coward's *Blithe Spirit* in New York, and became one of Truman Capote's favorite actresses when she appeared in his *Grass Harp*, an experience he remembered so fondly that he insisted that she appear in the filmization of his short story "Miriam" when it was incorporated into Frank Perry's *Trilogy* in 1969.

"What Millie has in her work," Tenn told me, "is what every writer craves, which is loving detail. Millie's work is utterly seamless, and yet it never appears overcontrolled or artificial. You never see the work; only the result."

"It's funny you should bring that up," Millie told me, "because when I was working with Ralph Richardson in *The Waltz of the Toreadors*, I had a difficult part, but I loved it. I once told Ralph that the work was torture, but divine." When I asked what made the part difficult for her, she winced again, and admitted that she hated to talk about acting. "I just think it's so impossible. I get sent these books where actors are interviewed and go on and on about approaching a role or analyzing an emotion, and I feel they might as well let me watch them have their teeth cleaned. You pour yourself, all that you are and all that you can spare, into the role that has been written, and you use your script as your guide. Your director is your guide to the script, and if you're lucky, both you and the director are headed in the right direction. That is that. Everything else merely happens." She then related how, after one especially good performance, Richardson had asked her how she had accomplished a particular dance step that had as its denouement a line reading that always tickled him. "And I said, 'Oh, Ralph, I don't know,' and he tried to have me reproduce it, and it utterly failed. Outside of the context of that play, without our other actors, and without the param-eters that Harold Clurman had set for us, nothing made sense, nothing worked. Ralph, heartbroken, looked at me and said, 'Never mind.' Well, I felt awful, like a truly bad actress. Then, the next night, the scene went beautifully, perfect, heavenly. Backstage, Ralph said, 'Millie, you got it right out there. Why not for me?' And I said, 'Ralph, it happened when it was supposed to.' And that's all I want to say about acting."

For many, Millie is known for her reprise of her Broadway role in the film version of *Barefoot in the Park,* for which she won an Oscar nomination, and for her role opposite Helen Hayes in the television series *The Snoop Sisters,* for which she won an Emmy, and she is still spoken of with admiration for her work. But no one seemed to capture her special appeal better than Tenn, when he said: "Detail upon detail upon detail. An accretion of apt movements and sounds that add up to an utterly real moment in time. You don't see huge explosions of theatricality in her work, just tiny flashes of humanity."

Millie's eyes welled up when I read her those words. "I never even knew that Tennessee knew my name! And to say something like that! That is enough for me."

NOTHING WAS EVER enough for Jo Van Fleet. According to Barbara Baxley, who had known her since she—Baxley—was a young girl, this may have been because Jo was recognized as a good actress at an early age, and she continued in her quest despite great resistance from her parents, who felt a theatrical career was beneath a proper and intelligent woman. "So anger and rage and a sense of 'Look at me now, folks' energized everything she did," Baxley told me, and it may help to explain her ease in parts requiring both great strength and cynicism. "When she was most sour," Baxley quipped, "she was most Jo."

And yet Jo had her supporters. Herbert Berghof thought her both a marvelous actress and a potential teacher. Berghof's wife, Uta Hagen, told me that "Jo was good, but Jo was always unstable, so Herbert gave her responsibilities he felt she could handle, which is to say they were limited. Jo used to call me and beg to teach with us here [at HB Studio in Greenwich Village], and right when I would feel sorry for her and might imagine that I could have her do something, she would say, 'It's time they were taught by a *real* actress,' and I would calmly hang up the phone."

Jo was cast in *Camino Real,* in 1953, as Marguerite Gautier, and her scene was not working particularly well. "Gadg [Kazan] alienated his affections from that play very early on," Tenn told me, "and he adopted a very lax attitude toward the whole enterprise. I had troubles with Jo's scene, and I literally and figuratively threw up my hands. I was not in a healthy frame of mind then, and Jo saw this and volunteered to work on her own scene herself. Well, by God, she went away and typed up some pages, making her the lead of course, but from those pages I was able to construct her part anew, and it was much stronger. I could see she was happy to have control over a part, and a production, and she was very easy to work with."

"Jo is tragic," Kazan told me, "and to mention her name in some settings is to see an entire group of people shudder. She seemed—and seems—hell-bent on destroying herself, and I do not know why. To direct her was often a grueling challenge, for while she wanted desperately to be true to the part, she intrinsically believes that she is smarter than everyone else on the set, including the director and the playwright. Many times she pushed me away, muttering, 'I know, dammit! I know what to do!' I put up with it, but more often than not, others decided that once was enough."

Jo earned a Tony Award in 1954 for her work in Horton Foote's *The*

"Epically devious" with both her talent and her attentions, Jo Van Fleet was an actress Tennessee loved to watch, write for, talk to about plays; but her company was, as he put it, "hellish, black with rage."

Trip to Bountiful, then an Oscar for her work with Kazan in *East of Eden.* "My persistent direction of Jo," Kazan told me, "was '*Tight, tight.* Keep it *tight,* Jo,' and I think she had migraines for a month keeping herself so rigid and constricted, but she was brilliant. Run her scenes and it's always amazing." Jo was equally strong in Kazan's *Wild River,* but after her cameo as Paul Newman's dying mother in *Cool Hand Luke,* she worked only a handful of times. Her last leading role onstage was in 1962, in *Oh Dad, Poor Dad, Momma's Hung You in the Closet and I'm Feelin' So Sad,* and Jerome Robbins, the director of that play, told me that he thought Jo was capable of becoming a major actress. "I thought she was larger than life, eccentric, a great leading character actress," he told me, "and I thought that maybe America would finally have its own Edith Evans, or a grainier, meaner Ruth Gordon. But for every good moment Jo had, she had to produce three equally horrendous ones that would shatter a performance or alienate the entire company." When I told Jo that Robbins thought her potentially a great actress, she yelled out, "Fuck him! He never called me, never sent me a dime, never even sent me a goddamn chicken potpie from Zabar's! Him with all his money! So I reject that completely. If he really meant that, he would feed me."

Time—its passage, its effects, its value—fascinated and frightened Tenn. There was the time that was helpful and healing, as when one takes stock of a situation, thinks things out, perhaps takes a nap. Far more often there was the ravaging time, which took away opportunity and health. Time was money, time was health, time was everything. Again, that analogy to trains, swiftly moving, keeping to their own ceaseless, uncaring schedules: "And heading to a station near you!" he would cackle. "All of my women—in my plays, of course, but I think in my life as well—are frantic, preternaturally aware of this train heading toward them called time, and utterly unaware of who's going to be getting on or getting off. Youth: heading out of town! Illness: incoming! Work: out of town! New opportunities: service interrupted!"

Tenn would giggle uproariously at these proclamations, seemingly unaware that others might be discomfited by them. Then again, he thought Blanche DuBois was the funniest female character in modern American theater, and that Billie Dawn, the character immortalized by Judy Holliday in Garson Kanin's *Born Yesterday* wasn't nearly so entertaining. "I mean, when they take her away at the end, I think it's hysterical that she pops right back into her games. She hasn't lost a thing, except her hold on reality. And what," he always asked when the subject arose, "has reality ever done for anybody?"

To be constantly aware of time and its effects made Tenn—and Tenn's women—jittery, agile at dodging reality and responsibilities, adept at adopting new strategies of living. The most effective foundation that he felt could be placed underneath this shaky edifice we call life was desire, which he felt was nothing more than prayer.

"I was sent to a monastery once," Tenn said, and he enjoyed my shock of his being in such a setting. "Now calm down," he said, chuckling. "I was sent there after one of my many travails, mental and physical, and it was believed that it might help me. This was during my rush toward Catholicism, which I felt was my only alternative to death or madness. It was during this sojourn, as they insisted upon calling it, that I realized how much fear we all carry, how fear is the fuel in all of our engines. And when fear motivates us, we tend to fall into a repetitious recitation of requests. When a friend of mine was mugged in New York in the seventies (and who wasn't?), she just said, over and over, 'No, please, no, please, no, please no,' which was merely her prayer to survive that situation. When I was in the hospital, waiting to see if I indeed would die, I actually wanted my mother and Frank, one of whom was useless and the other dead. My desire wasn't actually to have them with me, but to again feel whatever comfort I might have known with them. But mainly—youth and health! Bring them back!"

The women of Tenn's plays spoke in a pattern that he felt mirrored his own habits when he was afraid. "Not so much when I'm drunk, you see," he admitted, "because, of course, I am then not myself, but a medicated person who responds in a wholly different manner than a real person, an honest person. But when I am fully aware, I babble and charm and cajole, and so do my characters."

Tenn noted Blanche's endless nattering about literature, life, clothing—anything—to ward off not only inspection by those who might be observing her, but also time's endless choreography into our space. "Oh, God," Tenn would laugh, "I used to believe that if I just created enough, just laughed enough, I could hold back the demons of time, and the effects they visit upon us. What was that great quote by Thornton Wilder?" (He was thinking of "He who is happy is forever out of time's grasp.") "Oh, let me tell you, I looked for happiness, and happy times are as consuming as the bad times; they just use you up to a different tempo."

Maggie of *Cat on a Hot Tin Roof* was, in Tenn's mind, a supplicant crouched, mentally and at times physically, in a perpetual and penitential prayer. "The need for love, physical and emotional, was so strong in Maggie, and in me, that it consumes her life and her mind, and everything she does or says, is clouded, as with a cheap perfume, with this desire, this prayer, for Brick's love, for Big Daddy's support, for Big Mama's understanding and aid, and for Sister Woman's respect. This longing, this infernal, annoying longing, which we all must disguise as—charm? beauty? wit? talent? I chose to make Maggie alluring and fertile, frantically fertile, and those are the only amulets she has in her long prayer. But in her speech, I made her plead for her moments with those characters, for her redemption, so to speak, and it is my prayer that speaks through Maggie.

"I turned to Catholicism because, at an advanced artery of illness in my life, I felt I had run out of options, had used up my privileges at the other troughs of redemption," Tenn told me. "However, I remain, at heart, and in style, an Episcopalian, those words, desires, and rhythms pounded upon and within me by the merciless taskmaster who was my grandfather. And when I find that I'm in arrears, it is those prayers that I turn to, those words, those rhythms. In fact, the words are meaningless; it is the rhythms, the intent, that comfort me, and when I wandered into churches on foreign soil, the prayers, uttered in tongues unknown to me, nonetheless offered comfort."

At that moment, despite a day of alcohol and numerous infusions of pills, Tenn began to quote those prayers that gave him most comfort, particularly this one: "O Gracious Father, who opennest Thine hand and fillest all things living with plenteousness; We beseech Thee of thine infinite goodness to hear us, who now make our prayers and supplications unto thee . . ."

"I immediately reach for those prayers when I find myself bound by the results of my poor intentions," Tenn told me. "I wish I had reached for those prayers more frequently than I reached for pills or liquor or flesh, but *that* story has been written."

"That train has left the station?" I asked.

"Very good," Tenn chuckled, "and precisely the point you should have reached."

JO VAN FLEET CLAIMED never to pray, at least not to God. However, she admitted that when she was most despondent, she often felt she could do nothing but call out in anger or fear, often finding comfort in the exhaustion that resulted from the consistent badgering of . . . "Of what?" I asked her. "Forces beyond our control," Jo replied. "Fate, I imagine."

Jo never admitted to using alcohol, even as I would sit and watch her consume one of the huge bottles of inexpensive white wine she kept in her apartment. If I mentioned the wine she had already had that evening, she would blame me. "I'm only drinking because you're my guest. I don't keep wine in this house."

Prior to the Fourth of July celebrations of 1990, Jo told me she would like to get together with me to "do something." This was not an idea I relished, as previous meetings with her had not turned out to be pleasant, and she enjoyed creating a scene. Jo liked dining at a diner then at the corner of Broadway and West Seventy-ninth Street, clad only in the mink coat she had purchased for the premiere of *I'll Cry Tomorrow*. She made no effort to keep the coat around her nude, aged body. If clerks were inattentive or lines too long at the few stores she frequented, Jo would simply steal the handful of items she had collected. The store owners witnessed this and did nothing; they felt sorry for her and turned away during the commission of her crimes.

One day, Jo called my number and left nearly twenty messages for me. When I played them back and wrote them down, I didn't hear the words of a drunk woman growing increasingly angry with me for not being available. I heard a prayer.

"This is Jo Van Fleet. I would really, really like to not be alone tomorrow. Do you think you could be with me tomorrow? Tomorrow will be really terrible for me if I'm alone, again. This is Jo Van Fleet, and I'm always alone. Why do I have to be alone? You're not alone? Do you want to be with me? Would you like to get together with me? I don't want to be alone. Please don't let me be alone. This is Jo Van Fleet. I'm still alone. I still haven't heard from you. I need to hear from you. This is Jo Van Fleet. If we could just get together, I think I would be well enough to get on with things. I think I could feel better. I can't be alone. Can you come over? This is Jo Van Fleet. If I could just hear your voice,

I would feel better. I wouldn't even care if you couldn't come over. But I can't be alone. Please don't let me be alone."

"She had an evil about her that vibrated," Jerome Robbins would tell me, even as he admitted that when he directed her he felt he was witnessing one of "the greatest theatrical talents we would have, but one that wasn't properly harnessed."

"I would be happy," Jo told me once, "if just one person—one person!—would admit to me what I was. A great actress. Somebody!"

On one of our walks, Jo told me she needed some things from a drugstore. The store we entered, now long replaced, was at Broadway and Eightieth Street. Jo moved through the aisles with agonizing slowness (she was both tired and drunk), but she finally made it to the register and placed her few things in front of the bored cashier. When Jo attempted to pay for her items with a check, the cashier asked for some identification. Jo reached into her tote bag, hauled out her Oscar, and proudly and loudly slammed it on the counter. "*This* is who *I* am!"

Jo's check was accepted, and she was happier that day than I had ever seen her.

WHILE JO VAN FLEET'S identity crisis revolved around her recognition as someone of merit (both by herself and by others), Mildred Natwick seemed to perpetually ask herself who she was, ever had been, or was meant to be. Jo's rage stemmed from her sense that she was a talented, intelligent actress who had been mistreated and abandoned, while Millie was a grateful actress who wondered if she had done, or could do, enough to fulfill her destiny.

Jo was perpetually angry; Millie was unceasingly happy, upbeat, bemused. Nothing was ever presented to Jo that couldn't serve as proof that life was utterly miserable and untenable; nothing appeared to Millie that wasn't a blessing, and further proof that life was merely the raw material that was presented to us for the crafting of our identities.

When Jo walked about Manhattan, she was passing the locations of past triumphs and humiliations, both of which served to set her off in a rage. When Millie moved about Manhattan, she was, first and foremost, grateful that she was still ambulatory. "I take nothing for granted," she once told me, "and I feel that that's why nothing I ever really needed has ever been taken from me." Life was full of conflicts for Millie, but she refused to see them as evil or debilitating. One of her favorite quotes from Mary Baker Eddy was as imprinted on her brain as the Episcopalian prayers had been on Tenn's: "Hold thought steadfastly to the enduring, the good, and the true, and you will bring these into your experience proportionably to their occupancy of your thoughts." When I asked her one day how she managed to avoid the pettiness that had engulfed so many others in her profession, she replied, "I guess I just didn't see anything that would force me to debase myself or someone else. I was lucky enough to find a means of seeing things that were real and things that weren't real. I discarded the unreal."

SITTING IN THE ROOM at the Royal Orleans, reflecting on Jo Van Fleet, Tenn became decidedly morose, morbid. He rose from the bed and looked out the window for a long stretch of time. I asked what was wrong. "Jo has brought into my mind Rachel Roberts," Tenn told me. Two years before our meeting, in late summer 1980, Rachel Roberts had committed suicide, in Los Angeles, by swallowing a caustic substance—believed to be Drano or some other toxic drain cleaner—and had then been propelled by pain to crash through a glass pane and die, scratched and scalded, in her verdant backyard. "Brilliant women destroying themselves," Tenn said. "Rachel called women—brilliant women—late in the night, hectoring them for having values, standards, the good sense to avoid her. I loved her, but, I realize now, I avoided her as I avoided Jo: you cannot sustain their company for long, even as you long for their talents."

Tenn returned to the bed and told me he wanted to dictate some ideas he had for a profile of Rachel Roberts.

"This will be a tale of gifts that went begging. This will be a tale of gifts that burn and decimate and move swiftly to the next area of destruction. This will be a tale of Rachel Roberts."

Employing the style of Marguerite Duras and the biography of Rachel Roberts, an actress of "diabolical brilliance, a suicide, a Cassandra of the arts," Tenn thought he had the beginning of a profile, an exploration. "I did not care for my autobiography," Tenn told me. "The true story of my life is one that should be told through my influences—

those I utilized well and those I failed to utilize at all. I never have and I never will exist without the gifts—shared and studied—of a remarkable group of women.

"Much like Jo Van Fleet, Rachel could find little satisfaction in her talent, and absolutely none in the venues in which it was presented. Resentment was a perfume that surrounded her, cloaked her, made breathing in her presence difficult. Some of this was deserved, I suppose, but I have come to see the effects—the poisonous effects—of holding a grudge, harboring resentments, judging every act, gesture, karmic flip of the cards. There is no way to be gracious in the face of injustice, I imagine, and Rachel was so much better than her material or her memory will reveal, and the few acts of benevolence that were shown to her she chose to destroy. So do we cast her aside? Do we dismiss her as a difficult woman who got what she deserved? Do we fail to study and marvel at her gifts simply because to do so would reveal too many unpalatable truths about talent and its cultivation and its strength and its standing in the world?

"I think that we want to believe that happiness, or, at best, satisfaction, accrues to those who have given us pleasure or elucidation or inspiration. Our work can do this for us, but it requires an understanding both of the art and of ourselves for this to exist. Rachel did not possess this understanding; Rachel did not enjoy her own presence unless she was in the process of working, and working well, on a part in a good play with a cast from whom she could garner experience and respect and a decent drink at the end of the day. She expected too much too often, but her diabolical demands led to her extraordinary work, even as it made her passive hours—the quiet, nonworking hours—so hellish."

Tenn had photographs of Rachel Roberts tucked into a journal, along with several pages of notes that had been torn from various pads and notebooks.

"Her eyes see everything and like nothing.

"Such a hard jaw, purpose and hunger and power to move forward.

"Hers is a face in front of the open door that holds the bad news, the fateful telegram, the unfaithful lover locked in the arms of another. She has always just been given the news that none of us has the strength to hear. She tries to hear it, but it destroys her.

"She swallowed a corrosive substance, silencing the voice, stopping the heart, sizzling the brain, but long before she ventured into her kitchen and found that brightly advertised cleaning agent and swallowed it, she had swallowed so many bitter things: the truth about our theater, our culture, our world. She had come to see how we lie to ourselves and to each other about what will be, what will come, what will happen if we do the right things or if we fight to make things better or if we just give up.

"She seemed to know the score, and there is something to be said for the divinity of ignorance.

"I saw Rex Harrison not long after her self-murder, that Isadora-like dance she choreographed that ended in shattered glass and silence. I wanted to know if she had truly hated herself that much, that fervently. No, he told me, forever unflappable, so smooth—she had hated *us* that much, and that acidic toast was her final fuck-you to the world that had so disappointed her. She had married him in the belief that fame and money and good wines and good linens and a castle in the hills could make her happy, make her matter, shove her to a place she belonged—the center of attention.

"Myths. Delusions. How many corrosive things had she swallowed in the villa in the hills? How many have I swallowed? Have we all swallowed?

"I never hated her, and she never disappointed me. I think it is safe to say that she never disappointed an audience or a playwright or an actor who had high standards and a thick skin. Yes, she would call in the night and hector and criticize: she knew all of my flaws and my weaknesses and my own travel kit of myths and delusions. She was always correct, and she was always able to tell me how I could improve myself. I didn't want to hear it, and I didn't have the strength, the will, the courage to take her advice or to see the damage I had done, but she offered it, she was right, and she was angry.

"There is no way to do things well and gently and consistently. There can be no satisfaction anywhere and with anything until we can accept the flawed and unique prisoners we are—prisoners to our memories and the distinct mechanisms we have for sharing them. I do not have this gift—a sort of faith is what it is. Rachel didn't have it either. I have her face in my memory and that voice and that brutal detail she brought to her work and to her life and to every conversation we ever had.

"We let her down. She destroyed herself. There is no happy ending here and harsh reminders of what awaits some of us. I feel the incredible need for some reason to apologize to her. I will write words, plays, memorials.

"I will try, however I can, to throw some light her way."

Tenn concluded his comments, then retreated to the bathroom.

AS THE YEARS PASSED, I saw less and less of Jo. In fact, I don't know when she moved from the Riverside Drive apartment, and I was shocked to pick up *The New York Times* on that summer day in 1996 to see that she had died in a hospital in Queens. I did not attend her funeral service at the Actors Studio, but I was told that her son read from the notes I had given her from my meetings with Tenn.

And yet I would see Jo still making her arduous walks about the neighborhood, and she was confused as the neighborhood changed, as the reasonably priced Greek diner gave way to the posh takeout shop, as her drugstore gave way to a GNC health store. Every day, at virtually the same time, she would walk in and tell the perplexed staff what used to reside in that space and tell them who she was. She became the resident crazy lady, but a counterperson at Zabar's told me that they often gave her free food because she was so poor. Jo was not, in fact, poor: her pensions, and those of her husband, who died in late 1990, were sufficient to support her. But many of us, myself included, continued to leave her food or money or books, always imploring her doorman not to tell her who had left them.

And yet . . . As we were cleaning up Barbara Baxley's apartment after her death, Oli Brubeck, one of Barbara's oldest friends, noticed that there were messages on the answering machine, and she decided to listen to them. Most were from before Barbara's death, calls from friends, confirmations of appointments, but finally, at the end of the tape was a small, sad voice that said, "Oh, Barbara, I'm so sorry you died." It was Jo Van Fleet.

As Elia Kazan told me after we spoke of Jo's obituary in the *Times,* "We mustn't cry for her death, but for her life." I still see her, however, that time with her husband in his hospital room, and even if the performance meant more to her than to him, even if it might have been for her pleasure alone, I remember it as the time she had some sense of peace and control.

MILLIE ATTENDED services at the Third Church of Christ, Scientist on Park Avenue. She invited me to join her for services one Sunday, and afterward we went to a small restaurant that she liked. Millie was in a grave mood on that Sunday, and it was alarming, because while it was common for her to be serious, she had never been so mordant. The previous time I had seen Millie had been at the memorial service for Helen Hayes, and I had assumed that her mien on that day had been due to the grief she felt at the death of a close friend. But I now saw that there was an unraveling effect taking place within and upon Millie, as if she were literally falling apart, and she moved at times like a marionette whose strings had been snipped or loosened. She was still clearheaded and firm and precise, but even her voice had changed, as had her ideas on a few things.

"These women all seem to know what they wanted or what they wanted to do," she told me in her new apartment, which was a smaller version of her previous penthouse, but still sunny and bright, although today its tenant seemed anything but. "I think I knew, from Christian Science, what I could be and should be, and I used that as my guide to living, as a means to see how I was growing. I could demonstrate to myself how well I was doing by how well I was overcoming any false notions I had as to who and what I was, as well as what others were. Yet I still feel that I didn't fully develop, except as a student of Christian Science and, perhaps, as an actress. I used to have long conversations with Katharine Cornell about this, but after Guthrie died [in 1961], we didn't see each other as much, and our relationship grew more polite and accidental. I still loved her, and I still felt her to be the closest thing to a mentor, but the relationship changed. I never could fully divulge how I felt, or about what I wanted to accomplish, but she knew that I was being as truthful with her as I could be.

"Finally, one night, she said that it was difficult to be truly oneself if that self couldn't find acceptance, if to be what you really were born to be was somehow alien to others or might keep you from functioning at all. Katharine Cornell was a beautiful woman, loved as an actress even by those who only saw pictures of her, because she epitomized what an actress in that day was. She was charming and warm and she surrounded herself with people who never felt as special as they did when in her presence. That is not my presentation to the world. I feel that if I had been true to my emotions and had loved the people I had wanted in the way that I wanted, I would have been seen as sad or sinister, when I don't feel—and cannot feel—that love, honest affection, can make a person either of those things. Katharine told me that this was how she kept at bay anything negative that might exist in her personality, or that might cause her embarrassment. If she immediately turned her attentions to the work or to her friends and guests, the focus would no longer be on her. No one could hurt her or expose her.

"I did not have her gifts," Millie continued, "so I put on the mantle of Christian Science and chose to keep myself healthy and pure and of service to others, and to also keep myself from becoming bitter about any lost opportunities I might have suffered. I think you know what I'm telling you. Love whomever you wish, and be generous and open. We place so many spiritual values—golden lights, heavenly views, healing powers—on so many things, but we withhold it from anything that strikes us as odd or alien or costly." Millie's sweet smile returned. "I wonder now what Katharine Cornell might have been, what *I* might have been, if I had the courage to face my feelings and *still* be healthy, pure, and of service to others."

I admitted that I had no answers for her, and Tenn had never alluded to any secret self that might have existed within Mildred Natwick. Millie changed the subject, and we continued our visit. The conversation I had with Millie was not, I think, prompted by any dire feelings she might have had about impending death (she lived for another sixteen months), but rather by a sort of reckoning that some of the other women endured when they cleaned out homes and closets and memories, and came across another person they had once known or been.

In our final phone conversations, Millie continued to be upbeat and helpful and curious about anything she encountered, but she was no longer taking her walks, and she missed them. It was not, however, within Millie to bemoan anything, so she quickly added that she had plenty to enjoy right in her apartment, so I shouldn't feel sorry for her.

Tenn had said, "I wonder if the people we admire and love see themselves as we see them? I'm always surprised when someone I idolize turns out to be as big a mess as I am, but I'm always delighted when I find out that, like me, they have their alternate selves, who walk beside them through life, reminding them of what might be, or could be, or should be. Keep the trains running, honey!"

I walk Millie's routes on occasion, up and down the East Side, thinking of her, and when I see certain addresses or intersections, I'll be reminded of a conversation we might have had, and the quotes she felt inspired to share, and which she used for so long to hide what she felt was the unacceptable Mildred Natwick.

"May love and peace cheer your course."

"Become conscious for a single moment that Life and intelligence are purely spiritual."

"We should examine ourselves and learn what is the affection and purpose of the heart, for in this way only can we learn what we honestly are."

And her favorite:

"What we love determines what we are."

Sixteen

TENN HAD TOLD ME that the ability to succeed in the theater—and life, for that matter—often depended on a person's ability to withstand whatever had been presented, smile, and say thank you. "The vast majority of expressions of gratitude," he told me, "are uttered immediately before a retreat."

We found a café near the hotel and sat at a table for four, spreading the bags and pads generously. "Tell me," Tenn said, pushing his glasses up to the top of his head. "What is your exact, your *precise,* definition of faith?"

I had no definition, precise or otherwise, of faith on that day in 1982, and I do not have one today. Neither did Tenn. This was his point, I soon realized, but he wanted to prepare me for the "thicket of nonsense" I was about to enter, the sticky but potentially fascinating field of myth and delusion I would be finding—on his behalf, he understood—discovering if he mattered, if he could survive, if he rested in the memories of the people he used as inspiration, as one of his own systems of faith.

Tenn looked at me and began a series of confessions.

The young boy had hugged a radio in the dark and had hidden in the hallways of rectories and churches and had heard the sorrows and the desires of so many people, and it was all, he realized, fantasy, myth.

"The life, our lives," he told me, present some unalterable and authentic facts. We are born to particular people at particular times in particular places. Geography holds us to a certain, dull reality for a period of time, but the desire to matter, to be noticed and to contribute something, to rise above the mere facts that have been typed onto certificates and into our biological destinies, soon leads us to manufacture our own reality, our own personas.

At a young age, all of us, Tenn believed, begin the act of creating the people we will become, and we use, in this eternal production, whatever tools we may need.

As a child Tenn had the church, which was a theater, whose players gave him characters, structure, the earliest system of organization he would know. People married and found Christ and died and were buried at particular times, in certain cycles. The young Tennessee Williams believed that there was a season of death, because he remembered that certain times of the year seemed flush with funerals and mourning and prayers and houses full of food and recriminations. There were certain types of cakes and vegetable dishes that forever connoted death to Tenn, and he would refuse them. "A Lane cake," he told me, "or a particular cake of a shiny white, with boiled icing, meant someone had died in the night," he remembered, and the woman carrying it down the street, its frosting slightly sweating in the heat, was headed for the church or the house of the survivors or a union hall that might now bear bunting or be full of dour relatives and coworkers. "I would follow," he remembered, "and I would be welcomed. I was the pastor's little grandson, and some of my family would be there shortly, and I would soon hear the biography of the deceased." These biographies rose up from grief and guilt and anger and the fear of time lost. The time knot, that massive serpent that crushed life and energy and desire, had come for someone else, and Tenn heard the fear in the voices. A funeral service was the circling of the wagons, with prayers and perhaps pink frosting and the hope of eternal salvation, but, Tenn insisted, "there was still a dead body in the room, and the knot had tightened."

There was discussion of the dead person's values and contributions, and Tenn remembered his family often marveling at the revisions the deceased had undergone in the period of time from life to diagnosis to death to ecclesiastical celebration. "If you want to truly be reformed," his grandfather was once overheard saying to a group of friends, "it's best to up and die. It does wonders for the soul and the heart and the affections offered."

All of our biographies, Tenn told me, are born out of fear, are crafted as we jump out of the range of the time knot, cheat it and avoid it. It is unbearable to believe that we may be unnoticed or unloved, so we become what we must to get what we need.

We are born into one identity and we soon learn if we landed on the right side of the tracks, if we fell into the laps of the right people and the better situations. We can jiggle this reality a bit by means of faith. The rustic of the people turn to faith in churches that urge cleanliness of mind and body and a release from the bonds of the earth, of cruel reality, by speaking in tongues, through the agency of God and his many angels, who give wisdom to those who lack food or heat or teeth. These are God's children who may not matter in the city council or in their schools, but they have a high standing in the "better world."

The Episcopalians of Tenn's upbringing were refined people and Christians: they knew their place and it was good. They had no need for superstition, because life had been, for the most part, good to them. They had the nicer homes in the nicer neighborhoods, went to good schools, saw the church as social, a fire around which to gather and commiserate, plan the future, contribute, matter. The Methodists and the Baptists were rural and poor and mean—they needed their God and their faith, harsh and judgmental, to put things in perspective: God had chosen his people, and their respective itineraries of loss and despair and triumph, a scanty sheet of events for which they were to be resigned and grateful while searching for "signs" of what it meant and how they could matter by living with and overcoming whatever it presented. The Catholics lived submerged in myth and its beauty and the fabulist faith that they were covered by a sky full of their own angels and their own God, who knew the numbers of hairs in their heads and who rejoiced that they had joined the true faith and were headed, candle by candle, bead by bead, to their rightful place by His side.

These were the faiths that Tenn and his peers had presented to them, and he sipped at each of their troughs. As he aged and looked around and met other people, he found that there were other means of mattering, and the ability to lie and to craft new identities led to new churches, beliefs, systems of survival. Spirit guides, charts of the sun and the moon, angel visits. Perhaps a guru, and not a God, was called for: Someone hip and corporeal who knew your centers of pain and could coddle and compliment you. "Faith," Tenn told me, "is the perpetual act of making things work. Fitting what has been given to you into a narrative that pleases you." Psychiatry presented itself as a religion for those who placed the primary emotions and incentives in the brain—not the soul or the heart, those tertiary organs. It was chemicals and malformations that determined our moods and our destinies, our happiness and productivity. Talk about it or medicate it.

Salvation awaits those who seek it.

Fame and money were belief systems as well, and Tenn began a list of those who had subsumed their talents to the pursuit of both. "They are narcotics," Tenn told me, "as powerful as any I've tried, and every bit as pernicious. They offer their benefit and they exact their cost at precisely the same moment."

Sex was a church in which Tenn had literally and figuratively knelt, and it burned away as quickly as the youth and beauty that are the costs of admission.

Luchino Visconti would have nothing to do with the concept of any organized set of beliefs, save one. As he explained to Tenn, look to the cultures for revelations: "Visconti invited me into an extended aesthetic and cultural orgasm, training my eye for the color and intricacy of every available moment and every type of person," Tenn said. "What I learned, and what I want to pass on to you, is this: I must urge you to expand yourself and spend time with people not of your country. The French will teach you what you should hate. The Italians will teach you how to adequately love what you should. The Latins will teach you the majesty of superstition and instinct. The people of Nordic extraction teach us how to clean things and bear up. The Japanese lead us to extremity. Africans will teach you the mystical aspects of the earth, and how to draw power from them. And your American heritage? It has given you the appetite and the entitlement to be rapacious and to take all of these things from all of these people and to hope to be whole."

The pages filled up, my pen kept racing to capture Tenn's thoughts, and the coffee kept coming, and Tenn kept on with his pilgrimages to the tiny restroom in the rear of the café.

Tenn returned and asked me to look at the list of topics he had written. The first on the list was "Navigation."

"Perfect," he said, and went off, again, to the restroom. "Kim Stanley," he said as he walked off, and he turned to make sure I had written the name down.

On each of the days we had spent together, Tenn had made references to Kim Stanley. Notes had been scribbled, her name invoked, his eyes rolled in remembrance of time he had spent with her. "Kim is the best of times and the worst of times," Tenn quipped, "all at the same time, every time."

A wild and violent woman, with a quick mind and a memory that was at one time remarkable, Stanley had every one of her spigots turned to full force at all times, and damage appeared wherever she rested or cast her gaze. "Kim could not believe that any progress could have been made, in her best interests, until there was serious damage to be found," Tenn told me. "Serious physical and emotional damage, at which point she felt that her job had been done; she had made her impact."

Stanley was a tireless and inventive fabulist, and her family history and catalog of experiences varied frequently. The narrative changed to suit her daily need, and she required, at all times, an audience, which was there not only to pay her attention, but to offer, for her many stories, a summation, a defense of her actions, praise for her achievement.

If she was to be believed, Stanley was the daughter of one academic and the niece and cousin of many others, learned and rigid men who forced their erudition and expertise and bodies upon her at an early age. When I made contact with Stanley, in her home on Hillcrest in Los Angeles, she held to this story, made easier to tell, she claimed, by years of therapy and silence and the freedom that certain deaths in a family bring to the survivors.

"I was made, I believe, for abuse," she told me. "I don't know if this is something that was decided upon by a God or by fate. It was decided by men, who saw an opportunity and took it. It is what men do." She stressed the final five words slowly and deliberately, emphasizing each word, then repeating them, then laughing. "I have not had a good time on this earth with men," she continued. "I was given their abuse for years, and I then went to them, stupidly and blindly and eagerly, for their acceptance and their acknowledgment of what they had done to me. I chained myself to an awful Catherine wheel of rage and booze and sex and protracted scenes of surrender and forgiveness. I have sought out to reform myself thousands of times."

In the biography she chose to share with me, Kim Stanley spent

A self-confessed fabulist, Kim Stanley, seen here in
the 1960s, when she was spending a lot of time with
Tennessee, was a brilliant actress and a "tortured
woman" who, according to Tennessee, put off
the work required of her until she was terrified of
attempting it again. She once told him that she would
rather jump out of a plane than step on a stage.

her childhood in Texas and New Mexico, hot, dry climates where, she
remembered, she dressed lightly, moved quickly, and routinely defended
her ideas and her body. "I was sexual very early," she told me. "I was led
to believe that this was a natural thing among intelligent and enlight-
ened people. It was a need, like the dip in the pool you needed to survive
the afternoon, or the drinks that would help you sleep through the hot
night." Panties were placed in the icebox, a cool towel placed on the
neck, and her father, her brothers, perhaps a cousin might visit her, to
get through the "beastly night," she recalled. "All the nights then, and
all the nights since," she said, "have been beastly." Dinner conversations were debates on literature, biology, physics, history. "I had a good

Kim Stanley saw Katharine Cornell in a 1940s
traveling production and decided that she was
what all actresses should look like. In the hot,
dusty Texas town in which Cornell appeared, she
was cool and collected and unafraid. "I looked at
my mess of a life," Stanley said, "and decided that
I wanted to move through it like her."

mind," she told me. "I still have a good mind. It's full of horrible and
outrageous things, but it's good. It's helped me to survive."

Stanley told me that she earned a master's degree from a school in
New Mexico—when it was not in Texas. A brilliant student, she studied
a program of varied subjects, majoring, she insisted, in biography. "I
wanted to learn about other people's lives," she told me. "I wanted to
know points of departure, means of escape. I could escape mentally by
remembering things I'd read, snatches of song, but now I wanted to get
away, to plan and execute an actual means of escape from where I was."

The lives of actresses fascinated Stanley, and she read their biographies and articles in magazines like *Theatre Arts,* and she claimed
to have seen Katharine Cornell when the actress toured Texas in the
early 1940s. "Oh, I followed her across the state!" Stanley exulted. "I
thought she was so beautiful, so composed. We sat and sweltered in

our seats, but she glided across the stage, gorgeously costumed, dry as a bone, beautiful, every syllable perfect. I could see the words on the page she had memorized." Stanley went to bed each night, alone or with uninvited guests, imagining a blank page onto which she affixed facts learned, dreams pursued, revenge sought. Tenn had his mental theater, and Kim Stanley had her psychic diary, which she kept until her death. After seeing Cornell on the stage, Stanley imagined herself beautiful and well arranged, proper. It was inconceivable to Stanley that a person of Katharine Cornell's bearing might ever be used as she had been. "The blame began," Stanley told me. "I had been the sort of person, the sort of undeserving, aberrant person who should always earn her place by being smart or pretty or funny or useful in ways devised by men in the hot night." Katharine Cornell, or any well-preserved and well-presented person, would not be treated so badly.

"Katharine Cornell got me out of the mind-set I had known in Texas," Stanley confessed, "but I came to despise her style of acting. It wasn't real, it wasn't about real people. It was entertainment. Yokels like me, at that point, who had never seen anything like her, could be removed, for a moment, from our real lives and imagine something else, but I wanted to be a character in plays that made people realize that somewhere, right now, there was a girl in a bedroom making lists on a mental sheet of paper of how to survive and escape and be something else, someplace else. I then fell in love with Vivien Leigh. All the things I work so hard to achieve—truth, detail, emotional honesty—Vivien Leigh walked on the stage with. Katharine Cornell overwhelmed me when I was a young girl and I saw her onstage, because I had never seen anyone so pretty and cool and composed. Vivien Leigh had the assurance of Katharine Cornell, an ability to bring a profound light on a stage or press it into film, and then scare the hell out of you with some emotional truths that were so intense you wanted to look away. I did a couple of plays—*Chéri* and *A Far Country*—and I needed a particular look, a particular and exact way of looking and moving, and I would think of her and the way she removed a glove while breaking your heart or sauntered across a stage while planning the most diabolical revenge. I think she was remarkable, and she got me through some of those bad years. She gave me a fantasy or two."

Stanley spent time in California, ultimately claiming that such places as the Pasadena Playhouse held no interest for her. "I was bigger, even then, than the Pasadena Playhouse," she boasted, "so I went to New York. It was inevitable. My relationship with New York was like the relationship between Blanche and Stanley. When I got off that bus and hit that pavement, I said to that city, 'We've both known this was bound to happen!' I was where I belonged."

She lived in squalor—hot, small rooms that she rented by the week, with bedbugs and shared bathrooms, but she didn't care. By day she modeled for Jacques Fath and Pierre Balmain. "I had a good figure and blond hair," she told me, "and that's all you needed for the kinds of shows I did. No one got too close to you, so they couldn't see that I'd been up all night, reading or drinking or fooling around. They couldn't see that I sometimes ran out of the apartment without putting on makeup. They were looking at the dresses, these awful buyers for stores all across the country, they weren't looking at our faces." Sometimes they did look at the faces and they sought contact. "They were good for a dinner and a twenty," Stanley told me. "They thought we were glamorous and had spectacular lives, and I made them believe that I did. I told them about plays I'd been in, which of course had not been written yet, and offers made that were entirely imaginary. I was acting, you see. I was training myself, and they, these men from Nebraska and Kansas and Florida and Michigan, could put aside their own mean and little lives, with their wives and mortgage payments and ledgers and spend some time with an actress. I would get a steak and a night in a clean hotel. These were my first acting jobs."

Tenn remembered that when he met Stanley, not long after the premiere of *A Streetcar Named Desire*, she seemed very extreme, very odd. "I was not aware of such a thing as a beatnik or a hippie at that time," he told me, "but that is the best description I can offer of the woman I met at that time—disheveled, very opinionated, wildly inappropriate in her expressions of feelings and desires. I was amused by her, but I also wanted to guard myself against her. She was clearly dangerous."

Kim picked up jobs in touring companies, repertory theaters. She picked up a husband, a fellow actor, but this arrangement did nothing to curtail her ravenous interest in the company of men. "I was out there all the time," she told me, "like I was still at that dinner table with my father, making my points, making my case, trying to get his attention. I just went around looking for a man who would treat me as I thought I should be treated. I had a series of scenarios in my mind of how I *should* be treated, of how conversations ought to proceed, but I kept finding the same men and the same outcomes." This began to change for Stanley when she studied with Lee Strasberg at the Actors Studio, and she found a man who would, at last, listen to her, argue with her, give her the benefit of the doubt. Strasberg affirmed her talent and her intelligence, but he also lured her closer to him by offering advice, training, secrets that would open her up to becoming a better actress, a better person. "He was my guru, my church, my salvation," Stanley told me. "It would later fall apart, and there would be the great Reformation of my life that resembled Martin Luther's. I renounced Lee Strasberg, but that came years after I submitted to him completely."

Marlon Brando befriended Stanley at roughly the same time as her conversion to the tenets of the Actors Studio. Although Brando's name is one that is routinely highlighted on the roster of Studio alumni, he pointedly told me that he owed nothing to Lee Strasberg or to the place that the Studio became during its peak years in the 1950s. "If you like what I do, what I've done," he told me, "then lay your thanks at the feet of Elia Kazan and Stella Adler. They were my teachers. They kept me focused and in sight of the shore from which I always drifted. I liked a lot of the people who studied with Lee, but I never believed in him or trusted him."

Strasberg held a particular power over women who had suffered some trauma, physical or sexual, in their early years, and who now sought some comfort from a paternal influence who could make them feel safe and smart and special. "He fed on the weakest of egos," Kazan told me. "It was terribly predictable, but then Lee was among the most predictable of all people I've ever met. His machinery was exposed when in operation, and he gathered about him those who would completely surrender to him, body and soul, and those whose fame would elevate him. That is Lee Strasberg. That is all you need to know."

Tenn did not hold as harsh a view of Strasberg, but he offered a puny endorsement. "Look, the building existed," he told me. "It was built by Kazan and Clurman, with some janitorial assistance from Cheryl Crawford and Robert Lewis, minor lights who affixed themselves to two giants, two revolutionaries. Those people, for me, are the true Actors Studio, and they had bolder agendas to follow. Strasberg was the one who stayed behind, dragged along on the long tails left by greater men. He was very intelligent, very well read, and actors are not terribly bright,

Lee Strasberg was for many—and particularly for Kim
Stanley—an acting teacher, a guru, a best friend, and a
lover. "I didn't think I could do anything—anything at
all—without his approval," Stanley said.

on the whole, and the actors who sought Lee's counsel were particularly rough, hard, blank slates with a bright, sharp need to be avenged,
somehow, through their work." This was, of course, something with
which Tenn could relate: there was anger in his work as well, and he was
attracted to the angry energy he always found at the Studio.

"My anger was constructed, worked out, smoothed over in a room
where I was alone, and my demons were on paper," he told me, "but at
the Studio, there was shared space—in a former church, God help us,
with all the attendant ghosts and memories—and a leader, a flawed
guru, urging everyone to expose themselves, their weaknesses, their

desires, and to use them in the development of actors and plays and lives. I found it fascinating but evil."

Kim Stanley adored the Studio, and she adored Lee Strasberg. "Lee took the mental diary I had," she told me, "looked at what I had written on the pages, and put it on real pieces of paper, and he put them at the top of his priorities. I had never lived on a schedule before, and he gave me one. There were classes, there were auditions, there were rounds to be made. He gave a shape to my days and to my mind. He told me what I should eat, how to take care of myself. He loved me and he *made love* to me. There was nothing furtive or hurried or deep in the night about his affection."

Stanley got jobs and her work was noticed, but it wasn't until she began to attend Strasberg's private sessions, as well as therapy sessions with a psychiatrist of his choosing, that her work became the emotionally intense, almost unbearable experience people now describe.

The first stage performance of Kim Stanley's that Tenn could recall was in a short-lived production of *The Chase*, written by Horton Foote, and starring Kim Hunter, who invited him. "Horton Foote writes very deft and sentimental rough drafts of plays," Tenn told me. "If you stuck some gingham on Linda Loman and put some oilcloth on the table, and then rather than have Willy kill himself at the end, you have a pie baked or a little boy comforted after a nightmare or a criticism retracted, you could refashion *Death of a Salesman* into a Horton Foote play. He never cares or reaches for the truth of a play, a big moment, the reality of things. He reaches for the truth of an anecdote, a passing feeling. Old, sad people ignored. Loveless women seeking attention and affection. He writes *précis*, not plays. I don't know if his study of Christian Science has done this to him, but the sadness of his plays burns off quickly, through song or faith or sugary will or misunderstanding. A false mysticism hangs over his rooms like an odor of cooking or heat or decay. I find his plays to be remarkably like Mexican food. The ingredients— beans, rice, meat—are either rolled in soft flour or plopped on rigid flour. Whatever you order, you bite into it and you realize there is no difference. The presentation has changed, but the ingredients remain the same."

Stanley, however, performed as if the play held for her the truths of the ages, and it was not impressive to Tenn. "It was too much spread across too little," he remembered, "but it was the work of a good actress in the wrong play. She had been given no direction, or perhaps the director realized that she was the most interesting thing on the stage and gave her over to her intentions." Hunter performed simply and appropriately and gave an intelligent performance, but Stanley seemed to burn with some undiagnosed fever. It was a style—if one could call it that—that Stanley would replicate when she was cast the following year in William Inge's *Picnic.* Tenn saw the production many times, firmly rooted in his competition with Inge, but also intrigued by the work of Stanley and Eileen Heckart. "Eileen Heckart would escape me," Tenn recalled. "I never had the opportunity to write anything for her, to work with her, but her work in that play was very real, very troubling." As an aging schoolteacher, desperate for marriage, even to the flabby, unimpressive salesman to whom she's anchored, Heckart spared neither herself nor her audiences any unattractive aspects of her character's grasping nature. "I think that a great deal of that play's success came from the pathos of her performance," Tenn stated, still unable to attribute anything to its playwright, while Kim, as a tomboyish, bookish girl, was "neurasthenic, agitated, gasping." Years later, when Tenn wrote *Suddenly, Last Summer,* he thought of Stanley in the creation of Catherine, the young woman who has seen too much, which she remembers all too vividly, and whose only salvation lay in the scalpel of a surgeon, who is called to lobotomize her, to eradicate her past and her biography. "That is Kim," Tenn remembered. "Now try to imagine that character wedged onto the stage of a play set in homespun, corn-fed Kansas, where a bevy of horny women lust after cakes and a wandering stud."

Tenn could not imagine how a high-school student could have endured or witnessed so much trauma, but the scars were presented by Stanley, in the body language of a girl repeatedly beaten or criticized, and particularly in the speech patterns: a rush of words, a deep intake of breath, the threat of hyperventilation. During the prime of her talents, from 1953 to 1964, Tenn witnessed Kim Stanley on the stage, on television, and in two films, and he was alternately amazed and repulsed by what he saw. "Kim had the capacity to elevate trivial plays," Tenn told me, "and I never understood why she spent so much time in plays that were simply not good, simply not deserving of her talents." Elia Kazan believed that she sought minor plays deliberately, as some extremely talented actresses often have as their closest friend a decidedly less gifted actress. "It gives them ballast," Kazan believed. "They have a confidence with a lesser actress, a lesser play. They are not challenged. They can continue in the confidence of their gifts because no one—certainly not the script—is challenging them, pushing them toward higher goals." Stanley devoted herself to several plays by Horton Foote, among them *A Young Lady of Property,* which was presented by *Philco Television Playhouse* in 1953, and *The Traveling Lady,* televised by *Studio One in Hollywood* in 1957. Both survive. Tenn described the former program to me, and recalled that it was his first introduction to Joanne Woodward, who has a supporting part as Stanley's best friend. Playing a starstruck young girl, almost always without parental supervision, and dreaming of imminent stardom, Stanley radiates a manic energy that was difficult for Tenn to take. By the conclusion of the piece, when Stanley sits on a swing, clutching the chains holding the contraption together, you expect her to tear it apart or to render her hands bloody. She is out of control. Four years later, in *The Traveling Lady,* Stanley has her bearings, and Tenn was terribly moved by this young mother, her frightened child by her side, waiting for her husband, who is soon to be released from prison. The life she hopes for, for which she has made preparations, will never occur, and you know this from the first scene, from her first nervous giggle and hand to her hair, perpetually making herself presentable, proper—not the wife of a convict and a drunk. "The play is pure soap opera," Tenn stated, "something out of a ladies' magazine, but Kim was overwhelming. I felt that she was actively holding back her fear, her disappointment, her immense sadness, and of course it ultimately appeared, and it was wonderful, and horrible, and real.

"The primary identifying characteristic of Kim's work," Tenn told me, "is a suppressed emotion, a manic attack just beneath the surface, a willful pushing down of bile and memory. If this tsunami of rage can be countered by some modicum of comedy"—as in Inge's *Bus Stop*—"or a direct line of motivation, as when she played Maggie"—in the London premiere of *Cat on a Hot Tin Roof*—"there is great effectiveness. Both her character and the actress playing it are working against and with something—a strong text, recognizable emotions, forces beyond her control. But in most of the plays Kim chose to work with, there is nothing but Kim, nothing but emotional excess, undisciplined and messy and with no suitable outlet."

Tenn believed that Kim's talent would have grown and been fully

Kim Stanley as Maggie the Cat in the London premiere of *Cat on a Hot Tin Roof,* in 1958. Seen here with Paul Massie as Brick, Stanley confessed that she only got the part "half right," because she could not trust herself enough to admit how much she had in common with the character. Twenty-five years later, she would be Big Mama in a television version of the play. "And that I got," Stanley confessed.

served if she had taken his advice and tackled greater challenges in plays that "were as big as she was," that would have forced her to rise to situations that required more than the tricks she had learned and kept applying to every part. There was talk at some point of her being in a production of Congreve's *Way of the World,* as either Millamant or Lady Wishfort, wherever her weight was when rehearsals began. Plays by Shaw and Pirandello were offered to her, too, at a time when her name would have sold tickets, but she refused them.

She tried to explain this to me.

"When I was acting on the stage," she told me, "I was operating on a series of exercises that Lee had provided to me. My audience was always comprised of three people: my mother, my father, and Lee. I ignored the hundreds of people out there in the seats, and I ignored anything that might have been in the subtext of the plays I was doing. Everything I did was an attempt to have my father and my mother notice who I was and what I had become and what had been done to me, and for Lee to see that I was strong and I had overcome all of these obstacles, these terrible moments in my life, and had brought them to the stage, had made them into a truth that people could see. I wasn't Katharine Cornell gliding across a stage, composed and serene, with pear-shaped vowels and a caring husband in the wings, but I was a real person, hurt and hurting and trying to make some sense of things."

No matter the play?

"No matter the play," she told me. "The play is irrelevant, the text doesn't matter. My story was the primary one, slipped under and between every action and every character. That was my motivation, and that is what Lee gave me to work with."

And?

"And I now see how incredibly fucked up that was—and is," she told me.

"Kim Stanley worked very hard—and very well—on improving my spiritual life," Tenn said. Stanley introduced him to the writings of Martin Buber, a philosopher whose worldview was uncannily similar to Stanley's idea of acting, of artistic purity. "Acting is constant discovery," Kim told me, "and it requires an acute awareness, but it also requires a foundation that is bigger than we are, and Buber drew me toward that foundation. I wanted Tennessee to stand on that foundation—any foundation—and know that he was safe to write and to live. I wanted him to stop reacting—I wanted us both to stop reacting—in the dangerous, unbalanced way we always did, and I thought Buber could help him with this."

Stanley's favorite quote from Buber: "I do not accept any absolute formulas for living. No preconceived code can see ahead to everything that can happen in a man's life. As we live, we grow and our beliefs change. They must change. So I think we should live with this constant discovery. We should be open to this adventure in heightened awareness of living. We should stake our whole existence on our willingness to explore and experience."

I asked Stanley what the quote meant to her. "When I found that quote, it helped me to realize that I couldn't rely on Lee Strasberg—or anyone—to tell me how to act. I could not rely on any therapist to tell me what dreams meant or what imagery there was in my life or how it might be controlled by me. I saw that I could not remain the frightened, angry girl terrified in her bed at night, waiting for abuse that I some- how felt I deserved. I realized that the foundation on which I should be standing and from which I could begin a heightened awareness of living was my responsibility. I *was* the foundation. And Tennessee was his foundation, and I hoped that I—with my shattered background and my shared addictions and patterns—could be the one to lead him to that foundation."

By the time I came to know Kim Stanley, she had made several attempts to curb her alcoholism and to quell her anger. With the memo- rized words of Martin Buber, she came to believe that "the world is not comprehensible, but it is embraceable: through the embracing of one of its beings," a maxim that helped her to deal with her past and her parents. The study of Buber also helped her to realize that sin could not be uprooted from the human soul—only forgiven and repeatedly dealt with, studied. "I had studied every inch of my psyche," Stanley admit- ted, "but toward the goal of achieving something on the stage. I now wanted to achieve something in the here and now, in real time. I wanted to be a good mother to my children; I wanted to function in the world without drugs or alcohol." Stanley was appalled at the arrogance and the abuse she had displayed so fruitfully in the years she was working: she rarely completed her commitment to a play, leaving amid lawsuits and enraged ticket holders. "I had allowed myself to believe that my talent was a privilege that only a few were entitled to share or to see," she told me. "I felt no responsibility to any writer or director or actor. I was beholden only to my talent, to the use of it in a performance that was then laid out for that audience of three." However, of that audience of three, only one person—Lee Strasberg—was in attendance. The oth- ers were spectral, even if they sparked most of the rage that fueled her performances.

Kim Stanley's dependence on and respect for Lee Strasberg began to wane when she came to realize that he did not have the slavish devo- tion to his own teachings that he forced upon his students. "There were the canonical teachings," Stanley remembered, "the same quotes, the same advisements, over and over. The private sessions where he told me, over and over, that *I* had failed. He had not failed. The Method had not failed. It was exactly like the people in churches who can never feel comfort from the sermons: it is always their fault; it is always a failure of faith, of application."

In the early 1960s, at precisely the same time Elia Kazan was preparing his Repertory Theatre of Lincoln Center, Lee Strasberg announced the formation of the Actors Studio Theatre, which would be the culmination of everything he had ever hoped to achieve: a devoted company of actors taking on the great plays and utilizing the Method as fashioned and taught by Lee Strasberg. Edward Albee's *Who's Afraid of Virginia Woolf?* was considered by many to be the ideal play to launch this new enterprise; instead, the Actors Studio Theatre, in Stanley's words, devoted itself to "dead or very bad playwrights," opening its first season with Eugene O'Neill's *Strange Interlude,* appropriately enough a play about the wonders of analysis and self-awareness ("right up Lee's alley," Stanley cracked), and concluding with Randall Jarrell's adaptation of Chekhov's *Three Sisters,* which would star both Stanley and Geraldine Page.

Opinions vary on the production of *The Three Sisters.* Eva Le Gallienne called it a "mess, the after-effects of a huge accident, in which victims are racing about, frightened, confused, unaware of their surroundings." Uta Hagen, who might have felt some resentment toward a fellow acting teacher, was amazed that a cast of talented actors, "people whose worth I knew, whose talents were unmistakable," were "so adrift. There was no cohesion at all in the production. You could not imagine that anyone in the play was related, or had even met each other before."

The Three Sisters had its admirers, however. The reviews were, for the most part, positive, and Kazan enviously noted that in its first season, the Actors Studio Theatre was far more successful than his own efforts at Lincoln Center. "It looked as if we would fail," Kazan told me, "and Lee would have the national theater that our country has always needed. I never felt that Lee deserved to have that happen for him, not merely because I disliked the man and thought his talents slim and poorly utilized, but because I knew that he could never sustain the effort, could never hold together the people required to have such a theater happen. I knew he would alienate everyone."

Strasberg did just that when *The Three Sisters* was performed in London, at the Aldwych Theatre, in 1965, and was savagely dismissed by British audiences and critics. "It was horrible," Stanley remembered, "and we deserved the abuse. The story you heard—and probably still hear—around the Studio is that the British didn't supply us with the proper rehearsal space, or the stage of the theater was poorly conceived, or the lighting board was insufficient. Well, the problem was the arrogance of the company, which felt that our greatness was both obvious and settled: we only had to show up and show those stuffy British actors and theatergoers how theater was done, what real emotion and experience looked like. We ignored the rehearsals we obviously needed. We prepared nothing. We had been told—and we believed—that we were great."

Stanley could survive the brickbats that were thrown her way after the *Three Sisters* debacle, but she was not prepared for Strasberg's treatment of the company. "It was entirely our fault," Stanley remembered. "He stood on the stage of that theater the morning after the opening and told us the critics and the audiences were correct: We were horrible." Strasberg took no responsibility for the production, and proceeded to lay the blame on the company. "Here was my teacher," Stanley remembered, "the man who had asked me, forced me, to trust him, to reveal to him everything about myself, in whom I had put my complete trust, and he was disowning all of us, criticizing all of us."

Barbara Baxley and George C. Scott offered verbal responses to Strasberg, tough and combative, and Scott even physically threatened him. Stanley was in a daze. "I am now grateful for that realization," she said. "My eyes were opened. I saw that I had done everything wrong, I had botched everything. I had never understood what acting or the theater was all about."

At the conclusion of her time in *The Three Sisters,* Kim Stanley was in her early forties, but a visit to her physician revealed her to be in a state of medical crisis: she was severely overweight, her "blood numbers" were astronomical, and there was evidence, even then, of liver damage. "I was in terrible shape," she recalled. "I was young, but I looked old, and I felt ancient." Unable and unwilling to work, Stanley retreated to books, finding solace in a particular quote by Buber, which she shared, at one point, with Tenn: "To be old can be glorious if one has not unlearned how to begin."

The drinking continued, as did a dependence on Seconal and Nembutal, but eventually Stanley found direction for her talents and her energies through teaching. "I failed miserably at Santa Fe," she told me, referring to her tenure at the College of Santa Fe, where she managed to lure Maureen Stapleton for a production of *Waiting for Godot,* but where she also directed Greer Garson in a production of *The Madwoman of Chaillot,* which she played, according to Stanley, "exactly as if she were Auntie Mame. That was the nadir."

After teaching in New York for a number of years, heavily subsidized by friends, including Tenn, she moved to Los Angeles, where her home served as her acting studio. "I discovered something fascinating," she told me. "I had read biographies of actresses, and I had read plays, and my thoughts were always of escape—from home, from myself, from whatever despair I had to endure. I read books and plays again and I did not find escape: I found revelations. My point should never have been to remove myself from the life into which I had been born, but to come to terms with it. My point should never have been to overturn the relationships I had with people who abused me, but to repair and forgive them, and everything I ever needed for those acts is in works of literature and music and art, and of course they are also all within, and art takes you within, gives you some parameters for moving around inside yourself and figuring things out."

The sharing of oneself through writing or acting or painting always involves the sharing of one's data, including our most intense data—the fears, the regrets, the hopes. But we need to apply a process to our biographies before we commit them to the page or the workshop or the rehearsal room. Think of it as a cleansing process or the burning down of materials needed to make gold—fires to the fear. Remove the biography from the merely personal and apply it to something bigger than yourself, beyond yourself. The act of sharing must begin. Steps must be gentle.

After nearly two decades of inactivity, Kim Stanley returned to acting. "I wanted to see how I would do it with my new mind and my new eyes and my new legs," she told me. "I wasn't as strong as I had been, and I had limitations—physical limitations—that I hadn't had before, but I was so much clearer than I had been before. I understood what being an actress meant in a way I hadn't before."

Stanley was well received in the film biography *Frances,* in which she appeared with one of her students, Jessica Lange. "Jessie was ballast for me," Stanley told me. "She knew the rudiments of filmmaking, as I didn't. I had always gone into my character and expected—demanded—that I be followed. I had never thought to learn how a film was made, or how people conserved and utilized their energies. I felt like that young girl just beginning my studies again." Stanley earned an Oscar nomination for her performance, her second. (Her first, in 1965, had been for *Séance on a Wet Afternoon,* when she lost, incongruously, to Julie Andrews for *Mary Poppins.*)

As part of the great reclamation project she had undertaken, Stanley resumed long phone calls with Tenn, and she sought out the advice of people she had once ridiculed or openly rebuked. Phone calls were made to Eva Le Gallienne, who accepted them with curiosity and confusion, wherein Stanley apologized for her vehement dismissal of all that Le Gallienne had stood for. "It is terribly confusing to accept such a phone call," Le Gallienne remembered. "I had no idea I had held such a place in Kim Stanley's mind for so long," she recalled, "or that I had annoyed her so. Now I learned that she felt she had been wrong, and she told me all that she had learned from my example." Stanley hoped to create a theater, a company of players, to examine and exalt and mount the great plays, and she looked to Le Gallienne for advice. When these phone calls took place, Le Gallienne was in her late eighties and Stanley in her late sixties, but both believed that the dreams discussed were possible to attain, if only Stanley could stop drinking. "We talked about alcoholism," Le Gallienne told me, "and she was looking for nostrums, hopes, plans, and I had to tell her that there is only one way, only one means of victory over alcohol. You stop using it. Period. It's difficult, I assure you, but it is the only way." The advice offered seemed dry and less than inspirational to Stanley, but she kept trying to put the drinking behind her. "You cannot remove from your life the situations that cause you to drink," Stanley told me, "so I was trying to reeducate my mind so that the same situations wouldn't lead me to crave the slow, sweet death that alcohol brought me."

Stanley was involved in re-education until the day she died.

She came to forgive Lee Strasberg. "He was a great teacher," she told me, "even if he was not a great man or a great director. He had an extraordinary eye for detail, and an extraordinary ear. He could see and hear your weaknesses and your needs, and he could tell when you were lying. He took these gifts into places and situations he shouldn't have, but I was not a passive person. I was his willing victim and partner. I profited, in bizarre and painful ways, from our times together. I wish

I had been more fully present for my work in those years, those good years when I got work, but I was hidden beneath layers of anger and alcohol and this insane form of analysis Lee and I had constructed."

Tenn had told me that I would need to learn the art of navigation. He also told me that it was an art very few had mastered, that almost everyone he had known failed, significantly, in its execution. "Choices are offered," he said, "avenues opened, and you take the step and you wait to see what you'll find on this particular journey. None of us knows what the right thing to do is, not even at all times in hindsight, but it is better to be prepared for the journey, to have the Dopp kit of the pre-pared traveler, to be a smart pilgrim."

I last spoke to Kim Stanley in 1999, at a time when she was riddled with health problems and obsessed with problems that were visiting her grandchildren and friends. One of her salvations, she told me, was the study of plays, particularly those in which she had appeared. She read in amazement Lillian Hellman's *Montserrat*, Inge's *Picnic* and *Bus Stop* and *Natural Affection*, Anita Loos's *Chéri*, O'Neill's *A Touch of the Poet*, Arthur Laurents's *A Clearing in the Woods*, various versions of *The Three Sisters*. She imagined taking on these roles again, investing them with the person she now was, with the clarity she now possessed. "I had gifts," she told me, "but so frequently they were poorly applied, badly used. I now have a mental theater, like Tennessee's, and I can place myself on its stage and imagine that I'm assuming these roles again, from a better perspective."

She rediscovered Shaw and Beckett and Pinter, and she forced her-self to read all of the works of Edward Albee, an act that represented great courage for her, since she had humiliated herself at a rehearsal for the film version of *A Delicate Balance*, where, in the company of the film's director, Tony Richardson, and her costars, Paul Scofield, Katha-rine Hepburn, Lee Remick, Joseph Cotten, and Betsy Blair, she chose to reveal, in her estimation, the true "alcoholic and beastly and bestial nature" of the character Claire.

"I was out of control," she remembered, "and I was drunk, and I was angry. I chose to let everyone in the room know that this was not merely a play. This nightmare of a person was alive and well and in their midst." Writhing on the floor, drooling, touching herself, Stanley turned a reading into something "out of Bosch." Her good friend Tony

Richardson was forced to fire her, after both Scofield and Hepburn lodged complaints. Scofield refused to speak to or about Stanley in our conversations, but when Hepburn was told that Stanley still felt remorse and shame about the incident, she offered a response.

Asking me to take dictation from her, Hepburn urged me to tell Kim Stanley that "we all have, I assure you, moments in our lives that offer us pain and enlightenment. You are far too talented to waste your time and your energy on a moment that is gone, that is forgotten, that has taught you something. At the end of the day—at the end of all the days—we have precisely what we need to move on and do what we must."

I read the words to Stanley over the phone, and she asked me to type them up and send them to her. When she received them, she called and told me that she was aware of so many blocks that had been removed from her path, from her vision. "I can finally see and move as I should," she told me. "This is what I wish for everyone. It's what I always wanted to give to my students. It's the purest state of being, to always be moving forward, open and aware."

Marlon Brando had a desire to reconnect with Stanley, whose talent he admired so much and about whom he was most frequently asked. "What was so remarkable about Kim?" Brando responded to me late one night:

When she was truly focused and properly challenged, she had the ability to transmit the reality of human agitation, anguish, elation, concentration better than anyone else. There was a sense of embarrassment in watching Kim when everything worked, because you felt you were violating the confidences of a vulnerable woman, reading the pages of a diary carelessly left open for other eyes. She had the effect—on me, at any rate—of peeling layer after layer apart, from her soul outward, and this must have been exhausting. She is a brilliant actress who was tragically denied a long career—a career deserving of her talent. I would do Kim a dishonor, I think, if I pitied her. The past is gone, yes, but the past is full of Kim's brilliance, and I think we—I think you—need to remind people of what they didn't see and can't understand. When people ask about Kim, I talk about things that no longer exist, in my opinion: passion, genius, truth, danger, fearless exploration. Maybe someone like Kim wasn't meant to last long on the stage—it may be too much for most to handle. Many an actor walks—lamely, I might add—in lanes she hacked free, cleared, paved, and then left, and they have not been suitably tended since.

I read Marlon's words to Stanley over the phone, and she was stunned, awed. However, she only responded to one aspect of Brando's praise. "I just don't see the passion as much as I used to," she told me. "I see the dream and the aching want, but I don't see the hungry passion to give up everything else to become a warrior of the art of acting. Religious orders remind me of how I lived when I first began to realize the challenge that was ahead of me. I think a student—a good student—needs to show some penitential study and understanding before they look out and expect some applause and affirmation. I don't see as many students ready for the long haul as I used to, and I don't know if my vision is failing or if the students are failing. But it has me down."

"Navigation," Tenn told me, "is not only where you move, but how, and what you take with you." There was a look at the clock on the wall of the café, another visit to the restroom, and then Tenn returned and removed the envelope from the shopping bag. He slid it across the table to me and asked me to read it. I had, of course, already read it, but I looked over its essentials again. Checkout times, limousine confirmation, flight numbers.

"Let's try to make something of this as quickly as possible," Tenn suggested. "I don't know what we've accomplished so far. I don't know that I've been of any help to you, but I feel that both of us, in our own ways, are staring down roads, looking for some direction. Let's stay with that."

I do not remember if Tenn asked me at that point if I wanted him to continue our discussion. I cannot find the words in my notes, but I do find that I wrote, "It is coming to an end, whatever this has been, and I don't know what I have or what it adds up to being, or what I'm supposed to do with it."

But I stayed. We continued talking.

Seventeen

ENN AND I RETURNED to the "secondary" room he had secured at the Royal Orleans, and found it had been cleaned, the piles of papers and notes, shirt boards and paper plates, neatly placed on the dresser and the two bedside tables. Tenn asked me to collect them into one pile so that we could go over them "one last time," to excavate what we could. He turned on the television set, working with the remote control to bring the volume to the precise point that would allow him to look at its images and "listen for voices" and still talk to me and listen to me read to him. He asked me to call room service and order two buckets of ice ("the large ones," he insisted, "not the precious ones from banquet services"), a pitcher ("stainless steel, not crystal or glass") of iced tea, unsweetened, for both of us, a pitcher ("of any derivation") of orange juice, a bottle of Scotch ("they know my brand"), and anything I might wish to eat. "But please," he implored, "don't let it possess an odor. I'm feeling sensitive to scent today."

He then went into the bathroom, keeping the door open. As I called room service, I watched him pull a hand towel from a rung on the wall and neatly place it on the porcelain counter, spreading and patting it as if it were flour. When it was in position, bearing no bumps or wrinkles, he reached into his carrying case and placed on it several glassine envelopes and a large prescription bottle, amber-colored, bearing no label.

When the towel was covered with these items, resembling a quickly improvised altar bearing a highly improbable Eucharist, Tenn reached behind him with his left foot and slammed the door shut.

I could not decide at that point if he had wanted me to see this routine: with all of the visits to bathrooms and dark corners and doorways, it had been obvious to me what he might be doing, but he had been careful never to let me see him in the act of using any drug that might be "prohibitive," as he described them. When I had seen him taking pills, he had told me they were for his blood pressure or his glaucoma or a degenerative disease "related, in a tertiary way, to the connective tissue." (Carrie Nye told me that, on those rare occasions when Tenn would attempt to dry out or rest or undergo a full physical examination, his treatment was always for "conjunctivitis.")

When he came out of the bathroom, Tenn pulled the shades in the room, extinguished every light except for the lamp that was closest to his position on the bed, where he sat, padded from behind, pasha-like, by every pillow from the bed, the closet, and a cushion from one of the chairs in the room. I pulled a chair close to the bed and watched as he placed a moist washcloth over his forehead and eyes. His face was a vivid pink, sweaty, but the rest of his body still showed no signs of sweating, even though he complained of the heat. The thermostat in the room was set to its lowest level, but he continued to complain that the room was too warm. He was silent for several minutes, and he did not move or speak when our room-service order was delivered. He asked for a glass of water, with lots of ice, and a tumbler of Scotch.

With his face still partially covered by the washcloth, Tenn asked me if I had ever used cocaine. I told him I had, twice, in the summer after high school.

"Did you like it?" he asked. I told him I had.

"And you haven't used it since?" he asked. I told him I hadn't, because I felt I couldn't afford it, financially or physically.

"It is a wonderful, miserable means of temporary happiness," Tenn told me, still beneath his mask. "It is so clarifying, so healing—in the instant. It is the finest representation of God I have imagined, one I might never have conceived if I hadn't felt it for myself. I spent so many years—and I still spend so much time—appealing to God, whatever he may ultimately be revealed to be, asking for signs, for aid, for comfort, for understanding, for inspiration. I'm calmed, I'm reassured, I buy a little time, a little corner where inspiration or arousal or awareness may visit, but in minutes or hours or days I'm back in the same state, full of wonder and fear, and I return to my God, and to my 'gods,' the pills and the powders. An endless cycle."

He removed the washcloth and told me of a night in Key West when he had Truman Capote as his houseguest. The night had been hot, but still comfortable, and the old friends had walked the streets of the old, salty town that Tenn loved so much. They had enjoyed drinks and food, black beans he remembered being as shiny as onyx, pompano in a bag that the waiters had burst with great panache, eliciting silly squeals from Truman, who, on that evening, had been amusing, free of resentment, absent of envy.

The two had returned to Tenn's home, where Truman offered the end to the evening and "the beginning of the rest of that night, and the rest of my days." An enormous bag, normally used for the storage of frozen foods, was plopped on the coffee table. "Treats!" Truman had cooed. Tenn had no idea how to present or display the cocaine, and had only a cheese platter, used at the occasional party, on which to serve the "dessert." The plate had to be clean, it had to be smooth, it had to be slick. These were the directives shouted by Truman, and Tenn set about washing and patting down the platter, offering it to Truman for inspection, placing it, with painful precision, painstaking adjustment, in the dead center of a coffee table, where the two of them then sat, talking and laughing, passing the platter, back and forth, all night long. They spoke of sentences, phrases, words. Getting the ball rolling. Dropping a word, dropping a memory.

Tenn and Truman began a game, one they had come to believe might be a writer's myth, something writers should do, might have considered doing, but never had: offering a word, a sentence, and having their partner take it from there.

A line of cocaine, a line of prose.

Tenn tried to remember some of the lines from that night.

"There were cerulean skies on the night when I killed my son, this I remember," Truman opened.

"I was looking at the skies," Tenn offered, "because I could not look at what I had done."

"But it had been something I had needed—and wanted—to do for some time," Truman bounced back.

Tennessee envied Truman Capote his success in placing essays in various magazines for high fees. While there was often friction in their relationship, Tennessee recalled that his friend was "a wonderful, traveling show for a long time."

"I know that you will not understand my reasons, or me [right now], but you will," Tenn replied.

"All of us, you see," Truman offered, "do what we must. At the conclusion of any tale—moral or otherwise—everyone did precisely as they pleased."

The game continued, interrupted by observations on peers and friends and plans, but it grew tiresome, silly, strained. Tenn's head began to pound—a fissure, he thought, had opened right in the center of his forehead. The only solution was to snort more, to "feed the animal." Tenn looked over at Truman, crouched over the platter, inhaling one line, then another, then another, a marathon of ingestion. Tenn held out his hand for the platter, for more, for relief. Truman began to offer the platter, but when it was only inches from Tenn's hand, he snatched it away, positioned it on the coffee table again, and leaned over it. "I'm not happy yet," Truman announced, and snorted two more enormous lines, "railroad tracks," Tenn told me, "to oblivion."

Tenn sat up slightly and looked at me. "I want you to understand something," he said, "and I have no way of knowing if this will mean anything to you, now or ever, but there are only two modes in which I have been happy: when I have been deep in my work, and when I have been willfully insensitive. Those are the only states of being I know of that can render a person—*this* person—happy."

Tenn put on his glasses, picked up the television remote control, and began flipping through the channels. He would point the remote at the television and violently press on the buttons, in the belief, perhaps, that the force of his gesture is all that would move the channels, bring on more images, more sounds. Tenn asked for paper, anything on which he could write. I had my booklets, a legal pad. "Something clean," he said. "For me." There was nothing in the room—nothing immediately visible—that did not already bear writing, doodles, scratches. I opened the drawers of the dresser and found several pages of hotel stationery. I gave them to Tenn, who placed them on a New Orleans phone directory, which he positioned on his knees. He sat silent for a moment, then began clicking the channels.

A soap opera. Forty-six seconds, and a dismissive snort.

A movie commercial, a soap commercial, a game show. Three minutes and a grimace.

A movie, from the early seventies, on a cable channel. Tenn paused, watched, smiled. He reached for his pen.

He was faking the fog.

"WHEN DID YOU turn to this act?" I asked. "When did you start faking the fog?"

Tenn paused for a moment, put aside the paper on which he was writing, and began to think. "It was in that same year, 1973, when things began to change terribly for me," he replied. "When I found I could no longer talk to or understand actresses—people in general. I can live, I suppose, without inspiration or input from others, but I can't survive without a woman to talk to me and through me." Like the lonely man who has no female company in his life and looks at photographs or videos, manufactures a fantasy life with idealized women whom he can

Ellis Rabb, a man described by Carrie Nye as a hybrid of stork, magician, and lost unicorn, was chosen to direct a twenty-fifth-anniversary production of *A Streetcar Named Desire*, a decision Tennessee described as catastrophic.

mold and love and move, Tenn had turned to these "distant, divine" representations.

"I had a sort of creative breakdown in 1973," Tenn continued. "Beyond all of the things that were happening in my personal life, I had a horrible and divisive and explicit moment in that year when I began to be unable to do what I wanted to do and always had done." He asked for another Scotch, visited the bathroom, and promised to tell me about it.

Back on the bed, Scotch in hand, Tenn told me that he had approached the twenty-fifth-anniversary revival of *Streetcar* with excitement and no small amount of hope. It would be produced by the Repertory Theatre of Lincoln Center and directed by Ellis Rabb, the man who had brought into being the Association of Producing Artists (APA)/Phoenix Repertory Company, and Tenn initially felt good about handing his play over to this "Memphis-born man, queer and bold and manic." Tenn's knowledge of Rabb was provided primarily by Carrie Nye, a good friend to both men, Southern and impetuous, who loved and understood Rabb, and by Eva Le Gallienne, who had inspired him to create the APA and who had worked with the company. One of its productions, in 1968, had been Ionesco's *Exit the King,* in which Rabb directed Le Gallienne: Tenn saw it, and it led him to believe that prior to the curtain's rise he had been poisoned by bad food or injected with some new and wild drug. "There was no inherent logic or truth to the production," Tenn remembered, "and I suddenly recalled that this was a perpetual problem with all of the work coming out of the APA. There was simply no control, or there was only the worst sort of control—a fastidious detail to drapes and clothes and juvenile humor. There was no thread, that thread of which I always speak and for which I always look, that has to hold a company or a play together."

Tenn thought the company itself odd, full of people he felt might have been unable to work anywhere else, difficult to cast, impossible to hold in the thought, but all slavishly devoted to Rabb. The only times Tenn had enjoyed the work of the company was in its comedies, light fare that Rabb injected with style and allowed to move at a fast pace. "Empty calories," Tenn said. "Froth and meringue. At these things the company excelled, but I couldn't imagine that Rabb could do anything worthwhile with *Streetcar.*"

It was Le Gallienne who persuaded Tenn to reconsider his harsh assessment of Rabb, even as she admitted that she had serious problems with his lack of discipline, his crippling depression, his tendency to disappear and to relinquish control of his work. "Can you believe that I heard this litany of concerns and *still* proceeded?" Tenn asked me in wonder. "I held to Le Gallienne's plea that I give this man, this man she claimed she loved, a chance to redeem himself, to reclaim a talent in which she believed."

"I would do it for you," she had said to Tenn, a sentiment that moved and enraged him, but which nonetheless led him to accept Rabb as his director, which meant that he automatically accepted his former wife and "artistic channel," Rosemary Harris, as Blanche DuBois. "And Rosemary Harris pushed me toward the fog," Tenn told me. "She was the first actress I ever met with whom I could share nothing, offer nothing, expect nothing. I entered an alternate universe."

Blanche DuBois and Amanda Wingfield, in Tenn's biased belief, were roles that greatly tested the actresses who stepped into them. "They require a great deal of self-examination," he explained. "They insist that

Rosemary Harris was a beautiful and talented actress,
but Tennessee wanted a friend and a companion during
the production of *Streetcar,* and the reserved, private
Harris did not have time for him.

you have a heart, and one that you are unafraid to place in the service
of a part that will expose you in every way, that will show everyone how
you, the actress, judge and accept the fate given to these women. I did
not write these parts—or any parts—with the express purpose of taxing women, but each time I see these plays produced, I can see that a
woman has been placed in a position she might not be able to handle."

Tenn did not believe that Rosemary Harris could handle Blanche
DuBois.

By the time she took on the role, Harris and Rabb had terminated
their marriage, had concluded what Le Gallienne called a "silly charade," but there remained an interdependence between the two that
Tenn found baffling until he found it enraging. "There was a cult
around Ellis Rabb," Tenn told me. "The company acquiesced to him on
every matter, even as they walked about on eggshells that the sensitive
man might bolt, might go on a bender, might meet a captivating boy,

might decide the show might not be in his best interests." The mere fact that Rabb repeatedly referred to *Streetcar* as a "show" disturbed the playwright, but Tenn also confessed that he was not in his right mind, not on steady feet that year. "I needed consolation," he admitted, "and I needed to hear that this play, that any play I had written, mattered and had consequence and deserved to be produced, and I simply didn't get it." Instead, he heard, by phone and in meetings he characterized as "bizarre, even by my standards," what Rabb intended with the play. "He spoke in filmic terms—he wanted wipes and bleeds and blackouts." He envisioned gauze, membranous fabrics that would cover portions of the stage and at times the characters. This was meant to suggest the occlusion of mental illness, a shattered sensibility. None of this would have been alarming to Tenn, except for the fact that Rabb had yet to describe what *Streetcar* meant to him, what it was about, what it was saying. "I think it's a good idea to ask your directors—your potential directors—what your play is about. I have a feeling if I had asked this question of Rabb, he would have told me what I came to suspect to be the truth: *Streetcar* was about giving Rosemary Harris what she wanted."

Tenn had seen Harris in several of her roles at the APA—in *Man and Superman, Judith, You Can't Take It with You*—and in her Tony Award–winning role in *The Lion in Winter*. "I thought her skillful but cold, the type of actress you see if you go to Chichester or any of the other provincial companies in England. They hit their marks, they have a solidity that is admirable, but they do not set your heart or your mind ablaze." Margaret Leighton, an actress on whom Tenn greatly depended for her tart advice on plays and the requirements of working with actresses, called Tenn to offer advice on Harris. "She told me that Harris was a scullery worker who had put on the clothes of her mistress. The house was vacated for a vacation, and the help, like something out of Genet or, to be less brutal, in a Renoir film, had gone through the clothes and accessories of the owners of the house, their employers, and had dressed up and were walking about, eating the food and sitting in the good chairs and speaking in plummy tones as if the house was theirs. This was all good and fun and fair, but in the end the help can't pay the mortgage or the utility bills or the grocer. They cannot sell the house and move on to a new life. They are stuck in the pathetic role of playing a part they can never have. 'This, my darling,' Leighton told me, 'is Rosemary Harris. The maid has assumed the leadership of the house—in this instance, *your* house.' "

Tenn paused. "And this," he told me, "is what I walked into."

Both Le Gallienne and Nye, however, let it be known that Tenn went into rehearsals for *Streetcar* in a foul mood. "He was irritable, quick to rage, ready to quit," Nye remembered. "He went into every meeting, every reading, every rehearsal looking for flaws, and he found them. Of course, you find them everywhere. I asked him if he hadn't had doubts about Jessica Tandy, if he hadn't at first vetoed the idea of Kazan casting her." Tenn agreed with Nye, but added the pathetic rejoinder, "But Jessie always liked me. I could talk to her."

This, according to Le Gallienne, was the primary problem: Tenn could not get close to Rosemary Harris, found no comfort in her company, and was offered no flattery or consolation from her. "Rosemary is a cold woman," Le Gallienne told me, "very private and guarded, but she is a good actress. I thought it foolish that she undertook such a great and exhausting part under the direction of a man from whom she was now divorced, with whom she had a tortured history, but I believe that she went into that part with every intention of giving it everything she had, of making it work."

Tenn went to her several times, looking for the friend he needed, an actress to whom he could talk, with whom he could examine the contours of one of his women. He was met with firm and icy resistance.

When I met Ellis Rabb in 1992, and when I was employed, briefly, as his assistant for a production he was mounting of Paul Osborn's *Morning's at Seven*, he told me that he was met almost daily with the same question from Tenn: "What is wrong with your wife? Why doesn't she like me?" Rabb would calmly explain that Harris *respected* him greatly, but her relationship was with the part; there was no time for friendship.

"In retrospect," Rabb told me, "it was idiotic of me to have pursued that play at that time, but Le G was right: it was my reformation. My hoped-for reformation." Plagued by manic depression, alcoholic binges, and periods of doubt that left him "paralyzed, speechless, dumb," Rabb's marriage to Harris had ended, and so had the APA. "I met with Le G," he told me, "and I told her the state I was in. I was brutally honest, and she responded by being brutally honest with me. I had not behaved well in the past. I had not honored the theater in general, or my theater, and

Eva Le Gallienne and Rosemary Harris in the 1975
production of *The Royal Family,* a summing up of the
affection that could exist in and around Ellis Rabb and
the work he fostered. It was Le Gallienne who urged
Tennessee to accept both Ellis Rabb and Rosemary
Harris for the 1973 revival of *Streetcar,* believing that
the duo would bring good things to the play.

my role in my theater, with any degree of dignity or sacrifice. Le G was
very big on sacrifice. She would tell us that a mother is said to lose a
tooth with each pregnancy—things are needed for the child, the developing baby, and they are pulled from the mother. The teeth suffer. She
told me that I had not made the proper sacrifices. I had lost nothing in
the pursuit of good theater, only in the pursuit of my own pleasures, and
she was right. I had abdicated, as she put it, and I would only become

the director and the actor I was born to be by committing myself to greater assignments, test myself, push myself. Lose some teeth."

Rabb worked to limit his alcohol, and he searched for plays that would tax him, and in those years at Lincoln Center he extended himself with works by Gorky and Shakespeare and, to his highest satisfaction, Tennessee Williams. "It had always been my dream to direct his plays," Rabb told me, sitting in a restaurant and ordering a Salty Dog, the drink of choice for Le G, and one he drank in her honor. "I understood his plays. I saw myself in *The Glass Menagerie* because my mother is a vivid dreamer, a woman who lived ambitiously and happily through me, and I saw myself in *Streetcar*. I identify with Blanche, and I recognize her nervousness, her need to fashion a life, real only to her, to survive and to impress."

Born to a comfortable family in Memphis in 1930, one that indulged his love of plays and films and music, Rabb devised a theme, a mantra, a philosophy while still in college: make yourself indispensable to someone as quickly as possible. "I came to New York and looked for someone or someplace to which I could give myself, offer myself, and do everything." This would be the original Phoenix Theatre, and the two someones were Norris Houghton and T. Edward Hambleton. Under their guidance Rabb did everything: he acted, he read the plays that were sent to the company, he auditioned actors, he built and painted sets, he learned how lights worked, how costumes were built, and he took tickets. "I completely gave myself to them, of course, but to the theater as a whole. I saw every play and musical. I met and talked to actors and directors and designers. I would drive to the country to see actors in repertory companies in Massachusetts and Connecticut. I learned how they had their own philosophies—how companies operated and thought; how they took a play you might think you knew terribly well and present it in a way that was truthful to the text, but that nonetheless opened your eyes to an entirely new way of looking at it, hearing it." Tall and handsome, with piercing bright eyes and a mellifluous voice that Tenn, even at his angriest, found soothing and calming, Rabb shared with Tenn a belief in the voices of actors, particularly women, and he designed plays with them in mind. "I heard my company," Rabb told me. "I wanted a symphony on that stage. I did not want them to sound phony; I did not want them working their vocal organs simply to hear themselves. I wanted beauty of sound. I wanted strong, well-orchestrated voices to serve as the platters on which I could serve plays that we all loved."

Rosemary Harris had a voice that Rabb loved. Hers was a masticating voice, with something wonderful, perhaps a caramel or something equally buttery and warm, being worked in that pert little mouth. "Rosemary was probably what I wished I could have been in the theater," Rabb told me. "As dysfunctional and as odd as that sounds, I think it is true. I looked at her and I thought: 'If I were this pretty young actress with that marvelous voice, I would play the following roles,' and I started listing them. I was very bold with her, as you can be when you are utterly sure of what you want with a person. If I had been in pursuit of Rosemary for her love and her body and her undying commitment to me and to the family of children we were bound to create, I would have been a mess. I would not have been able to talk to her. What I wanted instead was her theatrical body. Let me costume it, let me direct it in plays that will showcase what I already see in you. Our children will be plays and a company of actors. I could commit to that, and so could she. We might never have had the honesty to say to ourselves and to each other what we were doing when we married, but I think we both knew what we were getting into and what we were getting. We were establishing for ourselves careers and lives we had both dreamed about."

Rabb and Harris were married in 1960, and approximately one year later, while on a flight in a noisy airplane, Rabb had the epiphany of creating a repertory company. Over the din of the engines, Rabb announced his intention. "That's nice," Harris replied, and went back to her book. "Rosemary did not believe in demonstrations of support or affection. In fact, she is not capable of them, but her 'That's nice' was the warmest thing she had ever said to me, and may remain the warmest." Rabb and I both wondered how Tenn might have felt about the casting of Harris if the playwright had known of this interaction. A lack of enthusiasm was as lethal to Tenn as a lack of beauty or charm or talent.

The APA began to make a name for itself quickly and Tenn began to imagine that they could do a good job with *Camino Real*. Rabb, however, had no interest in mounting that play, and instead hoped for a revival of either *The Glass Menagerie* or *Streetcar,* and, in 1973, he found a way to create his own version of the latter.

"MY FIRST MEETING with Tennessee was wonderful," Rabb remembered. "Funny and easy and full of talk about the look of the play. If he had any doubts about how I saw the play, he did not express them at that meeting." Tenn was taken with the handsome Rabb, and he had learned from the scenic designer Rouben Ter-Arutunian, with whom he had once enjoyed some "carnal abrasion," that Rabb was an ardent lover, amply endowed. "Our first meeting at Lincoln Center," Rabb told me, "after this charming meeting, and all of these phone calls about his play, and he walks up to me, in front of several people—my company, people involved with Lincoln Center—and he says, in a loud voice, 'Rouben Ter-Arutunian tells me you're hung!' Well, it's a line from a farce. I can laugh at it now, but at the time I was horrified. It demoralized me. I knew immediately that he did not take me seriously, that he didn't take the entire enterprise seriously."

Harris read the part, early in rehearsals, with the confidence and control of someone who had played it before, who had already come to every conclusion as to who and what her character was, and this is exactly the way Tenn came to feel she behaved through the run of the play. "There was no element of surprise in her Blanche," he remembered. "The vowels were perfect, the catches in the throat timed like a train schedule, but there was no heart, there was no peril. Blanche must always appear to be ready to break, as well as ready to reassemble and try a new tactic to survive. If I had to give an actress only one salient fact about Blanche, it is this: she is utterly unsure of herself and her surroundings. She has no faith in anything or anyone around her. Well, Rosemary Harris is the epitome of an actress utterly sure of her abilities and her charms and her control over her director—if that director is her ex-husband, Ellis Rabb—and I never felt for one moment that her Blanche was in grave danger, was at the edge, ready to topple. Her Blanche struck me as one who was basically fine, perhaps distraught, going through a phase. She acted as if she were a fat and happy cat who had just consumed a large platter of cream and was now lolling about, showing her extended belly, and waiting to have it patted."

Tenn took his doubts to Rabb, but the director was now so uncomfortable with the playwright that he tended to dismiss him. "I think I shut down a bit," Rabb confessed. "I just poured my energy into the design of the play, into helping Rosemary feel stronger. You know, she was in knots as well. She felt Tennessee was judging her; she could tell that he wanted something from her that she wasn't comfortable providing: friendship, company, constant uplift. She needed those things from me. She did not have them to give."

Rabb admits that there was an especially tight sense of control with the production. "In the past," he told me, "I had let too many things come undone. I had relegated too many things to too many people. I was trying to be a good director and a good adult and take control of this play and become the director I hoped to be. And I was surrounded by people who admired and supported me, and Tennessee was unrealistic and out of control and demanding. Were we right? Were we sympathetic? I have no idea, but I still think we were right not to let him assume control of the production."

Tenn made calls to old friends Maureen Stapleton and Elia Kazan. "It was just a jug of wine, a lot of bread, and my fat ass," Maureen quipped, "and I thought it was going to be a reunion of friends, but it turned into a real rant about Ellis Rabb and Rosemary Harris and these robots he had working for him. I tried to be what Tenn needed at that point: a sympathetic ear and shoulder to get plastered on. I realized that wasn't all he needed. He needed to be redefined. He needed to be comforted. He needed to be reassured that his work would survive, that he would survive. The revival of this play—all of those revivals that year—were nice in their way, but it was the first realization for Tenn that he might be a playwright in the past tense, that he might not have a future."

Elia Kazan, the director Tenn trusted the most, had been sent every play he had written all throughout the 1960s and into the early 1970s, with Tenn always hoping and asking for both his commitment to direct and his advice. Kazan always refused the first, but was generous with the second. "Look at those plays written in the years before that revival, and you'll see where his mind was," Kazan told me. "They really aren't plays, but dialogues, diatribes. Someone is essentially saying, begging, 'Look at me. Notice me. I am human and I am here,' and a play, of sorts, is assembled around it, smuggled in and around a rant. The plays weren't working, and I think Tenn felt terribly threatened."

Tenn was not relating well to women on the pages of his plays or to those with whom he was working. To executives at Lincoln Center, he suggested firing Harris and replacing her with Claire Bloom, an idea that was dismissed. "It was insane," Rabb said. "Here we were working and moving toward an opening, and Tenn was upstairs trying to recast or close down the show."

Tenn called Jessica Tandy and asked for her advice. She recalled that she was busy and in the midst of several things, but nonetheless made the time for her friend, and they had a stressful dinner. "He wanted me to go and see Rosemary Harris and explain the part to her," she told me. "A ludicrous idea, and one I rejected immediately. I told him that you cannot do that to an actress. I told him that he had to trust Rosemary to come to the Blanche that she could give him, and I believed that she would be fine. But Tenn wanted a big scene, a revision, a conversion that would turn the play around to his liking."

"He wanted a friend," Maureen Stapleton said, "a lot of friends; a friend on every corner, but really a friend in his leading actress. He wanted her to look at him with adoration. He wanted her to walk around the city with him and tell him how the part he wrote had changed her life and her view of the theater. He wanted Rosemary Harris to give him the devotion he thought was going to Ellis Rabb. Well, welcome to the world, honey. The allocation of affection is not fair, and it doesn't always run in our favor. It was not a great time to tell Tenn to grow up, but I think that's what I did. Let's just say there were not dark, sweet nights spent in my bed talking things out during that time. He was pissed at everyone."

"A writer has to matter," Tenn told me, "and I no longer mattered. I even began to revisit the plays of Bill Inge." Tenn had spoken at great length of Inge's plays, had outlined the plots for me, had been enraged that they so closely resembled his own; but now he confessed that together, "Bill and I make an ideal playwright. He constructs beautifully. His intentions are good and sound. I can build the plays up, put some meat on the bones of the little fish he provides." No one could convince Tenn that he was wasting his time and his energies. No one could tell him that one bad experience with one actress didn't mean that his days of communication were over, that he would never know happiness in the theater again.

Maria St. Just knew that the only thing that would help her friend was a new project, one that would compel him to work, to think about things, to look at himself. There was no play in the works, nothing that "needed me," as he put it, so he committed himself to writing a memoir, the book of his life, full of memories of encounters that had worked, of women who had walked from the fog and found him, walked with him.

"I didn't go into it thinking I was writing a biography," Tenn told me. "It was a summation, it was my statement of self. I wanted to share myself with others, but I also wanted to know who I was, who I had been, what I had done. I had lost track of how I had worked and believed and felt when things worked, when plays happened, when I had had the gift of friendship." Tenn spent months on the book, showed pages to friends, rewrote passages, both to refine them and to bring forth from them what he most wanted: the writer who had once known how to do it, "had known how to share a human soul with other humans; who had known how to communicate."

Tenn thought of the process as an extensive confession, a harsh self-examination, a fearless inventory.

He would do it again. He could do it again. I could help him.

Eighteen

"K ATHARINE HEPBURN, Turtle Bay" had been written on several pieces of paper in Tenn's possession, and he admitted that he liked to write it out, over and over, as a young girl might do with her name enhanced by the surname of her boyfriend. Tenn remembered receiving the first card from Hepburn, with those words written on the back flap of the envelope, and in his ignorance of that Manhattan neighborhood, he imagined the ruddy, angular actress on the banks of a creek, reading, barking orders to the wilds of nature to do her bidding, to be wonderful all of a sudden for her benefit. This "willful, wonderful rapid stylist" had seductively circled Tenn for years before they ultimately worked together, on the film version of *Suddenly, Last Summer,* a property delivered "partially stillborn but still screaming" to screenwriter Gore Vidal and director Joseph L. Mankiewicz, a marriage, Tenn admitted, that was decidedly odd, but not quite as odd as the casting of Hepburn as Mrs. Venable, a woman who was, in Tenn's words, "an authentic gem, a diamond of great size and worth, but deeply flawed, flawed perhaps beyond the human eye, but stuck in a diadem of dime-store junk."

Tenn recalled with mordant humor the description provided by Mankiewicz of the play he had agreed to direct: "Rich, crazy, over-dressed bitch in New Orleans seeks to have a young woman lobotomized, because she has witnessed the bitch's queer son involved in sodomy, and then cannibalized by local youths he has propositioned. The doctor craves the truth, a cure, and the funds this woman can provide." Tenn laughed and remembered that he felt that the director (who was also a screenwriter Tenn admired) had adequately summed up his one-act play. Mankiewicz, for reasons not made clear to Tenn, did not choose to write the screenplay, and the assignment went to Vidal, whose work was "perfectly fine," according to Tenn; but the film did not make him happy. "You have to consider the time," Tenn told me, and he recounted the late 1950s for me, a time in his life when he began to understand that talents and bodies and loyalties wane and wither and disappear. The country in which he lived seemed perpetually in peril—by virtue of Soviet menace or disease or cultural atrophy; baby girls fell into wells and dead Irish girls spoke to the living—and while Tenn's bank accounts were swelling to the point that he required regular maintenance of his funds, his emotional wealth, he recalled, was niggardly, "dribs and drabs and psychic IOUs." Tenn's relationship with Frank Merlo was unraveling, and he began to have difficulty with actors, producers, directors. Although Elia Kazan agreed, in 1959, to direct *Sweet Bird of Youth,* the experience was angry and left both men unhappy—with their work and with the state of their relationship. "There was a desiccation that was setting in with Tennessee," Kazan told me. "Imagine a band of rubber, a strap of sorts, dry and extended. You know it will snap and crack and become useless, and that process had begun for Tennessee. The suspense was in waiting for his responses, and ultimately for the snapping, the unraveling of the man."

Unable to sleep without assistance, Tenn began to heavily use sleeping pills, prescribed for him by a small retinue of doctors or given to him by friends, among them Kim Stanley and Maureen Stapleton, both of whom remembered—and regretted—their steady supply to their friend. In the mornings, up early to swim and to brew coffee and to face the task of writing, Tenn found himself logy and out of sorts, so he began to use amphetamines on a regular basis, whereas in the past they had been, as he put it, "dangerous candy, a treat to spark things up, to keep the thread going."

Tenn felt bloated and heavy and slow, as if his blood had turned to glue, and he found that the amphetamines, "the glorious rush," only gave him an hour or two of lightness and swiftness, after which he would begin again to fall to the earth, to drift downward. His eyes and nose and mouth were painfully dry, and the habit of flicking his tongue across and through his lips, like a manic lizard, began at this time.

"I had a fantasy at that time," he told me, "of being submerged in a cool liquid and calming my entire head down. Of having my blood replaced. Of being replenished." Tenn felt similarly in our time together, complaining of his swollen feet and burning ankles and heels, his dry eyes and mouth, the perpetual weight, "the cross of addiction," that bore down upon him. "I dwell upon my physical limitations at that time," he told me, "so that you will understand why I was so eager to spend time with Katharine Hepburn. I believed that somehow she would inspire and invigorate me as the pills occasionally could." Tenn subjected himself, as he put it, to a brutally clammy climate in London and a set on which he was not particularly welcome or needed to bask in something he hoped Hepburn might provide.

"I cannot be trusted to give you an adequate summation of that time," Tenn told me. "I would be interested in knowing how Kate felt about it. I would be curious to hear what her impressions might have been."

I did not think that Katharine Hepburn would respond to my letters, and if she did, I did not think that she would agree to see me. My earliest knowledge of her was that she was diabolically private, secretive, not interested in discussing things or looking back, but I was determined to honor Tenn's directions, and so I set about finding her. My old, red-clad copy of *Who's Who in America* listed 201 Bloomfield Avenue in Hartford, Connecticut, as her address, but Marian Seldes assured me that it was best to write to her at the Turtle Bay apartment; she also promised to tell Hepburn about me and my plans.

I had included my telephone number in my letter, and less than a week after I had sent it, I received a phone call from her. And there she was on the line. Surprised. Delighted. Exasperated. She could not imagine, could not understand at all what Tennessee might have seen in her, could have learned from her. The phone call appeared to be taking on the shape of so many calls from actresses, in which they expressed their gratitude and their love of Tennessee, but then begged off discussing him or pursuing anything at all. Hepburn, however, set about to ascertain what I might want, how I might obtain it, when I might be free to pursue what she called "this fascinating, foolish task ahead of you."

What, I asked her, was foolish about the task?

"Well," she said, laughing, "I think it's pretty damn foolish to come to *me,* for instance, to try and understand Tennessee Williams. To go to any actress and to try to decide what, if anything, matters, but . . ." Her sentence wandered off.

"Listen," she said. "Do you know my literary agent?" I told her I didn't.

"Oh, well, never mind," at which point she looked through notes or books or calendars and gave me a date for coming to see her—at the Turtle Bay apartment that Tenn had thought about so many times. I told her about his image of the home he thought she might live in.

"Oh, well," she replied, "you're going to be quite disappointed. No lakes or ponds or wildlife here, but I'll show you where he sat, and I'll try to make some sense out of what it is you're doing."

She told me she had finished writing another book, her autobiography.

"It's fascinating," she said, "and maddening."

I was about to reply, but she had hung up.

I had been told that it was in my best interests to arrive punctually at Hepburn's home. Both Marian Seldes and her husband, Garson Kanin, who, with his first wife and writing partner, Ruth Gordon, had created three of the Tracy-Hepburn films, told me to arrive "prepared," and I wasn't sure what they meant. They did not clarify the term too well; they only reiterated that one should be prepared and at one's best when in the company of Katharine Hepburn.

I had mailed to Hepburn some of Tenn's comments about her, but she specifically asked me to bring them for our visit, and I had copies with me. On the advice of Jessica Tandy, I arrived perfectly clean, with no scent of anything—perfume, city filth, food—on my person. "I have always found her to be a clean-slate sort of person," Tandy told me. "Clean, precise, detailed." Ellis Rabb had told me that she had positioned above her dressing-room mirror a quote from Nabokov, "Caress the detail, the divine detail," so I was rested and clear and ready to offer details or to be detailed.

I arrived at the house at the precise time that had been requested, and after one ring of the doorbell, the door swiftly flew open and Katharine Hepburn stood there, colorful and alert.

"I was right *here* when you rang!" she exclaimed. "Perfect! A good start. Now wait a minute." She was carrying a large shopping bag full of papers, and I had clearly interrupted the journey she had planned for them. She looked about a bit and then threw them into the dining room and made a gesture toward the bag as if to say "Stay there!" She then turned to me and asked if I needed or wanted anything. A drink? Something to eat? A tour? A trip to the bathroom? I told her I needed nothing.

"Perfect! Let's get right on to this," and I followed her up a narrow staircase to a bright, white-walled room, comfortable, with the windows open to a crisp breeze, even though it was late in June. "You! Sit there! Tennessee sat there once. Not in that chair, but in that space." I sat in a chair directly across from her and she looked at me strongly. She paused for a moment and then said, "Now *who* all is involved in this project you've begun?"

Most actresses wish to know the names of the members of the company she is keeping, and Hepburn was avaricious in her desire to know to whom I had spoken, what they were like, and what their response had been to Tenn's comments and to my questions. She was fearless in offering her opinions of the people on my list, and her exclaiming "Oh, well!" when a name was mentioned meant that I should watch myself. Her greatest generosity was in recognizing and praising the talent of others, and she offered concise and sharp summations of each and every person.

Jessica Tandy? "Oh, she's marvelous. Seemingly weak but granite and grace fused together." Maureen Stapleton? "Wonderful actress; funny; a mess." Kim Stanley? "Tragic. A great talent and a willful, public suicide." Barbara Baxley? "Trouble. Troubled within and looking to make trouble around her. To make her feel comfortable, at home, I suppose." Edward Albee? "Closed. Doors shut. Brilliant but buried somewhere I can't reach." Marian Seldes? "Well, I may change my opinion of her, given that she brought you to me, but I adore her. Disciplined and devoted. *Slavish.*" Geraldine Page? "The type of actress I would have liked to have been; the sort of person I tend to avoid." Helen Hayes? "Well, what can you say about Helen Hayes? She's no longer one of *us*, is she? She's like the color blue or ore or Benjamin Moore paint. She exists, she is used, she serves a purpose. What is there to discuss?" Stella Adler? "Beyond me. Brilliant. Wise. Regal. I wish she would act more and pontificate less."

On the Venice set of David Lean's *Summertime* (1955). "I wish I could move through life with her ease," Tennessee told me.

Hepburn was delighted to learn that I did not use tape recorders, and she wanted to know why I did not. I told her that the subject and I invariably became obsessed with the machine, stared at it, checked on it, and our conversation grew slack in detail because we believed, and hoped, that it was all being recorded on tape. I told her about the tape literally coming unspooled in the apartment of Mildred Natwick, the brown, snakelike material oozing out of the machine and onto Natwick's coffee table.

"Mildred Natwick! My God, you spoke to Mildred Natwick? What on *earth* did *she* have to say?"

I told Hepburn that it would be difficult to condense all that Natwick had told me, at which point she interrupted to demand that I tell her the *best* thing Natwick had told me. I told Hepburn that Natwick refused to be limited by lack or despair or troubles of any kind, and her reaction to anything was to say, boldly and cheerfully, "Let's make as little of this as quickly as possible."

"Perfect! I love that. I love Mildred Natwick, and she's quite right. Now . . . what did Tennessee tell you about *me*?"

I drew out my papers. Hepburn, in white pants and a crisp chambray shirt, had her leg up on a table and her left hand on her chin. During my reading to her, she frequently adjusted lamps, moved books on a table, readjusted pencils in a mug, but she made a point of keeping her gaze on me at almost every second. She did not interrupt my reading of Tenn's version of this person he idolized called Katharine Hepburn, but she often emitted a loud, sharp snort, a humorous editorial comment, and whenever I looked at her, she would motion for me to continue. I read it to her as she commanded: clearly, loudly, and exactly as I had written it down and remembered it.

Katharine Hepburn: Goethe in Gingham.

She cannot enter a room quietly or make a statement that doesn't have within it a tiny but lethal explosion of truth. A shock effect, of course, but true nonetheless, worthy of attention, yes, but worthier still of one's thought. Not really all that tall, but she appears to be so, through posture and both a sense of entitlement and of purpose—she is always moving toward a goal, an end, an explanation, an end to some nonsense. Work achieved; a sense of satisfaction; beginning again. This is her Holy Trinity, I think, while mine was a bit more exotic, darker, confused, overdone. Analysis to her was not conducted in sessions with doctors or experiments with pills and injections or through prayer to some supernal overseer, but through work. Whatever she wanted to find—and whatever she ultimately did find—came through work, through the seeking. Knowledge is nestled deep within the marble that is life, and she relentlessly hammers away at it, chipping away all that is superfluous and silly until she can see what she needs, admires it, uses it, cares for it. Like the axiom attributed to Goethe, Kate understands the magic and the power that begins and survives through boldness. For her there is nothing holier than the sacrificial act of making that leap toward the creation of something: a part in a play or a film; the reading of a book important to her; the creation of a meal; the conquering of a task. I toil in a church festooned with the images and the intentions of saints, their progressions noted and offered to us as examples of how to accept and apply all that has been given to us. Exemplification, my mother always told me, is what we are here for. I cannot find a reason to make my own leaps in the lives of Mary or Veronica or Bridget or any of the Theresas, but I can look upon this vivid woman, scornful of limits and blockage, and move toward the edge of whatever I need to do, to achieve, to exemplify.

On an index card Tenn had written: "Katharine Hepburn has one goal. One bar of soap for face, hair, teeth, body. A bar of soap big and white, like the pale judgment. Pressed against her body to get it going in the morning. The pale judgment awaits me in the morning, looking for me to press myself against it. To come clean."

In conversation with me: "I went to Kate in a form of supplication. I was unhappy and I didn't feel well, and I was divorced from this play of mine, which was now the film of other men, the property of other men, and I had my check from the film people, and I had my curiosity piqued at being on the set with such beautiful and vibrant people, but I was in terrible pain. Everything hurt, and things were beginning to be blurred for me. I did not have that clear intention that Kate always had, and I went to her, foolish and fulsome, to learn from her, to be guided by her, and she was a busy and committed actress. She had no time for my fears and my complaints, but she received me. She *received* me in the truest sense of that word. There was nothing holy or reverent about our time together; there was great laughter and a number of arguments. There were no secrets or covenants. But what I came away with I could have used effectively and persistently and been a better writer and a better friend and a better person—if I had had the courage and the discipline. That," he told me, no less than three times, "she gave me: The knowledge that I, and I alone, had to be and should be responsible for myself. For my talent and for my ankles and my dry mouth and blistered lips and itchy eyes. For my bad back and my bad intentions and my maddening ability to see the poison in the fruit and the sniper in the trees. To be, at all times, an adult."

For most of his life, Tenn had been surrounded by—had chosen to be surrounded by—women of a volatile nature, skittish, manic, tuned at times to a frequency no one else could hear or decipher. These were women with whom he felt comfortable, finding solace in their inability to function any better than he did, their tendency to foster appetites similar to his, to veer toward the illegal and the immobilizing. "You can talk deep into the night with a crazy woman," Tenn confided to me, "but you can't get the groceries with one, or meet a deadline, or get the lights turned back on, or take yourself to the doctor on time, or meet with someone who might produce or publish your work. They work against the grain of productivity and function. They howl at a moon of entertainment, endless and garish, but they are never a foundation upon which one can operate or from which one can propel oneself toward work or action."

The initial and predominant model of such a woman was, of course, his mother, a frantic fabulist, industrious with invention and denial, but never boring, whether she was creating stories about her ancestors or devising threats in the sounds of the wind or the whispers of Negroes on the streets of St. Louis. Edwina not only believed that the fruit was poisoned, but she had an idea who might have planted the cyanide or the curare within the flesh, and the snipers were on the roofs and in the bushes and they were placed there to prevent her from claiming the truth of things, which only she knew and had the presence of mind to share. "I grew up in a psychic circus," Tenn told me, with more wonder than anger or regret. "There was confetti in the air and it was madness, ideas floating in the wind of my mother's invention and madness, like my leaves of invention and illness. There was shit in the sawdust of that circus, but it was all self-produced and allowed to remain there. It was a dirty house, not to appearances, of course: my mother would have nothing but a neat and proper home. It was dirty in spirit, cluttered. Not evil; just terribly unfocused and misguided."

This was what Tenn believed all women must be, and he learned to navigate the world with his mother as his guide. Charm, guile, lies, hysteria. When I asked Tenn what his mother had given to him that had served him well, he had replied with those four words, qualities and attributes from which had sprung the other gift she had bestowed upon him: his ability to tell stories, to construct four walls around any situation and to get a woman talking and moving and aiming for release.

Talent, he told me, does not originate purely: it derives from something else, as a pearl or coal does, as pain must. Talent is the result of some friction, consistent and substantial, and the defense a person devises against it becomes a painting or a poem or a play. Or a tantrum. "The line between art and bad behavior is terribly fine," he told me. "Something that is of some use to others can arise, or simply a means of getting attention or a particular reaction. You need to know how to discern the difference in yourself and others."

Tenn's earliest memories of his own navigation involved his bed in various homes. The bed in which he was sick and was comforted by his mother, who brought him ginger ale and soup and magazines he was allowed to cut apart, finding images that appealed to him, settings into which he would have loved to disappear and belong. A bed to which his mother would come and read to him, acting out parts and editorializing. The bed in which he would lie at night, hugging his radio and listening to the stories of others, which he could imagine being a part of, or improving. The bed in which he lay, deprived of his radio by his angry father, and listening to the sounds of the neighbors—arguments, laughter, music from down the street, a train's whistle, a boat's horn, a dog barking, a baby crying. Trying to determine how far or near they might be, and what might be going on around them, creating a story. Imagining himself walking one block, two blocks, one mile, four miles to get to the dog or the baby or the river. Remembering the houses he might find on the way, the trees, the scent of the flowers at particular intersections.

His earliest acts of navigation all held the same motive: to calm down his home and his mother. "I wanted to make everything safe and calm for my mother," he told me. "For me as well, of course, but I knew that I was with her, bound to her, made of her, belonging to her. I felt I had to be prepared for some imminent and immediate departure from those homes and those cities. I needed to know the streets and the means of escape. I needed to be funny and wise and strong and quick."

And yet the escape, when it was needed, was provided by his mother. Tenn had an early memory, from when he was very young, of his father striking him across the face, leaving him red and burning, and sending him to bed to cry and rage and listen. But the night air brought no sounds, and his interior map was out of sorts that night: he could not foresee how he might get out of the house and down the street and reach the train or the river. There were loud arguments between his mother and his father until he fell into a defensive sleep . . . only to be awakened by his frantic mother. "She pulled me close to her," he remembered, "and I could smell her perfume and her hair spray and I could feel the softness of her cheek. My head rested perfectly on her shoulder, and we were heading out of the house."

Tenn could not remember where they were headed or where they wound up, but he could remember his mother's quick steps and her perfume and her cheek and her manic wobble down the sidewalk and her words, repeated over and over like a prayer in his ear: "You're safe, baby. You're safe, baby." A lie, surely—there was no safety in that house or on those streets or in the arms of that woman—but that was the story and that was a means to be calmed and they were on the move.

"We were navigating," he told me, "but it was precarious. I loved her and I knew she was trying to protect me, to get me away from anything that might harm me, but I wanted, and I needed, a stable woman, a stable person." Tenn had searched for years for that person, had come close to finding such a person, and he believed that it might be Katharine Hepburn. "So I brought all of this baggage, all of this drama, all of this pain right to her," he told me, "and I asked her to help me sort it out, to make some sense of it. It was ludicrous, but it was what I needed and wanted, and it brought me some of the same comfort as that run in the night with my mother."

Katharine Hepburn cried easily—and strenuously. When I had finished reading her these notes, she was waving her hands across her face, embarrassed. She asked me to stop and to give her some time. "I had no idea," she told me, quietly. "I wish I had known that he wanted me to help him. I wish I could have."

In a matter of minutes, Hepburn had concluded our first visit, with a promise for another, at which time she would tell me her side of the events concerning her and Tennessee Williams. I was aware that I was being rushed out of her home.

Several days later I received a letter from Hepburn in which she wrote: "Too bad Tennessee never told me that—I thought he was   is and always will be remarkable—"

I assumed that the letter might be the end of our relationship, but two days later, I received a call from her.

She had thought a great deal about this project of mine, and she had some things to say.

I noticed that Katharine Hepburn was at her freest when a dessert was served and consumed: a large bowl of ice cream delighted and released her, and she barely noticed or spoke to the woman who brought the trays into the room; she waved her away peremptorily and offered me a bowl. I noted that the bowls were like those at Brennan's in New

Katharine Houghton Hepburn

VII - 9 - 1990

Dear Jim Grissom --
     Too bad Tennessee
never told me that --
     I thought he was
-- is and always will be
remarkable --

Katharine Hepburn was easily moved—a fact she tried very hard to hide. After my first visit to her home, when she cried upon hearing how Tennessee felt about her, she sent me this note.

Orleans, one of the restaurants to which Tenn and I had gone one day, where the bowls of bread pudding were the size of a German shepherd's head.

"I would *like* that restaurant," Hepburn said, snorting and enjoying the ice cream. I resented the eating times with Hepburn because I felt that we weren't talking, but it was during these times that she shared her sharpest opinions of some of the people Tenn had admired.

"I had no idea that Tennessee was so enamored of Ruth Chatterton," she told me one evening. "She was a good actress, very stylish, but there was something about her that led me to believe she would just disappear."

"From?"

"From the stage, from the screen, from memory," Hepburn replied. "She liked to be married, I think. She liked clothes and travel, and she started to write. I think she wanted a type of life that wasn't the type of life an actress needs to live, *has* to live."

I asked her what type of life that would be.

"Look," she said, "nothing happens by accident or fate or luck. Everything happens by design, and most of those women on your list—on Tennessee's list—made very conscious decisions about their lives and about their actions in their careers to become good and to become some sort of inspiration to people. It is a struggle—a perpetual struggle—to do anything worthwhile, to earn anything from what you do. Nothing *happens*. Effort is made and it is rewarded. No gift falls upon anyone. It's dug out of someone, worked on, tried out, reworked, toned. It takes a lot of strength and determination to be ready to keep doing good work. This is what I remember Tennessee writing about me, right?"

I told her that Tenn had envied her upbringing, and had often dreamed of having the New England childhood she must have had. Some of the photos Tenn had clipped, and some of the homes he imagined moving about and living in, had been in Connecticut, New Hampshire, Vermont—names that seemed to him exotic, superior.

"Doesn't everyone feel that way?" Hepburn replied. "I loved my family and my childhood, and I still love New England, but I sometimes wonder how things might have been—what I might have become—if I'd been born in some exotic place like New Orleans, or a flat, dry place like Texas or Oklahoma. I would have been odd and determined wherever I had happened to live."

"No dreams when you were growing up?" I asked.

"Well, what the hell does that mean?" she retorted. "Do you mean while sleeping? Or looking up in the sky? No, I'm not much of a dreamer."

"No cutting of pictures or journal keeping?"

"God, no," she shot back. "I don't believe in there being too much time between the realization of what you want to do and doing it. Tennessee talks of threads, tying us to people and to things. Short threads are best, I think. You think it and you do it. You dream it and you do it. You love someone, you keep them close." Hepburn leaned forward, placing both hands on her knees, and shot me a stern look. "I'm so tired of the term 'victim,'" she said. "Everybody's a victim. I'm not talking about the tragedies of the world, in which people truly are victimized:

I'm talking about everyday activities in which people enjoy crying out about their status as a victim. Everybody has been abused or betrayed or deliberately set out on a course of failure. This is such bullshit, I don't even know what to say. Our failures emanate from within us; my failures are my own damned fault. I can't look at a man or a woman or a studio or the mores of a certain time and say, 'Well, I was a victim of that person or that time.' No, I might have allowed them to lead me to believe that I was unsuitable or unattractive or untalented. And I never let them, so I was never a victim. And this is not because I'm so smart—anyone can adopt this philosophy and do quite well in life. Refuse to be a victim. Learn from the unfortunate incident—failed audition, being fired, losing at love, being born in the wrong place or at the wrong time—and do something about it, and then succeed at the next go-round. I can't even turn on the television or look at a newsstand now without seeing the latest victim. I find people horribly boring, I must say. I think they must enjoy their acute ability to enjoy and promote their failure."

Her conversations with me, slightly argumentative and always pushing away too much curiosity, generally continued in this way; but on that one evening, sated by ice cream, I again brought up the meeting between Tenn and Hepburn, when he felt so tired and heavy and wanted her advice on how to live and how to come to grips with one's history.

"I wanted Tenn—I wanted everybody—to simplify things and just get on with their work, do what they were meant to do. I needed to understand that part and that director and those other actors, and Tennessee needed to write and sort out his life. In the notes Tennessee gave you, you mention the single bar of soap. Well, that came from my father, who taught me well. You keep asking questions and posing situations—just as Tennessee did—and I keep thinking of my father: A man whose sink had on it one big bar of durable, good soap. And that bar of soap was used for cleaning, shaving, and brushing his teeth. It worked fine; it was fast; it was economical. He could then get on with his day. I think we clutter our minds and our lives in a way people would have liked for my father to clutter his toilet. There is too much clutter and too much thinking and too much devising. I think you need to be true to your work and your friends—these should be small circles. People who have too many friends tend to have too few ideas, I find, and they cover up their disappointment with parties and chatter and movement. Focus on working well and being there for you, your work, and your friends. One bar of soap. Taught me a lot."

A pause.

"Tennessee worried too much," she continued, "and he felt that the answer to his problem was somewhere outside of himself, outside of his friends. He loved women, and that is wise, but we could only do so much. He wanted an example, but he never realized that he was an example to me—so brilliant and sharp and funny. I'm not any of those things. I'd like to be. I pretend to be. He was so extraordinary by birth and by effort, but he was a victim, or chose to see himself as one. He foolishly believed that I had escaped any sort of doubt in my life, and that my flawless past, as he saw it, could rub off on him.

"You sit down and you begin to think about your past and all that you've done with it," Hepburn admitted, "and you *are* going deep and close to the experiences, but to see it properly, you need a greater perspective, so you pull away and you take your life in sections. You think of yourself in your twenties. Later you think of yourself in terms of relationships, and you think 'the Cukor years' or the 'Spencer Tracy years' or 'the MGM years.' From that great distance, looking at yourself moving among all those other people and doing whatever you were doing, you find that it has a line—a time line—but to understand it, to fully understand it, you need to move in closer, and so you think—I had to think—about particular experiences or events or emotions. I had to chop it up, or edit it. No one wanted the *entire* time line, least of all me.

"You know," she continued, "I think what I wanted to tell you—what I've been meaning to tell you—and probably what I told Tennessee all those years ago—is that it's perfectly acceptable to take that long view and study your life and your actions, but I think it's a bit foolish to study it too much. Tennessee used the term 'navigation' to describe it for you, and one doesn't move too much or too far if you spend a lot of time analyzing everything you see along the way. You see some things and you use them or you don't, you like them or you don't, but the point, I think, is to get where you're going, and to spend the time getting there preparing for what you'll find, for what you'll need to do. Tennessee was so caught up in finding the meaning of things that I think he stopped moving, he stopped advancing, to use the term he kept talking about.

"There really isn't as much mystery to the world and the people

Katharine Hepburn, on the set of *Suddenly, Last Summer*, 1959. Tennessee sought her out for advice and to use as an example of living well and right, but she was not eager to be a teacher to him. "So talented and so needy," she said. "I could never understand why he didn't see how much he was loved."

in it," she continued. She smiled and she got up and began walking around the room. I thought the interview might be over, but she was only stretching her legs, after which she called down the stairs for a drink. She asked if I wanted one, but I declined. "Smart move, I guess," she quipped.

She sat back down and continued.

"Whatever is complicated about people, in my opinion, is entirely self-created," she said. "Life is often difficult, it certainly calls for some crafty navigation, but I don't find it at all mysterious or needing support systems or myths to get through it. Life is work, so you do your work and you do it well. This will require study and hard work and attention and stamina. That is all. Life is friendship, so you care for your friends and look after them and keep in touch. Some of them fall away; you find you have nothing in common with them any longer. Some of them die. You miss them and you remember them. That is all. I don't know why Tennessee needed to know what the *plan* was. I never looked for a plan, I can assure you. I looked for a *way*: a way to act, to do what I wanted, to live as I pleased. I didn't make lists or scatter notes about. I just did it.

"I also think that Tennessee thought his talent would save him. Well, it's not enough to be talented. There's a lot of talent out there, but it's owned by lazy, stupid, or essentially boring people. You can't just be talented: You have to be terribly smart and energetic and ruthless. You also have to become necessary to people, by working hard and well and bringing more than your bones and your skin to the project. Don't just show up. Transform the work, yourself, and everybody around you. Be needed. Be interesting. Be something no one else can be—and consistently."

She became a bit more animated as she continued. "Perhaps it is different for a writer. I'd have to admit that I have no concept of how they gather their ideas and get them into a script. I don't, but I was aggravated—I'm still aggravated, as you can see—that Tennessee was so caught up in the meaning of things, the getting through things, the remembering of all the things, big and small, that had happened to him and to those he liked and cared about."

I realized that the interview was over, but she merely stared at me, and I began to put my papers together, but she stopped me and asked me to read a particular portion of Tenn's notes that I had not sent to her, but which had been described to her by Marian Seldes. The notes dealt with Tenn's devotion to and need for women in his life, which he found baffling. "Why did he find it baffling?" Hepburn asked. I read her the notes.

So here we are—here I am—perpetually seeking the amatory affections and affirmations of men, while my heart, the very core of my soul, responds to, needs, reaches out for female company, friendship, communion. You know, I have never been betrayed by a woman. I can see now that my mother lied to protect both of us. Sins of creativity and escape, I suppose. Her anger was something she believed might construct a cocoon that could protect both of us. But betrayal? Never.

Now the men in my life—the men in the lives of all inverted men—will betray you and look away if your jacket is the wrong shade in the wrong material. They'll cast you aside if a single curd of fat graces your body, a wrinkle creases the fabric from which they hope to make a shawl of prayer and possession.

Perhaps because I want the best from women—soul and love and warmth and friendship and loyalty—it is what I receive. The life and desirability of the physical attributes are placed on our bodies with clocks ticking and gravity pulling with a mighty vengeance. But the heart and the soul—if surrounded by women—grow, swell, reach out perpetually for surcease and sharing.

A desirable man is the one who subsumes what he has been given by women, witnessed of women.

And here I am—here we are—looking at the legs and the smiles of those who don't care what we think or write or can do with a bundle of words and a couple of women. And when they reject and hurt us, we run back to the circle of women who surround us, prop us up, lead us back to the pale judgment, the blank page, the surface to which we apply our souls.

This is called irony, honey. Look into it.

Hepburn laughed as I finished the notes, raised her eyebrows, and quipped that "a lot of that is true," but then she was off on another thought. "I refuse to believe that love or affection can be defined," she said, "because we may feel and think differently in a year or two or after a bad experience next Thursday. And then someone walks into your life and you feel great affection for them. How do you define that? Why should you? Just feel it! Just enjoy it! Just express it! But people want to define it; they want to define everything. Tennessee had to have everything mapped out, understood. If I had known that about him—if he had brought those concerns in those notes to me—I would have told him that the plan belongs to him; the plan is waiting for your hand to write it and your heart to believe it. Our lives cannot be dictated by the feelings of others, no matter how painful those feelings may be, or how much harm they may inflict upon us. I can't understand why Tennessee—why so many people—don't have the faith in themselves or what they do or what they believe. Why are they always weakened by others?

"I will respect you till the day you die if you believe in things and stand up for them, but if you move into my space and try to tell me how I should feel, how I should love, how I should believe, well, I'll cut you down like lumber. And I wish I could have told Tennessee Williams to just cut down those people—and those thoughts—that kept him so frozen, so heavy, so afraid."

Hepburn walked me out of the house and strongly patted my shoulder. She thanked me for coming, for including her in the book, and asked that I stay in touch. But she was clearly done with the entire project.

"Love the man," she told me, "but study the work. Work cures everything, and work explains everything." Had I met Hepburn in time to take a message to Tenn, she would have told him, "To work is all. You were put here to work." "Tennessee only wanted to be loved," she said, "and he was: He just looked toward the wrong places, at the wrong things." She paused, smiled, then added, "He had terrific taste in friends."

Several days later I received another letter from Hepburn. Enclosed in it, on a small card, was her recipe for brownies.

"I HAD WAYS of getting to my room," Tenn told me. "I might become sick, or terribly tired, or consumed with the studies required of me the next day in school. I would banish myself to my room, and my mother, allied with my anxiety, might bring my dinner to me, a cool hand to the forehead, strength for the night." Strength was needed, because Tenn's father was addicted to the experience of criticizing his son. "He needed to diminish me so that his own stature would improve," Tenn remembered. "His own silhouette had been diminished and distorted by so many humiliations and exertions that I was his only means of affirmation, the only human to whom he could submit himself for comparison and feel both superior and abusive."

From the earliest age, the deepest memory, Tenn recalled that his father considered him a burden, a drain on the family's emotions and finances, an embarrassment. His father hated his attempts at writing, his "gallivanting" in backyards with Rose, putting on plays or imitating neighbors or film stars; the images that Tenn painstakingly clipped and saved and pasted into notebooks or on cardboard would periodically disappear, thrown away by his disapproving father, who castigated the sissy for wasting his time and making a mess of things. Before he had entered grade school, Tenn knew, from his father's insistence, that he must eventually obtain a good job with benefits and good people and the opportunity to "advance."

A lover of words, Tenn looked up the word "advance" in the dictionary. He could recall snatches of what he had read: "to rise beyond the elementary or introductory." Clearly, he recalled, this was the phase of development in which he was trapped with his family, a limbo not unlike that awaiting unsaved babies, an uncomfortable, unknowing state of being, devoid of sight and sound and touch. "That was home," Tenn told me.

Another definition: "to be developed beyond the initial stage or process." This was clearly the young Thomas Lanier Williams, born into a family of simpletons and savages, aware of things either beyond the imagination or beneath the contempt of his relations or peers, and hoping to escape.

Yet another definition: "to be much evolved from an early ancestral archetype." This is what Tenn wanted to be more than anything else. It was what he felt his father could never be. "He arrived at his own home," Tenn remembered, "and anywhere he went, I would imagine, intent on despoiling what was pleasant or calm or moving forward. He thrived on fear and power; he relished the barbaric. He enjoyed shouting at the radio when fights or other gladiatorial events were broadcast, praying for blood or injury or aborted careers. Limbs and lives destroyed. Adventure! Excitement! All at the expense of others. Drinking and demanding things of my mother and my sister. Judging the attempts—the pitiful but heartfelt attempts—my mother made around the house, to make it more appealing, as best she could on his niggardly contributions."

There was a regular dance in the household, Edwina and Cornelius Williams circling each other warily, angrily, words and décor thrown at each other in some attempt at communication. At some point the energy would be directed at Tenn, who waited, poised over a pad of paper or a book, or clutching his radio. Depending on the anger his father possessed, the item to which Tenn devoted himself would be destroyed or criticized or hidden away from him until he "improved."

"And here I am," Tenn told me. "I am seventy-one years old, and I am still trying to understand what my father wanted me to improve, what he wanted me to become. I realize now that he simply didn't understand me, couldn't believe that I was his son, that I was somehow created to honor or care for him." The earliest statement Tenn could remember coming to him from his father—and uttered to others in his presence—was that he was not *right*. There was something odd about the boy. *Something off.* Something within him needed to be slapped off or away, or the same unseemly something could be remedied by something better, more appropriate being pounded into him.

In order to function at all, Tenn believed, all people, not merely those who wished to write or act or paint or sing, must develop for themselves a support system comprised of myths tested by them and found to be effective. Most find comfort and a sense of purpose and a level of care under the supervision of a God or gods who have inspired or personally delivered to the mere mortals below a plan of action, a means of advancement, via canonical texts or visions or through the agency of fellow humans who are imbued with the spirit or propelled by the example of their chosen leader. As a child Tenn had roamed the halls of rectories and had overheard the means of atonement and acceptance and advancement and had found them lacking. "I turned to clipped photographs and radio dramas," he told me. "I preferred the morals and the lineaments of whatever story I could project into that imagined situation, those rooms of my dreaming. I know that I lifted characters and dialogue and contours from my 'real' life, and then placed them within what became my actual and my preferred life, and it was here." With the final statement, Tenn again poked a finger into my forehead.

"There is no salvation," he said. "There is no being saved. There is no 'Eureka!' moment. There is no Cassandra in the closet who will appear and ask the probing questions. There is within your mind all that you will ever be and all that you will ever need. I always felt this way, but I was never brave enough to face this fact and live entirely by my own counsel. I needed and I sought out the myths of my choosing."

Tenn had also come to believe that all of us are caught on that train he had mentioned to me, the train mistakenly jumped upon in haste, with badly marked directions, and we looked out the windows and realized we were headed in the wrong direction, or that people we would rather emulate or love or study were on the opposite track, better appointed, prepared, armed with itineraries that had a stated destination and the accommodations that would provide comfort and safe delivery. "I felt that way as I pursued my life in the theater," Tenn told me, "but my mother felt the same way, ironing doilies or cutting crusts off sandwiches or entertaining her friends in the front room. There was a present person; there was conversation. Deep in her mind, however, she was young and pretty and destined for a good and envied life, a life of purpose and demands that her creativity and humor could fill. She dreamed her way through her life. I am dreaming my way through my own. I talk to you now, but I keep seeing pages filling up with my handwriting or the words I've typed, in pica. Plays, essays, descriptions. On one track I'm dreaming of working again and being happy and being productive, and on another I'm at the task of writing, and I can make myself believe that I'm working. My mother did this: washing dishes but also dancing at the beautiful lake, with lights sparkling on the dappled water. Warding off the blows of my father, but actually taking on the final scenes of *Medea* and waiting for the applause. Living alone with her three wayward, badly wired, and confused children, stretching every nerve and every penny, but actually awaiting the attentions of the best men in town, who would deliver her from her penury and her pinched heart."

Two trains. Juggling of the gods.

"I left the God of my childhood," Tenn continued, "and I offered my soul and my allegiance to a variety of gods. There was the god of beauty and order, which I found in photographs of interiors designed by Dorothy Draper and Cedric Gibbons. There was no oilcloth or soiled damask or venetian blinds in those settings, and I believed that there was peace there. I would only later learn that the bright sheen of lacquer and marble could also house hatred and anger and abuse. I did not know that then, so I transported myself to those places and saw my mother and my sister in those chairs and in those doors and looking out those windows, happy and advancing in the right direction.

"That god fell by the wayside when I began to love the sound and the shape of words and sentences. I heard words first, over the radio and from the movie screen, and I always wondered where they came from and how they looked. After I learned to read, I imagined them, black on a white background, sometimes in the typefaces of the screen credits, bold and orderly, offering shape and style to every situation. Even in situations with those people who populated my life, I listened to what they said and could see the words, which I then paginated and indented to my satisfaction. When I began to write, I liked the length and the weight of sentences, the way a word looked or sounded or felt to me in particular placement. Then words went above and within the pictures I'd clipped. I had demoted my earlier god, who was now, with me, in service to the word.

"I talk to you about all of these women because they are like ambulatory, fleshly emblems of my beliefs. Think of them, if it helps, as if they were a human gallery of examples of a truly catholic—use the small *c*—Stations of the Cross. I gain nothing at all by focusing on the pains and betrayals of Jesus Christ, a fiction comprised of any number of myths that man, from the first and darkest of caves, fashioned for himself, a savior, a father, a buddy out there in the wild maneuverings of life, smoothing the rough edges, looking out for his well-being, furnishing a place in some Edenic hostel, comfortable and safe and eternal. However, I can imagine myself walking through a cathedral, designed by my desire and my imagination and my memory, and on the walls I might find Lillian Gish or Marian Seldes or Katharine Cornell. Ruth Chatterton or Pola Negri or Gloria Swanson. Ida Lupino or Barbara Stanwyck or Laurette Taylor. Examples. The sweetness and the devotion—the dogged persistence, cloaked in kindness—that Lillian and Marian and Katharine exhibited to me. The toughness and the carnal gaits of Stanwyck and Lupino. The scrubbed and sparse aestheticism of Katharine Hepburn and Frances Sternhagen. The brutal intelligence and fiery will of Estelle Parsons and Madeleine Sherwood. The flamboyant denial of fact and colorful poses of Elaine Stritch and Ruth Gordon. The earthly worthlessness but artistic supremacy of ethereal monsters like Geraldine Page and Kim Stanley. The judicious and frighteningly bright allegiance and intelligence of Marla Tucci, perpetually supplicating so that others might shine around her, so that life can flourish, even if her art suffers. Bring me saints who can compare with these lives! Bring me examples that would better suit my life, or any life!"

Tenn asked me if I had the rosary. I handed it to him.

"This thing, this series of beads," he said, holding it above his head, "has no meaning for me, serves as no sacrament, until I invest these beads with those women and men and events that give some foundation, some bones, to the fleshly man that I am. The bones and the beads prop me up, keep me upright and ambulatory, and give me some sense of what I'm doing. What I should be doing."

To one of the beads he added two names: Frank Merlo and Yasujiro Ozu.

TENN TOLD ME that in that "awful year of 1963," as Frank Merlo died of lung cancer in the apartment they shared, which now smelled of sour spit and sweat and the bursts of Mitsouko that a well-meaning maid insisted on spraying over the rooms, he was notified of the death of the Japanese film director Yasujiro Ozu. Dead at the age of sixty, dead in fact on his birthday, from cancer, Tenn found himself thinking of the man, whom he did not know, but whose films he had loved, and about whom he had argued with the writer Yukio Mishima, who had deplored Ozu's films and who had forced Tenn to defend them. Mishima did not care for the severity and the simplicity of the films: he wanted color and boldness in his art and in his life, and he found the films of Ozu to be tight and dry and airless. Tenn agreed with Mishima that life is colorful and bold and messy, and art should express that; but life is also almost always impossible to handle, and those simple tasks in the films of Ozu—tea, an orderly home, silent moments on a hill with a child— are the moments we all need to apply contours to the events the day presents to us. From the films of Ozu Tenn learned that everything, every solitary thing that comes into our life and our consciousness, is all that we will ever have, and it is the only inventory in which we can search for supplies. Our memories can only be built from the things and the people and the places that we see and hear and smell and love and discard or save, and in this ceaseless rush of stimulus we often need the vase of flowers to arrange, the pet to stroke, the tea to boil, the scented bath, as well as time to stop and think and attach to that memory whatever we might need to hold it and use it and share it.

Mishima agreed, and said he would reconsider the man who was Yasujiro Ozu. It was Mishima who contacted Tenn to let him know that Ozu's grave bore the inscription *mu*, a Japanese word meaning nothingness. This disturbed Tenn until Mishima explained that in the many obituaries and tributes that had been written for Ozu, it was revealed that the director believed, most strongly, in *mono no aware*, or an awareness of the impermanence of things. Life, Mishima told Tenn, truly is swift and unforgiving, and beauty and meaning are ours only if we can recognize them and snatch them and pass them along to others.

Tenn took this conversation with Mishima and "subsumed it, held it deep within me," and it would help him to write and think about Frank Merlo and what the man had meant to him and done for him. He remembered a day, during rehearsals of *Cat on a Hot Tin Roof,* when tempers flared, scenes sagged, and actors failed to make eye contact with the playwright. Elia Kazan and Roger Stevens, one of the play's producers, wanted substantial changes made to the text, and Tenn was unsure and unhappy about the direction the play was taking. Whenever Kazan brought up the deletions and the changes he had requested, Tenn would turn to Frank, who sat deep in the theater.

On this particular day that Tenn was remembering, voices were raised and an ultimatum was delivered: Tenn would make the changes to the play or the play would not open in New York. Angry and exhausted, he said nothing and looked out into the theater: Frank was not in his seat. Tenn calmly told Kazan and Stevens that he was leaving for the day, and with their voices yelling after him, he left, hailed a cab, and went to his apartment, where Frank sat.

"I yelled at him brutally," Tenn remembered. "I told him that I needed him, and never more than at that time, in that theater. I went straight to his deeply Italian, deeply Catholic core and reminded him that Jesus Christ Himself, at his lowest moment, had chastised his disciples for leaving him, asking if they could not spare him one hour. Well, I needed Frank at that hour."

Tenn told me that he needed me at this particular hour of his life, for a very particular purpose. He asked me to stay with him and be there for him and his dream, his "crazy dream": to have one more hour with his father.

TENN'S FATHER BECAME a character that he imagined placing in rooms of his own invention, moving about in stories that were as manic and angry as the ones he could remember, but in others that were tinged with some of the memories of happier times in younger days that his mother shared with friends or at Tenn's bedside when he was sick. The man in those stories was ambitious and romantic, and Tenn came to see that a life with Edwina and three decidedly odd and curious children had sapped him of anything but the incentive to perpetually provide and forbear. "All the sermons of my childhood," Tenn told me, "all the pamphlets and all the books that told you how to buck up and get on and survive, talked of the need to bear and forbear. Acceptance, they insisted, led to advancement. But my father and my mother found themselves immobile and growing heavy and going nowhere, and that nest of anger must have been impossible to bear for him." Tenn imagined that his father came into that house and was aware of the scattering of children who did not welcome him, did not want him, who resented the allocation of air and space given to him, and he could imagine his rage. Tenn's father often complained of being a salesman on the road, going to cities so rustic and removed that the telephone poles and the wires didn't even reach them, back-country people with no interest in him or his wares; but he went on, coming home to rest and have his clothes laundered, the scents of liquor and sweat removed, and he faced only resentment from everyone around him.

"And one day he was gone," Tenn said, "and I hated him for that, too. I hated him for hitting me and hating me and forcing me to become something other than what I was, but I came, in time, to see that he was absolutely my father, just as only Edwina could be my mother. I am their son in every way, and my father is the dreamer, the inconsistent, impossible, wandering poet that I have become. I dream as my mother did, but my mother had no movement in her. There was no advancement within her—her dreams were internal and suppressed by rage, fueled by denial. My father, however, took action, and his dreams were in his feet, and he moved away from a situation he could no longer handle. I took my thoughts and my dreams and put them into words that made their way to paper, and he took to the streets. He got away. He *navigated* in the truest sense of the word, and I came, in my way, to understand him and love him."

Tenn did not study his own plays, although he confessed that every year or so, he tried to reread *The Glass Menagerie* and *A Streetcar Named Desire*, the two plays that he felt came to him most clearly, and which are most clearly based on his parents and the "dance" they held with each other for so long. "I think that there may be elements of me in Tom and Blanche," he told me, "but I look at those plays now and I see my mother as Amanda and my father as Tom. I look at *Streetcar* and I

Stella Adler fascinated Tennessee from the time
he first saw her photograph in a magazine during
her years with the Group Theatre. "Her intellect
arose from the page," he told me, and later in life
her intellect helped him, somewhat, to gather
strength and write again—"to keep at it," he said.

see my mother and my father, having their dance and simultaneously
upholding and destroying illusions."

Stella Adler, a strong influence on Tenn's life, was, like Hepburn, not
terribly interested in the lives of artists she admired: her admonition to
Tenn was always to show her the work, and she would then know all
she needed to know—all she cared to know—about the person who
created it. Adler believed she could study and deconstruct and direct
and perform the plays of writers like Ibsen and Chekhov and Shaw and
Shakespeare and keep unearthing new things, and she exhorted Tenn to
do the same. Tenn's decline as a writer, in Adler's opinion (one she personally expressed to Tenn), came when he lost his interest in the works
of other writers, in the actions of the theater—when he submitted to
the devices, alcohol and drugs, that he believed helped him to survive.

When Adler was heard to exclaim, "Who will take care of Tennessee now?" he was not hurt or angered: he wanted it to be Adler who took care of him.

"That would be the day," Maureen Stapleton quipped. "Stella Adler was not going to lie in a bed with Tenn and talk things out. She would never do as I did, and let him drink and keep talking about demons and overhead camera shots—she would have put him to work." The ministrations of Stella Adler came with an ultimatum, and it was repeatedly given to Tenn: clean yourself up and get back to work. She promised to stand by him and look at whatever he wrote and offer whatever help he might need.

"But I couldn't do it," Tenn admitted. "I had the meetings with her, but my condition was not acceptable to her—or rather, it was not acceptable to what I knew she expected. Whatever condition I might have been in when I went to Hepburn for her aid, it was far worse when I went to Stella. The heaviness was *extreme,* and my head, and the dreams within it, were scary and gelatinous. Words and thoughts made no sense as I wrote them. It was through sheer will and massive editing that I was able to get anything out at all, and no one, least of all Stella, should have seen what that encompassed."

The meetings with Adler did have an effect on Tenn, and it was noticed by Elia Kazan. "Tennessee was reading so many different playwrights," he remembered, "and when he would bump into me, and several times when he called me, he would be full of questions about plays, particularly those I might have directed or acted in. He became terribly obsessed with Clifford Odets, and asked me so many questions about him, about his working habits, his methods."

Tenn had become obsessed—in a fashion that would have pleased Hepburn—with work, with what he called "the architecture of artistic desire." Tenn explained to me why the architecture of Clifford Odets had been so important to him.

"It is imperative that one should never begin to write anything," he told me, "for anyone, or for any venue, until something both monumental and rudimentary is at stake, and what is more monumental and rudimentary—and fragile and temporary and capricious—than our very existence? Our very reality? Our purpose, our worth, our identity?

"I am always asking my characters, and they are always asking themselves, who they are," Tenn continued, "and this is absolutely necessary for day-to-day survival, because we cannot perform any functions until we answer that essential question. Who will ultimately care what happens to a particular character until we know who and what they are?

"Clifford Odets taught me a great deal about identity," Tenn continued, "because his characters are so vividly examined and understood and loved by their creator. Intensely realized. Odets will not simply indicate, for example, that a character is male and poor and desperate; he will extrapolate until we see that this character is male and poor and desperate and unloved and trapped and American. His characters unfold before you as if you were watching an onion peeled away layer by layer, and all around him you suddenly see that there are still other layers—home, country, family, society—that must either be shed or used as protection from the onslaughts that life inevitably and without mercy presents to us.

"Amazingly," Tenn said, smiling, "he is to me a positive writer, no matter how tragic the circumstances, because no matter how pitiful the circumstances of his children—which is how we must see our characters—I am always left with the very vivid idea—the hope—that within us all, within the most horrific of circumstances, we will find, within or about one of our layers, the means to communicate, to defend, to love, to persevere.

"It is easy and acceptable to dismiss his works as proletarian," Tenn told me, "and I might have done so myself at some point, but I am proud to realize that, no matter my trappings, I am very much an Odets character—male, poor, and desperate, American, and yet, amazingly, positive. Positive and fighting and—this is the loveliest of his qualities, and, I would hope, mine—perpetually able to share, no matter how puny my treasures become or remain."

In his earliest years in New York, Tenn would not only spend time in movie theaters; he also snuck into theaters to watch other plays coming to life, and he persistently pursued Odets. "I was terribly attracted to him," Tenn confessed. "To his talent, and to him. He had the most wonderful hands, and I became, for a time, convinced that the quality of one's writings was proportional to the hands of the writer. Odets also had a beautiful mouth and a quick laugh and an intense gaze. I came to feel that he knew quite well what I was up to."

The ease with which Odets painted his characters, their passions, and Tenn's memories of the writer's personal magnetism and intensity inspired his play *Stairs to the Roof,* which owed, in his estimation, a great deal to *Awake and Sing!* "I had had a failure," Tenn remembered, "and I felt that *I* was a failure at that point as a writer and a man. Odets had had success as a writer and as a man, and he, more than any other young playwright at that time, spoke to me and excited me. His aesthetic fingerprints are all over *Menagerie,* and when it is properly directed and performed, I think you can hear the fast and urgent humor, the desperation, the airless rooms, and the sad hope of those two women, growing, at the play's curtain, as dim as the apartment."

An original thought and an original voice had come to Tenn when he began to write *Streetcar, Summer and Smoke,* and *Camino Real,* a sort of fever-dream narrative that came to him as he kept following the characters that had visited him, or as he looked at works of art that had inspired him. "I wrote those plays as if perpetually on a final deadline," he told me, "always acting as if I needed money to get a loved one out of jail, or money to get me out of an unfriendly country. I worked a lot in that time under the belief that I would be dead or incapacitated at any moment, and it brings a certain texture to the work, but it can wreak havoc on your soul and your body. I now believe it's better not to write in a state of anger. I think it works to be angry *about* something, a condition or the treatment given to someone, a character you come to love; but a general anger, which is what I operated beneath for so long in my fifties and early sixties—as I fought against the declivity in my talents and my health—was not good for the writing."

He paused for a moment, then looked at me. "I would like to rewrite a great many of those plays now," he said. "To get them right. And I think I can do it now."

TENN STOOD and looked at the notes on the bed. "We don't have much more time," he told me. "I need to read and study more plays, from all times and from all types of writers, and find out how they work, how they're built. I may soon be in a position, in a condition, to ask Stella for her help, to really place a play, and all its parts, in front of me cleanly and plainly."

There were two playwrights that Tenn was studying most intently, the two he loved the most, personally and artistically: John Guare and Edward Albee, both of whom he termed "terminal and magical." In the notes on that bed, I found comments about both men, and I copied some of them, those that could be deciphered. Of Guare, Tenn had written, "I want to work and to walk about with Guare eyes. Wonder and urgency. I think I always had in common with John my terminal vision, seeing everything as if for both the first and the last time, which allows one to invest anything with powerful, mystical, deeply emotional power."

Every walk past a particular building, Tenn instructed, could be the last. That pond over there—what if fate or blindness or relocation made it unavailable to you? "Items of subjective beauty," Tenn called them, and our pasts are full of them; our present life is crowded with them as well, but we are generally unaware of their existence, much less their worth, until they gain entrance into what he called an "amber-hued past, that closet of psychic bric-a-brac" to which we repair when we want to remember, or to lick or bind wounds, or, as Tenn insisted, "to find out what you are."

"Own all of what you see this day," Tenn had told me on one of our earlier walks around New Orleans, "and it will be of worth to you some other day." He had pointed to a woman in a vivid green coat and told me that I would have that color as a marker, a directional device back to this moment, this memory, this time we were having. There were smells and sounds all around us that were being placed in our inventories, our creative DNA, that would serve as levers to the feelings that would lead us to write. "This," Tenn demonstrated, opening his arms to encompass our surroundings, "is *living*, and it is writing, the present act of accumulating the material we are compelled, required, to use in our work. And *life* is the inventory of everything we've felt and seen and heard: our inventory of subjective beauty; items that have traveled with and alongside this act of living, of surviving, questioning, and coping, and which we reflect upon and fondle and remember and honor with our work.

"And John Guare seems to be alongside and with me as I live, as I gather and hoard my inventory, and I think it is because he taps into something I don't have in my amber-hued closet, but which I have sought and misplaced, sought and abused, sought and misunderstood, sought and overlooked with stupidity and fleshly misallocation. He has had a family," Tenn continued, "and he has shared it with us. The pond we pass, the color that serves as marker, these become our property. What we own, we carry, and whether we marry and have children, or write symphonies or plays, we deliver our property, our inventory, to those with whom we live and work and love and abuse. I have always wanted a family, a group of people—Christ, one person!—who might say to me, 'Stop crying, you fool, and come home to the people who love you. Come crouch in safety in our collective amber-hued closet. It's ours; it's here to be shared.'

"Our experiences, our families, our fears, our items of beauty—all locked in our DNA, which we splatter over our actions and our work. I now have membership in that Guare family. I can feel I've walked past his ponds and buildings, and I can feel, as he did, that I loved them too long, I didn't want to leave, and I don't want to leave."

Tenn paused, inhaled deeply, then laughed. "But," he said, "I live with his family, because mine only gave me a history, but they failed to offer me any shelter or comfort. That is something John has given me—that and an idea of where to begin and how to do it again."

BOTH EDWARD ALBEE and John Guare were "mountains, mighty cliffs of talent one sees in awe and climbs with some trepidation." Tenn felt more comfort with Guare because his mountain was covered with welcoming and soft greenery, while Albee had built with his words a jagged, wounding, vertiginous challenge. "You take on Albee," Tenn warned me, "with equipment of survival, to keep you alert and alive on your journey, but Guare's journey is like one you take while drunk: you laugh, you feel invincible, you feel elated, giddy. And then, at some point, you become aware of the heights you've reached, or you gain some sobriety in the fresh airs of his intellect and imagination, and you come awake, shattered, horrified . . . and stranded alone in a high, lonely place."

John Guare's talent was one that came to Tenn as if it were an over-exuberant puppy, out of control, full of affection, and utterly dependent on the reaction of the lap he's landed on. "I don't mean to imply that Guare, the writer, is out of control," Tenn added, "only that his talent is presented with full force. It hits me in a way that fills me with glee and also with an overwhelming sense of self-consciousness, as if it were unearned affection, or loving attention that calls attention to your double chin or the zit you've been hoping no one will notice."

Guare's plays appeared to Tenn in retrospect as if they were mammoth boxes designed by Joseph Cornell, with each compartment detailing a life in full development or disintegration. "Lives, you will learn," Tenn advised, "are perpetually in varying degrees of growth and decay, as are the people who have been cast in them, and I've come to see that a grab bag of myths is necessary for either providing the strength to grow or to stanch the wounds and cloak the odor of decay." Guare's characters may harbor cancer or mental illness or a staggering lack of self-worth, all of which they conceal or contain with particular myths that are in the arsenals of everyone, whether in Sunnyside, Queens; the Upper East Side of Manhattan; Hollywood; Mississippi; or an African veldt. "The human condition is maddeningly uniform," Tenn told me, laughing, "and no one escapes it. One of our most potent—our most visceral—myths is that some or all of the human experience is avoided, softened, abridged, or transferred by means of beauty, money, faith, good works, or chemical alchemy."

The Joseph Cornell artifact that Tenn imagined Guare's work to be was lacquered with liberal doses of the many myths that propel the characters trapped in its compartments, or "niches," as Tenn called them. "I prefer the idea of a niche," he admitted, "because I think of a niche as self-created, self-invented, a sinecure necessary for survival, and Guare's characters are all singularly diligent in their delusion, their survival, their self-destruction." Guare's plays are constructed with a merciless eye and a masterly sense of proportion and pacing. Within Tenn's memories were the uncomfortable sensations of feeling his soul rotting along with Kate Reid's breast in *Bosoms and Neglect,* his brain "oozing out of my head both from the batterings of life and the frustration of using that organ to no good effect" in tandem with Katherine Helmond, as Bananas, in the original production of *The House of Blue Leaves.* His most amazing and alarming reaction to a Guare play came with the original production, in 1977, of *Landscape of the Body,* a viewing that dramatically altered his concept of both theater and his role as an artist within it. It was within this play that he faced a sense of identity that was both an epiphany and a judgment, and with those characters, all of whom were on a journey toward "understanding what mattered and if they were part of that scene," Tenn came to re-evaluate himself, personally and professionally, and he realized that the many notes and index cards on which he had scribbled his characters and his intentions, his goals and his dreams, his "moral inventory built by magpie," were misguided and false. *Landscape of the Body* had led Tenn to try to figure out his identity, his "person" and to go to the most frightening place he could imagine.

What is that place?

"Never go there without a *very* strong sense of identity," Tenn told me.

Where?

"That most frightening of all places," Tenn continued, "the one I mentioned to you earlier today: the intersection of desire and aptitude."

That place. That corner which, like so many corners in Tenn's past, held what he needed. In Tenn's mind, and on his mental map, this corner housed Guare and Albee.

"The love that I feel for Edward Albee extends far beyond his work," Tenn told me, returning to the bed and leaning against a small pile of pillows. "I think that his is the most extraordinary talent to emerge in the last thirty years. I have admired other plays, and other writers, but his work is emotionally dangerous and stunningly beautiful. I can't think of any other writer who has managed to combine the lean and the lapidary. He understands to a shocking degree the ravages both of love and of love denied. His command of the language is far beyond me. My words come from some instinctual dictionary that responds to fear and rage, but he has a full command of the language and can therefore achieve more with less effort.

"You can see that I feel it is important that his work be studied. His is work from which you can learn, but the love of which I spoke derives from the fact that Edward remains the only playwright who truly acknowledged me and my work, and that is a great honor, especially considering his greater abilities. That I should have been noticed by this man, that I should have been of some aid, means a great deal to me. While others write my obituary and perpetually recalculate my worth and my gifts, he has always been loyal in his respect, and he has waved at me across some rocky seas."

Edward Albee came to Tenn's attention in the late fifties, when Tenn was urged to see a production of *The Zoo Story,* and what he loved about that one-act play ("danger and beauty and sexuality welded together as tightly as a fist") was further displayed three years later, in 1962, when Tenn saw, by his own estimation five times, *Who's Afraid of Virginia Woolf?* "The dance of people caught in a nest of poor choices and unfulfilled needs, a dance I know all too well, was on that stage," Tenn remembered. "I felt invaded by that play, purloined. I felt that someone had gotten into my head and my heart and my notes and had written the play I would have liked to have written. Bill Inge had the ability to write plays or scenes of plays that appeared to have been influenced by our conversations or by dreams I had had or by ideas I had entertained, but *Virginia Woolf* was the first play I ever sat through shivering, because someone had rushed ahead of me and done something I would have liked to have done, but had neither the talent nor the courage to do so."

Tenn endured Albee's adaptations of Carson McCullers's *Ballad of the Sad Café*, which was difficult because he felt the playwright was veering away from that intersection he was meant to dominate and devoting his time and his gifts to the work of another writer, one Tenn had known and loved. "I knew the shape of that novel," he told me. "I knew what she had intended and I knew what she felt she had failed to provide in that novel, so the play—the experience of watching that play—was odd and unpleasant, even though it was skillfully done." *Tiny Alice* and *A Delicate Balance* both devastated him, because both were, to him, plays about shattered families: the one to which we submit our souls in hope of salvation (the church) and the one into which we are born and in which we hope to find safety.

"Edward and I both exist now in a lacuna that is reserved for the writers the world feels no use for," Tenn said, "but I feel confident that we will again be heard and understood, and I have no doubt that should I again have a place of respect in the theater, it will be because Edward's hand was offered in helping me from this lacuna. Elia Kazan once told me that perhaps writers are abandoned because, through our work, readers are educated, they become wise to things they never considered before, and now they feel entirely beyond us, or utterly afraid of us. I want you to know that I believe that the corruption of the artist begins when he fails to acknowledge the work of his brethren," Tenn told me. "I now understand that the theater is so much greater than all of us, still so capable of so much, that we are all needed not only to ensure its survival, but to ensure its relevance."

Tenn sat up and looked through the notes at the foot of the bed. He failed to find what he was searching for, so he walked, none too steadily, to the desk, where he flipped through some pages that he had fastened

Irene Worth was one of Tennessee's "spiritual saviors," a great actress but also a woman who shared with him poetry, quotations that might help ease his mental strain, and a deliciously witty, almost "evil," imagination. Here, she is about forty years old.

with a paper clip. Eventually, he found what he was looking for, and read it me with the paper clip clenched in his teeth. "I always feel that Edward has placed upon his stage these gorgeously buffed suits of armor—our fellow men, encased in defense and delusion, and they gleam before us, objects of awe and art, but they are, to our surprise, empty. Utterly empty. And baby, to array such beauty before our eyes, shining and lovely and . . . empty? Well, that is tragedy in my book. Beautiful tragedy." He cast his eyes farther down the page and read on.

"Irene Worth had a beautiful analogy, as she should. Beautiful woman, beautiful actress, beautiful analogy. She heard me out on my description of Edward's plays, but she thought I was wrong. 'No,' she said. 'I see Edward's plays as lovely mirrors,'" she told Tenn, and to me she elaborated. "Baroque, perhaps, rarely rococo, but lovely. Ornate, heavy, of a craftsmanship we no longer see. We are lured by the frame of this mirror, but our eyes eventually graze toward the subject, which is ourselves, and the reflection is distorted, ugly, frightening. The frame is gorgeous, but the glass bows and distends, until you move the subject at its center, physically and emotionally and dramatically, and the reflection is sometimes perfect and clear, sometimes lovely, with a little deception of placement and lighting, sometimes cruelly exposing."

"It is not a mirror for the weak of spirit," Tenn said, "but I have been happy to step in front of it, to step into it, and I hold on to that frame not only for its beauty, of promises of what might be, but for balance, for strength."

The sun was rising, and we could see it through the curtains. Our time was over.

"Baby, I need to get to sleep," Tenn said. I stood and immediately wondered if I would be able to walk out of the room, much less drive to Baton Rouge. I was exhausted, dizzy. I began to collect my papers.

"You'll gather your strength," Tenn said, "and I'll gather mine, and we'll begin the journey. We'll go to these women and begin our work together."

He gave me a hug, strong and lingering, and whispered in my ear, "You'll be fine. Everything will turn out perfectly."

Tenn walked me to the door, smiled, and then closed me out of the room. I was in a hall that was utterly silent.

I walked several blocks to where I had parked my car. The sun was rising, but it was an overcast day: it looked more like dusk than dawn. I drove out of the city and found that I had the type of exhaustion that rendered me hyperalert: every bird that flew overhead led me to jerk my head toward it, and every car horn left me lurching. At a diner in the small town of LaPlace, I pulled over and went in. The diner was old and well-known in Louisiana and offered gumbo and a vast array of pies. I sat in the diner drinking coffee and reading over the notes I had taken, collating and ordering them. I became transfixed by a rotating display of desserts and lost track of time.

Once week before Thanksgiving of 1982, Tenn called me at home. It was nearly ten o'clock at night, and I answered the phone.

"Dixie!"

We had not seen each other for nearly two months, and I had not known how or where to reach him. I had begun to think that our "assignment" might never happen.

"When will you be coming to New York?" he asked. I did not know. I was taking classes and looking for ways to earn the money to make a trip to see him.

"I can get you up here," he told me. "That's not a problem."

I did not want to take his money, and there was no discussion of what, exactly, we would do once I got to New York, but he remained excited about looking up the people whose names he had given me, of deciphering his notes, and revisiting plays he and others had written. To "figure things out," he kept saying.

He wanted to know if I still had the rosary and if I used it. I told him I had and I thought about the people whose names were assigned to the beads. He asked me to consider calling some of those "beaded" people and asking them to offer their own prayers. I wrote this down, followed by three exclamation points.

"Call me when you have a chance," he said. He gave me the phone number of his apartment at Manhattan Plaza, as well as the number of the Hotel Elysée. "You can almost always find me at those places. And let me know when you can get here."

I did not call Tenn, but I began a letter to him, asking what it was he wanted me to do. I needed to know precisely what this assignment was, and how I might possibly find these people and approach them with Tenn's questions and comments. I read and reread the letter, and I did not like the tone of it: I was dismissive, dubious. I did not send the letter.

Tenn called my home a week before Christmas, but I did not know about the call until he called me again in the final week of January. My father had a habit—infuriating to me and my mother—of not writing down phone messages. We would come home and he would tell us that we had been called by several people, and when we asked who, he always replied, cheerily, that he didn't remember. "Name some names," he would say, and we would have to run through the names of those who might have called. On that particular day, my father only mentioned that "a man" had called, very friendly, and wanted to know how we all were doing and to have me call.

When Tenn phoned me in January, he told me about the call and that my father sounded "perfectly nice." He reminded me that mothers provide dreams but fathers provide "feet and energy: the engine to leave." Tenn asked me if I had tried to reach any of the people on the rosary beads. I told him I had not. Tenn reminded me that he could provide me with phone numbers and addresses, introductions, but he wanted to get started, he wanted to reach out to those people. He wanted to find out if he had mattered, and to see if he could write again.

I told him I would get to work on it.

I shared my notes with Marian Seldes. She was astounded by what she found within them, and she told me I should get to New York; I should get to Tenn. I told her of Tenn's drinking and drug use, the fears I had of being in New York City, where I knew few people, and being on this odd assignment with a man I admired but did not trust. In New Orleans, no matter how strange or frightening things might have become, I knew that my car was parked nearby. I could escape.

"There will be a right time," she told me.

On February 11, 1983, I came home from school and my job. My father told me there had been messages, and he proudly pointed to a pad he had placed by the telephone. There were five names on the pad, one of them reading "10."

"Who is that?" my father asked.

"A friend," I told him.

I had never told my mother or my father about the days spent with Tennessee Williams. As far as they knew, I had been with friends, carousing in New Orleans. I still did not feel comfortable telling them about my desire for a writing life and about my time with Tenn.

"What does the message mean?" my father asked.

I looked at the pad and under the "10," in my father's neat and distinctive handwriting, were the words "Be my witness."

"What does it mean?" my father asked again.

I told my father about Tennessee and our time together, about our assignment, about the rosary, and about the people he wanted me to meet, about the people he wanted to affirm him as a writer and as a man and as a friend.

"You have to call him," my father told me. "You have to do this."

"I know," I told him. "I know."

BY THE END of the month, Tennessee Williams was dead. I was told of his passing by my father, who greeted me when I came home for dinner. My father wanted to know if I had ever returned his phone call; if I had

"When all of this is over," Tennessee told me as our visits came to an end, "I want you to remember that I am a writer. Above all else, I'm a writer, and writing is all I really care about."

ever made plans to go to him and help him. Yes, I lied, we were in the midst of those plans. I lied to my father out of shame and guilt—both for my failure to respond to Tenn and for my inability to share with my father my dream of being a writer, of becoming someone who mattered, of providing to Tenn—to any friend—one sacred hour. For the rest of his life, my father and I could share our regret at my not being present for Tennessee Williams, and it may have been the one subject on which we agreed.

I began to think that there was now a way I could provide this sacred hour to Tenn. Tenn understood boundaries, safe places, what he called "the right mood for the right outcomes." He always sought out new notebooks and pads and clean pieces of paper to get started, and he needed music in the background to get the fog rolling. "Nothing like the drama of a clean slate, a fresh start," he had said. "Remember Pavese," he always said. " 'The only joy in the world is to begin.' One day it will happen," he told me. "A place that is safe and strong and right for the fog. All of us," he told me, "are seeking a home, and I don't mean where we were born, or where we now live and have things, but where we can do the big things, the right things. Where we belong, where we fit, where we're loved."

IN THE FALL of 1988, my father told me, with nothing to prompt him but the belief that I needed to leave Baton Rouge and begin my own life, that it was not too late to be a witness to Tennessee Williams; it was not too late to honor his request and to repay the time he had spent with me. I had let down a man who might not have considered me a friend, but who needed one. "Nothing will be right," my father told me, "until you do this. You're honor-bound to do this." Attached to a small mirror in my bedroom was a portion of T. S. Eliot's *Four Quartets* that Tenn had quoted to me, and which contained a dream of his—of finding meaning and a home:

> *Home is where one starts from. As we grow older*
> *The world becomes stranger, the pattern more complicated*
> *Of dead and living. Not the intense moment*
> *Isolated, with no before and after,*
> *But a lifetime burning in every moment . . .*

Tennessee Williams wanted to get home, my father reminded me, and I could honor his wish by capturing "burning moments" with those people who had mattered to him, who had gotten him up in the morning and in front of the pale judgment.

"Be his witness," my father told me.

My father provided the money for me to move to New York in March of 1989, to begin what he called "getting the man home." He made the time right, safe, and sound: his great gift to me, and one for which, I now realize, I never thanked him.

Acknowledgments

Follies of God exists because Tennessee Williams took the time to read and answer a letter sent to him from a twenty-year-old rube in Louisiana. I was that rube. For reasons we will never know or understand, Tenn chose to arrive in the French Quarter and offer me an astonishing assignment. It took nearly three decades and a great deal of patience on the part of more than a hundred people to complete this assignment, but I must admit that I would do it all over again. The subjects in this book have my eternal gratitude for braving the vast no-man's-land of my good intentions.

I have compiled a list of people who were generous with their time and their memories—about Tennessee Williams, of course, but so much more, and what they gave to me infused the book, and I am thankful to them: Yuki Abe, Ellen Adler, Karen Akers, Eileen Atkins, Sylvia Connie Atkins, Kaye Ballard, Anne Bancroft, Barbara Barrie, Barbara Bel Geddes, Betsy Blair, Ronee Blakley, Chris Boneau, Marlon Brando, Dave Brubeck, Iola Brubeck, Betty Buckley, Ellen Burstyn, Zoe Caldwell, Dixie Carter, Florence Chaney, Stockard Channing, Candy Clark, Patricia Clarkson, Tandy Cronyn, Mart Crowley, Agnes de Mille, Sandy Dennis, Colleen Dewhurst, Fernanda Eberstadt, Patricia Elliott, Robert Emmett, Andy Ensor, Barbara Feldon, John Fiedler, Fionnula Flanagan, Ruth Ford, John Gielgud, Anita Gillette, Joanna Gleason, Martha Graham, Lee Grant, Ruth Gordon, John Guare, Tammy Grimes, Alec Guinness, Christina Haag, Uta Hagen, Julie Harris, Roy Harris, Fayette Hauser, Polly Holliday, Dennis Hopper, Janis Ian, Albert Innaurato, Carmen Irizarry, Anne Jackson, Carol Kane, Garson Kanin, Frances Kazan, Anne Kaufman, Lila Kedrova, Thomas Keith, Deborah Kerr, Richard Kilbourne, Shirley Knight, Carole Laskey, Judith Light, Sidney Lumet, Norris Mailer, Marsha Mason, Marlane Gomard Meyer, Duane Michals, Don Millington, Rosemary Murphy, Peg Murray, Vivian Nathan, Paul Newman, Carrie Nye, Jack O'Brien, Tom Oppenheim, Angelica Page, Betsy Palmer, Estelle Parsons, Arthur Penn, Alice Playten, Sian Phillips, Harold Pinter, Ellis Rabb, Lynn Redgrave, Beah Richards, Doris Roberts, David Rothenberg, Sam Rudy, Katherine Sands, Joan Micklin Silver, Anna Sokolow, Maria St. Just, Louise Sorel, Beatrice Straight, Elaine Stritch, Elizabeth Taylor, Sada Thompson, Maria Tucci, Susan Tyrrell, Joan Vaill Thorne, Nanette Varian, Eli Wallach, Nicholas Fox Weber, Elizabeth Wilson, Lanford Wilson, Donald Windham, Joanne Woodward, Irene Worth. Special mention belongs to Ron and Howard Mandelbaum of Photofest, not only for bringing forth an abundance of images, but for not batting an eye when I requested a Kir Royale when asked if I wanted something to drink. They are clearly invaluable and rare people.

Tennessee spoke a lot about Dopp kits one needs on the road, and I had mine, as well as the people who helped me to stock them: Winnie Grissom, Sue Grissom, Robert Grissom, Wanda Smith, Kim Criswell, Molly Haskell, Andrew Sarris, Phyllis Nagy, Sally Kirkland, Edith Soloway, Allie Mulholland, Ron Raines, David Pittu, Alec Burnham, and Rose Byrnes. The principal source of sanity and sustenance was, always will be, and is Dr. Dale Atkins. There were survival jobs along the way, but I was luckier than most. I was employed by women wise and generous and understanding and inspiring: Evelina Emmi Rector of Ecce Panis, Amy Scherber of Amy's Bread, and Daryl Roth, a producer and lover of theater and people beyond compare. Three of the subjects in this book became cherished friends: Marian Seldes, Lois Smith, and Frances Sternhagen. Without their generosity and belief in me and my work, all those subjects might never have shown up and started talking . . . and talking. There were women in Baton Rouge, Louisiana—actresses—who prepared me for the two decades of talking: Barbara Chaney Molstedt, Lenore Evans Banks, and Patricia Snow.

I will never forget another belle of the South who taught me how to think in a new way: Patricia White Hardee. I am also grateful for two remarkable teachers who taught me about the art of reading and writing: Barbara O'Rourk and Patricia Geary.

Two talented men believed in this book when it was a pile of notes and dreams, and their help was invaluable. Thank you so much Donald Wiese and David Ebershoff for the guidance, the insight, and the company.

Edward Hibbert of Donadio & Olson believed in the book and brought it to Victoria Wilson at Alfred A. Knopf, and it all came together, in all the best ways. With or without a contract, I am going to insist that I have Wilson's eye for the rest of my life. I am also grateful to the help offered by Victoria's staff: Carmen Johnson, Daniel Schwartz, and Audrey Silverman, publishing tyros from Central Casting —if I ran Central Casting.

I hope that I have been a sufficient witness to Tennessee Williams and to the women he truly believed were among the greatest inventions of God. I do remember, however, that Tenn warned me that trying to understand and fully appreciate the gifts of women was a vast and eternal undertaking, and I remain on the job. I also have a dream similar to one Tenn shared with me: "If I should make it to Heaven—and I'm working on It—I will do as I always do: I will look for a woman to explain it to me, experience it with me. And then I'll find my mother and tell her what I've learned. And we'll laugh. And I'll be home—again."

Index

The initials TW refer to Tennessee Williams. Page numbers in *italics* refer to illustrations.